Engaging Videos explore a variety of business topics related to the theory students are learning in class. **Exercise Quizzes** assess students' comprehension of the concepts in each video.

92%   **92%**   **92%**

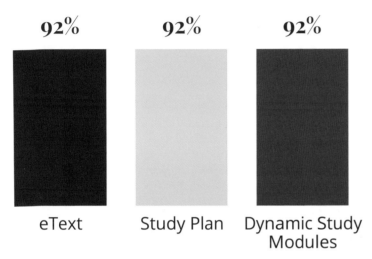

eText   Study Plan   Dynamic Study Modules

% of students who found learning aid helpful

Dynamic Study Modules use the latest developments in cognitive science and help students study chapter topics by adapting to their performance in real time.

Pearson eText enhances student learning with engaging and interactive lecture and example videos that bring learning to life.

The **Gradebook** offers an easy way for you and your students to see their performance in your course.

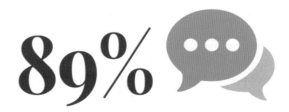

89%

of students would tell their instructor to keep using MyLab Marketing

For additional details visit: www.pearson.com/mylab/marketing

In Memoriam:
Warren J. Keegan 1936–2014

     —MCG

TENTH EDITION
GLOBAL EDITION

GLOBAL
MARKETING

Mark C. Green
Simpson College

Warren J. Keegan
Late, Pace University

Pearson

Harlow, England • London • New York • Boston • San Francisco • Toronto • Sydney • Dubai • Singapore • Hong Kong
Tokyo • Seoul • Taipei • New Delhi • Cape Town • Sao Paulo • Mexico City • Madrid • Amsterdam • Munich • Paris • Milan

Vice President, Business, Economics, and UK Courseware: Donna Battista
Director of Portfolio Management: Stephanie Wall
Executive Portfolio Manager: Lynn M. Huddon
Editorial Assistant: Rachel Chou
Content Producer, Global Editions: Pooja Aggarwal
Acquisitions Editor, Global Editions: Ishita Sinha
Senior Project Editor, Global Editions: Daniel Luiz
Media Producer, Global Editions: Jayaprakash Kothandapani
Manufacturing Controller, Production, Global Editions: Kay Holman
Vice President, Product Marketing: Roxanne McCarley
Senior Product Marketer: Becky Brown
Product Marketing Assistant: Marianela Silvestri
Manager of Field Marketing, Business Publishing: Adam Goldstein
Field Marketing Manager: Nicole Price
Vice President, Production and Digital Studio, Arts and Business: Etain O'Dea

Director, Production and Digital Studio, Business and Economics: Ashley Santora
Managing Producer, Business: Melissa Feimer
Content Producer: Michelle Zeng
Operations Specialist: Carol Melville
Design Lead: Kathryn Foot
Manager, Learning Tools: Brian Surette
Senior Learning Tools Strategist: Emily Biberger
Managing Producer, Digital Studio and GLP: James Bateman
Managing Producer, Digital Studio: Diane Lombardo
Digital Studio Producer: Monique Lawrence
Digital Studio Producer: Alana Coles
Full Service Project Management: Michelle Alojera, Gowri Duraiswamy, SPi Global
Interior Design: SPi Global
Cover Design: Paromita Banerjee and Lumina Datamatics, Inc.
Cover Art: Anastasiia Guseva/Shutterstock

Pearson Education Limited
KAO Two
KAO Park
Hockham Way
Harlow
CM17 9SR
United Kingdom

and Associated Companies throughout the world

Visit us on the World Wide Web at: www.pearsonglobaleditions.com

ISBN 10: 1-292-30402-2
ISBN 13: 978-1-292-30402-1

British Library Cataloguing-in-Publication Data

A catalogue record for this book is available from the British Library

10 9 8 7 6 5 4 3 2 1

Typeset in Times LT Pro by SPi Global Publisher Services.

Printed in Malaysia (CTP-VVP)

Brief Contents

Contents

Preface

We are proud that this Tenth Edition of *Global Marketing* marks more than two decades of publication success. In this new edition, as in prior editions, we take an environmental and strategic approach to global marketing by outlining the major dimensions of the global business environment. We also provide a set of conceptual and analytical tools that prepare students to successfully apply the 4Ps when pursuing careers in global marketing or related areas.

Guided by our experience using the text in undergraduate and graduate classrooms and in corporate training seminars, we have revised, updated, and expanded *Global Marketing*. One of our challenges in developing a new edition of *Global Marketing* is the rate of change in the global business environment. Yesterday's impossibility becomes today's reality; new companies explode onto the scene; company leadership changes abruptly. In short, any book can be quickly outdated by events. Even so, we set out to create a compelling narrative that captures the unfolding drama that is in inherent in marketing in the globalization era.

When *Principles of Global Marketing* first appeared in 1996, we invited readers to "look ahead" to such developments as the ending of America's trade embargo with Vietnam, Europe's new single market, Daimler AG's Smart car, Volkswagen's global ambitions, and Whirlpool's expansion into emerging markets. This newly revised edition also surveys important current developments in the international arena, including Britain's tortuous path towards Brexit, China's ascendance on the world stage, evolving trade relations in the Trump era, achievements by entrepreneurs such as Jack Ma, plus much more.

We are passionate about the subject of global marketing; if our readers detect a note of enthusiasm in our writing, then we have been successful. Our goal for all ten editions has been the same: to write a book that is authoritative in content yet relaxed and assured in style and tone. One instructor using the Ninth Edition wrote us to say, "I love the text, and really like the way it engages students. That is invaluable." We believe that you will find latest edition of *Global Marketing* to be the most engaging, up-to-date, relevant, useful text of its kind.

We recommend pairing the Tenth Edition with Pearson's MyLab Marketing. MyLab Marketing is a teaching and learning platform that empowers you to reach every student. By combining content from *Global Marketing* with digital tools and a flexible platform, MyLab Marketing personalizes the learning experience and will help your students learn and retain key course concepts while developing skills that future employers are seeking in their candidates.

New to This Edition

As with previous editions, the Tenth Edition offers up-to-date, original insights into the complexities and subtleties of shifts in the external environment and their implications for global marketers. Specific updates and revisions include:

- More than fifty percent of the chapter-opening vignettes and related end-of-chapter cases are new to the Tenth Edition. Cases retained from the prior edition have also been revised and updated for this new edition.
  - Revised and updated end-of-chapter cases include Case 1-2, "McDonald's Expands Globally While Adjusting Its Local Recipe"; Case 1-3, "Apple versus Samsung: The Battle for Smartphone Supremacy Heats Up"; Case 10-1, "Google"; Case 11-1, "Global Automakers Target Low-Income Consumers"; Case 16-1, "IKEA."
  - New cases in the Tenth Edition include Case 2-1, "India's Economy at the Crossroads: Can Prime Minister Narendra Modi Deliver *Acche Din*?"; Case 3-1, "Breaking Up Is Hard to Do: Britons Contemplate 'Brexit'"; Case 4-1, "Cotton, Clothing Consumption, Culture: From Small Beginnings to a Global Cultural System"; Case 5-1, "Travis Kalanick and Uber"; Case 7-2, "The 'Bubbling' Tea Market"; Case 12-1, "Welcome to the World of Fast Fashion"; Case 15-1, "How Do You Like Your Reality? Virtual? Augmented? Mixed?"

● New discussion of social media is integrated throughout the Tenth Edition. Chapter 15, "Global Marketing and the Digital Revolution," has been thoroughly revised and updated to include discussion of location-based mobile platforms, cloud computing, tablets, wearable devices, autonomous mobility, and other cutting-edge topics.

● In addition, most chapters contain sidebar features on the following themes: Emerging Markets Briefing Book; Entrepreneurial Leadership, Creative Thinking, and the Global Startup; and The Cultural Context.

  ● Among the entrepreneurs profiled in these sidebars are Kevin Systrom (Instagram); Reed Hastings (Netflix); Daniel Ek (Spotify); Oscar Farinetti (Eataly); Elon Musk (Tesla); Jack Ma (Alibaba), Sir James Dyson (Dyson), and Brian Chesky and Joe Gebbia (Airbnb).

  ● The Entrepreneurial Leadership, Creative Thinking, and the Global Startup sidebars also contain expanded coverage of digital entrepreneurship, including financial technology ("fintech"), in this Tenth Edition.

● All tables containing key company, country, and industry data have been updated. Examples include Table 2-3, "Index of Economic Freedom"; all the income and population tables in Chapters 3 and 7; Table 10-2, "The World's Most Valuable Brands"; Table 13-1, "Top 25 Global Marketers"; and Table 13-2, "Top 20 Global Advertising Agency Companies."

● The discussion of the BRICS nations has been updated to incorporate the impact of slowing growth in China and the volatility of commodity prices.

● Income and population data in Chapter 3 have been reorganized for improved clarity, comparability, and visual impact.

● More infographics have been incorporated into the text to enhance clarity and visual appeal.

Solving Teaching and Learning Challenges

Today's Millennial and Generation Z students are networked and technology-savvy. They have access to more content across more platforms than previous generations. Many are also taking on substantial debt loads as they pursue their college degrees. For these and other reasons, it is important to give them a textbook that is "worth the money," and that provides an experience that is rewarding and motivates them to "keep reading."

We have been gratified to receive positive feedback from students who have benefited from college courses in which *Global Marketing* was the required text. The following student comments suggest that *Global Marketing* does exactly that:

"The textbook is very clear and easy to understand."
"An excellent textbook with many real-life examples."
"The authors use simple language and clearly state the important points."
"This is the best textbook that I am using this term."
"The authors have done an excellent job of writing a text that can be read easily."

The Tenth Edition helps students develop cross-cultural awareness and engage with issues relating to sustainability and corporate social responsibility. The new edition also profiles some of the most innovative thinkers and entrepreneurial leaders of the modern era.

Each chapter opens with a brief case study introducing a company, a country, a product, or a global marketing issue that directly relates to chapter themes and content. The cases were written with the same objectives in mind: to raise issues that will encourage student interest and learning; to stimulate class discussion; to give students a chance to apply theory and concepts while developing critical-thinking skills; and to enhance the classroom experience for students and instructors alike. Every chapter and case has been classroom-tested in both undergraduate and graduate courses.

Throughout the text, we have added scores of current examples of global marketing practice as well as quotations from global marketing practitioners and industry experts. Organizational Web sites are referenced for further student study and exploration.

We have benefited tremendously from adopter feedback and input; we also continue to draw on our direct experience in key world regions. The result is a text that addresses your needs and the needs of instructors in every part of the world.

Developing Employability Skills

Employers at global companies want to know that the people they hire understand and can think critically about contemporary issues such as the dynamics of globalization and growth opportunities in emerging markets. One MBA student wrote to say that reading *Global Marketing* for coursework in 2017 provided her with a competitive advantage when pursuing a new career opportunity. She said, "I used many of the text's theories during my interview process, and I incorporate the lessons learned on a daily basis as I work with our offices in 12+ locations around the world!"

The Tenth Edition addresses current global trends and issues, including the economic disruption and social disruption that are among the forces at work in the world today. The resulting shifts in global market opportunities and threats are important themes in this revision, as are the rise of economic nationalism and populism. Terms such as *austerity, capital flight, currency wars, double-dip recession, global imbalances, global rebalancing, quantitative easing (QE), secular stagnation, sovereign-debt crisis,* and *negative interest rates* appear regularly in the business news. New terms such as *tax inversion* are now part of the conversation as well.

Recent research findings have been integrated into each chapter of *Global Marketing* to help students be conversant in the most current conversations that are happening in this field. For example, our thinking about the benefits of globalization has been influenced by Richard Baldwin's 2016 book, *The Great Convergence: Information Technology and the New Globalization.* As Baldwin notes, the process of removing constraints on the costs of moving goods, people, and ideas began in the late 19th century. The first wave of globalization was driven by the falling costs of water transport (e.g., ocean-going freighters) and land transport (e.g., the railroads). In keeping with the theory of competitive advantage, this meant that countries with manufacturing prowess benefited by trading with countries whose primary outputs were agricultural production. The current wave of globalization has resulted in part from the digital revolution that allows supply chains to stretch around the world.

Instructor Teaching Resources

The following supplements are available with this text:

Supplements available to instructors at www.pearsonglobaleditions.com	Features of the Supplement
Instructor's Manual authored by Kerry Walsh from University of South Florida	• Chapter-by-chapter summaries • Examples and activities not in the main book • Teaching outlines • Teaching tips • Solutions to all questions and problems in the book

Supplements available to instructors at www.pearsonglobaleditions.com	Features of the Supplement
Test Bank authored by Mahmood Khan from Pamplin College of Business, Virginia Tech	4,000 multiple-choice, true/false, short- answer, and graphing questions with these annotations: • Difficulty level (1 for straight recall, 2 for some analysis, 3 for complex analysis) • Type (Multiple-choice, true/false, short-answer, essay • Topic (The term or concept the question supports) • Learning outcome
	• AACSB learning standard (Written and Oral Communication; Ethical Understanding and Reasoning; Analytical Thinking; Information Technology; Interpersonal Relations and Teamwork; Diverse and Multicultural Work; Reflective Thinking; Application of Knowledge) Page number in the text
Computerized TestGen	TestGen allows instructors to: • Customize, save, and generate classroom tests • Edit, add, or delete questions from the Test Item Files • Analyze test results • Organize a database of tests and student results.
PowerPoints authored by Jill Solomon from University of South Florida	Slides include all the graphs, tables, and equations in the textbook. PowerPoints meet accessibility standards for students with disabilities. Features include, but not limited to: • Keyboard and Screen Reader access • Alternative text for images • High color contrast between background and foreground colors

Acknowledgments

I am indebted to the many colleagues, friends, and adopters who carefully read and critiqued individual manuscript sections and chapters. Their comments improved the clarity and readability of the text. In particular, I would like to thank Steven J. Archambault, James A. Baggett, Hunter Clark, Frank Colella, Dave Collins, Diana Dickinson, Mark Freyberg, Lora Friedrich, Alexandre Gilfanov, Carl Halgren, Kathy Hill, Mark Juffernbruch, David Kochel, Peter Kvetko, Keith Miller, Gayle Moberg, Christopher "Kit" Nagel, Alexandre Plokhov, Chatt Pongpatipat, Yao Lu Swanson, David Wolf, and Thomas Wright.

Many individuals were instrumental in helping us secure permissions, and I want to acknowledge everyone who "went the extra mile" in supporting this revision. I would especially like to thank Nicholas Arnold, Meredith Corporation; Jane Bachmann, DuPont; John Baloff, ATI Amplifier Technologies; Jeremy Banks, banxcartoons; William Bassett, Kikkoman; Julien Benatar, Pandora; Chris Boyens, Deere & Company; Paul Button, Jill Camp, Kohler; Lee Carter, Mower; Buzz Delano, Delano Associates; Kirk Edmondson, Lexus Advanced Business Development; Jemma Gould, IPG; Mandy Guss, Las Cruces; Jennifer Hall, Champagne Bureau, USA; Emma Hamm, Subaru; Sean Higgins, Forrester Research; David Johnson, Meredith Corporation; Allison Joyce, Allison Joyce Photojournalism; Tom Kingsbury, Bridgestone Americas, Inc.; Denise Lavoie, Henkel; Ilana McCabe, QVC Inc.; Edward Linsmier, Edward Linsmier Photography; Mike Lovell, Meredith Corporation; Katherine Miller, Nucor; Brad Miller, New Balance Athletic Shoe, Inc.; Morgan Molinoff, Edelman; Kerry Ann Nolan, Subaru; Meghan Reutzel, GoDaddy; Lenore Rice, Seibert & Rice; Michael Ross, Michael Ross Photography; Vivian Santangelo, Meredith Corporation; Mara Seibert, Seibert & Rice; Greg Selfe, Two Sides UK; Lindsy Shrewsberry, STIHL USA; Brady Spangenberg, BASF; Katie Szadziewska, McArthurGlen; and Vibhav Valdore, Bridgestone Latin America.

Colleagues and adopters at several institutions contributed material to this revision and made helpful suggestions. Thanks to Professor Steven Archambault, Cal-Poly Pomona University, and Professor Christopher "Kit" Nagel of Concordia University–Irvine, for suggestions that we incorporated in Chapter 2 and Chapter 8. Lora Friedrich, Professor of Sociology at Simpson College, and Chatt Pongpatipat, Assistant Professor of Marketing at Saginaw Valley State University, contributed the Chapter 7 sidebar about Thailand. Paul Button created a wonderful new set of infographic maps for Chapter 3. Thanks also to my daughter, Lauren Konrad, for additional last-minute help with infographic design.

I would also like to thank the many present and former students at Simpson College and the University of Iowa who have offered feedback on previous editions of *Global Marketing,* contributed case studies, and suggested improvements. These include Han Wang's contributions to the Chapter 7 opening case on segmenting the Chinese luxury market. Glynis Gallagher, a University of Iowa graduate, contributed a wonderful Chapter 2 case about her experience as a contracts analyst at Cargill. Brady Spangenberg wrote in detail about his vocational journey to BASF in a new case in Chapter 6. Simpson alumna Beth Dorrell graciously offered her expertise on export documentation. Mikkel Jakobsen wrote about his first job in global marketing for Case 8-2.

The students in my international marketing course at CIMBA Italy worked collaboratively on the issue of tourism in Venice. Hats off to Kaleb Beckett, Luci Boat, Leslie Bourland, Lauren Camerieri, Lucas Commodore, Jeff Dellinger, Chris Duncan, Jacque Ford, Brian Fry, Glynis Gallagher, Katie Greif, Kim Halamicek, Harper Hier, Jake Hirsch, Mike Johnson, Sarah Jones, Josh Kroll, Sean Miller, Chris Nucero, Mark Parmalee, Jack Roeder, Chris Shonkwiler, Slava Sinitsyn, and Chloe Suh. All were enthusiastic participants in the project and our work together in Italy made a lasting impression on me.

It was a great pleasure working with the Pearson team that managed the production of this edition. Thanks to: Stephanie Wall, Editor-in-Chief; Lynn M. Huddon, Executive Portfolio Manager; and Michelle Zeng, Content Producer, for their continued support. The production moved along smoothly, thanks to our friends at SPi Global. These include Anna Iremedio and Michelle Alojera, Content Production Managers; Maya Lane, Rights and Permissions Project Manager; Gowri Duraiswamy, Senior Project Manager. Kudos also to our photo researcher, Jason Acibes, for demonstrating once again that "every picture tells a story." Thanks also to the marketing team for the fantastic work on marketing support materials, and to the entire Pearson sales team for helping promote the book in the field. I also want to acknowledge the contributions of Mahmood Khan for in-depth updates to the TestBank, Kerry Walsh for her fine work on the Instructor's Manual, and Jill Solomon for preparing a new set of PowerPoint slides.

Mark C. Green
September 2018

Global Edition Acknowledgments

Pearson would like to thank the following people for their work on the Global Edition:

Contributors

Ayantunji Gbadamosi, University of East London
Ronan Jouan de Kervenoael, Sabancı Üniversitesi
Stefania Paladini, Birmingham City University
Hamed Shamma, The American University in Cairo
Muneeza Shoaib
Diane and Jon Sutherland

Reviewers

David Ahlstrom, The Chinese University of Hong Kong
Lynn Kahle, Technical University of Denmark
Goh See Kwong, Taylor's University
Tan Wei Lan, Taylor's University

PART ONE
INTRODUCTION

1 Introduction to Global Marketing

LEARNING OBJECTIVES

1-1 Use the product/market growth matrix to explain the various ways a company can expand globally.

1-2 Describe how companies in global industries pursue competitive advantage.

1-3 Compare and contrast a single-country marketing strategy with a global marketing strategy (GMS).

1-4 Identify the companies at the top of the Global 500 rankings.

1-5 Explain the stages a company goes through as its management orientation evolves from domestic and ethnocentric to global and geocentric.

1-6 Discuss the driving and restraining forces affecting global integration today.

CASE 1-1
The Global Marketplace Is Also Local

Consider the following proposition: *We live in a global marketplace.* Apple iPhones, Burberry trench coats, Caterpillar earthmoving equipment, Facebook, LEGO toys, McDonald's restaurants, Samsung HDTVs, and Swatch watches are found practically everywhere on the planet. Global companies are fierce rivals in key markets. For example, American auto industry giants General Motors and Ford are locked in a competitive struggle with Toyota, Hyundai, and other global Asian rivals as well as European companies such as Volkswagen. U.S.-based Intel, the world's largest chip maker, competes with South Korea's Samsung. In the global smartphone market, Apple (United States), Motorola (China), and Samsung are dominant players. The globalization of the appliance industry means that Bosch, Electrolux, Haier Group, LG, and Whirlpool all compete for precious retail floor space and consumer awareness and preference.

Now consider a second proposition: *We live in a world in which markets are local.* In China, for example, Yum! Brands' East Dawning fast-food chain competes with local restaurants such as New Asia Snack and Haidi Lao. Likewise, the best-selling smartphone in China isn't marketed by Samsung or Apple. In fact, the top four smartphone brands in China—Huawei, Vivo, Oppo, and Xiaomi—are all from domestic producers.

In Taiwan, 85C has overtaken Starbucks as the largest chain of coffee shops. In India, Dunkin' Donuts goes head-to-head with local chain Mad Over Doughnuts. In Poland, many consumers frequent small, family-owned shops rather than huge stores operated by France's Carrefour and U.K.–based Tesco.[1] In Southeast Asia, Uber jockeys for position with ride-hailing service Grab. Similarly, Brazilian companies such as Natura Cosméticos and O Boticário compete with Avon for direct-sale customers. Across Latin America, e-commerce giants eBay and Amazon compete with local market leader MercadoLibre.

Exhibit 1-1 Salvatore Ferragamo, based in Florence, Italy, is one of the world's leading fashion brands. Ferragamo and other companies in the luxury sector face challenges as consumer habits change. Historically, the luxury shopper was brand loyal and had an eye for classic designs. Now, many shoppers pursue the "next big thing" via online retail channels.
Source: Roussel Bernard/Alamy Stock Photo.

The "global marketplace versus local markets" paradox lies at the heart of this textbook. In later chapters, we will investigate the nature of local markets in more detail. For now, however, we will focus on the first part of the paradox. Think for a moment about brands and products that are found throughout the world. Ask the average consumer where this global "horn of plenty" comes from, and you'll likely hear a variety of answers. It's certainly true that some brands—McDonald's, Dos Equis, Swatch, Waterford, Ferragamo, Volkswagen, and Burberry, for instance—are strongly identified with a specific country. In much of the world, Coca-Cola and McDonald's are recognized as iconic American brands, just as Ferragamo and Versace are synonymous with classic Italian style (see Exhibit 1-1).

However, for many other products, brands, and companies, the sense of identity with a specific country is becoming blurred. Which brands are Japanese? American? Korean? German? Indian? Can you name the corporate owner of the Nokia smartphone brand? When is a Japanese car *not* a Japanese car? Even U.S. President Donald Trump appeared to be unaware of the global nature of the automobile business when, in 2017, he threatened to slap tariffs on German cars sold in the United States. Consider:

- In 2016, BMW produced 411,000 vehicles at its plant in South Carolina. More than two-thirds of the plant's production is exported, making BMW America's top auto exporter.
- A Mercedes-Benz plant in Alabama produces 300,000 cars annually.
- For several years, the top-selling "American" car (assembled in the United States with at least 75 percent domestic content) was the Toyota Camry.

At the end of this chapter, you will find the rest of Case 1-1. Taken together, the two parts give you the opportunity to learn more about the global marketplace and test your knowledge of current issues in global marketing. You may be surprised at what you learn!

(1-1) Introduction and Overview

◀ **1-1** Use the product/market growth matrix to explain the various ways a company can expand globally.

As the preceding examples illustrate, the global marketplace finds expression in many ways. Some are quite subtle; others are not. While shopping, you may have noticed more multilanguage labeling on your favorite products and brands. Chances are you were one of the millions of people around the world who tuned in to television coverage of the World Cup Soccer championship in 2018. On the highway, you may have seen a semitrailer truck from FedEx's Global Supply Chain Services fleet. Or perhaps you are one of the hundreds of millions of Apple iTunes customers who got a free download of U2's 2014 album *Songs of Innocence*—whether you wanted it or not! When you pick up a pound of Central American coffee at your favorite café, you will find that some beans are labeled Fair Trade Certified.

The growing importance of global marketing is one aspect of a sweeping transformation that has profoundly affected the people and industries of many nations during the past 160 years. International trade has existed for centuries. Beginning in 200 B.C., for example, the legendary Silk Road was a land route connecting China with Mediterranean Europe. From the mid-1800s to the early 1920s, with Great Britain the dominant economic power in the world, international trade flourished. However, a series of global upheavals, including World War I, the Bolshevik Revolution, and the Great Depression, brought that era to an end. Then, following World War II, a new era began. Unparalleled expansion into global markets by companies that previously served only customers located in their respective home countries is one hallmark of this new global era.

Four decades ago, the phrase *global marketing* did not exist. Today, businesspeople use global marketing to realize their companies' full commercial potential. That is why, no matter whether you live in Asia, Europe, North America, or South America, you may be familiar with the brands mentioned in the opening paragraphs of this chapter. However, there is another, even more critical reason why companies need to take global marketing seriously: survival. A management team that fails to understand the importance of global marketing risks losing its domestic business to competitors with lower costs, more experience, and better products.

But what is global marketing? How does it differ from "regular" marketing as it is typically practiced and taught in an introductory course? **Marketing** can be defined as the activity, set of institutions, and processes for creating, communicating, delivering, and exchanging offerings that have value for customers, clients, partners, and society at large.[2] Marketing activities center on an organization's efforts to satisfy customer wants and needs with products and services that offer competitive value. The **marketing mix** (the four Ps of product, price, place, and promotion) represents the contemporary marketer's primary tools in achieving this goal. Marketing is a universal discipline, as applicable in Argentina as it is in Zimbabwe.

This book is about *global marketing*. An organization that engages in **global marketing** focuses its resources and competencies on global market opportunities and threats. A fundamental difference between regular marketing and global marketing is the scope of activities. A company that engages in global marketing conducts important business activities outside the home-country market. The scope issue can be conceptualized in terms of the familiar product/market matrix of growth strategies (see Table 1-1). Some companies pursue a *market development strategy*, which involves seeking new customers by introducing existing products or services to a new market segment or to a new geographical market. Global marketing can also take the form of a *diversification strategy* in which a company creates new product or service offerings targeting a new segment, a new country, or a new region.

Starbucks provides a good case study of a global marketer that can simultaneously execute all four of the growth strategies shown in Table 1-1:

Market penetration: Starbucks is building on its loyalty card and rewards program with a smartphone app that enables customers to pay for purchases electronically. The app displays a bar code that the customer can scan.

Market development: Starbucks entered Italy in 2018, starting with a 25,000-square-foot flagship Reserve Roastery in Milan. Walking distance from the landmark Duomo, the Roastery will offer pastries by local bakery Princi as well as the aperitivo beverages that are so popular throughout Italy.[3]

Product development: Starbucks created a new instant-coffee brand, Via, to enable its customers to enjoy coffee at the office and other locations where brewed coffee is not available. After a successful launch in the United States, Starbucks rolled out Via in Great

TABLE 1-1 Product/Market Growth Matrix

		Product Orientation	
		Existing Products	New Products
Market Orientation	**Existing markets**	Market penetration strategy	Product development strategy
	New markets	Market development strategy	Diversification strategy

Britain, Japan, South Korea, and several other Asian countries. Starbucks also recently introduced its first coffee machine. The Versimo allows Starbucks' customers to "prepare their favorite beverages at home."

Diversification: In 2011, Starbucks dropped the word "Coffee" from its logo. It recently acquired a juice maker, Evolution Fresh; the Bay Bread bakery, and tea retailer Teavana Holdings. Next up: Revamping select stores so they can serve as wine bars and attract new customers in the evening.[4]

To get some practice applying the matrix shown in Table 1-1, create a product/market growth matrix for another global company. IKEA, LEGO, and Walt Disney are all good candidates for this type of exercise.

Companies that engage in global marketing frequently encounter unique or unfamiliar features in specific countries or regions of the world. In China, for example, product counterfeiting and piracy are rampant. Companies doing business there must take extra care to protect their intellectual property and deal with "knockoffs." In some regions of the world, bribery and corruption are deeply entrenched. A successful global marketer understands specific concepts and has a broad and deep understanding of the world's varied business environments.

The global marketer also must understand the strategies that, when skillfully implemented in conjunction with universal marketing fundamentals, increase the likelihood of market success. And, as John Quelch and Katherine Jocz assert, "The best global brands are also the best local brands." That is, managers at global companies understand the importance of local excellence.[5] This book concentrates on the major dimensions of global marketing. A brief overview of marketing is presented next, although the authors assume that the reader has completed an introductory marketing course or has equivalent experience.

(1-2) Principles of Marketing: A Review

◄ **1-2** Describe how companies in global industries pursue competitive advantage.

As defined in the previous section, marketing is one of the functional areas of a business, distinct from finance and operations. Marketing can also be thought of as a set of activities and processes that, along with product design, manufacturing, and transportation logistics, compose a firm's **value chain**. Decisions at every stage, from idea conception to support after the sale, should be assessed in terms of their ability to create value for customers.

For any organization operating anywhere in the world, the essence of marketing is to surpass the competition at the task of creating perceived value—that is, to provide a superior value proposition—for customers. The **value equation** is a guide to this task:

$$\text{Value} = \text{Benefits} / \text{Price (money, time, effort, etc.)}$$

The marketing mix is integral to the value equation because benefits are a combination of the product, the promotion, and the distribution. As a general rule, value, as the customer perceives it, can be increased in these ways. Markets can offer customers an improved bundle of benefits or lower prices (or both!). Marketers may strive to improve the product itself, to design new channels of distribution, to create better communications strategies, or a combination of all three.

Marketers may also seek to increase value by finding ways to cut costs and prices. Nonmonetary costs are also a factor, and marketers may be able to decrease the time and effort that customers must expend to learn about or seek out the product.[6] Companies that use price as a competitive weapon may scour the globe to ensure an ample supply of low-wage labor or access to cheap raw materials. Companies can also reduce prices if costs are low because of process efficiencies in manufacturing or because of economies of scale associated with high production volumes.

Recall the definition of a market: *people or organizations that are both able and willing to buy*. To achieve market success, a product or brand must measure up to a threshold of acceptable quality and be consistent with buyer behavior, expectations, and preferences. If a company is able to offer a combination of superior product, distribution, or promotion benefits *and* lower prices than the competition does, it should enjoy an extremely advantageous position. Toyota, Nissan, and other Japanese automakers made significant gains in the American market in the 1980s by creating a superior value proposition: They offered cars with higher quality, better mileage, and lower prices than those made by General Motors, Ford, and Chrysler.

Today, the auto industry is shifting its attention to emerging markets such as India and Africa. Renault and its rivals are racing to offer middle-class consumers a new value proposition: high-quality vehicles that sell for the equivalent of $10,000 or less. On the heels of Renault's success with the Dacia Logan have come the $2,500 Nano from India's Tata Motors and a $3,000 Datsun from Nissan (see Case 11-1).

Achieving success in global marketing often requires persistence and patience. Following World War II, some of Japan's initial auto exports were market failures. In the late 1960s, for example, Subaru of America began importing the Subaru 360 automobile and selling it for $1,297. After *Consumer Reports* judged the 360 to be unacceptable, sales ground to a halt. Similarly, the Yugo automobile achieved a modest level of U.S. sales in the 1980s (despite a "don't buy" rating from a consumer magazine) because its sticker price of $3,999 made it the cheapest new car available. Low quality was the primary reason for the market failure of both the Subaru 360 and the Yugo.[7] The Subaru story does have a happy ending, however, due in no small measure to the company's decades-long efforts to improve its vehicles. In fact, each year, *Consumer Reports* puts Subaru near the top of its quality rankings, in the same league with Lexus, Mazda, Toyota, and Audi.[8] History has not been so kind to the Yugo: It ended up on *Time* magazine's list of the "50 Worst Cars of All Time."

Even some of the world's biggest, most successful companies stumble while pursuing global opportunities. Walmart's exit from the German market was due, in part, to the fact that German shoppers could find lower prices at "hard discounters" such as Aldi and Lidl. In addition, many German consumers prefer to go to several small shops rather than seek out the convenience of a single, "all-in-one" store located outside a town center. Likewise, U.K.-based Tesco's attempts to enter the U.S. market with its Fresh & Easy stores failed, in part, because U.S. consumers were unfamiliar with the private-label goods that made up much of the merchandise stock. And, in 2015, American "cheap chic" retailer Target terminated its operations in Canada, a victim of missteps in terms of store locations and pricing. The cost for closing 133 stores: more than $5 billion.

Competitive Advantage, Globalization, and Global Industries

When a company succeeds in creating more value for customers than its competitors do, that company is said to enjoy **competitive advantage** in an industry.[9] Competitive advantage is measured relative to rivals in specific industry sectors. For example, your local laundromat is in a local industry; its competitors are local. In a national industry, competitors are national. In a global industry—consumer electronics, apparel, automobiles, steel, pharmaceuticals, furniture, and dozens of other sectors—the competition is, likewise, global (and, in many industries, local as well). Global marketing is essential if a company competes in a global industry or one that is globalizing.

The transformation of formerly local or national industries into global ones is part of a broader economic process of *globalization*, which Jagdish Bhagwati defines as follows:

> Economic globalization constitutes integration of national economies into the international economy through trade, direct foreign investment (by corporations and multinationals), short-term capital flows, international flows of workers and humanity generally, and flows of technology.[10]

From a marketing point of view, globalization presents companies with tantalizing opportunities—and challenges—as executives decide whether to offer their products and services everywhere. At the same time, globalization presents companies with unprecedented opportunities to reconfigure themselves. As John Micklethwait and Adrian Wooldridge put it, the same global bazaar that allows consumers to buy the best that the world can offer also enables producers to find the best partners.[11]

For example, globalization is presenting significant marketing opportunities for professional sports organizations such as the National Basketball Association, the National Football League, and Major League Soccer (see Exhibit 1-2). As Major League Soccer commissioner Don Garber noted, "In the global culture the universal language is soccer. That's the sweet spot. If it weren't for the shrinking world caused by globalization, we wouldn't have the opportunity we have today."[12]

Exhibit 1-2 The National Football League (NFL) promotes American football globally. The NFL is focusing on a handful of key markets, including Canada, China, Germany, Japan, Mexico, and the United Kingdom. Every fall, banners are draped over London's Regent Street to create awareness of the International Series games played before sellout crowds at Wembley Stadium and Twickenham.
Source: Alena Kravchenko/Shutterstock.

Is there more to a global industry than simply "global competition"? Definitely. As defined by management guru Michael Porter, a **global industry** is one in which competitive advantage can be achieved by integrating and leveraging operations on a worldwide scale. Put another way, an industry is global to the extent that a company's industry position in one country is interdependent with its industry position in other countries. Indicators of globalization include the ratio of cross-border trade to total worldwide production, the ratio of cross-border investment to total capital investment, and the proportion of industry revenue generated by companies that compete in all key world regions.[14] One way to determine the degree of globalization in an industry sector is to calculate the ratio of the annual value of global trade in the sector—including the value of components shipped to various countries during the production process—to the annual value of industry sales. In terms of these metrics, the consumer electronics, apparel, automobile, and steel industries are highly globalized.[15]

Achieving competitive advantage in a global industry requires executives and managers to maintain a well-defined strategic focus. **Focus** is simply the concentration of attention on a core business or competence. The importance of focus for a global company is evident in the following comment by Helmut Maucher, former chairman of Nestlé SA:

> Nestlé is focused: We are food and beverages. We are not running bicycle shops. Even in food we are not in all fields. There are certain areas we do not touch. For the time being we have no biscuits [cookies] in Europe and the United States for competitive reasons, and no margarine. We have no soft drinks because I have said we either buy Coca-Cola or we leave it alone. This is focus.[16]

Sometimes, however, company management may choose to initiate a change in focus as part of an overall strategy shift. Even Coca-Cola has been forced to sharpen its focus on its core beverage brands. Following sluggish sales for that company in 2000 and 2001, former chairman and chief executive Douglas Daft formed a new alliance with Nestlé that jointly developed and marketed coffees and teas. Daft also set about the task of transforming Coca-Cola's Minute Maid unit into a global division that markets a variety of juice brands worldwide. As Daft explained:

> We're a network of brands and businesses. You don't just want to be a total beverage company. Each brand has a different return on investment, is sold differently, drunk for different reasons, and has different managing structures. If you mix them all together, you lose the focus.[17]

"We believe a company can only think in one set of terms. If you are premium, you have to focus on it."[13]

Helmut Panke, former chairman, Bayerische Motoren Werke (BMW) AG

Exhibit 1-3 The Dragon Bridge in Da Nang is a major tourist attraction. The LED lighting is provided by Philips.
Source: Huu Dai Trinh/Alamy Stock Photo.

Examples abound of corporate executives addressing the issue of focus, often in response to changes in the global business environment. In recent years, Bertelsmann, Colgate, Danone, Electrolux, Fiat, Ford, Fortune Brands, General Motors, Harley-Davidson, Henkel, LEGO, McDonald's, Royal Philips, Toshiba, Vivendi, and many other companies have stepped up their efforts to sharpen their strategic focus on core businesses and brands.

Specific actions can take a number of different forms; in addition to alliances, these can include mergers, acquisitions, divestitures, and folding some businesses into other company divisions (see Table 1-2). At Royal Philips, CEO Frans van Houten has shed the electronics and engineering units; instead of marketing TV sets and VCRs, today's Philips is focused on three sectors: health care, lighting, and consumer lifestyle (see Exhibit 1-3). Major changes in the organizational structure such as these must also be accompanied by changes in corporate culture.[18]

Value, competitive advantage, and the focus required to achieve them are universal in their relevance, and they should guide marketing efforts in any part of the world. Global marketing requires attention to these issues on a worldwide basis and utilization of a business intelligence system capable of monitoring the globe for opportunities and threats. A fundamental premise of this book can be stated as follows: Companies that understand and engage in global marketing can offer more overall value to customers than companies that do not have such understanding. Many business managers and pundits share this conviction. In the mid-1990s, for example, C. Samuel Craig and Susan P. Douglas noted:

> Globalization is no longer an abstraction but a stark reality.... Choosing not to participate in global markets is no longer an option. All firms, regardless of their size, have to craft strategies in the broader context of world markets to anticipate, respond, and adapt to the changing configuration of these markets.[19]

Companies in a range of industries are "going global." For example, three Italian furniture companies have joined together to increase sales outside of Italy and ward off increased competition from Asia. Luxury goods purveyors such as LVMH and Prada Group provided the model for the new business entity, which unites Poltrona Frau, Cassina, and Cappellini.[20] Hong Kong's Tai

TABLE 1-2 Strategic Focus

Company/Headquarters	Divestiture/Buyer
General Electric (United States)	Appliance division, sold to Haier (China) for $5.4 billion (2016); NBC Universal, sold to Comcast for $30 billion (2009).
Vivendi (France)	Activision Blizzard videogame unit, management buyout for $8.2 billion (2013).
Unilever (United Kingdom/Netherlands)	American pasta sauce business, sold to Mizkan Group (Japan) for $2.15 billion (2014).
IBM (United States)	Microelectronics division, sold to Global Foundries for $1.5 billion (2014).

Ping Carpets International is also globalizing. Top managers have been dispersed to different parts of the world; while the finance and technology functions are still in Hong Kong, the marketing chief is based in New York City and the head of operations is in Singapore. As company director John Ying noted, "We're trying to create a minimultinational."[21]

Many gains can be ascribed to globalization. Hundreds of millions of people have been lifted from poverty and have joined the middle class. In countries where globalization has raised wages, living standards have improved. Even so, popular sentiment has been shifting, and a note of caution is in order. A mounting body of evidence indicates that the gains from globalization have not been evenly distributed. A disproportionate amount of wealth has flowed to the "have lots" and "have yachts," with not enough going to the "have nots." U.S. President Donald Trump's "America First" agenda is just one example of the way some nations are retreating into protectionism and isolation. Some industry observers have noted that we are entering a new era of "globalization in reverse."

(1-3) Global Marketing: What it is and What it isn't

◀ **1-3** Compare and contrast a single-country marketing strategy with a global marketing strategy (GMS).

The discipline of marketing is universal. It is natural, however, that marketing practices will vary from country to country for the simple reason that the countries and peoples of the world are different. These differences mean that a marketing approach that has proved successful in one country will not *necessarily* succeed in another country. Customer preferences, competitors, channels of distribution, and communication media may differ. An important managerial task in global marketing is learning to recognize the extent to which it is possible to extend marketing plans and programs worldwide, as well as the extent to which adaptation is required.

The way a company addresses this task is a manifestation of its **global marketing strategy (GMS)**. In single-country marketing, strategy development addresses two fundamental issues: choosing a target market and developing a marketing mix. The same two issues are at the heart of a firm's GMS, although they are viewed from a somewhat different perspective (see Table 1-3). *Global market participation* is the extent to which a company has operations in major world markets. *Standardization versus adaptation* is the extent to which each marketing mix element is standardized (i.e., executed the same way) or adapted (i.e., executed in different ways) in various country markets. For example, Nike recently adopted the slogan "Here I am" for its pan-European clothing advertising targeting women. The decision to drop the famous "Just do it" tagline in the region was based on research indicating that college-age women in Europe are not as competitive about sports as men are.[22]

GMS has three additional dimensions that pertain to marketing management. First, *concentration of marketing activities* is the extent to which activities related to the marketing mix (e.g., promotional campaigns or pricing decisions) are performed in one or a few country

TABLE 1-3 Comparison of Single-Country Marketing Strategy and Global Marketing Strategy

Single-Country Marketing Strategy	Global Marketing Strategy
Target market strategy	Global market participation
Marketing mix development	Marketing mix development
Product	Product adaptation or standardization
Price	Price adaptation or standardization
Promotion	Promotion adaptation or standardization
Place	Place adaptation or standardization
	Concentration of marketing activities
	Coordination of marketing activities
	Integration of competitive moves

THE CULTURAL CONTEXT

"1-2-3-4!" 40 Years of Punk Rock, 1976–2016

Rock music has often served as a cultural manifestation of youth movements. In 1960's "swinging London," for example, the Beatles, the Rolling Stones, and other British Invasion bands set new trends in sound and style. On the other side of the Atlantic Ocean, American rock groups such as the Grateful Dead and the Jefferson Airplane gave voice to the era's political and social turmoil during the "Summer of Love."

In 1976, a new sound emerged. Punk rock was both a musical and a cultural movement. On the musical side, it represented a visceral reaction to, and repudiation of, the prevailing musical styles and tastes of the time. Giant stadium concerts by English progressive rock bands such as Genesis, Pink Floyd, and Yes had become overblown spectacles. Southern California soft-rock, a genre popularized by the Eagles, Linda Ronstadt, and singer-songwriter Jackson Browne, was equally distasteful to the punks.

Punk also offered an outlet for the voices of disenfranchised young people and an opportunity to rebel against the establishment. In the United Kingdom in the mid-1970s, the country's economic stagnation meant there were few job opportunities for young people—as well as their elders. The government's decision to conserve coal supplies resulted in power shortages and mandatory three-day working weeks. During the same time period, New York City was in social and economic decline. In the summer of 1976, a serial killer known as the Son of Sam was terrorizing the area. Across America, the energy crisis meant rising prices for gasoline and shortages.

It was in this musical and economic context that young people in both the United States and the United Kingdom discovered that it was relatively easy to learn to play two or three guitar chords. Even better, punk's "DIY" ethos meant that musicianship was often beside the point. Who needs technique? Who cares what the notes are?

In the United States, punk scenes sprang up on both coasts. Forest Hills, New York, was the breeding ground for the Ramones. Seymour Stein, the Sire Records chief who signed the band to his label, says simply, "New York City needed an infusion." At the legendary CBGB ("Country Bluegrass Blues") music club in New York's East Village, the Ramones shared the stage with the Talking Heads, Blondie, and other new bands that were part of the local art-rock scene.

Key to the Ramones' sound was concise pop songwriting; many songs ranged in length from a mere two minutes (or less) to under three minutes. The look was important, too; the band members carefully cultivated an outcast image by wearing black leather biker jackets and ripped jeans. None of the four was actually named Ramone. Even so, the band was often referred to as "Da Brudders."

On the U.S. West Coast, a punk scene took shape when bands such as X and Black Flag were formed in Los Angeles. As John Doe, bassist and vocalist for X, recalls, "Rock and roll needed to be hit upside the head!" Despite being dismissed by the mainstream rock world, punk flourished in L.A. as a minority movement in clubs such as the Mask.

In the United Kingdom, the Sex Pistols burst onto the scene in 1976. The Clash, X-Ray Spex and a host of others followed and quickly gained fame and notoriety (see Exhibit 1-4). In July 1976, the Ramones played a landmark show at the Roundhouse in London that some observers credit with sparking the U.K. punk movement. In November 1976, the Sex Pistols released their debut single, "Anarchy in the UK," on the EMI label.

The following month, the Sex Pistols caused a national furor by swearing on-camera during a live interview with Thames Television presenter Bill Grundy. When Grundy asked what the band had done with its £40,000 advance from EMI, guitarist Steve Jones replied, "We f**kin' spent it, didn't we?" The following day, the headline in *The Daily Mirror* trumpeted, "The Filth and the Fury!" Grundy was fired. (The entire spectacle can viewed on YouTube.)

Vivian Goldman, a former features editor who covered punk for *Sounds*, a weekly British music paper, notes that punk's relevance and impact continue today. "In Indonesia, Russia, South Africa, and elsewhere, people use punk to rage against the system," she said recently. "Punk's rebel consciousness represents a flag for a new way of thinking."

Sources: Peter Aspden, "Infamy in the UK," *Financial Times* (June 11–12, 2016), p. 14; Anna Russell, "Punk Takes London by Storm, Again," *The Wall Street Journal* (March 25, 2016), p. D6; "Musical Milestones: Celebrating 40 Years of the Ramones," Conference Presentation, SXSW Music, Film, and Interactive, March 17, 2016; "No Future: 1976 and the Birth of Punk in the UK," Conference Presentation, SXSW Music, Film, and Interactive, March 16, 2016; Mikal Gilmore, "The Curse of the Ramones: How a Band of Misfits Launched Punk Rock," *Rolling Stone* (April 21, 2016), pp. 42–48+; Tom DeSavia and John Doe, *Under the Big Black Sun: A Personal History of L.A. Punk* (Boston, MA: Da Capo Press, 2016); Tim Jackson, *Virgin King: Inside Richard Branson's Business Empire* (London, UK: Harper Collins Publishers, 1995), Chapter 3, "Broken Bottles."

Exhibit 1-4 Among punk's positive social effects was the empowerment of women. For example, Exene Cervenka fronted L.A. punk band X, and Poly Styrene (shown here) was the singer for London's X-Ray Spex.
Source: Pictorial Press Ltd/Alamy Stock Photo.

locations. Second, *coordination of marketing activities* refers to the extent to which marketing activities related to the marketing mix are planned and executed interdependently around the globe. Third, *integration of competitive moves* is the extent to which a firm's competitive marketing tactics in different parts of the world are interdependent. The GMS should enhance the firm's performance on a worldwide basis.[23]

The decision to enter one or more particular markets outside the home country depends on a company's resources, its managerial mind-set, and the nature of opportunities and threats. Today, most observers agree that Brazil, Russia, India, China, and South Africa—five emerging markets known collectively as BRICS—represent significant growth opportunities. Mexico, Indonesia, Nigeria, and Turkey—the so-called MINTs—also hold great potential. Throughout this text, marketing issues in these countries are highlighted in "Emerging Markets Briefing Book" boxes.

We can use Burberry as a case study in global marketing strategy. This U.K.-based luxury brand is available in scores of countries, and Burberry's recent expansion plans emphasize several geographical areas (see Exhibit 1-5). First are the BRICS nations, where growing numbers of middle-class consumers are developing a taste for luxury brands. Second is the United States, which is dotted with shopping malls whose managers are anxious to entice crowd-pulling luxury goods retailers by sharing fit-out costs and offering attractive, rent-free periods. Under former CEO Angela Ahrendts, Burberry's marketing mix strategy included the following elements:

Product: Intensify focus on accessories. Boost sales of handbags, belts, and accessories—products whose sales are less cyclical than sales of clothing. Burberry Bespoke allows customers to design their own coats.

Price: "Affordable luxury" is central to the value proposition: more expensive than Coach, less expensive than Prada.

Place: Burberry is opening more independent stores in key U.S. cities, including flagship stores in Los Angeles, San Francisco, and New York; it is also expanding in London and Hong Kong. Such locations generate more than half the company's revenue and profit.[24]

Promotion: Encourage advocacy and sharing via social media and online channels such as Twitter, Instagram, and www.artofthetrench.com. Launch Burberry Acoustic to enhance brand relevance and to provide exposure for emerging music talent via www.burberry.com/acoustic.

As you can see in Table 1-3, the next part of the GMS involves the concentration and coordination of marketing activities. At Burberry, haphazard growth had led to a federation of individual operations. Company units in some parts of the world didn't talk to each other. In some cases, they

Exhibit 1-5 Thomas Burberry is credited with inventing gabardine fabric in the 1850s, paving the way for creation of the trench coat. England's Burberry Group celebrated its 160th anniversary in 2016. The Burberry trademark is registered in more than 90 countries.
Source: Oli Scarff/Getty Images.

competed *against* each other, and sometimes designed their own products for their own markets and wouldn't share ideas with other parts of the business. During her tenure as CEO, Angela Ahrendts was very clear in articulating her core strategic vision: Leverage the Franchise. In other words: "One company, one brand."[25]

When Christopher Bailey became CEO in 2014, he set about refining and updating Ahrendts' strategies with an approach he called "Inspire with the Brand." Bailey used data analytics to leverage consumer insights gleaned from Burberry's strong digital presence and its worldwide network of brick-and-mortar stores to project a consistent brand voice.[26] Collaborations with musicians also became integral to Bailey's strategy; he even designed the sequined gown global superstar Adele wore on her 2016 world tour! Bailey also embraced multichannel marketing, adding more mobile marketing to the existing mix of retail and wholesale channels.

An Italian businessman, Marco Gobetti, took over as Burberry's CEO in 2017. He faces a number of new challenges to the company's global marketing strategy, including the declining popularity of department store shopping in the United States and slowing sales of luxury goods in China.[27]

The issue of standardization versus adaptation in global marketing has been at the center of a long-standing controversy among both academicians and business practitioners. Much of the controversy dates back to Professor Theodore Levitt's 1983 article "The Globalization of Markets" in the *Harvard Business Review*. Levitt argued that marketers were confronted with a "homogeneous global village." He advised organizations to develop standardized, high-quality world products and market them around the globe by using standardized advertising, pricing, and distribution. Some well-publicized failures by Parker Pen and other companies that had tried to follow Levitt's advice brought his proposals into question. The business press frequently quoted industry observers who disputed Levitt's views. As Carl Spielvogel, chairman and CEO of the Backer Spielvogel Bates Worldwide advertising agency, told *The Wall Street Journal* in the late 1980s, "Theodore Levitt's comment about the world becoming homogenized is bunk. There are about two products that lend themselves to global marketing—and one of them is Coca-Cola."[28]

Global marketing is the key to Coke's worldwide success—but that success was *not* based on a total standardization of marketing mix elements. For example, Coca-Cola achieved success in Japan by spending a great deal of time and money to become an insider; the company built a complete local infrastructure with its sales force and vending machine operations. Coke's success in Japan is a function of its ability to achieve global localization, by being as much of an insider as a local company, yet still reaping the benefits that result from world-scale operations. Although the Coca-Cola Company has experienced a recent sales decline in Japan, that country remains a key market that accounts for about 20 percent of total worldwide operating revenues.[29]

What does the phrase *global localization* really mean? In a nutshell, it means that a successful global marketer must have the ability to "think globally and act locally." Kenichi Ohmae summed up this paradox as follows:

> The essence of being a global company is to maintain a kind of tension within the organization without being undone by it. Some companies say the new world requires homogeneous products—"one size fits all"—everywhere. Others say the world requires endless customization—special products for every region. The best global companies understand it's neither and it's both. They keep the two perspectives in mind simultaneously.[30]

As we will see many times in this book, *global* marketing may include a combination of standard (e.g., the actual product itself) and nonstandard (e.g., distribution or packaging) approaches. A global product may be the same product everywhere and yet different. Global marketing requires marketers to think and act in a way that is both global *and* local by responding to similarities and differences in world markets.

But it is important to bear in mind that "global localization" is a two-way street, and that there is more to the story than "think globally, act locally." Many companies are learning that it is equally important to *think locally and act globally*. In practice, this means that companies are discovering the value of leveraging innovations that occur far from headquarters and transporting them back home. For example, McDonald's restaurants in France don't look like McDonald's restaurants elsewhere. Décor colors are muted, and the golden arches are displayed more subtly. After seeing the sales increases posted in France, some American franchisees began undertaking similar renovations. As *Burger Business* newsletter editor Scott Hume has noted, "Most of the

"The more things globalize, the more people want to affiliate with everything that is local. This has led to unbelievable fragmentation."[31]

Peter Ter Kulve, Chief Transformation Officer, Unilever

"One of the top-level lessons is that we have done much more local market customization in India than we did in China."[33]

Jeff Bezos, CEO, Amazon

TABLE 1-4 Think Locally/Act Globally

Company/Headquarters Country	Product
Cinnabon/USA	Cinnabon customers in Central and South America prefer dulce de leche. Products developed for those regions are being introduced in the United States, where the Hispanic population is a key segment.[35]
Starbucks/USA	Starbucks opened an experimental store in Amsterdam that serves as a testing ground for new design concepts such as locally sourced and recycled building materials. The best concepts will be extended to other parts of Europe. *Fast Company* magazine included Liz Muller, Director of Creative Design at Starbucks, in its "Most Creative People 2013" ranking.
Kraft Foods/USA	Tang drink powder became a $1 billion brand as regional managers in Latin America and the Middle East moved beyond orange (the top-seller) into popular local flavors such as mango and pineapple. Kraft plans to reboot Tang in the U.S. market using lessons learned abroad.[36]

interesting ideas of McDonald's are coming from *outside* the U.S. McDonald's is becoming a European chain with stores in the U.S."[32] (see Case 1-2).

These reverse flows of innovation are not occurring just between developed regions such as Western Europe and North America. The growing economic power of China, India, and other emerging markets means that many innovations originate there (see Table 1-4). For example, Nestlé, Procter & Gamble, Unilever, and other consumer products companies are learning that low-cost products with less packaging developed for low-income consumers also appeal to cost-conscious consumers in, say, Spain and Greece (see Exhibit 1-6).[34]

The Coca-Cola Company supports its Coke, Fanta, and Powerade brands with marketing mix elements that are both global and local. Dozens of other companies also have successfully pursued global marketing by creating strong global brands, in various ways. In consumer electronics, Apple is synonymous with hardware and software integration, ease of use, cutting-edge innovation, and high-tech design. In appliances, Germany's reputation for engineering and manufacturing excellence is a source of competitive advantage for Bosch (see Exhibit 1-7). Italy's Benetton utilizes a sophisticated distribution system to quickly deliver the latest fashions to its worldwide network of stores. The backbone of Caterpillar's global success is a network of dealers who

Exhibit 1-6 For Nestlé, innovation is the key to its expanded presence in emerging markets such as Thailand, Sri Lanka, and Mali. Recently, Nestlé introduced mobile coffee carts from which vendors sell single servings of Nescafé brand coffee. Some of these innovations are being transferred to high-income countries in Europe and elsewhere.
Source: adrian arbib/Alamy.

Exhibit 1-7 MILAN - ITALY - APRIL 2012: Salone internazionale del mobile 2012, furniture fair, Bosch.
Source: A. Astes/Alamy Stock Photo.

support the company's promise of "24-hour parts and service" anywhere in the world. As these examples indicate, there are many different paths to success in global markets. In this book, we do *not* propose that global marketing is a knee-jerk attempt to impose a totally standardized approach on marketing around the world. Instead, a central issue in global marketing is how to tailor the global marketing concept to fit particular products, businesses, and markets.[37]

As shown in Table 1-5, McDonald's global marketing strategy is based on a combination of global and local marketing mix elements. For example, a vital element in McDonald's business model is a restaurant system that can be set up virtually anywhere in the world. McDonald's offers core menu items—hamburgers, french fries, and soft drinks—in most countries, and the company also customizes menu offerings in accordance with local eating customs. The average price of a Big Mac in the United States is $5.28. By contrast, in China, Big Macs sell for the equivalent of $3.17. In absolute terms, Chinese Big Macs are cheaper than American ones. But is it a fair comparison? Real estate costs vary from country to country, as do per capita incomes.

TABLE 1-5 Examples of Effective Global Marketing: McDonald's

Marketing Mix Element	Standardized	Localized
Product	Big Mac	McAloo Tikka potato burger, Chicken Maharaja Mac (India); Rye McFeast (Finland); Adagio (Italy)
Promotion	Brand name	Slang nicknames—for example, Mickey D's (United States, Canada), Macky D's (United Kingdom, Ireland), Macca's (Australia), Mäkkäri (Finland), MakDo (Philippines), McDo (France)
	Advertising slogan "i'm lovin' it"	*"Venez comme vous êtes"* ("Come as you are") television ad campaign in France. Various executions show individuals expressing different aspects of their respective personalities. One features a young man dining with his father. The ad's creative strategy centers on sexual freedom and rebellion: The father does not realize that his son is gay.
Place	Freestanding restaurants in high-traffic public areas	McDonald's Switzerland operates themed dining cars on the Swiss national rail system; McDonald's is served on the Stena Line ferry from Helsinki to Oslo; home delivery (India)
Price	Average price of Big Mac is $5.28 (United States)	$5.91 (Norway); $3.17 (China)

The approach to global marketing that a company adopts will depend on industry conditions, shifting economic realities, and its source or sources of competitive advantage. For example:

Harley-Davidson's motorcycles are perceived around the world as *the* all-American bike. Should Harley-Davidson start manufacturing motorcycles in a low-wage country such as Thailand?

The success of Honda and Toyota in world markets was initially based on exporting cars from factories in Japan. Today, both companies operate manufacturing and assembly facilities in the Americas, Asia, and Europe. From these sites, the automakers both supply customers in the local market and export their products to the rest of the world. For example, each year Honda exports tens of thousands of Accords and Civics from U.S. plants to Japan and dozens of other countries. Will European consumers continue to buy Honda vehicles exported from America? Will American consumers continue to snap up American-built Toyotas?

Uniqlo, a division of Japan's Fast Retailing, operates approximately 850 stores in Japan and 300 stores in 12 overseas countries. The company sources 90 percent of its clothing from China. Uniqlo currently has 46 stores in the United States; its plans call for a total of 200 U.S. stores by 2020. Can the company achieve its goal of reaching $50 billion in sales by 2020, thereby becoming the world's number 1 apparel retailer?

The answer to these questions is: It all depends. Although Harley-Davidson's competitive advantage is based, in part, on its "Made in the USA" positioning, the company has shifted some production outside the United States. India's 100 percent tariff on imported motorcycles prompted Harley-Davidson to launch production in the state of Haryana in 2011. To further capitalize on market opportunities in Asia, and to avoid import tariffs that can go as high as 60 percent, the company recently opened a manufacturing facility in Thailand.[38]

Toyota's success in the United States was originally attributable to its ability to transfer world-class manufacturing skills—"the Toyota Way"—to its U.S. plants while using advertising to inform prospective customers that American workers build the Avalon, Camry, and Tundra models, with many components purchased from American suppliers. The U.S. market generates approximately two-thirds of Toyota's profits. However, in its drive to become the world's top automaker, Toyota's insular corporate culture and focus on cost cutting compromised overall product quality. Under the leadership of Akio Toyoda, the company has rebounded. It sold 10.2 million cars in 2016 and posted record profits; an innovative production system, dubbed Toyota New Global Architecture, is designed to ensure that Toyota can respond quickly to market changes in any part of the world.[39]

As noted, about one-fourth of Uniqlo's 1,200 stores are located outside Japan; key country markets include the United States, China, Russia, Singapore, and South Korea. Shoppers have responded favorably to Uniqlo's colorful designs and the high service standards for which Japanese retailers are famous. According to A. T. Kearney's 2016 Global Retail Development Index, China is the number 1–ranked emerging market opportunity for retail. In China, Uniqlo's management team selectively targets cities with high population densities such as Beijing and Shanghai (see Exhibit 1-8).[40]

▶ **1-4** Identify the companies at the top of the Global 500 rankings.

(1-4) The Importance of Global Marketing

The largest single market in the world in terms of national income is the United States, representing roughly 25 percent of the total world market for all products and services. U.S. companies that wish to achieve their maximum growth potential must "go global," however, because 75 percent of world market potential is outside their home country. Management at Coca-Cola clearly understands this; about 75 percent of the company's operating income and two-thirds of its operating revenue are generated outside North America.

Non-U.S. companies have an even greater motivation to seek market opportunities beyond their own borders; their opportunities include the 325 million people in the United States. For example, even though the dollar value of the home market for Japanese companies is the third largest in the world (after the United States and China), the market *outside* Japan is 90 percent of the world potential. For European countries, the picture is even more dramatic. Even though Germany is the largest single-country market in Europe, 94 percent of the world market potential for German companies is outside Germany.

Many companies have recognized the importance of conducting business activities outside their home country. Industries that were essentially national in scope only a few years ago are dominated today by a handful of global companies. In most industries, the companies that will survive and prosper in the twenty-first century will be global enterprises. Some companies that fail to formulate adequate responses to the challenges and opportunities of globalization will be absorbed by more dynamic, visionary enterprises. Others will undergo wrenching transformations and, if their efforts succeed, will emerge from the process greatly transformed. Some companies will simply disappear.

Each year, *Fortune* magazine compiles a ranking of the 500 largest service and manufacturing companies by revenues.[41] Walmart stands atop the 2016 Global 500 rankings, with revenues of

Exhibit 1-8 Japan's Fast Retailing competes with global companies such as Inditex (Spain), H&M (Sweden), and Gap (U.S.). Fast Retailing founder Tadashi Yanai intends to create the world's biggest apparel retail operation by 2020.
Source: August_0802/ Shutterstock.

$486 billion; it currently generates only about one-third of its revenues outside the United States. However, global expansion is key to Walmart's growth strategy. In all, 5 companies in the top 10 compete in the oil or energy sectors. Toyota and Volkswagen, the only global automakers in the top 10, are locked in a fierce competitive struggle as the German company rebounds from a scandal involving its diesel engines.

Examining the size of individual product markets, measured in terms of annual sales, provides another perspective on global marketing's importance. Many of the companies identified in the *Fortune* rankings are key players in the global marketplace.

(1-5) Management Orientations

◀ **1-5** Explain the stages a company goes through as its management orientation evolves from domestic and ethnocentric to global and geocentric.

The form and substance of a company's response to global market opportunities depend greatly on its management's assumptions or beliefs—both conscious and unconscious—about the nature of the world. The worldview of a company's personnel can be described as ethnocentric, polycentric, regiocentric, or geocentric—collectively known as the EPRG framework.[42] This orientation may change over time. Management at a company with a prevailing ethnocentric orientation may, for example, consciously make a decision to move in the direction of geocentricism.

Ethnocentric Orientation

A person who assumes that his or her home country is superior to the rest of the world is said to have an **ethnocentric orientation**. Ethnocentrism is sometimes associated with attitudes of national arrogance or assumptions of national superiority; it can also manifest itself as indifference to marketing opportunities outside the home country. Company personnel with an ethnocentric orientation see only similarities in markets and *assume* that products and practices that succeed in the home country will succeed anywhere.

At some companies, the ethnocentric orientation means that opportunities outside the home country are largely ignored. Such companies are sometimes called *domestic companies*. Ethnocentric companies that conduct business outside the home country can be described as *international companies*; they adhere to the notion that the products that succeed in the home country are superior. This point of view leads to a **standardized or extension approach** to marketing based on the premise that products can be sold everywhere without adaptation.

As the following examples illustrate, an ethnocentric orientation can take a variety of forms:

Nissan's earliest exports were cars and trucks that had been designed for mild Japanese winters; the vehicles were difficult to start in many parts of the United States during the cold winter months. In northern Japan, many car owners would put blankets over the hoods of their cars. Nissan's assumption was that Americans would do the same thing. As a Nissan spokesman said, "We tried for a long time to design cars in Japan and shove them down the American consumer's throat. That didn't work very well."[43]

Until the 1980s, Eli Lilly and Company operated as an ethnocentric company: Activity outside the United States was tightly controlled by headquarters, and the focus was on selling products originally developed for the U.S. market.[44]

For many years, executives at California's Robert Mondavi Corporation operated the company as an ethnocentric international entity. As former CEO Michael Mondavi explained, "Robert Mondavi was a local winery that thought locally, grew locally, produced locally, and sold globally.... To be a truly global company, I believe it's imperative to grow and produce great wines in the world in the best wine-growing regions of the world, regardless of the country or the borders."[45]

The cell phone divisions of Toshiba, Sharp, and other Japanese companies prospered by focusing on the domestic market. When handset sales in Japan slowed a few years ago, the Japanese companies realized that Nokia, Motorola, and Samsung already dominated key world markets. Atsutoshi Nishida, president of Toshiba, noted, "We were thinking only about Japan. We really missed our chance."[46]

In the ethnocentric international company, foreign operations or markets are typically viewed as being secondary or subordinate to domestic ones. (We are using the term *domestic* to mean the country in which a company is headquartered.) An ethnocentric company operates under the assumption that headquarters' "tried-and-true" knowledge and organizational capabilities can be applied in other parts of the world. Although this assumption can sometimes work to a company's advantage, valuable managerial knowledge and experience in local markets may go unnoticed. Even if customer needs or wants diverge from those in the home country, those differences are often ignored at headquarters.

Sixty years ago, most business enterprises—and especially those located in a large country like the United States—could operate quite successfully with an ethnocentric orientation. Today, however, ethnocentrism is one of the major internal weaknesses that must be overcome if a company is to transform itself into an effective global competitor.

Polycentric Orientation

The **polycentric orientation** is the opposite of ethnocentrism. The term *polycentric* describes management's belief or assumption that each country in which a company does business is unique. This assumption lays the groundwork for each subsidiary to develop its own unique business and marketing strategies so as to succeed; the term *multinational company* is often used to describe such a structure. This point of view leads to a **localized or adaptation approach** that assumes products must be adapted in response to different market conditions. Examples of companies and business units with a polycentric orientation include the following:

> At Procter & Gamble, one of Pampers' many problems in the 1990s was that various regional groups and 80-plus country teams were all acting independently. P&G executives knew they had to address the issue in Pampers' two biggest organizations, Pampers Europe (run by an Austrian) and Pampers North America (run by an American). The two executives were not collaborating, thereby stifling any potential for their organizations to cooperate in solving the global challenges Pampers faced in research and development, design, manufacturing, and marketing.[48]

> Unilever, the Anglo-Dutch consumer products company, once exhibited a polycentric orientation. For example, its Rexona deodorant brand had 30 different package designs and 48 different formulations. Advertising was also executed on a local basis. Top management spent a decade changing Unilever's strategic orientation by implementing a reorganization plan that centralizes authority and reduces the power of local country managers.[49]

Regiocentric Orientation

In a company with a **regiocentric orientation**, a region becomes the relevant geographic unit; management's goal is to develop an integrated regional strategy. What does *regional* mean in this context? A U.S. company that focuses on the countries included in the North American Free Trade Agreement (NAFTA)—namely, the United States, Canada, and Mexico—has a regiocentric orientation. Similarly, a European company that focuses its attention on Europe is regiocentric. Some companies serve markets throughout the world, but do so on a regional basis. Such a company could be viewed as a variant of the multinational model discussed previously.

For decades, a regiocentric orientation prevailed at General Motors: Executives in different parts of the world—Asia-Pacific and Europe, for example—were given considerable autonomy when designing vehicles for their respective regions. Company engineers in Australia, for example, developed models for sale in the local market. One result of this approach was that a total of 270 different types of radios were being installed in GM vehicles around the world. As GM Vice Chairman Robert Lutz told an interviewer in 2004, "GM's global product plan used to be four regional plans stapled together."[50]

Geocentric Orientation

A company with a **geocentric orientation** views the entire world as a potential market and strives to develop integrated global strategies. A company whose management has adopted a geocentric orientation is sometimes known as a *global* or *transnational company*.[51] During the past several years, long-standing regiocentric policies at GM, such as those just discussed, have been replaced by a geocentric approach. Among other changes, the new policy calls for engineering jobs to be assigned on a worldwide basis, with a global council based in Detroit determining the allocation of the company's $7 billion annual product development budget. One goal of the geocentric approach: to save 40 percent in radio costs by using a total of 50 different radios.

It is a positive sign that, at many companies, management realizes the need to adopt a geocentric orientation. However, the transition to new structures and organizational forms can take time to bear fruit. As new global competitors emerge on the scene, management at long-established industry giants such as GM must face up to the challenge of organizational transformation. More than a decade ago, Louis R. Hughes, a GM executive, said, "We are on our way to becoming a transnational corporation." Basil Drossos, former president of GM de Argentina, echoed his colleague's words: "We are talking about becoming a global corporation as opposed to a multinational company; that implies that the centers of expertise may reside anywhere they best reside."[53] In 2008, Toyota sold more vehicles worldwide than GM for the first time. When GM emerged from bankruptcy in 2009, it did so as a smaller, leaner company.

A global company can be further described as one that either pursues a strategy of serving world markets from a single country, or sources globally for the purposes of focusing on specific country markets. In addition, global companies tend to retain their association with a particular headquarters country. Until recently, Harley-Davidson served world markets from the United States exclusively. Similarly, all the production for luxury fashion marketer Tod's takes place in Italy.

By contrast, Uniqlo sources its apparel from low-wage countries; a sophisticated supply chain ensures timely delivery to its network of stores. Benetton pursues a mixed approach, sourcing some of its apparel from Italy and some from low-wage countries. Harley-Davidson, Tod's, Uniqlo, and Benetton may all be thought of as global companies.

Transnational companies serve global markets and use global supply chains, which often results in a blurring of national identity. A true transnational would be characterized as "stateless." Toyota and Honda are two examples of companies that exhibit key characteristics of transnationality. At global and transnational companies, management uses a combination of standardized (extension) and localized (adaptation) elements in the marketing program. A key factor that distinguishes global and transnational companies from their international or multinational counterparts is *mind-set*: At global and transnational companies, decisions regarding extension and adaptation are not based on assumptions, but rather made on the basis of ongoing research into market needs and wants.

One way to assess a company's "degree of transnationality" is to compute an average of three ratios: (1) sales outside the home country to total sales, (2) assets outside the home country to total assets, and (3) employees outside the home country to total employees. Viewed in terms of these metrics, Nestlé, Unilever, Royal Philips Electronics, GlaxoSmithKline, and the News Corporation can also be categorized as transnational companies. Each is headquartered in a relatively small home-country market—a fact of life that has compelled the company's management to adopt a regiocentric or geocentric orientation to achieve revenue and profit growth.

The geocentric orientation represents a synthesis of ethnocentrism and polycentrism; it is a "worldview" that sees similarities and differences in markets and countries and seeks to create a global strategy that is fully responsive to local needs and wants. A regiocentric manager might be said to have a worldview on a regional scale; the world outside the region of interest will be viewed with an ethnocentric or a polycentric orientation, or a combination of the two. However, research suggests that many companies are seeking to strengthen their regional competitiveness rather than move directly to develop global responses to changes in the competitive environment.[54]

The ethnocentric company is centralized in its marketing management; the polycentric company is decentralized; and regiocentric and geocentric companies are integrated on a regional or global scale, respectively. A crucial difference among the various orientations is the underlying assumption for each. The ethnocentric orientation is based on a belief in home-country superiority. The underlying assumption of the polycentric approach is that there are so many differences in cultural, economic, and marketing conditions in the world that it is futile to attempt to transfer experience across national boundaries. A key challenge facing organizational leaders today is managing a company's evolution beyond an ethnocentric, polycentric, or regiocentric orientation to a geocentric one. As noted in one highly regarded book on global business, "The multinational solution encounters problems by ignoring a number of organizational impediments to the implementation of a global strategy and underestimating the impact of global competition."[55]

"These days everyone in the Midwest is begging Honda to come into their hometown. It is no longer viewed as a 'Japanese' company, but a 'pro-American-worker corporation' flush with jobs, jobs, jobs."[52]

Douglas Brinkley, Professor of History, Tulane University

ENTREPRENEURIAL LEADERSHIP, CREATIVE THINKING, AND THE GLOBAL STARTUP

Kevin Systrom and Mike Krieger, Instagram

Kevin Systrom and Mike Krieger are entrepreneurs. They developed an innovative product, created a brand, and cofounded a company to market it. By applying the basic tools and principles of modern marketing, the two Stanford University graduates have achieved remarkable success.

As is true with many entrepreneurs, Systrom's idea was based on his recognition of a problem that needed to be solved and his own needs and wants. Systrom had a passion for photography, and also appreciated the potential of social media. He hit upon an idea for a location-based photo-sharing app that he dubbed Burbn (after his favorite distilled spirit). He then recruited Krieger, who was working on his own app called Meebo. Krieger liked Systrom's idea, but the two agreed that Burbn was overloaded with functionality. Realizing that "There has to be a better way," the duo stripped out everything but the photo-sharing function, which they conceptualized as an "instant telegram" (see Exhibit 1-9).

In October 2010, Systrom and Krieger launched Instagram on Apple's App Store. Within two years, the photo-filtering and photo-sharing app had 30 million users. Soon thereafter, the platform was also launched on the Android and Windows Phone platforms.

Systrom's insight was that, even in prehistoric times, people communicated visually. Today, Instagram makes visual information accessible, just as Gutenberg's printing press made the printed word more accessible. Instagram's popularity is due in part to the dozens of filters that users can apply to their photos (the idea for filters came from Systrom's girlfriend Nicole).

In 2012, Facebook acquired Instagram for $1 billion. Today, Instagram has more than 600 million users who upload approximately 100 million photographs and videos each day; only 20 percent of users are in the United States. In 2016, Instagram generated more than $1.5 billion in revenues from mobile ads.

Social-media savvy companies in the luxury goods industry have been quick to embrace Instagram. To justify their products' high prices, managers of luxury brands need to help consumers understand the craftsmanship and heritage that are integral to the brand stories. Using photo images and videos, companies can take consumers "behind the scenes" and show the process by which luxury products are made by skilled artisans.

Nearly two-thirds of Instagram users use the app to learn about products and brands. Companies can leverage parent Facebook's powerful data and online advertising tools to reach different segments— say, current versus potential luxury consumers—by inserting targeted, photography-based ads in their respective Instagram feeds. One such segment is known as "Henrys," referring to younger Millennials who are described as "high earning, not rich yet."

Food is another category that is driving Instagram's popularity; to date, users have "IG-ed" (i.e., Instagrammed) more than 200 million posts with the hashtag #food. In response to this trend, social-media–conscious hospitality managers in London, New York, and other food-centric cities are taking steps to ensure that a restaurant's interior design, menus, and dishes lend themselves to Instagram posts. These range from Michelin-approved restaurants with posh addresses to Mexican-themed chains that feature burritos wrapped in branded foil. The most popular color? "Millennial Pink." Recent trending food items include "freakshakes" and "unicorn lattes."

Two new Instagram features, Stories and Live, launched in August 2016; they allow users to upload short video clips, live feeds, and photos that disappear within 24 hours. The features proved to be so addictive that parent company Facebook added similar functionality to WhatsApp, Messenger, and Facebook. Some critics have observed that, with Stories, Instagram was simply copying Snapchat. Systrom disagrees. To him, execution trumps originality. Stories "clearly provides unique value to people that they're not getting elsewhere," he says.

The music industry's embrace of Instagram and Stories illustrates Systrom's point. Musicians and bands of all types—from global superstars like Adele and Beyoncé to indie artists seeking to break through—are using the platform to connect with fans in an organic way. According to Nielsen, Instagram users spend more time listening to music and are likely to pay for streaming music services than nonusers. Artists use Stories and Live to announce new releases and tours, and to provide behind-the-scenes looks at the creative process. Popular posts can quickly go viral, allowing record companies and the artists themselves to see the impact on music sales.

Sources: John Paul Titlow, "How Instagram Became the Music Industry's Secret Weapon," *Fast Company* (September 29, 2017); Deepa Seetharaman, "A Copycat? No, Call It Competition," *The Wall Street Journal* (May 31, 2017), p. B5; Deepa Seetharaman, "'Efficiency Guru' Sharpens Instagram," *The Wall Street Journal* (April 14, 2017), p. B4; Deepa Seetharaman Natalie Whittle, "A Square Meal: How Restaurants Are Courting the Instagram Crowd," *FT Magazine* (April 7, 2017); Alexandra Wolfe, "Weekend Confidential: Kevin Systrom," *The Wall Street Journal* (July 2–3, 2016), p. C11; Hannah Kuchler, "Snap Happy: Instagram Rolls out Carpet for Fashion Brands," *Financial Times—FT Special Report: The Business of Luxury* (May 23, 2016), p. 2; Murad Ahmed, "The Camera-Shy Half of Instagram's Founding Duo," *Financial Times* (November 24, 2015), p. 10.

Exhibit 1-9 Stanford University graduates Kevin Systrom and Mike Krieger are Instagram's co-founders.
Source: CHRISTIE HEMM KLOK/The New York Times/Redux.

(1-6) Forces Affecting Global Integration and Global Marketing

◀ **1-6** Discuss the driving and restraining forces affecting global integration today.

The remarkable growth of the global economy over the past 65 years has been shaped by the dynamic interplay of various driving and restraining forces. During most of those decades, companies from different parts of the world in different industries achieved great success by pursuing international, multinational, or global strategies. During the 1990s, changes in the business environment presented numerous challenges to established ways of doing business. Today, despite calls for protectionism as a response to the changing political environment, global marketing continues to grow in importance. This is because, even today, driving forces have more momentum than restraining forces. The forces affecting global integration are shown in Figure 1-1.

Driving Forces

Regional economic agreements, converging market needs and wants, technological advances, pressure to cut costs, pressure to improve quality, improvements in communication and transportation technology, global economic growth, opportunities for leverage, and innovation and entrepreneurship all represent important driving forces; any industry subject to these forces is a candidate for globalization.

MULTILATERAL TRADE AGREEMENTS   For years, a number of multilateral trade agreements have accelerated the pace of global integration. NAFTA expanded trade among the United States, Canada, and Mexico. The General Agreement on Tariffs and Trade (GATT), which was ratified by more than 120 nations in 1994, created the World Trade Organization (WTO) to promote and protect free trade. In Europe, the expanding membership of the European Union has lowered boundaries to trade within the region. The creation of a single currency zone and the introduction of the euro have led to increased intra-European trade in the twenty-first century.

CONVERGING MARKET NEEDS AND WANTS AND THE INFORMATION REVOLUTION   A person studying markets around the world will discover cultural universals as well as differences. The common elements in human nature provide an underlying basis for the opportunity to create and serve global markets. The use of the word *create* is deliberate here. Most global markets do not exist in nature; marketing efforts must create them. For example, no one *needs* soft drinks— and yet today in some countries, per capita soft drink consumption *exceeds* water consumption. Marketing has driven this change in behavior, so that the soft drink industry is now a truly global one. Today, consumer needs and wants around the world are converging as never before, which in turn creates an opportunity for global marketing. Multinational companies pursuing strategies of product adaptation run the risk of failing to be successful against global competitors that have recognized opportunities to serve global customers.

The information revolution—what some refer to as the "democratization of information"—is one reason for the trend toward convergence. This revolution is fueled by a variety of technologies, products, and services, including satellite dishes; globe-spanning TV networks such as CNN and MTV; widespread access to broadband Internet; and Facebook, Twitter, YouTube, and other social media. Taken together, these communication tools mean that people in the remotest corners of the globe can compare their own lifestyles and standards of living with those of people in other countries. In regional markets such as Europe and Asia, the increasing overlap of advertising across national boundaries and the greater mobility of consumers have created opportunities for marketers to pursue pan-regional product positioning. The Internet is an even stronger driving force: When a company establishes a site on the Internet, the company automatically becomes

FIGURE 1-1 Driving and Restraining Forces Affecting Global Integration

global. In addition, the Internet allows people everywhere in the world to reach out to one another and to companies around the globe, buying and selling a virtually unlimited assortment of products and services.

TRANSPORTATION AND COMMUNICATION IMPROVEMENTS   The time and cost barriers associated with distance have fallen tremendously over the past 100 years. The jet airplane revolutionized travel and communication by making it possible for people to go around the world in less than 48 hours. Tourism enables people from many countries to see and experience the newest products sold abroad. In 1970, 75 million passengers traveled internationally; according to figures compiled by the International Air Transport Association, that figure increased to nearly 3.8 billion passengers in 2016.

One essential characteristic of the effective global business is face-to-face communication among employees and between a company and its customers. Modern jet travel made such communication feasible. Today's information technology allows airline alliance partners such as United and Lufthansa to sell seats on each other's flights, thereby making it easier for travelers to get from point to point. Meanwhile, the cost of international data, voice, and video communication has fallen dramatically over the past several decades. Today, Skype and FaceTime are powerful new communication channels. They are the latest in a series of innovations—including fax, e-mail, video teleconferencing, Wi-Fi, and broadband Internet—that enable managers, executives, and customers to link up electronically from virtually any part of the world without traveling at all.

A similar revolution has occurred in transportation technology. The costs associated with physical distribution, in terms of both money and time, have been greatly reduced in recent years. The per-unit cost of shipping automobiles from Japan and Korea to the United States by specially designed auto-transport ships is less than the cost of overland shipping from Detroit to either U.S. coast. Another key innovation has been the increased utilization of 20- and 40-foot metal containers that can be transferred from trucks to railroad cars to ships.

PRODUCT DEVELOPMENT COSTS   The pressure for globalization is intense when new products require major investments and long periods of development time. The pharmaceutical industry provides a striking illustration of this driving force. According to the Pharmaceutical Research and Manufacturers Association, the cost of developing a new drug in 1976 was $54 million. Today, the process of developing a new drug and securing regulatory approval to market it can take 14 years, and the average total cost of bringing a new drug to market is estimated to exceed $400 million.[56] Such costs must be recovered in the global marketplace, because no single national market is likely to be large enough to support investments of this size.

In the face of this reality, Pfizer, Merck, GlaxoSmithKline, Novartis, Bristol-Myers Squibb, Sanofi-Aventis, and other leading pharmaceutical companies have little choice but to engage in global marketing. As noted earlier, however, global marketing does not necessarily mean operating everywhere; in the pharmaceutical industry, for example, seven countries account for 75 percent of sales. As shown in Table 1-6, demand for pharmaceuticals in Asia is expected to exhibit double-digit growth in the next few years. Seeking to tap that opportunity and to reduce development costs, Novartis and its rivals are establishing research and development (R&D) centers in China.[57]

TABLE 1-6   **World Pharmaceutical Market by Region**

	2012	2007–2012	2012–2017
	Market Size (US$ billions)	CAGR* (%)	Forecast CAGR (%)
North America	$348.7	3.0%	0.7–3.7%
Europe	222.8	2.4	−0.4 to 2.6
Asia/Africa/Australia	168.3	15.0	11.4–14.4
Japan	112.1	3.0	1.7–4.7
Latin America	72.5	12.0	10–13
Total world	962.1	5.3	5.3

* Compound annual growth rate.
Source: Based on IMS Health Market Prognosis. Courtesy of IMS Health.

QUALITY   Global marketing strategies can generate more revenues and higher operating margins that, in turn, support design and manufacturing quality. For example, a global company and a domestic company may each spend 5 percent of their sales on R&D, but the global company may have many times the total revenue of the domestic company because it serves the world market. It is easy to understand how John Deere, Nissan, Matsushita, Caterpillar, and other global companies have achieved world-class quality (see Exhibit 1-10). Global companies "raise the bar" for all competitors in an industry.

When a global company establishes a benchmark in quality, competitors must quickly make their own improvements and come up to par. For example, starting in the 1960s, U.S. auto manufacturers saw their market share erode as Japanese carmakers built strong reputations based on their products' quality and durability. Although the U.S. companies have since made great strides in quality, Detroit now faces a new threat from a U.S. company: Tesla's all-electric cars have frequently been at or near the top of the quality and safety rankings for several years.

WORLD ECONOMIC TRENDS   Prior to the global economic crisis that began in 2008, economic growth had been a driving force in the expansion of the international economy and in the growth of global marketing for three reasons. First, economic growth in key developing countries creates market opportunities that provide a major incentive for companies to expand globally. Thanks to rising per capita incomes in India, China, and elsewhere, the growing ranks of middle-class consumers have more money to spend than in the past. At the same time, slow growth in industrialized countries has compelled management to look abroad for opportunities in nations or regions with high rates of growth.

Second, economic growth has reduced resistance that might otherwise have developed in response to the entry of foreign firms into domestic economies. When a country such as China is experiencing rapid economic growth, policymakers are likely to look more favorably on outsiders. A growing country means growing markets; there is often plenty of opportunity for everyone. As a consequence, it is possible for a "foreign" company to enter a domestic economy and establish itself without threatening the existence of local firms. The latter can ultimately be strengthened by the new competitive environment. Without economic growth, however, global enterprises may take business away from domestic ones. In this kind of environment, domestic businesses are more likely to seek governmental intervention to protect their local positions. Predictably, the most recent economic crisis has created new pressure on policymakers in emerging markets to protect domestic markets.

The worldwide movement toward free markets, deregulation, and privatization is a third driving force. The trend toward privatization is opening up formerly closed markets; tremendous

Exhibit 1-10 With annual sales of $26 billion, Moline, Illinois–based Deere & Company is the world's leading manufacturer of farm equipment. Deere has benefited from booming worldwide demand for agricultural commodities; demand for tractors has been especially strong in Brazil, China, India, and other emerging markets.
Source: Courtesy of John Deere.

opportunities are being created as a result. In their book, Daniel Yergin and Joseph Stanislaw described these trends as follows:

> It is the greatest sale in the history of the world. Governments are getting out of businesses by disposing of what amounts to trillions of dollars of assets. Everything is going—from steel plants and phone companies and electric utilities to airlines and railroads to hotels, restaurants, and nightclubs. It is happening not only in the former Soviet Union, Eastern Europe, and China but also in Western Europe, Asia, Latin America, and Africa—and in the United States.[58]

For example, when a nation's telephone company is a state monopoly, the government can require it to buy equipment and services from national companies. In contrast, an independent company that needs to maximize shareholder value has the freedom to seek vendors that offer the best overall value proposition, regardless of nationality. Privatization of telephone systems around the world created significant opportunities for telecommunications equipment suppliers such as Sweden's Ericsson; Alcatel-Lucent, a Franco-American company; and Canada-based Nortel Networks. After years of growth, however, most telecom suppliers experienced slower growth as customers cut their spending in the face of the global recession. In 2009, Nortel Networks filed for bankruptcy; in the wake of this move, it auctioned off thousands of patents to an alliance of companies including Apple and Microsoft.

LEVERAGE A global company possesses the unique opportunity to develop leverage. In the context of global marketing, **leverage** means some type of advantage that a company enjoys by virtue of the fact that it has experience in more than one country. Leverage allows a company to conserve resources when pursuing opportunities in new geographical markets. In other words, it enables a company to expend less time, less effort, and/or less money. Four important types of leverage are experience transfers, scale economies, resource utilization, and global strategy.

Experience Transfers A global company can leverage its experience in any market in the world. It can draw upon management practices, strategies, products, advertising appeals, or sales or promotional ideas that have been market tested in one country or region and apply them in other comparable markets. For example, Whirlpool has considerable experience in the United States dealing with powerful retail buyers such as Lowe's and Best Buy. Most European appliance retailers have plans to establish their own cross-border "power" retailing systems. As former Whirlpool CEO David Whitwam explained, "When power retailers take hold in Europe, we will be ready for it. The skills we've developed here are directly transferable."[60]

Chevron is another example of a global company that gains leverage through experience transfers. As H. F. Iskander, general manager of Chevron's Kuwait office, explains:

> Chevron is pumping oil in different locations all over the world. There is no problem we have not confronted and solved somewhere. There isn't a rock we haven't drilled through. We centralize all that knowledge at our headquarters, analyze it, sort it out, and that enables us to solve any oil-drilling problem anywhere. As a developing country you may have a national oil company that has been pumping your own oil for 20 years. But we tell them, "Look, you have 20 years of experience, but there's no diversity. It is just one year of knowledge 20 times over." When you are operating in a multitude of countries, like Chevron, you see a multitude of different problems and you have to come up with a multitude of solutions. You have to, or you won't be in business. All those solutions are then stored in Chevron's corporate memory. The key to our business now is to tap that memory, and bring out the solution that we used to solve a problem in Nigeria in order to solve the same problem in China or Kuwait.[61]

Scale Economies The global company can take advantage of its greater manufacturing volume to obtain traditional scale advantages within a single factory. Also, finished products can be manufactured by combining components manufactured in scale-efficient plants in different countries. Japan's giant Matsushita Electric Company is a classic example of global marketing in action; it achieved scale economies by exporting VCRs, televisions, and other consumer electronics products throughout the world from world-scale factories in Japan. The importance of manufacturing scale has diminished somewhat as companies implement flexible manufacturing techniques and

> "If we were going to be world-class, we needed to pull together and leverage our global assets around the world to create a powerhouse 'One Ford.' It's exactly why we are here."[59]
>
> Alan Mulally, former CEO, Ford Motor Company

invest in factories outside the home country. Nevertheless, scale economies were clearly a cornerstone of many Japanese companies' success in the 1970s and 1980s.

Leverage from scale economies is not limited to manufacturing. Just as a domestic company can achieve economies in staffing by eliminating duplicate positions after an acquisition, so a global company can achieve the same economies on a global scale by centralizing functional activities. The larger scale of the global company also creates opportunities to improve corporate staff competence and quality.

RESOURCE UTILIZATION A major strength of the global company is its ability to scan the entire world to identify people, money, and raw materials that will enable it to compete most effectively in world markets. For a global company, it is not problematic if the value of the "home" currency rises or falls dramatically, because there really is no such thing as a home currency. The world is full of currencies, and a global company seeks financial resources on the best available terms. In turn, it uses them where there is the greatest opportunity to serve a need at a profit.

GLOBAL STRATEGY The global company's greatest single advantage can be its global strategy. A global strategy is built on an information system that scans the world business environment to identify opportunities, trends, threats, and resources. When opportunities are identified, the global company adheres to the three principles identified earlier: It leverages its skills and focuses its resources to create superior perceived value for customers and achieve competitive advantage. *The global strategy is a design to create a winning offering on a global scale.* This takes great discipline, much creativity, and constant effort. The reward is not just success; it's survival.

For example, French automaker Renault operated for many years as a regional company. During that time, its primary struggle was a two-way race with Peugeot Citroën for dominance in the French auto industry. However, in an industry dominated by Toyota and other global competitors, Chairman Louis Schweitzer had no choice but to formulate a global strategy. Initiatives included acquiring a majority stake in Nissan Motor and Romania's Dacia. Schweitzer has also invested $1 billion in a plant in Brazil and spent hundreds of millions of dollars in South Korea.[62]

A note of caution is in order: A global strategy is no guarantee of ongoing organizational success. Companies that cannot formulate or successfully implement a coherent global strategy may lose their independence. InBev's acquisition of Anheuser-Busch at the end of 2008 is a case in point. Some globalization strategies do not yield the expected results, as seen in the unraveling of the DaimlerChrysler merger and the failure of Deutsche Post's DHL unit to penetrate the U.S. domestic package delivery market.

The severe downturn in the business environment in the early years of the twenty-first century wreaked havoc with strategic plans. This proved true for established global firms as well as newcomers from emerging markets that had only recently come to prominence on the world stage. For example, at Swiss-based ABB, Mexico's Cemex, and UK supermarket chain Tesco, the ambitious global visions of the respective chief executives were undermined by expensive strategic bets that did not pay off.[63] Although all three companies survived, they are smaller, more focused entities than before.

INNOVATION AND ENTREPRENEURSHIP Worldwide, new companies are forming. In India, Mexico, Spain, Vietnam, and many other countries, entrepreneurship is flourishing. So, what is an entrepreneur? Management guru Peter Drucker used the term to describe someone who introduces innovations. Entrepreneurs, by definition, are always pioneers in introducing new products and services. According to Drucker:

> They are people with exceptional abilities who seize opportunities that others are oblivious to or who create opportunities through their own daring and imagination.... Innovation is the specific instrument of entrepreneurship. Innovation is the act that endows resources with a new capacity to create wealth.... Through innovation, entrepreneurs create new satisfactions or new consumer demand.[64]

Italy's Emilia Romagna region is a good example of a place with a distinguished record of entrepreneurship. It is home to some of the world's most famous brands, including Ferrari, YOOX, Datalogic, and Technogym.[65] In this text, we will survey some of the most dynamic developments in global entrepreneurship so that readers will develop a better understanding of the importance of innovative leadership and creative thinking.

Restraining Forces

Despite the impact of the driving forces identified previously, several restraining forces may slow a company's efforts to engage in global marketing. In addition to the market differences discussed earlier, important restraining forces include management myopia, organizational culture, national controls, and opposition to globalization. As we have noted, in today's world the driving forces predominate over the restraining forces. That is why the importance of global marketing is steadily growing.

MANAGEMENT MYOPIA AND ORGANIZATIONAL CULTURE   In many cases, management simply ignores opportunities to pursue global marketing. A company that is "nearsighted" and ethnocentric will not expand geographically. Anheuser-Busch, the brewer of Budweiser beer, lost its independence after years of focusing primarily on the domestic U.S. market. Myopia is also a recipe for market disaster if headquarters attempts to dictate when it should listen. Global marketing does not work without a strong local team that can provide information about local market conditions.

In companies where subsidiary management "knows it all," there is no room for vision from the top. Conversely, in companies where headquarters management is all-knowing, there is no room for local initiative or an in-depth knowledge of local needs and conditions. Executives and managers at successful global companies have learned how to integrate global vision and perspective with local market initiative and input. A striking theme emerged during interviews conducted by one of the authors with executives of successful global companies—namely, respect for local initiative and input by headquarters executives, and the corresponding respect for headquarters' vision by local executives.

NATIONAL CONTROLS   Every country protects the commercial interests of its local enterprises by maintaining control over market access and entry into both low- and high-tech industries. Such control ranges from a monopoly controlling access to tobacco markets to national government control of broadcast, equipment, and data transmission markets. Today, tariff barriers have been largely removed in high-income countries, thanks to the WTO, GATT, NAFTA, and other economic agreements.

Even so, **nontariff barriers (NTBs)** are still very much in evidence. NTBs are nonmonetary restrictions on cross-border trade, such as food safety and labeling rules and other bureaucratic obstacles. For example, the European Union prohibits the use of generic terms such as "Parmesan" for dairy imports to protect cheese producers in Italy. NTBs have the potential to make it difficult for companies to gain access to some individual country and regional markets.

OPPOSITION TO GLOBALIZATION   To many people around the world, globalization and global marketing represent a threat. The term *globaphobia* is sometimes used to describe an attitude of hostility toward trade agreements, global brands, or company policies that appear to result in hardship for some individuals or countries while benefiting others.

Globaphobia manifests itself in various ways, including protests or violence directed at policymakers or well-known global companies (see Exhibit 1-11). Opponents of globalization include politicians, labor unions, college and university students, national and international nongovernmental organizations (NGOs), and others. *Shock Doctrine* author Naomi Klein has been an especially outspoken critic of globalization.

Two prominent examples of this restraining force are the election of Donald Trump in the United States and the Brexit vote in the United Kingdom. Shortly after being sworn in as the 45th U.S. president, Trump pulled the United States out of the Transatlantic Trade and Investment Partnership (TTIP) as well as the Trans-Pacific Partnership (TPP). He also campaigned on a pledge to revise or withdraw from NAFTA. Meanwhile, U.K. Prime Minister Theresa May was working to finalize "divorce" arrangements for the United Kingdom's withdrawal from the European Union.

In the United States, the perception that globalization has depressed the wages of American workers and resulted in the loss of both blue- and white-collar jobs helped Trump win the 2016

Exhibit 1-11 American fashion icon Ralph Lauren created the official uniforms that Team USA wore at the opening and closing ceremonies of the 2012 Olympics in China. Controversy erupted after it was revealed that the uniforms—navy blazers, white trousers and skirts, and berets—were "Made in China" rather than in the United States. Critics linked the outsourcing story to the broader issue of the loss of manufacturing jobs in America. Perhaps not surprisingly, the uniforms for the 2016 Summer Games in Rio were "Made in the USA."
Source: Leonard Zhukovsky/Shutterstock.

presidential election. Even prior to the election, there was a growing suspicion that the world's advanced countries—starting with the United States—were reaping a disproportionate amount of the rewards of free trade. As an unemployed miner in Bolivia put it, "Globalization is just another name for submission and domination. We've had to live with that here for 500 years and now we want to be our own masters."[66]

(1-7) Outline of This Book

This book has been written for students and businesspeople interested in global marketing. Throughout the book, we present and discuss important concepts and tools specifically applicable to global marketing.

The book is divided into five parts. Part One consists of Chapter 1, an overview of global marketing and the basic theory of global marketing.

Chapters 2 through 5 make up Part Two, in which we cover the environment of global marketing. Chapter 2 and Chapter 3 examine economic and regional market characteristics, including the locations of income and population, patterns of trade and investment, and stages of market development. In Chapter 4, we examine social and cultural elements, and in Chapter 5 we present the legal, political, and regulatory dimensions.

Part Three is devoted to topics that must be considered when approaching global markets. We cover marketing information systems and research in Chapter 6. Chapter 7 discusses market segmentation, targeting, and positioning. Chapter 8 surveys the basics of importing, exporting, and sourcing. We devote Chapter 9 to various aspects of global strategy, including strategy alternatives for market entry and expansion.

In Part Four, we examine the global context of marketing mix decisions. Guidelines for making product, price, channel, and marketing communications decisions in response to global market opportunities and threats are presented in detail in Chapters 10 through 14. Chapter 15 explores the ways that the Internet, e-commerce, and other aspects of the digital revolution are creating new opportunities and challenges for global marketers.

The two chapters in Part Five address issues of corporate strategy and leadership, in the twenty-first century. Chapter 16 includes an overview of strategy and competitive advantage. Chapter 17 addresses some of the leadership challenges facing the chief executives of global companies. In addition, this chapter examines the organization and control of global marketing programs as well as the issue of corporate social responsibility.

Summary

Marketing is an organizational function and a set of processes for creating, communicating, and delivering value to customers and for managing customer relationships in ways that benefit the organization and its stakeholders. A company that engages in *global marketing* focuses its resources on global market opportunities and threats. Successful global marketers such as Nestlé, Coca-Cola, and Honda use familiar *marketing mix* elements—the four Ps—to create global marketing programs. Marketing, R&D, manufacturing, and other activities compose a firm's *value chain*; firms configure these activities to create superior customer value on a global basis. The *value equation* ($V = B/P$) expresses the relationship between value and the marketing mix.

Global companies also maintain strategic *focus* while relentlessly pursuing *competitive advantage*. The marketing mix, value chain, competitive advantage, and focus are universal in their applicability, irrespective of whether a company does business only in its home country or has a presence in many markets around the world. However, in a *global industry*, companies that fail to pursue global opportunities risk being pushed aside by stronger global competitors.

A firm's *global marketing strategy (GMS)* can enhance its worldwide performance. The GMS addresses several issues. First is the nature of the marketing program in terms of the balance between a *standardized (extension) approach* to the marketing mix elements and a *localized (adaptation) approach* that is responsive to country or regional differences. Second is the *concentration of marketing activities* in a few countries or the dispersal of such activities across many countries. Companies that engage in global marketing can also engage in *coordination of marketing activities*. Finally, a firm's GMS addresses the issue of *global market participation*.

The importance of global marketing today can be seen in the company rankings compiled by *The Wall Street Journal*, *Fortune*, the *Financial Times*, and other publications. Whether ranked by revenues or some other measure, most of the world's major corporations are active regionally or globally. The size of global markets for individual industries or product categories helps explain why companies "go global." Global markets for some product categories represent hundreds of billions of dollars in annual sales; other markets are much smaller. Whatever the size of the opportunity, successful industry competitors find that increasing revenues and profits means seeking markets outside the home country.

Company management can be classified in terms of its orientation toward the world: *ethnocentric*, *polycentric*, *regiocentric*, or *geocentric*. These terms reflect progressive levels of development or evolution. An ethnocentric orientation characterizes *domestic* and *international companies*; international companies pursue marketing opportunities outside the home market by extending various elements of the marketing mix. A polycentric worldview predominates at a *multinational company*, whose country managers operate autonomously adapt the marketing mix. When management moves to integrate and coordinate activities on a regional basis, the decision reflects a regiocentric orientation. Managers at *global* and *transnational companies* are geocentric in their orientation and pursue both extension and adaptation strategies in global markets.

The dynamic interplay of several driving and restraining forces shapes the importance of global marketing. Driving forces include market needs and wants, technology, transportation and communication improvements, product costs, quality, world economic trends, recognition of opportunities to develop *leverage* by operating globally, and innovation and entrepreneurship. Restraining forces include market differences, management myopia, organizational culture, and national controls such as *nontariff barriers (NTBs)*.

Discussion Questions

1-1. What are the basic goals of marketing? Are these goals relevant to global marketing?

1-2. What is meant by "global localization"? Is Coca-Cola a global product? Explain.

1-3. How does Michael Porter's five forces competition model create a platform for achieving competitive advantage in the global market? Why is it necessary for some companies to change their strategic focus?

1-4. U.K.-based Burberry is a luxury fashion brand that appeals to both genders and to all ages. To improve Burberry's competitiveness in the luxury goods market, CEO Marco Gobetti must update the marketing program put in place by his predecessor. The strategy should address key markets that Burberry will participate in, as well as the integration and coordination of marketing activities. Research recent articles about Burberry and discuss Burberry's GMS.

1-5. Outline the challenges facing a business moving from a single country to global marketing.

1-6. Describe the differences among ethnocentric, polycentric, regiocentric, and geocentric management orientations.

1-7. Describe the four strategies in the product/market growth matrix. Explain how a financial institution may use these strategies to grow its global business.

1-8. Identify and briefly describe some of the restraining forces that impede the growth of global marketing.

1-9. Each July, *Fortune* publishes its Global 500 listing of the world's largest companies. You can find the current rankings online at www.fortune.com/global500/. Alternatively, you can consult the print edition of *Fortune*. Browse through the list and choose any company that interests you. Compare its 2017 ranking with the most recent ranking. Has the company's ranking changed? Consult additional sources (e.g., magazine articles, annual reports, the company's Web site) to get a better understanding of the factors and forces that contributed to the company's move up or down in the rankings. Write a brief summary of your findings.

1-10. Some of the United Kingdom's best-known high-street retailers have seen their markets and profits dwindle or even disappear over the past decade or more. Electrical retailer Comet was founded in 1933 and in 2008 it had a turnover in excess of $2.6 billion. By 2012, all of its 6,500 workers across 240 stores were out of work. Clinton Cards opened their first store in 1968. At one time it had 25 percent of the greeting cards market in the United Kingdom and had 1,100 stores. It went into administration in 2012. Other notable high-street failures include the video games retailer Game, the book and music retailer Borders, the film and video-game rental firm Blockbuster, and most recently, the toy-store chain Toys "R" Us and the electronics retailer Maplin, both of which failed in 2018. Research the reasons behind these failures and recommend a course of action for a retail chain that might find itself in the same situation in the future.

CASE 1-1 *Continued (refer to page 24)*

The Global Marketplace

Now that you have an overview of global marketing, it's time to test your knowledge of global current events. Some well-known companies and brands are listed in the left-hand column. The question is: In which country is the parent corporation located? Possible answers are shown in the right-hand column. Write the letter corresponding to the country of your choice in the space provided; each country can be used more than once. Answers follow.

1. Firestone Tire & Rubber	a. Germany
2. Ray-Ban	b. France
3. Rolls-Royce	c. Japan
4. RCA	d. Great Britain
5. Budweiser	e. United States
6. Ben & Jerry's Homemade	f. Switzerland
7. Gerber	g. Italy
8. Miller Beer	h. Sweden
9. Rollerblade	i. Finland
10. Case New Holland	j. China
11. Weed Eater	k. Netherlands
12. Holiday Inn	l. Belgium
13. Wild Turkey bourbon	m. India
14. ThinkPad	n. Brazil
15. Wilson Sporting Goods	o. South Korea
16. Right Guard	p. Thailand
17. BFGoodrich	
18. Jaguar	
19. Burger King	
20. Jenny Craig	
21. The Body Shop	
22. Titleist	
23. Swift	
24. Gaggia	
25. Church's English shoes	
26. American Standard Brands	
27. Chicken of the Sea tuna	

Answers

1. Japan (Bridgestone)   **2.** Italy (Luxottica SpA)   **3.** Germany (Volkswagen)   **4.** China (TTE)   **5.** Belgium (Anheuser-Busch InBev)   **6.** Great Britain/Netherlands (Unilever)   **7.** Switzerland (Nestlé)   **8.** Great Britain (SABMiller)   **9.** Italy (Benetton)**10.** Italy (Fiat)**11.** Sweden (AB Electrolux)**12.** Great Britain (InterContinental Hotels Group PLC)**13.** Italy (Campari)**14.** China (Lenovo)**15.** Finland (Amer Group)**16.** Germany (Henkel)**17.** France (Michelin)**18.** India (Tata Motors)**19.** Brazil (3G Capital)   **20.** Switzerland (Nestlé)   **21.** France (L'Oréal)   **22.** South Korea (Fila Korea)   **23.** Brazil (JBS)   **24.** Netherlands (Philips)   **25.** Italy (Prada Group)   **26.** Japan (Lixil Corp)   **27.** Thailand (Thai Union Frozen Products PCL)

Discussion Questions

1-11. Anheuser-Busch (A-B), which has been described as "an American icon," is now owned by a company based in Belgium. Responding to reports that some consumers planned to boycott Budweiser products to protest the deal, one industry observer said, "Brand nationality is all about where it was born, and also the ingredients of that beer and how they make the beer. Basically, it doesn't matter who owns it. We are in a global world right now." Do you agree?

1-12. Anheuser-Busch has long enjoyed a reputation as a very desirable place to work. Executives were awarded well-appointed corporate suites and traveled on corporate jets; many had secretaries as well as executive assistants. When managers took commercial flights, they flew first class. Most employees received beer for free and could count on donations of beer and merchandise for community events. Tickets to St. Louis Cardinals home baseball games were also used as a marketing tool. A-B spent heavily on advertising and promotion; various advertising agencies produced about 100 new ads for A-B each year. Given these facts, which changes, if any, would you expect A-B's new owners to make? Why?

1-13. In 2009, Italy's Fiat acquired a 20 percent stake in Chrysler, another iconic American company. In January 2014, Fiat completed the acquisition and Chrysler is now a subsidiary of Fiat. Are you familiar with Fiat? What do you think CEO Sergio Marchionne hoped to accomplish with this pair of deals? How might Chrysler benefit from the alliance?

1-14. Ben & Jerry's Homemade is a quirky ice cream marketer based in Burlington, Vermont. Founders Ben Cohen and Jerry Greenfield are legendary for their enlightened business practices, which include a three-part mission statement: product mission, financial mission, and social mission. When the company was acquired by consumer products giant Unilever, some of the brand's loyal customers were alarmed. What do you think was the source of their concern?

CASE 1-2
McDonald's Expands Globally While Adjusting Its Local Recipe

McDonald's Corporation is a fast-food legend whose famous golden arches can be found at more than 37,000 locations in 118 different countries. The company is the undisputed leader in the quick-service restaurant (QSR) segment of the hospitality industry, with more than twice the system-wide revenues of Burger King. McDonald's built its reputation by promising and delivering three things to customers: inexpensive food with consistent taste regardless of location; quick service; and a clean, familiar environment.

The company was also a pioneer in the development of convenience-oriented features such as drive-through windows and indoor play areas for children. Today, thanks to memorable advertising and intensive promotion efforts, McDonald's is one of the world's most valuable brands: In 2017, Interbrand ranked it as the world's number 12 brand overall (Apple has been number 1 for several years running). The golden arches are said to be the second-most-recognized symbol in the world, behind the Olympic rings. In 2014, McDonald's was named Creative Marketer of the Year at the Cannes Lions International Festival of Creativity.

Despite these successes, the company faces competitive attacks from several directions. During the 1990s, a wide range of upscale food and beverage purveyors arrived on the scene. For example, consumers began flocking to Starbucks coffee bars, where they spend freely on lattes and other coffee-based specialty drinks. The "fast-casual" segment of the industry, which includes companies such as Baja Fresh, Chipotle Mexican Grill, Panera Bread, and Cosi, is attracting customers seeking higher-quality menu items in more comfortable surroundings. Millennials, in particular, began shunning McDonald's and seeking out alternative fast-dining options such as Five Guys, a "better burger" chain that features freshly cut fries made from locally sourced potatoes.

Meanwhile, Subway overtook McDonald's as the restaurant chain with the most outlets in the United States. McDonald's U.S. menu offerings had grown rapidly, and, some would say, quality and service had suffered. Some industry observers also suggested that, in terms of both food offerings and marketing, McDonald's was losing touch with modern American lifestyles.

Until recently, the picture appeared brighter outside the United States. Thanks to changing lifestyles around the globe, more people are embracing the Western-style fast-food culture (see Exhibit 1-12). McDonald's responded to this opportunity by stepping up its rate of new unit openings. McDonald's International is organized into three geographic regions: (1) Europe; (2) Asia-Pacific, Middle East, and Africa (APMEA); and (3) Other Countries. In 2005, the offices of the country heads for Europe and Asia were moved from the U.S. headquarters to their respective regions; now, for example, the head of APMEA manages his business from Hong Kong. Commenting on the change, Ken Koziol, vice president of worldwide restaurant innovation, explained, "McDonald's was built on a strong foundation of a core menu that we took around the world but we need to make sure we are more locally relevant. Taste profiles and desires are changing."

Asia-Pacific

The Indian market holds huge potential for McDonald's. In 1996, the company formed a joint venture with an Indian partner, Vikram Bakshi, and opened restaurants in New Delhi and Bombay. In Delhi, McDonald's competes with Nirula's, a QSR chain with multiple outlets; in addition, hundreds of smaller regional chains can be found throughout India. The U.S.-based Subway chain opened its first Indian location in 2001; Pizza Hut, KFC, and Domino's Pizza have also entered this market.

Exhibit 1-12

Source: Hasan Jamali/AP Wide World Photos.

Indian demand for meals from the major food chains is growing at a double-digit rate; annual total sales exceed $1 billion. With those trends in mind, McDonald's identifies strategic locations for its restaurants in areas with heavy pedestrian traffic, such as the shopping street in Bandra in the Bombay suburbs. Other restaurant locations include a site near a college in Vile Parle and another opposite the Andheri train station; in all, McDonald's India operated more than 400 locations at the end of 2017.

Because the Hindu religion prohibits eating beef, McDonald's developed the Chicken Maharaja Mac specifically for India. Despite protests from several Hindu nationalist groups, the first McDonald's attracted huge crowds to its site near the Victoria railway terminal; customers included many tourists from across India and from abroad as well as locals commuting to and from work.

McDonald's has worked steadily to prove that it is sensitive to Indian tastes and traditions. As is true throughout the world, McDonald's emphasizes that most of the food ingredients it uses—as much as 95 percent—are produced locally. In addition, to accommodate vegetarians, each restaurant has two separate food preparation areas. The "green" kitchen is devoted to vegetarian fare such as the spicy McAloo Tikki potato burger, Pizza McPuff, and Paneer Salsa McWrap. Even the mayonnaise is made without eggs on this side of the kitchen. Meat items, in contrast, are prepared on the red side of the kitchen. Some of the new menu items developed for India are now being introduced in Europe and the United States.

McDonald's and other fast-food operators have also been instrumental in providing employment opportunities to Indian women. On a global basis, female participation in the work force is disproportionately low. Two-thirds of India's female labor force works in agriculture. Employers in the fast-food sector have discovered that women employees tend to be friendly and loyal, which is important for quick-serve restaurants. To reassure conservative parents, McDonald's invites them to visit restaurant locations to see firsthand that their daughters are working in a safe environment for a company that respects women.

China is currently home to the world's largest McDonald's; China is also the fastest-growing market in terms of the number of new restaurant openings. The first Chinese location opened in mid-1992 in central Beijing, a few blocks from Tiananmen Square. By 2016, McDonald's had more than 2,700 restaurants in China. The restaurants purchase 95 percent of their supplies, including lettuce, from local sources.

Prior to 2016, the corporate parent owned two-thirds of the McDonald's stores in China. However, a food-safety scare caused a short-term dip in sales and profitability. In search of improved profitability and flexibility, McDonald's launched an initiative dubbed "Vision 2022" as the blueprint for expanding outside China's largest cities. In a key strategic move, CEO Steve Easterbrook sold a controlling stake in all 2,700 Chinese stores to a state-run company, Citic, and a U.S.-based private equity group. The sale marked McDonald's transition to an all-franchise business model in China. As part of the deal, the new partners will build more than 1,000 new McDonald's stores.

Western Europe

The golden arches are a familiar sight in Europe, particularly in France, Germany, and the United Kingdom. There is even a four-star Golden Arch hotel in Zurich. Overall, Europe contributes about 40 percent of both revenue and operating income for the company, making it a key world region for McDonald's.

France's tradition of culinary excellence makes it a special case in Europe; French dining options range from legendary three-star Michelin restaurants to humble neighborhood bistros. From the time McDonald's opened its first French outlet in 1972, policymakers and media commentators have voiced concerns about the impact of fast food on French culture. Even so, with more than 1,400 locations, France today represents McDonald's second-largest European market (Germany ranks number 1).

Nevertheless, controversy has kept the company in the public eye. For example, some French citizens objected when McDonald's became the official food of the World Cup finals that were held in France in 1998. In August 1999, a sheep farmer named Jose Bové led a protest against construction of the 851st French McDonald's near the village of Millau. The protesters used construction tools to dismantle the partially finished structure. Bové told the press that the group had singled out McDonald's because, in his words, it is a symbol of America, "the place where they not only promote globalization and industrially produced food but also unfairly penalize our peasants." At one point, executives at McDonald's France even ran an ad in *Femme Actuelle* magazine suggesting that children should eat only one meal at McDonald's per week.

McDonald's French franchisees experience some of the same competitive pressures facing the U.S. units; there are also culturally distinct differences. For example, the French are obsessed with bread. Local bistro operators have enjoyed great success selling fresh-baked baguettes filled with ham and brie, effectively neutralizing McDonald's advantage of fast service and low prices. In response, McDonald's rolled out the McBaguette, a burger made with local Charolais beef and topped with French cheese and mustard.

In addition, executives hired an architecture firm to develop new restaurant designs and reimage the French operations. A total of eight different themes were developed; many of the redesigned restaurants have hardwood floors and exposed brick walls. Signs have muted colors rather than featuring the chain's signature red and yellow, and the golden arches are displayed more subtly. Overall, the restaurants don't look like McDonald's restaurants elsewhere.

The first redesigned restaurant was located on the Champs-Élysées on a site previously occupied by a Burger King; called "Music," the restaurant provides diners with the opportunity to listen to music on iPods and watch music videos on TV monitors. In some locations, lime green Danish designer armchairs have replaced plastic seats. As McDonald's locations in France have undergone style makeovers, some franchisees have reported sales increases of 10 to 20 percent. Encouraged by these results, McDonald's has embarked on an ambitious program to refurbish several thousand outlets in various countries.

> "The tastes of the urban, upwardly mobile Indian are evolving, and more Indians are looking to eat out and experiment. The potential Indian customer base for a McDonald's or a Subway is larger than the size of entire developed countries."
>
> Sapna Nayak, food analyst at Raobank India

Central and Eastern Europe

January 31, 2015, marked the 25th anniversary of McDonald's arrival in the Soviet Union. The first Moscow McDonald's was built on Pushkin Square, near a major metro station just a few blocks from the Kremlin. It has 700 indoor seats and another 200 outside. It boasts 800 employees and features a 70-foot counter with 27 cash registers, equivalent to 20 ordinary McDonald's restaurants rolled into one. For its 20th-birthday celebration, the Pushkin Square location offered customers a "buy one, get one free" hamburger promotion; accordion-wielding musicians provided background music.

Khamzat Khazbulatov was selected to manage the first restaurant; today, he is CEO of McDonald's Russia. At present, there approximately 600 McDonald's restaurants in Russia, and the company employs more than 35,000 people. To ensure a steady supply of high-quality raw materials, the company built McComplex, a huge, $50 million processing facility on the outskirts of Moscow. McDonald's also worked closely with local farmers to boost yields and quality. Now the facility has been turned over to private companies that today provide 80 percent of the ingredients used in Russia. For example, Wimm-Bill-Dann supplies dairy products to McDonald's; in 2002, it became the first Russian company to be listed on the New York Stock Exchange. Overall, 100,000 people are employed by companies in McDonald's supply chain.

Ukraine and Belarus are among the other countries in Eastern Europe with newly opened restaurants. The first Ukrainian McDonald's opened in Kiev in 1997; by 2007, the chain had expanded to 57 locations in 16 cities. Plans call for as many as 100 restaurants, for a total investment of $120 million.

The marketing environment in the region became notably more complicated in 2014. Russian President Vladimir Putin annexed a region in Ukraine called Crimea, forcing McDonald's to close its three restaurants there. After Moscow-backed rebels initiated military action in Ukraine in 2014, the United States, Germany, and other Western nations imposed trade sanctions on Russia. In retaliation, Russian consumer-safety officials descended on numerous McDonald's locations and cited them for alleged food safety, sanitation, and financial violations. Those issues were subsequently resolved, and in the last few years McDonald's has expanded into new Russian territories such as Siberia.

McDonald's has also set its sights on Central Europe, where plans call for hundreds of new restaurants to be opened in Croatia, Slovakia, Romania, and other countries. In 2010, McDonald's Czech Republic restaurants featured a special lineup of New York–themed sandwiches that were promoted with the iconic "I Heart NY" logo. Advertisements promised, "Another burger each week"; the offerings included Wall Street Beef ("grilled beef, cheese, crispy bacon, fresh lettuce and onion with BBQ sauce on an oval bun topped with sesame seeds") and Broadway Chicken.

"AND WE DON'T THINK MUCH OF YOUR STUPID TOYS, EITHER."

Source: Jeremy Banx/Banx Cartoons.

Refocusing on the U.S. Market

When Jim Cantalupo became McDonald's CEO in 2002, he took the extraordinary step of calling a summit meeting of senior creative personnel from 14 advertising agencies representing the company's 10 largest international markets. Foremost among them was New York–based DDB Worldwide, the lead agency on the McDonald's account that handles advertising in dozens of countries, including Australia, the United States, and Germany. In addition, Leo Burnett is responsible for ads targeting children. McDonald's marketing and advertising managers from key countries were also summoned to the meeting at company headquarters in Oak Brook, Illinois. As Larry Light, then global chief marketing officer for McDonald's, noted, "Creative talent is a rare talent, and creative people don't belong to geographies, to Brazil or France or Australia. We're going to challenge our agencies to be more open-minded about sharing between geographies."

Charlie Bell, a former executive at McDonald's Europe who was promoted to chief operating officer, didn't mince words about the company's advertising. "For one of the world's best brands, we have missed the mark," he said before the summit meeting. In June 2002, the company announced that "i'm lovin' it" would be the new global marketing theme; the copy was proposed by Heye & Partner, a DDB Worldwide unit located in Germany. The phrase remains the company's global tag line today.

After Jim Skinner was named chief executive officer in 2004, he instituted a "Plan to Win" initiative to increase McDonald's momentum. The core idea was to make McDonald's "better, not just bigger." Skinner identified five main drivers of McDonald's: people, products, place,

price, and promotion. The results of the initiative were very positive. For example, *Consumer Reports* lauded the company's efforts to upgrade its coffee program. Consumers embraced "better-for-you" menu items such as salads and sandwiches. McDonald's is also striving to be more environmentally conscious by using less plastic packaging and recycling more. Denis Hennequin, the executive in charge of European operations, is pleased with the results of his reimaging campaign. He said, "I'm changing the story. We've got to be loyal to our roots, we have to be affordable, we have to be convenient…but we have to add new dimensions."

McDonald's total stock return for the three-year period 2007 through 2009 was the highest among the 30 companies that make up the Dow Jones Industrial Average—a remarkable performance, given the difficult economic environment. The company's strong financial results gave it the resources to move forward with a remodeling initiative for its U.S. restaurants. The price tag: a whopping $1 billion. The upgrades were partly a response to the positive results from revamped European operations; the makeover also reflects the influence of modern retail design principles used by Apple, Starbucks, and other trendsetters. By 2015, most of McDonald's 14,350 U.S. restaurants had been updated.

> "For a market leader, they've been really aggressive in a pretty fundamental way, but at the same time not losing the core of who McDonald's is."
>
> Kevin Lane Keller, Professor of Marketing, Tuck School of Business, Dartmouth College

McDonald's executives are intent on creating a modern, streamlined environment that will encourage customers to stay longer and spend more. Some of the changes are dramatic: Gone are the red roofs and splashes of neon yellow that many associate with iconic spokes-clown Ronald McDonald. The new color palette includes subtle shades of orange, yellow, and green. Also on tap: softer lighting and comfortable, stylish new furniture. As Jim Carras, a senior U.S. executive, noted, "McDonald's has to change with the times. And we have to do so faster than we ever have before."

New Challenges at Home for the New Bosses

Despite winning accolades for its marketing creativity and investing significant sums in upgrades, McDonald's faces several challenges in its home market. After taking over the CEO position in 2012, Don Thompson was under constant pressure from public health activists alleging that the company is a major contributor to the wave of obesity striking the United States. In addition, animal rights activists continued to protest the treatment of animals by McDonald's suppliers. Also, the issue of pay inequality and the minimum wage came to the fore in the United States. Activists targeted the company for paying low wages; the current minimum wage in the United States is $7.25 per hour. McDonald's responded by noting that the company provides that all-important "first job" for many Americans.

Equally worrying was the worst sales slump in more than a decade, indicative that consumer tastes were changing in the United States. Pledging that McDonald's would "listen to the customer," Thompson authorized the rapid rollout of a menu innovation called "Create Your Taste." The system allowed customers to bypass the counter and go directly to a kiosk to customize orders for a hamburger or chicken sandwich on a tablet. Executives acknowledged that the new platform would take some of the "fast" out of the customer experience; it cannot be used with the drive-through, and the custom sandwiches are more expensive than the traditional offerings. However, with its eye on speed and convenience, McDonald's rolled out another innovation: It adopted Apple Pay to allow customers to pay for their purchases with their smartphones.

Don Thompson retired in 2015 after his initiatives failed to reignite sales. Upon his departure, Steve Easterbrook assumed the job of CEO, pledging that he would spearhead McDonald's transformation into a "modern, progressive burger company." Easterbrook, who is British, had spent several years engineering a turnaround in McDonald's U.K. business. Among other things, he objected to the venerable *Oxford English Dictionary's* definition of a "McJob" as "an unstimulating, low-paid job."

One of Easterbrook's first acts as CEO was to commission a study to determine where McDonald's had gone wrong. The research indicated that McDonald's core customers had defected to rival burger chains such as Wendy's and Burger King. Part of the attraction was value-oriented promotional pricing such as "5 items for $4" Deal Meals. Easterbrook responded by cutting McDonald's prices on coffee and soft drinks and launching "all-day breakfast." Responding to Wendy's brand pledge that its burgers are "fresh, never frozen," McDonald's is replacing the frozen beef patties in its Quarter Pounder sandwich with fresh ones. The CEO is also spending more than $1 billion to overhaul stores in the United States as well as France, Germany. and other key country markets.

Discussion Questions

1-15. Identify the key elements in McDonald's global marketing strategy. Despite a slowdown in global fast-food consumption, McDonald's continues to be a success story. What is the key to its success? Does McDonald's think globally and act locally? Does it also think locally and act globally?

1-16. Do you think government officials in developing countries such as Russia, China, and India welcome McDonald's? Do consumers in these countries welcome McDonald's? Why or why not?

1-17. Is it realistic to expect that McDonald's—or any well-known company—can expand globally without occasionally making mistakes or generating controversy? Why do antiglobalization protesters—and sometimes government officials—target McDonald's?

1-18. Assess the changes McDonald's has made to its marketing strategy in the United States and around the world.

Visit the Web Site

**See www.mcdonalds.com
for a directory to country-specific sites.**

Sources: Anna Nicolaou, "Flipping the Fortunes of Burgers," *Financial Times—FT Big Read: US Food and* Beverage (November 27, 2017), p. 11; Preetika Rana, "Fast-Food Jobs Attract Women in India," *The Wall Street Journal* (December 27, 2016), p. B3; Julie Jargon, "McDonald's Is Losing the Burger War," *The Wall Street Journal* (October 7, 2016), pp. A1, A10; Wayne Ma, Rick Carew, and Kane Wu, "McDonald's Hunts for a Partner in China," *The Wall Street Journal* (October 4, 2016), pp. B1, B6; Julie Jargon, "From the Grill: Ways to Rescue McDonald's," *The Wall Street Journal* (December 24, 2014), p. B8; James Marson and Julie Jargon, "Moscow Advances on McDonald's," *The Wall Street Journal* (August 21, 2014), pp. B1, B2; Maureen Morrison, "Is McDonald's Losing That Lovin' Feeling?" *Advertising Age* (February 20, 2012), pp. 1, 20; Marion Issard, "To Tailor Burgers for France, McDonald's Enlists Baguette," *The Wall Street Journal* (February 24, 2012), p. B4; Bruce Horovitz, "McDonald's Revamps Stores to Look More Upscale," *USA Today* (May 8, 2011), pp. 1B, 2B; Andrew E. Kramer, "Russia's Evolution, as Seen Through the Golden Arches," *The New York Times* (February 2, 2010), p. B3; Janet Adamy, "As Burgers Boom in Russia, McDonald's Touts Discipline," *The Wall Street Journal* (October 16, 2007), pp. A1, A17; Jenny Wiggins, "Burger, Fries, and a Shake-Up," *Financial Times* (January 27, 2007), p. 7; Steven Gray, "Beyond Burgers: McDonald's Menu Upgrade Boosts Meal Prices and Results," *The Wall Street Journal* (February 18–19, 2006), pp. A1, A7; Jeremy Grant, "Golden Arches Bridge Local Tastes," *Financial Times* (February 9, 2006), p. 10.

CASE 1-3
Apple versus Samsung: The Battle for Smartphone Supremacy Heats Up

When Steve Jobs died in October 2011, the world lost one of the towering figures of the modern business era (see Exhibit 1-14). Apple, the company Jobs cofounded, was a pioneer in the consumer electronics world; its key product introductions included the Apple II (1977), the Macintosh (1984), the iPod and iTunes (2001), the Apple Store (2001), the iPhone (2007), and the iPad (2009). At the time of Jobs's death, Apple was the most valuable tech company in the world. By September 2012, Apple stock had soared to record levels, with its price briefly rising above $700 per share. In addition, Apple had amassed more than $100 billion in cash, most of it held abroad as foreign earnings. Meanwhile, once-dominant tech industry giants such as Nokia, Sony, Dell, and BlackBerry were struggling.

Despite strong 2012 sales for the iPhone 5, industry observers began to wonder whether Apple's hot streak of hit product introductions was starting to cool. Apple's reputation was based on its proven ability to disrupt existing markets (e.g., the music and telecommunications industries) and to create new markets through the introduction of technical and design innovations. However, some viewed the 2012 launch of the iPhone 5 as an evolutionary step rather than a revolutionary breakthrough. In fact, many consumers opted to buy the slower, cheaper iPhone 4 or 4S rather than upgrade to the iPhone 5. Without Jobs, who was considered by many to be the heart and soul of the company, were Apple's best days behind it?

Exhibit 1-14 Apple cofounder Steve Jobs wore many hats during his illustrious career, including inventor, entrepreneur, CEO, and visionary technologist. He was also a master showman, a storyteller, and marketing genius. His appearances at product launches are the stuff of legend, and under his guidance Apple's must-have products—including the iPod, the iPhone, and the iPad—were, simply put, the epitome of "cool."
Source: Paul Sakuma/Associated Press.

The Competitive Threat

As growth in the key smartphone sector began to slow, Apple's most formidable competitor was Samsung Electronics, a division of Korean industrial giant Samsung Group, whose products range from semiconductors to household appliances to smartphones. Samsung's popular Galaxy series of phones are powered by Android, an operating system developed by Google. Some Galaxy models, including the Galaxy Note (also known as a "phablet"), have larger screens than the iPhone—a point of difference that has helped drive sales of those devices. The rivalry between Apple and Samsung has been heated, with the two sides squaring off in court over alleged patent infringement.

China and Europe are two of Samsung's key markets; in 2012, the company launched the Galaxy S III in Europe. In 2013, however, Samsung staged a lavish event at Radio City Music Hall in New York to launch the Galaxy S4. Why the change? As J. K. Shin, the executive in charge of Samsung's mobile business, noted, "We're a global player in the smartphone market and a global company, and the U.S. is an important market for us. . . . I'm not satisfied with our U.S. market share."

In many developing countries, there is strong demand for inexpensive mobile phones. Some Android-based models from Samsung and other companies sell for much less than Apple's cheapest models. For many years, Apple did not offer a lower-cost version of the iPhone. In the United States, wireless carriers such as Verizon and AT&T subsidized the price of the iPhone for consumers who signed multiyear service contracts—a factor that explained why an American iPhone 5 sold for $199. By contrast, in other countries consumers paid the full, unsubsidized price of the iPhone but were not tied to a contract. Moreover, the iPhone 5 was the same in every world market. By contrast, Samsung made several versions of the Galaxy S4—using different processors, for example—to suit the needs of different regions.

Not surprisingly, smartphone makers are setting their sights on China, India, and other emerging markets. For example, Greater China, which includes China, Hong Kong, and Taiwan, is now Apple's second-largest market. In 2013, Cook announced that China Mobile, the largest carrier in the region and the world's largest carrier overall, would begin selling the iPhone. Apple faces strong competition from local competitors such as Oppo and Xiaomi; Oppo's R9 bested the iPhone 6 as the top-selling smartphone in 2016. Distribution is critical, and Cook is aggressively expanding the number of outlets in China that sell iPhones.

As growth in China and Europe slows, India, the number 2 smartphone market, is becoming increasingly important. Here, however, Apple's 3 percent market share means that it lags far behind Samsung and Chinese producers in terms of smartphone shipments. Two-thirds of the phones sold in India cost less than $180. By contrast, Indian consumers pay about $300 for an iPhone 5S, the older model that Apple launched in 2013. These devices are sold through small, independent retailers; for entry-level buyers, Apple's Web site offers only the iPhone SE and iPhone 6. In May 2017, Apple began manufacturing the SE in India, bringing the price down to approximately $325. Local manufacturing will also allow Apple to open its own flagship stores in India.

Famously, Steve Jobs downplayed the importance of formal market research, saying that consumers don't know what they want. By contrast, Samsung Electronics relies heavily on market research; it has 60,000 staff members working in dozens of research centers in China, Great Britain, India, Japan, the United States, and elsewhere. Samsung designers have backgrounds in such diverse disciplines as psychology, sociology, and engineering. Researchers track trends in fashion and interior design. Also, Samsung spends more on advertising and promotion than does Apple.

The Post-Jobs Era Begins

In the months following Jobs's death, Cook made a number of key strategic decisions. For example, he authorized the introduction of the iPad mini, a product that Jobs had opposed. It quickly became a bestseller. In fall 2013, in conjunction with the launch of the iPhone 5s and iOS 7, a long-rumored lower-priced iPhone model was unveiled. The iPhone 5c featured a plastic case and was available in several colors; the price was approximately $100 lower than that of the new iPhone 5s. The 5c was designed to appeal especially to consumers in emerging markets who could not afford a top-of-the-line smartphone.

China represented a major opportunity, with a catch: Estimates of the market's potential were tempered by the rapid emergence of low-cost handsets from Chinese manufacturers such as Xiaomi. As Cook noted in an interview with *Bloomberg Businessweek*, "We never had an objective to sell a low-cost phone. Our primary objective is to sell a great phone and a great experience, and we figured out a way to do it at a lower cost."

Cook made key personnel decisions as well. Scott Forstall, the executive in charge of iOS mobile software, was fired. In his place, Cook named chief designer Jonathan Ive and software executive Craig Federighi. Going forward, Ive, who had been senior vice president for industrial design, will be responsible for the "look and feel"—in other words, the user interface—for the iPhone and iPad. When Cook, Ive, and Federighi appeared together on the cover of *Bloomberg Businessweek* in fall 2013, commentators noted that Steve Jobs would have never shared the spotlight in this manner. In another key appointment, Angela Ahrendts, the highly regarded CEO of Burberry PLC, was recruited to take over Apple's retail operations.

Apple's Marketing Communications Problem

Cook and his team also addressed the issue of Apple's marketing communications. It was widely reported that Phil Schiller, Apple's senior vice president for global marketing, was concerned that Apple's advertising had lost its edge. Apple had a long-standing relationship with a single agency: Los Angeles-based Chiat/Day, which had created the legendary "1984" television spot that launched the original Macintosh. In the 1990s, that agency, now known as TBWA/Chiat/Day, created the iconic "Think Different" campaign. However, a "Genius Bar" campaign timed to coincide with the 2012 Olympics was deemed a failure. In a subsequent e-mail to TBWA, Schiller admitted that he was impressed by arch-rival Samsung's 2013 Super Bowl ad; by contrast, he noted, Apple was "struggling to nail a compelling [creative] brief on iPhone."

The marketing issue was pushed to the forefront during the Academy Awards broadcast in spring 2014. Oscar host Ellen DeGeneres took a star-studded selfie (featuring Bradley Cooper, Jennifer Lawrence, and Brad Pitt, among others) with a Samsung Galaxy phone and posted it on Twitter. The post then made social media history after being retweeted more than 3.5 million times. It turns out that DeGeneres is an iPhone owner; however, Samsung had paid $20 million to sponsor the broadcast. Although there was some disagreement among industry insiders about the monetary value the publicity the stunt generated, most agreed that Samsung had gotten the better of Apple. Writing in *Advertising Age*, Mark Bergen summed up the situation bluntly when he noted, "Samsung is simply out-innovating its archrival when it comes to marketing."

Spurred into action, Cook and Schiller authorized the formation of an in-house advertising agency at Apple. The company is hiring top talent from some of the ad industry's best agencies to staff it. The in-house team has been tasked with creating new ads; it will compete against TBWA/Media Arts Lab, as TBWA is now known, in a process known as a "creative shootout." Schiller has also beefed up Apple's roster of agencies that specialize in digital marketing.

CEO Tim Cook Asserts Himself

By mid-2014, it was clear that CEO Tim Cook was stepping out of the shadow of his legendary predecessor (see Exhibit 1-15). In a move designed to make Apple's common stock more affordable to investors, Cook authorized a seven-for-one stock split. Simply put, if an investor held 50 shares of the stock at a price of, say $500 per share before the split, after the split the investor would have 350 shares of stock priced at $71.43 per share.

In May 2014, Cook announced that Apple was acquiring Beats Electronics for $3 billion. The deal brought two more key personnel into the Apple fold—namely, hip-hop star Dr. Dre and music mogul Jimmy Iovine. The two had founded Beats in 2006 to market premium headphones; by the time the deal was announced in May 2014, the duo had also launched an online music streaming service, Beats Radio. Both Dre and Iovine were added to the roster of Apple executives, and it was expected that their close ties to the music industry would be an asset. Moreover, the deal reflected the growing importance of wearable technology; many believed that "fashion electronics" products such as Beats' $399 headphones were poised for explosive growth.

In September 2014, CEO Cook and his team introduced the iPhone 6 and iPhone 6 Plus, both of which featured larger screens than earlier iPhones. Apple Pay, a key feature of the new devices, promised to usher in a new era of secure mobile payments. Cook also presided over the launch of a new wearable device, the Apple Watch, in 2015.

In 2016, the iPhone 7 and the larger iPhone 7 Plus went on sale. Their launch coincided with the recall of Samsung's Galaxy Note 7, a situation that helped drive sales and revenues at Apple. Even so, trouble spots were apparent. In China, for example, Apple's handsets were losing ground to local brands including Huawei, Oppo, and Vivo.

Even as the iPhone continued to generate significant profits, Cook set the strategic goal of doubling revenues from Apple's services business, including the App Store and Apple Music, to $50 billion by 2020. To help achieve that goal, Apple began to experiment with original video programming. As Apple Music chief Jimmy Iovine said, "A music service needs to be more than a bunch of songs and a few playlists. I'm trying to help Apple Music be an overall movement in popular culture." Among its projects: *Carpool Karaoke*, based on talk show host James Corden's popular feature, and *Planet of the Apps* from will.i.am.

Apple and Autonomous Cars

In 2014, word began to circulate that Apple was developing autonomous-driving technology for a new generation of automobiles. Project Titan, as the initiative was known, involved machine learning, artificial intelligence (AI), and other advanced technologies. Established automakers, including Ford and GM, were also speeding up their development efforts in this area in order to catch industry pioneer Tesla. For example, GM acquired Cruise Automation, an autonomous-car startup; GM has also deployed more than 300 Chevrolet Bolt EVs. Ford invested $1 billion in Argo AI. Meanwhile, other tech companies were jumping into the fray. Waymo, a division of Google, has been working on driverless-car technology since 2009. In 2016, Waymo launched a partnership with Fiat Chrysler Automobiles (FCA). Ride-sharing pioneer Uber also has projects in development.

The iPhone Turns 10

In 2017, anticipation was running high for the 10th-anniversary edition of Apple's iconic iPhone. At Apple's Worldwide Developers conference in June 2017, Apple launched ARKit, a technology platform that enables developers to create new apps for the next-generation iOS 11. LEGO and IKEA are two of the first companies to develop augmented-reality (AR) apps. The IKEA app, for example, allows furniture shoppers to use the iPhone's camera to visualize 3D images of IKEA furniture superimposed on different rooms in their homes and apartments. Some industry observers also predict that Apple will build AR technology and sensors into eyeglasses, in which case users would not need to have access to their phones to utilize the AR feature. iOS 11 was released at the end of September 2017.

Analysts had predicted a mammoth upgrade "supercycle," fueled in part by rumors of major form-factor changes such as a cutting-edge OLED (organic light-emitting diode) screen. The new phone was designed to support both augmented reality and virtual reality technologies as well as artificial intelligence.

On September 12, 2017, CEO Cook took the stage at the Steve Jobs Theater in Apple Park, the company's new $5 billion campus, to launch the new line of phones. These devices included the iPhone 8 ($699) and iPhone 8 Plus ($799). The special-edition iPhone X, starting at $999, reflected Apple's strategy of charging its most brand-loyal customers premium prices for hardware upgrades as the smartphone category entered the mature phase of the product life cycle.

In 2018, the company launched HomePod, a $349 home speaker powered by Apple's Siri voice assistant. Within the tech industry, some viewed the HomePod as Apple's "late-to-the-game" response to Amazon's wildly popular Echo digital assistant. Echo's artificial-intelligence capabilities allow it to respond to the vocal prompt "Alexa," followed by a verbal command or question. Despite the fact that Amazon commands roughly 70 percent of the market, Apple CEO Cook insists that the key to HomePod's success will be a feature Echo lacks: high-quality music playback capability. "We're hitting on something people will be delighted with. It's gonna blow them away. It's gonna rock the house," Cook says.

Discussion Questions

1-19. Are you an iOS user or an Android user? Which brand of smartphone did you buy, and why?

1-20. Do you think Apple can continue to grow by developing breakthrough products that create new markets, as it did with the iPod, iPhone, and iPad?

1-21. How has Samsung's global marketing strategy enabled it to compete so effectively against Apple?

1-22. Assess the prospects for the global success of HomePod.

1-23. Do you think Apple should develop self-driving cars (i.e., hardware) or focus on self-driving systems (i.e., software)?

1-24. Which uses for an AI-enabled iPhone can you think of?

1-25. More than 1.3 billion Apple devices are in use worldwide. The company's goal is to achieve 100 percent renewable energy and to generate and source 4 gigawatts of new clean energy by 2020. **Dig deeper**: What is the update on this initiative? Conduct some exploratory research, and write a short essay or present a brief oral report on your findings. Remember to cite your sources!

Sources: Saritha Rai, "Finally, a Cheap(ish) iPhone," *Bloomberg Businessweek* (June 19, 2017), pp. 30–32; Megan Murphy, "Tim Cook on Apple's Future—And His Legacy," *Bloomberg Businessweek* (June 19, 2017), p. 54; Lucas Shaw and Alex Webb, "A Star Is Born," *Bloomberg Businessweek* (May 1–7, 2017), pp. 22–24; Tim Bradshaw, "Apple Grapples with iPhone Retreat in China," *Financial Times* (February 2, 2017), p. 13; Ann-Christine Diaz and Maureen Morrison, "For Apple, Marketing Is a Whole New Game," *Advertising Age* (June 9, 2014), pp. 12–14+; Sam Grobart, "What, Us Worry?", *Bloomberg Businessweek* (September 19–25, 2013);

Sam Grobart, "Think Colossal: How Samsung Became the World's No. 1 Smartphone Maker," *Bloomberg Businessweek* (April 1–7, 2013), pp. 58–64; Yun-Hee Kim, "Samsung Targets Apple's Home Turf," *The Wall Street Journal* (March 15, 2013), pp. B1, B4; Dhanya Ann Thoppil, "In India, iPhone Lags Far Behind," *The Wall Street Journal* (February 27, 2013), pp. B1, B4; Brian X. Chen, "Challenging Apple's Cool," *The*

New York Times (February 11, 2013), pp. B1, B6; Anton Troianovski, "Fight to Unseat iPhone Intensifies," *The Wall Street Journal* (January 25, 2013), pp. B1, B6; Rolfe Winkler, "Apple's Power Within," *The Wall Street Journal* (December 7, 2013), p. C1; Josh Tyrangiel, "Tim Cook's Freshman Year," Cover Story, *Bloomberg Businessweek* (September 10–26, 2012), pp. 62–75.

Notes

[1] Jan Cienski, "The Man Who Bet on Tradition," *Financial Times* (January 14, 2015), p. 12.

[2] American Marketing Association. www.ama.org/AboutAMA/Pages/Definition-of-Marketing.aspx. Accessed June 19, 2015.

[3] Rachel Sanderson, "Starbucks's Shot at Selling Espresso to the Italians," *Financial Times* (February 28, 2017), p. B8.

[4] Bruce Horovitz, "Starbucks Remakes Its Future with an Eye on Wine and Beer," *USA Today* (October 22, 2010), p. 1B.

[5] Quelch, John A., and Katherine E. Jocz. *All Business is Local: Why Place Matters More Than Ever in a Global, Virtual World.* New York: Portfolio/Penguin, 2012.

[6] With certain categories of differentiated goods, including designer clothing and other luxury products, higher price is often associated with increased value.

[7] The history of the Subaru 360 is documented in Randall Rothman, *Where the Suckers Moon: The Life and Death of an Advertising Campaign* (New York, NY: Vintage Books, 1994), p. 4.

[8] "Best and Worst Car Brands," *Consumer Reports* (April 2018), p. 12.

[9] Jay Barney notes that "a firm is said to have a competitive advantage when it is implementing a value-creating strategy not simultaneously being implemented by any current or potential competitors." See Jay Barney, "Firm Resources and Sustained Competitive Advantage," *Journal of Management* 17, no. 1 (1991), p. 102.

[10] Jagdish Bhagwati, *In Defense of Globalization* (New York, NY: Oxford University Press, 2004), p. 3.

[11] John Micklethwait and Adrian Wooldridge, *A Future Perfect: The Challenge and Hidden Promise of Globalization* (New York, NY: Crown Publishers, 2000), p. xxvii.

[12] Grant Wahl, "Football vs. Fútbol," *Sports Illustrated* (July 5, 2004), pp. 68–72.

[13] Scott Miller, "BMW Bucks Diversification to Focus on Luxury Models," *The Wall Street Journal* (March 20, 2002), p. B4.

[14] Vijay Govindarajan and Anil Gupta, "Setting a Course for the New Global Landscape," *Financial Times—Mastering Global Business*, part I (1998), p. 3.

[15] Diana Farrell, "Assessing Your Company's Global Potential," *Harvard Business Review* 82, no. 12 (December 2004), p. 85.

[16] Elizabeth Ashcroft, "Nestlé and the Twenty-First Century," Harvard Business School Case 9-595-074, 1995. See also Ernest Beck, "Nestlé Feels Little Pressure to Make Big Acquisitions," *The Wall Street Journal* (June 22, 2000), p. B4.

[17] Betsy McKay, "Coke's 'Think Local' Strategy Has Yet to Prove Itself," *The Wall Street Journal* (March 1, 2001), p. B6.

[18] Tony Barber, "Culture Change Is Pivotal as Philips Sheds Its Old Skin," *Financial Times* (July 5, 2013), p. 14.

[19] C. Samuel Craig and Susan P. Douglas, "Responding to the Challenges of Global Markets: Change, Complexity, Competition, and Conscience," *Columbia Journal of World Business* 31, no. 4 (Winter 1996), pp. 6–18.

[20] Gabriel Kahn, "Three Italian Furniture Makers Hope to Create a Global Luxury Powerhouse," *The Wall Street Journal* (October 31, 2006), p. B1.

[21] Phred Dvorak, "Big Changes Drive Small Carpet Firm," *The Wall Street Journal* (October 30, 2006), p. B3.

[22] Aaron O. Patrick, "Softer Nike Pitch Woos Europe's Women," *The Wall Street Journal* (September 11, 2008), p. B6.

[23] Shaoming Zou and S. Tamer Cavusgil, "The GMS: A Broad Conceptualization of Global Marketing Strategy and Its Effect on Performance," *Journal of Marketing* 66, no. 4 (October 2002), pp. 40–56.

[24] Paul Sonne and Kathy Gordon, "Burberry Refocusing on World's Big Cities," *The Wall Street Journal* (November 8, 2012), p. B9.

[25] Angela Ahrendts, "Burberry's CEO on Turning an Aging British Icon into a Global Luxury Brand," *Harvard Business Review* 91, no. 1/2 (January–February 2013), pp. 39–42.

[26] Vanessa Friedman, "Christopher Bailey Reveals His Plan for Burberry," *The New York Times* (November 13, 2014).

[27] Mark Vandevelde, "Burberry at Creative Crossroads as Bailey Quits," *Financial Times* (November 1, 2017), p. 17.

[28] Joanne Lipman, "Ad Fad: Marketers Turn Sour on Global Sales Pitch Harvard Guru Makes," *The Wall Street Journal* (May 12, 1988), p. 1.

[29] Chad Terhune, "Coke Tries to Pop Back in Vital Japan Market," *The Wall Street Journal* (July 11, 2006), pp. C1, C3.

[30] William C. Taylor and Alan M. Webber, *Going Global: Four Entrepreneurs Map the New World Marketplace* (New York, NY: Penguin Books USA, 1996), pp. 48, 49.

[31] Saabira Chaudhuri, "Nipped by Upstarts, Unilever Decides to Imitate Them," *The Wall Street Journal* (January 3, 2018), p. A8.

[32] Greg Farrell, "McDonald's Relies on Europe for Growth," *Financial Times* (April 20, 2010).

[33] Simon Mundy, "Amazon to Deliver $3 bn Investment in India," *Financial Times* (June 8, 2016), p. 10.

[34] Louise Lucas, "New Accent on Consumer Tastes," *Financial Times* (December 14, 2010), p. 14.

[35] Leslie Kwoh, "Cinnabon Finds Sweet Success in Russia, Mideast," *The Wall Street Journal* (December 26, 2012), p. B5.

[36] E. J. Schultz, "To the Moon and Back: How Tang Grew to Be a Billion-Dollar Global Brand," *Advertising Age* (June 16, 2011), p. 13.

[37] John A. Quelch and Edward J. Hoff, "Customizing Global Marketing," *Harvard Business Review* 64, no. 3 (May–June 1986), p. 59.

[38] Neil Gough, "An Overseas Kick-Start," *The New York Times* (May 24, 2017), pp. B1, B4.

[39] Kana Inagaki, "Rebirth of a Brand," *Financial Times* (June 5, 2015), p. 5.

[40] Mayumi Negishi, Dana Mattioli, and Ryan Dezember, "Japan's Uniqlo Sets Goal: No. 1 in the U.S.," *The Wall Street Journal* (April 12, 2013), p. B7. See also Hiroyuki Kachi and Kenneth Maxwell, "Uniqlo Woos the World But Falters at Home," *The Wall Street Journal* (October 12, 2012), p. B8.

[41] The complete list can be found online at www.fortune.com/global500/.

[42] Adapted from Howard Perlmutter, "The Tortuous Evolution of the Multinational Corporation," *Columbia Journal of World Business* (January–February 1969).

[43] Norihiko Shirouzu, "Tailoring World's Cars to U.S. Tastes," *The Wall Street Journal* (January 1, 2001), pp. B1, B6.

[44] T. W. Malnight, "Globalization of an Ethnocentric Firm: An Evolutionary Perspective," *Strategic Management Journal* 16, no. 2 (February 1995), p. 125.

[45] Robert Mondavi, *Harvests of Joy: My Passion for Excellence* (New York, NY: Harcourt Brace & Company, 1998), p. 333.

[46] Martin Fackler, "A Second Chance for Japanese Cell Phone Makers," *The New York Times* (November 17, 2005), p. C1.

[47] Franck Riboud, "Think Global, Act Local," *Outlook* no. 3 (2003), p. 8.

[48] Jim Stengel, *Grow: How Ideals Power Growth and Profit at the World's Greatest Companies* (New York, NY: Crown Business, 2011), p. 167.

[49] Deborah Ball, "Too Many Cooks: Despite Revamp, Unwieldy Unilever Falls Behind Rivals," *The Wall Street Journal* (January 3, 2005), pp. A1, A5.

[50] Lee Hawkins, Jr., "New Driver: Reversing 80 Years of History, GM Is Reining in Global Fiefs," *The Wall Street Journal* (October 6, 2004), pp. A1, A14.

[51] Although the definitions provided here are important, to avoid confusion we will use the term *global marketing* when describing the general activities of global companies. Another note of caution is in order: Usage of the terms *international*, *multinational*, and *global* varies widely. Alert readers of the business press are likely to recognize inconsistencies; usage does not always reflect

the definitions provided here. In particular, companies that are (in the view of the authors as well as numerous other academics) global are often described as *multinational enterprises* (MNEs) or *multinational corporations* (MNCs). The United Nations prefers the term *transnational company* rather than *global company*. When we refer to an "international company" or a "multinational," we will do so in a way that maintains the distinctions described in the text.

[52]Douglas Brinkley, "Hoosier Honda," *The Wall Street Journal* (July 18, 2006), p. A14.

[53]Rebecca Blumenstein, "To Cut Costs, GM Is Adding Four Near-Identical Facilities," *The Wall Street Journal* (August 4, 1997).

[54]Allan J. Morrison, David A. Ricks, and Kendall Roth, "Globalization versus Regionalization: Which Way for the Multinational?" *Organizational Dynamics* (Winter 1991), p. 18.

[55]Michael A. Yoshino and U. Srinivasa Rangan, *Strategic Alliances: An Entrepreneurial Approach to Globalization* (Boston, MA: Harvard Business School Press, 1995), p. 64.

[56]Joseph A. DiMasi, Ronald W. Hansen, and Henry G. Grabowski, "The Price of Innovation: New Estimates of Drug Development Costs," *Journal of Health Economics* 22, no. 2 (March 2003), p. 151.

[57]Nicholas Zamiska, "Novartis to Establish Drug R&D Center in China," *The Wall Street Journal* (November 11, 2006), p. A3.

[58]Daniel Yergin and Joseph Stanislaw, *The Commanding Heights* (New York, NY: Simon & Schuster, 1998), p. 13.

[59]Bill Vlasic, "Ford's Bet: It's a Small World after All," *The New York Times* (January 9, 2010), p. B1.

[60]William C. Taylor and Alan M. Webber, *Going Global: Four Entrepreneurs Map the New World Marketplace* (New York, NY: Penguin USA, 1996), p. 18.

[61]Thomas L. Friedman, *The Lexus and the Olive Tree* (New York, NY: Anchor Books, 2000), pp. 221–222.

[62]John Tagliabue, "Renault Pins Its Survival on a Global Gamble," *The New York Times* (July 2, 2000), Section 3, pp. 1, 6; Don Kirk and Peter S. Green, "Renault Rolls the Dice on Two Auto Projects Abroad," *The New York Times* (August 29, 2002), pp. W1, W7.

[63]Joel Millman, "The Fallen: Lorenzo Zambrano; Hard Times for Cement Man," *The Wall Street Journal* (December 11, 2008), p. A1.

[64]Peter F. Drucker, *Innovation and Entrepreneurship* (New York, NY: Harper & Row, 1985), p. 19.

[65]Rachel Sanderson, "Bologna's Creative Hub Powers Revival," *Financial Times* (December 13, 2017), p. 8.

[66]Larry Rohter, "Bolivia's Poor Proclaim Abiding Distrust of Globalization," *The New York Times* (October 17, 2003), p. A3.

PART TWO

THE GLOBAL MARKETING ENVIRONMENT

2 The Global Economic Environment

LEARNING OBJECTIVES

2-1 Identify and briefly explain the major changes in the world economy that have occurred during the past 100 years.

2-2 Compare and contrast the main types of economic systems that are found in different regions of the world.

2-3 Explain the categories of economic development used by the World Bank, and identify the key emerging country markets at each stage of development.

2-4 Discuss the significance of balance of payments statistics for the world's major economies.

2-5 Identify world leaders in merchandise and services trade, and explain how currency exchange rates impact a company's opportunities in different parts of the world.

CASE 2-1

India's Economy at the Crossroads: Can Prime Minister Narendra Modi Deliver *Acche Din*?

During the global recession crisis years from 2008 to 2012, India's economy was in dismal shape. Average annual economic growth was stalled at about 4 percent, inflation was running in double digits, and foreign companies were being blindsided by substantial tax bills. Prime Minister Manmohan Singh and Finance Minister Pranab Mukherjee lacked the capacity to tame inflation, secure financing for much-needed infrastructure improvements, or deliver wheat and rice to India's poor. In short, the economic policies of the ruling Congress Party were ineffective.

Today, India's economy is a combination of good news and bad news. The good news: For several years, India was the world's fastest-growing large economy, posting annual gross domestic product (GDP) increases ranging from 7 percent to 8 percent. By 2017, however, as India commemorated the 70th anniversary of its independence from Great Britain, growth had slowed. Meanwhile, other macroeconomic issues continue to loom large. For one thing, the Indian economy isn't creating enough jobs to absorb the 1 million Indians who enter the job market each month. In addition, as capital expenditures have fallen, so has consumer confidence.

Narendra Modi, the Bharatiya Janata Party's (BJP) candidate, was elected prime minister in 2014. He immediately launched a number of modernization initiatives, including one titled "Make in India" (see Exhibit 2-1). During his first two years in office, Modi loosened investment restrictions and embarked on a global public relations tour to reach out to foreign investors. His efforts paid off. Between March 31, 2015, and March 31, 2016, foreign direct investment (FDI) in India totaled $40 billion, a 29 percent increase compared with the year ended March 31, 2014.

Exhibit 2-1 Shortly after taking office in May 2014, Indian Prime Minister Narendra Modi launched an initiative to attract more foreign manufacturing to his country. Manufacturing currently accounts for only 16 percent of India's economic output; the government is intent on increasing that figure to 25 percent. To reach that goal, India plans to create 100 million new jobs by 2022.
Source: Partha Sarkar/Xinhua/Alamy.

Despite such progress, Modi faces the daunting task of working with opposition politicians who are blocking his attempts at economic reform. For example, Modi was forced to drop a key piece of legislation that would have made it easier for companies to acquire land for greenfield investment. The measure was tabled after negative publicity and opposition from rural voters. Some observers assert that the prime minster still needs to deliver some additional "Big Bang" liberalization measures to further renew India's economy.

Will Modi be able to make good on his campaign pledges and deliver real economic reform? Or, in the end, will his efforts just amount to lots of talk and very little action? Case 2-1 describes the challenges facing India today and Modi's efforts to jump-start the economy. (When you are done reading the chapter, study the case and answer the discussion questions.) Needless to say, the current state of India's economy has created both challenges and opportunities for global marketers.

The situation in India illustrates vividly the dynamic, integrated nature of today's economic environment. Recall the basic definition of a market: people or organizations with needs and wants and the willingness and ability to buy or sell. As noted in Chapter 1, many companies engage in global marketing in an effort to reach new customers outside their home countries and thereby increase sales, profits, and market share. Brazil, Russia, India, China, and South Africa deserve special mention; collectively referred to as BRICS, these five country markets are especially dynamic and represent important opportunities.[1] The BRICS nations and other emerging markets are also nurturing companies that are challenging established global giants at home and abroad.

This chapter identifies the most salient characteristics of the world economic environment, starting with an overview of the world economy. We then present a survey of economic system types, a discussion of the stages of market development, and an explanation of the concept known as balance of payments. Foreign exchange is discussed in the final section of the chapter. Throughout the chapter, we consider the implications of the recent worldwide economic downturn on global marketing strategies.

2-1 The World Economy—Overview of Major Changes

◀ **2-1** Identify and briefly explain the major changes in the world economy that have occurred during the past 100 years.

The world economy has changed profoundly since the end of World War II.[2] Perhaps the most fundamental change is the emergence of global markets: Responding to new opportunities, global competitors have steadily displaced or absorbed local competitors in many markets. Concurrently, the integration of the world economy has increased significantly. Economic integration stood at 10 percent at the beginning of the twentieth century; today, it is approximately 50 percent. Integration is particularly striking in the European Union (EU) and the North American Free Trade Area (NAFTA). However, as noted in the last chapter, protectionism and nationalism are emerging forces in some countries that may slow the pace further integration.

Just 75 years ago, the world was far less integrated than it is today. As evidence of the changes that have taken place, consider the automobile. Cars with European nameplates such as Renault, Citroën, Peugeot, Morris, Volvo, and others were once radically different from the American cars from Chevrolet, Ford, or Plymouth or the Japanese models from Toyota or Nissan. They were local cars built by local companies using local supply chains, mostly destined for local or regional markets. Even today, global and regional auto companies make cars for their home-country car buyers that are not marketed abroad.

For automakers BMW, Ford, Honda, Hyundai, Kia, and Toyota, however, the global car has become a reality. The changes in their products reflect organizational changes as well. The world's largest automakers have, for the most part, evolved into global companies. Supply chains now stretch around the globe. Ford is a case in point: In 2008, the company unveiled an updated version of the Fiesta that is being marketed throughout the world. As Mark Fields, an executive vice president at Ford, explained, "We've had cars with the same name, like Escort and Focus, but the products themselves were very regional. This is a real shift point for us in that it's a real global car."[3]

During the past two decades, the world economic environment has become increasingly dynamic; change has been dramatic and far-reaching. To achieve success, executives and marketers must take into account the following new realities:[4]

Capital movements have replaced trade as the driving force of the world economy.

Production has become "uncoupled" from employment.

The world economy dominates the scene; individual country economies play a subordinate role.

The 100-year struggle between capitalism and socialism that began in 1917 is largely over.

The growth of e-commerce diminishes the importance of national barriers and forces companies to reevaluate their business models.

The first change is the increased volume of capital movements. The dollar value of world trade in goods was $16.5 trillion in 2015. However, the Bank for International Settlements has calculated that foreign exchange transactions worth approximately $5 trillion are booked *every day*. This works out to more than $1 quadrillion annually, a figure that far surpasses the dollar value of world trade in goods and services.[5] An inescapable conclusion resides in these data: Global capital movements far exceed the dollar volume of global trade. In other words, *currency trading represents the world's largest market*.

The second change concerns the relationship between productivity and employment. To illustrate this relationship, it is necessary to review some basic macroeconomics. **Gross domestic product (GDP)**, a measure of a nation's economic activity, is calculated by adding consumer spending (*C*), investment spending (*I*), government purchases (*G*), and net exports (*NX*):

$$GDP = C + I + G + NX$$

Economic growth, as measured by GDP, reflects increases in a nation's productivity. Until the economic crisis of the late 2000s, employment in manufacturing had remained steady or declined while productivity continued to grow. Employment rates declined in countries where a bubble economy of misallocated resources in housing and real estate collapsed. In the United States, manufacturing's share of GDP declined from 19.2 percent in 1989 to 13 percent in 2009.[6] In 2011, approximately 9 percent of the U.S. workforce was employed in manufacturing; in 1971, that figure had been 26 percent. During that 40-year period, productivity increased dramatically.

Similar trends can be found in many other major industrial economies. In the United Kingdom, for example, manufacturing accounts for only 8 percent of the country's total employment, compared with 24 percent in 1980.[7] Manufacturing represents only 10 percent of the U.K. economy; key sectors include automobiles, aerospace, and pharmaceuticals. One recent study of 20 large economies found that between 1995 and 2002, more than 22 million factory jobs were eliminated. Manufacturing is not in decline; rather, it is *employment* in manufacturing that is in decline.[8] Creating new job opportunities is one of the most important tasks facing policymakers today.

The third major change in the world economic environment is the emergence of the world economy as the dominant economic unit. Company executives and national leaders who recognize this reality have the greatest chance of success. For example, the real secret of the economic success of Germany and Japan is the fact that business leaders and policymakers focus on world markets and their respective countries' competitive positions in that world economy. This change has brought two questions to the fore: How does the global economy work, and who is in charge? Unfortunately, the answers to these questions are not clear-cut.

The fourth change is the end of the Cold War. The demise of communism as an economic and political system can be explained in a straightforward manner: Communism is not an effective economic system. The overwhelmingly superior performance of the world's market economies has given leaders in socialist countries little choice but to renounce their ideology. A key policy change in such countries has been the abandonment of futile attempts to manage national economies with a single central plan. This policy change frequently goes hand in hand with governmental efforts to foster increased public participation in matters of state by introducing democratic reforms.

Finally, the personal computer revolution and the advent of the Internet era have in some ways diminished the importance of national boundaries. Worldwide, an estimated 1 billion people use personal computers. In the so-called Information Age, barriers of time and place have been subverted by a transnational cyberworld that functions "24/7." Alibaba, Amazon.com, eBay, Facebook, Google, Instagram, Netflix, Snapchat, Spotify, Twitter, and YouTube are just a sampling of the companies that are pushing the envelope in this Web 3.0 world.

> "Only an outbreak of protectionist policies or a sharp rise in international shipping costs could slow or temporarily reverse manufacturing's declining share of employment in the United States."[9]
>
> Steven J. Davis, Professor of Economics, University of Chicago

(2-2) Economic Systems

◀ **2-2** Compare and contrast the main types of economic systems that are found in different regions of the world.

Traditionally, economists identified four main types of economic systems: market capitalism, centrally planned socialism, centrally planned capitalism, and market socialism. As shown in Figure 2-1, this classification was based on the dominant method of resource allocation (market versus command) and the dominant form of resource ownership (private versus state). Thanks to globalization, however, economic systems are harder to categorize within the confines of a four-cell matrix. More robust, descriptive criteria include the following:[10]

Type of economy.   Is the nation an advanced industrial state, an emerging economy, a transition economy, or a developing nation?

Type of government.   Is the nation ruled by a monarchy, a dictatorship, or a tyrant? Is there an autocratic, one-party system? Is the nation dominated by another state, or is it a democracy with a multiparty system? Is it an unstable or terrorist nation?

Trade and capital flows.   Is the nation characterized by almost completely free trade or incomplete free trade, and is it part of a trading bloc? Is there a currency board, or are there exchange controls? Is there no trade, or does the government dominate trade possibilities?

FIGURE 2-1 Economic Systems

	Resource Allocation	
	Market	Command
Private	Market capitalism	Centrally planned capitalism
State	Market socialism	Centrally planned socialism

Resource Ownership

The commanding heights.   Are these sectors (e.g., the transportation, communications, and energy sectors) state owned and operated? Is there a mix of state and private ownership? Are they all private, with or without controlled prices?

Services provided by the state and funded through taxes.   Are pensions, health care, and education provided? Pensions and education but not health care? Do privatized systems dominate?

Institutions.   Is the nation characterized by transparency, standards, the absence of corruption, and the presence of a free press and strong courts? Or is corruption a fact of life and the press controlled by the government? Are standards ignored and the court system compromised?

Markets.   Does the nation have a free market system characterized by high-risk/high-reward entrepreneurial dynamism? Is it a free market that is dominated by monopolies, cartels, and concentrated industries? Is it a socialized market with cooperation among business, government, and labor (but with little entrepreneurial support)? Or is planning, including price and wage controls, dominated by the government?

Market Capitalism

Market capitalism is an economic system in which individuals and firms allocate resources and production resources are privately owned. Simply put, consumers decide which goods they desire and firms determine what and how much of those goods to produce; the role of the state in market capitalism is to promote competition among firms and to ensure consumer protection. Today, market capitalism is widely practiced around the world, most notably in North America and the European Union (EU) (see Table 2-1).

It would be a gross oversimplification, however, to assume that all market-oriented economies function in an identical manner. Economist Paul Krugman has remarked that the United States is distinguished by its competitive, "wild free-for-all," and decentralized initiative. By contrast, outsiders sometimes refer to Japan as "Japan Inc." This label can be interpreted in different ways, but it basically refers to a tightly run, highly regulated economic system that is also market oriented.

Centrally Planned Socialism

At the opposite end of the spectrum from market capitalism is **centrally planned socialism**. In this type of economic system, the state has broad powers to serve the public interest as it sees fit. State planners make "top-down" decisions about which goods and services are produced and in which quantities; consumers can spend their money on what is available. Government ownership of entire industries as well as individual enterprises is characteristic of centrally planned socialism. Because demand typically exceeds supply in this model, the elements of the marketing mix are not used as strategic variables.[11] Little reliance is placed on product differentiation, advertising, or promotion; to eliminate "exploitation" by intermediaries, the government also controls distribution.

The clear superiority of market capitalism in delivering the goods and services that people need and want has led to its adoption in many formerly socialist countries. Thus, the socialist

TABLE 2-1 **Western Market Systems**

Type of System	Key Characteristics	Countries
Anglo-Saxon model	Private ownership; free enterprise economy; capitalism; minimal social safety net; highly flexible employment policies	United States, Canada, Great Britain
Social market economy model	Private ownership; "social partners" orientation that includes employer groups, unions, and banks; unions and corporations are involved in government, and vice versa; inflexible employment policies	Germany, France, Italy
Nordic model	Mix of state ownership and private ownership; high taxes; some market regulation; generous social safety net	Sweden, Norway

ideology, which was developed in the nineteenth century by Marx and perpetuated in the twentieth century by Lenin and others, has been resoundingly refuted. As William Greider wrote two decades ago:

> Marxism is utterly vanquished, if not yet entirely extinct, as an alternative economic system. Capitalism is triumphant. The ideological conflict first joined in the mid-nineteenth century in response to the rise of industrial capitalism, the deep argument that has preoccupied political imagination for 150 years, is ended.[13]

For decades, the economies of China, the former Soviet Union, and India functioned according to the tenets of centrally planned socialism. Today, however, all three countries are engaged in economic reforms characterized, in varying proportions, by increased reliance on market resource allocation and private ownership. Even as China's leaders attempt to maintain control over society, they acknowledge the importance of economic reform. At a recent assembly, leaders of the Chinese Communist Party asserted that reform "is an inevitable road for invigorating the country's economy and promoting social progress, and a great pioneering undertaking without parallel in history."

Centrally Planned Capitalism and Market Socialism

In reality, market capitalism and centrally planned socialism do not exist in "pure" form. In most countries, to a greater or lesser degree, command and market resource allocation are practiced simultaneously, as are private and state resource ownership. The role of government in modern market economies varies widely. An economic system in which command resource allocation is utilized extensively in an overall environment of private resource ownership can be called **centrally planned capitalism**. A fourth variant, **market socialism**, is also possible in which market-allocation policies are permitted within an overall environment of state ownership.

In Sweden, for example, where the government controls two-thirds of all expenditures, resource allocation is more "voter" oriented than "market" oriented. Also, as indicated in Table 2-2, the Swedish government has significant holdings in key business sectors. Thus, Sweden's "welfare state" is based on a hybrid economic system that incorporates elements of both centrally planned socialism and capitalism. The Swedish government is embarking on a privatization plan that calls for selling its stakes in some of the businesses listed in Table 2-2.[14] For example, in 2008 Vin & Spirit was sold to France's Pernod Ricard for $8.34 billion.

As noted previously, China is an example of state-directed socialism. However, China's communist leadership has given considerable freedom to businesses and individuals in the Guangdong Province to operate within a market system. Today, China's private sector accounts for approximately 70 percent of national output. Even so, state enterprises still receive more than two-thirds of the credit available from the country's banks.

Market reforms and nascent capitalism in many parts of the world are creating opportunities for large-scale investments by global companies. Indeed, Coca-Cola returned to India in 1994, two decades after being forced out by the government. A new law allowing 100 percent foreign ownership of enterprises helped pave the way for Coke's renewed efforts in that country. By contrast, Cuba stands as one of the last bastions of the command allocation approach. Daniel Yergin and Joseph Stanislaw sum up the situation this way:

> "Countries with planned economies have never been part of economic globalization. China's economy must become a market economy."[12]
>
> Long Yongtu, chief WTO negotiator for China

TABLE 2-2 Examples of Government Resource Ownership in Sweden

Company	Industry Sector	State Ownership %
TeliaSonera	Telecommunications	45
SAS	Airline	21*
Nordea	Banking	20
OMX	Stock exchange	7
Vin & Spirit	Alcohol	100**

*The Danish and Norwegian governments each own 14 percent.
**Sold in 2008.

> Socialists are embracing capitalism, governments are selling off companies they had national-
> ized, and countries are seeking to entice multinational corporations expelled just two decades
> earlier. Today, politicians on the left admit that their governments can no longer afford the
> expansive welfare state. . . . The decamping of the state from the "commanding heights" marks
> a great divide between the twentieth and twenty-first centuries. It is opening the doors of many
> formerly closed countries to trade and investment, and vastly increasing the global market.[15]

The Washington, D.C.–based Heritage Foundation, a conservative think tank, takes a more conventional approach to classifying economies: It compiles data from a survey of more than 180 countries that are ranked by degree of economic freedom (see Table 2-3). A number of key economic variables are considered in the rankings: trade policy, taxation policy, government consumption of economic output, monetary policy, capital flows and foreign investment, banking policy, wage and price controls, property rights, regulations, and the black market. Hong Kong and Singapore (see Exhibit 2-2) are currently ranked first and second in terms of economic freedom; Cuba, Venezuela, and North Korea are ranked lowest. Coincidentally, Cuba and North Korea are the only two countries where Coca-Cola is not available through authorized channels!

The market opportunity in Cuba has changed considerably recently (see Exhibit 2-3). In December 2014, with two years left in his administration, then-U.S. President Barack Obama took executive action: He announced that the United States and Cuba were renewing diplomatic

Exhibit 2-2 Home to the world's second-busiest port, Singapore has long been an important trade hub in Southeast Asia. The city-state is now being remade as a cultural destination. Because developers are running out of real estate, small, new projects are heading underground, as in the Ngee Ann Shopping Mall shown here.
Source: Rick Piper Photography/Alamy.

Exhibit 2-3 In March 2016, rock 'n' roll legends the Rolling Stones played their first-ever concert in Havana, Cuba. Singer Mick Jagger led the 500,000 attendees in a sing-along during the Stones classic "You Can't Always Get What You Want."
Source: Ernesto Mastrascusa/LatinContent/Getty Images.

TABLE 2-3 Index of Economic Freedom—2017 Rankings

Free
1. Hong Kong
2. Singapore
3. New Zealand
4. Switzerland
5. Australia

Mostly Free
6. Estonia
7. Canada
8. United Arab Emirates
9. Ireland
10. Chile
11. Taiwan
12. United Kingdom
13. Georgia
14. Luxembourg
15. Netherlands
16. Lithuania
17. United States
18. Denmark
19. Sweden
20. Latvia
21. Mauritius
22. Iceland
23. South Korea
24. Finland
25. Norway
26. Germany
27. Malaysia
28. Czech Republic
29. Qatar
30. Austria
31. Macedonia
32. Macau
33. Armenia
34. Botswana

Moderately Free
35. Brunei Darussalam
36. Israel
37. Colombia
38. Uruguay
39. Romania
40. Japan
41. Jamaica
42. Kazakhstan
43. Peru
44. Bahrain
45. Poland

46. Kosovo
47. Bulgaria
48. Cyprus
49. Belgium
50. Malta
51. Rwanda
52. Vanuatu
53. Jordan
54. Panama
55. Thailand
56. Hungary
57. Slovakia
58. Philippines
59. Saint Vincent and the Grenadines
60. Turkey
61. Kuwait
62. Saint Lucia
63. Costa Rica
64. Saudi Arabia
65. Albania
66. El Salvador
67. Dominica
68. Azerbaijan
69. Spain
70. Mexico
71. Fiji
72. France
73. Tonga
74. Guatemala
75. Côte d'Ivoire
76. Dominican Republic
77. Portugal
78. Namibia
79. Italy
80. Paraguay
81. South Africa
82. Oman
83. Montenegro
84. Indonesia
85. Seychelles
86. Morocco
87. Trinidad and Tobago
88. Swaziland
89. Kyrgyz Republic
90. Bahamas
91. Uganda
92. Bosnia and Herzegovina

Mostly Unfree
93. Burkina Faso
94. Cambodia
95. Croatia
96. Benin
97. Slovenia
98. Nicaragua
99. Serbia
100. Honduras
101. Belize
102. Mali
103. Gabon
104. Belarus
105. Tanzania
106. Guyana
107. Bhutan
108. Samoa
109. Tajikistan
110. Moldova
111. China
112. Sri Lanka
113. Madagascar
114. Russia
115. Nigeria
116. Cabo Verde
117. Democratic Republic of Congo
118. Ghana
119. Guinea-Bissau
120. Senegal
121. Comoros
122. Zambia
123. Tunisia
124. São Tomé and Príncipe
125. Nepal
126. Solomon Islands
127. Greece
128. Bangladesh
129. Mongolia
130. Barbados
131. Mauritania
132. Micronesia
133. Laos
134. Lesotho
135. Kenya
136. The Gambia
137. Lebanon
138. Togo

139. Burundi
140. Brazil
141. Pakistan
142. Ethiopia
143. India
144. Egypt
145. Sierra Leone
146. Burma
147. Vietnam
148. Uzbekistan
149. Malawi
150. Cameroon
151. Central African Republic
152. Papua New Guinea
153. Kiribati
154. Niger
155. Iran
156. Argentina
157. Maldives

Repressed
158. Mozambique
159. Haiti
160. Ecuador
161. Liberia
162. Chad
163. Afghanistan
164. Sudan
165. Angola
166. Ukraine
167. Timor-Leste
168. Bolivia
169. Guinea
170. Turkmenistan
171. Djibouti
172. Algeria
173. Timor-Leste
174. Equatorial Guinea
175. Zimbabwe
176. Eritrea
177. Republic of Congo
178. Cuba
179. Venezuela
180. North Korea

Not Ranked
Iraq

Libya
Liechtenstein

Somalia
Syria

Yemen

Source: Adapted from Terry Miller and Kim R. Holmes, *2017 Index of Economic Freedom* (Washington, DC: Heritage Foundation and Dow Jones & Company, 2017), available at www.heritage.org/index (accessed January 1, 2018).

relations. Within weeks of the announcement, embassies were reestablished. However, full normalization of trade relations can come only after the U.S. Congress repeals the embargo.

At the end of 2017, a spokesperson for John Deere indicated that shipments of farm tractors from the United States to Cuba were scheduled to begin soon. In addition, Caterpillar announced the opening of a distribution center in the Mariel Special Economic Development Zone. However, there is a possibility that Obama's successor, President Donald Trump, will reverse course and once again prohibit U.S. companies from doing business in Cuba.

A high correlation exists between the degree of economic freedom and the extent to which a nation's mixed economy is market oriented, although the criteria for the ranking have been subject to some debate. For example, author William Greider has observed that the authoritarian state capitalism practiced in Singapore deprives the nation's citizens of free speech, a free press, and free assembly. Indeed, Singapore once banned the import, manufacture, and sale of chewing gum, because discarded wads of gum were making a mess in public places. Today, gum is available at pharmacies; before buying a pack, however, consumers must register their names and addresses. Greider notes, "Singaporeans are comfortably provided for by a harshly autocratic government that administers paranoid control over press and politics and an effective welfare state that keeps everyone well housed and fed, but not free."[16] As Greider's observation makes clear, some aspects of "free economies" bear more than a passing resemblance to command-style economic systems.

2-3 Stages of Market Development

▶ **2-3** Explain the categories of economic development used by the World Bank, and identify the key emerging country markets at each stage of development.

At any point in time, individual country markets are at different stages of economic development. The World Bank has developed a four-category classification system that uses per capita **gross national income (GNI)** as a basis for categorizing countries (see Table 2-4). The income definition for each of the stages is derived from the World Bank's lending categories, and countries within a given category generally have a number of characteristics in common. Thus, the stages provide a useful basis for global market segmentation and target marketing.

"In a global market, you're not going to gain your profit by sitting tight in the United States in a flat and declining market. You're going to make your money in China and Russia and India and Brazil."[17]

Tom Pirko, president of BevMark, commenting on InBev's acquisition of Anheuser-Busch

Two decades ago, a number of countries in Central Europe, Latin America, and Asia were expected to experience rapid economic growth. The list of these *big emerging markets* (BEMs) included China, India, Indonesia, South Korea, Brazil, Mexico, Argentina, South Africa, Poland, and Turkey.[18] Today, much attention is focused on opportunities in Brazil, Russia, India, China, and South Africa. As previously noted, these five countries are collectively known as BRICS. Experts predict that the BRICS nations will be key players in global trade even as their track records on human rights, environmental protection, and other issues come under closer scrutiny by their trading partners. The BRICS government leaders will also come under pressure at home as their developing market economies create greater income disparity. For each of the stages of economic development discussed here, special attention is given to the BRICS countries.

TABLE 2-4 Stages of Market Development

Income Group by per Capita GNI	2016 GDP ($ millions)	2016 GNI per Capita ($)	World GDP (%)	2016 Population (millions)
High-income countries (OECD)				
GNI per capita ≥ $12,236	48,557,000	41,208	64	1,190
Upper-middle-income countries				
GNI per capita ≥ $3,956 to ≤ $12,235	20,624,000	8,177	27	2,579
Lower-middle-income countries				
GNI per capita ≥ $1,006 but ≤ $3,955	6,263,000	2,079	8	3,012
Low-income countries				
GNI per capita ≤ $1,005	402,000	612	1	659

Note: OECD, Organisation for Economic Co-operation and Development.

Low-Income Countries

Low-income countries have a GNI per capita of $1,005 or less. Countries at this income level share the following general characteristics:

1. Limited industrialization and a high percentage of the population engaged in agriculture and subsistence farming
2. High birth rates, short life expectancy
3. Low literacy rates
4. Heavy reliance on foreign aid
5. Political instability and unrest
6. Concentration in Africa south of the Sahara

Approximately 9 percent of the world's population resides in countries included in this economic category. Many low-income countries have such serious economic, social, and political problems that they represent extremely limited opportunities for investment and operations. Some, such as Burundi, are no-growth economies, with a high percentage of the population living at the national poverty line. Others were once relatively stable countries with growing economies that have become divided by political struggles. The result is an unstable environment characterized by civil strife, flat incomes, and considerable danger to residents. Countries embroiled in civil wars are dangerous areas; most companies find it prudent to avoid them.

Other low-income countries have rebounded sharply after years of ethnic turmoil and internal strife. For example, Rwanda's per-capita GNI increased 100 percent in the decade from 2006 to 2016. President Paul Kagame is investing heavily to bring about economic transformation. A new convention center in Kigali is designed to lure business to the capital city and increase tourism to the country overall (see Exhibit 2-4). Kagame has laid out an ambitious growth agenda dubbed Vision 2050, and he envisions raising the country's per capita income to $4,035 by 2035. Critics have noted that government-linked businesses known as "partystatals" dominate some industry sectors in Rwanda; however, the president denies that his ruling Rwandan Patriot Front is trying to take over the economy.[19]

With per capita income of less than $700, Ethiopia is another poor country located in sub-Saharan Africa. However, Ethiopians have enjoyed more than a decade of double-digit economic expansion. Buoyed by foreign investment from China, several industrial parks have opened in the past few years. This has paved the way for garment workers to earn the equivalent of $45 per month making garments for global brands such as J Crew and Burberry. Hong Kong–based TAL Apparel has opened a factory in one of the industrial parks. Roger Lee, chief executive of TAL, recently summed up the advantages of Ethiopia: "We were looking for a country that has a sufficient available workforce, is sufficiently near a seaport for exports, low enough wage levels . . . and duty-free access to the key U.S. and European markets."[20]

Exhibit 2-4 Rwanda's gleaming new $300 million convention center is integral to President Paul Kagame's strategy for economic growth. Other investments include a new $800 million airport and special economic zones to attract investment.
Source: MARCO LONGARI/AFP/ Getty Images.

Exhibit 2-5 BRCK is a tech company based in Kenya. The company's breakthrough product, a surge-resistant Internet router with an 8-hour battery, sells for $250. Although low-income African nations are the primary target market for the devices, tech-savvy consumers in Europe and the United States have also snapped up BRCKs. A new product, the Kio Kit, is an affordable educational package that provides digital content to students studying in remote areas. The company has also launched Moja, a free public Wi-Fi network.
Source: SIMON MAINA/AFP/Getty Images.

Lower-Middle-Income Countries

The United Nations designates 50 countries in the bottom ranks of the low-income category as **least-developed countries (LDCs)**; the term is sometimes used to contrast them with **developing countries** (i.e., upper ranks of low-income plus lower-middle- and upper-middle-income countries) and **developed countries** (high-income countries). **Lower-middle-income countries** have a GNI per capita between $1,006 and $3,955. Consumer markets in these countries are expanding rapidly. Vietnam (GNI per capita $2,050), Indonesia ($3,400), and others in this group represent an increasing competitive threat as they mobilize their relatively cheap—and highly motivated—labor forces to serve the world market. The developing countries in the lower-middle-income category have a major competitive advantage in mature, standardized, labor-intensive light industry sectors such as footwear, textiles, and toys. Case in point: Vietnam and Indonesia are the top two countries in terms of line employee head count in Nike's worldwide network of more than 500 contractor factories.

With a 2016 GNI per capita of $1,680, India has transitioned out of the low-income category and now is classified as a lower-middle-income country. In 2017, India commemorated the 70th anniversary of its independence from Great Britain. For many decades, economic growth was weak. Indeed, as the 1990s began, India was in the throes of an economic crisis: Inflation was high, and foreign exchange reserves were low. Country leaders opened India's economy to trade and investment and dramatically improved market opportunities.

During this era, Manmohan Singh was placed in charge of India's economy. Singh, former governor of the Indian central bank and finance minister, believed that India had been taking the wrong road. Accordingly, he set about dismantling the planned economy by eliminating import licensing requirements for many products, reducing tariffs, easing restrictions on foreign investment, and liberalizing the rupee.

Yashwant Sinha, the country's former finance minister, once declared that the twenty-first century would be "the century of India." His words appear prescient: India is now home to a number of world-class companies with growing global reach, including Infosys, Mahindra & Mahindra, Tata, and Wipro. Meanwhile, the list of global companies operating in India is growing longer. They include Benetton, Cadbury, Coca-Cola, DuPont, Ericsson, Fujitsu, IBM, L'Oréal, MTV, Staples, Unilever, and Walmart, among others. India's huge population base also presents attractive opportunities for automakers. Suzuki, Hyundai, General Motors, and Ford are among the global car manufacturers doing business in India.

"As the saying goes, if you are not manufacturing in China or selling in India, you are as good as finished."[21]

Dipankar Halder, Associate Director, KSA Technopak, India

Two of the smaller countries from the former Soviet Union, Tajikistan and Uzbekistan, also fall into the lower-middle income categories. Sometimes lumped into a regional group known as "the Stans," they invite closer study on both an individual and regional basis. Incomes in these countries are low, there is considerable economic hardship, and the potential for disruption is certainly high. Are they problem cases, or are they attractive opportunities with good potential for economic growth? These countries represent an obvious risk–reward trade-off; some companies have taken the plunge, but many others are still assessing whether they ought to join the pioneers.

Table 2-3 ranks Uzbekistan quite low in terms of economic freedom. This is one indication of a risky business environment in a lower-middle-income country. Perhaps that helps explain why there are no Western fast-food chains in Uzbekistan—no Starbucks, no McDonald's! The good news is that, in the last few years, Uzbekistan has transitioned from "repressed" in the index to "mostly unfree." And, as befits a nation whose cities were once important trade hubs on the Silk Road, there are market opportunities here. For example, GM is the top car company in Uzbekistan; in 2013, GM Uzbekistan produced its two-millionth car. Overall, this Central Asian country is one of GM's 10 largest markets worldwide! Moreover, Uzbekistan stands to gain from China's infrastructure investment in neighboring Kazakhstan.

Russia's economy has slipped from the high-income category to the upper-middle-income tier; it stands at number 114 in the 2017 economic freedom rankings. The pace of Russia's economic recovery has lagged that in other emerging markets. With the collapse in oil prices, the Kremlin's search for new sources of revenue to fund its budget outlays has created tension between government ministries and business. In fact, some observers have asked whether Russia should still be included in the BRICS grouping. Pundits debated whether President Vladimir Putin would run for a fourth term as elections loomed in 2018.

Upper-Middle-Income Countries

Upper-middle-income countries, also known as *industrializing* or *developing countries*, are those with GNI per capita ranging from $3,956 to $12,235. In these countries, the percentage of the population engaged in agriculture drops sharply as people move to the industrial sector and the degree of urbanization increases. Chile, Malaysia, Mexico, Venezuela, and many other countries in this stage are rapidly industrializing. They have high literacy rates and strong education systems; wages are rising, but they are still significantly lower than in the advanced countries. Innovative local companies can become formidable competitors and help contribute to their nations' rapid, export-driven economic growth.

Brazil ($8,840 GNI per capita in 2016), Russia ($9,720), China ($8,260), and South Africa ($5,480) are the four BRICS nations that currently fall into the upper-middle-income category. Brazil is the largest country in Latin America in terms of the size of its economy, population, and geographic territory. Brazil also boasts the richest reserves of natural resources in the hemisphere; China, Brazil's top trading partner, has an insatiable appetite for iron ore and other commodities.

Government policies aimed at stabilizing Brazil's macroeconomy yielded a decade of impressive results: Brazil's GNI grew steadily between 2003 and 2013. During the same period, tens of millions of Brazilians joined the middle class as their incomes and living standards increased.[23] Needless to say, this trend was a boon to global companies doing business in Brazil, which include Electrolux, Fiat, Ford, General Motors, Nestlé, Nokia, Raytheon, Toyota, Unilever, and Whirlpool (see Exhibit 2-7). More recently, Brazil's economy has been negatively impacted by a series of scandals known as *Lavo Jato* ("Car Wash") involving government and business leaders.

As is typical for countries at this stage of development, Brazil is a study in contrasts. Grocery distribution companies use logistics software to route their trucks; meanwhile, horse-drawn carts are still a common sight on many roads. To keep pace with the volatile financial environment of the early 1990s, many local retailers invested in sophisticated computer and communications systems. They use sophisticated inventory management software to maintain financial control. Thanks to Brazil's strength in computers, the country's outsourcing sector is growing rapidly.[24] Former French President Jacques Chirac underscored Brazil's importance on the world trade scene when he noted, "Geographically, Brazil is part of America. But it's European because of its culture and global because of its interests."[25]

"It may feel like the temperature has only risen a couple of degrees so far, but this heralds the end of India's economic Ice Age."[22]

Vivek Paul, vice chairman, Wipro

EMERGING MARKETS BRIEFING BOOK

Myanmar Is Open For Business

Myanmar is a low-income country in Southeast Asia with a population of 52 million people. After gaining independence from Great Britain in 1948, the country was ruled for decades by a military junta. In 2003, the U.S. government imposed a trade embargo on Myanmar, effectively slamming the door on opportunities for American businesses in that country.

In 2011, however, the country formerly known as Burma abruptly changed course. For starters, Myanmar's citizens elected a president, Thein Sein. Other political and economic changes swiftly followed: Political prisoners have been released, and press censorship has been abolished.

Encouraged by Myanmar's transition from dictatorship toward economic openness and democracy, many Western governments have lifted sanctions such as bans on the country's imports. These actions have opened the doors to global companies, and Coca-Cola, General Electric (GE), MasterCard, Mitsubishi, Nestlé, Visa, and many others have begun setting up operations in Myanmar (see Exhibit 2-6). Indeed, foreign investment has skyrocketed, from a modest $208 million in 2000 to $850 million in 2011. Coca-Cola alone has pledged to invest $200 million by 2018.

However, those global giants will be playing catch-up. Why? During years of Western sanctions, companies in China, Japan, and other Asian countries maintained a presence in Myanmar. That fact is paying dividends today. Mitsubishi is a case in point. This company established an export office in Yangon years ago. As Mitsuo Ido, Mitsubishi's general manager, notes, "Japan and Myanmar have had a long relationship, and Japanese companies are now very interested in increasing their involvement here. Myanmar people are very similar to Japanese in some ways."

U.S. President Barack Obama made a quick visit to Myanmar at the end of 2012. Even now, however, some sanctions remain in place. These include sanctions targeting "Specially Designated Nationals," who had ties to the former military regime, such as businessman Zaw.

Much remains to be done to improve life in Myanmar. Ethnic conflict is rife; the fledgling government is struggling to achieve peace and stability in the face of protests. In addition, Myanmar's economic and physical infrastructures have serious shortcomings. The legal system is undeveloped, and workers lack training. Mobile telecommunications networks need upgrades; most Western cell phones don't work in Myanmar. According to the Asian Development Bank, only about one-fourth of Myanmar's population has access to reliable electricity, and power shortages and outages are not unusual. Despite these obstacles, the country's rich gas and oil reserves represent a major opportunity for GE; Total, a French energy giant; and other companies.

It remains to be seen whether the "gold rush" in Myanmar will yield big successes. Years ago, some companies that attempted to capitalize on new opportunities in Russia and Vietnam ended up losing a lot of money. Moreover, corruption is rampant in Myanmar, and many former military leaders have secured licenses in banking and other services. Global soft drinks titan Coca-Cola finds itself competing with inexpensive soft drinks such as Blue Mountain Cola and Fantasy Orange. Even so, some business owners in Myanmar worry that foreigners will dominate key business sectors. An executive at a New York–based investment firm summed up the opportunity this way: "If I was 25 years old and single, I'd just go there. It's just ready for takeoff."

Sources: Shibani Mahtani, "Gap to Make Old Navy, Banana Republic Apparel in Myanmar," *The Wall Street Journal* (June 6–7, 2014), p. B3; Laura Meckler, "Obama Challenges Myanmar on Visit," *The Wall Street Journal* (November 20, 2012), p. A8; Patrick Barta, "Final Frontier: Firms Flock to Newly Opened Myanmar," *The Wall Street Journal* (November 12, 2012), p. A1; Michiyo Nakamoto and Gwen Robinson, "Japan Looks for Early Lead in Myanmar Race," *Financial Times* (October 1, 2012), p. 6; Patrick Barta, "Myanmar Concerns Remain, U.S. Envoy Says," *The Wall Street Journal* (August 20, 2012), p. A7; "Myanmar Is Next Real Thing for Coke," *Financial Times* (June 15, 2012), p. 16; Simon Hall, "Energy Titans Look to Myanmar," *The Wall Street Journal* (June 8, 2012), p. B6; David Pilling and Gwen Robinson, "Myanmar: A Nation Rises," *Financial Times* (December 3, 2010), p. 6.

Exhibit 2-6 An employee takes a call as customers purchase jewelry at a gold shop in Yangon, the former capital of Myanmar. Myanmar's economy is set for growth as sweeping political, economic, and financial reforms raise hopes of a renaissance for the impoverished nation. Now that trade sanctions have been lifted, global companies in a variety of industries are moving quickly to formulate and implement market-entry strategies.
Source: Ye Aung Thu/AFP/Getty Images.

Exhibit 2-7 Nestlé has invested tens of millions of dollars to build several plants in the Brazilian state of Rio de Janeiro. This $83 billion facility in Tres Rios opened in 2011. It produces milk products and was designed with environmental sustainability in mind. Coffee, cookies, noodles, and other items that Nestlé produces locally are adapted to suit Brazilian tastes and pocketbooks. As Ivan Zurita, CEO of Nestlé Brasil, noted, "In our country there are 30 million people considered too poor to be consumers, and we have come to the conclusion that regionalization will speed up our competitiveness in terms of cost and greater operational efficiency."
Source: visicou/Shutterstock.

In 2016, Russia slipped from the high-income category as its per capita GNI decreased from $14,840 in 2013 to $9,720 (upper-middle income). Overall, Russia's economic situation rises and falls as the price of oil fluctuates. The current slump in world oil prices has impacted Russia, as have international sanctions. Strong local companies have appeared on the scene, including Wimm-Bill-Dann Foods, Russia's largest dairy company; PepsiCo acquired it in 2011. However, corruption in Russia is pervasive, and the bureaucracy often creates a mountain of red tape for companies such as Diageo, Mars, McDonald's, Nestlé, and SAB Miller.

China is the third BRICS nation in the upper-middle-income category; its GNI per capita was $8,260 in 2016. China represents the largest single destination for foreign investment in the developing world. Attracted by the country's vast size and market potential, companies in Asia, Europe, and North and South America are marking China as a key target in their global strategies. Shenzhen and other special economic zones have attracted billions of dollars in foreign investment. Despite the ongoing market reforms, however, Chinese society lacks a democratic foundation.

China is a case study in how to jump-start a nation's economic growth. Leveraging the country's central planning economic model, the government poured money into infrastructure improvements such as highways, railways, and ports. Soon, China's economy was growing at a double-digit pace. The beneficiaries of this economic boom included companies in Australia, Brazil, Indonesia, and other countries that export goods to China. Avon, Coca-Cola, Dell, Ford, General Motors, Honda, HSBC, JPMorgan Chase, McDonald's, Motorola, Procter & Gamble, Samsung, Siemens AG, Toyota, and Volkswagen were among the scores of global companies that began actively pursuing opportunities in China.

In 2007, just prior to the global economic crisis, the message from the Chinese government began to change. As words like "unsteady," "unbalanced," and "uncoordinated" began to pop up in key political speeches, China watchers sensed that change was in the wind. For years, China's economic growth has been built on exports and low-wage manufacturing. More recently, GDP growth has begun to weaken. A new leadership team is in place, and Beijing is shifting from an external focus to an internal one in an effort to deal with urgent problems related to the country's infrastructure, bribery, and corruption.

Meanwhile, China is moving to become less reliant on exports. To achieve this goal, consumption by Chinese citizens must increase. President Xi Jinping's ambitious infrastructure plan, known variously as the "Belt and Road Initiative" (BRI) and "One Belt One Road," revives the ancient Silk Road trade route. Beijing has also launched a new industrial strategy dubbed "Made in China 2025." The aim is for China to become a world leader in advanced industries such as

"If you want to do well globally today, you have to first be successful in China, and we're already here."[26]

Daniel Kirchert, co-founder, Byton (electric vehicle company)

Exhibit 2-8 Leaders of the BRICS nations met at a summit in Xiamen in 2017 (from left): Brazilian President Michel Temer, Russian President Vladimir Putin, Chinese President Xi Jinping, South African President Jacob Zuma, and Indian Prime Minister Narendra Modi.
Source: PIB/Alamy Stock Photo.

robotics and electric vehicles. However, Beijing's state involvement in industry is one reason why the World Trade Organization (WTO) has still not granted China "market economy" status.

South Africa joined the BRICS group in 2011. In 2017, the Chinese president welcomed leaders from the other four BRICS nations to a summit in Xiamen (see Exhibit 2-8). One topic of discussion at this meeting was the opening of the Africa Regional Centre, funded by the BRICS-supported National Development Bank. The Centre will serve as a source of financing for infrastructure development and other projects. South Africa hosted the tenth BRICS summit in Johannesburg in 2018, providing President Jacob Zuma with an opportunity attract more direct investment in the African continent as a whole.[27]

Lower-middle- and upper-middle income countries that achieve the highest sustained rates of economic growth are sometimes referred to collectively as **newly industrializing economies (NIEs)**. Overall, NIEs are characterized by greater industrial output than developing economies; heavy manufacturing operations and refined products account for an increasing proportion of their exports. Goldman Sachs, the firm that developed the original BRIC framework more than a decade ago, has identified a new country grouping called Next-11 (N11). Five of the N11 countries are considered NIEs: three lower-middle-income countries (Egypt, Indonesia, and the Philippines) and two upper-middle-income countries (Mexico and Turkey). Among these five countries, Egypt, Indonesia, and the Philippines have posted positive GDP growth over the past several years.

Marketing Opportunities in LDCs and Developing Countries

Despite the many problems in LDCs and developing countries, it is possible to nurture long-term market opportunities there. Today, Nike produces and sells only a small portion of its output in China, but when the firm refers to China as a "2-billion-foot market," it clearly has the future in mind. C. K. Prahalad and Allen Hammond have identified several assumptions and misconceptions about the "bottom of the pyramid" (BOP) that need to be corrected:[28]

Mistaken assumption #1: The poor have no money.   In fact, the aggregate buying power of poor communities can be substantial. In rural Bangladesh, for example, villagers spend considerable sums to use village phones operated by local entrepreneurs.

Mistaken assumption #2: The poor are too concerned with fulfilling basic needs to "waste" money on nonessential goods.   In fact, consumers who are too poor to purchase a house do buy "luxury" items such as television sets and gas stoves to improve their lives.

Mistaken assumption #3: The goods sold in developing markets are so inexpensive that there is no room for a new market entrant to make a profit.   In fact, because the poor often pay higher prices for many goods, there is an opportunity for efficient competitors to realize attractive margins by offering quality and low prices.

Mistaken assumption #4: People in BOP markets cannot use advanced technology. In fact, residents of rural areas can and do quickly learn to use cell phones, PCs, and similar devices.

Mistaken assumption #5: Global companies that target BOP markets will be criticized for exploiting the poor. In fact, the informal economies in many poor countries are highly exploitative. A global company offering basic goods and services that improve a country's standard of living can earn a reasonable return while benefiting society.

Despite the difficult economic conditions in parts of Southeast Asia, Latin America, Africa, and Eastern Europe, many nations in these regions will evolve into attractive markets. One role of marketing in developing countries is to focus resources on the task of creating and delivering products that are best suited to local needs and incomes. Appropriate marketing communications techniques can also be applied to accelerate acceptance of these products. Marketing can be the link that relates resources to opportunity and facilitates need satisfaction on the consumer's terms.

An interesting debate in marketing is whether it has any relevance to the process of economic development. Some people believe that marketing is relevant only in affluent, industrialized countries, where the major problem is directing society's resources into ever-changing output or production to satisfy a dynamic marketplace. In the less-developed country, the argument goes, the major problem is the allocation of scarce resources toward obvious production needs. Efforts should therefore focus on production and ways to increase output, rather than on customer needs and wants.

Conversely, it can be argued that the process of focusing an organization's resources on environmental opportunities is a process of universal relevance. The role of marketing—to identify people's needs and wants and to focus individual and organizational efforts so as to respond to those needs and wants—is the same in all countries, irrespective of the level of economic development. When global marketers respond to the needs of rural residents in emerging markets such as China and India, they are also more likely to gain all-important government support and approval.

For example, pursuing alternative energy sources is important for two reasons: the lack of coal reserves in many countries and the concerns that heavy reliance on fossil fuels contributes to global warming. Similarly, people everywhere need affordable, safe drinking water. Recognizing this fact, Nestlé launched Pure Life bottled water in Pakistan. The price was set at about 35 cents per bottle, and advertising promised, "Pure safety. Pure trust. The ideal water." Pure Life quickly captured 50 percent of the bottled water market in Pakistan; the brand has since been rolled out in dozens of other low-income countries.[30] The Coca-Cola Company recently began to address dietary and health needs in low-income countries by developing Vitango, a beverage product that can help fight anemia, blindness, and other ailments related to malnutrition.

There is also an opportunity to help developing countries join the Internet economy. Intel Chairman Craig Barrett has been visiting villages in China and India and launching programs to provide Internet access and computer training to the residents there. One aspect of Intel's World Ahead initiative is the development of a $550 computer that is powered by a car battery. Similarly, Hewlett-Packard engineers are working to develop solar-powered communication devices that can link remote areas to the Internet.[31] Meanwhile, an initiative called One Laptop Per Child embarked on a program to develop a laptop computer that governments in developing countries can buy for $100.

Global companies can also contribute to economic development by finding creative ways to preserve old-growth forests and other resources while creating economic opportunities for local inhabitants. In Brazil, for example, Daimler AG works with a cooperative of farmers who transform coconut husks into natural rubber to be used in auto seats, headrests, and sun visors. French luxury goods marketer Hermès International has created a line of handbags called "Amazonia" made of latex extracted by traditional rubber tappers. Both Daimler and Hermès are responding to the opportunity to promote themselves as environmentally conscious while appealing to "green"-oriented consumers. As Isabela Fortes, director of a company in Rio de Janeiro that retrains forest workers, notes, "You can only prevent forest people from destroying the jungle by giving them viable economic alternatives."[32]

"Sustainable energy pioneers who focus on the base of the pyramid could set the stage for one of the biggest bonanzas in the history of commerce, since extensive adoption and experience in developing markets would almost certainly lead to dramatic improvements in cost and quality."[29]

Stuart L. Hart and Clayton M. Christensen

ENTREPRENEURIAL LEADERSHIP, CREATIVE THINKING, AND THE GLOBAL STARTUP

Blake Mycoskie, TOMS

Blake Mycoskie is an entrepreneur. He created a brand, developed several innovative products, and started a company to market them using an innovative business design. By applying the basic tools and principles of modern marketing, Mycoskie has achieved remarkable success.

As is true with many entrepreneurs, Mycoskie's innovative idea was based on his recognition of unmet needs. In this particular case, the needs were not his own; rather, they were the needs of children whose parents could not afford to buy shoes.

While competing on the reality TV show *The Amazing Race* in 2002, Mycoskie and his sister found themselves in Argentina. Although they lost the contest (by a mere 4 minutes!), Mycoskie was captivated by the local people and culture. He returned to Argentina in 2006 for a vacation. Using his own powers of direct observation, he could see that a lightweight canvas shoe called the *alpargata* was very popular in Argentina. He also noted that many of the local children had no shoes; many suffered from foot disease as a result of going barefoot.

Back home in the United States, Mycoskie started thinking about how he could help the disadvantaged people he had seen. One key decision: Instead of setting up a nonprofit organization, he started a for-profit business, based on a "sell one, give one away" business design. He set up a shoe company, TOMS, with a unique business model and social mission: Each time a customer buys a pair of TOMS, the company donates a pair of shoes to a child in need. This business model has become known as "One-for-One" or "B1G1" ("Buy One, Give One"); Mycoskie's title is "Chief Shoe Giver." In fact, Mycoskie insists TOMS is not a shoe company. Rather, he defines his business as "one-for-one," and the company's mission as improving lives (see Exhibit 2-9).

Exhibit 2-9 Blake Mycoskie is founder and Chief Shoe Giver at TOMS. He pioneered a business design called "one-for-one" that aims to improve the lives of those in need and promote economic development.
Source: Aristidis Vafeiadakis/ZUMA Press, Inc./Alamy.

Mycoskie's business design put him at odds with some of his advisors, who urged him to give a percentage of profits, or perhaps donate one pair for every three pairs sold. Undeterred, Mycoskie was intent on giving away as many pairs as possible, while giving shoe customers, which the company calls "supporters," an intimate "one-for-one" experience.

Mycoskie next turned his attention to the urgent need for eye care in developing countries. Partnering with the Seva Foundation, he introduced TOMS sunglasses in 2011, pledging to donate funds for eye care and surgery for every pair purchased. Instead of a logo, each pair of frames features three painted stripes. As Mycoskie explains, every stripe tells a story: The outside stripes represent the bond between the purchaser and the person in need, while the middle stripe represents TOMS, which brought the other two together.

In 2014, Mycoskie extended the TOMS brand to a third category: premium coffee. While on a trip to Africa, Mycoskie realized that coffee farmers required a lot of water to wash coffee beans. Also, clean drinking water was in very short supply in many villages. He was struck by the irony that the countries that supply the world with the best coffee don't have adequate water for their own people. Mycoskie partnered with Water For People, a nonprofit organization whose mission is to ensure that everyone has access to a safe, continuous supply of water. The result was TOMS Roasting Company, which sells coffee beans at Whole Foods stores and other select locations. For every bag of coffee beans purchased, TOMS donates one week of clean water to a person in need.

What's next for TOMS? As the company reached its 10-year anniversary in 2015, it began to transition from being a wholesaler by opening brick-and-mortar stores. These retail locations currently account for only 5 percent of company sales, but Mycoskie envisions that share increasing to 25 percent within a few years. By embedding itself in local communities, TOMS will be better able to "start a movement," as company executives put it. If supporters want to stop in at a store just to use the Internet or have a cup of coffee, that's fine with TOMS.

TOMS is experimenting with new media to help encourage customer loyalty. For example, all associates (sales staff) have the opportunity to go on giving trips after they have worked at the company for one year. A giving trip to Peru was filmed and supporters can view the event using an Oculus virtual reality (VR) headset. Even as the company searches for ways to operationalize such leading-edge communication tools in today's tech environment, it offers TOMS supporters a new way to participate in the TOMS brand experience.

Sources: Blake Mycoskie, "TOMS and the Future of the One-for-One Movement," SXSW Presentation, March 2014; Blake Mycoskie, *Start Something That Matters* (New York, NY: Random House, 2011); Andrew Adam Newman, "'Buy One, Give One' Spirit Imbues an Online Store," *The New York Times* (November 5, 2013), p. B7; Mark Hornickel, "Fit for the Sole," *Northwest Alumni Magazine* (Fall 2013), pp. 10–13; Carly Gillis, "TOMS Announces Eyewear as Next 'One for One' Product," *The Huffington Post* (June 7, 2011).

High-Income Countries

High-income countries, also known as *advanced, developed, industrialized,* or *postindustrial countries,* are those with a GNI per capita of $12,236 or higher. With the exception of a few oil-rich nations, the countries in this category reached their present income level through a process of sustained economic growth.

The phrase *postindustrial countries* was first used by Daniel Bell of Harvard to describe the United States, Sweden, Japan, and other advanced, high-income societies. In his 1973 book *The Coming of the Post-Industrial Society,* Bell drew a distinction between the industrial and postindustrial stages of country development that went beyond mere measures of income. Bell's thesis was that the sources of innovation in postindustrial societies are derived increasingly from the codification of theoretical knowledge rather than from "random" inventions. When a country reaches this level, the service sector accounts for more than half of national output, the processing and exchange of information become increasingly important, and knowledge trumps capital as the key strategic resource.

In addition, in a postindustrial society, intellectual technology is more important than machine technology, and scientists and professionals play a more dominant role than do engineers and semiskilled workers. Further, postindustrial societies exhibit an orientation toward the future and stress the importance of interpersonal relationships in the functioning of society. Taken together, these forces and factors spell big sociological changes for the work and home lives of the residents of postindustrial nations.

Product and market opportunities in a postindustrial society are heavily dependent upon new products and innovations. Ownership levels for basic products are extremely high in most households. As a consequence, organizations seeking to grow often face a difficult task if they attempt to expand their share of existing markets. Alternatively, they can endeavor to create new markets. Today, for example, global companies in a range of communication-related industries are seeking to create new e-commerce markets for interactive forms of electronic communication. A case in point is Barry Diller's Expedia Inc.; the world's largest online travel company, it includes the Expedia, Orbitz and Travelocity brands. Diller also founded IAC/InterActiveCorp, which owns Vimeo; the Match.com, OkCupid, and Tinder dating sites; the Web magazine *Daily Beast*; and other Internet businesses.[33]

In 2009, the *Financial Times* Stock Exchange (FTSE) upgraded South Korea's economic status from "emerging" to "developed." The change is consistent with the World Bank's ranking and reflects South Korea's emergence as a global powerhouse. It is the 11th-largest economy by GDP, and a major importer and exporter. South Korea is home to Samsung Electronics, LG Group, Kia Motors Corporation, Daewoo Corporation, Hyundai Corporation, and other well-known global enterprises. Instead of erecting substantial barriers to free trade, South Korea initiated major reforms in its political and economic systems in response to the "Asian flu" (i.e., the 2009 economic crisis in Asia, which coincided with an influenza pandemic originating in the region).

Even so, investors note the political risk posed by North Korea's aggressiveness and the missile tests ordered by President Kim Jung Un. Another concern is inconsistent treatment of foreign investors by the government. For example, authorities recently raided the local offices of French retailer Carrefour. Adding to the uncertainty is U.S. President Donald Trump's pledge to overturn the U.S./Korea Free Trade Agreement.

Seven high-income democracies—the United States, Japan, Germany, France, Britain, Canada, and Italy—comprise the **Group of Seven (G-7)**. Finance ministers, central bankers, and heads of state from the seven nations have worked together for more than a quarter of a century in an effort to steer the global economy in the direction of prosperity and to ensure monetary stability. Whenever a global crisis looms—be it the Latin American debt crisis of the 1980s or Russia's struggle to transform its economy in the 1990s or the economic crisis in Greece in 2007–2008—representatives from the G-7 nations gather and try to coordinate policy (see Exhibit 2-10).

Starting in the mid-1990s, Russia began attending the G-7 summit meetings. In 1998, Russia became a full participant, giving rise to the **Group of Eight (G-8)**. Russia's membership was suspended in 2014 after President Vladimir Putin annexed the Crimean peninsula (see

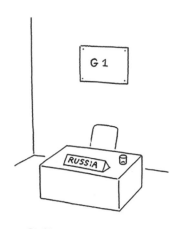

Exhibit 2-11
Source: Jeremy Banx/Banx Cartoons.

Exhibit 2-11 and Case 5-1). The **Group of Twenty (G-20)** was established in 1999; it is composed of finance ministers and central bank governors from 19 countries plus the European Union. The G-20 includes developing nations such as Argentina, Brazil, India, Indonesia, and Turkey; Russia remains a member.

Another institution to which high-income countries belong is the **Organisation for Economic Co-operation and Development** (OECD; www.oecd.org). The 35 nations that belong to the OECD believe in market-allocation economic systems and pluralistic democracy. The organization has been variously described as an "economic think tank" and a "rich-man's club"; in any event, the OECD's fundamental task is to "enable its members to achieve the highest sustainable economic growth and improve the economic and social well-being of their populations." The OECD evolved from a group of European nations that worked together after World War II to rebuild the region's economy; it is headquartered in Paris. Canada and the United States have been members since 1961, while Japan joined in 1964. Evidence of the increasing importance of the BRICS group is the fact that Brazil, Russia, India, and China have all formally announced their intention to join the OECD. To become members of this organization, applicants must demonstrate progress toward economic reform.

Representatives from OECD member nations work together in committees to review economic and social policies that affect world trade. The secretary-general presides over a council that meets regularly and has decision-making power. Committees of specialists from member countries provide a forum for discussion of trade and other issues. Consultation, peer pressure, and diplomacy are the keys to helping member nations candidly assess their own economic policies and actions. The OECD publishes country surveys and an annual economic outlook.

Recently, the OECD has become more focused on global issues, social policy, and labor market deregulation. For example, it has addressed the vexing problem of bribery: In 1997, it passed a convention that requires members to cooperate when pursuing bribery allegations. In the 20-plus years since this agreement entered into force, Germany, France, and other countries have adopted antibribery laws. Prosecutors from various countries are doing a better job of collaborating across borders, with one case against Siemens AG resulting in a record $1.6 billion fine.[34]

Marketing Implications of the Stages of Development

The stages of economic development described previously can serve as a guide to marketers in evaluating **product saturation levels,** or the percentage of potential buyers or households that own a particular product. George David is the former CEO of United Technologies; its business units include Otis Elevators. David explained the significance of product saturation to his former business as follows:

> We measure elevator populations in countries as units installed per thousand people. And in China, the number today is about one half an elevator per thousand people. In most countries of the world outside of the U.S., people live in elevator and storied apartment houses. It's true all over Europe, all over Asia, South America, certainly true in China. And in a mature market like Europe, the installed population is about six elevators per thousand people. And so we're on our way to some portion of six.[35]

As this comment suggests, product saturation levels for many products are low in emerging markets. For example, while Indian consumers have 700 million debit cards, only 700,000 retail outlets in India had card machines in 2016. Overall, India has one card machine for every 1,785 people. By contrast, in Europe the ratio is one machine per 119 people; China has one machine for every 60 people. In the United States, the corresponding figures are one machine for every 25 people.[36]

Automobile ownership exhibits similar disparity. In India, just 8 out of every 1,000 adults own a car.[37] In Russia, 200 people out of 1,000 own cars; in Germany, the figure is 565 out of 1,000.[38] Low levels of vehicle ownership are one reason Myanmar represents an attractive market opportunity for global automakers (see "Myanmar Is Open for Business").

The global market for French Champagne provides another example. Following the Brexit vote in 2016, the British pound fell in value relative to the euro. That translated into higher prices for premium imported bubbly in the United Kingdom, the number 2 export market by sales behind the United States. As budget-conscious British shoppers opt for English sparkling wines or Italian Prosecco, French Champagne producers have been compelled to seek more growth elsewhere. Again, relative product saturation levels show the opportunity. In 2016, Champagne producers shipped two bottles per person in France, one bottle per capita in Switzerland, and one-half bottle per person in Great Britain. As for the United States, shipments totaled just 0.07 bottle per person—less than half a glass. Conclusion: Americans should be popping more Champagne corks![39]

(2-4) Balance of Payments

◄ 2-4 Discuss the significance of balance of payments statistics for the world's major economies.

The **balance of payments** is a record of all economic transactions between the residents of a country and the rest of the world. U.S. balance of payments statistics for the period 2012 to 2016 are shown in Table 2-5. International trade data for the United States is available from the U.S. Bureau of Economic Analysis (www.bea.gov); the bureau's interactive Web site enables users to generate customized reports. The International Monetary Fund's *Balance of Payments Statistics Yearbook* provides trade statistics and summaries of economic activity for all countries in the world.[40]

The balance of payments is divided into the current and capital accounts. The **current account** is a broad measure that includes **merchandise trade** (i.e., manufactured goods) and **services trade** (i.e., intangible, experience-based economic output) plus certain categories of financial transfers such as humanitarian aid. A country with a negative current account balance has a **trade deficit**; that is, the outflow of money to pay for imports exceeds the inflow of money from sales of exports. Conversely, a country with a positive current account balance has a **trade surplus**.

The **capital account** is a record of all long-term direct investment, portfolio investment, and other short- and long-term capital flows. The minus signs signify outflows of cash. For example, in Table 2-5, line 2 shows an outflow of more than $2.2 trillion in 2016 that represents payment for U.S. merchandise imports. (Entries not shown in Table 2-5 represent changes in net errors and omissions, foreign liabilities, and reserves.) These are the entries that constitute the balance of payments balance. In general, a country accumulates reserves when the net of its current and capital account transactions shows a surplus; it gives up reserves when the net shows a deficit. The important fact to recognize about the overall balance of payments is that it is always in balance, although imbalances do occur in subsets of

TABLE 2-5 U.S. Balance of Payments, 2012–2016 (US$ millions)

	2012	2013	2014	2015	2016
A. Current Account	**−426,198**	**−349,543**	−373,800	−434,598	−451,685
1. Goods Exports	1,561,540	1,592,784	1,632,639	1,510,757	1,455,704
2. Goods Imports	−2,303,785	−2,294,453	−2,374,101	−2,272,612	2,208,211
3. *Balance on Goods*	−742,095	−701,669	−741,462	−761,855	−752,507
4. Services: Credit	654,850	687,410	710,565	753,150	752,507
5. Services: Debit	−450,360	−462,134	−477,428	−491,740	−504,654
6. *Balance on Services*	204,490	225,276	233,138	261,410	247,714
7. *Balance on Goods and Services*	−537,605	−476,392	−508,324	−500,445	−504,793
B. Capital Account	**6,904**	**−412**	**−45**	**−42**	**−59**

Source: www.bea.gov. Accessed December 1, 2017.

the overall balance. For example, a commonly reported balance is the trade balance on goods (line 3 in Table 2-5).

A close examination of Table 2-5 reveals that the United States regularly posts deficits in both the current account and the trade balance in goods. The U.S. trade deficit reflects a number of factors, including the high volume of trade with China, a seemingly insatiable consumer demand for imported goods, and the enormous cost of military operations in the Middle East and Afghanistan.

Table 2-6 shows a record of goods and services trade between the United States and the BRIC countries for 2011. A comparison of lines 4 and 5 in Table 2-5 and Table 2-6 shows a bright spot from the U.S. perspective: The United States has maintained a services trade surplus with much of the rest of the world. Overall, however, the United States posts balance of payments deficits while important trading partners, such as China, have surpluses.

China has more than $3 trillion in foreign reserves, more than any other nation. It offsets its trade surpluses with an outflow of capital, while the United States offsets its trade deficit with an inflow of capital. China and other countries with healthy trade surpluses are setting up *sovereign wealth funds* to invest some of the money. As trading partners, U.S. consumers and businesses own an increasing quantity of foreign products, while foreign investors own more U.S. land, real estate, and government securities. Foreign-owned U.S. assets total $2.5 trillion; China currently owns about $1.2 trillion in U.S. treasury bonds. As Ha Jiming, an economist with China's largest investment bank, noted, "One trillion is a big amount, but it is also a hot potato."[41] A key focus of U.S. President Trump's trade policy is America's trade deficit with China, which pushed past the $300 billion mark in 2013.

TABLE 2-6 U.S. Goods and Services Trade with China, India, and Brazil 2016 (US$ millions)

	China	India	Brazil
1. U.S. Goods Exports to	115,988	21,624	30,022
2. Goods Imports from	−463,288	−46,125	−24,620
3. *Balance on Goods*	−347,290	−24,501	*5,402*
4. U.S. Services Exports to	54,157	20,632	24,338
5. Services Imports from	−16,139	−25,808	−6,797
6. *U.S. Balance on Services*	*38,018*	−5,175	*17,541*
7. *U.S. Balance on Goods and Services*	−309,272	−29,676	*22,944*

Source: www.bea.gov. Accessed December 1, 2017.

(2-5) Trade in Merchandise and Services

◀ **2-5** Identify world leaders in merchandise and services trade, and explain how currency exchange rates impact a company's opportunities in different parts of the world.

Thanks in part to the achievements of the General Agreement on Tariffs and Trade (GATT) and the WTO, world merchandise trade has grown at a faster rate than world production since the end of World War II. Put differently, import and export growth has outpaced the rate of increase in GNI. According to figures compiled by the WTO, the dollar value of world merchandise trade in 2015 totaled $16.5 trillion, a modest downturn after several years of growth as trade recovered to pre–economic crisis levels. The top exporting and importing countries are shown in Table 2-7.

In 2003, Germany surpassed the United States as the world's top exporter. German manufacturers of all sizes have benefited from global economic growth because they provide the motors, machines, vehicles, and other capital goods that are required to build factories and country infrastructures; worldwide, machinery and transport equipment constitute approximately one-third of global exports. Overall, approximately two-thirds of Germany's exports go to other EU nations; France is the number 1 country destination, while the United States ranks second. Today, exports generate 40 percent of Germany's GDP, and 9 million jobs are export related. In addition, annual sales by the foreign subsidiaries of German-based companies are $1.5 billion.[43] To ensure that local companies keep pace with the rate of digital disruption and opportunities associated with the Internet of Things, the German government recently announced an action program dubbed Industrie 4.0, whose centerpiece is a shift toward decentralized "smart" manufacturing.

In 2009, China leapfrogged Germany in the global merchandise export rankings (see Table 2-7). China's top-place ranking underscores its role as an export powerhouse: The country has demonstrated continued economic strength by achieving double-digit export growth. Chinese exports have surged since China joined the WTO in 2001; in fact, policymakers in several countries are pressuring Beijing to boost the value of the yuan in an effort to stem the tide of imports.

The fastest-growing sector of world trade is trade in services—and it is also one of the major issues in trade relations between the high- and lower-income countries. Services include travel and entertainment; education; business services such as accounting, advertising, engineering, investment banking, and legal services; and royalties and license fees that represent payments for intellectual property.

As a group, low-, lower-middle, and even upper-middle-income countries are lax in enforcing international copyrights and protecting intellectual property and patent laws. Countries that export service products such as computer software, music, and video entertainment suffer a loss of income when these rights are not enforced. According to the Global Software Piracy Study conducted each year by the Business Software Alliance, annual worldwide losses due to software piracy amount to approximately $62.7 billion. In China alone, software piracy cost the industry an estimated $8.8 billion in lost sales in 2013.

The United States is the world's leading services trader. The United Kingdom ranks second, with services accounting for 45 percent of that country's total exports. More than one-third of the U.K. services exports go to the EU; the trade in services is a key issue as the United Kingdom proceeds with its plans to exit the EU.[44]

As shown in Figure 2-2, U.S. services exports in 2016 totaled more than $750 billion, or nearly half of total U.S. exports. The U.S. services surplus (service exports minus imports) stood at $247 billion. This surplus partially offset the U.S. merchandise trade deficit of $758 billion in 2016. Bottom line: The United States runs an annual trade deficit of $0.5 trillion. It is this figure in particular that President Trump has promised to address with his vision of "America First."

TABLE 2-7 Top Exporters and Importers in World Merchandise Trade, 2015 (US$ billions)[42]

Leading Exporters	2015	Leading Importers	2015
1. China	$2,274	1. United States	$ 2,308
2. United States	1,504	2. China	1,681
3. Germany	1,329	3. Germany	1,050
4. Japan	624	4. Japan	648
5. Netherlands	567	5. United Kingdom	625

Source: www.wto.org. Accessed December 1, 2017.

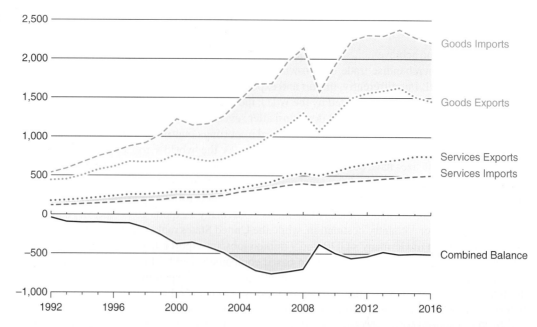

FIGURE 2-2 U.S. Trade Balance on Services and on Merchandise Trade (US$ billions)

Source: www.bea.gov. Accessed December 1, 2017.

Many economists, however, argue that trade deficits should not be used as an indication of an economy's strength, or lack thereof.

Overview of International Finance

Foreign exchange makes it possible for a company in one country to conduct business in other countries with different currencies. However, foreign exchange is an aspect of global marketing that involves certain financial risks, decisions, and activities that are completely different from those facing a domestic marketer. Moreover, those risks can be even higher in developing markets such as Thailand, Malaysia, and South Korea. When a company conducts business within a single country or region with customers and suppliers paying in the same currency, there is no exchange risk. All prices, payments, receipts, assets, and liabilities are in the given currency. In contrast, when conducting business across boundaries in countries with different currencies, a company is thrust into the turbulent world of exchange risk.

The foreign exchange market consists literally of a buyer's and a seller's market where currencies are traded for both spot and future delivery on a continuous basis. As noted earlier in the chapter, $5 trillion in currencies is traded every day. The *spot* market is for immediate delivery; the market for future delivery is called the *forward* market. This is a true market where prices are based on the combined forces of supply and demand that come into play at the moment of any transaction.

Who are the participants in this market? First, a country's central bank can intervene in currency markets by buying and selling currencies and government securities in an effort to influence exchange rates. Recall that China currently holds trillions of dollars in U.S. treasury securities. Such purchases help ensure that China's currency is relatively weak compared to the U.S. dollar.[45] Second, some of the trading in the foreign exchange market takes the form of transactions needed to settle accounts for the global trade in goods and services. For example, because Porsche is a German company, the dollars spent on Porsche automobiles by American car buyers must be converted to euros. Finally, currency speculators also participate in the foreign exchange market.

Devaluation can result from government action or an economic crisis; whatever the cause, devaluation is reduction in the value of a nation's currency against other currencies. For example, in August 1998 the Russian economy imploded. The ruble plunged in value, and the government defaulted on its foreign debt obligations. Many Russians faced wage cuts and layoffs; savings were wiped out as banks collapsed. In the decade that followed, however, Russia's economy made a rapid recovery. Real GDP doubled, in part because import price increases caused by the ruble's devaluation stimulated local production. As one economist noted, "The crash of '98 really cleaned out the macroeconomy."[46] But in 2014, it was "déjà vu all over again." As world oil prices crashed below $50 per barrel, the ruble was in free fall once again.

In 2014, the European Central Bank (ECB) embarked on a course of action that resulted in a decline of the euro's value. Using a tool known as *quantitative easing*, the ECB began buying tens of billions of euros' worth of government bonds each month, greatly increasing the supply of euros. As the supply expanded, the euro's value declined significantly. Just a few years ago, one euro was equal to $1.35. By early 2015, the exchange rate was €1 equals $1.13. While the stronger dollar was good news for U.S. tourists traveling in Europe, U.S. businesses faced significant losses when euro sales were converted into dollars at the new exchange rate.

To the extent that a country sells more goods and services abroad than it buys, there will be a greater demand for its currency and a tendency for that currency to appreciate in value—unless the government pursues foreign exchange policies that do not allow the currency to fluctuate. In international economics, such policies are called *mercantilism* or *competitive-currency politics* because they favor domestic industries at the expense of foreign competitors. During the past few years, the Chinese government has been criticized for keeping China's currency undervalued to support exports. Faced with escalating rhetoric from politicians in the United States and elsewhere, Beijing has responded by adopting a policy of **revaluation** to allow the yuan to strengthen against the dollar and other currencies.[47] Between 2006 and 2008, the yuan appreciated by approximately 20 percent.

What effect would a stronger Chinese currency have? The impacts would be felt both domestically and globally. In the broadest sense, a stronger renminbi (or yuan, as the Chinese currency is called) should help rebalance the global economy. In other words, China's economic growth would be less dependent on the United States and other countries continuing to snap up its exports. Chinese consumers and companies would enjoy increased purchasing power as imported goods became more affordable. This would put downward pressure on China's consumer price index, helping Beijing meet its goal of keeping inflation under control. Global automakers such as BMW, General Motors, and Volkswagen that assemble cars in China from imported parts would reap the benefits of lower costs.

Table 2-8 shows how fluctuating currency values can affect financial risk, depending on the terms of payment specified in the contract. Suppose, at the time a deal is made, the exchange rate is €1.10 equals $1.00. How is a U.S. exporter affected if the dollar strengthens against the euro (e.g., €1.25 equals $1.00) and the contract specifies payment in dollars? What happens if the dollar weakens (e.g., €0.85 equals $1.00)? Conversely, what if the European buyer contracts to pay in euros rather than dollars?

Given that currencies fluctuate in value, a reasonable question to ask is whether a particular currency is overvalued or undervalued compared with another currency. Recall from the chapter discussion that a currency's value can reflect government policy (as in the case of China) or market forces. One way to approach the question is to compare world prices for a single well-known product: McDonald's Big Mac hamburger. *The Economist* magazine's Big Mac Index is a "quick and dirty" way of determining which of the world's currencies are weak or strong. The underlying assumption is that the price of a Big Mac in any world currency should, after being converted to dollars, equal the price of a Big Mac in the United States. (Similar indexes have been proposed based on the price of Starbucks coffee and IKEA furniture.[48])

A country's currency would be overvalued if the Big Mac price (converted to dollars) is higher than the U.S. price. Conversely, a country's currency would be undervalued if the converted Big Mac price is lower than the U.S. price. Economists use the concept of purchasing power parity (PPP) when adjusting national income data to improve comparability. For example, let's take as given that the average U.S. price of a Big Mac is $5.06; in China, the price is 19.19 yuan. If we divide 19.19 by 6.78 (the yuan/dollar exchange rate), we get 2.83. Because this converted price is less than the U.S. price, the yuan must be undervalued. In other words, based on the average U.S. price for a Big Mac, the yuan/dollar exchange rate ought to be 3.79 to $1 (19.19 ÷ 3.79 = 5.06) rather than 6.78 to $1.[49] Make sure you understand that if the exchange rate changes from 6.78 yuan to the dollar to 3.79 yuan to the dollar, the yuan has strengthened relative to the dollar.

TABLE 2-8 **Exchange Risks and Gains in Foreign Transactions**

Foreign Contract Exchange Rates	$1,000,000 Contract		€1,100,000 Contract	
	U.S. Seller Receives	European Buyer Pays	U.S. Seller Receives	European Buyer Pays
€1.25 = $1	$1,000,000	€1,250,000	$880,000	€1,100,000
€1.10 = $1	$1,000,000	€1,100,000	$1,000,000	€1,100,000
€1.00 = $1	$1,000,000	€1,000,000	$1,100,000	€1,100,000
€0.85 = $1	$1,000,000	€850,000	$1,294,118	€1,100,000

Economic Exposure

Economic exposure reflects the impact of currency fluctuations on a company's financial performance. It can come into play when a company's business transactions result in sales or purchases denominated in foreign currencies. Diageo, for example, faces economic exposure to the extent that it accepts payment for exports of Scotch whisky at one exchange rate but actually settles its accounts at a different exchange rate.[50] Obviously, economic exposure is a critical issue for Nestlé, as 98 percent of that company's annual sales occur outside Switzerland.

Among countries in the euro zone, GlaxoSmithKline, Daimler AG, BP, Sanofi-Aventis, Royal Dutch Shell, and AstraZeneca all generate more than one-third of total sales in the U.S. market. Given the volatility of the dollar relative to the euro, all of these companies face potential economic exposure. Conversely, GE generates 45 percent of its revenues in the domestic U.S. market and only 14 percent in Europe, so the relative extent of GE's exposure is less than that of the European companies just listed. Even so, GE does face economic exposure. For example, in a 2014–2015 Securities and Exchange Commission filing, the company noted, "The effects of a stronger U.S. dollar compared to mainly the euro, Brazilian real, and Canadian dollar, decreased consolidated revenues by $4.9 billion."[51]

In dealing with the economic exposure introduced by currency fluctuations, a key issue is whether the company can use price as a strategic tool for maintaining its profit margins. Can the company adjust prices in response to a rise or fall of foreign exchange rates in various markets? That depends on the price elasticity of demand. The less price-sensitive the demand, the greater the flexibility a company has in responding to exchange rate changes. In the late 1980s, for example, Porsche raised prices in the United States three times in response to the weak dollar. The result: Porsche's U.S. sales dropped precipitously, from 30,000 vehicles in 1986 to 4,500 vehicles in 1992. Clearly, U.S. luxury car buyers were exhibiting elastic demand curves for pricey German sports cars!

Managing Exchange Rate Exposure

It should be clear from this discussion that accurately forecasting exchange rate movements is a major challenge. Over the years, the search for ways of managing cash flows to eliminate or reduce exchange rate risks has resulted in the development of numerous techniques and financial strategies. For example, it may be desirable to sell products in the company's home-country currency. When this is not possible, techniques are available to reduce both transaction and operating exposure.

Hedging exchange rate exposure involves establishing an offsetting currency position such that the loss or gain of one currency position is offset by a corresponding gain or loss in some other currency. This practice is common among global companies that sell products and maintain operations in different countries. For example, Porsche now relies on currency hedging rather than price increases to boost pretax profits on sales of its automobiles. This automaker manufactures all of its cars in Europe, but generates about 45 percent of its sales in the United States. Thus, Porsche faces economic exposure stemming from the relative value of the dollar to the euro. Porsche is "fully hedged"; that is, it takes currency positions to protect all earnings from foreign exchange movements.[52]

If company forecasts suggest that the value of the foreign currency will weaken against the home currency, it can hedge to protect against potential transaction losses. Conversely, when it is anticipated that the foreign currency will appreciate (strengthen) against the home currency, then a gain can be expected on foreign transactions when revenues are converted into the home currency. Given this expectation, the best decision may be not to hedge at all. (The operative word is "may"—many companies hedge anyway unless management is convinced the foreign currency will strengthen.) Porsche has profited by (correctly) betting on a weak dollar.

External hedging methods for managing both transaction and translation exposure require companies to participate in the foreign currency market. Specific hedging tools include forward contracts and currency options. *Internal hedging methods* include price adjustment clauses and intracorporate borrowing or lending in foreign currencies. The **forward market** is a mechanism for buying and selling currencies at a preset price for future delivery. If it is known that a certain amount of foreign currency will be paid out or received at some future date, a company can insure itself against exchange loss by buying or selling forward. With a forward contract, the company can lock in a specific fixed exchange rate for a future date, thereby immunizing itself against the loss (or gain) caused by the exchange rate fluctuation. By consulting sources such as the *Financial Times, The Wall Street Journal*, or www.ozforex.com, it is possible to determine exchange rates on any given day. In addition to spot prices, 30-, 60-, and 180-day forward prices are quoted for dozens of world currencies.

Companies use the forward market when the currency exposure is known in advance (e.g., when a firm contract for sale of a good exists). In some situations, however, companies are not certain about the future foreign currency cash inflow or outflow. Consider the risk exposure of a U.S. company that bids for a foreign project but won't know until sometime later if it will be awarded the project. The company needs to protect the dollar value of the contract by hedging the *potential* foreign currency cash inflow that will be generated if the company turns out to be the winning bidder. In such an instance, forward contracts are not the appropriate hedging tool.

A foreign currency **option** is the best approach for dealing with such situations. A **put option** gives the buyer the right—but not the obligation—to sell a specified number of foreign currency units at a fixed price, up to the option's expiration date. (Conversely, a **call option** is the right—but not the obligation—to buy the foreign currency.) In the example of bidding for the foreign project, the company can take out a put option to sell the foreign currency for dollars at a set price in the future. In other words, the U.S. company locks in the value of the contract in dollars. Thus, if it wins the bid, the company's future foreign currency cash inflow has been hedged by means of the put option. If it is *not* awarded the project, the company can trade the put option in the options market without exercising it. Remember, options are rights, not obligations. The only money the company stands to lose is the difference between what it paid for the option and what it receives upon selling it.

Financial officers of global firms can avoid economic exposure altogether by demanding a particular currency as the payment for their foreign sales. As noted, a U.S-based company might demand U.S. dollars as the payment currency for its foreign sales. This, however, does not eliminate currency risk; it simply shifts that risk to the customers. In common practice, companies typically attempt to invoice exports (receivables) in strong currencies and invoice imports (payables) in weak currencies. However, in today's highly competitive world market, such practice may reduce a company's competitive edge.

Summary

The economic environment is a major determinant of global market potential and opportunity. In today's global economy, capital movements are the key driving force, production has become uncoupled from employment, and capitalism has vanquished communism. Based on patterns of resource allocation and ownership, the world's national economies can be categorized as *market capitalism*, *centrally planned capitalism*, *centrally planned socialism*, and *market socialism*. The final years of the twentieth century were marked by a transition toward market capitalism in many countries that had been centrally controlled. Nevertheless, great disparity still exists among the nations of the world in terms of economic freedom.

Countries can be categorized in terms of their stage of economic development: *low income*, *lower-middle income*, *upper-middle income*, and *high income. Gross domestic product (GDP)* and *gross national income (GNI)* are commonly used measures of economic development. The 50 poorest countries in the low-income category are sometimes referred to as *least-developed countries (LDCs)*. Upper-middle-income countries with high growth rates are often called *newly industrializing economies (NIEs)*. Several of the world's economies are notable for their fast growth; for example, the *BRICS* nations include Brazil (lower-middle income), Russia (upper-middle income), India (low income), China (lower-middle income), and South Africa (upper-middle income). The *Group of Seven (G-7)*, the *Group of Eight (G-8)*, the *Group of Twenty (G-20)*, and the *Organisation for Economic Co-operation and Development (OECD)* represent efforts by high-income nations to promote democratic ideals and free market policies throughout the rest of the world. Most of the world's income is located in Japan and Greater China, the United States, and Western Europe; companies with global aspirations generally have operations in all three areas. Market potential for a product can be evaluated by determining *product saturation levels* in light of income levels.

A country's *balance of payments* is a record of its economic transactions with the rest of the world; this record shows whether a country has a *trade surplus* (value of exports exceeds value of imports) or a *trade deficit* (value of imports exceeds value of exports). Trade figures can be further divided into *merchandise trade* and *services trade* accounts; a country can run a surplus in both accounts, a deficit in both accounts, or a combination of the two. Although the U.S. merchandise trade deficit was $752 billion in 2016, the United States enjoys an annual services trade surplus. Overall, the United States is a debtor; China enjoys an overall trade surplus and serves as a creditor nation.

Foreign exchange provides a means for settling accounts across borders. The dynamics of international finance can have a significant impact on a nation's economy as well as the fortunes of individual companies. Currencies can be subject to *devaluation* or *revaluation* as a result of actions taken by a country's central bank. Currency trading by international speculators can also lead to devaluation. When a country's economy is strong or when demand for its goods is high, its currency tends to appreciate in value. When currency values fluctuate, global firms face various types of economic exposure. Firms can manage exchange rate exposure by *hedging*.

Discussion Questions

2-1. The seven criteria for describing a nation's economy introduced at the beginning of this chapter can be combined in a number of different ways. For example, the United States can be characterized as follows:

Type of economy: advanced industrial state
Type of government: democracy with a multiparty system
Trade and capital flows: incomplete free trade and part of a trading bloc
The commanding heights: mix of state and private ownership
Services provided by the state and funded through taxes: pensions and education, but not health care
Institutions: transparency, standards, no corruption, a free press, and strong courts
Markets: free market system characterized by high-risk/high-reward entrepreneurial dynamism

Use these seven criteria (page 66) to develop a profile of one of the BRICS nations, or any other country that interests you. What implications does this profile have for marketing opportunities in the country?

2-2. Briefly describe the five major transformations affecting the global economic environment since the Second World War. What is the one common theme that features among the changes?

2-3. What are the main features of market capitalism and centrally planned socialism? What has led to the adoption of a market capitalist system among many former socialist countries?

2-4. The Heritage Foundation's Index of Economic Freedom is not the only ranking that assesses countries in terms of successful economic policies. For example, the World Economic Forum (WEF; www.weforum.org) publishes an annual Global Competitiveness Report; in the 2017–2018 report, the United States ranked 2rd, according to the WEF's metrics. By contrast, Sweden was in 7th place. According to the Index of Economic Freedom's rankings for 2017, the United States and Sweden are in 17th and 19th place, respectively. Why are the rankings so different? Which criteria does each index consider?

2-5. When the first edition of this textbook was published in 1996, the World Bank defined "low-income country" as one with per capita income of less than $501. In 2003, when the third edition of *Global Marketing* appeared, "low income" was defined as $785 or less in per capita income. As shown in Table 2-4, $1,005 is the current "low-income" threshold. The other stages of development have been revised in a similar manner. How do you explain the trend in the definition of income categories during the past 20 years?

2-6. Your friend owns an import-and-export company and is worried that the value of the local currency has underperformed in comparison to all regional currencies in recent months. How would you advise your friend on the use of hedging in managing exchange rate exposure?

2-7. The prices of general products and services fluctuate, but there are marked differences in prices across the world. A small bottle of water costs $3.29 in Switzerland but only $0.19 in Tunisia. How does your country measure up in terms of the price of products and services? The website Numbeo.com was launched in April 2009 and has comparison prices across a broad range of products and services in a number of countries. Choose ten products or services at random and see how your country compares in terms of price. Apart from price, what other factors should be considered?

CASE 2-1 *Continued (refer to page 63)*

India's Economy at the Crossroads: Can Prime Minister Narendra Modi Deliver *Acche Din*?

In mid-2015, Modi announced several policy changes that were designed to open India's economy even further to foreign investment. One change grants foreign single-brand retailers a three-year grace period for complying with local-content rules requiring that at least 30 percent of manufactured materials in the products they sell are sourced in India. Tech retailers offering "cutting-edge" or "state-of-the-art" products have an additional five years to comply.

Foreign Investment Increases

This policy change paves the way for Apple to open its own stores in the world's second-largest smartphone market. Apple currently has an approximately 3 percent market share in India. Apple requested an exemption from the local-sourcing requirements, and a government panel ruled in the company's favor. However, India's finance minister and the Foreign Investment Promotion Board rejected the panel's findings, thwarting Apple's retail plans for the near future.

Amazon is another tech company that is targeting India for its growth potential. In doing so, Amazon India is competing with entrenched local e-commerce companies including Flipkart and Snapdeal. The key to success, according to CEO Jeff Bezos, will be local market customization. This approach embodies lessons learned in Amazon's failure to penetrate China's e-commerce market. In India, Amazon will accept payment in cash for shoppers who don't use credit or debit cards. Also, customers can shop using tablets installed in local shops.

One challenge is that Indian regulations prevent Amazon from using an "inventory-led" business model. In essence, Amazon cannot sell its own goods, but rather must adhere to a "marketplace model" in which the technology platform brings buyers and sellers together. Also, no single vendor is allowed to account for more than 25 percent of products sold. In spite of such restrictions, Amazon's investment in India has totaled approximately $5 billion to date.

In addition to retail, other sectors of the Indian market are being liberalized. For example, foreign investors will now be allowed to have 100 percent ownership of Indian airlines; previously, ownership stakes by foreign investors were limited to 49 percent. In the defense sector, full foreign ownership of arms-related projects will also be allowed. U.S.-based Boeing is taking advantage of the new rules to form a partnership with India's Tata Advanced Systems to make aircraft frames.

The Innovation Imperative

Fostering innovation is another of Modi's imperatives, though achieving success on this front will require changing the nature of Indian capitalism. Indeed, in the World Bank's 2015 Ease of Doing Business index, India's ranking improved four points, to 130. In the World Economic Forum's 2015–2016 rankings of global competitiveness, India ranks 55, one step above Vietnam. High on Modi's agenda is improving education for girls and providing more opportunities for women.

> "Value creation comes where different businesses collide, not within businesses themselves."[53]
>
> Anand Mahindra, Mahindra Group

Another important element of the recent initiatives is "Digital India," Modi's plan to provide more high-speed Internet access throughout India. In September 2015, an audience of 18,000 people attended a town-hall style meeting with Facebook's Mark Zuckerberg and the prime minister at the SAP Arena in San Jose, California. Many in the audience were Indian-born Facebook employees who greeted the prime minister with chants of "Modi! Modi!" Modi told the crowd, "We are an $8 billion economy today. My dream is to become a $20 trillion economy." At the time of the meeting, Modi had more than 15 million Twitter followers and more than 30 million Facebook likes.

Thanks to booming sales of low-cost smartphones, approximately one-third of India's population—some 425 million people—is now connected to the Internet. Local e-commerce startups such as Quikr and Snapdeal offer app-based services in Hindi and other local languages. Baidu, a Chinese e-commerce company, is following suit. Some of these companies feature content translated from English with the aid of machine-learning software. Other Indian companies, such as social networking site ShabdaNaragi and news aggregator Dailyhunt, are creating or sharing content that is native in local Indian languages.

Wipro, Infosys, and Tata Consultancy Services (TCS) are currently India's Big Three information technology companies. Starting in the 1980s, these companies benefited from the outsourcing trend that saw Western companies taking advantage of India's low-cost, highly educated labor force. Call centers were one key industry; another was installation and maintenance of computer software systems.

Today, Wipro, Infosys, TCS, and other Indian IT companies are navigating the global shift in IT spending. Competitive threats—and opportunities—are coming from all sides. For example, cloud-based services from Amazon and Microsoft threaten to disrupt the traditional IT services that have long been a bright spot in India's economy. Some cloud-services companies are focused on specific sectors; an example is U.K.-based Equiniti Financial Services, whose customers include both individuals and organizations. At the same time, companies such as IBM and Accenture are expanding their IT services offerings.

Demonetization: Modi Clamps Down on "Black Money"

In November 2016, Prime Minister Modi made a bold move: He announced that, overnight, the government was canceling the country's Rs500 ($7.66) and Rs1000 currency notes. The move was designed to curb various forms of "black money" obtained through black market transactions and other illegal activities such as corruption or currency counterfeiting. "Black money" also includes money earned legally but not declared as taxable income.

Before the change, roughly 80 percent of consumer transactions in India were conducted in cash. After Modi's announcement, Indians had a short window of opportunity to deposit the canceled bank notes in their bank accounts or exchange them for new currency. The move basically "demonetized" about 86 percent of the currency—worth a total of $220 billion—circulating through India's economy. It also provided opportunities for fintech startups such as mobile payments provider Paytm.

Some critics noted that "shock treatment" of this type had previously occurred only in countries experiencing hyperinflation or economic collapse. Why, the critics asked, was Modi resorting to such a drastic measure when India's GDP was growing at a rate of 7 percent? Swapan Dasgupta, a member of India's parliament, had this answer: "It's motivated by a philosophy which is that if you want India to be a meaningful player on the world economic stage you've got to take tough measures."

TABLE 2-9 GST Categories

Tax Rate (%)	Items Included (Partial List)
0	Milk; fruit; children's picture books and coloring books; raw coffee beans
3	Gold
5	Packaged food; clothing costing less than Rs 1,000 ($15.50); roasted coffee beans; railway transport; small restaurants without air conditioning
12	Toothpaste; umbrellas; mobile phones; medium-sized restaurants without air conditioning
18	Cookies; cakes, restaurants with air conditioning
28	Chewing gum; deodorant; shampoo; instant coffee

New Tax Regime

In July 2017, Modi's government launched a new national sales tax system, which included the Goods and Services Tax (GST). The GST was designed to eliminate some of the abundant red tape that kept a damper on India's economic growth. Previously, products could be taxed at different rates in different Indian states. Instead of a single national sales tax rate, the new system includes six rates, ranging from 0 percent to 28 percent (see Table 2-9). Mass-consumption goods are taxed at the lowest rates. In contrast, luxury cars, tobacco, chewing tobacco, and carbonated soft drinks will be taxed at "sin tax" rates approaching 300 percent. Some categories, including property and alcoholic beverages, are not included in the GST and will be subject to tax at the state level.

Discussion Questions

2-8. Social activists and political opponents in India have voiced objection to Modi's economic liberalization initiatives. What do you think is the nature of some of these objections?

2-9. Do you think Modi's large number of social media "likes" and "followers" are indicative of his potential to achieve economic reform?

2-10. Assess Modi's two main economic reforms—namely, demonetization and tax reform.

2-11. What must Wipro, Infosys, TCS, and other companies in India's IT sector do to avoid being victimized by new trends in technology?

Sources: Simon Mundy, "Bangalore's Finest Eye the Storm Beyond the Cloud," *Financial Times* (July 6, 2016), p. 16; Amy Kazmin, "Modi Hopes Investment Easing Will See India Fly," *Financial Times* (June 22, 2016), p. 6; Rajesh Roy, "India Move Could Help Apple Run Own Stores," *The Wall Street Journal* (June 21, 2016), pp. B1, B2; Simon Mundy, "India Phone Apps Learn the Vernacular to Reach New Customers," *Financial Times* (June 14, 2016), p. 18; Victor Mallet, "Modi Struggles to Realise Indian Dreams," *Financial Times* (May 16, 2016), p. 4; Jason Overdorf, "Hopes of Business-Friendly Reforms Fade Away in India," *USA Today* (March 1, 2016), p. 5B; Victor Mallet, "Air of Caution as Modi Faces Defining Year," *Financial Times* (January 13, 2016), p. 4; John D. Stoll, "Detroit Remains Foreign Car Makers' Mecca," *The Wall Street Journal* (January 11, 2016), pp. B1, B4; Jessica Guynn, "India's Modi Gets a 'Like' at Facebook HQ," *USA Today* (September 28, 2015), p. 2B; Amy Kazmin, "Indian Farmers Dig In over Modi 'Land Grab,'" *Financial Times* (February 26, 2015), p. 5.

CASE 2-2
A Day in the Life of a Contracts Analyst at Cargill

Glynis Gallagher works as a contracts analyst at Cargill Risk Management, which is a business unit within Cargill. Based in Wayzata, Minnesota, Cargill celebrated its 150th anniversary in 2015. Cargill is a truly global company: With operations in more than 60 countries, it markets food, agricultural, financial, and industrial products and services to customers worldwide. The company is one of the world's top grain traders. In addition, it has global beef operations, and it does business in starches and sweeteners as well. Cargill also processes steel and de-icing salt. Its revenues totaled $109,699 billion in 2017, making Cargill the largest privately owned company in the United States.

Cargill is committed to feeding the world in a responsible way, while also reducing its environmental impact and improving the communities where its employees live and work. Writing in the introduction to his 1979 book *Merchants of Grain*, author Dan Morgan noted:

Grain is the only resource in the world that is even more central to modern civilization than oil. It goes without saying that grain is essential to human lives and health. . . . As America became the center of the planetary food system, trade routes were transformed, new economic relationships took shape, and grain became one of the foundations of the postwar American Empire.

Today, as the saying goes, "You can't walk down the grocery aisle without seeing something Cargill has been involved with in one way or another." A recent article in *Forbes* described the scope of the company's operations:

Cargill, the $135 billion (fiscal year 2014 sales) family-owned food behemoth dominates all roads between the world's farms and your dinner plate. . . . Since the company was founded in 1865, the core of its business has always been trading commodities—buying, storing, shipping and selling the crops farmers grow around the world.

Commodities processing is a high-volume, low-margin business; Cargill crushes large quantities of soybeans each day. Because the company is privately held, Cargill can pursue long-term investment opportunities in many global markets. For example, it has had a major presence in India and other emerging markets for decades. The company has made large investments in cocoa, sugar, and food innovation.

The career path of Greg Page, former Cargill CEO and current executive chairman, shows the range of job opportunities Cargill offers its employees. After graduating from college, Page took a trainee position in the Feed Division. In subsequent years, he held a number of positions in the United States and Singapore. He was also involved with the startup of a poultry processing facility in Thailand. Today, Cargill exports roughly 100 million metric tons of chicken from Thailand every year.

Gallagher graduated from a large Midwestern university in 2012 with a major in marketing. She spent fall semester of her senior year studying in northern Italy. Many of her business courses helped prepare her for her current role. She recalls, "Although I never took a course focused on derivatives and trading exclusively, my math and finance courses gave me a solid foundation in order to understand portfolio exposures, fee schedules, and financing options we utilize every day. My marketing courses have allowed me to use this data in a more customer-focused approach on a daily basis."

Cargill Risk Management is part of Financial Services, one of Cargill's six platforms that comprise 65 business units. Cargill, through Cargill Risk Management, is a registered limited designation swap dealer with the U.S. Commodities Futures Trading Commission (CFTC). Gallagher must make sure that everything she does for customers complies with CFTC swap dealing guidelines. Cargill and other commodities trade houses are industry members of the Commodity Markets Council, a trade group that serves as a liaison between companies and the government.

Gallagher is a contracts analyst. She says, "I have always been interested in law. Becoming a contracts analyst in such a regulated industry allowed me to gain exposure to contractual language, legal requirements, and the regulatory environment. For example, if you do not set up a contract properly, you are opening yourself up to unnecessary risk." As Gallagher explains, "In today's highly regulated and changing business environment, it is essential to protect yourself while completing business transactions. Being part of this facet of the business is a daily challenge. It pushes me outside of my comfort zone to understand a basic question—namely, what is the true risk here for Cargill?"

As noted previously, Cargill Risk Management is a limited designated swap dealer. What's a "swap"? Swaps, also known as over-the-counter (OTC) transactions, can be complex financial structures that derive their value from something else—a futures contract, for example. Swaps are traded in direct negotiation between buyer and seller; they represent a $700 trillion market. Who uses swaps? Gallagher's business unit services a variety of customers, including farmers, major airlines, food companies, investment funds, oil companies, and many others.

Gallagher's business unit works with its customers to provide commodities hedges through swaps and structured products. The commodities in question are often agricultural commodities such as grains (e.g., corn, wheat, and soybeans), as well as beef and other animal proteins. Cargill also deals in metals and energy. Hedging is a financial strategy that allows a customer to lock in the price for a specific commodity purchase in the future. An important part of Gallagher's job is to work diligently to understand customers' business objectives, and to ensure contractual terms are aligned with these strategies. The Cargill team assists customers by creating tailored risk management solutions to reduce risks and uncertainty by having more diversified hedging portfolios.

Consider the following example: When a large restaurant chain purchases cooking oil, it must manage budgets and margins to ensure profitability. When the price of oil seeds—a commodity—increases, the company needs to find a way to offset this increase instead of passing along the cost to its customers in the form of higher prices. Of course, market volatility and cost swings are difficult to predict—so how is the restaurant chain able to do this? Helping customers answer this question is an important part of Gallagher's team's job.

Summing up her experience, Gallagher says, "I enjoy working with our customers in more than 60 countries throughout the world. With 16 global offices, I am exposed to different cultures and business practices that challenge me to think globally. Understanding where the customer is coming from allows me to succeed in helping them understand and navigate this complex field. Ultimately, I am part of the process which allows enterprises ranging from huge corporations to small farmers succeed in managing their overall risk."

Discussion Questions

2-12. What knowledge and skills are required to be successful as a contracts analyst?

2-13. What do you think is the best part of Gallagher's job? The most challenging part?

2-14. What does Gallagher's career profile tell you about the importance of professionalism and a good work ethic at a company such as Cargill?

2-15. Cargill engages in a wide range of sustainability initiatives, including ensuring access to food; preventing food waste; supporting urban agriculture; and participating in the Non-GMO Project. **Dig deeper:** Choose one of these topics, conduct some exploratory research, and write a short essay or present a brief oral report on your findings. Remember to cite your sources!

Sources: Jacob Bunge, "Demographic Destiny 2050—Chicken to Feed the World," *The Wall Street Journal* (December 5–6, 2015), pp. C1, C2; Gregory Meyer and Neil Hume, "Cargill Set to Keep It in the Family 150 Years On," *Financial Times* (April 20, 2015), p. 18; Dan Alexander, "Faster Food: Inside Cargill's Plan to Make the World's Biggest Food Business Even Bigger," *Forbes* (November 24, 2014), pp. 44–48; Dan Morgan, *Merchants of Grain* (New York, NY: Penguin Books, 1979); Scott Kilman, "Bountiful Harvest: Giant Cargill Resists Pressure to Go Public as It Pursues Growth," *The Wall Street Journal* (January 9, 1997), pp. A1, A4.

Notes

[1]The "BRIC" designation first appeared in a 2001 report published by Goldman Sachs, the New York–based investment bank, hedge fund, and private equity firm.

[2]Numerous books and articles survey this subject—for example, Lowell Bryan et al., *Race for the World: Strategies to Build a Great Global Firm* (Boston, MA: Harvard Business School Press, 1999). See also Thomas Piketty, *Capital in the Twenty-First Century* (Cambridge, MA: Belknap Press, 2014).

[3]Bill Vlasic, "Ford Introduces One Small Car for a World of Markets," *The New York Times* (February 15, 2008), p. C3.

[4]William Greider offers a thought-provoking analysis of these new realities in *One World, Ready or Not: The Manic Logic of Global Capitalism* (New York, NY: Simon & Schuster, 1997).

[5]Tom Lauricella, "Currency Trading Soars," *The Wall Street Journal* (September 1, 2010), p. A1.

[6]Another economic indicator, *gross national income* (GNI), comprises GDP plus income generated from nonresident sources. A third metric, *gross national product* (GNP), is the total value of all final goods and services produced in a country by its residents and domestic business enterprises, plus the value of output produced by citizens working abroad, plus income generated by capital held abroad, minus transfers of net earnings by global companies operating in the country. GDP also measures economic activity; however, GDP includes *all* income produced within a country's borders by its residents and domestic enterprises as well as foreign-owned enterprises. Income earned by citizens working abroad is *not* included. For example, Ireland has attracted a great deal of foreign investment, and foreign-owned firms account for nearly 90 percent of Ireland's exports. This helps explain the fact that, in 2016, Ireland's GDP totaled $304 billion while GNI was $247 billion. As a practical matter, GNP, GDP, and GNI figures for many countries will be roughly the same.

[7]Brian Groom, "Balance and Power," *Financial Times* (July 22, 2010), p. 7.

[8]Jon E. Hilsenrath and Rebecca Buckman, "Factory Employment Is Falling World-Wide," *The Wall Street Journal* (October 20, 2003), p. A2. Some companies have cut employment by outsourcing or subcontracting nonmanufacturing activities such as data processing, accounting, and customer service.

[9]Tracey Taylor, "A Label of Pride That Pays," *The New York Times* (April 23, 2009), p. B4.

[10]The authors are indebted to Professor Emeritus Francis J. Colella, Department of Economics, Simpson College, for suggesting these criteria.

[11]Peggy A. Golden, Patricia M. Doney, Denise M. Johnson, and Jerald R. Smith, "The Dynamics of a Marketing Orientation in Transition Economies: A Study of Russian Firms," *Journal of International Marketing* 3, no. 2 (1995), pp. 29–49.

[12]Nicholas R. Lardy, *Integrating China into the Global Economy* (Washington, DC: Brookings Institution, 2003), p. 21.

[13]William Greider, *One World, Ready or Not: The Manic Logic of Global Capitalism* (New York, NY: Simon & Schuster, 1997), p. 37.

[14]Joel Sherwood and Terence Roth, "Defeat of Sweden's Ruling Party Clears Way for Sales of State Assets," *The Wall Street Journal* (September 19, 2006), p. A8.

[15]Daniel Yergin and Joseph Stanislaw, "Sale of the Century," *Financial Times Weekend* (January 24–25, 1998), p. I.

[16]William Greider, *One World, Ready or Not: The Manic Logic of Global Capitalism* (New York, NY: Simon & Schuster, 1997), pp. 36–37. See also John Burton, "Singapore's Social Contract Shows Signs of Strain," *Financial Times* (August 19–20, 2006), p. 3.

[17]Sarah Theodore, "Beer Has Big Changes on Tap," *Beverage Industry* (September 2008), p. 24.

[18]For an excellent discussion of BEMs, see Jeffrey E. Garten, *The Big Ten: The Big Emerging Markets and How They Will Change Our Lives* (New York, NY: Basic Books, 1997).

[19]John Aglionby and David Pilling, "Slow Growth Blurs Rwanda's Vision," *Financial Times* (September 12, 2017), p. 7.

[20]John Aglionbi, "Ethiopia Bids to Become the Last Development Frontier," *Financial Times* (July 4, 2017), p. 9.

[21]Saritha Rai, "Tastes of India in U.S. Wrappers," *The New York Times* (April 29, 2003), p. W7.

[22]Manjeet Kirpalani, "The Factories Are Humming," *Businessweek* (October 18, 2004), pp. 54–55.

[23]Joe Leahy, "Brazil Needs to Be Wary as It Enjoys Success Amid 'Insanity,'" *Financial Times* (August 3, 2011), p. 2.

[24]Antonio Regalado, "Soccer, Samba and Outsourcing?" *The Wall Street Journal* (January 25, 2007), p. B1.

[25]Matt Moffett and Helene Cooper, "Silent Invasion: In Backyard of the U.S., Europe Gains Ground in Trade, Diplomacy," *The Wall Street Journal* (September 18, 1997), pp. A1, A8.

[26]Charles Clover and Sherry Fei Ju, "China's Larger-Than-Life Electric Car Ambitions," *Financial Times* (February 2, 2018), p. 15.

[27]Patrick McGroarty, "South Africa Trade Hits Bump," *The Wall Street Journal* (March 25, 2013), p. A11.

[28]Adapted from C. K. Prahalad and Allen Hammond, "Serving the World's Poor, Profitably," *Harvard Business Review* 80, no. 9 (September 2002), pp. 48–57.

[29]Stuart L. Hart and Clayton M. Christensen, "The Great Leap: Driving Innovation from the Base of the Pyramid," *MIT Sloan Management Review* 44, no. 1 (Fall 2002), p. 56.

[30]Ernest Beck, "Populist Perrier? Nestlé Pitches Bottled Water to World's Poor," *The Asian Wall Street Journal* (June 18, 1999), p. B1.

[31]Jason Dean and Peter Wonacott, "Tech Firms Woo 'Next Billion' Users," *The Wall Street Journal* (November 3, 2006), p. A2. See also David Kirkpatrick, "Looking for Profits in Poverty," *Fortune* (February 5, 2001), pp. 174–176.

[32]Miriam Jordan, "From the Amazon to Your Armrest," *The Wall Street Journal* (May 1, 2001), pp. B1, B4.

[33]Scott McCartney, "Behind Your Online Travel Booking with Barry Diller," *The Wall Street Journal* (July 14, 2016), pp. D1, D2.

[34]Jenny Wiggins, "Brands Make a Dash into Russia," *Financial Times* (September 4, 2008), p. 10.

[35]Russell Gold and David Crawford, "U.S., Other Nations Step up Bribery Battle," *The Wall Street Journal* (September 12, 2008), pp. B1, B6.

[36]Kiran Stacey, "Card Machine Queue Frustrates Merchants," *Financial Times* (December 6, 2016), p. 17.

[37]Amy Chozik, "Nissan Races to Make Smaller, Cheaper Cars," *The Wall Street Journal* (October 22, 2007), p. A12.

[38]Lukas I. Alpert, "Russia's Auto Market Shines," *The Wall Street Journal* (August 30, 2012), p. B3.

[39]Saabira Chaudhuri, "Champagne Loses Its Sparkle in U.K.," *Financial Times* (March 21, 2017), p. B2.

[40]Balance of payments data are available from a number of different sources, each of which may show slightly different figures for a given line item.

[41]Richard McGregor, "The Trillion Dollar Question: China Is Grappling with How to Deploy Its Foreign Exchange Riches," *Financial Times* (September 25, 2006).

[42]www.wto.org/english/res_e/statis_e/its2013_e/its13_world_trade_dev_e.pdf. Accessed February 14, 2015.

[43]Bertrand Benoit and Richard Milne, "Germany's Best-Kept Secret: How Its Exporters Are Beating the World," *Financial Times* (May 19, 2006), p. 11.

[44]Valentina Romei, "The 'Dark Matter That Matters' in Trade with EU," *Financial Times* (December 18, 2017), p. 2.

[45]Mark Whitehouse, "U.S. Foreign Debt Shows Its Teeth as Rates Climb," *The Wall Street Journal* (September 25, 2006), p. A9.

[46]Damian Paletta and John W. Miller, "China, U.S. Square off over Yuan," *The Wall Street Journal* (October 7, 2010), p. A10.

[47]David J. Lynch, "Russia Brings Revitalized Economy to the Table," *USA Today* (July 13, 2006).

[48]"When the Chips Are Down," *Economist.com* (accessed December 1, 2010).

[49]The authors acknowledge that the PPP theory–based Big Mac Index is simplistic; as noted in this section, exchange rates are also affected by interest rate differentials and monetary and fiscal policies—not just prices.

[50]John Willman, "Currency Squeeze on Guinness," *Financial Times—Weekend Money* (September 27–28, 1997), p. 5.

[51]"About General Electric," *GE 2015 Form 10-K*, p. 30.

[52]Stephen Power, "Porsche Powers Profit with Currency Play," *The Wall Street Journal* (December 8, 2004), p. C3.

[53]James Crabtree, "India's Tycoons Still Believe in the Notion That Big Is Beautiful," *Financial Times* (November 4, 2015), p. 14.

3

The Global Trade Environment

LEARNING OBJECTIVES

3-1 Explain the role of the World Trade Organization in facilitating global trade relations among nations.

3-2 Compare and contrast the four main categories of preferential trade agreements.

3-3 Explain the trade relationship dynamics among signatories of the North American Free Trade Agreement.

3-4 Identify the four main preferential trade agreements in Latin America and the key members of each.

3-5 Identify the main preferential trade agreements in the Asia-Pacific region.

3-6 Describe the various forms of economic integration in Europe. What is Brexit, and what are the implications for Great Britain's relationship with Europe.

3-7 Describe the activities of the key regional organizations in the Middle East.

3-8 Identify the issues for global marketers wishing to expand in Africa.

CASE 3-1

Breaking Up Is Hard to Do: Britons Contemplate "Brexit"

"Should we stay or should we go?" That was the question on the minds of voters who went to the polls in June 2016 to decide whether the United Kingdom of Great Britain and Northern Ireland would remain in the European Union (EU). The issue was complicated by the election of Jeremy Corbyn, a far-left candidate, as leader of the Labor Party in September 2015. Britain was also witnessing the rise of populist movements, as evidenced by the fact that nearly 4 million people voted for the anti-EU U.K. Independence Party (UKIP). UKIP's leader, Nigel Farage, had long been a vocal critic of the EU.

Disillusionment was also evident among members of the Tory party who had opposed Britain's initial inclusion in the EU, which dated to 1973. In the 1990s, some Tories had also opposed Britain's participation in the Maastricht treaty that established Europe's Single Market.

In 2013, Prime Minister David Cameron, a member of the Conservative party, had announced that he was calling a referendum on the issue. At the time, Cameron was convinced that, after sufficient public debate, most U.K. citizens would opt for the status quo. By the time the referendum was put to a vote three years later, however, the opposition movement had gathered considerable momentum and rhetoric on both sides became heated. When the votes were tallied, the "Exit" camp prevailed: The United Kingdom would leave the EU.

As a member of the EU, the United Kingdom has access to a free, open market of nearly 500 million people. For that reason alone, many members of the U.K. business community were

Exhibit 3-1 Opinions continue to be divided between those in favor of "Leave" and those in the "Remain" camp following the Brexit vote in June 2016.
Source: Chris Ratcliffe/Bloomberg via Getty Images.

firmly in the "Remain" camp. The Confederation of British Industry (CBI) was against leaving; the trade group produced a study suggesting that 1 million jobs and £100 billion in national income would be lost by 2020. Rolls-Royce Motor Cars and Airbus have major manufacturing operations in the United Kingdom; executives at both companies warned that a "Leave" vote would have negative consequences on employment and competitiveness.

Other companies shied away from the debate, no doubt for fear of alienating their customers on the European continent. One notable exception: Sir James Dyson, the industrialist best known for his vacuum cleaners, was a Leave supporter. In his view, British companies are being "bullied and dominated" by Germany.

For their part, "Euro-skeptics" and other members of the Leave movement were convinced that their country could thrive economically outside of the EU framework (see Exhibit 3-1). There was a shared sense among some in this group that "faceless bureaucrats" in Brussels were creating mountains of red tape that hampered U.K. business. Moreover, some people believed that British politicians avoided making key policy decisions by deferring to the EU. As one jokester put it, "Nothing of use has come out of Brussels since the sprout!"

Since World War II, nations have had tremendous interest in furthering the cause of economic cooperation and integration. Such agreements can be *bilateral* in nature; that is, a trade deal can be negotiated between two nations. However, multilateral trade agreements also occur at the regional and global levels. The euro zone, and the larger, 28-nation EU to which 19 euro-zone countries also belong, exemplify regional economic integration. The "Brexit" vote in the United Kingdom, the world's fifth-largest economy and the second-largest economy in the EU, represents a step backward from such integration.

Our survey of the world trade environment begins at the global level with the World Trade Organization (WTO) and its predecessor, the General Agreement on Tariffs and Trade (GATT). Next, the four main types of bilateral and regional preferential trade agreements (PTAs) are identified and described. An introduction to individual countries in the world's major market regions follows; each section also includes detailed discussion of the specific preferential trade agreements in which those countries participate. Important marketing issues in each region are also discussed. Several important emerging country markets were described in Chapter 2; in this chapter, special attention will be given to individual country markets that were not previously discussed.

(3-1) The World Trade Organization and GATT

◄ **3-1** Explain the role of the World Trade Organization in facilitating global trade relations among nations.

The year 2017 marked 70 years since the enactment of the **General Agreement on Tariffs and Trade (GATT)**, a treaty among nations whose governments agreed, at least in principle, to promote trade among members. GATT was intended to be a multilateral, global initiative, and GATT negotiators did succeed in liberalizing world merchandise trade. GATT was also an organization that handled 300 trade disputes—many involving food—during its half-century of existence. GATT itself had no enforcement power (the losing party in a dispute was entitled to ignore the ruling), and the process of dealing with disputes sometimes stretched on for years. Little wonder, then, that some critics referred to GATT as the "General Agreement to Talk and Talk."

The successor to GATT, the **World Trade Organization (WTO)**, came into existence on January 1, 1995. From its base in Geneva, Switzerland, the WTO provides a forum for trade-related negotiations among its 164 members. The WTO's neutral trade experts also serve as mediators in global trade disputes (see Table 3-1). The WTO has a Dispute Settlement Body (DSB) that mediates complaints concerning unfair trade barriers and other issues among the WTO's member countries. During a 60-day consultation period, parties to a complaint are expected to engage in good-faith negotiations and reach an amicable resolution.

If that fails, the complainant can ask the DSB to appoint a three-member panel of trade experts to hear the case behind closed doors. After convening, the panel has nine months to issue its ruling.[1] The DSB is empowered to act on the panel's recommendations.

The losing party has the option of turning to a seven-member Appellate Body. If, after due process, a country's trade policies are found to violate WTO rules, the country is expected to change those policies. If changes are not forthcoming, the WTO can authorize trade sanctions against the loser. Final resolution of a dispute is not always swift, however: The European Union and the United States have spent more than a decade at the WTO trying to work out issues relating to aerospace subsidies.

Trade ministers representing the WTO member nations meet on a biennial basis to work on improving world trade. In 2017, that meeting took place in Buenos Aires. It remains to be seen whether the WTO will live up to expectations when it comes to additional major policy initiatives on such vexing issues as illegal fishing subsidies. Another issue is whether China should be classified as a market economy. The most recent round of WTO negotiations began in 2001; the talks collapsed in 2005, and attempts to revive them in the years since have not been successful. That is one reason why the focus of trade talks shifted to the Transatlantic Trade and Investment Partnership (TTIP) and Trans-Pacific Partnership (TPP; see Case 3-2). Following the election of U.S. President Donald Trump in 2016, the TTIP and TPP negotiations proceeded without the United States. Also, the Trump administration has blocked the process for filling vacancies on the WTO's Appellate Body.

"For the WTO process to work, countries have to start liberalizing policies in politically sensitive sectors."[2]

Daniel Griswold, Center for Trade Policy Studies, Cato Institute

▶ **3-2** Compare and contrast the four main categories of preferential trade agreements.

3-2 Preferential Trade Agreements

The WTO promotes free trade on a global basis; however, countries in each of the world's regions are seeking to liberalize trade within their own regions. A **preferential trade agreement (PTA)** is a mechanism that confers special treatment on select trading partners. By favoring certain countries, such agreements frequently discriminate against other countries. For that reason, it is customary for countries to notify the WTO when they enter into preferential trade agreements. In

TABLE 3-1 Recent WTO Cases

Countries Involved in the Dispute	Nature of the Dispute
United States versus China	In 2016, the United States filed a complaint that Chinese export duties on a range of extractive commodities gave its own manufacturers access to key materials at market-distorting prices.
European Union versus United States	In 2014, the EU filed a complaint that the government of Washington state violated international trade rules by extending tax incentives to Boeing for in-state manufacture of the 777x jetliner.
Antigua and Barbuda versus the United States	In 2003, Antigua filed suit charging that by prohibiting Internet gambling, the United States was violating global trade agreements. In 2004, the WTO ruled in favor of Antigua.

recent years, the WTO has been notified of approximately 300 preferential trade agreements. Few fully conform to WTO requirements; none, however, has been disallowed.

Free Trade Area

A **free trade area (FTA)** is formed when two or more countries agree to eliminate tariffs and other barriers that restrict trade. When trading partners successfully negotiate a **free trade agreement (also abbreviated FTA)**, the ultimate goal of which is to have zero duties on goods that cross borders between the partners, it creates a free trade area. In some instances, duties are eliminated on the day the agreement takes effect; in other cases, duties are phased out over a set period of time. Countries that belong to an FTA can maintain independent trade policies with respect to third countries. **Rules of origin** discourage the importation of goods into the member country with the lowest external tariff for transshipment to one or more FTA members with higher external tariffs; customs inspectors police the borders between members.

For example, because Chile and Canada established an FTA in 1997, a Canadian-built Caterpillar grader tractor imported into Chile would not be subject to duty. If the same piece of equipment was imported from a factory in the United States, the importer would pay about $13,000 in duties. Could Caterpillar send the U.S.-built tractor to Chile by way of Canada, thereby allowing the importer to avoid paying the duty? No, because the tractor would bear a "Made in the U.S.A." certificate of origin indicating it was subject to the duty. Little wonder, then, that the U.S. government negotiated its own bilateral free trade agreement with Chile that entered into force in 2003.

According to the Business Roundtable, to date several hundred FTAs have been negotiated globally. Overall, more than 50 percent of global trade takes place among nations linked by FTAs, a figure that increases as more agreements are negotiated. Additional examples of FTAs include the European Economic Area, a free trade area that includes the EU plus Norway, Liechtenstein, and Iceland; the Group of Three (G-3), an FTA encompassing Colombia, Mexico, and Venezuela; and the Closer Economic Partnership Agreement, an FTA between China and Hong Kong.

In October 2011, the U.S. Congress finally ratified the United States' long-delayed FTAs with South Korea, Panama, and Colombia. Also on tap: the Comprehensive Economic and Trade Agreement (CETA), which would eliminate most tariffs on the trade in goods between Canada and the European Union. As is often the case with such agreements, there has been considerable opposition to CETA in Europe (see Exhibit 3-2).

Exhibit 3-2 Activists opposed to the Comprehensive Economic and Trade Agreement staged a protest in Vienna in September 2016.
Source: JOE KLAMAR/AFP/Getty Images.

Customs Union

A **customs union** represents the logical evolution of an FTA. In addition to eliminating internal barriers to trade, members of a customs union agree to the establishment of **common external tariffs (CETs)**. In 1996, for example, the EU and Turkey initiated a customs union in a move that boosted two-way trade above the average annual level of $20 billion. The arrangement called for the elimination of tariffs averaging 14 percent, which added $1.5 billion each year to the cost of European goods imported by Turkey.

A customs union between Great Britain and the EU was one widely discussed scenario as Brexit negotiations commenced in 2017 (see Case 3-1). Such a deal would allow Britain to negotiate its own trade terms in the services and agriculture sectors; the EU would set any external tariffs on goods. This arrangement would be modeled on the existing customs union between Turkey and the EU. The downside for Great Britain would be the inability to independently negotiate tariff reductions with the United States and China, two important trading partners.

Other customs unions discussed in this chapter are the Andean Community, the Central American Integration System (SICA), the Common Market of the South (Mercosur), and the Caribbean Community and Common Market (CARICOM).

Common Market

A **common market** is the next level of economic integration. In addition to the removal of internal barriers to trade and the establishment of common external tariffs, the common market allows for free movement of factors of production, including labor and capital. The Andean Community, SICA, and CARICOM, which currently function as customs unions, may ultimately evolve into true common markets.

Economic Union

An **economic union** builds upon the elimination of internal tariff barriers, the establishment of common external barriers, and the free flow of factors. It seeks to coordinate and harmonize economic and social policies within the union to facilitate the free flow of capital, labor, and goods and services from country to country. An economic union is a common marketplace not only for goods but also for services and capital. For example, so that professionals can work anywhere in the EU, the members must harmonize their practice licensing so that a doctor or lawyer qualified in one country may practice in any other EU member country.[3]

The full evolution of an economic union would involve the creation of a unified central bank; the use of a single currency; and common policies on agriculture, social services, welfare, regional development, transport, taxation, competition, and mergers. A true economic union requires extensive political unity, which makes it similar to a nation. The next phase of integration for nations that were members of fully developed economic unions would be the formation of a central government that would bring together independent political states into a single political framework. The EU is approaching its target of completing most of the steps required to become a full economic union, with one notable setback: Despite the fact that 16 member nations ratified a proposed European Constitution, the initiative was derailed after voters in France and the Netherlands voted against the measure. Table 3-2 and Figure 3-1 compare the various forms of regional economic integration.

TABLE 3-2   Forms of Regional Economic Integration

Stage of Integration	Elimination of Tariffs and Quotas Among Members	Common External Tariff (CET) and Quota System	Elimination of Restrictions on Factor Movements	Harmonization and Unification of Economic and Social Policies and Institutions
Free trade area	Yes	No	No	No
Customs union	Yes	Yes	No	No
Common market	Yes	Yes	Yes	No
Economic union	Yes	Yes	Yes	Yes

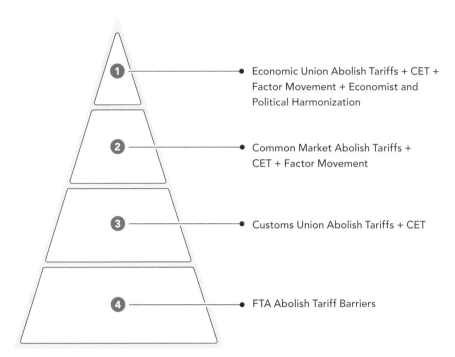

FIGURE 3-1 Hierarchy of Preferential Trade Agreements
Source: Paul Button, based on data from The World Bank.

1. Economic Union Abolish Tariffs + CET + Factor Movement + Economist and Political Harmonization

2. Common Market Abolish Tariffs + CET + Factor Movement

3. Customs Union Abolish Tariffs + CET

4. FTA Abolish Tariff Barriers

(3-3) North America

◀ **3-3** Explain the trade relationship dynamics among signatories of the North American Free Trade Agreement.

North America, which includes Canada, the United States, and Mexico, constitutes a distinctive regional market. The United States combines great wealth, a large population, vast geographical space, and plentiful natural resources in a single national economic and political environment and presents unique marketing characteristics. It is home to more global industry leaders than any other nation in the world; U.S. companies are the dominant producers in the computer, software, aerospace, entertainment, medical equipment, and jet engine industry sectors.

Although Canada has few major global manufacturers, train and plane maker Bombardier is one success story (see Exhibit 3-3). The company has high hopes for its newest corporate jet, the Global 7000. Blackberry (formerly known as Research in Motion), a one-time leader in cellphones, is also based in Canada.

Mexico is gaining a reputation as a manufacturing center; for example, it is the world's number 1 producer of flat-screen TV sets. Carlos Slim, head of telecommunications giant América Móvil, is one of the world's richest men.

Exhibit 3-3 Bombardier, one of Canada's premier companies, builds aircraft for both the business jet and commercial jet markets. In fact, Bombardier Aerospace is the world's third-largest civil aircraft manufacturer. Another business unit, Bombardier Transportation, produces rail equipment.
Source: Stefano Politi Markovina/Alamy.

FIGURE 3-2 United States' Top Import/Export Partners

Source: Paul Button, based on data from The World Bank.

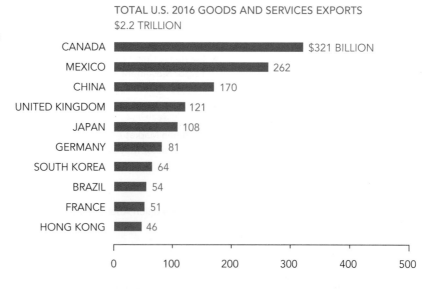

TOTAL U.S. 2016 GOODS AND SERVICES EXPORTS
$2.2 TRILLION

- CANADA — $321 BILLION
- MEXICO — 262
- CHINA — 170
- UNITED KINGDOM — 121
- JAPAN — 108
- GERMANY — 81
- SOUTH KOREA — 64
- BRAZIL — 54
- FRANCE — 51
- HONG KONG — 46

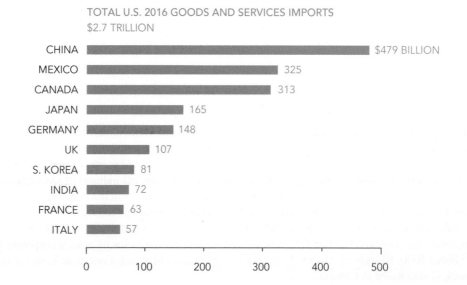

TOTAL U.S. 2016 GOODS AND SERVICES IMPORTS
$2.7 TRILLION

- CHINA — $479 BILLION
- MEXICO — 325
- CANADA — 313
- JAPAN — 165
- GERMANY — 148
- UK — 107
- S. KOREA — 81
- INDIA — 72
- FRANCE — 63
- ITALY — 57

In 1988, the United States and Canada signed a free-trade agreement (U.S.–Canada Free Trade Agreement [CFTA]), and the Canada–U.S. Free Trade Area formally came into existence in 1989. More than $650 billion in goods and services now flow between Canada and the United States each year, in what is the biggest trading relationship between any two single nations in the world. Canada takes 20 percent of U.S. exports and the United States buys approximately 85 percent of Canada's exports. Figure 3-2 illustrates the economic integration of North America: Canada is the United States' number 1 trading partner, China is second, and Mexico ranks third.

American companies have more funds invested in Canada than in any other country. Many U.S. manufacturers, including General Electric (GE) and IBM, use their Canadian operations as major global suppliers for some product lines. By participating in the Canadian auto market, U.S. automakers gain greater economies of scale. The CFTA, which was fully implemented when all duties were eliminated effective January 1998, has created a true continental market for most products.

In 1992, representatives from the United States, Canada, and Mexico concluded negotiations for the **North American Free Trade Agreement (NAFTA)**. The agreement was approved by both houses of the U.S. Congress and became effective on January 1, 1994. The result is a free

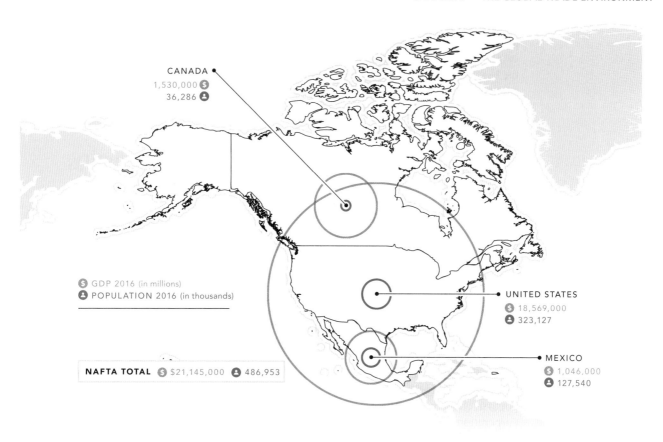

CANADA •
1,530,000 $
36,286 👤

$ GDP 2016 (in millions)
👤 POPULATION 2016 (in thousands)

UNITED STATES
$ 18,569,000
👤 323,127

NAFTA TOTAL $ $21,145,000 👤 486,953

MEXICO
$ 1,046,000
👤 127,540

FIGURE 3-3 NAFTA Income and Population
Source: Paul Button, based on data from The World Bank.

trade area with a combined population of more than 486 million people and a total gross domestic product (GDP) of more than $21 trillion (see Figure 3-3).

Why does NAFTA create a free trade area as opposed to a customs union or a common market? The governments of all three nations pledge to promote economic growth through tariff elimination and expanded trade and investment. At present, however, there are no common external tariffs among the NAFTA partners, nor have restrictions on labor and other factor movements been eliminated.

Annual two-way trade between the United States and Mexico has passed the $500 billion mark; more than $1 billion in goods crosses the border each day. The agreement does leave the door open for discretionary protectionism, however. An insufficient number of checkpoints means that cargo may sit for long periods on trucks at bottleneck points such as Tijuana, a key hub for manufacturing. For this reason, some companies choose not to manufacture their products in Mexico. It is estimated that every minute of delay at the border costs the United States $100 million and 500 lost jobs.[4]

Two key issues, illegal immigration and trade, came to the fore during Donald Trump's U.S. presidential campaign. Candidate Trump promised to "build a wall" along the U.S.–Mexico border and repeal NAFTA, which he famously denounced as "the worst trade deal ever." Following his election, President Trump threatened to make good on his NAFTA pledge while pro-trade legislators tried to persuade him to negotiate a new, improved agreement. The president was targeting America's $70 billion trade deficit with Mexico, much of it attributable to the auto industry.

To advance his agenda, the Trump administration put forth a series of "poison pill" proposals that some observers feared were designed to ensure NAFTA's collapse. One demand was that the free-trade agreement "sunset" (i.e., automatically be ended and reopened to negotiation) every five years. Another was to guarantee that 50 percent of the content of duty-free auto production in North America would be sourced in the United States. A third proposal would scrap NAFTA's dispute resolution process, which is designed to ensure that contracts cannot be unilaterally terminated.

In fall 2018, the three countries agreed to replace NAFTA with a new trade pact known as the U.S. Mexico Canada Agreement. Winners included the U.S. automobile industry, which will continue to use complex supply chains linking the three countries. Canada prevailed in its efforts to retain use of an independent panel as a means of dispute resolution.

(3-4) Latin America: SICA, Andean Community, Mercosur, and CARICOM

▶ **3-4** Identify the four main preferential trade agreements in Latin America and the key members of each.

Latin America includes the Caribbean and Central and South America (because of NAFTA, Mexico is grouped with North America). The allure of the Latin American market has been its considerable size and huge resource base. After an extended period of no growth, crippling inflation, increasing foreign debt, protectionism, and bloated government payrolls, the countries of Latin America have begun the process of economic transformation. Balanced budgets are a priority in the region, and privatization is under way. Free markets, open economies, and deregulation have begun to replace the policies of the past. In many countries, tariffs that sometimes reached as high as 100 percent or more have been lowered to 10 to 20 percent.

With the exception of Cuba, most elected governments in Latin America are democratic. Nevertheless, widespread skepticism about the benefits of participating fully in the global economy is apparent in most Latin American countries. As left-leaning politicians who follow in the ideological footsteps of Venezuela's late President Hugo Chávez become more popular, concern is growing that free market forces may lose momentum in the region. Global corporations are watching these developments closely. They are encouraged by import liberalization, the prospects for lower tariffs within subregional trading groups, and the potential for establishing more efficient regional production. Many observers envision a free trade area throughout the hemisphere. The four most important preferential trading arrangements in Latin America are the Central American Integration System (SICA), the Andean Community, the Common Market of the South (Mercosur), and the Caribbean Community and Common Market (CARICOM).

Central American Integration System

Central America is trying to revive its common market, which was originally set up in the early 1960s. The five original members—El Salvador, Honduras, Guatemala, Nicaragua, and Costa Rica—decided in July 1991 to reestablish the Central American Common Market (CACM). Efforts to improve regional integration gained momentum with the granting of observer status to Panama. In 1997, with Panama as a member, the group's name was changed to the **Central American Integration System** (*Sistema de la Integración Centroamericana* [SICA]; see Figure 3-4).

The Secretariat for Central American Economic Integration, headquartered in Guatemala City, helps to coordinate the progress toward a true Central American common market. Common rules of origin have been adopted by the partners, allowing for more free movement of goods among SICA countries. SICA countries agreed to conform to a common external tariff of 5 to 20 percent for most goods by the mid-1990s; many tariffs had previously exceeded 100 percent. Starting in 2000, import duties converged to a range of 0 to 15 percent.

In 2006 and 2007, implementation of the Central American Free Trade Agreement with the United States created a free trade area known as DR-CAFTA that includes five SICA members (El Salvador, Honduras, Guatemala, Nicaragua, and Costa Rica; Panama is excluded) plus the Dominican Republic. Implementation has been slow, but some changes have already taken effect. For example, 80 percent of U.S. goods and more than half of U.S. agricultural products can now be imported into Central America on a duty-free basis. Benefits to Central American companies include a streamlining of export paperwork and the adoption of an online application process. The region will attract more foreign investment as investors see reduced risk thanks to the clearer rules. In Costa Rica alone, foreign direct investment increased by 15 percent from 2012 to 2013.

FIGURE 3-4 SICA Income and Population
Source: Paul Button, based on data from The World Bank.

Exhibit 3-4 The Panama Canal is one of the world's most important shipping routes. Its enlargement means that the canal can accommodate a new generation of huge cargo vessels.
Source: Moises Castillo/ASSOCIATED PRESS.

For a long time, myriad Central American companies have operated in the "shadow economy," with many commercial transactions going unreported. In the mid-2000s, for example, undocumented economic activity in Guatemala and El Salvador amounted to roughly 50 percent of GDP. Government tax revenues should increase as companies join the formal economy to take advantage of CAFTA's benefits.[5]

Critics of the agreement note that signatory countries are not obliged to comply with international labor standards such as those established by the International Labor Organization (ILO). The negative repercussions, these critics say, include low wages and poor working conditions.

One of the most exciting projects in the region is the enlargement of the Panama Canal, which celebrated its centennial in 2014. A new generation of mega-sized cargo freighters now passes through the canal. Port improvements are also under way on the east coast of the United States as Miami and other cities get ready to handle more and bigger ships (see Exhibit 3-4).

Despite some progress having been made, attempts to achieve integration in Central America remain uncoordinated, inefficient, and costly. Tariffs still exist on imports of products—sugar, coffee, and alcoholic beverages, for example—that are also produced in the importing country. As one Guatemalan analyst remarked more than a decade ago, "Only when I see Salvadoran beer on sale in Guatemala and Guatemalan beer on sale in El Salvador will I believe that trade liberalization and integration is a reality."[6]

Andean Community

The four-nation **Andean Community** (*Comunidad Andina* [CAN]; see Figure 3-5), which includes Bolivia, Colombia, Ecuador, and Peru, celebrates its 50th anniversary in 2019. Chile and Venezuela were once members as well; Chile withdrew in 1976, and Venezuela in 2006. Policymakers in the four remaining members have agreed to lower tariffs on intragroup trade and to work together to decide which products each country should produce. Common external tariffs have been established, marking the transition to a true customs union. At the same time, foreign goods and companies have been kept out as much as possible. One Bolivian described the unfortunate result of this lack of competition in the following way: "We had agreed, 'You buy our overpriced goods and we'll buy yours.'"[7] Overall, the region's rural residents and urban poor have become frustrated and impatient with the lack of economic progress. As one Andean scholar put it in the early 2000s, "After 10 or 15 years of operating with free-market policies, paradise hasn't come. People start wondering if the gospel was as good as advertised."[8]

Competing ideologies help explain why intraregional trade is not yielding more benefits. Notably, Peru and Colombia are pursuing growth via capitalism, whereas the governments in Ecuador and Bolivia have socialist leanings.

There are bright spots, however. Starting in the early 1990s, the Andean Trade Promotion and Drug Eradication Act allowed Andean Community members to export flowers to the United States on a duty-free basis. The U.S. Congress passed the act to encourage Latin American farmers to cultivate ornamental flowers rather than plants that are the basis of the illegal drug trade. However, the act expired at the end of 2013; for Peru and Colombia, the flower trade is covered by bilateral trade agreements. Although Ecuador's duty-free status was extended, President Rafael Correa is opposed to free trade talks with the United States.

Meanwhile, blessed with a location near the equator and Andean elevations that receive plenty of sun, Ecuador's cut-flower industry continues to generate hundreds of millions of dollars in export sales each year. Nevado Roses, Agrocoex, and other sustainability-minded producers have adopted fair-trade practices and policies; these companies, in turn, have been embraced by retailers and consumers seeking ethically sourced products. The majority of Ecuador's flower harvest is exported to the United States, though significant quantities are exported to Italy, Russia, Germany, and Canada as well.

Peru is benefiting from surging demand and high prices for maca, a native vegetable root crop that grows at high altitudes and whose origins can be traced back to pre-Incan times (see Exhibit 3-5). Thanks to a centuries-old reputation based on its medicinal qualities—as an aphrodisiac and, more recently, as a cancer-fighting agent—maca has become a hot commodity in China and Japan. In the United States, organic maca is marketed at Whole Foods stores as an "Incan superfood." Anxious to retain control of this valuable agricultural export, officials at Peru's National Commission Against Biopiracy have ramped up efforts to prevent maca seeds from being smuggled out of the country for cultivation elsewhere.[9]

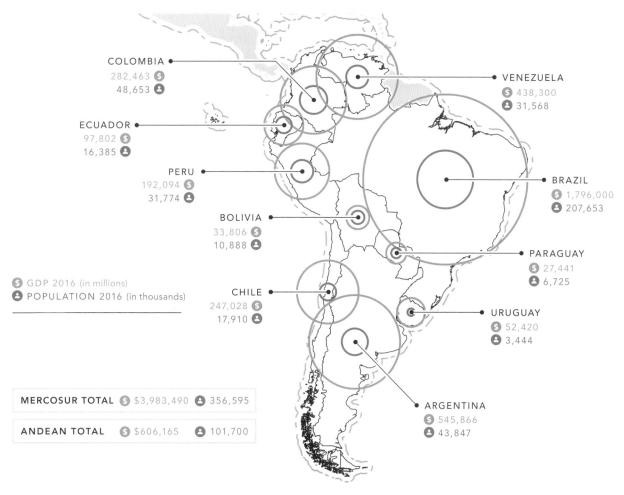

COLOMBIA •
282,463 Ⓢ
48,653 Ⓟ

VENEZUELA •
Ⓢ 438,300
Ⓟ 31,568

ECUADOR •
97,802 Ⓢ
16,385 Ⓟ

PERU •
192,094 Ⓢ
31,774 Ⓟ

BRAZIL •
Ⓢ 1,796,000
Ⓟ 207,653

BOLIVIA •
33,806 Ⓢ
10,888 Ⓟ

PARAGUAY •
Ⓢ 27,441
Ⓟ 6,725

Ⓢ GDP 2016 (in millions)
Ⓟ POPULATION 2016 (in thousands)

CHILE •
247,028 Ⓢ
17,910 Ⓟ

URUGUAY •
Ⓢ 52,420
Ⓟ 3,444

| **MERCOSUR TOTAL** | Ⓢ $3,983,490 | Ⓟ 356,595 |
| **ANDEAN TOTAL** | Ⓢ $606,165 | Ⓟ 101,700 |

ARGENTINA •
Ⓢ 545,866
Ⓟ 43,847

FIGURE 3-5 Mercosur and Andean Community Income and Population
Source: Paul Button, based on data from The World Bank.

Exhibit 3-5 Peruvian maca has been cultivated high in the Andes for millennia. It is highly sought after in China, where it is viewed as a substitute for wild ginseng.
Source: age fotostock/SuperStock.

Common Market of the South (Mercosur)

March 2016 marked the 25th anniversary of the signing of the Asunción Treaty, which signified the agreement by the governments of Argentina, Brazil, Paraguay, and Uruguay to form the **Common Market of the South** (*Mercado Común del Sur*, **or Mercosur**; see Figure 3-5). These four countries agreed to begin phasing in tariff reform on January 1, 1995. Internal tariffs were eliminated, and CETs of 20 percent or less were established. In theory, goods, services, and factors of production will ultimately move freely throughout the member countries; until this goal is achieved, however, Mercosur will actually operate as a customs union rather than as a true common market. Today, about 90 percent of goods are traded freely, but individual members of Mercosur can charge both internal and external tariffs when it suits the respective government.

Much depends on the successful outcome of this experiment in regional cooperation. The early signs were positive, as trade between the four full member nations grew dramatically during the 1990s. Nevertheless, the region has experienced a series of financial crises since Mercosur was established. For example, Brazil's currency was devalued in 1995 and again in 1999.

Argentina provides a case study in how a country can emerge from an economic crisis as a stronger global competitor. Argentina's economy minister responded to the financial crisis of 2001–2002 by implementing emergency measures that included a 29 percent currency devaluation for exports and capital transactions. Argentina was allowed to break from the CET and raise duties on consumer goods.

The crisis had a silver lining: Virtually overnight, Argentina's wine exports to the United States were worth four times more when dollar revenues were converted into pesos. The currency devaluation also made Argentine vineyard property cheaper for foreign buyers. Low prices for land, inexpensive labor, and ideal growing conditions for the Malbec grape have combined to make Argentina's wine industry a major player in world markets. As one winemaker noted, "You can make better wine here for less money than anywhere in the world."

New challenges loom, however. For example, in the late 2000s, the dollar's weakness relative to the euro meant that winemakers were paying 25 percent more for oak aging barrels imported from France.[10] Argentina's current president, Mauricio Macri, has laid out an ambitious program of economic reforms, which include a simplified corporate tax code and pension reform aimed at cutting the government's budget deficit.

The trade agreement landscape in the region continues to evolve. In 1996, Chile became an associate member of Mercosur. Policymakers opted against full membership because Chile already had lower external tariffs than the rest of Mercosur; ironically, full membership would have required raising them. (In other words, Chile participates in the free trade area aspect of Mercosur, not the customs union.) Chile's export-driven success makes it a role model for the rest of Latin America as well as for Central and Eastern Europe.

In 2004, Mercosur signed a cooperation agreement with the Andean Community; as a result, Bolivia, Colombia, Ecuador, and Peru have become associate members. The EU is Mercosur's number 1 trading partner; Mercosur is negotiating with the EU to establish a free trade area. Jean-Claude Juncker, the president of the European Commission, is pushing to complete a deal to demonstrate that the EU is "open for business." Notably, beef farmers in Ireland and France are opposed to this agreement on the grounds that low-cost exports from Brazil and Argentina will harm them; similar objections come from EU agricultural producers whose crops are used to produce ethanol.[12]

As noted earlier, Venezuela withdrew from the Andean Community in 2006; President Hugo Chávez declared the community "dead" after Peru and Colombia began negotiating FTAs with the United States. Although Venezuela was on track to become a full member of Mercosur, its membership was suspended for failure to adhere to the group's economic and democratic principles.

For many years Venezuela reaped the rewards of booming demand and high prices for oil; in fact, oil revenues account for 75 percent of its exports. Its late president, Chávez, was a self-proclaimed revolutionary firebrand. After being elected in 1998, he proclaimed that his vision for Venezuela was "socialism for the twenty-first century."

"The boom in the export of commodities to countries such as China and India has led to the emergence of Latin American countries with a large consumer demand. Agreements such as Mercosur facilitate trade within the region of products with higher levels of added value."[11]

Mauricio Claveria, Abeceb Consultancy, Argentina

A decade ago, Venezuela offered significant market opportunities for global companies such as Cargill, Chevron, ExxonMobil, Ford, Kellogg, 3M, and Toyota.[13] As the country became mired in economic and political turmoil, however, the government led by President Nicolás Madura seized the General Motors plant in Valencia and nationalized a Cargill grain-processing facility. Today, food shortages are a fact of daily life in Venezuela, annual inflation is approaching 5,000 percent, and the government has been forced to restructure its $150 billion foreign debt to forestall default.[14]

Caribbean Community and Common Market (CARICOM)

CARICOM was formed in 1973 as a movement toward unity in the Caribbean. It replaced the Caribbean Free Trade Association (CARIFTA), which had been founded in 1965. The members of this organization are Antigua and Barbuda, Bahamas, Barbados, Belize, Dominica, Grenada, Guyana, Haiti, Jamaica, Montserrat, St. Kitts and Nevis, St. Lucia, St. Vincent and the Grenadines, Suriname, and Trinidad and Tobago. The population of the entire 15-member CARICOM is approximately 17 million (see Figure 3-6).

To date, CARICOM's main objective has been to achieve a deepening of economic integration by means of a Caribbean common market. However, CARICOM was largely stagnant during its first two decades of existence. At its annual meeting in July 1991, member countries agreed to speed integration; a customs union was established with common external tariffs. At the 1998 summit meeting, leaders from the 15 countries agreed to move quickly to establish an economic union with a common currency. A study of the issue suggested, however, that

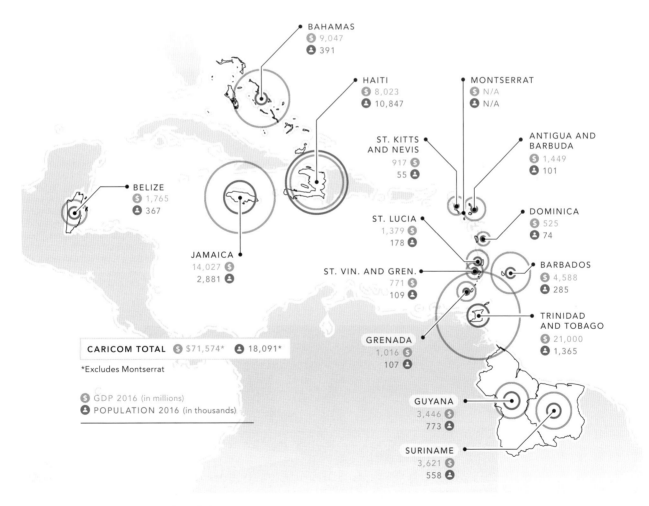

FIGURE 3-6 CARICOM Income and Population
Source: Paul Button, based on data from The World Bank.

EMERGING MARKETS BRIEFING BOOK

Brazil

As the data in Figure 3-5 clearly show, Brazil is an economic powerhouse in South America. Brazil has the largest geographical territory and the largest population in the region. It has emerged on the world stage as a strong exporter, and its rapid economic growth has given Brazilian policymakers a greater presence on the global stage and more clout at global trade talks.

One symbol of Brazil's new role in the global economy is Embraer, a jet aircraft manufacturer (see Exhibit 3-6). Specializing in regional jets that seat between 37 and 124 passengers, Embraer has won orders from a variety of carriers. A cornerstone of Embraer's strategy is its management's policy of sourcing the best components available anywhere in the world. This approach, known as reverse outsourcing, has proved its worth in the development of new models such as the E-170/175. In that program, more than one dozen partners, including GE and Honeywell, shared the development risks in exchange for a percentage of revenue from aircraft sales. To sell more regional jets to China, Embraer has also established a $50 million joint venture with China Aviation Industry Corporation.

In the United States alone, more than 850 Embraer jets are currently in service. The reason is simple: It is a huge market. As Paulo Cesar Silva, Embraer's top executive for Commercial Aviation, notes, "For us, North America is—and will continue to be—the most important market in terms of the potential to sell new products here. Aviation in North America is about 40 percent of aviation in the world." Embraer is also aggressively pursuing the defense sector with its light attack aircraft, the Super Tucano. The U.S. military has expressed interest, and orders have come in from Colombia, Indonesia, and other nations.

Brazil's agricultural sector is also a leading exporter. Brazil is the world's number 1 exporter of beef, coffee, orange juice (check the label on your orange juice carton), and sugar. Annual coffee bean production totals 40 million 60-kilo bags—one-third of the world total. JBS is the world's largest meat processor. Brazil is also rapidly gaining a reputation as a producer of sugar-based ethanol fuel. Says Ermor Zambello, manager of the Grupo Farias sugar mill, "Globalization has made us think more about foreign markets. Now, we have more of a global outlook, and we are concerned about global production."

The central issue in the stalled Doha Round of WTO negotiations was agriculture. Brazil and India are taking the lead of the Group of Twenty developing nations calling for agricultural sector reform. For example, the average tariff on Brazil's exports to the 34 Organisation for the Economic Co-operation and Development (OECD) nations is 27 percent.

Government subsidies are also a key issue. In the EU, government spending accounts for approximately one-third of gross farm receipts; in the United States, the government provides about one-fourth of gross farm receipts. By contrast, Brazil farm support spending amounts to only 3 percent of farm receipts.

Moving forward, Brazil faces a number of other challenges. Repercussions are still being felt from *Lava Jato* ("Car Wash"), a massive corruption scandal that ensnared politicians and top officials at Brazil's national oil company. Former president Luiz Inácio Lula da Silva was convicted on corruption charges and sentenced to prison. In the wake of the scandal, Brazil's current president, Michel Temer, is privatizing a wide range of state-owned businesses.

Despite improvements made prior to the country's hosting of the 2016 Summer Olympics, Brazil's infrastructure remains woefully underdeveloped. Significant investment is required to improve highways, railroads, and ports. Businesspeople speak of "the Brazil cost," a phrase that refers to delays related to excessive red tape.

Trade with China is presenting both opportunities and threats. In 2009, China surpassed the United States to become Brazil's top trading partner and is investing tens of billions of dollars in the country. China's explosive economic growth has created great demand for soybeans, iron ore, and other Brazilian commodity exports. However, Brazilian manufacturers in light-industry sectors such as toys, eyeglasses, and footwear are facing increased competition from low-priced Chinese imports.

Sources: Joe Leahy, Andres Schipani, and Lucy Hornby, "'Suddenly Everything Is for Sale,'" *Financial Times* (November 14, 2017), p. 9; Ben Mutzabaugh, "Brazil's Embraer Jets Are Sized Just Right," *USA Today* (July 6, 2012), pp. 1B, 2B; Joe Leahy, "In Search of More High-Flyers," *Financial Times* (April 17, 2012), p. 10; Joe Leahy, "The Brazilian Economy: A High-Flyer Now Flags," *Financial Times* (January 11, 2012), p. 7; Antonia Regalado, "Soccer, Samba, and Outsourcing?", *The Wall Street Journal* (January 25, 2007), pp. B1, B8; David J. Lynch, "Brazil Hopes to Build on Its Ethanol Success," *USA Today* (March 29, 2006), pp. 1B, 2B; David J. Lynch, "China's Growing Pull Puts Brazil in a Bind," *USA Today* (March 21, 2006), pp. 1B, 2B; David J. Lynch, "Comeback Kid Embraer Has Hot New Jet, and Fiery CEO to Match," *USA Today* (March 7, 2006), pp. 1B, 2B; David J. Lynch, "Brazil's Agricultural Exports Cast Long Shadow," *USA Today* (March 10, 2006), pp. 1B, 2B.

Exhibit 3-6 Embraer is the world's fourth-largest aircraft manufacturer, but is second only to Canada's Bombardier in the regional aircraft sector.
Source: Alexandre Meneghini/AP Images.

the limited extent of intraregional trade would limit the potential gains from lower transaction costs.[15]

In the past few years, a trade dispute between the United States and Antigua and Barbuda has raised some eyebrows. Until recently, Antigua's online gambling industry generated more than $3 billion annually. However, after Washington clamped down on Internet poker sites, Antigua's revenues slumped. Believing that the United States was violating international law, Antigua appealed to the WTO. The trade body ruled in favor of Antigua, and gave it the right to sell various types of U.S. intellectual property, including software and DVDs, without compensating the trademark and copyright owners.[16]

The English-speaking CARICOM members in the eastern Caribbean are also concerned with defending their privileged trading position with the United States. That status dates to the Caribbean Basin Initiative (CBI) of 1984, which promoted export production of certain products by providing duty-free U.S. market access to 20 countries, including members of CARICOM. Recently, CBI members requested that the CBI be expanded. The Caribbean Basin Trade Partnership Act, which went into effect on October 1, 2000, exempts textile and apparel exports from the Caribbean to the United States from duties and tariffs.

3-5 Asia-Pacific: The Association of Southeast Asian Nations

◀ **3-5** Identify the main preferential trade agreements in the Asia-Pacific region.

The **Association of Southeast Asian Nations (ASEAN)** was established in 1967 as an organization for economic, political, social, and cultural cooperation among its member countries. Brunei, Indonesia, Malaysia, the Philippines, Singapore, and Thailand were the original six members. Vietnam became the first Communist nation in the group when it was admitted to ASEAN in July 1995. Cambodia and Laos were admitted at the organization's 30th anniversary meeting in July 1997. Burma (known as Myanmar by the ruling military junta) joined in 1998, following delays related to the country's internal politics and human rights record (see Figure 3-7). The original six members are sometimes referred to as ASEAN-6.

Both individually and collectively, ASEAN countries are active in regional and global trade. ASEAN's top trading partners include Japan, the EU, China, and the United States. A few years ago, ASEAN officials realized that having broad common goals was not enough to keep the association alive. Although the ASEAN member countries are geographically close, they have historically been divided in many respects. One problem was the strict need for consensus among all members before proceeding with any form of cooperative effort. An ASEAN Free Trade Area (AFTA) has finally become a reality, thanks to recent progress at achieving intraregional tariff reductions among the six founding ASEAN members. ASEAN's leaders are now working to establish a fully integrated, single-market ASEAN Economic Community by 2015.

Recently, Japan, China, and Korea were informally added to the member roster; some observers call this configuration "ASEAN + 3." When the roster expanded again to include Australia, New Zealand, and India, it was dubbed "ASEAN + 6." This group is now working to establish an East Asian Community, with the first step being the establishment of an East Asian Free Trade Area.[17] Although China's participation has met with some opposition, China's dynamic growth and increasing power in the region required a response. Collectively, ASEAN participants must seek new avenues for economic growth that are less dependent on exporting goods and services to the West. A central challenge is the fact that, despite generating roughly one-third of global GNP, the ASEAN countries are currently in widely varying stages of development.[18]

January 1, 2010, marked the formal establishment of a new China/ASEAN FTA. Encompassing 1.9 billion people, the new FTA removes tariffs on 90 percent of traded goods among the partners. Overall, the FTA should benefit the region; Malaysia, for example, should experience an increase in commodity exports such as palm oil and rubber. Other ASEAN industry sectors stand to be hurt by a flood of low-cost Chinese imports. Thailand's leaders were so concerned about the impact of this possibility on the country's steel and textile industries that it asked for a delay in lifting tariffs.[19]

18,000

The number of islands that comprise Indonesia

1.2 million

The number of bicycles that Cambodia exports to the EU duty free each year. Cambodia's status falls under GSP (Generalized System of Preferences).

$61/month

Minimum wage in Cambodia

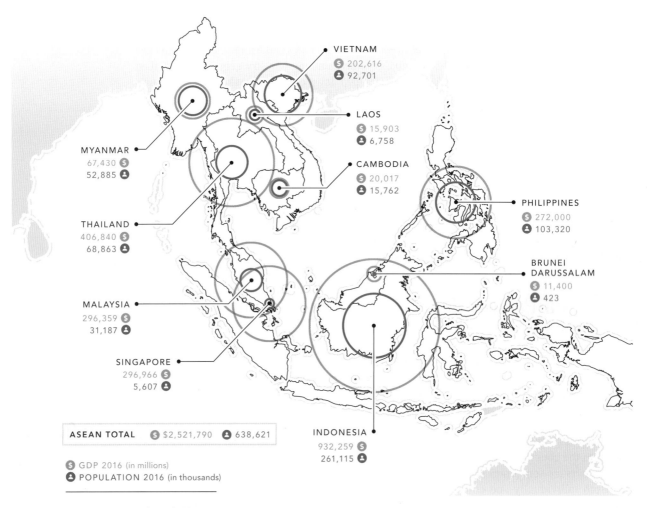

FIGURE 3-7 ASEAN Income and Population
Source: Paul Button, based on data from The World Bank.

Singapore represents a special case among the ASEAN nations. Once a British colony, it has become a vibrant, 240-square-mile industrial power. Singapore has an extremely efficient infrastructure—the Port of Singapore is the world's second-largest container port (Hong Kong's ranks first)—and a standard of living second in the region only to Japan's. Singapore's 5.4 million citizens have played a critical role in the country's economic achievements by readily accepting the notion that "the country with the most knowledge will win" in global competition. Excellent training programs and a 95 percent literacy rate help explain why Singapore has more engineers per capita than the United States. Singapore's Economic Development Board has also actively recruited businesses to operate in the country. The companies that have been attracted to Singapore read like a "Who's Who" of global marketing and include General Motors, Hewlett-Packard, IBM, Koninklijke Philips, Procter & Gamble, and Apple; in all, more than 3,000 companies have operations or investments in Singapore.

Singapore alone accounts for more than one-third of U.S. trading activities with ASEAN countries; U.S. merchandise exports to Singapore in 2014 totaled $30.5 billion, while imports totaled $16.5 billion. Singapore is closely tied with its neighbors in terms of economic activity, with more than 32 percent of its imports ultimately being reexported to other Asian countries. At the same time, Singapore's efforts to fashion a civil society have gained the country some notoriety: Crime is nearly nonexistent, but only because of the severe treatment of criminals by the long-ruling People's Action Party.

Marketing Issues in the Asia-Pacific Region

The 10 ASEAN nations are slated to launch an economic bloc called the ASEAN Economic Community (AEC). Although tariffs have been cut in the region, nontariff barriers—including cumbersome labor laws, lack of harmonization in product standards, and bureaucracy—are some of the

Exhibit 3-7 At the 25nd annual APEC meeting in November 2017 in Da Nang, policymakers from 11 nations conducted negotiations on the Trans-Pacific Partnership without the participation of the United States.
Source: APEC Summit Pool/Alamy Stock Photo.

issues that have yet to be resolved. ASEAN is not a customs union, so import/export activities are conducted with different procedures. As a result, goods can languish in ports for weeks while documents are reviewed and approved. Much work remains to be done before the AEC evolves into a customs union or common market.[20]

Another regional group is the Asia-Pacific Economic Cooperation (APEC), a forum that brings 19 leaders together each fall to discuss issues of mutual interest (see Exhibit 3-7). In 2017, APEC met in Da Nang; in a speech at a business conference, U.S. President Trump outlined his vision for free and open trade in what he termed the "Indo-Pacific region."

(3-6) Western, Central, and Eastern Europe

3-6 Describe the various forms of economic integration in Europe. What is Brexit, and what are the implications for Great Britain's relationship with Europe.

The countries of Western Europe are among the most prosperous in the world. Despite the fact that there are significant differences in income between the north and the south and obvious differences in language and culture, the once-varied societies of Western Europe have grown remarkably alike. Even so, enough differences remain that many observers view Western Europe in terms of three tiers. Many Britons view themselves as somewhat apart from the rest of the continent; Euro-skepticism is widespread in that country, and the United Kingdom still has problems finding common ground with historical rivals Germany and France. Meanwhile, across the English Channel, Greece, Italy, Portugal, and Spain have struggled mightily to overcome the stigma of being labeled "Club Med nations," "peripheral economies," and other derogatory descriptions by their northern neighbors. Indeed, as noted in Case 3-2, these Southern European countries have been at the center of the sovereign debt crisis.

The European Union

The European Union (EU) is home to some of the world's most famous consumer brands, including Heineken (Netherlands), H&M (Sweden), LEGO (Denmark), L'Oréal (France), Nutella (Italy), and Zara (Spain). Some EU nations, including France, Germany, Spain, and Sweden, rely heavily on exports of machinery, motor vehicles, and transportation equipment. Other countries, including Greece, export relatively few manufactured goods and are heavily dependent on tourism.

The origins of the EU can be traced back to the 1958 Treaty of Rome. The six original members of the European Community (EC), as the group was called then, were Belgium, France, Holland, Italy, Luxembourg, and West Germany. In 1973, Great Britain, Denmark, and Ireland were admitted, followed by Greece in 1981 and Spain and Portugal in 1986. Beginning in 1987, the 12 countries that were EC members set about the difficult task of creating a genuine single

THE CULTURAL CONTEXT

Bhutan and GNH (Gross National Happiness)

When Britain's Prince William visited Bhutan in 2016 with his wife Catherine, the Duchess of Cambridge, the world got a rare glimpse into a country that has been called the "forbidden kingdom." Why "forbidden?" For one thing, the country's leaders limit tourism; only about 57,000 foreign visitors traveled to Bhutan in 2015. One hopes that the royal couple were able to glean some insights into their host country's secret regarding happiness.

Bhutan is a kingdom of 754,000 people in the Himalaya Mountains (see Exhibit 3-8). Per capita GNI is approximately $2,330; using this figure as a metric, Bhutan is included in the ranks of lower-middle-income nations. However, for the past several decades, Bhutan has relied on another measure besides economic growth to assess its success—namely, gross national happiness (GNH).

It has been argued that indicators such as GDP and GNI per capita are inadequate when explaining a nation's well-being. For example, China's GDP has doubled twice since 1990, yet ordinary Chinese citizens do not appear any happier today than they were when the country's leaders began transitioning to a free market economy. If increased income and consumption don't correlate with happiness, then what does? According to some economists and policymakers, supplemental indicators that measure factors such as social progress, quality of life, and sustainability are needed.

The GNH Index includes both objective and subjective indicators: psychological well-being, time use, community vitality, culture, health, education, environmental diversity, living standards, and governance. As Lyonpo Jigmi Thinley, home minister of Bhutan, explained, "We have to think of human well-being in broader terms. Material well-being is only one component. That doesn't ensure that you're at peace with your environment and in harmony with each other."

Not surprisingly, there is some disagreement among social scientists regarding the best way to define, track, and measure such intangibles as happiness and quality of life. In Britain, for example, officials have developed a summary of "sustainable development indicators" that include measures of traffic, pollution, and crime. In another approach, survey participants report the feelings they experience as they go about their daily routines, with these activities ranging from paying bills to participating in sports activities. In France, former President Nicolas Sarkozy established the Commission on the Measurement of Economic Performance and Social Progress to address issues related to national well-being.

Meanwhile, officials in Bhutan have launched a number of initiatives to promote happiness in the kingdom. For example, teachers are rotated between rural and urban areas to ensure all schoolchildren have access to a top-quality education. As Thakur S. Powdyel, an official at Bhutan's Ministry of Education, puts it, "The goal of life should not be limited to production, consumption, more production, and more consumption. There is no necessary relationship between the level of possession and the level of well-being."

With the global economic crisis as a backdrop, a first-ever Happiness Congress was held in Madrid in the fall of 2010. The Congress was sponsored by the Coca-Cola Company, which uses the tagline "Open Happiness" in its global advertising. The global beverage giant also established the Coca-Cola Institute of Happiness in Spain after research indicated that Spanish consumers associate Coke, more than any other brand, with happiness.

Minister Thinley from Bhutan was the keynote speaker at the Congress; his address was titled "Happiness in Difficult Times." As Thinley told attendees, "Our economic models are greatly, deeply flawed. They are not sustainable." The 7th International Congress was held in November 2017 in Thimphu, Bhutan.

Sources: Kai Schultz, "In Bhutan, Happiness Index as Gauge for Social Ills," *The New York Times* (January 28, 2017), p. A6; "Forbidden Kingdom," *CBS Sunday Morning* (April 17, 2016); Jody Rosen, "Higher State of Being," *New York Times Style Magazine: Travel* (November 2, 2014), pp. 144–151; Richard Easterlin, "When Growth Outpaces Happiness," *The New York Times* (September 28, 2012), p. A31; Tim Harford, "Happiness: A Measure of Cheer," *Financial Times* (December 27, 2010), p. 5; Victor Mallet, "Bhutan and Coke Join Hands for Happiness," *Financial Times* (October 23, 2010); Andrew C. Revkin, "A New Measure of Well-Being from a Happy Little Kingdom," *The New York Times* (October 6, 2005).

Exhibit 3-8 GNH (gross national happiness), rather than GNP (gross national product), guides policy in Bhutan. Some critics argue that promoting happiness in the Himalayan state has resulted in some negative consequences. For example, the emphasis on the Buddhist culture shared by the majority of the population has caused resentment among the Nepalese minority living in the south.
Source: dpa picture alliance/Alamy Stock Photo.

market in goods, services, and capital. In other words, the goal was to create a true economic union. Adopting the Single European Act by the end of 1992 was a major EC achievement; the Council of Ministers adopted more than 200 pieces of legislation and regulations to make the single market a reality.

The objective of the European project, as it has been called, is to harmonize national laws and regulations so that goods, services, people, and money can flow freely across country boundaries. January 1, 1993, marked the dawn of the new economic era that turned 25 in 2018. Finland, Sweden, and Austria officially joined the EU on January 1, 1995. (In November 1994, voters in Norway rejected a membership proposal.) Evidence that this is more than a free trade area, customs union, or common market is the fact that citizens of member countries are now able to freely cross borders within the union. The EU is encouraging the development of a community-wide labor pool; it is also attempting to shake up Europe's cartel mentality by handing down rules of competition patterned after U.S. antitrust law. Improvements to highway and rail networks are now being coordinated as well.

For the past 15 years, EU enlargement was an important story in the region. Cyprus, the Czech Republic, Estonia, Hungary, Poland, Latvia, Lithuania, Malta, the Slovak Republic, and Slovenia became full EU members on May 1, 2004. Bulgaria and Romania joined in 2007; Croatia, the newest member, joined on July 1, 2013. As shown in Figure 3-8, the 28 nations of the EU are home to 500 million people and constitute the world's largest economy, with

○ GDP 2016
○ POPULATION 2016

FIGURE 3-8 The 28-Nation EU: Income and Population (Pre-Brexit)

Source: Paul Button, based on data from The World Bank.

#	COUNTRY	GDP 2016 (in millions)	POP. 2016 (in thousands)
1	AUSTRIA	$386,428	8,747
2	BELGIUM	466,366	11,348
3	BULGARIA	52,395	7,127
4	CROATIA	50,425	4,170
5	CYPRUS	19,802	1,170
6	CZECH REPUBLIC	192,925	10,561
7	DENMARK	306,143	5,731
8	ESTONIA	23,137	1,316
9	FINLAND	236,785	5,495
10	FRANCE	2,806,000	66,030
11	GERMANY	3,467,000	82,667
12	GREECE	194,559	10,747
13	HUNGARY	124,343	9,818
14	IRELAND	294,054	4,773
15	ITALY	$1,850,000	60,600
16	LATVIA	27,677	1,960
17	LITHUANIA	42,739	2,872
18	LUXEMBOURG	59,948	583
19	MALTA	10,949	437
20	NETHERLANDS	770,845	17,018
21	POLAND	469,509	37,948
22	PORTUGAL	204,565	10,325
23	ROMANIA	186,691	19,705
24	SLOVAK REPUBLIC	89,552	5,429
25	SLOVENIA	43,991	2,064
26	SPAIN	1,232,000	46,444
27	SWEDEN	511,000	9,903
28	UNITED KINGDOM	2,619,000	64,637

EU28 TOTAL	16,738,828	509,625

EU27 TOTAL (EXCLUDES UK)	14,119,828	444,988

Exhibit 3-9 In March 2017, protesters in Rome staged an anti-EU demonstration as government leaders marked the 60th anniversary of the Treaty of Rome.

Source: Allessandro Bianchi/Reuters Pictures.

more than $16 trillion in combined GDP. As discussed in the chapter opening case, the EU28 will become the EU27 when Brexit is triggered in 2019 and Great Britain leaves the EU (see Exhibit 3-9).

The 1992 signing of the **Maastricht (Netherlands) Treaty** set the stage for the creation of the economic and monetary union that includes a European central bank and the euro, the single European currency. The treaty entered into force in November 1993; in May 1998, Austria, Belgium, Finland, Ireland, the Netherlands, France, Germany, Italy, Luxembourg, Portugal, and Spain were chosen as the 11 charter members of the **euro zone**. The United Kingdom was a notable holdout; it never joined the euro zone.

The single-currency era, which officially began on January 1, 1999, has brought many benefits to companies in the euro zone, such as eliminating costs associated with currency conversion and exchange rate uncertainty. The euro existed as a unit of account until January 1, 2002, when actual coins and paper money were issued and national currencies such as the French franc were withdrawn from circulation. Greece joined the euro zone in 2001; Slovenia became the 13th member on January 1, 2007. Today, 19 EU countries are also members of the euro zone including the following countries (see Exhibit 3-10):

Cyprus and Malta, 14th and 15th members, joined January 1, 2008

Slovakia, 16th member, joined January 1, 2009

Estonia, 17th member, joined January 1, 2011

Latvia, 18th member, January 1, 2014

Lithuania, 19th member, joined January 1, 2015

For several years following the global financial crisis, the future of the euro zone appeared to be in doubt. There was widespread concern of a possible "Grexit" (i.e., Greece leaving the euro zone). Thanks in part to a stimulus program by the European Central Bank and in part to structural reforms undertaken in several countries, economic output is now expanding across the euro zone. Disparities remain, such as stubborn double-digit unemployment in Spain, Italy, and Greece. In addition to boosting employment, many euro zone nations need to find ways to improve productivity.

Exhibit 3-10 Lithuania joined the euro zone on January 1, 2015.
Source: Alfredas Pliadis/Xinhua/Alamy Stock Photo.

Marketing Issues in the EU

The European Commission establishes directives and sets deadlines for their implementation by legislation in individual nations. The business environment in Europe has undergone considerable transformation since 1992, with significant implications for all elements of the marketing mix:[21]

Product: **Harmonization**, which means that content and other product standards that varied among nations have been brought into alignment. As a result, companies have an opportunity to reap the benefits of various economies by reducing the number of product adaptations.

Price: A more competitive environment. **Transparency** has been improved in the euro zone because the single currency makes it easier to compare prices for the same product in different countries.

Promotion: Common guidelines on TV broadcasting; uniform standards for TV commercials.

Distribution: Simplification of transit documents; elimination of customs formalities at border crossings.

Case Europe, for example, manufactures and markets farm machinery. When it introduced the Magnum tractor in Europe in 1988, it offered 17 different versions because of different countries' regulations regarding placement of lights and brakes. Thanks to harmonization, Case offers the current model, the Magnum MX, in one version. However, because different types of implements and trailers are used in different countries, the MX is available with different kinds of hitches.[22]

The advent of the euro on January 1, 1999, brought about more changes. Customers' ability to directly compare prices in the euro zone has forced many companies to review their pricing policies. The marketing challenge is to develop strategies to take advantage of opportunities in one of the largest, wealthiest, most stable markets in the world. Corporations must therefore assess the extent to which they can treat the region as one entity and consider how to change their organizational policies and structures to adapt to and take advantage of a unified Europe.

The enlargement of the EU will further impact marketing strategies. For example, food safety laws in the EU are different from those in some Central European countries. As a result, Coca-Cola had to delay launching its Powerade sports drink and other beverage products to deal with these disparities; specifically, Polish and EU food law require the use of different ingredients. In addition to the harmonization of laws, the very size of the expanded EU offers opportunities. For example, Procter & Gamble executives foresee that in the event of shortages in a particular country, they will be able to shift products from one market to another. A 28- (or 27-) nation EU also allows for more flexibility in the placement of factories.

At the same time, some challenges have emerged from the EU's expansion. For example, South American banana growers now face 75 percent tariffs on exports to the new EU countries; previously, tariffs on bananas were virtually nonexistent. Also, because tariffs and quotas protect sugar production in the EU, both consumers and food producers such as Kraft will face rising costs.[23]

Central and Eastern Europe

Because they are in transition, the markets of Central and Eastern Europe present interesting opportunities and challenges. Global companies view the region as an important new source of growth, and the first company to penetrate a country market often emerges as the industry leader. Exporting has been favored as a market-entry mode, but direct investment in the region is on the rise. With wage rates much lower than those in Greece, Italy, Portugal, and Spain, this region offers attractive locations for low-cost manufacturing in light-industry sectors. For example, a shoe manufacturer in Italy might source some of its lower-cost lines in Slovenia.

January 1, 2015, marked the launch of the Eurasian Economic Union (EEU) integrating the economies of Russia, Belarus, and Kazakhstan. Kyrgyzstan and Armenia have also joined the EEU since then. Russian President Vladimir Putin views the EEU as a cornerstone of Russian economic growth. However, with the ruble's collapse in the wake of falling oil prices, Belarus has reinstated some customs controls.

One study examined the approaches utilized by 3M International, McDonald's, Koninklijke Philips, Henkel, Südzucker AG, and several other companies operating in Central Europe. Consumers and businesses in the region are eagerly embracing well-known global brands that were once available only to government elites and others in privileged positions. The study found a high degree of standardization of marketing program elements; in particular, the core product and brand elements were largely unchanged from those used in Western Europe. Consumer companies generally target high-end segments of the market and focus on brand image and product quality; industrial marketers concentrate on opportunities to do business with the largest firms in a given country.[24]

3-7 The Middle East

> **3-7** Describe the activities of the key regional organizations in the Middle East.

The Middle East includes 16 countries: Afghanistan, Bahrain, Cyprus, Egypt, Iran, Iraq, Israel, Jordan, Kuwait, Lebanon, Oman, Qatar, Saudi Arabia, Syria, the United Arab Emirates (UAE, which include Abu Dhabi and Dubai), and Yemen. The majority of the population in this region is Arab, a large percentage is Persian, and a small percentage is Jewish. Persians and most Arabs share the same religion, beliefs, and Islamic traditions, making the population 95 percent Muslim and 5 percent Christian and Jewish.

Despite this apparent homogeneity, many differences exist. Middle Eastern countries are distributed across the Index of Economic Freedom discussed in Chapter 2; the United Arab Emirates ranks the highest in terms of freedom, at 8; next is Qatar (29), and then Israel (36). Bahrain is ranked at 44, while Saudi Arabia ranks 64th. By contrast, Iraq and Syria are not ranked, due to the ongoing conflict and economic disruption in both countries. Moreover, the Middle East does not have a single societal type with a typical belief, behavior, and tradition. Each capital and major city in the Middle East has a variety of social groups that can be differentiated on the basis of religion, social class, education, and degree of wealth.

The price of oil drives business in the Middle East. Seven of the countries have historically enjoyed high revenues from the sale of oil: Bahrain, Iran, Iraq, Kuwait, Oman, Qatar, and Saudi Arabia hold significant world oil reserves. Oil revenues have widened the gap between poor and rich nations in the Middle East, and the disparities contribute to political and social instability in the area.

Saudi Arabia, a monarchy with 22 million people and 25 percent of the world's known oil reserves, remains the most important market in this region. However, as the price of oil has dropped sharply on world markets, and with Iran ramping up oil production now that international sanctions against that country have been lifted, Saudi Arabia's leaders must find new sources of revenue in a "post-oil economy." Saudi Vision 2030 is the government's plan for economic change.

One goal is to boost tourism. Oil revenues currently account for 39 percent of Saudi GDP, compared with less than 3 percent for tourism.[25] In 2017, Crown Prince Mohammed bin Salman unveiled ambitious plans for a $500 billion economic zone on the Red Sea coast known as Neom, which is intended to attract foreign investment in key sectors such as robotics and renewable energy.

In 2011, the region was rocked by demonstrations and protests that have been described as "the Arab awakening" and "the Arab spring." The governments of Tunisia and Egypt were overthrown, civil war broke out in Libya, and Syria's regime cracked down on insurgent activists. Elsewhere in the region, leaders were forced to make economic and political concessions.

Prior to the uprisings, Syria had been a case study in the slow pace of change coming to the Middle East. Citing China's success at opening its economy while maintaining social control, President Bashar al-Assad took steps to move Syria away from a rigid socialist economic model. Private banks opened for business, a stock market was established, and possessing foreign currency became legal for Syrian citizens. Ties with the West began improving, too; U.S. President Barack Obama lifted some sanctions and named an ambassador to Syria. Entrepreneurs with ties to Syria began returning from Lebanon and the United States, a trend that helped spark a consumer culture. In Damascus, signs of economic rebirth included a Ford dealership, a KFC restaurant, and Benetton boutiques.[26] Currently, however, Syria is embroiled in a civil war as rebel forces try to overthrow President al-Assad.

Cooperation Council for the Arab States of the Gulf

The key regional organization in the Middle East, commonly referred to as the **Gulf Cooperation Council (GCC)**, was established in 1981 by Bahrain, Kuwait, Oman, Qatar, Saudi Arabia, and the United Arab Emirates (see Figure 3-9 and Exhibit 3-11). These six countries hold about 45 percent of the world's known oil reserves, but their production amounts to only 18 percent of world oil output. Ironically, Saudi Arabia and several other Middle Eastern countries post current account deficits, largely because they must import most of the goods and services that their citizens consume.

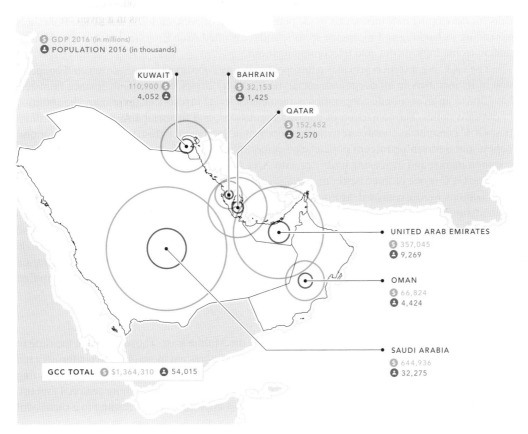

FIGURE 3-9 GCC Income and Population

Source: Paul Button, based on data from The World Bank.

Exhibit 3-11 The six nations of the Gulf Cooperation Council, shown here meeting in Doha, Qatar, are striving to speak with one voice about the crises that have rocked the Middle East. For example, member nations are divided over the appropriate response to the political turmoil in Egypt, Libya, and Syria. Qatar supports the Muslim Brotherhood, while Saudi Arabia and the United Arab Emirates consider the group to be a threat to regional stability.

Source: 506 collection/Alamy Stock Photo.

In 2017, an unprecedented diplomatic crisis began to fold in the Middle East. In an effort spearheaded by Saudi Arabia and the UAE, the GCC accused Qatar of providing a refuge for terrorists. Qatar denies the allegations. Even so, Egypt joined GCC members Saudi Arabia, UAE, and Bahrain in closing their banking sectors to Qatar and restricting travel and trade with that country. Kuwait and Oman have opted to remain neutral. The boycott has resulted in a heightened state of economic uncertainty even as Qatar pours some $200 billion into infrastructure improvements in preparation for its hosting of the 2022 World Cup.

Historically, the GCC countries have been heavily dependent on oil revenues to pay for their imports; with the collapse of oil prices, efforts toward economic diversification and job creation are gaining traction. As noted earlier, Saudi Arabia has launched Saudi Vision 2030, which calls for developing new businesses in the petrochemical, cement, and iron industries. Bahrain is expanding its banking and insurance sectors, and the United Arab Emirates is focusing on information technology, media, and telecommunications.

The GCC organization provides a means of realizing coordination, integration, and cooperation of its members in all economic, social, and cultural affairs. Persian Gulf finance ministers have drawn up an economic cooperation agreement covering investment, petroleum, the abolition of customs duties, harmonization of banking regulations, and financial and monetary coordination. GCC committees coordinate trade development in the region, industrial strategy, agricultural policy, and uniform petroleum policies and prices. Current goals include establishing an Arab common market and increasing trade ties with Asia.

The GCC is one of three newer regional organizations in the Middle East. In 1989, two other organizations were established. Morocco, Algeria, Mauritania, Tunisia, and Libya banded together in the Arab Maghreb Union (AMU); Egypt, Iraq, Jordan, and North Yemen created the Arab Cooperation Council (ACC). Many Arabs see their new regional groups—the GCC, ACC, and AMU—as embryonic economic communities that will foster the development of inter-Arab trade and investment. The newer organizations are likely to lead more quickly to economic integration and reform than does the Arab League, which consists of 22 member states and has a constitution that requires unanimous decisions.

Marketing Issues in the Middle East

Connection is a key word in conducting business in the Middle East. Those who take the time to develop relationships with key business and government figures are more likely to cut through red tape than those who do not. A predilection for bargaining is culturally ingrained, and the visiting businessperson must be prepared for some old-fashioned haggling. Establishing personal rapport, mutual trust, and mutual respect are essentially the most important factors leading to a successful business relationship. Decisions are usually not made by correspondence or telephone. The Arab businessperson does business with the individual, not with the company. Also, most social customs are based on the Arab male-dominated society. Thus, women are usually not part of the business or entertainment scene for traditional Muslim Arabs.

 Africa

◄ **3-8** Identify the issues for global marketers wishing to expand in Africa.

The African continent is an enormous landmass with a territory of 11.7 million square miles; the United States would fit inside Africa about three and a half times. It is not really possible to treat Africa as a single economic unit. The 54 nations on the continent can be divided into three distinct areas: the Republic of South Africa; North Africa; and sub-Saharan, or Black, Africa, which is located between the Sahara in the north and the Zambezi River in the south. With 1.3 percent of the world's wealth and 15 percent of its population, Africa is considered a developing region. Average per capita income ranges from $1,505 in the sub-Saharan countries to $7,800 in the North Africa/Middle East region. Many African nations are former European colonies, and the EU remains the continent's most important trading partner.

The Arabs living in North Africa are differentiated politically and economically from the populace in the rest of Africa. The six northern nations are richer and more developed than those located in the sub-Saharan region, and several—notably Libya, Algeria, and Egypt—benefit from substantial oil reserves. The Middle East and North Africa are sometimes viewed as a regional entity known as "Mena"; when oil prices soared, the International Monetary Fund (IMF) encouraged Mena policymakers to invest the petrodollar windfall in infrastructure improvements as a way of sustaining economic growth.[27] With the collapse of oil prices, governments in the area are working to reduce their reliance on oil revenues and their public aid levels. The economies of non-oil-based, "emerging Mena" countries, which include Jordan, Lebanon, Morocco, and Tunisia, have also performed well in recent years.

Economic Community of West African States

The Treaty of Lagos establishing the **Economic Community of West African States (ECOWAS)** was signed in May 1975 by 16 states with the object of promoting trade, cooperation, and self-reliance in West Africa. The original members were Benin, Burkina Faso, Cabo Verde, Côte d'Ivoire, the Gambia, Ghana, Guinea, Guinea-Bissau, Liberia, Mali, Mauritania, Niger, Nigeria, Senegal, Sierra Leone, and Togo; Mauritania left the group in 2002 (see Figure 3-10). In 1980, the member countries agreed to establish a free trade area for unprocessed agricultural products and handicrafts. Tariffs on industrial goods were also to be abolished, although implementation delays occurred on this front.

By January 1990, tariffs on numerous items manufactured in ECOWAS member states had been eliminated. The organization installed a computer system to process customs and trade statistics and to calculate the loss of revenue resulting from the liberalization of intercommunity trade. In June 1990, ECOWAS adopted measures to create a single monetary zone in the region by 1994.

Despite such achievements, economic development has occurred unevenly in the region. In recent years, Ghana has performed impressively, propelled by deals related to its oil, gas, and mineral sectors. China has signed deals with the region that are worth $15 billion.[28] By contrast, Liberia and Sierra Leone are still experiencing political conflict and economic decline.

East African Community

Kenya, Uganda, Tanzania, Rwanda, and Burundi are the five nations that make up the world's newest common market (see Figure 3-10). The East African Community's origins date back more than 40 years, but only since 1999 has substantial progress been made toward its integration and cooperation. Today's East African Community has evolved through several of the stages listed in Table 3-2. In 2005, a customs union was implemented. The formation of the common market in 2010 resulted in the free movement of people, goods and services, and capital within the community. Members also intend to move swiftly to establish an economic union. The first step will be creating a monetary union; the goal is to introduce a common currency within ten years. There is even talk about forming a single nation. As one observer noted, "The idea of a United States of East Africa is less far-fetched than it was before."[29]

FIGURE 3-10 ECOWAS, SADC, and East African Community Income and Population

Source: Paul Button, based on data from The World Bank.

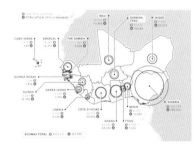

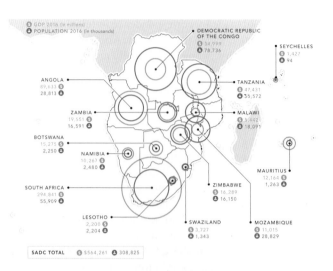

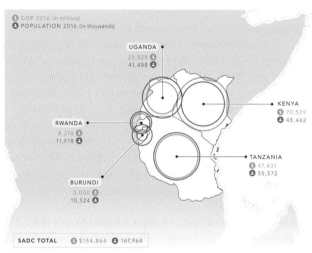

Southern African Development Community

In 1992, the **Southern African Development Community (SADC)** superseded the South African Development Coordination Council as a mechanism by which the region's black-ruled states could promote trade, cooperation, and economic integration. The members of SADC are Angola, Botswana, Democratic Republic of Congo (formerly Zaire), Lesotho, Malawi, Mauritius, Mozambique, Namibia, South Africa, Seychelles, Swaziland, Tanzania, Zambia, and Zimbabwe (see Figure 3-10). South Africa joined the community in 1994; it represents about 75 percent of the income in the region and 86 percent of intraregional exports. The SADC's ultimate goal is a fully developed customs union; in 2000, an 11-nation free trade area was finally established (Angola, the Democratic Republic of Congo, and Seychelles are not participants).

South Africa and the EU signed a Trade, Development, and Cooperation Agreement (TDCA) in 2000; two-way trade and foreign direct investment have increased substantially since then. Meanwhile, other SADC members are concerned that this arrangement provides European global companies with a base from which to dominate the continent.

South Africa, Botswana, Lesotho, Namibia, and Swaziland also belong to the Southern African Customs Union (SACU).

Marketing Issues in Africa

In 2000, U.S. President George W. Bush signed the African Growth and Opportunities Act (AGOA) into law (see www.trade.gov/agoa/). Under the rubric of "trade, not aid," the law is designed to support African nations that make significant progress toward economic liberalization. African companies will find it easier to gain access to financing from the U.S. Export–Import Bank; AGOA also represents a formal step toward a U.S.–Africa free trade area.[30] One of the act's key provisions grants textile and apparel manufacturers in Kenya, Lesotho, and Mauritius free access to the U.S. market for as much as $3.5 billion in exports each year. As Benjamin Kipkorir, Kenya's ambassador to the United States, observed a decade ago, "Every country that has industrialized, starting from England in the eighteenth century, began with textiles. We'd like to do the same thing."

Under the Agreement on Textiles and Clothing negotiated during the Uruguay Round of GATT negotiations, global textile quotas were eliminated in 2005. Nevertheless, the textile provision in AGOA is controversial. The United States imports nearly $100 billion in textiles and apparel each year. The largest share—more than 40 percent—originates in China, with the balance coming from other parts of Asia plus Latin America and Africa. Wary U.S. legislators from textile-producing states fear job losses among their constituents.

Despite such initiatives, only about 3 percent of annual foreign direct investment goes to Africa. Even so, some Persian Gulf states now appear bent on creating closer ties with Africa, investing billions of dollars in key sectors such as infrastructure, agriculture, and telecommunications. For example, Dubai World, a state-owned company, is negotiating a deal in Nigeria's energy sector that could be valued at several billion dollars. Dubai also funded construction of a container terminal that opened recently in Djibouti. The largest terminal of its kind in sub-Saharan Africa, it will be managed by DP World, a subsidiary of Dubai World. Such investments are welcome at a time when investors in Europe, stung by economic losses in the developed world, are cutting their spending. In the words of Djibouti President Ismaïl Guelleh, "What the Arabs are doing for us is what colonialists should have done for Africa."[31]

Summary

This chapter examines the environment for world trade, focusing on the institutions and regional cooperation agreements that affect trade patterns. The multilateral *World Trade Organization*, created in 1995 as the successor to the *General Agreement on Tariffs and Trade*, provides a forum for settling disputes among member nations and tries to set policy for world trade. The world trade environment is also characterized by *preferential trade agreements* among smaller numbers of countries on regional and subregional bases. These agreements can be conceptualized on a continuum of increasing economic integration.

Free trade areas such as the one created by the *North American Free Trade Agreement (NAFTA)* represent the lowest level of economic integration. The purpose of a *free trade agreement (FTA)* is to eliminate tariffs and quotas. *Rules of origin* are used to verify the country from which goods are shipped. A *customs union*, such as Mercosur, represents a further degree of integration in the form of *common external tariffs*. In a *common market*, such as the Central American Integration System (SICA) and the East African Community, restrictions on the movement of labor and capital are eased in an effort to further increase integration. An *economic union*, such as the EU, the highest level of economic integration, is achieved by unification of economic policies and institutions. *Harmonization*, the coming together of varying standards and regulations, is a key characteristic of the EU.

Other important cooperation arrangements include the Association of Southeast Asian Nations (ASEAN) and the Gulf Cooperation Council (GCC). In Africa, the two main cooperation agreements are the Economic Community of West African States (ECOWAS) and the South African Development Community (SADC).

Discussion Questions

3-1. Explain the relationship between a free trade agreement and the rules of origin.

3-2. What were the issues faced by members of ASEAN in recent years? Identify the new member countries of ASEAN + 3 and ASEAN + 6.

3-3. How would you assess the effectiveness of the Eurasian Economic Union?

3-4. Identify a regional economic organization or agreement in each of the following areas: Latin America, Asia-Pacific, Western Europe, Central Europe, the Middle East, and Africa.

3-5. Several key dates mentioned in the chapter are listed here. Can you identify the event associated with each? (The answers follow.)

January 1, 1994

January 1, 1995

January 1, 1999

January 1, 2002

May 1, 2004

January 1, 2007

January 1, 2009

January 1, 2011

July 1, 2013

January 1, 2014

January 1, 2015

Answers: January 1, 1994—NAFTA becomes effective; January 1, 1995—WTO becomes the successor to GATT; January 1, 1999—introduction of the euro as a unit of account; January 1, 2002—euro currency goes into circulation; May 1, 2004—EU enlargement to 25 members; January 1, 2007—Romania and Bulgaria join the EU; January 1, 2009—Slovakia becomes the 16th member of the euro zone; January 1, 2011—Estonia becomes the 17th member of the euro zone; July 1, 2013—Croatia joins the EU; January 1, 2014—Latvia joins the euro zone; January 1, 2015—Lithuania joins the euro zone.

CASE 3-1   *(Continued from page 95)*

Breaking Up Is Hard to Do: Britons Contemplate "Brexit"

Having called the national referendum, Prime Minister Cameron initiated negotiations with EU officials about the future of the United Kingdom's continued participation in the regional bloc. His goal was to convince the EU to make certain concessions that would make the "Remain" option more appealing to voters. Among the reforms was a measure to restrict welfare benefits offered to certain EU nationals coming to the United Kingdom.

For the most part, politicians, diplomats, and institutions outside the United Kingdom were lending their voices to the "Remain" argument. For example, U.S. President Barack Obama, plus the leaders of Canada, New Zealand, and Australia, all urged voters to cast "In" ballots. In fact, on a visit to London in April 2016, Obama disagreed with the view that an "Out" vote would allow Britain to play a bigger role in the global arena. In fact, the U.S. president said, being part of the EU actually amplified Britain's voice around the world.

In lieu of EU membership, several alternative options would be available to the United Kingdom. First, the United Kingdom could retain privileged access to the EU's single market by joining Iceland, Lichtenstein, and Norway in the European Economic Area (EEA). Second, the United Kingdom could enter into a bilateral free-trade agreement with the EU; Canada has a similar arrangement. As a third option, the United Kingdom could pursue trade with the EU under its current membership in the World Trade Organization.

Those in the "Remain" camp argued that any of these alternatives would result in substantial decrease in the United Kingdom's GDP.

The U.K. Treasury's chief economist produced reports on the short-term and long-term impact of a "Leave" vote, factoring in the various alternatives. George Osborne, the Chancellor of the Exchequer (as the U.K. finance minister is called), said that in the worst-case "Leave" scenario, more than 800,000 jobs could be lost in the long term. In the short term—two years after leaving—520,000 jobs would be lost. The Treasury report estimated that, under the free-trade agreement option, annual economic output would fall 6.2 percent. Thus, by 2030, the average British households would be worse off by an estimated £4,300 ($6,665).

Despite these warnings, some politicians from Cameron's own Conservative Party broke ranks with the prime minister and his cabinet. Former London mayor Boris Johnson and justice minister Michael Gove, among others, both argued for "Out."

Immigration, Terrorism, and the Migrant Crisis

As the migrant crisis expanded in 2016, Michael Gove, the Conservative politician, asserted that EU rules hindered the efforts of Britain's security forces to keep terror suspects out of the country. Another concern: If Turkey joined the EU, some of its 76 million people would join the wave of migrants seeking new opportunities in Britain. While Germany, one of the strongest EU members, favors unconditional free movement of people, some policymakers emphasized the need for flexibility to impose conditions on immigration. Questions were raised about the impact on the United Kingdom outside of the EU framework.

Exhibit 3-12 Theresa May was Prime Minster of the United Kingdom from 2016 to 2019 and led the Brexit negotiations with the EU during that period.
Source: Drop of Light/Shutterstock.

Trade with Non-EU Countries

If Vote Leave movement prevailed, the United Kingdom would be outside the framework of the Transatlantic Trade and Investment Partnership (TTIP; see Case 3-2). The country would then be forced to negotiate separate, bilateral trade deals with the United States and other countries that currently have agreements with the EU. Likewise, the EU has signed free-trade agreements with Singapore, Vietnam, and South Korea. The FTA with South Korea was implemented in 2011; since then, U.K. exports to South Korea have increased 30 percent. "Remain" advocates noted that there are more advantages when the United Kingdom is part of a wider trade relationship.

Voter Demographics

One thing was clear in the run-up to the June 23, 2016, referendum vote: There was a split along voters based on age. Voters age 18–24, who grew up in the EU era, were in favor of "Remain." By contrast, many older voters, who were nostalgic for the pre-EU years, intended to vote "Leave." Many members of this demographic, especially those with lower levels of formal education, viewed globalization as a threat rather than an opportunity. Brexit supporters were heartened by research showing that older voters were more likely to go to the polls than younger ones.

The Voters Spoke: Leave

In the end, those voting "Leave" won the day. The immediate aftermath of the referendum was a political shakeup. Prime Minster David Cameron, the man who had called for the referendum, announced that he would step down. Saying that his work was done, Nigel Farage resigned as leader of UKIP. After brief maneuvering by several potential candidates, including Boris Johnson, the former mayor of London, and Energy Minister Andrea Leadom, Theresa May emerged as the new leader of the Conservative Party.

As home secretary starting in 2010, May had proved to be a formidable presence in a political arena traditionally dominated by men. Some observers compared her favorably with Margaret Thatcher, the "Iron Lady" who had served as prime minister in the 1980s. Others compared May's no-nonsense, efficient political style to that of German Chancellor Angela Merkel. May vowed to "make Brexit a success," but also pledged not to start the formal Brexit process until 2017.

Industry Impact

In the late fall of 2016, Nissan announced that it would produce two new SUV models at its plant in Sunderland. The announcement came after Prime Minister May provided assurances to Nissan executives that the automaker would be protected from any negative Brexit consequences. The plant, located in northeast England, is very important to the nation's economy. It is the United Kingdom's largest auto manufacturing plant, employing 7,000 people and producing 500,000 vehicles annually. What is more, some 80 percent of the production is exported, meaning that access to the European market is a critical factor for Nissan's success.

Theresa May in Number 10 Downing Street

As prime minister, May advocated a "hard Brexit"; in her words, "No Brexit deal is better than a bad deal." Hoping to bolster the Conservative majority in Parliament, in April 2017 May called a "snap" election for the House of Commons. As it turned out, when voters went to the polls in June, they did not deliver the additional parliamentary seats that May had anticipated. This state of affairs forced May to back off on some of her plans for Brexit negotiations, which were to be completed by March 2019. The "Queen's Speech," written by the Prime Minister but delivered by Queen Elizabeth II two weeks after the snap election, contained eight bills pertaining to a "softer" Brexit. In particular, May's legislative program included a Great Repeal bill to convert EU legislation into U.K. law and bills to establish frameworks for customs and trade.

Questions for the Future

Once the U.K. political landscape had settled, the focus shifted to the risks and opportunities facing the nation. Many questions loomed. Would London lose its status as a leading global banking center? How could the United Kingdom continue to benefit from workers entering from the EU while at the same time reducing immigration?

As Christmas 2017 approached, it appeared a breakthrough had been reached in the "divorce settlement." Following the implementation of Brexit in March 2019, there will be a two-year "transition period" that will allow all parties to adjust to the new realities. Prime Minister Theresa May agreed that the United Kingdom would pay the EU approximately €40 billion. This represented a shift: Previously,

"I COULDN'T HELP NOTICE WE DIDN'T WIN THE NOBEL PRIZE FOR ECONOMICS."

Source: Banx Cartoons.

the United Kingdom had responded to the multibillion-euro payment demand by saying that the EU could "go whistle." Agreement was also reached concerning the rights of EU citizens residing in the United Kingdom as well as U.K. citizens residing in the EU.

Looking ahead, the two sides began to address issues pertaining to trade. Would the United Kingdom leave the single market and the customs union? If so, how would trade be conducted? Also, which kind of border would be established between Northern Ireland (part of the United Kingdom) and the Republic of Ireland (part of the EU)?

Discussion Questions

3-6. If you had been eligible to vote in the referendum, would you have voted "In" or "Out"? What is the basis for your answer?

3-7. What would it mean for the Unite Kingdom to remain in the "EU customs union"?

3-8. As this edition went to press, there was uncertainty about whether there would be a "hard exit," a "soft exit," or "no exit." Where do things stand currently?

Sources: Lloyd Dorfman, "Brexit Would Damage Important Trade Links with Asia," *The Daily Telegraph* (May 24, 2016), p. 2; Philip Stevens, "Brexit May Break Britain's Tory Party," *Financial Times* (April 22, 2016), p. 9; Chris Giles, "Economics That Lie Behind Treasury's Dire Warning," *Financial Times* (April 19, 2016), p. 2; Jason Douglas, "U.K. Exit's Impact on Jobs Could Roil EU," *The Wall Street Journal* (April 18, 2016), p. A2; Jenny Gross, "Cameron Defends Draft EU Deal," *The Wall Street Journal* (February 4, 2016), p. A14; "Can the UK Economy Survive Brexit?", Panel Discussion, Battle of Ideas (October 18, 2015), London.

CASE 3-2
Can Global Trade Talks Survive in an Era of Populism and Protectionism?

As the second decade of the twenty-first century came to a close, optimism about global trade talks began to wane. The United States and several Asian countries had spent years working on the details of a trade framework known as the Trans-Pacific Partnership (TPP). The goal was an ambitious one: to create a free trade area that would lead to long-term economic growth. Meanwhile, the United States and the European Union (EU) were *also* in negotiations to create a separate free trade area. As with the TPP, the goal of the Transatlantic Trade and Investment Partnership (TTIP) was to kick-start economic growth among the member nations.

Transatlantic Trade and Investment Partnership

The United States and the EU have the world's largest trading relationship, with their two-way trade in goods and services amounting to more than $1 trillion annually. Nevertheless, the share of trade between the regions had been declining for years, as both sides have increasingly focused on trade in goods and services to China and other Asian countries.

In an effort to increase U.S.–EU economic integration, negotiators sought to forge a "transformative, 21st-century agreement" that would boost the volume of two-way U.S.–EU trade. The rationale was straightforward: A free trade agreement (FTA) that generated more trade would boost economies for all parties. In the United States, business leaders pressed then-President Barack Obama to pursue more

trade deals. In Europe, German Chancellor Angela Merkel, former British Prime Minister David Cameron, and other leaders were pushing for a new agreement that would create new avenues for job creation and economic growth across the region.

In 2016, two key events had a direct impact on the future of the TTIP. The first was the British vote for Brexit; the United Kingdom had been one of the strongest advocates of an expanded trade relationship with the United States (see Case 3-1). Shortly after the "Leave" vote prevailed, Prime Minister Cameron resigned. The second pivotal event was the election in November 2016 of Donald Trump as president of the United States. During his campaign, Trump consistently spoke out against trade liberalization. Another presidential hopeful, Bernie Sanders, also included anti-trade rhetoric in his campaign.

As noted in Chapter 2, Europe desperately needs to find new sources of economic growth. What better way to do so than to sign an FTA with the United States? That is exactly what European leaders were asking as talks got under way between leaders on both sides of the Atlantic. Even though tariffs on goods imports and exports average only about 3 percent, the volume of the two-way trade between the United States and the EU is very large—some $500 billion in goods alone. If tariffs were eliminated, even a small increase in trade could yield substantial benefits. As an executive at GE explained, "This could be the biggest, most valuable free-trade agreement by far, even if it produces only a marginal increase in trade."

Complicating the trade talks was increasing friction between the two sides. Some European businesses complained that they had been hurt by Western trade sanctions imposed on Russia after President Vladimir Putin annexed Crimea and launched military operations in Ukraine. By contrast, it was noted, U.S. business interests had not been materially affected by this move. Meanwhile, the EU stepped up its actions against American tech giants. For example, Apple was ordered to pay €13 billion in back taxes, and Google was fined €2.4 billion for antitrust violations.

Major differences separate the two sides. One key sticking point is agriculture. For example, the EU restricts the import of most genetically modified crops, which are common in the United States. Tariff reduction is another key issue. Although tariffs between the trading partners currently average between 2 and 3 percent, further reduction could result in significant savings.

A third issue concerns a variety of regulations that hamper cross-border investment and purchasing. Such regulations are sometimes called nontariff barriers, and many observers argue that they are harder to remove than tariff barriers. The various types of nontariff restrictions create bureaucratic obstacles that affect a variety of industries. For example, the EU would like an easing of restrictions on U.S. government purchases of European goods, but that matter is complicated because some of those buying decisions are made at the state level, and some states have passed "Buy American" laws. For its part, as noted earlier, Europe has blocked imports of genetically modified agricultural products such as corn and soy.

Another issue concerns product labeling. Some food companies that market dairy products in the United States use terms such as "Parmesan" on their labeling. According to EU law, the name "Parmesan" should apply only to a cow's-milk cheese known as "Parmigiano–Reggiano" that is produced using traditional methods in the Parma/Reggio region of Italy. The Italian cheese bears symbols for protected geographical indication (PGI) and protected designation of origin (PDO). The only ingredients besides milk in true Parmigiano–Reggiano are salt and an enzyme. By contrast, Kraft 100% Grated Parmesan Cheese contains cellulose powder (for a smooth texture), potassium sorbate (a preservative), and other ingredients. Because of EU regulations, Kraft cannot sell its cheese in Europe.

Another contentious issue is a cultural one. In parts of Europe, some hold the view that American cultural exports—Hollywood movies, for example—overwhelm the works of local film producers. This perspective prompted European policymakers to demand "carve-outs" that exempt certain industries from the trade pact. In France, for example, the motion picture industry receives state subsidies, and broadcasters are required to comply with quotas for the amount of programming that originates in Europe. Digital media would also be exempt. Not surprisingly, some critics have denounced the proposed carve-outs as blatant protectionism; in contrast, supporters suggest they are legitimate ways to preserve cultural diversity.

By 2017, with President Donald Trump pulling the United States out of the deal, it appeared that the TTIP negotiations would not be resumed. Instead, the EU was focusing on bilateral trade agreements with Japan, Australia, and New Zealand, as well as new deals with Mercosur and Canada.

The Trans-Pacific Partnership

In 2005, Brunei, Chile, New Zealand, and Singapore signed an agreement pledging to eliminate all tariffs among the trade partners by 2015. A decade later, signatories to the proposed free trade pact, known as the Trans-Pacific Partnership, included Australia, Canada, Japan, Malaysia, Mexico, Peru, the United States, and Vietnam. According to the International Monetary Fund, goods exports by the 12 nations negotiating the TPP accounted for about 40 percent of the world total.

Impetus for U.S. involvement gained momentum under President George W. Bush. U.S. President Obama viewed the TPP as a means of increasing American exports. The president was also under pressure to create more jobs for U.S. workers. In 2015, Obama scored a legislative victory when Congress granted him "fast-track" authority to negotiate trade deals.

Despite the policymakers' best intentions, today less than 10 percent of the U.S. workforce is engaged in manufacturing. Author Beth Macy's best-selling book *Factory Man* chronicled the plight of the furniture industry in states such as North Carolina and Virginia where jobs have been lost to Chinese competition. Another recent book, *Janesville: An American Story*, won the 2017 *Financial Times* and McKinsey Business Book of the Year Award. In it, author Amy Goldstein tells how the local community was disrupted by General Motors' decision to close its assembly plant in Janesville, Wisconsin.

In a painful twist, some evidence suggested that implementation of the TPP could result in a loss of manufacturing jobs. For example, New

Source: Jeremy Banx/Banx Cartoons.

Balance Athletics produces 7 million pairs of athletic shoes annually at its plant in Maine. It is the only major company that still manufactures athletic shoes in its headquarters country. Even so, the company must source more than 20 million pairs from factories in China, Indonesia, the United Kingdom, and Vietnam to meet the demand of its U.S. customers. As Matthew LeBretton, head of public affairs at New Balance, explained, from a purely financial point of view, it is more profitable to source shoes in low-wage countries. However, management at New Balance believes that having some of its products "Made in America" is important to the company's brand story. The venerable 990 line of running shoes is a case in point.

Another issue was China's concern that TPP represented an American strategy of "containment"—that is, an attempt to neutralize China's growing influence in the Asia-Pacific region. This concern increased after Japan joined the group. China responded by proposing an alternative trading bloc known as the Regional Comprehensive Economic Partnership (RCEP). The RCEP would deepen ties with the 10-nation ASEAN group as well as several other Pacific Rim nations. Chinese president Xi Jinping has also proposed a multilateral Free Trade Area of Asia Pacific (FTAAP) that would include the United States.

In January 2017, U.S. President Trump signed an executive order withdrawing the United States from the TPP. Candidate Trump, pledging an "America First" administration, had criticized the proposed free-trade pact on the grounds that it created jobs in low-wage nations at the expense of the U.S. manufacturing sector. Some observers, such as the president of the United Steelworkers, praised the president's move. By contrast, farm groups were disappointed that American agricultural producers would be missing out on new export market opportunities.

Policymakers in the remaining 11 TPP countries were committed to reviving the talks without the United States. Japanese Prime Minister Shinzo Abe referred to the group as "Ocean's Eleven," a reference to the 2001 Hollywood movie. At the 2017 APEC meeting in Da Nang, Vietnam, it was announced that a tentative agreement had been reached on a new version of the pact, which was now called the Comprehensive and Progressive Agreement for Trans-Pacific Trade.

Meanwhile, it was apparent that, in the future, the U.S. president would give preference to negotiating new trade deals on a bilateral basis rather than along broader regional lines. President Trump's protectionist stance also heralded a more confrontational approach to key trading partners and the prospect of renegotiating or even canceling existing trade deals such as NAFTA.

Discussion Questions

3-9. Which critical-thinking issues are raised by this case?

3-10. Are you in favor of dropping U.S. tariffs on footwear, even if it means some New Balance employees might lose their jobs?

3-11. Do you agree with President Trump's decision to withdraw the United States from TTIP and TPP?

3-12. Assess the prospects for regional integration in the Asia-Pacific region.

Sources: Shawn Donnan, "Globalization Marches on without Trump," *Financial Times* November 7, 2017), p. 11; Shawn Donnan, "Pacific Trade Deal a Hard Sell for Obama," *Financial Times* (June 12, 2015), p. 3; Shawn Donnan, "Hard Sell," *Financial Times* (June 9, 2014), p. 5; Brian Spegele and Thomas Catan, "China Suggests Shift on U.S.-Led Trade Pact," *The Wall Street Journal* (June 1–2, 2013), p. A6; James Kanter, "European Parliament Approves Resolution Limiting the Scope of a Free-Trade Pact," *The New York Times* (May 24, 2013), p. B7; David Dreier, "China Belongs in the Pacific Trade Talks," *The Wall Street Journal* (April 12, 2013), p. A11; Yuka Hayashi, "'Abenomics' Plan for Growth in Japan: Free-Trade Talks," *The Wall Street Journal* (March 15, 2013), p. A8; Hiroko Tabuchi, "Japan to Enter Talks on Pacific Trade," *The New York Times* (March 16, 2013), p. B3; Philip Stephens, "Transatlantic Free Trade Promises a Bigger Prize," *Financial Times* (February 15, 2013), p. 11; Stephen Fidler, "Trans-Atlantic Trading Partners Barter over Rules," *The Wall Street Journal* (February 14, 2013), p. A11; Sudeep Reddy, "Broad Trade Deal on Table," *The Wall Street Journal* (February 14, 2013), p. A1; Matthew Dalton and Stephen Fidler, "U.S. Considers Opening Ambitious Trade Talks with EU," *The Wall Street Journal* (December 24, 2012), p. A7; Jack Ewing, "US, Europe trade deal may come to the forefront", Business Standard (November 27, 2012); Larry Olmsted, "Most Parmesan Cheese in America Is Fake, Here's Why," *Forbes* (November 19, 2012); Eric Martin, "New Balance Wants Its Tariffs, Nike Doesn't," *Bloomberg Businessweek* (May 7, 2012), pp. 14–15; Yuka Hayashi and Tom Barkley, "Japan's Bid to Join Asian Trade Pact Faces a Leery U.S.," *The Wall Street Journal* (February 7, 2012), p. A9; John D. McKinnon, "Bush Pushes Trans-Pacific Free Trade," *The Wall Street Journal* (January 24, 2008), p. A3.

Exhibit 3-13 Trade ministers and delegates from the remaining 11 members of the Trans-Pacific Partnership at the TPP ministerial meeting that was held during the 2017 Asia-Pacific Economic Cooperation (APEC) leaders summit in Danang, Vietnam.
Source: Na Son Nguyen/ASSOCIATED PRESS.

"Globalization is a force. It exists. The question is whether we want to use trade agreements to shape it, or whether we want to just sit and be shaped by it."

Mike Froman, former U.S. trade representative

Notes

1. Scott Miller, "Global Dogfight: Airplane Battle Spotlights Power of a Quirky Court," *The Wall Street Journal* (June 1, 2005), pp. A1, A14.

2. Scott Miller, "Trade Talks Twist in the Wind," *The Wall Street Journal* (November 8, 2005), p. A14.

3. Gabriele Steinhauser, "A Rocky Road to Economic Union," *The Wall Street Journal* (June 9–10, 2010), p. A9.

4. John Paul Rathbone, "Bottleneck at Frontier Chokes Opportunities to Boost Trade," *Financial Times* (June 28, 2013), p. 2.

5. Adam Thomson, "Trade Deal Has Hidden Qualities," *Financial Times Special Report: Central America Finance & Investment* (September 19, 2008), p. 3.

6. Johanna Tuckman, "Central Americans Start to Act Together," *Financial Times* (July 9, 1997), p. 4.

7. "NAFTA Is Not Alone," *The Economist* (June 18, 1994), pp. 47–48.

8. Marc Lifsher, "The Andean Arc of Instability," *The Wall Street Journal* (February 24, 2003), p. A13.

9. William Neuman, "Vegetable Spawns Larceny and Luxury in Peru," *The New York Times* (December 7, 2014), pp. A9, A15.

10. David J. Lynch, "Golden Days for Argentine Wine Could Turn a Bit Cloudy," *USA Today* (November 16, 2007), pp. 1B, 2B.

11. Viñcent Bevins, "A Dream Disrupted," *Financial Times—International Business Insight, Part Four: Latin America* (November 23, 2010), p. 8.

12. Jim Brunsden and Alan Beattie, "Farmers' Resistance Tests EU Drive for South American Trade Deal," *Financial Times* (November 3, 2017), p. 7.

13. David J. Lynch, "Venezuelan Consumers Gobble Up U.S. Goods," *USA Today* (March 28, 2007), pp. 1B, 2B.

14. John Paul Rathbone and Robin Wigglesworth, "Caracas Plays Its Last Cards," *Financial Times—FT Big Read: Latin America* (November 22, 2017), p. 9.

15. Myrvin L. Anthony and Andrew Hughes Hallett, "Is the Case for Economic and Monetary Union in the Caribbean Realistic?" *World Economy* 23, no. 1 (January 2000), pp. 119–144.

16. Bruce Einhorn, "A Caribbean Headache for Obama's New Trade Rep," *Bloomberg Businessweek* (May 3, 2013), p. 13.

17. Bernard Gordon, "The FTA Fetish," *The Wall Street Journal* (November 17, 2005), p. A16.

18. James Hookway, "Asian Nations Push Ideas for Trade," *The Wall Street Journal* (October 26, 2009), p. A12.

19. Liz Gooch, "In Southeast Asia, Unease over Free Trade Zone," *The New York Times* (December 28, 2009), p. B1.

20. Jeremy Grant, "Business Warns of Barriers for Trading Bloc," *Financial Times* (February 20, 2015), p. 5.

21. G. Guido, "Implementing a Pan-European Marketing Strategy," *Long Range Planning* (Vol. 5, 1991), p. 32.

22. George Russell, "Marketing in the 'Old Country': The Diversity of Europe Presents Unique Challenges," *Agri Marketing* 37, no. 1 (January 1999), p. 38.

23. Scott Miller, "Trading Partners Meet New EU," *The Wall Street Journal* (May 4, 2004), p. A17.

24. Arnold Shuh, "Global Standardization as a Success Formula for Marketing in Central Eastern Europe," *Journal of World Business* 35, no. 2 (Summer 2000), pp. 133–148.

25. Margherita Stancati, "A Jump in Saudi Tourism," *The Wall Street Journal* (July 16-17, 2016), p. C3.

26. Jay Solomon, "Syria Cracks Open Its Frail Economy," *The Wall Street Journal* (September 1, 2009), pp. A1, A12.

27. Victoria Robson, "Window of Opportunity," *Middle East Economic Digest* 49, no. 18 (May 6, 2005), p. 6.

28. Will Connors, "China Extends Africa Push with Loans, Deal in Ghana," *The Wall Street Journal* (September 24, 2010), p. A15.

29. Josh Kron, "African Countries Form a Common Market," *The New York Times* (July 2, 2010), p. B2. See also William Wallis, "Enthusiasm for EAC Not Matched by Results," *Financial Times Special Report: Doing Business in Kenya* (November 26, 2010), p. 1.

30. Andrew England, "Producers Pin Hope on AGOA Trade Pact to Drive Exports," *Financial Times* (August 6, 2014), p. 3.

31. Margaret Coker, "Persian Gulf States Bet on Africa Despite Downturn," *The Wall Street Journal* (February 24, 2009), p. A9.

4 Social and Cultural Environments

LEARNING OBJECTIVES

4-1 Define *culture* and identify the various expressions and manifestations of culture that can impact global marketing strategies.

4-2 Compare and contrast the key aspects of high- and low-context cultures.

4-3 Identify and briefly explain the major dimensions of Hofstede's social values typology.

4-4 Explain how the self-reference criterion can affect decision making at global companies, and provide a step-by-step example of a company adapting to conditions in a global market.

4-5 Analyze the components of diffusion theory and its applicability to global marketing.

4-6 Explain the marketing implications of different social and cultural environments around the globe.

CASE 4-1
Cotton, Clothing Consumption, Culture: From Small Beginnings to a Global Cultural System

Cotton has been a major part of trade across many parts of the world for centuries. It is produced on a commercial scale in 80 countries and provides a livelihood to about 100 million farmers, and another 250 million people in related industries benefit from it. The oldest-known cotton bolls, dated to approximately 3600 BCE, were discovered in a cave in Tehuacán Valley in Mexico, but evidence for the earliest use of cotton for clothing can be traced to the fifth millennium BCE in ancient India.

Cotton was introduced to Britain in the 1690s by the East India Company, and by the end of the 19th century, it was dominating the world's textile industry. The history of cotton production would be incomplete without due reference to the inventions from the 1770s that made the mass production of cotton possible: the spinning jenny, the spinning mule, and the water frame. These inventions transformed the British Midlands into a profitable manufacturing hub, and cotton products became a central symbol of national identity in Britain.

In the present day, the global importance of cotton in apparel continues to soar. The textile industry in India in particular is expected to grow and reach around $221 billion by 2020, but the trend is visible all over the world. In Europe, for instance, evidence shows that cotton fabrics have become popular among various consumer groups. While the demands for children's cotton apparel are being met, other age groups are also increasingly being catered to in response to their growing demand for cotton clothing. Cotton permeates the entire socio-cultural context of the society in various countries all over the world.

This rise in popularity of cotton is not without its problems. Prominent among them is uncertainty about its availability, as reported by the International Cotton Advisory Committee. Cotton inventories are reportedly hitting their lowest point in comparison to 2011–12 figures. This is a global challenge beyond the scope of an individual organization or a particular consumer group. Despite these prospects, the consumption rate of cotton remains unabated.

The growth in consumption of cotton all over the world, the instability of the production cycle, and the activities of major fashion companies such as Inditex, H&M, and Marks & Spencer all illustrate the ways that socio-cultural environments impact marketing opportunities and dynamics around the globe. This chapter focuses on the forces that shape and affect individual, group, and corporate behavior in the marketplace.

We start with a general discussion of the basic aspects of culture and society and the emergence of a twenty-first-century global consumer culture. Next, several useful conceptual frameworks for understanding culture are presented, including Hall's concept of high-and low-context cultures, Maslow's hierarchy of needs, Hofstede's cultural typology, the self-reference criterion, and diffusion theory. The chapter also cites specific examples of the impact of culture and society on the marketing of both consumer and industrial products.

Clearly, cotton's popularity is on the rise around the world. It remains to be seen, however, how the rise in consumption can be balanced with increased production. You will have the opportunity to explore the issue in the continuation of the case at the end of the chapter. The discussion questions at the end of the case will give you a chance to reflect further on "lessons learned."

Society, Culture, and Global Consumer Culture

▶ **4-1** Define *culture* and identify the various expressions and manifestations of culture that can impact global marketing strategies.

Both differences and similarities characterize the world's cultures, meaning that the task of the global marketer is twofold. First, marketers must study and understand the cultures of the countries in which they will be doing business. Second, they must incorporate this understanding into the marketing planning process. In some instances, strategies and marketing programs will have to be adapted to the local culture; however, marketers should also take advantage of shared cultural characteristics and avoid unneeded and costly adaptations of the marketing mix.

Any systematic study of a new geographic market requires a combination of tough-mindedness and open-mindedness. While marketers should be secure in their own convictions and traditions, an open mind is required to appreciate the integrity and value of other ways of life and points of view.

Put simply, people must overcome the prejudices that are a natural result of the human tendency toward ethnocentricity. Although "culture shock" is a normal human reaction to the new and unknown, successful global marketers strive to comprehend human experience from the local point of view. One reason cultural factors challenge global marketers is that many of these factors are hidden from view. Because culture is a learned behavior passed on from generation to generation, it can be difficult for outsiders to fathom. However, as they endeavor to understand cultural factors, outsiders gradually become insiders and develop cultural empathy. There are many different paths to the same goals in life: The global marketer understands this and revels in life's rich diversity.

Anthropologists and sociologists have offered scores of different definitions of culture. As a starting point, **culture** can be understood as "ways of living, built up by a group of human beings, that are transmitted from one generation to another." A culture acts out its ways of living in the context of *social institutions*, including family, educational, religious, governmental, and business institutions. Those institutions, in turn, function to reinforce cultural norms. Culture also includes both conscious and unconscious values, ideas, attitudes, and symbols that shape human behavior and that are transmitted from one generation to the next. Organizational anthropologist Geert Hofstede defines *culture* as "the collective programming of the mind that distinguishes the members of one category of people from those of another."[1] A particular "category of people" may constitute a nation, an ethnic group, a gender group, an organization, a family, or some other unit.

Some anthropologists and sociologists divide cultural elements into two broad categories: material culture and nonmaterial culture. The former is sometimes referred to as the *physical component* or *physical culture*; it includes physical objects and artifacts created by humans such as clothing and tools. Nonmaterial culture (also known as *subjective* or *abstract culture*) includes intangibles such as religion, perceptions, attitudes, beliefs, and values. It is generally agreed that the material and nonmaterial elements of culture are interrelated and interactive. Cultural anthropologist George P. Murdock studied material and nonmaterial culture and identified dozens of "cultural universals," including athletic sports, body adornment, cooking, courtship, dancing, decorative art, education, ethics, etiquette, family feasting, food taboos, language, marriage, mealtime, medicine, mourning, music, property rights, religious rituals, residence rules, status differentiation, and trade.[2]

It is against this background of traditional definitions that global marketers should understand a key worldwide sociocultural phenomenon of the early twenty-first century:[3] Consumption has become the hallmark of postmodern society. As cultural information and imagery flow freely across borders via satellite TV, the Internet, and other communication channels, new global consumer cultures are emerging. Persons who identify with these cultures share meaningful sets of consumption-related symbols. Some of these cultures are associated with specific product categories; marketers speak of "coffee culture," "credit-card culture," "fast-food culture," "pub culture," "soccer/football culture," and so on. This cosmopolitan culture, which is composed of various segments, owes its existence in large part to a wired world in which there is increasing interconnectedness of various local cultures. It can be exploited by **global consumer culture positioning (GCCP)**, a marketing tool that will be explained in more detail in Chapter 7. In particular, marketers can use advertising to communicate the notion that people everywhere consume a particular brand or to appeal to human universals.

Attitudes, Beliefs, and Values

If we accept Hofstede's notion of culture as "the collective programming of the mind," then it makes sense to learn about culture by studying the attitudes, beliefs, and values shared by a specific group of people. An **attitude** is a learned tendency to respond in a consistent way to a given object or entity. Attitudes are clusters of interrelated beliefs. A **belief** is an organized pattern of knowledge that an individual holds to be true about the world. Attitudes and beliefs, in turn, are closely related to values. A **value** can be defined as an enduring belief or feeling that a specific mode of conduct is personally or socially preferable to another mode of conduct.[4] In the view of Hofstede and others, values represent the deepest level of a culture and are present in the majority of the members of that particular culture.

Some specific examples will allow us to illustrate these definitions by comparing and contrasting attitudes, beliefs, and values. The Japanese, for example, strive to achieve cooperation, consensus, self-denial, and harmony. Because these all represent feelings about modes of conduct, they are *values*. Japan's monocultural society reflects the *belief* among the Japanese that they are unique in the world. Many Japanese, especially young people, also believe that the West is the source of important fashion trends. As a result, many Japanese share a favorable *attitude* toward American brands. Within any large, dominant cultural group, there are likely to be **subcultures**— that is, smaller groups of people with their own shared subset of attitudes, beliefs, and values. Values, attitudes, and beliefs can also be surveyed at the level of any "category of people" that is embedded within a broad culture. For example, if you are a vegetarian, then eating meat represents a mode of conduct that you and others who share your views avoid. Subcultures often represent attractive niche marketing opportunities.

Religion

Religion is an important source of a society's beliefs, attitudes, and values. The world's major religions include Buddhism, Hinduism, Islam, Judaism, and Christianity; the last includes Roman Catholicism and numerous Protestant denominations. Examples abound of religious tenets, practices, holidays, and histories directly impacting the way people of different faiths react to global marketing activities. For example, Hindus do not eat beef, which means that McDonald's does not serve hamburgers in India (see Case 1-2). In Muslim countries, Yum! Brands successfully promotes KFC in conjunction with religious observances. In the Islamic world, Ramadan is a time of fasting that begins in the ninth month of the Islamic calendar. In Indonesia, home to the world's largest Muslim population, KFC uses Ramadan-themed outdoor advertising to encourage Indonesians to come to the restaurants at buka puasa, the end of each day's fast. Business at KFC Indonesia's 500 units increases as much as 20 percent during Ramadan.

When followers of a particular religion believe they have been offended, the response can sometimes be tragic (see Exhibit 4-2). In the aftermath of the September 2001 terrorist attacks in New York and Washington, D.C., and the subsequent U.S. military actions in the Middle East and Afghanistan, some Muslims have tapped into anti-American sentiment by urging a boycott of American brands. One entrepreneur, Tunisian-born Tawfik Mathlouthi, launched a soft drink brand, Mecca-Cola, as an alternative to Coca-Cola for Muslims living in the United Kingdom and France. The brand's name is both an intentional reference to the holy city of Islam and an ironic swipe at Coca-Cola, which Mathlouthi calls "the Mecca of capitalism." London's *Sunday Times* called Mecca-Cola "the drink now seen as politically preferable to Pepsi or Coke."[5] In 2003, Qibla Cola (the name comes from an Arabic word for "direction") was launched in the United Kingdom. Founder Zahida Parveen hoped to reach a broader market than Mecca-Cola by positioning the brand "for any consumer with a conscience, irrespective of ethnicity or religion."[6]

Exhibit 4-2 In 2014, jihadist gunmen opened fire at the Paris office of Charlie Hebdo, a satirical weekly that had published cartoon images of the Prophet Muhammed. Seventeen people were killed in the attack.
Source: Richard Milnes/Alamy.

Aesthetics

Within every culture, there is an overall sense of what is beautiful and what is not beautiful, what represents good taste as opposed to tastelessness or even obscenity, and so on. Such considerations are matters of **aesthetics**. Global marketers must understand the importance of *visual aesthetics* embodied in the color or shape of a product, label, or package. Likewise, different parts of the world perceive *aesthetic styles*—various degrees of complexity, for example—differently. Aesthetic elements that are attractive, appealing, and in good taste in one country may be perceived in an entirely different way in another country.

In some cases, a standardized color can be used in all countries; examples include Caterpillar Yellow, the trademark of the earthmoving equipment company and its licensed outdoor gear. Likewise, Cadbury has trademarked the color purple for its chocolate confectionary packaging. In surveys about color preferences, 50 percent of respondents indicate blue is their favorite—and it is favored by a wide margin over the next-preferred color. The use of blue dates back millennia; artisans in ancient Egypt, China, and Mayan civilizations all worked with the color after the advent of mining led to the extraction of minerals containing blue pigment. Because it was rare and expensive, blue came to be associated with royalty and divinity.[7] Today, Tiffany Blue is a trademarked color that the luxury goods marketer uses on its gift bags and boxes. When Prince William and his family visit other European royalty, blue is a frequent wardrobe choice (see Exhibit 4-3).

Because color perceptions can vary among cultures, adaptation to local preferences may be required. Such perceptions should be taken into account when making decisions about product packaging and other brand-related communications. In highly competitive markets, inappropriate or unattractive product packaging may put a company or brand at a distinct disadvantage. New color schemes may also be needed because of a changing competitive environment.

There is nothing inherently "good" or "bad" about any color of the spectrum; all associations and perceptions regarding color arise from culture. Red is a popular color in most parts of the world: Besides being the color of blood, in many countries red is tied to centuries-old traditions of viticulture and winemaking. One eight-country study of color perceptions found that red is associated with perceptions such as "active," "hot," and "vibrant"; in most countries studied, it also conveys meanings such as "emotional" and "sharp."[8] As such, red has positive connotations in many societies. In contrast, in Korea, it is taboo to write a person's name in red ink. Why? Because traditionally, red was used to record the names of the deceased. Blue, because of its associations with sky and water, has an elemental connotation with undertones of dependability, constancy,

Exhibit 4-3 Members of the British royal family make diplomatic tours during which their wardrobe choices often reflect cultural awareness. When the Duke and Duchess of Cambridge arrived in Germany in 2017, the duchess wore Prussian blue; Prince William wore a matching tie.
Source: KAY NIETFELD/AFP/Getty Images.

and eternity. White connotes purity and cleanliness in the West, but is often associated with death, mourning, and funerals in China and other parts of Asia. Attitudes are changing quickly among the younger generation, however; today, many Chinese women rent white wedding gowns and pose for photos with their friends to commemorate graduating from university![9]

Another research team concluded that gray connotes inexpensive in China and Japan, whereas it is associated with high quality and high cost in the United States. The researchers also found that the Chinese associate brown with soft drink labels and perceive the color as connoting a beverage that tastes good; in contrast, South Korean and Japanese consumers associate yellow with soft drinks that "taste good." For Americans, the color red has those associations.[10]

Music is an aesthetic component of all cultures and is accepted as a form of artistic expression and a source of entertainment. In one sense, music represents a "transculture" that is not identified with any particular nation. For example, rhythm, or movement through time, is a universal aspect of music. But music is also characterized by considerable stylistic variation with regional or country-specific associations. For example, bossa nova rhythms are associated with Argentina; samba with Brazil; salsa with Cuba; reggae with Jamaica; merengue with the Dominican Republic; and blues, driving rock rhythms, hip-hop, and rap with the United States. Sociologists have noted that national identity derives in part from a country's indigenous or popular music; a unique music style can "represent the uniqueness of the cultural entity and of the community."[11]

Music provides an interesting example of the "think globally, act locally" theme of this book. Musicians in different countries draw from, absorb, adapt, and synthesize transcultural music influences, as well as country-specific ones, as they create hybrid styles such as Polish reggae or Italian hip-hop. Motti Regev describes this paradox as follows:

> Producers of and listeners to these types of music feel, at one and the same time, participants in a specific contemporary, global-universal form of expression *and* innovators of local, national, ethnic, and other identities. A cultural form associated with American culture and with the powerful commercial interests of the international music industry is being used in order to construct a sense of local difference and authenticity.[12]

Because music plays an important role in advertising, marketers must understand which style is appropriate to use in their campaigns in a given national market. Although background music can be used effectively in broadcast commercials, the type of music appropriate for a commercial in one part of the world may not be acceptable or effective in another part. Government restrictions must also be taken into account. In China, authorities have the power to dictate which songs can be marketed and performed, as the Rolling Stones can attest. Rock music journalism must also conform to state mandates, as the publisher of *Rolling Stone* magazine learned (see Exhibit 4-4).

Dietary Preferences

Cultural influences are also quite apparent in food preparation and consumption patterns and habits. Need proof? Consider the following examples:

- Domino's Pizza, the world's largest pizza-delivery company, pulled out of Italy because Italians perceived its product to be "too American." In particular, the tomato sauce was too bold and the toppings were too heavy. Domino's had better luck in India, where it localized its recipes with offerings that include pizza keema do pyaaza, peppy paneer, and five peppers.[13] Today, Domino's is the largest foreign fast-food chain in India, with more than 700 stores.
- When Dunkin' Donuts opened its first Indian outlets in 2012, morning business was slow because most Indians eat breakfast at home. Success finally came after the company introduced a new menu item: Original Tough Guy Chicken Burgers.[14]

These examples underscore the fact that a solid understanding of food-related cultural preferences is important for any company that seeks to market food or beverage products globally. Titoo Ahluwalia, chairman of a market research firm in Mumbai, has pointed out that local companies can also leverage superior cultural understanding to compete effectively with large foreign firms: "Indian companies have an advantage when they are drawing from tradition. When it comes to food, drink, and medicine, you have to be culturally sensitive."[15] Companies that lack such

Exhibit 4-4 The March 2006 inaugural issue of *Rolling Stone*'s Chinese edition featured local rocker Cui Jian on the cover. Global superstars U2 were also profiled.
Source: Frederic J. Brown/AFP/Getty Images.

sensitivity are bound to make marketing mistakes. To avoid this kind of problem, when Subway expanded into India, the company chose two U.S.-educated Indian brothers to help open stores and supervise operations.

Although some food preferences remain deeply embedded in culture, plenty of evidence suggests that global dietary preferences are converging. Over the past half century, the fast-food culture has gained increased acceptance around the world. Heads of families in many countries are pressed for time and are disinclined to prepare home-cooked meals. Millennials, who are open to different cultures and lifestyles, are experimenting with different foods. In addition, the global tourism boom has exposed travelers to pizza, pasta, and other ethnic foods. Shorter lunch hours and tighter budgets are forcing workers to find a place to grab a quick, cheap bite before returning to work. As food-related cultural differences become less relevant, such convenience products are likely to be purchased wherever consumers' disposable incomes are high enough to afford them (see Exhibit 4-5).

As we have seen, such processes can also provoke a nationalist backlash. To counteract the exposure of its young citizens to *le Big Mac* and other American-style fast foods, the French National Council of Culinary Arts designed a course on French cuisine and "good taste" for elementary school students. The director of the council is Alexandre Lazareff. In his book *The French Culinary Exception*, Lazareff warned that France's tradition of *haute cuisine* is under attack by the globalization of taste. More generally, Lazareff spoke out against perceived challenges to France's culinary identity and way of life. His concerns are not unjustified: While McDonald's continues to open new restaurants in France (today there are more than 1,100 outlets), the number of traditional bistros and cafés has declined steadily for years. Despite McDonald's success, the French have coined a new buzzword, *le fooding*, to express the notion that the nation's passion for food goes beyond mere gastronomy:

> To eat with feeling in France is to eat with your head and your spirit, with your nose, your eyes, and your ears, not simply your palate. *Le fooding* seeks to give witness to the modernity and new reality of drinking and eating in the twenty-first century.... Everything is *fooding* so long as audacity, sense, and the senses mix.[16]

Language and Communication

The diversity of cultures around the world is also reflected in language. A person can learn a great deal about another culture without leaving home by studying its language and literature; such study is the next-best thing to actually living in another country. Linguists have divided

Exhibit 4-5 SPAM, the iconic brand of canned ham, is a reliable, if unglamorous, pantry staple in American households. SPAM is so deeply embedded in American food culture that there is even a SPAM Museum in Austin, Minnesota, home to parent company Hormel Foods Corporation.

In South Korea, SPAM is regarded as a delicacy, often packaged in gift sets for holiday giving. It turns out that SPAM is a favorite of Chloe Kim, the American gold medalist in snowboarding at the 2018 Winter Olympics in PyeongChang, South Korea.

Source: Jodi Cobb/National Geographic Image Collection/Alamy.

the study of *spoken* or *verbal* language into four main areas: syntax (rules of sentence formation), semantics (system of meaning), phonology (system of sound patterns), and morphology (word formation). *Unspoken* or *nonverbal* communication includes gestures, touching, and other forms of body language that supplement spoken communication. (Nonverbal communication is sometimes called the silent language.) Both the spoken and unspoken aspects of language are included in the broader linguistic field of *semiotics*, which is the study of signs and their meanings.

In global marketing, language is a crucial tool for communicating with customers, suppliers, channel intermediaries, and others. The marketing literature is full of cringe-worthy anecdotes about blunders such as embarrassing pronunciations of product names and inept translations of advertising copy. As you can see from Figure 4-1, pronunciation subtleties associated with certain Chinese characters can trip up well-meaning gift giving in China. For example, it would be a bad sign to give an umbrella to a business acquaintance because it would be the equivalent of hoping that his or her business fails.

In China, Dell had to find a meaningful interpretation of "direct sales," the phrase that describes the company's powerful business model. A literal translation results in *zhi xiao*, which is the Chinese term for "illegal pyramid marketing schemes." To counteract the negative connotation, Dell's sales representatives began using the phrase *zhi xiao ding gou*, which translates as "direct orders."[17] Similarly, a team of translators was tasked with compiling a dictionary to help fans of American football in China understand the game (see Figure 4-2).

When the British/American retail-development firm BAA McArthurGlen sought approval for a U.S.-style factory outlet mall in Austria, local officials wanted to know, "Where's the factory?" To win approval for the project, McArthurGlen was forced to call its development a "designer outlet center." Another linguistic issue: The American making the marketing pitch incorrectly rendered the name "Nike"—a prospective anchor tenant at the proposed outlet center—when speaking to French audiences. Summoning his rudimentary language skills, the American assumed that the shoemaker's name would be pronounced "NEEK" in French. Imagine his dismay when a sympathetic colleague took him aside and told him that the correct pronunciation was "NIk" (rhymes with "bike"). It turns out that "NEEK" is not just the "F-word" in French; it is the "F-word" in the sense of "fornicating with animals"![18]

THE CULTURAL CONTEXT

Globe to Globe: Shakespeare Around the World

Why would a small troupe of actors and a handful of stage managers take it upon themselves to produce an English-language version of *Hamlet* in every country on the planet over the course of two years? "I'll tell you why . . . ," says Hamlet in Act 2, Scene 2 of Shakespeare's play. Former Globe Theatre Artistic Director Dominic Dromgoole offers this concise explanation: "*Hamlet* is of benefit to everyone."

The Globe to Globe world tour began in April 2014, the 450th anniversary of the Bard's birth, and wrapped up on London's South Bank in 2016, the 500th anniversary of his death. Convinced that everyone, everywhere, has a right to see Shakespeare's play, Dromgoole characterizes his goal of providing a unique cultural exchange alternatively as both "mad" and "utterly affirming."

How can a centuries-old play be relevant to today's audiences? Despite the obstacles presented by the play's early modern English vocabulary, the dialogue draws people in. At the original Globe Theatre in London, many members of the audience stood ("groundlings") and there was no cover over the stage. Bathed in natural light, actors looked out at audience members and addressed them directly. The same was true in the modern staging. "That's what Shakespeare is all about," says Dromgoole. "When Hamlet asks questions, you know you are being spoken to."

In addition, the architecture of the play translates well to many cultures. The opening scene with two nervous soldiers on the battlements at Elsinore castle is a good example. "People everywhere understand it," Dromgoole says. Then, of course, there is the appearance of a ghost—also universally recognized.

As another example, Dromgoole points to the scene in which a young man who is seething with rage confronts Claudius, a smooth-talking, practiced politician. Audiences lock into the scene literally and directly, even if the nuances of language are lost. As Naeem Hayat, one of the actors who portrayed Hamlet, says, "Direct communication opens up Hamlet's humanity."

In a textbook example of "markets are global, markets are local," the show changed from country to country according to the dictates of different venues. In Spain, for example, the play was presented in an opera house. In Djibouti, the performance took place in front of the Red Sea.

Hamlet's meaning also took on a local resonance that varied from one country to another. For example, when the play was staged in Phnom Penh, Cambodia, Dromgoole saw a connection between Claudius and the notorious Khmer Rouge revolutionary Pol Pot. At the United Nations in New York City, Dromgoole linked Ophelia's father Polonius to the functionaries who go about their tasks of diplomacy with modest virtue. In a Middle Eastern country, some audience members interpreted the play as an indictment of a monarchy beset by corruption. The company also performed in refugee camps harboring migrants from war-torn countries such as Syria (see Exhibit 4-6).

Sources: Dominic Dromgoole, *Hamlet, Globe to Globe: Taking Shakespeare to Every Country in the World* (London, UK: Canongate, 2017); "Alas Poor Dominic," Presentation by Dominic Dromgoole and Naeem Hayat, *Financial Times* Weekend Festival, London (September 2, 2017); Steven Greenblatt, "Their Hours upon the Stage," *The New York Times Sunday Book Review* (April 23, 2017), p. BR 1; Harriet Fitch Little, "Home and Away: The Globe to Globe Hamlet Project," *Financial Times* (April 22, 2016).

Exhibit 4-6 One performance took place at Calais Jungle, a camp for displaced migrants who hoped to enter the United Kingdom via the Eurotunnel.
Source: Anthony Devlin/PA Wire URN:25420563/Associated Press.

book   umbrella   clock

FIGURE 4-1 In China, it is bad luck to give a book, an umbrella, or a clock as a gift. Why? The character for "book" is pronounced *shu*, which sounds like "I hope you lose (have bad luck)." "Umbrella" (*san*) sounds like "to break into pieces or fall apart." "Clock" (*zhong*) sounds like "death" or "the end."

Anheuser-Busch and Miller Brewing both experienced market failures in the United Kingdom because of their use of the phrase "light beer" in their marketing campaigns; this phrase was understood as meaning "reduced alcohol levels" rather than "fewer calories." Now Miller Lite is marketed in Europe as "Miller Pilsner."[19]

Phonology and morphology can also come into play. Colgate discovered that in Spanish, *colgate* is a verb form that means "go hang yourself." IKEA is known for product names based on Scandinavian cities and children's names. However, in Thailand, the furniture giant had to hire linguists and native speakers to help render product names in Thai. The reason? The names for products such as the Redalen bed and Jättebra (a flower pot) had sexual connotations when pronounced in Thai. The solution: The team of native speakers proposed vowel and consonant changes to certain names so they would not sound offensive.[20]

Whirlpool spent considerable sums of money on brand advertising in Europe, only to discover that consumers in Italy, France, and Germany had trouble pronouncing the company's name.[21] Conversely, Renzo Rosso deliberately chose "Diesel" for a new jeans brand because, as he once noted, "It's one of the few words pronounced the same in every language." Rosso has built Diesel into a successful global youth brand and one of Italy's top fashion success stories; the company's annual sales revenues exceed $1.2 billion.[22]

Technology is providing interesting new opportunities for exploiting linguistics in the name of marketing. For example, young people throughout the world are using cell phones to send text messages; it turns out that certain number combinations have meanings in particular languages. For example, in Korean the phonetic pronunciation of the numerical sequence 8282, "Pal Yi Pal Yi," means "hurry up," while 7179 ("Chil Han Chil Gu") sounds like "close friend." Also, as many digital-savvy young teens in Korea can attest, 4 5683 968 can be interpreted as "I love you."[23] Korean marketers are using these and other numerical sequences in their advertising.

One impact of globalization on culture is the diffusion of the English language around the globe. Today, more people speak English as a second language than there are people whose native language is English. Nearly 85 percent of the teenagers in the EU are studying English. Despite the fact that Sony is headquartered in Japan, the company makes it clear to job applicants

blitz
突袭:猛撞
(四分卫)一种
防守技术

gambling kickoff
赌博踢

short kick
短开球

punt
凌空踢球

capture and kill
'擒杀'

successfully capture the quarterback
成功地擒抱四分卫

play action
假跑真传

Hail Mary pass
长传到达阵区

touchdown
持球触地

FIGURE 4-2 Thanks to a team of academics who compiled an encyclopedia of American football terms, Chinese sports fans should have a better understanding of NFL games. For example, the Chinese translation for *blitz* is "lightning war against the quarterback." *Onside kick* is rendered as "gambling kickoff" or "short kick," while *punt* is "give up and kick it back." The authors of *The American Football Encyclopedia* also interpreted *sack* as "capture and kill" or "capture the quarterback"; *play action* is "pass after fake run." *Hail Mary pass* translates as "miracle long pass," and *touchdown* is "hold the ball and touch the ground."

in any part of the world that it does not consider English to be a "foreign language." The same is true for Finland's Nokia. Matsushita introduced a policy that requires all managers to pass an English-language-competency test before being considered for promotion. This move came after top management at Matsushita concluded that a staid, exclusively Japanese corporate culture was eroding the company's competitiveness in the global market. The English-language requirement is a potent symbol that this Japanese company is focusing on globalizing its operations.[24]

The challenges presented by nonverbal communication are perhaps even more formidable. For example, Westerners doing business in the Middle East must be careful not to reveal the soles of their shoes to hosts or pass documents with the left hand. In Japan, bowing is an important form of nonverbal communication that has many nuances. People who grow up in the West tend to be verbal; those from Asia exhibit behavior that places more weight on nonverbal aspects of interpersonal communication. In the East, it is expected that people will pick up on nonverbal cues and intuitively understand meanings without being told.[25] Westerners must pay close attention not only to what they hear but also to what they see when conducting business in such cultures.

Deep cultural understanding that is based in language can be an important source of competitive advantage for global companies. The aggressive expansion of Spain's Telefónica in Latin America provides a case in point. As Juan Villalonga, former chairman of Telefónica, noted, "It is not just speaking a common language. It is sharing a culture and understanding friendships in the same way."[26]

Several important communication issues related to culture may arise. One is *sequencing*, which concerns whether the discussion goes directly from point A to point B or seems to go off on tangents. Another is *phasing*, which pertains to whether certain important agenda items are discussed immediately or after the parties have taken some time to establish rapport. According to two experts on international negotiations, several distinctly American tactics are frequently employed during negotiations that may be effective with other Americans, but require modification when dealing with people from other cultural backgrounds. In any communication situation, speakers offer a variety of cues that can help astute observers understand the speaker's mind-set and mental programming. Here are some examples:[27]

> Americans typically want to "go it alone." As a result, they may be outnumbered in a negotiation situation.

> Many Americans like to "lay their cards on the table." However, in some contexts, it is important to build rapport and *not* "get to the point" immediately.

> Americans tend to talk too much and to talk when they should be listening and observing. In some cultures, long silences are valued. Nonverbal communication cues can be just as important as words.

Such "unwritten rules" of communication are found in other cultures as well. In the United Kingdom, for example, sociologist Kate Fox has identified the "polite procrastination rule" governing workplace encounters and meetings. Rather than getting down to business right away, meetings often begin with small talk about mundane topics such as traffic and weather. Fox recounts interviewing a Canadian businessman on assignment in Great Britain who noted the following:

> I wish someone had warned me about this earlier. I had a meeting the other day and they'd all been dithering and talking about the weather and making jokes about the M25 for what seemed like half an hour, so I suggested maybe we could get started on the contract and they all looked at me like I'd farted or something! Like, how could I be so crass?[28]

It turns out that the English predilection for "weather-speak" is characterized by several unwritten "grammar" rules. For example, native speakers of British English intuitively comply with, and demonstrate competence with, the "reciprocity rule" (i.e., when someone comments on the weather, one must reply) and the "agreement rule" (i.e., if someone says "Oooh, it's cold," one must concur), among others. This observation, Fox points out, "tells us quite a lot about Englishness."

Marketing's Impact on Culture

Universal aspects of the cultural environment represent opportunities for global marketers to standardize some or all elements of a marketing program. The astute global marketer often discovers that much of the apparent cultural diversity in the world turns out to be different ways of accomplishing the same thing. Shared preferences for convenience foods, disposable products, popular music, and movies in North America, Europe, Latin America, and Asia suggest that many consumer products have broad—even universal—appeal.

In recent times, increasing travel and improving communications have contributed to a convergence of tastes and preferences in a number of product categories. The greater opportunities for cultural exchange and the globalization of culture have been seized upon, and even significantly accelerated, by companies that have seized opportunities to find customers around the world. Nevertheless, the impact of marketing and, more generally, of global capitalism on culture can be controversial. For example, sociologist George Ritzer and others lament the "McDonaldization of culture," which, they say, occurs when global companies break down cultural barriers while expanding into new markets with their products. As Ritzer noted:

> Eating is at the heart of most cultures and for many it is something on which much time, attention and money are lavished. In attempting to alter the way people eat, McDonaldization poses a profound threat to the entire cultural complex of many societies.[29]

Fabien Ouaki is living proof that persons outside of academe and government have also joined the battle against McDonaldization. Ouaki is the former managing director of Tati, a legendary French discount retailer with a flagship store in Paris. In the late 1990s, Ouaki opened new stores in select countries, including the United States. Ouaki, the son of the company founder, once claimed that "personal revenge" was one motivation for entering the U.S. market. "As a Frenchman, it makes me sick to see kids crying to go see 'Titanic,' eat at McDonald's, or drink Coke. I want to see New Yorkers crying to have a Tati wedding dress," he said.[31]

Similarly, the international Slow Food movement boasts tens of thousands of members worldwide. Slow Food grew out of a 1986 protest over the opening of a McDonald's on a popular plaza in Rome; every two years, Slow Food stages a Salone del Gusto in Italy that showcases traditional food preparation. As a spokesperson said, "Slow Food is about the idea that things should not taste the same everywhere."[32] In 2016, in celebration of the 30th anniversary of the Slow Food movement, the Terra Madre Salone del Gusto gastronomy exposition was spread across various locations in Torino (see Exhibit 4-7).

> "A great cook tells his story, not that of his neighbor or what he has seen on television. The future is 'glocal' cooking, both global and local."[30]
>
> Alain Ducasse, Louis XV restaurant, Monaco

Exhibit 4-7 According to event organizers, the challenge of Terra Madre Salone del Gusto 2016 was political, cultural, and social: To assert that good, clean and fair food is a human right. Attendees sampled artisanal meats, cheeses, breads, and much more.
Source: Marco Imazio/Alamy Stock Photo.

▶ 4-2 Compare and contrast the key aspects of high- and low-context cultures.

(4-2) High- and Low-Context Cultures

Edward T. Hall has suggested the concept of high and low context as a way of understanding different cultural orientations.[33] In a **low-context culture**, messages are explicit and specific; words carry most of the communication power. In a **high-context culture**, less information is contained in the verbal part of a message, while much more information resides in the context of communication, including the background, associations, and basic values of the communicators. In general, high-context cultures function with much less legal paperwork than is deemed essential in low-context cultures. Japan, Saudi Arabia, and other high-context cultures place a great deal of emphasis on a person's values and position or place in society. In such cultures, the granting of a business loan is more likely to be based on "who you are" than on formal analysis of pro forma financial documents.

In a low-context culture, such as the United States, Switzerland, or Germany, deals are made with much less information about the character, background, and values of the participants. Much more reliance is placed on the words and numbers in the loan application. By contrast, Japanese companies, such as Sony, traditionally paid a great deal of attention to the university background of a new hire; preference would be given to graduates of Tokyo University. Specific elements on a résumé, by comparison, were less important.

In a high-context culture, a person's word is his or her bond. Because such as culture emphasizes obligations and trust as important values, there is less need to anticipate contingencies and provide for external legal sanctions. Shared feelings of obligation and honor take the place of impersonal legal sanctions—which helps explain the importance of long and protracted negotiations that never seem to get to the point. Part of the purpose of negotiating, for a person from a high-context culture, is to get to know the potential partner.

For example, insisting on competitive bidding can cause complications in low-context cultures. In a high-context culture, the job is given to the person who will do the best work and whom one can trust and control. In a low-context culture, one tries to make the specifications so precise that the threat of legal sanction forces a builder, for example, to do a good job. As Hall has noted, a builder in Japan is likely to say, "What has that piece of paper got to do with the situation? If we can't trust each other enough to go ahead without it, why bother?"

Although countries can be classified as high or low context in terms of their overall tendency, exceptions do arise with regard to specific subcultures. Consider the United States, a low-context culture with subcultures that operate in the high-context mode. The world of the central banker, for example, is a "gentleman's" world—that is, a high-context culture. Even during the most hectic day of trading in the foreign exchange markets, a central banker's word is sufficient for him or her to borrow millions of dollars. In a high-context culture, there is trust, a sense of fair play, and a widespread acceptance of the rules of the game as it is played. Table 4-1 summarizes some of the ways in which high- and low-context cultures differ.

TABLE 4-1 High- and Low-Context Cultures

Factors or Dimensions	High Context	Low Context
Lawyers	Less important	Very important
A person's word	Is his or her bond	Is not to be relied upon; "get it in writing"
Responsibility for organizational error	Taken by highest level	Pushed to lowest level
Space	People breathe on each other	People maintain a bubble of private space and resent intrusions
Time	Polychronic—everything in life must be dealt with in terms of its own time	Monochronic—time is money; linear—one thing at a time
Negotiations	Are lengthy—a major purpose is to allow the parties to get to know each other	Proceed quickly
Competitive bidding	Infrequent	Common
Country or regional examples	Japan, Middle East	United States, Northern Europe

(4-3) Hofstede's Cultural Typology

◀ **4-3** Identify and briefly explain the major dimensions of Hofstede's social values typology.

Organizational anthropologist Geert Hofstede was introduced earlier in this chapter in a discussion of his widely quoted definition of culture. Hofstede is also well known for research studies of social values that suggest the cultures of different nations can be compared in terms of five dimensions (see Table 4-2).[34] Hofstede notes that three of the dimensions refer to expected social behavior, the fourth dimension is concerned with "man's search for Truth," and the fifth reflects the importance of time (for more information, visit www.geert-hofstede.com).

The first dimension is a reflection of the degree to which individuals in a society are integrated into groups. In **individualistic cultures**, each member of society is primarily concerned with his or her own interests and those of his or her immediate family. In contrast, in **collectivistic cultures**, all of society's members are integrated into cohesive in-groups. High individualism is a general aspect of culture in the United States and Europe; low individualism is characteristic of Japanese and other Asian cultural patterns.

The second dimension, **power distance**, is the extent to which the less powerful members of a society accept—even expect—power to be distributed unequally. Hong Kong and France are both high-power-distance cultures; low power distance characterizes Germany, Austria, the Netherlands, and Scandinavia.

Uncertainty avoidance, the third dimension in Hofstede's model, is the extent to which the members of a society are uncomfortable with unclear, ambiguous, or unstructured situations. Members of uncertainty-avoiding cultures may resort to aggressive, emotional, intolerant behavior; they are characterized by a belief in absolute truth. Members of uncertainty-accepting cultures (e.g., Denmark, Sweden, Ireland, and the United States) are more tolerant of persons whose opinions differ from their own.

TABLE 4-2 **Hofstede's Five Dimensions of National Culture**

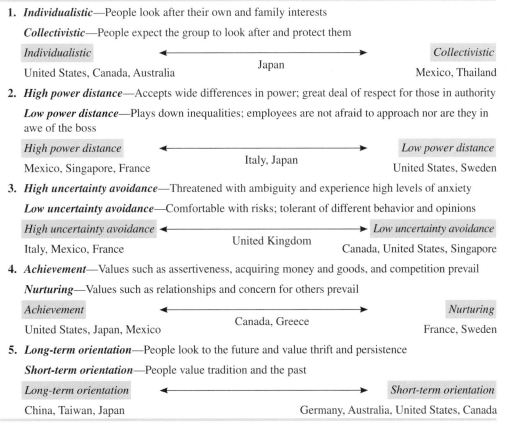

1. *Individualistic*—People look after their own and family interests

    Collectivistic—People expect the group to look after and protect them

Individualistic	← Japan →	*Collectivistic*
United States, Canada, Australia		Mexico, Thailand

2. *High power distance*—Accepts wide differences in power; great deal of respect for those in authority

    Low power distance—Plays down inequalities; employees are not afraid to approach nor are they in awe of the boss

High power distance	← Italy, Japan →	*Low power distance*
Mexico, Singapore, France		United States, Sweden

3. *High uncertainty avoidance*—Threatened with ambiguity and experience high levels of anxiety

    Low uncertainty avoidance—Comfortable with risks; tolerant of different behavior and opinions

High uncertainty avoidance	← United Kingdom →	*Low uncertainty avoidance*
Italy, Mexico, France		Canada, United States, Singapore

4. *Achievement*—Values such as assertiveness, acquiring money and goods, and competition prevail

    Nurturing—Values such as relationships and concern for others prevail

Achievement	← Canada, Greece →	*Nurturing*
United States, Japan, Mexico		France, Sweden

5. *Long-term orientation*—People look to the future and value thrift and persistence

    Short-term orientation—People value tradition and the past

Long-term orientation	← →	*Short-term orientation*
China, Taiwan, Japan		Germany, Australia, United States, Canada

Source: Stephen P. Robbins and Mary Coulter, *Management*, 12th ed. (Upper Saddle River, NJ: Pearson Education, 2014), 87.

Achievement, the fourth dimension, describes a society in which men are expected to be assertive, competitive, and concerned with material success and women fulfill the role of nurturer and are concerned with issues such as the welfare of children. **Nurturing**, by contrast, describes a society in which the social roles of men and women overlap, with neither gender exhibiting overly ambitious or competitive behavior. Japan and Austria rank highest in masculinity; Spain, Taiwan, the Netherlands, and the Scandinavian countries have some of the lowest ratings on this dimension.

Hofstede's research convinced him that, although these four dimensions yield interesting and useful interpretations, they do not provide sufficient insight into possible cultural bases for economic growth. Hofstede was also disturbed by the fact that *Western* social scientists had developed the surveys used in the research. Because many economists had failed to predict the explosive economic development of Japan and the "Asian tigers" (i.e., South Korea, Taiwan, Hong Kong, and Singapore), Hofstede surmised that some cultural dimensions in Asia were eluding the researchers. This methodological problem was remedied by a Chinese Value Survey (CVS) developed by Chinese social scientists in Hong Kong and Taiwan.

The CVS data supported the first three "social behavior" dimensions of culture: power distance, individualism/collectivism, and achievement/nurturing. Uncertainty avoidance, however, did not show up in the survey results. Instead, the CVS revealed a dimension, **long-term orientation (LTO)** versus **short-term orientation**, that had eluded Western researchers.[35] Hofstede interpreted this dimension as concerning "a society's search for virtue," rather than truth. The dimension assesses the sense of immediacy within a culture—that is, whether gratification should be immediate or deferred. Long-term values include *persistence* (perseverance), defined as a general tenacity in the pursuit of a goal. *Ordering relationships* by status reflects the presence of societal hierarchies, and *observing this order* indicates the acceptance of complementary relations. *Thrift* manifests itself in high savings rates. Finally, *a sense of shame* leads to sensitivity in social contacts.

By studying Hofstede's work, marketers can gain insights to guide them in a range of activities, including developing products, interacting with business partners, and conducting sales meetings. For example, understanding the time orientation of one's native culture compared to that of others is crucial (see Table 4-1). In Brazil, India, Japan, and Mexico, building a relationship with a potential business partner takes precedence over transacting the deal. As they say in Latin America, "*Uno no vive para trabajar . . . Uno trabaja para vivir!*" ("One doesn't live to work . . . one works to live!"). Conducting business in this region of the world should never come at the expense of enjoying life. People from cultures that emphasize the short term must adapt to the slower pace of business in some countries with a longer-term orientation.

Similarly, the Japanese notion of *gaman* ("persistence") provides insight into the willingness of Japanese corporations to pursue research and development (R&D) projects for which the odds of short-term success appear low. When Sony licensed the newly invented transistor from Bell Laboratories in the mid-1950s, for example, the limited high-frequency yield (sound output) of the device suggested to American engineers that the most appropriate application would be for a hearing aid. However, *gaman* meant that Sony engineers were not deterred by the slow progress of their efforts to increase the yield from their investment. As Sony cofounder Masaru Ibuka recalled, "To challenge the yield is a very interesting point for us. At that time no one recognized the importance of it." Sony's persistence was rewarded when company engineers eventually made the yield breakthrough that resulted in a wildly successful global product—the pocket-sized transistor radio.[36]

The power distance dimension reflects the degree of trust among members of society. The higher the power distance index (PDI), the lower the level of trust. Organizationally, high PDI finds expression in tall, hierarchical designs; a preference for centralization; and relatively more supervisory personnel. In cultures where respect for hierarchy is high, subordinates may have to navigate through several layers of assistants to get to the boss. In such cultures, superiors may easily intimidate lower-level employees. Research has suggested that, when evaluating alternatives for entering global markets, companies in high-PDI cultures prefer sole ownership of subsidiaries because it provides them with more control. Conversely, companies in low-PDI cultures are more apt to use joint ventures.[37]

J. Byrne Murphy learned about power distance and the differences between U.S.-style individualism and the French style when he was negotiating to build the first American-style designer outlet mall in France. As he recounts in his book *Le Deal*:

> In France, there always seemed to be more glory for those who pursued solo endeavors. . . . Individualism seemed always to be loudly proclaimed, while the praise for team effort seemed to me to be distinctly muted.
>
> I saw this national trait play itself out regularly in our weekly managers meetings. I'd always end each meeting with my exhortation to coordinate all efforts between departments to ensure that there would be no time lost, no surprises.
>
> But there were always surprises.
>
> Each week I'd leave the team meeting full of optimism that this time we were all in the same boat, all coordinated, all members of one disciplined crew team, all pulling our oars together, all moving rapidly forward in a straight line. And the next week I'd realize I was not only full of optimism but also of naiveté. Because I'd discover we weren't in the same boat. We weren't in any boat. A more accurate analogy was that they were running in a footrace, each in separate lanes. Marketing in Lane 1, Sales in Lane 2, Finance in Lane 3, and so on. And as each runner sprinted through the week, they didn't look left or right, or even acknowledge there were other runners. . . .
>
> "Why," I continued to ask myself, "do they all think so differently? Why can't they coordinate their own actions before problems arise?"

Ultimately, Murphy realized that he would have to change his own behavior patterns. He resolved to explain to his managers the American concept of teamwork within the French context; after he did, the project moved forward more smoothly.[38]

Steelcase, a U.S. company that makes office furniture, also uses data about national cultures. Its 11-nation study was used as input to the design process for global customers. Among its findings:[39]

Short term versus long term: Enduring relationships are more valued in India and China than in the United States.

Cooperative (feminine) behaviors versus competitive (masculine) behaviors: Flexible work arrangements such as telecommuting are becoming more common in the Netherlands. By contrast, in India, professionals rarely work from home.

Collectivistic versus individualistic: Expressing the strength of a corporate institution is important in Southern Europe, so lobbies in office buildings tend to be grandiose.

(4-4) The Self-Reference Criterion and Perception

◀ **4-4** Explain how the self-reference criterion can affect decision making at global companies, and provide a step-by-step example of a company adapting to conditions in a global market.

As described earlier in this chapter, a person's perception of market needs is framed by his or her own cultural experience. A framework for systematically reducing perceptual blockage and distortion was developed by James Lee and published in the *Harvard Business Review* in 1966. Lee termed the unconscious reference to one's own cultural values the **self-reference criterion (SRC)**. To address this problem and eliminate or reduce cultural myopia, he proposed a systematic, four-step framework:

1. Define the problem or goal in terms of home-country cultural traits, habits, and norms.
2. Define the problem or goal in terms of host-country cultural traits, habits, and norms. Make no value judgments.
3. Isolate the SRC influence and examine it carefully to see how it complicates the problem.
4. Redefine the problem without the SRC influence and solve for the host-country market situation.[40]

The Walt Disney Company's decision to build a theme park in France provides an excellent vehicle for understanding SRC. While planning their entry into the French market, how might Disney executives have done things differently by using the steps of SRC? Let's start at step 1 and examine Disney's home-country norms; then we will proceed with the remaining steps to see which cultural adapt ations should have been made.

Step 1 Disney executives believe there is virtually unlimited demand for American cultural exports around the world. Evidence includes the success of McDonald's, Coca-Cola, Hollywood movies, and American rock music. Disney has a stellar track record in exporting its American management system and business style (see Exhibit 4-8). Tokyo Disneyland, a virtual carbon copy of the park in Anaheim, California, has been a runaway success. Disney policies prohibit sale or consumption of alcohol inside its theme parks.

Step 2 Europeans in general, and the French in particular, are sensitive about American cultural imperialism. Consuming wine with the midday meal is a long-established custom. Europeans have their own real castles, and many popular Disney characters come from European folk tales.

Step 3 The significant differences revealed by comparing the findings in steps 1 and 2 suggest strongly that the needs upon which the American and Japanese Disney theme parks were based do not exist in France. A modification of this design is needed for European success.

Step 4 This would require the design of a theme park that is more in keeping with French and European cultural norms—that is, allowing the French to put their own identity on the park.

The lesson that the SRC teaches is that a vital, critical skill of the global marketer is unbiased perception—that is, the ability to see what is so in a culture. Although this skill is as valuable at home as it is abroad, it is critical to the global marketer because of the widespread tendency toward ethnocentrism and the use of the SRC. The SRC can be a powerful negative force in global business, and forgetting to check for it can lead to misunderstanding and failure. While planning Euro Disney, former Disney Chairman Michael Eisner and other company executives were blinded by a potent combination of their own prior success and ethnocentrism. Clearly, this approach was not the best one. Today, the park is known as Disneyland Paris; a second venue, Walt Disney Studios Park, was launched in 2002 to encourage multi-day visits. Although it is a top tourist destination, the venture has experienced financial losses in all but a handful of years. Avoiding the SRC requires a person to suspend assumptions based on prior experience and success and to be prepared to acquire new knowledge about human behavior and motivation.

Exhibit 4-8 Disneyland Shanghai opened its doors on June 6, 2016. The specific date—6/16/2016—was chosen for a reason: "Six" sounds like the word *liu* in Chinese, and means "smooth."
Source: Ng Han Guan/Associated Press.

ENTREPRENEURIAL LEADERSHIP, CREATIVE THINKING, AND THE GLOBAL STARTUP

Huda Kattan, Huda Beauty

Huda Kattan is one of a new breed of entrepreneurs and influencers. Born in the United States to an Iraqi immigrant family settled in Oklahoma, she was bullied for much of her childhood because of her ethnicity to the point that she began to go by the name Heidi in school. After turning 12, to boost her self-confidence and fit in better, she started using make-up. It was an introduction to a lifelong passion as well as a means of re-embracing her identity: it would lead her to begin calling herself Huda again, and years later, that would be the name of her own make-up brand: Huda Beauty.

Make-up remained her abiding interest when she settled in Dubai with her husband and a career in finance. She found that there were no bloggers who looked like her—Mediterranean or Middle Eastern—or could offer the kind of make-up inspiration she needed. She decided to start her own website that would offer beauty tips, make-up tutorials, how-to videos and skin-care regimes—a space for women to explore and share their ideas about beauty.

The blog was a huge success, spurring Huda and her sisters in 2013 to launch Huda Beauty in Dubai. She started selling more beauty products on her website and, crucially, on Instagram, where she currently has more than 35 million followers. Instagram was still an emerging trend and in its early stages in the Middle East, and Kattan's decision to explore its possibilities for her business is a good reflection of how entrepreneurs can synchronize their marketing strategy with changing cultures for better success. Kattan has admitted that Instagram was the catalyst in spurring the growth of her brand, allowing her to connect with and inspire people around the world.

As of 2018, the brand has brought in at least $200 million each year in revenue and now sells around 140 beauty products, from eye lashes to lip gloss. Huda Beauty's products are not only sold through its online channel but also in more than 900 stores in the United States and in 600 stores around the world. The net worth of Kattan's beauty empire is around $550 million, and she has made it to Forbes' list of America's Richest Self-Made Women, joining the ranks of Oprah Winfrey and Kylie Jenner.

As one of the pioneers among new influencers, Huda has become an inspiration to businesswomen in the Middle East as well as the rest of the world. Social media influencers like Huda have had a huge impact on the beauty market in the United Arab Emirates; many more customers now use beauty products, and per-capita spending on them in the country rose to $228 million in 2017 from $168 million in 2010.

Beauty brands that have a strong social media presence tend to keep their consumers engaged. This requires a digitally connected user and follower base. As social media platforms continue to be very popular as a means of expression and learning in Saudi Arabia and the United Arab Emirates, this has never been a problem there. In fact, thanks to its large expat population and high levels of disposable incomes, the United Arab Emirates is an ideal market for beauty brands and has welcomed many international retail stores, including Sephora, Kiko Milano, Anastasia Beverly Hills, and Nars.

As Huda Kattan was familiar with the traditions and culture of her country, she was able to incorporate them extensively within the representation of her brand and craft her products accordingly. She also saw that make-up is a way of making a statement—and thereby empowering—for women in the Middle East. However, as is the case for many other entrepreneurs, Huda Kattan's success is also based on global accessibility and opportunities provided by the Internet to reach out to and engage with a wider range of people from different parts of the world.

Sources: S. McClear, "Why Huda Kattan Is One of Beauty's Most Influential Women," *Allure*, June 28, 2017, https://www.allure.com/story/huda-kattan-profile; Z. Mejia, "How This Self-Made Millionaire and Instagram Star Built Her Billion-Dollar Beauty Brand," *CNBC Make It*, October 29, 2018, https://www.cnbc.com/2018/10/29/how-self-made-millionaire-huda-kattan-built-her-billion-dollar-beauty-brand.html; C. Sorvino, "How Huda Kattan Built a Billion-Dollar Cosmetics Brand With 26 Million Followers," *Forbes*, July 11, 2018, https://www.forbes.com/sites/chloesorvino/2018/07/11/huda-kattan-huda-beauty-billion-influencer/#615bf1da6120; C. Wischhover, "How Entrepreneur and Beauty Sensations Huda Kattan Handles Intsa-fame", *Fashionista*, October 20, 2017, https://fashionista.com/2015/11/huda-kattan-beauty-blogger.

Exhibit 4-9 Huda Beauty emerged out of a desire to create a space for women to explore and share their ideas about beauty.
Source: Brian Chase/Shutterstock.

▶ **4-5** Analyze the components of diffusion theory and its applicability to global marketing.

4-5 Diffusion Theory[41]

Hundreds of studies have described the process by which an individual adopts a new idea. Sociologist Everett Rogers reviewed these studies and discovered a pattern of remarkably similar findings. Rogers then distilled the research into three concepts that are extremely useful to global marketers: the adoption process, characteristics of innovations, and adopter categories. Taken together, these concepts constitute Rogers's **diffusion of innovation** framework.

An innovation is something new. When applied to a product, "new" can mean different things. In an absolute sense, once a product has been introduced anywhere in the world, it is no longer an innovation, because it is no longer new to the world. Relatively speaking, however, a product already introduced in one market may be an innovation elsewhere because it is new and different for the targeted market. Global marketing often entails just such product introductions. Managers find themselves marketing products that may be, simultaneously, innovations in some markets and mature or even declining products in others.

The Adoption Process

One of the basic elements of Rogers's diffusion theory is the concept of an **adoption process**—the mental stages through which an individual passes from the time of his or her first knowledge of an innovation to the time of product adoption or purchase. Rogers suggests that an individual passes through five different stages in proceeding from first knowledge of a product to the final adoption or purchase of that product: awareness, interest, evaluation, trial, and adoption.

1. *Awareness:* In the first stage, the customer becomes aware for the first time of the product or innovation. Studies have shown that at this stage, impersonal sources of information such as mass-media advertising are most important. An important early communication objective in global marketing is to create awareness of a new product through general exposure to advertising messages.
2. *Interest:* During this stage, the customer is interested enough to learn more. The customer has focused his or her attention on communications relating to the product and will engage in research activities and seek out additional information.
3. *Evaluation:* In this stage the individual mentally assesses the product's benefits in relation to present and anticipated future needs and, based on this judgment, decides whether to try it.
4. *Trial:* Most customers will not purchase expensive products without the "hands-on" experience marketers call a "trial." A good example of a product trial that does not involve purchase is the automobile test drive. For health care products and other inexpensive consumer packaged goods, a trial often involves actual purchase. Marketers frequently induce a trial by distributing free samples. For inexpensive products, an initial single purchase is defined as a trial.
5. *Adoption:* At this point, the individual either makes an initial purchase (in the case of the more expensive product) or continues to purchase—adopts and exhibits brand loyalty to— the less expensive product.

Studies show that as a person moves from evaluation through a trial to adoption, personal sources of information are more important than impersonal sources. It is during these stages that sales representatives and word of mouth become major persuasive forces affecting the decision to buy.

Characteristics of Innovations

In addition to describing the product adoption process, Rogers identified five major **characteristics of innovations**. These factors, which affect the rate at which innovations are adopted, are relative advantage, compatibility, complexity, divisibility, and communicability.

1. *Relative advantage:* How a new product compares with existing products or methods in the eyes of customers. The perceived relative advantage of a new product versus existing products is a major influence on the rate of adoption. If a product has a substantial relative advantage vis-à-vis the competition, it is likely to gain quick acceptance. When compact disc players were first introduced in the early 1980s, industry observers predicted that only audiophiles would care enough about digital sound—and have enough money—to purchase them.

In reality, the sonic advantages of CDs compared to LPs were obvious to the mass market; as prices for CD players plummeted, the 12-inch black vinyl LP was rendered virtually extinct in less than a decade. (But vinyl is making a comeback!)

2. *Compatibility:*   The extent to which a product is consistent with existing values and past experiences of adopters. The history of innovations in international marketing is replete with failures caused by the lack of compatibility of new products in the target market. For example, the first consumer VCR, the Sony Betamax, ultimately failed because it could record for only 1 hour. Most buyers wanted to record movies and sports events; thus they shunned the Betamax in favor of VHS-format VCRs, which could record 4 hours of programming.

3. *Complexity:*   The degree to which an innovation or new product is difficult to understand and use. Product complexity is a factor that can slow down the rate of adoption, particularly in developing country markets with low rates of literacy. In the 1990s, dozens of global companies developed new, interactive, multimedia consumer electronics products. Complexity was a key design issue; it was a standing joke that in most households, VCR clocks flashed "12:00" because users didn't know how to set them. To achieve mass success, new products have to be as simple to use as, for example, slipping a prerecorded DVD into a DVD player.

4. *Divisibility:*   The ability of a product to be tried and used on a limited basis without great expense. Wide discrepancies in income levels around the globe result in major differences in preferred purchase quantities, serving sizes, and product portions. For example, CPC International's Hellmann's mayonnaise was simply not selling in U.S.-size jars in Latin America, but sales took off after the company placed the mayonnaise in small plastic packets. The plastic packets were within the food budgets of local consumers, and they required no refrigeration—another plus.

5. *Communicability:*   The degree to which the benefits of an innovation or the value of a product may be communicated to a potential market. A new digital cassette recorder from Philips was a market failure, in part because advertisements did not clearly communicate the fact that the product could make CD-quality recordings using new cassette technology while still playing older, analog tapes.

Adopter Categories

Adopter categories are classifications of individuals within a market on the basis of innovativeness. Hundreds of studies of the diffusion of innovation demonstrate that, at least in the Western world, adoption is a social phenomenon that is characterized by a normal distribution curve (see Figure 4-3).

Five categories have been assigned to the segments of this normal distribution. The first 2.5 percent of people to purchase a product are defined as innovators; the next 13.5 percent are early adopters; the next 34 percent are the early majority; the next 34 percent are the late majority; and the final 16 percent are laggards. Studies show that innovators tend to be venturesome, more

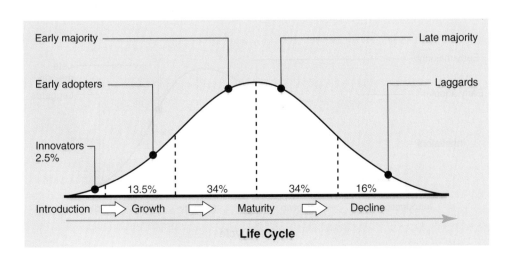

FIGURE 4-3 Adopter Categories

cosmopolitan in their social relationships, and wealthier than those who adopt products later. Early adopters are the most influential people in their communities, even more so than the innovators. Thus, the early adopters are a critical group in the adoption process, and they have great influence on the early and late majorities, who account for the bulk of the adopters of any product. Several characteristics of early adopters stand out: They tend to be younger, with higher social status, and in a more favorable financial position than later adopters. They must be responsive to mass-media information sources and must learn about innovations from these sources, because they cannot simply copy the behavior of innovators.

One of the major reasons for the normal distribution of adopter categories is the *interaction effect*—that is, the process through which individuals who have adopted an innovation influence others. Adoption of a new idea or product is the result of human interaction in a social system. If the first adopter of an innovation or new product discusses it with two other people, and each of those two adopters passes the new idea along to two other people, and so on, the resulting distribution yields a normal bell shape when plotted.[42]

Diffusion of Innovations in Pacific Rim Countries

Based on a cross-national comparison of the United States, Japan, South Korea, and Taiwan, Takada and Jain presented evidence that different country characteristics—in particular, culture and communication patterns—affect diffusion processes for room air conditioners, washing machines, and calculators. Proceeding from the observation that Japan, South Korea, and Taiwan are high-context cultures with relatively homogeneous populations, whereas the United States is a low-context, heterogeneous culture, Takada and Jain surmised that Asia would show faster rates of diffusion than the United States (see Figure 4-4).

A second hypothesis supported by the research was that adoption would proceed more quickly in markets where innovations were introduced relatively late. Presumably, the lag time would give potential consumers more opportunity to assess the relative advantages, compatibility, and other product attributes. Takada and Jain's research has important marketing implications. These authors noted: "If a marketing manager plans to enter the newly industrializing countries (NICs) or other Asia markets with a product that has proved to be successful in the home market, the product's diffusion processes are likely to be much faster than in the home market."[43]

▶ **4-6** Explain the marketing implications of different social and cultural environments around the globe.

(4-6) Marketing Implications of Social and Cultural Environments

The various cultural factors described earlier can exert important influences on marketing of consumer and industrial products around the globe; thus, they must be recognized and incorporated into a global marketing plan. **Environmental sensitivity** reflects the extent to which products must be adapted to the culture-specific needs of different national markets. A useful approach

FIGURE 4-4 Asian Hierarchy for Diffusion of Innovation

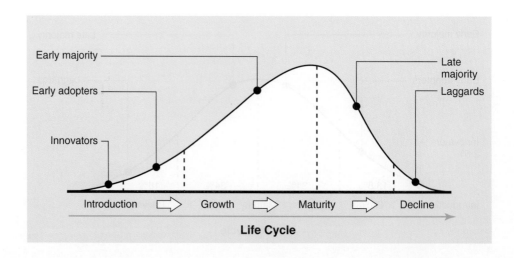

is to view products as being located on a continuum of environmental sensitivity. At one end of the continuum are environmentally insensitive products that do not require significant adaptation to the environments of various world markets. At the other end of the continuum are products that are highly sensitive to different environmental factors. A company with environmentally insensitive products will spend relatively less time determining the specific and unique conditions of local markets because the product is basically universal. The greater a product's environmental sensitivity, the greater the need for managers to address country-specific economic, regulatory, technological, social, and cultural environmental conditions.

The sensitivity of products can be represented on a two-dimensional scale, as shown in Figure 4-5. The horizontal axis shows environmental sensitivity, and the vertical axis the degree for product adaptation needed. Any product exhibiting low levels of environmental sensitivity—integrated circuits, for example—belongs in the lower left of the figure. Intel has sold more than 100 million microprocessors because a chip is a chip anywhere around the world. Moving to the right on the horizontal axis, the level of sensitivity increases, as does the amount of adaptation needed. Computers exhibit moderate levels of environmental sensitivity; for example, variations in country voltage requirements require some adaptation. In addition, the computer's software documentation should be in the local language.

At the upper right of Figure 4-5 are products with high environmental sensitivity. Food sometimes falls into this category because it is sensitive to climate and culture. As we saw in the McDonald's case at the end of Chapter 1, this fast-food giant has achieved great success outside the United States by adapting its menu items to local tastes. General Electric's turbine equipment may also appear on the high-sensitivity end of the continuum; in many countries, local equipment manufacturers receive preferential treatment when bidding on national projects.

Research studies show that, independent of social class and income, culture is a significant influence on consumption behavior and durable goods ownership.[44] Consumer products are probably more sensitive to cultural differences than are industrial products. Abraham Maslow, a psychologist who studied human motivation, developed a hierarchy of needs ranging from the most basic needs to the more abstract. Hunger is a basic physiological need in Maslow's hierarchy; humans share a biological imperative to obtain a meal, but what we *want* to eat can be strongly influenced by culture. Evidence from the front lines of the marketing wars suggests that food is probably the most sensitive category of consumer products. The ongoing controversy about genetically modified organisms (GMOs) in the food supply is a case in point. American consumers are generally accepting of foods containing GMO ingredients; Europeans are much less accepting.

Thirst, like hunger, shows how needs differ from wants. Humans all have a biological imperative to secure hydration to sustain life (see Exhibit 4-10). As is the case with food and cooking,

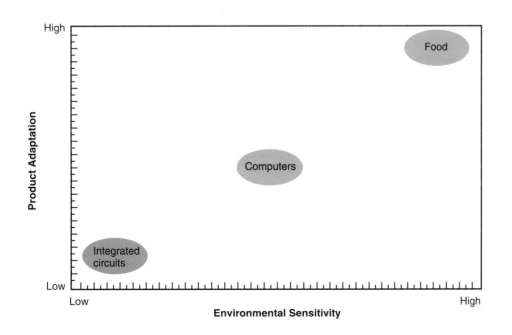

FIGURE 4-5 Environmental Sensitivity Versus Product Adaptation

Exhibit 4-10 In countries where water from the tap or well may be contaminated, bottled water is a convenient alternative. The fastest growth in the industry is occurring in developing countries; in the past five years, bottled water consumption has tripled in India and more than doubled in China. Many consumers also choose bottled water as an alternative to other beverage choices. However, the Earth Policy Institute and other groups view bottled water as an overpriced, wasteful extravagance. The International Bottled Water Association disagrees with that view. A spokesman said, "We're an on-the-go society demanding convenient packaging and consistent quality, and that's what bottled water provides."
Source: Gurinder Osan/AP Images.

however, the particular liquids people *want* to drink can be strongly influenced by culture. Coffee is a beverage category that illustrates the point. Coffee has been consumed for centuries on the European continent. By contrast, Britain has historically been a nation of tea drinkers, a legacy of the East India Company's exploits in India and China. Britons from all walks of life ascribe a variety of medicinal properties to "a nice cup of tea," and the custom of taking afternoon tea is firmly entrenched in British culture.[45] In the 1970s, tea outsold coffee by a ratio of 4 to 1.

Brits who did drink coffee tended to buy it in instant form, because the preparation of instant coffee is similar to that of tea. By the 1990s, however, Britain was experiencing an economic boom and an explosion of new nightclubs and restaurants. Trendy Londoners looking for a nonpub "third place" found it in the form of Seattle Coffee Company cafés. An instant success after the first store was opened by coffee-starved Americans in 1995, by 1998 Seattle Coffee had 65 stores around London. Starbucks bought the business from Seattle Coffee's founders for $84 million. Today, Starbucks has overcome the challenge of high real estate prices and has more than 345 company-operated cafés in the United Kingdom.[46]

Summary

Culture, a society's "programming of the mind," has both a pervasive and a changing influence on each national market environment. Global marketers must recognize the influence of culture and be prepared to either respond to it or change it. Human behavior is a function of a person's own unique personality and that person's interaction with the collective forces of the particular society and culture in which he or she has lived. In particular, *attitudes*, *values*, and *beliefs* can vary significantly from country to country. Also, differences pertaining to religion, *aesthetics*, dietary customs, and language and communication can affect local reaction to a company's brands or products as well as the ability of company personnel to function effectively in different cultures. A number of concepts and theoretical frameworks provide insights into these and other cultural issues.

Cultures can be classified as *high* or *low context*; communication and negotiation styles can, in turn, differ from country to country. Hofstede's social values typology helps marketers understand culture in terms of *power distance*, *individualism* versus *collectivism*, *achievement* versus *nurturing*, *uncertainty avoidance*, and *long-term* versus *short-term orientation*. By understanding the *self-reference criterion*, global marketers can overcome people's unconscious tendency for perceptual blockage and distortion.

Rogers's classic study on the *diffusion of innovation* helps explain how products are adopted over time by different *adopter categories*. The *adoption process* that consumers go through can be divided into a multistage *hierarchy of effects*. Rogers's findings concerning the *characteristics of innovations* can also help marketers successfully launch new products in global markets. Research has suggested that Asian adopter categories differ from those found in the Western model. An awareness of *environmental sensitivity* can help marketers determine whether consumer and industry products must be adapted to the needs of different markets.

Discussion Questions

4-1. Compare "material culture" and "nonmaterial culture." Why is it important for global marketers to understand the relationship between them?

4-2. What is the difference between a low-context culture and a high-context culture? Name a country that is an example of each type and offer evidence for your answer.

4-3. How important is the self-reference criterion to global marketers in analyzing culture?

4-4. Briefly explain the social research of Everett Rogers on the topics of diffusion of innovation, characteristics of innovations, and adopter categories. How does the adoption process in Asia differ from the traditional Western model?

CASE 4-1 *Continued (refer to page 129)*

Cotton, Clothing Consumption, Culture: From Small Beginnings to a Global Cultural System

Cotton and Clothing across Cultures

Cotton is an integral part of clothing in societies and cultures across the world. It is crucial to cotton-producing countries as well as to those importing it. According to estimates, cotton supplies more than 70 percent of clothing used by men and boys; meanwhile, 60 percent of women's garments have cotton fibers and 40 percent of their clothing are made from 100 percent cotton. It is also used in industrial products such as zipper tapes, wall coverings, bookbinding, medical supplies, and tarpaulins.

To some extent, clothing—cotton or otherwise—can be used to differentiate one national culture from another, in terms of individualism, collectivism, power distance, and other dimensions per Hofstede's framework. In fact, it is one of the core indicators that determine levels of enculturation and acculturation. In enculturation, which involves learning about one's own culture, clothing and attire become a means of fulfilling this process. For instance, parents introduce their children to a way of dressing that they have likely adopted in relation to their specific cultural settings. By extension, cotton can play a significant role in this.

When people travel abroad or interact with another cultural system, they undergo acculturation, which is about learning other people's cultures. For example, a study on clothing acculturation among Black African women in London showed that women in a new cultural context tend to acquire the clothing consumption patterns of others. However, the study also noted the influence of other factors, such as religion, age, and weather conditions. Moreover, social factors also play a significant role in how people embrace the mode of dressing in the host cultural system. While, on one hand, the study showed that women's clothing becomes reflective of their acculturation in the host cultural system, there are times when their clothing reflects a sense

of nostalgia. This occurs when the clothes they choose to wear are in some way representative of their home culture (Africa, in this case) in their host cultural environment (the United Kingdom) during special cultural events like weddings, naming ceremonies, etc. that bring them together as an ethnic group. In addition, most of these women tend to be immigrants concentrated in the country's cosmopolitan centers, further encouraging the use of clothing that reminds them of their home countries.

Given the link between cotton and clothing, cotton's influence and impact on every facet of the socio-cultural dimensions of the global marketing system cannot be overstated.

Cotton's Supply Chain

There are three main types of cotton: conventional, organic, and genetically modified (GM). Conventional cotton is vulnerable to a large number of pests and heavily dependent on the use of agrochemicals. GM cotton, on the other hand, is from produced using biotechnology and usually generates higher yields. Meanwhile, organic cotton—so defined because of its low impact on the environment—is one of the most popular of all the organic fibers. The production systems associated with organic cotton reduce the use of fertilizers and toxic and persistent pesticides; they also replenish and maintain soil fertility while building biologically diverse agriculture.

Meanwhile, the popularity of cotton all over the world shows in the numbers. In 2010–11, about 219,000 farmers in 20 countries, including China, the United States, Burkina Faso, Brazil, and India, grew organic cotton. This number can only have increased since then, reacting to major developments in virtually all dimensions of the global marketing environment. This period has witnessed population shifts, technological advancement, and economic growth, all of which have been hugely influential in the dynamics of cotton production and consumption over the years and will surely introduce further significant changes to the system.

Global cotton production in 2017 is reported at 120.86 million bales, but it is important to note that there have been instances where production figures have dwindled but the popularity of cotton for consumption has remained strong. For instance, a report by the United States Department of Agriculture (USDA) estimates that world cotton consumption will exceed production in the year 2019–20. Although the report states that world cotton production will increase to 126.5 million bales in that year, this will represent a fall of 6.9 percent compared to previous records. On the other hand, the world cotton consumption for the same period is estimated at 125.5 million bales, an increase of 1.5 percent over the previous year.

Based on their role in satisfying the world's demand for cotton, India, China, and the United States are the largest producers, responsible for over half of the total production volume in the world. Cotton is essential to the thriving textile industry in the United States; about 7.5 million bales of cotton are used by its textile mills annually. These are used in several forms in the country: approximately 57 percent is converted into apparel, about a third is used in home furnishings, and the rest is largely used in industrial cotton-based products. Although China is the leading producer of cotton, it uses most of the cotton grown internally; the United States is the second-largest producer of cotton and ships between 40 and 60 percent of it to other nations. This is a noteworthy dynamic in terms of the global supply chain of cotton.

Drivers of Cotton Consumption

Cotton is the world's most commonly used natural fiber, and 2.5 percent of the world's arable land is used to grow it. But what makes cotton so popular around the world? One of the main reasons is its versatility. As we have seen, it is widely used not only in clothing and homeware but also for industrial purposes. In clothing, cotton is notably good for moisture control because of its absorbent properties. Cotton also finds uses in all weather conditions, and clothes made from cotton are hypo-allergic, which means that they do not irritate the skin (this is why clothing for babies, who have especially sensitive skin, is often made out of cotton). Cotton clothing is durable too; it can withstand the pressures of washing by hand as well as by machine, and it does not require extended washing periods. Cotton clothing is also less likely to be toxic than synthetic fibers. Finally, cotton clothing is comfortable, hence its common use in underwear and undershirts.

Beyond apparel, cotton is also used to make fishnets, archival paper, and other products that are vital for businesses and organizations irrespective of size, sector, or location. Cottonseed serves as fodder for cattle and can be crushed to make oil, which is used not only in cooking but also as input for the production of several other products, such as margarine, soap, cosmetics, and pharmaceuticals. The USDA's report cited previously shows that the prices of cotton prices were competitive compared to polyester, and this trend is expected to continue for the year 2018–19.

Fair Treatment for Producers

The discourse on ethics, sustainability, and the environment now pervades a range of sectors, including manufacturing, retailing, and services. A number of issues link cotton to sustainability, including ethical consumerism in relation to cotton usage and production, the clothing industry, and the use of toxic pesticides. Among the most prominent of these are fair treatment for stakeholders involved in cotton production and sustainable practices relating to cotton as a product.

Fair trade is a major socio-cultural issue. Criticism has been leveled at some countries, including China, Burkina Faso, Pakistan, and India, with respect to allegations of forced labor in cotton production. One example is Uzbekistan, where coercion is allegedly used not only to force farmers to grow cotton but also to press over one million citizens from other professions, including doctors and teachers, into picking cotton for a few weeks every year. A related issue of great concern in the production of cotton is child labor. According to the International Labor Organization (ILO), some cotton-producing countries engage children in manual harvesting, weeding, irrigation, crop protection, hybridization, and ginning. The ILO identifies poverty, a weak legislative

Exhibit 4-11 An organic cotton label is a noteworthy badge of pride in global fashion marketing.
Source: Andrey_Popov/Shutterstock.

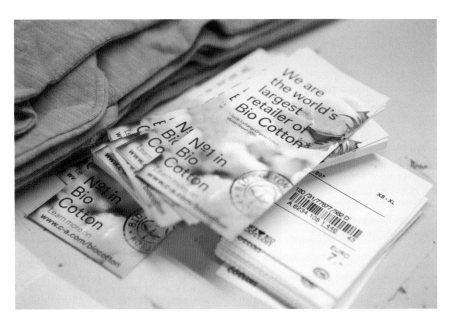

Exhibit 4-12 Organic cotton fashion items are favorites of environmental conscious consumers, even at a premium price.
Source: Mile 91/C & A Foundation/Alamy Stock Photo

environment, local social norms, migration, barriers to education, and cheap and compliant labor as some of the factors that contribute to child labor in the countries where it is rampant. Efforts are being led by the ILO to curb these practices in cotton-producing countries.

Like all crops, cotton needs water, and the production of cotton goods needs still more. For example, producing a pair of jeans that weighs 800 grams requires 8,000 liters of water. By and large, the average water footprint of cotton fabric is 10,000 liters per kilogram annually. This, of course, contributes to water scarcity and has larger implications for the planet. Take Indian cotton as an example: the water it takes to grow the cotton that the country exports could serve the needs of 85 percent of its people. The crop not only uses 2.5 percent of the world's cultivated land but also 16 percent of its insecticides, which surpasses the requirements of other major crops. Attention is being increasingly focused on GM cotton. According to the International Service for the Acquisition of Agri-Biotech Applications, GM cotton constitutes 64 percent of cotton grown in 2016, and it is expected that this number will continue to grow, as many of the high-street clothing companies have pledged toward more sustainability in their sourcing. In May 2017, Tesco, F&F, ASOS, Sainsbury's, Levi, and Kering signed the Sustainable Cotton Communique, which set a target for sourcing 100 percent sustainable cotton by 2025. Meanwhile, H&M and FatFace have committed to achieving this even earlier, by 2020. These figures indicate the advances in the responsible source network on business ethics. The clamor for companies to "go clean" on ethical production of cotton is an ongoing phenomenon sustained by the media, NGOs, and other campaigners. For instance, an article by Jane Turner in *Ethical Consumer* titled "The Ethics of Cotton Production" lays out a metric to rate companies on their compliance to sustainability. As described in this article, If any firm does not source 100 percent organic cotton or fails to be 100 percent fair trade, it will lose half a mark in the "Ethical Consumers' Pollution" and "Toxic and Controversial Technologies" categories.

Cotton Moves Upmarket

Although the idea of organic cotton started several years ago with just a few countries looking for ways to contribute to environmental sustainability, the record of companies following this trend is improving. Organizations are now embracing the idea of being certified to traceability standards like Organic Exchange, while a good number of the cotton manufacturers also adhere to the Global Organic Textile Standard (GOTS), which relates to textile processing stages and good labor provisions. Organic fiber is now being used in several products such as fabrics, home furnishings, blankets, bathrobes, and towels. It is also becoming commonplace in care items like make-up removal pads, ear swabs, and sanitary products. Organic cotton is, of course, also used in several types and styles of clothing. It is particularly appealing to the growing segment of eco-conscious consumers who are willing to pay a premium for greener products.

Cashing in on Higher Cotton Consumption

Fashion is one of the most dynamic elements of modern socio-cultural systems, and many fashion companies all over the world seek to leverage this. For example, the top five fashion companies in the world based on their revenue in 2018 were U.S. giants L Brands and Gap, with revenues of $12.6 billion and $15.9 billion, respectively; and Fast Retailing Co., at $18.2 billion; H&M, at $22.7 billion, and Inditex, at $28.8 billion. How do these brands thrive in the turbulent global marketing environment? The answer lies in their focus on meeting the dynamic needs of their customers all over the world. As people's taste for cotton clothing continues to grow each year, it is reasonable to expect that these companies will continue to benefit by serving their customers throughout the global market.

Meanwhile, other fashion companies are exploring the consumers' interest in cotton as well. Brands like Marks & Spencer, Tesco, Asos, and Burberry have been cited as particularly engaged in issues of sustainability and fair wages. They have recognized that consumers are not only interested in the usual product-related attributes like how to wash the apparel and whether it shrinks after washing; they are looking at the products' production procedures, like whether it meets ISO9000/14000 or OekoTEx Standard 100. Studies indicates that consumers who are highly knowledgeable show a more positive attitude to organic clothing and are willing to pay as much as 50 percent more to acquire them.

Discussion Questions

4-5. To what extent does the consumption of cotton differentiate particular cultural contexts from others?

4-6. The marketing records of the fashion retailers highlighted in the case suggest that cotton clothing is a major success. What do you think should be done by these and organizations in related businesses to ensure that this success is maintained and built upon in the future?

4-7. The case indicates that some cotton-producing countries need to improve their ethical standards. What measures do you think could be put in place to ensure significant improvement on this front and in global sustainable cotton production?

4-8. Assume you have been invited to speak on the topic "Global Cotton Consumption: The Good, the Bad, and the Ugly." What key points would you cover?

4-9. Do you think the adoption process in Roger's product diffusion theory is applicable to cotton-related products? Justify your standpoint with examples.

Sources: J.H. Fewkes, "Living in the Material World: Cosmopolitanism and Trade in Early Twentieth Century Ladakh," *Modern Asian Studies*, 46(2) (2012), pp. 259–281; T. Roy, "Consumption of Cotton Cloth in India, 1795–1940," *Australian Economic History Review*, 52(1) (2012), pp. 61-84; L. Fayet and W. J. Vermeulen, "Supporting Smallholders to Access Sustainable Supply Chains: Lessons from the Indian Cotton Supply Chain," *Sustainable Development*, 22(5) (2014), pp. 289–310; A. Khare and G. Varshneya, "Antecedents to Organic Cotton Clothing Purchase Behaviour: Study on Indian Youth," *Journal of Fashion Marketing and Management: An International Journal*, 21(1) (2017), pp. 51–69; B. Menapace, "Cotton Prices Could Reach Five-Year High Next Year—What Increased Costs, Environmental Impacts and More Mean for Apparel," *Promo Marketing Magazine*, April 4, 2018, https://magazine.promomarketing.com/article/cotton-prices-trends-availability-popularity (accessed March 4, 2019); K. Oh and L. Abraham, "Effect of Knowledge on Decision Making in the Context of Organic Cotton Clothing," *International Journal of Consumer Studies*, 40(1) (2016), pp. 66–74, History of Cotton, http://www.historyofclothing.com/textile-history/history-of-cotton/ (accessed March 4, 2019); S. Olanubi, "Top Five Largest Fashion Retailers in the World," *Tharawat Magazine*, November 15, 2018, https://www.tharawat-magazine.com/facts/top-5-largest-fashion-clothing-retailers-world/#gs.3b2l8f (accessed March 28, 2019); ILO, "Child Labour in Cotton: A Briefing" (2016), http://www.ilo.org/ipec/Informationresources/WCMS_IPEC_PUB_29655/lang--en/index.htm (accessed March 27, 2019); Organic Trade Association, "Organic Cotton Facts," https://ota.com/sites/default/files/indexed_files/Organic-Cotton-Facts.pdf (accessed March 28, 2019); C. Hopley, "A History of the British Cotton Industry," *British Heritage Travel*, July 29, 2006, https://britishheritage.com/british-textiles-clothe-the-world (accessed March 28, 2019); USDA, "USDA's 94th Annual Agricultural Outlook Forum: The Roots of Prosperity," February 22–23, 2018, https://www.usda.gov/oce/forum/2018/commodities/Cotton.pdf (accessed March 28, 2019); A. Gbadamosi, "Acculturation: An Exploratory Study of Clothing Consumption among Black African Women in London (UK)," *Journal of Fashion Marketing and Management: An International Journal*, 16(1), pp. 5–20; USDA, "USDA's 95th Annual Agricultural Outlook Forum: Growing Locally, Selling Locally," February 22, 2019, https://www.usda.gov/oce/forum/2019/outlooks/Cotton.pdf (accessed March 28, 2019); S. Laville, "Six UK Fashion Retailers Fail to Cotton On to Sustainability," *The Guardian*, January 31, 2019, https://www.theguardian.com/fashion/2019/jan/31/six-uk-fashion-retailers-fail-to-cotton-on-to-sustainability-environment (accessed March 28, 2019); J. Turner, "The Ethics of Cotton Production," *Ethical Consumer*, August 11, 2017, https://www.ethicalconsumer.org/fashion-clothing/ethics-cotton-production (accessed March 28, 2019); JVC Groups, "6 Reasons Why You Should Wear Cotton Made Clothing," December 26, 2018, https://www.jvgroup.in/6-reasons-why-you-should-wear-cotton-clothing/ (accessed March 28, 2019); S. Howell, (n.d.) "How Much of the World's Clothing Is Made from Cotton?", https://www.livestrong.com/article/1001371-much-worlds-clothing-made-cotton/ (accessed March 28, 2019); "Cotton: Statistics and Facts," *Statista*, https://www.statista.com/topics/1542/cotton/ (accessed March 28, 2019).

CASE 4-2
Dubai's Evolution from a Fishing Village to the Host of Expo 2020

Located along the shoreline of the Persian Gulf and emerging from the sands of the Arabian Desert is one of the world's fastest-growing cities—Dubai, in the United Arab Emirates. The population of Dubai is around 3 million, of which 85 percent are expatriates and only 15 percent are native Emiratis. People from over 200 nationalities reside in Dubai, and a majority of the city's population is in the age group of 25 to 54 years because of this mostly young working expatriate demographic.

Although the city now brims with skyscrapers and boasts some of the world's most amazing structures, it used to be little more than a fishing village, and its people depended for their livelihood on fishing, pearl diving, boat building, and providing lodging to gold, spice, and textile traders journeying across the desert. Gold, spices, and traditional textiles are still the cultural ornaments that represent Dubai's history and are popular in their *souqs*. Traditionally, these *souqs* were open markets in narrow streets, and they have been showcased in many tourism videos (like Dubai Tourism's award-winning #BeMyGuest campaign, which we discuss later) as an ingrained part of the city's heritage with special cultural and economic significance for its people.

With the discovery of oil in the 1950s and 1960s, Dubai's development and economy received a huge boost, and various projects were initiated to establish the city as a leading trading hub. This started Dubai's transformation from a small port city into a modern, cosmopolitan city. On December 2, 1971, the Emirate of Dubai joined its five neighboring emirates—Abu Dhabi, Sharjah, Ajman, Umm Al Quwain, and Fujairah—to form the United Arab Emirates. The seventh emirate, Ras Al Khaimah, joined the federation one year later. Since its formation, the country has been progressing at a rapid pace and its leadership has undertaken various developmental efforts to reduce its dependence on oil and diversify its economy.

Over the last four decades, Dubai has also successfully built a mix of diversified economic drivers, including information technology, real estate, construction, finance and trade, tourism and hospitality, and aviation. Such diversification has fueled the growth of the emirate and has increased its global popularity as a place to visit. The development and progress made in the commercial and financial sector of the city, along with its growth in trade, logistics, tourism, and real estate have contributed to Dubai's emergence as a business hub.

Tourism is one of the main pillars of this diversified economy. In 2018, Dubai was the world's sixth most-visited city after Hong Kong, Bangkok, London, Paris, and Singapore, with the size of its tourism sector reaching around $30 billion. At 2.1 million, Indian travelers represented the largest group of tourists to Dubai, accounting for nearly 13 percent of the total number of tourists. This was followed by tourists from Saudi Arabia and the United Kingdom. These countries have been considered traditional markets that contribute significantly to increasing tourism in Dubai. Dubai has also started targeting newer markets, with campaigns running in 44 additional markets since 2017. As a result, there has been an increase in the number of tourists from other countries, like Russia, Germany, and China. According to *Khaleej Times*, Chinese tourism to Dubai showed a year-over-year increase of 41.4 percent between 2016 and 2017.

The government of Dubai has also established various free zones across the city that have promoted foreign investment and business activity. This has encouraged global business tourists to visit Dubai and explore the opportunities it offers. Many people, particularly from Southeast Asia, travel to Dubai seeking business and employment opportunities, drawn by its booming economy and promises of high income and standards of living.

Dubai's growth as one of the top tourist destinations in the world is especially impressive considering that it is a small city surrounded by sand, with a climate where summer temperatures rise as high as 50° Celsius. Despite this, Dubai's popularity around the world and reputation as one of best tourist destinations continues to rise. Dubai presents a perfect meeting place between East and West, a vibrant, modern city that proudly wears its culture and traditions and offers activities and experiences for people of all ages, cultures, and interests. Dubai wants to establish an image as an open, inclusive, and tolerant city that welcomes people from every part of the globe.

Dubai's award-winning #BeMyGuest campaign also captures this inclusive spirit. With iconic Bollywood celebrity Shah Rukh Khan as its ambassador, the campaign showcases the vibrance, diversity, culture, and range of activities and opportunities that it has to offer. In the campaign, Khan introduces the city's various attractions, including its traditional markets, fine dining, luxury shopping, sports, and beaches. The campaign shows how people of different ages, nationalities, ethnicities, and interests enjoy their time in Dubai, feeling right at home and always finding something catering to their interests. Each segment highlights Dubai's welcoming spirit and offers a glimpse into its culture, infrastructure, range of activities, investment in art and entertainment, etc.

Dubai is also the region's entertainment hub, with attractions such as the world's tallest building, Burj Khalifa; the world's only seven-star hotel, Burj Al Arab; Dubai Mall, which is one of the world's biggest; and The Palm Dubai, an artificial island. Dubai will soon also have the largest Ferris wheel, named Ain Dubai.

Dubai organizes a number of art exhibitions and events that attract artists from all over the world. Its concerts, events, movie launches, and promotions are not only popular among Indian tourists but also cater to a large proportion of the expatriate population. In fact, besides India, Dubai has become the second most popular center for Bollywood events.

Dubai is a hub for thrill seekers too. From zip lining, to para gliding, to sky diving, to water sports, to desert safaris, Dubai has a huge range of activities to offer. This range of offerings is also reflected in its amusement parks, such as IMG Worlds of Adventure, the world's largest indoor theme park, and Dubai Parks and Resorts, which includes three different parks within it: Motiongate Dubai, Legoland Dubai, and Bollywood Parks Dubai. One of the most popular tourist activities in Dubai is the desert safari, which involves camping, dune bashing, buggy rides, traditional cuisine, belly dancing, and other local activities.

Another key factor that adds to Dubai's attractiveness is its modern and glamorous retail sector and hotels. Dubai is a shopper's paradise: there are over 65 malls catering to a population of only 3 million, and they host some of the best stores in the world. One of the most popular shopping locations for tourists is the Gold Souq, which has more than 300 retailers. Gold shopping is extremely popular with shoppers around the world but especially among visitors from the wider Middle East and South Asia.

Dubai also offers some of the world's top-class hotels, including 104 five-star hotels. The UAE hospitality sector is expected to reach $7.6 billion by 2022 at a compounded annual growth rate (CAGR) of 8.5 percent between 2017 and 2022. The city caters to niche as well as mass tourism, and it plans to increase its affordable hotel options.

Beaches and water parks in Dubai can be enjoyed throughout the year due to its warm temperatures. Its coastline stretches across thousands of miles and has been beautifully developed with beachfront projects like Jumeirah Beach Residence, LaMer, Blue Waters, and Palm Jumeirah as well as exotic hotels like Atlantis and Four Seasons. Dubai is also popular for its night life, offering some of the best bars and pubs in the world.

Exhibit 4-13 Dubai has undertaken efforts to diversify its economy to reduce dependency on oil and transform itself into one of the world's top tourist destinations.
Source: Anna Om/Shutterstock.

Dubai's strategic location adds benefits to its status as a trading and aviation hub. Dubai International Airport has taken the title of "World's Busiest Airport" from London Heathrow for the number of international passengers that visit or pass through it. Nearly two-thirds of the world's population are within an eight-hour flight to Dubai, and a third are within a four-hour flight from Dubai. This makes Dubai a major aviation hub, especially between Europe and Asia. Dubai International Airport offers connections and flights to 240 destinations and is the base of Emirates, the world's largest long-haul carrier.

Dubai's aviation sector was a key area that the government of Dubai wanted to diversify into, as it would create more jobs and also increase tourism. The growth of the sector has been spurred by the open-skies policy, huge infrastructure projects, heavy investments, and an investor-friendly business environment. It is forecasted that the aviation sector will contribute 37.5 percent of Dubai's GDP (gross domestic product) by 2020 and nearly 45 percent of GDP by 2030.

At present, Dubai is all set to host the Expo 2020, which will involve 190 participating countries and be the largest event ever hosted by an Arab country. It is expected that around 25 million people will visit the expo between October 2020 and April 2021. Since Dubai won the right to host the expo in 2013, it has been preparing a celebration of a lifetime. The main theme of Expo 2020 is "Connecting Minds, Creating the Future," and with the youth as its main focus, it aims to lay foundations for innovations, partnerships, and business opportunities for future generations around the world. Expo 2020 will present a valuable opportunity to explore potential areas of partnerships and collaboration, and the governments of Dubai and the United Arab Emirates hope that it will demonstrate to the world that the country celebrates diversity by welcoming different cultures, traditions, identities, and collaborations. Expo 2020 will also emphasize tradition: a team of young students has developed a welcome message based on a traditional Emirati greeting, "Hayakum." One of the students remarked, "I am excited to welcome people for the Expo 2020 and to say 'Hayakum' to everyone. I would like to introduce the visitors to the Expo and tell them about my country's past, present, and future."

Experts believe that Expo 2020 will have long-term benefits for Dubai. Indeed, its economic impact was felt as early as 2013, when Dubai was awarded the right to host it, leading to an increase in its stock index and GDP. More than 275,000 jobs will be created, and demand will receive a significant boost in all key sectors, including real estate, tourism, hospitality, retail, education, technology, manufacturing, and healthcare.

Thanks to its many projects, events, and investments, Dubai's tourist appeal continues to grow and will continue to play a vital role as one of the main drivers of its economy. A key factor bolstering tourism in Dubai has been is its visa initiative, which has made access very smooth for visitors. Other growth drivers for its tourism include customized marketing programs, campaigns with celebrity ambassadors, and promotion of Dubai's tourism on digital and multimedia platforms. With its ability to offer something for everyone across the global market, Dubai seems well on its way to record 20 million tourists by 2020.

Exhibit 4-14 At one of Dubai's open souqs, or traditional markets, traders sell textiles, gold, and spices.
Source: Naki Kouyioumtzis/Pearson Education Ltd.

Discussion Questions

4-10. What role do cultural and social factors play in building Dubai's tourism appeal? How well do you think Dubai has managed to bring the East and the West together?

4-11. Indian tourists account for the biggest segment of total tourism in Dubai. Discuss the role of Bollywood and other factors that attract Indian tourists to Dubai.

4-12. Comment on the growth of Dubai as a tourist destination and how other economic drivers have contributed to it.

4-13. Dubai aims to increase the number of tourists from beyond its tradition markets. What changes, if any, will be needed in its targeting and communication strategy to encourage tourists from non-traditional markets?

4-14. Discuss the role of Expo 2020 in further boosting Dubai's tourism. Will Dubai be able to sustain its gains in tourism after the expo?

Sources: Waheed Abbas, "Dubai's Tourism Appeal Continues to Flourish," *Khaleej Times* (August 2, 2018); "Shah Rukh Khan Is Back with 2019's 'Be My Guest' Campaign," *Khaleej Times* (February 26, 2019); "Come Explore Shahrukh Khan's Dubai, #BeMyGuest" (video), https://www.visitdubai.com; Afshin Molavi, "Is Dubai a Model for Economic Diversification in the Persian Gulf?" CNN (June 5, 2018); Dania Saadi, "Economic Diversification and Expo 2020 to Shield Dubai from Oil Price Rout," *The National* (June 26, 2016); Ashraf Mishrif and Harun Kapetanovic, *Dubai's Model of Economic Diversification* (Gulf Research Centre Cambridge, 2018); Nigel Green, "Expo 2020 Will Boost Dubai Economy for Decades," *Khaleej Times* (November 12, 2018); Andrew R. Goetz, *The Airport as an Attraction: The Airport City and Aerotropolis Concept* (Air Transport: A Tourism Perspective, Elsevier Inc., 2019) pp. 217–232; "Dubai Expo 2020 Highlights," http://www.dubaicityguide.com; Sarah Diaa, "Oil Prices to Echo in Aviation Sector Around Second Quarter of 2015," *Gulf News* (December 30, 2014); "Aviation to Contribute $53.1b to Dubai's Economy in 2020," *Gulf News*, November 17, 2014, https://gulfnews.com/business/aviation/aviation-to-contribute-531b-to-dubais-economy-in-2020-1.1413852; Jennifer Aguinaldo, "Aviation to Account for 45 per cent of Dubai GDP by 2030," *MEED*, May 17, 2017, https://www.meed.com/aviation-to-account-for-45-per-cent-of-dubai-gdp-by-2030/; James Chen, "Gulf Tiger," July 11, 2018, Investopedia, https://www.investopedia.com/terms/g/gulf-tiger.asp; "How Dubai Became a Global Destination for Trade Shows," TGP, March 29, 2017, https://tgp.ae/how-dubai-became-a-global-destination-for-trade-shows/.

Notes

[1]Geert Hofstede and Michael Harris Bond, "The Confucius Connection: From Cultural Roots to Economic Growth," *Organizational Dynamics* (Spring 1988), p. 5.

[2]George P. Murdock, "The Common Denominator of Culture," in *The Science of Man in the World Crisis*, Ralph Linton, ed. (New York, NY: Columbia University Press, 1945), p. 145.

[3]The following discussion is adapted from Dana L. Alden, Jan-Benedict Steenkamp, and Rajeev Batra, "Brand Positioning through Advertising in Asia, North America, and Europe: The Role of Global Consumer Culture," *Journal of Marketing* 63, no. 1 (January 1999), pp. 75–87.

[4]Milton Rokeach, *Beliefs, Attitudes, and Values* (San Francisco, CA: Jossey-Bass, 1968), p. 160.

[5]Bill Britt, "Upstart Cola Taps Anti-War Vibe," *Advertising Age* (February 24, 2003), p. 1. See also Digby Lidstone, "Pop Idols," *Middle East Economic Digest* (August 22, 2003), p. 4.

[6]Meg Carter, "New Colas Wage Battle for Hearts and Minds," *Financial Times* (January 8, 2004), p. 9.

[7]Natalie Angier, "True Blue Stands out in an Earthy Crowd," *The New York Times* (October 23, 2012), pp. D1, D3. See also Natalie Angier, "Blue through the Centuries: Sacred and Sought After," *The New York Times* (October 23, 2012), p. D3.

[8]Thomas J. Madden, Kelly Hewett, and Martin S. Roth, "Managing Images in Different Cultures: A Cross-National Study of Color Meanings and Preferences," *Journal of International Marketing* 8, no. 4 (2000), p. 98.

[9]Te-Ping Chen, "In China, Women Graduates Are Married to Gowns, Not Caps," *The Wall Street Journal* (July 2, 2014), pp. A1, A12.

[10]Laurence E. Jacobs, Charles Keown, Reginald Worthley, and Kyung-I Ghymn, "Cross-Cultural Colour Comparisons: Global Marketers Beware!" *International Marketing Review* 8, no. 3 (1991), pp. 21–30.

[11]Martin Stokes, *Ethnicity, Identity, and Music: The Musical Construction of Place* (Oxford, UK: Berg, 1994).

[12]Motti Regev, "Rock Aesthetics and Musics of the World," *Theory, Culture & Society* 14, no. 3 (August 1997), pp. 125–142.

[13]Amy Kamzin, "Domino's Deadline to Deliver," *Financial Times* (January 18, 2013), p. 10.

[14]Preetika Rana, "In India, Forget Doughnuts, It's Time to Make the Tough Guy Chicken Burger," *The Wall Street Journal* (November 29–30, 2014), p. A1.

[15]Fara Warner, "Savvy Indian Marketers Hold Their Ground," *The Wall Street Journal Asia* (December 1, 1997), p. 8.

[16]Jacqueline Friedrich, "All the Rage in Paris? Le Fooding," *The Wall Street Journal* (February 9, 2001), p. W11.

[17]Evan Ramstad and Gary McWilliams, "Computer Savvy: For Dell, Success in China Tells Tale of Maturing Market," *The Wall Street Journal* (July 5, 2005), pp. A1, A8.

[18]Recounted in J. Byrne Murphy, *Le Deal* (New York, NY: St. Martins, 2008), pp. 60–61.

[19]Dan Bilefsky and Christopher Lawton, "In Europe, Marketing Beer as 'American' May Not Be a Plus," *The Wall Street Journal* (July 21, 2004), p. B1.

[20]James Hookway, "IKEA's Products Make Shoppers Blush in Thailand," *The Wall Street Journal* (June 5, 2012), pp. A1, A16.

[21]Greg Steinmetz and Carl Quintanilla, "Tough Target: Whirlpool Expected Easy Going in Europe, and It Got a Big Shock," *The Wall Street Journal* (April 10, 1998), pp. A1, A6.

[22]Renzo Rosso / Alice Rawsthorn, "A Hipster on Jean Therapy," *Financial Times* (August 20, 1998), p. 8.

[23]Meeyoung Song, "How to Sell in Korea? Marketers Count the Ways," *The Wall Street Journal* (August 24, 2001), p. A6.

[24]Kevin Voigt, "At Matsushita, It's a New Word Order," *Asian Wall Street Journal Weekly* (June 18–24, 2001), p. 1.

[25]See Anthony C. Di Benedetto, Miriko Tamate, and Rajan Chandran, "Developing Strategy for the Japanese Marketplace," *Journal of Advertising Research* (January–February 1992), pp. 39–48.

[26]Tom Burns, "Spanish Telecoms Visionary Beholds a Brave New World," *Financial Times* (May 2, 1998), p. 24.

[27]John L. Graham and Roy A. Heberger, Jr., "Negotiators Abroad—Don't Shoot from the Hip," *Harvard Business Review* 61, no. 4 (July–August 1983), pp. 160–168.

[28]Kate Fox, *Watching the English: The Hidden Rules of English Behavior* (Boston. MA: Nicholas Brealey Publishing, 2014), p. 287.

[29]George Ritzer, *The McDonaldization Thesis* (London, UK: Sage Publications, 1998), p. 8.

[30]Rosa Jackson, "Michelin Men," *Financial Times* (November 24/25, 2012), p. R8.

[31]Amy Barrett, "French Discounter Takes Cheap Chic World-Wide," *The Wall Street Journal* (May 27, 1998), p. B8.

[32]Christine Muhlke, "A Slow Food Festival Reaches out to the Uncommitted," *The New York Times* (September 3, 2008), p. D12. See also Alexander Stille, "Slow Food's Pleasure Principles," *The Utne Reader* (May/June 2002), pp. 56–58.

[33]Edward T. Hall, "How Cultures Collide," *Psychology Today* (July 1976), pp. 66–97.

[34]Geert Hofstede and Michael Harris Bond, "The Confucius Connection: From Cultural Roots to Economic Growth," *Organizational Dynamics* (Spring 1988), p. 5.

[34]In some articles, Hofstede refers to this dimension as "Confucian dynamism" because it is highest in Japan, Hong Kong, and Taiwan.

[36]Masaru Ibuka / James Lardner, *Fast Forward: Hollywood, the Japanese, and the VCR Wars* (New York, NY: NAL Penguin, 1987), p. 45.

[37]Scott A. Shane, "The Effect of Cultural Differences in Perceptions of Transaction Costs on National Differences in the Preference for International Joint Ventures," *Asia Pacific Journal of Management* 10, no. 1 (1993), pp. 57–69.

[38]J. Byrne Murphy, *Le Deal* (New York, NY: St. Martin's Press, 2008), p. 109.

[39]Christina Larson, "Office Cultures: A Global Guide," *Bloomberg Businessweek* (June 17, 2013), p. 15.

[40]James A. Lee, "Cultural Analysis in Overseas Operations," *Harvard Business Review* (March–April 1966), pp. 106–114.

[41]This section draws from Everett M. Rogers, *Diffusion of Innovations* (New York, NY: Free Press, 1962).

[42]For an excellent application and discussion of adopter categories, see Malcolm Gladwell, *The Tipping Point* (New York, NY: Little, Brown, 2000), Chapter 6.

[43]Hirokazu Takada and Dipak Jain, "Cross-National Analysis of Diffusion of Consumer Durable Goods in Pacific Rim Countries," *Journal of Marketing* 55 (April 1991), pp. 48–53.

[44]Charles M. Schaninger, Jacques C. Bourgeois, and Christian W. Buss, "French–English Canadian Subcultural Consumption Differences," *Journal of Marketing* 49 (Spring 1985), pp. 82–92.

[45]Kate Fox, *Watching the English: The Hidden Rules of English Behavior* (Boston, MA: Nicholas Brealey Publishing, 2014), p. 437.

[46]Deborah Ball, "Lattes Lure Brits to Coffee," *The Wall Street Journal* (October 20, 2005), pp. B1, B6. See also Marco R. della Cava, "Brewing a British Coup," *USA Today* (September 16, 1998), pp. D1, D2.

5

The Political, Legal, and Regulatory Environments

LEARNING OBJECTIVES

5-1 Understand the elements of a country's political environment that can impact global marketing activities.

5-2 Define *international law* and describe the main types of legal systems found in different parts of the world.

5-3 Understand the most important business issues that can lead to legal problems for global marketers.

5-4 Describe the available alternatives for conflict resolution and dispute settlement when doing business outside the home country.

5-5 In general terms, outline the regulatory environment in the European Union.

CASE 5-1
Travis Kalanick and Uber

Travis Kalanick is an entrepreneur who has achieved a level of success and notoriety rarely matched in the modern era. Kalanick is cofounder of Uber Technologies, the parent company of the wildly popular Uber ride-sharing service.

Kalanick, along with friend and cofounder Garrett Camp, launched the Uber service in San Francisco in 2010. By now, most people are familiar with the way Uber works: Customers download the Uber app to a smartphone and set up an account that includes mobile payment information. Then, when the customer needs a ride, he or she opens the app and types in a destination. The app's GPS identifies the customer's current location and calculates an estimated fare, distance, and trip time to the destination. If the fare is acceptable, the customer then requests a car and driver.

By the end of 2014, Uber had raised venture capital that valued the company at nearly $40 billion! The service was available in more than 250 cities worldwide, and some industry observers hailed the company as a prime example of digital technology disrupting an established industry. Uber's rapid growth was another example that the "sharing economy," also known as "collaborative consumption," was gaining traction, as evidenced by the success of Lyft (an Uber competitor), room rental service Airbnb, and others.

However, Uber has encountered resistance as its popularity has grown. In London and other major cities, drivers have staged demonstrations and mass protests against what they claim is unfair competition from unregulated drivers. Several cities, including Brussels, Miami, and Las Vegas, have banned Uber. In Brussels, a court fines drivers who use the service. Uber has been paying the fines and providing legal support. Regulators in Germany succeeded in obtaining a temporary injunction banning the service; after a series of appeals and counter-appeals, the injunction was lifted.

Exhibit 5-1 Protests against Uber have been staged in Spain, France, the United Kingdom, and other countries.
Source: Lora Grigorova/NEWZULU/CrowdSpark/Alamy Stock Photo.

The European Commission, the executive arm of the EU, conducted an inquiry to determine whether Uber was an "information-society service company," as Uber maintained, or the equivalent of a taxi service, as the French government alleged (see Exhibit 5-1).

Kalanick's company provides a case study of the impact that the political, legal, and regulatory environments can have on international trade and global marketing activities. Each of the world's national governments regulates trade and commerce with other countries and attempts to control the access outside enterprises have to their country's national resources. Every country has its own unique legal and regulatory system that affects the operations and activities of the global enterprise, including the global marketer's ability to address market opportunities and threats. Laws and regulations constrain the cross-border movement of products, services, people, money, and know-how. The global marketer must attempt to comply with each set of national—and, in some instances, regional—constraints. The fact that laws and regulations are frequently ambiguous and continually changing hampers these efforts. And, in the case of Uber, new technologies are evolving at a faster pace than laws and regulations can follow.

In this chapter, we consider the basic elements of the political, legal, and regulatory environments of global marketing, including the most pressing current issues, and offer some suggestions for dealing with those issues. Some specific topics—such as rules for exporting and importing industrial and consumer products; standards for health and safety; and regulations regarding packaging, labeling, advertising, and promotion—are examined in later chapters devoted to individual marketing mix elements.

5-1 The Political Environment

◀ **5-1** Understand the elements of a country's political environment that can impact global marketing activities.

Global marketing activities take place within the **political environment** of governmental institutions, political parties, and organizations through which a country's people and rulers exercise power. As we saw in Chapter 4, each nation has a unique culture that reflects its society. Each nation also has a *political culture* that reflects the relative importance of the government and legal system and provides a context within which individuals and corporations understand their relationship to the political system. Any company doing business outside its home country should carefully study the political culture in the target country and analyze salient issues arising from the political environment. These issues include the governing party's attitude toward sovereignty, present and future levels of political risk, tax policies, the threat of equity dilution, and the risk of expropriation.

Nation-States and Sovereignty

Sovereignty can be defined as supreme and independent political authority. A century ago, U.S. Supreme Court Chief Justice Melville Fuller said, "Every sovereign state is bound to respect the independence of every other sovereign state, and the courts in one country will not sit in judgment on the acts of government of another done within its territory." The late Richard Stanley, founder and former president of the Stanley Foundation, offered the following concise description:

> A sovereign state was considered free and independent. It regulated trade, managed the flow of people into and out of its boundaries, and exercised undivided jurisdiction over all persons and property within its territory. It had the right, authority, and ability to conduct its domestic affairs without outside interference and to use its international power and influence with full discretion.[1]

Government actions taken in the name of sovereignty occur in the context of two important criteria: a country's stage of development, and the political and economic systems in place in the country.

As outlined in Chapter 2, the economies of individual nations may be classified as industrialized, newly industrializing, or developing. Many governments in developing countries exercise control over their nations' economic development by passing protectionist laws and regulations. Their primary objective is to encourage economic development by protecting emerging or strategic industries in the home country, but government leaders can also engage in cronyism and provide favors for family members or "good friends."

Conversely, when many nations reach advanced stages of economic development, their governments declare that (in theory, at least) any practice or policy that restrains free trade is illegal. Antitrust laws and regulations are established to promote fair competition. Advanced-country laws often define and preserve a nation's social order; these laws may extend to political, cultural, and even intellectual activities and social conduct.

In France, for example, laws forbid the use of foreign words such as *le weekend* or *le marketing* in official documents. Also, a French law that went into effect in 1994 required that at least 40 percent of the songs played by popular radio stations be in the French language. The rationale? To protect against an "Anglo-Saxon cultural invasion." In 2016, the quota was reduced to 35 percent, as Daft Punk and other French recording artists released music with English-language lyrics to appeal to a global audience. Companies that may be affected positively or negatively by legislative acts sometimes use advertising as a vehicle for expressing their positions on issues (see Exhibit 5-2).

We also noted in Chapter 2 that most of the world's economies combine elements of market and nonmarket systems. The sovereign political power of a government in a predominantly nonmarket economy reaches quite far into the economic life of a country. Cuba is a case in point. By contrast, in a capitalist, market-oriented democracy, that power tends to be much more constrained. A current global phenomenon in both nonmarket and market structures is the trend toward privatization, which reduces direct governmental involvement as a supplier of goods and services in the country's economy. In essence, each act of privatization moves a nation's economy further in the free market direction.

This trend can be traced to the late Margaret Thatcher's economic policies in the 1980s when she was British prime minister. British Airways, British Petroleum, British Steel, and Rolls-Royce were some of the companies that were privatized under so-called Thatcherite economics. The policy was highly controversial: Some pilloried the prime minister for visiting misery on Great Britain, while others hailed her for taking bold steps to spur the economy. More recently, the economic crisis in the EU prompted Italy's government to sell 5.7 percent of its stake in Enel,

Motherhood, apple pie and GATT

Quick, name something supported by Presidents Clinton, Bush and Reagan; 450 leading American economists, including four Nobel laureates; the National Governors Association; the Consumers Union; the Business Roundtable, and many others.

Motherhood? Apple pie? Well, probably. But there's no doubt that each of those individuals and organizations supports GATT, the General Agreement on Tariffs and Trade. What's known as the Uruguay Round of GATT, an accord that took 117 countries more than seven years to negotiate, is now awaiting approval by Congress.

The agreement will reduce import tariffs worldwide by an average of 40 percent and cover new areas such as agriculture, intellectual property and some services — areas of importance to the U.S. economy. It could generate as much as $5 trillion in new worldwide commerce by 2005.

In the words of former President Ronald Reagan: "In trade, everyone ends up a winner as markets grow." We've seen evidence of that this year since the North American Free Trade Agreement (NAFTA) went into effect January 1. Despite negative predictions to the contrary, trade is up, consumer prices are down and massive layoffs just haven't happened.

While the GATT tariff reductions are smaller than those for NAFTA, the number of countries involved and the size of their trade flows are much larger. GATT's effect on the U.S. alone will be five times that of NAFTA.

We hope the enacting legislation is approved before Congress adjourns for the year — and without any financing features that would hurt the companies GATT is intended to help.

What will GATT mean for the U.S.?

First, it's important to note that international trade represents about a quarter of U.S. gross domestic product, or GDP — the value of what the nation produces. Over the last five years, exports accounted for half of U.S. economic growth. More than 10.5 million U.S. workers owe their jobs directly or indirectly to the export of goods or services, and another 500,000 to 1.4 million jobs — at higher-than-average pay — are predicted from GATT.

The Treasury Department estimates that the long-range benefits of this GATT accord will amount to $100 billion to $200 billion a year in added income to the U.S., or $1,700 per family. Other studies predict increases to the GDP as high as 1.2 percent. Agricultural exports alone are expected to rise by as much as $8.5 billion a year in the next decade.

What makes GATT such a boon to the U.S.?

■ Foreign countries on average have more trade restrictions and tariffs on U.S. goods than the U.S. does on theirs. GATT will reduce tariffs and level the playing field.

■ GATT will, for the first time, protect "intellectual property" like patents, trademarks and copyrights. That'll help U.S. computer-software, entertainment, high-tech and pharmaceutical industries, to name a few.

■ Also for the first time, GATT will open markets for service industries like accounting, advertising, computer services, construction and engineering.

■ GATT will open markets for U.S. agricultural products.

So let's call our mothers, cut ourselves a slice of apple pie and let our senators and representatives know we want the GATT legislation passed this year.

Mobil®

Exhibit 5-2 Many global companies use corporate advertising to advocate their official position on trade-related issues. In the mid-1990s, Mobil mounted an advocacy campaign that addressed a number of topics of public interest, including trade issues, clean air, alternative fuels, and health care reform. This op-ed urged the U.S. Congress to approve GATT.

Source: Courtesy of Exxon Mobil Corporation.

the country's largest power utility. The Italian government is also considering selling part of its stake in Eni, an energy company. Italy's debt totals more than $2 trillion, and the government is seeking ways to raise millions of euros.

Some observers believe global market integration is eroding national economic sovereignty. Economic consultant Neal Soss noted, "The ultimate resource of a government is power, and we've seen repeatedly that the willpower of governments can be overcome by persistent attacks from the marketplace."[2] Is this a disturbing trend? If the issue is framed in terms of marketing, the concept of exchange comes to the fore: Nations may be willing to give up sovereignty in return for something of value. If countries can increase their share of world trade and increase national income, perhaps they will be willing to cede some sovereignty.

In Europe, individual EU countries gave up the right to have their own currencies, ceded the right to set their own product standards, and have made other sacrifices in exchange for improved market access. The Brexit issue can be viewed as a mandate by Britons to regain some of what their nation lost to the "collective sovereignty" of the EU28.

Separatist and secessionist movements are also undercutting the traditional sovereignty of the nation-state. Within Italy, for example, voters in the Lombardy and Veneto regions in the wealthy north are increasingly reluctant to provide the tax base for subsidizing the poorer south.[4] Such intra-country regionalism is also seen Spain, where Catalonia has sought greater economic independence and the right to become a sovereign state. Meanwhile, in Scotland, calls for independence from the United Kingdom continue to be heard.

> "The country may lag behind in some respects, but it has a 1,000 year history, and Russia will not trade its sovereignty for anything."[3]
>
> Russian President Vladimir Putin

> "What we will no longer do is enter into large trade agreements that tie our hands, surrender our sovereignty, and make meaningful enforcement practically impossible."
>
> "Trump Pitches 'America First' Trade Policy at Asia-Pacific Gathering", The New York Times Company (November 10, 2017)

Political Risk

Political risk is the possibility of a change in a country's political environment or government policy that would adversely affect a company's ability to operate effectively and profitably. As Ethan Kapstein, a professor at INSEAD, has noted:

> Perhaps the greatest threats to the operations of global corporations, and those that are most difficult to manage, arise out of the political environment in which they conduct their business. One day, a foreign company is a welcome member of the local community; the next day, opportunistic politicians vilify it.[5]

Political risk can deter a company from investing abroad. Put another way, when a high level of uncertainty characterizes a country's political environment, the country may have difficulty attracting foreign investment.

As Professor Kapstein has pointed out, executives often fail to conceptualize political risk because they have not studied political science—which means they have not been exposed to the issues that students of politics ask about the activities of global companies. (A strong argument for a liberal arts education!) The modern corporation is coming under increasing scrutiny from business and government leaders as well as the general public; the same is true of free-market capitalism in general. This trend can be viewed as contributing to political risk.

Without a doubt, current events must be part of the corporate information agenda; for example, business managers need to stay apprised of the formation and evolution of political parties as well as the public's perception of political institutions. The emergence of far-right parties such as the Alternative for Germany (AfD), whose success in the 2017 national elections has been described as a "political earthquake," is a case in point.[6] Other potential disruptors of continental Europe's established political order include Austria's Freedom Party, France's National Front, and the Party for Freedom in the Netherlands.

> "If you want to be in growing markets you have to assume and expect some volatility. You can't be in growth markets without presuming there will be risks."[7]
>
> Jørgen Buhl Rasmussen, CEO, Carlsberg

Valuable sources of current-events information include the *Financial Times*, *The Economist*, and other daily and weekly business periodicals. The Economist Intelligence Unit (EIU; www.eiu.com), the Geneva-based Business Environment Risk Intelligence (BERI; www.beri.com), and the PRS Group (www.prsgroup.com) publish up-to-date political risk reports on individual country markets. Note that these commercial sources vary somewhat in the criteria they consider to constitute political risk. For example, BERI focuses on societal and system attributes, whereas the PRS Group focuses more directly on government actions and economic functions (see Table 5-1).

TABLE 5-1   Categories of Political Risk

EIU	BERI	PRS Group
War	Fractionalization of the political spectrum	Political turmoil probability
Social unrest	Fractionalization by language, ethnic, and/or religious groups	Equity restrictions
Orderly political transfer	Restrictive/coercive measures required to retain power	Local operations restrictions
Politically motivated violence	Mentality (xenophobia, nationalism, corruption, nepotism)	Taxation discrimination
International disputes	Social conditions (including population density and wealth distribution)	Repatriation restrictions
Change in government/pro-business orientation	Organization and strength of forces for a radical government	Exchange controls
Institutional effectiveness	Dependence on and/or importance to a major hostile power	Tariff barriers
Bureaucracy	Negative influences of regional political forces	Other barriers
Transparency or fairness	Societal conflict involving demonstrations, strikes, and street violence	Payment delays
Corruption	Instability as perceived by assassinations and guerilla war	Fiscal or monetary expansion
Crime		Labor costs
		Foreign debt

Source: Adapted from Llewellyn D. Howell, *The Handbook of Country* and *Political Risk Analysis*, 2nd ed. (East Syracuse, NY: The PRS Group, 1998).

As noted in Case 5-2, the political maneuverings of the Russian government create a high level of political risk for companies that seek to do business in that country. During his first two terms as Russia's president (2000–2008), Vladimir Putin implemented reforms in an effort to pave the way for Russia's membership in the World Trade Organization (WTO) and to attract foreign investment. He also created an environment of uncertainty for foreign companies. In 2010, Paul Melling, a partner at the law firm of Baker & McKenzie, explained, "Many multinationals are thinking long and hard about how big their company in Russia ought to be—the bigger the company, the bigger the risk."[8] In 2018, Putin was elected to a fourth term as president, and the level of political risk remains elevated owing to tense relations between the White House and the Kremlin.

Meanwhile, the current political climate in the rest of Central and Eastern Europe is still characterized by varying degrees of uncertainty. In the Economic Intelligence Unit's Political Instability Index rankings, Hungary, Albania, and Latvia are identified as having moderate levels of risk. Hungary and Latvia have already achieved upper-middle-income status. Now that Latvia has joined the euro zone, it is expected that lower interest rates will promote further economic growth. Moreover, political winds continue to shift in in the region: Poland and Hungary are two examples of countries that have recently elected populist governments. Common themes include opposition to adopting the euro, concern about welcoming migrants, and resistance to deeper integration with the EU.

Albania's progress in transitioning to a market economy has attracted investment from abroad. Moreover, products that are labeled "Made in Albania" are finding acceptance in global markets. The evidence can be seen in the success of DoniAnna, a shoe manufacturer that was founded by Albanian entrepreneur Donika Mici.[9] Diligent attention to risk assessment throughout the region should be ongoing to determine when the risk has decreased to levels acceptable to management.

Companies can purchase insurance to offset potential risks arising from the political environment. In Japan, Germany, France, Britain, the United States, and other industrialized nations, various agencies offer investment insurance to corporations doing business abroad. The Overseas Private Investment Corporation (OPIC; www.opic.gov) provides various types of political risk insurance to U.S. companies; in Canada, the Export Development Corporation performs a similar function.

Taxes

Governments rely on tax revenues to fund social services, to support their military forces, and to cover other expenditures. Unfortunately, government taxation policies on the sale of goods and services frequently motivate companies and individuals to profit by *not* paying taxes. For example, in China, import duties have dropped since the country joined the WTO. Even so, many goods are still subject to double-digit duties plus a 17 percent value-added tax (VAT). As a result, significant quantities of oil, cigarettes, photographic film, personal computers, and other products are smuggled into China. In some instances, customs documents are falsified to undercount goods in a shipment; the Chinese military has allegedly escorted goods into the country as well.

Ironically, global companies can still profit from the practice; it has been estimated, for example, that 90 percent of the foreign cigarettes sold in China are smuggled in. For Philip Morris, this means annual sales of $100 million to distributors in Hong Kong, which then smuggle the smokes across the border.[10] High excise and VAT taxes can also encourage legal cross-border shopping as consumers go abroad in search of good values. In Great Britain, for example, the Wine and Spirit Association estimates that, on average, cars returning from France are loaded with 80 bottles of wine.

The diverse geographical activity of the global corporation also requires that special attention be given to tax laws. The issue is especially acute in the tech sector; many companies make efforts to minimize their tax liability by shifting the location in which they declare income. Facebook, Amazon, Google, and Apple are some of the companies that have shifted profits earned from intellectual property to low-tax jurisdictions such as Ireland and Luxembourg. In addition, tax minimization by foreign companies doing business in the United States costs the U.S. government billions of dollars each year in lost revenue. After the 2016 U.S. presidential election, companies looked to the Trump administration for broad-based tax reform. They were rewarded with a major tax cut that was passed in December 2017.

THE CULTURAL CONTEXT

EU to Global Companies: "Pay Your Taxes!"

As Benjamin Franklin famously said, "In this world nothing can be said to be certain, except death and taxes." For global companies, the taxation issue is complicated by the fact that corporate tax rates vary widely around the world. Until recently, the United States had one of the world's highest corporate taxes: 35 percent. When combined with state and local taxes, the rate for businesses rose to 39.1 percent. By contrast, Ireland's corporate tax rate is only 12.5 percent.

Corporate tax reform was just one item on the agenda of U.S. President Donald Trump. Authorities have been stepping up their efforts to collect taxes from a range of global companies, including Amazon, Apple, Fiat Chrysler Automotive (FCA), and Starbucks. Members of the Organisation for Economic Co-operation and Development (OECD) and the Group of Twenty (G-20) are also working to reform tax rules.

In fall 2017, Margrethe Vestager, the EU's competition commissioner, announced that Amazon would have to pay €250 million in back taxes after the European Commission ruled that the online giant's Luxembourg operations had benefited from illegal state aid over a 10-year period. In 2004, Amazon had shifted certain intellectual property (IP) into a non-taxable holding company in Luxembourg that collected IP royalties from operations in Europe and then paid the parent company. The Brussels-based Commission alleged that the arrangement allowed Amazon to shift as much as three-fourths of its European profits into the holding company, thereby reducing its tax bill. As Vestager explained, under EU law, individual EU states cannot selectively grant tax benefits to some global companies but not others. Not surprisingly, Amazon denied any wrongdoing.

The previous year, in 2016, the Commission ruled that Ireland had granted Apple illegal tax advantages, and ordered the country to recover €13 billion in back taxes. Both Apple and Ireland disagreed with the Commission's findings; Apple CEO Tim Cook called the investigation and the resulting ruling "total political crap." After Apple refused to pay, the Commission referred the case to the European Court of Justice (ECJ; see Table 5-5).

In the United Kingdom, where the corporate tax rate is 19 percent, legislation passed in 2015 was aimed at cracking down on transfer pricing—that is, intra-corporate transfers among different units of the same company. One of the first targets was Google, which had been investigated for diverting profits to its European headquarters in Ireland. The United Kingdom is the tech giant's second-largest market (the United States is number 1), and Google was found to have paid only £20.5 million in taxes on 2013 revenues of £5.6 billion. Although Google was not accused of tax evasion, the company was ordered to pay £130 million in back taxes. Even so, George Osborne, the authority who crafted the deal that became known as the "Google tax," faced considerable backlash from critics who felt Google had gotten off lightly (see Exhibit 5-3).

With corporate tax structures and policies becoming high-profile political issues on both sides of the Atlantic, Netflix and eBay also got caught up in the controversy. For example, eBay was found to have reported one set of 2016 revenue figures to U.K. tax authorities, while recording different figures in its U.S. filings. As for Netflix, €22 million in fees from its 6.5 million U.K. subscribers were posted as 2016 revenue to parent company Netflix International BV in the Netherlands. According to an outside analysis, the streaming giant's 2016 U.K. revenues actually amounted to more than $500 million.

In fall 2017, data compiled by Her Majesty's Revenue & Customs (HMRC) were made public; they indicated that global companies had avoided 2016 tax obligations of as much as £5.8 billion. That amount was 50 percent higher than had previously been assumed.

Meanwhile, the U.S. Congress was hard at work hammering out a tax reform bill for President Donald Trump to sign before the end of the year. One of the measures would impose an excise tax of 20 percent on transfer payments, referring to cross-border purchases by a U.S. company from any of its foreign subsidiaries. Transactions with subsidiaries in the United States would not be subject to the levy; the measure reflected Trump's pronouncements about putting "America First." Several European finance ministers denounced the proposed tax as discriminatory and a potential violation of WTO rules.

Sources: Madison Marriage, "Tax Lost to Multinationals Shifting Profits Overseas Climbs to £5.8bn," *Financial Times* (October 25, 2017), p. 1; Rochelle Toplensky, "Tech Giants Hit by EU Tax Crackdown," *Financial Times* (October 5, 2017), p. 17; Tom Fairless and Shayndi Raice, "Firms Drawn to U.K. for Tax Deals," *The Wall Street Journal* (July 29, 2014), p. C3; Kiuz Hoffman and Hester Plumridge, "Race to Cut Taxes Fuels Urge to Merge," *The Wall Street Journal* (July 14, 2014), pp. A1, A2; Hester Plumridge, "EU Tax Inquiry Adds to Deals Buzz," *The Wall Street Journal* (June 16, 2014), p. B8; Michelle Hanlon, "The Lose–Lose Tax Policy Driving Away U.S. Business," *The Wall Street Journal* (June 12, 2014), p. A15; Vanessa Houlder and Vincent Boland, "The Irish Inversion," *Financial Times* (April 30, 2014), p. 9.

Exhibit 5-3 Europeans have responded negatively to some of the policies of tech firms such as Uber and Airbnb. Protests have also erupted over allegations that Apple and other firms have not paid their fair share of taxes.
Source: Anthony DEPERRAZ/NEWZULU/CrowdSpark/Alamy Stock Photo.

Seizure of Assets

The ultimate threat that a government can impose on a company is seizing its assets. **Expropriation** refers to governmental action to dispossess a foreign company or investor. Compensation is generally provided, albeit often not in the "prompt, effective, and adequate" manner provided for by international standards. If no compensation is provided, the action is referred to as **confiscation**.[11] International law is generally interpreted as prohibiting any act by a government to take foreign property without compensation. **Nationalization** is generally broader in scope than expropriation; it occurs when the government takes control of some or all of the enterprises in a particular industry. International law recognizes nationalization as a legitimate exercise of government power, as long as the act satisfies a "public purpose" and is accompanied by "adequate payment" (i.e., payment that reflects fair market value of the property).

In 1959, for example, the newly empowered Castro government nationalized property belonging to American sugar producers in retaliation for new American import quotas on sugar. Castro offered compensation in the form of Cuban government bonds, which was adequate under Cuban law. Because Cuban-owned sugar producers were not nationalized, the U.S. State Department viewed this particular act as discriminatory and the compensation offered as inadequate.[12] More recently, the late Venezuelan President Hugo Chávez nationalized Electricidad de Caracas, a utility company, and CANTV, a telecommunications provider. The Venezuelan government paid AES Corporation $739.3 million for Electricidad de Caracas; Verizon Communications received $572 million for its stake in CANTV.[13]

Short of outright expropriation or nationalization, the phrase *creeping expropriation* has been applied to limitations on economic activities of foreign firms in particular countries. These limitations have involved repatriation of profits, dividends, royalties, and technical assistance fees from local investments or technology arrangements. Other issues include increased local content requirements, quotas for hiring local nationals, price controls, and other restrictions affecting return on investment. Global companies have also suffered discriminatory tariffs and nontariff barriers that limit market entry of certain industrial and consumer goods, as well as discriminatory laws on patents and trademarks. Intellectual property restrictions have had the practical effect of eliminating or drastically reducing protection of pharmaceutical products.

In the mid-1970s, Johnson & Johnson (J&J) and other foreign investors in India had to submit to a host of government regulations to retain majority equity positions in companies they had already established. Many of these rules were later copied in whole or in part by Malaysia, Indonesia, the Philippines, Nigeria, and Brazil. By the late 1980s, after a "lost decade" in Latin America characterized by debt crises and low gross national product (GNP) growth, lawmakers reversed many of these restrictive and discriminatory laws. The goal was to again attract foreign direct investment and badly needed Western technology. The end of the Cold War and the restructuring of political allegiances contributed significantly to these changes.

When governments expropriate foreign property, a number of impediments can limit actions to reclaim that property. For example, according to the U.S. Act of State Doctrine, if the government of a foreign state is involved in a specific act, the U.S. courts will not get involved. Instead, representatives of expropriated companies may seek recourse through arbitration at the World Bank's International Centre for Settlement of Investment Disputes (ICSID). It is also possible to buy expropriation insurance from either a private company or a government agency such as OPIC.

The expropriation of copper companies operating in Chile in the early 1970s shows the effect that companies can have on their own fate. Companies that strenuously resisted government efforts to introduce home-country nationals into the company management were expropriated outright; those companies that made genuine efforts to follow Chilean guidelines were allowed to remain under joint Chilean–U.S. management.

(5-2) International Law

International law may be defined as the rules and principles that nation-states consider binding upon themselves. International law pertains to property, trade, immigration, and other areas that have traditionally been under the jurisdiction of individual nations. International law applies only to the extent that countries are willing to assume all rights and obligations in these areas.

5-2 Define *international law* and describe the main types of legal systems found in different parts of the world.

The roots of modern international law can be traced back to the seventeenth-century Peace of Westphalia. Early international law was concerned with waging war, establishing peace, and handling other political issues such as diplomatic recognition of new national entities and governments.

Although elaborate international rules gradually emerged—covering, for example, the status of neutral nations—the creation of laws governing commerce proceeded on a state-by-state basis in the nineteenth century. International law still has the function of upholding order, although in a broader sense than laws dealing with problems arising from war. At first, international law was essentially an amalgam of treaties, covenants, codes, and agreements. As trade grew among nations, order in commercial affairs assumed increasing importance. The law had originally dealt only with nations as entities, but a growing body of law rejected the idea that only nations could be subject to international law.

Paralleling the expanding body of international case law in the twentieth and twenty-first centuries, new international judiciary organizations have contributed to the creation of an established rule of international law: the Permanent Court of International Justice (1920–1945); the International Court of Justice (ICJ; www.icj-cij.org), which is the judicial arm of the United Nations and was founded in 1946; and the International Law Commission, established by the United States in 1947 (see Exhibit 5-4). Disputes arising between nations are issues of *public international law*, and they may be taken before the ICJ (also known as the World Court), located in The Hague. As described in the supplemental documents to the United Nations Charter, Article 38 of the ICJ Statute concerns international law:

> The Court, whose function is to decide in accordance with international law such disputes as are submitted to it, shall apply:
>
> a. international conventions, whether general or particular, establishing rules expressly recognized by the contesting states;
>
> b. international custom, as evidence of a general practice accepted as law;
>
> c. the general principles of law recognized by civilized nations;
>
> d. subject to the provisions of Article 59, judicial decisions and the teachings of the most highly qualified publicists of the various nations, as subsidiary means for the determination of rules of law.

Exhibit 5-4 Located in The Hague, the International Court of Justice (ICJ) is the judicial arm of the United Nations. The court's 15 judges are elected to 9-year terms. The primary function of the ICJ is to settle disputes among different countries according to international law. The ICJ also offers advice on legal issues submitted by various international agencies.
Source: Ankor Light/Shutterstock.

Other sources of modern international law include treaties, international customs, judicial case decisions in the courts of law of various nations, and scholarly writings. What happens if a nation allows a case against it to be brought before the ICJ and then refuses to accept a judgment against it? The plaintiff nation can seek recourse through the United Nations Security Council, which can use its full range of powers to enforce the judgment.

Common Law versus Civil Law

Private international law is the body of law that applies to disputes arising from commercial transactions between companies based in different nations. As noted, the laws governing commerce emerged gradually, leading to a major split in legal systems among various countries.[14] The story of law in the Western world can be traced to two sources: Rome, from which the continental European civil-law tradition originated, and English common law, from which the U.S. legal system originated.

A **civil-law country** is one in which the legal system reflects the structural concepts and principles of the Roman Empire in the sixth century.

> For complex historical reasons, Roman law was received differently and at vastly different times in various regions of Europe, and in the nineteenth century each European country made a new start and adopted its own set of national private-law codes, for which the *Code Napoleon* of 1804 was the prototype. But the new national codes drew largely on Roman law in conceptual structure and substantive content. In civil-law countries, the codes in which private law is cast are formulated in broad general terms and are thought of as completely comprehensive, that is, as the all-inclusive source of authority by reference to which every disputed case must be referred for decision.[15]

"To understand *stare decisis*, you have to understand English common law. To understand English common law, you have to understand where England came from—the Norman Conquest, the Vikings, the Romans . . ."[16]

U.S. Supreme Court Justice Clarence Thomas

In a **common-law country**, many disputes are decided by reliance on the authority of past judicial decisions (cases). A common-law legal system is based on the concept of precedent, sometimes called *stare decisis*. Precedent is the notion that past judicial decisions on a particular issue are binding on a court when that same issue is presented later. This description is somewhat cryptic, because it is easier to observe the operation of precedent than to define it. Nevertheless, precedent and *stare decisis* represent the fundamental principles of common-law decision making.

In its origins, the legal system of the United States was substantially influenced by English law. The English and American systems are common law in nature; that is, the law is pronounced by courts when there are no statutes to follow. Common-law systems are distinguishable from the civil-law systems found in much of Europe. Although much of contemporary American and English law is legislative in origin, the law inferred from past judicial decisions is equal in importance to the law set down in codes. Common-law countries often rely on codification in certain areas—the U.S. Uniform Commercial Code (UCC) is one example—but these codes are not the all-inclusive, systematic statements found in civil-law countries.

The UCC, which has been fully adopted by 49 U.S. states, codifies a body of specifically designed rules covering commercial conduct. (Louisiana has adopted parts of the UCC, but its laws are still heavily influenced by the French civil code.) The host country's legal system—that is, common or civil law—directly affects the form a legal business entity will take. In common-law countries, companies are legally incorporated by state authority. In civil-law countries, a contract between two or more parties who are fully liable for the actions of the company forms a company.

The United States, 9 of Canada's 10 provinces, and other former colonies with an Anglo-Saxon history founded their systems on common law. Historically, much of continental Europe was influenced by Roman law and, later, the Napoleonic Code (see Exhibit 5-5). Asian countries are split on this issue: India, Pakistan, Malaysia, Singapore, and Hong Kong are common-law jurisdictions, whereas Japan, Korea, Thailand, Indochina, Taiwan, Indonesia, and China are civil-law jurisdictions. The legal systems in Scandinavia are mixed, displaying some civil-law attributes and some common-law attributes. Today, the majority of countries have legal systems based on civil-law traditions.

Exhibit 5-5 Civil-law systems rely more heavily on statutes and codes, such as the Napoleonic Code of 1804, in deciding cases. From these code provisions, abstract principles are recognized and then applied in specific cases. By contrast, common-law courts find abstract principles in particular cases and then generalize what the law is from those principles.
Source: L F File/Shutterstock.

As various countries in Eastern and Central Europe have wrestled with establishing legal systems in the post-Communist era, a struggle of sorts has broken out, with consultants representing both common-law and civil-law countries trying to influence the process. In much of Central Europe, including Poland, Hungary, and the Czech Republic, the German civil-law tradition prevails. As a result, banks not only take deposits and make loans, but also engage in the buying and selling of securities.

In contrast, in Eastern Europe, and particularly in Russia, the U.S. system has had greater influence. Germany has accused the United States of promoting a system so complex that it requires legions of lawyers to interpret it. The U.S. response: The German system is outdated.[17] In any event, the constant stream of laws and decrees issued by the Russian government creates an unpredictable, evolving legal environment. Specialized publications such as Anatoly Zhuplev's *Doing Business in Russia: A Concise Guide* are important resources for anyone doing business in Russia or in the 11 other nations that comprise the Commonwealth of Independent States.

Islamic Law

The legal system in many Middle Eastern countries is identified with the laws of Islam, which are associated with "the one and only one God, the Almighty."[18] In **Islamic law**, the *sharia* is a comprehensive code governing Muslim conduct in all areas of life, including business. The code is derived from two sources. First is the Koran, the Holy Book written in Arabic that is a record of the revelations made to the Prophet Mohammed by Allah. The second source is the Hadith, which is based on the life, sayings, and practices of Muhammad. In particular, the Hadith spells out the products and practices that are *haram* (forbidden). The orders and instructions found in the Koran are analogous to code laws; the guidelines of the Hadith correspond to common law. Any Westerner doing business in Malaysia or the Middle East should have, at minimum, a rudimentary understanding of Islamic law and its implications for commercial activities. Brewers, for example, must refrain from advertising beer on billboards or in local-language newspapers.

5-3 Understand the most important business issues that can lead to legal problems for global marketers.

(5-3) Sidestepping Legal Problems: Important Business Issues

Clearly, the global legal environment is very dynamic and complex, so the best course to follow is to get expert legal help. Nevertheless, the astute, proactive marketer can do a great deal to prevent conflicts from arising in the first place, especially concerning issues such as establishment, jurisdiction, patents and trademarks, antitrust, licensing and trade secrets, bribery, and advertising and other promotion tools. Chapter 13 and Chapter 14 discuss regulation of specific promotion activities.

Jurisdiction

Company personnel working abroad should understand the extent to which they are subject to the jurisdiction of host-country courts. **Jurisdiction** pertains to global marketing insofar as it concerns a court's authority to rule on particular types of issues arising outside of a nation's borders or to exercise power over individuals or entities from different countries. Employees of foreign companies working in the United States must understand that U.S. courts have jurisdiction to the extent that the company can be demonstrated to be doing business in the state in which the court sits. The court may examine whether the foreign company maintains an office, solicits business, maintains bank accounts or other property, or has agents or other employees in the state in question.

One trade-related dispute in which jurisdiction played an important role pitted Volkswagen AG against General Motors. After Volkswagen hired GM's worldwide head of purchasing, José Ignacio López de Arriortúa, in 1992, his former employer accused him of taking trade secrets to his new company. Volkswagen accepted U.S. court jurisdiction in the dispute, although the company's lawyers requested that the U.S. District Court in Detroit transfer the case to Germany.

Intellectual Property: Patents, Trademarks, and Copyrights

Patents and trademarks that are protected in one country are not necessarily protected in another, so global marketers must ensure that all forms of intellectual property are registered in each country where business is conducted. A **patent** is a formal legal document that gives an inventor the exclusive right to make, use, and sell an invention for a specified period of time. Typically, the invention represents an "inventive leap" that is "novel" or "nonobvious." A **trademark** is defined as a distinctive mark, motto, device, or emblem that a manufacturer affixes to a particular product or package to distinguish it from goods produced by other manufacturers (see Exhibit 5-6 and Exhibit 5-7). A **copyright** establishes ownership of a written, recorded, performed, or filmed creative work.

The Champagne region in France is world famous for producing sparkling wines. In some countries, including the United States, the use of the word "Champagne" is permitted on labels of sparkling wines that are not produced in the region. Due to international trade agreements, consumer rights laws, and legal precedents, more than 110 countries require wines labeled "Champagne" to come exclusively from Champagne. Such protection assures consumers about the origin and authenticity of the products they buy; in other words, a wine labeled "Champagne" would only come from Champagne, France.

In 2005, representatives from several wine regions in the United States and the EU signed a Joint Declaration to Protect Wine Place & Origin. The organization now has members from more than nine countries spanning North America, Europe, and Australia. A 2006 Wine Accord signed by the United States and EU bans the misuse of 16 region names, including Champagne, by wine producers that request the use of these names on labels after March 2006 for wines that do not originate in those places. Wine producers that misused these region names prior to that date are still permitted to do so.

Infringement of intellectual property can take a variety of forms. **Counterfeiting** is the unauthorized copying and production of a product. An *associative counterfeit*, or *imitation*, uses a product name that differs slightly from a well-known brand but is close enough that consumers will mistake it for the genuine product (see Exhibit 5-8). Another type of counterfeiting is *piracy*, the unauthorized publication or reproduction of copyrighted work. Counterfeiting and piracy are particularly important in industries such as motion pictures, recorded music, computer software, and textbook publishing. Companies in these industries produce products that can be easily duplicated and distributed on a mass basis.

The United States, in particular, has a vested interest in intellectual property protection around the globe, because it is home to many companies in the industries just mentioned.

"We have confidence in international law. When you invent something, it is necessary immediately to defend your creativity with intellectual patents. Italy has one of the poorest records in Europe with regard to patents. We need to educate businessmen about this."[19]

Mario Moretti Polegato, chairman, Geox (Italy's biggest shoe company)

Exhibit 5-6 Kimberly-Clark Corporation markets Kleenex brand tissues and is the registered trademark owner. Trademarks and other forms of intellectual property are valuable assets; this ad, which appeared in *Advertising Age* magazine, serves notice that Kimberly-Clark is protecting its investment in the Kleenex brand name. Companies take this type of action to prevent brand names from becoming generic terms.
Source: Courtesy, Kimberly-Clark Corp. All Rights Reserved.

However, the United States faces significant challenges in countries such as China. As one expert has noted:

> Current attempts to establish intellectual property law, particularly on the Chinese mainland, have been deeply flawed in their failure to address the difficulties of reconciling legal values, institutions, and forms generated in the West with the legacy of China's past and the constraints imposed by its present circumstances.[20]

In the United States, where patents and trademarks are registered with the federal Patent and Trademark Office, the patent holder retains all rights for the life of the patent even if the product is not produced or sold. The Trademark Act of 1946, also known as the Lanham Act, covers trademarks in the United States. President Ronald Reagan signed the Trademark Law Revision Act into law in November 1988; this act makes it easier for companies to register new trademarks. Patent and trademark protection in the United States is very good, and U.S. law relies on the precedent of previously decided court cases for guidance.

To register a patent in Europe, a company has the option of filing on a country-by-country basis or applying to the European Patent Office in Munich for patent registration in a specific number

Exhibit 5-7 The Champagne region in France is world famous for producing sparkling wines.
Learn more at www.champagne.com.
Source: Champagne, USA.

Exhibit 5-8 Many counterfeit products produced in China have garbled English names, such as clothing from "Hugo Bsos," a "Haiyatt Hotel," and "Spoony," a misspelling of the popular Peanuts character.
Source: Greg Baker/AP Images.

of countries. A third option will soon be available: The Community Patent Convention will make it possible for an inventor to file for a patent that is effective in the 27 signatory nations. Currently, patent procedures in Europe are quite expensive, in part because of the cost of translating technical documents into all the languages of the EU countries; as of mid-2004, the translation issue remained unresolved.[21] In July 1997, in response to complaints, the European Patent Office instituted a 19 percent reduction in the average cost of an eight-country patent registration.

The United States recently joined the World Intellectual Property Organization (WIPO). Governed by the Madrid agreement of 1891 and the more flexible 1996 **Madrid Protocol**, the WIPO system allows trademark owners to seek protection in as many as 74 countries with a single application and fee (see Exhibit 5-9).

Companies sometimes find ways to exploit loopholes or other unique opportunities offered by patent and trademark laws in individual nations. Sometimes, individuals register trademarks in local country markets before the actual corporate entity files for trademark protection. For example, Starbucks filed for trademark protection in 1997 in Russia but did not open any cafés there. Sergei Zuykov, an attorney in Moscow, filed a petition in court in 2002 to cancel Starbucks' claim to the brand name because it had not been used in commerce. Technically, Zuykov was merely taking advantage of provisions in Russia's civil code; even though he has been denounced as a "trademark squatter," he was not violating the law. Zuykov then offered to sell Seattle-based Starbucks its name back for $600,000![22]

The U.S. Patent and Trademark Office recently granted the Cuban government a trademark for Havana Club rum. This has resulted in a legal dispute between two global distilled-spirits marketing giants (see Exhibit 5-10). Bacardi Ltd., which is based in the Bahamas, was once a Cuban company. Bacardi sells its own Havana Club liquor in the U.S. market; this rum is produced in Puerto Rico. Bacardi acquired the rights to the brand from the Arechabala family, who fled Cuba in 1960 with the original recipe after Fidel Castro nationalized their company.

Since 1993, France's Pernod Ricard has operated a 50-50 joint venture with the Cuban government to produce Havana Club in Cuba, from Cuban sugar cane, for sale outside the United States. Pernod Ricard argues that its brand is authentic because it is a product of climate and growing conditions unique to Cuba, where the Havana Club logo is found in a variety of non-alcoholic products, including drinking glasses, T-shirts, and souvenirs. The new ruling opens the

Exhibit 5-9 Headquartered in Geneva, Switzerland, the World Intellectual Property Organization (WIPO) is one of 16 specialized subunits of the United Nations. WIPO's mission is to promote and protect intellectual property throughout the world. WIPO views intellectual property as a critical element in economic development; it has created illustrated booklets that explain trademarks, copyright, and other intellectual property issues in a straightforward, easy-to-understand manner. Local agencies can access and print the booklets directly from WIPO's Internet site.

Source: Trademarks Comic Book (2004). World Intellectual Property Organization.

Exhibit 5-10 Americans may soon be able to buy "Made in Cuba" Havana Club rum following a ruling by the U.S. Patent and Trademark Office. An ongoing legal dispute pits Bacardi Ltd. against Pernod Ricard; both claim rights to the Havana Club brand.
Source: ADALBERTO ROQUE/AFP/Getty Images.

way for Cuban-made Havana Club rum, which ranks number 1 in global rum consumption, to be marketed in the United States.[23]

International concern about intellectual property issues in the nineteenth century resulted in two important agreements. The first is the International Convention for the Protection of Industrial Property. Also known as the Paris Union or Paris Convention, the convention dates to 1883 and is now honored by nearly 100 countries. This treaty facilitates multicountry patent registrations by ensuring that once a company files in a signatory country, the company will be afforded a "right of priority" in other countries for 1 year from the date of the original filing. A U.S. company wishing to obtain foreign patent rights must apply to the Paris Union within 1 year of filing in the United States or risk a permanent loss of patent rights abroad.[24]

In 1886, the International Union for the Protection of Literary and Artistic Property was formed. Also known as the Berne Convention, this landmark agreement focuses on copyright protection. References to the convention pop up in some unexpected places. For example, sharp-eyed fans of *The Ellen DeGeneres Show* on the CBS television network will see the following message appear as the final credits roll:

> Country of publication United States of America. WAD Productions, Inc. is the author of this film/motion picture for purposes of Article 15 (2) of the Berne Convention and all national laws giving in effect thereto.

Two other treaties deserve mention. The Patent Cooperation Treaty (PCT) has more than 100 contracting states, including Australia, Brazil, France, Germany, Japan, North Korea, South Korea, the Netherlands, Switzerland, the Russian Federation and other former Soviet republics, and the United States. The members constitute a union that provides certain technical services and cooperates in the filing, searching, and examination of patent applications in all member countries.

The European Patent Office administers applications for the European Patent Convention, which is effective in the EU and Switzerland. An applicant can file a single patent application covering all the convention states; the advantage is that the application will be subject to only one procedure of grant. Although national patent laws remain effective under this system, approved patents are effective in all member countries for a period of 20 years from the filing date.

In recent years, the U.S. government has devoted considerable diplomatic effort to improving the worldwide environment for intellectual property protection. For example, China agreed to accede to the Berne Convention in 1992; on January 1, 1994, China became an official signatory of the PCT. Now, more than two decades later, Chinese companies are aggressively building their own patent portfolios. In 2015, two of the top three companies filing applications under the PCT were Chinese (see Table 5-2). Significant numbers of patents often signal that a company is a leader in innovation: As illustrated in Exhibit 5-11, DuPont has more than 7 million patents.

Effective June 7, 1995, in accordance with the General Agreement on Tariffs and Trade (GATT), new U.S. patents are granted for a period of 20 years from the filing date. Previously,

TABLE 5-2 Companies Filing the Most International Patent Applications under PCT, 2015

Company	Country	Number of Patent Applications Filed
1. Huawei Technologies	China	3,898
2. Qualcomm	United States	2,442
3. ZTE	China	2,155
4. Samsung Electronics	South Korea	1,683
5. Mitsubishi Electric	Japan	1,593
6. Telefonaktiebolaget LM Ericsson	Sweden	1,481
7. LG Electronics	South Korea	1,457
8. Sony	Japan	1,381
9. Koninklijke Philips	Netherlands	1,378
10. Hewlett-Packard Development	United States	1,310

Source: World Intellectual Property Organization.

Exhibit 5-11 New products and innovations are the lifeblood of DuPont.
Source: Courtesy of DuPont.

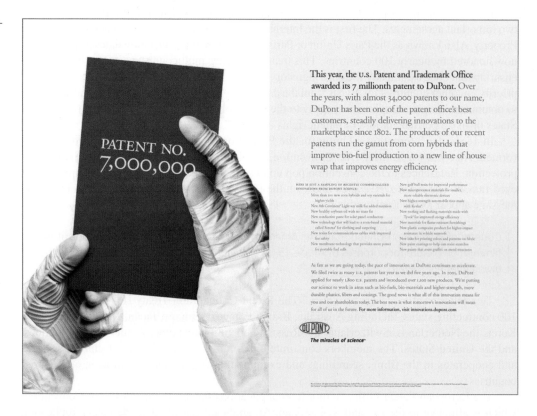

patents were valid for a 17-year term that began after they were granted. Thus, U.S. patent laws are now harmonized with those in the EU as well as Japan. Even with the changes, however, patents in Japan are narrower than those in the United States. As a result, companies such as Caterpillar have been unable to protect critical innovations in Japan because products very similar to those made by U.S. companies can be patented without fear of infringement.[25]

Another key issue is global patent protection for software. Although copyright law protects the computer code, it does not apply to the idea embodied in the software. Beginning in 1981, the U.S. Patent and Trademark Office extended patent protection to software. In the United States alone, Microsoft has tens of thousands of patents, of which the majority are software related. In Europe, software patents were not allowed under the Munich Convention; in June 1997, however, the EU indicated it was ready to revise patent laws so they would cover software.[26]

In 2011, the U.S. government overhauled the patent system once again with the passage of the American Innovation Act. This act addressed the problem of so-called patent trolls who file multiple patent applications with the intent of getting large tech companies such as Facebook, Apple, and Google to pay large sums to settle patent claims. A new entity, the Patent Trial and Appeal Board, was created to expedite the process of resolving patent infringement cases. Some observers have noted that the push-back on patent protection has led to a decline of U.S. investment in life sciences and software.[27]

Antitrust

Antitrust laws in the United States and other countries are designed to combat restrictive business practices and to encourage competition. Agencies such as the U.S. Federal Trade Commission, Japan's Fair Trade Commission (FTC), and the European Commission enforce antitrust laws (see Exhibit 5-12). Some legal experts believe that the pressures of global competition have resulted in an increased incidence of price-fixing and collusion among companies. As then FTC Chairman Robert Pitofsky said, "For years, tariffs and trade barriers blocked global trade. Now those are falling, and we are forced to confront the private anticompetitive behavior that often remains."[28]

A recent rash of antitrust actions brought in the United States against foreign companies has raised concerns that the United States is violating international law as well as the sovereignty of other nations. The U.S. antitrust laws are a legacy of the nineteenth-century trust-busting era and are intended to maintain free competition by limiting the concentration of economic power. The Sherman Act of 1890 prohibits certain restrictive business practices, including fixing prices, limiting production, allocating markets, and engaging in any other scheme designed to limit or avoid competition. The law applies to the activities of U.S. companies outside U.S. boundaries as well as to foreign companies conducting business in the United States.

In a precedent-setting case, a U.S. court found Nippon Paper Industries guilty of conspiring with other Japanese companies to increase fax paper prices in the United States. The Japanese government denounced the U.S. indictment of Nippon Paper in December 1995 as a violation of international law and Japan's sovereignty. The meetings at which pricing strategies were allegedly discussed took place outside the United States; a U.S. federal judge struck down the indictment, ruling that the Sherman Act does not apply to foreign conduct. However, a federal appeals court in Boston reversed the decision. In his opinion, U.S. Circuit Judge Bruce Selya wrote, "We live in an age of international commerce, where decisions reached in one corner of the world can reverberate around the globe."[29]

For the past four decades, the competition authority of the European Commission has had the power to prohibit agreements and practices that prevent, restrict, and distort competition. The Brussels-based Commission has jurisdiction over European-based companies as well as non-European-based ones that generate significant revenues in Europe, such as Google and Microsoft. For example, the Commission can block a proposed merger or joint venture, approve it with only minor modifications, or demand substantial concessions before granting approval. The Commission begins with a preliminary study of a proposed deal; serious concerns can lead to an in-depth investigation lasting several months.

Since the mid-1990s, when Mario Monti became Europe's antitrust chief, the Commission has taken an increasingly activist approach (Monti's nickname was "Super Mario"). In 2009, for example, Intel was fined $1.2 billion for antitrust violations. In 2017, following a seven-year investigation, competition commissioner Margrethe Vestager fined Alphabet Inc.'s Google unit €2.42 billion ($2.72 billion) for abusing its dominance in search (see Exhibit 5-13). Specifically, the Commission accused the tech giant of stifling competition by promoting its own Google Shopping comparison-shopping service over alternative services offered by rivals such as Foundem.co.uk.[30] Meanwhile, the Commission has two other antitrust cases pending against Google.

There have also been calls on both sides of the Atlantic for regulators to challenge the dominance of online retailing giant Amazon. For example, during the 2016 U.S. presidential campaign, candidate Donald Trump singled out the company for criticism, complaining, "Amazon is controlling so much." Amazon's admirers point out that, despite—or perhaps because of—its size, Amazon is a "consumer first" company that offers low prices on some 400 million different products. The broader question is whether existing antitrust laws and regulations need to be

Exhibit 5-12 Advanced Micro Devices (AMD) is the world's second-largest supplier of microprocessors for PCs and servers and is recognized as a technology innovation leader. The dominant market leader, Intel, has held a constant market share, in the 80–90 percent range, over the years. AMD filed a lawsuit against Intel in U.S. Federal Court, claiming Intel uses its dominant market power to stifle or exclude competition and engage in anticompetitive behavior around the globe. Full-page ads were deployed to describe Intel's conduct.
Source: Advanced Micro Devices (AMD).

revised to reflect the Internet age. Some observers want companies such as Facebook and Google to be regulated as public utilities!

Table 5-3 summarizes some recent joint ventures, mergers, and other global business deals that have been subject to review by antitrust authorities in various regions of the world.

Because the interstate-trade clause of the Treaty of Rome applies to trade with third countries, a company must be aware of the conduct of its affiliates. The European Commission also exempts certain cartels from Articles 85 and 86 of the treaty in an effort to encourage the growth of important businesses. The intent is to allow European companies to compete on an equal footing

Exhibit 5-13 Margrethe Vestager is the European Commissioner for Competition. Summing up her core beliefs, she says, "Politics should give all people opportunities and enable them to make free choices."
Source: Alexandros Michailidis/Shutterstock.

with Japan and the United States. In some instances, individual country laws in Europe apply to specific marketing mix elements. For example, some countries permit selective or exclusive product distribution. However, European Community law can take precedence.

In one case, Consten, a French company, had exclusive French rights to import and distribute consumer electronics products from the German company Grundig AG. Consten sued another French firm, charging the latter with bringing "parallel imports" into France illegally; that is, Consten charged that the competitor had bought Grundig products from various foreign suppliers without Consten's knowledge and was selling them in France. Although Consten's complaint was upheld by two French courts, the Paris Court of Appeals suspended the judgment, pending a ruling by the European Commission on whether the Grundig–Consten arrangement violated Articles 85 and 86 of the Treaty of Rome. The Commission eventually ruled against Consten on the grounds that "territorial protection proved to be particularly damaging to the realization of the Common Market."[31]

In some instances, companies or entire industries have been able to secure exemption from antitrust rules. In the airline industry, for example, OneWorld and Star Alliance are separate alliances in which competing airlines can share computer codes and set prices jointly. Similarly, the European Commission permitted United International Pictures (UIP), a joint venture between Paramount, Universal, and MGM/UA, to cut costs by collaborating on motion picture distribution

TABLE 5-3 Antitrust Rulings

Companies Involved	Global Antitrust Review	Antitrust Review in the United States
Acquisition of SABMiller by InBev (Belgium/Brazil), 2016, $101 billion	Deal was approved in China but SABMiller must sell its stake in Snow	Approved; InBev required to sell MillerCoors
Acquisition of Anheuser-Busch (United States) by InBev (Belgium/Brazil), 2008, $52 billion	Deal was approved in China but the company is prohibited from pursuing Huaran Snow or Beijing Yanjing	Approved; InBev required to sell Labatt USA
Acquisition of Honeywell (United States) by GE (United States), 2001, $40 billion	Deal was vetoed on grounds that the merged firm would be stronger than competitors in aviation equipment	Deal was on track for approval, subject to conditions
Joint venture between music businesses of EMI Group PLC (Great Britain) and Time Warner (United States), 2000, $20 billion	EU regulators expressed concern that the new EMI–Time Warner would dominate the growing market for digital music distribution	Deal was scrapped in October 2000 before regulatory review began.

Source: Compiled by the authors.

ENTREPRENEURIAL LEADERSHIP, CREATIVE THINKING, AND THE GLOBAL STARTUP

James Dyson, Dyson

Sir James Dyson is a British entrepreneur (see Exhibit 5-14). He has developed a wide range of innovative products, started a company to manufacture and market them, and built a global brand. By applying the basic tools and principles of modern marketing, Dyson has achieved remarkable success. In fact, he was knighted in 2006!

As is true with many entrepreneurs, Dyson's original idea was based on his recognition of a problem that needed to be solved and his own needs and wants. Simply put, he was frustrated with the way traditional vacuum cleaners functioned: As disposable bags filled with dust, the units lost suction. He said to himself, "There has to be a better way."

With this point in mind, Dyson developed a bagless vacuum; the first model, called the G-Force, was priced at $2,000. After the vacuum was awarded the 1991 International Design Fair Prize in Japan, Dyson was in business.

Fast-forward to today, and Dyson employs 9,000 people and generates nearly $3 billion in revenue each year. Over the last quarter century the company has launched a steady stream of premium-priced new products, including hair dryers, the AirBlade line of electric hand dryers, and variations on the original bagless vacuum cleaner.

The road has not always been smooth; some new product launches have not panned out. For example, the company stopped manufacturing its CR01 Contrarotator washing machines due to high production costs. According to Dyson, there is no stigma attached to failure: "As long as you are learning something," he says. One thing he learned from the washing machine experience: Charge higher prices!

In 2011, Dyson's company introduced a handheld, bagless, cordless vacuum, even though market research did not show a need for such a product. The technology involved required nearly 200,000 hours to develop and resulted in more than 100 patents. Dyson says, "You can't ask your customers to tell you what to do next. They don't know. That's our job." Armed with that insight, the company now offers a whole range of handheld vacuums, including the V6 Mattress vacuum ("removes allergens and bacteria") and the 360 Eye robot vacuum.

Although the United States is Dyson's top market, Asia accounts for more than half of the company's profits. Japan is Dyson's number 2 market, and China is showing rapid growth. The market opportunity in the latter case is due in part to the aspirations and spending habits of China's growing middle class. Also, ownership of domestic appliances in China is currently in the low single digits. Because Asian homes typically have hard floors rather than carpet, Dyson developed the V6 Fluffy cordless vacuum with a rotating fabric head for the market. In true "Think local, act global" fashion, the Fluffy is now a best-seller in the West as well.

Thanks to Dyson's core competencies in high-speed motors and batteries, the company recently announced that it will develop an electric vehicle (EV). The estimated cost? About £1 billion to develop the battery technology, and another £1 billion to develop the car, including the chassis.

Industry observers expect that Dyson will eventually leverage its battery expertise to use solid-state batteries in its EV program. Compared to lithium ion batteries, the advantages of using this technology include faster charging and longer driving range. Even so, it is anticipated that the first vehicle, which has a planned product launch in 2020 or 2021, will be powered by lithium batteries. A manufacturing site in the United Kingdom is under consideration, as are sites in China, Malaysia, and Singapore.

Sources: Alexandra Wolfe, "Weekend Confidential: James Dyson," *The Wall Street Journal* (December 9–10, 2017), p. C11; Michael Pooler and Peter Campbell, "Dyson Makes Dust Fly with Electric Vehicle Plans," *Financial Times* (September 30–October 1, 2017), p. 19; Michael Pooler and Peter Campbell, "Dyson Looks to Extend Midas Touch to Tomorrow's Vehicles," *Financial Times* (September 28, 2017), p. 18; Tom Hancock, "Dyson Aims to Build on Sales with R&D Center in China," *Financial Times* (May 26, 2017), p. 17; John Gapper and Tanya Powley, "'All Inventors Are Maniacs,'" *Financial Times* (April 11–12, 2015), pp. 17–18.

Exhibit 5-14 James Dyson. One of Dyson's newest products is the Airwrap, a curling iron with a detachable head that can be swapped out with attachments for curling, drying or smoothing.
Source: The Asahi Shimbun/ Getty Images.

in Europe. However, in 1998, the commission reversed itself and notified the three studios that they had to distribute their films independently in Europe.[32]

A **cartel** is a group of individual companies that collectively set prices, control output, or take other actions to maximize profits. For example, the group of oil-producing countries known as Organization of the Petroleum Exporting Countries (OPEC) is a cartel. In the United States, most cartels are illegal. One notable exception, however, has a direct impact on global marketing: A number of the world's major shipping lines, including the U.S.-based Sea-Land Service and Denmark's A. P. Moller/Maersk line, have enjoyed exemptions from antitrust laws since the passage of the Shipping Act of 1916. This law was originally enacted to ensure reliability; today, it has been estimated that the cartel results in shipping prices that are 18 percent higher than they would be if shippers set prices independently. Attempts in recent years to change the law have been unsuccessful.[33]

Licensing and Trade Secrets

Licensing is a contractual agreement in which a licensor allows a licensee to use patents, trademarks, trade secrets, technology, or other intangible assets in return for royalty payments or other forms of compensation. U.S. laws do not regulate the licensing process per se as do technology-transfer laws in the EU, Australia, Japan, and many developing countries. The duration of the licensing agreement and the amount of royalties a company can receive are considered a matter of commercial negotiation between licensor and licensee, and there are no government restrictions on remittances of royalties abroad. Important considerations in licensing include which assets a firm may offer for license, how to price the assets, and whether to grant only the right to "make" the product or the rights to "use" and to "sell" the product as well. The right to sublicense is another important issue. As with distribution agreements, decisions must also be made regarding exclusive or nonexclusive arrangements and the size of the licensee's territory.

To prevent the licensee from using the licensed technology to compete directly with the licensor, the latter may try to limit the licensee to selling only in its home country. The licensor may also seek to contractually bind the licensee to discontinue use of the technology after the contract has expired. In practice, host-government laws and even U.S. antitrust laws may make such agreements impossible to obtain. Licensing is thus a potentially dangerous action: It may be instrumental in creating a competitor. For this reason, licensors should be careful to ensure that their own competitive positions remain advantageous—which requires constant innovation.

As noted, licensing agreements can come under antitrust scrutiny. In one case, Bayer AG granted an exclusive patent license for a new household insecticide to S. C. Johnson & Sons. The German firm's decision to license was based in part on the time required for obtaining approval for the insecticide from the U.S. Environmental Protection Agency (EPA), which had stretched to 3 years. Bayer decided it made better business sense to let the U.S. firm deal with regulatory authorities in return for a 5 percent royalty on sales. However, a class-action suit filed against the companies alleged that the licensing deal would allow Johnson to monopolize the $450 million home insecticide market.

At this point, the U.S. Justice Department stepped in, calling the licensing agreement anticompetitive. In a statement, Anne Bingaman, then head of the Justice Department's antitrust unit, said, "The cozy arrangement that Bayer and Johnson maintained is unacceptable in a highly concentrated market." Bayer agreed to offer licenses to any interested company on better terms than the original contract with Johnson. Johnson agreed to notify the U.S. government of any future pending exclusive licensing agreements for household insecticides. Further, if Bayer was party to any such agreements, Bayer agreed that the Justice Department had the right to veto them. The reaction from the legal community was negative. One Washington lawyer who specializes in intellectual property law noted that the case "really attacks traditional licensing practices." As Melvin Jager, president of the Licensing Executives Society, explained, "An exclusive license is a very valuable tool to promote intellectual property and get it out into the marketplace."[34]

What happens if a licensee gains knowledge of the licensor's trade secrets? *Trade secrets* are confidential information or knowledge that has commercial value and is not in the public domain and for which steps have been taken to keep it secret. Trade secrets may include manufacturing processes, formulas, designs, and customer lists. To prevent disclosure, the licensing of unpatented trade secrets should be linked to confidentiality contracts with each employee who has access to the protected information. In the United States, trade secrets are protected by state law rather than federal statute; most states have adopted the Uniform Trade Secrets Act (UTSA). The U.S. law provides trade secret liability against third parties that obtain confidential information through an intermediary. Remedies include damages and other forms of relief.

The 1990s saw widespread improvements in laws pertaining to trade secrets. Several countries adopted trade secret statutes for the first time. Mexico's first statute protecting trade secrets became effective on June 28, 1991; China's first trade secret law took effect on December 1, 1993. In both countries, the new laws were part of broader revisions of intellectual property laws. Japan and South Korea have also amended their intellectual property laws to include trade secrets. In addition, many countries in Central and Eastern Europe enacted laws to protect trade secrets.

When the North American Free Trade Agreement (NAFTA) became effective on January 1, 1994, it marked the first international trade agreement with provisions for protecting trade secrets. This milestone was quickly followed by the Agreement on Trade-Related Aspects of Intellectual Property Rights (TRIPs), which resulted from the Uruguay Round of GATT negotiations. The TRIPs agreement requires signatory countries to protect against acquisition, disclosure, or use of trade secrets "in a manner contrary to honest commercial practices."[35] Despite these formal legal developments, in practice, enforcement is the key issue. Companies transferring trade secrets across borders should seek information about not only the existence of legal protection but also the risks associated with lax enforcement.

Bribery and Corruption: Legal and Ethical Issues

History does not record a burst of international outrage when Charles M. Schwab, head of Bethlehem Steel at the beginning of the twentieth century, presented a $200,000 diamond and pearl necklace to the mistress of Czar Alexander III's nephew.[36] In return for that consideration, Bethlehem Steel won the contract to supply the rails for the Trans-Siberian railroad. Today, in the post-Soviet era, emerging opportunities in Central and Eastern Europe are again luring global companies. However, in Poland, Hungary, and elsewhere, nationalist governments are increasingly hostile to foreign companies. When awarding state contracts, for example, politicians in the region sometimes favor powerful local businesspeople with close ties to the government. Which kind of ties? In some cases, bribery may be involved.

Bribery is the corrupt business practice of demanding or offering some type of consideration—typically in the form of cash payments—when negotiating business deals. While most countries have anticorruption laws that prohibit bribery, enforcement is often lax. That is not the case in the United States. Employees of U.S. companies in particular are constrained by U.S. government policies of the post-Watergate age. Transparency International (www.transparency.org) compiles an annual report ranking countries in terms of a Corruption Perceptions Index (CPI), where the "cleanest" score is 100. The 2016 ranking of countries with the highest and lowest CPI scores is shown in Table 5-4.

TABLE 5-4   2016 Corruption Rankings

Rank/Country	2016 CPI Score	Rank/Country	2016 CPI Score
1. Denmark	90	166. Venezuela	17
1. New Zealand	90	168. Guinea-Bissau	16
3. Finland	89	169. Afghanistan	15
4. Sweden	88	170. Libya	14
5. Switzerland	86	170. Sudan	14
6. Norway	85	170. Yemen	14
7. Singapore	84	173. Syria	13
8. Netherlands	83	174. North Korea	12
9. Canada	82	175. South Sudan	11
10. Germany	81	176. Somalia	10

Note: Transparency International's Corruption Perceptions Index (CPI) scores countries on their perceived levels of public-sector corruption on a scale from 0 (highly corrupt) to 100 (very clean).
Source: Adapted from 2016 Corruption Rankings. Copyright 2016 Transparency International: the global coalition against corruption. For more information, visit www.transparency.org.

In the United States, the **Foreign Corrupt Practices Act (FCPA)** is a legacy of the Watergate scandal during Richard Nixon's presidency. In the course of his investigation, the Watergate special prosecutor discovered that hundreds of American companies had made undisclosed payments to foreign officials, totaling hundreds of millions of dollars. Congress unanimously passed the act, which President Jimmy Carter signed into law in 1977.

Administered by the Department of Justice (DOJ) and the Securities and Exchange Commission (SEC), the FCPA is concerned with disclosure and prohibition. Regarding disclosure, the act requires publicly held companies to institute internal accounting controls. The prohibition part makes it a crime for U.S. corporations to bribe an official of a foreign government or political party to obtain or retain business. Payments to third parties are also prohibited when the company has reason to believe that part or all of the money will be channeled to foreign officials.

The U.S. business community immediately began lobbying for changes to the FCPA, complaining that the statute was too vague and so broad in scope that it threatened to severely curtail U.S. business activities abroad. President Ronald Reagan signed amendments to the statute into law in 1988 as part of the Omnibus Trade and Competitiveness Act. Among the changes were exclusions for "grease" payments to low-level officials to cut red tape and expedite "routine governmental actions" such as clearing shipments through customs, securing permits, or getting airport passport clearance to leave a country.

Convictions for FCPA violations carry severe jail sentences and substantial fines. The law is worded quite broadly and has plenty of gray areas; even so, in 2009 and 2010 the U.S. Justice Department collected $2 billion in fines and penalties.[37] A company cannot pay or reimburse fines incurred by "rogue" employees; the rationale is that individuals commit such crimes. As noted on the Justice Department's Web site:

> The following criminal penalties may be imposed for violations of the FCPA's anti-bribery provisions: corporations and other business entities are subject to a fine of up to $2,000,000; officers, directors, stockholders, employees, and agents are subject to a fine of up to $100,000 and imprisonment for up to five years. Moreover, under the Alternative Fines Act, these fines may be actually quite higher—the actual fine may be up to twice the benefit that the defendant sought to obtain by making the corrupt payment. You should also be aware that fines imposed on individuals may not be paid by their employer or principal.[38]

In addition, this law does not let a person do indirectly (e.g., through an agent, joint venture partner, or other third party) what it prohibits directly.

Rolls-Royce (the aircraft engine manufacturer, not the luxury car brand) is one well-known company that has run afoul of antibribery laws in the United States and elsewhere. The U.K.-based firm has businesses in a variety of sectors, including civil aviation. Its energy business was sold to Germany's Siemens in 2014, but prior to the sale, there was evidence of multiple offenses that occurred in Brazil, Kazakhstan, Nigeria, and Russia. Rolls-Royce agreed to pay a £671 million ($919 million) fine to the United Kingdom, the United States, and Brazil. In exchange, the company was not prosecuted on criminal charges. However, several former Rolls-Royce employees charged by the U.S. Department of Justice with conspiring to violate the FCPA ultimately pleaded guilty.[39]

Some critics of the FCPA decry it as a regrettable display of moral imperialism. At issue is the extraterritorial sovereignty of U.S. law. It is wrong, according to these critics, to impose U.S. laws, standards, values, and mores on American companies and citizens worldwide. As one legal expert pointed out, this criticism has one fundamental flaw: There is no nation in which the letter of the law condones bribery of government officials. Thus, the standard set by the FCPA is shared, in principle at least, by other nations.[40]

Another criticism of the FCPA is that it puts U.S. companies in a difficult position relative to foreign competitors, especially those in Japan and Europe. Several opinion polls and surveys of the business community have revealed the widespread perception that the act adversely affects U.S. businesses overseas. In contrast, some academic researchers have concluded that the FCPA has *not* negatively affected the export performance of U.S. industry. However, a U.S. Commerce Department report prepared with the help of U.S. intelligence services indicated that in 1994 alone, bribes offered by non-U.S. companies were a factor in 100 business deals valued at $45 billion. Foreign companies prevailed in 80 percent of those deals.[42] Although accurate statistics are

"Corruption is probably the most immediate threat and difficulty that any business faces in Russia—and the trend is increasing."[41]

Carlo Gallo, business risk consultant

hard to come by, the rankings shown in Table 5-4 highlight some areas of the world where bribery is still rampant.

The existence of bribery as a fact of life in world markets will not change just because the U.S. Congress condemns it. Bribery payments are considered a deductible business expense in many European countries. According to one estimate, the annual price tag for illegal payments by German firms alone is more than $5 billion. Still, increasing numbers of global companies are adopting codes of conduct designed to reduce illegal activities. Moreover, in May 1997, the OECD adopted a formal standard against bribery by drafting a binding international convention that makes it a crime for a company bidding on a contract to bribe foreign officials. The OECD's antibribery convention (officially known as the Convention on Combating Bribery of Foreign Public Officials in International Business Transactions) went into effect in 1999. The OECD is also working on a smaller scale to create so-called islands of integrity. The goal is to achieve transparency at the level of an individual deal, with all the players pledging not to bribe.[43]

Investigative reporters often file stories regarding bribery or other forms of malfeasance. In emerging countries, journalists may themselves become targets if they criticize the rich or powerful (see Case 5-2). When companies operate abroad in the absence of home-country legal constraints, they face a continuum of choices concerning company ethics. At one extreme, they can maintain home-country ethics worldwide with absolutely no adjustment or adaptation to local practice. At the other extreme, they can abandon any attempt to maintain company ethics and adapt entirely to local conditions and circumstances as company managers perceive them in each local environment. Between these extremes, one approach that companies may select is to utilize varying degrees of an extension of home-country ethics. Alternatively, they may adapt in varying degrees to local customs and practices.

What should a U.S. company do if competitors are willing to offer a bribe? Two alternative courses of action are possible. One is to ignore the expectation for bribery and act as if it does not exist. The other is to recognize the existence of bribery and evaluate its effect on customers' purchase decisions as if it were just another element of the marketing mix. The overall value of a company's offer must be as good as, or better than, the competitor's overall offering, bribe included. It may be possible to offer a lower price, a better product, better distribution, or better advertising to offset the value added by the bribe. The best line of defense is to have a product that is clearly superior to that of the competition. In such a case, a bribe should not sway the purchase decision. Alternatively, clear superiority in service and in local representation may tip the scales in the company's desired direction.

▶ **5-4** Describe the available alternatives for conflict resolution and dispute settlement when doing business outside the home country.

(5-4) Conflict Resolution, Dispute Settlement, and Litigation

The degree of legal cooperation and harmony in the EU is unique and stems, in part, from the existence of code law as a common bond. Other regional organizations have made far less progress toward harmonization. As a result, countries vary in their approach toward conflict resolution. The United States has more lawyers than any other country in the world and is arguably the most litigious nation on earth. In part, this is a reflection of the low-context nature of American culture and the spirit of confrontational competitiveness. Other factors can contribute to differing attitudes toward litigation. For example, in many European nations, class-action lawsuits are not allowed. Also, European lawyers cannot undertake cases on a contingency fee basis. Change is now in the air, though, as Europe experiences a broad political shift away from its traditional embrace of "the welfare state."[44]

Conflicts inevitably arise in business everywhere, but they are especially likely when different cultures come together to buy, sell, establish joint ventures, compete, and cooperate in global markets. For American companies, the dispute with a foreign party is frequently in the home-country jurisdiction. Such an issue can be litigated in the United States, where the company and its attorneys might be said to enjoy "home-court" advantage. Litigation in foreign courts is a vastly more complex undertaking, partly because of differences in language, legal systems, currencies, and traditional business customs and patterns.

In addition, problems may arise from differences in procedures relating to discovery. In essence, *discovery* is the process of obtaining evidence to prove claims and determining which evidence may be admissible in which countries under which conditions. A further complication is the fact that judgments handed down in courts in another country may not be enforceable in the home country. For all these reasons, many companies prefer to pursue arbitration before proceeding to litigation.

Alternatives to Litigation for Dispute Settlement

In 1995, the Cuban government abruptly canceled contracts with Endesa, a Spanish utility company. Rather than seek restitution in a Cuban court, Endesa turned to the International Arbitration Tribunal in Paris, seeking damages of $12 million. Endesa's actions illustrate how alternative dispute resolution (ADR) methods allow parties to resolve international commercial disputes without resorting to the court system. Formal arbitration is one means of settling international business disputes outside the courtroom. **Arbitration** is a negotiation process that the two parties have, by prior agreement, committed themselves to using. It is a fair process in the sense that the parties using it have created it themselves. Generally, arbitration involves a hearing of the parties before a three-member panel; each party selects one panel member, and those two panel members in turn select the third member. The panel renders a judgment that the parties agree in advance to abide by.

The most important treaty regarding international arbitration is the 1958 New York Convention on the Recognition and Enforcement of Foreign Arbitral Awards. Also known as the New York Convention, the treaty currently has 157 signatory countries, including China. The framework created by the New York Convention is important for several reasons. First, when parties enter into agreements that provide for international arbitration, the signatory countries can hold the parties to their pledge to use arbitration. Second, after arbitration has taken place and the arbitrators have made an award, the signatories recognize and can enforce the judgment. Third, the signatories agree that there are limited grounds for challenging arbitration decisions. The grounds that are recognized are different from the typical appeals that are permitted in a court of law.

Some firms and lawyers inexperienced in the practice of international commercial arbitration approach the arbitration clauses in a contract as "just another clause." However, the terms of every contract are different and, therefore, no two arbitration clauses should be the same. Consider, for example, the case of a contract between an American firm and a Japanese one. If the parties resort to arbitration, where will it take place? The American side will be reluctant to go to Japan; conversely, the Japanese side will not want to arbitrate in the United States. An alternative, "neutral" location—Singapore or London, for example—must be considered and specified in the arbitration clause. In which language will the proceedings be conducted? If no language is specified in the arbitration clause, the arbitrators themselves will choose.

In addition to location and language, other issues must be addressed in relation to the arbitration process. For example, if the parties to a patent-licensing arrangement agree in the arbitration clause that the validity of the patent cannot be contested, such a provision may not be enforceable in some countries. Which country's laws will be used as the standard for invalidity? Pursuing such an issue on a country-by-country basis would be inordinately time-consuming. In addition, there is the issue of acceptance: By law, U.S. courts must accept an arbitrator's decision in patent disputes; in other countries, there is no general rule of acceptance.

To reduce delays owing to disputed issues, one expert suggests drafting arbitration clauses with as much specificity as possible. To the extent possible, for example, patent policies in various countries should be addressed; arbitration clauses may also include a provision that all foreign patent issues will be judged according to the standard of home-country law. Another provision could forbid the parties from commencing separate legal actions in other countries. The goal is to help the arbitration tribunal zero in on the express intentions of the parties.[45]

For decades, business arbitration has also been promoted through the International Court of Arbitration at the Paris-based International Chamber of Commerce (ICC; www.iccwbo.org). The ICC recently modernized some of its older rules. However, because it is such a well-known organization, it has an extensive backlog of cases. Overall, the ICC has gained a reputation for being slower, more expensive, and more cumbersome than some arbitration alternatives. As U.S. involvement in global commerce grew dramatically during the post–World War II period, the American Arbitration Association (AAA) also became recognized as an effective institution within which to resolve disputes. In 1992, the AAA signed a cooperation agreement with China's Beijing Conciliation Center.

Another agency for settling disputes is the Swedish Arbitration Institute of the Stockholm Chamber of Commerce. This agency frequently handles disputes between Western and Eastern European countries and has gained credibility for its evenhanded administration. However, a favorable ruling from the arbitration tribunal is one thing; an enforced ruling is another. For example, Canada's IMP Group took its case against a Russian hotel development partner to Stockholm and was awarded $9.4 million. When payment was not forthcoming, IMP's representatives took matters into their own hands: They commandeered an Aeroflot jet in Canada and released it only after the Russians paid up![46]

Other arbitration alternatives have proliferated in recent years. In addition to those already mentioned, active centers for arbitration exist in Vancouver, Hong Kong, Cairo, Kuala Lumpur, Singapore, Buenos Aires, Bogotá, and Mexico City. A World Arbitration Institute was established in New York; in the United Kingdom, the Advisory, Conciliation and Arbitration Service (ACAS) has achieved great success in handling industrial disputes. An International Council for Commercial Arbitration (ICCA) was established to coordinate the far-flung activities of arbitration organizations; it meets in different locations around the world every four years.

The United Nations Commission on International Trade Law (UNCITRAL; www.uncitral. org) has also been a significant force in the area of arbitration. Its rules have become more or less standards, as many of the organizations just named have adopted them with some modifications. Many developing countries, for example, long held prejudices against the ICC, AAA, and other developed-country organizations. Representatives of developing nations assumed that such organizations would be biased in favor of multinational corporations. For this reason, developing nations insisted on settlement of disputes in national courts, which was unacceptable to many multinational firms. This was especially true in Latin America, where the Calvo Doctrine required disputes arising with foreign investors to be resolved in national courts under national laws. The growing influence of the ICCA and UNCITRAL rules, coupled with the proliferation of regional arbitration centers, has contributed to changing attitudes in developing countries and resulted in the increased use of arbitration around the world.

▶ **5-5** In general terms, outline the regulatory environment in the European Union.

(5-5) The Regulatory Environment

The **regulatory environment** of global marketing consists of a variety of governmental and nongovernmental agencies that enforce laws or set guidelines for conducting business. These regulatory agencies address a wide range of marketing issues, including price control, valuation of imports and exports, trade practices, labeling, food and drug regulations, employment conditions, collective bargaining, advertising content, and competitive practices. As noted in *The Wall Street Journal*:

> Each nation's regulations reflect and reinforce its brand of capitalism—predatory in the U.S., paternal in Germany, and protected in Japan—and its social values. It's easier to open a business in the U.S. than in Germany because Germans value social consensus above risk-taking, but it's harder to hire people because Americans worry more about discrimination lawsuits. It's easier to import children's clothes in the U.S. than [in] Japan because Japanese bureaucrats defend a jumble of import restrictions, but it's harder to open bank branches across the U.S. because Americans strongly defend state prerogatives.[47]

In most countries, the influence of regulatory agencies is pervasive, and an understanding of how they operate is essential to protect business interests and advance new programs. Executives at many global companies are realizing they need to hire lobbyists to represent their interests and to influence the direction of the regulatory process. For example, in the early 1990s, McDonald's, Nike, and Toyota didn't have a single representative in Brussels—but today these and other companies have several people representing their interests to the European Commission. U.S. law firms and consulting firms also have sharply increased their presence in Brussels; in an effort to gain insight into EU politics and access to its policymakers, some have hired EU officials. In all, there are currently approximately 15,000 lobbyists in Brussels representing some 1,400 companies and nonprofit organizations from around the world.[48]

Regional Economic Organizations: The EU Example

The overall importance of regional organizations such as the WTO and the EU was discussed in Chapter 3. The legal dimensions are important, however, and will be briefly mentioned here. The Treaty of Rome established the European Community (EC), the precursor to the EU. This treaty created an institutional framework in which a council (the Council of Ministers) serves as the main decision-making body, with each country member having direct representation. The other three main institutions of the community are the European Commission, the EU's executive arm; the European Parliament, the legislative body; and the European Court of Justice.

The 1987 Single European Act amended the Treaty of Rome and provided strong impetus for the creation of a single market beginning January 1, 1993. Although technically the target was not completely met, approximately 85 percent of the newer recommendations were implemented into national law by most member states by the target date, resulting in substantial harmonization. A relatively new body known as the European Council (a distinct entity from the Council of Ministers) was formally incorporated into the EC institutional structure by Article 2 of the 1987 act. Composed of heads of member states plus the president of the European Commission, the European Council's role is to define general political guidelines for the union and provide direction on integration-related issues such as monetary union.[49] Governments in Central and Eastern European countries that hope to join the EU are currently getting their laws in line with those of the EU.

The Treaty of Rome contains hundreds of articles, several of which are directly applicable to global companies and global marketers. Articles 30 through 36 establish the general policy referred to as "Free Flow of Goods, People, Capital and Technology" among the member states. Articles 85 through 86 contain competition rules, as amended by various directives of the 20-member EU Commission. The Commission is the administrative arm of the EU; from its base in Brussels, it proposes laws and policies, monitors the observance of EU laws, administers and implements EU legislation, and represents the EU to international organizations.[50] Commission members represent the union rather than their respective nations.

The laws, regulations, directives, and policies that originate in the EU Commission must be submitted to the European Parliament for an opinion and then passed along to the European Council for a final decision. Once the Council approves a prospective law, it becomes union law, which is somewhat analogous to U.S. federal law. Regulations automatically become law throughout the EU; directives include a time frame for implementation by legislation in each member state. For example, in 1994 the Commission issued a directive regarding use of trademarks in comparative advertising. Individual member nations of the EU worked to implement the directive; in the United Kingdom, the 1994 Trade Marks Act gave companies the right to apply for trademark protection of smells, sounds, and images and also provided improved protection against trademark counterfeiting.

With the rise of the single market, many industries are facing new regulatory environments. The European Court of Justice (ECJ) is the EU's highest legal authority (see Exhibit 5-15). As the sole arbiter of EU law, it is responsible for ensuring that EU laws and treaties are interpreted uniformly throughout the union. Based in Luxembourg, it consists of two separate tribunals. The senior body is known as the Court of Justice; a separate entity, the Court of First Instance, hears cases involving commerce and competition (see Table 5-5).

Although the European Court of Justice plays a role similar to that of the U.S. Supreme Court, there are important differences. The European court cannot decide which cases it will hear, and it does not issue dissenting opinions. The court exercises jurisdiction over a range of civil matters involving trade, individual rights, and environmental law. For example, the ECJ can assess damages against countries that fail to introduce directives by the date set. The court also hears disputes that arise among the EU's 28 member nations on trade issues such as mergers, monopolies, trade barriers and regulations, and exports. In addition, the ECJ is empowered to resolve conflicts between national law and EU law. In most cases, EU law supersedes national laws of individual European countries.

Marketers must be aware, however, that national laws should always be consulted. National laws may be *stricter* than EU law, especially in such areas as competition and antitrust. To the extent possible, EU law is intended to harmonize national laws to promote the purposes defined in Articles 30 through 36. The goal is to bring the lax laws of some member states up to designated minimum standards, but more restrictive positions may still exist in some national laws.

For example, Italy recently introduced the Reguzzoni-Versace Law, which is intended to regulate trade in textiles, leather, and footwear. It states that if at least two stages of production—there are four stages altogether—occur in Italy, a garment can be labeled "Made in Italy." In addition, the country or countries in which the remaining production stages take place must be identified. Reguzzoni-Versace was *supposed* to enter into force October 1, 2010, but Brussels objected on the grounds that the law conflicts with Article 34, which prohibits national measures providing restrictions to trade in the EU. In the view of EU regulators, the Reguzzoni-Versace Law is "protectionist" and more stringent than EU law, which requires only that one main production stage take place in Europe.[55]

Another recent case in Italy involved the University of Florence, which was sued by a lecturer from Belgium on grounds of discrimination. The Italian court was required to determine whether the facts of the case indicated that Italian law had been applied equally to both Italian and foreign academics. If the court found national law had, in fact, been applied equally, the case would end there. If not, the case would go on to the ECJ, which would make a ruling based on EU laws prohibiting discrimination on the basis of nationality.

TABLE 5-5 Recent Cases before the European Court of Justice/General Court of the European Union[51]

Country/Plaintiffs Involved	Issue
Taxi drivers (Spain)/Uber (United States)	The Court ruled that Uber is a transportation company. Uber had sought to be classified as a tech company.
Parfümerie Akzente (Germany)/Coty (United States)	The Court upheld the decision by American beauty products company to prohibit its authorized German distributor from selling Coty's brands on Amazon.de.[52]
EU/Ireland	EU Competition Minister Margrethe Vestiger sought to force Ireland to collect €13 billion in back taxes from Apple.
Facebook (Ireland)/privacy advocate Max Schrems	In 2015, the Court struck down the Safe Harbor Act following publication of documents leaked by Edward Snowden about surveillance by the U.S. National Security Agency.
Chocoladefabriken Lindt & Sprüngli AG (Switzerland)/Franz Hauswirth GmbH (Austria)	Lindt markets gold-foil–wrapped chocolate Easter bunnies (Goldhase), for which it owns a trademark. Lindt sued Hauswirth for trademark infringement after the Austrian company began marketing its own foil-wrapped bunny. The Austrian Supreme Court asked the ECJ to rule on "bad faith" in trademark matters.[53]
L'Oréal (France)/Bellure (France)	Perfume marketer L'Oréal sued rival Bellure for marketing "knockoff" perfume that mimicked the bottles, packaging, and fragrances of L'Oréal's brands. The ECJ ruled in favor of L'Oréal on the grounds that the similarity of Bellure's products to L'Oréal's constituted an unfair advantage. The Court of Appeal later upheld the ECJ's decision.[54]

Summary

The political environment of global marketing is the set of governmental institutions, political parties, and organizations that are the expression of the people in the nations of the world. In particular, anyone engaged in global marketing should have an overall understanding of the importance of *sovereignty* to national governments. The political environment varies from country to country, and *political risk* assessment is crucial. It is also important to understand a particular government's actions with respect to taxes and seizures of assets. Historically, the latter have taken the form of *expropriation*, *confiscation*, and *nationalization*.

The legal environment consists of laws, courts, attorneys, legal customs, and practices. *International law* comprises the rules and principles that nation-states consider binding upon themselves. The countries of the world can be broadly categorized as having either *common-law* legal systems or *civil-law* legal systems. The United States and Canada and many former British colonies are common-law countries; most other countries are civil-law countries. A third system, *Islamic law*, predominates in the Middle East. Some of the most important legal issues pertain to *jurisdiction*, antitrust, and licensing. In addition, *bribery* is pervasive in many parts of the world; the *Foreign Corrupt Practices Act (FCPA)* applies to American companies operating abroad. Intellectual property protection is another critical legal issue. *Counterfeiting* is a major problem in global marketing; it often involves infringement of a company's *copyright*, *patent*, or *trademark* ownership. When legal conflicts arise, companies can pursue the matter in court or use *arbitration*.

The regulatory environment consists of agencies, both governmental and nongovernmental, that enforce laws or set guidelines for conducting business. Global marketing activities can be affected by a number of international or regional economic organizations; in Europe, for example, the EU makes laws governing member states. The WTO will have a broad impact on global marketing activities in the years to come.

Although all three environments—political, legal, and regulatory—are complex, astute marketers plan ahead to avoid situations that might result in conflict, misunderstanding, or outright violation of national laws.

Discussion Questions

5-1.   Why should global marketers be concerned by the various kinds of infringement on intellectual property?

5-2.   Briefly explain the meaning of "expropriation," "confiscation," and "nationalization." What options are available for global companies to mitigate potential risks such as these?

5-3.   There are an increasing number of international judicial institutions that produce decisions and opinions on a variety of matters related to international relations and trade. These international courts no longer restrict themselves to settling disputes; they have adopted a role in what could be described as global governance. Why is fair and impartial justice at the international level so important?

5-4.   Establishing jurisdiction in international legal disputes is a tricky problem. How is jurisdiction usually established?

CASE 5-1   (Continued from page 161)
Travis Kalanick and Uber

One dramatic incident occurred in India, where Uber was banned in the Delhi region after a driver was accused of sexually assaulting a female passenger. Uber issued a statement expressing sympathy for the victim; Kalanick vowed to work more closely with the Indian government to improve procedures for conducting background checks of prospective drivers. Even so, it turned out that company executives had allegedly mishandled some of the victim's medical records.

From the start, Kalanick seemed to relish locking horns with lawmakers. As he told *The Wall Street Journal* in 2013, "We don't have to beg for forgiveness because we are legal. But there's been so much corruption and so much cronyism in the taxi industry and so much regulatory capture that if you ask permission for something that's already legal, you'll never get it. There's no upside to them."

By 2017, Uber was valued at $68 billion—but the company's rapid growth had been accompanied by considerable negative publicity. These included the company's use of so-called Greyball software that allowed drivers to deny rides to passengers who worked for legal authorities. A number of top executives left the company. In addition, during a taxi strike at New York's John F. Kennedy airport, the company's surge pricing kicked in, and unhappy customers launched a #DeleteUber social media firestorm against the ride-sharing pioneer for price gouging.

Perhaps most troubling were allegations of sexism and sexual harassment at the company. These revelations came to light in February 2017 when a software engineer named Susan Fowler published a blog post in which she described the sexual harassment that she had endured at Uber. By the end of 2017, the #MeToo social media campaign by silence breakers had gained considerable momentum and ended the careers of several powerful figures from politics, media, and the entertainment industry.

More broadly, Ms. Fowler's act of speaking out was just one facet of growing public and government concern over the power of Big Tech companies such as Amazon and Google. Some observers noted that the "fourteen values" that guided the Uber organization—for example, "let builders build," "always be hustling," and "principled confrontation"—had created a toxic corporate culture.

To help address these issues at Uber, the company hired Frances Frei, a professor of service management at the Harvard Business School. Her title: Senior Vice President for Leadership and Strategy. Frei was tasked with overhauling Uber's corporate culture. To do so, she began teaching management skills that she says had been lacking as the company pursued ambitious growth goals. In her view, one of Uber's problems was that it underinvested in its people.

Another key figure is Chief Brand Officer Bozoma Saint John (see Exhibit 5-16). Hired by Kalanick in the summer of 2017, Saint John had an outstanding track record as a marketer at Pepsi, Beats Audio, and Apple Music. At Uber, she moved quickly to create local advertising tie-ins with the National Football League featuring Uber drivers who are sports fans driving friends to the stadium on game day. A second tie-in, with the National Basketball League, launched nationally. In Saint

John's view, the campaign, dubbed "Rolling with the Champion" and featuring ESPN SportsCenter co-anchor Cari Champion, positioned the Uber brand as "the official ride of pop culture."

A New Leader Steps In

In June 2017, founder Travis Kalanick stepped down as Uber's CEO. A 14-person executive team, including Professor Frei, ran the company until a new boss could be recruited. The new CEO, Dara Khosrowshahi, came on board in September 2017. He immediately set about the task of rebuilding trust in the brand among the general public as well as with government authorities. Khosrowshahi acknowledged that the company's notoriety had damaged its reputation and came at a cost. In an open letter, he wrote, "On behalf of everyone at Uber globally, I apologize for the mistakes we've made."

Transport for London Cracks Down

After just a few weeks on the job, Khosrowshahi was confronted by a new challenge: In fall 2017, Transport for London (TfL), the British regulatory authority, announced that it would not renew Uber's license. The agency had issued Uber its first permit to operate in London in 2012; the city quickly became one of Uber's most important markets. In 2013, Uber launched UberX, a lower-cost ride-hailing service, which TfL classified as a minicab service that used "private-hire vehicles." Thus, in London, Uber was competing with the city's iconic black cabs as well as swelling the numbers of minicabs.

The TfL revoked Uber's permit on the grounds that the company was not "fit and proper" to operate in London. In doing so, the regulatory authority identified four concerns relating to corporate responsibility and governance. One focused on passenger safety; the TfL faulted Uber for lax reporting of crimes committed by drivers. The TfL also alleged that Uber did not follow the correct procedures for obtaining medical certificates for drivers and for conducting criminal background checks. Finally, the agency raised the issue of use of the Greyball software. Uber responded to all four issues. It noted, for example, that it was the TfL's responsibility to ensure that background checks had been performed before it issued licenses to drivers.

In November 2017, Uber suffered another setback. A judge at an employment tribunal in London ruled that Uber's 50,000 U.K. drivers were, in fact, employees rather than independent contractors. If the ruling stands, it will have far-reaching implications for a variety of technology apps that are integral to the so-called gig economy. In Uber's case, it would lead to higher costs by requiring the company to pay drivers the minimum wage as well as make provisions for holiday pay, national insurance contributions, and additional taxes.

Trade Secrets and Data Breaches

Meanwhile, back in the United States, Uber faced a trial to defend itself against charges of stealing trade secrets. The suit had been brought

Exhibit 5-16 Bozoma Saint John.
Source: Steve Jennings/Stringer/Getty Images.

by Waymo, the autonomous vehicle unit of Google parent Alphabet. Lawyers for Waymo alleged that a former employee, Anthony Levandowski, downloaded thousands of confidential documents prior to leaving to start Otto, a self-driving truck venture.

Some of the documents included details about Waymo's proprietary work on LiDAR, a laser-based sensor technology that is integral to autonomous mobility. In August 2016, Uber acquired Otto. The suit was settled in early 2018, with Uber agreeing to give Waymo stock worth $245 million. Uber also agreed to use only its own technology in its autonomous vehicles program.

Another revelation during the trade secrets trial concerned a shadowy "marketplace analytics team" at Uber whose role was to gather information, including trade secrets, about foreign competitors. According to the evidence presented at the trial, the team had used self-deleting messages to avoid creating a paper trail.

There was still more bad news to come. Near the end of November 2017, Khosrowshahi announced that one year previously Uber had suffered a data breach in which hackers stole the names, e-mail addresses, and telephone numbers of 50 million Uber passengers and 7 million drivers. At the time, the company did not report the breach to authorities, opting instead to pay the hackers $100,000 on the condition that they delete the stolen data. Data privacy authorities in the United States and elsewhere launched investigations into Uber's handling of the situation. Critics noted that Uber's response to the cyber hack was yet another example of the company's self-defeating corporate culture.

Lyft Gets a Lift

The turmoil surrounding Uber has provided an opportunity for Lyft, the rival U.S.-based ride-sharing company. Cofounders John Zimmer and Logan Green are confident that their company has the necessary controls in place to ensure good corporate governance and enable it to avoid the type of pitfalls Uber created for itself.

Even as Lyft's driver-friendly corporate culture enabled it to take market share from Uber in the United States, it was targeting key cities for international expansion. For example, Lyft launched operations in Toronto, and top management held a series of meetings with TfL regulators concerning expanding in London.

Discussion Questions

5-5. Despite the negative publicity surrounding Uber, consumers continue to utilize the company's services. Is this surprising?

5-6. Is ride-hailing likely to become a commodity service? If so, how will companies such as Lyft and Uber differentiate themselves in the market?

5-7. Do you think either Uber or Lyft will emerge as the leading global ride-hailing brand? Or will the sector be characterized by local and regional brands such as China's Didi or India's Ola?

Sources: Sarah O'Conner, Aliya Ram, and Leslie Hook, "Uber 'Workers' Ruling Deals Blow to Gig Economy," *Financial Times* (November 11–12, 2017), p. 18; Leslie Hook, "Fixing Uber: The Professor Dismantling a Rotten Culture," *Financial Times* (September 11, 2017), p. 12; Newly Purnell, "Uber Hits Resistance as It Expands in Asia," *The Wall Street Journal* (December 4, 2014), p. B7; Julie Weed, "In Turnabout, Some Companies Are Rating Their Customers," *The New York Times* (December 2, 2014), p. B7; John Aglioby and Sally Davies, "Taxis Protest against Hailing Apps," *Financial Times* (June 12, 2014), p. 4; L. Gordon Crovitz, "Uber Shocks the Regulators," *The Wall Street Journal* (June 16, 2014), p. A13; Kara Swisher, "Man and Uber Man," *Vanity Fair* (December 2014), pp. 146, 148, 150; Andy Kessler, "Travis Kalanick: The Transportation Trustbuster," *The Wall Street Journal* (January 26, 2013), p. A13.

CASE 5-2
Putin's Russia versus the West: Cold War 2.0?

On November 7, 2017, people in Russia and around the world paused to observe the 100th anniversary of the Bolshevik revolution and the creation of the Soviet Union. Following Vladimir Lenin's death in the early 1920s, Josef Stalin seized the levers of power and engineered his country's economic transformation from a nation of impoverished peasants into a modern industrial power. In doing so, Stalin created a totalitarian police state. Soviet industrialization helped the Allies defeat Nazi Germany in World War II, after which Stalin embarked on expansionist policies that laid the groundwork for a Cold War with the West.

Nikita Khrushchev became the new leader upon Stalin's death in 1953. In 1956, he famously pounded a shoe on a podium at the United Nations and warned the West, "We will bury you!" The following year, the Soviet Union launched a dog into orbit aboard the Sputnik 2 spacecraft, heating up the space race with the United States.

Despite such achievements, by the mid-1970s the country's leadership was dominated by an aging Politburo, and the Soviet Union had slipped into a state of stagnation and decay. After Ronald Reagan won the 1980 U.S. presidential election, he was determined to win the Cold War. When the Kremlin tried to achieve parity with the United States on defense spending, the Soviet Union was soon bankrupt.

The Cold War effectively ended in 1991, after Mikhail Gorbachev's reform-oriented policies of *glasnost* and *perestroika* led to the dissolution of the Soviet Union. In the twenty-first century, Russia continues to be transformed by political and economic change. In 2000, Vladimir Putin was elected president. When President Putin hosted the Group of Eight Summit in St. Petersburg in 2006, the moment marked Russia's arrival on the world stage. Putin took advantage of the opportunity to present his country in a positive light. The public relations effort included a two-hour television broadcast during which Putin answered questions submitted from around the world via the Internet. Putin was also *Time* magazine's 2007 "Man of the Year."

In 2006, flush with dollars from oil exports, the Russian government lifted all currency controls and made the ruble freely convertible in world markets. Although per capita gross national income (GNI) in Russia is only $9,720, Russian shoppers spend billions each year on luxury goods, tourism, and foreign real estate. Today, affluent Russians can shop at boutiques that offer Versace, Burberry, Bulgari, and other exclusive brands.

Despite the positive publicity, the phrases *managed democracy* and *state capitalism* have been used to describe the arbitrary exercise of state power in Russia. The Kremlin limits foreign investment in strategic industries such as oil; the term *renationalization* has been applied to the process by which state-owned enterprises (SOEs) acquire their rivals. Terms such as *crony capitalism* and *kleptocracy* refer to the rampant corruption and bribery prevalent among Putin loyalists.

In May 2012, Putin was elected to a third term as Russia's president. Soon, he found himself at the center of several controversies that unsettled the international community. First, the government arrested and jailed members of an all-female art collective after they sang an anti-Putin rock song in an Orthodox cathedral. Members of the feminist punk rock band Pussy Riot were arrested following a brief performance at the Christ the Savior cathedral in Moscow (see Exhibit 5-17). The band was known for its anti-Putin stance and provocative lyrics; one of the band's songs is titled "Holy Mary, Blessed Virgin, Drive Putin Away." Three of the band's members—Maria Alyokhina, Yekaterina Samutsevich, and Nadezhda Tolokonnikova—were charged with "hooliganism motivated by religious hatred." After a lengthy legal process, Alyokhina and Tolokonnikova were sentenced to two-year prison terms in a remote part of Siberia; Samutsevich was acquitted. In December 2013, in the run-up to the Winter Olympics in Sochi, President Putin pardoned the women and they were released from prison.

Also in 2012, after Ukraine began negotiating a trade deal with the European Union, Putin threatened to impose sanctions. In March 2014, Putin angered the West by annexing Crimea, a region that had been considered part of Ukraine. A few months later, after pro-Russian separatists launched a military campaign in Ukraine, the West turned the tables and threatened Russia with sanctions. Tragically, in July, a separatist missile downed a Malaysian airliner over Ukrainian airspace, killing everyone on board. Then, as 2014 came to an end, the global price of oil dropped below $60 per barrel and the Russian ruble plunged in value.

Faced with a financial crisis and a test of his political will, Putin blamed the West for Russia's problems. Then-U.S. President Barack Obama responded by observing that Russia's problem is that it doesn't produce any products that people want to buy. Despite—or perhaps because of—such rhetoric, Putin remains extremely popular with the Russian people. Indeed, many Russians agreed when Putin asserted that the collapse of the Soviet Union was "one of the greatest geopolitical catastrophes of the twentieth century for Russia and Russians." Some observers have suggested that a new Cold War era is dawning.

The Economic and Political Environments in Russia

There is other evidence that the political environment in Russia is precarious. Anna Politkovskaya, a reporter for Russia's *Novaya Gazeta* ("New Paper"), often filed stories critical of President Vladimir Putin. On October 7, 2006, assailants gunned down Politkovskaya as she returned from a shopping trip. Since 2000, more than a dozen journalists have been murdered in Russia. Observers note that Russia's independent press suffered as the Kremlin tightened control in anticipation of the 2008 presidential election.

Revenues from the fuel and energy sectors translate into government spending that consumes a whopping 40 percent of GDP. A related problem is the fact that Russia's energy industry is dominated by a handful of huge conglomerates. The men who run these companies are known as *oligarchs*; at one time, Yukos Oil's Mikhail Khodorkovsky, Sibneft's Roman Abramovich, and their peers were among Russia's ultra-rich elite. However, there was widespread resentment among the Russian citizenry about the manner in which the oligarchs had gained control of their respective companies. In 2003, the Putin government sent a message to the oligarchs by arresting Khodorkovsky and several of his peers. In 2010, after having spent 7 years in prison, Khodorkovsky was sentenced to another 13.5 years of incarceration after a Moscow court found him guilty of money laundering and embezzlement. Many observers viewed the verdict as evidence of the Russian government's desire to maintain an iron grip on the economy.

Russia faces other problems as well. Its entrenched bureaucracy is a barrier to increased economic freedom. Further, the banking system remains fragile and is in need of reform. Yevgeny Yasin, a former economy minister and an advocate of liberal reforms, noted recently, "The Russian economy is constrained by bureaucratic shackles. If the economy is to grow, these chains must be dropped. If we can overcome this feudal system of using power, we will create a stimulus for strong and sustainable economic growth and improve the standards of living."

Exhibit 5-17 Disguised in bright balaclavas, the all-female art collective known as Pussy Riot appears on Red Square in Moscow. In 2012, after attempting to perform an anti-Kremlin song in an Orthodox cathedral, three of the activists were arrested and convicted of "anti-religious hooliganism." Two of the women were sent to prison; the third was released. The group's members maintain that their work is intended to transform Russian society for the better. President Putin pardoned the prisoners prior to the 2014 Winter Olympics in Sochi.
Source: Denis Sinyakov/Reuters.

The Marketing Opportunity: Do the Rewards Outweigh the Risks?

Despite the political risk, a number of global companies have been seeking to capitalize on Russia's improved economic climate. PepsiCo, whose operations date back to the Soviet era, has a cumulative investment of more than $4 billion in the country. As noted in Case 1-2, McDonald's has opened hundreds of restaurants since 1990. BP, Carlsberg, Coca-Cola, Danone SA, General Motors, IKEA, Salvatore Ferragamo, and Yum!Brands are some of the other companies with footholds in Russia.

IKEA, the global furniture retailer, has opened dozens of new stores across Russia. However, after Russian bureaucrats allegedly sought bribes, the company had to lease diesel generators to ensure a stable supply of electricity. In 2010, IKEA announced that it was halting construction of a $1 billion mall and would focus on its existing stores. France's Auchan and German retail chains Rewe and Metro are targeting the grocery market. By contrast, Carrefour and U.K.-based Tesco do not yet have a market presence due to the perceived risks. Walmart recently closed its Moscow office.

Moscow's Strained Relationship with Washington

Even before the crisis in Ukraine, Washington's relationship with Moscow had been growing more strained. In December 2012, President Obama signed the Russia and Moldova Jackson-Vanik Repeal and Sergei Magnitsky Rule of Law Accountability Act. The first part of the law normalized trade relations with Russia and Moldova by repealing Jackson-Vanik, a law dating to the mid-1970s. At that time, the Soviet Union was a "non-market economy" that restricted the right of its citizens to emigrate abroad; Jackson-Vanik denied most-favored-nation trading status to any country that blocked emigration rights. After the Soviet Union broke apart in 1991, Russia transitioned to a market economy, and today its citizens are free to travel abroad and emigrate. Moreover, Russia joined the WTO in 2012. For these reasons, Jackson-Vanik is no longer relevant.

The second part of the law is concerned with civil rights issues in Russia at the present time. Sergei Magnitsky was a Russian lawyer who uncovered evidence that Russian government officials had stolen $230 million in tax payments made by the Heritage Capital Management investment firm. When Magnitsky went public with his allegations in 2008, he was arrested. He died in jail under suspicious circumstances in November 2009. The law calls for the U.S. government to identify by name Russian officials believed to be complicit in Magnitsky's death; those persons will not be allowed to enter the United States and any assets held in the United States have been frozen.

A Tough Environment: The One–Two Punch of Plunging Oil Prices and Sanctions

The Kremlin was steadfast in asserting its right to annex Crimea and in denying that it was supporting the separatists. Even so, the European Union, the United States, Australia, Canada, and Norway moved to impose sanctions on a variety of Russia's industry sectors. Russia responded by banning imports of Western food products (see Exhibit 5-18).

As the ruble's value fell through most of 2014, European firms began to feel the effects. Carlsberg, the Danish brewer, generates most of its revenues in Russia. France's Danone, which has two-dozen Russian dairy plants and 13,000 employees, experienced reduced demand for milk. As 2014 came to an end, IKEA announced price increases. After raising the price of the iPhone 6 by 25 percent, Apple temporarily halted online sales of the hot-selling device. Russian consumers rushed to change rubles to dollars and euros and to buy big-ticket items such as big-screen TVs and luxury cars.

Election Meddling and Lobbying to Overturn the Magnitsky Law

Following the election of Donald Trump to the U.S. presidency in November 2016, Washington's relationship with Moscow took a bizarre turn. As it turned out, prior to the election, members of the Trump family had met with Russian officials who claimed to have information that would negatively impact the election chances of Democrat presidential candidate Hillary Clinton.

Throughout his campaign, Trump asserted that he would be able to, in his words, "get along" with President Vladimir Putin and reset America's relationship with Russia. Despite these assurances, the Kremlin's support for Syria's President Bashar al-Assad was a constant source

Exhibit 5-18 A Russian ban on European imports has resulted in excess supplies of milk, apples, and other agricultural products.
Source: JANEK SKARZYNSKI/AFP/Getty Images.

of tension between the United States and Russia. At a G-20 conference in 2016, Trump had a private meeting with Putin without any of his U.S. staff members present. Some observers were concerned that in such an encounter Putin, a former intelligence official, might find a way to set a trap for Trump.

As it turns out, the sanctions have been a boon for Russia's agricultural sector. In many instances, Russian consumers have little choice but to "buy local." As a result, Russian Aquaculture, a producer of farmed salmon, has expanded to keep up with booming demand. In addition to winning domestic market share, Russian agricultural producers are increasing their exports. For example, grain production has reached record levels. In 2016, Russian wheat exports surpassed those of the United States, and Russia was on track to pass the EU as the world's number 1 grain exporter in 2017.

Conclusion

Today, even as relations between the West and Russia are at their lowest point in decades, Russia's dependence on a single commodity for the bulk of its export earnings is easing. Repercussions—both negative and positive—from the sanctions imposed after the crisis in Ukraine and the 2016 U.S. election continue to reverberate. Despite upbeat talk of creating a Silicon Valley–type development in suburban Moscow, some observers have begun asking whether it is time to take the "R" out of "BRICS."

Which emerging market should take its place? Indonesia is the top choice. The new acronym could be BIIC; an alternative would be BICI.

As Richard Shaw, an investment advisor, noted, BICIS ("BEE-chees") "is catchy—kind of like an Italian purse."

Discussion Questions

5-8. Discuss why the Putin government decided to pursue legal action against the members of Pussy Riot.

5-9. What impact will the Magnitsky law have on the political and legal environment in Russia?

5-10. Russia hosted the 2018 World Cup, with matches held in St. Petersburg, Kaliningrad, and other cities. Did the event generate favorable publicity that enhanced Russia's standing on the world stage? Or was the press coverage negative?

5-11. As the chief marketing officer of a global company, would you recommend establishing operations in Russia?

Sources: Henry Foy, "Sanctions Spur Growth in Russian Agriculture," *Financial Times* (September 4, 2017), p. 17; Courtney Weaver, "Freedom Fighter," *Financial Times Life & Arts* (December 15–16, 2012), p. 23; Melena Ryzik, "Carefully Calibrated for Protest," *The New York Times* (August 26, 2012), p. AR1; John Thornhill and Geoff Dyer, "Death of a Lawyer," *Financial Times Life & Arts* (July 28–29, 2012), pp. 2–3; Anatol Lieven, "How the Rule of Law May Come Eventually to Russia," *Financial Times* (December 6, 2010), p. 11; Roben Farzad, "The BRIC Debate: Drop Russia, Add Indonesia?" *BusinessWeek* (November 18, 2010); Neil Buckley, "From Shock Therapy to Retail Therapy: Russia's Middle Class Starts Spending," *Financial Times* (October 31, 2006), p. 13; David Lynch, "Russia Brings Revitalized Economy to the Table," *USA Today* (July 13, 2006), pp. 1B, 2B; Guy Chazan, "Kremlin Capitalism: Russian Car Maker Comes under Sway of Old Pal of Putin," *The Wall Street Journal* (May 19, 2006), pp. A1, A7; Greg Hitt and Gregory L. White, "Hurdles Grow as Russia, U.S. Near Trade Deal," *The Wall Street Journal* (April 12, 2006), p. A4.

Notes

[1]Richard Stanley, *Changing Concepts of Sovereignty: Can the United Nations Keep Pace?* (Muscatine, IA: Stanley Foundation, 1992), p. 7.

[2]Karen Pennar, "Is the Nation-State Obsolete in a Global Economy?" *BusinessWeek* (July 17, 1995), p. 80.

[3]Kathrin Hille, "Putin Sidesteps Celebration of Bolshevik Revolution," *Financial Times* (October 26, 2017), p. 4.

[4]Rachel Sanderson, "Italy's Richest Regions Back Call for Greater Autonomy," *Financial Times* (October 24, 2017), p. 4.

[5]Ethan Kapstein, "Avoiding Unrest in a Volatile Environment," *Financial Times—Mastering Uncertainty, Pt I* (March 17, 2006), p. 5.

[6]Guy Chazan, "'Left Behind' Voters Propel AfD in East Germany," *Financial Times* (September 27, 2017), p. 8.

[7]Richard Milne, "Carlsberg Takes a Sobering Look at Russia," *Financial Times* (August 12, 2014), p. 14.

[8]Courtney Weaver, "The Price of a Presence in Russia," *Financial Times* (July 26, 2010), p. 2B.

[9]Dan Bilefsky, "Intrepid Shoe Executive Casts Lot with Albania," *The New York Times* (October 8, 2009), p. B6.

[10]Craig S. Smith and Wayne Arnold, "China's Antismuggling Drive to Hurt U.S. Exporters That Support Crackdown," *The Wall Street Journal* (August 5, 1998), p. A12.

[11]Franklin R. Root, *Entry Strategies for International Markets* (New York, NY: Lexington Books, 1994), p. 154.

[12]William R. Slomanson, *Fundamental Perspectives on International Law* (St. Paul, MN: West Publishing, 1990), p. 356.

[13]David J. Lynch, "Venezuelan Consumers Gobble up U.S. Goods Despite Political Tension," *USA Today* (March 28, 2007).

[14]Much of the material in this section is adapted from Randall Kelso and Charles D. Kelso, *Studying Law: An Introduction* (St. Paul, MN: West Publishing, 1984).

[15]Harry Jones, "Our Uncommon Common Law," *Tennessee Law Review* 30 (1975), p. 447.

[16]Gregory Maggs, "Conversation with Clarence Thomas," C-SPAN (February 15, 2018).

[17]Mark M. Nelson, "Two Styles of Business Vie in East Europe," *The Wall Street Journal* (April 3, 1995), p. A14.

[18]Adapted from Mushtaq Luqmani, Ugur Yavas, and Zahir Quraeshi, "Advertising in Saudi Arabia: Content and Regulation," *International Marketing Review* 6, no. 1 (1989), pp. 61–63. MCB UP Limited 1989.

[19]Tony Barber, "'Patents Are Key' to Taking on China," *Financial Times* (July 25, 2006), p. 2.

[20]William P. Alford, *To Steal a Book Is an Elegant Offense: Intellectual Property Law in Chinese Civilization* (Stanford, CA: Stanford University Press, 1995), p. 2.

[21]Frances Williams, "Call for Stronger EU Patent Laws," *Financial Times* (May 22, 1997), p. 3.

[22]Andrew Kramer, "He Doesn't Make Coffee, But He Controls 'Starbucks' in Russia," *The New York Times* (October 12, 2005), pp. C1, C4.

[23]Tripp Mickel, "U.S. Move Reignites Cuba Rum Fight," *The Wall Street Journal* (January 15, 2016), p. B1.

[24]Franklin R. Root, *Entry Strategies for International Markets* (New York, NY: Lexington Books, 1994), p. 113.

[25]John Carey, "Inching toward a Borderless Patent," *BusinessWeek* (September 5, 1994), p. 35.

[26]Richard Pynder, "Intellectual Property in Need of Protection," *Financial Times* (July 7, 1998), p. 22.

[27]Rana Foroohar, "A Better Patent System Will Spur Innovation," *Financial Times* (September 4, 2017), p. 11.

[28]John R. Wilke, "Hunting Cartels: U.S. Trust-Busters Increasingly Target International Business," *The Wall Street Journal* (February 5, 1997), p. A10.

[29]John R. Wilke, "U.S. Court Rules Antitrust Laws Apply to Foreigners," *The Wall Street Journal* (March 19, 1997), p. B5.

[30]Kim Hjelmgaard, "Google Fined Record-Setting $2.72 Billion over EU Rules," *USA Today* (June 28, 2017), p. 3B.

[31]Detlev Vagts, *Transnational Business Problems* (Mineola, NY: Foundation Press, 1986), pp. 285–291.

[32]Alice Rawsthorn and Emma Tucker, "Movie Studios May Have to Scrap Joint Distributor," *Financial Times* (February 6, 1998), p. 1.

[33]Anna Wilde Mathews, "Making Waves: As U.S. Trade Grows, Shipping Cartels Get a Bit More Scrutiny," *The Wall Street Journal* (October 7, 1997), pp. A1, A8.

[34]Brigid McMenamin, "Eroding Patent Rights," *Forbes* (October 24, 1994), p. 92.

[35]Salem M. Katsh and Michael P. Dierks, "Globally, Trade Secrets Laws Are All over the Map," *National Law Journal* 17, no. 36 (May 8, 1995), p. C12.

[36]Much of the material in this section is adapted from Daniel Pines, "Amending the Foreign Corrupt Practices Act to Include a Private Right of Action," *California Law Review* (January 1994), pp. 185–229.

[37]John Bussey, "The Rule of Law Finds Its Way Abroad—However Painfully," *The Wall Street Journal* (June 24, 2011), p. B1.

[38]www.justice.gov/criminal/fraud/fcpa/docs/lay-persons-guide.pdf. Accessed June 1, 2011.

[39]Peggy Hollinger, "Charges Revealed over Rolls-Royce Bribery Scheme," *Financial Times* (November 9, 2017), p. 18.

[40]Daniel Pines, "Amending the Foreign Corrupt Practices Act to Include a Private Right of Action," *California Law Review* (January 1994), p. 205.

[41]Rebecca Bream and Neil Buckley, "Investors Still Drawn to Russia Despite Pitfalls," *Financial Times* (December 1, 2006), p. 21.

[42]Amy Borrus, "Inside the World of Greased Palms," *BusinessWeek* (November 6, 1995), pp. 36–38.

[43]José Ángel Gurría, "Rich Must Set the Example of Bribery," *Financial Times* (September 13, 2006), p. 5.

[44]Charles Fleming, "Europe Learns Litigious Ways," *The Wall Street Journal* (February 24, 2004), p. A17.

[45]Bruce Londa, "An Agreement to Arbitrate Disputes Isn't the Same in Every Language," *Brandweek* (September 26, 1994), p. 18. See also John M. Allen, Jr., and Bruce G. Merritt, "Drafters of Arbitration Clauses Face a Variety of Unforeseen Perils," *National Law Journal* 17, no. 33 (April 17, 1995), pp. C6–C7.

[46]Dorothee J. Feils and Florin M. Sabac, "The Impact of Political Risk on the Foreign Direct Investment Decision: A Capital Budgeting Analysis," *Engineering* 45, no. 2 (2000), p. 129.

[47]Bob Davis, "Red-Tape Traumas: To All U.S. Managers Upset by Regulations: Try Germany or Japan," *The Wall Street Journal* (December 14, 1995), p. A1.

[48]Raphael Minder, "The Lobbyists Take Brussels by Storm," *Financial Times* (January 26, 2006), p. 7. See also Brandon Mitchener, "Standard Bearers: Increasingly, Rules of Global Economy Are Set in Brussels," *The Wall Street Journal* (April 23, 2002), p. A1.

[49]Klaus-Dieter Borchardt, *European Integration: The Origins and Growth of the European Union* (Luxembourg: Office for Official Publications of the European Communities, 1995), p. 30.

[50]Klaus-Dieter Borchardt, *The ABC of Community Law* (Luxembourg: Office for Official Publications of the European Communities, 1994), p. 25.

[51]Formerly known as the Court of First Instance.

[52]Rochelle Toplensky, "Upmarket Brands Win Online Sales Ban," *Financial Times* (December 7, 2017), p. 16.

[53]Charles Forelle, "Europe's High Court Tries on a Bunny Suit Made of Chocolate," The Wall Street Journal (June 11, 2009), p. A1.

[54]Michael Peel, "L'Oréal in Legal Victory over Rival," Financial Times (June 18, 2009), p. 3.

[55]David Segal, "Is Italy Too Italian?" *The New York Times* (July 31, 2010), p. B1.

6

Global Information Systems and Market Research

LEARNING OBJECTIVES

6-1 Discuss the roles of information technology, management information systems, and big data in a global company's decision-making processes.

6-2 Describe the various sources of market information, including direct perception.

6-3 Identify the individual steps in the traditional market research process,

and explain some of the ways global marketers adapt them.

6-4 Compare the way a multinational firm organizes the marketing research effort with the way a global or transnational firm approaches the organizing issue.

6-5 Explain how information's role as a strategic asset affects the structure of global corporations.

CASE 6-1
Nestlé Middle East's Investment in Market Research

Nestlé Middle East has enjoyed a reputation for innovation and creativity that goes back years, with the company motto of "Good Food, Good Life" serving as a promise that Nestlé is committed to delivering. The Switzerland-based food-and-beverage company has a wide range of products including bottled water, ice cream, chocolate, dairy products, and baby food, and it is recognized for its high quality, superior taste, and nutritional value. In the Middle East alone, Nestlé has over 60 products, and despite formidable competitors like Procter and Gamble (P&G), Coca-Cola, and Unilever vying for the same space, Nestlé manages to retain a good market share by focusing on nutritional value and a healthy lifestyle.

Exhibit 6-1 Nestlé is a global brand employing over 308,000 people in 447 factories and with operations in nearly every country on the map. It founded Nestlé Middle East in 1997 and has been operating successfully in the region for the past 80 years. It has invested more than $400 million in the Middle East and now owns and operates 18 factories and 16 offices.
Source: Fitria Ramli/Shutterstock.

Nestlé SA has come a long way from its humble beginnings in the late 19th century in Vevey, Switzerland. It operates successfully in more than 80 countries with the help of intensified market research and has developed a diverse portfolio of products. Nestlé's products include Maggi, KitKat, Cerelac, and Nescafé. The company today boasts of more than 5,500 cups of Nescafé instant coffee being consumed every second, with different varieties catering to different tastes and preferences around the globe.

Nestlé operates successfully in more than 80 countries with the help of intensified market research and has developed a diverse portfolio of products. Nestlé acts as a regional hub in the Middle East, catering to the needs of 13 countries and a total population of 220 million. Nestlé Middle East was founded in1997 in Jebel Ali Free Zone, Dubai, and at present, it owns and operates 18 factories and 16 offices in the region, employing more than 13,000 people across all operations. Over the last five years, Nestlé Middle East has invested more than $400 million in research and development and in the establishment of factories in high growth markets. To learn more about the way Nestlé invests and conducts research, turn to the continuation of Case 6-1 at the end of this chapter.

When researching any market, marketers must know where to go in order to obtain information, what subject areas to investigate and what data to seek, the different ways to acquire it, and the various types of analyses that would contribute to a better understanding of consumers with important insights into their framework. It is the marketer's good luck that a veritable cornucopia of market information is available on the Internet. A few keystrokes can yield literally hundreds of articles, research findings, and websites that offer a wealth of information about a particular country's market. Even so, marketers must do their homework if they are to make the most of modern information technology. First, they need to understand the importance of information technology and marketing information systems as strategic assets. Second, they should have a general understanding of the formal market research process. Finally, they should know how to manage the marketing information collection system and the marketing research effort. These topics are the focus of this chapter.

▶ **6-1** Discuss the roles of information technology, management information systems, and big data in a global company's decision-making processes.

6-1 Information Technology, Management Information Systems, and Big Data for Global Marketing

Information technology (IT) refers to an organization's processes for creating, storing, exchanging, using, and managing information. A **management information system (MIS)** provides managers and other decision makers with a continuous flow of information about company operations. MIS is a broad term that can be used to refer to a system of hardware and software that a company uses to manage information. An MIS should provide a means for gathering, analyzing, classifying, storing, retrieving, and reporting relevant data. The term **big data** refers to extremely large data sets that can be subjected to computational analysis to reveal patterns and trends (see Exhibit 6-2).

Big data and big data analytics have long been the province of astronomers, meteorologists, and other members of the scientific community. Only recently have big data collection and analysis been applied to business situations. In particular, the exploding popularity of Facebook and other social media platforms has resulted in a wealth of big data. Of course, much of that data may be redundant or irrelevant, for a simple reason: The cost of data collection has dropped so dramatically that a company can amass scads of data irrespective of a particular question, problem, or purpose that its marketers might have.

A case in point is video-streaming pioneer Netflix, which has collected more than 10 billion movie ratings from subscribers. Netflix also gathers demographic data about all its subscribers, including age, gender, and place of residence. Netflix knows, for example, that some 20-something males have viewing habits that many people would associate with 70-year-old females, and vice versa. Netflix managers must determine how to use the ratings in conjunction with demographic information and viewership data so that new subscribers enjoy a better content-discovery experience.

As the Netflix example illustrates, gathering data is not an end in itself, but rather a means to an end. Confronted with mountains of data that include user-generated content, often from a variety of sources, marketers must be able to determine what matters and what doesn't. Metaphorically speaking, this calls for separating the wheat from the chaff, or, as a data scientist might put it, separating the signal from the noise. A company's trove of data, which includes a great deal of "noise," must be converted into information ("signal") by eliminating statistical redundancy and

Exhibit 6-2 Coca-Cola's Freestyle vending machines utilize "micro-dosing technology" that allows for 170 possible drink combinations. User data generated by the units prompted Coca-Cola to develop a new flavor: Cherry Sprite.
Source: Roberto Machado Noa/LightRocket via Getty Images.

corruption. Finally, by applying data analytics to the problem that needs to be solved or the question that needs to be answered, marketers can arrive at insights that are interpretable and relevant. Those insights can be used to improve decision making (see Figure 6-1).

One component of a firm's MIS is a business intelligence (BI) network that helps managers make decisions. The major objective of the BI network is

> to enable interactive access to data, enable manipulation of these data, and to provide managers and analysts with the ability to conduct appropriate analysis. By analyzing historical and current data, situations, and performances, decision makers get valuable insights upon which they can base more informed and better decisions.[2]

Global competition, together with the advent of the big data era, intensifies the need for effective MIS and business intelligence that are accessible throughout the company. As Jean-Pierre Corniou, former chief information officer (CIO) at Renault, noted:

> My vision is to design, build, sell, and maintain cars. Everything I do is directly linked to this, to the urgent need to increase turnover, margins, and brand image. Every single investment and expense in the IT field has to be driven by this vision of the automotive business.[3]

Many companies with global operations have made significant investments in their IT infrastructure in recent years. Such investments are typically directed at upgrading a company's legacy computer hardware and software. Amazon Web Services (AWS), Microsoft, SAP, Oracle, and IBM are some of the beneficiaries of this trend. All of these companies are global enterprises,

> "We are positioning ourselves as a data company. We have half a billion customers with us with shopping intentions and a method to pay. We know who they are, what they want, what they hate."[1]
>
> Daniel Zhang, CEO, Alibaba

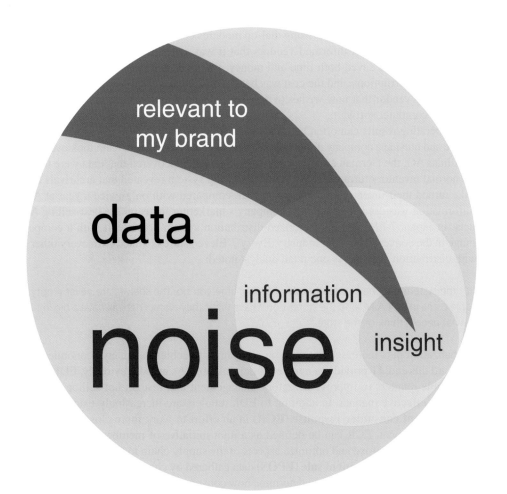

FIGURE 6-1 Relationship Between Data, Information, and Insight.

and many of their customers are global as well. Vendors of complex software systems can find it difficult to achieve 100 percent customer satisfaction. Thomas Siebel, founder of Siebel Systems, explains how his company met this challenge:

> Siebel Systems is a global company, not a multinational company. I believe the notion of the multinational company—where a division is free to follow its own set of business rules—is obsolete, though there are still plenty around. Our customers—global companies like IBM, Zurich Financial Services, and Citicorp—expect the same high level of service and quality, and the same licensing policies, no matter where we do business with them around the world. Our human resources and legal departments help us create policies that respect local cultures and requirements worldwide, while at the same time maintaining the highest standards. We have one brand, one image, one set of corporate colors, one set of messages, across every place on the planet.[4]

Unlike the public Internet, an **intranet** is a private network that allows authorized company personnel or outsiders to share information electronically in a secure fashion without generating mountains of paper. Intranets, in conjunction with a state-of-the-art IT system, can serve as a 24-hour nerve center. Through their use, Amazon, FedEx, Google, Netflix, Spotify, Walmart, and other companies can operate as *real-time enterprises* (RTEs). The RTE model is growing in popularity as more executives and managers realize leveraging big data via advanced analytics can be a source of competitive advantage.

An **electronic data interchange (EDI)** system allows a company's business units to submit orders, issue invoices, and conduct business electronically with other company units as well as with outside companies. One of the key features of EDI is that its transaction formats are universal, which enables computer systems at different companies to "speak the same language." Walmart is legendary for its sophisticated EDI system. For years, vendors had received orders from the giant retailer on personal computers using dial-up modems connected to third-party transmission networks. In 2002, Walmart informed vendors that it was switching to an Internet-based EDI system. The switch has saved both time and money; the modem-based system was susceptible to transmission interruptions, and the cost was between \$0.10 and \$0.20 per thousand characters transmitted. Any vendor that now wishes to do business with Walmart must purchase and install the necessary computer software.[5]

Poor operating results can often be traced to insufficient data and information about events both inside and outside a company. For example, when a new management team took over the U.S. unit of Adidas AG, the German athletic shoemaker, the team discovered that data were not available on normal inventory turnover rates. A new reporting system revealed that archrivals Reebok and Nike turned their inventories five times a year, compared with only twice a year at Adidas. This information was used to tighten the company's marketing focus on the best-selling Adidas products. In Japan, 7-Eleven's computerized distribution system provides it with a competitive advantage in the convenience store industry. Every 7-Eleven store is linked with every other store and with distribution centers. As one retail analyst noted:

> With the system they have established, whatever time you go, the shelves are never empty. If people come in at 4 A.M. and the stores don't have what they want, that will have a big impact on what people think of the store.[6]

Globalization puts increased pressure on companies to achieve as many economies as possible. Toward this end, IT provides a number of helpful tools. As noted previously, EDI links with vendors enable retailers to improve inventory management and restock hot-selling products in a timely, cost-effective manner. In addition to EDI, retailers are increasingly using a technique known as **efficient consumer response (ECR)** in an effort to work more closely with vendors on stock replenishment. ECR can be defined as a joint initiative of members of a supply chain working together to improve and optimize aspects of the supply chain to benefit customers. ECR systems utilize **electronic point of sale (EPOS)** data gathered by checkout scanners to help retailers identify product sales patterns and determine how consumer preferences vary with geography. Although currently more popular in the United States, the ECR system is gaining traction in

Europe. Companies such as Carrefour, Metro, Coca-Cola, and Henkel have all embraced ECR. Supply-chain innovations such as radio frequency identification tags (RFID) are likely to provide increased momentum for the use of ECR.

EPOS, ECR, and other IT tools are also helping businesses improve their ability to target consumers and increase loyalty. The trend among retailers is to develop customer-focused strategies that will personalize and differentiate the business. In addition to point-of-sale (POS) scanner data, loyalty programs such as Tesco's Clubcard, which use electronic smartcards, provide retailers with important information about shopping habits. **Customer relationship management (CRM)** is an important business tool that helps companies leverage the data they collect through such systems.

Although industry experts offer varying descriptions and definitions of CRM, the prevailing view is that CRM is a philosophy that values two-way communication between the company and the customer. Every point of contact ("touchpoint" in CRM-speak) that a company has with a consumer or business customer—via a Web site, a warranty card, a sweepstakes entry, a payment on a credit card account, or an inquiry to a call center—offers an opportunity to collect data. Likewise, every time a Spotify user clicks "play," a data point is generated. CRM tools allow companies to determine which customers are most valuable and to react in a timely manner with customized product and service offerings that closely match customer needs. If implemented correctly, CRM can make employees more productive and enhance corporate profitability; it also benefits customers by providing value-added products and services.

A company's use of CRM can manifest itself in various ways. In the hotel industry, for example, CRM can take the form of front-desk staff who monitor, respond to, and anticipate the needs of repeat customers. A visitor to Amazon.com who buys the latest Taylor Swift CD encounters CRM when he or she gets the message "Frequently Bought with the Item You Added: Ed Sheeran's *X* and Sam Smith's *In the Lonely Hour*." CRM can also be based on the click path that a Web site visitor follows. In this case, however, Internet users may be unaware that a company is tracking their behaviors and interests.

One challenge of using CRM is integrating data into a complete picture of the customer and his or her relationship to the company and its products or services—a perspective sometimes referred to as a "360-degree view of the customer." This challenge is compounded for global marketers. Their subsidiaries in different parts of the world may use different customer data formats, and commercial CRM products may not support all the target languages. In view of such issues, industry experts recommend implementing global CRM programs in phases.

The first phase could focus on a specific task such as *sales force automation* (SFA); this term refers to a software system that automates routine aspects of sales and marketing functions such as lead assignment, contact follow-up, and opportunity reporting. While Salesforce.com is a key player in this space, Microsoft Dynamics CRM and Oracle Siebel CRM on Demand are among the other vendors offering SFA. An SFA system can also analyze the cost of sales and the effectiveness of marketing campaigns. Some SFA software can assist with quote preparation and management of other aspects of a sales campaign, such as mass mailings and conference or convention attendee follow-up.

For example, an important first step in implementing a CRM system could be to utilize SFA software from a company such as Oracle. The objective at this stage of the CRM effort would be to provide sales representatives in all country locations with access via an Internet portal to sales activities throughout the organization. To simplify the implementation, the company could require that all sales activities be recorded in English. Subsequently, marketing, customer service, and other functions could be added to the system.[7]

Privacy issues related to data collection and use vary widely from country to country. In the EU, for example, a Directive on Data Collection has been in effect since 1998. Companies that use CRM to collect data about individual consumers must satisfy the regulations in each of the EU's 28 member countries. There are also restrictions about sharing such information across national borders. In 2000, the U.S. Department of Commerce and the EU concluded a Safe Harbor agreement that established principles for privacy protection for companies that wish to transfer data to the United States from Europe.

However, in 2013, following revelations by Edward Snowden about U.S. intelligence activities, an Austrian activist named Max Schrems brought suit in the European Court of Justice (ECJ)

THE CULTURAL CONTEXT

Tesco's Clubcard

As the number 1 supermarket chain in the United Kingdom, Tesco is "the one to beat." Tesco's management team faces the constant challenge of staying ahead of fast-growing competitors. These include local chains such as Sainsbury as well as Asda, which is owned by retail giant Walmart.

One of the keys to Tesco's success is a loyalty program tied to its Clubcard. Signing up for the program is easy: Shoppers fill out applications (either at the store or online) that include questions regarding family demographics and dietary preferences. The 15 million households with Clubcards represent 80 percent of Tesco's customer base. Shoppers present their cards at checkout and are awarded two points for every £1 spent (see Exhibit 6-3).

For every 100 points accumulated, shoppers receive a £1 voucher that can be redeemed for future grocery purchases or used with airline frequent-flyer programs. Tesco also partners with other retailers such as Pizza Express, where vouchers are worth four times their face value. Needless to say, the Clubcard is a hit with university students! Tesco also offers different incentives to different segments; for example, high spenders are offered vouchers that are worth triple points when redeemed on certain categories of merchandise.

The Clubcard program actually does more than allow Tesco to reward its customers: It provides Tesco's IT team with a clear picture of what is selling, what isn't selling, and where the gaps are in its product assortment. The Clubcard program is managed by Dunnhumby, an independent consultancy located near London. Each product in the database is scored on price and dozens of other dimensions. As an example of the value of the Clubcard program, Dunnhumby cofounder Clive Humby points to wine sales:

> In the wine department, we could see that people were trading up to stuff Tesco didn't stock. At Christmas, people wanted to buy "posh" wine; those who usually bought cheap wine went from spending £2.99 a bottle to £5.99 a bottle—

but where were the people who should have been trading up from £5.99 to £7.99? They were at [specialty wine store] Oddbins because Tesco didn't have a full-enough range.

Dunnhumby groups Tesco customers into various clusters based on the similarity of the contents of their shopping carts. For example, analysts have dubbed one segment "Finer Foods"; it comprises time-deprived, affluent customers who choose upscale products. When the data indicated that these shoppers weren't buying fine wine or cheese at Tesco, the company upgraded its offerings and introduced a house brand bearing the "Tesco's Finest" label. By contrast, traditional shoppers are "Makers" who buy ingredients to prepare home-cooked meals. They gravitate toward Tesco's lower-priced "Tesco Value" products such as beer, baked beans, canned tomatoes, and noodles.

By combining household information with weekly purchase behavior data, Tesco is able to tailor promotions to specific customer segments. Did a shopper buy diapers for the first time? Tesco sends that household coupons for baby wipes and beer. Why beer? New dads who are staying home with the baby can't get out to the local pub as often as they once did, so they stock up on beer to consume at home.

Clubcard also gives Tesco a tactical advantage over Walmart's Asda stores. Walmart's value proposition is very clear: low prices. To prevent the most value-conscious shoppers from defecting, Tesco mined its database to identify Clubcard users who bought the lowest-priced grocery items. Managers identified several hundred items that the value hunters bought regularly; prices on those items were then lowered. The result: The shoppers stayed with Tesco instead of switching to Asda. Tesco currently leads Asda in share of U.K. grocery sales by a margin of two to one.

Sources: Elizabeth Rigby, "Fresh Horizons Uneasily Scanned," *Financial Times* (September 19, 2010), p. 8; Andrea Felsted, "Tesco Takes Clubcard Route to Buoyant Sales," *Financial Times* (January 12, 2010), p. 13; Andrea Felsted, "Tesco Experiments with Clubcard," *Financial Times* (September 8, 2010), p. 10; Cecilie Rohwedder, "Stores of Knowledge: No. 1 Retailer in Britain Uses "Clubcard" to Thwart Wal-Mart," *The Wall Street Journal* (June 6, 2006), pp. A1, A16.

Exhibit 6-3 Tesco's Clubcard is a loyalty program that the U.K.-based grocery store chain uses to reward customers; shoppers receive points based on purchase amounts. Points are converted to vouchers that can be redeemed for merchandise. Tesco also uses Clubcard to collect data on shopping preferences and patterns. Clubcard has been rolled out in many of Tesco's international locations, including Poland.
Source: Leon Neal/AFP/Getty Images.

arguing that Facebook lacked adequate safeguards to protect user information from U.S. intelligence services. The result: The collapse of the U.S.–EU Safe Harbor agreement. Regulators in the EU, increasingly frustrated by their inability to enforce data protection laws, decided to take aim at Facebook and other U.S. "Big Tech" companies that control much of the data being generated worldwide. A new law, the General Data Protection Regulation (GDPR), entered into force in 2016 and became enforceable against U.S. and other non-EU companies on May 25, 2018. The GDPR covers a variety of privacy-related issues, including protection of personal data, data subjects, and data processing.[8]

Databases called **data warehouses** are frequently an integral part of a company's CRM system. Data warehouses can serve other purposes as well. For example, they can help retailers with multiple store locations fine-tune their product assortments at specific venues. Company personnel, including persons who are not computer specialists, can access data warehouses via standard Web browsers. Teradata, Oracle, IBM, and SAP are among the leading data warehouse vendors.

These examples show just some of the ways that IT and big data are affecting global marketing. However, EDI, ECR, EPOS, SFA, CRM, and other aspects of IT do not simply represent marketing issues; rather, they are organizational imperatives. The tasks of designing, organizing, and implementing systems for business intelligence and information gathering must be coordinated in a coherent manner that contributes to the organization's overall strategic direction. Modern IT tools provide the means for a company's marketing information system and research functions to provide relevant information in a timely, cost-efficient, and actionable manner.

Overall, then, the global organization has the following needs:

- An efficient, effective system that will scan and digest published sources and technical journals in the headquarters country as well as in all countries in which the company has operations or customers.
- Daily scanning, translating, digesting, abstracting, and electronic inputting of information into a market intelligence system. Today, thanks to advances in IT, full-text versions of many sources are available online as PDF files. Print documents can easily be scanned, digitized, and added to a company's information system.
- Expanding information coverage in other regions of the world.

(6-2) Sources of Market Information

◀ **6-2** Describe the various sources of market information, including direct perception.

Although environmental scanning is a vital source of information, research has shown that executives at the headquarters of global companies obtain as much as two-thirds of the information they need from *personal sources*. A great deal of external information comes from executives based abroad in company subsidiaries, affiliates, and branches. These executives are likely to have established communication with distributors, consumers, customers, suppliers, and government officials. A striking feature of the global corporation—and a major source of its competitive strength—is the role that executives abroad play in acquiring and disseminating information about the world environment. Headquarters-based executives generally acknowledge that company executives overseas are the people who know best what is going on in their areas.

The information issue exposes one of the key weaknesses of a domestic company: Although more attractive opportunities may be present outside existing areas of operation, they are likely to go unnoticed by inside sources in a domestic company because the scanning horizon tends to end at the home-country border. Similarly, a company with limited geographical operations may be at risk because internal sources abroad tend to scan only the information about their own countries or regions.

Direct sensory perception provides a vital background for the information that comes from human and documentary sources. Direct perception gets all the senses involved. It means seeing, feeling, hearing, smelling, or tasting for oneself to find out what is going on in a particular country, rather than getting secondhand information by hearing or reading about a particular issue. Some information is easily available from other sources, but sensory experience of it is needed for it to

Exhibit 6-4 Judith McKenna became President and CEO of Walmart Iin February 2018. Despite Walmart's enormous size, McKenna focuses on "TNTs" - "tiny, noticeable things."
Source: Julio Cortez/Associated Press.

sink in. Often, the background information or context one gets from observing a situation can help fill in the big picture. For example, Walmart's first stores in China stocked a number of products—extension ladders and giant bottles of soy sauce, for example—that were inappropriate for local customers. Joe Hatfield, Walmart's top executive for Asia, began roaming the streets of Shenzhen in search of ideas. His observations paid off: When Walmart's giant store in Dalian opened in April 2000, a million shoppers passed through its doors in the first week (see Exhibit 6-4). They snapped up products ranging from lunch boxes to pizza topped with corn and pineapple.[9] When Jim Stengel was chief marketing officer at Procter & Gamble, he moved his managers away from a preoccupation with research data to a wider view based on direct perception. As Stengel noted:

> We often find consumers can't articulate it. That's why we need to have a culture where we are understanding. There can't be detachment. You can't just live away from the consumer and the brand and hope to gain your insights from data or reading or talking to academics. You have to be experiential. And some of our best ideas are coming from people getting out there and experiencing and listening.[10]

Direct perception can also be important when a global player dominates a company's domestic market. Such was the case with Microsoft and its Xbox video game system, which was launched in a market dominated by Sony. Cindy Spodek-Dickey, Microsoft's group manager for national consumer promotions and sponsorships, took Xbox "on the road" with various promotional partners such as the Association of Volleyball Professionals (AVP). At AVP tournaments in different cities, spectators (and potential customers) had the opportunity to visit the Xbox hospitality tent to try out the new system. At one tournament event, Spodek-Dickey explained the importance of informal market research:

> What are the other sponsors doing? What's the crowd into? What brands are they wearing? How are they interacting with our property? I'll stop them as they come out of the tent and say: "What do you think? What do you like about Xbox? What do you think of your PlayStation?" It's mother-in-law research. I wouldn't want to stake a $10 million ad campaign on it, but I think it keeps you credible and real. When you start to hear the same feedback, three, four, five times, you'd better be paying attention. . . . I believe it is part of any good marketer's job to be in touch with their audience and their product. There's no substitute for face-to-face, eye-to-eye, hand-to-hand.[12]

"Case studies from the footwear industry show the importance of direct perception in identifying market opportunities. Diego Della Valle is CEO of Tod's; Mario Moretti Polegato heads Geox; and Blake Mycoskie founded TOMS. What they have in common is that all three were traveling abroad, viewing and experiencing the world, when inspiration struck."[11]

Mark C. Green, Professor of Marketing, Simpson College

(6-3) Formal Market Research

▶ **6-3** Identify the individual steps in the traditional market research process, and explain some of the ways global marketers adapt them.

Information is a critical ingredient in formulating and implementing a successful marketing strategy. As described earlier, a marketing information system should produce a continuous flow of information. **Market research**, by contrast, is the project-specific, systematic gathering of data. The American Marketing Association defines *marketing research* as "the activity that links the consumer, customer, and public to the marketer through information."[13] In **global market research**, this activity is carried out on a global scale. The challenge of global market research is to recognize and respond to the important national differences that influence the way information can be obtained. These include cultural, linguistic, economic, political, religious, historical, and market differences.

Michael Czinkota and Ilkka Ronkainen note that the objectives of international market research are the same as the objectives of domestic research. However, they have identified four specific environmental factors that may require international research efforts to be conducted differently than domestic research. First, researchers must be prepared for new parameters of doing business. Not only will there be different requirements, but the ways in which rules are applied may differ as well. Second, "cultural megashock" may occur as company personnel come to grips with a new set of culture-based assumptions about conducting business. Third, a company entering more than one new geographic market faces a burgeoning network of interacting factors; research may help prevent psychological overload. Fourth, company researchers may have to broaden their definition of competitors in international markets to include competitive pressures that would not be present in the domestic market.[15]

Market research can be conducted in two different ways. First, a company may design and implement a study with in-house staff. Alternatively, it may use an outside firm specializing in market research. In global marketing, a combination of in-house and outside research efforts is often advisable. Many outside firms have considerable international expertise; some specialize in particular industry segments. According to the American Marketing Association, global market research revenues for the top 25 research companies totaled $22.5 billion in 2015.[16] The Nielsen Company is the world's largest market research organization; it is the source of the well-known Nielsen TV ratings for the U.S. market. Nielsen Media Research International also provides media measurement services in more than 40 global markets. Other research specialists are the Kantar Group (brand awareness and media analysis), IMS Health (pharmaceutical and health care industries), and Germany's GfK SE (custom research and consumer tracking).

> "Traditional research concentrated on the 'what.' Now we are trying to establish the 'why.' We are not asking what consumers think about products and ideas but focusing on what makes them tick."[14]
>
> Simon Stewart, marketing director, Britvic

The process of collecting data and converting it into useful information can be quite detailed, as shown in Figure 6-2. In the discussion that follows, we will focus on eight basic steps: information requirements, problem definition, choosing the unit of analysis, examining data availability, assessing the value of research, research design, data analysis, and interpretation and presentation.

Step 1: Information Requirements

The late Thomas Bata was a self-described "shoe salesman" who built the Bata Shoe Organization into a global empire that is now based in Switzerland. Legend has it that the Czech-born, Swiss-educated Bata once fired a salesman who, upon returning from Africa, reported that there was no opportunity to sell shoes there because everyone walked around barefoot. According to this story, Bata hired another salesman who understood that, in fact, Africa represented a huge untapped market for shoes. This anecdote underscores the fact that direct observation must be linked to unbiased perception and insight. However, as many marketers will acknowledge, it can be difficult to alter entrenched consumer behavior patterns.

Formal research often is undertaken after a problem or opportunity has been identified. A company may need to supplement direct perception with additional information to determine whether a particular country or regional market does, in fact, offer good growth potential. What proportion of potential customers can be converted into *actual* customers? Is a competitor making inroads in one or more important markets around the world? Is research on local taste preferences required to determine whether a food product must be adapted? A truism of market research is that a problem well defined is a problem half-solved. Thus, regardless of the particular situation that sets the research effort in motion, the first two questions a marketer should ask are "What information do I need?" and "Why do I need this information?" Table 6-1 lists various subject categories that may require research.

Step 2: Problem Definition

As noted in Chapter 4, when a person's home-country values and beliefs influence the assessment of a foreign culture or country, the self-reference criterion (SRC) is at work. The SRC tendency underscores the importance of understanding the cultural environments of global markets, as the following examples illustrate:

- When Mattel first introduced Barbie in Japan, managers assumed that Japanese girls would find the doll's design just as appealing as American girls did. They didn't.

FIGURE 6-2 Market Research Process

Source: Adapted from V. Kumar, *International Marketing Research,* 1st edition, © 2000. Pearson Education, Inc., Upper Saddle River, NJ.

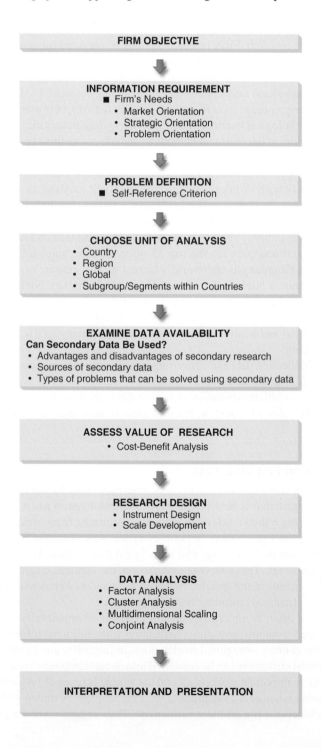

TABLE 6-1 Subject Agenda Categories for a Global Marketing Information System

Category	Coverage
1. Market potential	Demand estimates, consumer behavior, review of products, channels, communication media
2. Competitor information	Corporate, business, and functional strategies; resources and intentions; capabilities
3. Foreign exchange	Balance of payments, interest rates, attractiveness of country currency, expectations of analysts
4. Prescriptive information	Laws, regulations, rulings concerning taxes, earnings, dividends in both host and home countries
5. Resource information	Availability of human, financial, physical, and information resources
6. General conditions	Overall review of sociocultural, political, and technological environments

- When the Walt Disney Company opened Disneyland Paris, park employees were expected to comply with a detailed written code regarding personal appearance. The goal was to ensure that guests received the kind of experience associated with the Disney name. The French workers, however, considered the code to be an insult to French culture, individualism, and privacy.

As these examples show, managers sometimes make decisions based on home-country marketing success that can turn out to be wrong when applied globally. Marketers might also assume that a marketing program that is successful in one country market can be applied to other country markets in the region. Consider again the case of Disney's theme park business. Although Disneyland Japan was a huge success from opening day, the $3.2 billion Hong Kong Disneyland that opened in 2005 was less successful. This was due, in part, to the fact that visitors from mainland China had limited familiarity with traditional Disney "face characters" such as Snow White. As Jay Rasulo, president of Disney's park and resort division, noted, "People from the mainland don't show up with the embedded 'Disney software' like at other parks."[17]

When approaching global markets, it is best to have "eyes wide open." In other words, marketers must be aware of the impact that SRC and other cross-cultural assumptions can have. Such awareness can have several positive effects. First, it can enhance management's willingness to conduct market research in the first place. Second, an awareness of SRC can help ensure that the research effort is designed with minimal home-country or second-country bias. Third, it can enhance management's receptiveness to research findings—even if they contradict "tried-and-true" marketing experience in other markets.

Step 3: Choosing the Unit of Analysis

The next step involves the need to identify in which part(s) of the world the company should be doing business and to find out as much as possible about the business environment in the area(s) identified. These issues are reflected in the subject agenda categories in Table 6-1. The unit of analysis may be a single country, or it may be a region such as Europe or South America. In some instances, the marketer is interested in a segment that is global. Countrywide data are not required for all market-entry decisions; in some cases, a specific city, state, or province may be the relevant unit of analysis. For example, a company that is considering entering China may focus initially on Shanghai. Located in the Jiangsu province, Shanghai is China's largest city and main seaport. Because Shanghai is a manufacturing center, has a well-developed infrastructure, and is home to a population with a relatively high per capita income, it would be the logical focus of a market research effort.

Step 4: Examining Data Availability

The first task at this stage is to answer several questions regarding the availability of data. Which type of data should be gathered? Can **secondary data**—for example, data available in company files, the library, industry or trade journals, or online databases—be used? When does management need the information to make a decision regarding market entry? Marketers must address these issues before proceeding to the next step of the research process. Using data that are readily available saves both money and time: A formal market study can cost hundreds of thousands of dollars and take many months to complete.

A low-cost approach to market research and data collection begins with desk research. In other words, "The key to creating a cost-effective way of surveying foreign markets is to climb on the shoulders of those who have gone before."[18] Suppose a marketer wants to assess the basic market potential for a particular product. To make this determination, secondary sources are a good place to start. Clipping services, company or public libraries, online databases, government census records, and trade associations are just a few of the data sources that can be tapped with minimal effort and cost. Data from these sources already exist. Such data are known as *secondary data* because they were not gathered for the specific project at hand. *Statistical Abstract of the United States* is just one of the annual publications issued by the U.S. government that contains myriad facts about international markets.

The U.S. government's most comprehensive source of world trade data is the National Trade Data Base (NTDB), an online resource from the Department of Commerce. The Bureau of Economic Analysis (www.bea.gov) and the Census Bureau (www.census.gov) are excellent online resources for foreign trade, economic indicators, and other current and historical data. Trade data for the European Union are available from Eurostat (epp.eurostat.ec.europa.eu). Most countries compile estimates of gross national product (GNP), gross domestic product (GDP), consumption, investment, government expenditures, and price levels. Demographic data indicating the population size, distribution of population by age category, and rates of population growth are also readily available. Market information from export census documents compiled by the Department of Commerce on the basis of shippers' export declarations is available as well. Formerly known as "ex-decs" or SEDs, these Electronic Export Information (EEI) forms must be filled out for any export valued at $2,500 or more. Another important source of market data is the Foreign Commercial Service.

Many countries have set up Web sites to help small firms find opportunities in world markets. For example, the Canadian Trade Commissioner Service (www.tradecommissioner.gc.ca) is a service supported by Foreign Affairs, Trade and Development Canada. Its Web site offers information about international markets and provides export assistance.

These suggestions do not exhaust the types of data available, however. A single source, *The Statistical Yearbook of the United Nations*, contains global data on agriculture, mining, manufacturing, construction, energy production and consumption, internal and external trade, railroad and air transport, wages and prices, health, housing, education, communication infrastructure, and availability of mass communication media. The U.S. Central Intelligence Agency publishes *The World Factbook*, which is revised yearly. Other important sources of data are the World Bank, the International Monetary Fund, and Japan's Ministry of International Trade and Industry (MITI). *The Economist* and the *Financial Times* regularly compile comprehensive surveys of regional and country markets and include them in their publications. Data from these sources are generally available in both print and electronic form.

How can such data be useful? Take industrial growth patterns as one example. Because they generally reveal consumption patterns, production patterns are helpful in assessing market opportunities. Additionally, trends in manufacturing production indicate potential markets for companies that supply manufacturing inputs. At the early stages of growth in a country, when per capita incomes are low, manufacturing centers on such necessities as food and beverages, textiles, and other forms of light industry. As incomes rise, the relative importance of these industries declines as heavy industry begins to develop.

A word of caution is in order at this point: Remember that data are compiled from various sources, some of which may not be reputable. Even when the sources are reputable, there is likely to be some variability from source to source. Anyone using data should be clear on exactly what the data are measuring. For example, studying income data requires understanding whether one is working with GNP or GDP figures. Also, anyone using the Internet as an information source should evaluate the credibility of the person(s) responsible for the Web site. Moreover, as Czinkota and Ronkainen note,[19] secondary data may support the decision to pursue a market opportunity outside the home country, but such data are unlikely to shed light on specific questions: What is the market potential for our furniture in Indonesia? How much does the typical Nigerian consumer spend on soft drinks? Now that German law no longer requires that the "Der Grûne Punkt" trademark appear on product packaging, what effect, if any, will dropping the logo have on consumer purchasing behavior in Germany?

Syndicated studies published by private research companies are another source of secondary data and information (the word *syndicated* comes from the newspaper and television industries and refers to the practice of selling articles, cartoons, or guest columns, or programming to a number of different organizations). For example, MarketResearch.com (www.marketresearch.com) sells reports on a wide range of global business sectors, including consumer goods, food and beverages, and life sciences. The company partners with hundreds of research firms to offer a comprehensive set of reports. Although a single report can cost thousands of dollars, a company may be able to get the market information it needs without incurring the greater costs associated with conducting primary research.

Step 5: Assessing the Value of Research

When data are not available through published statistics or studies, management may wish to conduct further study of the individual country market, region, or global segment. However, collecting information costs money. Thus, the marketing research plan should also spell out what this information is worth to the company in dollars (or euros, or yen, or some other currency) compared with what it would cost to collect it. What will the company gain by collecting these data? What would be the cost of not getting the data that could be converted into useful information? Research requires an investment of both money and managerial time, and it is necessary to perform a cost–benefit analysis before proceeding further. In some instances, a company will pursue the same course of action no matter what the research reveals. Even when more information is needed to ensure a high-quality decision, a realistic cost estimate of a formal study may reveal that the cost to perform research is simply too high.

The many small markets around the world pose a special problem for the researcher. The relatively low profit potential in smaller markets justifies only modest expenditures for marketing research, so the global researcher must devise techniques and methods that keep expenditures in line with the market's profit potential. The researcher is often pressured to discover economic and demographic relationships that can lead to estimates of demand based on a minimum of information. It may also be necessary to use inexpensive survey research that sacrifices some elegance or statistical rigor to achieve results within the constraints of the smaller market research budget.

Step 6: Research Design

As indicated in Figure 6-2, if secondary data can be used, the researcher can go directly to the data analysis step. Suppose, however, that data are not available through published statistics or studies; in addition, suppose that the cost–benefit analysis indicated in step 5 has been performed and that the decision has been made to carry on with the research effort. **Primary data** are gathered through original research pertaining to the particular problem identified in step 1. At this point, it is time to establish a research design.

Global marketing guru David Arnold offers the following guidelines regarding data gathering:[20]

- Use multiple indicators rather than a single measure. This approach will decrease the level of uncertainty for decision makers. As the saying goes, "There are three sides to every story: your side, my side, and the truth." A land surveyor can pinpoint the location of a third object given the known location of two objects. This technique, known as *triangulation*, is equally useful in global market research.
- Individual companies should develop customized indicators specific to the industry, product market, or business model. Such indicators should leverage a company's previous experience in global markets. For example, in some developing markets, Mary Kay Cosmetics uses the average wage of a female secretary as a basis for estimating income potential for its beauty consultants.
- Always conduct comparative assessments in multiple markets; do not assess a particular market in isolation. Comparative assessment enables management to develop a "portfolio" approach in which alternative priorities and scenarios can be developed. For example, to better understand Czech consumers in general, a company might also conduct research in nearby Poland and Hungary. By contrast, if a brewing company wished to learn more about beer consumption patterns in the Czech Republic, it might also conduct research in Ireland and Germany, where per capita beer consumption is high.
- Observations of purchasing patterns and other behavior should be weighted more heavily than reports or opinions regarding purchase intention or price sensitivity. Particularly in developing markets, it is difficult to accurately survey consumer perceptions.

With these guidelines in mind, the marketer must address a new set of questions and issues in primary data collection. Should the research effort be geared toward quantitative, numerical data that can be subjected to statistical analysis, or should qualitative techniques be used? In global market research, it is advisable for the plan to call for a mix of techniques. For consumer products, qualitative research is especially well suited to accomplish the following tasks:[21]

- To provide consumer understanding; to "get close" to the consumer
- To describe the social and cultural contexts of consumer behavior, including cultural, religious, and political factors that impact decision making
- To identify core-brand equity and "get under the skin" of brands
- To "mine" the consumer and identify what people really feel

ISSUES IN DATA COLLECTION   The research problem may be more narrowly focused on marketing issues, such as the need to adapt products and other mix elements to local tastes and to assess demand and profit potential. Demand and profit potential, in turn, depend in part on whether the market being studied can be classified as existing or potential. *Existing markets* are those in which customer needs are already being served by one or more companies. In many countries, data about the size of existing markets—in terms of dollar volume and unit sales—are readily available. In some countries, however, formal market research is a relatively new phenomenon and data are scarce.

In recent years, McKinsey & Company, Gartner Group Asia, and Grey China Advertising have been very active in China. For example, using focus groups and other techniques, Grey China gathers a wealth of information about attitudes and buying patterns that it publishes in its Grey China Base Annual Consumer Study. Recent findings point to growing concerns about the future, Westernization of grocery purchases, growing market saturation, increasingly discerning customers, and a rise in consumer willingness to try new products. Even with such data collection efforts, however, data gathered by different sources may be inconsistent. What is the level of soft drink consumption in China? Euromonitor International estimates consumption at 23 billion liters, whereas Coca-Cola's in-house marketing research team places the figure at 39 billion liters. Likewise, CSM, a Chinese television-rating agency, estimates the TV-advertising market at $2.8 billion per year, but Nielsen Media Research puts this figure closer to $7.5 billion.[22]

In such situations, and in countries where such data are not available, researchers must first estimate the market size, the level of demand, or the rate of product purchase or consumption. A second research objective in existing markets may be assessment of the company's overall competitiveness in terms of product appeal, price, distribution, and promotional coverage and effectiveness. Researchers may be able to pinpoint a weakness in the competitor's product or identify an underserved or unserved market segment. The minivan and sport-utility vehicle segments of the auto industry illustrate the opportunity that an existing market can present. For years, Chrysler dominated the U.S. minivan segment, for which annual sales at one time totaled nearly 1.2 million vehicles. Most global marketers compete in this segment, although a number of models have been discontinued due to declining sales. For example, Toyota introduced its Japanese-built Previa in the United States in 1991; critics mocked the teardrop styling and dismissed it as being underpowered. For the 1998 model year, the Previa was replaced with the American-built Sienna. To ensure that the Sienna suited American tastes, Toyota designers and engineers studied Chrysler minivans and duplicated key features such as numerous cup holders and a second sliding rear door on the driver's side.

In some instances, there is no existing market to research. Such *potential markets* can be further subdivided into latent and incipient markets. A **latent market** is, in essence, an undiscovered segment. It is a market in which demand would materialize *if* an appropriate product were made available. In a latent market, demand is zero before the product is introduced. In the case of existing markets, such as the one for minivans previously described, the main research challenge is to understand the extent to which the competition fully meets customer needs. As J. Davis Illingworth, an executive at Toyota Motor Sales USA, explained, "I think the American public will look at Sienna as an American product that meets their needs."[23] With latent markets, initial success is not based on a company's competitiveness, but rather depends on the prime-mover advantage—that is, a company's ability to uncover the opportunity and launch a marketing program that taps the latent demand. This is precisely what Chrysler achieved by single-handedly creating the minivan market.

Sometimes, traditional market research is not an effective means for identifying latent markets. As Peter Drucker has noted, the failure of U.S. companies to successfully commercialize fax machines—an American innovation—can be traced to research that indicated no potential demand for such a product. The problem, in Drucker's view, stems from the typical survey question for a product targeted at a latent market. Suppose a researcher asks, "Would you buy a telephone accessory that costs upward of $1,500 and enables you to send, for $1 a page, the same letter the post office delivers for $0.25?" On the basis of economics alone, the respondent most likely will answer, "No."

According to Drucker, Japanese companies are the leading sellers of fax machines today because their understanding of the market was not based on survey research. Instead, they reviewed the early days of mainframe computers, photocopy machines, cell phones, and other information and communications products. The Japanese companies realized that, judging only by the initial costs associated with buying and using these new products, the prospects of market acceptance were low. However, each of these products became a huge success after people began to use them. This realization prompted the Japanese companies to focus on the market for the *benefits* provided by fax machines, rather than the market for the machines themselves. By looking at the success of courier services such as FedEx, they realized that, in essence, the fax machine market already existed.[24]

To illustrate Drucker's point, consider the case of Red Bull energy drink. Dietrich Mateschitz hired a market research firm to assess the market potential for his creation. In the tests, consumers reacted negatively to the taste, the logo, and the brand name. Mateschitz ignored the research, and Red Bull is now a $2 billion brand. As Mateschitz explains, "When we first started, we said there is no existing market for Red Bull, but Red Bull will create it. And this is what finally became true."[26]

An **incipient market** is a market that will emerge if a particular economic, demographic, political, or sociocultural trend continues. A company is not likely to succeed if it offers a product in an incipient market before the trends have taken root. After the trends have had a chance to gain traction, the incipient market will become latent and, later, existing. The concept of incipient markets can also be illustrated by the impact of rising income on demand for automobiles and other expensive consumer durables. As per capita income rises in a country, the demand for automobiles will also rise. Therefore, if a company can predict a country's future rate of income growth, it can also predict the growth rate of its automobile market.

For example, to capitalize on China's rapid economic growth, Volkswagen, Peugeot, Chrysler, and other global automakers have established in-country manufacturing operations. China even has incipient demand for imported exotic cars; in early 1994, Ferrari opened its first showroom in Beijing. Because of a 150 percent import tax, China's first Ferrari buyers were entrepreneurs who had profited from China's increasing openness to Western-style marketing and capitalism. By the end of the 1990s, demand for luxury cars had grown at a faster rate than anticipated.[27] Today, annual passenger vehicle sales in China have passed the 20 million unit mark. Clearly, China represents a very attractive market opportunity for carmakers.

In the past, some companies had concluded that China had limited potential for their products. For example, in 1998, U.K.-based retailer Marks & Spencer closed its office in Shanghai and tabled plans to commence operations there. Commenting to the press, a spokesperson directly addressed the issue of whether the company viewed China as an incipient market:

> After 3 years of research, we have come to the conclusion that the timing is not right. The majority of our customers are from middle-income groups. But, our interest is in Shanghai, and the size of the middle-income group, although it is growing, is not yet at a level that would justify us opening a store there.[28]

Within a decade, however, China's emerging middle class represented an attractive opportunity. Marks & Spencer opened its first store in Shanghai in 2008; by 2017, there were 10 stores. However, when its sales stalled, the company pulled out of China for the second time. Part of the problem: low brand awareness, plus the fact that many Chinese shoppers prefer "fast-fashion" brands such as Zara and H&M.[29]

RESEARCH METHODOLOGIES Survey research, interviews, consumer panels, observation, and focus groups are some of the tools used to collect primary market data. These are the same tools

"At that time, Japanese women almost never used mascaras because, by nature, they have very straight, short and thin lashes. We designed mascara that was able to lengthen and curl lashes. It was a huge success. We would never have seen that in a focus group."[25]

Jean-Paul Agon, Chairman and CEO, L'Oréal, discussing the decision to relaunch the Maybelline makeup brand in Japan with mascara

"Data regresses to the mean. Something that's really original, really authentic, it's probably not going to score that well because people have a knee-jerk reaction against new things."[30]

James Gilmore, coauthor, *Authenticity: What Consumers Really Want*

used by marketers whose activities are not global, though some adaptations and special considerations for global marketing may be required.

Survey research utilizes questionnaires designed to elicit quantitative data ("How much would you buy?"), qualitative responses ("Why would you buy?"), or both. Survey research is often conducted by means of a questionnaire distributed through the mail, asked over the telephone, or asked in person. Many good marketing research textbooks provide details on questionnaire design and administration.

In global market research, a number of survey design and administration issues may arise. When using the telephone as a research tool, it is important to remember that what is customary in one country may be impossible in others because of infrastructure differences, cultural barriers, or other reasons. For example, telephone directories or lists may not be available; also, important differences may exist between urban dwellers and people in rural areas. In China, for example, the Ministry of Information Industry reports that 77 percent of households in coastal areas have at least one fixed-line telephone; in rural areas, that proportion is only 40 percent.

At a deeper level, culture shapes attitudes and values in a way that directly affects people's willingness to respond to interviewer questions. Open-ended questions may help the researcher identify a respondent's frame of reference. In some cultures, respondents may be unwilling to answer certain questions or may intentionally give inaccurate answers.

Recall that step 2 of the global market research process calls for identifying possible sources of SRC bias. This issue is especially important in survey research: SRC bias can originate from the cultural backgrounds of those designing the questionnaire. For example, a survey designed and administered in the United States may be inappropriate in non-Western cultures even if it is carefully translated. This is especially true if the person designing the questionnaire is not familiar with the SRC. A technique known as *back-translation* can help increase comprehension and validity; it requires that, after a questionnaire or survey instrument is translated into a particular target language, it is translated once again, this time into the original language by a different translator. For even greater accuracy, *parallel translations*—two versions by different translators—can be used as input to the back-translation. The same techniques can ensure that advertising copy is accurately translated into different languages.

A **consumer panel** is a sample of respondents whose behavior is tracked over time. For example, a number of companies, including the Nielsen Media Research unit of Netherlands-based VNU, AGB, GfK, and TNS, conduct television audience measurement (TAM) by studying the viewing habits of household panels. Broadcasters use audience share data to set advertising rates; advertisers such as Procter & Gamble, Unilever, and Coca-Cola use the data to choose programs during which to advertise. In the United States, Nielsen has enjoyed a virtual monopoly on viewership research for half a century. For years, however, the four major U.S. television networks have complained that they lose advertising revenues because Nielsen's data collection methods undercount viewership. Nielsen has responded to these concerns by upgrading its survey methodology; the company now uses an electronic device known as a **peoplemeter** to collect national audience data. Peoplemeter systems are currently in use in dozens of countries around the world, including China; Nielsen is also rolling out peoplemeters to collect local audience viewership data in key metropolitan markets such as New York City.

When **observation** is used as a data collection method, one or more trained observers (or a mechanical device such as a video camera) watch and record the behavior of actual or prospective buyers. The research results are then used to guide marketing managers in their decision making. For example, after Volkswagen's U.S. sales began to slump, the company launched "Moonraker," an 18-month effort designed to help its engineers, marketers, and design specialists better understand American consumers. Despite the presence of a design center in California, decision makers at headquarters in Wolfsburg, Germany, generally ignored feedback from U.S. customers. As Stefan Liske, director of product strategy at VW, acknowledged, "We needed a totally different approach. We asked ourselves, 'Do we really know everything about this market?'" The Moonraker team visited the Mall of America in Minneapolis and the Rock and Roll Hall of Fame in Cleveland; they also spent spring break in Florida observing college students.

The experience was an eye-opener. As one designer explained, "In Germany, it's all about driving, but here, it's about everything *but* driving. People here want to use their time in other ways, like talk on their cell phone." Another member of the team, an engineer, shadowed a single mom as she took her kids to school and ran errands. The engineer noted that American drivers need

"You can't go out and ask people what they need or want because they don't know. The whole trick is to come out with a product and say, 'Have you thought of this?' and hear the consumer respond, 'Wow! No, I hadn't.' If you can do that, you're on."[31]

David Lewis, chief designer, Bang & Olufsen

a place to store a box of tissues and a place to put a bag of fast food picked up at a drive-through window. "I began thinking about what specific features her car needed. It was about living the customer's life and putting ourselves in their place," he said.[32]

A marketer of breakfast cereals might send researchers to preselected households at 6 A.M. to watch families go about their morning routines. The client could also assign a researcher to accompany family members to the grocery store to observe their behavior under actual shopping conditions. The client might wish to know about the shoppers' reactions to in-store promotions linked to an advertising campaign. The researcher could record comments or discretely take photographs. Of course, companies using observation as a research methodology must be sensitive to concerns about privacy issues. A second problem with observation is *reactivity*, which is the tendency of research subjects to behave differently for the simple reason that they know they are under study. Additional examples of observation-based studies include the following:

- To gain insights for product and package design improvements, Procter & Gamble sent video crews into 80 households in the United Kingdom, Italy, Germany, and China. P&G's ultimate goal was to amass an in-house video library database. Stan Joosten, an IT manager, noted, "You could search for 'eating snacks' and find all [the] clips from all over the world on that topic. Immediately, it gives you a global perspective on certain topics."[33]
- Michelle Arnau, a marketing manager for Nestlé's PowerBar brand, attended the 2004 New York City Marathon to see how runners were using single-serve packets of PowerGel. Arnau observed that runners typically tore off the top with their teeth and attempted to consume the gel in a single squeeze without breaking their stride. Designers at Nestlé then created an improved package with an upside-down, triangular-shaped top that is narrow enough to control the flow of the gel but also fits into the athlete's mouth.[34]

In **focus group** research, a trained moderator facilitates discussion of a product concept, a brand's image and personality, an advertisement, a social trend, or another topic with a group of 6 to 10 people. Global marketers can use focus groups to arrive at important insights. For example:

- In the mid-1990s, Whirlpool launched a successful advertising campaign in Europe that featured fantasy characters such as a drying diva and a washing-machine goddess. Before adapting the campaign for the United States and Latin America, the company conducted focus groups. Nick Mote, Whirlpool's worldwide account director at France's Publicis advertising agency, said, "We've had some incredible research results. It was just like somebody switched the lights on."[35]
- In Singapore, focus groups of young teens were used to help guide development of Coca-Cola's advertising program. As Karen Wong, Coke's country marketing director for Singapore, explained, "We tested everything from extreme to borderline boring: body-piercing all over, grungy kids in a car listening to rock music and head-banging all the way. Youth doing things that youth in America do." Some participants found much of Coke's imagery to be too rebellious. As one young Singaporean remarked, "They look like they're on drugs. And if they're on drugs, then how can they be performing at school?" Armed with the focus group results, Coca-Cola's managers devised an ad campaign for Singapore that was well within the bounds of societal approval.[36]

A typical focus group meets at a facility equipped with recording equipment and a two-way mirror, behind which representatives of the client company observe the proceedings. The moderator can utilize a number of approaches to elicit reactions and responses, including projective techniques such as visualization and role plays. When using a projective technique, the researcher presents open-ended or ambiguous verbal stimuli to a subject. Presumably, when responding, the subjects will "project"—that is, reveal—any unconscious attitude, needs, or biases. By analyzing the responses, researchers are better able to understand how consumers perceive a particular product, product concept, brand, or company.

Visualization is especially appropriate and effective for companies wishing to create breakthrough or disruptive innovations. Suppose a consumer electronics company wants to generate ideas for a new home theater system. In the focus group, the moderator attempts to erase all stimuli

ENTREPRENEURIAL LEADERSHIP, CREATIVE THINKING, AND THE GLOBAL STARTUP

Daniel Ek, Spotify

Daniel Ek is an entrepreneur who developed an innovative service and started a company called Spotify to market it. By applying the basic tools and principles of modern global marketing, Ek achieved remarkable success (see Exhibit 6-5).

As is true with many entrepreneurs, Ek's idea was based on his own needs and wants. In the late 1990s, he discovered Napster, the original file-sharing Web site for music. Ek recalls, "Napster changed my life. You could search for any band, and there it was. It allowed me to listen to all this music that I never knew existed." Ultimately, the courts ordered Napster to shut down for infringing intellectual property rights.

Within a few years of Napster's demise, a number of legal music-subscription services appeared on the scene, including Rhapsody, MOG, and a legal version of Napster. Meanwhile, Apple created the market for paid, legal music downloads with its iTunes Store. Undeterred by the competitive landscape, Ek was convinced that "there had to be a better way" to learn about new music and share music with others while also compensating songwriters and performers. Ek's insight was to tap the power of social media—specifically Facebook—for music sharing.

As a young man growing up in Sweden, Ek benefitted from a government program designed to ensure that most households had computers. At home, he was exposed to both music and technology; by the time he was 14 years old, he was earning as much as $15,000 per month designing Web pages. When he was 16, Ek applied for a job at Google but was turned away with the advice, "Come back when you have a degree." Ek briefly attended Sweden's Royal Institute of Technology, but dropped out to start Tradedoubler, an Internet marketing company.

After taking time off to do some soul searching, Ek decided to start a music streaming company; the result was Spotify. From his base in Sweden, Ek expanded across Europe and, in 2011, he launched the service in the United States. By mid-2017, Spotify had 140 million users with on-demand access to more than 30 million songs. Spotify's business model is built on the "freemium" pricing strategy. Several service tiers are available. The service is free for listeners who are willing to listen to ads. Student subscribers pay $4.99 per month; otherwise, individual subscriptions cost $9.99 per month. Family plans are available for $14.99 per month. Apple Music offers similar pricing, but without the free tier.

Spotify gathers a great deal of data from its listeners. First-time subscribers provide basic demographic and geographic data such as age, gender, and country of residence. In addition, every time a user hits the "play" button, data are generated. Spotify uses these data to improve the listening experience for its subscribers, many of whom are Millennials. What's more, Spotify users have created more than 1.5 billion playlists; the different names tell Spotify a great deal about the listening context—for example, "coffeehouse," "exercise," and so on.

Among the challenges facing Spotify today as it expands globally is the difficulty of licensing songs on a country-by-country basis. As Ek notes, "That doesn't really work in this Internet world where a song made here in Sweden might be shared with someone in Ukraine." A related issue is rights holder compensation. Even though Spotify pays hundreds of millions of dollars—about 70 percent of its revenues—in royalties and licensing fees, many artists have criticized Spotify for not paying them enough. In addition, Apple Music is on track to surpass Spotify in terms of paid U.S. subscribers.

Sources: Anne Steele, "Apple Nips at Spotify's Lead," The Wall Street Journal (February 5, 2018), p. A9; Johannes Ledel and John Stoll, "Boss Talk: Spotify—Eating Google's Lunch and Loving It," The Wall Street Journal (August 27, 2013), p. B7; Jefferson Graham, "Daniel Ek Wants to Turn You on to New Music," USA Today (February 20, 2013), p 1B.

Exhibit 6-5 Daniel Ek is the Swedish entrepreneur who started Spotify, the popular on-demand music streaming service. For a song that receives 1 million plays, Spotify pays out fees totaling $6,000 to $8,000; the money is split between record labels, artist, songwriters, and publishers.

Source: norazaminayob/ Shutterstock.

by dimming the lights. Participants close their eyes and lie down on pillows or comfortable surfaces. The moderator speaks quietly and gently:

> Picture yourself lying comfortably in a hammock on a lovely spring day. Gaze intently at a tree, then focus on one leaf, and watch it turn from green to white, like a movie screen, where you can project anything that you want. Picture whatever is your perfect place, and put yourself and anyone else you desire into the scene. Now imagine you're watching and hearing your favorite program. Maybe Kerry Washington is once again saving the White House in *Scandal*. How are you seeing the image? What furniture or equipment—if any— do you see? What else is in the room? What size is the image? Who else is there?

After further questions of this type, the moderator guides the participants back to the "here and now" by suggesting that the scene they are visualizing is fading until the screen is white, the tree leaf turns from white back to green, and then they see the whole tree again. The participants open their eyes, sit up, take a pad of paper, and record in words and pictures as much as possible of what they experienced. These experiences are shared with the group, and can serve as springboards for new home entertainment concepts.

Many variations on the role-play technique exist, which can be used to uncover insights for innovation. The quest to reveal these hidden points often takes the form of an ideation workshop. A consumer may have unmet needs or wants that she hasn't conveyed directly because she's not consciously aware of them. Those needs may emerge during role plays; the technique is projective because the consumer projects onto others what she can't (or won't) see in herself. Perhaps a variety of psychological factors—such as motivations, attitudes, or fears—contribute to whether a consumer accepts or rejects a product. In addition, when participants in a role play act out each minute step in a process, the researchers may notice something that is incongruous or unconscious that can lead to a product improvement.

For example, managers at a home-care products company might participate in a role play that also involves consumers. Before the focus group is convened, each manager on the client team is briefed about a consumer who has been recruited. Then, the managers meet in a group and each one role-plays his or her consumer using a particular product. In other words, they "walk" in the consumers' shoes, with the goal of understanding and predicting consumers' behavior and interactions with the product. Then the actual consumers arrive at the session and perform the task with the product. The managers from the client company can see for themselves how well or poorly they role-played their respective consumers. In this case, the managers witness first-hand what they got right or wrong, and why.

As example, suppose an automaker convenes a focus group to assess car-buying preferences among a segment consisting of twenty-somethings. The researcher might ask participants to describe a party where various automotive brands are present. What is Nissan wearing, eating, and drinking? Which kind of sneakers does Honda have on? What are their personalities like? Who's shy? Who's loud? Who gets the girl (or guy)? Interactions among group members can result in synergies that yield important qualitative insights that are likely to differ from those based on data gathered through more direct questioning.

For example, executives at the ABC Family channel realized that they needed to rebrand the network after research revealed the associations that viewers made with the name. As Karey Burke, vice president for programming and development, explained:

> We saw a psychographic study of what sort of person audiences thought different channels would be. MTV was a "cool teenager," the CW was a "thoughtful college student," and ABC Family was a "Midwestern housewife." That's not what we were.[37]

Within a few months, the channel was renamed Freeform.

Focus groups, visualization, and role plays yield qualitative data that do not lend themselves to statistical projection. Such data suggest, rather than confirm, hypotheses; also, qualitative data tend to be directional rather than conclusive. Such data are extremely valuable in the exploratory phase of a project and are typically used in conjunction with data gathered via observation and other methods.

SCALE DEVELOPMENT   Market research requires assigning some type of measure, ranking, or interval to a response. To take a simple example of measurement, a *nominal scale* is used to establish the identity of a survey element. For example, male respondents could be labeled "1" and female respondents could be labeled "2." Scaling can also entail placing each response in some kind of continuum; a common example is the Likert scale, which asks respondents to indicate whether they "strongly agree" with a statement, "strongly disagree," or whether their attitude falls somewhere in the middle. In a multicountry research project, it is important to have *scalar equivalence*, which means that two respondents in different countries with the same value for a given variable receive equivalent scores on the same survey item.

Even with standard data-gathering techniques, the application of a particular technique may differ from country to country. Matthew Draper, vice president at New Jersey–based Total Research Corporation, cites "scalar bias" as a major problem: "There are substantial differences in the way people use scales, and research data based on scales such as rating product usefulness on a scale of 1 to 10 is therefore frequently cluttered with biases disguising the truth." For example, while the typical American scale would equate a high number such as 10 with "most" or "best" and 1 with "least," Germans prefer scales in which 1 is "most/best." Also, while American survey items pertaining to spending provide a range of figures, Germans prefer the opportunity to provide an exact answer.[38]

SAMPLING   When collecting data, researchers generally cannot administer a survey to every possible person in the designated group. A sample is a selected subset of a population that is representative of the entire population. The two best-known types of samples are probability samples and nonprobability samples. A probability sample is generated by following statistical rules that ensure each member of the population under study has an equal chance—or probability—of being included in the sample. The results of a probability sample can be projected to the entire population with statistical reliability reflecting sampling error, degree of confidence, and standard deviation.

In contrast, the results of a nonprobability sample cannot be projected with statistical reliability. One form of nonprobability sample is a *convenience sample*. As the name implies, with this type of sample researchers select people who are easy to reach. For example, in one study that compared consumer shopping attitudes in the United States, Jordan, Singapore, and Turkey, data for the latter three countries were gathered from convenience samples recruited by an acquaintance of the researcher. Although data gathered in this way are not subject to statistical inference, they may be adequate to address the problem defined in step 1. In this study, for example, the researchers were able to identify a clear trend toward cultural convergence in shopping attitudes and customs that cut across modern industrial countries, emerging industrial countries, and developing countries.[39]

To obtain a *quota sample*, the researcher divides the population under study into categories; a sample is then taken from each category. The term *quota* refers to the need to make sure that enough people are chosen in each category to reflect the overall makeup of the population. For example, assume a country's population is divided into six categories according to monthly income, as follows:

Percentage of population	10%	15%	25%	25%	15%	10%
Earnings per month	0–9	10–19	20–39	40–59	60–69	70–100

If it is assumed that income is the characteristic that adequately differentiates the population for study purposes, then a quota sample would include respondents of different income levels in the same proportion as they occur in the population—that is, 15 percent with monthly earnings from 10 to 19, and so on.

Step 7: Data Analysis[40]

The data collected up to this point must be subjected to some form of analysis if they are to be useful to decision makers. Although a detailed discussion is beyond the scope of this text, a brief overview of data analysis is in order. First, the data must be prepared—the term *cleaned* is sometimes used—before further analysis is possible. They must be logged and stored in a central location or database. When research has been conducted in various parts of the world, this process of rounding up data can pose some difficulties. Are data comparable across samples so that multicountry analysis can be performed? Some amount of editing may be required; for example, some responses may be missing or difficult to interpret. Next, questionnaires must be coded. Simply put, coding involves identifying the respondents and the variables. Finally, some data adjustment may be required.

Data analysis continues with *tabulation*—that is, the arrangement of data in tabular form. Researchers may wish to determine various things: the mean, median, and mode; range and standard deviation; and the shape of the distribution (e.g., that of a normal curve or not). For nominally scaled variables such as "male" and "female," a simple cross-tabulation may be performed.

Suppose, for example, that Nielsen Media Research surveyed video gamers to determine how they feel about products (e.g., soft drinks) and advertisements (e.g., a billboard for a cell phone) embedded in video games. Nielsen could use cross-tabulation to separately examine the responses of male and female subjects to see if their responses differ significantly. If females are equally or more positive in their responses than males, video game companies could use this information to persuade consumer products companies to pay to have select products targeted at women featured as integral parts of the games. Researchers can use various relatively simple statistical techniques such as hypothesis testing and chi-square testing; advanced data analysis such as analysis of variance (ANOVA), correlation analysis, and regression analysis can also be used.

If the researcher is interested in the interactions among variables, *interdependence techniques* such as factor analysis, cluster analysis, and multidimensional scaling can be used to study these aspects of the data. **Factor analysis** can be used to transform large amounts of data into manageable units; specialized computer programs perform data reduction by "distilling out" from a multitude of survey responses a few meaningful factors that underlie attitudes and perceptions. Factor analysis is useful in psychographic segmentation studies and can also be used to create perceptual maps.

In this form of analysis, variables are not classified as dependent or independent. Instead, subjects are asked to rate specific product benefits on five-point scales. Table 6-2 shows a hypothetical scale that Google might use to assess consumer perceptions of a new smartphone. Although the scale shown in Table 6-2 lists 10 characteristics/benefits, factor analysis will generate *factor*

TABLE 6-2 Hypothetical Scales for Obtaining Consumer Perceptions of Google Pixel 2 Smartphone

Instructions: Please rate this product on the following product characteristics or benefits.

Variables (Product Characteristics/Benefits)	Low 1	2	3	4	High 5
1. Long battery life	—	—	—	—	—
2. Many apps available	—	—	—	—	—
3. 4G Internet access	—	—	—	—	—
4. Thin case	—	—	—	—	—
5. Intuitive interface	—	—	—	—	—
6. Music storage capacity	—	—	—	—	—
7. Large display screen	—	—	—	—	—
8. Fits hand comfortably	—	—	—	—	—
9. Works anywhere in the world	—	—	—	—	—
10. Fast processing speed	—	—	—	—	—

loadings that enable the researcher to determine which two or three factors underlie the benefits. In this way, factor analysis results in data reduction. For the smartphone, the researcher might label the factors "easy to use" and "stylish." The computer doing the analysis will also output *factor scores* for each respondent; respondent 1 might have a factor score of .35 for the factor identified as "easy to use"; respondent 2 might have a factor score of .42, and so on. When all respondents' factor scores are averaged, Google's position on a perceptual map can be determined (see Figure 6-3). Similar determinations can be made for other smartphone brands.

Cluster analysis allows the researcher to group variables into clusters that maximize within-group similarities and between-group differences. This type of analysis shares some characteristics of factor analysis: It does not classify variables as dependent or independent, and it can be used in psychographic segmentation. Cluster analysis is well suited to global market research because it can help establish similarities and differences among local, national, and regional markets of the world. Such analysis can also be used to perform benefit segmentation and to identify new product opportunities.

Multidimensional scaling (MDS) is another technique for creating perceptual maps. When the researcher is using MDS, the respondent is given the task of comparing products or brands, one pair at a time, and judging them in terms of similarity. The researcher then infers the dimensions that underlie these judgments. MDS is particularly useful when there are many alternatives from which to choose—soft drink, toothpaste, or automotive brands, for instance—and when consumers may have difficulty verbalizing their perceptions. To create a well-defined perceptual map, a minimum of eight products or brands should be used.

For example, suppose that a luxury goods marketer such as Coach initiates a study of consumer perceptions of global luxury brands. There are many luxury brands to choose from; some (including Coach) have outlet stores featuring discounted merchandise, and some offer "flash sales" offering selected styles for a limited time. Some brands, including Michael Kors and Ralph Lauren, offer lower-priced but highly profitable "diffusion" lines in addition to high-end collections. Some luxury goods firms, including Louis Vuitton, distribute their goods exclusively through company-owned retail stores; for Burberry and other brands, channel strategy includes wholesale operations.

Consumers may differentiate one designer brand from another in various ways: how easy it is to purchase each brand, how visible each brand is, whether the brand offers diffusion lines, and so on. To the researcher, this might represent an underlying perceptual dimension of "ubiquitous versus rare." Table 6-3 shows a five-point similarity judgment scale for eight designer brands.

TABLE 6-3 **MDS Study Inputs: Similarity Judgment Scales for Pairs of Luxury Brands**

	Very Similar				Very Different
	1	2	3	4	5
Burberry/Gucci	—	—	—	—	—
Burberry/Coach	—	—	—	—	—
Burberry/Michael Kors	—	—	—	—	—
Burberry/Tod's	—	—	—	—	—
Burberry/Dolce & Gabbana	—	—	—	—	—
Burberry/Dior	—	—	—	—	—
Burberry/Bottega Veneta	—	—	—	—	—
Gucci/Coach	—	—	—	—	—
Gucci/Michael Kors	—	—	—	—	—
Gucci/Tod's	—	—	—	—	—
Gucci/Dolce & Gabbana	—	—	—	—	—
Gucci/Dior	—	—	—	—	—
Gucci/Bottega Veneta	—	—	—	—	—

Figure 6-4 shows the position of the eight brands on the "ubiquity" dimension for a hypothetical respondent. The figure shows that Burberry and Coach are perceived as the most similar while Coach and Dior are the farthest apart.

The responses help marketers understand which brands in a particular category—luxury fashion brands in this example—are in direct competition with each other and which are not. The responses are used as input into a computer running an MDS program; the output is a perceptual map such as that shown in Figure 6-5. Once the computer has generated the map, the marketer examines the positions of different brands and infers the dimensions, which in this case are "ubiquity/rarity" and "exclusivity/accessibility." Coach's high ranking in terms of accessibility could be attributed in part to a pricing strategy that includes the lowest-priced entry-level handbag. Coach's position on the ubiquity dimension would be a function of the brand's multiple company-owned retail and outlet stores, wide availability at department stores, and the Poppy diffusion line.

This type of study could help Coach and other luxury goods marketers respond to new industry realities, which include a shift in the perception of what constitutes luxury and the increasing fragmentation of consumer tastes. Some of these changes in the market are driven by increasing opportunities in China and other emerging markets.[41] Such a map would also be helpful to, say, an up-and-coming fashion designer hoping to launch a new line. Perhaps the designer could find an optimal ubiquity/accessibility balance and fit in the gap between Burberry, Coach, and Ralph Lauren.

Dependence techniques assess the interdependence of two or more dependent variables with one or more independent variables. Conjoint analysis is an example of a dependence technique that is useful in both single market and global market research. Let us illustrate this with an

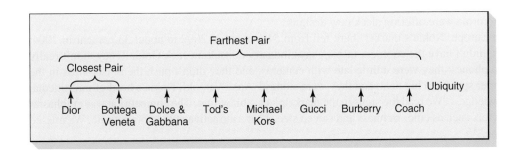

FIGURE 6-4 Hypothetical One-Dimensional Illustration of Similarity Judgments for Luxury Brands

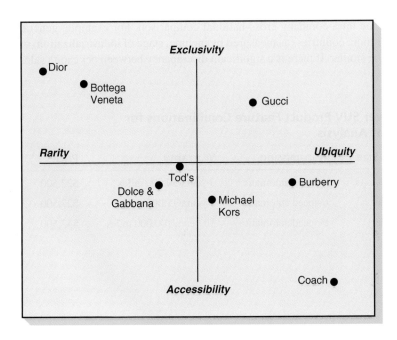

FIGURE 6-5 Hypothetical MDS-Based Perceptual Map for Luxury Fashion Brands

example from the SUV category of the automotive industry. Suppose Kia's new-product team has performed an MDS study and created a perceptual map similar to the one shown in Figure 6-4. The next task is to select an ideal position and then identify specific product features that match up with the desired positioning. To so, the researchers must determine the relative importance of a product's *salient attributes* in consumer decision making—that is, the relevance or importance that consumers attach to a product's qualities or properties. If the target position is "smooth, car-like ride with sports handling," the team must determine relevant physical product characteristics (e.g., 6-cylinder engine, 6-speed transmission). The team must also determine other characteristics (e.g., price, mileage, warranty) that consumers most prefer. Each attribute should be available in different levels—for example, a 5-year or 10-year warranty.

Conjoint analysis is a tool that researchers can use to gain insights into the combination of features that will be most attractive to consumers; it is assumed that features affect both perception and preferences. Table 6-4 shows a listing of possible features—a total of 36 combinations in this case. In a full-profile approach, each of these combinations (e.g., 6-cylinder engine, 6-speed automatic transmission, 5-year warranty, $27,500) is printed on an index card, and consumers are asked to rank them in order by preference. Conjoint analysis then determines the values or *utilities* of the various levels of product features and plots them graphically. Because the number of combinations can overwhelm subjects and lead to fatigue, it is sometimes preferable to use a pair-wise approach that allows subjects to consider two attributes at a time.

Better marketing research might have helped Nokia in its struggle to maintain leadership in the highly competitive global cellular phone market. Nokia focused on the functionality and features of its phones, even as consumer tastes and preferences were shifting to trendy styling and features such as cameras and large color screens. For years, Nokia manufactured only "candy bar" phones; because executives believed that the shape was a signature of the Nokia brand, the company did not offer flip (clamshell), slide, or swivel styles. Meanwhile, Sony, LG, Samsung, and Motorola were offering sleek new designs.

In Europe, Nokia's market share fell from 51 percent in 2002 to about 33 percent in 2004. "Nokia didn't have the coolness factor," says industry consultant Jack Gold. "They didn't really do flip phones; they were a little late with cameras, and they didn't push them. Coolness in the consumer space is a big deal, and they were stodgy." Ansii Vanjoki, Nokia's head of multimedia, acknowledges, "We read the signs in the marketplace a bit wrong. The competition was emphasizing factors such as color richness and screen size. That's attractive at the point of sale. We missed that one."[42]

COMPARATIVE ANALYSIS AND MARKET ESTIMATION BY ANALOGY   One of the unique opportunities in global marketing analysis is to conduct comparisons of market potential and marketing performance in different country or regional markets at the same point in time. A common form of comparative analysis is the intra-company cross-national comparison. For example, general market conditions in two or more countries (as measured by income, stage of industrialization, or some other indicator) may be similar. If there is a significant discrepancy between per capita sales

TABLE 6-4   Crossover SUV Product Feature Combinations for Conjoint Analysis

	Engine Size	Transmission	Warranty	Price
Level 1	4-cylinder	4-speed automatic	3 years/50,000 miles	$22,500
Level 2	6-cylinder	6-speed automatic	5 years/75,000 miles	$27,500
Level 3	8-cylinder	8-speed automatic	10 years/100,000 miles	$32,500

of a given product in the countries, the marketer might reasonably research that gap and determine which actions need to be taken. Consider the following examples:

- Campbell is the world's largest soup company, commanding approximately 80 percent of the U.S. canned soup market. However, the company has a presence in only 6 percent of the world's soup markets. Russians eat 32 billion servings of soup each year, and the Chinese consume *300* billion! By contrast, Americans eat 15 billion servings each year. Sensing a huge opportunity, Campbell CEO Douglas Conant dispatched teams to observe Russian and Chinese habits.[43]
- Cadbury, the British confectionary company owned by Kraft Foods, estimates that the chocolate market in India is worth approximately $465 million per year. By contrast, annual chocolate sales are $4.89 billion in Britain, which has one-tenth the population of India. Cadbury executives believe the Indian market for confections and chocolate will grow at more than 12 percent annually.[44]
- In India, only 10 percent of men who shave use Gillette razors. Worldwide, 50 percent of male shavers use Gillette products. To achieve greater penetration in India, Gillette rolled out a no-frills brand that costs 15 rupees—about 34 cents. The Gillette Guard has a lighter handle that is cheaper to produce, it lacks the lubrication strip found in Gillette's more expensive razors, and replacement blades cost only 5 rupees (11 cents).[45]

In these examples, data are, for the most part, available for assessing the source and scale of these market discrepancies. In other situations, global marketers may find that certain types of desired data are unavailable for a particular country market, especially in developing-country markets. If this is the case, it is sometimes possible to estimate market size or potential demand by analogy. Drawing an *analogy* is simply stating a partial resemblance. For example, Germany and Italy both have flagship automakers—Volkswagen and Fiat, respectively. A less well-known flagship automaker is Russia's AvtoVAZ. So, we could say that "AvtoVAZ is to Russia what Volkswagen is to Germany and Fiat is to Italy." Statements such as this are analogies. Analogy reduces the unknown by highlighting the "commonness" of two different things."[47]

According to David Arnold, there are four possible approaches to forecasting by analogy:[48]

- Data are available on a comparable product in the same country.
- Data are available on the same product in a comparable country.
- Data are available on the same product from an independent distributor in a neighboring country.
- Data are available about a comparable company in the same country.

Time-series displacement is an analogy technique based on the assumption that an analogy between markets exists in different time periods. Displacing time is a useful form of market analysis when data are available for two markets at different levels of development. The time-displacement method requires a marketer to estimate when two markets are at similar stages of development. For example, the market for Polaroid instant cameras in Russia at the present time is comparable to the instant camera market in the United States in the mid-1960s. By obtaining data on the factors associated with demand for instant cameras in the United States in 1964 and in Russia today, as well as actual U.S. demand in 1964, one could estimate the current potential for these products in Russia.

Step 8: Interpretation and Presentation

The report based on the market research must be useful to managers as input to the decision-making process. Whether the report is presented in written form, orally, or electronically via video, it must relate clearly to the problem or opportunity identified in step 1. Generally, it is advisable

> "Truffles are to the earth as oysters are to the sea. They capture the very essence of their habitat."[46]
>
> Chef patron Jacob Kenedy, Boca di Lupa

for major findings to be summarized concisely in a memo that indicates the answer or answers to the problem first proposed in step 1. Many managers are uncomfortable with research jargon and complex quantitative analysis. To overcome their resistance, results should be clearly stated and provide a basis for managerial action. Otherwise, the report may end up on the shelf, where it will gather dust and serve as a reminder of wasted time and money.

As the data provided by the corporate information systems and market research become increasingly available on a worldwide basis, it becomes possible to analyze marketing expenditures' effectiveness across national boundaries. Managers can then decide where they are achieving the greatest marginal effectiveness for their marketing expenditures and can adjust expenditures accordingly.

▶ **6-4** Compare the way a multinational firm organizes the marketing research effort with the way a global or transnational firm approaches the organizing issue.

(6-4) Headquarters' Control of Market Research

An important issue for the global company is where to locate control of the organization's research capability. The difference between a multinational, polycentric company and a global, geocentric company on this issue is significant. In the multinational company, responsibility for research is delegated to the operating subsidiary. In contrast, the global company delegates responsibility for research to operating subsidiaries but retains overall responsibility and control of research as a headquarters' function. A key difference between single-country market research and global market research is the importance of comparability. In practice, this means that the global company must ensure that research is designed and executed so as to yield comparable data.

Simply put, *comparability* means that the results can be used to make valid comparisons between the countries covered by the research.[49] To achieve this goal, the company must inject a level of control and review of marketing research at the global level. The director of worldwide marketing research must respond to local conditions as he or she develops a research program that can be implemented on a global basis. The research director must pay particular attention to whether data gathered are based on emic analysis or etic analysis. These terms, which come from anthropology, refer to the perspective taken in the study of another culture. **Emic analysis** is similar to ethnography in that it attempts to study a culture from within, using its own system of meanings and values. **Etic analysis** is "from the outside"; in other words, it is a more detached perspective that is often used in comparative or multicountry studies. In a particular research study, an etic scale would entail using the same set of items across all countries. This approach enhances comparability, but means that some precision is inevitably lost.

By contrast, an emic study would be tailored to fit a specific country; inferences about cross-cultural similarities based on emic research have to be made subjectively. Consider, for example, Coca-Cola's experience in China when it launched fruit-flavored bottled teas. After the launch failed, the drinks giant commissioned an ethnographic study that revealed two key insights. First, Coca-Cola's U.S. headquarters is in Atlanta, Georgia. The researchers discovered that tea with added sweeteners and flavors is associated with pleasure and indulgence, especially when enjoyed with afternoon barbeques that are customary in the warm Southern states. The context helps explain the popularity of fruit flavors and added sugar. By contrast, in China, tea has different associations; its essence is subtraction, rather than addition of sugar and flavorings. Christian Madsbjerg described these findings in a recent book:

> Tea—like meditation—is a tool in Chinese culture for revealing the true self. The experience should take away irritants and distractions like noise, pollution, and stress. It wasn't until Coke incorporated this fundamentally different understanding of the "tea experience" that their bottled products gained significant market share.[50]

A good compromise is to use a survey instrument that incorporates elements of both types of analysis. It is likely that the marketing director will end up with a number of marketing programs

TABLE 6-5 Worldwide Marketing Research Plan

Research Objective	Country Cluster A	Country Cluster B	Country Cluster C
Identify market potential			X
Appraise competitive intentions		X	X
Evaluate product appeal	X	X	X
Study market response to price	X		
Appraise distribution channels	X	X	X

tailored to clusters of countries that exhibit within-group similarities. The agenda of a coordinated worldwide research program might look like the one in Table 6-5.

The director of worldwide research should not simply direct the efforts of country research managers. Instead, his or her job is to ensure that the corporation achieves maximum results worldwide from the total allocation of its research resources. Accomplishing this feat requires that personnel in each country are aware of research being carried out in the rest of the world and are involved in influencing the design of their own in-country research as well as the overall research program. Ultimately, the director of worldwide research is responsible for the overall research design and program. It is his or her job to take inputs from the entire world and produce a coordinated research strategy that generates the information needed to achieve global sales and profit objectives.

(6-5) The Marketing Information System as a Strategic Asset

◀ **6-5** Explain how information's role as a strategic asset affects the structure of global corporations.

The advent of the transnational enterprise means that boundaries between the firm and the outside world are dissolving. Marketing has historically been responsible for managing many of the relationships across those boundaries. The boundaries between marketing and other functions are also dissolving, and the traditional notion of marketing as a distinct functional area within the firm may be giving way to a new model. Likewise, the process of marketing decision making is changing, largely because of the changing role of information from a support tool to a wealth-generating, strategic asset.

Many global firms are creating flattened organizations with less hierarchical and less centralized decision-making structures. Such organizations facilitate the exchange and flow of information among departments that previously may have operated as autonomous "silos." The more information intensive the firm, the greater the degree to which marketing is involved in activities traditionally associated with other functional areas. In such firms, parallel processing of information takes place.

Information intensity in the firm has an impact on perceptions of market attractiveness, competitive position, and organizational structure. The greater a company's information intensity, the more the traditional product and market boundaries are likely to shift. In essence, companies increasingly face new sources of competition from other firms in historically noncompetitive industries, particularly if those other firms are also information intensive. Diverse firms now find themselves in direct competition with each other. They offer essentially the same products as a natural extension and redefinition of their traditional product lines and marketing activities. Today, when marketers speak of "value added," the chances are they are not referring to unique product features. Rather, the emphasis is on the information exchanged as part of customer transactions, much of which cuts across traditional product lines.

Summary

Information is one of the most basic ingredients of a successful marketing strategy. A company's *management information system (MIS)* and *intranet* provide decision makers with a continuous flow of information. *Information technology* is profoundly affecting global marketing activities by allowing managers to access and manipulate data to assist in decision making. *Electronic data interchange (EDI)*, *electronic point of sale (EPOS)* data, *efficient consumer response (ECR)*, *customer relationship management (CRM)*, and *data warehouses* are some of the new tools and techniques available. The global marketer must scan the world for information about opportunities and threats and make information available via a management information system.

Formal *market research*—the project-specific, systematic gathering of data—is often required before marketers make key decisions. *Global market research* links customers and marketers through information gathered on a global scale. The research process begins when marketers define the problem and set research objectives; this step may entail assessing whether a particular market should be classified as *latent* or *incipient*. A research plan specifies the relative amounts of qualitative and quantitative information desired. Information is collected using either primary or *secondary data* sources. In today's wired world, the Internet has taken its place alongside more traditional channels as an important secondary information source. In some instances, the cost of collecting primary data may outweigh the potential benefits. Secondary sources are especially useful for researching a market that is too small to justify a large commitment of time and money.

If collection of primary data can be justified on a cost–benefit basis, research can be conducted via *survey research*, *personal interviews*, *consumer panels*, *observation*, and *focus groups*. Before collecting data, researchers must determine whether a probability sample is required. In global marketing, careful attention must be paid to issues such as eliminating cultural bias in research, accurately translating surveys, and ensuring data comparability in different markets. A number of techniques are available for analyzing survey data, including *factor analysis*, *cluster analysis*, *multidimensional scaling (MDS)*, and *conjoint analysis*. Research findings and recommendations must be presented clearly. A final issue is how much control headquarters will have over research and the overall management of the organization's information system. To ensure comparability of data, the researcher should utilize both *emic* and *etic* approaches.

Discussion Questions

6-1. Describe the global marketer's considerations and adjustments of research methodologies when conducting research.

6-2. For a number of years, sales were falling in Argentina for Aguas Danone. They desperately needed to understand their customers, identify market opportunities and find a new product. Suggest how market segmentation helped the business succeed.

6-3. Outline the basic steps of the market research process.

6-4. What are some of the issues faced by the global market researcher while using a survey?

6-5. Coach has been described as "a textbook lesson on how to revitalize a brand." The same could be said for Burberry, the British fashion goods company discussed in Chapter 1. Locate some articles about Burberry and read about the research its management has conducted and the formula it used to polish the brand. Are the approaches evident at Burberry and Coach similar? Are they competitors?

6-6. Below is a table similar to Table 6-3 that contains eight sports sedan nameplates. You can perform a rudimentary analysis along the lines of multidimensional scaling by ranking them by similarity. Do some research on the different models and see which pair you find to be the most similar. Which pair is the most different? Using these eight brands, create a rough perceptual map. What dimensions would you use to label the axes?

MDS STUDY INPUTS: SIMILARITY JUDGMENT SCALES FOR PAIRS OF SPORT SEDANS

	Very Similar				Very Different
	1	2	3	4	5
BMW328i/Volvo S60	—	—	—	—	—
BMW328i/Acura TL	—	—	—	—	—
BMW328i/Cadillac ATS	—	—	—	—	—
BMW328i /Audi A4	—	—	—	—	—
BMW328i/Mercedes-Benz C250	—	—	—	—	—
BMW328i/Lexus IS	—	—	—	—	—
BMW328i/Infiniti G37	—	—	—	—	—
Volvo S60/Acura TL	—	—	—	—	—
Volvo S60/Cadillac ATS	—	—	—	—	—
Volvo S60/Audi A4	—	—	—	—	—
Volvo S60/Mercedes-Benz C250	—	—	—	—	—
Volvo S60/Lexus IS	—	—	—	—	—
Volvo S60/Infiniti G37	—	—	—	—	—

CASE 6-1   *(Continued from page 197)*

Nestlé Middle East's Investment in Market Research

In 2015, Nestlé Middle East's total revenue, from a range of 60 products, was $2.4 billion. Nestlé gains the consumer's trust not only by considering serious concerns over the quality of food and the variety it serves to its consumers, but also by investing in research labs to ensure that they exceed food safety and quality requirements. The Middle East is an important market globally and has been identified as a potential growth market with a lot of opportunities.

In March 2019, Nestlé Middle East announced that the number of women in management or senior leader roles had risen from 16 percent to 30 percent over the last eight years. This was a crucial step for the company's goal of improving gender balance across all its offices around the world. Another recent investment is the advanced Sensory Lab Unit for Renovation–Innovation of Products (SLURP), located in Dubai. This lab is fitted with high-end technological facilities to serve as a center of expertise for advanced sensory profiling analyses on shelf-stable dairy, coffee, and confectionery products.

Nestlé believes that investing in factories is extremely important as they support and facilitate research in various ways. As a market, the Middle East does not have homogenous consumers. Different countries have different tastes and preferences; the Middle East comprises 22 different countries with varying economies, cultures, and belief systems. Manufacturing products locally allows Nestlé to adapt to the cultural needs and preferences of the local markets and accelerate the delivery of fresher products to the consumer. Any new information gathered from the market can be implemented effectively in a timely manner. According to Nestlé, manufacturing products locally along with timely implementation of information gives them a prime advantage over their competition. Nestlé has thus followed this practice for many of their manufacturing plants in the Middle East.

In March 2018, the company announced its intention to make 100 percent of its packaging reusable or recyclable by 2025. This initiative was introduced across the business with the goal of ensuring that none of the packaging or plastics is sent to a landfill. In February 2019, Nestlé Middle East announced that it was offering $50,000 to the individual who comes up with a simple and economic way of checking daily levels of vitamin D deficiencies, a problem common across the Middle East and one that Nestle aims to address with a permanent solution. This will include developing a product portfolio that provides the ideal daily amount of vitamin D, phosphate, calcium, and other nutrition that is critical for the body. The company also plans to launch a long-term scientific health study of vitamin D deficiency in the Middle East and North Africa.

With health awareness on the rise, Nestlé is focusing not just on expansion but also on making its products healthier. It is planning to reduce salt, saturated fats, and sugar in new as well as existing products.

The United Arab Emirates is not the only country where Nestlé is interested in investing. In January 2019, Nestlé opened its new Bonjorno coffee factory in Egypt with an investment of $14 million. The new factory has a direct workforce of about 240, along with 7,000 indirect jobs. The state-of-the-art factory was designed to meet their aim of supplying to the entire Egyptian market. This was made possible after Nestlé acquired Caravan Marketing Company SAE in January

2017. Nestlé has been investing in Egypt for over 100 years and now operates three factories with 3,500 direct employees.

Nestlé continues to expand in emerging markets and is currently using the popularly positioned products (PPP) model to drive growth in the region. In order to target emerging consumers who are entering the cash economy and buying branded goods for the first time, Nestlé's PPPs are adapted to meet the consumers' needs in terms of price, accessibility, and formats (such as single-serve packets). In Egypt, research conducted on behalf of the food service industry is used for Nestlé's professional strengthening. Moreover, since consumption on-the-go and out-of-home is steadily on the rise, there is scope for developing Nestlé's coffee-machine vending business.

Satisfaction of the needs of consumers, from "emerging consumers" to "those looking for premium products," is a priority, and Nestlé continuously strives to fill this gap. The Egyptian Revolution, also known as the Revolution of January 25, did not stop Nestlé's investment; a week after the uprising it publicized a $160-million program for improvements across its manufacturing and distribution along with investment in skills over the next three to five years. Nestlé Egypt aims to attract and adapt to the cultural change in an innovative way. For instance, it launched a new nutrition initiative called "Healthy Kids," an educational scheme that aims to increase nutritional awareness and promote a healthy lifestyle. By the end of 2016, the program had reached over 650,000 children and trained around 2,000 teachers across 1,025 schools in 12 governorates.

Finally, Nestlé is very keen on different marketing-research-based projects like understanding the nutritional needs of its consumers in order to accelerate the development of products with an improved nutrition profile at the right price in emerging markets. For example, in 2012, in Nestlé entered into a research partnership with scientists

Exhibit 6-6 Nestlé manufactures its products locally to adapt to the cultural needs and preferences of local markets and deliver fresh products faster.

Source: gudkovandrey/123rf.com.

Exhibit 6-7 Nestlé Egypt's "Healthy Kids" scheme aims to increase nutritional awareness and promote a healthy lifestyle.
Source: Design Pics Inc./Alamy Stock Photo

coordinated by the Council for Scientific and Industrial Research, a part of the South African government's Department for Science and Technology. The partnership allows scientists to explore and make extensive use of Nestlé's research capabilities and expertise in nutrition, food science, and food safety. Moreover, part of Nestlé's global research and development efforts focuses on discovering new bioactive ingredients. Biodiversity is very important, and some of the research will work on studying how to make use of locally sourced ingredients to create foods that provide health benefits. Researchers have examined these ingredients' effectiveness in targeting different tissues and in promoting health overall.

Discussion Questions

6-7. Critically examine Nestlé's positioning model.

6-8. Discuss the importance of investment in research with regard to the Nestlé case.

6-9. Explain the different ways in which market research can be used to satisfy consumers.

Sources: "A Word from the Chairman and CEO," Nestlé Middle East, www.nestle-me.com/en/aboutus; "Fact Sheet," Nestlé Middle East (2010), www.nestle.com/assetlibrary/Documents/Library/Events/2010-Inauguration-of-a-new-factory-in-Dubai/Fact_Sheet_2010_Nestle_Middle_East_EN_FINAL.pdf; "FMCG Companies Tap Middle East Growth," Warc (May 8, 2013), www.warc.com/Content/News/FMCG_companies_tap_Middle_East_growth.content?ID=efe6d4d4-bd8c-44b7-9e1b-9700051a3718&q; "Nestlé Opens New USD 136 Million Factory in Dubai," Nestlé (2010), www.nestle.com/media/newsandfeatures/nestle-opens-new-factory-dubai; "Nestlé Invests CHF 160m and Creates 500 New Jobs in Egypt," Nestlé (2010), www.nestle.com/media/newsandfeatures/nestle-invests-chf-160m-and-creates-500-new-jobs-in-egypt; "Nestlé Egypt: The New Egypt," *Business Excellence* (November 25, 2011), www.bus-ex.com/article/nestl%C3%A9-egypt; "Nestlé Partners with South African Scientists," *New Food Magazine* (March 6, 2012), www.newfoodmagazine.com/7099/news/nestle-partners-with-south-african-scientists/; "Egypt Factory Investment as Appetite for Ice Cream Soars," Nestlé (2013), www.nestle.com/Media/NewsAndFeatures/Ice-Cream-Egypt.

CASE 6-2
A Day in the Life of a Business Systems and Analytics Manager

Brady Spangenberg leads a team that oversees the critical business information technology (IT) systems, transaction and customer data, business intelligence reporting, and strategic analytics for the U.S. sales organization of BASF Agricultural Solutions. Headquartered in Ludwigshafen, Germany, BASF is one of the world's largest integrated chemical manufacturers and suppliers. With approximately 114,000 employees in more than 80 countries, BASF supplies chemistry-based products and solutions to business partners in nearly every part of the world. BASF's global advertising tagline, "We create chemistry," highlights the corporate mission to combine economic success with environmental protection and social responsibility.

Based in BASF Agricultural Solutions Headquarters in Research Triangle Park, North Carolina, Spangenberg and his team focus primarily on supporting the company's U.S. agriculture product portfolio. The Agricultural Solutions division has something to offer nearly every grower and farming operation in America. Examples of key brands and uses include Armezon Pro herbicide for early season weed control in corn (see Exhibit 6-8), Priaxor fungicide for foliar ("leaf-related") disease control in soybeans and cotton, and even Nealta miticide for mite control in almond orchards. That is what makes Spangenberg's job both fun and challenging at the same time. One day, he and his team are formatting county-level data about California almond acreage. (Fun fact:

Approximately 80 percent of the world's almond supply is produced in California's Central Valley.) The next day they are updating counts of independent and co-op chemical retailers across the Midwest.

The customer base is as complex as U.S. agriculture itself, comprising vastly different crops, cropping systems, distribution channels (some consisting of two steps, others including three steps), and grower entities (corporate versus individual owned and operated). Another fun fact: The United States had 318.2 million acres of farmland in production in 2017, and experts predict that by 2019 soybeans will have surpassed corn as the number 1 crop by acreage.

The Business Systems and Analytics team relies on structured customer hierarchies and market segmentation strategies to help the BASF Agricultural Solutions organization make sense of historical trends, current sales activities, and potential future opportunities. The work is structured into three main pillars and follows a path that starts with data cleaning and ends with delivering insights and predictions:

In a role like Spangenberg's, it's not a cliché to say that every workday is different, presenting new challenges and opportunities. The most difficult aspect is figuring out how to balance managing the day-to-day operational tasks—such as verifying third-party-reported point-of-sale transactions—with longer-term strategic work such as 10-year market forecasting. While both activity types have significant data and analytics components, they also require a substantial amount of human intervention and finesse.

"Data problems are actually people problems first," Spangenberg says. "Solving an IT infrastructure issue or analytics request means that we have to understand the people using that information first. What are their priorities and their concerns? What are they trying to accomplish? Once we know those things, we can more quickly and easily provide a solution."

That's where Spangenberg relies on his academic training in the humanities. He earned a BA degree in English and religion from a small liberal arts college in the Midwest and then went on to complete MA and PhD degrees in comparative literature at Purdue University in West Lafayette, Indiana. With that type of training, Spangenberg's most logical career path would have been to become a college professor. Although he pursued that angle for a time, he also remembers, "I always had this voice in my head saying, 'What if this literature professor thing doesn't work out? What skills do I have to support me and my family?'"

That nagging concern drove him to continuously work on his "professional hedges"—namely, those skills and job opportunities that could differentiate him in a crowded marketplace. As part of that quest, he sought to improve all the "basics" that he learned during his high school and undergraduate studies.

As a college student, Spangenberg audited German 101 and German 102 and spent the summers after his junior and senior years studying at language institutes in Germany. After finishing his

Exhibit 6-8 BASF's Armezon Pro herbicide for early season weed control in corn is one of the products Spangenberg's customers rely on.

Source: BASF Corporation.

Improved business tools for improved understanding, greater efficiency and better insights

Customer Knowledge Center	Reporting	Analytics
Improve business predictability through better, cleaner data	Improve business steering through more standardized, repeatable reporting	Improve business agility through insightful analytics and guidance

undergraduate studies, he earned two graduate degrees in comparative literature at Purdue University and also spent an exchange year at the Albert Ludwig University of Freiburg.

Throughout his post-graduate education, Spangenberg continued to refine his German language skills, tutored at the Purdue Writing Center (home of the well-known Purdue Online Writing Lab), learned business communication, studied abroad, tried his hand (unsuccessfully) at stock market investing, contributed to digital projects and blogs, threw himself into grammar and rhetoric, and even applied for a Fulbright Scholarship ("Rejected!"). Those elements, diverse as they were, made him ready for the day when a friend recommended that he apply for a global communications position with BASF Agricultural Solutions in Germany.

Including his studies, Spangenberg has spent nearly five years living and working abroad in Germany. Those experiences became some of the most exciting and adventurous of his and his family's lives, yet they were also, at times, some of the most frustrating and secluded. For anyone considering the possibility of working abroad, Spangenberg offers some practical advice based on his five-plus years' experience:

- *Financial basics:*   Make sure you (or your company) have plans in place for your banking, taxes (your home country and host country of residence), currency exchange, credit, and insurance (health, life, liability).

- *Language skills for all the "little" situations:*   Most of your coworkers and other professionals (e.g., doctors, bankers, managers) will speak and understand English, but don't assume the same for the Internet/telecommunications installer, office IT support, gym manager, doctor's receptionist, apartment custodian, or hairstylist. Knowing enough of the target language to get by in these little situations goes a long way toward your overall enjoyment and satisfaction abroad. It also helps you build rapport with host country nationals, because they see you have made the effort to "meet them halfway" by working on your language skills.

- *Company culture and networking:*   Go out of your way to meet people in the company and around town. Ask what they do, how to be successful, how to avoid pitfalls and faux pas, and which activities they enjoy in their free time. Remember that you are the "outsider" in these situations, so the longer you wait for others to come talk to you, the more isolated you'll start to feel.

At the end of the day, Spangenberg found that working abroad presents many of the same opportunities and challenges as working at home. The best advice he ever received became something of a family motto: "When you're at home, you dream of adventure; when you're on an adventure, you dream of home."

No matter where in the world the job position is located, Spangenberg has found some commonalities in regard to the nature of work and employee expectations, which he now includes as agenda items for monthly team meetings. Take creativity, for example. As automation becomes increasingly prevalent in agriculture and other industry sectors, it is incumbent on every employee to produce more creative solutions and strategies to stay ahead of the curve. This principle has an inverse as well: Which operational, mundane tasks can be automated or delegated? As Spangenberg says, "We need to be creative enough to look for solutions but also self-assured enough to start moving things off our plate."

Communication is also critically important. Spangenberg continues, "If you can't communicate your analysis, problem, or subject matter, then you won't capture—or hold—anyone's attention. Communication goes beyond writing or speaking skills. It's really the ability to decide—often on the fly—how to structure and present an argument, concept, or need."

So, what does Spangenberg look for when hiring new team members? A positive attitude is key, as is the ability to deal with failure. Spangenberg offers the following advice to new hires: Be willing to learn and be willing to fail. New things and questions will always come along, and managing them requires that employees adapt quickly. Those who have the passion and interest to learn will generally thrive, as will those with a positive attitude, because that perspective helps them to move on from failure or quickly react to critical feedback

Given the rapid pace of change in agriculture, critical thinking skills are important as well. As Spangenberg notes, "Sometimes you're presented with a problem in the real world that doesn't have an easy solution. In other words, it's not a textbook problem! So, you have to be quick on your feet and not constantly bugging your manager to ask about the next step you should take. They hired you for a reason."

Finally, what advice would Spangenberg offer to recent college graduates or those looking to move up the corporate ladder? "Anticipation, intentionality, and having the end in mind," he says. "If people are intentional and can anticipate their next steps, then they will save the company a lot of headaches in the future. It also keeps team members happier to be able to think that their work is having an impact on the bigger picture."

"This also applies to personal goals," Spangenberg says. "If someone has a goal, or has the end in mind, it will keep him or her on the path that is moving forward. This is also called 'foresight.'" In other words, spend time imagining what the future will be like, which problems might arise, and how you might start solving them now. Spangenberg concludes, "By the time your manager identifies a problem for you to 'work on,' it's likely too late."

Discussion Questions

6-10. What knowledge and skills are required to be successful as a business systems and analytics manager?

6-11. What do you think is the best part of Spangenberg's job? The most challenging part?

6-12. What does Spangenberg's career profile tell you about the importance of professionalism and a good work ethic at a company such as BASF?

6-13. BASF engages in a wide range of environmental protection and sustainability initiatives, including membership in the voluntary Responsible Care initiative for chemical companies. **Dig deeper:** Conduct some exploratory research on these initiatives at BASF, and write a short essay or make an oral in-class presentation on your findings.

6-14. In light of the recent global economic downturn, should Lew Frankfort's strategy for expanding in China be revised?

6-15. MyLab Marketing Only—comprehensive writing assignment for this chapter.

Notes

[1] John Thornhill, "Single-Minded Leader behind a Supercharged Empire," *Financial Times* (September 4, 2017), p. 24.

[2] Efraim Turban, Ramesh Sharda, Jay E. Aronson, and David King, *Business Intelligence: A Managerial Approach* (Upper Saddle River, NJ: Pearson Education, 2008), p. 9.

[3] Jean-Pierre Corniou, "Bringing Business Technology out into the Open," *Financial Times—Information Technology Review* (September 17, 2003), p. 2.

[4] Bronwyn Fryer, "High-Tech the Old-Fashioned Way: An Interview with Tom Siebel of Siebel Systems," *Harvard Business Review* (March 2001), pp. 118–125. In 2006, Siebel Systems merged with Oracle.

[5] Ann Zimmerman, "To Sell Goods to Walmart, Get on the Net," *The Wall Street Journal* (November 21, 2003), pp. B1, B6.

[6] Bethan Hutton, "Japan's 7-Eleven Sets Store by Computer Links," *Financial Times* (March 17, 1998), p. 26.

[7] Gina Fraone, "Facing up to Global CRM," *eWeek* (July 30, 2001), pp. 37–41.

[8] Tim Bell, "GDPR: What Does It Mean for U.S. Business in the EU?" Solo Session, SXSW Interactive (March 12, 2018).

[9] Peter Wonacott, "Walmart Finds Market Footing in China," *The Wall Street Journal* (July 17, 2000), p. A31.

[10] Gary Silverman, "How May I Help You?" *Financial Times* (February 4–5, 2006), p. W2.

[11] Mark C. Green, "Entrepreneurship, Italian Style." Paper presented at Schumptoberfest Conference on Innovation and Entrepreneurship in the Liberal Arts, Grinnell College (October 2012).

[12] Kenneth Hein, "We Know What Guys Want," *Brandweek* (November 14, 2002), p. M48.

[13] Peter D. Bennett, ed., *Dictionary of Marketing Terms*, 2nd ed. (Chicago, IL: American Marketing Association, 1995), p. 169.

[14] Louise Lucas, "Up Close and Personal Brands," *Financial Times* (October 14, 2010), p. 13.

[15] Michael R. Czinkota and Ilkka A. Ronkainen, "Market Research for Your Export Operations: Part I—Using Secondary Sources of Research," *International Trade Forum* 30, no. 3 (1994), pp. 22–33.

[16] Michael Brereton and Diane Bowers, "The 2016 AMA Gold Global Top 25 Report," *Marketing News*. www.ama.org, accessed March 1, 2018.

[17] Merissa Marr and Geoffrey A. Fowler, "Chinese Lessons for Disney," *The Wall Street Journal* (June 12, 2006), p. B1.

[18] Michael R. Czinkota and Ilkka A. Ronkainen, "Market Research for Your Export Operations: Part I—Using Secondary Sources of Research," *International Trade Forum* 30, no. 3 (1994), p. 22.

[19] Michael R. Czinkota and Ilkka A. Ronkainen, "Market Research for Your Export Operations: Part II—Conducting Primary Marketing Research," *International Trade Forum* 31, no. 1 (1995), p. 16.

[20] David Arnold, *The Mirage of Global Markets* (Upper Saddle River, NJ: Financial Times Prentice Hall, 2004), pp. 41–43.

[21] John Pawle, "Mining the International Consumer," *Journal of the Market Research Society* 41, no. 1 (1999), p. 20.

[22] Gabriel Kahn, "Chinese Puzzle: Spotty Consumer Data," *The Wall Street Journal* (October 15, 2003), p. B1.

[23] Kathleen Kerwin, "Can This Minivan Dent Detroit?" *BusinessWeek* (February 3, 1997), p. 37.

[24] Peter F. Drucker, "Marketing 101 for a Fast-Changing Decade," *The Wall Street Journal* (November 20, 1990), p. A17.

[25] Adam Jones, "How to Make up Demand," *Financial Times* (October 3, 2006), p. 8.

[26] Kerry A. Dolan, "The Soda with Buzz," *Forbes* (March 28, 2005), p. 126.

[27] Jason Leow and Gordon Fairclough, "Rich Chinese Fancy Luxury Cars," *The Wall Street Journal* (April 12, 2007), pp. B1, B2.

[28] James Harding, "Foreign Investors Face New Curbs on Ownership of Stores," *Financial Times* (November 10, 1998), p. 7.

[29] Tom Hancock, "Marks and Spencer Retreats from Mainland China," *Financial Times* (April 1, 2017), p. 11.

[30] Charles Duhigg, "Yoplait Battles the Greeks," *The New York Times* (June 26, 2017), p. B3.

[31] Deborah Steinborn, "Talking about Design," *The Wall Street Journal—The Journal Report: Product Design* (June 23, 2008), p. R6.

[32] Gina Chon, "VW's American Road Trip," *The Wall Street Journal* (January 4, 2006), pp. B1, B9.

[33] Emily Nelson, "P&G Checks out Real Life," *The Wall Street Journal* (May 17, 2001), pp. B1, B4.

[34] Deborah Ball, "The Perils of Packaging: Nestlé Aims for Easier Openings," *The Wall Street Journal* (November 17, 2005), p. B1.

[35] Katheryn Kranhold, "Whirlpool Conjures up Appliance Divas," *The Wall Street Journal* (April 27, 2000), p. B1.

[36] Cris Prystay, "Selling to Singapore's Teens Is Tricky," *The Wall Street Journal* (October 4, 2002), p. B4.

[37] Scott Porch, "Sex and the Single Girl, for Millennials," *The New York Times* (July 2, 2017), p. 13.

[38] Jack Edmonston, "U.S., Overseas Differences Abound," *Business Marketing* (January 1998), p. 32.

[39] Eugene H. Fram and Riad Ajami, "Globalization of Markets and Shopping Stress: Cross-Country Comparisons," *Business Horizons* 37, no. 1 (January–February 1994), pp. 17–23.

[40] Parts of this section are adapted from Glen L. Urban, John R. Hauser, and Nikhilesh Dholakia, *Essentials of New Product Management* (Upper Saddle River, NJ: Prentice Hall, 1987), Chapters 6 and 7.

[41] Parts of this section were adapted from Vanessa Friedman, Rachel Sanderson, and Scheherazade Daneshkhu, "Luxury's New Look," *Financial Times* (December 24, 2012), p. 5.

[42] Nelson D. Schwartz and Joan M. Levinstein, "Has Nokia Lost It?" *Fortune* (January 24, 2005), pp. 98–106.

[43] Bruce Horovitz, "CEO Nears 10-Year Goal to Clean up a Soupy Mess," *USA Today* (January 26, 2009), pp. 1B, 2B.

[44] Sonya Misquitta, "Cadbury Redefines Cheap Luxury," *The Wall Street Journal* (June 8, 2009), p. B4.

[45] Ellen Byron, "Gillette's Latest Innovation in Razors: The 11-Cent Blade," *The Wall Street Journal* (October 1, 2010), p. B1.

[46]Ben McCormack, "Truffle Hunting: The Best London Restaurants to Enjoy White Truffles," *The Telegraph* (October 31, 2016), p. 4.

[47]Ikujiro Nonaka and Hirotaka Takeuchi, *The Knowledge-Creating Company* (Cambridge, MA: Harvard Business School Press, 1995), p. 67. As Nonaka and Takeuchi explain, "Metaphor and analogy are often confused. Association of two things through metaphor is driven mostly by intuition and holistic imagery and does not aim to find differences between them. On the other hand, association through analogy is carried out by rational thinking and focuses on structural/functional similarities between two things. . . . Thus analogy helps us understand the unknown through the known."

[48]David Arnold, *The Mirage of Global Markets* (Upper Saddle River, NJ: Financial Times Prentice Hall, 2004), pp. 41–43.

[49]V. Kumar, *International Marketing Research* (Upper Saddle River, NJ: Prentice Hall, 1999), p. 15.

[50]Christian Madsbjerg, *Sensemaking: The Power of the Humanities in the Age of the Algorithm* (New York, NY: Hachette Books, 2017), p. 118.

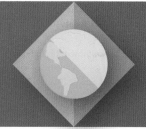

7

Segmentation, Targeting, and Positioning

LEARNING OBJECTIVES

7-1 Identify the variables that global marketers can use to segment global markets, and give an example of each.

7-2 Explain the criteria that global marketers use to choose specific markets to target.

7-3 Understand how global marketers use a product–market grid to make targeting decisions.

7-4 Compare and contrast the three main target market strategy options.

7-5 Describe the various positioning options available to global marketers.

CASE 7-1
Segmenting the Chinese Luxury Goods Market

Global marketers are flocking to China, attracted by the country's population of more than 1.3 billion people. In addition to a rapidly growing middle class, China is home to increasing numbers of millionaires and billionaires. Thanks to the rising aspirations and purchasing power of these groups, Chinese consumers as a whole buy more luxury goods than consumers of any other nationality. Dozens of Chinese cities have populations of more than 1 million people. In so-called first-tier coastal cities such as Shanghai, Shenzhen, and Beijing, as well as in second-tier cities in the country's interior, Chinese consumers can flaunt their wealth by purchasing French wine, Italian designer clothes, and German luxury cars (see Exhibit 7-1).

Global marketers are fueling corporate growth by targeting China's economic elite; when they do, they discover that a "one-size-fits-all" strategy will not work. Several distinct segments can be discerned among China's richest "1 percent." These include the super-elite, the newly rich, and high-level government officials. To learn more about these segments, and the opportunities and challenges of reaching them, turn to the continuation of Case 7-1 at the end of the chapter.

The efforts by global companies to connect with wealthy Chinese consumers highlight the importance of skillful global market segmentation and targeting. **Global market segmentation** is the process of identifying and categorizing groups of customers and countries according to common characteristics. **Targeting** involves evaluating the segments and focusing marketing efforts on a country, region, or group of people that has significant potential to respond. Such targeting reflects the reality that a company should identify those consumers it can reach most effectively, efficiently, and profitably. Finally, proper **positioning** is required to differentiate the product or brand in the minds of target customers.

Exhibit 7-1 Ford has repositioned its Lincoln division as The Lincoln Motor Company. Lincoln recently began selling the MKZ sedan, the MKC crossover, and other luxury models in China. To differentiate the Lincoln brand in this market, the company is creating a retail network that has a boutique feeling. Company executives believe that a focus on personalized attention and service and other amenities will allow Lincoln to attract wealthy Chinese car buyers.
Source: Ng Han Guan/Associated Press.

Global markets can be segmented according to buyer category (e.g., consumer, enterprise, government, education), age, gender, income, and a number of other criteria. Segmentation and targeting are two separate but closely related go-to-market activities. Together, they serve as the link between market needs and wants and the tactical decisions by managers to develop marketing programs and value propositions that meet the specific needs of one or more segments. Segmentation, targeting, and positioning are all examined in this chapter.

(7-1) Global Market Segmentation

◀ **7-1** Identify the variables that global marketers can use to segment global markets, and give an example of each.

Global market segmentation has been defined as the process of identifying specific segments—whether they be country groups or individual consumer groups—of potential customers with homogeneous attributes who are likely to exhibit similar responses to a company's marketing mix.[1] Marketing practitioners and academics have been interested in global market segmentation for several decades. In the late 1960s, one observer suggested that the European market could be divided into three broad categories—international sophisticate, semi-sophisticate, and provincial—solely on the basis of consumers' presumed receptivity to a common advertising approach.[2] Another writer suggested that some themes—for example, the desire to be beautiful, the desire to be healthy and free of pain, and the love between mother and child—are universal and could be used in advertising around the globe.[3]

Consider the following examples of market segmentation:

- The market for computers and related products can be divided into home users, corporate ("enterprise") users, and educational users. In 2014, Hewlett-Packard split into two companies. Hewlett Packard Enterprises markets servers and data storage services to the business-to-business market; HP Inc. (with the familiar blue circle logo) focuses on the consumer market for PCs and printers.
- After convening worldwide employee conferences to study women's shaving preferences, Schick-Wilkinson Sword introduced a shaving system for women that

features a replaceable blade cartridge. Intuition, as the system is known, incorporates a "skin-conditioning solid" that allows a woman to lather and shave her legs simultaneously. Intuition is a premium product targeted directly at users of Venus, Gillette's three-blade razor system for women.[4]

- Dove, a division of Unilever, traditionally targeted women with its Dove-branded skin-care products. In 2010, the company launched a new brand, Men+Care. The move prompted marketers at rival-brand Old Spice to launch humorous TV ads poking fun at guys who use "lady-scented body wash"—a clear jab at Dove.

- GM's original market-entry strategy for China called for targeting government and company officials who were entitled to a large sedan-style automobile. Today, GM's lineup for China includes the Buick Excelle GT, targeted at the country's middle class, and the Buick Verano.

Four decades ago, Professor Theodore Levitt advanced the thesis that consumers in different countries increasingly seek variety and that the same new segments are likely to show up in multiple national markets. Thus, ethnic or regional foods such as sushi, falafel, or pizza might be in demand anywhere in the world. Levitt suggested that this trend, known variously as the *pluralization of consumption* and *segment simultaneity*, provides an opportunity for marketers to pursue one or more segments on a global scale. Frank Brown, former president of MTV Networks Asia, acknowledged this trend in explaining MTV's success in Asia despite a business downturn in the region: "When marketing budgets are tight, advertisers look for a more effective buy, and we can deliver a niche audience with truly panregional reach," he said.[5] Authors John Micklethwait and Adrian Wooldridge sum up the situation this way:

> The audience for a new recording of a Michael Tippett symphony or for a nature documentary about the mating habits of flamingos may be minuscule in any one country, but round up all the Tippett and flamingo fanatics around the world, and you have attractive commercial propositions. The cheap distribution offered by the Internet will probably make these niches even more attractive financially.[6]

Global market segmentation is based on the premise that companies should attempt to identify consumers in different countries who share similar needs and desires. Of course, the fact that significant numbers of pizza-loving consumers are found in many countries does not mean that they are eating the exact same thing. In France, for example, Domino's serves pizza with goat cheese and strips of pork fat known as *lardoons*. In Taiwan, toppings include squid, crab, shrimp, and pineapple; Brazilians can order their pies with mashed bananas and cinnamon. As Patrick Doyle, executive vice president of Domino's international division, explains, "Pizza is beautifully adaptable to consumer needs around the world, simply by changing the toppings."[7]

A. Coskun Samli developed a useful approach to global market segmentation that compares and contrasts "conventional" versus "unconventional" wisdom.[8] For example, conventional wisdom might assume that consumers in Europe and Latin America are interested in World Cup soccer, whereas those in America are not. Unconventional wisdom would note that the "global jock" segment exists in many countries, including the United States.[9] Similarly, conventional wisdom might assume that, because per capita income in India is about $1,670, all Indians have low incomes. Unconventional wisdom would note the presence of a higher-income, middle-class segment. As Sapna Nayak, a food analyst at Raobank India, noted, "The potential Indian customer base for a McDonald's or a Subway is larger than the size of entire developed countries."[10] A similar situation is found in China, where there is considerable income disparity between western and eastern provinces. For example, per capita income in Shanghai Municipality is 47,710 yuan, whereas residents of Gansu are much poorer.[11]

Contrasting Views of Global Segmentation

As we have noted many times in this book, global marketers must determine whether a standardized or an adapted marketing mix will best serve consumers' wants and needs. By performing market segmentation, marketers can generate the strategic insights needed to devise the most effective approaches. The process of global market segmentation begins with the choice of one or more variables to use as a basis for grouping customers. Common variables include demographics, psychographics, behavioral characteristics, and benefits sought. It is also possible to cluster different national markets in terms of their environments—for example, the presence or absence of government regulation in a particular industry—to establish groupings.

Demographic Segmentation

Demographic segmentation is based on measurable characteristics of populations, such as income, population, age distribution, gender, education, and occupation. A number of global demographic trends—fewer married couples, smaller family size, changing roles of women, and higher incomes and living standards, for example—have contributed to the emergence of global market segments. The following are several key demographic facts and trends from around the world:

- Southeast Asia's population numbers 600 million, 70 percent of whom are younger than the age of 40.
- India has the youngest demographic profile among the world's large nations. Two-thirds of its population is younger than age 35. This youthful segment is expected to deliver a "demographic dividend" by serving as a key driver of economic growth.
- In the European Union (EU), the number of consumers age 16 and younger is rapidly approaching the number of consumers age 60 and older.
- Half of Japan's population will be age 50 years or older by 2025.
- By 2030, 20 percent of the U.S. population—70 million Americans—will be age 65 years or older versus 13 percent (36 million) today.
- America's three main ethnic groups—African/Black Americans, Hispanic Americans, and Asian Americans—represent a combined annual buying power of $3.5 trillion.
- The United States is home to 28.4 million foreign-born residents with a combined income of $233 billion.

Statistics such as these can provide valuable insights to marketers who are scanning the globe for opportunities. As noted in Chapter 4, for example, Disney hopes to capitalize on the huge number of young people—and their parents' rising incomes—in India as a means to extend its brand. Managers at global companies must be alert to the possibility that marketing strategies will have to be adjusted in response to the aging of the population and other demographic trends. For example, consumer products companies will need to convene focus groups consisting of people age 50 years or older who are nearing retirement. These same companies will also have to target Brazil, Mexico, Vietnam, and other developing-country markets to achieve their growth objectives in the years to come.

Demographic changes can create opportunities for marketing innovation. In France, for example, two entrepreneurs began rewriting the rules of retailing years before Sam Walton founded the Walmart chain. Marcel Fournier and Louis Defforey opened the first Carrefour ("crossroads") hypermarket in 1963. At the time, France had a fragmented shop system that consisted of small, specialized stores with only about 5,000 square feet of floor space, such as the *boulangerie* and the *charcuterie*. The shop system was part of France's national heritage, and shoppers developed personal relationships with a shop's proprietor. However, time-pressed, dual-parent-working families had less time to stop at several stores for daily shopping. The same trend the Carrefour entrepreneurs noted in France was also occurring in other countries. By 1993, Carrefour SA was a global chain with $21 billion in sales and a market capitalization of $10 billion. Sales totaled $83 billion in 2016, and today Carrefour operates more than 12,200 stores in 35 countries. As Adrian Slywotzky has noted, it was a demographic shift that provided the opportunity for Fournier and Defforey to create a novel, customer-matched, cost-effective business design.[12]

Demographic change has also been a driving force behind the renaissance of shopping malls in the United States. The first enclosed mall opened in 1956; 50 years later, retail experts were using terms like "dying culture" to describe American shopping malls. Although America boasts approximately 1,500 malls, many have closed as the Internet has brought the world's stores into American homes. However, today's entrepreneurs are discovering opportunities in the changing face of America. For example, the Hispanic population in the Atlanta area quadrupled between 1990 and 2000. This change prompted real estate broker José Legaspi to renovate a blighted mall in Atlanta and rechristen it Plaza Fiesta. The mall attracts more than 4 million visitors each year;

many are Hispanic families who gather to listen to mariachi bands, relax, and, of course, shop. Legaspi has worked his magic in other locations, including the Panorama Mall in suburban Los Angeles (see Exhibit 7-2).[13]

SEGMENTING GLOBAL MARKETS BY INCOME AND POPULATION   When a company charts a plan for global market expansion, it often finds that income is a valuable segmentation variable. After all, a market consists of those customers who are willing and *able* to buy. For cigarettes, soft drinks, candy, and other consumer products that have a low per-unit cost, population is often a more valuable segmentation variable than income. Nevertheless, for a vast range of industrial and consumer products offered in global markets today, income is a valuable and important macro indicator of market potential. About two-thirds of world gross national income (GNI) is generated in the Triad (i.e., North America, Europe, and the Pacific Rim); by comparison, only 12 percent of the world's population is located in Triad countries.

The concentration of wealth in a handful of industrialized countries has significant implications for global marketers. After segmenting potential markets in terms of a single demographic variable—income—a company can reach the most affluent markets by targeting fewer than 20 nations: half the EU, North America, and Japan. By doing so, however, the marketers are *not* reaching almost 90 percent of the world's population! A word of caution is in order here. Data about income (and population) have the advantage of being widely available and inexpensive to access. However, management may unconsciously "read too much" into such data. In other words, while providing some measure of market potential, such macro-level demographic data should not necessarily be used as the sole indicator of presence (or absence) of a market opportunity. This is especially true when an emerging country market or region is being investigated.

Ideally, gross domestic product (GDP) and other measures of national income converted to U.S. dollars should be calculated on the basis of purchasing power parities (PPP; i.e., what the currency will buy in the country of issue) or through direct comparisons of actual prices for a given product. This approach provides an actual comparison of the standards of living in the countries of the world. Table 7-1 ranks the top 10 countries in terms of 2016 per capita income; it also provides the respective figure adjusted for purchasing power parity. Although the United States ranks sixth in per capita income, it ranks ninth in terms of standard of living, as measured by what money can buy.[14] By most metrics, the U.S. market is enormous: $18.6 trillion in national income and a population that passed the 300 million milestone in 2006. Little wonder, then, that so many non-U.S. companies target and cater to American consumers and organizational buyers!

Exhibit 7-2 Hispanic Americans accounted for more than half of the U.S. population's growth during the first decade of the 2000s. The number of Hispanic families with household incomes of $50,000 or more is also growing rapidly. According to Pew Research Center, Hispanics will represent approximately $1.7 trillion in annual buying power by 2020. Clearly, this segment of the U.S. population is very attractive to marketers.
Source: Photo by Emily Berl.

TABLE 7-1   Per Capita Income, 2016*

	2016 GNI per Capita	2016 Income Adjusted for Purchasing Power
1. Norway	$82,440	$62,550
2. Switzerland	81,240	63,660
3. Luxembourg	71,470	70,430
4. Denmark	56,990	51,100
5. Iceland	56,990	52,490
6. United States	56,810	58,700
7. Sweden	54,590	50,030
8. Australia	54,420	45,970
9. Singapore	51,880	85,190
10. Ireland	51,760	56,870

*Ranking omits countries for which 2016 data were not available—for example, Monaco, Liechtenstein, and Qatar.

A case in point is Mitsubishi Motors, which had begun redesigning its Montero Sport sport utility vehicle (SUV) with the goal of creating a "global vehicle" that could be sold worldwide with little adaptation. Then the design program changed course: The new goal was to make the vehicle more "American" by providing more interior space and more horsepower. Hiroshi Yajima, a Mitsubishi executive in North America, attributed the change to the vibrancy and sheer size of the American auto market. "We wouldn't care if the vehicle didn't sell outside the U.S.," he said.[15] The Montero was sold in the United States until 2004, when it was superseded by the Endeavor. The Endeavor, manufactured in Illinois, was part of Mitsubishi's "Project America" program, which focuses on producing cars targeting the U.S. market without concern for the preferences of drivers in export markets. The program is paying off: Mitsubishi's current SUV offering, the Outlander, has a "Recommended" rating from the influential *Consumer Reports*.

Despite having comparable per capita incomes, other industrialized countries are nevertheless quite small in terms of *total* annual income (see Table 7-2). In Sweden, for example, per capita GNI is about $54,480; however, Sweden's smaller population—9.9 million—means that, in relative terms, its market is limited. This helps explain why Ericsson, IKEA, Volvo, and other Swedish companies have looked beyond their borders for significant growth opportunities.

While Table 7-1 highlights the differences between straightforward income statistics and the standard of living in the world's most affluent nations, such differences can be even more pronounced in less-developed countries. A visit to a mud house in Tanzania will reveal many of the things that money can buy: an iron bed frame, a corrugated metal roof, beer and soft drinks,

TABLE 7-2   Top 10 Nations Ranked by GDP, 2016

Country	GDP (in millions)
1. United States	$18,589,000
2. China	11,199,000
3. Japan	4,939,000
4. Germany	3,467,000
5. United Kingdom	2,619,000
6. France	2,465,000
7. India	2,264,000
8. Italy	1,850,000
9. Brazil	1,796,000
10. Canada	1,530,000

bicycles, shoes, photographs, radios, and televisions. What Tanzania's per capita income of $900 does not reflect is the fact that instead of utility bills, Tanzanians have the local well and the sun. Instead of nursing homes, tradition and custom ensure that families will take care of the elderly at home. Instead of expensive doctors and hospitals, villagers may utilize the services of witch doctors and healers.

In industrialized countries, a significant portion of national income consists of the value of goods and services that would be free in a poor country. Thus, the standard of living in low- and lower-middle-income countries is often higher than income data might suggest; in other words, the *actual* purchasing power of the local currency may be much higher than that implied by exchange values. For example, the per capita income average for China of $8,250 equals 51,645 Chinese yuan at an exchange rate of 6.26 yuan = US$1.00. But 51,645 yuan will buy much more in China than $8,250 will buy in the United States. Adjusted for PPP, per capita income in China is estimated to be $15,500—an amount nearly twice as high as the unadjusted figure suggests.

Similarly, calculated in terms of purchasing power, per capita income in mainland Tanzania is approximately $2,740. Indeed, a visit to the capital city of Dar es Salaam reveals that stores are stocked with televisions and fashion items, and businesspeople can be seen negotiating deals using their smartphones. At the Kariakoo market, vendors conduct business via mobile money transactions instead of cash (see Exhibit 7-3). In fact, the World Bank reports that Tanzania has the most mobile money accounts per 1,000 adults of any African country.[16]

In 2016, the 10 most populous countries in the world accounted for 60 percent of the total world income; the 5 most populous countries accounted for approximately 46 percent of that total (see Table 7-3). Although population is not as concentrated as income, there is, in terms of size of nations, a pattern of considerable concentration. The concentration of income in the high-income and large-population countries means that a company can be "global" by targeting buyers in 10 or fewer countries. World population now exceeds 7 billion; at the present rate of growth, it will reach 12 billion by the middle of the century. Simply put, global population will probably double during the lifetimes of many students using this textbook.

As noted previously, for products whose price is low enough, population is a more important variable than income in determining market potential. Thus, China and India, with populations exceeding 1.3 billion people in each country, represent attractive target markets. In a country like India, one segmentation approach would call for serving the existing mass market for inexpensive consumer products. Kao, Johnson & Johnson, Procter & Gamble, Unilever, and other packaged goods companies are targeting and developing the India market, lured in part by the presence of hundreds of millions of customers who are willing and able to spend a few cents for a single-use pouch of shampoo and other personal-care products.

McDonald's global expansion illustrates the significance of both income and population on marketing activities. As noted in Case 1-2, McDonald's operates in 118 countries. What

Exhibit 7-3 Mobile money is replacing cash as a means of exchange in Tanzania, where most of the population is unbanked.

Source: iStock Unreleased/Getty Images.

TABLE 7-3 The 10 Most Populous Countries, 2016

Global Income and Population	2016 Population (millions)	Percentage of World Population	2016 GDP (billions)	2016 per Capita GNI	Percentage of World GDP
World Total	**7,422**	**100.00%**	**$75,544**	**$10,298**	**100.0%**
1. China	1,378	19%	11,199	8,250	15.0%
2. India	1,324	18%	2,264	1,670	3.0%
3. United States	323	4.4%	18,589	56,180	25.0%
4. Indonesia	261	3.5%	934	3,400	1.0%
5. Brazil	207	2.8%	1,796	8,840	2.0%
6. Pakistan	193	2.6%	283	1,510	0.4%
7. Nigeria	185	2.5%	405	2,450	0.5%
8. Bangladesh	162	2.2%	221	1,330	0.3%
9. Russian Federation	144	1.9%	1,280	9,720	1.7%
10. Mexico	127	1.7%	1,046	9,040	1.4%

this figure conceals, however, is that 80 percent of McDonald's restaurants are located in nine country markets: Australia, Brazil, Canada, China, France, Germany, Japan, the United Kingdom, and the United States. These nine countries generate nearly 75 percent of the company's total revenues. Eight of these countries appear in the top 10 rankings shown in Table 7-2; however, only three appear in the Table 7-3 population rankings. At present, the restaurants in the company's approximately 100 non-major-country markets contribute less than 20 percent of McDonald's operating income. McDonald's is counting on an expanded presence in China and other high-population-country markets to drive corporate growth in the twenty-first century.

In rapidly growing economies, marketers must take care when using income, population, and other macro-level data during the segmentation process. For example, marketers should keep in mind that national income figures such as those cited for China and India are averages. Using averages alone, it is possible to underestimate a market's potential: Fast-growing, higher-income segments are present in both China and India. As Harold L. Sirkin, James W. Hemerling, and Arindam K. Bhattacharya point out in *Globality*, the income disparity in China and India is reflected in the diversity of their huge populations. In China, this diversity manifests itself in eight major languages and several dialects and minor languages; in addition, 30 Chinese cities have populations of 2 million people or more. Sirkin and his coauthors write:

> Mandarin is the dominant language in the main cities of northern China, while Cantonese is the dominant language in the south, particularly in Hong Kong. And behind each language is a unique regional history, culture, and economy that collectively give rise to radical differences in tastes, activities, and aspirations.
>
> Such differences present a major challenge for companies in the most fundamental of go-to-market activities: segmenting the population to understand motivations, expectations, and aspirations—and estimating how much spending power each segment has. It makes the term "mass market" almost meaningless. Yes, there is a mass of consumers in the rapidly developing economies, but they can hardly be addressed en masse, at least not through one set of product propositions or one campaign of spoken or written communications.[17]

The same is true in India, where more than 10 percent of the population can be classified as "upper middle class." Pinning down a demographic segment may require additional information; according to some estimates, India's middle class totals 300 million people. However, if one defines the middle-class segment more narrowly as "households that own cars, computers, and washing machines," the figure would be much lower.

According to one Indian expert, India's population can be further segmented to include a "bike" segment of 25 million households in which telephones and motorbikes are present. However, the vast majority of India's population comprises a "bullock cart" segment whose

"Urban India is getting saturated. In the cities, everyone who can afford a television has one. If you want to maintain high growth, you have to penetrate into rural India."[18]

K. Ramachandran, chief executive, Philips Electronics India

households lack most modern conveniences but typically own a television.[19] And, how can a global company "act local" when "local" is very diverse? As Amit Agarwal, head of Amazon India, notes, "There's so little standardization: Every region has something that defines it. It's like 25 different countries."[20] The lesson is clear: To avoid being misled by averages, do not *assume* homogeneity.

AGE SEGMENTATION   Age is another useful demographic variable in global marketing. One global segment based on demographics is **global teens**, young people between the ages of 12 and 19. Teens, by virtue of their shared interests in fashion, music, and a youthful lifestyle, exhibit consumption behavior that is remarkably consistent across borders. As Renzo Rosso, creator of the Diesel brand and investor in Italy's H-Farm innovation incubator, explains, "A group of teenagers randomly chosen from different parts of the world will share many of the same tastes."[21] Young consumers may not yet have conformed to cultural norms; indeed, they may be rebelling against them. This fact, combined with shared universal wants, needs, desires, and fantasies (for name-brand, novelty, entertainment, trendy, and image-oriented products), makes it possible to reach the global teen segment with a unified marketing program.

This segment is attractive both in terms of its size (approximately 1.3 billion people) and its multi-billion-dollar purchasing power. According to London-based trend consultancy LS:NGlobal, the U.S. teen market represents roughly $200 billion in annual buying power; the United Kingdom's 7.5 million teens spend more than $10 billion each year.[22] Coca-Cola, Benetton, Swatch, and Sony are some of the companies pursuing the global teen segment. The global telecommunications revolution is a critical driving force behind the emergence of this segment. Global media such as MTV, Facebook, and Twitter are perfect vehicles for reaching this segment. Meanwhile, satellites are beaming Western programming and commercials to millions of viewers in China, India, and other emerging markets.

Another global segment is the **global elite**, affluent consumers who are well traveled and have the money to spend on prestigious products with an image of exclusivity (see Exhibit 7-4). Although this segment is often associated with older individuals who have accumulated wealth over the course of a long career, it also includes movie stars, musicians, elite athletes, entrepreneurs, and others who have achieved great financial success at a relatively young age. China is

Exhibit 7-4 Rolls-Royce, the automaker whose name is synonymous with exclusive luxury, sells approximately 1,000 vehicles each year. The company has operations in 47 countries; the United States accounts for roughly one-third of the overall market. The carmaker also sells to customers in key emerging country markets such as Cambodia, India, Indonesia, Nigeria, and Vietnam.
Source: PORNCHAI KITTIWONGSAKUL/AFP/ Getty Images.

home to 18,000 such individuals, which means it ranks number 2 overall worldwide. This segment of the Chinese population is expected to grow 40 percent in the next 5 years (see Case 7-1).

The global elite's needs and wants are spread over various product categories: durable goods (luxury automobiles such as Rolls-Royce and Mercedes-Benz), nondurables (upscale beverages such as Cristal champagne and Grey Goose vodka), and financial services (American Express Gold and Platinum cards). Prices for the flagship Rolls-Royce Phantom start at about $400,000; the typical buyer is an individual with an ultra-high net worth including more than $30 million in liquid assets. The introduction of the new $250,000 Ghost has jump-started sales for Rolls-Royce. Potential buyers can download an iPhone app that allows them to create their own vehicles. As one industry analyst noted recently, "One of the things that Rolls-Royce has been particularly good at is not corrupting its brand in the name of growth or profit."

GENDER SEGMENTATION   For obvious reasons, segmenting markets by gender is an approach that makes sense for many companies. Less obvious, however, is the need to ensure that opportunities for sharpening the focus on the needs and wants of one gender or the other do not go unnoticed. Although some companies—fashion designers and cosmetics companies, for example—market primarily or exclusively to women, other companies offer different lines of products to both genders.

For example, in 2015, Nike generated $5.7 billion in global sales of women's shoes and apparel. Nike executives believe the company's global women's business is poised for big growth, with sales expected to increase to $11 billion by 2020. The recent growth in this segment is due in large part to women's increased interest in fitness and the athleisure trend. Nike's recent advertising campaign, keyed to the theme #betterforit, encouraged women to share their fitness goals on social media.[23]

In Europe, Levi Strauss is also sharpening its focus on women. In 2003, the company opened its first boutique for young women, Levi's for Girls, in Paris. As Suzanne Gallacher, associate brand manager for Levi's in Europe, the Middle East, and Africa, noted, "In Europe, denim is for girls."[24] The company's move is part of a broader strategy to boost Levi Strauss's performance in the face of strong competition from Calvin Klein and Gap in the United States and from Topshop and Diesel in Europe. Gallacher predicts that if Levi's for Girls succeeds in France, similar stores will be opened in other European countries.

Psychographic Segmentation

Psychographic segmentation involves grouping people in terms of their attitudes, values, and lifestyles. The data used to classify individuals are obtained from questionnaires that require respondents to indicate the extent to which they agree or disagree with a series of statements. Psychographics is primarily associated with SRI International, a market research organization whose original Values and Lifestyles (VALS) and updated VALS 2 analyses of consumers are widely known. For years, Nokia relied heavily on psychographic segmentation of mobile phone users; its most important segments were Poseurs, Trendsetters, Social Contact Seekers, and Highfliers. By carefully studying these segments and tailoring products to each, Nokia once commanded 40 percent of the world's market for mobile communication devices.[25] Ultimately, Nokia's market share declined due to intense competition from a new generation of Apple and Android-based phones.

Porsche AG, the German sports car maker, turned to psychographics after experiencing a worldwide sales decline from 50,000 units in 1986 to about 14,000 units in 1993. Its U.S. subsidiary, Porsche Cars North America, already had a clear demographic profile of its typical customer: a 40-plus-year-old male college graduate whose annual income exceeded $200,000. A psychographic study showed that, demographics aside, Porsche buyers could be divided into several distinct categories. Top Guns, for example, buy Porsches and expect to be noticed; for Proud Patrons and Fantasists, in contrast, such conspicuous consumption is irrelevant. Porsche used the profiles to develop advertising tailored to each type. As Richard Ford, Porsche's vice president of sales and marketing, noted: "We were selling to people whose profiles were diametrically opposed." The results were impressive; Porsche's U.S. sales improved nearly 50 percent after a new advertising campaign was launched.[26]

Porsche is not the only global automobile marketer to use psychographic segmentation in combination with other segmentation variables. In some instances, however, the marketers reach a segment that they weren't necessarily targeting. For the past decade, Fiat, GM, Kia, Toyota, and other car makers have targeted U.S. Millennials, a segment that encompasses 80 million tech-savvy twenty- and thirty-somethings. As shown in Exhibit 7-5, recent entrants in the subcompact car market such as the Chevy Sonic, Toyota Scion, Fiat 500, and Kia Soul were designed with hip styling cues and features that clearly distinguished them from "typical" cars. Marketing communications (including Kia's breakdancing hamsters) were targeted squarely at Millennials. As it turns out, American Baby Boomers—the cohort born between 1946 and 1964—have been snapping up the funky-looking cars. The size and purchasing power of the Boomer generation makes this group hard for automakers to ignore: In 2012, they accounted for 40 percent of new car sales. By contrast, car buyers age 18 to 34 accounted for only 12 percent of new car purchases.[27]

As these examples illustrate, just as people of the same age don't necessarily have the same attitudes, people in one age bracket sometimes share attitudes and tastes with those in other age brackets. Sometimes it is preferable to market to a mind-set rather than to a particular age group; in such an instance, psychographic studies can help marketers arrive at a deeper understanding of consumer behavior than is possible with traditional segmentation variables such as demographics.

Psychographic market profiles are available from a number of different sources; companies may pay thousands of dollars to use these studies. In the Big Data era, Facebook and other tech firms can leverage their competitive advantages in mining social media data to provide answers to questions and arrive at insights about consumer behavior and technology trends around the globe. The analytics approaches typically involve a mix of qualitative and quantitative techniques and cut across the various segmentation bases discussed in this chapter.

Consider, for example, the behavior of online shoppers in the specialty retail category. Many retailers offer consumers the option to browse and buy online as well as to shop in physical stores; these companies often embed Facebook's Pixel code in their Web sites. In one study, Facebook collected data to identify cues and signals about the online behavior of 1.6 million online shoppers over a 1-month period in 2017. The company's consumer insights team divided the population into several categories, including Shopping Mavens, Informed Mobilizers, Fashion Enthusiasts, Opportunistic Shoppers, Social Savvies, and Online Reluctants. Segmentation bases from online behavior in the study included things like "average total days on brand site before purchase" and "average number of pages viewed each day on site." Insights about Shopping Mavens (representing approximately 10 percent of the total) included "the information on a brand or retailer's Web site inspires me" and "I am very passionate about shopping specialty retail." Compare that to the attitude of an Online Reluctant, whose attitude might be "Online you can't physically touch the product." Retailers can use these and other insights to optimize their advertising campaigns and tailor the overall marketing program to each segment.[28]

The segmentation and targeting approach used by a company can vary from country to country. In Europe, Levi Strauss now relies heavily on gender segmentation. By contrast, former CEO Phil

Exhibit 7-5 Music is an important part of the appeal of the Kia Soul ads that feature breakdancing hamsters. For example, Kia licensed Motörhead's song "Ace of Spades" for a recent ad launching the new Soul Turbo. Kia has also licensed songs by Lady Gaga, Maroon 5, and other top artists.
Source: Raymond Boyd/Getty Images.

EMERGING MARKETS BRIEFING BOOK

Segmenting the Thai Tourism Market

The Kingdom of Thailand is known as the "Land of Smiles." Tourism brochures are chock-full of gorgeous images of mountains and sunny beaches. Tourism currently accounts for about 10 percent of Thailand's GNP, generating an estimated $50 billion in revenues in 2017. One-fourth of the 40 million foreign tourists who visit each year are Chinese.

Yet, for many years, there has been a dark side to Thailand's tourist industry. Prostitution and sex tourism long flourished in the country. The tourist sex trade had its roots in the Vietnam War era; some U.S. soldiers were based in Thailand, others traveled there on leave. After the war ended and the majority of Americans left, the sex trade continued in Pattaya and other cities because of the amount of money it generated. Men still account for roughly 60 percent of foreign visitors.

Today, Thai government programs aim to limit the sex trade by improving the country's transportation infrastructure and redeveloping crowded city areas. At the same time, the Tourism Authority of Thailand (TAT) has developed a series of promotional campaigns aiming to reposition Thailand and change public perceptions. "Amazing Thailand" and "Unseen Thailand" are among the campaign themes in recent years. Currently, TAT is targeting two distinct segments: gay and lesbian couples, and Muslim families.

Buddhism is the dominant religion in Thailand, and slightly less than 5 percent of the population is Islamic. Even so, sociologist Lora Friedrich, an American who has spent many years in Thailand, notes that the country has always had a "Muslim-friendly" infrastructure. Prayer rooms are available at shopping malls, resorts, and beaches; and many restaurants have *halal*-certified kitchens. Malaysia, where nearly two-thirds of the population practices Islam, is among the top 10 countries sending tourists to Thailand. For its part, Malaysia is the number 1 destination for Muslim tourists. Interestingly, while Saudi Arabia, the United Arab Emirates, Sri Lanka, and Egypt are *not* in the top 10 as far as number of tourists visiting Thailand, tourists from these countries are the top spenders.

"Go Thai. Be Free" is the theme of a government-sponsored campaign targeting gay and lesbian travelers (see Exhibit 7-6). Gay couples have, on average, higher household incomes than heterosexual couples. Gay tourists frequently gather on Silom Road, an area in Bangkok with myriad dance clubs, gay bars, and restaurants. It's easily accessible by the city's Skytrain mass transit system. Visitors are also attracted to special events such as the Songkran Festival, held every year on April 13, 14, and 15. Celebrating the traditional Thai New Year, the festival is embraced by both gay and straight tourists. The event is known as the water splashing festival; anyone who wants to stay dry should stay home! Western holidays such as Halloween, Christmas, and New Year's Eve/Day are also celebrated in Thailand. "Thai people like to celebrate and have fun," says Bangkok native Dr. Chatt Pongpatipat.

Fazal Bahardeen is CEO of Crescentrating, a Singapore-based company that ranks countries on the basis of hospitality toward Muslims. Noting that Thais are an "inherently hospitable people," Bahardeen emphasizes the fact that foreign tourists care about how and where they spend their money. He says, "I keep telling tourist organizations, 'It's Marketing 101. Why would you want to go to a place that doesn't welcome you?'"

Sources: The authors are indebted to Dr. Lora Friedrich, Professor of Sociology, Simpson College, and Dr. Chatt Pongpatipat, Assistant Professor of Marketing, Saginaw Valley State University. *Additional sources:* Trefor Moss, "Thais Love Chinese Tourism—to a Point," *The Wall Street Journal* (February 16, 2018), p. A10; Burhan Wazir, "Halal Holidays Boost Muslin Visitor Numbers," *Financial Times Special Report: Turkey & The Arab World* (September 28, 2017), p. 5; James Hookway and Wilawan Watcharasakwet, "Bangkok Takes on a Major Makeover," *The Wall Street Journal* (October 12, 2016), p. C3; Thomas Fuller, "Thais Cast a Wide Net for Diverse Tourists," *The New York Times* (August 3, 2013), p. 12; Fuller, "A City Known for Sex Tries to Broaden Its Appeal," *The New York Times* (September 17, 2010), p. A9; Krittinee Nuttavuthisit, "Branding Thailand: Correcting the Negative Image of Sex Tourism," *Place Branding and Public Democracy* 3 (2007), pp. 21–30.

Exhibit 7-6 Thailand's tourism industry generates an estimated $1.6 billion each year by welcoming gay and lesbian travelers. Likewise, Thailand ranks high on the list of "*halal*-friendly destinations" for Muslim vacationers.
Source: Amble Design/Shutterstock.

Marineau believed that a psychographic segmentation strategy was the key to revitalizing the venerable jeans brand in its home market. Marineau's team identified several different segments, including Fashionistas, Trendy Teens, Middle-Aged Men, and Budget Shoppers. The goal was to create different styles of jeans at different price points for each segment and to make them available at stores ranging from Walmart to Neiman Marcus.[29] Likewise, Sony Electronics, a unit of Sony Corp. of America, undertook a reorganization of its marketing function. Traditionally, Sony had approached marketing from a product category point of view. It changed its philosophy so that a new unit, the Consumer Segment Marketing Division, would be responsible for getting closer to consumers in the United States (see Table 7-4).[30] Which variables did Sony use to develop these categories?

Behavior Segmentation

Behavior segmentation can focus on whether people buy and use a product, as well as how often and how much they use or consume. In today's social-media–saturated environment, behavior segmentation can also be based on big data that reflect online engagement with a brand or a company. Consumers can be categorized in terms of **usage rates**: heavy, medium, light, or nonuser. Consumers can also be segmented according to **user status**: potential users, nonusers, ex-users, regulars, first-timers, or users of competitors' products.

Marketers sometimes refer to the **80/20 rule** when assessing usage or engagement rates. This rule (also known as the *law of disproportionality* or *Pareto's law*) suggests that, for example, 80 percent of a company's revenues or profits are accounted for by 20 percent of a firm's products or customers. As noted earlier, nine country markets generate nearly 80 percent of McDonald's revenues. And, as you learned in Case 6-1 about the music business, 5 percent of recording artists account for 95 percent of all artist-related Facebook engagement. So, one challenge facing an emerging or "undiscovered" artist seeking to build his or her career in the music industry is how to increase audience size on Facebook, Twitter, and other online platforms—maybe drop a new single every month to generate online buzz?

Benefit Segmentation

Global **benefit segmentation** focuses on the numerator of the value equation—the B in $V = B/P$. This approach is based on marketers' superior understanding of the problem a product solves, the benefit it offers, or the issue it addresses, regardless of geography. Food marketers, for example, are finding success creating products that can help parents create nutritious family meals with a minimal investment of time. Campbell Soup is making significant inroads into Japan's $500 million soup market as time-pressed homemakers place a premium on convenience. Marketers of health and beauty aids also use benefit segmentation. Many toothpaste brands are straightforward cavity fighters, and as such they reach a very broad market. However, as consumers become more concerned about whitening, sensitive teeth, gum disease, and other oral care issues, marketers are developing new toothpaste brand extensions suited to the different sets of perceived needs.

Demographic trends are also creating opportunities for food products with medicinal benefits. The World Health Organization predicts that, by 2050, 22 percent of the world's population will

TABLE 7-4 Sony's U.S. Consumer Segments

Segment	Description
Affluent	High-income consumers
CE Alphas	Early adopters of high-tech consumer electronics products, irrespective of age
Zoomers	55 years old or older
SoHo	Small office/home office
Families	35 to 54 years old
Young professionals/D.I.N.K.S.	Dual income, no kids, 25 to 34 years old
Gen Y	Younger than 25 years old (includes tweens, teens, college students)

Exhibit 7-7 Only a handful of FDA-approved drugs are available to treat Alzheimer's patients in the United States. Some patients have sought alternative therapies such as Axona, a medical food. In Alzheimer's patients, the brain loses its ability to metabolize glucose; Axona provides an alternative "brain fuel" known as ketones.
Source: Courtesy of Accera, Inc.

be age 60 or older—today, that proportion is only 12 percent. According to Euromonitor International, the global market for foods that offer health benefits is currently worth about $600 billion in annual sales. Nestlé is in the vanguard of companies that are expanding offerings in the health-food category, for which the 60–and-older demographic is a key target. The giant Swiss company recently established two new subsidiaries, Nestlé Health Science SA and the Nestlé Institute of Health Sciences, that will focus on products known as "medical foods," "functional foods," and "nutraceuticals." The goal is to create new food products that target diseases. Nestlé recently acquired CM&D Pharma, a U.K.-based startup that has developed a chewing gum that offers relief from kidney disease. Nestlé also bought a stake in Accera; this company makes Axona, a prescription medical food intended for the clinical dietary management of mild to moderate Alzheimer's disease (see Exhibit 7-7).[31]

Ethnic Segmentation

In many countries, the population includes ethnic groups of significant size. In the United States, for example, the three major ethnic segments are African/Black Americans, Asian Americans, and Hispanic Americans. Each segment shows great diversity and can be further subdivided. For example, Asian Americans include Thai Americans, Vietnamese Americans, and Chinese Americans, and each of these groups speaks a different language.

America's Hispanic population shares a common language but can also be segmented by place of origin: the Dominican Republic, Cuba, Central America, South America, Puerto Rico, and, of course, Mexico. The Hispanic American segment comprises more than 55 million people, representing nearly 17 percent of the total U.S. population and nearly $2 trillion in annual buying power. As a group, Hispanic Americans are hardworking and exhibit strong family and religious orientations. However, the different segments are very diverse, and marketers need to beware of falling into the trap of thinking "All Hispanics are the same." Some call the new face of opportunity the "$1 trillion Latina." Indeed, the United States is home to 24 million women of Hispanic heritage; 42 percent are single, 35 percent are heads of households, and 54 percent are employed.

From a marketing point of view, the various Hispanic American segments represent a great opportunity. Companies in a variety of industry sectors, including food and beverages, consumer durables, and leisure and financial services, are recognizing the need to include these segments when preparing marketing programs for the United States. Almost two decades ago, companies based in Mexico began zeroing in on opportunities to the north. Three Mexican retailers—Famsa, Grupo Gigant SA, and Grupo Comercial Chedraui SA—all opened stores in the United States. As Famsa President Humberto Garza Valdez explained at the grand opening of a store in San Fernando, California, "We're not coming to the U.S. to face big companies like Circuit City or Best Buy. Our focus is the Hispanic market."[32]

Modelo Especial is a Mexican beer brand that has successfully capitalized on its heritage to target Hispanic Americans while also appealing to the "Mercado General." The brand was

"The aim is to target a new demographic that we call Generation M: Multicultural, Mobile, and Millennial."[33]

Cesar Conde, Chairman, NBC Universal Telemundo Enterprises

first introduced in the United States in 1982; today, Latinos account for 50 percent of its sales volume. Gradually, over the course of several decades, various aspects of Latino culture have been widely embraced in the United States, as evidenced by the mainstream popularity of artists such as Jennifer Lopez and Pitbull. In addition, the marketing team at Constellation Brands, which distributes Modelo Especial, attributes the brand's mainstream appeal today in part to the fact that urban Millennial consumers are generally open to different cultures and lifestyles.[34] Moreover, Modelo benefits from the fact that its brand-loyal consumers are "hyper-social" users of new media. Tumblr is the social media site of choice for the beer's parent company, where posts include "beer recipes" for Latino-style cocktails.

The preceding discussion outlined the ways global companies (and the research and advertising agencies that serve them) use market segmentation to identify, define, understand, and respond to customer wants and needs on a worldwide basis. In addition to the segmentation variables previously discussed, new segmentation approaches are being developed in response to today's rapidly changing business environment. For example, the widespread adoption of the Internet and other new technologies creates a great deal of commonality among global consumers. These consumer subcultures are composed of people whose similar outlooks and aspirations create a shared mind-set that transcends language and national differences. Consumer products giant Procter & Gamble is one company that is attuned to the changing times. As Melanie Healey, former president of P&G's Global Health and Feminine Care unit, noted, "We're seeing global tribes forming around the world that are more and more interconnected through technology."[35]

▶ **7-2** Explain the criteria that global marketers use to choose specific markets to target.

(7-2) Assessing Market Potential and Choosing Target Markets or Segments

After segmenting the market by one or more of the criteria just discussed, the next step is to assess the attractiveness of the identified segments.[36] This part of the process is especially important when sizing up emerging country markets as potential targets. It is at this stage that global marketers should be mindful of several potential pitfalls associated with the market segmentation process.

First, there is a tendency to overstate the size and short-term attractiveness of individual country markets, especially when estimates are based primarily on demographic data such as income and population. For example, while China, India, Brazil, and other emerging markets undoubtedly offer potential in the long run, management must realize that short-term profit and revenue growth objectives may be hard to achieve. During the 1990s, Procter & Gamble and other consumer packaged goods companies learned this lesson in Latin America. By contrast, the success of McDonald's Russia during the same period is a case study in the rewards of persistence and long-term outlook.

A second trap that global marketers can set for themselves is to target a country because shareholders or competitors exert pressure on management not to "miss out" on a strategic opportunity. Recall from Chapter 2, for example, the statement by India's former finance minister that the twenty-first century will be "the century of India." Such pronouncements can create the impression that management must "act now" to take advantage of a limited window of opportunity.

Third, there is a danger that management's network of contacts will emerge as a primary criterion for targeting. The result can be market entry based on convenience rather than on rigorous market analysis. For example, a company may enter into a distribution agreement with a non-national employee who wants to represent the company after returning to his or her home country. The issue of choosing the right foreign distributor is discussed in detail in Chapter 12.

With these pitfalls in mind, marketers can utilize three basic criteria for assessing opportunity in global target markets: current size of the segment and anticipated growth potential, competition, and compatibility with the company's overall objectives and the feasibility of successfully reaching a designated target.

Current Segment Size and Growth Potential

Is the market segment currently large enough to present the company with the opportunity to make a profit? If the answer is "no" today, does it have significant growth potential to make it attractive in terms of the company's long-term strategy? Consider the following facts about India:

- India is the one of the world's fastest-growing mobile phone markets. This market is expanding at a double-digit annual rate, with millions of new subscribers added every month. In mid-2008, India had 261 million cell phone users; that number approached 650 million by the end of 2016. However, only 300 million of those users own a smartphone.

- Approximately 3 million cars are sold each year in India. In absolute terms, this is a relatively small number—but it also means that Indian's light-vehicle market has more than doubled in size over the past decade.

- Approximately 70 percent of India's population is younger than the age of 35. This segment is increasingly affluent, and today's young, brand-conscious consumers are buying $100 Tommy Hilfiger jeans and $690 Louis Vuitton handbags. Mohan Murjani owns the rights to the Tommy Hilfiger brand in India. Commenting on the country's decade-long economic boom, he notes, "Aspirationally, things changed dramatically. What we were seeing was huge growth in terms of consumers' assets, in terms of their incomes and in terms of their spending power through credit."[37]

As noted earlier, one of the advantages of targeting a market segment globally is that although the segment in a single-country market might be small, even a narrow segment can be served profitably if that same segment exists in several countries. The billion-plus members of the global MTV Generation are a case in point. Moreover, by virtue of its size and purchasing power, the global teen segment is extremely attractive to consumer goods companies. In the case of a huge country market such as India or China, segment size and growth potential may be assessed in a different manner.

From the perspective of a consumer packaged goods company, for example, low incomes and the absence of a distribution infrastructure offset the fact that 75 percent of India's population lives in rural areas. The appropriate decision may be to target urban areas only, even though they are home to only 25 percent of the population.

Visa's strategy in China perfectly illustrates this criterion as it relates to demographics, but also highlights the difficulty of penetrating the Chinese market in times of rapid technological change. Visa targeted persons with monthly salaries equivalent to $300 or more. The company predicted that, by the early 2010s, that demographic could include as many as 200 million people. At the time, only 1 percent of the Chinese population owned a credit card. However, the Chinese people generally have negative attitudes about incurring debt; in addition, government regulations made it difficult for Visa's entry. Meanwhile, mobile payment technology exploded in popularity, as consumers embraced Alibaba's Alipay and Tencent's WeChat Pay (see Exhibit 7-8). Now, Visa and rival Mastercard are launching their own mobile payment apps.[38]

Exhibit 7-8 Alipay and WeChat pay are the preferred mobile payments platforms in China, commanding more than 90 percent of the market. Chinese consumers prefer using their phones as digital wallets rather than paying in cash.

Source: Visual China Group/Getty Images.

TABLE 7-5 Global Automakers Targeting the U.S. Market with SUVs

Automaker	Selected SUV Model	Country of Assembly or Manufacture	Year Introduced
Porsche	Cayenne	Germany	2003
Volkswagen	Touareg	Slovakia	2004
Honda	CR-V	Japan	1995
Toyota	RAV-4	Japan	1994
Kia	Sorento	South Korea	2003
BMW	X5	United States	2000
Mercedes-Benz	ML 350	United States	2003

Thanks to a combination of favorable demographics and lifestyle-related needs, the United States has been a very attractive market for foreign automakers. For example, demand for SUVs exploded during the 1990s. From 1990 to 2000, SUV sales tripled, growing from nearly 1 million units in 1990 to 2 million units in 1996 and passing 3 million sold in 2000. Why are these vehicles so popular? Primarily it is the security of four-wheel drive and the higher clearance for extra traction in adverse driving conditions. These vehicles also typically have more space for hauling cargo.

Reacting to high demand for the Jeep Cherokee, Ford Explorer, and Chevy Blazer, manufacturers from outside the United States introduced models of their own at a variety of price points (see Table 7-5). Dozens of SUV models have become available as Toyota, Mazda, Honda, Kia, Nissan, Rover, BMW, Mercedes, Volkswagen, and other global automakers have targeted American buyers. Many manufacturers offer various SUV styles, including full-size, mid-size, compact, and crossover versions. Even as growth in SUV sales slows in the United States, SUVs are growing in popularity in many other countries. In China, for example, SUVs account for approximately 40 percent of auto imports and represent the fastest-growing sector in the auto industry. In 2008, GM started exporting its popular Escalade to China; the sticker price is the equivalent of about $150,000.

Potential Competition

A market segment or country market characterized by strong competition may be a segment to avoid. However, if the competition is vulnerable in terms of price or quality disadvantages, it is possible for a market newcomer to make significant inroads. Over the past several decades, for example, Japanese companies in a variety of industries have targeted the U.S. market despite the presence of entrenched domestic market leaders. Some of the newcomers proved to be extremely adept at segmenting and targeting; as a result, they made significant inroads. In the motorcycle industry, for example, Honda first created the market for small-displacement dirt bikes. The company then moved upmarket with bigger bikes targeted at casual riders whose psychographic profiles were quite different from those of the hard-core Harley-Davidson rider. In document imaging, Canon outflanked Xerox by offering compact desktop copiers and targeting department managers and secretaries. Similar examples can be found in earthmoving equipment (Komatsu versus Caterpillar), photography (Fuji versus Kodak), and numerous other industries.

By contrast, many examples can be cited of companies whose efforts to develop a position in an attractive country market ended in failure. For example, Germany's DHL tried to enter the U.S. package-delivery market in 2003; to achieve scale, DHL acquired Airborne Express. However, management underestimated the dominance of the entrenched incumbents FedEx and UPS. DHL finally withdrew from the United States market in 2008 after losses totaling nearly $10 billion. Likewise, Walmart pulled out of South Korea and Germany after failing to find the right positioning and product mix.

Virgin chief executive Richard Branson learned important lessons in the mid-1990s when he launched Virgin Cola, directly targeting Coca-Cola's core market (see Exhibit 7-9). In his book *Business Stripped Bare: Adventures of a Global Entrepreneur*, Branson recalls:

Exhibit 7-9 Virgin Group chief Sir Richard Branson has an uncanny knack for generating publicity. He has crossed the Atlantic Ocean by hot-air balloon and by speedboat—both ventures sponsored by Virgin, of course. In 1998, Branson famously rode into New York's Times Square on a military tank and crushed a pile of Coca-Cola cans for the launch of Virgin Cola. For Virgin Cola's Japanese launch, Branson donned a costume for a public appearance in Tokyo.
Source: PA Images/Alamy Stock Photo.

> Starting a soft-drinks war with Coca-Cola was crazy. It was one of our highest profile business mistakes.... We somehow contrived to blind ourselves completely to the power and the influence of a global brand that epitomizes the strength and reach of American capitalism.[39]

Feasibility and Compatibility

If a market segment is judged to be large enough, and if strong competitors are either absent or deemed to be vulnerable, then the final consideration is whether a company can and should target that market. The feasibility of targeting a particular segment can be negatively impacted by various factors. For example, significant regulatory hurdles may limit market access. This issue is especially important in China today. Other marketing-specific issues can also arise. In India, for example, 3 to 5 years of work is required to build an effective distribution system for many consumer products. This fact may serve as a deterrent to foreign companies that would otherwise be attracted by the apparent potential of India's large population.[40]

Managers must decide how well a company's product or business model fits the country market in question. Alternatively, if the company does not currently offer a suitable product, can it develop one? To make this decision, a marketer must consider several criteria:

- Will adaptation be required? If so, is this move economically justifiable in terms of the expected sales volume?
- Will import restrictions, high tariffs, or a strong home-country currency drive up the price of the product in the target-market currency and effectively dampen demand?
- Is it advisable to source locally? In many cases, reaching global market segments requires considerable expenditures for distribution and travel by company personnel. Would it make sense to source products in the country for export elsewhere in the region?

Finally, it is important to address the question of whether targeting a particular segment is compatible with the company's overall goals, brand image, or established sources of competitive advantage. For example, BMW is one of the world's premium auto brands. Should BMW add a minivan to its product lineup? For now, management is responding to other competitive opportunities and threats. In 2013, BMW unveiled the i-Series electric sedan as an alternative for drivers shopping for a plug-in car such as the Tesla Model S. Meanwhile, Maserati is taking aim at BMW's 5 Series: The Italian company has unveiled a $65,000 "entry-level" model. Management hopes that the appeal of Italian chic paired with a Ferrari engine will prove irresistible to luxury car buyers.[41]

A Framework for Selecting Target Markets

As one can infer from this discussion, it would be extremely useful to have formal tools or frameworks available when assessing emerging country markets. Table 7-6 presents a market selection framework that incorporates some of the elements just discussed. Suppose an American company has identified China, Russia, and Mexico as potential country target markets. The table shows the countries arranged in declining rank by market size. At first glance, China might appear to hold the greatest potential simply on the basis of size. However, the competitive advantage of our hypothetical firm is 0.07 in China, 0.10 in Russia, and 0.20 in Mexico. Multiplying the market size and competitive advantage index yields a market potential of 7 in China, 5 in Russia, and 4 in Mexico.

The next stage in the analysis requires an assessment of the various market access considerations. In Table 7-6, all these conditions or terms are reduced to an index number of terms of access, which is 0.50 for China, 0.35 for Russia, and 0.90 for Mexico. In other words, the "market access considerations" are more favorable in Mexico than in Russia or China. At present, market conditions are perilous in Russia due to sanctions imposed by the United States and Europe in response to Russia's interference in Ukraine. Also, Russian President Vladimir Putin has proved to be mercurial and unpredictable. Multiplying the market potential by the terms of access index suggests that Mexico, despite its small size, holds greater market potential than China or Russia.

Although the framework in Table 7-6 should prove useful as a preliminary screening tool for intercountry comparisons, it does not go far enough in terms of assessing actual market potential. Global marketing expert David Arnold has developed a framework that goes beyond demographic data and considers other, marketing-oriented assessments of market size and growth potential. Instead of a "top-down" segmentation analysis beginning with, for example, income or population data from a particular country, Arnold's framework is based on a "bottom-up" analysis that begins at the product-market level.

As shown in Figure 7-1, Arnold's framework incorporates two core concepts: marketing model drivers and enabling conditions. **Marketing model drivers** are key elements or factors required for a business to take root and grow in a particular country market environment. The drivers may differ depending on whether a company serves consumer or industrial markets. Does success hinge on establishing or leveraging a brand name? In Vietnam, for example, Procter & Gamble promotes its Tide detergent brand as "Number 1 in America." Or is distribution the key element? Or a tech-savvy sales staff? Marketing executives seeking an opportunity must arrive at insights into the true driving force(s) that will affect success for their particular product market.

Enabling conditions are structural market characteristics whose presence or absence can determine whether the marketing model can succeed. For example, in India, refrigeration is not widely available in shops and market food stalls. This factor creates challenges for Nestlé and Cadbury as they attempt to capitalize on Indians' increasing appetite for chocolate confections. Although Nestlé's KitKat and Cadbury's Dairy Milk bars have been reformulated to better withstand the heat, the absence or rudimentary nature of refrigeration hampers the companies' efforts to ensure their products are in saleable condition.

After marketing model drivers and enabling conditions have been identified, the third step is for management to weigh the estimated costs associated with entering and serving the market against the potential short- and long-term revenue streams. Does this segment or country market merit entry now? Or would it be better to wait until specific enabling conditions are established?

The issue of timing is often framed in terms of the quest for **first-mover advantage**; the conventional wisdom suggests that the first company to enter a market has the best chance of becoming the market leader. Examples from the annals of global marketing that appear to support

TABLE 7-6 Market Selection Framework

Market (population)	Market Size	Competitive Advantage		Market Potential	Terms of Access	Market Potential
China (1.3 billion)	100	0.07	=	7	0.50	3.5
Russia (143 million)	50	0.10	=	5	0.35	1.7
Mexico (122 million)	20	0.20	=	4	0.90	3.6

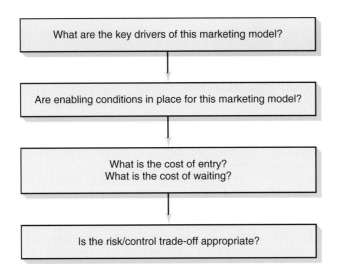

FIGURE 7-1 Screening Criteria for Market Segments
Source: David Arnold, *The Mirage of Global Markets: How Globalizing Companies Can Succeed as Markets Localize."*
© 2004 Reprinted by permission of Pearson Education, Inc. Upper Saddle River, NJ.

this notion include the Coca-Cola Company, which established itself globally during World War II. However, there are also first-mover *disadvantages*. The first company to enter a market often makes substantial investments in marketing, only to find that a late-arriving competitor reaps some of the benefits from its efforts.

Ample evidence suggests that late entrants into global markets can also achieve success. One way they do this is by benchmarking established companies and then outmaneuvering them, first locally and then globally. Jollibee, the Philippines-based fast-food chain whose business model was influenced by McDonald's, is a case in point. Late movers can also succeed by developing innovative business models. This approach was used by Stephen Millar, chief executive of Australian wine producer BRL Hardy. Millar's insight was that no leading global brand had emerged in the wine business; in other words, there was no equivalent to Coca-Cola in the wine business. During the 1990s, Millar established Hardy as a leading global brand. He accomplished this by moving on several fronts. First, he took control of the sales function. Second, he made sure Hardy's wines were crafted to appeal to a broader demographic than "wine snobs," who tend to favor bottles from France and Italy. Third, he supplemented Hardy's line of Australian wines with selected brands from other countries. In 2002, Hardy sold 20 million cases of wine worldwide; today, it is one of the world's top 10 wine companies.[42]

One way to determine the marketing model drivers and enabling conditions is to create a product–market profile. The profile should address some or all of the following basic questions:

1. Who buys our product or brand?
2. Who does not buy our product or brand?
3. What need or function does our product serve? Does our product or brand address that need?
4. Is there a market need that is not being met by current product or brand offerings?
5. What problem does our product solve?
6. What are customers currently buying to satisfy the need, or solve the problem, that our product targets?
7. What price are they paying for the product they are currently buying?
8. When is our product purchased?
9. Where is our product purchased?

(7-3) Product–Market Decisions

◄ **7-3** Understand how global marketers use a product–market grid to make targeting decisions.

The next step in assessing market segments is a company review of current and potential product offerings in terms of their suitability for the country market or segment. This assessment can be performed by creating a product–market grid that maps markets as horizontal rows on a spreadsheet and products as vertical columns. Each cell represents the possible intersection of a product and a market segment. In the case of the candy companies discussed earlier, both Nestlé

EMERGING MARKETS BRIEFING BOOK

Middle Eastern Airlines Target Lucrative Global Markets

Are you shopping for a flight between Chicago and Bangkok? Frankfort and Singapore? Toronto and Dubai? Your first thought might be to book your trip on a home-country carrier such as United, Lufthansa, or Air Canada, all of which are members of the Star Alliance partnership. These days, however, your choices also include Emirates Airline, which is based in the United Arab Emirates (UAE). Etihad Airways, based in the emirate of Abu Dhabi, and Qatar Airways have also been expanding their international operations (see Exhibit 7-10).

All three Middle Eastern carriers are government owned. Thanks to international open-skies agreements negotiated by the U.S. State Department, these and other foreign carriers can now fly in and out of the United States much more frequently than they did in the past. Germany also has opened its market. By contrast, in Canada, where air treaties are more restrictive, the Middle Eastern carriers have less penetration in terms of number of weekly flights.

Deregulation of the airline industry in the United States has resulted in more consumer choice and lower prices, among other benefits for passengers. As Emirates and other Middle Eastern carriers penetrate more deeply into the world's largest aviation market, they are becoming known for very high-quality in-flight service. All offer a limited number of first-class suites to address the needs of the elite travel segment. And, blessed with prime geographic locations, the "Gulf Three" carriers have collectively earned the nickname "superconnectors" because their respective hubs can link so many air travelers.

The newcomers are spending lavishly on advertising and promotional events to build brand awareness. For example, Emirates Airline sponsored the 2014 U.S. Open tennis championship, and it is the official airline of the San Francisco Symphony. The Persian carriers have also booked a large number of orders for jumbo jets from Boeing and Airbus, meaning they will have plenty of capacity on long-haul flights. In fact, the number of seats available on flights originating in the United States has increased dramatically in the past few years. Meanwhile, Dubai International Airport rivals London's Heathrow in terms of the number of international passengers who pass through this facility.

At the same time, the Middle Eastern newcomers have encountered some opposition. United Continental, American Airlines, and Delta have filed complaints with the U.S. government that the state-owned carriers benefit from substantial government subsidies. According to the complaint, subsidies, along with tax exemptions and access to low-cost airport services, allow the carriers to sell seats at below cost in the United States and other markets.

All three Gulf carriers have experienced other barriers to growth as well. For example, Qatar's bookings dropped dramatically after four of its Middle Eastern neighbors initiated an air and sea blockade in June 2017. Bahrain, Egypt, Saudi Arabia, and the UAE imposed the embargo amid allegations that Qatar harbored terrorists. Meanwhile, Etihad's strategy of investing in struggling carriers faltered, with Air Berlin and Alitalia going into receivership. And Emirates Airline, the oldest of the three, saw declining passenger traffic due to immigration restrictions in the United States as well as a ban on in-cabin laptop computers—later lifted—on flights into the United States.

Sources: Tanya Powley and Simeon Kerr, "A Hard Landing for High Flyers," *Financial Times Big Read: Middle East Aviation* (September 6, 2017), p. 9; Susan Carey, "Gulf Airlines Force Question: Join or Fight?" *The Wall Street Journal* (March 17, 2015), pp. B1, B4; Susan Carey, "Persian Gulf Airlines' Service Wins U.S. Fans," *The Wall Street Journal* (March 17, 2015), p. B4; Susan Carey, "U.S. Airlines Clash over Rivals from Persian Gulf," *The Wall Street Journal* (February 24, 2015), pp. B1, B5; Scott McCartney, "Airlines Compete to Become First in First Class," *The Wall Street Journal* (December 17, 2014), p. D3; Ben Mutzabaugh, "Lufthansa Looks to Make Bigger Mark on U.S. Market," *USA Today* (November 17, 2014), p. 5B; Scott McCartney, "Now Landing: Tough Challengers—Emirates, Etihad, and Qatar Accelerate Their Push to Win U.S. Fliers," *The Wall Street Journal* (November 6, 2014), p. D1.

Exhibit 7-10 Emirates Airline and other carriers based in the Middle East are targeting flyers in the United States and other key markets.

Source: pio3/Shutterstock.

and Cadbury determined that a liquid chocolate confection would be one way to address the issue of India's hot weather. The companies are also working to improve the enabling conditions for selling traditional chocolate treats by supplying coolers to merchants.

Table 7-7 shows a product–market matrix for Lexus. Toyota launched the Lexus brand in 1989 with two sedan models. In market segmentation terms, the luxury car buyer Lexus hoped to attract is associated with an upper-income demographic. In 1996, Lexus launched its first SUV. The decision to enter the SUV product–market intersection represented the brand management's desire to reach upper-income consumers whose lifestyles required something other than a luxury sedan. In 2012, Lexus offered a total of 11 different models in the United States; these included the top-of-the line LX 470 luxury utility vehicle, the LS 430 luxury sedan, and, at the entry level, the IS series. Lexus vehicles are marketed in more than 60 countries; the United States is the number 1 market. In an odd twist, in Japan, the vehicles were sold for years under the Toyota nameplate; the line was relaunched under the Lexus brand in 2005.[43]

Toyota management intends to build Lexus into a global luxury brand; worldwide 2016 sales totaled 677,615 vehicles. To achieve its ultimate goal, Lexus has to target Germany, the largest market in Europe, where 4 in 10 vehicles sold are luxury models. Approximately 15 million cars are sold in Europe each year, and Germany accounts for nearly one-fourth of the total. At the beginning of 2013, there were about 25,000 registered Lexus vehicles in Germany; by comparison, total vehicle registrations for Mercedes and BMW exceeded 6.8 million. Can Lexus succeed on the home turf of two of the world's leading luxury car makers?

Armed with the understanding that local brands account for more than 90 percent of German auto sales in the premium segment, Lexus has made significant product adaptations. For example, because Germans want the option of buying vehicles with diesel engines, Lexus developed new diesel models as well as a gas–electric hybrid engine for the RX series. Note that in Europe, Lexus offers the top-of-the-line LX 470 SUV in only one country: Russia. Can you explain this situation? How do the model offerings vary among the BRICS countries?

(7-4) Targeting and Target Market Strategy Options

◀ **7-4** Compare and contrast the three main target market strategy options.

After evaluating the identified segments in terms of the three criteria presented earlier—segment size and growth rate, potential competition, and feasibility—a company must decide whether it will pursue a particular opportunity. Not surprisingly, in global marketing one fundamental decision concerns which country or regional market(s) to enter. For example, Hershey, the U.S.-based confectionary company, recently targeted the United Kingdom, Europe, and the Middle East, where Mars and Kraft are the dominant players. Previously, Hershey's business was concentrated in North and South America and Asia. Consider also the following examples of targeting:

- The global home furnishings market can be segmented in terms of gender. Approximately 70 percent of IKEA's customers are women.
- India's vehicle market can be segmented into scooter and motorcycle drivers and those who can afford a vehicle with four wheels. The target market for Tata Motors' Nano microcar is two-wheeled drivers who are willing and able to upgrade to four wheels. When the Nano was launched in April 2009, Ratan Tata predicted sales of 20,000 vehicles per month.
- American car buyers can be segmented by age. Toyota's Scion (now discontinued) was targeted at Generation Y—twenty-somethings who were buying their first car.

If the decision is made to proceed, an appropriate targeting strategy must be developed. The three basic categories of target marketing strategies are standardized marketing, concentrated marketing, and differentiated marketing.

Standardized Global Marketing

Standardized global marketing is analogous to mass marketing in a single country. It involves creating the same marketing mix for a broad mass market of potential buyers. Standardized global marketing, also known as *undifferentiated target marketing*, is based on the premise that a mass market exists around the world. In addition, that mass market is served with a marketing mix of standardized elements. Product adaptation is minimized, and a strategy of intensive distribution

TABLE 7-7 2012 Product–Market Grid for Lexus, Selected Country Markets

Country Segment	Lexus Brand										
	IS	RX	CT	LS	GS	IS C	IS F	LX	ES	LFA	HS
Asia											
China	X	X	X	X	X	X		X	X	X	
Hong Kong	X	X	X	X	X	X				X	
Taiwan	X	X	X	X	X	X	X	X	X		
India											
North America											
Canada	X	X	X	X	X	X	X	X	X	X	X
United States	X	X	X	X	X	X	X	X	X	X	X
Latin America											
Brazil	X			X					X		
Europe											
Austria	X	X	X	X	X	X	X				
Belgium	X	X	X	X	X	X	X				
Denmark	X	X	X		X						
Finland	X	X	X	X	X	X	X				
France	X	X	X	X	X	X	X			X	
Germany	X	X	X	X	X	X	X			X	
Great Britain	X	X	X	X	X	X	X			X	
Greece	X	X	X		X						
Ireland	X	X	X	X		X	X				
Netherlands	X	X	X	X	X	X	X				
Portugal	X	X	X		X	X	X				
Russia	X	X	X	X	X	X	X	X	X		
Sweden	X	X	X	X	X	X	X				
Switzerland	X	X	X	X	X	X	X				
Middle East											
Israel	X	X	X	X	X	X					
United Arab Emirates	X	X	X	X	X	X	X	X	X	X	
Kuwait	X	X	X	X	X	X	X	X	X	X	
Saudi Arabia	X	X	X	X	X	X	X	X	X		

Source: Used by permission of Toyota Motor Corporation.

ensures that the product is available in the maximum number of retail outlets. The appeal of standardized global marketing is clear: lower production costs. The same is true of standardized global communications.

Concentrated Global Marketing

The second global targeting strategy, concentrated target marketing, involves devising a marketing mix to reach a **niche**. A niche is simply a single segment of the global market. In cosmetics, Estée Lauder, Chanel, and other cosmetics marketers have used this approach successfully to target the upscale, prestige segment of the market. As Leonard Lauder remarked recently, "The founders, who were my parents, had two very simple ideas: product quality and narrow distribution to high-end retailers. We never went mass."[44]

Concentrated targeting is also the strategy employed by the hidden champions of global marketing: companies unknown to most people that have succeeded by serving a niche market that exists in many countries. These companies define their markets narrowly and strive for global depth rather than national breadth. For example, Germany's Winterhalter is a hidden champion in the dishwasher market, but the company has never sold a dishwasher to a consumer, hospital, or school. Instead, it focuses exclusively on dishwashers and water conditioners for hotels and restaurants. As Jürgen Winterhalter noted, "The narrowing of our market definition was the most important strategic decision we ever made. It is the very foundation of our success in the past decade."[45]

Differentiated Global Marketing

The third target marketing strategy, **differentiated global marketing**, represents a more ambitious approach than concentrated target marketing. Also known as **multisegment targeting**, this approach entails targeting two or more distinct market segments with multiple marketing mix offerings. This strategy allows a company to achieve wider market coverage. For example, Danone SA, the French food products company, targets consumers in developed countries with premium brands such as Evian and Badoit mineral water and the Dannon and Activia yogurt brands. When he was Danone's CEO, Franck Riboud also focused on developing markets. In Bangladesh, Shoktidoi is an inexpensive yogurt brand sold by local women. In Senegal, Danone's offerings include 50-gram packets of Dolima drinkable yogurt that sell for 50 cents.[46] Positioning, which we discuss in the next section, is key to successful execution of this strategy (see Exhibit 7-11).

As Riboud has noted, different brands within any one of the company's multiple product lines are positioned differently. In its line of bottled waters, for example, Evian's positioning associates the brand with health and beauty—a promise of youthful looks through drinking water. Marketing communications for the Volvic brand utilize the same creative strategy, but the appeal and creative execution focus on energy through replenishing the body during or after physical exertion. The two brands don't cannibalize each other, because they're positioned as promoting different qualities.[47]

In the cosmetics industry, Unilever pursues differentiated global marketing strategies by targeting both ends of the perfume market. Unilever targets the luxury market with Calvin Klein and Elizabeth Taylor's Passion; Wind Song and Brut are its mass-market brands. Mass marketer

Exhibit 7-11 The positioning of PepsiCo's Lifewtr brand is based on the belief that "art ignites inspiration, and inspiration is as essential as water."

Source: Mike Coppola/Getty Images

Procter & Gamble, known for its Old Spice and Incognito brands, also embarked upon this strategy with its 1991 acquisition of Revlon's EuroCos, marketer of Hugo Boss for men and Laura Biagiotti's Roma perfume. In the mid-1990s, it launched a new prestige fragrance, Venezia, in the United States and several European countries. Currently, Procter & Gamble also markets Envy, Rush, and other Gucci fragrances as a licensee of the Italian fashion house.

▶ **7-5** Describe the various positioning options available to global marketers.

(7-5) Positioning

The term *positioning* is attributed to marketing gurus Al Ries and Jack Trout, who first introduced it in a 1969 article published in *Industrial Marketing* magazine. As noted at the beginning of the chapter, positioning refers to the act of differentiating a brand in customers' minds in relation to competitors in terms of attributes and benefits that the brand does and does not offer. Put differently, positioning is the process of developing strategies for "staking out turf" or "filling a slot" in the mind of target customers.[48]

Positioning is frequently used in conjunction with the segmentation variables and targeting strategies discussed previously. For example, Unilever and other consumer goods companies often engage in differentiated target marketing, offering a full range of brands within a given product category. Unilever's various detergent brands include All, Wisk, Surf, and Persil; each is positioned slightly differently. In some instances, extensions of a popular brand can also be positioned in different ways. Colgate's Total toothpaste is positioned as the brand that addresses a full range of oral health issues, including gum disease. In most parts of the world, Total is available in several formulations, including Total Advanced Clean, Total Clean Mint Paste, and Total Whitening Paste. Effective positioning differentiates each variety from the others.

In the decades since Ries and Trout first focused attention on the importance of the concept, marketers have utilized a number of general positioning strategies. These include positioning by attribute or benefit, quality and price, use or user, or competitor.[49] Recent research has identified three additional positioning strategies that are particularly useful in global marketing: global consumer culture positioning, local consumer culture positioning, and foreign consumer culture positioning.

Attribute or Benefit

A frequently used positioning strategy exploits a particular product attribute, benefit, or feature. Economy, reliability, and durability are frequently used attribute/benefit positions. Volvo automobiles are known for solid construction that offers safety in the event of a crash. By contrast, BMW is positioned as "the ultimate driving machine," a reference that signifies high performance. In the ongoing credit card wars, Visa's long-running advertising theme "It's Everywhere You Want to Be" drew attention to the benefit of worldwide merchant acceptance. In global marketing, it may be deemed important to communicate the fact that a brand is imported, an approach known as *foreign consumer culture positioning* (FCCP).

Quality and Price

A positioning strategy based on quality and price can be thought of in terms of a continuum from high fashion/quality and high price to good value (rather than "low quality") at a reasonable price. A legendary print ad campaign for Belgium's Stella Artois beer included various executions that positioned the brand at the premium end of the market. One ad juxtaposed a cap pried off a bottle of Stella with a close-up of a Steinway piano. The tagline "Reassuring expensive" was the only copy; upon close inspection of the Steinway, the reader could see that one of the keys was broken because it had been used to open the bottle! InBev, the world's biggest brewer in terms of volume, markets the Stella Artois brand. While Stella is regarded as an "everyday" beer in its local market of Belgium, the marketing team at InBev has repositioned it as a premium global brand.[50]

At the high end of the distilled spirits industry, marketers of imported vodkas such as Belvedere and Grey Goose have successfully positioned their brands as super-premium entities selling for twice the price of premium ("ordinary") vodka. Ads for several export vodka brands emphasize their national origins, demonstrating how FCCP can reinforce quality and price positioning. Marketers sometimes use the phrase "transformation advertising" to describe advertising that seeks to change the experience of buying and using a product—in other words, the product benefit—to justify a higher-price/quality position. Presumably, buying and drinking Grey Goose (from France), Belvedere (Poland), or Ketel One (the Netherlands) is a more gratifying consumption experience than buying and drinking a "bar brand" such as Popov (who knows where it's made?).

Use or User

Another positioning strategy represents how a product is used or associates the brand with a user or class of users. For example, to capitalize on the global success and high visibility of the *Lord of the Rings* trilogy, Gillette's Duracell battery unit ran print and TV ads proclaiming that when on location in remote areas of New Zealand, *Rings* director Peter Jackson and his crew used Duracell exclusively. Likewise, Max Factor makeup is positioned as "the makeup that makeup artists use." Pulsar watch associates the brand with a handsome man who is "addicted to reality TV" and enjoys reading Dostoevsky.

Competition

Implicit or explicit reference to competitors can provide the basis for an effective positioning strategy. For example, when Anita Roddick started The Body Shop International in the 1970s, she emphasized the difference between the principles pursued by "mainstream" health and beauty brands and those of her company. The Body Shop brand stands for natural ingredients, no animal testing, and recyclable containers. In addition, the company sources key ingredients via direct relationships with suppliers throughout the world; sustainable sourcing and paying suppliers fair-trade prices are integral to the brand's essence. Moreover, Roddick abandoned the conventional industry approach of promising miracles; instead, women are given realistic expectations of what health and beauty aids can accomplish.

Dove's "Campaign for Real Beauty" broke new ground by positioning the brand around a new definition of beauty. The campaign was based on research commissioned by Silvia Lagnado, Dove's global brand director. The research indicated that, worldwide, only 2 percent of women considered themselves to be beautiful. Armed with this insight, Ogilvy & Mather Worldwide's office in Dusseldorf developed the concept that was the basis of the Real Beauty campaign. To strengthen the connection between this campaign and Dove's products, Dove launched a Web community in 2008. Visitors to the site could watch "Fresh Takes," a miniseries that aired on MTV, as well as seek medical advice on skin care.[51]

Global, Foreign, and Local Consumer Culture Positioning

As noted in Chapter 4 and discussed briefly in this chapter, global consumer culture positioning is a strategy that can be used to target various segments associated with the emerging global consumer culture.[52] **Global consumer culture positioning (GCCP)** is defined as a strategy that identifies a brand as a symbol of a particular global culture or segment. It has proved to be an effective strategy for communicating with global teens, cosmopolitan elites, globe-trotting laptop warriors who consider themselves members of a "transnational commerce culture," and other groups. For example, Sony's brightly colored "My First Sony" line is positioned as *the* electronics brand for youngsters around the globe with discerning parents. Philips' current global corporate image campaign is keyed to the theme "Sense and Simplicity." Benetton uses the slogan "United Colors of Benetton" to position itself as a brand concerned with the unity of humankind. Heineken's strong brand equity around the globe can be attributed in good measure to a GCCP strategy that reinforces consumers' cosmopolitan self-images.

Certain categories of products lend themselves especially well to GCCP. High-tech and high-touch products are both associated with high levels of customer involvement and by a shared "language" among users.[53] *High-tech products* are sophisticated, technologically complex, and/or difficult to explain or understand. When shopping for them, consumers often have specialized needs or interests and rational buying motives. High-tech brands and products are frequently evaluated in terms of their performance against established, objective standards. Portable MP3 players, cell phones, personal computers, home theater audio/video components, luxury automobiles, and financial services are some of the high-tech product categories for which companies have established strong global positions. Buyers typically already possess—or wish to acquire—considerable technical information. Generally speaking, for example, computer buyers in all parts of the world are equally knowledgeable about Pentium microprocessors, 500-gigabyte

Exhibit 7-12 This Portuguese-language Bridgestone print ad underscores the point that although Bridgestone is a global company, it is a local one as well. Translation: "There is only one thing better than a Japanese tire. A Japanese tire made in Brazil. Made in Brazil with Japanese technology."
Source: Bridgestone Americas Tire Operations, LLC.

hard drives, software RAM requirements, and high-resolution flat-panel displays. High-tech global consumer positioning also works well for special-interest products associated with leisure or recreation. Fuji bicycles, Adidas sports equipment, and Canon cameras are examples of successful global special-interest products. Because most people who buy and use high-tech products "speak the same language" and share the same mind-set, marketing communications should be informative and emphasize performance-related attributes and features to establish the desired GCCP (see Exhibit 7-12).

By contrast, when shopping for *high-touch products*, consumers are generally energized by emotional motives rather than rational ones. Consumers may feel an emotional or spiritual connection with high-touch products, the performance of which is evaluated in subjective, aesthetic terms rather than objective, technical terms. Acquisition of high-touch products may represent an act of personal indulgence, reflect the user's actual or ideal self-image, or reinforce interpersonal relationships between the user and family members or friends. High-touch products appeal to the senses more than the intellect; if a product comes with a detailed user's manual, it's probably high tech rather than high touch.

Luxury perfume, designer fashions, and fine champagne are all examples of high-touch products that lend themselves to GCCP. Some high-touch products are linked with the joy or pleasure found in "life's little moments." Ads that show friends chatting over a cup of coffee in a café or someone's kitchen put the product at the center of everyday life. As Nestlé has convincingly demonstrated with its Nescafé brand, this type of high-touch, emotional appeal is understood worldwide.

> "Chinese companies are certainly growing but they haven't yet acquired the skills that make their Western peers so successful in 'high tech and high touch' industries."[54]
>
> Pankaj Ghemwat, Professor of Global Strategy, IESE Business School, Barcelona

A brand's GCCP can be reinforced by the careful selection of the thematic, verbal, or visual components that are incorporated into advertising and other communications. For marketers seeking to establish a high-touch GCCP, leisure, romance, and materialism are three themes that cross borders well. For high-tech products such as global financial services, professionalism and experience are advertising themes that work well. In the early 1990s, for example, Chase Manhattan bank launched a $75 million global advertising campaign geared to the theme "Profit from experience." According to Aubrey Hawes, a vice president and corporate director of marketing for the bank, Chase's business and private banking clients "span the globe and travel the globe. They can only know one Chase in their minds, so why should we try to confuse them?"[55] Presumably, Chase's target audience is sophisticated enough to appreciate the subtlety of the copywriter's craft—"profit" can be interpreted as either a noun ("monetary gain") or a verb ("reap an advantage").

In some instances, products may be positioned globally in a "bipolar" fashion as both high tech and high touch. This approach can be used when products satisfy buyers' rational criteria while evoking an emotional response. For example, audio/video components from Denmark's Bang & Olufsen (B&O), by virtue of their performance and elegant styling, are perceived as both

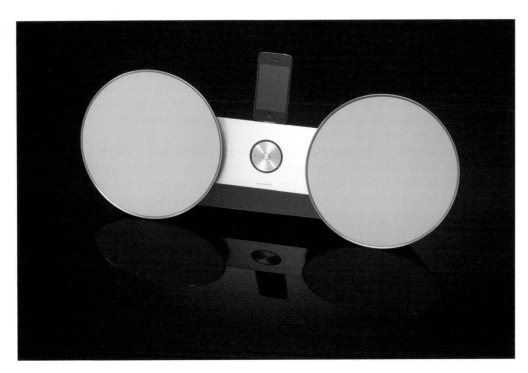

Exhibit 7-13 Renowned worldwide for Danish craftsmanship and innovation, Bang & Olufsen is a textbook example of high-touch, high-tech global brand positioning. At left is Bang & Olufsen's BeoPlay A8 speaker dock. One reviewer called it "a truly exceptional product . . . the coolest and most 'now' product B&O has made for years."
Source: David Caudery/Tap Magazine via Getty Images.

high tech (i.e., advanced engineering and sonically superior) and high touch (i.e., sleek, modern design; see Exhibit 7-13). As former CEO Torben Ballegaard Sørensen explained, "Our brand is about feeling good at home, or where you feel at home—in a car or in a hotel. When daily life is cluttered, you can come home to a system that works and is tranquil. It cocoons you."[56]

Apple became the world's most valuable tech company by combining state-of-the-art technical performance with a fashion orientation that allows users to view their iPods, iPhones, and Apple Watches as extensions of themselves. Apple positions its products on the basis of both performance and design (writing in the *Financial Times*, a reviewer called the iPod "an all-time design classic"). Positioning itself as a luxury brand with the 2015 launch of its watch, Apple segmented the market by offering three pricing tiers: the $349 Sport model; a mid-tier model with a stainless steel case; and an Edition model priced at $10,000. Similarly, in 2017, Apple launched the iPhone 8 ($699), the iPhone 8 Plus ($799), and the iPhone X ($999).

To the extent that English is the primary language of international business, mass media, and the Internet, one can make the case that English signifies modernism and a cosmopolitan outlook. Therefore, the use of English in advertising and labeling throughout the world is another way to achieve GCCP. Benetton's tagline "United Colors of Benetton" appears in English in all of the company's advertising. The implication is that fashion-minded consumers everywhere in the world shop at Benetton. English is often used as a marketing tool in Japan. Even though a native English speaker would doubtless find the syntax to be muddled, it is the symbolism associated with the use of English that counts, rather than the specific meanings that the words might (or might not) convey.

Another way to reinforce a GCCP is to use brand symbols whose interpretation defies association with a specific country culture. Examples include Nestlé's "little nest" logo with an adult bird feeding its babies, the Nike swoosh, and the Mercedes-Benz star.

The marketing strategy known as **foreign consumer culture positioning (FCCP)** associates the brand's users, use occasions, or production origins with a foreign country or culture. A long-running campaign for Foster's Brewing Group's U.S. advertising proudly trumpeted the brand's national origin; print ads featured the tagline "Foster's. Australian for beer," while TV and radio spots were keyed to the theme "How to speak Australian." Needless to say, these ads were not used in Australia itself! Advertising for Constellation Brands' Modelo brand is identified more generally with Latin America. The "American-ness" of Levi jeans, Marlboro cigarettes, American Apparel clothing, and Harley-Davidson motorcycles—sometimes conveyed with subtlety, sometimes not—enhances their brands' appeal to cosmopolitans around the world and offers opportunities for FCCP.

IKEA, the home furnishings retailer based in Sweden, wraps itself in the Swedish flag—literally. Inside and out, IKEA's stores are decorated in the national colors of blue and yellow. To reinforce the chain's Scandinavian heritage—and to encourage shoppers to linger—many stores feature cafeterias in which Swedish meatballs and other foods are served! Sometimes, brand names suggest an FCCP, even though a product is of local origin. For example, the name "Häagen-Dazs" was made up to imply a Scandinavian origin for the product, even though an American company launched the ice cream. Conversely, a popular chewing gum in Italy marketed by Perfetti bears the brand name "Brooklyn."

Marketers can also utilize **local consumer culture positioning (LCCP)**, a strategy that associates the brand with local cultural meanings, reflects the local culture's norms, portrays the brand as consumed by local people in the national culture, or depicts the product as locally produced for local consumers. An LCCP approach can be seen in Budweiser's U.S. advertising; ads featuring the iconic Clydesdale horses, for example, associate the brand with small-town American culture. Researchers studying television advertising in seven countries found that LCCP predominated, particularly in ads for food, personal nondurables, and household nondurables.

Summary

The global environment must be analyzed before a company pursues expansion into new geographic markets. Through *global market segmentation*, a company can identify and group customers or countries according to common needs and wants. *Demographic segmentation* can be based on country income and population, age, ethnicity, or other variables. *Psychographic segmentation* groups people according to attitudes, interests, opinions, and lifestyles. *Behavior segmentation* utilizes *user status* and *usage rate* as segmentation variables. *Benefit segmentation* is based on the benefits buyers seek. *Global teens* and *global elites* are two examples of global market segments.

After marketers have identified segments, the next step is *targeting*: The identified groups are evaluated and compared, and one or more segments with the greatest potential are selected. The groups are then evaluated on the basis of several factors, including segment size and growth potential, competition, and compatibility and feasibility. Target market assessment also entails a thorough understanding of the *product market* in question and determining *marketing model drivers* and *enabling conditions* in the countries under study. The timing of market entry should take into account whether a *first-mover advantage* is likely to be gained. After evaluating the identified segments, marketers must decide on an appropriate targeting strategy. The three basic categories of global target marketing strategies are *standardized global marketing*, *niche marketing*, and *multisegment targeting*.

Positioning a product or brand to differentiate it in the minds of target customers can be accomplished in various ways: *positioning by attribute or benefit*, *positioning by quality/price*, *positioning by use or user*, and *positioning by competition*. Global consumer culture positioning (*GCCP*), *foreign consumer culture positioning* (*FCCP*), and *local consumer culture positioning* (*LCCP*) are additional strategic options in global marketing.

Discussion Questions

7-1. During the World Economic Forum's Global Agenda Council on Ageing in 2015, Arnaud Bernaert, the head of Global Health and Healthcare Industries, called on businesses to target people of ages 60 and over. Describe how the automobile, telecommunications, and real estate companies have transformed some of their products or services in targeting the elderly market.

7-2. Describe the various forms of behavioral segmentation and describe the emergence of the global teens and global elites' segments.

7-3. Explain the marketing basis of psychographic segmentation.

7-4. What is positioning? Identify the different positioning strategies presented in the chapter, and give examples of companies or products that illustrate each.

7-5. Two closely related positioning strategies are the country-of-origin positioning strategy and consumer culture positioning strategy. What are these strategies, and how do they differ?

CASE 7-1 *Continued (refer to page 236)*

Segmenting the Chinese Luxury Goods Market

Diego Della Valle, chief executive of Italian luxury goods marketer Tod's, has witnessed firsthand the luxury sector's explosive growth in China. In a recent interview, Della Valle noted that China has upended traditional models of the way luxury markets evolve. In the "waterfall" or "cascade" model, a luxury brand's reputation would mature over the course of many years. The reason is simple: Elite, wealthy customers would be the first to purchase high-quality, high-end brands. The middle class would aspire to own those same brands, but only at a later time would they acquire them. In a similar manner, lower-income consumers would aspire to the luxury goods that the middle class had acquired; later, some in the lower-income tier would be able to buy select luxury brands.

Today, Della Valle notes, huge numbers of Chinese consumers are simultaneously demanding luxury goods. The challenge is to maintain an image of exclusivity in the face of exploding popularity. Tod's and other luxury goods marketers are working hard to understand the Chinese luxury consumer. One thing the marketers have discovered is that the millions of newly wealthy Chinese consumers can be divided into several segments: the super-elite, the newly rich, and government officials.

Super-Elite

The first segment, the "super-elite" or "extremely rich," consists of individuals who seized entrepreneurial opportunities in the 1980s when Beijing instituted economic reform policies and began to open China's market. A typical member of this segment is educated, influential, and well respected in Chinese society. These individuals started businesses and now, decades later, number among China's economic elite.

For example, 61-year-old Jianlin Wang has a net worth of more than $15 billion. He is chairman of the Dalian Wanda group, which is a powerful force in Chinese real estate. Wang is the richest man in China, and ranked No. 56 in *Forbes* magazine's 2014 rankings of the world's billionaires. His company currently operates dozens of shopping centers, and is developing plans for a new theme park. Yan Jiehe is another member of the super-elite; a former high school teacher, he rose to prominence by restructuring some of China's poor-performing state-owned enterprises. Pacific Construction Group, the company he founded, is China's largest privately owned construction company.

Newly Rich

The second segment, the "newly rich," consists of Chinese whose wealth, like that of the super-elite, dates back only one generation. In contrast to the super-elite, however, the newly rich typically grew up in rural areas and do not have college educations. While in their 20s, some members of this group moved to large cities seeking new opportunities. Largely self-taught, this group improved their skills by reading and immersing themselves in self-study. After joining the urban workforce, they climbed the corporate ladder and ultimately rose to leadership positions. Not as affluent as the super-elite, this segment spends selectively as well as splurges.

A variation on the newly rich were those Chinese who exhibited little desire to move to the city. Instead, they stayed in the provinces, where they exploited the local natural resources and thereby accumulated wealth on a par with the super-elite. The term *méi laoban* ("coal boss" or "coal baron") was coined to describe rich mine owners from Shanxi Province, where abundant coal reserves are found.

Despite—or because of—their humble origins, members of this group sometimes engage in freewheeling spending and conspicuous consumption. The term *tuhao* is a popular way for Chinese to mock this type of consumer behavior. *Tu* literally means "dirt," but in common usage it has taken on the connotation of "vulgar" or "unrefined." *Hao's* translation of "rich" is an extension of its original meaning as "bullying" or "despotic." In sum, *tuhao* is a pejorative term that roughly translates as "uncultured rich" and is sometimes applied to *méi laoban* and others with a penchant for profligate spending tied to uncouth behavior.

With these definitions in mind, imagine witnessing the following scene:

> A Chinese couple is shopping at the New York City flagship store of French luxury goods marketer Hermès. The man is a *méi laoban*, the woman his *Xiao San* (Chinese slang for the third woman in a marriage, usually a young woman seeking money from an older married man). The couple is shopping for Hermès's iconic Birkin bag, a limited-production item priced at $10,000 or more. The *Xiao San* has a Birkin on each arm, and can't decide which one she likes better. The *méi laoban* says, "Buy both, buy both, it's just another truck of coal, it's nothing."

Both types of newly rich invest heavily in their children's educations, due in large part to the fact that they themselves did not go to college. (In fact, the term "rich redneck" is sometimes applied to this segment as a put-down.) There is a sense among the newly rich that they neither command the respect nor have the influence of the super-elite. Anxious for their children to earn respect, parents in the newly rich segment aspire to send their children abroad to attend college.

In 2017, there were 350,755 Chinese students enrolled in U.S. educational programs, including secondary schools, undergraduate studies, and graduate school. Chinese students represent one-third of the total international student population in the United States, and their numbers have tripled over the past decade. The most popular programs for these students are STEM ("science, technology, engineering, mathematics") and business administration and marketing. The University of Southern California is currently the number 1 destination for students from China. India, South Korea, Saudi Arabia, and Canada also send tens of thousands of students to the United States each year.

Government Officials

The third luxury subsegment consists of government officials, ranging from senior officials ("tigers") to petty bureaucrats ("flies"). Gift-giving is deeply embedded in 5,000 years of Chinese culture and history. Historically, there is a sales spike in demand for luxury goods each March, when thousands of Communist Party delegates converge on Beijing for annual meetings. Lower-level officials seek favor with superiors by giving Hermès scarves, handbags from Louis Vuitton or Gucci, or Montblanc pens. Overall, government officials account for an estimated 50 percent of luxury goods sales. Chinese businessmen seeking government contracts, business licenses, or tax breaks also buy luxury gifts for government officials. In addition, cash gifts enable the recipients to buy Swiss watches, jewelry, designer clothes, or imported sport utility vehicles.

The result of this behavior has been rampant corruption in China's bureaucracy. In recent years, President Xi Jinping has targeted this group by cracking down on lavish spending, which has dampened demand for some luxury goods. Although bribery is against the law in China, the law is not enforced consistently. To protect their customers, luxury goods companies are discreet. Managers at some stores keep special accounts and use code names for government officials. Sometimes a middleman, rather than the gift-giver, makes the purchase. For example, a private businessman might use his credit card to make the purchase. He then passes the gift off to a government official, who in turn gives it to the ultimate recipient. Thus, the purchase process is sometimes a two-person activity: One person, the gift-giver, selects the gift; the second person pays for it.

Shopping Behavior Varies by Segment

The extremely rich favor luxury brands that reflect the buyers' superior taste. For example, a Louis Vuitton handbag with its iconic monogram would be too commonplace. Instead, this customer would prefer a handbag from Bottega Veneta that offers renowned Italian craftsmanship but signals the brand identity more discreetly. The extremely rich consumer also shops for luxury goods abroad while on business trips or when vacationing. This segment was an early adopter of Apple's iPhone; even before Apple established stores on the mainland, the extremely rich purchased the phones in Hong Kong, the United States, and the United Kingdom.

The newly rich shopper, by contrast, is not as knowledgeable about luxury brands and does not seek out information about them. Coming from a frugal background, this shopper is aware that less-exclusive brands can be purchased for reasonable prices; even so, newly rich shoppers also want a reward for years of hard work. "Practical" luxury brands such as Louis Vuitton, Gucci, and Chanel are the right choice. The exception would be the *tuhao* variant of the newly rich, who would be more status conscious and more likely to make extravagant purchases.

Government officials, the third segment, must be strategic; officials can't flaunt purchases that they can't afford on their state salaries. "Accessible luxury" brands such as Coach are the ideal purchase for this group. This segment also favors group shopping trips arranged by travel agencies. The agency takes care of transportation, accommodations, and other logistical issues; the tourists get to focus on shopping. According to the Paris Tourism Office, nearly 2 million Chinese tourists visited Paris in 2016, where they spent more than €1 billion. Tour buses regularly stop at Galeries Lafayette and other popular destinations in the French capital. Overall, the average Chinese tourist on such trips spends $5,000.

Lincoln's Focus on the Chinese Market

Executives at Ford and the Lincoln Motor Company acknowledge that the Chinese market is critical for the revitalization of the Lincoln nameplate. The Lincoln Continental, out of production since 2002, was once the vehicle of choice for U.S. presidents and Hollywood stars. According to Kumar Galhotra, former group vice president for Lincoln and chief marketing officer for Ford Motor Company, focus groups in China repeatedly use the word "presidential"—for example, referring to John F. Kennedy—when describing Lincoln's heritage and image.

The latest generation of Continental was designed specifically to appeal to wealthy Chinese who can afford chauffeurs. Interior options include premium materials such as Alcantara suede. Now that Beijing has lifted the one child per family limit, some buyers are looking for a vehicle that can carry children as well as grandparents. And, with the Chinese government restricting the number of cars on the road in an effort to reduce pollution, the decision a first-time luxury car buyer makes becomes critical.

Galhotra notes that managers at Lincoln's Chinese dealerships are always on the lookout for ways to enhance the customer experience and build relationships with buyers. One observation: The name of Lincoln's top-of-the-line SUV, the MKX, is hard for Chinese speakers to pronounce. Therefore, starting in 2019, the name will be the Lincoln Nautilus. The localization approach is clearly working: Lincoln's sales in China increased from 32,558 in 2016 to almost 50,000 in 2017.

Discussion Questions

7-6. Compare and contrast the various segments of Chinese luxury consumers and customers profiled in the case.

7-7. How have luxury goods brands responded to President Xi Jinping's crackdown on corruption?

7-8. Why do so many Chinese parents want their children to study at foreign universities?

7-9. Assess the prospects for success for the Lincoln Motor Company's entry in the China market.

Sources: Phoebe Wall Howard, "Lincoln's Leader in China Adapts to Selling Luxury SUVs," *USA Today* (December 15, 2017), p. 6B; Brook Larmer, "The New Kids," *The New York Times Magazine* (February 5, 2017), pp. 40–45; Brian Groom, "Fears over Loss of Billions from Overseas Students," *Financial Times—FT Special Report: Destination North of England* (April 15, 2016), p. 2; Te-Ping Chen, "China Curbs Elite Programs Aimed at Overseas Study," *The Wall Street Journal* (December 21, 2015), p. A19; Bill Vlasic, "Chinese Tastes and American Heritage Inspire New Continental," *The New York Times* (March 30, 2015), p. B2; Laurie Burkitt and Alyssa Abkowitz, "Corruption Crackdown a Boon for Lingerie," *The Wall Street Journal* (February 14–15, 2015), p. B4; Scott Cendrowski, "China's Baddest Billionaire Builder," *Fortune* (July 7, 2014), pp. 105–114; Joseph B. White and Mike Ramsey, "Ford's China Beachhead for Lincoln," *The Wall Street Journal* (April 18, 2014), p. B6; David Gelles, "Bringing Luxury, Fast, to China's Cities," *The New York Times* (September 11, 2014), pp. B1, B8; Amy Qin, "Yet Another Way to Mock China's Rich," *The New York Times* (October 15, 2013), p. 14; Tim Higgins, "Chinese Students Major in Luxury Cars," *Bloomberg Businessweek* (December 23, 2013), pp. 23–25; David Barboza, "For Bribing Officials, Chinese Give the Best," *The New York Times* (March 14, 2009), p. A4.

CASE 7-2
The "Bubbling" Tea Market

Tea has been in the limelight recently thanks to increasing global demand, especially in emerging economies like China and India. China, India, Kenya, and Sri Lanka are some of the largest producers of tea in the world. An popular beverage among all socio-economic classes, tea is also popular in other Asia-Pacific countries like Thailand, Japan, Singapore, Hong Kong, and Australia. In most of these markets, offering tea to welcome guests is part of cultural hospitality.

Tea is regarded as the second most-consumed liquid after water. The global increase in tea consumption can be attributed to the health and wellbeing benefits commonly associated with the beverage and its popularity as a lifestyle product. Other factors include growing tea-consuming populations, an increase in disposable income, lifestyle changes, the growing size of the food and beverage industry, a new variety of flavors, innovations in packaging, and industrialization. Tea has also become a specialty beverage due to a global culture of tea cafés and tea houses, which has also encouraged restaurants to add more tea options to their menus. This has propelled tea into the luxury segment, with companies like Singapore-based TWG Tea converting the high-end teahouse concept into a $120 million business and expanding their business operations to Europe.

According to statista.com, the global tea market is expected to record significant growth. In 2017, the estimated worth of the global tea market was $49.46 billion, and it is expected to reach $73.13 billion by 2024, growing at a compounded annual growth rate (CAGR) of 4.5 percent between 2018 and 2024.

In terms of revenue, the Asia-Pacific region is expected to lead the global tea market. However, a rising preference for tea has been exhibited in North America as well, where consumer preferences are shifting from carbonated drinks to healthier options. The Middle East and Africa region is forecasted to show significant growth between 2017 and 2023. The European tea market is also expected to exhibit impressive growth, with demand primarily driven by the premium tea segment and a variety of flavors catering to the preferences of those with more disposable income.

Mint tea is in high demand in North Africa, while black tea is more popular in the Middle East region. China is the largest tea producer (worth approximately $11.33 billion) and has an annual consumption of about 0.57 kg per person. The largest number of tea consumers are in Turkey, Ireland, the United Kingdom, Russia, and Morocco: the Turks consume an average of 3.16 kg per person per year; the Irish, 2.19 kg; and the British, 1.94 kg.

The global tea market is competitive, and a number of large companies operate in the industry. Big players in the market include Tata Global Beverages, Kusmi Tea, Davids Tea, and Unilever, but the many small- and medium-sized suppliers constitute a large portion of the market. The tea market can be segmented in many ways: packaging, users, distribution, and type. There are several different kinds of tea packaging, including loose tea, paper bags, aluminum tins, tea bags, and plastic boxes. Of these, the tea bag segment was the fastest growing in 2017 and enjoyed a considerable market share. The typical channels through which tea is sold include hypermarkets, supermarkets, specialty stores, convenience stores, online channels, and other channels. For tea products, traditional retail channels—supermarkets and hypermarkets—are the most popular. Based on types of users, the tea market can be divided into household and commercial segments. The commercial segment is anticipated to grow rapidly owing to

increasing industrialization, a rising number of hotels and restaurants, and increasing penetration of specialty tea cafés. Geographically, the tea market is analyzed across North America, Europe, Asia-Pacific, and LAMEA (the Latin America, Middle East, and Africa region).

Based on the type of tea, the market can broadly be classified into black, green, oolong, and herbal (or fruit). Of the total tea production in the world, the majority produced is black tea, at 60 percent, followed by green, at 30 percent. In terms of revenue, the black tea segment accounted for the largest market share in 2017, mainly because of its high production and continuous developments within the category. However, the green tea segment is anticipated to grow at the highest rate between 2018 and 2023 owing to its increasing adoption across the world. The increasing popularity of green tea is based on its supposed health benefits, such as a boosted immune system and weight loss. Asia-Pacific shows the highest growth rate for green tea, followed by North America.

In the sub-segment of flavored tea, bubble tea, also known as pearl tea, boba tea, and tapioca tea, has become very popular around the world over the last two decades. Created in the 1980s by Liu Han-Chieh Hien at her Chun Shui Tang teahouse in Taichung, Taiwan, bubble tea is a fun and interesting drink that uses some traditional and some very non-traditional tea ingredients, including its signature chewy tapioca balls. The main drivers of the bubble tea segment are its cost-effective pricing and alleged health benefits, though critics are quick to note that it contains preservatives, food coloring, and a high amount of sugar. Typically, it uses black or oolong tea, milk, fruit flavors, a sweetener, and a chewy Taiwanese cuisine ingredient called QQ, which become the tapioca balls in the tea. The tea is freshly made with milk and sugar and then shaken with ice in a cocktail shaker, creating the bubbly froth that gives the tea its name. In 2016, the global bubble tea market was estimated to be $1.957 billion and was projected to reach $3.214 billion by 2023, with a CAGR of 7.4 percent between 2017 and 2023.

To keep up with this growth and to target a wider customer base, the bubble tea industry spends more on developing new flavors and creating more varieties. The aim is to enhance and differentiate the bubble tea–drinking experience and appeal to different tastes. Countries like China and India show a lot of potential for growth of the bubble tea markets. Looking at the huge opportunity in India, Malaysian bubble tea company Tealive announced its collaboration with one of India's leading franchise development companies, World Iconic Brands Hospitality Pvt. Ltd. (WIB), in 2018. WIB was given franchisee rights to open 140 stores in the New Delhi, Mumbai, and Bengaluru between 2018 and 2023. Tealive believes that India, which is primarily a tea-loving nation, is ready for more creative and modern tea-drinking experiences. Along with the international brands, local Indian brands are also entering the bubble tea segment.

An example of the successful international expansion of bubble tea comes from the Taiwanese bubble tea brand Coco Fresh Tea & Juice, which is now one of the leading bubble tea brands in the world. Coco was founded by Tommy Hung in 1997 in Taipei, Taiwan, and has since rapidly entered international markets through the franchising model. Today, it has more than 2,500 store locations in China, Hong Kong, the United States, Thailand, Indonesia, Philippines, South Africa, South Korea, and Canada. Although bubble tea is their best-selling item, they also sell fresh tea, milk tea, fruit tea, yogurt drinks, coffee, and other beverages. To ensure more consistency in its brand image, CoCo supports its franchisees around the world through professional training programs, innovative products, evaluation systems, and its experienced management team. CoCo believes that the brand must continuously innovate and update itself to maintain its success and build a sustainable, profitable business.

Exhibit 7-14 The tea industry continues to grow in developed as well as developing markets, expanding into new segments like bubble tea.
Source: mama_mia/Shutterstock.

The growth in the overall tea market will continue to be fueled by changing demographics and lifestyles around the world. In developed markets, where increasing sales volume is more difficult, premiumization will contribute to value growth in the industry. In developing markets, a mix of factors like population growth, income levels, affordability, and lifestyle changes will continue to drive growth. As the middle class grows and greater urbanization takes place in emerging markets, adoption of different types of tea will continue, boosting consumption in the overall tea market. The popularity of tea houses and cafes, new formats and flavors of tea, convenience, availability, and versatility have changed the tea-drinking experience. Making tea more "special" and a more premium product creates room for more brands with different propositions to be created. As more and more differentiation takes place within the tea market segment, targeting, positioning, and the marketing mix will become more important.

Discussion Questions

7-10. Consider the different tea markets around the world. What are the main growth drivers of the global tea industry?

7-11. Discuss the segmentation of the global tea industry. With more tea products and varieties being introduced, do you think the sales growth of the industry will be sustainable?

7-12. The coffee industry has big brands like Starbucks, Tim Hortons, Nescafé, and Second Cup. How important is branding and positioning for the tea industry?

7-13. Do you think the bubble tea segment will continue to grow? What can international brands like Coco and Tealive do to strength their global positions?

Sources: "The Basics to Successfully Marketing Your Bubble Tea Shop," Bossen (October 31, 2017), https://www.bossenstore.com/blogs/blog/the-basics-to-successfully-marketing-your-bubble-tea-shop; R. Trieu, "Three Taiwanese Bubble Tea Chains Race to California," stenoodie (August 24, 2017), https://stenoodie.com/tag/worlds-largest-bubble-tea-brand/; Allied Market Research, "Global Bubble Tea Market Expected to Reach $3,214 Million by 2023—Allied Market Research," Ciston PR Newsire (April 13, 2018), https://www.prnewswire.com/news-releases/global-bubble-tea-market-expected-to-reach-3214-million-by-2023---allied-market-research-679632513.html; J. John, "Global Tea Market Will Reach USD 49,456.52 Million by 2024," Zion Market Research (August 08, 2018), https://globenewswire.com/news-release/2018/08/08/1549020/0/en/Global-Tea-Market-Will-Reach-USD-49-456-52-Million-by-2024-Zion-Market-Research.html; Nusra, "How Bubble Tea Market in India Is Likely To Become Bigger," Franchise Holding India, Limited IN (May 5, 2018), https://www.franchiseindia.com/restaurant/How-Bubble-Tea-Market-in-India-is-Likely-to-Become-Bigger.11026; Allied Market Research, "Tea Market Size, Share, Trends and Industry Analysis—2023," https://www.alliedmarketresearch.com/tea-market; Credence Research website, https://www.credenceresearch.com/industry/automotive-and-transportation-market; Lindsey Goodwin, "Explore the Various Types of Bubble Tea," *The Spruce Eats*, May 9, 2019, https://www.thespruceeats.com/types-of-bubble-tea-766451; CoCo Fresh Tea & Juice, "About CoCo," http://en.coco-tea.com/our-brand.

Notes

[1] Salah S. Hassan and Lea Prevel Katsanis, "Identification of Global Consumer Segments: A Behavioral Framework," *Journal of International Consumer Marketing* 3, no. 2 (1991), p. 17.

[2] John K. Ryans, Jr., "Is It Too Soon to Put a Tiger in Every Tank?" *Columbia Journal of World Business* (March–April 1969), p. 73.

[3] Arther C. Fatt, "The Danger of 'Local' International Advertising," *Journal of Marketing* 31, no. 1 (January 1967), pp. 60–62.

[4] Charles Forelle, "Schick Puts a Nick in Gillette's Razor Cycle," *The Wall Street Journal* (October 3, 2003), p. B7.

[5] Magz Osborne, "Second Chance in Japan," *Ad Age Global* 1, no. 9 (May 2001), p. 28.

[6] John Micklethwait and Adrian Wooldridge, *A Future Perfect: The Challenge and Hidden Promise of Globalization* (New York, NY: Crown Publishers, 2000), p. 198.

[7] Neil Buckley, "Domino's Returns to Fast Food's Fast Lane," *Financial Times* (November 26, 2003), p. 10.

[8] A. Coskun Samli, *International Consumer Behavior* (Westport, CT: Quorum, 1995), p. 130.

[9] Robert Frank, "When World Cup Soccer Starts, World-Wide Productivity Stalls," *The Wall Street Journal* (June 12, 1998), pp. B1, B2; Daniela Deane, "Their Cup Runneth Over: Ethnic Americans Going Soccer Crazy," *USA Today* (July 2, 1998), p. 13A.

[10] Saritha Rai, "Tastes of India in U.S. Wrappers," *The New York Times* (April 29, 2003), p. W7.

[11] "Rich Province, Poor Province," *The Economist* (October 1, 2016), p. 11.

[12] Adrian Slywotzky, *Value Migration* (Cambridge, MA: Harvard Business School Press, 1996), p. 37.

[13] Miriam Jordan, "Mall Owners Woo Hispanic Shoppers," *The Wall Street Journal* (August 14, 2013), p. C1.

[14] For a more detailed discussion, see Malcolm Gillis et al., *Economics of Development* (New York, NY: Norton, 2001), pp. 37–40.

[15] Norihiko Shirouzu, "Tailoring World's Cars to U.S. Tastes," *The Wall Street Journal* (January 1, 2001), p. B1.

[16] John Aglionby, "Tanzania's Fintech and Mobile Money Transform Business," *Financial Times* (July 13, 2016), p. 8.

[17] Harold L. Sirkin, James W. Hemerling, and Arindam K. Bhattacharya, *Globality: Competing with Everyone from Everywhere for Everything* (New York, NY: Boston Consulting Group, 2008), p. 117.

[18] Chris Prystay, "Companies Market to India's Have-Littles," *The Wall Street Journal* (June 5, 2003), p. B1.

[19] Sundeep Waslekar, "India Can Get Ahead If It Gets on a Bike," *Financial Times* (November 12, 2002), p. 15.

[20] Andrew Hill, "Multinationals Ignore India's Bottom Billion at Their Peril," *Financial Times* (October 31, 2016), p. 10.

[21] Alice Rawsthorn, "A Hipster on Jean Therapy," *Financial Times* (August 20, 1998), p. 8.

[22] Lucie Greene, "Pretty, Posh, and Profitable," *Financial Times* (May 14–15, 2011), p. 19.

[23] Hadley Malcolm, "How Nike Plans to Turn Women's Fitness into an $11 Billion Empire," *USA Today* (November 9, 2015), p. B1.

[24] John Tagliabue, "2 Sexes Separated by a Common Levi's," *The New York Times* (September 30, 2003), p. W1.

[25] John Micklethwait and Adrian Wooldridge, *Future Perfect: The Challenge and Hidden Promise of Globalization* (New York, NY: Crown Business, 2000), p. 131.

[26] Alex Taylor III, "Porsche Slices up Its Buyers," *Fortune* (January 16, 1995), p. 24.

[27] Christina Rogers, "Who's Buying 'Young' Cars? Seniors," *The Wall Street Journal* (August 14, 2013), p. B1.

[28] Helen Crossley and Yini Guo, "Reading Signals: The New Segmentation," Panel Presentation, SXSW Interactive, March 11, 2018.

[29] Sally Beatty, "At Levi Strauss, Trouble Comes from All Angles," *The Wall Street Journal* (October 13, 2003), pp. B1, B3.

[30] Tobi Elkin, "Sony Marketing Aims at Lifestyle Segments," *Advertising Age* (March 18, 2002), pp. 1, 72.

[31] John Revill, "Nestlé Seeks Foods to Treat Disease," *The Wall Street Journal* (April 13, 2016), pp. B1, B2. see also John Revill, "Nestlé Buys U.S. Maker of 'Brain Health' Shake," *The Wall Street Journal* (July 20, 2012), p. B1.

[32]Joel Millman, "Mexican Retailers Enter U.S. to Capture Latino Dollars," *The Wall Street Journal* (February 8, 2001), p. A18.

[33]Shannon Bond, "Networks Revamp Content in Hispanic Ratings War," *Financial Times* (September 18, 2017), p. 19.

[34]E.J. Schultz, "Modelo Especial Goes for Mainstream Audience with National Campaign," *Advertising Age* (March 6, 2015), p. 2.

[35]Carol Hymowitz, "Marketers Focus More on Global 'Tribes' Than on Nationalities," *The Wall Street Journal* (December 10, 2007), p. B1.

[36]Parts of the following discussion are adapted from David Arnold, *The Mirage of Global Markets* (Upper Saddle River, NJ: Pearson Education, 2004), Chapter 2.

[37]Eric Bellman, "As Economy Grows, India Goes for Designer Goods," *The Wall Street Journal* (March 27, 2007), pp. A1, A17. See also Christina Passariello, "Beauty Fix: Behind L'Oréal's Makeover in India: Going Upscale," *The Wall Street Journal* (July 13, 2007), pp. A1, A14.

[38]Alyssa Abkowitz, "The Cashless Society Has Finally Arrived—In China," *The Wall Street Journal* (January 4, 2018), pp. A1, A8.

[39]Richard Branson, *Business Stripped Bare: Adventures of a Global Entrepreneur* (London, UK: Virgin Books, 2010), p. 178.

[40]Khozem Merchant, "Sweet Rivals Find Love in a Warm Climate," *Financial Times* (July 24, 2003), p. 9.

[41]Tommaso Ebhardt, "Maserati Woos Drivers Bored with BMW," *Bloomberg Businessweek* (July 8, 2013), pp. 21–22.

[42]Christopher A. Bartlett and Sumantra Ghoshal, "Going Global: Lessons from the Late Movers," *Harvard Business Review* 78, no. 2 (March–April 2000), pp. 138–140. See also Christopher Lawton, "Aussie Wines Star at Spirits Marketer Constellation Brands," *The Wall Street Journal* (January 16, 2004), pp. B1, B4.

[43]Jathon Sapsford, "Toyota Introduces a New Luxury Brand in Japan: Lexus," *The Wall Street Journal* (August 3, 2005), pp. B1, B5.

[44]Natasha Singer, "What Would Estée Do?" *The New York Times* (March 26, 2011), p. BU 1.

[45]Hermann Simon, *Hidden Champions: Lessons from 500 of the World's Best Unknown Companies* (Boston, MA: Harvard Business School Press, 1996), p. 54.

[46]Christina Passariello, "Danone Expands Its Pantry to Woo the World's Poor," *The Wall Street Journal* (June 29, 2010), p. A1.

[47]"Think Global, Act Local," *Outlook* 3 (2003), p. 9.

[48]Al Ries and Jack Trout, *Positioning: The Battle for Your Mind* (New York, NY: Warner Books, 1982), p. 44.

[49]David A. Aaker and J. Gary Shansby, "Positioning Your Product," *Business Horizons* 25, no. 2 (May–June 1982), pp. 56–62.

[50]"Head to Head," *The Economist* (October 29, 2005), pp. 66–69.

[51]Suzanne Vranica, "Can Dove Promote a Cause and Sell Soap?" *The Wall Street Journal* (April 10, 2008), p. B6.

[52]The following discussion is adapted from Dana L. Alden, Jan-Benedict Steenkamp, and Rajeev Batra, "Brand Positioning through Advertising in Asia, North America, and Europe: The Role of Global Consumer Culture," *Journal of Marketing* 63, no. 1 (January 1999), pp. 75–87.

[53]Teresa J. Domzal and Lynette Unger, "Emerging Positioning Strategies in Global Marketing," *Journal of Consumer Marketing* 4, no. 4 (Fall 1987), pp. 26–27.

[54]Pankaj Ghemawat and Thomas M. Hout, "Softening the 'Red Edge,'" *The Wall Street Journal* (October 10, 2008), p. B4.

[55]Gary Levin, "Ads Going Global," *Advertising Age* (July 22, 1991), p. 42.

[56]John Gapper, "When High Fidelity Becomes High Fashion," *Financial Times* (December 20, 2005), p. 8.

8 Importing, Exporting, and Sourcing

LEARNING OBJECTIVES

8-1 Compare and contrast export selling and export marketing.

8-2 Identify the stages a company goes through, and the problems it is likely to encounter, as it gains experience as an exporter.

8-3 Describe the various national policies that pertain to exports and imports.

8-4 Explain the structure of the Harmonized Tariff System.

8-5 Describe the various organizations that participate in the export process.

8-6 Identify home-country export organization considerations.

8-7 Identify market-country export organization considerations.

8-8 Discuss the various payment methods that are typically used in trade financing.

8-9 Identify the factors that global marketers consider when making sourcing decisions.

CASE 8-1
East-Asian Countries: Export-Led Growth for Economic Success

Few countries have witnessed economic growth as sustained and incredible as the East-Asian countries have over the last 30 years. If the 21st century will be defined as the Asian Century, then the key to this achievement can be traced back to Japan's recipe for economic success. Soon after 1860, when the country was forced to open its borders, Japan's traditional cotton textile industry was wiped out by European goods. By 1914, however, the country was selling half of its automated cotton-spinner-produced yarn abroad, accounting for about a quarter of the global cotton yarn exports. This phenomenon represents the two competing theories of economic development in international trade: import-substitution industrialization (ISI) and export-led growth. ISI is a model of trade and economic growth where a country reduces its share of imported goods by locally producing as much as it can. In a model of export-led growth, a country specializes completely or substantially in export production. These products are usually goods in which the country enjoys comparative advantage.

Which one of these models is more suitable for assuring sustainable and balanced economic growth? This is an age-old debate. There is some factual evidence that low- and middle-income free trade countries have higher economic growth on average. This is why many governments previously advocating ISI began liberalizing trade by the mid-1980s.

Following Japan's astounding growth, the Asian Tigers adopted its trade models. China opened four special economic zones (SEZs) in 1979, and the coastal cities of Shenzhen and Zhuhai became

Exhibit 8-1 Instead of closing up their economies, several countries in East Asia adopted trade policies that promoted exports in targeted industries. After witnessing Japan's astonishing growth before and after World War II, Hong Kong, Singapore, South Korea, and Taiwan, the so-called Asian Tigers, replicated the model for trade and economic growth in the 1960s and 1970s. Since then, the Asian markets have been booming despite periods with financial instabilities, with Hong Kong leading the race.
Source: Imagemore Co., Ltd.

centers of global manufacturing for export production. China is by far the largest export economy in the world. In 2017, China exported $2.41 trillion and imported $1.54 trillion, with a positive trade balance of $873 billion.

Some economists have warned about the limitations of this model, especially during periods of general economic depressions or slumps, and the 2008–2009 global economic crisis has shown some proof of it. Exports from Asia in 2017 reached estimated $6.398 trillion in 2017. This was a 1.7 percent increase since 2013 but a 2.4 percent fall compared to 2016—not bad for a controversial model of growth! Learn more in the continuation of Case 8-1 at the end of the chapter.

This chapter provides an overview of import–export basics. We begin by explaining the difference between export selling and export marketing. Next is a survey of organizational export activities. An examination of national policies that support exports and/or discourage imports follows. After a discussion of tariff systems, we introduce key export participants. The next section provides an overview of organizational design issues as they pertain to exporting.

This is followed by a section devoted to material that can be extremely useful to undergraduates who are majoring in international business and international marketing: export financing and payment methods. For many students, that all-important first job may be in the import–export department. A familiarity with documentary credits and payment-related terminology can help you make a good impression during a job interview and, perhaps, lead to a job as an export/import coordinator. The chapter ends with a discussion of outsourcing, a topic that is becoming increasingly important as companies in many parts of the world cut costs by shifting both blue-collar and white-collar work to nations with low-wage workforces.

(8-1) Export Selling and Export Marketing: A Comparison

◀ **8-1** Compare and contrast export selling and export marketing.

To better understand importing and exporting, it is important to distinguish between **export selling** and **export marketing**. First, export selling does not involve tailoring the product, the price, or the promotional material to suit the requirements of global markets. Also, the only marketing mix element that differs is the "place"—that is, the country where the product is sold. The export selling approach may work for some products or services; for unique products with little or no international competition, such an approach is feasible. Similarly, companies new to exporting may initially experience success with selling. Even today, the managerial mind-set in many companies still favors export selling. However, as companies mature in the global marketplace or as new competitors enter the picture, export *marketing* becomes necessary.

Export marketing targets the customer in the context of the total market environment. The export marketer does not simply take the domestic product "as is" and sell it to international customers. Instead, to the export marketer, the product offered in the home market represents a starting point. This product is then modified as needed to meet the preferences of international target markets; for example, this is the approach the Chinese have adopted in the U.S. furniture market. Similarly, the export marketer sets prices to fit the marketing strategy and does not merely extend home-country pricing to the target market. Charges incurred in export preparation, transportation, and financing must be taken into account in determining prices. Finally, the export marketer adjusts strategies and plans for communication and distribution to fit the market. In other words, effective communication about product features or uses to buyers in different export markets may require creating brochures with different copy, photographs, or artwork. As the vice president of sales and marketing of one manufacturer noted, "We have to approach the international market with *marketing* literature as opposed to *sales* literature."

Export marketing is the integrated marketing of goods and services that are destined for customers in international markets. Export marketing requires:

1. An understanding of the target market environment
2. The use of marketing research and identification of market potential
3. Decisions concerning product design, pricing, distribution channels, advertising, and communications—the marketing mix

After the research effort has zeroed in on potential markets, there is no substitute for a personal visit to size up the market firsthand and begin the development of an actual export-marketing program. A market visit should accomplish several things. First, it should confirm (or contradict) assumptions and research regarding market potential. Second, the company representative should gather the additional data necessary to reach the final go or no-go decision regarding an export-marketing program. Certain kinds of information simply cannot be obtained from secondary sources. For example, an export manager or international marketing manager may have a list of potential distributors provided by the U.S. Department of Commerce. In addition, he or she may have corresponded with distributors on the list and formed some tentative idea of whether they meet the company's international criteria. Even so, it is difficult to negotiate a suitable arrangement with international distributors without actually meeting face-to-face to allow each side to appraise the capabilities and character of the other party. Third, a visit to the export market should enable the company representative to develop a marketing plan in cooperation with the local agent or distributor. This plan should cover the necessary product modifications, pricing, advertising and promotion expenditures, and a distribution plan. If the plan calls for investment, agreement on the allocation of costs must also be reached.

As shown in Exhibit 8-2, one way to visit a potential market is through a **trade show** or a state- or federally sponsored **trade mission**. Each year hundreds of trade fairs, usually organized around a product category or industry, are held in major markets. By attending these events, company representatives can conduct market assessment, develop or expand markets, find distributors or agents, or locate potential end users. Perhaps most important, attending a trade show enables company representatives to learn a great deal about competitors' technology, pricing, and depth of market penetration. For example, exhibits often offer product literature with strategically useful technological information. Overall, company managers or sales personnel should be able to get a good general impression of competitors in the marketplace as they try to sell their own company's product.

Exhibit 8-2 Milan is widely regarded as the design capitol of the world. The year 2016 marked the 55th anniversary of Salon Internazionale del Mobile di Milano ("Milan Furniture Fair"), the world's largest furniture and home furnishings trade fair. Every April, some 2,000 vendors and 300,000 visitors from more than 160 countries converge on Milan to share the latest designs. Many Italian industrial designers are recognizing the necessity of expanding outside the home market. To do that, exports will be key.
Source: Courtesy Salone del Mobile.Milano/ Photo by Andrea Mariani.

(8-2) Organizational Export Activities

◄ **8-2** Identify the stages a company goes through, and the problems it is likely to encounter, as it gains experience as an exporter.

Exporting is becoming increasingly important as companies in all parts of the world step up their efforts to supply and service markets outside their national boundaries.[1] Research has shown that exporting is essentially a developmental process that can be divided into the following distinct stages:

1. The firm is unwilling to export; it will not even fill an unsolicited export order. This may be due to perceived lack of time ("too busy to fill the order") or to apathy or ignorance.
2. The firm fills unsolicited export orders but does not pursue unsolicited orders. Such a firm is an export seller.
3. The firm explores the feasibility of exporting (this stage may bypass stage 2).
4. The firm exports to one or more markets on a trial basis.
5. The firm is an experienced exporter to one or more markets.
6. After this success, the firm pursues country- or region-focused marketing based on certain criteria (e.g., all countries where English is spoken or all countries where it is not necessary to transport by water).
7. The firm evaluates global market potential before screening for the "best" target markets to include in its marketing strategy and plan. *All* markets—domestic and international—are regarded as equally worthy of consideration.

The probability that a firm will advance from one stage to the next depends on several different factors. Moving from stage 2 to stage 3 depends on management's attitude toward the attractiveness of exporting and their confidence in the firm's ability to compete internationally. However, *commitment* is the most important aspect of a company's international orientation. Before a firm can reach stage 4, it must receive and respond to unsolicited export orders. The quality and dynamism of management are important factors that can lead to such orders. Success in stage 4 can lead a firm to stages 5 and 6. A company that reaches stage 7 is a mature, geocentric enterprise that is relating global resources to global opportunity. To reach this stage requires management with vision and commitment.

One study noted that export procedural expertise and sufficient corporate resources are required for successful exporting.[2] An interesting finding was that even the most experienced exporters express lack of confidence in their knowledge about shipping arrangements, payment procedures, and regulations. The same study also showed that, although profitability is an important expected benefit of exporting, other advantages include increased flexibility and resiliency and improved ability to deal with sales fluctuations in the home market. Although research generally supports the proposition that the probability of being an exporter increases with firm size, it is less clear whether

TABLE 8-1 Potential Export Problems

Logistics	Servicing Exports
Arranging transportation	Providing parts availability
Transport rate determination	Providing repair service
Handling documentation	Providing technical advice
Obtaining financial information	Providing warehousing
Distribution coordination	Sales promotion
Packaging	Advertising
Obtaining insurance	Sales effort
Legal procedures	Marketing information
Government red tape	Foreign market intelligence
Product liability	Locating markets
Licensing	Trade restrictions
Customs/duty	Competition overseas
Contract	
Agent/distributor agreements	

export intensity—that is, the ratio of export sales to total sales—is positively correlated with firm size. Table 8-1 lists some of the export-related problems that a company typically faces.

▶ 8-3 Describe the various national policies that pertain to exports and imports.

(8-3) National Policies Governing Exports and Imports

It is hard to overstate the impact of exporting and importing on the world's national economies. In 1997, for example, total imports of goods and services by the United States passed the $1 trillion mark for the first time; in 2017, the combined total was $2.9 trillion. European Union (EU) imports, counting both intra-EU trade and trade with non-EU partners, totaled more than $3 trillion. Trends in both exports and imports reflect China's pace-setting economic growth in the Asia-Pacific region. Exports from China have grown significantly in the years since China joined the World Trade Organization (WTO). As shown in Table 8-2, Chinese apparel exports surpass those of other countries by a wide margin. Historically, China protected its own producers by imposing double-digit import tariffs, but these tariffs have been reduced as China has sought to comply with WTO regulations.

Needless to say, representatives of the apparel, footwear, furniture, and textile industries in many countries are deeply concerned about the impact that increased trade with China will have on these sectors. As this example suggests, one word can summarize national policies toward exports and imports: contradictory. For centuries, nations have combined two opposing policy attitudes toward the movement of goods across national boundaries. On the one hand, nations directly encourage exports; on the other hand, they generally restrict the flow of imports.

Government Programs That Support Exports

To see the economic boost that can come from a government-encouraged export strategy, consider Japan, Singapore, South Korea, and the so-called Greater China or "China triangle" market, which includes Taiwan, Hong Kong, and the People's Republic of China. After recovering from the destruction of its economy during World War II, Japan became an economic superpower as a direct result of export strategies devised by the Ministry for International Trade and Industry (MITI). The four tigers—Singapore, South Korea, Taiwan, and Hong Kong—learned from the Japanese experience and built strong export-based economies of their own. Although Asia's "economic bubble" burst in 1997 as a result of uncontrolled growth, Japan and the tigers are moving forward in the twenty-first century at a more moderate rate. China, an economy unto itself, has attracted increased foreign

TABLE 8-2   Top 10 Clothing Exporters 2016 (U.S.$ billions)

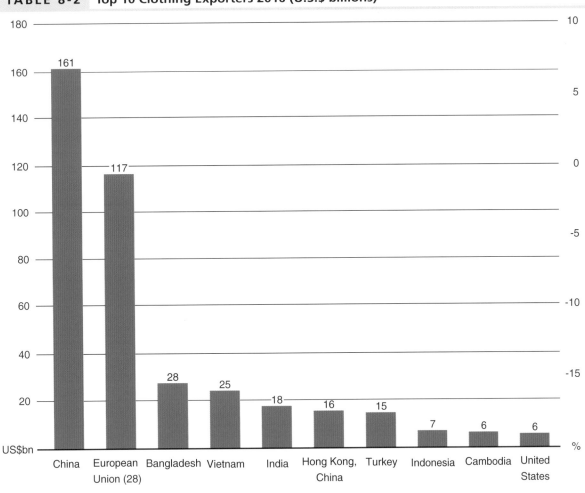

investment from Daimler AG, General Motors (GM), Hewlett-Packard, and scores of other companies that are setting up production facilities to support local sales, as well as exports to world markets.

Any government concerned with trade deficits or economic development should focus on educating firms about the potential gains from exporting. Policymakers should also remove bureaucratic obstacles that hinder company exports. This is true at the national, regional, and local government levels. In India, for example, leaders in the state of Tamil Nadu gave Hyundai permission to operate its plant around the clock, making it the first Hyundai operation anywhere in the world to operate on a 24-hour basis (see Exhibit 8-3).[3]

Exhibit 8-3 A worker finishes a K-Series engine at the Maruti Suzuki assembly line in Gurgaon, India. Maruti Suzuki is one of India's leading auto manufacturers. However, foreign investment in the automotive sector is exploding as Ford, Honda, Nissan, Toyota, and other companies rush to capitalize on growing Indian demand for passenger cars.
Source: Gurinder Osan/Associated Press.

Governments commonly use four activities to support and encourage firms that engage in exporting: tax incentives, subsidies, export assistance, and free trade zones.

Tax incentives treat earnings from export activities preferentially either by applying a lower tax rate to earnings from these activities or by refunding taxes already paid on income associated with exporting. The tax benefits offered by export-conscious governments include varying degrees of tax exemption or tax deferral on export income, accelerated depreciation of export-related assets, and generous tax treatment of overseas market development activities.

From 1985 until 2000, the major tax incentive for exporters under U.S. law was the **foreign sales corporation (FSC)**, through which American exporters could obtain a 15 percent exclusion on earnings from international sales. Big exporters benefited the most from the arrangement; Boeing, for example, saved approximately $100 million per year, and Eastman Kodak saved nearly $40 million annually. However, in 2000 the WTO ruled that any tax break that was contingent on exports amounted to an illegal subsidy. Accordingly, the U.S. Congress has set about the task of overhauling the FSC system; failure to do so would entitle the EU to impose up to $4 billion in retaliatory tariffs. Potential winners and losers from a change in the FSC law are lobbying furiously. One proposed version of a new law would benefit GM, Procter & Gamble, Walmart, and other U.S. companies with extensive manufacturing or retail operations overseas. By contrast, Boeing would no longer benefit. As Rudy de Leon, a Boeing executive in charge of government affairs, noted, "As we look at the bill, the export of U.S. commercial aircraft would become considerably more expensive."[4]

Governments also support export performance by providing outright **subsidies**, which are direct or indirect financial contributions or incentives that benefit producers. Subsidies can severely distort trade patterns when less competitive but subsidized producers displace competitive producers in world markets. Organisation for Economic Co-operation and Development (OECD) members spend nearly $400 billion annually on farm subsidies; currently, total annual farm support in the EU is estimated at $100 billion. With approximately $40 billion in annual support, the United States has the highest subsidies of any single nation. Agricultural subsidies are particularly controversial because, although they protect the interests of farmers in developed countries, they work to the detriment of farmers in developing areas such as Africa and India.

The EU has undertaken an overhaul of its **Common Agricultural Policy (CAP)**, which critics have called "as egregious a system of protection as any" and "the single most harmful piece of protectionism in the world."[5] In May 2002, much to Europe's dismay, U.S. President George W. Bush signed a $118 billion farm bill that actually *increased* subsidies to American farmers over a 6-year period. The Bush administration took the position that, despite the increases, overall U.S. subsidies were still lower than those in Europe and Japan; Congress voted to extend the farm bill for another 5 years.

Another means of supporting exporters is by extending *governmental assistance* to exporters. Companies can avail themselves of a great deal of government information concerning the location of markets and credit risks. Assistance may also be oriented toward export promotion. Government agencies at various levels often take the lead in setting up trade fairs and trade missions designed to promote sales to foreign customers.

The export–import process often entails red tape and bureaucratic delays, especially in emerging markets such as China and India. In an effort to facilitate exports, countries are designating certain areas as **free trade zones (FTZ)** or **special economic zones (SEZ)**. In geographic entities, manufacturers benefit from simplified customs procedures, operational flexibility, and a general environment of relaxed regulations.

Governmental Actions to Discourage Imports and Block Market Access

Measures such as tariffs, import controls, and a host of nontariff barriers are designed to limit the inward flow of goods. **Tariffs** can be thought of as the "three Rs" of global business: rules, rate schedules (duties), and regulations of individual countries. ("Tariff" is an ancient trading term derived from the Arabic word "ta'rif", which means "information" or "notification.")[6] Duties on individual products or services are listed in the schedule of rates (see Table 8-3). One expert on global trade defines **duties** as "taxes that punish individuals for making choices of which their governments disapprove."[7]

TABLE 8-3 Examples of Trade Barriers

Country/Region	Tariff Barriers	Nontariff Barriers
European Union	16.5% antidumping tariff on shoes from China, 10% on shoes from Vietnam	Quotas on Chinese textiles
China	Tariffs as high as 28% on foreign-made auto parts	Expensive, time-consuming procedures for obtaining pharmaceutical import licenses

As noted in earlier chapters, a major U.S. objective in the Uruguay Round of General Agreement on Tariffs and Trade (GATT) negotiations was to improve market access for U.S. companies with major U.S. trading partners. When the Uruguay Round ended in December 1993, the United States had secured reductions or total eliminations of tariffs on 11 categories of U.S. goods exported to the EU, Japan, five of the European Free Trade Association (EFTA) nations (Austria, Switzerland, Sweden, Finland, and Norway), New Zealand, South Korea, Hong Kong, and Singapore. The categories affected included equipment for the construction, agricultural, medical, and scientific industry sectors, as well as steel, beer, brown distilled spirits, pharmaceuticals, paper, pulp and printed matter, furniture, and toys. Most of the remaining tariffs were phased out over a 5-year period. A key goal of the ongoing Doha Round of WTO trade talks is the reduction in agricultural tariffs, which currently average 12 percent in the United States, 31 percent in the EU, and 51 percent in Japan.

Developed under the auspices of the Customs Cooperation Council (now the World Customs Organization), the **Harmonized Tariff System (HTS)** went into effect in January 1989 and has since been adopted by the majority of trading nations. Under this system, importers and exporters have to determine the correct classification number for a given product or service that will cross borders. With the Harmonized Tariff Schedule B, the export classification number for any exported item is the same as the import classification number. Also, exporters must include the Harmonized Tariff Schedule B number on their export documents to facilitate customs clearance. Accuracy, especially in the eyes of customs officials, is essential. The U.S. Census Bureau compiles trade statistics from the HTS system. Any HTS with a value of less than $2,500 is not counted as a U.S. export. However, *all* imports, regardless of value, are counted.

In spite of the progress made in simplifying tariff procedures, administering a tariff is an enormous burden. People who work with imports and exports must familiarize themselves with the different classifications and use them accurately. Even a tariff schedule of several thousand items cannot clearly describe every product traded globally. Plus, the introduction of new products and new materials used in manufacturing processes creates new problems. Often, determining the duty rate on a particular article requires assessing how the item is used or determining its main component material. Two or more alternative classifications may have to be considered.

A product's classification can make a substantial difference in the duty applied. For example, is a Chinese-made *X-Men* action figure a doll or a toy? For many years, dolls were subject to a 12 percent duty when imported into the United States; the rate was 6.8 percent for toys. Moreover, action figures that represent nonhuman creatures such as monsters or robots were categorized as toys and, therefore, qualified for lower duties than human figures that the Customs Service classified as dolls. Duties on both categories have been eliminated; however, the Toy Biz subsidiary of Marvel Enterprises spent nearly 6 years on an action in the U.S. Court of International Trade to prove that its *X-Men* action figures do not represent humans. Although the move appalled many fans of the mutant superheroes, Toy Biz hoped to be reimbursed for overpayment of past duties made when the U.S. Customs Service had classified imports of Wolverine and his fellow figures as dolls.[8]

One of the most controversial aspects of U.S. Donald Trump's "America First" policy was his decision to impose tariffs on imports of steel and aluminum (see Exhibit 8-4). Opponents of this policy—including trade partners and some U.S. industry leaders—argue that the tariffs will negatively impact the U.S. economy and invite retaliation from abroad.

A **nontariff barrier (NTB)** is any measure other than a tariff that is a deterrent or obstacle to the sale of products in a foreign market. Also known as *hidden trade barriers*, NTBs include quotas, discriminatory procurement policies, restrictive customs procedures, arbitrary monetary policies, and restrictive regulations.

Exhibit 8-4 President Donald Trump's decision to impose tariffs on steel and aluminum imports was hailed by some an important step toward reversing unemployment in America's Rust Belt.
Source: DAVID HECKER/EPA-EFE/ Shutterstock.

A **quota** is a government-imposed limit or restriction on the number of units or the total value of a particular product or product category that can be imported. Generally, quotas are designed to protect domestic producers. In 2005, for example, textile producers in Italy and other European countries were granted quotas on 10 categories of textile imports from China. The quotas, which were scheduled to run through the end of 2007, were designed to give European producers an opportunity to prepare for increased competition.[9]

Discriminatory procurement policies can take the form of government rules, laws, or administrative regulations requiring that goods or services be purchased from domestic companies. For example, the Buy American Act of 1933 stipulates that U.S. federal agencies and government programs must buy goods produced in the United States. The act does not apply if domestically produced goods are not available, if the cost is unreasonable, or if "buying local" would be inconsistent with the public interest. Similarly, the Fly American Act states that U.S. government employees must fly on domestic carriers whenever possible.

Customs procedures are considered restrictive if they are administered in a way that makes compliance difficult and expensive. For example, the U.S. Department of Commerce might classify a product under a certain harmonized number; Canadian customs may disagree. The U.S. exporter may have to attend a hearing with Canadian customs officials to reach an agreement. Such delays cost time and money for both the importer and the exporter.

Discriminatory exchange rate policies distort trade in much the same way as selective import duties and export subsidies. As noted earlier, some Western policymakers have argued that China is pursuing policies that ensure an artificially weak currency. Such a policy has the effect of giving Chinese goods a competitive price edge in world markets.

Finally, **restrictive administrative** and **technical regulations** can create barriers to trade. These may take the form of antidumping regulations, product size regulations, and safety and health regulations. Some of these regulations are intended to keep out foreign goods; others are directed toward legitimate domestic objectives. For example, the safety and pollution regulations being developed in the United States for automobiles are motivated almost entirely by legitimate concerns about highway safety and pollution. However, an effect of these regulations has been to make it so expensive to comply with U.S. safety requirements that some automakers have withdrawn certain models from the market. Volkswagen, for example, was forced to stop selling diesel automobiles in the United States for several years.

As discussed in earlier chapters, there is a growing trend to remove all such restrictive trade barriers on a regional basis. The largest single effort was undertaken by the EU and resulted in

ENTREPRENEURIAL LEADERSHIP, CREATIVE THINKING, AND THE GLOBAL STARTUP

Oscar Farinetti, Eataly

Oscar Farinetti is an entrepreneur. He developed an innovative retail concept, Eataly, and started a company to market it. By applying the basic tools and principles of modern global marketing, Farinetti has achieved remarkable success. As is true with many entrepreneurs, Farinetti's idea was based on a crucial insight about his native country. His hometown is Alba, the birthplace of the Slow Food movement and the source of world-famous white truffles. Farinetti also owns two wineries in the Barolo appellation, which is renowned for its red wines. Farinetti realized that Italy's two great resources, its artistic heritage and its biodiversity, represented an opportunity for innovation.

Farinetti made a fortune when he sold UniEuro, the appliance company that evolved from his family's supermarket, for €500 million. Guided by the principle that it is important to "put a little poetry" into his personal endeavors, he turned his attention from washing machines to food. This was a natural move, considering that the root of Farinetti's family name is *farina*, the Italian word for flour. A turning point for Farinetti was a visit to Istanbul's Grand Bazaar, where he was captivated by the sights, sounds, and smells.

Starting in 2007 with a single location in Turin, Italy, Farinetti now presides over a far-flung global empire of Eataly megastores that celebrate all things Italian (see Exhibit 8-5). Armed with the tagline "Italy is Eataly," Farinetti has opened more than 25 stores in major cities such as Chicago, Dubai, and New York City. In addition to the original store in Turin, there are now numerous other locations in Italy as well.

Eataly gourmet supermarkets, and the restaurants tucked inside them, are helping Italian food producers during Italy's ongoing recession. Overall, Italy's retail sector has pursued very little international expansion; by contrast, other European supermarket chains such as Tesco (United Kingdom), Metro (Germany), and Carrefour (France) took local products and brands with them as they expanded around the globe.

Some Italian food brands, such as Ferrero (Nutella) and Barilla (pasta), are well known throughout the world. However, many of Italy's food companies, which represent about 15 percent of the country's overall economy, lack the money or the managerial expertise to export. As noted in Chapter 3, Italy boasts myriad product categories that carry designations such as Denominazione Origine Controllata e Garantita (DOCG) and Denominazione Origine Protetta (DOP). Such a designation means, for example, that cheese marketed as Parmigiano-Reggiano can only be made from cow's milk from a certain part of Italy. Eataly's success has helped small-scale, artisanal wine, cheese, and prosciutto producers to reach new customers who are willing to pay premium prices for Italian quality and authenticity.

Many observers note that the "Made in Italy" movement got an additional boost from the 2015 World Expo in Milan. The theme of the Expo was "Feeding the Planet. Energy for Life." Perhaps not surprisingly, the Italian Pavilion showcased Italy's national food culture. Needless to say, Eataly was present at the 2015 Expo: Eataly Milan Smeraldo opened months before the Expo itself.

Farinetti is optimistic about Italy's future. "We need to double tourism in Italy, we can double our export of food and agriculture products, we need to open up other industries of fashion, design, industrial manufacturing. And if we manage this we will bring the country to another renaissance," he says.

Sources: Manuela Mesco, "Corporate News: Prices Pinch Prosciutto Trade," *The Wall Street Journal* (January 2, 2015), p. B3; Elisabeth Rosenthal, "The Fantasy Italy," *The New York Times Sunday Review* (August 3, 2014), p. 3; Robert Camuto, "Eataly: A Revolutionary Approach to Italian Food and Wine," *Wine Spectator* (April 30, 2013), pp. 30–33+; Rachel Sanderson, "Food: The New Frontier for Italian Luxury," *Financial Times* (December 23, 2014), p. 5; Rachel Sanderson, "Matteo Renzi's Favourite Deli Man," *Financial Times* (May 28, 2014), p. 10.

Exhibit 8-5 After analyzing the Italian food market, Oscar Farinetti realized that there were plenty of large stores with wide selections but low quality and low prices. There were also small stores with small selections but high quality and high prices. With Eataly, Farinetti offers consumers the best of both worlds: a wide selection of high-quality products with reasonable prices.
Source: Piero Oliosi/Polaris/Newscom.

THE CULTURAL CONTEXT

International Education for Chinese Students = Service Exports for Host Countries

As noted in Chapter 7, newly affluent Chinese parents invest heavily in their children's educations, due in large part to the fact that many of the parents themselves did not go to college. (In fact, the term "rich redneck" is sometimes applied to this segment as a put-down.) There is a sense among some families that they neither command the respect nor have the influence of China's super-elite. Anxious for their children to earn respect, many parents enroll them in private international schools in China, starting as early as kindergarten. Alternatively, many students take international classes at public schools. In either case, wealthy Chinese parents are under enormous social pressure to ensure that their children get an international education, starting at the K–12 level.

Of course, international education is expensive. However, since 2000, average household wealth in China has increased 600 percent. As a consequence, more Chinese parents are both willing and able to invest in their children's educations.

Many of these same parents aspire to send their children abroad to attend college (see Exhibit 8-6). Australia, Japan, Germany, the United Kingdom, and the United States are favorite destinations. In the United States alone, 350,755 Chinese students were enrolled in U.S. higher education institutions in 2017. That figure represents one-third of the total international student population in the United States and is triple the number of a decade ago. The University of Southern California is currently the number 1 destination for students from China. India, South Korea, Saudi Arabia, and Canada also send tens of thousands of students to the United States each year.

One reason that Chinese and other international students are welcome at colleges and universities around the world is that they generally pay higher tuition charges, and they frequently pay those fees in cash. Such students are viewed by educational institutions as important revenue sources, especially in the United States where declining enrollments and growing concerns about student debt are affecting many colleges and universities. In fact, in any given calendar year, international students contribute more than $35 billion to the U.S. economy. One barrier to extending financial aid to Chinese students is the absence of any mechanism to check the credit scores of the parents.

Until recently, business schools in North America and Europe offering MBA programs benefited from an influx of Chinese students. The reason was simple: Applicants perceived Western MBA programs to be superior to those available at home. Indeed, for many years, the majority of Chinese who studied abroad were graduate students. That situation is changing now, and the number of undergraduate students has surpassed the number of graduate students. One reason for this trend: A growing number of Chinese institutions have received accreditation, including the China Europe International Business School (CEIBS) in Shanghai. As a result, many Chinese students seeking graduate degrees are opting to "go local."

Meanwhile, concern is mounting that Beijing is using "soft power" to extend its influence in schools and universities by sponsoring an initiative known as the Confucius Institute. The Confucius Institute is administered by Hanban, which is affiliated with China's education ministry. With a presence in more than 140 countries, the officially stated mission of the Confucius Institute is to promote the study of the Chinese language. The initiative is welcomed on many campuses where budgets are stretched and language programs have been curtailed. However, critics say that the Confucius Institutes allow the Chinese government to present a carefully scripted picture of China today.

Sources: Bei Guo and Zhengyu Huang, "Chinese Students in America," Solo Session, SXSW Interactive, Austin, Texas (March 13, 2018); Emily Feng, "Academics Fear Spread of China's Soft Power on West's Campuses," *Financial Times* (October 30, 2017), p. 6; Joshua Chaffin, "'Tiger Mums' Look to UK's First English–Chinese Primary School," *Financial Times* (October 9, 2017), p. 3; Jonathan Moules, "WeChat Replaces Textbooks in MBA Classrooms," *Financial Times* (October 2, 2017), p. 15; Jonathan Moules, "Business Advantage Brings China's Students Home," *Financial Times* (September 25, 2017), p. 15; Brook Larmer, "The New Kids," *The New York Times Magazine* (February 5, 2017), pp. 40–45; Brian Groom, "Fears over Loss of Billions from Overseas Students," *Financial Times—FT Special Report: Destination North of England* (April 15, 2016), p. 2; Te-Ping Chen, "China Curbs Elite Programs Aimed at Overseas Study," *The Wall Street Journal* (December 21, 2015), p. A19; Te-Ping Chen and Melissa Korn, "Colleges Pay a Price for Foreign Students," *The Wall Street Journal* (October 1, 2015), pp. A1, A14.

Exhibit 8-6 Chinese students study abroad to gain a wider perspective, to find a better educational environment, and to enrich their knowledge. Many return to China after receiving their degrees. These students showed their support for President Xi Jinping during his visit to Manchester, England, in 2015.
Source: Richard Stonehouse/Getty Images.

TABLE 8-4   Sample Rates of Duty for U.S. Imports

	Column 1	Column 2
General	Special	Non-NTR
1.5%	Free (A, E, IL, J, MX)	30%
	0.4% (CA)	

A: Generalized System of Preferences
E: Caribbean Basin Initiative (CBI) Preference
IL: Israel Free Trade Agreement (FTA) Preference
J: Andean Agreement Preference
MX: North American Free Trade Agreement (NAFTA) Canada Preference
CA: NAFTA Mexico Preference

the creation of a single market starting January 1, 1993. The intent of this agreement was to have one standard for all of Europe's industry sectors, including automobile safety, drug testing and certification, and food and product quality controls. The introduction of the euro has also facilitated trade and commerce within the euro zone.

 Tariff Systems

◀ **8-4** Explain the structure of the Harmonized Tariff System.

Tariff systems provide either a single rate of duty for each item, applicable to all countries, or two or more rates, applicable to different countries or groups of countries. Tariffs are usually grouped into two classifications.

The **single-column tariff** is the simplest type of tariff: a schedule of duties in which the rate applies to imports from all countries on the same basis. Under the **two-column tariff** (see Table 8-4), column 1 includes "general" duties plus "special" duties indicating reduced rates determined by tariff negotiations with other countries. Rates agreed upon by "convention" are extended to all countries that qualify for **normal trade relations (NTR)** (formerly most-favored nation [MFN]) status within the framework of the WTO. Under the WTO, nations agree to apply their most favorable tariff or lowest tariff rate to all nations—subject to some exceptions—that are signatories to the WTO. Column 2 shows rates for countries that do not enjoy NTR status.

Table 8-5 shows a detailed entry from Chapter 89 of the Harmonized Tariff System pertaining to "Ships, Boats, and Floating Structures" (for explanatory purposes, each column has been identified with an alphabet letter). Column A contains the heading-level numbers that uniquely identify each product. For example, the product entry for heading level 8903 is "Yachts and other vessels for pleasure or sports; rowboats and canoes." Subheading level 8903.10 identifies "Inflatable"; 8903.91 designates "Sailboats with or without auxiliary motor." These six-digit numbers are used by more than 100 countries that have signed on to the HTS. Entries can extend to as many as 10 digits, with the last 4 digits used on a country-specific basis for each nation's individual tariff and data collection purposes. Taken together, columns E and F correspond to column 1 in Table 8-4, and column G corresponds to column 2 in Table 8-4.

The United States has given NTR status to some 180 countries around the world, so the name is really a misnomer. Only North Korea, Iran, Cuba, and Libya are excluded, showing that NTR is really a political tool more than an economic one. In the past, China had been threatened with the loss of NTR status because of alleged human rights violations. The landed prices of its exports—the cost after the goods have been delivered to a port, unloaded, and passed through customs—would have risen significantly had this threat been carried through. Thus, many Chinese products would have been priced out of the U.S. market. However, the U.S. Congress granted China permanent NTR as a precursor to its joining the WTO in 2001. Table 8-6 illustrates what a loss of NTR status would have meant to China.

A **preferential tariff** is a reduced tariff rate applied to imports from certain countries. GATT prohibits the use of preferential tariffs, with three major exceptions. First are historical preference arrangements such as the British Commonwealth preferences and similar arrangements that existed before GATT. Second, preference schemes that are part of a formal economic integration

TABLE 8-5   Chapter 89 of the Harmonized Tariff System

A	B	C	D	E	F	G
8903		Yachts and other vessels for pleasure or sports; rowboats and canoes				
8903.10.00		Inflatable		2.4%	Free	
					(A, E, IL, J, MX)	
					0.4% (CA)	
		Valued over $500				
	15	With attached rigid hull	No			
	45	Other	No			
	60	Other	No			
8903.91.00		Other:		1.5%	Free	
		Sailboats, with or without auxiliary motors			(A, E, IL, J, MX)	
					0.3% (CA)	

A: Generalized System of Preferences
E: Caribbean Basin Initiative (CBI) Preference
IL: Israel Free Trade Agreement (FTA) Preference
J: Andean Agreement Preference
MX: North American Free Trade Agreement (NAFTA) Canada Preference
CA: NAFTA Mexico Preference

treaty, such as free trade areas or common markets, are excluded. Third, industrial countries are permitted to grant preferential market access to companies based in less-developed countries.

The United States is now a signatory to the GATT customs valuation code, and U.S. customs value law was amended in 1980 to conform to the GATT valuation standards. Under the code, the primary basis of customs valuation is "transaction value." As the term implies, *transaction value* is defined as the actual individual transaction price paid by the buyer to the seller of the goods being valued. In instances where the buyer and the seller are related parties (e.g., when Honda's U.S. manufacturing subsidiaries purchase parts from Japan), customs authorities have the right to scrutinize the transfer price to make sure it is a fair reflection of market value. If there is no established transaction value for the good, alternative methods that are used to compute the customs value sometimes result in increased values and, consequently, increased duties. In the late 1980s, the U.S. Treasury Department began a major investigation into the transfer prices charged by the Japanese automakers to their U.S. subsidiaries. It contended that the Japanese paid virtually no U.S. income taxes because of their "losses" on the millions of cars they imported into the United States each year.

During the Uruguay Round of GATT negotiations, the United States successfully sought a number of amendments to the Agreement on Customs Valuations. Most important, the United States wanted clarification of the rights and obligations of importing and exporting countries in

TABLE 8-6   Tariff Rates for China, NTR versus Non-NTR

	NTR	Non-NTR
Gold jewelry, such as plated neck chains	6.5%	80%
Screws, lock washers, misc. iron/steel parts	5.8%	35%
Steel products	0–5%	66%
Rubber footwear	0	66%
Women's overcoats	19%	35%

Source: U.S. Customs Service.

cases where fraud was suspected. Two overall categories of products were frequently targeted for investigation. The first included exports of textiles, cosmetics, and consumer durables; the second included entertainment software such as videotapes, audiotapes, and compact discs. Such amendments improve the ability of U.S. exporters to defend their interests if charged with fraudulent practices. The amendments were also designed to encourage nonsignatories, especially developing countries, to become parties to the agreement.

Customs Duties

Customs duties are divided into categories based on how they are calculated: as a percentage of the value of the goods (ad valorem duty), as a specific amount per unit (specific duty), or as a combination of both of these methods. Before World War II, specific duties were widely used and the tariffs of many countries, particularly those in Europe and Latin America, were extremely complex. During the past half-century, the trend has been toward the conversion to ad valorem duties.

As noted, an **ad valorem duty** is expressed as a percentage of the value of goods. The definition of customs value varies from country to country. An exporter is well advised to secure information about the valuation practices applied to his or her product in the country of destination, so that the exporter can price that product to be competitive with local producers. In countries adhering to GATT conventions on customs valuation, the customs value is the value of cost, insurance, and freight (CIF) at the port of importation. This figure should reflect the arm's-length price of the goods at the time the duty becomes payable.

A *specific duty* is expressed as a specific amount of currency per unit of weight, volume, length, or other unit of measurement—for example, "50 cents U.S. per pound," "$1.00 U.S. per pair," or "25 cents U.S. per square yard." Specific duties are usually expressed in the currency of the importing country, but there are exceptions, particularly in countries that have experienced sustained inflation.

Both ad valorem and specific duties are occasionally set out in the customs tariff for a given product. Usually, the applicable rate is the one that yields the higher amount of duty, although sometimes the lower amount is specified. Compound or mixed duties provide for specific, plus ad valorem, rates to be levied on the same articles.

Other Duties and Import Charges

Dumping, which is the sale of merchandise in export markets at unfair prices, is discussed in detail in Chapter 11. To offset the impact of dumping and to penalize guilty companies, most countries have introduced legislation providing for the imposition of **antidumping duties** if injury is caused to domestic producers; such duties take the form of special additional import charges equal to the dumping margin. Antidumping duties are almost invariably applied to products that are also manufactured or grown in the importing country. In the United States, antidumping duties are assessed after the U.S. Commerce Department finds a foreign company guilty of dumping and the International Trade Commission (ITC) rules that the dumped products injured American companies.

Countervailing duties (CVDs) are additional duties levied to offset subsidies granted in the exporting country. In the United States, CVD legislation and procedures are very similar to those pertaining to dumping. The U.S. Commerce Department and the ITC jointly administer both the CVD and antidumping laws under provisions of the Trade and Tariff Act of 1984. Subsidies and countervailing measures received a great deal of attention during the Uruguay Round of GATT negotiations. In 2001, the ITC and the U.S. Commerce Department imposed both countervailing and antidumping duties on Canadian lumber producers. The CVDs were intended to offset subsidies to Canadian sawmills in the form of low fees for cutting trees in forests owned by the Canadian government. The antidumping duties on imports of softwood lumber, flooring, and siding were applied in response to complaints by U.S. producers that the Canadians were exporting lumber at prices below their production cost.

Several countries, including Sweden and some other members of the EU, apply a system of **variable import levies** to certain categories of imported agricultural products. If the prices of imported products would undercut the prices of domestic products, these levies raise the price of imported products to the domestic price level. **Temporary surcharges** have also been introduced from time to time by certain countries, such as the United Kingdom and the United States, to provide additional protection for local industries and, in particular, in response to balance of payments deficits.

▶ **8-5** Describe the various organizations that participate in the export process.

(8-5) Key Export Participants

Anyone with responsibilities for exporting should be familiar with some of the entities that can assist with various export-related tasks. Some of these entities, including foreign purchasing agents, export brokers, and export merchants, have no assignment of responsibility from the client. Others, including export management companies, manufacturers' export representatives, export distributors, and freight forwarders, are formally assigned responsibilities by the exporter.

Foreign purchasing agents are variously referred to as the *buyer for export*, *export commission house*, or *export confirming house*. These agents operate on behalf of, and are compensated by, an overseas customer known as a *principal*. They generally seek out a manufacturer whose price and quality match the specifications of their principal. Foreign purchasing agents often represent governments, utilities, railroads, and other large users of materials. These agents do not offer the manufacturer or exporter a stable volume of business, except when long-term supply contracts are agreed upon. Purchases may be completed as domestic transactions, with the purchasing agent handling all export packing and shipping details, or the agent may rely on the manufacturer to handle the shipping arrangements.

The **export broker** receives a fee for bringing together the seller and the overseas buyer. Although this fee is usually paid by the seller, sometimes the buyer pays it. The broker takes no title to the goods and assumes no financial responsibility. A broker usually specializes in a specific commodity, such as grain or cotton, and is less frequently involved in the export of manufactured goods.

Export merchants are sometimes referred to as *jobbers*. These marketing intermediaries identify market opportunities in one country or region and make purchases in other countries to fill these needs. An export merchant typically buys unbranded products directly from the producer or manufacturer, then brands the goods and performs all other marketing activities for them, including distribution. For example, an export merchant might identify a good source of women's boots in a factory in China. The merchant might then purchase a large quantity of the boots and market them in, for example, the EU or the United States.

An **export management company (EMC)** is an independent marketing intermediary that acts as the export department for two or more manufacturers (principals) whose product lines do not compete with each other. Although the EMC usually operates in the name of its principals for export markets, it may also operate in its own name. This company may act as an independent distributor, purchasing and reselling goods at an established price or profit margin. Alternatively, it may act as a commissioned representative, taking no title and bearing no financial risks in the sale. According to one survey of U.S.-based EMCs, the most important activities for export success are gathering marketing information, communicating with markets, setting prices, and ensuring parts availability. The same survey ranked export activities in terms of degree of difficulty; analyzing political risk, sales force management, setting pricing, and obtaining financial information were found to be the most difficult to accomplish. One of the study's conclusions was that the U.S. government should do a better job of helping EMCs and their clients analyze the political risk associated with foreign markets.[10]

Another type of intermediary is the **manufacturer's export agent (MEA)**. Much like an EMC, the MEA can act as an export distributor or as an export commission representative. However, the MEA does not perform the functions of an export department, and the scope of its market activities is usually limited to a few countries.

An **export distributor** does assume financial risk as part of the export process. Because this party usually represents several manufacturers, it is sometimes known as a *combination export manager*. The export distributor usually has the exclusive right to sell a manufacturer's products in all or some markets outside the country of origin. The distributor pays for the goods and assumes all financial risks associated with the foreign sale; it also handles all shipping details. The agent ordinarily sells at the manufacturer's list price abroad; compensation comes in the form of an agreed percentage of the list price. The distributor may operate in its own name or in the manufacturer's name.

Unlike an export distributor, the **export commission representative** assumes no financial risk. The manufacturer assigns some or all foreign markets to the commission representative. The manufacturer carries all accounts, although the representative often provides credit checks and arranges financing. Like the export distributor, the export commission representative handles several accounts; hence, it is also known as a *combination export management company*.

The **cooperative exporter**, sometimes called a *mother hen*, a *piggyback exporter*, or an *export vendor*, is an export organization of a manufacturing company retained by other independent manufacturers to sell their products in foreign markets. Cooperative exporters usually operate as export distributors for other manufacturers, but in special cases they operate as export commission representatives. They are regarded as a form of export management company.

Freight forwarders are licensed specialists in traffic operations, customs clearance, and shipping tariffs and schedules; simply put, they can be thought of as travel agents for freight. Minnesota-based C. H. Robinson Worldwide is one such company. Freight forwarders seek out the best routing and the best prices for transporting freight; they also assist exporters in determining and paying fees and insurance charges. When necessary, forwarders may do export packing as well. They usually handle freight from the port of export to the overseas port of import. In addition, they may move inland freight from the factory to the port of export and, through affiliates abroad, handle freight from the port of import to the customer. Moreover, freight forwarders perform consolidation services for land, air, and ocean freight. Because they contract for large blocks of space on a ship or airplane, they can resell that space to various shippers at a rate lower than is generally available to individual shippers dealing directly with the export carrier.

A licensed forwarder receives brokerage fees or rebates from shipping companies for booked space. Some companies and manufacturers engage in freight forwarding or some portion of it on their own, but they may not, under law, receive brokerage from shipping lines.

(8-6) Organizing for Exporting in the Manufacturer's Country

◀ **8-6** Identify home-country export organization considerations.

Home-country issues involve deciding whether to assign export responsibility inside the company or to work with an external organization specializing in a product or geographic area. Most companies handle export operations within their own in-house export organization. Depending on the company's size, responsibilities for this function may be incorporated into an employee's domestic job description. Alternatively, these responsibilities may be handled as part of a separate division or organizational structure. The possible arrangements for handling exports include the following:

1. As a part-time activity performed by domestic employees.
2. Through an export partner affiliated with the domestic marketing structure that takes possession of the goods before they leave the country.
3. Through an export department that is independent of the domestic marketing structure.
4. Through an export department within an international division.
5. For multidivisional companies, each of the preceding options is available.

A company that assigns a sufficiently high priority to its export business will establish an in-house organization. It then faces the question of how to organize this function effectively. The most appropriate approach depends on two things: the company's appraisal of the opportunities in export marketing and its strategy for allocating resources to markets on a global basis. It may be possible for a company to make export responsibility part of a domestic employee's job description. The advantage of this arrangement is obvious: It is a low-cost arrangement requiring no additional personnel. However, this approach can work only under two conditions: (1) The domestic employee assigned to the task must be thoroughly competent in terms of product and customer knowledge and (2) that competence must be applicable to the target international market(s). The key issue underlying the second condition is the extent to which the target export market is different from the domestic market. If customer circumstances and characteristics are similar, the requirements for specialized regional knowledge are reduced.

The company that chooses not to perform its own marketing and promotion in-house has numerous external export service providers from which to choose. As described previously, these options include EMCs, export merchants, export brokers, combination export managers, manufacturers' export representatives or commission agents, and export distributors. Because these terms and labels may be used inconsistently, we urge the reader to check and confirm the specific services performed by a particular independent export organization.

▶ **8-7** Identify market-country export organization considerations.

(8-7) Organizing for Exporting in the Market Country

In addition to deciding whether to rely on in-house or external export specialists in the home country, a company must make arrangements to distribute its products in the target market country. Every exporting organization faces one basic decision: To what extent do we rely on direct market representation as opposed to representation by independent intermediaries?

The two major advantages to direct representation in a market are control and communications. Direct market representation enables decisions concerning program development, resource allocation, or price changes to be implemented unilaterally. Moreover, when a product is not yet established in a market, special efforts are necessary to achieve sales. The advantage of direct representation is that the marketer's investment ensures that these special efforts will be undertaken. In contrast, with indirect or independent representation, such efforts and investment are often not forthcoming; in many cases, there is simply not enough incentive for independents to invest significant time and money in representing a product. The other great advantage of direct representation is that the possibilities for feedback and information from the market are much greater. This information can vastly improve export-marketing decisions concerning product, price, communications, and distribution.

Note that direct representation does not mean that the exporter is selling directly to the consumer or customer. In most cases, direct representation involves selling to wholesalers or retailers. For example, the major automobile exporters in Germany and Japan rely upon direct representation in the U.S. market in the form of their distributing agencies, which are owned and controlled by the manufacturing organization. The distributing agencies then sell products to franchised dealers.

In smaller markets, it is usually not feasible to establish direct representation because the low sales volume does not justify the cost. Even in larger markets, a small manufacturer usually lacks adequate sales volume to justify the cost of direct representation. Whenever sales volume is small, use of an independent distributor is an effective method of sales distribution. Finding "good" distributors can be the key to export success.

▶ **8-8** Discuss the various payment methods that are typically used in trade financing.

(8-8) Trade Financing and Methods of Payment[11]

The need for a company to be paid for its export sales should be obvious. Yet, many who are new to international trade consider this issue only as an afterthought. Experienced exporters and importers (sellers and buyers) consider the financial and shipping terms of a transaction to be a normal part of any negotiation. In fact, settling the details of a transaction is a valuable act of discipline for all parties to limit future misunderstandings or conflicts. The credit and collection functions are both art and science and require ongoing senior management oversight. There is no "one size fits all" approach to trade finance. Naturally, from a marketing perspective, a firm needs to ensure its terms of sale are competitive.

Selling across borders is inherently riskier than selling within one's home country. Managers may have only limited understanding of topics covered in previous chapters of this book, including language, cultural differences, and foreign political environments. Another reality is that, outside of the OECD economies, a firm will have no effective legal recourse if difficulties arise. Those engaging in international trade must manage the central risks of "nonpayment" and "nonperformance" by their business partners—situations where the exporter might not receive payment for its goods or where the importer might not receive what had been promised. Fortunately, the international banking system plays a critical role in enabling successful international commerce by reducing these transaction risks. Before taking up a discussion of banking's role, however, we need to highlight two basic methods of payment: cash with order and open account.

Cash with order (CWO) presents the least transaction risk to the exporter. In this payment arrangement, the exporter sends the importer a **pro-forma invoice** [a Latin term meaning "before the fact" or "for the sake of form"] with the details and costs of a future shipment. The financial figures and other information are nonbinding, but will be reflected in the future actual invoice. After receiving this "proforma," the importer then sends its purchase order with prepayment

(CWO) to the exporter. While beneficial to the exporter, this presents risks for the importer: Although the importing firm has sent funds to the exporter, it has no assurance of shipment.

Open account payment presents the greatest transaction risk to the exporter. In this arrangement, the importer sends a purchase order to the exporter, which then produces, ships, and subsequently invoices the importer for the shipment. The importer then remits payment to the exporter via wire transfer. While beneficial to the importer, this scheme is risky for the exporter because, even though it has made the requested shipment, there is no assurance of payment.

Letters of Credit

While the CWO and open account payment methods both carry risks, they may be used when two companies have a longstanding, mutually beneficial relationship with each other. However, for most firms entering cross-border business with a new commercial partner, the risks of nonpayment or nonperformance are simply too great, and failure could put their companies at risk.

This is where the banking system helps manage the risk via a key document called the **letter of credit (L/C)** (also known as a *documentary credit*). An L/C substitutes a bank's creditworthiness for that of the importer. From the exporter's perspective, if it ships and "performs" under an L/C, it can rely on the full faith and credit of that bank for payment—not the creditworthiness of the buyer. At the same time, the importer is not obligated to pay for the shipment unless and until the exporter has performed under the terms specified in the L/C. Performance is demonstrated when the exporter provides the buyer's bank with a *documentary package*. This agreed-upon set of documents, which are listed in the L/C, collectively demonstrates that the exporter has performed as agreed.

The importer's bank is known as the "issuing" or "opening" bank. At the request of the buyer, it "opens" an L/C "in favor of" the exporter, which is thereafter referred to as the "beneficiary." In some instances, the opening bank may require the importer to deposit funds or provide collateral against the L/C because the bank is, in essence, extending its own credit on behalf of the importer. However, if there is an established relationship between the bank and the importer, this requirement may be waived. The now-opened L/C is sent to the exporter's bank, which then advises the exporter that an L/C has been opened in its favor. The exporter's bank is referred to as the "negotiating" or "advising" bank.

The most common type of L/C is an **irrevocable letter of credit**. As the name implies, the bank issuing the L/C cannot cancel ("revoke") or modify the L/C terms without obtaining approval from both the exporter and the importer. The key point, from the exporter's perspective, is that even if the importer subsequently cancels the order or fails to pay for the merchandise, the opening bank remains obligated to pay the exporter so long as the exporter has fulfilled the terms given in the L/C.

If the exporter desires (at its prerogative), it can secure an extra layer of protection (for a fee) by asking its advising bank to confirm the L/C of the opening bank. Such a confirmation adds the full faith and credit of the exporter's bank on top of the existing pledge by the importer's bank. If the buyer's opening bank ultimately does not or cannot pay—due, for example, to government-imposed currency controls—the exporter is still guaranteed payment by its own bank. In this scenario, the exporter is said to be operating under a **confirmed irrevocable letter of credit**. Bank fees for opening an L/C vary by country and commercial risk, but can range from $1/8\%$ to 1% of the total credit. Banks charge similar fees for confirming an L/C.

After being satisfied that it can perform under the L/C terms, the exporter will produce and ship the product to the importer. The exporter then assembles the group of documents listed in the L/C. As noted earlier, the L/C includes an agreed-upon (by buyer and seller) list of documents that will be considered evidence of the seller's performance. This documentary package often includes commercial invoices, drafts, packing lists, certificates of insurance, certificates of origin, and ocean bills of lading (which represent title to the shipment). The documentary package and the L/C are sent via the advising (or now confirming) bank and "presented" to the buyer's opening bank. The buyer's bank reviews the documentary package and, if all is in order, will "honor" the credit.

If the transaction is conducted under a *sight draft*, the bank will promptly transfer payment to the beneficiary. If the exporter had agreed to extended credit terms, the draft in the documentary package would be a *time draft* and the bank would remit payment after that agreed-upon period. At this point, for the importer to take possession of the shipment, the opening bank will arrange for the buyer to make its payment, either at sight or at the later time given in the time draft. Upon the importer paying the opening bank or signing a *promissory note* (pledging to make the future payment), the bank will release the documentary package to the buyer. This package includes the ocean bills of lading (and thus title to the goods), enabling the importer to take possession of those goods from the freight carrier. In this process, it is important to note that banks operate only against documents—not on handshakes, contracts, or the shipment's physical move.

Documentary Collections (Sight or Time Drafts)

Over time, an exporter and an importer may establish a good working relationship and decide to move to a simpler, less-complicated form of payment called **documentary collection**. Engaging in such an arrangement requires the exporter to balance the high risk of shipping under open account against the burdensome but low risk of operating under an L/C. Banks are again involved as intermediaries, but provide no guarantees or credit. With a documentary collection, using either a sight draft or time draft, the exporter produces and ships the ordered product. The documentary package, including a draft, is sent to the exporter's correspondent bank (working on behalf of the exporter) in the buyer's country. The importer goes to the bank and makes payment per the terms specified in the draft. In the case of a sight draft (a process known as *documents against payment*), title to the goods passes to the importer when it makes payment to the bank and the bank releases the shipping documents (including bills of lading representing title to the goods). Again, this is separate from the physical movement of the goods.

For the exporter, a higher-risk variation involves a time draft (a process known as *documents against acceptance*). In this case, the exporter would again send a draft and documentary package to its correspondent bank. There, the buyer signs and thus "accepts" the time draft (now a formal obligation for payment at a future date) in exchange for the document package from the correspondent bank. When the accepted time has elapsed, the correspondent bank collects and relays the payment from the importer.

Neither of these options protects the exporter from a buyer that cancels a shipment or refuses to pay. Also, *documents against acceptance* has the added risk of a buyer taking physical possession without payment.

Navigating the Real World: A Brief Case Study

While operating under an L/C is often preferred, in some markets that arrangement is not possible. Bayer, a leader in global life sciences and pharmaceuticals, manages a complex non-L/C payment process to provide vital medicines to the people of Venezuela. Bayer's production costs are based in hard-currency countries, so it ultimately needs hard currency to cover those costs. Yet, in Venezuela, its medicines are purchased in bolivars, the country's volatile and rapidly depreciating currency. Moreover, Nicolás Maduro's government has imposed stringent currency controls. How, then, does Bayer manage payments for its medicines in Venezuela?

In a multistep process, Bayer sells to the Venezuelan government's national health insurance plan and receives payment in bolivars. Bayer then has to negotiate with the government to change those bolivars into U.S. dollars (or euros) at various levels of exchange (there are even different rates among medicines). Once the payment is converted, Bayer still needs government permission to transfer the money out of the country. These hard-currency payments from the government are arranged under a form of *documents against acceptance*. Title to the medicines (shown in the documents) is passed to the government when it signs ("accepts") a Bayer time draft that stipulates the future negotiated payment date, currency amount, and future bolivar/dollar exchange rate.

Naturally, Bayer's preference would be to operate under an L/C—but that would offend the government and might lead to having company officers arrested and their families harassed. A further complication is that, at times, the government simply defaults. Bayer, the beneficiary, then must renegotiate terms with the government to convert the documents against acceptance into Venezuelan government bonds denominated in U.S. dollars with yet another maturity date. Unfortunately, the government offers such bonds only at a discount from the original agreed-upon payment.

Once the bonds are received, Bayer immediately sells them at yet a further discount, resulting in receipts that are 25 to 35 percent below the original invoice. Given Venezuela's high rate of inflation—more than 800 percent in 2017—and the falling value of the bolivar, Bayer's management focus is on cash flow and the timely receipt of receivables, and less on the absolute amounts received. Despite this major difficulty, Bayer's senior management remains committed to the market and recognizes their ethical obligation to support society's health care. Bayer, and many other global firms, look forward to the day when Venezuela's political and economic environments become more stable. Dieter Weinand, head of Bayer Pharma notes, "Each set of countries, customers, and intermediaries requires a unique approach. Credit and collection is an art and science unto itself and it takes an army of people to do this work."

Navigating the Real World: Another Brief Case Study

Subaru's history in the United States provides another good case study in the importance of L/Cs. Today, Subaru is a highly regarded global brand. Fifty years ago, however, it was a different story. In the late 1960s, entrepreneurs Malcolm Bricklin and Harvey Lamm set up Subaru of America (SOA) in Cherry Hill, New Jersey, and began importing the Subaru 360 from Japan. The parent company, Fuji Heavy Industries, initially agreed to a 5-year commitment. When Bricklin and Lamm asked to extend the agreement in perpetuity, Fuji insisted on several concessions. As described by Randall Rothenberg:

> All payment, the manufacturer told Subaru of America, must now be made up front. If the Americans could not get the cash from their dealers, then they would have to get the money from banks. S.O.A., the new contract read, could "order vehicles or equipment only upon the presentation to Fuji of an irrevocable letter of credit to cover the invoice price and in some cases freight for all items ordered." The letters of credit would be opened the moment Fuji placed vehicles on the boats in Yokohama, and would be payable no later than 180 from the shipment date.[12]

For several months, U.S. sales of the 360 boomed. Then, in April 1969, *Consumer Reports* road-tested the 360 and rated it "Unacceptable"; demand for the vehicle evaporated. SOA's dealers quit ordering (and paying for) additional cars, so Bricklin and Lamm had no funds to pay Fuji ("up front," as noted above). Fuji then collected on the L/Cs; SOA could not reimburse the banks, and defaulted on its credit agreements. The bad credit history meant that no banks would provide letters of credit; SOA was at risk of having its import agreement canceled. Ultimately, Malcolm Bricklin was forced out of the company. Subaru of America found new sources of financing, and began assembling a dealer network in rural America. The rest, as the saying goes, is history: Today Subaru has some of the best reviewed, best-selling cars on the market.

Additional Export and Import Issues

In the post–September 11 business environment in the United States, national security concerns have resulted in increased scrutiny of imports into the country. A number of initiatives have been launched to ensure that international cargo cannot be used for terrorism. One such initiative is the Customs Trade Partnership Against Terrorism (C-TPAT). As noted on the U.S. Customs and Border Protection Web site:

> C-TPAT recognizes that U.S. Customs and Border Protection (CBP) can provide the highest level of cargo security only through close cooperation with the ultimate owners of the international supply chain such as importers, carriers, consolidators, licensed customs brokers, and manufacturers. Through this initiative, CBP is asking businesses to ensure the integrity of their security practices and communicate and verify the security guidelines of their business partners within the supply chain.

CBP is responsible for screening import cargo transactions; the goal of C-TPAT is to secure voluntary cooperation from supply-chain participants in an effort to reduce inspection delays. Organizations that are C-TPAT certified are entitled to priority status for CBP inspections.

Another issue with imports and exports is *duty drawback*—that is, refunds of duties paid on imports that are processed or incorporated into other goods and then reexported. Drawbacks have long been used in the United States to encourage exports. However, when NAFTA was negotiated, the U.S. trade representative agreed to restrict drawbacks on exports to Canada and Mexico. As the United States negotiates new trade agreements, some industry groups are lobbying in favor of keeping drawbacks.[13] Duty drawbacks are also common in protected economies and represent a policy instrument that aids exporters by reducing the price of imported production inputs. China was required to remove duty drawbacks as a condition for joining the WTO. As duty rates around the world fall, the drawback issue will become less important.

▶ **8-9** Identify the factors that global marketers consider when making sourcing decisions.

8-9 Sourcing

In global marketing, the issue of customer value is inextricably tied to the **sourcing decision**: whether a company makes or buys its products as well as *where* it makes or buys its products. **Outsourcing** means shifting production jobs or work assignments to another company to cut costs. When the outsourced work moves to another country, the terms *global outsourcing* and *offshoring* are sometimes used. In today's competitive marketplace, companies are under intense pressure to lower costs; one way to do this is to locate manufacturing and other activities in China, India, and other low-wage countries. And why not? Many consumers do not know where the products they buy—athletic shoes, for example—are manufactured (see Exhibit 8-7). It is also true that, as Case 1-1 in Chapter 1 indicated, people often can't match corporate and brand names with particular countries.

In theory, this situation bestows great flexibility on companies. However, in the United States the sourcing issue has become highly politicized. At election time, candidates tap into Americans' fears and concerns over a "jobless" economic recovery. The first wave of nonmanufacturing outsourcing primarily affected **call centers**, sophisticated telephone operations that provide customer support and other services to in-bound callers from around the world; call centers also perform outbound services such as telemarketing (see Exhibit 8-8). Now, however, outsourcing is expanding and includes white-collar, high-tech service-sector jobs. Workers in low-wage countries are performing a variety of tasks including completing tax returns, processing insurance claims, performing research for financial services companies, reading medical scans and X-rays, and drawing up architectural blueprints. American companies that transfer work abroad are finding

Exhibit 8-7 Vietnam is home to dozens of state-run textile and apparel manufacturers that export $1 billion in clothing and footwear each year. The country's garment sector produces merchandise for Nike, Zara, The Limited, and other popular brands. Recently, Vietnam's National Textile-Garment Group (Vinatex) began working with Western consultants to transform the structure and culture of its affiliated companies.
Source: Richard Vogel/Associated Press.

Exhibit 8-8 In Mumbai, India, and other locations, call centers such as this one specialize in "long-distance" or "arm's-length" services. India's well-educated workforce and the growing availability of broadband Internet connections mean that more Western service jobs and industries are subject to global outsourcing. Among the tasks being outsourced to India are medical record transcription, tax return preparation, and technical writing. In fact, the book you are reading was typeset in Chennai, Tamil Nadu, India.
Source: David Pearson/Alamy Stock Photo.

TABLE 8-7 Top 30 Country Destinations for Outsourcing

Region	Countries
Americas	Argentina, Brazil, Chile, Colombia, Costa Rica, Mexico, Panama, Peru
Asia-Pacific	Bangladesh, China, India, Indonesia, Malaysia, Philippines, Sri Lanka, Thailand, Vietnam
Europe, Middle East, and Africa	Bulgaria, Czech Republic, Egypt, Hungary, Mauritius, Morocco, Poland, Romania, Russia, Slovakia, South Africa, Turkey, Ukraine

themselves in the spotlight. Table 8-7 lists the top 30 country destinations for global outsourcing, as determined by the Gartner Group.

As this discussion suggests, the decision of where to locate key business activities depends on factors besides cost. There are no simple rules to guide sourcing decisions. Thus the sourcing decision is one of the most complex and important decisions faced by a global company. Several factors may figure into the sourcing decision: management vision, factor costs and conditions, customer needs, public opinion, logistics, country infrastructure, the political environment, and exchange rates.

Source: Cartoon Features Syndicate.

Management Vision

Some chief executives are determined to retain some or all manufacturing in their home country. The late Nicolas Hayek was one such executive. When he was head of the Swatch Group, Hayek presided over the spectacular revitalization of the Swiss watch industry. The Swatch Group's portfolio of brands includes Blancpain, Omega, Breguet, Rado, and, of course, the inexpensive Swatch brand itself. Hayek demonstrated that the fantasy and imagination of childhood and youth could be translated into breakthroughs that allow mass-market products to be manufactured in high-wage countries side by side with handcrafted luxury products. The Swatch story is a triumph of engineering, as well as a triumph of the imagination. The challenge going forward: winning the business of customers—especially young ones—who do not believe that they need to own a traditional timepiece (see Exhibit 8-9).[14]

Similarly, top management at Canon has chosen to maintain a strategic focus on high-value-added products rather than manufacturing location. The company aims to keep 60 percent of its manufacturing at home in Japan. The company offers a full line of office equipment, including popular products such as printers and copiers; it is also one of the top producers of digital cameras. Instead of increasing the level of automation in its Japanese factories, the company has transitioned from assembly lines to so-called cell production.[15]

Exhibit 8-9 Jay-Z is a brand ambassador for Swiss watchmaker Hublot. Hublot's limited-edition watch, Shawn Carter by Hublot, was available in black ($17,900) and yellow gold ($33,900). A total of 350 were made; all were sold.
Source: Paul Martinka/Polaris/Newscom.

"Twenty years ago we were in the process of moving every appliance manufacturing job to China or Mexico. But when I open up the safe under my desk I can't find the pennies that we have saved. . . . So the next generation of products are going to be made in the U.S."[16]

Jeff Immelt, former CEO, General Electric

Factor Costs and Conditions

Factor costs are land, labor, materials, and capital costs (remember Economics 101!). Labor includes the cost of workers at every level: manufacturing and production, professional and technical, and management. Direct labor costs in basic manufacturing today range from less than $1 per hour in the typical emerging country to $6 to $12 per hour in the typical developed country. In certain industries in the United States, direct labor costs in manufacturing exceed $20 per hour without benefits. German hourly compensation costs for production workers in manufacturing are 160 percent of those in the United States, whereas those in Mexico are a fraction of those in the United States.

Volkswagen's business environment includes a significant wage differential between Mexico and Germany, the strength of the euro, and growing worldwide demand for compact and subcompact vehicles. Taken together, these factors dictate a Mexican manufacturing facility that builds models destined for the United States, China, Europe, and other key markets. Assembly-line wages for Mexican workers start at about $40 per day; by contrast, German auto workers average $60 per hour in pay and benefits. Volkswagen has invested $1 billion to design and produce the next-generation Jetta at a sprawling plant in Mexico City. Next up: The company will build a $1.3 billion plant to produce its popular Audi Q5 SUV. Volkswagen, Honda, Nissan, and other global automakers also benefit from the fact that Mexico has 45 free trade agreements (FTAs) with North America, Europe, Japan, and most of the countries of South America. These FTAs cut the costs of importing components as well as exporting finished vehicles. In addition, Mexico's car industry is now well developed and the labor pool is highly skilled and productive.[17]

Do lower wage rates demand that a company relocate 100 percent of its manufacturing to low-wage countries? Not necessarily. During his tenure as chairman at Volkswagen, Ferdinand Piech improved his company's competitiveness by convincing unions to accept flexible work schedules. For example, during peak demand, employees work 6-day weeks; when demand slows, factories produce cars only 3 days per week. Labor costs in nonmanufacturing jobs are also dramatically lower in some parts of the world. For example, a software engineer in India may receive an annual salary of $12,000; by contrast, an American with the same education and experience might earn $80,000.

Besides labor, the other factors of production are land, materials, and capital. The costs of these factors depend on their availability and relative abundance. Often, the differences in factor costs will offset each other so that, on balance, companies have a level field in the competitive arena. For example, some countries have abundant land, and Japan has abundant capital. These advantages partially offset each other. When this is the case, the critical factor is management, professional, and worker team effectiveness.

The application of advanced computer controls and other new manufacturing technologies has reduced the proportion of labor relative to capital for many businesses. In formulating a sourcing strategy, company managers and executives should also recognize the declining importance of direct manufacturing labor as a percentage of total product cost. It is certainly true that, for many companies in high-wage countries, the availability of cheap labor is a prime consideration when choosing manufacturing locations; this is why China has become "the world's workplace." However, it is also true that direct labor cost may be a relatively small percentage of the total production cost. As a result, it may not be worthwhile to incur the costs and risks of establishing a manufacturing activity in a distant location.

Customer Needs

Although outsourcing can help reduce costs, sometimes customers are seeking something besides the lowest possible price. A few years ago, for example, Dell rerouted some of its call center jobs back to the United States after complaints from key business customers that Indian tech support workers were offering scripted responses and having difficulty answering complex problems. In such instances, the need to keep customers satisfied justifies the higher cost of home-country support operations.

Logistics

In general, the greater the distance between the product source and the target market, the greater the time delay for delivery and the higher the transportation cost. However, innovation and new transportation technologies are cutting both time and dollar costs related to logistics. To facilitate global delivery, transportation companies such as CSX Corporation are forming alliances and becoming an important part of industry value systems. Manufacturers can take advantage of intermodal services that allow containers to be transferred among rail, boat, air, and truck carriers. In Europe, Latin America, and elsewhere, the trend toward regional economic integration means fewer border controls, which greatly speeds up delivery times and lowers costs.

Despite these overall trends, a number of specific issues pertaining to logistics can affect the sourcing decision. For example, since the 2001 terrorist attacks, importers have been required to send electronic lists of cargo to the U.S. government prior to shipping goods to the United States. The goal is to help the U.S. Customs Service identify high-risk cargo that could be linked to the global terror network. In 2014, a work slowdown at West Coast ports cost the U.S. economy an estimated $2 billion per day. Such incidents can delay shipments by weeks or even months.

"Supply Chain 101 says the most important thing is continuity of supply. When you establish a supply line that is 12,000 miles long, you have to weigh the costs of additional inventory and logistics costs versus what you can save in terms of lower costs per unit or labor costs."[18]

Norbert Ore, Institute for Supply Management

Country Infrastructure

To present an attractive setting for a manufacturing operation, it is important that a country's infrastructure be sufficiently developed to support manufacturing and distribution. Infrastructure requirements will vary by company and by industry, but, at a minimum, they will include power, transportation and roads, communications, service and component suppliers, a labor pool, civil order, and effective governance. In addition, companies must have reliable access to foreign exchange for the purchase of necessary materials and components from abroad. Additional requirements include a physically secure setting where work can be done and from which products can be shipped.

A country may have cheap labor, but does it have the necessary supporting services or infrastructure to support a high volume of business activities? Many countries offer these conditions, including Hong Kong, Taiwan, and Singapore. In scores of other low-wage countries, however, the infrastructure is woefully underdeveloped. In China, a key infrastructure weakness is the "cold chain," a food industry term for temperature-controlled trucks and warehouses. According to one estimate, an investment of $100 billion will be required to modernize China's cold chain.[19] Meanwhile, the Chinese government is spending hundreds of millions of dollars on a superhighway system that will eventually connect all 31 of China's provinces. When the project is completed in 2020, China will have approximately 53,000 miles of paved expressway—more than the roads system of the United States.

Infrastructure improvement is a key issue in other emerging markets as well. In India, for example, it takes 8 days for cargo traveling by truck between Kolkata and Mumbai to make the trip of 1,340 miles![20] Likewise, one of the challenges of doing business in the new

Russian market is an infrastructure that is woefully inadequate to handle the increased volume of shipments.

Political Factors

As discussed in Chapter 5, political risk is a deterrent to investment in local sourcing. Conversely, the lower the level of political risk, the less likely it is that an investor will avoid a country or market. The difficulty of assessing political risk is inversely proportional to a country's stage of economic development: All other things being equal, the less developed a country, the more difficult it is to predict political risk. The political risk of the Triad countries, for example, is quite limited as compared to that of a less-developed country in Africa, Latin America, or Asia. The recent rapid changes in Central and Eastern Europe and the dissolution of the Soviet Union have clearly demonstrated the risks *and* opportunities resulting from political upheavals.

Other political factors may weigh on the sourcing decision. For example, with protectionist sentiment on the rise, the U.S. Senate passed an amendment that would prohibit the U.S. Treasury and the Department of Transportation from accepting bids from private companies that use offshore workers. In a highly publicized move, the state of New Jersey changed a call center contract that had shifted jobs offshore. About one dozen jobs were brought back to the state—at a cost of nearly $900,000.

Market access is another type of political factor. If a country or a region limits market access because of local content laws, balance of payments problems, or any other reason, it may be necessary to establish a production facility within the country itself. For instance, the Japanese automobile companies invested in U.S. plant capacity because of concerns about market access. By producing cars in the United States, they have a source of supply that is not exposed to the threat of tariff or import quotas. Market access also figured heavily in Boeing's decision to produce airplane components in China. China ordered 100 airplanes valued at $4.5 billion; in return, Boeing is making investments and transferring engineering and manufacturing expertise.[21]

Foreign Exchange Rates

"Ultimately, the best strategy is to build vehicles in the markets where we sell them."[22]

Takahiko Ijichi, senior managing director, Toyota

In deciding where to source a product or locate a manufacturing activity, managers must take into account foreign exchange rate trends in various parts of the world. Exchange rates are so volatile today that many companies pursue global sourcing strategies as a way of limiting exchange-related risk. At any point in time, what has been an attractive location for production may become much less attractive due to exchange rate fluctuation. For example, *endaka* is the Japanese term for a strong yen. In 2010, the yen strengthened to a 15-year high, trading at ¥85/$1. For every 1 yen increase relative to the American dollar, Canon's operating income declines by 6 billion yen! As noted earlier, Canon's management is counting on research-and-development investment to ensure that its products deliver superior margins that offset the strong yen. Also, Canon and other Japanese companies have become less reliant on the U.S. market as demand in emerging markets has increased.

The dramatic shifts in price levels of commodities and currencies are a major characteristic of the world economy today. Such volatility argues for a sourcing strategy that provides alternative country options for supplying markets. Thus, if the dollar, the yen, or the mark becomes seriously overvalued, a company with production capacity in other locations can achieve competitive advantage by shifting its production among several different sites.

Summary

A company's first business dealings outside the home country often take the form of exporting or importing. Companies should recognize the difference between *export marketing* and *export selling*. By attending *trade shows* and participating in *trade missions*, company personnel can learn a great deal about new markets.

Governments use a variety of programs to support exports, including tax incentives, subsidies, and export assistance. Governments also discourage imports with a combination of *tariffs* and *nontariff barriers*. A *quota* is one example of a nontariff barrier. Export-related policy issues include the status of *foreign sales corporations (FSCs)* in the United States, Europe's *Common Agricultural Policy (CAP)*, and *subsidies*. Governments establish *free trade zones* and *special economic zones* to encourage investment.

The *Harmonized Tariff System (HTS)* has been adopted by most countries that are actively involved in export–import trade. *Single-column tariffs* are the simplest type of tariffs; *two-column tariffs* include special rates such as those available to countries with *normal trade relations (NTR)* status. Governments can also impose special types of duties, including *antidumping duties*, which are imposed on products whose prices government officials deem too low, and *countervailing duties (CVDs)*, which are designed to offset government subsidies.

Key participants in the export–import process include *foreign purchasing agents*, *export brokers*, *export merchants*, *export management companies*, *manufacturer's export agents*, *export distributors*, *export commission representatives*, *cooperative exporters*, and *freight forwarders*.

A number of export–import payment methods are available. A transaction begins with the issue of a *pro-forma invoice* or some other formal document. A basic payment instrument is the *letter of credit (L/C)*, which ensures payment from the buyer's bank. *Documentary collection* is option that involves using either a *sight draft* or a *time draft*. Sales may also be made using *cash with order (CWO)* and sales on open account, or a consignment agreement.

Exporting and importing are directly related to management's *sourcing decisions*. Concern is mounting in developed countries about job losses linked to *outsourcing* jobs, both skilled and unskilled, to low-wage countries. A number of factors determine whether a company makes or buys the products it markets as well as where it makes or buys those products.

Discussion Questions

8-1. Briefly explain the issues of potential export problems with regards to logistics.

8-2. Describe the stages a company typically goes through as it learns about exporting.

8-3. Identify and explain the roles of some of the key participants involved in the exporting process.

8-4. What is a trade mission, and why might it be crucial in developing trade?

8-5. What are duty drawbacks, and which types of economy are likely to use them?

8-6. What is the difference between an L/C and other forms of export–import financing? Why do sellers often require L/Cs in international transactions?

CASE 8-1 *(Continued from page 267)*
The Hong Kong Trade and Investment Hub

The Hong Kong Special Administrative Region (HKSAR) has a central place in the East Asian production and distribution channels as one of the leading regional distribution centers (RDCs) together with Shanghai, Shenzhen, and Singapore. A former British territory handed over to China in 1997 but still preserving a fairly autonomous and independent economy (according to the formula "one country, two systems"), it is one of the principal export-led growth Asian economies.

Hong Kong is the world's seventh-largest trading economy as of 2017, has the highest foreign direct investment (FDI) after China, and is often the first port of call for Western companies approaching Asian markets for exporting as well as sourcing. More than anything else, it offers a very sophisticated service economy; services account for more than 90 percent in terms of contribution. Hong Kong's GDP is based on four main sectors: trading and logistics (21.5 percent of GDP in 2018), tourism (4.5 percent), financial services (18.9 percent), and professional services of various kinds (12.2 percent).

What makes Hong Kong so attractive? History aside, there are many important factors that appeal to a company when it decides to go global and enter Asian markets, which are now acknowledged as engines of world growth.

First of all, Hong Kong is a free trade zone in the sense that all products, with the exception of specific items like tobacco and spirits, enjoy zero taxes in imports and exports. This has allowed a series of advantages, such as the offshoring of manufacturing to the neighboring Guangdong province in China since the 1970s. Outputs are sent to Hong Kong for packaging, advertising, and further re-exports.

A rapid look at the Hong Kong Trade and Development Centre's trade statistics will show that the majority of the HK SAR's exports actually comprise re-exports of imported products from China and abroad. Hong Kong's total exports were about $533.1 billion in 2018, while re-exports accounted for $527.2 billion. China, unsurprisingly, is the main supplier of imports, but many countries benefit from the free-trade regime. In the case of China, this relationship has become easier since the Closer Economic Partnership Arrangement (CEPA). This treaty, signed in 2004 (and the first of its kind to be signed between the two entities), is now a building block of the progressively closer integration of Hong Kong's economy with the Chinese mainland, not only in the traditional manufacturing and logistics sectors but also in services, which are generally off-limits for foreign companies. As a result of CEPA's provisions, Hong Kong suppliers are enjoying preferential treatment when entering the mainland market in various service areas and can also have professional titles and qualifications recognized in China.

Hong Kong's infrastructure has a major role to play in its success in international trade and investments. Hong Kong as a city has an impressive network for exhibitions and conventions. It is considered one of the most efficient and organized cities in the world, with locations like the Hong Kong Convention and Exhibition Centre (HKCEC) in the main business district, the Asia World-Expo near the international airport, and the Hong Kong International Trade and Exhibition Centre in the Kowloon area. According to government statistics, the exhibition business generated nearly 77,000 jobs in 2016 and accounted for 2.1 percent of Hong Kong's GDP, which has continued to grow steadily. Almost 40,000 companies were exhibited in 2018 in one of Hong Kong's numerous trade fairs, with the number of visitors reaching 1.9 million (around one-fifth of the whole Hong Kong population); the sector also attracts high-value visitors that spend on accommodation and meals.

All these factors contribute to the creation of a very positive environment for external trade logistics, which is where Hong Kong's specialty lies. A veritable trade hub, Hong Kong is now a key component in Asian supply chains, and its deep-water port is one of the world's most competitive. It has the world's busiest airport for international cargo as of 2017 and the fifth busiest container port after Shanghai, Singapore, Shenzen and Ningbo-Zhoushan, with 20.77 million TEU[23] in 2017. Hong Kong International Airport (HKIA) at Chek Lap Kok is the busiest cargo gateway and was reportedly the eighth busiest passenger airport in the world in 2018. The deep-water port was the world's most important for container traffic from 1987 to 1989, then from 1992 to 1997, and later from 1999 to 2004, and it operates nine container terminals in three locations: Kwai Chung, Stonecutters Island, and Tsing Yi. There are many important operators here, including Modern Terminals Ltd., Hongkong International Terminals Ltd., COSCO Information

& Technology (H.K.) Ltd., Dubai Port International Terminals Ltd., and Asia Container Terminals Ltd.

Many Western companies have started using Hong Kong not only as a hub but also as a location to showcase brands that will be sold later in Chinese markets (especially in fashion). Hong Kong is a city of references for mainland customers, who increasingly visit the SAR for shopping sprees. More than 58.4 million visitors were recorded in 2017, with Mainland Chinese accounting for 44.4 million of the total.

Nevertheless, challenges await Hong Kong. The SAR is a late starter compared to, say, Singapore or Taiwan, when it comes to trade partnerships, which are progressively becoming a fundamental tool in international trade. Hong Kong has seven free trade associations: Mainland China (June 2003), New Zealand (March 2010), the European Free Trade Association (EFTA) (June 2011), Chile (September 2012), Macao (October 2017), the Association of Southeast Asia Nations (ASEAN) (November 2017), and Georgia (June 2018). It has also finished FTA negotiations with Maldives and Australia. The partnership with the ASEAN bloc is only in its inception. Furthermore, given its free port status, Hong Kong has less to offer in terms of tariff cuts. However, because of its privileged status with China and its strengths in financial and legal services, odds are that the Hong Kong SAR will maintain its position as one of the world's leading trading economies.

Discussion Questions

8-7. What are the elements that make Hong Kong so successful in terms of external trade?

8-8. Analyze the role of the exhibition industry in Hong Kong.

8-9. Using the sources provided as well as online research, illustrate the main features of Hong Kong as a logistics hub, especially regarding its deep-water port.

8-10. Why are Western companies increasingly using Hong Kong to showcase their products?

8-11. What are the main challenges awaiting Hong Kong in its efforts to remain one of the world's largest trading economies?

Sources: Hong Kong Trade and Development Centre, research.hktdc.com; CEPA Partnership Agreement, www.tid.gov.hk/english/cepa/cepa_overview.html; World Bank Statistics on Container Port Traffics in TEU Statistics, data.worldbank.org/indicator/IS.SHP.GOOD.TU; Hong Kong International Airport, www.hongkongairport.com/eng/index.html.

CASE 8-2
Turkish Cars: The Big Picture

Over the last few years, the automotive sector has become Turkey's leading source of exports, accounting for $31 billion, or 15 percent, of Turkey's total export revenue. Over the last decade, the market has been dominated by four main producers, representing 85 percent of the production: Ford Otosan, Oyak-Renault, and Tofas-Fiat, which are partnerships between Turkish and foreign car makers, and Toyota, which is wholly owned by Japan. In 2017, Turkey was estimated to be the 14th largest producer worldwide, having earned that rank by exporting 83.3 percent of its total production. Foreign direct investment has been the main means of entry into the sector. Between 2000 and 2017, original equipment manufacturers invested $14 billion in Turkey.

Turkey became the fifth largest producer in Europe by the end of 2017. However, there is yet to be an automotive brand completely owned by a Turkish company. While Turkey aims to produce and develop a local brand by 2023, sourcing all the components and technologies from within the country is highly unlikely despite the availability of technological infrastructure (research and development centers and high-level universities) and accumulation of skills owing to a globalized economy and the role of automotive imports. It should be noted, however, that there are no brands in this sector with absolute local sourcing within the country of production. As such, it may not be a drawback for Turkey to not have its own car brand; it has instead been opting to encourage further cooperation with major global manufacturers, with particular focus on electric batteries and design development, and to develop a brand that imports some of the required components. Automobile ownership per capita over the last decade has increased considerably in Turkey, with a current level of 142 cars per 1,000 people compared to ownership in France and Germany, where there were approximately 479 and 555 cars per 1,000 people, respectively, in 2017.

Yet there are several challenges worldwide that keep Turkey from achieving its annual export target. A recession in the global economy since 2008 has negatively affected external demand. The decreasing value of the Turkish lira against the euro and the dollar adversely affected the sector and exporters, as other currencies also lost against the dollar (especially in emerging markets). Interestingly, the change in exchange rates causes imported input prices to rise, thereby increasing export prices. Moreover, foreign luxury carmakers like BMW, Audi, VW, Mercedes, Jaguar Land Rover, and Porsche reap huge profits by selling luxury cars in Turkey despite heavy import taxes. In addition, import prices of car parts and raw material (such as steel and energy) along with the luxury car sector (comprising vehicles not made in Turkey) are canceling out the positive effects of car exports on the balance of payment. In 2012, incentives were introduced by the Ministry of Economy for the automobile sector to become a global player by 2023. In a bid to raise the sector's annual exports to $75 billion (from $21.5 billion in 2014) over the next decade, Turkey began offering tax breaks of up to 60 percent and incentives like deductions on employee costs in the hopes of attracting investment in the automotive sector. In the same year, however, a hike in the special consumption tax (SCT) from 84 percent to 130 percent on engines of two liters and over took the sector by surprise. Reacting to the rise in the SCT and the global financial crisis, local automotive sales dropped from the beginning of 2012, with an annual market contraction estimated at around 15 percent year-on-year. Additionally, other factors must be considered: (a) although consumer loan applications (car credit) have not decreased much, the number of approved requests has as banks are more selective now, and (b) inflation and hikes in unemployment were also noted in many reports as reasons for falling purchases.

Looking ahead, Turkey's automotive sector is expected to heavily depend on exports of finished products and imports of components and technological knowhow. With Europe slowly recovering from the 2008 economic crisis, a moderate rise in demand is expected.

Domestically, as indicated above, the number of cars per 1,000 residents is still low, allowing production to be redirected toward the home market, depending on credit and general economic conditions. Turkey manufactured 1.55 million vehicles and exported more than 1.3 million vehicles in 2018. Looking forward, there is a continued downward pressure on the production front largely due to the high increases in production over the past few years. It is expected that production will remain flat for two or three years. Exports continue to be an important part of the equation. The value of the euro against the dollar is a significant factor; higher exchange rates lower demand for imported cars in Turkey and increase demand for domestically produced vehicles. Government-sponsored scrappage schemes have also been effective. The government has also offered incentives on hybrid and diesel engine investments. A new prototype is expected to be introduced by 2019 to go into production in 2021.

This case demonstrates the importance of having a good understanding of country-specific factors, macro-factors, local legislation, and political strategy while dealing with international businesses. Working in the automotive sector in Turkey entails operating on an international level on a daily basis while dealing with both internal and external changes in the ecosystem. When working in the transportation industry, it is easy to forget the big picture. Although the process may seem overwhelming—with specific jargon such as container load (CL), rate request, transit times, hazardous declarations, estimated time of departure (ETD) and estimated time of arrival (ETA), storage/disposal charges, letter of credit, shippers export declaration (SED), and bill of lading (B/L)—together with an array of agents—from vessel operating common carrier to local customs, trade associations and part suppliers networks—it is important to remember the counterintuitive factors that enhance or hinder import/export potentials.

Discussion Questions

8-12. Based on the complexities and challenges discussed in the case, what industry knowledge and skills are required to be successful as an export coordinator, especially in the automotive sector?

8-13. What do you think is the hardest type of macro-environmental factor to obtain? How can you keep it up to date?

8-14. If you were working in the automotive industry in Turkey, what would your next move be?

Notes

[1] This section relies heavily on Warren J. Bilkey, "Attempted Integration of the Literature on the Export Behavior of Firms," *Journal of International Business Studies* 8, no. 1 (1978), pp. 33–46. The stages are based on Rogers's adoption process. See Everett M. Rogers, *Diffusion of Innovations* (New York, NY: Free Press, 1995).

[2] Masaaki Kotabe and Michael R. Czinkota, "State Government Promotion of Manufacturing Exports: A Gap Analysis," *Journal of International Business Studies* 23, no. 4 (Fourth Quarter 1992), pp. 637–658.

[3] Anand Giridharadas, "Foreign Automakers See India as Exporter," *The New York Times* (September 12, 2006), p. C5.

[4] Edmund L. Andrews, "A Civil War within a Trade Dispute," *The New York Times* (September 20, 2002), pp. C1, C2.

[5] John Micklethwait and Adrian Wooldridge, *A Future Perfect: The Challenge and Hidden Promise of Globalization* (New York, NY: Crown Publishers, 2000), p. 261.

[6] Ben Zimmer, "Tariff: From Arab Trade's Bygone Days," *The Wall Street Journal* (May 5–6, 2018), p. C4.

[7] Edward L. Hudgins, "Mercosur Gets a 'Not Guilty' on Trade Diversion," *The Wall Street Journal* (March 21, 1997), p. A19.

[8] Neil King, Jr., "Is Wolverine Human? A Judge Answers 'No'; Fans Howl in Protest," *The Wall Street Journal* (January 20, 2003), p. A1.

[9] Juliane von Reppert-Bismarck and Michael Carolan, "Quotas Squeeze European Boutiques," *The Wall Street Journal* (October 22, 2005), p. A9.

[10] Donald G. Howard, "The Role of Export Management Companies in Global Marketing," *Journal of Global Marketing* 8, no. 1 (1994), pp. 95–110.

[11] The authors thank Professor Christopher "Kit" Nagel, Concordia University-Irvine School of Business, for his contributions to this section.

[12] Randall Rothenberg, *Where the Suckers Moon: The Life and Death of an Advertising Campaign* (New York, NY: Vintage Books, 1995), pp. 47–51.

[13] R. G. Edmonson, "Drawback under Attack at USTR," *The Journal of Commerce* (August 11–17, 2003), p. 21.

[14] Matthew Dalton, "Time Runs out for Swiss Watch Industry," *The Wall Street Journal* (March 13, 2018), p. A8.

[15]Sebastian Moffett, "Canon Manufacturing Strategy Pays off with Strong Earnings," *The Wall Street Journal* (January 4, 2004), p. B3.

[16]Jeremy Lemer, "GE Plans to Return to U.S.-Made Products," *Financial Times* (October 19, 2010), p. 17.

[17]Nicolas Casey, "In Mexico, Auto Plants Hit the Gas," *The Wall Street Journal* (November 20, 2012), pp. A1, A12. See also Adam Thomson, "Car Exports Power Mexico to Recovery," *Financial Times* (October 19, 2010), p. 17.

[18]Barbara Hagenbaugh, "Moving Work Abroad Tough for Some Firms," *USA Today* (December 3, 2003), p. 2B.

[19]Jane Lanhee Lee, "China Hurdle: Lack of Refrigeration," *The Wall Street Journal* (August 30, 2007), p. A7.

[20]Harold L. Sirkin, James W. Hemerling, and Arindam K. Bhattacharya, *Globality: Competing with Everyone from Everywhere for Everything* (New York, NY: Boston Consulting Group, 2008), p. 23.

[21]Jeff Cole, Marcus W. Brauchli, and Craig S. Smith, "Orient Express: Boeing Flies into Flap over Technology Shift in Dealings with China," *The Wall Street Journal* (October 13, 1995), pp. A1, A11. See also Joseph Kahn, "Clipped Wings: McDonnell Douglas's High Hopes for China Never Really Soared," *The Wall Street Journal* (May 22, 1996), pp. A1, A10.

[22]Jonathan Soble and Lindsay Whipp, "Yen's March Spoils the Party for Japan's Exporters," *Financial Times* (August 10, 2010), p. 14.

[23]TEU stands for twenty-foot equivalent unit, which is used to measure cargo capacity.

9

Global Market-Entry Strategies: Licensing, Investment, and Strategic Alliances

---

LEARNING OBJECTIVES

9-1 Explain the advantages and disadvantages of using licensing as a market-entry strategy.

9-2 Compare and contrast the different forms that a company's foreign investments can take.

9-3 Discuss the factors that contribute to the successful launch of a global strategic partnership.

9-4 Identify some of the challenges associated with partnerships in developing countries.

9-5 Describe the special forms of cooperative strategies found in Asia.

9-6 Explain the evolution of cooperative strategies in the twenty-first century.

9-7 Use the market expansion strategies matrix to explain the strategies used by the world's biggest global companies.

CASE 9-1
AB InBev and SABMiller: A Match Made in (Beer) Heaven?

South African Breweries (SAB) PLC had a problem. The company owned more than 100 breweries in 24 countries. South Africa, where SAB had a commanding 98 percent share of the beer market, accounted for approximately 14 percent of annual revenues. However, most of its brands, which include Castle Lager, Pilsner Urquell, and Carling Black Label, were sold on a local or regional basis; none had the global status of, say, Heineken, Amstel, or Guinness. Nor were the company's brands well known in the key U.S. market, where a growing number of the "echo boom"—the children of the nation's 75 million Baby Boomers—were reaching drinking age.

In the early 2000s, then-CEO Graham Mackay embarked on a buying spree; over the course of 14 years, Mackay negotiated dozens of merger, acquisition, and joint-venture deals. Before long, SAB-Miller had operations in nearly 80 countries. For example, Mackay bought Philip Morris's Miller Brewing unit. The $3.6 billion deal created SABMiller, the world's number 2 brewer in terms of production volume; Anheuser-Busch InBev ranked first. Miller operates nine breweries in the United States, where

Exhibit 9-1 Two decades ago, South African Breweries was a local company that dominated its domestic market. Using joint ventures and acquisitions, the company expanded into the rest of Africa as well as key emerging markets such as China, India, and Central Europe. Today, SABMiller is a global brewer whose portfolio still includes local brands. For example, Kilimanjaro is popular in Tanzania, where the competition includes brands from Diageo-owned East African Breweries such as Tusker and Serengeti. SABMiller's merger with Anheuser-Busch InBev created the world's largest brewer.
Source: Fabian von Poser/imageBROKER/Alamy Stock Photo.

its flagship brand, Miller Lite, has struggled to maintain market share. Among the challenges facing SABMiller was to revitalize the Miller Lite brand in the United States and then to launch Miller in Europe as a premium brand.

SABMiller's relentless pursuit of global market opportunities began under the leadership of CEO Mackay and continues with current CEO Alan Clark (see Exhibit 9-1). The actions of both executives illustrate the fact that most firms face a broad range of strategic options. In the last chapter, we examined exporting and importing as ways to exploit global market opportunities. However, for SABMiller and other brewers, exporting their brands (in the conventional sense) is just one way to "go global." In this chapter, we go beyond exporting to discuss several additional entry mode options that form a continuum. As shown in Figure 9-1, the levels of involvement, risk, and financial reward increase as a company moves from market-entry strategies such as licensing to joint ventures and, ultimately, various forms of investment.

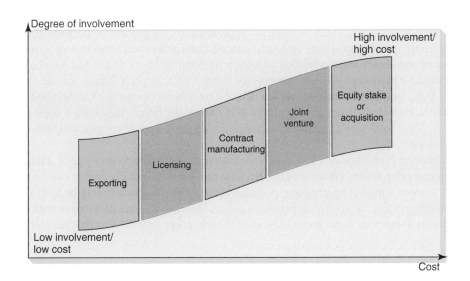

FIGURE 9-1 Investment Cost/Level of Involvement of Market-Entry Strategies

(Continued)

When a global company seeks to enter a developing-country market, an additional strategy issue that must be addressed is whether to replicate, without significant adaptation, the strategy that served the company well in developed markets. You will learn more about the strategic options available to the brewing industry in the continuation of Case 9-1 at the end of the chapter.

To the extent that the objective of entering the market is to achieve penetration, executives at global companies are well advised to consider embracing a mass-market mind-set. This may well mandate an adaptation strategy.[1] Formulating a market-entry strategy means that management must decide which option or options to use in pursuing opportunities outside the home country. The particular market-entry strategy that company executives choose will depend on their vision, their attitude toward risk, the availability of investment capital, and the amount of control sought.

▶ **9-1** Explain the advantages and disadvantages of using licensing as a market-entry strategy.

(9-1) Licensing

Licensing is a contractual arrangement whereby one company (the licensor) makes a legally protected asset available to another company (the licensee) in exchange for royalties, license fees, or some other form of compensation.[2] The licensed asset may be a brand name, company name, patent, trade secret, or product formulation. Licensing is widely used in the fashion industry. For example, the namesake companies associated with Giorgio Armani, Hugo Boss, and other global design icons typically generate more revenue from licensing deals for jeans, fragrances, and watches than from their high-priced couture lines. Organizations as diverse as Disney, Caterpillar Inc., the National Basketball Association, and Coca-Cola also make extensive use of licensing. Even though none is an apparel manufacturer, licensing agreements allow them to leverage their brand names and generate substantial revenue streams. As these examples suggest, licensing is a global market-entry and expansion strategy with considerable appeal. It can offer an attractive return on investment for the life of the agreement, provided that the necessary performance clauses are included in the contract. The only cost is signing the agreement and policing its implementation.

> "That [Presidential Seal] t-shirt was like having a huge international hit record. Everyone knows it. And if we hadn't done it, the bootleggers would have done it for us. A licensing deal gets done and it's all passive income promoting the band."[3]
>
> Marky Ramone, drummer for punk icons The Ramones, on the importance of merchandise licensing deals for recording artists

Two key advantages are associated with licensing as a market-entry mode. First, because the licensee is typically a local business that will produce and market the goods on a local or regional basis, licensing enables companies to circumvent tariffs, quotas, or similar export barriers discussed in Chapter 8. Second, when appropriate, licensees are granted considerable autonomy and are free to adapt the licensed goods to local tastes.

Disney's success with licensing is a case in point. Disney licenses its trademarked cartoon characters, names, and logos to producers of clothing, toys, and watches for sale throughout the world. This practice allows Disney to create synergies based on its core theme park, motion picture, and television businesses. Its licensees are allowed considerable leeway to adapt colors, materials, or other design elements to local tastes.

According to the international Licensing Industry Merchandisers Association (LIMA), worldwide sales of licensed goods totaled $263 billion in 2016. LIMA also has reported that the United States and Canada account for approximately 60 percent of licensed goods sales.[4] For example, yearly worldwide sales of licensed Caterpillar merchandise now approach $2.1 billion, as consumers make a fashion statement by donning boots, jeans, and handbags bearing the distinctive black-and-yellow Cat label (see Exhibit 9-2). Stephen Palmer was the chief executive of U.K.-based Overland Ltd., which held the worldwide license for Cat-branded apparel in the 2000s. He noted, "Even if people here don't know the brand, they have a feeling that they know it. They have seen Caterpillar tractors from an early age. It's subliminal, and that's why it's working."[5]

Licensing is also associated with several disadvantages and opportunity costs. First, licensing agreements offer limited market control. Because the licensor typically does not become involved in the licensee's marketing program, potential returns from marketing may be lost. The second disadvantage is that the agreement may have a short life if the licensee develops its own know-how and begins to innovate in the licensed product or technology area. In a worst-case scenario (from

Exhibit 9-2 Cat's flagship store in the City Center Mall, Isfahan, Iran. Top-selling merchandise includes footwear and clothing.
Source: Eric Lafforgue/Art in All of Us/Corbis/Getty Images.

the licensor's point of view), licensees—especially those working with process technologies—can develop into strong competitors in the local market and, eventually, into industry leaders. Indeed, licensing, by its very nature, enables a company to "borrow"—that is, leverage and exploit—another company's resources. A case in point is Pilkington, which saw its leadership position in the glass industry erode in the 1990s as Glaverbel, Saint-Gobain, PPG, and other competitors achieved higher levels of production efficiency and lower costs. In 2006, Pilkington was acquired by Japan's Nippon Sheet Glass.[6]

Perhaps the most famous example of the opportunity costs associated with licensing dates back to the mid-1950s, when Sony cofounder Masaru Ibuka obtained a licensing agreement for the transistor from AT&T's Bell Laboratories. Ibuka dreamed of using transistors to make small, battery-powered radios. However, the Bell engineers with whom he spoke insisted that it was impossible to manufacture transistors that could handle the high frequencies required for a radio; they advised him to try making hearing aids instead. Undeterred, Ibuka presented the challenge to his Japanese engineers, who then spent many months improving high-frequency output. Sony was not the first company to unveil a transistor radio; a U.S.-built product, the Regency, featured transistors from Texas Instruments and sported a colorful plastic case. It was Sony's high-quality, distinctive approach to styling and marketing savvy, though, that ultimately translated into world-wide success.

When the licensee applies the lessons learned from the licensor to its own advantage in this way, companies may find that the upfront easy money obtained from licensing turns out to be a very expensive source of revenue. To prevent a licensor-competitor from gaining a unilateral benefit, licensing agreements should provide for a cross-technology exchange among all parties. At the absolute minimum, any company that plans to remain in business must ensure that its license agreements include a provision for full cross-licensing (i.e., the licensee must share its developments with the licensor).

Overall, the licensing strategy must be designed to ensure ongoing competitive advantage for the licensor. For example, license arrangements can create export market opportunities and open the door to low-risk manufacturing relationships. They can also speed diffusion of new products or technologies.

Special Licensing Arrangements

Companies that use **contract manufacturing** provide technical specifications to a subcontractor or local manufacturer. The subcontractor then oversees production. Such arrangements offer several advantages. First, the licensing firm can specialize in product design and marketing, while transferring responsibility for ownership of manufacturing facilities to contractors and subcontractors. Other advantages include limited commitment of financial and managerial resources and quick entry into target countries, especially when the target market is too small to justify significant investment.[7] One disadvantage is that companies may open themselves to public scrutiny and criticism if workers in contract factories are poorly paid or labor in inhumane circumstances. To circumvent such problems with their public image, Timberland and other companies that source in low-wage countries are using image advertising to communicate their corporate policies on sustainable business practices.

Franchising is another variation of licensing strategy. A franchise is a contract between a parent company/franchiser and a franchisee that allows the franchisee to operate a business developed by the franchiser in return for a fee and adherence to franchise-wide policies and practices. For example, South Africa-based Nando's is a casual dining chain specializing in Portuguese-style chicken served with spicy peri-peri sauce (see Exhibit 9-3).

Franchising has great appeal to local entrepreneurs who are anxious to learn and apply Western-style marketing techniques. Franchising consultant William Le Sante suggests that would-be franchisers ask the following questions before expanding overseas:

> "One of the key things licensees bring to the business is their knowledge of the local marketplace, trends, and consumer preferences. As long as it's within the guidelines and standards, and it's not doing anything to compromise our brand, we're very willing to go along with it."[8]
>
> Paul Leech, chief operating officer, Allied Domecq Quick Service Restaurants

- Will local consumers buy your product?
- How tough is the local competition?
- Does the government respect trademark and franchiser rights?
- Can your profits be easily repatriated?
- Can you buy all the supplies you need locally?
- Is commercial space available and are rents affordable?
- Are your local partners financially sound and do they understand the basics of franchising?[9]

By addressing these issues, franchisers can gain a more realistic understanding of global opportunities. In China, for example, regulations require foreign franchisers to directly own two or more stores for a minimum of 1 year before franchisees can take over the business. Intellectual property protection is also a concern in China; U.S. President Donald Trump has made this issue a key element in trade negotiations with Beijing.

The specialty retailing industry favors franchising as a market-entry mode. The U.K.-based Body Shop has more than 3,200 stores in 66 countries; franchisees operate the majority of them. (In 2017, the Brazil's Natura Cosméticos acquired The Body Shop from L'Oréal.) Franchising is also a cornerstone of global growth in the fast-food industry; McDonald's reliance on franchising to expand globally is a case in point. The fast-food giant has a well-known global brand name and a business system that can be easily replicated in multiple country markets. As a crucial part of its success, McDonald's headquarters has learned the wisdom of leveraging local market knowledge by granting franchisees considerable leeway to tailor restaurant interior designs and menu offerings to suit country-specific preferences and tastes (see Case 1-2). Generally speaking, however, franchising is a market-entry strategy that is typically executed with less localization than is licensing.

When companies do decide to license, they should sign agreements that anticipate more extensive market participation in the future. Insofar as is possible, a company should keep its options and paths open for other forms of market participation. Many of these forms require investment and give the investing company more control than is possible with licensing.

Exhibit 9-3 This Nando's store in London's Soho neighborhood incorporated Pride colors in the brand's logo that features Barci the chicken. The company uses franchising as a global market-entry strategy.
Source: DrimaFilm/Shutterstock.

9-2 Investment

9-2 Compare and contrast the different forms that a company's foreign investments can take.

After companies gain experience outside the home country via exporting or licensing, the time often comes when executives desire a more extensive form of participation. In particular, the desire to have partial or full ownership of operations outside the home country can drive the decision to invest. **Foreign direct investment (FDI)** figures reflect investment flows out of the home country as companies invest in or acquire plants, equipment, or other assets. FDI allows companies to produce, sell, and compete locally in key markets. Examples of FDI abound: Honda built a $550 million assembly plant in Greensburg, Indiana; Hyundai invested $1 billion in a plant in Montgomery, Alabama; IKEA has spent nearly $2 billion to open stores in Russia; and South

Korea's LG Electronics purchased a 58 percent stake in Zenith Electronics (see Exhibit 9-4). Each of these arrangements represents FDI.

The final years of the twentieth century were a boom time for cross-border mergers and acquisitions. The trend continues today: Worldwide FDI totaled $1.9 trillion in 2016. The United States is the number 1 destination for direct investment; acquisitions alone accounted for $366 billion of FDI in 2016. Canada is the source of the largest share of U.S.-bound FDI, followed by the United Kingdom, Ireland, and Switzerland. Investment in emerging and fast-growing regions has also expanded rapidly in the past few decades. For example, as noted in earlier chapters, investment interest in the BRICS (Brazil, Russia, India, China, and South Africa) nations is increasing, especially in the automobile industry and other sectors critical to the countries' economic development.

Exhibit 9-4 Fiskars, based in Finland, is famous for premium-quality cutlery. The company is perhaps best known for its scissors with the iconic orange handles. Fiskars has expanded its brand portfolio via investment; its 2015 acquisition of WWRD included Waterford and Wedgewood.
Source: Fiskars Brand, Inc.

Foreign investments may take the form of minority or majority shares in joint ventures, minority or majority equity stakes in another company, or outright acquisition. A company may also choose to use a combination of these entry strategies by acquiring one company, buying an equity stake in another, and operating a joint venture with a third. For example, in recent years, United Parcel Service (UPS) has made numerous investments and acquisitions that have focused on logistics, trucking, and e-commerce companies.

Joint Ventures

A joint venture with a local partner represents a more extensive form of participation in foreign markets than either exporting or licensing. Strictly speaking, a **joint venture** is an entry strategy for a single target country in which the partners share ownership of a newly created business entity.[10] This strategy is attractive for several reasons. First and foremost is the sharing of risk. By pursuing a joint venture entry strategy, a company can limit its financial risk as well as its exposure to political uncertainty. Second, a company can use the joint-venture experience to learn about a new market environment. If it succeeds in becoming an insider, it may later increase the level of commitment and exposure. Third, joint ventures allow partners to achieve synergy by combining different value-chain strengths. For example, one company might have in-depth knowledge of a local market, an extensive distribution system, or access to low-cost labor or raw materials. Such a company might link up with a foreign partner possessing well-known brands or cutting-edge technology, manufacturing know-how, or advanced process applications. Alternatively, a company that lacks sufficient capital resources might seek partners to jointly finance a project. Finally, a joint venture may be the only way to enter a country or region if government bid award practices routinely favor local companies, if import tariffs are high, or if laws prohibit foreign control but permit joint ventures.

The disadvantages of joint venturing can be significant. The partners in the joint venture must share both rewards and risks. The main disadvantage associated with joint ventures is that a company incurs very significant control and coordination cost issues when working with a partner. (However, in some instances, country-specific restrictions limit the share of capital that can be injected by foreign companies.)

A second disadvantage is the potential for conflict between partners. These disagreements often arise out of cultural differences, as was the case in a failed $130 million joint venture between Corning Glass and Vitro, Mexico's largest industrial manufacturer. The venture's Mexican managers sometimes viewed the Americans as being too direct and aggressive; the Americans believed their partners took too much time to make important decisions.[11] Such conflicts can multiply when the venture is formed among several different partners. Disagreements about third-country markets where partners view each other as actual or potential competitors can lead to "divorce." To avoid this unhappy outcome, it is essential to work out a plan for approaching third-country markets as part of the venture agreement.

A third issue, also noted in the discussion of licensing, is that a dynamic joint-venture partner can evolve into a stronger competitor. Many developing countries are very forthright about their desire to pursue this goal. As Yuan Sutai, a member of China's Ministry of Electronics Industry, told *The Wall Street Journal* more than 20 years ago, "The purpose of any joint venture, or even a wholly-owned investment, is to allow Chinese companies to learn from foreign companies. We want them to bring their technology to the soil of the People's Republic of China."[12] General Motors (GM) and South Korea's Daewoo Group formed a joint venture in 1978 to produce cars for the Korean market. By the mid-1990s, GM had helped Daewoo improve its competitiveness as an auto producer, but Daewoo chairman Kim Woo-Choong terminated the venture because its provisions prevented the export of cars bearing the Daewoo name.[13]

As one global marketing expert warns, "In an alliance you have to learn skills of the partner, rather than just see it as a way to get a product to sell while avoiding a big investment." Yet, compared with U.S. and European firms, Japanese and Korean firms seem to excel in their abilities to leverage new knowledge that comes out of a joint venture. For example, Toyota learned many new things from its partnership with GM—about U.S. supply and transportation and managing American workers—that Toyota subsequently applied at its Camry plant in Kentucky. Conversely, some American managers involved in the venture complained that the manufacturing expertise that Toyota brought to the table was not applied broadly throughout GM.

Investment via Equity Stake or Full Ownership

The most extensive form of participation in global markets is investment that results in either an equity stake or full ownership. An **equity stake** is simply an investment. If the investor owns fewer than 50 percent of the shares, it is a minority stake; ownership of more than half the shares makes it a majority. **Full ownership**, as the name implies, means the investor has 100 percent control. This may be achieved by a startup of new operations, known as **greenfield investment**, or by merger or acquisition of an existing enterprise.

In 2016, one of the largest merger and acquisition (M&A) deals was the proposed acquisition of American agricultural giant Monsanto by Germany-based Bayer for $66 billion. In March 2018, the EU gave its approval; the following month, the U.S. Justice Department did the same. Prior to the global financial crisis in the late 2000s, the media and telecommunications industry sectors were among the busiest for M&A worldwide. As illustrated by these and many other deals, ownership requires the greatest commitment of capital and managerial effort and offers the fullest means of participating in a market.

Companies may move from licensing or joint venture strategies to ownership in attempt to achieve faster expansion in a market, greater control, and/or higher profits. A quarter-century ago, Ralston Purina ended a 20-year joint venture with a Japanese company to start its own pet food subsidiary. Home Depot used acquisition to expand in China; in 2006, the home improvement giant acquired the HomeWay chain—only to discover that Chinese consumers did not embrace the big-box, do-it-yourself model. By the end of 2012, Home Depot had closed the last of its big-box stores in China; its two remaining Chinese retail locations are a paint-and-flooring specialty store and an interior design store.

If government restrictions prevent 100 percent ownership by foreign companies, the investing company will have to settle for a majority or minority equity stake. In China, the government usually restricts foreign ownership in joint ventures to a 51 percent majority stake. However, a minority equity stake may suit a company's business interests. For example, Samsung was content to purchase a 40 percent stake in computer maker AST. As Samsung manager Michael Yang noted, "We thought 100 percent would be very risky, because any time you have a switch of ownership, that creates a lot of uncertainty among the employees."[14]

In other instances, the investing company may start with a minority stake and then increase its share. In 1991, Volkswagen AG made its first investment in the Czech auto industry by purchasing a 31 percent share in Skoda. By 1995, Volkswagen had increased its equity stake to 70 percent, with the government of the Czech Republic owning the rest. Volkswagen acquired full ownership in 2000. By 2011, when Skoda celebrated the twentieth anniversary of its relationship with VW, the Czech automaker had evolved from a regional company to a global one, selling more than 750,000 vehicles in 100 countries.[15] Similarly, during the economic downturn of the late 2000s, Italy's Fiat acquired a 20 percent stake in Chrysler when the U.S. automaker was in bankruptcy proceedings. Fiat CEO Sergio Marchionne returned Chrysler to profitability and upped his company's stake first to 53.5 percent and then to 58.5 percent. Finally, in 2013, Fiat was set to acquire the remaining 41.5 percent and complete the full acquisition of Chrysler.[16]

Large-scale direct expansion by means of establishing new facilities can be expensive and require a major commitment of managerial time and energy. However, political or other environmental factors sometimes dictate this approach. For example, Japan's Fuji Photo Film Company invested hundreds of millions of dollars in the United States after the U.S. government ruled that Fuji was guilty of dumping (i.e., selling photographic paper at substantially lower prices than in Japan). As an alternative to greenfield investment in new facilities, acquisition is an instantaneous—and sometimes less expensive—approach to market entry or expansion. Although full ownership can yield the additional advantage of avoiding communication and conflict-of-interest problems that may arise with a joint venture or coproduction partner, acquisitions still present the demanding and challenging task of integrating the acquired company into the worldwide organization and coordinating activities.

EMERGING MARKETS BRIEFING BOOK

Auto Industry Joint Ventures in Russia

Russia represents a huge, barely tapped market for a variety of industries, and the number of joint ventures being formed there is increasing. In 1997, GM became the first Western automaker to begin assembling vehicles in Russia. To avoid hefty tariffs that would have pushed the street price of an imported Blazer to $65,000 or more, GM invested in a 25–75 joint venture with the government of the autonomous Tatarstan republic. That partnership, known as Elaz-GM, assembled Blazer sport-utility vehicles (SUVs) from imported components until the end of 2000. Young Russian professionals were expected to snap up the vehicles as long as the price was less than $30,000. However, after only 15,000 vehicles had been sold, market demand evaporated. At the end of 2001, GM terminated the joint venture. Some other recent joint venture alliances are outlined in Table 9-1.

GM achieved better results with a joint venture with AvtoVAZ, the largest car maker in Russia (see Exhibit 9-5). Founded in 1966 in Togliatti, a city on the Volga River, AvtoVAZ is home to Russia's top technical design center and also has access to low-cost Russian titanium and other materials. In the past, the company was best known for being inefficient and for producing the outdated, boxy Lada, whose origins date back to the Soviet era. GM originally intended to assemble a stripped-down, reengineered car based on its Opel model. But market research revealed that a "Made in Russia" car would be acceptable only if it sported a very low sticker price; the same research pointed GM toward an opportunity to put the Chevrolet nameplate on a redesigned domestic model.

Developed with $100 million in funding from GM, the Chevrolet Niva was launched in fall 2002. Within a few years, however, the joint venture was struggling as AvtoVAZ installed a new management team that had the personal approval of then President Vladimir Putin. The Russian government owns 25 percent of AvtoVAZ; in 2008, Renault paid $1 billion for a 25 percent stake. Renault's contribution consisted of technology transfer—specifically, its "B-Zero" auto platform—and production equipment. That same year, Russians bought a record 2.56 million vehicles. When Russian auto sales collapsed as the global economic crisis deepened, however, AvtoVAZ was pushed close to bankruptcy. More than 40,000 workers were laid off, and Moscow was forced to inject $900 million into the company.

In 2009, an American, Jeffrey Glover, was sent from GM's Adam Opel division in Germany to run the Russian joint venture. By 2011, when AvtoVAZ celebrated its 45th anniversary, Russian automobile sales had rebounded. In 2012, annual sales reached pre-crisis levels of 3 million vehicles. Indeed, industry analysts predicted that Russia would surpass Germany as Europe's top auto market by 2014. And the Niva? More than 500,000 have been sold since 2002. As Jim Bovenzi, president of GM Russia explains, "Ten years ago, this was a difficult decision for GM. It was the first time in the 100-year history of the company that we would produce a fully locally designed and produced product, but when we look back now, it was the right decision."

More recent events in Russia have put a damper on GM's outlook. By 2016, the volume of car sales had dropped to half of the 2012 level. As a result, Russia is no longer on track to surpass Germany as Europe's top car market. New car sales in Russia have dropped significantly. The ruble's decline in value and Russia's military incursions in Crimea and Ukraine prompted GM to slash production and cut jobs. Despite the turmoil, GM is maintaining the AvtoVAZ joint venture. And, to cut costs and take advantage of the weak ruble, GM is sourcing more components from local suppliers.

Prior to the crisis, the Russian market for imported premium vehicles was also growing as the number of households that could afford luxury products exhibited rapid growth. Porsche (a division of Volkswagen) and BMW both expanded the number of their dealerships in Russia. Rolls-Royce (owned by BMW) now has two dealerships in Moscow; the only other city in the world with two dealerships is New York City. In addition, Nissan is assembling the Infiniti FX SUV in St. Petersburg. Even so, the weak ruble means that imports are much more expensive than in the past.

By 2017, as the country emerged from recession, there were signs that sales were recovering. AvtoVAZ returned to profitability. Some plants that had been shuttered, including a Mitsubishi Motors plant in Kaluga, were brought back online.

Sources: Henry Foy and Peter Campbell, "Carmakers Gear up for Recovery in Russia," *Financial Times* (September 29, 2017), p. 20; Jason Chow and James Marson, "Renault Tries to Fix Russian Misadventure," *The Wall Street Journal* (April 11, 2016), pp. A1, A10; James Marson, "CEO under Fire at Russian Car Giant," *The Wall Street Journal* (March 5–6, 2016), pp. B1, B4; William Boston and Sarah Sloat, "GM Slices Jobs and Output in Russia," *The Wall Street Journal* (September 14, 2014), p. B6; Anatoly Temkin, "The Land of the Lada Eyes Upscale Rides," *Bloomberg Businessweek* (September 17, 2012), pp. 28–30; Luca I. Alpert, "Russia's Auto Market Shines," *The Wall Street Journal* (August 30, 2012), p. B3; John Reed, "AvtoVAZ Takes Stock of 45 Years of Ladas," *Financial Times* (July 22, 2011), p. 17; David Pearson and Sebastian Moffett, "Renault to Assist AvtoVAZ," *The Wall Street Journal* (November 28, 2009), p. A5; Guy Chazan, "Kremlin Capitalism: Russian Car Maker Comes under Sway of Old Pal of Putin," *The Wall Street Journal* (May 19, 2006), p. A1; Keith Naughton, "How GM Got the Inside Track in China," *BusinessWeek* (November 6, 1995), pp. 56–57; Gregory L. White, "Off Road: How the Chevy Name Landed on SUV Using Russian Technology," *The Wall Street Journal* (February 20, 2001), pp. A1, A8.

Exhibit 9-5 In the past, Russia was known as "the land of the Lada," a reference to a Soviet-era car of dubious distinction. Until recently, Russia was on track to surpass Germany as Europe's largest car market. Despite the current sales slump, GM is standing by its $100 million joint venture bet with AvtoVAZ.

Source: Evg Zhul/Shutterstock.

TABLE 9-1 Market Entry and Expansion by Joint Venture

Companies Involved	Purpose of Joint Venture
GM (USA), Toyota (Japan)	NUMMI, a jointly operated plant in Freemont, California (venture was terminated in 2009).
GM (USA), Shanghai Automotive Industry (China)	A 50–50 joint venture to build an assembly plant to produce 100,000 mid-sized sedans for the Chinese market beginning in 1997 (total investment of $1 billion).
GM (USA), Hindustan Motors (India)	A joint venture to build as many as 20,000 Opel Astras annually (GM's investment was $100 million).
GM (USA), governments of Russia and Tatarstan	A 25–75 joint venture to assemble Blazers from imported parts and, by 1998, to build a full assembly line for 45,000 vehicles (total investment of $250 million).
Ford (USA), Mazda (Japan)	AutoAlliance International 50–50 joint operation of a plant in Flat Rock, Michigan.
Ford (USA), Mahindra & Mahindra Ltd. (India)	A 50–50 joint venture to build Ford Fiestas in the Indian state of Tamil Nadu (total investment of $800 million).
Chrysler (USA), BMW (Germany)	A 50–50 joint venture to build a plant in South America to produce small-displacement, 4-cylinder engines (total investment of $500 million).

Source: Compiled by authors.

Table 9-2, Table 9-3, and Table 9-4 provide a sense of how companies in the automotive industry utilize a variety of market-entry options discussed previously, including equity stakes, investments to establish new operations, and acquisition. Table 9-2 shows that GM historically favored minority stakes in non-U.S. automakers; from 1998 through 2000, the company spent $4.7 billion on such deals, whereas Ford spent twice as much on acquisitions. Despite the fact that GM losses from the deals resulted in substantial write-offs, the strategy reflects management's skepticism about big mergers actually working. As former GM chairman and CEO Rick Wagoner said, "We could have bought 100 percent of somebody, but that probably wouldn't have been a good use of capital." Meanwhile, the company's

TABLE 9-2 Investment in Equity Stake

Investing Company (Home Country)	Investment (Share, Amount, Date)
Fiat (Italy)	Chrysler (United States, initial 20% stake, 2009; Fiat took Chrysler out of bankruptcy)
General Motors (USA)	Fuji Heavy Industries (Japan, 20% stake, $1.4 billion, 1999); Saab Automobiles AB (Sweden, 50% stake, $500 million, 1990; remaining 50%, 2000; following bankruptcy filing, sold Saab to Swedish consortium in 2009)
Volkswagen AG (Germany)	Skoda (Czech Republic, 31% stake, $6 billion, 1991; increased to 50.5%, 1994; currently owns 70% stake)
Ford (USA)	Mazda Motor Corp. (Japan, 25% stake, 1979; increased to 33.4%, $408 million, 1996; decreased stake to 13%, 2008; reduced to 3.5%, 2010)
Renault SA (France)	AvtoVAZ (Russia, 25% stake, $1.3 billion, 2008); Nissan Motors (Japan, 35% stake, $5 billion, 2000)

TABLE 9-3 Investment to Establish New Operations

Investing Company (Headquarters Country)	Investment (Location, Date)
Honda Motor (Japan)	$550 million auto-assembly plant (Indiana, United States, 2006)
Hyundai (South Korea)	$1.1 billion auto-assembly and manufacturing facility producing Sonata and Santa Fe models (Georgia, United States, 2005)
Bayerische Motoren Werke AG (Germany)	$400 million auto-assembly plant (South Carolina, United States, 1995)
Mercedes-Benz AG (Germany)	$300 million auto-assembly plant (Alabama, United States, 1993)
Toyota (Japan)	$3.4 billion manufacturing plant producing Camry, Avalon, and minivan models (Kentucky, United States); $400 million engine plant (West Virginia, United States)

TABLE 9-4 **Market Entry and Expansion by Acquisition**

Acquiring Company	Target (Country, Amount, Date)
Anheuser-Busch InBev (Belgium)	SABMiller (United Kingdom; $101 billion; 2016)
Tata Motors (India)	Jaguar Land Rover (United Kingdom, $2.3 billion, 2008)
Volkswagen AG (Germany)	Sociedad Española de Automóviles de Turismo (SEAT, Spain, $600 million, purchase completed in 1990)
Zhejiang Geely (China)	Volvo car unit (Sweden, $1.3 billion, 2010)

investments in minority stakes have paid off: The company enjoys scale-related savings in purchasing, it has gained access to diesel technology, and Saab produced a new model in record time with the help of Subaru.[17] Following its bankruptcy filing in 2009, GM divested itself of several noncore businesses and brands, including Saab. By the early 2010s, Saab Automobile itself had gone out of business.

What is the driving force behind many of these acquisitions? Globalization. In companies like Anheuser-Busch management realizes that the path to globalization cannot be undertaken independently. Two decades ago, management at Helene Curtis Industries came to a similar realization and agreed to be acquired by Unilever. Ronald J. Gidwitz, president and CEO, said, "It was very clear to us that Helene Curtis did not have the capacity to project itself in emerging markets around the world. As markets get larger, that forces the smaller players to take action."[18] Still, management's decision to invest abroad sometimes clashes with investors' short-term profitability goals—or with the wishes of members of the target organization (see Exhibit 9-6).

Several of the advantages of joint ventures also apply to ownership, including access to markets and avoidance of tariff and quota barriers. Like joint ventures, ownership permits important technology experience transfers and provides a company with access to new manufacturing techniques and intellectual property.

The alternatives discussed here—licensing, joint ventures, minority or majority equity stake, and ownership—are all points along a continuum of alternative strategies for global market entry and expansion. The overall design of a company's global strategy may call for combinations of exporting–importing, licensing, joint ventures, and ownership among different operating units. As an example, Avon Products uses both acquisition and joint ventures to enter developing markets. A company's strategy preference may also change over time. For example, Borden Inc. ended licensing and joint venture arrangements for branded food products in Japan and set up its own production, distribution, and marketing capabilities for dairy products. Meanwhile, in nonfood products, Borden has maintained joint-venture relationships with Japanese partners in flexible packaging and foundry materials.

"OK, but just suppose China *did* make a takeover move on our B-school."

Exhibit 9-6 As we have seen in previous chapters, China's growing economic clout has contributed to increased anti-globalization sentiment in various parts of the world. China offsets its huge trade surplus with the United States by investing in American securities and companies. As this cartoon implies, business schools may be next!

Source: Cartoon Features Syndicate.

Competitors within a given industry may pursue different strategies. Cummins Engine and Caterpillar both face very high costs—in the $300 to $400 million range—for developing new diesel engines suited to new applications, but the two companies vary in their strategic approaches to the world market for engines.

Cummins management looks favorably on collaboration; also, the company's relatively modest $6 billion in annual revenues presents financial limitations to engaging in acquisitions and some other approaches. Thus, Cummins prefers joint ventures. One of the biggest joint ventures between an American company and a Russian company linked Cummins with the KamAZ truck company in Tatarstan. The joint venture allowed the Russians to implement new manufacturing technologies while providing Cummins with access to the Russian market. Cummins also has joint ventures in Japan, Finland, and Italy.

Management at Caterpillar, by contrast, prefers the higher degree of control that comes with full ownership. The company has spent more than $2 billion on purchases of Germany's MaK, British engine maker Perkins, Electro-Motive Diesel, and others. Caterpillar's management believes that it is often less expensive to buy existing firms than to develop new applications independently. Also, Caterpillar is concerned about safeguarding proprietary knowledge that is basic to manufacturing in its core construction equipment business.[19]

▶ **9-3** Discuss the factors that contribute to the successful launch of a global strategic partnership.

(9-3) Global Strategic Partnerships

In Chapter 8 and the first half of this chapter, we surveyed the range of options—exporting, licensing, joint ventures, and ownership—traditionally used by companies wishing either to enter global markets for the first time or to expand their activities beyond present levels. However, recent changes in the political, economic, sociocultural, and technological environments of the global firm have combined to change the relative importance of those strategies. Trade barriers have fallen, markets have globalized, consumer needs and wants have converged, product life cycles have contracted, and new communications technologies and trends have emerged.

Although these developments provide unprecedented marketing opportunities, they also have strong strategic implications for the global organization and new challenges for the global marketer. Such strategies will undoubtedly incorporate—or may even be structured around—a variety of collaborations. Once thought of only as joint ventures, with the more dominant party reaping most of the benefits (or losses) of the partnership, cross-border alliances are taking on surprising new configurations and even more surprising players.

Why would any firm—global or otherwise—seek to collaborate with another firm, be it local or foreign? Today's competitive environment is characterized by unprecedented degrees of turbulence, dynamism, and unpredictability; thus global firms must respond and adapt to changing market conditions very quickly. To succeed in global markets, firms can no longer rely exclusively on the technological superiority or core competence that brought them past success. The disruption that is evident across a variety of industry sectors—from transportation to retailing to media to telecommunications—requires new vision and new approaches.

In the twenty-first century, firms must look toward new strategies that will enhance environmental responsiveness. In particular, they must pursue "entrepreneurial globalization" by developing flexible organizational capabilities, innovating continuously, and revising global strategies accordingly.[20] In the second half of this chapter, we will focus on global strategic partnerships. In addition, we will examine the Japanese *keiretsu* and various other types of cooperation strategies that global firms are using today.

The Nature of Global Strategic Partnerships

The terminology used to describe the new forms of cooperation strategies varies widely. The terms **strategic alliances**, **strategic international alliances**, and **global strategic partnerships (GSPs)** are frequently used to refer to linkages among companies from different countries to jointly pursue a common goal. This terminology can cover a broad spectrum of interfirm agreements, including joint ventures. Notably, the strategic alliances discussed here all share three characteristics (see Figure 9-2):[21]

1. The participants remain independent subsequent to the formation of the alliance.
2. The participants share the benefits of the alliance as well as control over the performance of assigned tasks.
3. The participants make ongoing contributions in technology, products, and other key strategic areas.

The number of strategic alliances has been growing at an estimated rate of 20 to 30 percent since the mid-1980s. This upward trend for GSPs comes, in part, at the expense of traditional cross-border mergers and acquisitions. Since the mid-1990s, a key force driving partnership formation has been the realization that globalization and the Internet will require new, intercorporate configurations (see Exhibit 9-7). Table 9-5 lists some examples of GSPs.

Like traditional joint ventures, GSPs have some disadvantages. Partners share control over assigned tasks, a situation that creates management challenges. Also, strengthening a competitor from another country can present a number of risks. However, there are compelling reasons for pursuing a strategic alliance. First, high product development costs in the face of resource constraints may force a company to seek one or more partners; this was part of the rationale

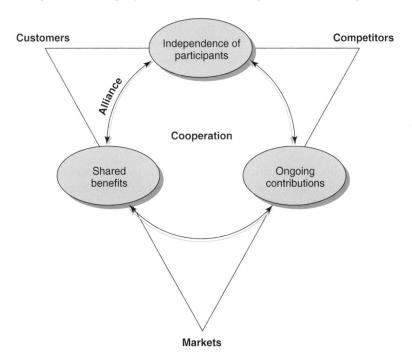

FIGURE 9-2 Three Characteristics of Strategic Alliances

Exhibit 9-7 Oneworld is a global network that brings together American Airlines and other carriers in a number of different countries. Passengers booking a ticket on any network member can easily connect with other carriers for smooth travel around the globe. A further benefit for travelers is the fact that AAdvantage frequent-flyer miles earned can be redeemed with any member of the network.
Source: First Class Photography/ Shutterstock.

TABLE 9-5 Examples of Global Strategic Partnerships

Name of Alliance or Product	Major Participants	Purpose of Alliance
Renault–Nissan–Mitsubishi Alliance	Groupe Renault, Nissan Motor, Mitsubishi Motors	Sharing vehicle platforms, cross-brand manufacturing, combine purchasing operations
S-LCD	Sony Corp., Samsung Electronics Co.	Produce flat-panel LCD screens for high-definition televisions
High-performance engines	Aston Martin and Mercedes-AMG	Mercedes-Benz's performance division produces 4.0-liter V8 engines for Aston-Martin
Star Alliance	Airberlin, American Airlines and US Airways, British Airways, Cathay Pacific, Finnair, Iberia, Japan Airlines, LAN, Malaysia Airlines, Qantas, Qatar Airways, Royal Jordanian, S7 Airlines, Sri Lankan Airlines, TAM Airlines	Create a global travel network by linking 15 member airlines and providing improved service for international travelers

for Sony's partnership with Samsung to produce flat-panel TV screens. Second, the technology requirements of many contemporary products mean that an individual company may lack the skills, capital, or know-how to go it alone.[22] This helps explain why Britain's iconic Aston-Martin has formed partnerships with Mercedes-Benz. The German company provides high-performance engines, cabin electronics, and infotainment systems. This means that Aston-Martin's engineers can focus on other design issues.[23] Third, partnerships may be the best means of securing access to national and regional markets. Fourth, partnerships provide important learning opportunities; in fact, one expert regards GSPs as a "race to learn." Professor Gary Hamel of the London Business School has observed that the partner that proves to be the fastest learner can ultimately dominate the relationship.

As noted earlier, GSPs differ significantly from the market-entry modes discussed in the first half of the chapter. Because licensing agreements do not call for continuous transfer of technology or skills among partners, such agreements are not strategic alliances.[24] Traditional joint ventures are basically alliances focusing on a single national market or a specific problem. The Chinese joint venture mentioned previously between GM and Shanghai Automotive fits this description; the basic goal is to make cars for the Chinese market. A true global strategic partnership, however, is different and is distinguished by five attributes.[25] S-LCD, Sony's strategic alliance with Samsung, offers a good illustration of each attribute.[26]

1. *Two or more companies develop a joint long-term strategy aimed at achieving world leadership by pursuing cost leadership, differentiation, or a combination of the two.* Samsung and Sony are jockeying with each other for leadership in the global television market. One key to profitability in the flat-panel TV market is being the cost leader in panel production. S-LCD is a $2 billion joint venture that produces 60,000 panels per month.

2. *The relationship is reciprocal. Each partner possesses specific strengths that it shares with the other; learning must take place on both sides.* Samsung is a leader in the manufacturing technologies used to create flat-panel TVs. Sony excels at parlaying advanced technology into world-class consumer products; its engineers specialize in optimizing TV picture quality. Jang Insik, Samsung's chief executive, says, "If we learn from Sony, it will help us in advancing our technology."[27]

3. *The partners' vision and efforts are truly global, extending beyond their home countries and home regions to the rest of the world.* Sony and Samsung are both global companies that market global brands throughout the world.

4. *The relationship is organized along horizontal, not vertical, lines. Continual transfer of resources laterally between partners is required, with technology sharing and resource pooling representing norms.* Jang and Sony's Hiroshi Murayama speak by telephone on a daily basis; they also meet face-to-face each month to discuss panel making.

5. *When competing in markets excluded from the partnership, the participants retain their national and ideological identities.* Samsung developed a line of high-definition televisions that use digital light processing (DLP) technology; Sony does not produce DLP sets.

When drawing up plans for a DVD player and home theater sound system to match the TV, a Samsung team headed by head TV designer Yunje Kang worked closely with the audio/video division. At Samsung, managers with responsibility for consumer electronics and computer products report to digital media chief Gee-sung Choi. All the designers worked side by side on open floors. According to a company profile, "the walls between business units are literally nonexistent."[28] By contrast, in recent years Sony has been plagued by a time-consuming, consensus-driven communication approach among divisions that have operated largely autonomously.

Success Factors

Assuming that a proposed alliance has these five attributes, it is necessary to consider six basic factors deemed to have significant impact on the success of GSPs: mission, strategy, governance, culture, organization, and management:[29]

1. *Mission*. Successful GSPs create win–win situations, in which participants pursue objectives on the basis of mutual need or advantage.
2. *Strategy*. A company may establish separate GSPs with different partners; strategy must be thought out upfront to avoid conflicts.
3. *Governance*. Discussion and consensus must be the norms. Partners must be viewed as equals.
4. *Culture*. Personal chemistry is important, as is the successful development of a shared set of values. The failure of a partnership between Great Britain's General Electric Company and Siemens AG was blamed in part on the fact that the former was run by finance-oriented executives, the latter by engineers.
5. *Organization*. Innovative structures and designs may be needed to offset the complexity of multicountry management.
6. *Management*. GSPs invariably involve a different type of decision making. Potentially divisive issues must be identified in advance and clear, unitary lines of authority established that will result in commitment by all partners.

Companies forming GSPs must keep these factors in mind. Moreover, four principles can be applied to guide successful collaborations. First, despite the fact that partners are pursuing mutual goals in some areas, partners must remember that they are competitors in others. Second, harmony is not the most important measure of success—some conflict is to be expected. Third, all employees, engineers, and managers must understand where cooperation ends and competitive compromise begins. Finally, as noted earlier, learning from partners is critically important.[30]

The issue of learning deserves special attention. As one team of researchers notes,

> The challenge is to share enough skills to create advantage vis-à-vis companies outside the alliance while preventing a wholesale transfer of core skills to the partner. This is a very thin line to walk. Companies must carefully select what skills and technologies they pass to their partners. They must develop safeguards against unintended, informal transfers of information. The goal is to limit the transparency of their operations.[31]

Alliances with Asian Competitors

Western companies may find themselves at a disadvantage in GSPs with an Asian competitor, especially if the latter's manufacturing skills are the attractive quality in the partnership. Unfortunately for Western companies, manufacturing excellence represents a multifaceted competence that is not easily transferred. Non-Asian managers and engineers must also learn to be more receptive and attentive—they must overcome the "not invented here" syndrome and begin to think of themselves as students, not teachers. At the same time, they must learn to be less eager to show off proprietary lab and engineering successes.

To limit transparency, some companies involved in GSPs establish a "collaboration section." Much like a corporate communications department, this department is designed to serve as a gatekeeper through which requests for access to people and information must be channeled. Such gatekeeping serves an important control function in guarding against unintended transfers.

A 1991 report by McKinsey and Company shed additional light on the specific problems of alliances between Western and Japanese firms.[32] Oftentimes, problems between partners have less to do with objective levels of performance than with a feeling of mutual disillusionment and missed opportunity. The study identified four common problem areas in alliances gone wrong. The first type of problem arises when each partner has a "different dream": The Japanese partner sees itself emerging from the alliance as a leader in its business or entering new sectors and building a new basis for the future; the Western partner seeks relatively quick and risk-free financial returns. Said one Japanese manager, "Our partner came in looking for a return. They got it. Now they complain that they didn't build a business. But that isn't what they set out to create."

A second area of concern is the balance between partners. Each must contribute to the alliance, and each must depend on the other to a degree that justifies participation in the alliance. The most attractive partner in the short run is likely to be a company that is already established and competent in the business but with the need to master, say, some new technological skills. The best long-term partner, however, is likely to be a less competent player or even one from outside the industry.

A third common cause of problems is "frictional loss" caused by differences in management philosophy, expectations, and approaches. All functions within the alliance may be affected, and performance is likely to suffer as a consequence. Speaking of his Japanese counterpart, a Western businessperson said, "Our partner just wanted to go ahead and invest without considering whether there would be a return or not." The Japanese partner stated, "The foreign partner took so long to decide on obvious points that we were always too slow." Such differences often lead to frustration and time-consuming debates that can stifle decision making.

Last, the study found that short-term goals can result in the foreign partner limiting the number of people allocated to the joint venture. Sometimes, those involved in the venture may work on only two- or three-year assignments. The result is "corporate amnesia"—that is, little or no corporate memory is built up on how to compete in Japan. The original goals of the venture will be lost as each new group of managers takes their turn. When taken collectively, these four problems will almost always ensure that the Japanese partner will be the only one in it for the long haul.

CFM International, GE, and Snecma: A Success Story

Commercial Fan Moteur (CFM) International, a partnership between GE's jet engine division and Snecma, a government-owned French aerospace company, is a frequently cited example of a successful GSP. GE was motivated to form this alliance, in part, by its desire to gain access to the European market so it could sell engines to Airbus Industrie; also, the $800 million in development costs was more than GE could risk on its own. While GE focused on system design and high-tech work, the French side handled fans, boosters, and other components. In 2004, the French government sold a 35 percent stake in Snecma; in 2005, Sagem, an electronics maker, acquired Snecma. The new business entity, known as Safran, had more than €13 billion ($18.7 billion) in 2016 revenues; slightly more than half was generated by the aerospace propulsion unit.[33]

The alliance got off to a strong start because of the personal chemistry between two top executives, GE's Gerhard Neumann and the late General René Ravaud of Snecma. The partnership continues to thrive despite each side's differing views regarding governance, management, and organization. Brian Rowe, senior vice president of GE's engine group, has noted that the French like to bring in senior executives from outside the industry, whereas GE prefers to bring in experienced people from within the organization. Also, the French prefer to approach problem solving with copious amounts of data, while Americans may take a more intuitive approach. Despite these philosophical differences, senior executives from both sides of the partnership have been delegated substantial responsibility.

Boeing and Japan: A Controversy

In some circles, GSPs have been the target of criticism. Critics warn that employees of a company that becomes reliant on outside suppliers for critical components will lose expertise and experience erosion of its engineering skills. Such criticism is often directed at GSPs involving U.S. and Japanese firms. For example, a proposed alliance between Boeing and a Japanese consortium to build a new fuel-efficient airliner, the 7J7, generated a great deal of controversy. The project's $4 billion price tag was too high for Boeing to shoulder alone. The Japanese were to contribute between $1 billion and $2 billion; in return, they would get a chance to learn manufacturing and marketing techniques from Boeing. Although the 7J7 project was shelved in 1988, a new wide-body aircraft, the 777, was developed with approximately 20 percent of the work subcontracted out to Mitsubishi, Fuji, and Kawasaki.[34]

Critics envision a scenario in which the Japanese use what they learn to build their own aircraft and compete directly with Boeing in the future—a disturbing thought considering that Boeing is a major exporter to world markets. One team of researchers developed a framework outlining the stages that a company can go through as it becomes increasingly dependent on partnerships:[35]

1. Outsourcing of assembly for inexpensive labor
2. Outsourcing of low-value components to reduce product price
3. Growing levels of value-added components move abroad
4. Manufacturing skills, designs, and functionally related technologies move abroad
5. Disciplines related to quality, precision manufacturing, testing, and future avenues of product derivatives move abroad
6. Core skills surrounding components, miniaturization, and complex systems integration move abroad
7. Competitor learns the entire spectrum of skills related to the underlying core competence

Yoshino and Rangan have described the interaction and evolution of the various market-entry strategies in terms of cross-market dependencies.[36] Many firms start with an export-based approach, as described in Chapter 8. Historically, the success of Japanese firms in the automobile and consumer electronics industries can be traced back to such an export drive. Nissan, Toyota, and Honda initially concentrated production in Japan, thereby achieving economies of scale.

Eventually, an export-driven strategy gives way to an affiliate-based one. The various types of investment strategies—equity stake, investment to establish new operations, acquisitions, and joint ventures—create operational interdependence within the firm. By operating in different markets, firms have the opportunity to transfer production from place to place in response to fluctuating exchange rates, resource costs, or other considerations. Although at some companies foreign affiliates operate as autonomous fiefdoms (the prototypical multinational business with a polycentric orientation), other companies realize the benefits that operational flexibility can bring.

The third and most complex stage in the evolution of a global strategy comes with management's realization that full integration and a network of shared knowledge from different country markets can greatly enhance the firm's overall competitive position. As company personnel opt to pursue increasingly complex strategies, they must simultaneously manage each new interdependency as well as the existing ones. The stages described here are reflected in the evolution of South Korea's Samsung Group, as described in Case 1-3.

(9-4) International Partnerships in Developing Countries

◀ **9-4** Identify some of the challenges associated with partnerships in developing countries.

Central and Eastern Europe, Asia, India, and Mexico offer exciting opportunities for firms that seek to enter gigantic and largely untapped markets. An obvious strategic choice for entering these markets is the strategic alliance. Like the early joint ventures between U.S. and Japanese firms, potential partners will trade market access for know-how. Other entry strategies are also possible. In 1996, for example, Chrysler and BMW agreed to invest $500 million in a joint-venture plant in Latin America capable of producing 400,000 small engines annually. Although then Chrysler chairman Robert Eaton was skeptical of strategic partnerships, he believed that limited forms of cooperation such as joint ventures make sense in some situations. Eaton knew that, outside of the domestic market, most car engines were smaller than 2.0 liters—a design in which Chrysler had little experience. As Eaton explained, "In the international market, there's no question that in many cases such as this, the economies of scale suggest you really ought to have a partner."[37]

Assuming that risks can be minimized and problems overcome, joint ventures in the transition economies of Central and Eastern Europe could evolve at a more accelerated pace than past joint ventures with Asian partners. On the one hand, a number of factors combine to make Russia an excellent location for an alliance: It has a well-educated workforce, and quality is very important to Russian consumers. On the other hand, several problems are frequently cited in connection with joint ventures in Russia—namely, organized crime, supply shortages, and outdated regulatory and legal systems in a constant state of flux. Despite the risks, the number of joint ventures in Russia is growing, particularly in the service and manufacturing sectors. In the early post-Soviet era, most of the manufacturing ventures were limited to assembly work, but higher value-added activities such as component manufacture are now being performed.

A Central European market with interesting potential is Hungary. Hungary already has the most liberal financial and commercial systems in the region. It has also provided investment incentives to Westerners, especially in high-tech industries. Like Russia, this former Communist economy does have its share of problems. Digital's recent joint-venture agreement with the Hungarian Research Institute for Physics and the state-supervised computer systems design firm Szamalk offers a case in point. Although the venture was formed so Digital would be able to sell and service its equipment in Hungary, the underlying impetus of the venture was to stop the cloning of Digital's computers by Central European firms.

▶ **9-5** Describe the special forms of cooperative strategies found in Asia.

(9-5) Cooperative Strategies in Asia

As we have seen in earlier chapters, Asian cultures exhibit collectivist social values; cooperation and harmony are highly valued in both personal life and the business world in Asia. Therefore, it is not surprising that some of Asia's biggest companies—including Mitsubishi, Hyundai, and LG—pursue cooperation strategies.

Cooperative Strategies in Japan: *Keiretsu*

Japan's *keiretsu* represent a special category of cooperative strategy. A *keiretsu* is an interbusiness alliance or enterprise group that, in the words of one observer, "resembles a fighting clan in which business families join together to vie for market share."[38] The *keiretsu* were formed in the early 1950s as regroupings of four large conglomerates—*zaibatsu*—that had dominated the Japanese economy until 1945. *Zaibatsu* were dissolved after the U.S. occupational forces undertook antitrust actions as part of the reconstruction following World War II.

Today, Japan's Fair Trade Commission appears to favor harmony rather than pursuing anticompetitive behavior. As a result, the U.S. Federal Trade Commission has launched several investigations of price-fixing, price discrimination, and exclusive supply arrangements. Hitachi, Canon, and other Japanese companies have also been accused of restricting the availability of high-tech products in the U.S. market. The Justice Department has considered prosecuting the U.S. subsidiaries of Japanese companies if the parent company is found guilty of unfair trade practices in the Japanese market.[39]

Keiretsu exist in a broad spectrum of markets, including the capital, primary goods, and component parts markets.[40] *Keiretsu* relationships are often cemented by bank ownership of large blocks of stock and by cross-ownership of stock between a company and its buyers and nonfinancial suppliers. Further, *keiretsu* executives can legally sit on one another's boards, share information, and coordinate prices in closed-door meetings of "presidents' councils." Thus, *keiretsu* are essentially cartels that have the government's blessing. Although not a market-entry strategy per se, *keiretsu* have played an integral role in the international success of Japanese companies as they sought new markets.

Some observers have disputed charges that *keiretsu* have an impact on market relationships in Japan and claim instead that the groups primarily serve a social function. Others acknowledge the past significance of preferential trading patterns associated with *keiretsu* but assert that these alliances' influence is now weakening. Although it is beyond the scope of this chapter to address these issues in detail, there can be no doubt that, for companies competing with Japanese companies or wishing to enter the Japanese market, a general understanding of *keiretsu* is crucial. Imagine, for example, what it would mean in the United States if an automaker (e.g., GM), an electrical products company (e.g., GE), a steelmaker (e.g., USX), and a computer firm (e.g., IBM) were interconnected, rather than separate, firms. Global competition in the era of *keiretsu* means that competition exists not only among products, but also among different systems of corporate governance and industrial organization.[41]

As the hypothetical example from the United States suggests, some of Japan's biggest and best-known companies are at the center of *keiretsu*. Several large companies with common ties to a bank are at the center of the Mitsui Group and the Mitsubishi Group. These and the Sumitomo, Fuyo, Sanwa, and DKB groups together make up the "big six" *keiretsu* (in Japanese, *roku dai kigyo shudan*, or "six big industrial groups"). The big six strive for a strong position in each major sector of the Japanese economy. Because intragroup relationships often involve shared stock holdings and trading relations, the big six are sometimes known as *horizontal keiretsu*.[42] Annual revenues in each group are in the hundreds of billions of dollars. In absolute terms, *keiretsu* represent only a small percentage of all Japanese companies. However, these alliances can effectively block foreign suppliers from entering the market and result in higher prices to Japanese consumers, while at the same time resulting in corporate stability, risk sharing, and long-term employment.

In addition to the big six, several other *keiretsu* have formed, bringing new configurations to the basic forms previously described. *Vertical* (i.e., supply and distribution) *keiretsu* are hierarchical alliances between manufacturers and retailers. For example, Matsushita controls a chain of National stores in Japan through which it sells its Panasonic, Technics, and Quasar brands. Approximately half of Matsushita's domestic sales is generated through the National chain, 50 to 80 percent of whose inventory consists of Matsushita's brands. Japan's other major consumer electronics manufacturers, including Toshiba and Hitachi, have similar alliances. (Sony's chain of stores is much smaller and weaker by comparison.) All are fierce competitors in the Japanese market.[43]

Another type of manufacturing *keiretsu* consists of vertical hierarchical alliances between automakers and suppliers and component manufacturers. Intergroup operations and systems are closely integrated, with suppliers receiving long-term contracts. Toyota has a network of about 175 primary suppliers and several thousand secondary suppliers. One such supplier is Koito; Toyota owns about one-fifth of Koito's shares and buys about half of its production. The net result of this arrangement is that Toyota produces approximately 25 percent of the sales value of its cars, compared with 50 percent for GM. The manufacturing *keiretsu* demonstrate the gains that, in theory, can result from an optimal balance of supplier and buyer power. Because Toyota buys a given component from several suppliers (some are in the *keiretsu*, some are independent), discipline is imposed down the network. Also, because Toyota's suppliers do not work exclusively for Toyota, they have an incentive to be flexible and adaptable.[44]

The *keiretsu* system ensures that high-quality parts are delivered on a just-in-time basis, a key factor in the high quality for which Japan's auto industry is renowned. However, as U.S. and European automakers have closed the quality gap, larger Western parts makers have begun building economies of scale that enable them to operate at lower costs than small Japanese parts makers. Moreover, the stock holdings that Toyota, Nissan, and others have in their supplier networks tie up capital that could be used for product development and other purposes.

After Renault took a controlling stake in Nissan, for example, a new management team from France headed by Carlos Ghosn began divesting the company's 1,300 *keiretsu* investments. Nissan shifted to an open-source bidding process for parts suppliers, some of which were not based in Japan.[45] Eventually, Honda and Toyota adopted a similar approach and began seeking bids from non-*keiretsu* component suppliers. That, in turn, led to collusion among auto-parts makers that saw an opportunity to set higher prices. Recent antitrust charges brought by the U.S. Department of Justice resulted in fines totaling approximately $1 billion for the colluding partners. Several Japanese auto-parts suppliers admitted that they had collaborated, and the Justice Department alleged that American car buyers paid higher prices for vehicles as a result.

Despite the sometimes problematic nature of the *keiretsu*, change comes slowly in Japan. As Mitsuhisa Kato, vice president for R&D at Toyota, said, "We feel a duty to protect our *keiretsu*. We are trying to incorporate more outside suppliers, but won't give up on our own way of doing business in Japan."[46]

HOW *KEIRETSU* AFFECT AMERICAN BUSINESS: TWO EXAMPLES   Clyde Prestowitz provides the following example to show how *keiretsu* relationships have a potential impact on U.S. businesses.

In the early 1980s, Nissan was in the market for a supercomputer to use in car design. Two vendors under consideration were Cray, the worldwide leader in supercomputers at the time, and Hitachi, which had no functional product to offer. When it appeared that the purchase of a Cray computer was pending, Hitachi executives called for solidarity; both Nissan and Hitachi are members of the same big six *keiretsu*, the Fuyo group. Hitachi essentially mandated that Nissan show preference to Hitachi, a situation that rankled U.S. trade officials. Meanwhile, a coalition within Nissan was pushing for a Cray computer; ultimately, thanks to U.S. pressure on both Nissan and the Japanese government, the business went to Cray.

Prestowitz describes the Japanese attitude toward this type of business practice:[47]

> It respects mutual obligation by providing a cushion against shocks. Today Nissan may buy a Hitachi computer. Tomorrow it may ask Hitachi to take some of its redundant workers. The slightly lesser performance it may get from the Hitachi computer is balanced against the broader considerations. Moreover, because the decision to buy Hitachi would be a favor, it would bind Hitachi closer and guarantee slavish service and future Hitachi loyalty to Nissan products . . . . This attitude of sticking together is what the Japanese mean by the long-term view; it is what enables them to withstand shocks and to survive over the long term.[48]

Because *keiretsu* relationships are crossing the Pacific and directly affecting the American market, U.S. companies have reason to be concerned with *keiretsu* outside the Japanese market as well. According to data compiled by Dodwell Marketing Consultants, in California alone *keiretsu* own more than half of the Japanese-affiliated manufacturing facilities. But the impact of *keiretsu* extends beyond the West Coast. Illinois-based Tenneco Automotive, a maker of shock absorbers and exhaust systems, does a great deal of worldwide business with the Toyota *keiretsu*. In 1990, however, Mazda dropped Tenneco as a supplier to its U.S. plant in Kentucky. Part of the business was shifted to Tokico Manufacturing, a Japanese transplant and a member of the Mazda *keiretsu*; a non-*keiretsu* Japanese company, KYB Industries, was also made a vendor. A Japanese auto executive explained the rationale behind the change: "First choice is a *keiretsu* company, second choice is a Japanese supplier, third is a local company."[49]

Cooperative Strategies in South Korea: *Chaebol*

South Korea has its own type of corporate alliance groups, known as *chaebol*. Like the Japanese *keiretsu*, *chaebol* are composed of dozens of companies, centered on a central bank or holding company, and dominated by a founding family. Compared to *keiretsu*, however, *chaebol* are a more recent phenomenon: It was only in the early 1960s that Korea's military dictator granted government subsidies and export credits to a select group of companies in the auto, shipbuilding, steel, and electronics sectors. In the 1950s, for example, Samsung was best known as a woolen mill. By the 1980s, Samsung had evolved into a leading producer of low-cost consumer electronics products. Today, Samsung Electronics' Android-powered Galaxy smartphone line is a worldwide best seller.

The *chaebol* were a driving force behind South Korea's economic miracle; gross national product (GNP) increased from $1.9 billion in 1960 to $238 billion in 1990. After the economic crisis of 1997–1998, however, South Korean President Kim Dae Jung pressured *chaebol* leaders to initiate reform. Prior to the crisis, the *chaebol* had become bloated and heavily in debt; within a few years, the *chaebol* were being transformed. Samsung diversified into pharmaceuticals and green energy, and LG Electronics moved into wastewater treatment. Samsung, LG, Hyundai, and other *chaebol* built their brands by developing high-value-added branded products supported by sophisticated advertising.[50]

Recently, questions about corporate governance have arisen after some *chaebol* leaders were accused of various offenses including colluding with politicians and corruption. In 2017, for example, a Korean court convicted Samsung heir Lee Jae-yong of bribing then-president Park Geun-hye. In an ironic twist, Park was elected in part on the basis of campaign pledges to rein in *chaebol* excesses. Observers hope that reform can increase transparency and corporate oversight and reduce the amount of economic power wielded by the *chaebol*. If that happens, it is hoped that Korea's millions of small- and mid-sized enterprises will be better positioned to boost employment and generate long-term economic growth.[51]

(9-6) Twenty-First-Century Cooperative Strategies

◀ **9-6** Explain the evolution of cooperative strategies in the twenty-first century.

One U.S. technology alliance, Sematech, is unique in that it is the direct result of government industrial policy. The U.S. government, concerned that key companies in the domestic semiconductor industry were having difficulty competing with Japan, agreed to subsidize a consortium of 14 technology companies beginning in 1987. Sematech originally had 700 employees, some permanent and some on loan from IBM, AT&T, Advanced Micro Devices, Intel, and other companies. The task facing the consortium was to save the U.S. chip-making equipment industry, in which manufacturers were rapidly losing market share in the face of intense competition from Japan. Although initially plagued by attitudinal and cultural differences among the different factions, Sematech eventually helped chip makers try new approaches with their equipment vendors. By 1991, the Sematech initiative, along with other factors such as the economic downturn in Japan, had reversed the market share slide of the U.S. semiconductor equipment industry.[52]

Sematech's creation heralded a new era in cooperation among technology companies. As the company has expanded internationally, its membership roster has likewise grown to include Advanced Micro Devices, Hewlett-Packard, IBM, Infineon, Intel, Panasonic, Qualcomm, Samsung, and STMicroelectronics. Companies in a variety of industries are pursuing similar types of alliances.

The "relationship enterprise" is another possible stage of evolution of the strategic alliance. In a relationship enterprise, groupings of firms in different industries and countries are held together by common goals that encourage them to act as a single firm. Cyrus Freidheim, former vice chairman of the Booz Allen Hamilton consulting firm, outlined an alliance that, in his opinion, might be representative of an early relationship enterprise. He suggests that within the next few decades, Boeing, British Airways, Siemens, TNT, and Snecma might jointly build several new airports in China. As part of the package, British Airways and TNT would be granted preferential routes and landing slots, the Chinese government would contract to buy all its aircraft from Boeing/Snecma, and Siemens would provide air traffic control systems for all 10 airports.[53]

More than the simple strategic alliances we know today, relationship enterprises will be super-alliances among global giants, with revenues approaching $1 trillion. They will be able to draw on extensive cash resources; circumvent antitrust barriers; and, with home bases in all major markets, enjoy the political advantage of being a "local" firm almost anywhere. This type of alliance is not driven simply by technological change, but rather reflects the political necessity of having multiple home bases.

Another perspective on the future of cooperative strategies correctly predicted the emergence of the virtual corporation. As described in a *BusinessWeek* cover story in the early 1990s, the virtual corporation "will seem to be a single entity with vast capabilities but will really be the result of numerous collaborations assembled only when they're needed."[54] On a global level, the virtual corporation could combine the twin competencies of cost-effectiveness and responsiveness; thus, it could pursue the "think globally, act locally" philosophy with ease. This approach, with its emphasis on just-in-time alliances, reflects the trend toward "mass customization." The same forces that are driving the formation of the digital *keiretsu*—high-speed communication networks, for example—are embodied in the virtual corporation. As noted by William Davidow and Michael Malone in their book *The Virtual Corporation*, "The success of a virtual corporation will depend on its ability to gather and integrate a massive flow of information throughout its organizational components and intelligently act upon that information."[55]

Why did the virtual corporation burst onto the scene in the early 1990s? Previously, firms lacked the technology needed to facilitate this type of data management. Today's distributed databases, networks, and open systems make possible the kinds of data flow required for the virtual corporation. In particular, these data flows permit superior supply-chain management. Ford provides an interesting example of how technology is improving information flows among the far-flung operations of a single company. Ford's $6 billion "world car"—known as the Mercury Mystique and Ford Contour in the United States and the Mondeo in Europe—was developed using an international communications network linking computer workstations of designers and engineers on three continents.[56]

TABLE 9-6   Market Expansion Strategies

		Market	
		Concentration	Diversification
Country	**Concentration**	1. Narrow focus	2. Country focus
	Diversification	3. Country diversification	4. Global diversification

▶ **9-7** Use the market expansion strategies matrix to explain the strategies used by the world's biggest global companies.

(9-7) Market Expansion Strategies

Companies must decide whether to expand by seeking new markets in their existing countries of operation or, alternatively, by seeking new country markets for already identified and served market segments.[57] These two dimensions in combination produce four **market expansion strategy** options, as shown in Table 9-6.

Strategy 1, **country and market concentration**, involves targeting a limited number of customer segments in a few countries. This is typically a starting point for most companies. It matches company resources and market investment needs. Unless a company is large and endowed with ample resources, this strategy may be the only realistic way to begin.

In strategy 2, **country concentration and market diversification**, a company serves many markets in a few countries. This strategy was implemented by many European companies that remained in Europe and sought growth by expanding into new markets. It is also the approach of the American companies that decide to diversify in the U.S. market as opposed to going international with existing products or creating new, global products. According to the U.S. Department of Commerce, the majority of U.S. companies that export limit their sales to five or fewer markets. This means that U.S. companies typically pursue strategy 1 or 2.

Strategy 3, **country diversification and market concentration**, is the classic global strategy whereby a company seeks out the world market for a product. The appeal of this strategy is that by serving the world customer, a company can achieve a greater accumulated volume and lower costs than any competitor and, therefore, have an unassailable competitive advantage. This is the strategy of the well-managed business that serves a distinct need and customer category.

Strategy 4, **country and market diversification**, is the corporate strategy of a global, multibusiness company such as Panasonic Corporation. Panasonic celebrated its 100th anniversary in 2018; the company's founder, Konosuke Matsushita, is an icon of twentieth-century business. Today, Panasonic is multicountry in scope, and its various business units and groups serve multiple consumer and business segments. Thus, at the level of corporate strategy, Panasonic may be said to be pursuing strategy 4. At the operating business level, however, managers of individual units must focus on the needs of the world customer in their particular global market. In Table 9-6, this is strategy 3—country diversification and market concentration. An increasing number of companies all over the world are beginning to see the importance of market share not only in the home or domestic market, but also in the world market. Success in overseas markets can boost a company's total volume and lower its cost position.

Summary

Companies that wish to move beyond exporting and importing can avail themselves of a wide range of *market-entry strategies*. Each strategy has distinct advantages and disadvantages associated with it; the alternatives can be ranked on a continuum representing increasing levels of investment, commitment, and risk. *Licensing* can generate revenue flow with little new investment; it can be a good choice for a company that possesses advanced technology, a strong brand image, or valuable intellectual property. *Contract manufacturing* and *franchising* are two specialized forms of licensing that are widely used in global marketing.

A higher level of involvement outside the home country may involve *foreign direct investment (FDI)*. This investment can take many forms. *Joint ventures* offer two or more companies the opportunity to share risk and combine value-chain strengths. Companies considering joint ventures must plan carefully and communicate with partners to avoid "divorce." FDI can also be used to establish company operations outside the home country through *greenfield investment*, acquisition of a minority or majority *equity stake* in a foreign business, or *full ownership* of an existing business entity through merger or outright acquisition.

Cooperative alliances known as *strategic alliances*, *strategic international alliances*, and *global strategic partnerships (GSPs)* represent an important market-entry strategy in the twenty-first century. GSPs are ambitious, reciprocal, cross-border alliances that may involve business partners in a number of different country markets. GSPs are particularly well suited to emerging markets in Central and Eastern Europe, Asia, and Latin America. Western businesspeople should also be aware of two special forms of cooperation found in Asia—namely, Japan's *keiretsu* and South Korea's *chaebol*.

To assist managers in thinking through the various alternatives, the four possible *market expansion strategies* can be represented in matrix form: *country and market concentration*, *country concentration and market diversification*, *country diversification and market concentration*, and *country and market diversification*. The preferred expansion strategy will reflect the company's stage of development (i.e., whether it is international, multinational, global, or transnational). The stage 5 transnational combines the strengths of the prior three stages into an integrated network to leverage worldwide learning.

Discussion Questions

9-1. What are the advantages and disadvantages of a joint venture as a global market-entry tool? Give examples of joint-venture companies from different countries that have ventured successfully.

9-2. According to Franchise Direct (www.franchisedirect.com), U.S. franchise businesses hold sixteen of the top twenty global franchise operations. Of the remaining four, three are French and the fourth is from the United Kingdom. The first Asian franchise operation in the top 100 is Kumon, a Japanese education franchise. Explain the continued success of Western franchises over Asian ones.

9-3. Explain the advantages and disadvantages of using a contract manufacturer.

9-4. What are *keiretsu*? How does this form of industrial structure affect companies that compete with Japan or that are trying to enter the Japanese market?

CASE 9-1 *(continued from page 298)*

AB InBev and SABMiller: A Match Made in (Beer) Heaven?

Market Entry Problems in Japan

SAB was not the only brewer seeking to expand its global presence. Anheuser-Busch's experience in Japan provided a case study in entry-mode options, and highlighted the advantages and disadvantages of the joint-venture approach.

Access to distribution is critical to success in Japan; Anheuser-Busch first entered that market by means of a licensing agreement with Suntory, which at the time was the smallest of Japan's four top brewers. Although Budweiser became Japan's top-selling imported beer brand within a decade, Bud's market share in the early 1990s was still less than 2 percent. Anheuser-Busch then created a joint venture with Kirin Brewery, the market leader. Anheuser-Busch's 90 percent stake in the venture entitled it to market and distribute beer produced in a Los Angeles brewery through Kirin's channels. Anheuser-Busch also had the option to use some of Kirin's brewing capacity to brew Bud locally.

For its part, Kirin was well positioned to learn more about the global market for beer from the world's largest brewer. By the end of the decade, however, Bud's market share hadn't increased and the venture was losing money. On January 1, 2000, Anheuser-Busch dissolved the joint venture and eliminated most of the associated job positions in Japan; it then reverted to a licensing agreement with Kirin. The lesson was clear: In Japan, it often makes more sense to give control to a local partner via a licensing agreement than to make a major investment.

Heineken

Netherlands-based Heineken is another brewer that, like SAB, has made the transition from a local brand to first a regional brand and then a global one. Today Heineken, in the iconic green bottle emblazoned with the red star, is sold in more countries than any other single brand. Heineken is an independent brewer, and the fourth generation of the founding Heineken family remains in control of the company. In 2014, Heineken turned down an acquisition offer from SABMiller.

The brand's popularity can be attributed in part to an advertising tagline from the 1970s and 1980s that has become legendary in the annals of marketing communications. At the time, Whitbread PLC, a brewer of English ales, distributed Heineken in the United Kingdom. The phrase "Heineken refreshes the parts other beers cannot reach" helped convert British consumers from traditional ales to Heineken's lager.

Following a game plan similar to SABMiller's strategy, Heineken CEO Jean-François van Boxmeer has invested more than $30 billion since the mid-2000s by making dozens of acquisitions. In doing so, he almost doubled the company's market coverage, which now extends to 70 countries. In addition to its namesake brew, today the company markets Amstel, Affligem (based in Belgium), Sol (Mexico), and Tiger (Singapore). Increased scale is one way the company helps reduce the costs of key commodity inputs such as malted barley and aluminum.

More Acquisitions

Consolidation in the brewing industry continued at a rapid pace in the 2000s. In 2004, Belgium's Interbrew merged with a Brazilian company, Ambev. The new entity was known as InBev; in 2008, InBev acquired Anheuser-Busch in a deal valued at $52 billion. After cementing its status as the world's largest brewer, Anheuser-Busch InBev, led by its CEO, Carlos Brito, made headlines again in 2016 when antitrust regulators approved a £79 billion ($101 billion) takeover bid for SABMiller. The deal is expected to result in annual cost savings of as much as $500 million for the behemoth.

At the time, approximately one-third of AB InBev's revenues were generated in the United States, where the top-selling brands include Bud Light and Budweiser. However, the company had virtually no presence in Africa. By contrast, SABMiller was experiencing growth in both sales and revenues in Africa. More generally, emerging markets account for about three-fourths of SABMiller's revenues. For example, Snow, a local Chinese brand, was SABMiller's sales volume leader. As noted in Chapter 5, however, to satisfy Chinese antitrust regulators, SABMiller was required to sell its stake in Snow before the acquisition could go through. The combined entity had $64 billion in 2017 revenue and commands nearly one-third of the global beer market.

Emerging Markets

Global brewers are also stepping up their marketing activities and making strategic investments in fast-growing emerging markets. A case in point is China, the world's largest beer market, with $6 billion in annual sales. As Sylvia Mu Yin, an analyst with Euromonitor, noted, "Local brewers are keen to explore strategic alliances with large multinational companies. At the same time, foreign companies are eager to sell to the 1.3 billion Chinese, but lack local knowledge." In particular, AB InBev is seeking deeper penetration with its Budweiser brand.

Vietnam is also attracting the attention of the major international brewing companies. With a population of 90 million people, Vietnam is a nation of beer drinkers and ranks fifth in per capita consumption in the Asia-Pacific region (Australia ranks number 1). In 2017, the Vietnamese government moved forward with plans to sell stakes in two key state enterprises. Hanoi Alcohol Beer and Beverages Corporation (Habeco), the third largest by sales, brews and markets the popular Hanoi Beer brand. Its larger rival, Sabeco, is based in Ho Chi Minh City and commands approximately 40 percent of the market with brands including 333 and Saigon Beer.

AB InBev, Carlsberg, Heineken, Thai Beverage, and Kirin Holdings were among the potential suitors eying both Vietnamese companies as potential investment targets. Heineken, whose Heineken and Tiger brands are popular in Vietnam, already owned a 5 percent stake in Sabeco. Danish brewer Carlsberg's stake in Habeco stood at 17 percent.

Africa: The Last Frontier

Heineken currently has operations in Ethiopia and Cote d'Ivoire. However, AB InBev's SABMiller unit has also set its sights on low-income consumers in Africa. According to industry forecasts, Africa's beer sector will grow by 5 percent annually; by contrast, beer consumption is declining in Europe and North America.

In Africa, brewers are cutting costs by negotiating deals with local governments to lower taxes on beer sales. Officials can often be persuaded with a two-pronged argument. First, the low-cost beers use local crops such as sorghum, so they create jobs locally. Second, legal, branded brews from well-known companies are a safer alternative to illegal home brew. One unintended consequence: As farmers switch from food crops such as corn and beans, prices for these and other consumer staples are increasing.

Back in the United States

Prior to the acquisition by AB InBev, SABMiller had introduced several local brands in its portfolio in the United States. The company set out to build Pilsner Urquell, the number 1 beer in the Czech Republic, into a national brand in the United States. Success in that effort would be the foundation for transforming Pilsner Urquell into a global premium brand to rival Heineken.

A pale lager, Pilsner Urquell has been produced at the Prazdroj brewery in Plzen ("Pilsen") since 1842. The brew has benefited from a trend that finds U.S. consumers graduating to craft beers that have stronger hops flavors. SABMiller's marketing program included training bartenders to ensure that each draft pour came with a thick head of foam.

In 2005, Colorado-based Adolph Coors merged with Canada's Molson. In 2008, to compete more effectively with AB InBev, SAB Miller and Molson Coors created a 50–50 joint venture called MillerCoors LLC. That venture, a combination of SABMiller's U.S. operations and those of Molson Coors Brewing, created the number 2 brewer in the United States. At the time, AB InBev commanded a nearly 49 percent share of the $100 billion U.S. beer market. Coors Light was the number 2 beer brand by volume; Miller Lite was number 4. Then, in 2016, following the SAB Miller and AB InBev deal, Molson Coors raised its stake in MillerCoors to full ownership as part of a $12 billion deal.

Discussion Questions

9-5. Why are AB InBev, Heineken, and other global brewers targeting emerging markets such as Vietnam?

9-6. Is the brewing industry local or global?

9-7. Why do so many licensing deals, mergers, and acquisitions occur in the brewing industry?

Sources: John Reed and Scheherazade Daneshkhu, "Big Brewers Work up Thirst for Vietnamese Beer," *Financial Times* (November 13, 2017), p. 18; Scheherazade Daneshkhu, "Jean-François van Boxmeer: The Refreshingly Expansive Leader," *Financial Times* (October 9, 2017), p. 24; Lindsay Whipp, "Beer Offer Brews Opportunity for Molson Coors," *Financial Times* (September 23, 2015), p. 14; Tripp Mickle, "MillerCoors Caught in a Downdraft," *The Wall Street Journal* (March 31, 2015), pp. B1, B2; Nicolas Bariyo and Peter Evans, "African Farmers Put Hope in Beer," *The Wall Street Journal* (March 12, 2015), p. B3; Scheherazade Daneshkhu, "A Psychologist

Who Thought His Way into the Beer Elite," *Financial Times* (June 9, 2014), p. 10; Paul Sonne, "With West Flat, Big Brewers Peddle Cheap Beer in Africa," *The Wall Street Journal* (March 20, 2013), p. A1; Sean Carney, "Posh Beer Flows in U.S.," *The Wall Street Journal* (October 19, 2010), p. B10; Chris Buckley, "Battle Shaping up for Chinese Brewery," *The New York Times* (May 6, 2004), pp. W1, W7; Maggie Urry and Adam Jones, "SABMiller Chief Preaches the Lite Fantastic," *Financial Times* (November 21, 2003), p. 22; Dan Bilefsky and Christopher Lawton, "SABMiller Has U.S. Hangover," *The Wall Street Journal* (November 20, 2003), p. B5;

Christopher Lawton and Dan Bilefsky, "Miller Lite Now: Haste Great, Less Selling," *The Wall Street Journal* (October 4, 2002), pp. B1, B6; Nicol Deglil Innocenti, "Fearless Embracer of Challenge," *Financial Times Special Report—Investing in South Africa* (October 2, 2003), p. 6; David Pringle, "Miller Deal Brings Stability to SAB," *The Wall Street Journal* (May 31, 2002), p. B6; Yumiko Ono, "Beer Venture of Anheuser, Kirin Goes Down Drain on Tepid Sales," *The Wall Street Journal* (November 3, 1999), p. A23; John Willman, "Time for Another Round," *Financial Times* (June 21, 1999), p. 15.

CASE 9-2
Jaguar's Passage to India

Jaguar, one of Britain's most iconic brands, celebrates its 85th anniversary in 2020. Jaguar's storied history can be traced back to the 1930s, when a factory was established at Castle Bromwich in Birmingham. In 1935, the first car bearing the Jaguar nameplate was produced.

During World War II, the factory was utilized for military production, and it was here that more than 10,000 of the legendary Spitfire single-engine fighter planes were produced. The Lancaster heavy bomber flown by the Royal Air Force was produced at Castle Bromwich as well. During the war, the exteriors of the brick buildings were covered in camouflage paint. Even so, German bombers inflicted heavy damage on the factory, which was quickly rebuilt.

In the decades following the war, production returned to automobiles, and the corporate structure underwent a series of changes. Once known as Swallow Sidecars (S.S.), the company formally adopted the Jaguar name in 1945. In the 1960s, Jaguar merged with British Motor Corporation, later known as British Motor Holdings (BMH). In 1962, the legendary Jaguar E-Type sports car was born.

In 1968, BMH merged with Leyland Motor Corporation. The new entity, known as British Leyland, manufactured several legendary British sports cars including the Austin, MG, and Triumph nameplates. Land Rover was also a unit of British Leyland.

British Leyland was nationalized in 1975; in other words, the British government took partial control of the company. In the 1980s, however, Prime Minister Margaret Thatcher's government reversed course, and British Leyland was privatized. In 1984, Jaguar was spun off from British Leyland as a stand-alone company.

Fast-forward a quarter of a century. In 2008, Tata Motors paid the Ford Motor Company $2.3 billion for Jaguar and Land Rover. The deal came about as Detroit's automakers faced one of the worst business environments in decades. The Big Three posted losses in the billions of dollars; by 2008, with the global recession and credit crunch causing a sharp decline in demand, executives from GM and Chrysler appealed to Congress for a bailout. Meanwhile, industry observers called for Ford to shed some of its luxury brands.

The Ford Acquisition

When Ford acquired Jaguar in 1989, the American company lacked a high-end luxury model. Executives were betting that they could leverage an exclusive nameplate by launching a new, less-expensive Jaguar line and selling it to more people. The challenge was to execute this strategy without diminishing Jaguar's reputation. Daniel Jones, a professor at the University of Cardiff and an auto industry expert, noted that the Ford name is synonymous with "bread and butter" cars.

Meanwhile, Land Rover, another iconic British nameplate, had also been nationalized and then privatized by the British government. BMW acquired the Land Rover business in 1994. Before the end of the decade,

however, heavy losses at the unit prompted BMW to look for a buyer. In 2000, Ford bought the business for $2.7 billion, with both Jaguar and Land Rover becoming part of Ford's Premier Automotive Group.

Ford's Japanese competitors, including Honda, Nissan, and Toyota, were pursuing a different strategy for moving upmarket: They launched new nameplates and upgraded their dealer organizations. Status- and quality-conscious car buyers embraced Lexus, Infiniti, and other new luxury sedans that offer high performance and outstanding dealer organizations.

Despite Jaguar's classy image and distinguished racing heritage, the cars were somewhat notorious for their unreliability. Gears sometimes wouldn't shift, headlights wouldn't light, and the brakes sometimes caught fire. Part of the problem could be traced to manufacturing.

To remedy the situation, Ford invested heavily to update and upgrade Jaguar's plant facilities and improve productivity. As a benchmark, Ford's manufacturing experts knew that German luxury car makers could build a vehicle in 80 hours; in Japan, the figure was 20 hours. If Jaguar were ever to achieve world-class manufacturing status, Jaguar's assembly time of 110 hours per car had to be drastically reduced.

As the 1990s came to an end, Jaguar introduced several new vehicles. In 1997, amid industry estimates that Ford's cumulative investment had reached $6 billion, Jaguar launched the $64,900 XK8 coupe and roadster. Styling cues clearly identified this model as the successor to Jaguar's legendary XK-E, or E-Type. In the spring of 1999, the S-Type sedan was introduced to widespread acclaim. One observer called the S-Type a "handsome car, instantly recognizable as a Jaguar, yet totally contemporary."

In 2001, the long-awaited "baby Jaguar," the $30,000 X-Type compact sports sedan, was unveiled. Company executives hoped to attract a new generation of drivers and capture a significant share of the entry-level luxury market dominated by the BMW 3-series and the Mercedes C-Class. The X-Type was built on the same platform as the Ford Contour.

The early signs were positive. In 2002, first-year sales of the X-Type boosted Jaguar's worldwide sales by 29 percent, with a record 130,000 vehicles being snapped up by buyers. Unfortunately, the company was not able to sustain the momentum. A backlash began to develop. For example, critics of the X-Type dismissed it as a "warmed-over Ford." Critics also found fault with Ford for failing to move Jaguar's styling forward enough. As one longtime Jaguar owner explained, "They lost their way in what the public wanted. Instead of making Jaguar a niche player, where it should be, they tried to go the mass-production route."

In 2005, bowing to pressures to move the venerable nameplate upmarket again, it was announced that the least expensive Jaguar model, the 2.5 liter X-Type, would be discontinued. In 2008, the curtain came down on Jaguar's two decades under American ownership.

> "For me, the revival of Jaguar Land Rover is because Ratan Tata owns it and he is a petrolhead. I've been to three Grand Prix and he was on the starting grid at all of them."[58]
>
> Sir James Dyson, inventor/ entrepreneur

The Tata Era Begins

Jaguar Land Rover's new owner, Tata Motors, faced challenges of its own. The global economic crisis led to a slump in demand for cars in India; in fact, in its first year of ownership, Tata Motors lost $500 million on Jaguar Land Rover (JLR). Then, as the global economy began to rebound, so did sales of luxury cars. As noted in Exhibit 9-8, Jaguar's XF and XJ sedans won rave reviews from auto critics; the XE, launched in 2015, quickly became the company's best-selling model. In short, two decades of restructuring by Ford were finally paying off under Tata's ownership. For the 2015–2016 model year, JLR sold 521,000 vehicles, up from 250,000 just a few years earlier.

John Edwards, brand director for Land Rover, noted, "Ford laid out a good foundation for us, but I think we are more nimble." For its part, Ford management didn't second-guess its decision to sell the Jaguar and Land Rover brands. As Lewis Booth, Ford's CFO, explained, "We didn't have enough capital resources to look after them. But we found an owner that had the resources to continue what we started."

Over the next few years, Jaguar showed the world how it had been putting those resources to use to improve quality and productivity. For example, Tata invested £500 million to enlarge the Jaguar factory in Castle Bromwich and a similar amount at a plant in nearby Solihull that produces Land Rovers.

On a production floor at Castle Bromwich, employees feed sheets of aluminum ("aluminium" in British English) and steel into giant die presses that stamp out body panels. Nearby, in the body assembly area, hundreds of industrial robots from Swiss engineering giant ABB perform spot welds, apply adhesive, and drive rivets. After the completed bodies are painted, logistics partner DHL ensures that deliveries of seats, auto glass, and instrument panels from outside vendors are routed to the final assembly hall on a just-in-time basis. The plant's D7a technology means that four different models can be produced on the same production line.

Eighty percent of Jaguar's production is exported, and the United States is a key market for these cars. For the 2014 model year, Jaguar launched an all-wheel-drive (AWD) version of the XF sedan; it was available with an optional V6 engine for the first time. These changes, it was hoped, would enhance the car's appeal to American buyers living in areas where winter snow and ice makes AWD a virtual necessity. Jaguar's most affordable model, the XE sport sedan, was launched at the Paris Auto Show in October 2014; production began the following spring.

In fall 2015, Jaguar rolled back prices on some of its cars by approximately 10 percent, and also announced a more comprehensive warranty. Despite these new-model introductions and other marketing

changes, overall sales of sedans and coupes were being eclipsed by demand for a vehicle Jaguar lacked—namely, an SUV. In spring 2016, Jaguar responded by launching the company's first SUV, the F-Pace. In short order, it became Jaguar's best-selling model.

In November 2016, the company raised the curtain on its first electric vehicle (EV), the £65,000 Jaguar I-Pace SUV, at the Los Angeles Motor Show. Some industry analysts noted that Jaguar's entry into the luxury EV category comes relatively late; Tesla is the dominant player with its Model S sedan and Model X SUV. Although Jaguar's identity is closely tied to its British heritage, the first-generation I-Pace is being assembled in a factory in Austria owned by Canadian carmaker Magna. The reason is straightforward: Jaguar's U.K. manufacturing operations are currently operating at 100 percent capacity.

Discussion Questions

9-8. Why has JLR prospered under the ownership of Tata Motors?

9-9. In 2016, Jaguar launched the second-generation XF sedan with a V6 engine and a 5-year, 60,000-mile warranty at a base price of $51,600. The new price represented a savings of approximately $5,100 from the previous model year. What is the rationale behind these changes?

9-10. Jaguar recently launched a new compact luxury crossover, the E-Pace, whose price tops out at nearly $50,000. Observers expect it to be a high-volume, profitable addition to the Jaguar lineup. What are its prospects for success?

9-11. What do you think are the biggest challenges facing the Jaguar and Land Rover brands in the next few years?

Sources: Peter Campbell, "JLR Moves into Glare of the Electric Spotlight," *Financial Times* (November 16, 2016), p. 16; Vikas Bajaj, "Burnishing British Brands," *The New York Times* (August 31, 2012), pp. B1, B4; Marietta Cauchi, "U.K. Car Factories Own the Road Again," *The Wall Street Journal* (March 26, 2014), p. B3; Vanessa Fuhrmans, "Cast-Off Car Brands Find a Road Back," *The Wall Street Journal* (April 6, 2011), pp. B1, B5; Bill Neill, "Jaguar XJ: The Hottest Cat on the Road," *The Wall Street Journal* (April 30, 2010), p. B8; Sharon Silke Carty, "Ford Plans to Park Jaguar, Land Rover with Tata Motors," *USA Today* (March 26, 2008), pp. 1B, 2B; Gordon Fairclough, "Bill Ford Jr.: For Auto Makers, China Is the New Frontier," *The Wall Street Journal* (October 27, 2006), p. B5; James Mackintosh, "Ford's Luxury Unit Hits Problems," *Financial Times* (October 24, 2006), p. 23; Silke Carty, "Will Ford Make the Big Leap?" *USA Today* (August 31, 2006), pp. 1B, 2B; James Mackintosh, "Jaguar Still Aiming to Claw Back Market Share," *Financial Times* (July 20, 2006), p. 14; "Reinventing a '60s Classic," *The Wall Street Journal* (May 5, 2006), p. W9; James R. Healy, "Cheapest Jags Get Kicked to the Curb," *USA Today* (March 29, 2005), p. 1B; Danny Hakim, "Restoring the Heart of Ford," *The New York Times* (November 14, 2001), pp. C1, C6.

Notes

[1]David Arnold, *The Mirage of Global Markets: How Globalizing Companies Can Succeed as Markets Localize* (Upper Saddle River, NJ: Prentice Hall, 2004), pp. 78–79.

[2]Franklin R. Root, *Entry Strategies for International Markets* (New York, NY: Lexington Books, 1994), p. 107.

[3]Cliff Jones, "How the Music Industry Cares More about Making Money Than Music," *FT Wealth* 47 (December 2017), p. 23.

[4]"LIMA Study: Global Sales of Retail Licensed Goods and Services Hit $262.9 Billion in 2016," (May 22, 2017). https://www.licensing.org/news/lima-study-global-retail-sales-of-licensed-goods-and-services-hit-us262-9-billion-in-2016/. Accessed March 1, 2018.

[5]Cecilie Rohwedder and Joseph T. Hallinan, "In Europe, Hot New Fashion for Urban Hipsters Comes from Peoria," *The Wall Street Journal* (August 8, 2001), p. B1.

[6]Charis Gresser, "A Real Test of Endurance," *Financial Times—Weekend* (November 1–2, 1997), p. 5.

[7]Franklin R. Root, *Entry Strategies for International Markets* (New York, NY: Lexington Books, 1994), p. 138.

[8]Sarah Murray, "Big Names Don Camouflage," *Financial Times* (February 5, 2004), p. 9.

[9]Eve Tahmincioglu, "It's Not Only the Giants with Franchises Abroad," *The New York Times* (February 12, 2004), p. C4.

[10]Franklin R. Root, *Entry Strategies for International Markets* (New York, NY: Lexington Books, 1994), p. 309.

[11]Anthony DePalma, "It Takes More Than a Visa to Do Business in Mexico," *The New York Times* (June 26, 1994), Section 3, p. 5.

[12]David P. Hamilton, "China, with Foreign Partners' Help, Becomes a Budding Technology Giant," *The Wall Street Journal* (December 7, 1995), p. A10.

[13]"Mr. Kim's Big Picture," *The Economist* (September 16, 1995), pp. 74–75.

[14]Ross Kerber, "Chairman Predicts Samsung Deal Will Make AST a Giant," *The Los Angeles Times* (March 2, 1995), p. D1.

[15]Andrew English, "Skoda Celebrates 20 Years of Success under VW," *The Telegraph* (April 19, 2011). See also Gail Edmondson, "Skoda, Volkswagen's Hot Growth Engine," *BusinessWeek* (September 14, 2007), p. 30.

[16]Sharon Terlep and Christina Rogers, "Fiat Poised to Absorb Chrysler," *The Wall Street Journal* (April 25, 2013), p. B1.

[17]James Mackintosh, "GM Stands by Its Strategy for Expansion," *Financial Times* (February 2, 2004), p. 5.

[18]Richard Gibson and Sara Calian, "Unilever to Buy Helene Curtis for $770 Million," *The Wall Street Journal* (February 19, 1996), p. A3.

[19]Peter Marsh, "Engine Makers Take Different Routes," *Financial Times* (July 14, 1998), p. 11.

[20]Michael Y. Yoshino and U. Srinivasa Rangan, *Strategic Alliances: An Entrepreneurial Approach to Globalization* (Boston, MA: Harvard Business School Press, 1995), p. 51.

[21]Kenichi Ohmae, "The Global Logic of Strategic Alliances," *Harvard Business Review* 67, no. 2 (March–April 1989), p. 145.

[22]Michael Y. Yoshino and U. Srinivasa Rangan, *Strategic Alliances: An Entrepreneurial Approach to Globalization* (Boston, MA: Harvard Business School Press, 1995), p. 5. For an alternative description, see Riad Ajami and Dara Khambata, "Global Strategic Alliances: The New Transnationals," *Journal of Global Marketing* 5, no. 1/2 (1991), pp. 55–59.

[23]Dan Neil, "2019 Aston Martin DB11 Volante: A Six-Figure Car That's Worth Every Penny," *The Wall Street Journal* (April 28, 2018), p. D11.

[24]Kenichi Ohmae, "The Global Logic of Strategic Alliances," *Harvard Business Review* 67, no. 2 (March–April 1989), p. 145.

[25]Michael A. Yoshino and U. Srinivasa Rangan, *Strategic Alliances: An Entrepreneurial Approach to Globalization* (Boston, MA: Harvard Business School Press, 1995), p. 6.

[26]Phred Dvorak and Evan Ramstad, "TV Marriage: Behind Sony–Samsung Rivalry, an Unlikely Alliance Develops," *The Wall Street Journal* (January 3, 2006), pp. A1, A6.

[27]Phred Dvorak and Evan Ramstad, "TV Marriage: Behind Sony–Samsung Rivalry, an Unlikely Alliance Develops," *The Wall Street Journal* (January 3, 2006), pp. A1, A6.

[28]Frank Rose, "Seoul Machine," *Wired* (May 2005).

[29]Howard V. Perlmutter and David A. Heenan, "Cooperate to Compete Globally," *Harvard Business Review* 64, no. 2 (March–April 1986), p. 137.

[30]Gary Hamel, Yves L. Doz, and C. K. Prahalad, "Collaborate with Your Competitors—and Win," *Harvard Business Review* 67, no. 1 (January–February 1989), pp. 133–139.

[31]Ibid., p. 136.

[32]Kevin K. Jones and Walter E. Schill, "Allying for Advantage," *The McKinsey Quarterly*, no. 3 (1991), pp. 73–101.

[33]Robert Wall, "Airbus–Safran Deal Aims to Cut Costs for Rockets," *The Wall Street Journal* (June 17, 2014), p. B3.

[34]John Holusha, "Pushing the Envelope at Boeing," *The New York Times* (November 10, 1991), Section 3, pp. 1, 6.

[35]David Lei and John W. Slocum, Jr., "Global Strategy, Competence-Building, and Strategic Alliances," *California Management Review* 35, no. 1 (Fall 1992), pp. 81–97.

[36]Michael A. Yoshino and U. Srinivasa Rangan, *Strategic Alliances: An Entrepreneurial Approach to Globalization* (Boston, MA: Harvard Business School Press, 1995), pp. 56–59.

[37]Angelo B. Henderson, "Chrysler and BMW Team up to Build Small-Engine Plant in South America," *The Wall Street Journal* (October 2, 1996), p. A4.

[38]Robert L. Cutts, "Capitalism in Japan: Cartels and Keiretsu," *Harvard Business Review* 70, no. 4 (July–August 1992), p. 49.

[39]Carla Rappoport, "Why Japan Keeps on Winning," *Fortune* (July 15, 1991), p. 84.

[40]Michael L. Gerlach, "Twilight of the *Keiretsu*? A Critical Assessment," *Journal of Japanese Studies* 18, no. 1 (Winter 1992), p. 79.

[41]Ronald J. Gilson and Mark J. Roe, "Understanding the Japanese Keiretsu: Overlaps between Corporate Governance and Industrial Organization," *The Yale Law Journal* 102, no. 4 (January 1993), p. 883.

[42]Kenichi Miyashita and David Russell, *Keiretsu: Inside the Hidden Japanese Conglomerates* (New York, NY: McGraw-Hill, 1996), p. 9.

[43]However, the importance of the chain stores is eroding due to increasing sales at mass merchandisers not under the manufacturers' control.

[44]"Japanology, Inc.—Survey," *The Economist* (March 6, 1993), p. 15.

[45]Norihiko Shirouzu, "U-Turn: A Revival at Nissan Shows There's Hope for Ailing Japan Inc.," *The Wall Street Journal* (November 16, 2000), pp. A1, A10.

[46]Chester Dawson and Brent Kendall, "Japan Probe Pops Car-Part Keiretsu," *The Wall Street Journal* (February 16–17, 2013), pp. B1, B4.

[47]For years, Prestowitz has argued that Japan's industry structure—*keiretsu* included—gives its companies unfair advantages. A more moderate view might be that any business decision must have an economic justification. Thus, a moderate would caution against overstating the effect of *keiretsu*.

[48]Clyde Prestowitz, *Trading Places: How We Are Giving Our Future to Japan and How to Reclaim It* (New York, NY: Basic Books, 1989), pp. 299–300.

[49]Carla Rappoport, "Why Japan Keeps on Winning," *Fortune* (July 15, 1991), p. 84.

[50]Christian Oliver and Song Jung-A, "Evolution Is Crucial to Chaebol Survival," *Financial Times* (June 3, 2011), p. 16.

[51]Bryan Harris, "Taking On Korea Inc" *Financial Times—FT Big Read: Corporate Governance* (September 13, 2017), p. 9. See also Song Jung-A, "Reform Vision Set out for Korea Conglomerates," *Financial Times* (January 20, 2017), p. 14.

[52]Robert D. Hof, "Lessons From Sematech," *MIT Technology Review* (July 25, 2011).

[53]"The Global Firm: R.I.P.," *The Economist* (February 6, 1993), p. 69.

[54]John Byrne, "The Virtual Corporation," *BusinessWeek* (February 8, 1993), p. 103.

[55]William Davidow and Michael Malone, *The Virtual Corporation: Structuring and Revitalizing the Corporation for the 21st Century* (New York, NY: HarperBusiness, 1993), p. 59.

[56]Julie Edelson Halpert, "One Car, Worldwide, with Strings Pulled from Michigan," *The New York Times* (August 29, 1993), Section 3, p. 7.

[57]This section draws on I. Ayal and J. Zif, "Market Expansion Strategies in Multinational Marketing," *Journal of Marketing* 43 (Spring 1979), pp. 84–94; and "Competitive Market Choice Strategies in Multinational Marketing," *Columbia Journal of World Business* (Fall 1978), pp. 72–81.

[58]John Gapper and Tanya Powley, "'All Inventors Are Maniacs,'" *Financial Times* (April 11/12, 2015), p. 18.

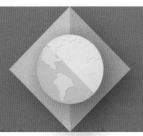

10

Brand and Product Decisions in Global Marketing

LEARNING OBJECTIVES

10-1 Review the basic product concepts that underlie a successful global marketing product strategy.

10-2 Compare and contrast local products and brands, international products and brands, and global products and brands.

10-3 Explain how Maslow's needs hierarchy helps global marketers understand the benefits sought by buyers in different parts of the world.

10-4 Outline the importance of "country of origin" as a brand element.

10-5 List the five strategic alternatives that marketers can utilize during the global product planning process.

10-6 Explain the new-product continuum and compare and contrast the different types of innovation.

CASE 10-1
Alphabet

Alphabet, the company formerly known as Google, has developed some of the world's premier technology products and services. Founded in 1998 by Larry Page and Sergei Brin with a focus on Internet searches, Alphabet's mission is connecting people with technology. The company's core search and ad-driven businesses are still called Google, the brand name recognized virtually everywhere. In Europe, for example, despite operating under the glare of regulatory scrutiny, Google accounts for 90 percent of online search traffic. Roughly one-third of annual global digital ad revenues go to Google.

Today, the company has grown far beyond its roots in search, which is one of the reasons for the corporate restructuring and name change that was announced in August 2015. Alphabet has developed an impressive product portfolio under the Google brand that includes consumer offerings such as Google+, the Google Play app store, Google Wallet, Google Chrome, and Google Chromecast. Alphabet has also made a number of strategic acquisitions, including video-sharing site YouTube and the Internet of Things thermostat brand Nest.

Alphabet serves its enterprise customers as well. For example, Samsung and several other handset manufacturers use its Android smartphone operating system. Google Fiber is bringing high-speed, one-gigabyte-per-second Internet service to a growing list of American cities. Google Analytics is a source of big data, and Google AdWords allows advertisers—both small and large—to bid for preferred placement on Web pages. The company also operates huge data centers throughout the world.

Exhibit 10-1 Alphabet is investing in "moonshot" innovations such as Project Loon, a network of stratospheric balloons that will bring Internet access to billions of people.
Source: CB2/ZOB/Supplied by WENN.com/Newscom.

Alphabet spends approximately $10 billion each year on research and development. X (formerly Google X), the company's semi-secret research division, is known as the Moonshot Laboratory. The name references its lofty mission: Staff members are working on "moonshot" projects that represent leading-edge technology leaps (see Exhibit 10-1). Astro Teller, the division's Rollerblade-wearing chief executive, has the title "Captain of Moonshots."

Another research group, Advanced Technology and Projects (ATAP), focuses on mobile applications. Among the many new products and services currently under development are self-driving cars; Wing, a delivery drone service; and wearable devices. To learn more about some of the challenges and opportunities facing managers in charge of Alphabet's diverse product and brand portfolio, turn to the continuation of Case 10-1 at the end of the chapter.

Alphabet's myriad product development initiatives illustrate the point that products and brands are perhaps the most crucial element of a company's marketing program; they are integral to the company's value proposition. In Part Three elsewhere in this text, we surveyed several topics that directly impact product strategy as a company approaches global markets. Input from a company's business intelligence network and market research studies guides the product development process. The market must be segmented, one or more target markets selected, and strong positioning established. Global marketers must also make decisions about exporting and sourcing; other market-entry strategies, such as licensing and strategic alliances, may be considered as well.

As we will see in Part Four, every aspect of a firm's marketing program, including pricing, distribution, and communication policies, must fit the product. This chapter examines the major dimensions of global product and brand decisions. First is a review of basic product and brand concepts, followed by a discussion of local, international, and global products and brands. Product design criteria are identified, and attitudes toward foreign products are explored. Then, strategic alternatives available to global marketers are presented. Finally, new-product issues in global marketing are discussed.

(10-1) Basic Product Concepts

◀ 10-1 Review the basic product concepts that underlie a successful global marketing product strategy.

The product *P* of the marketing mix is at the heart of the challenges and opportunities facing global companies today: Management must develop product and brand policies and strategies that are sensitive to market needs, competition, and the company's ambitions and resources on a global scale. Effective global marketing often entails finding a balance between the payoff from extensively adapting products and brands to local market preferences and the benefits that come from concentrating company resources on relatively standardized global products and brands.

A **product** is a good, service, or idea with both tangible and intangible attributes that collectively create value for a buyer or user. A product's *tangible* attributes can be assessed in physical terms, such as weight, dimensions, or materials used. Consider, for example, a flat-panel TV with an OLED screen that measures 42 inches across. The unit weighs 20 pounds, is 2.2 inches deep, features four high-definition media interface (HDMI) connections, has a built-in tuner capable of receiving high-definition TV signals over the air, and delivers a 4K screen resolution. These tangible, physical features and attributes translate into benefits that enhance the enjoyment of watching HDTV broadcasts and Blu-ray movies. Accessories such as wall mounts and floor stands enhance the value offering by enabling great flexibility in placing the set in a living room or home theater.

Intangible product attributes, including the status associated with product ownership, a manufacturer's service commitment, and a brand's overall reputation or mystique, are also important. When shopping for a new TV, many people want "the best": They want a TV loaded with features (tangible product elements), as well as one that is "cool" and makes a status statement (intangible product element).

Product Types

A frequently used framework for classifying products distinguishes between consumer and industrial goods. For example, Samsung offers products and services to both consumers and businesses worldwide. Consumer and industrial goods, in turn, can be further classified on the basis of criteria such as buyer orientation. Buyer orientation is a composite measure of the amount of effort a customer expends, the level of risk associated with a purchase, and buyer involvement in the purchase. The buyer orientation framework includes such categories as convenience, preference, shopping, and specialty goods. Electronics products are often high-involvement purchases, and many shoppers will compare several brands before making a decision. Products can also be categorized in terms of their life span (durable, nondurable, and disposable). Samsung and other electronics companies market products that are meant to last for many years; in other words, they are durable goods. As these examples from the electronics industry suggest, traditional product classification frameworks are fully applicable to global marketing.

Product Warranties

A warranty can be an important element of a product's value proposition. An **express warranty** is a written guarantee that assures the buyer that he or she is getting what he or she has paid for or that provides recourse in case a product's performance falls short of expectations. In global marketing, warranties can be used as a competitive tool to position a company in a positive way.

For example, in the late 1990s, Hyundai Motor America chief executive Finbarr O'Neill realized that many American car buyers perceived Korean cars as "cheap" and were skeptical about the Hyundai nameplate's reliability. Although the company had made significant improvements in the quality and reliability of its vehicles, consumer perceptions of the brand had not kept pace with the changes. O'Neill instituted a 10-year, 100,000-mile warranty program that represents the most comprehensive coverage in the auto industry. Concurrently, Hyundai launched several new vehicles and increased expenditures for advertising. The results have been impressive: Hyundai's U.S. sales jumped from approximately 90,000 vehicles in 1998 to nearly 665,000 vehicles in 2017. Hyundai has also overtaken Toyota as Europe's best-selling Asian car brand.

Packaging

Oftentimes, packaging is an integral element of product-related decisions. Packaging is an especially important consideration for products that are shipped to markets in far-flung corners of the world. The term *consumer packaged goods* (CPG) applies to a wide variety of products whose packaging is designed to protect or contain the product during shipping, at retail locations, and at the point of use or consumption. "Eco-packaging" is a key issue today, and package designers must address environmental issues such as recycling, biodegradability, and sustainable forestry.

Packaging also serves important communication functions: Packages (and the labels attached to them) offer communication cues that can influence consumers when making a purchase decision. Today, many industry experts agree that packaging must engage the senses, make an emotional connection, and enhance a consumer's brand experience. According to Bernd Schmitt, director of Columbia University's Center on Global Brand Leadership, "Packages are creating an experience for the customer that goes beyond the functional benefits of displaying and protecting the object."[1] Absolut Vodka, Altoids breath mints, and Godiva chocolates are a few examples of brands whose value proposition includes "experiential packaging."

Brewers, soft drink marketers, distillers, and other beverage firms typically devote considerable thought to ensuring that packages speak to consumers or provide some kind of benefit beyond simply holding liquid. For example, a critical element in the success of Corona Extra beer in export markets was management's decision to retain the traditional package design, which consists of a tall transparent bottle with "Made in Mexico" etched directly on the glass. At the time, the conventional wisdom in the brewing industry was that export beer bottles should be short, green or brown in color, with paper labels. In other words, the bottle should resemble Heineken's! The fact that consumers could see the beer inside the Corona Extra bottle made it seem more pure and natural. Today, Corona is the top-selling imported beer brand in the United States, Australia, Belgium, the Czech Republic, and several other countries.[2]

Coca-Cola's distinctive (and trademarked) contour bottle comes in both glass and plastic versions and helps consumers seek out the "real thing." The bottle design, which dates back to 1916, was intended to differentiate Coke from other soft drinks. The design is so distinctive that a consumer could even use his or her sense of touch to identify the bottle in the dark! The Coke example also illustrates the point that packaging strategies can vary by country and region. In North America, where large refrigerators are found in many households, one of Coca-Cola's packaging innovations is the Fridge Pack, a long, slender carton that holds the equivalent of 12 cans of soda. The Fridge Pack fits on a refrigerator's lower shelf and includes a tab for easy dispensing. In Latin America, by contrast, Coca-Cola executives intend to boost profitability by offering Coke in several different-sized bottles. Until recently, for example, 75 percent of Coke's volume in Argentina was accounted for by 2-liter bottles priced at $0.45 each. Now Coke has also introduced cold, individual-serving bottles priced at $0.33 that are stocked in stores near the front; unchilled, 1.25-liter returnable glass bottles priced at $0.28 are available on shelves farther back in the store.[3]

Other examples of packaging innovations include the following:

- Grey Goose, the world's top-selling super-premium vodka brand, was the brainchild of the late Sidney Frank. The owner of an importing business in New Rochelle, New York, Frank first devised the bottle design and name. Only then did he approach a distiller in Cognac, France, to create the actual vodka.[4]
- Nestlé's worldwide network of packaging teams contributes packaging improvement suggestions on a quarterly basis. Implemented changes include a plastic lid to make ice cream containers easier to open, slightly deeper indentations in the flat end of candy wrappers in Brazil that make them easier to rip open, and deeper notches on single-serve packets of Nescafé in China. Nestlé also asked suppliers to find a type of glue to make the clicking sound louder when consumers snap open a tube of Smarties-brand chocolate candies.[5]
- When GlaxoSmithKline launched Aquafresh Ultimate toothpaste in Europe, the marketing team wanted to differentiate the brand from category leader Colgate Total. Most tube toothpaste is sold in cardboard cartons that are stocked horizontally on store shelves. The team designed the Aquafresh Ultimate tube to stand up vertically. The tubes are distributed to stores in shelf-ready trays, and the box-free packaging saves hundreds of tons of paper each year.[6]

Labeling

One hallmark of the modern global marketplace is the abundance of multilanguage labeling that appears on many products. In today's self-service retail environments, product labels may be designed to attract attention, to support a product's positioning, and to help persuade consumers to buy. Labels can also provide consumers with various types of information. Obviously, care must be taken that all ingredient information and use and care instructions are properly translated.

The content of product labels may also be dictated by country- or region-specific regulations. Regulations regarding mandatory label content vary in different parts of the world; for example, the European Union now requires mandatory labeling for some foods containing genetically modified ingredients. Regulators in Australia, New Zealand, Japan, Russia, and several other countries have proposed similar legislation.

In the United States, the Nutrition Education and Labeling Act that went into effect in the early 1990s was intended to make food labels more informative and easier to understand. Today, virtually all food products sold in the United States must present, in a standard format, information regarding nutrition (e.g., calories and fat content) and serving size. The use of certain terms such as *light* and *natural* is also restricted.

Other examples of labeling in global marketing include the following:

- Mandatory health warnings on tobacco products are required in most countries.
- The American Automobile Labeling Act clarifies the country of origin, the final assembly point, and the percentages of the major sources of foreign content of every car, truck, and minivan sold in the United States (effective since October 1, 1994).
- Responding to pressure from consumer groups, in 2006 McDonald's began posting nutrition information on all food packaging and wrappers in approximately 20,000 restaurants in key markets worldwide. Executives indicated that issues pertaining to language and nutritional testing would delay labeling in 10,000 additional restaurants in smaller country markets.[7]
- Nestlé introduced Nan, an infant-formula brand that is popular in Latin America, in the American market. Targeted at Hispanic mothers, Nan's instructions are printed in Spanish on the front of the can. Competing brands have English-language labeling on the outside; Spanish-language instructions are printed on the reverse side.[8]
- In 2008, the United States enacted a country-of-origin labeling (COOL) law. The law requires supermarkets and other food retailers to display information that identifies the country from which meat, poultry, and certain other food products are sourced. France enacted a similar law in January 2017.

Aesthetics

In Chapter 4, the discussion of aesthetics included perceptions of color in different parts of the world. Global marketers must understand the importance of *visual aesthetics* embodied in the color or shape of a product, label, or package. Likewise, *aesthetic styles*, such as the degree of complexity found on a label, are perceived differently in different parts of the world. For example, it has been said that German wines would be more appealing in export markets if the labels were simplified. Put simply, aesthetic elements that are deemed appropriate, attractive, and appealing in a company's home country may be perceived differently—and to the product's detriment—elsewhere.

In some cases, a standardized color can be used in all countries; examples include the distinctive yellow color on Caterpillar's earthmoving equipment and its licensed outdoor gear, the red Marlboro chevron, and John Deere's signature green. In other instances, color choices should be changed in response to local perceptions. For example, as noted in Chapter 4, white is associated with death and bad luck in some Asian countries. When General Motors (GM) executives were negotiating with China for the opportunity to build cars there, they gave Chinese officials gifts from upscale Tiffany & Company in the jeweler's signature blue box. The Americans astutely replaced Tiffany's white ribbons with red ones because red is considered a lucky color in China and white has negative connotations (see the Emerging Markets Briefing Book sidebar later in the chapter).

Packaging aesthetics are particularly important to the Japanese. This point was driven home to the chief executive of a small U.S. company that manufactures an electronic device for controlling corrosion. After spending much time in Japan, the executive managed to secure several orders for the device. However, following an initial burst of success, Japanese orders dropped off; for one thing, the executive was told, the packaging was too plain. "We couldn't understand why we needed a five-color label and a custom-made box for this device, which goes under the hood of a car or in the boiler room of a utility company," the executive said. While waiting for the bullet train in Japan one day, the executive's local distributor purchased a cheap watch at the station and had it elegantly wrapped. The distributor asked the American executive to guess the value of the watch based on the packaging. Despite all that he had heard and read about the Japanese obsession with quality, it was the first time the American understood that, in Japan, "a book is judged by its cover." As a result, the company revamped its packaging, seeing to such details as ensuring that the strips of tape used to seal the boxes are cut to precisely the same length.[9]

 10-2 Compare and contrast local products and brands, international products and brands, and global products and brands.

(10-2) Basic Branding Concepts

A **brand** is a complex bundle of images and experiences in the customer's mind. Brands perform two important functions. First, a brand represents a promise by a particular company regarding a particular product; it is a type of quality certification. Second, brands enable customers to better organize their shopping experience by helping them seek out and find a particular product. Thus, an important brand function is to differentiate a particular company's offering from all other companies' offerings.

Customers integrate all their experiences of observing, using, or consuming a product with everything they hear and read about it. Information about products and brands comes from a variety of sources and cues, including advertising, publicity, word of mouth, sales personnel, and packaging. Perceptions of service after the sale, price, and distribution are also taken into account. The sum of these impressions is a **brand image**, defined as perceptions about a brand as reflected by brand associations that consumers hold in their memories.[10]

Brand image is one way that competitors in the same industry sector differentiate themselves. Take Apple and Samsung, for example. Both companies market smartphones. The late Steve Jobs, Apple's legendary cofounder and CEO, was a constant media presence and a master at generating buzz; the iPhone, iPad, and other Apple products generally receive stellar reviews for their sleek designs, powerful functionality, and user-friendly features. Apple's retail stores reinforce the brand's hip, cool image. By contrast, Samsung's brand image is more heavily skewed toward technology; few Samsung users are likely to know the name of the company's chief executive.

Another important brand concept is **brand equity**, which represents the total value that accrues to a product as a result of a company's cumulative investments in the marketing of the brand. Just as a homeowner's equity grows as a mortgage is paid off over the years, so brand equity grows as a company invests in the brand. Brand equity can also be thought of as an asset representing the value created by the relationship between the brand and its customers over time: The stronger the relationship, the greater the equity. For example, the value of global megabrands such as Coca-Cola and Marlboro runs in the tens of *billions* of dollars.[12] As outlined by branding expert Kevin Lane Keller, strong brand equity brings numerous benefits for the company:

- Greater loyalty
- Less vulnerability to marketing actions
- Less vulnerability to marketing crises
- Larger margins
- More inelastic consumer response to price increases
- More elastic consumer response to price decreases
- Increased marketing communication effectiveness[13]

Warren Buffett, the legendary American investor who heads Berkshire Hathaway, asserts that the global power of brands such as Coca-Cola and Gillette permits the companies that own them to set up a protective moat around their economic castles. As Buffett once explained, "The average company, by contrast, does battle daily without any such means of protection."[14] That protection often yields added profit because the owners of powerful brand names can typically command higher prices for their products than can owners of lesser brands. In other words, the strongest global brands have tremendous brand equity.

Companies develop logos, distinctive packaging, and other communication devices to provide visual representations of their brands. A logo can take a variety of forms, starting with the brand name itself. For example, the Coca-Cola brand is expressed in part by a *word mark* consisting of the words *Coke* and *Coca-Cola* written in a distinctive white script. The "wave" that appears on red Coke cans and bottle labels is an example of a *nonword mark logo*, sometimes known as a *brand symbol*. Nonword marks such as the Nike swoosh, the three-pronged Mercedes star, and McDonald's golden arches have the great advantage of transcending language and, therefore, are especially valuable to global marketers. To protect the substantial investment of time and money required to build and sustain brands, companies register brand names, logos, and other brand elements as trademarks or service marks. As discussed in Chapter 5, safeguarding trademarks and other forms of intellectual property is a key issue in global marketing.

Local Products and Brands

A **local product** or **local brand** is one that has achieved success in a single national market. Sometimes a global company creates local products and brands in an effort to cater to the needs and preferences of particular country markets. For example, Coca-Cola has developed several branded drink products for sale only in Japan, including a noncarbonated, ginseng-flavored beverage; a blended

"If you're into a certain brand, you expect a certain terminology and vocabulary. For brands, it's important to speak the language of the target audience."[11]

Ron Tolido, Global Chief Technology Officer for Insights and Data, Capgemini

"There is a strong local heritage in the brewing industry. People identify with their local brewery, which makes beer different from detergents or electronic products."[15]

Karel Vuursteen, chairman, Heineken

tea known as Sokenbicha; and the Lactia-brand fermented milk drink. In India, Coca-Cola markets bottled water under the Kinely brand. In contrast, the spirits industry often creates brand extensions to leverage popular brands without making large marketing expenditures. For example, Diageo PLC markets Gordon's Edge, a gin-based ready-to-drink beverage in the United Kingdom. Allied Domecq created TG, a brand flavored with Teacher's Scotch and guaraná, in Brazil.[16]

Local products and brands also represent the lifeblood of domestic companies. Entrenched local products and brands can present significant competitive hurdles to global companies that are seeking to enter new country markets. In China, for example, a sports-apparel company started by Olympic gold medalist Li Ning competes head to head with global powerhouse Nike. In developing countries, global brands are sometimes perceived as overpowering scrappy local ones. In some cases, growing national pride may result in a social backlash that favors local products and brands. In China, a local TV manufacturer, Changhong Electric Appliances, has generated a high degree of awareness among Chinese consumers by cutting prices and using patriotic advertising themes such as "Let Changhong hold the great flag of revitalizing our national industries."

White-goods maker Haier Group has also successfully fought off foreign competition and now accounts for 40 percent of China's refrigerator sales. In addition, Haier enjoys a 30 percent share of both the washing machine and air conditioner markets. Slogans stenciled on office walls delineate the aspirations of company president Zhang Ruimin: "Haier—Tomorrow's Global Brand Name" and "Never Say 'No' to the Market."[17] In 2002, Haier Group announced a strategic alliance with Taiwan's Sampo Group. The deal, valued at $300 million, called for each company to manufacture and sell the other's refrigerators and telecommunications products both globally and locally.

International Products and Brands

International products and **international brands** are offered in several markets in a particular region. For example, a number of "Euro products" and "Euro brands" such as Daimler's two-seat Smart car are available in Europe; the Smart was eventually launched in the United States as well. GM's experience with its Corsa model in the early 1990s provides a case study in how an international product or brand can be taken global. The Opel Corsa was a new model originally introduced in Europe. GM then decided to build different versions of the Corsa for China, Mexico, and Brazil. As David Herman, chairman of Adam Opel AG, noted, "The original concept was not that we planned to sell this car from the tip of Tierra del Fuego to the outer regions of Siberia. But we see its possibilities are limitless." GM calls the Corsa its "accidental world car."[18]

Honda had a similar experience with the Fit, a five-door hatchback built on the company's Global Small Car platform. Following Fit's successful Japanese launch in 2001, Honda rolled out the vehicle in Europe (where it is known as Jazz). Over the next few years, Fit was introduced in Australia, South America, South Africa, and China. The Fit model made its North American market debut in 2006.

Global Products and Brands

Globalization is putting pressure on companies to develop global products and to leverage brand equity on a worldwide basis. A **global product** meets the wants and needs of a global market. A true global product is offered in all world regions, including the Triad and in countries at every stage of development. A **global brand** has the same name and, in some instances, a similar image and positioning throughout the world. Some companies are well established as global brands. For example, when Nestlé asserts that it "Makes the very best," the quality promise is understood and accepted globally. The same is true for Gillette ("The best a man can get"), BMW ("The ultimate driving machine"), GE ("Imagination at work"), Harley-Davidson ("An American legend"), General Motors ("Find new roads"), and many other global companies (see Exhibit 10-2).

Former Gillette CEO Alfred Zeien explained his company's approach as follows:

> A multinational has operations in different countries. A global company views the world as a single country. We know Argentina and France are different, but we treat them the same. We sell them the same products, we use the same production methods, we have the same corporate policies. We even use the same advertising—in a different language, of course.[19]

Exhibit 10-2 In French ("*La perfection au masculin*"), German ("*Für das Besteim Mann*"), Italian ("*Il meglio di un uomo*"), Portuguese ("*O melhorpara o homem*"), or any other language, Gillette's trademarked brand promise is easy to understand.
Source: Joy Scheller/Avalon/Photoshot License Limited.

Zeien's remarks reflect the fact that Gillette creates competitive advantage by marketing global products and utilizing global branding strategies. The company reaps economies of scale associated with creating a single ad campaign for the world and the advantages of executing a single brand strategy. By contrast, Peter Brabeck-Letmathe, the former CEO of Nestlé, has a different perspective:

> We believe strongly that there isn't a so-called global consumer, at least not when it comes to food and beverages. People have local tastes based on their unique cultures and traditions—a good candy bar in Brazil is not the same as a good candy bar in China. Therefore, decision making needs to be pushed down as low as possible in the organization, out close to the markets. Otherwise, how can you make good brand decisions? A brand is a bundle of functional and emotional characteristics. We can't establish emotional links with consumers in Vietnam from our offices in Vevey.[20]

Whichever view prevails at headquarters, all global companies are trying to increase the visibility of their brands, especially in key markets such as the United States and China. Examples include Philips with its "Innovation and you" global image advertising and Siemens' recent "Siemens answers" campaign.

In the twenty-first century, global brands are becoming increasingly important. As one research team noted:

> People in different nations, often with conflicting viewpoints, participate in a shared conversation, drawing upon shared symbols. One of the key symbols in that conversation is the global brand. Like entertainment stars, sports celebrities, and politicians, global brands have become a lingua franca for consumers all over the world. People may love or hate transnational companies, but they can't ignore them.[21]

These researchers note that brands that are marketed around the world are endowed with both an aura of excellence and a set of obligations. Across the planet, consumers, corporate buyers, governments, activists, and other groups associate global brands with three characteristics, which consumers then use as a guide when making purchase decisions:

- *Quality signal.* Global brands compete fiercely with each other to provide world-class quality. A global brand name differentiates product offerings and allows marketers to charge premium prices.
- *Global myth.* Global brands are symbols of cultural ideals. As noted in Chapter 7, marketers can use global consumer culture positioning (GCCP) to communicate a brand's global identity and link that identity to aspirations in any part of the world.
- *Social responsibility.* Customers evaluate companies and brands in terms of how they address social problems and how they conduct business (see Exhibit 10-3).

Exhibit 10-3 Nucor is a steel company best known for its pioneering use of the minimill. Minimills produce steel by melting scrap in electric arc furnaces—a process that is much more efficient than the one used by traditional integrated steel producers. Nucor uses print and online media for an integrated general branding campaign featuring the tagline "It's our nature." This campaign is designed to raise awareness about the company's stance on a variety of issues, including the environment, energy conservation, sustainability, and the importance of creating a strong corporate culture.
Source: Nucor Corporation.

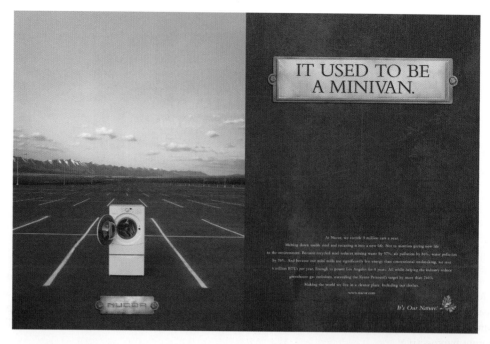

A global brand, however, is not the same thing as a global product. For example, personal stereos are a category of global product; Sony is a global brand. Many companies, including Sony, make personal stereos, but Sony created the category 30 years ago when it introduced the Walkman in Japan. The Sony Walkman is an example of **combination branding** or **tiered branding**, whereby a corporate name (Sony) is combined with a product brand name (Walkman). By using combination branding, marketers can leverage a company's reputation while developing a distinctive brand identity for a line of products. The combination brand approach can be a powerful tool for introducing new products. Although Sony markets a number of local products, the company also has a stellar track record as a global corporate brand, a creator of global products, and a marketer of global brands. For example, using the Walkman brand name as a point of departure, Sony created the Discman portable CD player and the Watchman portable TV. Sony's current global product brand offerings include Bravia brand HDTVs, Cyber-Shot digital cameras, PlayStation game consoles and portables, and the Xperia XZ smartphone.

Co-branding is a variation on combination branding in which two or more *different* company or product brands are featured prominently on product packaging or in advertising. When properly implemented, co-branding can engender customer loyalty and allow companies to achieve synergy. When done badly, it can confuse consumers and dilute brand equity. This approach works most effectively when the products involved complement each other. Credit card companies were the pioneers in the co-branding realm, so that today it is possible to use cards to earn frequent-flyer miles and discounts on automobiles. Another well-known example of co-branding is the Intel Inside campaign promoting both the Intel Corporation and its Pentium-brand processors in conjunction with advertising for various brands of personal computers.

Global companies can also leverage strong brands by creating **brand extensions**. This strategy entails using an established brand name as an umbrella when entering new businesses or developing new product lines that represent new categories to the company. British entrepreneur Richard Branson is an acknowledged master of this approach: The Virgin brand has been attached to a wide range of businesses and products (www.virgin.com). Virgin is a global brand, and the company's businesses include an airline, a railroad franchise, retail stores, movie theaters, financial services, and health clubs. Some of these businesses are global, and some are local. For example, Virgin Atlantic Airways flies to many global destinations, whereas Virgin Rail Group and Virgin Media operate only in the United Kingdom. The brand has been built on Branson's shrewd ability to exploit weaknesses in competitors' customer service skills, as well as his flair for self-promotion. Branson's business philosophy is that brands are built around reputation, quality, innovation, and price rather than image. Although Branson is intent on establishing Virgin as *the* British brand of the new millennium, some industry observers wonder if the brand has been spread too thin. Branson's newest ventures include spaceflight firm Virgin Galactic.

The history of the Sony Walkman illustrates the burden placed on visionary marketers to create global brands. Initially, Sony planned to market its personal stereo under three brand names. In their book *Breakthroughs!*, Ranganath Nayak and John Ketteringham describe how the global brand as we know it today came into being when famed Sony chairman Akio Morita realized that global consumers were one step ahead of his marketing staffers:

> At an international sales meeting in Tokyo, Morita introduced the Walkman to Sony representatives from America, Europe, and Australia. Within 2 months, the Walkman was introduced in the United States under the name "Soundabout"; 2 months later, it was on sale in the United Kingdom as "Stowaway." Sony in Japan had consented to the name changes because their English-speaking marketing groups had told them the name "Walkman" sounded funny in English. Nevertheless, with tourists importing the Walkman from Japan and spreading the original name faster than any advertising could have done, Walkman became the name most people used when they asked for the product in a store. Thus, *Sony managers found themselves losing sales because they had three different names for the same item.* Morita settled the issue at Sony's U.S. sales convention in May 1980 by declaring that, "funny or not," Walkman was the name everybody had to use.[22]

Table 10-1 shows the four combinations of local and global products and brands in matrix form. Each represents a different strategy; a global company can use one or more strategies as appropriate. Some global companies pursue strategy 1 by developing local products and brands for individual country or regional markets. Coca-Cola makes extensive use of this strategy: Its Georgia canned coffee in Japan is one example. Coca-Cola's flagship cola brand is an example of strategy 4. In South Africa, Coca-Cola markets Valpre brand bottled water (strategy 2). The global cosmetics industry makes extensive use of strategy 3: The marketers of Chanel, Givenchy, Clarins, Guerlain, and other leading cosmetics brands create different formulations for different regions of the world. However, the brand name and the packaging may be uniform everywhere.

Global Brand Development

Table 10-2 shows global brands ranked in terms of their economic value as determined by analysts at the Interbrand consultancy and Citigroup. To be included in the rankings, the brand has to generate approximately one-third of sales outside the home country; brands owned by privately held companies, such as Mars, are not included. Not surprisingly, technology giants Apple and Google occupy the top two spots. Coincidentally, Google also ranked number 3 in the 2017 Global Brand Simplicity Index compiled by Siegel+Gale; German discounter Aldi topped the rankings.[23]

The rankings show that strong brand management is being practiced by companies in a wide range of industries, from consumer packaged goods to electronics to automobiles. But even top brands have their ups and downs: When the 2012 rankings were released, Nokia had dropped out of the top 10. When he was president and CEO of Nokia, Stephen Elop partnered with Microsoft to develop a new generation of smartphones. Despite that collaboration, in the 2014 rankings, Nokia dropped out of the top 25 (see Exhibit 10-4). Following Microsoft's purchase of Nokia's Devices and Services business, Elop was named executive vice president of Microsoft Devices Group. HMD Global group is currently the owner of the Nokia smartphone brand.

Developing a global brand is not always an appropriate goal. As David Aaker and Erich Joachimsthaler note in the *Harvard Business Review*, managers who seek to build global brands must consider whether such a move fits well with their company or their markets. First, those managers must realistically assess whether anticipated scale economies will actually materialize.

TABLE 10-1 Product/Brand Matrix for Global Marketing

		Product	
		Local	Global
Brand	**Local**	1. Local product/local brand	2. Global product/local brand
	Global	3. Local product/global brand	4. Global product/global brand

TABLE 10-2 The World's Most Valuable Brands

Rank	Value ($ millions)	Rank	Value ($ millions)
1. Apple	184,154	14. Disney	40,772
2. Google	141,703	15. Intel	39,459
3. Microsoft	79,999	16. Cisco	31,930
4. Coca-Cola	69,733	17. Oracle	27,466
5. Amazon	64,796	18. Nike	27,021
6. Samsung	56,249	19. Louis Vuitton	22,919
7. Toyota	50,291	20. Honda	22,696
8. Facebook	48,188	21. SAP	22,635
9. Mercedes	47,829	22. Pepsi	21,491
10. IBM	46,829	23. H&M	20,488
11. GE	44,208	24. Zara	18,573
12. McDonald's	41,533	25. IKEA	18,472
13. BMW	41,521		

Source: Adapted from "Best Global Brands: 2017 Rankings," www.bestglobalbrands.com/2017/ranking/ (accessed March 1, 2018).

Second, they must recognize the difficulty of building a successful global brand team. Finally, managers must be alert to instances in which a single brand cannot be imposed on all markets successfully. Aaker and Joachimsthaler recommend that companies place a priority on creating strong brands in *all* markets through **global brand leadership**:

> Global brand leadership means using organizational structures, processes, and cultures to allocate brand-building resources globally, to create global synergies, and to develop a global brand strategy that coordinates and leverages country brand strategies.[24]

"People love the Uber product. They don't necessarily love the brand."[25]

Bozoma Saint John, chief brand officer, Uber

Mars Inc. confronted the global brand issue with its chocolate-covered caramel bar that was sold under a variety of national brand names, such as Snickers in the United States and Marathon in the United Kingdom. Management decided to transform the candy bar—already a global product—into a global brand. This decision entailed some risk, such as the possibility that consumers in the United Kingdom would associate the name Snickers with knickers, the British slang for a woman's undergarment. Mars also changed the name of its successful European chocolate biscuit from Raider to Twix, the same name used in the United States. In both instances, having a single brand name gave Mars the opportunity to leverage all of its product communications across national boundaries.

Exhibit 10-4 Annual global cellphone sales have passed the 1 billion units mark. Now, faced with saturated markets in the West, HMD Global, owner of the Nokia smartphone brand, and its competitors are looking to emerging markets for new customers. Robust economic growth and rising incomes mean that consumers in China, India, and other emerging markets can buy cellphones as status symbols. Many users are upgrading to new handsets with fashionable designs and the latest features, including myriad apps, wireless charging, and dual cameras.
Source: Jing Wei-Imaginechina/Associated Press.

Managers were forced to think globally about the positioning of Snickers and Twix—something that they had not been obliged to do when the candy products were marketed under different national brand names. The marketing team rose to the challenge; as Lord Saatchi described it:

> Mars decided there was a rich commercial prize at stake in ownership of a single human need: hunger satisfaction. From Hong Kong to Lima, people would know that Snickers was "a meal in a bar." Owning that emotion would not give them 100 percent of the global confectionery market but it would be enough. Its appeal would be wide enough to make Snickers the number-one confectionery brand in the world, which it is today.[26]

Table 10-3 lists the names of several global brands and describes the strategy behind the names. The following six guidelines can assist marketing managers in their efforts to establish global brand leadership:[27]

1. Create a compelling value proposition for customers in every market entered, beginning with the home-country market. A global brand begins with this foundation of value.
2. Before taking a brand across borders, think about all elements of brand identity and select names, marks, and symbols that have the potential for globalization. Give special attention to the Triad and BRICS nations.
3. Develop a company-wide communication system to share and leverage knowledge and information about marketing programs and customers in different countries.
4. Develop a consistent planning process across markets and products. Make a process template available to all managers in all markets.
5. Assign specific responsibility for managing branding issues to ensure that local brand managers accept global best practices. This can take a variety of forms, ranging from a business management team or a brand champion (led by senior executives) to a global brand manager or brand management team (led by middle managers).
6. Execute brand-building strategies that leverage global strengths and respond to relevant local differences.

Coke is perhaps the quintessential global product and global brand. Coke relies on similar positioning and marketing in all countries; it projects a global image of fun, good times, and enjoyment. The product itself, though, may vary to suit local tastes; for example, Coke increased the sweetness of its beverages in the Middle East, where customers prefer a sweeter drink. Also, prices may vary to suit local competitive conditions, and the channels of distribution may differ. In 2009,

TABLE 10-3   **Where Did That Name Come From?**

Company Name/HQ Country	History Behind the Name
Aldi (Germany)	"**Al**brecht **Di**scount," named for the two brothers who founded the company.
Alfa (Italy)	"Anonima Lombarda Fabbrica Automobili"
Alibaba (China)	"Everybody knows the story of Alibaba. He's a young man who is willing to help others."
Fiat (Italy)	"Fabbrica Italiana Automobil Torino"
Haribo (Germany)	**Ha**ns **Ri**egel Sr., **Bo**nn, named for the founder and the city where he lived.
IKEA (Sweden)	"**I**ngvar **K**amprad **E**lmtaryd **A**gunnaryd," named for founder's initials; the farm where he grew up; and name of hometown.
Kering (France)	Luxury goods firm formerly known as PPR. "Ker" means "home" in Brittany; "Kering" is pronounced like "caring" in English; name change intended to "soften company's image."
LEGO (Denmark)	"*Leg godt*" means "play well" in Danish.
Rimowa (Germany)	**Ri**chard **Mo**rszeck **Wa**renzichen; Richard is son of company founder Paul Morszeck
TOMS (USA)	Founder Blake Mycoskie shortened the name from "Shoes for a Better Tomorrow" and "Tomorrow's Shoes."

EMERGING MARKETS BRIEFING BOOK

China Gives Buick a New Lease on Life

GM's experience at home and abroad provides a good example of how a company's brand strategy must be adapted to cultural realities as well as the changing needs of the market. For example, in the 1990s GM was vying for the right to build a sedan in China. Company executives gave Chinese officials gifts from Tiffany's in the jeweler's signature blue boxes. However, the Americans replaced Tiffany's white ribbons with red ones: They recognized that red is considered a lucky color in China and white has negative connotations.

GM ultimately won government approval of its proposal and was given the opportunity to produce Buick sedans for government and business. Why was the Buick nameplate chosen from among GM's various vehicle brands? In an interview with *Fortune*, former GM CEO Rick Wagoner explained that the Chinese have a straightforward negotiation style. The Chinese wanted Buick; the American company suggested one of its global nameplates. The Chinese were adamant, saying, "We'd like you to use Buick." The Americans agreed, and a deal was struck.

Back at home, Buick's image has been in decline for decades. The average Buick buyer is 61 years old; this demographic stands in marked contrast to that served by, say, Volvo, whose average buyer is only 50. Buick was once a popular aspirational brand among American drivers; one advertising tagline asked, "Wouldn't you really rather have a Buick?" The line was designed to motivate a Ford owner to take a step up in class by choosing a Buick LeSabre or Riviera. Another headline read, "Want the Big buy for Big families?"

Unfortunately, by the mid-1980s, Buick had fallen victim to corporate consolidation and cost cutting. The resulting design and engineering overlap meant that some car buyers found it difficult to distinguish among models from GM's different divisions. A case in point: The Riviera, the Oldsmobile Toronado, and the Cadillac Eldorado were all very similar. Even the breakthrough design of the 1995 Riviera could not breathe new life into the brand; despite rave reviews (*Autoweek* said the new design was "bound to make waves

in the luxury coupe segment"), the Riviera model itself was retired in 1999.

By 2009, Buick's Chinese sales totaled 450,000, more than four times the U.S. sales figure. Moreover, the typical Buick owner in China is 35 years old. These facts help explain why the Buick nameplate is still in production. When the U.S. government took control of GM, it pressured GM chief Fritz Henderson to terminate Buick. Thanks to the brand's popularity in China, it was given a reprieve. Meanwhile, GM has phased out Oldsmobile, Pontiac, and Saturn. One auto analyst summarized the situation by noting, "In China, GM has played a local strategy. They left the people running Buick alone, and they were extremely successful in building the brand there."

Now the task facing the company's American marketing managers is to revitalize the Buick brand at home. New models such as the mid-sized Regal and the Verano compact sedan are integral to that effort. The Regal is built in Germany, and some early print ads positioned it as having European roots. For example, one ad suggested, "Listen closely and you might detect a German accent." As Craig Bierley, advertising and promotions director, told *Financial Times*, "The goal is about expanding the audience for the brand. Germany automatically says 'sports sedan' to people." In summer 2016, the Buick Envision, a midsize SUV, was launched in the United States. It is sure to be a case study in Buick's global strategy, for one simple reason: The Envision is the first Chinese-assembled mass-market vehicle sold in the United States (see Exhibit 10-5).

Sources: James R. Healey, "Buick Tries to Buff Away Its Image as Inefficient Carmaker," *USA Today* (June 22, 2012), pp. 1B, 2B; Sharon Terlep, "GM Seeks Sway in China," *The Wall Street Journal* (April 19, 2012), pp. B1, B2; Bernard Simon, "Out with the Old," *Financial Times* (October 18, 2010); Jens Meiners, "Chinese Takeout," *Car and Driver* (October 2010), pp. 31–32; John D. Stoll, "East Meets West," *The Wall Street Journal* (June 23, 2008), p. R5; Alex Taylor III, "China Would Rather Have Buicks," *Fortune* (October 4, 2004), p. 98; Matt DeLorenzo, "Cruising in Style," *Autoweek* (December 6, 1993), pp. 13–14.

Exhibit 10-5 GM's Buick brand is one of the top-selling nameplates in China. Overall, the Buick Division sold 1.4 million vehicles in 2017. In China, seven new Buick models launched in 2017 helped keep sales running at a brisk pace. This photo shows United States-bound Buick Envision SUVs ready to be loaded at a Chinese port.
Source: VCG/Getty Images.

Coke adopted the global advertising theme "Open Happiness." The previous slogan, "The Coke Side of Life," was also global but required adaptation in emerging markets such as Russia and China.[28] In 2016, Coke replaced "Open Happiness" with a new global tagline, "Taste the Feeling."

Summing up, the basic, underlying strategic principles that guide the management of the brand are the same worldwide. The issue is not exact uniformity but rather a more subtle question: Are we offering *essentially* the same product and brand promise? As discussed in the next few chapters, other elements of the marketing mix—for example, price, communications appeal and media strategy, and distribution channels—may vary as well.

(10-3) A Needs-Based Approach to Product Planning

◄ **10-3** Explain how Maslow's needs hierarchy helps global marketers understand the benefits sought by buyers in different parts of the world.

Coca-Cola, McDonald's, Singapore Airlines, Mercedes-Benz, and Sony are a few of the companies that have transformed local products and brands into global ones. The essence of marketing is finding needs and filling them. **Maslow's needs hierarchy**—a staple of sociology and psychology courses—provides a useful framework for understanding how and why local products and brands can be extended beyond home-country borders. Maslow proposed that people's desires can be arranged into a hierarchy of five needs.[29] As an individual fulfills needs at each level, he or she progresses to higher levels (Figure 10-1). At the most basic level of human existence, physiological and safety needs must be met. People need food, clothing, and shelter, and a product that meets these basic needs has potential for globalization.

Of course, the basic human need to consume food and drink for nutrition is not the same thing as wanting or preferring a Big Mac or a Coke. Before the Coca-Cola Company and McDonald's conquered the world, they built their brands and business systems at home. Because their products fulfilled basic human needs and because both companies are masterful marketers, they were able to cross geographic boundaries and build global brand franchises. At the same time, Coca-Cola and McDonald's have learned from experience that some food and drink preferences—China is a case in point—remain deeply embedded in culture.[30] Responding to those differences has meant creating local products and brands for particular country markets. Sony has prospered for a similar reason. Audio and video entertainment products fulfill important social functions. Throughout its history, Sony's corporate vision has called for developing new products, such as the transistor radio and the Walkman personal stereo, that fulfill the need for mobile entertainment.

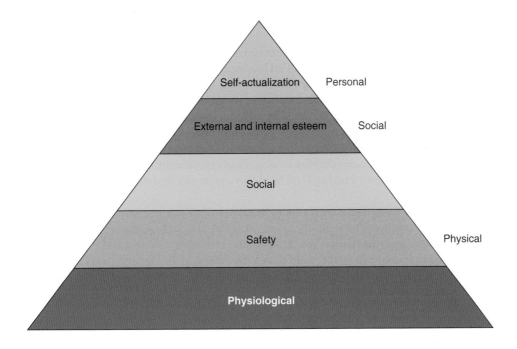

FIGURE 10-1 Maslow's Hierarchy of Needs

Source: A. H. Maslow, "A Theory of Human Motivation," in *Readings in Managerial Psychology*, Harold J. Levitt and Louis R. Pondy, eds. (Chicago, IL: University of Chicago Press, 1964), pp. 6–24. Original—*Psychological Review* 50 (1943).

Mid-level needs in Maslow's hierarchy of needs include self-respect, self-esteem, and the esteem of others. These social needs, which can create a powerful internal motivation driving demand for status-oriented products, cut across the various stages of country development. Gillette's Alfred Zeien understood this point quite well. Marketers in Gillette's Parker Pen subsidiary are confident that consumers in Malaysia and Singapore shopping for an upscale gift will buy the same Parker pen as Americans shopping at Neiman Marcus. "We are not going to come out with a special product for Malaysia," Zeien has said.[31] In Asia today, young women are taking up smoking as a status symbol—and showing a preference for Western brands such as Marlboro. At the same time, those smokers' needs and wants may be tempered by economic circumstances. Recognizing this reality, companies such as BAT create local brands that allow individuals to indulge their desire or need to smoke at a price they can afford to pay.

Luxury goods marketers are especially skilled at catering to esteem needs on a global basis. Rolex, Louis Vuitton, and Dom Perignon are just a few of the global brands that consumers buy in an effort to satisfy esteem needs. Some consumers flaunt their wealth by buying expensive products and brands that others will notice—a behavior referred to as *conspicuous consumption* or *luxury badging*. Any company with a premium product or brand that has proved itself in a local market by fulfilling esteem needs should consider devising a strategy for taking the product global.

Products can fulfill different needs in different countries. Consider the refrigerator as used in industrialized, high-income countries. The *primary function* of the refrigerator in these countries is related to basic needs as fulfilled in that society: storing frozen foods for extended periods; keeping milk, meat, and other perishable foods fresh between car trips to the supermarket; and making ice cubes.

In lower-income countries, by contrast, frozen foods are not widely available and home-makers shop for food daily, rather than weekly. In these markets, people are reluctant to pay for unnecessary features such as icemakers, because they are perceived as luxuries that require high income levels to support. The function of the refrigerator in a lower-income country is to store small quantities of perishable food for one day and to store leftovers for slightly longer periods. Because the needs fulfilled by the refrigerator are limited in these countries, a relatively small refrigerator is quite adequate.

In some developing countries, refrigerators have an important *secondary purpose* related to higher-order needs: They fulfill a need for prestige. In these countries, there is demand for the largest model available, which is prominently displayed in the living room rather than hidden in the kitchen (see Exhibit 10-6).

Today, some Indian companies are developing innovative new products that the country's poorest consumers can afford. For example, one company has created the Little Cool refrigerator. Selling for the equivalent of $70, the device is small and portable. It has only 20 parts, about one-tenth the number of parts that are found in conventional full-sized units.

Hellmut Schütte has proposed a modified hierarchy to explain the needs and wants of Asian consumers (see Figure 10-2).[33] Although the two lower-level needs are the same as in the traditional hierarchy, the three highest levels emphasize social needs. *Affiliation needs* in Asia are satisfied when an individual has been accepted by a group. In keeping with these needs, conformity with group norms becomes a key force driving consumer behavior. For example, when a cool new cell phone hits the market, every teenager who wants to fit in buys one. Understanding this drive, managers at Japanese companies develop local products specifically designed to appeal to teens. The next level is *admiration*, a higher-level need that can be satisfied through acts that command respect within a group.

At the top of the Asian hierarchy is *status*, the esteem of society as a whole. In part, attainment of high status is character driven, but the quest for status also leads to luxury badging. Support for Schütte's contention that status is the highest-ranking need in the Asian hierarchy can be seen in the geographic breakdown of the more than $200 billion global luxury goods market: Fully 20 percent of industry sales are generated in Japan alone, with another 22 percent of sales occurring in the rest of the Asia-Pacific region. Nearly half of all sales revenues of Italy's Gucci Group are generated in Asia.

"For Asians, face is very important, so you have to show you are up to date with the latest available product."[32]

Alan Chang, View Sonic (Taiwan), explaining the popularity of flat-panel TVs in Japan

"Every Chinese person has an iPhone now, even cooks and cleaners, so if rich people want to show their status, the best way is with an expensive toilet."[34]

Andy Yang, Ikahe Sanitary Ware, a subsidiary of Chinese manufacturer Megmeet, which makes a $2,000 smart toilet

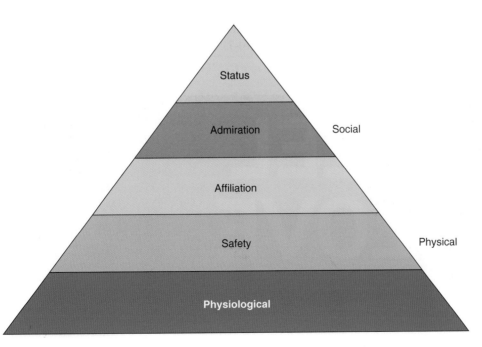

FIGURE 10-2 Maslow's Hierarchy: The Asian Equivalent

10-4 "Country of Origin" as a Brand Element

One of the facts of life in global marketing is that perceptions of and attitudes toward particular countries often extend to products and brands known to originate in those countries. Such perceptions contribute to the **country-of-origin effect**; they become part of a brand's image and contribute to brand equity. This is particularly true for automobiles, electronics, fashion, beer, recorded music, and certain food products.

Perceptions and attitudes about a product's origins can be either positive or negative. On the positive side, as one marketing expert pointed out in the mid-1990s, "'German' is synonymous with quality engineering, 'Italian' is synonymous with style, and 'French' is synonymous with chic."[36] Why is this still true today, especially in emerging markets? As Diego Della Valle, CEO of Italian luxury goods marketer Tod's, explains:

> "Made in Italy" will retain its luster because it is still the maximum guarantee of high quality for products such as ours. Like the French for perfume, the Swiss for watches. The Chinese do not want to buy "Made in China."[37]

The manufacturing reputation of a particular country can change over time. Studies conducted during the 1970s and 1980s indicated that the "Made in the USA" image had lost ground to the "Made in Japan" image. Today, however, U.S. brands are finding renewed acceptance globally. Examples include the Jeep Cherokee, clothing from Lands' End and American Apparel, and Budweiser beer, all of which are being successfully marketed with strong "USA" themes. Even so, companies must be able to back up their "Made in the USA" claims. For example, Shinola, a manufacturer based in Detroit, used the slogan "Where America is made" and "Made in Detroit" in its watch advertising. As it turns out, however, the watches are assembled in the United States from imported components. The United States Federal Trade Commission ruled that the company would have to amend its slogan to read "Built in Detroit using Swiss and imported parts."

Finland is home to Nokia, the one-time leader in cell phones that now focuses on telecommunications equipment. Nokia rose in stature from a local company to a global one in little more than a decade. However, as brand strategy expert Simon Anholt points out, other Finnish companies need to move quickly to capitalize on Nokia's success if Finland is to become a valuable nation-brand. For example, Raisio Oy's Benecol brand margarine has been shown to lower cholesterol levels. If large numbers of health-conscious consumers around the world embrace so-called nutraceutical products, Raisio and Benecol may become well-known brands and further raise Finland's profile on the global scene. Anholt also notes that Slovenia and other countries are "launch brands," in the sense that they lack centuries of tradition and foreign interaction upon which to build their reputations (see Exhibit 10-7):

> "China is complex and becoming more so. But 'Made in Germany' still carries great appeal here and if you prepare seriously, there are few limits to what you can achieve."[35]
>
> Christian Sommer, German Centre for Industry and Trade

Exhibit 10-7 Countries, like products, can be branded and positioned. For example, Slovenia recently launched an integrated brand image campaign that will be used by a variety of governmental and nongovernmental organizations. "Slovenian green" is the dominant color in the new logo. As the Government Communication Office explains, "It refers to the natural balance and calm diligence of Slovenes. One can feel Slovenia through the smell of the forest, the rushing of the creek, the fresh taste of water and the softness of wood. . . . "
Source: Embassy of the Republic of Slovenia.

For a country like Slovenia to enhance its image abroad is a very different matter than for Scotland or China. Slovenia needs to be launched: Consumers around the world first must be taught where it is, what it makes, what it has to offer, and what it stands for. This in itself represents a powerful opportunity: The chance to build a modern country brand, untainted by centuries of possibly negative associations.[38]

Since the mid-1990s, the "Made in Mexico" image has gained in stature as local companies and global manufacturers have established world-class manufacturing plants in Mexico to supply world demand. For example, Ford, GM, Nissan, Volkswagen, and other global automakers have established Mexican operations that produce nearly 2 million vehicles per year, three-fourths of which are exported.[39] Similarly, consumer attitudes toward "Made in Japan" have come a long way since the mid-1970s. What about "Made in China" or "Made in India"? China and India take great pride in their manufacturing capabilities but, generally speaking, consumer perception lags behind the reality. They face quite a challenge in shaping their brands: How do you change that image?[40]

In some product categories, foreign products have a substantial advantage over their domestic counterparts simply because of their "foreign-ness." Global marketers, in turn, recognize that they can capitalize on that situation by charging premium prices. The import segment of the beer industry is a case in point. In one study of American attitudes toward beer, subjects who were asked to taste beer with the labels concealed indicated a preference for domestic beers over imports. The same subjects were then asked to indicate preference ratings for beers in an open test with labels attached. In this test, the subjects preferred imported beer. Conclusion: The subjects' perceptions were positively influenced by the knowledge they were drinking an import. In 1997, thanks to a brilliant marketing campaign, Grupo Modelo's Corona Extra surpassed Heineken as the best-selling imported beer in America. With distribution in 150 countries, Corona is a textbook example of a local brand that has been built into a global powerhouse.

Scotland provides an interesting case study of a country that enjoys strong brand equity but is somewhat misunderstood. A study titled "Project Galore" was undertaken to discover which aspects of Scotland's equity could be leveraged for commercial advantage. Among other things, the researchers learned that high-quality goods and services such as whisky, wool, salmon, and golf courses were perceived as Scotland's core industries. In fact, Scotland's top export category is information technology! The researchers created a perceptual map that identified Scotland's four key values: integrity, tenacity, inventiveness, and spirit.[41] Similarly, other regions, countries, and cities use a variety of marketing tools to promoting business and economic development (see Exhibit 10-8).

> "Consider labels such as 'Made in Brazil' and 'Made in Thailand.' Someday they may be symbols of high quality and value, but today many consumers expect products from those countries to be inferior."[42]
>
> Christopher A. Bartlett and Sumantra Ghoshal

Exhibit 10-8 Las Cruces, New Mexico, is home to Spaceport America. From here, Virgin Galactic will offer civilian space flight services. Economic development managers for the City of Las Cruces devise marketing campaigns to attract individuals and organizations to the area by offering "Mountains of Opportunity."
Source: City of Las Cruces.

▶ **10-5** List the five strategic alternatives that marketers can utilize during the global product planning process.

(10-5) Extend, Adapt, Create: Strategic Alternatives in Global Marketing

To capitalize on opportunities outside the home country, company managers must devise and implement appropriate marketing programs. Depending on organizational objectives and market needs, a particular program may consist of extension strategies, adaptation strategies, or a combination of the two. A company that has developed a successful local product or brand can implement an **extension strategy** that calls for offering a product virtually unchanged (i.e., "extending" it) in markets outside the home country. A second option, known as an **adaptation strategy**, involves changing elements of design, function, or packaging in response to needs or conditions in particular country markets. Such a product strategy can be used in conjunction with extension or adaptation communication strategies. For example, this type of strategic decision faces executives at a company like Starbucks, who build a brand and a product/service offering in the home-country market before expanding into global markets. A third strategic option, **product invention**, entails developing new products "from the ground up" with the world market in mind.

Laws and regulations in different countries frequently lead to obligatory product design adaptations. This mandate may be seen most clearly in Europe, where one impetus for the creation of the single market was the desire to dismantle regulatory and legal barriers that prevented pan-European sales of standardized products. In particular, technical standards and health and safety standards created obstacles to marketing of such products. In the food industry, for example, there were 200 legal and regulatory barriers to cross-border trade within the European Union in 10 food categories. Among these were prohibitions or taxes on products with certain ingredients and different packaging and labeling laws. As these barriers are dismantled, there will be less need to adapt product designs, and many companies will be able to create standardized "Euro-products."

Despite the trend toward convergence in Europe, many product standards that remain on the books have not been harmonized. This situation can create problems for companies not based in EU member countries. For example, Dormont Manufacturing—appropriately based in Export, Pennsylvania—makes hoses that hook up to deep-fat fryers and similar appliances used in the food industry. Dormont's gas hose is made of stainless-steel helical tubing with no covering. British industry requirements call for galvanized metal annular tubing and a rubber covering; Italian regulations specify stainless-steel annular tubing with no covering. The cost of complying with these regulations effectively shuts Dormont out of the European market.[43]

Moreover, the European Commission continues to set product standards that force many non-EU companies to adapt their product or service offerings to satisfy domestic market regulations. For example, consumer safety regulations mean that McDonald's cannot include soft plastic toys in its Happy Meals in Europe. Microsoft has been forced to modify contracts with European software makers and Internet service providers to ensure that EU-based consumers have access to a wide range of technologies. The commission has also set stringent guidelines on product content as it affects recyclability. As Maja Wessels, a Brussels-based lobbyist for United Technologies Corporation (UTC), noted, "Twenty years ago, if you designed something to U.S. standards you could pretty much sell it all over the world. Now the shoe's on the other foot." Engineers at UTC's Carrier division have redesigned the company's air conditioners to comply with pending European recycling rules, which are tougher than U.S. standards.[44]

As noted in Chapter 1, the extension/adaptation/creation decision is one of the most fundamental issues addressed by a company's global marketing strategy. Although it pertains to all elements of the marketing mix, extension/adaptation is of particular importance in product and communications decisions. Earlier in the chapter, Table 10-1 displayed product and brand strategic options in matrix form. Figure 10-3 expands on those options: All aspects of promotion and communication—not just branding—are considered. Figure 10-3 shows four strategic alternatives available to Starbucks or any other company seeking to expand from its domestic base into new geographic markets.

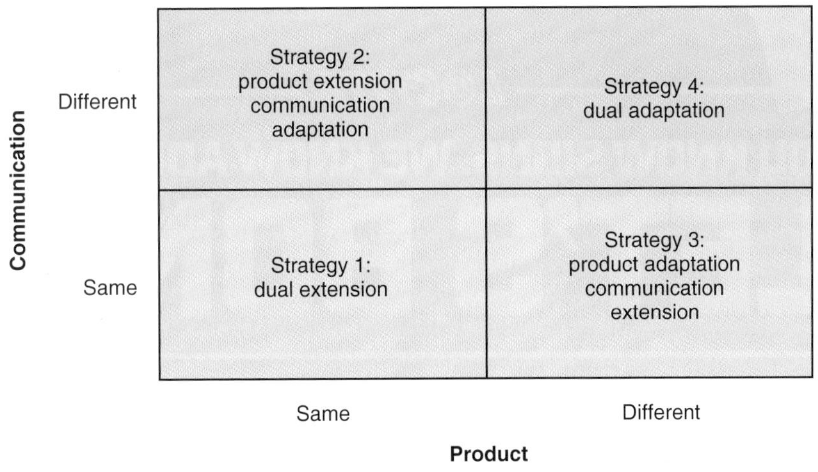

FIGURE 10-3 Global Product Planning: Strategic Alternatives

Companies in the international, global, and transnational stages of development all employ extension strategies. The critical difference is one of execution and mind-set. In an international company, for example, the extension strategy reflects an ethnocentric orientation and the *assumption* that all markets are alike. A global company such as Gillette does not fall victim to such assumptions; the company's geocentric orientation allows it to thoroughly understand its markets and consciously take advantage of similarities in world markets. Likewise, a multinational company utilizes the adaptation strategy because of its polycentric orientation and the assumption that all markets are different. By contrast, the geocentric orientation of managers and executives in a global company has sensitized them to actual, rather than assumed, differences between markets. The key, as one executive has noted, is to avoid being either "hopelessly local" or "mindlessly global."

Strategy 1: Product-Communication Extension (Dual Extension)

Many companies employ the **product-communication extension** strategy when pursuing global market opportunities. Under the right conditions, this is a very straightforward marketing strategy; it can be the most profitable approach as well. Companies pursuing this strategy sell the same product with essentially no adaptation, using the same advertising and promotional appeals used domestically, in two or more country markets or segments. For this strategy to be effective, the advertiser's message must be understood across different cultures, including those in emerging markets. Examples of the dual-extension strategy include the following:

- Apple launched its iPhone in the United States in mid-2007. In the following months, this product was gradually rolled out in several more markets, including France and the United Kingdom. When Apple brought its second-generation iPhone to market 1 year later, it was launched in 21 countries simultaneously.
- Henkel KGaA markets its Loctite-brand family of adhesive products globally using the dual-extension strategy (see Exhibit 10-9). The company's various lines—including medical adhesives and threadlockers—bear the Loctite brand name. Ads also include the Henkel corporate logo.

As a general rule, extension/standardization strategies are utilized more frequently with industrial (business-to-business) products than with consumer products. The reason is simple: Industrial products tend to be less deeply rooted in culture than are consumer goods. But if this is so, how can Apple—the consummate consumer brand—utilize the dual-extension strategy to such good effect? One explanation is that, as discussed in Chapter 7, the brand's high-tech, high-touch image lends itself to global consumer culture positioning.

Exhibit 10-9 Germany's Henkel is a global company that markets industrial and consumer products in three main categories: adhesives; laundry and home care; and beauty. The Loctite family of adhesives and sealants has a wide range of applications in the home as well as in medical and industrial settings. Henkel's portfolio also includes such popular consumer brands as Right Guard, Dial, Persil, and Purex.
Source: Henkel Corporation.

As these examples show, technology companies and industrial goods manufacturers should be especially alert to dual-extension possibilities. However, Henkel also markets hundreds of other glues, detergents, and personal-care products with different formulas and different brand names. Speaking about Loctite, former Henkel CEO Ulrich Lehner explained, "There aren't many products like that. Usually, you have to adapt to local tastes. You have to balance between local insight and centralized economies of scale. It's a constant battle."[45] Henkel's Persil brand laundry detergent is a case in point. Although the Persil name is used in more than two dozen countries, the same detergent is marketed as Dixan in Greece, Italy, and Cyprus. Wipp is the name used in Spain and China; in other markets, variants include Nadhif and Fab.

Strategy 2: Product Extension–Communication Adaptation

In some instances, a product or brand can be successfully extended to multiple country markets with some modification of the communication strategy. Research may have revealed that consumer perceptions about one or more aspects of the value proposition are different from country to country. It may also turn out that a product fills a different need, appeals to a different segment, or serves a different function in a particular country or region. Whatever the reason, extending the product while adapting the marketing communications program may be the key to market success. The appeal of the **product extension–communication adaptation** strategy is its relatively low cost of implementation. Because the product itself is unchanged, the company avoids additional expenditures for research and development (R&D), manufacturing setup, and inventory. Instead, the biggest costs associated with this approach stem from researching the market and revising advertising, sales promotion efforts, point-of-sale material, and other communication elements as appropriate.

Consider the following examples of product extension–communication adaptation:

- In Hungary, Slovakia, and other Central European countries, SABMiller positions Miller Genuine Draft as an international lifestyle brand (GCCP) rather than an American brand (foreign consumer culture positioning [FCCP]). The communication adaptation strategy was chosen after focus group research showed that many Europeans have a low regard for American beer.[46]
- Before executives at Ben & Jerry's Homemade launched their ice cream in the United Kingdom, the company conducted extensive research to determine whether the package design effectively communicated the brand's "super-premium" position. The research indicated that British consumers perceived the colors differently than U.S. consumers do. The package design was then changed, and Ben & Jerry's was launched successfully in the UK market.

- To promote its Centrino wireless chip, Intel launched a global ad campaign that features different combinations of celebrities. In print, TV, and online ads, one of the celebrities sits on the lap of a mobile computer user. The celebrities—including comedian John Cleese, actress Lucy Liu, and skateboard king Tony Hawk—were chosen because they are widely recognized in key world markets.[47]
- In the United States, Sony's TV ads for its Bravia high-definition TVs encourage viewers to log onto the Internet and choose different endings. In Europe, the ads are completely different: They feature bright images such as colored balls bouncing in slow motion. As Mike Fasulo, chief marketing officer at Sony Electronics, explains, "Consumer adoption as well as awareness of high-definition products, including our line of Bravia televisions, differs dramatically from region to region."[48]
- Targeting the 300 million farmers in India who still use plows harnessed to oxen, John Deere engineers created a line of relatively inexpensive, no-frills tractors. The Deere team then realized that the same equipment could be marketed to hobby farmers and acreage owners in the United States—a segment that the company had previously overlooked.[49]

Marketers of premium American bourbon brands such as Wild Turkey have found that images of Delta blues music, New Orleans, and Route 66 appeal to upscale drinkers outside the United States. However, images that stress bourbon's rustic, backwoods origins do not necessarily appeal to Americans. As Gary Regan, author of *The Book of Bourbon*, has noted, "Europeans hate Americans when they think of them as being the policemen of the world, but they love Americans when they think about blue jeans and bourbon and ranches."[51]

Likewise, Jägermeister schnapps is marketed differently in different key country markets. Chief executive Hasso Kaempfe believes that a diversity of images has been a key element in the success of Jägermeister outside of Germany, where the brown, herb-based concoction originated. In the United States, Jägermeister was "discovered" in the mid-1990s by the college crowd. In turn, Kaempfe's marketing team has capitalized on the brand's cult status by hiring "Jägerettes," girls who pass out free samples; the company's popular T-shirts and orange banners are also distributed at rock concerts. By contrast, in Italy, the brand's second-largest export market, Jägermeister is considered an up-market digestive to be consumed after dinner. In Germany, Austria, and Switzerland, where beer culture predominates, Jägermeister and other brands of schnapps have more traditional associations as a remedy for coughs and stomachaches, or as a "morning after" elixir.[52]

Jägermeister is an example of **product transformation**: The same physical product ends up serving a different function or use than that for which it was originally designed or created. In some cases, a particular country or regional environment will allow local managers a greater degree of creativity and risk taking when approaching the communication task.

> "I can think of very few truly global ads that work. Brands are often at different stages around the world, and that means there are different advertising jobs to do."[50]
>
> Michael Conrad, chief creative officer, Leo Burnett Worldwide

Strategy 3: Product Adaptation–Communication Extension

A third approach to global product planning is to adapt the product to local use or preference conditions while extending, with minimal change, the basic home-market communications strategy or brand name. This third strategy option is known as **product adaptation–communication extension**. For example:

- For many years, Ford sold the Escort, Focus, and other nameplates worldwide, though the vehicles themselves often varied from region to region. In 2010, Ford launched a new Focus model in the United States that has 80 percent shared content with the European Focus. The 20 percent adapted content reflects regulations such as bumper crash test standards.[53]
- When Kraft Foods launched Oreo-brand cookies in China in 1996, it used a product extension approach. Following several years of flat sales, Kraft's in-country marketing team launched a research study, which alerted the team to the fact that Oreos were too sweet for the Chinese palate and that the price—14 cookies for 72 cents—was too high. Oreos were then reformulated as a less-sweet, chocolate-covered, four-layer

wafer filled with vanilla and chocolate cream. Packages of the new wafer Oreo contain fewer cookies but sell for about 29 cents. Today, Oreo is the best-selling cookie brand in China.[54]

Kraft's experience with Oreos in China illustrates the process of changing from a product extension to a product adaptation strategy when an extension strategy does not yield the desired results. Conversely, managers at Ford, faced with strong competition from Toyota, Honda, and other automakers, are now seeking alternatives to product adaptation. In 2008, Ford unveiled the latest version of its Fiesta. It is designed to be manufactured in high volumes—as many as 1 million units annually—that can be sold worldwide with minimal adaptation. As former Ford CEO Mark Shields explained, "This is a real shift point for us in that it's a real global car."[55]

Strategy 4: Product-Communication Adaptation (Dual Adaptation)

Some companies may utilize a **product-communication adaptation (dual adaptation)** strategy. As the name of this strategy implies, both the product and one or more promotional elements are adapted for a particular country or region. Sometimes marketers discover that environmental conditions or consumer preferences differ from country to country; the same may be true of the function a product serves or consumer receptivity to advertising appeals. In cases where country managers who have been granted considerable autonomy order adaptations, they may be simply exercising their power to act independently. If headquarters tries to achieve intercountry coordination, the result can be, in the words of one manager, "like herding cats."

Consider Unilever's use of dual adaptation strategies. Unilever's Italian country managers discovered that, although Italian women spend more than 20 hours each week cleaning, ironing, and doing other tasks, they are not interested in labor-saving conveniences. The final result—a really clean, shiny floor, for example—is more important than saving time. For the Italian market, Unilever reformulated its Cif brand spray cleaner to do a better job on grease; several different varieties were also rolled out, as were bigger bottles. Television commercials portray Cif as strong rather than convenient.[56]

In another product line, Unilever's Rexona deodorant once had 30 different package designs and 48 different formulations. Advertising and branding were also executed on a local basis.[57] In the case of Cif in Italy, managers had boosted sales by making product and promotion improvements based on business intelligence findings. By contrast, the multiple formulations of the Rexona brand were, for the most part, redundant and unnecessary. To address such issues, in 1999, Unilever initiated Path to Growth, a program designed to reduce country-by-country tinkering with product formulations and packaging.

As noted previously, the four strategy alternatives are not mutually exclusive. In other words, a company can simultaneously utilize different product-communication strategies in different parts of the world. For example, Nike has built a global brand by marketing technologically advanced, premium-priced athletic shoes in conjunction with advertising that emphasizes U.S.-style, in-your-face brashness and a "Just Do It" attitude. In the huge and strategically important China market, however, this approach had several limitations.

For one thing, Nike's "bad boy" image is at odds with ingrained Chinese values such as respect for authority and filial piety. As a general rule, Nike advertisements in China do not show disruption of harmony; this is due, in part, to a government that discourages dissent. Price was another issue: A regular pair of Nike shoes cost the equivalent of $60–$78, while average annual family income in China ranges from approximately $200 in rural areas to $500 in urban areas. In the mid-1990s, Nike responded to these factors by creating a shoe that could be assembled in China specifically for the Chinese market using less expensive material and sold for less than $40. After years of running ads designed for Western markets by longtime agency Wieden & Kennedy, Nike hired Chinese-speaking art directors and copywriters working in WPP Group's J. Walter Thompson ad agency in Shanghai to create new advertising featuring local athletes; the ads were designed to appeal to Chinese nationalistic sentiments.[58]

Strategy 5: Innovation

Extension and adaptation strategies are effective approaches to many, but not all, global market opportunities. For example, they do not respond to markets where there is a need but not the purchasing power to buy either the existing product or an adapted product. Global companies are likely to encounter this situation when targeting consumers in India, China, and other emerging markets. When potential customers have limited purchasing power, a company may need to develop an entirely new product designed to address the market opportunity at a price point that is within the reach of the potential customer. The converse is also true: Companies in low-income countries that have achieved local success may have to go beyond mere adaptation by "raising the bar" and bringing product designs up to world-class standards if they are to succeed in high-income countries. **Innovation**, the process of endowing resources with a new capacity to create value, is a demanding but potentially rewarding product strategy for reaching mass markets in less-developed countries as well as important market segments in industrialized countries.

As an example of how innovation can be applied to meet the needs of low-income populations, consider two entrepreneurs, working independently, who recognized that millions of people around the globe need low-cost eyeglasses. Robert J. Morrison, an American optometrist, created Instant Eyeglasses. These glasses utilize conventional lenses, can be assembled in minutes, and sell for approximately $20 per pair. Joshua Silva, a physics professor at Oxford University, took a more high-tech approach and came up with glasses with transparent membrane lenses filled with clear silicone fluid. Using two manual adjusters, users can increase or decrease the power of the lenses by regulating the amount of fluid in them. Professor Silva is currently CEO of the Centre for Vision in the Developing World, whose mission is to sell low-cost, self-adjusting glasses in developing countries.[59]

An innovation strategy was also pursued by a South African company that licensed the British patent for a hand-cranked, battery-powered radio. The radio was designed by an English inventor responding to the need for radios in low-income countries. Consumers in these countries do not have electricity in their homes, and they cannot afford the cost of replacement batteries. His invention is an obvious solution to this problem: a hand-cranked radio. It is ideal for the needs of low-income people in emerging markets. Users simply crank the radio, and it will play for almost an hour on the charge generated by a short cranking session.

Sometimes manufacturers in developing countries that intend to go global also utilize the innovation strategy. For example, Thermax, an Indian company, had achieved great success in its domestic market with small industrial boilers. Engineers then developed a new design for the Indian market that significantly reduced the size of the individual boiler unit. The new design was not likely to succeed outside India, because the product's installation was complex and time-consuming. In India, where labor costs are low, relatively elaborate installation requirements are not an issue. The situation is different in higher-wage countries, where industrial customers demand sophisticated, integrated systems that can be installed quickly. The managing director at Thermax instructed his engineers to revise the design for the world market with ease of installation as a key attribute. The gamble paid off: Today, Thermax is one of the world's largest producers of small boilers.[60]

The winners in global competition are the companies that can develop products offering the most benefits and, in turn, creating the greatest value for buyers anywhere in the world. In some instances, value is not defined in terms of performance, but rather in terms of customer perception. Product quality is essential—indeed, it is frequently a given—but it is also necessary to support the product quality with imaginative, value-creating advertising and marketing communications. Most industry experts believe that a global appeal and a global advertising campaign are more effective in creating the perception of value than a series of separate national campaigns.

How to Choose a Strategy

Most companies seek product-communication strategies that optimize company profits over the long term. Which strategy for global markets best achieves this goal? There is no one right answer to this question. For starters, the considerations noted earlier must be addressed. In addition, managers run the risk of committing two types of errors regarding product and communication decisions. One error is to fall victim to the **"not invented here" (NIH) syndrome** and *ignore* decisions made by subsidiary or affiliate managers. Managers who behave in this way are essentially abandoning any effort to leverage product-communication policies outside the home-country market. The other error is to *impose* policies upon all affiliate companies based on the assumption that what is right for customers in the home market must also be right for customers everywhere.

To sum up, the choice of product-communication strategy in global marketing is a function of three key factors: (1) the product itself, defined in terms of the function or need it serves; (2) the market, defined in terms of the conditions under which the product is used, the preferences of potential customers, and customers' ability and willingness to buy; and (3) the adaptation and manufacturing costs to the company considering these product-communication approaches. Only after analysis of the product–market fit and of company capabilities and costs can executives choose the most profitable strategy.

▶ **10-6** Explain the new-product continuum and compare and contrast the different types of innovation.

(10-6) New Products in Global Marketing

The matrix shown in Figure 10-3 provides a framework for assessing whether extension or adaptation strategies can be effective. However, the four strategic options described in the matrix do not necessarily represent the best possible responses to global market opportunities. To win in global competition, marketers, designers, and engineers must think outside the box and create innovative new products that offer superior value worldwide. In today's dynamic, competitive market environment, many companies realize that continuous development and introduction of new products are keys to survival and growth. That is the point of strategy 5, product invention. Similarly, marketers should look for opportunities to create global advertising campaigns to support the new product or brand.

Identifying New-Product Ideas

What is a new product? A product's newness can be assessed in terms of its relation to those who buy or use it. Newness may also be organizational, as when a company acquires an existing product with which it has no previous experience. Finally, an existing product that is not new to a company may be new to a particular market.

The starting point for an effective worldwide new-product program is an information system that seeks new-product ideas from all potentially useful sources and channels these ideas to relevant screening and decision centers within the organization. Ideas can come from many sources, including customers, suppliers, competitors, company salespeople, distributors and agents, subsidiary executives, headquarters executives, documentary sources (e.g., information service reports and publications), and actual, firsthand observation of the market environment.

The three degrees of product newness can be represented in terms of a continuum, as shown in Figure 10-4. At one end of this continuum, the product may be radically new, in the form of an innovation that requires a significant amount of learning on the part of users. When such products are successful, they create new markets and new consumption patterns, and have a disruptive impact on industry structures. Sometimes referred to as **discontinuous innovations**, products that belong to this category of "new and different" represent a dramatic break with the past.[62] In short, they are game-changers.

For example, the revolutionary impact of videocassette recorders (VCRs) in the 1970s can be explained by the concept of time shifting: The VCR's initial appeal was that it freed TV viewers

> "The album changed the [music] business; cassette, 8-track, changed the business. CD, exploded the business. What was the next thing? MP3—cut the business in half. So that can happen at any time. No one knows."[61]
>
> Jimmy Iovine, Apple Music

FIGURE 10-4 New-Product Continuum

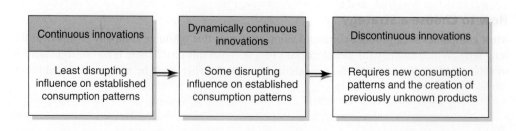

from the tyranny of network programming schedules—and allowed viewers to fast-forward past commercials! Likewise, the personal computer revolution that began three decades ago resulted in the democratization of technology. When they were first introduced, PCs were a discontinuous innovation that dramatically transformed the way users live and work. Apple's brilliant string of new-product introductions in the 2000s—the iPod (2001), the iPhone (2007), and the iPad (2010)—likewise represents a hat trick of discontinuous innovation.

An intermediate category of newness is less disruptive and requires less learning on the part of consumers; such products are called **dynamically continuous innovations**. Products that embody this level of innovation share certain features with earlier generations while incorporating new, breakthrough features that offer added value, such as a substantial improvement in performance or greater convenience. Such products cause relatively smaller disruptions in previously existing consumption patterns. The Sensor, SensorExcel, MACH3, and Fusion shaving systems represent Gillette's ongoing efforts to bring new technology to bear on wet shaving, an activity that is performed today pretty much as it has been for centuries.

The consumer electronics industry has been the source of many dynamically continuous innovations. Personal stereos such as Sony's Walkman provide music on the go, something that people had been accustomed to since the transistor radio was introduced in the 1950s; the innovation was a miniaturized playback-only cassette tape system. The advent of the compact disc in the early 1980s provided an improved music listening experience but didn't require significant behavioral changes. Similarly, much to the delight of couch potatoes everywhere, wide-screen, flat-panel HDTVs offer viewers significantly improved performance. It must be noted that HDTV owners do have to order a high-definition service tier from cable or satellite companies or have sufficient Wi-Fi bandwidth to stream programming in hi-def.

Most new products fall into a third category, **continuous innovation**. Such products are typically "new and improved" versions of existing ones and require less R&D expenditure to develop than dynamically continuous innovations. Because they represent incremental improvement, continuous innovations cause minimal disruption in existing consumption patterns and require the least amount of learning on the part of buyers. As noted previously, newness can be evaluated relative to a buyer or user. When a current PC user seeking an upgrade buys a new model with a faster processor or more memory, the PC can be viewed as a continuous innovation. In contrast, to a first-time PC user, the same computer represents a discontinuous innovation.

Consumer packaged goods companies and food marketers rely heavily on continuous innovation when rolling out new products. These often take the form of **line extensions**, such as new sizes, flavors, and low-fat versions.

New-Product Development

A major driver for the development of global products is the cost of product R&D. As competition intensifies, companies may discover they can reduce the cost of R&D for a product by developing a global product design. Often the goal is to create a single **platform**, or core product design element or component, that can be quickly and cheaply adapted to various country markets. As Christopher Sinclair noted during his tenure as president and CEO of PepsiCo Foods and Beverages International, "What you really want to do is look at the four or five platforms that can allow you to cut across countries, become a scale operator, and do the things that global marketers do."[63]

Even automobiles, which must meet national safety and pollution standards, are now designed with global markets in mind. With a global product platform, automakers can offer an adaptation of a global design as needed instead of creating unique designs for individual countries or geographic regions. The first-generation Ford Focus, launched in Europe at the end of 1998 and in the United States in 1999, was marketed globally with a minimum of adaptation. The chief program engineer on the Focus project was from Great Britain, the chief technical officer was German, the project manager was Irish, and an Anglo-Australian was chief designer. As part of the Ford 2000 initiative, approximately $1,000 per vehicle was cut out of the development cost.[65]

A standardized platform was also a paramount consideration when GM set about the task of redesigning its minivan in the 1990s. GM's globally minded board directed the design team to create a vehicle that would be popular in both the United States and Europe. Because roads in Europe are typically narrower and fuel is more expensive, the European engineers lobbied for a vehicle that was smaller than the typical minivan. By using lightweight metals such as magnesium for some components, vehicle weight was minimized, with a corresponding improvement in fuel

"With the Model 3, Elon Musk is aiming at a completely different demographic that has not shown interest in electric cars before. Unlike many of the company's existing customers, these are not people who can afford multiple vehicles, or who wear their eco-credentials on their sleeve."[64]

Michelle Krebs, analyst, Autotrader

ENTREPRENEURIAL LEADERSHIP, CREATIVE THINKING, AND THE GLOBAL STARTUP

Elon Musk and Tesla

Elon Musk is an entrepreneur. He has developed several innovative products and services, created new brands, and started companies to market his creations. By applying the basic tools and principles of modern marketing, Musk has achieved remarkable success.

As is true with many entrepreneurs, some of Musk's innovations are based on his insights into the possibilities and opportunities provided by the Internet. In 1995, he developed Zip2 Corporation, an online city guide for the new digital editions of *The New York Times* and *Chicago Tribune*. In 1999, Compaq Computer bought Zip2, making Musk an Internet millionaire.

That same year, Musk started X.com, an online banking service that incorporated Musk's e-mail address-based money transfer protocols. X.com, in turn, acquired Confinity, which had its own money transfer service called PayPal. Musk changed the name of the new combined entity to PayPal, and focused on online payment transfers. This service dovetailed perfectly with online auction pioneer eBay's needs for a secure payment system. In 2002, eBay bought PayPal for $1.5 billion. Musk's takeaway: a cool $165 million in eBay stock!

Next, Musk turned his attention to new projects. His interest in environmentalism and sustainability led him to cofound Tesla Motors. Based in Fremont, California, the company initially manufactured and marketed luxury sedans powered by lithium-ion batteries. The all-wheel-drive Tesla Model S carries a list price of approximately $75,000, but U.S. buyers are eligible for a $7,500 federal tax credit. By contrast, the $118,000 sticker price in China reflects a 25 percent import duty plus value-added taxes. Beijing has set a goal of having 5 million electric cars on the road by 2020. Sensing an opportunity, Musk plans to build a factory in China so that Tesla buyers will be eligible for tax credits on domestically produced electric vehicles.

In September 2015, Tesla began delivering the Model X, an $80,000 all-electric SUV with exotic gull-wing doors. Next up is the mass-market Model 3 (see Exhibit 10-10). With a base price of $35,000, the four-door sedan is integral to Musk's goal of building 500,000 cars annually by 2018.

Musk is also moving ahead with plans to build heavy-duty trucks and busses, all powered by batteries. The Semi, which Musk expects to launch in 2019, will have a range of 500 miles on a single charge. A key sales handle: The new trucks promise to be cheaper to operate per mile than conventional diesel trucks. Walmart and J. B. Hunt Transport Services have already placed orders.

Musk is also an innovator when it comes to the "place" (*P*) element of the marketing mix. He is pioneering a new business model of direct-to-the-customer selling, rather than relying on a network of independent dealers. To ensure a top-notch customer experience, Musk hired George Blankship, a former executive at Apple and Gap, as vice president of design and store development.

Just as General Electric founder Thomas Edison had to design a national electric grid to create market demand for his newly invented light bulb, Musk is building a network of charging stations for Tesla owners. More than 5,000 Supercharger stations are now available, mostly clustered in the United States, Western Europe, and China. The half-ton lithium-ion battery pack in the Model S represents about $15,000 of the cost of each vehicle. To bring that cost down, Musk is building a large-scale "Gigafactory" in Nevada that will eventually produce enough batteries each year to power 500,000 Tesla vehicles.

In fall 2017, it became apparent that Tesla was falling behind in its production goals for the Model 3. Instead of producing 5,000 units per week, as Musk had projected, only a few hundred vehicles were completed. Those vehicles had to be partially assembled by hand due to problems with some elements of the highly sophisticated automated assembly process.

Sources: Bob Tita, Tim Higgins, and Jennifer Smith, "Tesla Plays the Long Game with Semi," *The Wall Street Journal* (November 18–19, 2017), p. B3; Marco della Cava, "Musk Goes for Broke with Gigafactory," *USA Today* (March 3, 2014), p. 2B; Richard Waters, "Musk Pushes Tesla Dream Further Along the Road," *Financial Times* (July 22, 2016), p. 14; Scott Cendrowski, "Tesla's Big Gamble in China," *Fortune* (May 8, 2014), p. 72; Chris Woodyard, "'Gigafactory' Sets off 4-State Bidding War," *USA Today* (March 3, 2014), p. 2B; Kara Swisher and Walt Mossberg, "First Comes an Electric Car. Next, a Trip to Mars," *The Wall Street Journal* (June 3, 2013), p. D6; Myles Edwin Mangram, "The Globalization of Tesla Motors: A Strategic Marketing Plan Analysis," *Journal of Strategic Marketing* 20, no. 4 (June 2012), pp. 289–312; Joshua Davis, "Supercharged," Cover Story, *Wired* (October 2010), pp. 138–145.

Exhibit 10-10 Elon Musk, founder of Tesla and SpaceX, has plans to bring electric vehicles to the masses with the Model 3.
Source: dpa picture alliance/Alamy Stock Photo.

economy.[66] As it turned out, the resulting models—the Chevrolet Silhouette (United States), Opel Sentra (Germany), and Vauxhall Sintra (United Kingdom)—met with only limited success in their respective markets. The lesson: It is one thing to formulate a global strategy; it is quite another thing to execute it successfully!

Other design-related costs, whether incurred by the manufacturer or the end user, must also be considered. *Durability* and *quality* are important product characteristics that must be appropriate for the proposed market. In the United States and Europe, many car buyers do not wish to incur high service bills. Thus, the new Ford Focus was designed to be less expensive to maintain and repair. For example, engine removal takes only 1.5 hours, roughly half the time required to remove the engine in the discontinued Escort. In addition, body panels are bolted together rather than welded, and the rear signal lights are mounted higher so they are less likely to be broken in minor parking lot mishaps.

The International New-Product Department

As noted previously, a high volume of information flow is required to scan the horizon for new-product opportunities, and considerable effort is subsequently required to screen these opportunities to identify viable candidates for product development. The best organizational design for addressing these requirements is a new-product department. Managers in such a department engage in several activities. First, they ensure that all relevant information sources are continuously tapped for new-product ideas. Second, they screen these ideas to identify appropriate candidates for investigation. Third, they investigate and analyze these selected new-product ideas. Finally, they ensure that the organization commits resources to the most promising new-product candidates and is continuously involved in an orderly program of new-product introduction and development on a worldwide basis.

With the enormous number of possible new products, most companies establish screening grids to enable them to focus on the most appropriate ideas for investigation. The following questions are relevant to this task:

1. How big is the market for this product at various prices?
2. What are our competitors' likely moves in response to our activity with this product?
3. Can we market the product through our existing structure? If not, which changes will be required, and what costs will be incurred to make the changes?
4. Given estimates of potential demand for this product at the specified prices and estimated levels of competition, can we source the product at a cost that will yield an adequate profit?
5. Does this product fit our strategic development plan? (a) Is the product consistent with our overall goals and objectives? (b) Is the product consistent with our available resources? (c) Is the product consistent with our management structure? (d) Does the product have adequate global potential?

For example, the corporate development team at Virgin evaluates more than a dozen proposals each day from outside the company, as well as proposals from Virgin staff members. Brad Rosser, Virgin's former group corporate development director, headed the team for several years. When assessing new-product ideas, Rosser and his team looked for synergy with existing Virgin products, pricing, marketing opportunities, risk versus return on investment, and whether the idea "uses or abuses" the Virgin brand. Examples of ventures that have been given the green light are Virgin Jeans, a denim clothing store chain; Virgin Bride, a wedding consulting service; and Virgin Net, an Internet service provider.[67]

Testing New Products

The major lesson of new-product introduction outside the home market has been that whenever a product interacts with human, mechanical, or chemical elements, there is the potential for a surprising and unexpected incompatibility. Because almost *every* product matches this description, it is important to test a product under actual market conditions before proceeding with full-scale introduction. A test does not necessarily require a full-scale test-marketing effort, but may simply involve observing the actual use of the product in the target market.

Failure to assess actual use conditions can lead to big surprises, as Unilever learned when it rolled out a new detergent brand in Europe without sufficient testing. Unilever spent $150 million to develop the new detergent, which was formulated with a stain-fighting manganese complex molecule intended to clean fabrics faster at lower temperatures than competing products such as Procter & Gamble's (P&G) Ariel. Backed by a $300 million marketing budget, the detergent was launched in April 1994 as Persil Power, Omo Power, and other brand names. After a restructuring, Unilever had cut the time required to roll out new products in Europe from 3 years to 16 months. In this particular instance, the increased efficiency combined with corporate enthusiasm for the new formula resulted in a marketing debacle. Consumers discovered that some clothing items were damaged after being washed with Power. P&G, quick to capitalize on the situation, ran newspaper ads denouncing Power and commissioned lab tests to verify that the damage did, in fact, occur. Unilever chairman Sir Michael Perry called the Power fiasco "the greatest marketing setback we've seen." Unilever reformulated Power, but it was too late to save the brand. As a result of the product failure, the company lost the opportunity to gain share against P&G in Europe.[68]

Summary

The product is the most important element of a company's marketing program. Global marketers face the challenge of formulating coherent product and brand strategies on a worldwide basis. A *product* can be viewed as a collection of tangible and intangible attributes that collectively provide benefits to a buyer or user. A *brand* is a complex bundle of images and experiences in the mind of the customer. In most countries, *local brands* compete with *international brands* and *global brands*. A *local product* is available in a single country; an *international product* is available in several countries; a *global product* meets the wants and needs of a global market.

A global brand has the same name and a similar image and positioning in most parts of the world. Many global companies leverage favorable *brand images* and high *brand equity* by employing *combination (tiered) branding*, *co-branding*, and *brand-extension* strategies. Companies can create strong brands in all markets through *global brand leadership*. *Maslow's needs hierarchy* is a needs-based framework that offers a way of understanding opportunities to develop local and global products in different parts of the world. Some products and brands benefit from the *country-of-origin effect*. Product decisions must also address packaging issues such as labeling and *aesthetics*. Also, *express warranty* policies must be appropriate for each country market.

Product and communications strategies can be viewed within a framework that allows for combinations of three strategies: *extension strategy*, *adaptation strategy*, and *creation strategy*. Five strategic alternatives are open to companies pursuing geographic expansion: *product-communication extension*, *product extension–communication adaptation*, *product adaptation–communication extension*, *product-communication adaptation (dual adaptation)*, and *product invention (innovation)*. The strategic alternative(s) that a particular company chooses will depend on the product and the need it serves, customer preferences and purchasing power, and the costs of adaptation versus standardization. *Product transformation* occurs when a product that has been introduced into new country markets serves a different function or is used differently than originally intended. When choosing a strategy, management should consciously strive to avoid the *"not invented here" (NIH) syndrome*.

Global competition has put pressure on companies to excel at developing standardized product *platforms* that can serve as a foundation for cost-efficient adaptations. New products can be classified as *discontinuous*, *dynamically continuous*, or *continuous innovations* such as *line extensions*. A successful product launch requires an understanding of how markets develop—sequentially over time or simultaneously. Today, many new products are launched in multiple national markets as product development cycles shorten and product development costs soar.

Discussion Questions

10-1.   Describe the three classifications that may be given to a new product or idea.

10-2.   How do local, international, and global products differ? Cite examples.

10-3.   What are the key characteristics of durable, non-durable, and disposable products?

10-4. Which criteria should global marketers consider when making product design decisions?

10-5. How can buyer attitudes about a product's country of origin affect marketing strategy?

10-6. In 2018, consumer electronics company Lenovo topped a list of the most popular Chinese brands among people outside China. What challenges do Chinese brands face in the global market?

10-7. You have been asked by a supermarket chain to propose suitable packaging and labeling for a range of snack food products such as chocolate chip cookies, ginger snaps, crackers, peanut butter cookies, cereal bars, and granola bars. The packaged products are meant to be exported to its various supermarkets on the international market. You are required to highlight the key considerations on eco-packaging and labeling for the export market. You may consult additional online sources on packaging and labeling food items.

10-8. Hofstede's social values framework can be used to help explain the Asian version of Maslow's hierarchy. Which dimension from Table 4-2 is most relevant? In Chapter 4, we also noted the differences between innovation diffusion processes in Asia and the West. Review the discussion in the chapter. Can you relate it to Figure 10-1?

10-9. Compare and contrast the aesthetic elements of the different types of laundry detergent at the local supermarket. How does aesthetics influence your purchase decision?

CASE 10-1 *continued (refer to page 325)*

Google

Google's dominance in search and other online spaces allows it to collect vast amounts of data that help it deliver targeted advertising. In fact, advertising revenues from the Google unit accounted for more than 90 percent of Alphabet's $110 billion total revenues in 2017. However, as growth in the core advertising business slows, company executives are seeking to diversify Alphabet's revenue stream. Plans for some promising new products, including Google Glass, have been scaled back. Moreover, Google's ability to link its various Web sites to the search process has attracted the attention of antitrust regulators in Europe.

Android OS

In terms of global sales, smartphones that use Google's Android operating system account for roughly 80 percent of the market. Google provides Android—and its green Bugdroid brand mascot—free to handset and tablet manufacturers; Samsung, Motorola, HTC, and LG all use Android. One reason for Android's popularity is the fact that Samsung and other handset manufacturers offer a variety of screen sizes and price points.

By contrast, Apple's iOS is exclusive to the iPhone. Prior to 2014, the iPhone was not available in large screen sizes. Although the number of Android apps slightly exceeds the number for Apple, some developers prefer the iOS platform. One reason cited is the superior ease of use of Xcode, Apple's development environment, compared with Android's Eclipse. Also, the iOS customer base tends to be more affluent.

As mobile video games grow in popularity, Apple and Google are jockeying for dominance in the mobile space. Both companies offer game developers extra promotional support in exchange for exclusivity for new game titles. For example, Electronic Arts released "Plants vs. Zombies 2" on Apple's App Store two months before the title was made available for Android phones. One industry observer likens the competition to an "arms race for the best content."

Waymo

Phrases such as "autonomous functionality" and "robocars" are used to refer to cars and other vehicles that can operate without a human driver. Driverless technology is one example of the type of "moonshot" that Alphabet is aiming for. Audi, BMW, Daimler, GM, and other traditional car manufacturers are also racing to develop the technology, as are tech disrupters such as Uber.

Despite the competition, Alphabet believes that it will be, in management guru Peter Drucker's words, "the fustest with the mostest." The development process began in 2009; the company has invested more than $1 billion and its driverless cars have logged more than 3.5 million actual driving miles so far. Alphabet has created a separate business unit called Waymo, which has been conducting extensive tests at a research facility in California and in a suburb of Phoenix, Arizona (see Exhibit 10-11).

Many of Waymo's test vehicles are specially modified Chrysler minivans equipped with roof-mounted lasers. Although the technology originally cost about $75,000 per vehicle, engineers working on the project expect that figure to quickly fall. Data from the lasers are used to create a picture of a vehicle's surroundings. Those readings, plus information from sensors in the wheels and elsewhere, are fed into an onboard computer. Software then selects the appropriate speed and route.

Self-driving cars promise to address a number of problems related to the traditional automotive environment as we know it today. Many cities are prone to congestion and pollution from cars. Safety is an issue as well: More than 1 million people die in car crashes each year; in the United States alone, an estimated 94 percent of all accidents are attributed to human error. Self-driving cars, and shared mobility, potentially mean safe, reliable transportation for everyone. Of course, persuading people to give up control while riding in a self-driving vehicle may take a while.

Exhibit 10-11 Google's Waymo autonomous mobility unit is testing modified Lexus SUVs (shown here) and Fiat Chrysler minivans in Arizona and a few other states.
Source: dpa picture alliance/Alamy Stock Photo.

As Waymo works to perfect the technology, Alphabet's Google unit is competing with Apple in the automotive space on a more modest scale. Both companies are creating platforms for connecting their respective smartphone software with automotive in-dash systems that provide entertainment, maps, and other services. Music streaming, state-of-the-art voice recognition, and other functions are already standard equipment in many vehicles.

Although concerns have been raised that such advances will lead to distracted drivers, Google insists that the technology will make driving safer. Android Auto allows Android users to control the central screen in a car's dashboard; Apple's CarPlay does the same for users of its iOS. Each company has signed agreements with dozens of automakers that are now including the functionality in new vehicles. Many new car models support both Android Auto and CarPlay. At the same time, in an effort to avoid relying too heavily on Google and Apple, several manufacturers have formed a consortium that is developing proprietary technology called SmartDeviceLink.

Project Loon

More than one-third of the world's population does not have Internet access. Project Loon is Google's solution to that dilemma: The company has an ambitious plan to launch thousands of solar-powered, high-pressure aerial balloons that will circle the globe and connect to the Internet by means of a network of ground stations.

Project Loon is one example of Google's product strategy of investing in selected high-risk, high-potential "moonshot" innovations. The balloons—40 feet high and 50 feet wide—are designed to hover in the stratosphere at altitudes of 60,000 to 70,000 feet above earth. Each balloon can cover roughly 5,000 square kilometers of terrain. By crunching meteorological data from the U.S. National Oceanic and Atmospheric Administration, Google's engineers can adjust the balloons' altitude so that they take advantage of wind currents. The project team is currently tweaking the design to ensure that the balloons can stay aloft for weeks at a time.

In May 2017, Google launched balloons over Peru after the country experienced severe flooding. Later the same year, after Hurricane Maria ravaged Puerto Rico and knocked out cellular service, Google sent dozens of balloons to the region. Project Loon enabled customers of AT&T's 4 LTE network to send and receive texts and e-mails, as well as access the Internet. By applying machine learning technology to flight algorithms, engineers were able to keep the balloons clustered aloft over Puerto Rico for extended periods of time.

Google Fiber

As noted in the chapter introduction, Google Fiber provides lightning-fast Internet speeds. However, the service is currently available in only a dozen American cities. According to the Speedtest Global Index, in 2017 the United States ranked 11th in average fixed broadband speed (download speeds of about 75 Mbps). That ranking puts it between Lithuania and Hungary (Singapore ranks number 1, with average download speeds of about 150 Mbps). Although Google has already made a significant investment, its plans to create a national Google Fiber broadband network have been dialed back because of concerns by Alphabet about how much cash the venture is consuming.

Wearables

Google Glass, Google's Internet-connected eyewear, was once envisioned as a multibillion-dollar business. However, after less than rosy test market results, the project was moved out of X. Google Glass was expensive, relatively few apps were available for it, and the product was the target of a backlash from fashionistas, privacy advocates, and other critics. A new program, Google at Work, is aimed at finding applications in health care, manufacturing, and other workplace situations where employees need quick access to information while their hands are occupied with important tasks.

Google's next-generation high-tech eyewear product will be audio-centric and incorporate Google Home, the company's voice-activated speaker. Integral to the new glasses is an audio technique that was first demonstrated by an Italian physician in the sixteenth century. Known as bone conduction, its functionality is based on a basic feature of human physiology. In a nutshell, when a person speaks, the vibrations of the vocal cords are transmitted to the jawbone. Those vibrations, in turn, can be transmitted to a device such as eyeglasses that "recognize" speech.

The Android Wear 2.0 platform has been successfully incorporated into other consumer products such as the LG Watch Sport and the Moto 360 smartwatch. Meanwhile, Google has partnered with Swiss watchmaker TAG Heuer and semiconductor giant Intel on a new smart watch. One challenge facing Intel is the need to develop a chip that is efficient enough to support software functionality in a device with a very small battery.

Assistant Digital Helper

When the Assistant digital helper was launched in fall 2016, Google CEO Sundar Pichni said the goal was "a personal Google for each and every user." Assistant represents the culmination of years of research and investment in artificial intelligence (AI) and machine learning. The software is integrated in several new Google products, including Allo, a new messaging app; the Home voice-activated, Internet-connected speaker; and a new line of smartphones.

Pixel Phone

As previously noted, Google's Android is the dominant smartphone operating system; globally, more than 2 billion Android-powered handsets are in use. In the past, Google partnered with manufacturers such China's

Huawei and South Korea's LG on various models of Nexus-brand smartphones. However, Nexus sales lagged behind those of other brands. In October 2016, Google renewed its commitment to hardware when it debuted new handsets under the Pixel brand name. The base (5-inch display) Pixel retailed for $649, and introductory advertising featured the tagline "Phone by Google." The phones featured 12-megapixel cameras and software with artificial intelligence capabilities linked to Google Assistant. Although the initial sales were underwhelming, the next generation of Pixel phones was introduced in fall 2017.

Home Voice-Activated Speaker

Amazon's Alexa-powered Echo currently dominates the market for voice-activated, Internet-connected speakers. Home is Google's initial foray into the category. The parent company's expertise in search and personalization mean that Home can "voice match"—that is, recognize—individual household members. Meanwhile, other tech companies, including Apple and Sonos, have also launched smart speaker products.

Discussion Questions

10-10. Why was Google rebranded as Alphabet?

10-11. Apply the new-product continuum (Figure 10-4) to Google's Moonshot Factory. Which category of products and services is most evident in that organization's work?

10-12. Assess the prospects for driverless cars. Once the technology is perfected, which obstacles will Waymo have to overcome before autonomous mobility becomes widely adopted?

10-13. One goal for Alphabet's X division is to create a new money-making business that rivals Google in size and profitability but does not involve search functions. What do you think that will be?

Sources: Leslie Hook and Richard Waters, "Waymo Puts Driverless Car Project in Fast Lane," *Financial Times* (November 10, 2017), p. 17; Tim Bradshaw, "Amazon Bones up on History with 'Smart Glasses,'" *Financial Times* (September 27, 2017), p. 17; Richard Waters, "Alphabet Revolution Is Not as Simple as ABC," *Financial Times* (August 8, 2016), p. 17; Connor Dougherty, "They Promised Us Jet Packs," *The New York Times* (July 24, 2016), pp. B1, B4; Jessica Guynn, "Once a Moonshot, Google Fiber Grows into Reality," *USA Today* (July 20, 2016), p. 3B; Hannah Kuchler, "Bridging the Tech Divide," *Financial Times* (July 13, 2016), p. 10; Connor Dougherty, "Hoping Google's Lab Is a Rainmaker," *The New York Times* (February 16, 2015), pp. B1, B4; Richard Waters, "Google Aims to Eat Carmakers' Lunch," *Financial Times* (February 14–15, 2015), p. 10; Aaron M. Kessler and Brian X. Chen, "A Fight for the Dashboard," *The New York Times* (February 23, 2015), pp. B1, B2; Ian Sherr and Daisuke Wakabayashi, "Apple, Google: Game of Apps" *The Wall Street Journal* (April 21, 2014), pp. B1, B6; Steven Levy, "Google's Wi-Fi from the Sky," *Wired* (September 2013), pp. 126–131; Brad Stone, "Inside the Moonshot Factory," Cover Story, *Bloomberg Businessweek* (May 27, 2013), pp. 56-61.

Notes

[1] Queena Sook Kim, "The Potion's Power Is in Its Packaging," *The Wall Street Journal* (December 21, 2000), p. B12.

[2] Sara Silver, "Modelo Puts Corona in the Big Beer League," *Financial Times* (October 30, 2002), p. 26.

[3] Betsy McKay, "Coke's Heyer Finds Test in Latin America," *The Wall Street Journal* (October 15, 2002), p. B4.

[4] Christina Passariello, "France's Cognac Region Gives Vodka a Shot," *The Wall Street Journal* (October 20, 2004), p. B1.

[5] Deborah Ball, "The Perils of Packaging: Nestlé Aims for Easier Openings," *The Wall Street Journal* (November 17, 2005), p. B1.

[6] Clare Dowdy, "GlaxoSmithKline's New Toothpaste," *Financial Times* (August 11, 2011), p. 8.

[7] Steven L. Gray and Ian Brat, "Read It and Weep? Big Mac Wrapper to Show Fat, Calories," *The Wall Street Journal* (October 26, 2005), p. B1.

[8] Miriam Jordan, "Nestlé Markets Baby Formula to Hispanic Mothers in U.S.," *The Wall Street Journal* (March 4, 2004), p. B1.

[9] Nilly Landau, "Face to Face Marketing Is Best," *International Business* (June 1994), p. 64.

[10] Kevin Lane Keller, *Strategic Brand Management: Building, Measuring, and Managing Brand Equity* (Upper Saddle River, NJ: Prentice Hall, 1998), p. 93.

[11] Ming Liu, "Brands Seize on Artificial Intelligence," *Financial Times—FT Special Report: Watches & Jewellery* (November 11, 2017), p. 11.

[12] For a complete discussion of brand equity, see Kevin Lane Keller, *Strategic Brand Management: Building, Measuring, and Managing Brand Equity* (Upper Saddle River, NJ: Prentice Hall, 1998), Chapter 2.

[13] Kevin Lane Keller, *Strategic Brand Management: Building, Measuring, and Managing Brand Equity* (Upper Saddle River, NJ: Prentice Hall, 1998), p. 93.

[14] John Willman, "Labels That Say It All," *Financial Times—Weekend Money* (October 25–26, 1997), p. 1.

[15] John Willman, "Time for Another Round," *Financial Times* (June 21, 1999), p. 15.

[16] Deborah Ball, "Liquor Makers Go Local," *The Wall Street Journal* (February 13, 2003), p. B3.

[17] John Ridding, "China's Own Brands Get Their Acts Together," *Financial Times* (December 30, 1996), p. 6; Kathy Chen, "Global Cooling: Would America

Buy a Refrigerator Labeled 'Made in Quingdao'?" *The Wall Street Journal* (September 17, 1997), pp. A1, A14.

[18] Diana Kurylko, "The Accidental World Car," *Automotive News* (June 27, 1994), p. 4.

[19] Victoria Griffith, "As Close as a Group Can Get to Global," *Financial Times* (April 7, 1998), p. 21.

[20] Suzy Wetlaufer, "The Business Case Against Revolution," *Harvard Business Review* 79, no. 2 (February 2001), p. 116.

[21] Douglas B. Holt, John A. Quelch, and Earl L. Taylor, "How Global Brands Compete," *Harvard Business Review* 82, no. 9 (September 2004), p. 69.

[22] Adapted from P. Ranganath Nayak and John M. Ketteringham, *Breakthroughs! How Leadership and Drive Create Commercial Innovations That Sweep the World* (San Diego, CA: Pfeiffer & Company, 1994), pp. 128–129. See www.prnayak.org, where the whole of *Breakthroughs!* is available for free download.

[23] "Global Brand Simplicity Index 2017." www.siegelgale.com/siegelgale-unveils-seventh-annual-global-brand-simplicity-index-brands-that-embrace-simplicity-enjoy-increased-revenue-valuation-brand-advocacy-and-employee-engagement/. Accessed March 1, 2018.

[24] David Aaker and Erich Joachimsthaler, "The Lure of Global Branding," *Harvard Business Review* 77, no. 6 (November–December 1999), pp. 137–144.

[25] Leslie Hook, "Bozoma Saint John," *Financial Times—FT Weekend Magazine* (December 9/10, 2017), p. 28.

[26] Lord Saatchi, "Battle for Survival Favours the Simplest," *Financial Times* (January 5, 1998), p. 19.

[27] Warren J. Keegan, "Global Brands: Issues and Strategies," Center for Global Business Strategy, Pace University, Working Paper Series, 2002.

[28] Betsy McKay and Suzanne Vranica, "Coca-Cola to Uncap 'Open Happiness' Campaign," *The Wall Street Journal* (January 14, 2009), p. B6.

[29] A. H. Maslow, "A Theory of Human Motivation," in *Readings in Managerial Psychology*, Harold J. Levitt and Louis R. Pondy, eds. (Chicago, IL: University of Chicago Press, 1964), pp. 6–24.

[30] Jeremy Grant, "Golden Arches Bridge Local Tastes," *Financial Times* (February 9, 2006), p. 10.

[31] Louis Uchitelle, "Gillette's World View: One Blade Fits All," *The New York Times* (January 3, 1994), p. C3.

[32]Andrew Ward, Kathrin Hille, Michiyo Nakamoto, and Chris Nuttal, "Flat Out for Flat Screens: The Battle to Dominate the $29 bn Market Is Heating up But the Risk of Glut Is Growing," *Financial Times* (December 24, 2003), p. 9.

[33]Hellmut Schütte, *Consumer Behavior in Asia* (New York, NY: NYU Press, 998).

[34]Ben Bland, "China Manufacturing: Adapt or Die," *Financial Times—FT Big Read: China* (November 4, 2015), p. 7.

[35]Bertrand Benoit and Geoff Dyer, "The Mittelstand Is Making Money in the Middle Kingdom," *Financial Times* (June 6, 2006), p. 13.

[36]Dana Milbank, "Made in America Becomes a Boast in Europe," *The Wall Street Journal* (January 19, 1994), p. B1.

[37]Peter Aspden, "Diego Della Valle," *Financial Times* (August 12, 2011).

[38]Simon Anholt, "The Nation as Brand," *Across the Board* 37, no. 10 (November–December 2000), pp. 22–27.

[39]Elliot Blair Smith, "Early PT Cruiser Took a Bruising," *USA Today* (August 8, 2001), pp. 1B, 2B; see also Joel Millman, "Trade Wins: The World's New Tiger on the Export Scene Isn't Asian; It's Mexico," *The Wall Street Journal* (May 9, 2000), pp. A1, A10.

[40]Vanessa Friedman, "Relocated Labels," *Financial Times* (September 1, 2010), p. 5.

[41]Kate Hamilton, "Project Galore: Qualitative Research and Leveraging Scotland's Brand Equity," *Journal of Advertising Research* 40, nos. 1/2 (January–April 2000), pp. 107–111. *Galore* is one of two English words that are taken from Gaelic; the other is *whisky*.

[42]Christopher A. Bartlett and Sumantra Ghoshal, "Going Global: Lessons from Late Movers," *Harvard Business Review* 78, no. 2 (March–April 2000), p. 133.

[43]Timothy Aeppel, "Europe's 'Unity' Undoes a U.S. Exporter," *The Wall Street Journal* (April 1, 1996), p. B1.

[44]Brandon Mitchener, "Standard Bearers: Increasingly, Rules of Global Economy Are Set in Brussels," *The Wall Street Journal* (April 23, 2002), p. A1.

[45]Gerrit Wiesmann, "Brands That Stop at the Border," *Financial Times* (October 6, 2006), p. 10.

[46]Dan Bilefsky and Christopher Lawton, "In Europe, Marketing Beer as 'American' May Not Be a Plus," *The Wall Street Journal* (July 21, 2004), p. B1.

[47]Geoffrey A. Fowler, "Intel's Game: Play It Local, But Make It Global," *The Wall Street Journal* (September 30, 2005), p. B4.

[48]Jorge Valencia, "Sony Paints Lavish Hues to Sell LCDs," *The Wall Street Journal* (August 3, 2007), p. B3.

[49]Jenny Mero, "John Deere's Farm Team," *Fortune* (April 14, 2008), pp. 119–126.

[50]Vanessa O'Connell, "Exxon 'Centralizes' New Global Campaign," *The Wall Street Journal* (July 11, 2001), p. B6.

[51]Kimberly Palmer, "Rustic Bourbon: A Hit Overseas, Ho-Hum in the U.S.," *The Wall Street Journal* (September 2, 2003), p. B1.

[52]Bettina Wassener, "Schnapps Goes to College," *Financial Times* (September 4, 2003), p. 9.

[53]Joseph B. White, "One Ford for the Whole World," *The Wall Street Journal* (March 17, 2009), p. D2.

[54]Bruce Einhorn, "Want Some Milk with Your Green Tea Oreos?" *Bloomberg Businessweek* (May 7, 2012), pp. 25, 26.

[55]Bill Vlasic, "Ford Introduces One Small Car for a World of Markets," *The Wall Street Journal* (February 15, 2008), p. C3.

[56]Deborah Ball, "Women in Italy Like to Clean But Shun the Quick and Easy," *The Wall Street Journal* (April 25, 2006), pp. A1, A12.

[57]Deborah Ball, "Too Many Cooks: Despite Revamp, Unwieldy Unilever Falls Behind Rivals," *The Wall Street Journal* (January 3, 2005), pp. A1, A5.

[58]Sally Goll Beatty, "Bad-Boy Nike Is Playing the Diplomat in China," *The Wall Street Journal* (November 10, 1997), p. B1.

[59]Amy Borrus, "Eyeglasses for the Masses," *BusinessWeek* (November 20, 1995), pp. 104–105; Nicholas Thompson, "Self-Adjusted Glasses Could Be Boon to Africa," *The New York Times* (December 10, 2002), p. D6.

[60]Christopher A. Bartlett and Sumantra Ghoshal, "Going Global: Lessons from Late Movers," *Harvard Business Review* 78, no. 2 (March–April 2000), p. 137.

[61]Colin Stutz, "Jimmy Iovine Breaks Down What's Wrong with the Music Business," *Billboard* (November 29, 2017). Accessed December 15, 2017.

[62]The terminology and framework described here are adapted from Thomas Robertson, "The Process of Innovation and the Diffusion of Innovation," *Journal of Marketing* 31, no. 1 (January 1967), pp. 14–19.

[63]"Fritos' Round the World," *Brandweek* (March 27, 1995), pp. 32, 35.

[64]Richard Waters, "Tesla and Elon Musk's Moment of Truth with First Mass-Market Car," *Financial Times* (July 23, 2017), p. 11.

[65]Robert L. Simison, "Ford Hopes Its New Focus Will Be a Global Bestseller," *The Wall Street Journal* (October 8, 1998), p. B10.

[66]Rebecca Blumenstein, "While Going Global, GM Slips at Home," *The Wall Street Journal* (January 8, 1997), pp. B1, B4.

[67]Elena Bowes, "Virgin Flies in Face of Conventions," *Ad Age International* (January 1997), p. i4.

[68]Laurel Wentz, "Unilever's Power Failure a Wasteful Use of Haste," *Advertising Age* (May 6, 1995), p. 42.

11

Pricing Decisions

LEARNING OBJECTIVES

11-1 Review the basic pricing concepts that underlie a successful global marketing pricing strategy.

11-2 Identify the different pricing strategies and objectives that influence decisions about pricing products in global markets.

11-3 Summarize the various Incoterms that affect the final price of a product.

11-4 List some of the environmental influences that impact prices.

11-5 Apply the ethnocentric/polycentric/geocentric framework to decisions regarding price.

11-6 Explain some of the tactics global companies can use to combat the problem of gray market goods.

11-7 Assess the impact of dumping on prices in global markets.

11-8 Compare and contrast the different types of price fixing.

11-9 Explain the concept of transfer pricing.

11-10 Define *countertrade* and explain the various forms it can take.

CASE 11-1
Global Automakers Target Low-Income Consumers

In the 1950s and 1960s, the "space race" pitted the Soviet Union against the United States in an effort to explore outer space. Half a century later, the International Space Station is a collaborative effort involving Russia, the United States, and other nations. Meanwhile, a new "race" is under way—one that is much more "down to earth" and does not involve superpowers in different hemispheres jostling for geopolitical advantage. Rather, this twenty-first-century competition involves efforts by leading automakers in Asia, Europe, and the United States to create inexpensive cars that can be sold in huge volumes to consumers in India and other developing countries.

Renault, the French automotive group, was a pioneer in the low-price segment, with its Logan model; since it was first launched in 2004, more than 4 million units have been sold (see Exhibit 11-1). Initially, the Logan was produced at a single plant operated by Renault's Dacia affiliate in Romania. As Dacia chairman Luc-Alexandre Ménard explained, "At the time, we weren't too sure of what we would do with this car. It was meant to be a one-off, a Trojan horse to penetrate new markets in developing countries." Today, Logans are manufactured in several locations, including Iran, India, and Brazil; the cars are available for sale in dozens of countries.

Two other automakers have joined the race to bring low-cost cars to the emerging-market masses. In 2009, India's Tata Motors launched the Nano, a radical new design with a rock-bottom sticker price

Exhibit 11-1 The Dacia Logan is one element at the center of Renault chief Carlos Ghosn's low-price strategy. Some entry-level models don't have power steering or air conditioning; even so, the Logan brand has proved very popular in both emerging and developed countries. The Logan's success demonstrates a very simple marketing idea: Price sells cars. Many first-time buyers have discovered that they can own a new Logan for about the same price as a motorcycle.
Source: Grzegorz Czapski/Shutterstock.

of 1 lakh (equivalent to 100,000 rupees, or $2,500). The Nano has a rear-mounted, 2-cylinder engine that delivers 33 horsepower. The top speed is 60 miles per hour, and it delivers 50 miles per gallon of gas. Nissan revived the venerable Datsun nameplate in 2014 with the launch of the $6,400 Go hatchback. Like the Nano, the new Datsun's powertrain features a 2-cylinder engine mated to a manual transmission. Unlike the Nano, which has no air bags, Datsuns are available with a driver's-side air bag. Although sales have yet to meet expectations, the social media response to the relaunched Datsun in India has been overwhelmingly positive: On Facebook, @datsunindia has more than half a million "likes" and followers.

In general, two basic factors determine the boundaries within which prices should be set. The first is product cost, which establishes a *price floor*, or minimum price. Although pricing a product below the cost boundary is certainly possible, few firms can afford to pursue this tactic over the long run. Moreover, as we saw in Chapter 8, low prices in export markets can invite dumping investigations.

Second, prices for comparable substitute products create a *price ceiling*, or maximum price. In many instances, global competition puts pressure on the pricing policies and related cost structures of domestic companies. The imperative to cut costs—especially fixed costs—is one of the reasons for the growth of outsourcing. In some cases, local market conditions, such as low incomes, force companies to innovate by creating new products that can be profitably sold at low prices. For more on the auto industry's efforts to create low-cost cars, turn to the continuation of Case 11-1 at the end of the chapter.

Between the lower and upper boundaries for every product is an *optimum price*, which is a function of the demand for the product as determined by the willingness and ability of customers to buy it. In this chapter, we will first review basic pricing concepts and then discuss several pricing topics that pertain to global marketing. These include target costing, price escalation, and environmental considerations such as currency fluctuations and inflation. In the second half of the chapter, we will discuss gray market goods, dumping, price fixing, transfer pricing, and countertrade.

(11-1) Basic Pricing Concepts

◀ 11-1 Review the basic pricing concepts that underlie a successful global marketing pricing strategy.

Generally speaking, international trade results in lower prices for goods. Lower prices, in turn, help keep a country's rate of inflation in check. In a truly global market, the **law of one price** would prevail: All customers in the market could get the best product available for the best price. As Lowell Bryan and his collaborators note in *Race for the World*, a global market exists for certain products, such as crude oil, commercial aircraft, diamonds, and integrated circuits. All other things being equal, a Boeing 787 costs the same worldwide. By contrast, many consumer products made available around the world are actually offered in markets that are national rather than global in nature; that is, national competition in these markets reflects differences in factors such as costs, regulations, and the intensity of the rivalry among industry members.[1]

The beer market, for one, is extremely fragmented; even though Budweiser is the leading global brand, it commands less than 4 percent of the total market. The nature of the beer market explains why a six-pack of a global brand like Heineken varies in price by as much as 50 percent (adjusted for purchasing power parity, transportation, and other transaction costs) depending on where it is sold. In Japan, for example, the price is a function of the competition between Heineken, other imports, and four major national producers—Asahi, Kirin, Sapporo, and Suntory—which collectively command more than 90 percent of the market.

Because of these differences in national markets, the global marketer must develop pricing systems and pricing policies that take into account price floors, price ceilings, and optimum prices. A firm's pricing system and policies must also be consistent with other uniquely global opportunities and constraints. Many companies that are active in the 19 nations of the euro zone have adjusted to the new cross-border transparency of prices. Similarly, the Internet has made price information for many products available around the globe. Companies must carefully consider how customers in one country or region will react if they discover they are paying significantly higher prices for the same product than customers in other parts of the world.

Another important internal organizational consideration also exists besides cost. Within the typical corporation, there are many interest groups and, frequently, conflicting price objectives. Divisional vice presidents, regional executives, and country managers are all concerned about profitability at their respective organizational levels. Similarly, the director of global marketing seeks competitive prices in world markets. The controller and the financial vice president are concerned about profits. The manufacturing vice president seeks long production runs for maximum manufacturing efficiency. The tax manager is concerned about compliance with government transfer pricing legislation. Finally, company counsel is concerned about the antitrust implications of global pricing practices. Ultimately, the prices for a company's products generally reflect the goals set by members of the sales staff, product managers, corporate division chiefs, and/or the company's chief executive.

▶ **11-2** Identify the different pricing strategies and objectives that influence decisions about pricing products in global markets.

 Global Pricing Objectives and Strategies

Whether dealing with a single home-country market or multiple country markets, marketing managers must develop pricing objectives as well as strategies for achieving those objectives. Price is always an independent variable; as a marketing tactic, managers can raise, lower, or maintain prices as part of the overall marketing strategy. Nevertheless, a number of pricing issues are unique to global marketing. The pricing strategy for a particular product may vary from country to country; a product may be positioned as a low-priced, mass-market product in some countries and as a premium-priced, niche product in others. Stella Artois beer is a case in point: As noted in Chapter 7, it is a low-priced, "everyday" beer in Belgium, but a premium brand (advertising taglines have included "Perfection Has Its Price" and "Reassuringly Expensive") in export markets. Pricing objectives may also vary depending on a product's life-cycle stage and the country-specific competitive situation. In making global pricing decisions, it is also necessary to factor in external considerations such as the added cost associated with shipping goods over long distances across national boundaries. Moreover, the issue of global pricing can be fully integrated in the product design process, an approach widely used by Japanese companies.

Market Skimming and Financial Objectives

Price can be used as a strategic variable to achieve specific financial goals, including return on investment, profit, and rapid recovery of product development costs. When meeting financial criteria such as profit and maintenance of margins is the objective, the product must be part of a superior value proposition for buyers; in such a case, price is integral to the total positioning strategy. The **market skimming** pricing strategy is often part of a deliberate attempt to reach a market segment that is willing to pay a premium price for a particular brand or for a specialized or unique product (see Exhibit 11-2 and Exhibit 11-3).

Exhibit 11-2 Reebok dominates the footwear market in India, where its cricket shoes are a top seller. Reeboks are expensive: A shoe that costs Rs2,500 requires the equivalent of a month's salary for a junior civil servant.
Source: Tsering Topgyal/Associated Press.

Companies that seek competitive advantage by pursuing differentiation strategies or positioning their products in the premium segment frequently use market skimming. For example, LVMH and other luxury goods marketers that target the global elite market segment use skimming strategies (see Case 11-3). As Muktesh Pant, the first CEO of Reebok India, noted about aspirational buyers of the company's relatively high-priced shoes, "For Rs2,000 to Rs3,000, people feel they can really make a statement. It's cheaper than buying a new watch, for instance, if you want to

Exhibit 11-3 Canada's Imax Corporation is the world's premier provider of large-format motion picture projection technology. The company has identified 900 potential markets for new Imax theaters; two-thirds of those are global. China is Imax's fastest-growing market. As of mid-2016, there were 335 Imax theaters in China, and the company's recent deal with property and media giant Dalian Wanda calls for adding 150 more screens by 2022. Imax enjoys high brand awareness levels in China's Tier 1, Tier 2, and Tier 3 cities.
Source: Zhang Peng/LightRocket via Getty Images.

make a splash at a party. And though our higher-priced shoes put us in competition with things like refrigerators and cows, the upside is that we're now being treated as a prestigious brand."

The skimming pricing strategy is also appropriate in the introductory phase of the product life cycle, when both production capacity and competition are limited. By setting a high price, demand is limited to innovators and early adopters, who are willing and able to buy and who want to be among the first to own and use the product (see Exhibit 11-2). When the product enters the growth stage of the life cycle and competition increases, manufacturers start to cut prices. This strategy has been used consistently in the consumer electronics industry. Case in point: When Sony introduced the first consumer videocassette recorders (VCRs) in the 1970s, the retail price exceeded $1,000. The same was true when compact disc players were launched in the early 1980s. Within a few years, though, prices for these products dropped well below $500. Today, of course, VCRs and CD players are obsolete, DVD players have become commodities, and streaming audio and video platforms such as Spotify and Netflix dominate their respective industries.

A similar pattern is evident with high-definition televisions (HDTVs). In late 1998, HDTVs went on sale in the United States with prices starting at approximately $7,000. This price maximized revenue on limited volume and matched demand to available supply. Subsequently, prices for HDTVs dropped significantly as consumers became more familiar with the advantages of HDTV and as next-generation factories in Asia lowered costs and increased production capacity. In 2005, Sony surprised the industry by launching a 40-inch HDTV for $3,500; by the end of 2006, comparable HDTVs were selling for approximately $2,000. Today, sets with state-of-the-art display technology cost less than $1,000, and Sony's dominance has been eclipsed by Korean brands such as LG and Samsung. The challenge facing manufacturers now is to hold the line on prices; if they do not succeed, HDTVs may also become commoditized.

Penetration Pricing and Nonfinancial Objectives

Some companies are pursuing nonfinancial objectives with their pricing strategy. In particular, price can be used as a competitive weapon to gain or maintain market position. Market share or other sales-based objectives are frequently pursued by companies that enjoy cost-leadership positions in their industry. A **market penetration pricing strategy** calls for setting price levels that are low enough to quickly build market share. Historically, many companies that used this type of pricing were located in the Pacific Rim. Scale-efficient plants and low-cost labor allowed these companies to blitz the market.

A first-time exporter is unlikely to use penetration pricing, for a simple reason: Penetration pricing often means that the product may be sold at a loss for a certain length of time. Unlike Sony, many companies that are new to exporting cannot absorb such losses, nor are they likely to have the marketing system in place (including transportation, distribution, and sales organizations) that allows global companies like Sony to make effective use of a penetration strategy.

Companion Products: Captive ("Razors and Blades") Pricing

When formulating pricing strategies for products such as video game consoles, DVD players, and smartphones, it is necessary to view these products in a broader context. The biggest profits in the video industry come from sales of game software. In fact, Sony and Microsoft may actually lose money on each console, but the sales of hit video titles generate substantial revenues and profits that more than make up for the losses. Sony, Microsoft, and Nintendo also receive licensing fees from the companies that create the games. Moreover, typical households own only one or two consoles but dozens of games. Likewise, in the mobile phone business, substantial profits come from the services—things like apps, in-app purchases, and music downloads—that handset users purchase.

These examples illustrate the concept of *companion products*: A video game console has no value without video game software, and a DVD player has no value without movies available on DVD. Likewise, a razor handle has no value without blades. Thus, Gillette can sell a single Mach3 razor for less than $5—or even give the razor away for free—because it knows that over a period of years, the company will make significant profits from selling packages of replacement blades. As the saying goes, "If you make money on the blades, you can give away the razors."

For many years, companion products pricing has been the preferred strategy of Vodaphone, AT&T, and other cellular service providers. They buy handsets at prices set by Motorola, Nokia, and other manufacturers, and then subsidize the cost by offering significant discounts on (or even

"For us, 'Made in Italy' is so important, the quality and the artisans and the material is so important, that if we feel any kind of pressure on our profitability we will raise prices. We've found that as long as our quality is maintained the customers are willing to pay a premium."[2]

Marco Bizzari, chairman and CEO, Bottega Veneta

giving away) handsets to subscribers who sign long-term contracts. The carriers make up the price difference by charging additional fees for extras such as roaming, text messaging, and so on. However, this approach does not always work globally.

For example, in the United States, Apple's iPhone 5 was priced at the equivalent of $199 when combined with a 2-year phone service contract. In India and other markets, however, consumers don't like to be locked into long-term contracts. In addition, electronics imports are heavily taxed. That helps explain why the least-expensive iPhone, the SE, costs about $325, and an entry-level 16GB iPhone 6Ssells for the equivalent of $955. Moreover, Apple distributes the iPhone in India exclusively through stores operated by Airtel, an Indian carrier, and Vodaphone. Indian sales of the iPhone have been slow because consumers in that country tend to choose lower-priced models from Nokia and Samsung that are distributed through more retailers. In the product's early days, a significant number of $199 iPhone 5s made the trip from the United States to India in tourist luggage![3] Today, all the major handset manufacturers are designing lower-priced versions for emerging markets.

When Sony was developing the Walkman in the late 1970s, the company's initial plans called for a retail price of ¥50,000 ($249) to achieve break-even. Some executives, however, believed that a price of ¥35,000 ($170) was necessary to attract the all-important youth market segment. After the engineering team conceded that it could trim costs to achieve break-even volume at a price of ¥40,000, chairman Akio Morita pushed them further and insisted on a retail price of ¥33,000 ($165) to commemorate Sony's 33rd anniversary. At that price, even if the initial production run of 60,000 units sold out, the company would lose $35 per unit.

The marketing department was convinced the product would fail: Who would want a tape recorder that couldn't record? Even Yasuo Kuroki, the project manager, hedged his bets: He ordered enough parts for 60,000 units but had only 30,000 produced. Although sales were slow immediately following the Walkman's launch in July 1979, they exploded in late summer. The rest, as the saying goes, is marketing history.[4]

Target Costing[6]

Japanese companies have traditionally approached cost issues in a way that results in substantial production savings and products that are competitively priced in the global marketplace. Toyota, Sony, Olympus, and Komatsu are some of the well-known Japanese companies that use target costing. Researchers Robin Cooper and W. Bruce Chew have described this process, sometimes known as *design to cost*, as follows:

> Target costing ensures that development teams will bring profitable products to market not only with the right level of quality and functionality but also with appropriate prices for the target customer segments. It is a discipline that harmonizes the labor of disparate participants in the development effort, from designers and manufacturing engineers to market researchers and suppliers. . . . In effect, the company reasons backward from customers' needs and willingness to pay instead of following the flawed but common practice of cost-plus pricing.[7]

Western companies are beginning to adopt some of these money-saving ideas. Target costing was used in the development of Renault's Logan, a car that retails for less than $10,000 in Europe. Nissan also used target costing to develop a $3,000 Datsun (see Case 11-1). According to Luc-Alexandre Ménard, chief of Renault's Dacia unit, the design approach prevented technical personnel from adding features that customers did not consider absolutely necessary. For example, the first-generation Logan's side windows had relatively flat glass; curved glass is more attractive, but it adds to the cost. The Logan was originally targeted at consumers in Eastern Europe; to the company's surprise, it has proved popular in Germany and France as well.[8]

The target costing process begins with market mapping and product definition and positioning; this requires using concepts and techniques discussed in Chapter 6 and Chapter 7. The marketing team must do the following:

- Determine the segment(s) to be targeted, as well as the prices that customers in the segment will be willing to pay. Using market research techniques such as focus groups and conjoint analysis, the team seeks to better understand how customers will perceive product features and functionalities.

"Nobody buys a piece of hardware because they like hardware. They buy it to play movies or music content."[5]

Howard Stringer, former chairman, Sony Corporation

- Compute overall target costs with the aim of ensuring the company's future profitability.
- Allocate target costs to the product's various functions. Calculate the gap between the target cost and the estimated actual production cost. Think of debits and credits in accounting: Because the target cost is fixed, additional funds allocated to one subassembly team for improving a particular function must come from another subassembly team's funds.
- Obey the cardinal rule: If the design team can't meet the targets, the product should not be launched.

The target costing approach can be used with inexpensive consumer nondurables. In Mexico and other emerging markets, Procter & Gamble (P&G) managers know that workers are often paid a daily wage; its Mexican customers generally carry 5- and 10-peso coins. To keep prices of shampoo and detergent below, say, 11 or 12 pesos and still ensure satisfactory profit margins, P&G uses target costing (P&G calls it "reverse engineering"). Rather than create an item and then assign a price to it—the traditional cost-plus approach—the company first estimates what consumers in emerging markets can afford to pay. From there, product attributes and manufacturing processes are adjusted to meet various pricing targets. For example, to hold down the cost of its Ace Natural detergent, which is used to hand-wash clothes in Mexico, P&G reduced the product's enzyme content. The result: a product that costs a peso less than a single-use packet of regular Ace. In addition, the reformulated product is gentler on the skin.[9]

The target costing process can also go hand-in-hand with sourcing decisions. Consider the case of an Italian company that markets lifestyle and performance apparel and footwear. Manufacturing is Italy's strength, but labor costs in the country are high. In fact, the target price that consumers are willing to pay for some products is too low to allow for Italy-based production. Thanks to the Internet, consumers in all parts of the world are familiar with prices and will quickly identify price disparities. Likewise, retailers want an "equal price policy." The challenge for the Italian company is how to keep its industrial know-how without giving it away to an original equipment manufacturer (OEM) factory in, say, Romania or Slovenia.

Suppose the company is designing a new ski boot with advanced materials. When it comes to product development and R&D, the teams ask, "What does the high-end athlete need, no matter what the cost?" If product testers like the prototype, the concept is refined into a consumer product that is less radical so it can sell at the right price point.

Of course, consumers in different parts of the world have different needs. So, another challenge is to standardize as much as possible and make compromises with respect to versions destined for the United States versus the European Union versus Asia.

When all of these considerations are taken into account, the team arrives at a second design that will be accepted by consumers and be price efficient. In the ski boot example, the high-end, high-value-added version will be "Made in Italy" while the lower-priced consumer version will be "Made in Slovenia."

Calculating Prices: Cost-Plus Pricing and Export Price Escalation

Laptops, smartphones, tablets, and other popular consumer electronics products exemplify many characteristics of today's global supply chain: No matter what the brand—Acer, Apple, Dell, Samsung, or something else—components are typically sourced in several different countries, and the products themselves are assembled in China, Taiwan, or Japan. Within a matter of days, the goods are sent via air freight to the countries where they will be sold. As anyone who has studied managerial accounting knows, finished goods have a cost associated with the actual production. In global marketing, however, the total cost depends on the ultimate market destination, the mode of transport, tariffs, various fees, handling charges, and documentation costs. **Export price escalation** is the increase in the final selling price of goods traded across borders that reflects these factors. The following is a list of eight basic considerations for those whose responsibility includes setting prices on goods that cross borders:[10]

1. Does the price reflect the product's quality?
2. Is the price competitive given the local market conditions?
3. Should the firm pursue market penetration, market skimming, or some other pricing objective?
4. Which type of discount (trade, cash, quantity) and allowance (advertising, trade-off) should the firm offer its international customers?

5. Should prices differ with market segment?
6. Which pricing options are available if the firm's costs increase or decrease? Is demand in the international market elastic or inelastic?
7. Are the firm's prices likely to be viewed by the host-country government as reasonable? Exploitative?
8. Do the foreign country's dumping laws pose a problem?

Companies frequently use a method known as cost-plus or cost-based pricing when selling goods outside their home-country markets. **Cost-based pricing** is based on an analysis of internal (e.g., materials, labor, testing) and external costs. As a starting point, firms that comply with Western cost-accounting principles typically use the *full absorption cost method*; this defines the per-unit product cost as the sum of all past or current direct and indirect manufacturing and overhead costs.

Beyond this per-unit cost, when goods cross national borders, additional costs and expenses such as transportation, duties, and insurance are incurred. If the manufacturer is responsible for those costs, they, too, must be included (we discuss Incoterms in the next section). By adding the desired profit margin to the cost-plus figure, managers can arrive at a final selling price. It is important to note that in China and some other developing countries, many manufacturing enterprises are state run and state subsidized—a factor that makes it difficult to calculate accurate cost figures and opens a country's exporters to charges that they are selling products for less than the "true" cost of producing them. The recent controversy over Chinese-made solar panel exports is a case in point.

Companies using *rigid cost-plus pricing* set prices without regard to the eight considerations listed previously. They make no adjustments to reflect market conditions outside the home country. The obvious advantage of rigid cost-based pricing is its simplicity: Assuming that both internal and external cost figures are readily available, it is relatively easy to arrive at a quote. The disadvantage is that this approach ignores demand and competitive conditions in target markets; the risk is that prices will be set either too high or too low.

An alternative method, *flexible cost-plus pricing*, is used to ensure that prices are competitive in the context of the particular market environment. Experienced exporters realize that the rigid cost-plus approach can result in severe price escalation, with the unintended result that exports are priced at levels above what customers are willing or able to pay. Managers who utilize flexible cost-plus pricing are acknowledging the importance of the eight criteria listed earlier. Flexible cost-plus pricing sometimes incorporates the *estimated future cost method* to establish the future cost for all component elements. For example, the automobile industry uses palladium in catalytic converters. Because the market price of heavy metals is volatile and varies with supply and demand, component manufacturers might use the estimated future cost method to ensure that the selling price they set will enable them to cover their costs.

(11-3) Incoterms

11-3 Summarize the various Incoterms that affect the final price of a product.

Every commercial transaction is based on a contract of sale, and the trade terms in that contract specify the exact point at which the ownership of merchandise is transferred from the seller to the buyer and which party in the transaction pays which costs. The following activities must be performed when goods cross international boundaries:

1. Obtaining an export license, if required (In the United States, nonstrategic goods are exported under a general license that requires no specific permit.)
2. Obtaining a currency permit, if required
3. Packing the goods for export
4. Transporting the goods to the place of departure (which usually involves transport by truck or rail to a seaport or airport)
5. Preparing a land bill of lading
6. Completing necessary customs export papers
7. Preparing customs or consular invoices as required by the country of destination
8. Arranging for ocean freight and preparation
9. Obtaining marine insurance and certificate of the policy

ENTREPRENEURIAL LEADERSHIP, CREATIVE THINKING, AND THE GLOBAL STARTUP

Dr. Dre and Jimmy Iovine, Beats Electronics and Beats Music

Dr. Dre and Jimmy Iovine are entrepreneurs. Working as a team, they started a company, created a brand, developed an innovative product, and began to manufacture and market it. By applying the basic tools and principles of modern marketing, Dre and Iovine have achieved remarkable success. Along the way, they also became billionaires! As is true with many entrepreneurs, their breakthrough idea was based on their recognition of a problem that needed to be solved. Both were music industry veterans who identified an opportunity to develop high-quality consumer headphones that would enhance the music playback experience while also serving as a fashion accessory.

Dr. Dre (real name: Andre Young) is a well-known hip-hop recording artist who got his start in the music business as a DJ while growing up in the Compton, California, projects. After bursting into the public eye with gangsta rap pioneers NWA in the late 1980s, Dre started recording solo albums. His signature sound, a bass-heavy beat, had a significant impact on the burgeoning hip-hop scene. In addition to creating his own music, Dre's resume includes starting Death Row Records and Aftermath Entertainment. As label chief, Dre helped launch the careers of Snoop Dogg, Tupac Shakur, Eminem, 50 Cent, and many other artists.

Dre identified a problem that grew out of the surging popularity of DJ culture on the music scene. He was frustrated with the low-fidelity audio that music fans experienced when they listened to music on mobile devices such as iPods and laptops. As Dre explains, "I want to hear the music like I hear it in the clubs. I want to hear the same sounds the DJ hears."

Dre's business partner, Jimmy Iovine, is a true music industry mogul. He founded Interscope Records in 1990; by 2014, after more than two decades of producing hit records and making deals, he was chairman of Interscope Geffen A&M records. Iovine was also well known to television viewers as a regular for three seasons on the popular *American Idol* talent search show.

Dre and Iovine shared a passion for sonic integrity in music playback. After disassembling the ear buds that were standard equipment with portable music players and smartphones, the duo recognized that cheap components were the root cause of the lo-fi sound. Dre and Iovine formed Beats Electronics in 2006 and set about designing a premium headphone that would deliver the sound they wanted. Although other high-end headphone brands were already on the market, they were niche products aimed at audiophiles.

In 2008, the young company introduced the Studio line of Beats by Dr. Dre on-ear headphones, priced at $299 and featuring an embossed lowercase "b" on each ear cup. The bottom line: They sounded great, and they looked great, too. Almost overnight, Beats caught on with celebrities as well as the general public. The following year, Hewlett-Packard launched the Envy line of laptops that incorporated Beats audio technology for improved sound.

By 2013, Beats by Dr. Dre had grown into a $1 billion-plus global business and had become the top-selling brand in dozens of countries (see Exhibit 11-4). Meanwhile, Dre and Iovine were turning their attention to streaming music. They acquired online music service Mog in 2012. In 2014, in conjunction with Nine Inch Nails frontman Trent Reznor, they launched Beats Music, a subscription streaming service. Why launch a new service in an industry space dominated by Pandora, Spotify, and other competitors? According to Iovine, the new service was designed to do a better job of helping music lovers decide what to listen to.

Beats Music began life as a $10-per-month subscription service that offers users access to millions of songs. A key feature is curation: In contrast to services that rely primarily on data-driven computer algorithms, Beats staffers and guest programmers—human beings with ears, in other words—assist in the creation of playlists.

Sources: *The Defiant Ones*, Directed by Allen Hughes, Netflix, 2017; Matthew Garrrahan, "Hip-Hop's First Billionaire Mixes Beats with Business," *Financial Times* (May 31/June 1, 2014), p. 7; Ben Sisario, "Algorithm for Your Personal Rhythm," *The New York Times* (January 12, 2014), pp. 1, 24; Hannah Karp, "Beats Stars Sidle up to Apple," *The Wall Street Journal* (May 10–11, 2014), p. B3.

Exhibit 11-4 Dr. Dre became the first hip-hop billionaire when Beats, the company he cofounded with Jimmy Iovine, was acquired by Apple for $3 billion.
Source: Todd Williamson/Invision/Associated Press.

Who is responsible for performing these tasks? It depends on the terms of the sale. The internationally accepted terms of trade are known as International Commercial Terms, shortened to **Incoterms**. Incoterms are classified into four categories. **Ex-works (EXW)**, the sole "E-Term" or "origin" term among Incoterms, refers to a transaction in which the buyer takes delivery at the premises of the seller; the buyer bears all risks and expenses from that point on. In principle, ex-works affords the buyer maximum control over the cost of transporting the goods. Ex-works can be contrasted with several "D-Terms" ("post-main-carriage" or "arrival" terms). For example, under **delivered duty paid (DDP)**, the seller has agreed to deliver the goods to the buyer at the place the buyer names in the country of import, with all costs, including duties, paid. Under this contract, the seller is also responsible for obtaining the import license if one is required.

Another category of Incoterms is known as "F-Terms" or "pre-main-carriage terms." Because it is suited for all modes of transport, **free carrier (FCA)** delivery is widely used in global sales. Under FCA, transfer from seller to buyer occurs when the goods are delivered to a specified carrier at a specified destination. Two additional F-terms apply to sea and inland waterway transportation only. **Free alongside ship (FAS) named port** is the Incoterm for a transaction in which the seller places the shipment alongside, or available to, the vessel upon which the goods will be transported out of the country. The seller pays all charges up to that point. The seller's legal responsibility ends once the goods have been cleared for export; the buyer pays the cost of actually loading the shipment. FAS is often used with *break bulk cargo*, which is noncontainerized, general cargo such as iron, steel, or machinery (often stowed in the hold of a vessel rather than in containers on the deck). With **free on board (FOB) named port**, the responsibility and liability of the seller do not end until the goods—typically housed in containers—have cleared the ship's rail. As a practical matter, access to the terminal and harbor areas in many modern ports may be restricted; in such an instance, FCA should be used instead.

Several Incoterms are known as "C-Terms" or "main-carriage" terms. When goods are shipped **cost, insurance, freight (CIF) named port**, the risk of loss or damage to goods is transferred to the buyer once the goods have passed the ship's rail. In this sense, CIF is similar to FOB. However, with CIF, the seller has to pay the expense of transportation for the goods up to the port of destination, including the expense of insurance. If the terms of the sale are **cost and freight (CFR)**, the seller is not responsible for risk or loss at any point outside the factory.

Table 11-1 is a typical example of the kind of export price escalation that can occur when some of these costs are added to the per-unit cost of the product itself. In this example, a Des Moines–based distributor of agricultural equipment is shipping a container load of agricultural tires to Yokohama, Japan, through the port of Seattle. A shipment of tires that costs ex-works $45,000 in Des Moines ends up with a total retail price in excess of $66,000 in Yokohama. A line-by-line analysis of this shipment shows how price escalation occurs. First, there is the total shipping charge of $2,715, which is 6 percent of the ex-works Des Moines price. The principal component of this shipping charge is a combination of land and ocean freight totaling $1,475.

All import charges are assessed against the landed price of the shipment (CIF value). Note that there is no line item for duty in this example; no duties are charged on agricultural equipment sent to Japan, although duties may be charged in other countries. A nominal distributor markup of 10 percent ($4,925.46) actually represents 12 percent of the CIF Yokohama price because it is a markup not only on the ex-works price, but also on the freight and value-added tax (VAT) as well. Finally, a dealer markup of 25 percent adds up to $12,313.64 (27 percent) of the CIF Yokohama price. Like distributor markups, dealer markup is based on the total landed cost.

The net effect of this add-on, accumulating process is a total retail price in Yokohama of $66,493.67, or 147 percent of the ex-works Des Moines price. This example of price escalation is by no means an extreme case. Indeed, longer distribution channels or channels that require a higher operating margin, as are typically found in export marketing, can contribute to dramatic price escalation. Because of the layered distribution system in Japan, the markups in Tokyo could easily result in a price that is 200 percent of the CIF value.

An example of price escalation for a single product is shown in Table 11-2. A right-hand-drive Jeep Grand Cherokee equipped with a V8 engine ends up costing ¥5 million—roughly $50,000—in Japan. The final price represents 167 percent of the U.S. sticker price of $30,000.

Price escalation was also a major issue in China. Jeep established the first joint U.S./China auto operation in 1983; however, production ceased in 2006. Until recently, the Compass, Wrangler, and Cherokee models were all shipped from the United States and were subject to a

TABLE 11-1 Price Escalation: A 20-ft Container of Agricultural Equipment Shipped from Des Moines to Yokohama*

Item			Percentage of Ex-Works Price
Ex-works Des Moines		$45,000	100%
Inland and ocean freight from DSM to CY Yokohama	$1,475.00		4.44%
Bunker adjustment fee	300.00		0.67%
Destination charges	240.00		0.53%
Freight forwarding fee	150.00		0.33%
AES filing fee	25.00		0.06%
Total shipping charges	$2,715.00	$ 2,715.00	6.03%
Insurance (110% of CIF value)—$0.20 per $100		104.97	0.23%
Total CIF Yokohama value		$47,819.97	106.27%
VAT (3% of CIF value)		1,434.60	3.19%
Landed cost		49,254.57	109.45%
Distributor markup (10%)		4,925.46	10.95%
Dealer markup (25%)		12,313.64	27.36%
Total retail price		$66,493.67	147.76%

*This was loaded at the manufacturer's door, shipped by stack train to Seattle, and then transferred via ocean freight to Yokohama. Total transit time from factory door to foreign port was about 30 days.

25 percent import tariff. In dollar terms, the sticker price of a fully loaded Jeep Grand Cherokee SRT8 with a 6.4-liter V8 engine could top $200,000—more than triple the U.S. price of $62,790! No wonder Fiat Chrysler Automobiles (FCA) opted to start local production in 2015 (see Exhibit 11-5). FCA chief executive Sergio Marchionne has set a goal of tripling Jeep's sales in China to 500,000 units by 2018.[11]

These examples of cost-plus pricing show an approach that a beginning exporter might use to determine the CIF price. The same approach could also be used for differentiated products such as the Jeep Cherokee for which buyers are willing to pay a premium. As noted earlier, experienced global marketers are likely to take a more flexible approach and view price as a strategic variable that can help achieve marketing and business objectives (see Exhibit 11-5).[12]

From a practical point of view, a working knowledge of Incoterms can be a source of competitive advantage to anyone seeking an entry-level job in global marketing. A former export

TABLE 11-2 An American-Built Jeep Grand Cherokee Goes to Japan (estimates)

Item	Amount of Price Escalation	Total
Ex-works price	0	$30,000
Exchange rate adjustment	$2,100	$32,100
Shipping	$300	$32,400
Customs fees	$1,000	$33,400
Distributor margin	$3,700	$37,100
Inspection, accessories	$1,700	$38,800
Added options, prep	$3,000	$41,800
Final sticker price	$8,200	$50,000

Exhibit 11-5 Jeep enjoys high brand awareness in China, thanks in part to Jeep-branded clothing sold in specialty stores. Fiat Chrysler Automobile's market strategy for the brand includes restarting local production and doubling the number of dealers.
Source: Andy Wong/Associated Press.

coordinator at a U.S.-based company that markets industrial ink products, explains how terms of the sale affect price:[13]

> We actually use different Incoterms as incentives for larger orders. Instead of offering a "price break" price, we offer a better Incoterm based upon the size of a customer's order. We adhere to some general guidelines: Any order less than 1 ton is sold on an ex-works basis. Anything 1 ton or more is sold CIF port. All air freight is ex-factory. We will, of course, go to great lengths to ensure that our customers are happy. So, even though a product is sold ex-works, we'll often arrange shipping to destination port (CIF) or airport (CIP), or to the domestic port (FOB) and simply tag the freight cost onto the invoice. We end up with an ex-factory price, but a CIF or FOB invoice total. Sounds complicated, doesn't it? It keeps me busy arranging shipping.

(11-4) Environmental Influences on Pricing Decisions

◀ **11-4** List some of the environmental influences that impact prices.

Global marketers must deal with a number of environmental considerations when making pricing decisions. Among them are currency fluctuations, inflation, government controls and subsidies, and competitive behavior. Some of these factors work in conjunction with others; for example, inflation may be accompanied by government controls. Each is discussed in detail in the following paragraphs.

Currency Fluctuations

In global marketing, fluctuating exchange rates complicate the task of setting prices. As we noted in Chapter 2, currency fluctuations can create significant challenges and opportunities for any company that exports. Management faces different decision situations, depending on whether currencies in key markets have strengthened or weakened relative to the home-country currency. A weakening of the home-country currency swings exchange rates in a favorable direction: A producer in a weak-currency country can choose to cut export prices to increase market share, or maintain its prices and reap healthier profit margins. Overseas sales can result in windfall revenues when translated into the home-country currency.

It is a different situation when a company's home currency strengthens; this is an unfavorable turn of events for the typical exporter because overseas revenues are reduced when translated into the home-country currency. As an example, suppose the U.S. dollar weakens relative to the Japanese yen. This is good news for American companies such as Boeing, Caterpillar, and GE, but bad news for Canon and Olympus (and Americans shopping for cameras). Indeed, according to Teruhisa Tokunaka, chief financial officer of Sony, a 1-yen shift in the yen–dollar exchange rate can raise or lower the company's annual operating profit by 8 billion yen (see Figure 11-1).[14] These examples underscore the point that "roller-coaster" or "yo-yo"–style swings in currency values, which may move in a favorable direction for several quarters and then abruptly reverse, characterize today's business environment.

The degree of exposure varies among companies. Harley-Davidson exports most of its motorcycles from the United States. In every export market, the company's pricing decisions must take currency fluctuations into account. Similarly, 100 percent of German automaker Porsche's production takes place at home; Germany serves as its export base. However, for exports within the euro zone, Porsche is insulated from currency fluctuations.

In responding to currency fluctuations, global marketers can utilize other elements of the marketing mix besides price. In some instances, slight upward price adjustments due to the strengthening of a country's currency have little effect on export performance, especially if demand is relatively inelastic. Companies in the strong-currency country can also choose to absorb the cost of maintaining international market prices at previous levels—at least for a while. Other options include offering improved quality or after-sales service, improving productivity and cutting costs, and sourcing outside the home country.[15]

Companies using the rigid cost-plus pricing method described earlier may be forced to change to a more flexible approach. The use of the flexible cost-plus method to reduce prices in response to unfavorable currency swings is an example of a **market holding strategy** and is adopted by companies that do not want to lose market share. If, by contrast, large price increases are deemed unavoidable, managers may find that their products can no longer compete.

In the 3 years immediately after the euro zone was established, the euro declined in value more than 25 percent relative to the U.S. dollar. This situation forced American companies—in particular, small exporters—to choose from among the options associated with strong currencies. The strategy selected varied according to a company's particular circumstances. For example, Vermeer Manufacturing of Pella, Iowa, a midsized company with approximately $1 billion in annual sales, prices its products in euros for the European market. As 2000 came to an end, Vermeer had been forced to raise its European prices four times since the euro's introduction. Its subsidiary in the Netherlands pays employees in euros and also buys materials locally.

FIGURE 11-1 Value of U.S. Dollars versus Japanese Yen

Source: Based on data gathered by the Board of Governors of the Federal Reserve (www.federalreserve.gov).

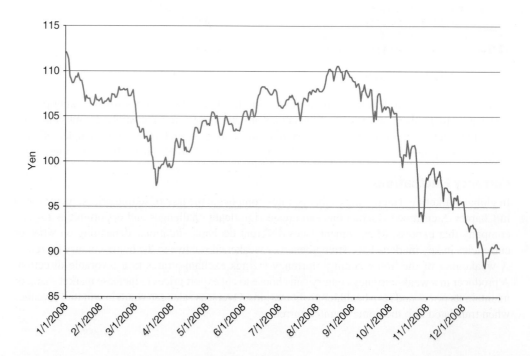

EMERGING MARKETS BRIEFING BOOK

Demand in Asia Drives Fine Wine Prices

As every student of microeconomics knows, when demand exceeds supply, prices tend to rise. The market for fine wine is a textbook example. Each year connoisseurs seek out wines from top estates such as France's Château Lafite Rothschild. A single bottle from a top vintage—for example, 2009—can cost $1,000 or more. The world's best wines need some time in the cellar and, as the years go by, the bottles appreciate in value.

Today, a set of new customers has joined the global wine culture: affluent collectors in China and other Asian countries (see Exhibit 11-6). Several factors have contributed to this trend. In 2008, the Hong Kong government reduced tariffs on wine imports from 40 percent to zero. Since then, a flourishing wine auction scene has emerged within the Special Administrative Region. Although mainland China still imposes ad valorem taxes on wine, hand-carried bottles crossing the border from Hong Kong are not taxed. Needless to say, this has created a business opportunity for entrepreneurial individuals to hire "mules" to transport wine to the mainland. Also not surprisingly, considering the prices consumers are paying, there is a brisk trade in counterfeit wine.

With the booming Chinese economy, well-heeled consumers and collectors in that country can't seem to get enough of Château Lafite and other wines. How many Chinese are willing and able to buy expensive wine? According to industry observers, the number is between 5,000 and 10,000. Chinese wine drinkers do their homework; they have been known to check out the tasting scores and prices of wines they have been served. This, of course, reflects the importance of status in Asian culture. Meanwhile, recession-weary buyers in Japan, the United States, and Europe are scaling back on their purchases of expensive wines. As one European wine exporter noted, "Every case of Château Lafite we purchase ends up in China."

Singapore and Indonesia are also vibrant markets for fine wine. Retail distribution in Singapore is streamlined compared to elsewhere, meaning that importers can sell directly to consumers. In addition, government regulations have been loosened somewhat, and two casinos have opened as part of the Resorts World Sentosa and Marina Bay Sands developments. Free-spending high rollers at these establishments want to drink the best. Demand for fine wine is growing in Indonesia as well, even though the hot, humid climate creates challenges for members of the wine trade hoping to keep wine in saleable condition.

Sources: Jason Chow, "French Wines Are Tough Sell," *The Wall Street Journal* (April 26, 2013), p. B1; Jancis Robinson, "China's Viticultural Revolution," *Financial Times—Life & Arts* (February 12–13, 2011), p. 4; Gideon Rachman, "China Reaps a Vintage European Crop," *Financial Times* (November 30, 2010), p. 13; Kimberly Peterson, "New Whine: China Pushes Bordeaux Prices Higher," *The Wall Street Journal* (September 15, 2010), pp. B1, B2; John Stimpfig, "Demand from China Fuels Spectacular Performance," *Financial Times Special Report: Buying and Investing in Wine* (June 19, 2010), p. 6; Robinson, "A Continent of Connoisseurs," *Financial Times* (May 15, 2010), p. 11; Laura Santini, "Wealthy Chinese Make Hong Kong a New Wine Hub," *The Wall Street Journal* (December 2, 2009), p. B9.

Exhibit 11-6 High auction prices in Hong Kong reflect skyrocketing Asian demand for top-rated French wines such as those from Château Lafite Rothschild. China is the most important export market for Bordeaux wine producers, accounting for more than one-third of that region's exports. Chinese investors are also snapping up top winemaking estates in France.
Source: Philippe Lopez/AFP/GettyImages.

By contrast, Stern Pinball of Melrose Park, Illinois, prices its machines in dollars in export markets. Company president Gary Stern's product strategy also reflects a strong-currency strategy: To offset the higher cost to European customers who must convert euros before paying in dollars, the company developed new features such as pinball machines that "speak" several European languages. It has also produced new products such as a soccer game themed to European interests as well as an Austin Powers game targeted at the United Kingdom. As Stern commented, "If I were bright enough to know which way the euro was going, I sure wouldn't be making pinball machines. I'd be trading currency."[16]

As noted earlier, price discrepancies across the euro zone have been disappearing because manufacturers are no longer be able to cite currency fluctuations as a justification for the discrepancies. **Price transparency** means that buyers are able to comparison shop easily because goods will be priced in euros as opposed to marks, francs, or lira. For several years, the European Commission published an annual report comparing automobile price differences in the European Union. Thanks in part to the Internet, price discrepancies have narrowed; in 2011, the commission discontinued the report.

Even in the euro zone, some automobile prices differ in various countries due to different standards for safety equipment and different tax levels. For example, Denmark and Sweden have a VAT of 25 percent, the highest rate in the European Union. Moreover, Denmark taxes luxury goods heavily. Taxes are also high in Finland, Belgium, Ireland, Austria, and Italy. Volkswagen has already begun to harmonize its wholesale prices for vehicles distributed in Europe.

Inflationary Environment

Inflation, or a persistent upward change in price levels, is a problem in many country markets. An increase in the money supply can cause inflation; in turn, inflation is often reflected in the prices of imported goods in a country whose currency has weakened. For example, following the Brexit vote in 2016, the British pound fell approximately 15 percent against the euro and other major currencies. That was a mixed blessing for producers of English sparkling wine. On the plus side, export prices for wines made in England were more attractive and boosted demand, while the price of Champagne imported from France to the United Kingdom increased. As for the downside, most English vintners buy winemaking equipment and supplies such as bottles from Europe, so they are paying higher prices.[18]

Spiraling commodities and raw materials costs may also put upward pressure on prices for a variety of goods. These are more than just theoretical issues for businesses. Indeed, understanding the dynamics affecting price and product decisions can help recent graduates respond to tough interview questions. For example, a prospective employer might ask how you would deal with increasing commodity costs. How would you respond, if asked?

Take chocolate, for example. Mondelez International's iconic Toblerone chocolate bars are produced in Berne, Switzerland, and exported to more than 120 countries. In January 2015, production costs jumped in Switzerland due to a significant drop in the value of the euro against the Swiss franc. Cocoa prices also have risen steadily over the past several years. How did the company respond? Rather than raise prices, it reduced the size of the chocolate bar (see Exhibit 11-7). Call it "shrinkflation!"

> "We believe that our customers—especially our European customers—are just as willing to pay in pounds and may have more access to British pounds than dollars."[17]
>
> Christine Russell, chief financial officer, Evans Analytical Group LLC, Santa Clara, California

Exhibit 11-7 Toblerone chocolate bars are available in different sizes and distributed through a variety of retail channels. The smaller bars, often sold by discounters, were recently "downsized" from 170 grams to 150 grams while the price stayed the same.
Source: Darren Staples/Reuters.

Higher prices for corn and wheat may force companies such as Kraft Foods to raise prices; as noted in Case 2-2, however, many global companies formulate and implement sophisticated commodity hedging strategies in an effort to avoid such price increases. Higher prices for copper, oil, and other commodities mean that managers at United Technologies must review pricing for the helicopters, jet engines, and air-conditioning systems the company makes. And, as anyone who shopped for clothes in the early 2010s can attest, prices for sweaters, jeans, and T-shirts increased sharply. The reason? Cotton inventories were low worldwide, and the price of cotton almost doubled.[19]

An essential requirement for pricing in an inflationary environment is the maintenance of operating profit margins. Inflation may require price adjustments for a simple reason: Rising costs must be covered by higher selling prices. Regardless of cost-accounting practices, if a company maintains its margins, it has effectively protected itself from the effects of inflation.

Sometimes inflationary forces arise out of changes in the political environment. For example, in early 2018, U.S. President Donald Trump announced tariffs of 10 percent on aluminum imports from China and several other nations. That was bad news for the beer industry; the U.S. beer market represents about $100 billion in annual sales of aluminum, much of it in the form of aluminum cans. A trade group called the Beer Institute estimated that the tariffs amount to a $347 million tax on the beverage industry by raising its variable costs.

An aluminum beer can costs about 10 cents to manufacture, so a 10 percent tariff on aluminum would boost the cost of each can by about a penny, or roughly 6 cents per six-pack. Marketing managers at AB InBev, the company that brews Bud Light, face a decision about whether they can pass on the increased cost to consumers without any decrease in demand for Bud Light and other brands. The question is, if tariffs lead to price increases, will Americans drink less beer? Will Bud Light fans exhibit elastic demand curves or inelastic demand curves?

Low inflation presents pricing challenges of a different type. With inflation in the United States in the low single digits in the late 1990s and strong demand forcing factories to run at or near capacity, companies should have been able to raise prices. However, the domestic economic situation was not the only consideration in pricing decisions made in that era. In the mid-1990s, excess manufacturing capacity in many industries, high rates of unemployment in many European countries, and the lingering recession in Asia made it difficult for companies to increase prices. As John Ballard, CEO of a California-based engineering firm, noted in 1994, "We thought about price increases. But our research of competitors and what the market would bear told us it was not worth pursuing." By the end of the decade, globalization, the Internet, a flood of low-cost exports from China, and a new cost-consciousness among buyers were also significant price-constraining factors.[20]

Government Controls, Subsidies, and Regulations

Governmental policies and regulations that affect pricing decisions include dumping legislation, resale price maintenance legislation, price ceilings, and general reviews of price levels. Government actions that limit management's ability to adjust prices can put pressure on margins. Under certain conditions, government actions may pose a threat to the profitability of a subsidiary operation. In a country that is undergoing severe financial difficulties and is in the midst of a financial crisis (e.g.,a foreign exchange shortage caused in part by runaway inflation), for example, government officials are under pressure to take some type of action. This was true in Brazil for many years. In some cases, governments take expedient steps such as selective or broad price controls.

When selective controls are imposed, foreign companies are more vulnerable to control than local ones, particularly if the outsiders lack the political influence over government decisions that local managers have. For example, Procter & Gamble encountered strict price controls in Venezuela in the late 1980s. Despite increases in the cost of raw materials, P&G was granted only about 50 percent of the price increases it requested; even then, months passed before permission to raise prices was forthcoming. As a result, by 1988, detergent prices in Venezuela were less than detergent prices in the United States.[21]

Government control can also take other forms. As discussed in Chapter 8, companies are sometimes required to deposit funds in a non-interest-bearing escrow account for a specified period of time if they wish to import products. In one case, Cintec International, an engineering firm that specializes in restoring historic structures, spent 8 years seeking the necessary approval from Egyptian authorities to import special tools to repair a mosque. In addition, the country's port authorities required a deposit of nearly $25,000 before they allowed Cintec to import diamond-tipped drills and other special tools. Why would Cintec's management accept such conditions? Cairo is the largest city in the Muslim world, and hundreds of its centuries-old historic structures are in need of refurbishment. By responding to the Egyptian government's demands with patience and persistence, Cintec was positioning itself as a leading contender for more contract work.[22]

Cash deposit requirements such as the one just described clearly create an incentive for a company to minimize the stated value of the imported goods; lower prices mean smaller deposits. Other government requirements that affect the pricing decision are profit transfer rules that restrict the conditions under which profits can be transferred out of a country. Under such rules, a high transfer price paid for imported goods by an affiliated company can be interpreted as a device for transferring profits out of a country.

Also discussed in Chapter 8 were government subsidies. As noted there, the topic of agricultural subsidies is a sensitive one in the current round of global trade talks. Brazil and a bloc of more than 20 other nations are pressing the United States to end agricultural subsidies. For example, the United States spends between $2.5 billion and $3 billion per year on cotton subsidies (the European Union spends the equivalent of $700 million), a fact that has contributed to delays in completing trade talks. Benin, Chad, Burkina Faso, and other countries complain that the subsidies keep U.S. cotton prices so low that the African nations lose $250 million each year in exports.[23] Brazil recently won its World Trade Organization (WTO) complaint against U.S. cotton subsidies. Meanwhile, in Uzbekistan, the government is finally beginning to address a human-rights abuse issue: For years, doctors, teachers, and students have been pressed into service during the cotton harvest.[24]

Government regulations can also affect prices in other ways. In Germany, for example, price competition was historically severely restricted in a number of industries, especially in the service sector. The German government's recent moves toward deregulation have improved the climate for market entry by foreign firms in a range of industries, including insurance, telecommunications, and air travel. Deregulation is also giving German companies their first experience of price competition in the domestic market. In some instances, deregulation represents a *quid pro quo* that will allow German companies wider access to other country markets.

For example, in the late 1990s, the United States and Germany completed an open-skies agreement that allows Lufthansa to fly more routes within the United States. At the same time, the German air market has been opened to competition. Thanks to newcomers like Air Berlin, Ryanair, and easyJet, air travel costs to and from Germany have fallen significantly. The past two decades have seen slow changes within the retail sector as well. The Internet and globalization have forced policymakers to repeal two archaic laws. The first, the *Rabattgesetz*, or Discount Law, limited discounts on products to 3 percent of the list price. The second, the *Zugabeverordung*, or Free Gift Act, banned companies from giving away free merchandise such as shopping bags.[25]

Competitive Behavior

Pricing decisions are bounded not only by cost and the nature of demand, but also by competitive action. If competitors do not adjust their prices in response to rising costs, management—even if acutely aware of the effect of rising costs on operating margins—will be severely constrained in its ability to adjust prices accordingly. Conversely, if competitors are manufacturing or sourcing in a lower-cost country, it may be necessary to cut prices to stay competitive.

In the United States, Levi Strauss & Company is under price pressure from several directions. First, Levi's face stiff competition from the Wrangler and Lee brands marketed by VF Corporation. A pair of Wrangler jeans retails for about $20 at JCPenney and other department stores, compared with about $30 for a pair of Levi's 501 jeans. Second, the two primary retail customers for Levi's, JCPenney and Sears, are aggressively marketing their own private-label brands. Finally, designer jeans from Calvin Klein, Polo, and Diesel are enjoying renewed popularity. Exclusive fashion brands such as 7 for All Mankind and Lucky retail for more than $100 per pair.

Outside the United States, thanks to the heritage of the Levi's brand and less competition, Levi's jeans command premium prices—$80 or more for one pair of 501 jeans. To support their prestige image, Levi's are sold in boutiques. Levi's non-U.S. sales represent about one-third of revenues but more than 50 percent of profits. In an attempt to apply its global experience and enhance the brand in the United States, Levi has opened a number of Original Levi's Stores in selected American cities. Despite such efforts, Levi rang up only $4.5 billion in sales in 2016, compared with $7.1 billion in 1996. More than a decade ago, the company closed six plants and moved most of its North American production offshore in an effort to cut costs.[26]

Using Sourcing as a Strategic Pricing Tool

The global marketer has several options for addressing the problem of price escalation or the environmental factors described in the last section. Product and market competition, in part, dictate the marketer's choices. Marketers of domestically manufactured finished products may be forced to switch to offshore sourcing of certain components to keep costs and prices competitive. In particular, China is quickly gaining a reputation as "the world's workshop." For example, U.S. bicycle companies such as Huffy are relying more heavily on production sources in China and Taiwan.

Another option is a thorough audit of the distribution structure in the target markets. A rationalization of the distribution structure can substantially reduce the total markups required to achieve distribution in international markets. Rationalization may include selecting new intermediaries, assigning new responsibilities to old intermediaries, or establishing direct marketing operations. For years, Toys 'R' Us successfully targeted the Japanese toy market by bypassing layers of distribution and adopting a warehouse style of selling similar to its U.S. approach. Toys 'R' Us was viewed as a test case of the ability of Western retailers—discounters, in particular—to change the rules of distribution. By early 2018, though, times had changed: Toys 'R' Us management announced the company was closing all of its 885 U.S. stores and was seeking a buyer for its international operations.

 ## 11-5 Global Pricing: Three Policy Alternatives

◀ **11-5** Apply the ethnocentric/polycentric/geocentric framework to decisions regarding price.

What pricing policy should a global company pursue? Recall that price is a strategic variable; pricing strategy can be developed using a rational, analytical approach or an intuitive one. For example, when Sydney Frank created Grey Goose vodka, he set the per-bottle price $10 higher than that of Stolichnaya or Absolut. Why? Because he could! Frank did not conduct any form of market analysis. Instead, he relied on instinct and insights gained during a long career in the liquor business. Similar examples of simple decision rules used in pricing include the following:

- "We have our competitor's price list on our desk . . . . We know exactly what our competitors charge for certain products, and we calculate accordingly."
- "We differentiate simply because there are some countries where we can get a better price. Then there are countries where we can't."[27]

Viewed broadly, a company has three positions it can take on worldwide pricing.

Extension or Ethnocentric Pricing

The first position, known as **extension or ethnocentric pricing**, calls for the per-unit price of an item to be the same no matter where in the world the buyer is located. In such instances, the importer must absorb freight and import duties. The extension approach has the advantage of extreme simplicity because it does not require information on competitive or market conditions for implementation. Its main disadvantage is that the ethnocentric approach does not respond to the competitive and market conditions of each national market and, therefore, does not maximize the company's profits in each national market or globally. When toymaker Mattel adapted U.S. products for overseas markets, for example, little consideration was given to the price levels that would result when U.S. prices were converted to local currency prices. As a result, Holiday Barbie and some other toys were overpriced in global markets.[28]

Similarly, Mercedes executives moved beyond an ethnocentric approach to pricing. As Dieter Zetsche, chairman of Daimler AG, noted, "We used to say that *we* know what the customer wants, and he will have to pay for it . . . we didn't realize the world had changed."[29] Mercedes got its wake-up call when Lexus began offering "Mercedes quality" for $20,000 less. After assuming the top position in the company in 1993, Mercedes CEO Helmut Werner boosted employee productivity, increased the number of low-cost outside suppliers, and invested in production facilities in the United States and Spain in an effort to move toward more customer- and competition-oriented pricing. The company also rolled out new, lower-priced versions of its E Class and S Class sedans.

Advertising Age immediately hailed management's new attitude for transforming Mercedes from "a staid and smug purveyor into an aggressive, market-driven company that will go bumper-to-bumper with its luxury car rivals—even on price."[30]

Apple learned an important lesson about the potential drawbacks of ethnocentric pricing in China, where many smartphone apps give users the ability to "tip" each other by sending yuan as an acknowledgment of user-created content. Apple's policy is to take 30 percent of fees generated by apps, and it initially applied this policy in China, where it considered "tipping" to be an in-app purchase. By contrast, Tencent Holding's popular WeChat app did not charge for tipping. In response to complaints about its own pricing, Apple changed its policy.[31]

Adaptation or Polycentric Pricing

The second policy, **adaptation or polycentric pricing**, permits subsidiary or affiliate managers or independent distributors to establish whatever price they believe is most appropriate in their market environment. There is no requirement that prices be coordinated from one country to the next. IKEA takes a polycentric approach to pricing: While it is company policy to have the lowest price on comparable products in every market, managers in each country set their own prices. These depend, in part, on local factors such as competition, wages, taxes, and advertising rates. Overall, IKEA's prices are lowest in the United States, where the company competes with large retailers. Prices are higher in Italy, where local competitors tend to be smaller, more upscale furniture stores than those in the U.S. market. Generally, prices are higher in countries where the IKEA brand is strongest. When IKEA opened its first stores in mainland China, the young professional couples who are the company's primary target segment considered the prices to be too high. Ian Duffy, an Englishman in charge of the stores, quickly increased the amount of Chinese-made furniture in the stores so that he could lower prices; today, the average Chinese customer spends ¥300—about $36—per visit.[32]

One recent study of European industrial exporters found that companies utilizing independent distributors were the most likely to utilize polycentric pricing. Such an approach is sensitive to local market conditions, but valuable knowledge and experience within the corporate system concerning effective pricing strategies are not brought to bear on each local pricing decision. Because the distributors or local managers are free to set prices as they see fit, they may ignore the opportunity to draw upon company experience. Arbitrage is also a potential problem with the polycentric approach: When disparities in prices between different country markets exceed the transportation and duty costs separating the markets, enterprising individuals can purchase goods in the lower-price country market and then transport them for sale in markets where higher prices prevail.

This is precisely what has happened in both the pharmaceutical and textbook publishing industries. Discounted drugs intended for patients with acquired immunodeficiency syndrome (AIDS) in Africa have been smuggled into the European Union and sold at a huge profit. Similarly, Pearson (which publishes this text), McGraw-Hill, Thomson, and other publishers typically set lower prices in Europe and Asia than in the United States. The reason is that the publishers use polycentric pricing: They establish prices on a regional or country-by-country basis using per capita income and economic conditions as a guide. (By the way, authors have no control over the prices that university bookstores and other retailers charge for textbooks. Trust us on this one!)

Geocentric Pricing

The third approach, **geocentric pricing**, is more dynamic and proactive than the other two. A company using geocentric pricing neither fixes a single price worldwide, nor allows subsidiaries or local distributors to make independent pricing decisions. Instead, the geocentric approach represents an intermediate course of action. Geocentric pricing is based on the realization that unique local market factors should be recognized when arriving at pricing decisions. These factors include local costs, income levels, competition, and the local marketing strategy. Price must also be integrated with other elements of the marketing program. The geocentric approach recognizes that price coordination from headquarters is necessary in dealing with international accounts and product arbitrage. This approach also consciously and systematically seeks to ensure that accumulated national pricing experience is leveraged and applied wherever relevant.

With geocentric pricing, local costs plus a return on invested capital and personnel fix the price floor for the long term. In the short term, however, headquarters might decide to set a market

> "The practice of selling U.S. products abroad at prices keyed to the local market is longstanding. It's not unusual, it doesn't violate public policy, and it's certainly not illegal."[33]
>
> Allen Adler, American Association of Publishers

penetration objective and price at less than the cost-plus return figure by using export sourcing to establish a market. This was the case described earlier with the Sony Walkman launch. Another short-term objective might be to arrive at an estimate of the market potential at a price that would be profitable given local sourcing and a certain volume of production. Instead of immediately investing in local manufacture, a decision might be made to supply the target market initially from existing higher-cost external supply sources. If the market accepts the price and product, the company can then build a local manufacturing facility to further develop the identified market opportunity in a profitable way. If the market opportunity does not materialize, the company can experiment with the product at other prices because it is not committed to a fixed sales volume by existing local manufacturing facilities.

(11-6) Gray Market Goods

◀ **11-6** Explain some of the tactics global companies can use to combat the problem of gray market goods.

Gray market goods are trademarked products that are exported from one country to another and sold by unauthorized persons or organizations. Consider the following illustration:

> Suppose that a golf equipment manufacturer sells a golf club to its domestic distributors for $200; it sells the same club to its Thailand distributor for $100. The lower price may be due to differences in overseas demand or ability to pay. Alternatively, the price difference may reflect the need to compensate the foreign distributor for advertising and marketing the club. But the golf club never actually makes it to Thailand: Instead, the Thailand distributor resells the club to a gray marketer in the United States for $150. The gray marketer can then undercut the prices charged by domestic distributors who paid $200 for the club. The manufacturer is forced to lower the domestic price or risk losing sales to gray marketers, driving down the manufacturer's profit margins. Additionally, gray marketers make liberal use of manufacturers' trademarks and often fail to provide warranties and other services that consumers expect from the manufacturer and its authorized distributors.[34]

This practice, known as **parallel importing**, occurs when companies employ a polycentric, multinational pricing policy that calls for setting different prices in different country markets. Gray markets can flourish when a product is in short supply, when producers employ skimming strategies in certain markets, or when the goods are subject to substantial markups. For example, in the European pharmaceuticals market, prices vary widely. In the United Kingdom and the Netherlands, parallel imports account for as much as 10 percent of the sales of some pharmaceutical brands. The Internet serves as a powerful tool that allows would-be gray marketers to access pricing information and reach customers.[35]

Gray markets impose several costs or consequences on global marketers, including the following:[36]

- *Dilution of exclusivity.* Authorized dealers are no longer the sole distributors. The product is often available from multiple sources and margins are threatened.
- *Free riding.* If the manufacturer ignores complaints from authorized channel members, those members may engage in free riding. In this practice, channel members may opt to take various actions to offset the downward pressure on margins, such as cutting back on presale service, customer education, and salesperson training.
- *Damage to channel relationships.* Competition from gray market products can lead to channel conflict as authorized distributors attempt to cut costs, complain to manufacturers, and file lawsuits against the gray marketers.
- *Undermining segmented pricing schemes.* As noted earlier, gray markets can emerge because of price differentials that result from multinational pricing policies. However, a variety of forces—including falling trade barriers, the information explosion on the Internet, and modern distribution capabilities—hamper a company's ability to pursue local pricing strategies.
- *Reputation and legal liability.* Even though gray market goods carry the same trademarks as goods sold through authorized channels, they may differ in quality, ingredients, or some other way. Gray market products can compromise a manufacturer's reputation and dilute

brand equity, as when prescription drugs are sold past their expiration dates or electronics equipment is sold in markets where it is not approved for use or where manufacturers do not honor warranties.

Sometimes, gray marketers bring a product produced in a single country—French Champagne, for example—into export markets in competition with authorized importers. The gray marketers sell at prices that undercut those set by the legitimate importers. In another type of gray marketing, a company manufactures a product in the home-country market as well as in foreign markets. In this case, products manufactured abroad by the company's foreign affiliate for sales abroad are sometimes sold by a foreign distributor to gray marketers. The latter then bring the products into the producing company's home-country market, where they compete with domestically produced goods.

As these examples show, the marketing opportunity that presents itself requires gray market goods to be priced lower than goods sold by authorized distributors or domestically produced goods. Clearly, buyers gain from lower prices and increased choice. In the United Kingdom alone, total annual retail sales of gray market goods are estimated to be in the billions of pounds Sterling.

A case in Europe resulted in a ruling that strengthened the rights of brand owners. Silhouette, an Austrian manufacturer of upscale sunglasses, sued the Hartlauer discount chain after the retailer obtained thousands of pairs of sunglasses that Silhouette had intended for sale in Eastern Europe. The European Court of Justice found in favor of Silhouette. In clarifying a 1989 directive, the court ruled that stores cannot import branded goods from outside the European Union and then sell them at discounted prices without permission of the brand owner. However, the *Financial Times* denounced the ruling as "bad for consumers, bad for competition, and bad for European economies."[37]

In the United States, gray market goods are subject to the Tariff Act of 1930. Section 526 of the act expressly forbids importation of goods of foreign manufacture without the permission of the trademark owner. However, because courts have considerable leeway in interpreting the act, one legal expert has argued that the U.S. Congress should repeal Section 526. In its place, a new law might require gray market goods to bear labels clearly explaining any differences between them and goods that come through authorized channels. Other experts believe that instead of changing the laws, companies should develop proactive strategic responses to gray markets. One such strategy would be improved market segmentation and product differentiation to make gray market products less attractive; another would be to aggressively identify and terminate distributors that are involved in selling to gray marketers.

> "The gray market is the biggest threat we have. You can't develop this market properly and make investments in retailing, merchandising, after-sales service and distribution without a legal market."[38]
>
> Pankaj Mohindroo, president, Indian Cellular Association

▶ **11-7** Assess the impact of dumping on prices in global markets.

(11-7) Dumping

Dumping is an important global pricing strategy issue. The General Agreement on Tariff and Trade's (GATT) 1979 antidumping code defined *dumping* as the sale of an imported product at a price lower than that normally charged in a domestic market or country of origin. In addition, many countries have their own policies and procedures for protecting national companies from dumping. For example, China has retaliated against years of Western antidumping rules by introducing rules of its own. China's State Council passed the Antidumping and Antisubsidy Regulations in March 1997. The Ministry of Foreign Trade and Economic Cooperation and the State Economic and Trade Commission have responsibility for antidumping matters.[39]

The U.S. Congress has defined *dumping* as an unfair trade practice that results in "injury, destruction, or prevention of the establishment of American industry." Under this definition, dumping occurs when imports sold in the U.S. market are priced either at levels that represent less than the cost of production plus an 8 percent profit margin or at levels below those prevailing in the producing country. The U.S. Commerce Department is responsible for determining whether products are being dumped in the United States; the International Trade Commission (ITC) then determines whether the dumping has resulted in injury to U.S. firms.

Many of the dumping cases in the United States involve manufactured goods from Asia and frequently target a single or very narrowly defined group of products. U.S. companies that claim to be materially damaged by the low-priced imports often initiate such cases. In 2000, the U.S.

> "Dumping is the single most immediate threat for the whole of the European steel industry. Excess steel capacity in a truly global market helps no one in the long term."[40]
>
> Geert van Poelvoorde, president, Eurofer

Congress passed the so-called **Byrd Amendment**; this law calls for antidumping revenues to be paid to U.S. companies harmed by imported goods sold at below-market prices.[41]

In Europe, the European Commission administers antidumping policy; a simple majority vote by the Council of Ministers is required before duties can be imposed on dumped goods. Six-month provisional duties can be imposed, while more stringent measures include definitive, 5-year duties. In the past, low-cost imports from Asia have been the subject of dumping disputes in Europe. Another issue concerned $650 million in annual imports of unbleached cotton from China, Egypt, India, Indonesia, Pakistan, and Turkey. One dispute pitted an alliance of textile importers and wholesalers against Eurocoton, which represents textile weavers in France, Italy, and other EU countries. Eurocoton supported duties as a means of protecting jobs from low-priced imports; the job issue was particularly sensitive in France. British textile importer Broome & Wellington maintained, however, that imposing duties would drive up prices and cost even more jobs in the textile finishing and garment industries.[42] In January 2005, the global system of textile quotas was abolished. Almost overnight, Chinese textile exports to the United States and Europe increased dramatically. Within a few months, the U.S. government had re-imposed quotas on several categories of textile imports; in the European Union, trade minister Peter Mandelson also imposed quotas for a period of 2 years.

Dumping was a major issue in the Uruguay Round of GATT negotiations. Many countries took issue with the U.S. system of antidumping laws, in part because historically the U.S. Commerce Department has almost always ruled in favor of the U.S. company that filed the complaint. For their part, U.S. negotiators were concerned that U.S. exporters were often targeted in antidumping investigations in countries with few formal rules for due process. The U.S. side sought to improve the ability of U.S. companies to defend their interests and understand the bases for rulings.

The result of the GATT negotiations was an agreement on interpretation of GATT Article VI. From the U.S. point of view, one of the most significant changes between the agreement and the 1979 code is the addition of a "standard of review" that will make it harder for GATT panels to dispute U.S. antidumping determinations. A number of procedural and methodological changes were also made. In some instances, these have the effect of bringing GATT regulations more in line with U.S. law. For example, in calculating the "fair price" for a given product, any sales of the product at below-cost prices in the exporting country are not included in the calculations; inclusion of such sales would have the effect of exerting downward pressure on the fair price. The agreement also aligned GATT standards with U.S. standards by prohibiting governments from penalizing differences between home-market and export-market prices of less than 2 percent.

To provide positive proof that dumping has occurred in the United States, the complainant must demonstrate that both price discrimination and injury occurred. *Price discrimination* is the practice of setting different prices when selling the same quantity of "like-quality" goods to different buyers. The existence of either one without the other is an insufficient condition to constitute dumping.

Companies concerned with running afoul of antidumping legislation have developed a number of approaches for avoiding these laws. One approach is to differentiate the product sold from that in the home market so it does not represent "like quality." An example is an auto accessory that one company packaged with a wrench and an instruction book, thereby changing the "accessory" to a "tool." The duty rate in the export market happened to be lower on tools, and the company also acquired immunity from antidumping laws because the package was not comparable to competing goods in the target market. Another approach is to make nonprice competitive adjustments in arrangements with affiliates and distributors. For example, credit can be extended, which essentially has the same effect as a price reduction.

11-8 Price Fixing

◄ **11-8** Compare and contrast the different types of price fixing.

In most instances, it is illegal for representatives of two or more companies to secretly agree to set similar prices for their products. This practice, known as **price fixing**, is generally held to be an anticompetitive act. Companies that collude in this manner are usually trying to ensure higher prices for their products than would generally be available if markets were functioning freely. In *horizontal price fixing*, competitors within an industry that make and market the same product conspire to keep prices high. For example, in 2011 the European Commission determined that P&G, Unilever, and Henkel had conspired to set prices for laundry detergent. The term *horizontal* applies in this instance because P&G and its co-conspirators are all at the same supply-chain "level" (i.e., they are manufacturers).

Vertical price fixing occurs when a manufacturer conspires with wholesalers or retailers (i.e., channel members at different "levels" from the manufacturer) to ensure certain retail prices are maintained. The European Commission once fined Nintendo nearly $150 million after it was determined that the video game company had colluded with European distributors to fix prices. During the 1990s, prices of Nintendo video game consoles varied widely across Europe. The devices were much more expensive in Spain than in Britain and other countries; however, distributors in countries with lower retail prices agreed not to sell to retailers in countries with higher prices.[43]

Another case of price fixing pitted DeBeers SA, the South African diamond company, against the United States. At issue were prices for industrial diamonds, not gemstones; however, DeBeers is a well-known name in the United States thanks to a long-running advertising campaign keyed to the tagline "A Diamond Is Forever." Because the company itself has no American retail presence, DeBeers diamonds are marketed in the United States by intermediaries. DeBeers executives reached a plea agreement and paid a $10 million fine in exchange for access to the U.S. market. As a spokesperson said in the months leading up to the plea, "The U.S. is the biggest market for diamond jewelry—accounting for 50 percent of global retail jewelry sales—and we would really, really like to resolve these issues."[44]

▶ 11-9 Explain the concept of transfer pricing.

(11-9) Transfer Pricing

Transfer pricing refers to the pricing of goods, services, and intangible property bought and sold by operating units or divisions of the same company. In other words, transfer pricing concerns *intracorporate exchanges*, which are transactions between buyers and sellers that have the same corporate parent. For example, Toyota subsidiaries both sell to, and buy from, each other. Transfer pricing is an important topic in global marketing because goods crossing national borders represent a sale; therefore, their pricing is a matter of interest both to the tax authorities, which want to collect a fair share of income taxes, and to the customs service, which wants to collect an appropriate duty on the goods. Joseph Quinlan, chief marketing strategist at Bank of America, estimates that U.S. companies have 23,000 overseas affiliates; approximately 25 percent of U.S. exports represent shipments by American companies to affiliates and subsidiaries outside the United States.

In determining transfer prices to subsidiaries, global companies must address a number of issues, including taxes, duties and tariffs, country profit transfer rules, conflicting objectives of joint-venture partners, and government regulations. Tax authorities such as the Internal Revenue Service (IRS) in the United States, Inland Revenue in the United Kingdom, and Japan's National Tax Administration Agency take a keen interest in transfer pricing policies.[45] Transfer pricing is proving to be a key corporate issue in Europe as the euro makes it easier for tax authorities to audit transfer pricing policies.

Three major alternative approaches can be applied to transfer pricing decisions. The approach used will vary with the nature of the firm, the products, the markets, and the historical circumstances of each case. A **market-based transfer price** is derived from the price required to be competitive in the global marketplace. In other words, it represents an approximation of an arm's-length transaction. **Cost-based transfer pricing** uses an internal cost as the starting point in determining price. This kind of transfer pricing can take the same forms as the cost-based pricing methods discussed earlier in the chapter. The way costs are defined may have an impact on tariffs and duties of sales to affiliates and subsidiaries. A third alternative is to allow the organization's affiliates to determine **negotiated transfer prices** among themselves. This method may be employed when market conditions are subject to frequent changes. Table 11-3 summarizes the ways that the different methods satisfy multiple managerial criteria.

Tax Regulations and Transfer Prices

Because global companies conduct business in a world characterized by different corporate tax rates, companies have an incentive to maximize income in countries with the lowest tax rates—Ireland is a prime example—and to minimize income in the United States and

TABLE 11-3 Comparison of Different Transfer Pricing Methods

Criteria	Market-Based	Cost-Based	Negotiated
Achieves goal congruence	Yes, when markets are competitive	Often, but not always	Yes
Motivates managerial effort	Yes	Yes, when based on budgeted costs	Yes
Useful for evaluating subunit performance	Yes, when markets are competitive	Difficult unless transfer price exceeds full cost	Yes, but transfer prices are affected by the negotiating skills of the buyer and the seller
Preserves subunit autonomy	Yes, when markets are competitive	No, because it is rule-based	Yes, because it is based on negotiations between subunits
Other factors	Markets may not exist or may be imperfect	Useful for determining the full cost of products; easy to implement	Bargaining and negotiations take time and may need to be reviewed as conditions change

Source: Adapted from Charles T. Horngren, Srikant M. Datar, George Foster, Madhav Rajan, and Christopher Ittner, *Cost Accounting: A Managerial Emphasis* (Upper Saddle River, NJ: Prentice Hall, 2009), p. 783.

other countries with high tax rates. As we discussed in Chapter 5, governmental regulatory agencies are well aware that Apple and other companies formulate strategies for tax planning and tax minimization.[46] In recent years, many governments have tried to maximize national tax revenues by examining company returns and mandating reallocation of income and expenses. Among the companies that have become involved in transfer pricing cases are the following:

- The IRS sought as much as $500 million in back taxes on earnings from Motorola's global operations that were allegedly booked incorrectly.
- The U.S. Labor Department filed a complaint against Swatch Group alleging that the Swiss watchmaker improperly used transfer pricing to evade millions of dollars in customs duties and taxes.[47]
- The U.S. government spent years attempting to recover $2.7 billion plus interest from pharmaceutical giant GlaxoSmithKline (GSK). The IRS charged that GSK did not pay enough tax on profits from Zantac, its hugely successful ulcer medication. Between 1989 and 1999, U.S. revenues from Zantac totaled $16 billion; the IRS charged that GSK's American unit overpaid royalties to the British parent company, thereby reducing taxable U.S. income. The case was scheduled for trial in 2007; however, in September 2006, GSK settled the case by agreeing to pay the IRS approximately $3.1 billion.[48]

Sales of Tangible and Intangible Property

Each country has its own set of laws and regulations for dealing with controlled intracompany transfers. Whatever the pricing rationale, executives and managers involved in global pricing policy decisions must familiarize themselves with the laws and regulations in the applicable countries. The pricing rationale must conform with the intention of these laws and regulations. Although the applicable laws and regulations often seem perplexingly inscrutable, ample evidence exists that most governments simply seek to prevent tax avoidance and to ensure fair distribution of income from the operations of companies doing business internationally.

Even companies that make a conscientious effort to comply with the applicable laws and regulations and that document this effort may find themselves in tax court. Should a tax auditor raise questions, executives must be able to make a strong case for their decisions. Fortunately, consulting services are available to help managers deal with the arcane world of transfer pricing. It is not unusual for large global companies to invest hundreds of thousands of dollars and hire international accounting firms to review transfer pricing policies.

▶ **11-10** Define *countertrade* and explain the various forms it can take.

11-10 Countertrade

In recent years, many exporters have been forced to finance international transactions by taking full or partial payment in some form other than money.[49] A number of alternative finance methods, known as *countertrade*, are widely used. In a **countertrade** transaction, a sale results in product flowing in one direction to a buyer; a separate stream of products and services, often flowing in the opposite direction, is also created. Countertrade generally involves a seller from the West and a buyer in a developing country; for example, the countries in the former Soviet bloc have historically relied heavily on countertrade. This approach, which reached a peak in popularity in the mid-1980s, is now used in some 100 countries. Within the former Soviet Union, countertrade flourished in the 1990s, following the collapse of the central planning system.

As one expert noted, countertrade flourishes when hard currency is scarce. Exchange controls may prevent a company from expatriating earnings; the company may be forced to spend money in-country for products that are then exported and sold in third-country markets. Historically, the single most important driving force behind the proliferation of countertrade was the decreasing ability of developing countries to finance imports through bank loans. This trend resulted in debt-ridden governments pushing for self-financed deals.[50]

Generally, several conditions affect the probability that some form of countertrade will be used.

- *The priority attached to the import.* The higher the priority, the less likely it is that counter-trade will be required.
- *The value of the transaction.* The higher the value, the greater the likelihood that counter-trade will be involved.
- *The availability of products from other suppliers.* If a company is the sole supplier of a differentiated product, it can demand monetary payment.

In the past decade, the debt crisis in Europe prompted some companies to consider using countertrade. German chemical giant BASF has a contingency plan to accept countertrade deals with Greek buyers in the agricultural sector. Such deals are not new for BASF; in Eastern Europe, for example, the company has accepted minerals as payment for its chemical products. Some customers in Brazil even pay with molasses! Fried-Walter Muenstermann, the CFO for BASF, says his company will be selective with new countertrade deals in Europe: "We don't need wine and olive oil."[51]

Two categories of countertrade are discussed here. Barter falls into one category; the mixed forms of countertrade, including counterpurchase, offset, compensation trading, and switch trading, belong in a separate category. They incorporate a real distinction from barter because the transaction involves money or credit.

Barter

The term **barter** describes the least complex and oldest form of bilateral, nonmonetized counter-trade. Simple barter is a direct exchange of goods or services between two parties. Although no money is involved, both partners construct an approximate shadow price for products flowing in each direction. To make these arrangements, companies sometimes seek outside help from barter specialists. For example, New York–based Atwood Richards engages in barter in all parts of the world. More often, distribution of the bartered items occurs directly between the trading partners, with no intermediary included.

In the annals of global marketing, PepsiCo was one of the highest-profile companies involved in barter deals. Pepsi has done business in the Soviet and post-Soviet market for decades. In the Soviet era, when the ruble could not be converted to dollars or other "hard" currencies, PepsiCo bartered soft drink syrup concentrate for Stolichnaya vodka. The vodka was exported to the United States by the PepsiCo Wines & Spirits subsidiary and marketed by M. Henri Wines. In the post-Soviet market economy, Russian rubles are freely convertible, and barter is no longer required. Today, Stolichnaya is imported and distributed by Stoli Group, a unit of Luxembourg-based SPI Group.

A cornerstone of the late Venezuelan president Hugo Chávez's economic policy was bartering oil to foster closer relations with other Latin American countries. Cuba sent doctors to Venezuela in exchange for oil; other countries "paid" for oil with bananas or sugar. More recently, shortages in goods have forced Venezuelans to barter for their daily needs using WhatsApp, Facebook, and Instagram. Sample trades: Pasta and sugar for diapers; flour for shampoo; and Colombian toilet paper for pantry staples.[52]

Counterpurchase

The **counterpurchase** form of countertrade, also termed *parallel trading* or *parallel barter*, is distinguished from other forms of countertrade in that each delivery in an exchange is paid for in cash. For example, Rockwell International sold a printing press to Zimbabwe for $8 million—but the deal went through only after Rockwell agreed to purchase $8 million in ferrochrome and nickel from Zimbabwe. It subsequently sold those ores on the world market.

The Rockwell–Zimbabwe deal illustrates several aspects of counterpurchase. Generally, products offered by the foreign principal are not related to the Western firm's exports and cannot be used directly by the firm. In most counterpurchase transactions, two separate contracts are signed. In one contract, the supplier agrees to sell products for a cash settlement (the original sales contract); in the other, the supplier agrees to purchase and market unrelated products from the buyer (a separate, parallel contract). The dollar value of the counterpurchase generally represents a set percentage—and sometimes the full value—of the products sold to the foreign principal. When the Western supplier sells these goods, the trading cycle is complete.

Offset

Offset is a reciprocal arrangement whereby the government in the importing country seeks to recover large sums of hard currency spent on expensive purchases such as military aircraft or telecommunications systems. In effect, the government is saying, "If you want us to spend government money on your exports, you must import products from our country." Offset arrangements may also involve cooperation in manufacturing, some form of technology transfer, placing subcontracts locally, or arranging local assembly or manufacturing equal to a certain percentage of the contract value.[53] In one deal involving offsets, Lockheed Martin sold F-16 fighters to the United Arab Emirates for $6.4 billion. In return, Lockheed Martin agreed to invest $160 million in the petroleum-related UAE Offsets Group.[54]

Offset may be distinguished from counterpurchase in that the latter is characterized by smaller deals over shorter periods of time.[55] Another major distinction between offset and other forms of countertrade is that the agreement is not contractual, but rather reflects a memorandum of understanding that sets out the dollar value of products to be offset and the time period for completing the transaction. In addition, there is no penalty on the supplier for nonperformance. Typically, requests range from 20 to 50 percent of the value of the supplier's product. Some highly competitive sales have required offsets exceeding 100 percent of the valuation of the original sale.

Offsets have become a controversial aspect of today's trade environment. To win sales in important markets such as China, global companies can face demands for offsets even when transactions do not involve military procurement. For example, the Chinese government requires Boeing to spend 20 to 30 percent of the price of each aircraft on purchases of Chinese goods. As former Boeing executive Dean Thornton once explained:

> "Offset" is a bad word, and it's against GATT and a whole bunch of other stuff, but it's a fact of life. It used to be 20 years ago in places like Canada or the UK, it was totally explicit, down to the decimal point. "You will buy 20 percent offset of your value." Or 21 percent or whatever. It still is that way in military stuff. [With sales of commercial aircraft], it's not legal so it becomes less explicit.[56]

Compensation Trading

Compensation trading, also called *buyback*, is a form of countertrade that involves two separate and parallel contracts. In one contract, the supplier agrees to build a plant or provide plant equipment, patents or licenses, or technical, managerial, or distribution expertise for a hard-currency down payment at the time of delivery. In the other contract, the supplier company agrees to take payment in the form of the plant's output equal to its investment (minus interest) for a period of as many as 20 years.

Essentially, the success of compensation trading rests on the willingness of each firm to be both a buyer and a seller. China has used compensation trading extensively. Egypt also used this approach to develop an aluminum plant. A Swiss company, Aluswiss, built the plant and also exports alumina (an oxide of aluminum found in bauxite and clay) to Egypt. Aluswiss takes back a percentage of the finished aluminum produced at the plant as partial payment for building the plant. As this example shows, compensation differs from counterpurchase in that the technology or capital supplied in the former is related to the output produced.[57] In counterpurchase, as noted earlier, the goods taken by the supplier typically cannot be used directly in its business activities.

Switch Trading

Also called *triangular trade* and *swap*, **switch trading** is a mechanism that can be applied to barter or countertrade. In this arrangement, a third party steps into a simple barter or other countertrade arrangement when one of the parties is not willing to accept all the goods received in a transaction. The third party may be a professional switch trader, a switch trading house, or a bank. The switching mechanism provides a "secondary market" for countertraded or bartered goods and reduces the inflexibility inherent in barter and countertrade. Fees charged by switch traders range from 5 percent of market value for commodities to 30 percent for high-technology items. Switch traders develop their own networks of firms and personal contacts and are generally headquartered in Vienna, Amsterdam, Hamburg, or London. If a party to the original transaction anticipates that the products received in a barter or countertrade deal will be sold eventually at a discount by the switch trader, the common practice is to price the original products higher, build in "special charges" for port storage or consulting, or require shipment by the national carrier.

Summary

Pricing decisions are a critical element of the marketing mix that must reflect costs, competitive factors, and customer perceptions regarding value of the product. In a true global market, the *law of one price* would prevail. Pricing strategies include *market skimming*, *market penetration*, and *market holding*. Novice exporters frequently use the cost-plus method when setting prices. International terms of a sale such as *ex-works*, *DDP*, *FCA*, *FAS*, *FOB*, *CIF*, and *CFR* are known as *Incoterms* and specify which party to a transaction is responsible for covering various costs. These and other costs lead to *export price escalation*, the accumulation of costs that occurs when products are shipped from one country to another.

Expectations regarding currency fluctuations, inflation, government controls, and the competitive situation must also be factored into pricing decisions. The introduction of the euro has impacted price strategies in the European Union because of the improved *price transparency* it supports. Global companies can maintain competitive prices in world markets by shifting production sources as business conditions change. Overall, a company's pricing policies can be categorized as *ethnocentric*, *polycentric*, or *geocentric*.

Several other pricing issues must be taken into account in global marketing. The possibility of *gray market goods* arises because price variations between different countries lead to *parallel imports*. *Dumping* is another contentious issue that can result in strained relations between trading partners. *Price fixing* among companies is anticompetitive and illegal. *Transfer pricing* is an issue because of the sheer monetary volume of intracorporate sales and because country governments are anxious to generate as much tax revenue as possible. Various forms of *countertrade* play an important role in today's global environment. *Barter, counterpurchase, offset, compensation trading*, and *switch trading* are the main countertrade options.

Discussion Questions

11-1. What are the basic factors that affect price in any market? Which considerations enter into the pricing decision?

11-2. What are some of the effects of "dumping" on the country of origin?

11-3. Identify some of the environmental constraints on global pricing decisions.

11-4. What are the differences between "horizontal price fixing" and "vertical price fixing"?

11-5. What is a transfer price? Why is it an important issue for companies with foreign affiliates? Why did transfer pricing in Europe take on increased importance in 1999?

11-6. How do the ethnocentric, polycentric, and geocentric pricing strategies differ? Which would you recommend to a company that has global market aspirations?

11-7. In November 2018, China launched its first ever anti-dumping investigation against Australia. The subject of the investigation was barley. The Australians had not been dumping excess barley production in China; the latter was angered by Australian moves to stop the practice. Why is dumping such an issue to a country like Australia?

11-8. Compare and contrast the different forms of countertrade.

CASE 11-1 *Continued (refer to page 359)* *Continued (refer to page 359)*
Global Automakers Target Low-Income Consumers

The Logan is a case study in driving down costs. Drivers turn on the ignition with an "old-fashioned," manual key; there is no cruise control. The windshield glass is nearly flat, which makes it less expensive to produce. The left and right outside mirrors are identical; the ashtrays are exactly the same as the ones used in another Renault model, the Espace. Similarly, Logan shares an engine and gearbox with Renault's Clio subcompact. For these and other components, high manufacturing volumes translate into economies of scale.

Production of the first Logan models began in Romania in 2004. The choice of an assembly site was dictated by simple economics: France's high labor rates and payroll taxes would have translated into an additional €1,000 ($1,400) cost per vehicle. The Logan was launched in India in April 2007 with a sticker price of about $10,000; the vehicle was manufactured by a joint venture between Renault and Mahindra & Mahindra (M&M), one of India's best-known industrial conglomerates. After a dispute between the partners, the joint venture was dissolved. Mahindra & Mahindra now produces Logans under a licensing agreement.

In 2008 a hatchback model, the Sandero, was introduced. It was followed in 2009 by the Duster sport-utility vehicle; the Lodgy debuted in 2012. In 2012, Renault sold a record 2.55 million vehicles, 25 percent of which were low-cost models. Sales were split roughly evenly between the Logan and entry-level Renault models. As it turned out, the geographic distribution of sales indicated that Renault's strategy was in trouble: Although the Logan was targeted at emerging markets, it was a big hit with consumers in affluent European countries.

How did this happen? Enterprising independent distributors bought Logans that were manufactured in Romania and exported them to France and other countries in Western Europe. This coincided with a shift in consumer attitudes; in light of the financial crisis happening at the time, it was not surprising that many young Europeans were of the opinion that cutting back on spending was a sensible thing to do. Indeed, surveys showed that a high proportion of twenty-something Europeans were "interested" or "very interested" in buying a low-cost car.

Nano

Even as Renault continued to refine its low-cost-car strategy, some in the industry were asking a tantalizing question: Could the auto companies come up with the optimal value proposition—small, no-frills, four-door cars that are safe to drive, stylish enough to appeal to the aspirations of first-time buyers, and yet sell for *half* the price of a Logan (or less)? Under the best of circumstances, creating such a vehicle would test the prowess of the world's best automotive engineers. The challenge was even more daunting in a business environment characterized by record prices for steel, resin, and other commodities and components. As the general manager for a sourcing and procuring company noted, "There are so many legacy costs built into a design, and trying to engineer those out is difficult. It's better to start with a clean sheet of paper and engineer low costs in."

Top executives at India's Tata Motors believed their company was up to the task, and the Nano is the evidence. The Nano's instrument panel is clustered in the middle of the dashboard so that Tata can offer both right- and left-hand-drive versions for export. Tata's target market is consumers in emerging markets who currently travel by scooter. Some environmentalists have warned about the negative impact of hundreds of thousands of new vehicles on India's already congested roads. Chairman Ratan Tata asserts that low-income families should be given access to the freedom that a car provides: "Should they be denied the right to independent transport?" he asks.

After an initial flurry of industry interest and positive press, the Nano program fell victim to bad luck and changing attitudes. For one thing, protesters objected to the location of the first assembly plant. After production finally began, there were several well-publicized incidents in which the cars caught fire. Many car buyers shopped the competition; one best-selling model was the $6,200 Maruti Suzuki Alto. It seemed that the market had spoken: Very few people wanted to be seen driving "the world's cheapest car." As Hormazd Sorabjee, editor of *India Autoweek*, noted, "The bottom of the pyramid continues to be where the action is, but the aspirations of people are moving up. People want to jump into something more substantial."

Industry analysts Arya Sen had a similar assessment. "Cars in India are aspirational, but this was positioned as a cheap product," he said.

Datsun

Tata Motors' announcement about the Nano galvanized Carlos Ghosn, Nissan's chief executive. Nissan's Datsun relaunch had Ghosn's full support: He was born in Brazil and didn't own a car until his late teens. To Ghosn, Datsun represented more than a business strategy or business model. Much more, in fact: It was a life mission, a make-or-break, billion-dollar decision that would determine his legacy and his reputation. In 2007, Ghosn convened a cadre of company executives known as the Nissan Exploratory Team and dispatched members to India to study what consumers there sought in a car.

Industry observers noted that the Datsun nameplate was very popular in the United States in the 1960s and 1970s. In 1981, executives decided to unify the two brands, so Datsun became Nissan. The result: Much confusion among consumers and a gradual erosion of Nissan's market position in the United States. The move is widely regarded as one of the worst decisions in the history of the automobile business.

In 2012, Yukitoshi Funo, an executive vice president at rival Toyota Motor Corporation, expressed doubts about Datsun's prospects: "It's a big mistake to think you can introduce a cheap car in emerging markets and be successful. People want a car they and their families can be proud of." His remarks proved to be prescient. When Datsun launched in India in March 2013, Ghosn predicted that Datsun and Nissan would have a combined 10 percent market share in India by 2016. As it turned out, sales were below expectations. One issue was low brand recognition for both Nissan and Datsun. Also, only a few

Datsun dealerships were opened, so Nissan dealers were recruited to carry the Datsun line. Consumers appeared to view Datsun as simply a stripped-down Nissan.

Discussion Questions

11-9. What is the key to the Logan's low price?

11-10. Do you think Tata will be able to save the Nano? Which steps should the company take?

11-11. Assess Carlos Ghosn's plans to revive the Datsun nameplate in India. Can a car that sells for $3,000 generate a profit for the parent company?

11-12. Low-cost cars such as the Nano and Datsun lack the multilayered safety and quality features required by regulators in high-income markets. Is it appropriate to create "bare-bones" cars with fewer safety features for emerging markets?

Sources: Simon Mundy, "Tata on Road to Recovery after Nano Disaster," *Financial Times* (March 13, 2018), p. 13; Santanu Choudhury, "Datsun's Second-Coming Sputters," *The Wall Street Journal* (February 12, 2015), p. B6; Henry Foy and James Crabtree, "Nissan Goes Back to the Future with Datsun," *Financial Times* (July 15, 2013), p. 16; Chester Dawson, "For Datsun Revival, Nissan Gambles on $3,000 Model," *The Wall Street Journal* (October 1, 2012), p. A1; Sebastian Moffett, "Renault's Low-Price Plan Turns Tricky," *The Wall Street Journal* (February 2, 2011), pp. B1, B2; Vikas Bajaj, "Tata's Nano, the Car That Few Want to Buy," *The New York Times* (December 10, 2010), p. B1; Simon Robinson, "The World's Cheapest Car," Time.com (January 10, 2008); Heather Timmons, "In India, a $2,500 Pace Car," *The New York Times* (October 12, 2007), pp. C1, C4; David Gauthier-Villars, "Ghosn Bets Big on Low-Cost Strategy," *The Wall Street Journal* (September 4, 2007), p. A8; John Reed and Amy Yee, "Thrills without Frills," *Financial Times* (June 25, 2007), p. 9; Christopher Condon, "The Birth of a Frankenstein Car," *Financial Times* (July 20, 2004), p. 12.

CASE 11-2
Global Consumer-Products Companies Target Low-Income Consumers

"Frugal engineering." "Indovation." "Reverse innovation." These are some of the terms that marketers at GE, Procter & Gamble, Siemens, and Unilever are using to describe efforts to penetrate more deeply into emerging markets. As growth in mature markets slows, executives and managers at many global companies are realizing that the ability to serve the needs of the world's poorest consumers will be a critical source of competitive advantage in the decades to come. Procter & Gamble CEO Robert McDonald set a strategic goal of introducing 800 million new consumers to the company's brands by 2015. Achieving this goal would require a better understanding of what daily life is like in, say, hundreds of thousands of rural villages in Africa, Latin America, and China.

Consider, for example, that two-thirds of the world's population—more than 4 billion people—live on less than $2 per day. This segment is sometimes referred to as the "bottom of the pyramid" and includes an estimated 1.5 billion people who live "off the grid." Such individuals have no access to electricity to provide light or to charge their cell phones. Often, a villager must walk several miles to hire a taxi for the trip to the nearest city with electricity—a trip that is costly in terms of both time and money.

This situation has provided an opportunity for companies to create innovative sources of renewable energy. Solutions include a small-scale,

roof-mounted, Chinese-made solar power system that costs $80, underground biogas chambers that generate electricity from cow manure, and scaled-down hydroelectric dams that can power a village from a local stream or river.

One of the most pressing issues at the bottom of the pyramid is access to basic infrastructure. Historically, government-owned power-generation facilities, including massive solar projects and wind farms, have been the norm in emerging markets such as India. However, it is often not cost-effective to extend the power grid into rural areas. In fact, according to the International Energy Agency, fewer than two-thirds of the rural residents in the world's developing nations have access to electricity. One problem with the new renewable energy systems is the lack of scale. Rural markets are dispersed, and distribution is not well established. As a result, many investors consider rural renewable energy initiatives to be too risky to warrant funding.

This situation may be changing in Africa, where nearly 600 million people are included in the "off-grid segment." For years, small-scale organizations such as Solar Sisters have worked at the individual level to help provide renewable energy sources. Now large global companies such as Philips Electronics, DuPont, and Siemens are testing solar-powered systems at the village level. The companies hope that government officials will purchase the systems and bring power to rural areas. The systems include solar panels for charging batteries and overhead home lighting and lanterns that use efficient LEDs. As Philips has discovered in its pilot program in South Africa, the money that villagers save by not buying kerosene can be spent on necessities such as bread. If the pilot programs are successful and win government funding, enough power will be available to enable village households to have refrigerators and radios.

Lack of scale and a shortage of capital are just two of the problems associated with reaching the world's poor. For consumer products, Professor Aneel Karnani of the Ross School of Business has identified another stumbling block to market success. "The biggest problem is that prices are too high. Companies overestimate the size of the market and end up selling to the middle class, not the poor," he says. But there is a potential upside: Even as shoppers in mature markets cut back on discretionary spending, consumer spending on basic items such as food and soap remains stable and relatively unaffected by trends in the broader global economy. However, after companies have created the right product at the right price, another potential problem presents itself: communicating product benefits and persuading low-income consumers to change long-entrenched behaviors by paying for new products and integrating them into their lifestyles. In short, it is not enough to simply launch a low-cost product; markets for that product must be created.

Nestlé's experience in emerging markets illustrates how a painstaking approach can yield positive results. Indonesia is a case in point. As the data in Table 7-3 indicate, Indonesia is the world's fourth most populous country. Even though per capita income is only $3,400 per year, Nestlé Indonesia generates annual revenues of $1 billion. The company has enjoyed consistent sales growth for Milo, a chocolate sports drink mix for children. It can be prepared hot or cold and sells for about 10 cents per serving. Crunch, another new chocolate product, is a bite-sized snack wafer that also sells for 10 cents per package. Nestlé's food engineers managed to keep the cost low by using existing production processes utilized for the company's breakfast cereal lines. Because the Crunch packaging is inflated, the wafers don't melt or break into pieces.

Nestlé has also successfully targeted low-income consumers in Latin America. With a population of 207 million people and a gross domestic product (GDP) of $1.8 trillion, Brazil dominates the region. Per capita income is $8,840, placing Brazil in the ranks of upper-middle-income countries. But averages can be deceiving: Some 30 million Brazilians qualify as "bottom-of-the-pyramid" consumers, and an estimated 16 million Brazilians live on less than $600 per year. In the mid-2000s, the president of Nestlé do Brasil initiated a regionalization program. Ivan Zurita knows that Brazil's vast geographical territory means that brand preferences will vary from region to region. There is no "one size fits all," single consumer profile in the country.

For example, northeastern Brazil is the poorest region in the country. There, Nestlé launched Leche Ideal, a powdered milk mix enriched with vitamins and iron that is sold in 200-gram packets that are easy to store. In the Brazilian state of Bahia, Nestlé opened a new plant in 2007 that has the capacity to produce 50,000 tons of food products each year. Crucially, the products can easily be adapted to local tastes, such as a smoother-tasting coffee. The success of the regionalization program in Brazil has prompted Nestlé executives to call for its expansion throughout the region. Zurita is confident that Nestlé can leverage its experience in Brazil to launch similar programs in Chile and other Latin American countries.

Other well-known global marketers are also capitalizing on the opportunity to serve low-income consumers. For example, Kraft recently opened its first plant in northeastern Brazil. Adidas has developed a sneaker priced at 1 euro that it hopes to sell in Bangladesh. Unilever's Cubitos are seasoning cubes that sell for as little as 2 cents each. Danone has developed a variety of products for emerging markets, including Dolima drinkable yogurt, Dany Xprime jelly pouches, and Milky Start milk porridge.

Not every company has been successful in targeting the low-income segment. For example, Procter & Gamble spent years developing PUR, a water purification powder that sells for 10 cents. Although market research indicated that villagers wanted clean water, PUR ultimately did not catch on with consumers. In the end, P&G chose to donate PUR to relief organizations and partner with other groups to educate villagers about the benefits of PUR.

Even as Procter & Gamble continues to target consumers at the bottom of the pyramid, its primary target is the middle-class consumer: a professional manager who lives in a modern high-rise apartment building and has enough discretionary income to dine out several times each month.

Procter & Gamble has also learned the value of local research and development programs. This is something that domestic companies in India and other emerging markets have recognized for a long time. In fact, as innovation guru Vijay Govindarajan has noted, "The biggest threat for U.S. multinationals is not existing competitors. It is going to be emerging-market competitors." In India, for example, entrepreneurial companies are creating a variety of low-cost products that meet the needs and fit the lifestyles of consumers at affordable prices.

> "Our innovation strategy is not just diluting the top-tier product for the lower-end consumer. You have to discretely innovate for every one of those consumers on that economic curve, and if you don't do that, you'll fail."
>
> Robert McDonald, former CEO and chairman, Procter & Gamble

One of these products is an improved $23 wood-burning stove created by a startup company called First Energy. Indian women spend many hours each day cooking, and there was a clear need for a stove that burned less wood and generated less smoke. The key was adapting technology used in power plants. Engineers at the Indian Institute of Science created a high-efficiency, perforated burning chamber equipped with a small fan. The engineers also found an innovative way to convert agricultural by-products into valuable resources: The new stove burns pellets made from corn husks and peanut shells.

Hindustan Unilever spent 4 years developing Pureit, a portable water purification system that costs $43. Rather than rely on traditional distribution channels, Unilever tapped its network of 45,000 sales representatives who demonstrate Unilever products in their own homes. The women follow up the demonstrations by delivering products door-to-door. Today, more than 3 million Indian homes have Pureit systems.

Godrej & Boyce Manufacturing offers Little Cool, a $70 portable refrigerator that uses minimal electricity. Only 20 percent of Indian households have refrigerators; to assess the opportunity, Godrej sent researchers to meet with farm families in rural India. The resulting product resembles a cooler with handles for easy transport. Instead of a power-hungry compressor, the units have cooling chips and fans. Because power outages are common in India, Little Cool can run on batteries, and it is heavily insulated so contents stay cool for hours.

Discussion Questions

11-13. Why are companies such as Siemens, GE, Nestlé, and Procter & Gamble targeting the "bottom of the pyramid"?

11-14. Review the Chapter 4 discussion of diffusion theory. How might an understanding of the characteristics of innovations help marketers succeed in emerging markets?

11-15. Which types of marketing communications may be necessary to launch an innovative product such as Procter & Gamble's PUR in emerging markets? Which changes in consumer attitudes and behavior are required for successfully launching a product such as PUR?

11-16. Which key concepts discussed in Chapter 1 apply to Nestlé's experience in Latin America?

Sources: Heidi Vogt, "Made in Africa: A Gadget Startup," *The Wall Street Journal* (July 10, 2014), pp. B1, B6; Tio Kermeliotis, "'Solar Sisters' Spreading Light in Africa," *Marketplace Africa,* www.cnn.com (January 2, 2013); Eric Bellman, "Multinationals Market to the Poor," *The Wall Street Journal* (July 24, 2012), p. B8; Patrick McGroarty, "Power to More People," *The Wall Street Journal Report: Innovations* (June 18, 2012), p. R4; "Catching up in a Hurry," *The Economist* (May 19, 2011), p. 32; Jennifer Reinhold, "Can P&G Make Money in Places Where People Earn $2 a Day?" *Fortune* (January 17, 2011), pp. 58–63; Christina Passariello, "Danone Expands Its Pantry to Woo the World's Poor," *The Wall Street Journal* (June 25, 2010), pp. A1, A16; James Lamont, "The Age of 'Indovation' Dawns," *Financial Times* (June 15, 2010), p. 17; Elisabeth Rosenthal, "African Huts Far from the Grid Glow with Renewable Power," *The New York Times* (December 25, 2010), p. A1; Erik Simanis, "At the Base of the Pyramid," *The Wall Street Journal* (October 26, 2009), p. R6; Eric Bellman, "Indian Firms Shift Focus to the Poor," *The Wall Street Journal* (October 21, 2009), p. A1; Carlos Adese, "In Good Taste: Nestlé Tweaks Products for Different Parts of Brazil—and Latin America—to Boost Sales," *Latin Trade* (July 1, 2007), p. 6.

CASE 11-3
LVMH and Luxury Goods Marketing

LVMH Moët Hennessy–Louis Vuitton SA is the world's largest marketer of luxury products and brands. Chairman Bernard Arnault has assembled a diverse empire of more than 60 brands, sales of which totaled €42.8 billion (about $50 billion) in 2017 (see Figure 11-2). Arnault, whom some refer to as "the pope of high fashion," recently summed up the luxury business as follows: "We are here to sell dreams. When you see a couture show on TV around the world, you dream. When you enter a Dior boutique and buy your lipstick, you buy something affordable, but it has the dream in it."

Decades ago, the companies that today make up LVMH were family-run enterprises focused more on prestige than on profit. Fendi, Pucci, and others sold mainly to a niche market composed of very rich clientele. However, as markets began to globalize, the small luxury players struggled to compete. When Arnault set about acquiring smaller luxury brands, he had three goals in mind. First, he hoped that the portfolio approach would reduce the risk exposure in fashion cycles. According to this logic, if demand for watches or jewelry declined, clothing or accessory sales would offset any losses. Second, he intended to cut costs by eliminating redundancies in sourcing and manufacturing. Third, he hoped that LVMH's stable of brands would translate into a stronger bargaining position when managers negotiated leases for retail space or bought advertising.

Sales of luggage and leather fashion goods, including the 163-year-old Louis Vuitton brand, account for 30 percent of LVMH's revenues (see Figure 11-2). The company's Selective Retailing group includes Duty Free Shoppers (DFS) and Sephora. DFS operates "travel retail" stores in international airports around the world; Sephora, which LVMH acquired in 1997, is Europe's second-largest chain of perfume and cosmetics stores. Driven by such well-known brands as Christian Dior, Givenchy, and Kenzo, perfumes and cosmetics generate nearly 15 percent of LVMH's revenues. LVMH's wine and spirits unit includes Dom Perignon, Moët & Chandon, Veuve Clicquot, and other prestigious Champagne brands.

Despite the high expenses associated with operating elegant stores and purchasing advertising space in upscale magazines, the premium retail prices that luxury goods command translate into handsome profits. The Louis Vuitton brand alone accounts for approximately 60 percent of LVMH's operating profit. Unfortunately for the company, unscrupulous operators have taken note of the high margins associated with Vuitton handbags, gun cases, and luggage displaying the distinctive beige-on-brown latticework LV monogram. Louis Vuitton SA spends $10 million annually battling counterfeiters in Turkey, Thailand, China, Morocco, South Korea, and Italy. Some of the money is spent on lobbyists who represent the company's interests in meetings with foreign government officials. Yves Carcelle, chairman of Louis Vuitton SA, recently explained, "Almost every month, we get a government somewhere in the world to destroy canvas, or finished products."

Another problem is a flourishing gray market. Givenchy and Christian Dior's Dune fragrance are just two of the luxury perfume brands that are sometimes diverted from authorized channels for sale at mass-market retail outlets. However, LVMH and other luxury goods marketers found a way to combat gray market imports into the United States. In March 1995, the U.S. Supreme Court let stand an appeals court ruling prohibiting a discount drugstore chain from selling Givenchy perfume without permission. Parfums Givenchy USA had claimed that its distinctive packaging should be protected under U.S. copyright law. The ruling has meant that Costco, Walmart, and other discounters cannot sell some imported fragrances without authorization.

Opportunities and Challenges in Asia

Asia has long been a key region for LVMH and its competitors. For decades Japan was the number 1 market, but today China's luxury market exhibits the strongest growth (see Exhibit 11-8). The financial turmoil in Asia in the late 1990s and the subsequent currency devaluations and weakening of the yen translated into lower demand for luxury goods. Because price perceptions are a critical component of luxury goods' appeal, LVMH executives made a number of adjustments in response to changing business conditions. For example, Patrick Choel, president of the perfume and cosmetics division, raised wholesale prices in individual Asian markets. The goal was to discourage discount retailers from stocking up on designer products and then selling them to down-market consumers. Also, expenditures on perfume and cosmetics advertising were reduced to maintain profitability in the face of a possible sales decline.

FIGURE 11-2 LVMH Operating Units
by 2017 Net Sales

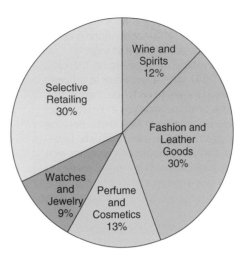

Exhibit 11-8 Louis Vuitton is opening
flagship stores in Shanghai, Beijing,
and other key cities in China.
Source: testing/Shutterstock.

"The big question for the
future is, will the Chinese
new entrant to the luxury
market choose a Louis Vuitton as her first bag, as she
has tended to do to date, or
that of another brand?"

Antoine Belge, luxury goods analyst, HSBC

Strategic Decisions at LVMH

Over the past decade, Arnault has leveraged his multibrand strategy by broadening the company's consumer base. In the late 1990s, Arnault sensed that cosmetics-buying habits were changing in key markets. He opened Sephora stores in New York, Chicago, and San Francisco in conjunction with a new Web site, Sephora.com. Today, there are more than 270 Sephora stores in the United States and Canada; the chain also has a presence in more than a dozen other countries, including China and Russia. Customers who visit Sephora USA stores are encouraged to wander freely and sample products on an open floor without waiting for sales clerks to assist them.

In 2001, Arnault paid more than $600 million for Donna Karan International and its trademarks. Arnault had tried without success to acquire Giorgio Armani; Donna Karan is LVMH's first American designer label. As Arnault noted, "What appealed to us is the fact that it is one of the best-known brand names in the world."

In January 2008, executives at Louis Vuitton announced a new corporate branding campaign using a 90-second ad slated to appear on cable and satellite television and in cinemas. This was something new in the luxury goods sector; generally, advertising budgets are limited and television time is viewed as too expensive. In addition, some in the industry believe that TV's status as a mass-marketing medium can undercut a luxury brand's aura of exclusivity. For Louis Vuitton executives, the hope was that audiences would connect with the brand's travel heritage. To achieve that connection, the company's ad agency proposed buying time on news channels that business travelers watch such as CNN. As Louis Vuitton marketing chief Pietro Beccari noted,

"It is supposed to touch our clientele and viewers in ways that perhaps other media will not touch. This is a way to say Louis Vuitton is different. It is something *éphémère*, but also something that stays."

Arnault has also turned his attention to emerging markets. Louis Vuitton entered India in 2002 with a boutique at a luxury hotel; now, Fendi, Tag Heuer, and Dior are open for business in that country as well. LVMH has a lock on prime locations at Emporio, an upscale shopping mall that opened recently in New Delhi. Because LVMH has a group presence in the mall, it can negotiate favorable lease rates for retail space. Arnault's expansion coincided with the September 2007 launch of *Vogue India*. Once again, thanks to LVMH's diverse brand portfolio, the company is able to buy large blocks of advertising space from the magazine's owner, Condé Nast India, at discounted prices.

The global economic crisis that gained traction in 2008 affected many retail sectors, and the luxury goods business was no exception. Overall purchases of luxury goods fell in the key U.S. market; sales slowed in Russia and other emerging markets as well. Although total sales in the luxury segment were expected to reach a record €175 billion ($218 billion) in 2008, industry observers expected the sales to drop significantly in 2009. For European-based luxury companies, there was some good news: The dollar was strengthening against the euro. As the 2008 holiday shopping season approached, many luxury goods makers reduced prices in the United States. At Chanel, the cuts ranged from 7 to 10 percent; as John Galantic, president of Chanel's U.S. unit, noted, "The dollar's recent strength has allowed us to pass on greater value to our customers." Louis Vuitton was a notable exception; during 2008, the company raised prices twice, resulting in an average increase of 10 percent. The price increases did not dampen sales; in fact, sales continued to increase.

Visit the Web Site

www.lvmh.com

A complete PowerPoint presentation of the current year's financial results is available on the LVMH Web site.

www.sephora.com

Discussion Questions

11-17. What were the possible risks of Louis Vuitton's first-ever television advertising campaign?

11-18. In fall 2011, the euro/dollar exchange rate was €1 = $1.35. By spring 2015, the dollar had strengthened to €1 = $1.10. Assume that a European luxury goods marketer cut the price of an $8,000 linen suit by 10 percent when launching its spring 2015 collection. How would revenues have been affected when dollar prices were converted to euros?

11-19. Louis Vuitton executives raised prices in the late 2000s, and sales continued to increase. What does this say about the demand curve of the typical Louis Vuitton customer?

11-20. Compare and contrast LVMH's pricing strategy with that of "accessible luxury" brands such as Coach.

Sources: Scheherazade Daneshkhu, "LVMH Faces Dilemma of Success," *Financial Times* (October 20/21, 2012), p. 11; Christina Passariello, "LVMH Sees Shift in China: Locals Go Abroad to Shop," *The Wall Street Journal* (April 19, 2012), pp. B1, B2; Rachel Dodes and Christina Passariello, "In Rare Move, Luxury-Goods Makers Trim Their Prices in U.S.," *The Wall Street Journal* (November 14, 2008), p. B1; Eric Pfanner, "Vuitton Is Embracing Medium of the Masses," *The New York Times* (January 30, 2008), p. C3; Passariello, "LVMH Books Passage to India for Vuitton, Dior, Fendi, Celine," *The Wall Street Journal* (May 8, 2007), pp. B1, B2; Lisa Bannon and Alessandra Galloni, "Brand Manager Deluxe," *The Wall Street Journal* (October 10, 2003), p. B1; John Carreyrou and Christopher Lawton, "Napoleon's Nightcap Gets a Good Rap from Hip-Hop Set," *The Wall Street Journal* (July 14, 2003), pp. A1, A7; Teri Agins and Deborah Ball, "Changing Outfits: Did LVMH Commit a Fashion Faux Pas Buying Donna Karan?" *The Wall Street Journal* (March 21, 2002), pp. A1, A8; Ball, "Despite Downturn, Japanese Are Still Having Fits for Luxury Goods," *The Wall Street Journal* "(April 24, 2001), pp. B1, B4; Bonnie Tsui, "Eye of the Beholder: Sephora's Finances," *Advertising Age* (March 19, 2001), p. 20; Lucia van der Post, "Life's Brittle Luxuries," *Financial Times* (July 18–19, 1998), p. I; Gail Edmondson, "LVMH: Life Isn't All Champagne and Caviar," *BusinessWeek* (November 10, 1997), pp. 108 ff.; Jennifer Steinhauer, "The King of Posh," *The New York Times* (August 17, 1997), Section 3, pp. 1, 10–11; David Owen, "A Captain Used to Storms," *Financial Times* (June 21–22, 1997), p. 13; Holly Brubach, "And Luxury for All," *The New York Times Magazine* (July 12, 1998), pp. 24–29.

Notes

[1] Lowell Bryan, *Race for the World: Strategies to Build a Great Global Firm* (Boston, MA: Harvard Business School Press, 1999), pp. 40–41.

[2] Rachel Sanderson, "Bottega Veneta Hits Luxury Sweet Spot," *Financial Times* (April 9, 2013), p. 17.

[3] Brian Caulfield, "iPhone's Pricing Problem in India," Forbes.com (November 18, 2008).

[4] Adapted from P. Ranganath Nayak and John M. Ketteringham, *Breakthroughs! How Leadership and Drive Create Commercial Innovations That Sweep the World* (San Diego, CA: Pfeiffer, 1994), pp. 124–127.

[5] Phred Dvorak and Merissa Marr, "Shock Treatment: Sony, Lagging Behind Rivals, Hands Reins to a Foreigner," *The Wall Street Journal* (March 7, 2005), p. A8.

[6] This section is adapted from Robin Cooper and W. Bruce Chew, "Control Tomorrow's Costs through Today's Designs," *Harvard Business Review* 74, no. 1 (January–February 1996), pp. 88–97. See also Robin Cooper and Regine Slagmulder, "Develop Profitable New Products with Target Costing," *Sloan Management Review* 40, no. 4 (Summer 1999), pp. 23–33.

[7] Robin Cooper and W. Bruce Chew, "Control Tomorrow's Costs through Today's Designs," *Harvard Business Review* 74, no. 1 (January–February 1996), pp. 88–97.

[8] Norihiko Shirouzu and Stephen Power, "Unthrilling But Inexpensive, the Logan Boosts Renault in Emerging Markets," *The Wall Street Journal* (October 14, 2006), pp. B1, B18.

[9] Ellen Byron, "Emerging Ambitions: P&G's Global Target: Shelves of Tiny Stores," *The Wall Street Journal* (July 16, 2007), p. A1.

[10] Adapted from "Price, Quotations, and Terms of Sale Are Key to Successful Exporting," *Business America* (October 4, 1993), p. 12.

[11] Eric Sylvers, "Jeep Slowly Gains Traction in China," *The Wall Street Journal* (December 21, 2016), pp. B1, B2. See also Keith Bradsher, "One Rub in Trade Negotiations: Why a Jeep Costs More in China," *The New York Times* (March 21, 2017), pp. BU1, BU4.

[12] Since the Uruguay Round of General Agreement on Tariffs and Trade (GATT) negotiations, Japan has lowered or eliminated duties on thousands of categories of imports. Japan's simple average most-favored-nation duty rate for 2017 was 4 percent; approximately 60 percent of tariff lines (including for most industrial products) were rated 5 percent or lower.

[13]Beth Dorrell, personal interview (December 20, 2008).

[14]Robert A. Guth, Michael M. Phillips, and Charles Hutzler, "On the Decline: As the Yen Keeps Dropping, a New View of Japan Emerges," *The Wall Street Journal* (April 24, 2002), pp. A1, A8.

[15]S. Tamer Cavusgil, "Pricing for Global Markets," *Columbia Journal of World Business* 31, no. 4 (Winter 1996), p. 69.

[16]Christopher Cooper, "Euro's Drop Is Hardest for the Smallest," *The Wall Street Journal* (October 2, 2000), p. A21.

[17]Emily Chasan, "Currencies Pose New Risks," *The Wall Street Journal* (August 14, 2012), p. B5.

[18]Alan Livsey, "Brexit Bonus for English Sparkling Winemakers," *Financial Times* (September 12, 2017), p. 5.

[19]John Shipman and Anjali Cordiero, "Dilemma over Pricing," *The Wall Street Journal* (October 20, 2010), pp. B1, B4.

[20]Lucinda Harper and Fred R. Bleakley, "Like Old Times: An Era of Low Inflation Changes the Calculus for Buyers and Sellers," *The Wall Street Journal* (January 14, 1994), p. A1. See also Jacob M. Schlesinger and Yochi J. Dreazen, "Counting the Cost: Firms Start to Raise Prices, Stirring Fear in Inflation Fighters," *The Wall Street Journal* (May 16, 2000), pp. A1, A8.

[21]Alecia Swasy, "Foreign Formula: Procter & Gamble Fixes Aim on Tough Market: The Latin Americans," *The Wall Street Journal* (June 15, 1990), p. A7.

[22]Scott Miller, "In Trade Talks, the Gloves Are Off," *The Wall Street Journal* (July 15, 2003), p. A12. See also James Drummond, "The Great Conservation Debate," *Financial Times Special Report—Egypt* (October 22, 2003), p. 6.

[23]Neil King, Jr., and Scott Miller, "Trade Talks Fail Amid Big Divide over Farm Issues," *The Wall Street Journal* (September 15, 2003), pp. A1, A18.

[24]Andrew Higgins, "The Ice Is Melting: Dismantling a Police State," *The New York Times* (April 2, 2018), p. A1.

[25]Greg Steinmetz, "Mark Down: German Consumers Are Seeing Prices Cut in Deregulation Push," *The Wall Street Journal* (August 15, 1997), pp. A1, A4; David Wessel, "German Shoppers Get Coupons," *The Wall Street Journal* (April 5, 2001), p. A1.

[26]Leslie Kaufman, "Levi Strauss to Close 6 U.S. Plants and Lay Off 3,300," *The New York Times* (April 9, 2002), p. C2.

[27]Barbara Stöttinger, "Strategic Export Pricing: A Long and Winding Road," *Journal of International Marketing* 9, no. 1 (2001), pp. 40–63.

[28]Lisa Bannon, "Mattel Plans to Double Sales Abroad," *The Wall Street Journal* (February 11, 1998), pp. A3, A11.

[29]Alex Taylor III, "Speed! Power! Status!" *Fortune* (June 10, 1996), pp. 46–58.

[30]Raymond Serafin, "Mercedes-Benz of the '90s Includes Price in Its Pitch," *Advertising Age* (November 1, 1993), p. 1.

[31]Li Yuan, "A Tip for Apple in China: Your Hunger for Revenue May Cost You," *The Wall Street Journal* (May 18, 2017), p. B1.

[32]Mei Fong, "IKEA Hits Home in China," *The Wall Street Journal* (March 3, 2006), pp. B1, B4. See also Eric Sylvers, "IKEA Index Indicates the Euro Is Not a Price Equalizer Yet," *The New York Times* (October 23, 2003), p. W1; and Paula M. Miller, "IKEA with Chinese Characteristics," *The China Business Review* (July–August 2004), pp. 36–38.

[33]Tamar Lewin, "Students Find $100 Textbooks Cost $50, Purchased Overseas," *The New York Times* (October 21, 2003), p. A16.

[34]Adapted from Perry J. Viscounty, Jeff C. Risher, and Collin G. Smyser, "Cyber Gray Market Is Manufacturers' Headache," *The National Law Journal* (August 20, 2001), p. C3.

[35]Perry J. Viscounty, Jeff C. Risher, and Collin G. Smyser, "Cyber Gray Market Is Manufacturers' Headache," *The National Law Journal* (August 20, 2001), p. C3.

[36]Kersi D. Antia, Mark Bergen, and Shantanu Dutta, "Competing with Gray Markets," *MIT Sloan Management Review* 46, no. 1 (Summer 2004), pp. 65–67.

[37]Peggy Hollinger and Neil Buckley, "Grey Market Ruling Delights Brand Owners," *Financial Times* (July 17, 1998), p. 8.

[38]Ray Marcelo, "Officials See Red over Handset Sales," *Financial Times* (October 3, 2003), p. 16.

[39]Lester Ross and Susan Ning, "Modern Protectionism: China's Own Antidumping Regulations," *China Business Review* (May–June 2000), pp. 30–33.

[40]Michael Pooler and Emily Feng, "Steel Industry Grapples with Curse of Oversupply," *Financial Times* (October 30, 2017), p. 17.

[41]Philip Brasher, "Clarinda Plant Takes Hit in Dispute over Imports," *The Des Moines Register* (November 16, 2005), p. D1.

[42]Neil Buckley, "Commission Faces Fight on Cotton 'Dumping,'" *Financial Times* (December 2, 1997), p. 5; Emma Tucker, "French Fury at Threat to Cotton Duties," *Financial Times* (May 19, 1997), p. 3.

[43]Paul Meller, "Europe Fines Nintendo $147 Million for Price Fixing," *The Wall Street Journal* (February 24, 2004), p. W1.

[44]John R. Wilke, "DeBeers Is in Talks to Settle Price-Fixing Charge," *The Wall Street Journal* (February 24, 2004), pp. A1, A14.

[45]Matthew Saltmarsh, "Tax Enforcers Intensify Focus on Multinationals," *The New York Times* (January 5, 2010), p. B3.

[46]Rochelle Toplensky, "Tech Giants Hit by EU Tax Crackdown," *Financial Times* (October 5, 2017), p. 17;

[47]Leslie Lopez and John D. McKinnon, "Swatch Faces Complaint over Taxes," *The Wall Street Journal* (August 13, 2004), p. B2.

[48]Susannah Rodgers, "GlaxoSmithKline Gets Big Tax Bill," *The Wall Street Journal* (January 8, 2004), p. A8.

[49]Many of the examples in this section are adapted from Matt Schaffer, *Winning the Countertrade War: New Export Strategies for America* (New York, NY: John Wiley & Sons, 1989).

[50]Pompiliu Verzariu, "Trends and Developments in International Countertrade," *Business America* (November 2, 1992), p. 2.

[51]Emily Chasan, "Currencies Pose New Risks," *The Wall Street Journal* (August 14, 2012), p. B5.

[52]"Venezuelans Barter Diapers for Food on Smartphones," Agence France-Presse (June 14, 2016).

[53]The commitment to local assembly or manufacturing under the supplier's specifications is commonly termed a *coproduction agreement*, which is tied to the offset but does not, in itself, represent a type of countertrade.

[54]Daniel Pearl, "Arms Dealers Get Creative with 'Offsets,'" *The Wall Street Journal* (April 20, 2000), p. A18.

[55]Patricia Daily and S. M. Ghazanfar, "Countertrade: Help or Hindrance to Less-Developed Countries?" *Journal of Social, Political, and Economic Studies* 18, no. 1 (Spring 1993), p. 65.

[56]William Greider, *One World, Ready or Not: The Manic Logic of Global Capitalism* (New York, NY: Simon & Schuster, 1997), p. 130.

[57]Patricia Daily and S. M. Ghazanfar, "Countertrade: Help or Hindrance to Less-Developed Countries?" *Journal of Social, Political, and Economic Studies* 18, no. 1 (Spring 1993), p. 66.

12 Global Marketing Channels and Physical Distribution

LEARNING OBJECTIVES

12-1 Identify and compare the basic structure options for consumer channels and industrial channels.

12-2 List the guidelines companies should follow when establishing channels and working with intermediaries in global markets.

12-3 Describe the different categories of retail operations that are found in various parts of the world.

12-4 Compare and contrast the six major international transportation modes and explain how they vary in terms of reliability, accessibility, and other performance metrics.

CASE 12-1
Welcome to the World of Fast Fashion

The world of global fast-fashion is like a three-way horse race. Spain's Inditex SA is the parent company of specialty retailer Zara; Sweden is home to Hennes & Mauritz AB, better known to shoppers as H&M; and Uniqlo is the flagship brand of Japan's Fast Retailing.

Part of the appeal of fast fashion is the low prices. Also attractive is the speed at which inventories are replenished and updated with affordable versions of the latest runway trends from the world's fashion capitals. The need for speed is fueled in part by social media. A key element for some fast-fashion brands is sourcing clothing from countries with low-cost labor in Asia and elsewhere. In Cambodia, for example, more than 400 garment factories are registered exporters.

However, some industry observers note that low prices actually carry high social and environmental costs. Chasing the latest trends means that shoppers often discard inexpensive garments after wearing them just a few times. This leads to a consumer mindset that clothing purchases are disposable, rather than long-term investments. Critics assert that unwanted clothing often ends up in landfills, and that the fast-fashion trend is not sustainable (see Exhibit 12-1).

For years, Tadashi Yanai, the founder of the Uniqlo ("Unique Clothing") chain, pursued a business model that differentiated his company from its European rivals. Uniqlo's focus was on everyday basics and a new-product development process that relied heavily on innovative materials.

Inditex is the world's largest fashion retailer, with more than 7,000 stores in 92 countries. In addition to Zara, its brands include Bershka, Pull & Bear, and Massimo Dutti. The company does not advertise, and its motto is "The company doesn't speak; the customer speaks for the company." Unlike some of its competitors, Inditex keeps nearly two-thirds of its production in Spain or neighboring countries.

Exhibit 12-1 Some critics assert that the fast fashion trend contributes to overproduction and a "throw-away" mentality. The result is vast quantities of discarded clothing as well as "deadstock" (out-of-season garments and unused textiles). This Saks Fifth Avenue window display by Vetements was designed to call attention to the problem.
Source: Michael Ross Photography.

Zara entered India in 2010, and today has more than 18 stores in that country; H&M has been in India since 2015. Global fashion trends are the mainstay in fast fashion. However, many women's fashions can be considered "racy" because they feature plunging necklines, deep backs, and exposed midriffs. An Indian company, Future Group, has invested in Cover Story, a brand of Western-style clothing with more-modest tailoring that better suits the tastes and needs of Indian shoppers. The clothes also feature brighter colors. In a perhaps unexpected twist, Cover Story has a design studio in London. As Future Group CEO Kishore Biyani explains, "You can't take on the Zara's and H&M's of the world sitting in India. You need to look and feel what they do to beat them at their own game."

Prior to 2017, H&M was growing at a torrid pace. Revenue growth was driven by store openings; today, the company has approximately 4,700 stores. However, profits have been stagnant, and the company is feeling pressure from several directions. Discount retailer Primark has lower prices, while some shoppers perceive Zara to offer higher quality. Moreover, online-only competitors, including Britain's Asos and Germany's Zalando, offer free shipping and generous return policies that lure customers away from brick-and-mortar stores. One industry analyst likens H&M's position to that of former industry titans such as Nokia, Ericsson, and IBM: All had successful business models until market conditions changed faster than their respective managements realized it.

Specialty retailers such as Zara, H&M, and Uniqlo are just three of the many elements that make up distribution channels around the globe. Today, global supply chains connect producers in all parts of the world, and sophisticated logistics are utilized to ensure the smooth flow through the system. The American Marketing Association defines a **channel of distribution** as "an organized network of agencies and institutions that, in combination, perform all the activities required to link producers with users to accomplish the marketing task."[1] Physical distribution is the movement of goods through channels; channels, in turn, are made up of a coordinated group of individuals or firms that perform functions that add utility to a product or service.

Distribution channels are one of the most highly differentiated aspects of national marketing systems. Retail stores vary in size from giant hypermarkets to small stores in Latin America called *pulperías*. The diversity of channels and the wide range of possible distribution strategies and market-entry options can present challenges to managers who are responsible for designing global marketing programs. Channels and physical distribution are crucial aspects of the total marketing program; without them, a great product at the right price and effective communications mean very little.

(12-1) Distribution Channels: Objectives, Terminology, and Structure

◀ **12-1** Identify and compare the basic structure options for consumer channels and industrial channels.

Marketing channels exist to create utility for customers. The major categories of channel utility are **place utility** (the availability of a product or service in a location that is convenient to a potential customer), **time utility** (the availability of a product or service when desired by a customer), **form utility** (the availability of the product processed, prepared, in proper condition, and/or ready to use), and **information utility** (the availability of answers to questions and general communication about useful product features and benefits). Because these utilities can be a basic source of competitive advantage and represent an important element of a firm's overall value proposition, choosing a channel strategy is one of the key policy decisions that management must make. For example, the Coca-Cola Company's global marketing leadership position is based in part on its ability to put Coke "within an arm's reach of desire"—in other words, to create place utility.

The starting point in selecting the most effective channel arrangement is a clear focus of the company's marketing effort on a target market and an assessment of the way(s) in which distribution can contribute to the firm's overall value proposition. Who are the target customers, and where are they located? What are their information requirements? What are their preferences for service? How sensitive are they to the product's or service's price? Moreover, each market must be analyzed to determine the cost of providing channel services.

What is appropriate in one country may not be always effective in another. Even marketers concerned with a single-country program should study channel arrangements in different parts of the world for valuable information and insight into possible new channel strategies and tactics. For example, retailers in Europe and Asia studied self-service discount retailing in the United States and then introduced the self-service concept in their own countries. Similarly, governments and business executives from many parts of the world have examined Japanese trading companies to learn from their success. Walmart's formula has been closely studied and adapted by competitors in the markets it has entered.

As mentioned previously, distribution channels are systems that link manufacturers to customers. Although channels for consumer products and industrial products are similar, there are also some distinct differences between them. In **business-to-consumer marketing** (also known as b-to-c or B2C marketing), consumer channels are designed to put products in the hands of people for their own use. By contrast, **business-to-business marketing** (also known as b-to-b or B2B marketing) involves industrial channels that deliver products to manufacturers or other organizations that then use them as inputs in the production process or in day-to-day operations. Intermediaries play important roles in both consumer and industrial channels. A **distributor** is a wholesale intermediary that typically carries product lines or brands on a selective basis. An **agent** is an intermediary who negotiates exchange transactions between two or more parties but does not take title to the goods being purchased or sold.

Consumer Products and Services

Figure 12-1 summarizes six channel structure alternatives for consumer products. The characteristics of both buyers and products have an important influence on channel design. The first alternative is to market directly to buyers via the Internet, mail order, various types of door-to-door

FIGURE 12-1 Marketing Channel Alternatives: Consumer Products

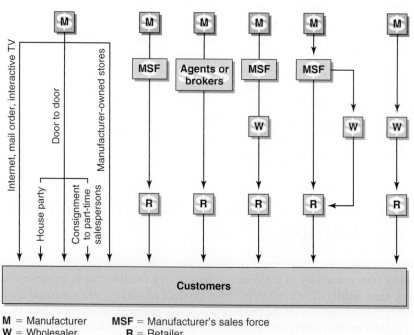

M = Manufacturer   MSF = Manufacturer's sales force
W = Wholesaler   R = Retailer

selling, or manufacturer-owned retail outlets. The other options use retailers and various combinations of sales forces, agents/brokers, and wholesalers. The number of individual buyers and their geographic distributions, incomes, shopping habits, and reactions to different selling methods frequently vary from country to country and may require different channel approaches.

Product characteristics such as degree of standardization, perishability, bulk, service requirements, and unit price have an impact as well. Generally speaking, channels tend to be longer (require more intermediaries) as the number of customers to be served increases and the price per unit decreases. Bulky products usually require channel arrangements that minimize shipping distances and the number of times products change hands before they reach the ultimate customer.

The Internet and related forms of new media are dramatically altering the distribution landscape. For example, eBay pioneered the **peer-to-peer marketing** (p-to-p) model, whereby individual consumers market products to other individuals. eBay's success was one reason that traditional merchants quickly recognized the Internet's potential. To sustain revenue growth, eBay began assisting large companies such as Disney and IBM in setting up online "storefronts" to sell items for fixed prices in addition to conducting b-to-c auctions. "As we evolved from auction-style bidding to adding Buy It Now, the logical next step for us was to give sellers a place to showcase their listings," said Bill Cobb, eBay's senior vice president for global marketing.[2] Some observers predict that interactive television (ITV) will also become a viable direct-distribution channel in the coming years as more households are wired with the necessary two-way technology. Time-pressed consumers in many countries are increasingly attracted to the time and place utility created by the Internet and similar new media technologies.

Low-cost mass-market products and certain services can be sold on a door-to-door basis via a direct sales force. Door-to-door and house-party selling is considered a mature channel in the United States; however, it is now growing in popularity elsewhere. For example, Orlando, Florida–based Tupperware has a sales force of 200,000 in Indonesia. Brand-conscious consumers there have embraced the company's plastic food-storage containers, and Tupperware's direct-sales business model gives it an advantage in a country with a limited retail infrastructure (see Exhibit 12-2). Today, Indonesia is Tupperware's biggest market. As former CEO and current executive chairman Rick Goings notes, "This is an incredible sweet spot for us. It's where the population of the world is. You cannot fight that."[3]

Exhibit 12-2 Tricia Stitzel became CEO of Tupperware in 2018. According to former CEO and current executive chairman Rick Goings, "The United States is less than 10 percent of our business. We happen to have our headquarters in the United States, but we're a global company."[4]

Source: Edward Linsmier Photography.

In 1995, Mary Kay entered the Chinese cosmetics market with its network of independent sales agents. After successfully penetrating China's first-tier cities, the company expanded into second- and third-tier locations.[5] In April 1998, China's state council imposed a blanket ban on all types of direct selling. Because the ban was aimed most directly at illegal pyramid schemes, several foreign companies, including Amway, Avon, Mary Kay, and Tupperware, were allowed to continue operations in China. However, they were forced to adapt their business models: Their sales agents had to be affiliated with brick-and-mortar retailers. Although the ban was lifted in 2005, because it had restricted competition, the handful of foreign direct-sales marketers that had maintained a presence in China had had a unique growth opportunity during the years the ban was in force. Mary Kay is a case in point: By 2011, Mary Kay's Chinese sales were more than 50 times higher than they had been in 1999. Today, Mary Kay has dozens of branch offices in China.

In Japan, the biggest barrier facing U.S. auto manufacturers isn't high tariffs, but rather the fact that half the cars that are sold each year are sold door-to-door. Toyota and its Japanese competitors do maintain showrooms, but they also employ more than 100,000 car salespeople. Unlike their American counterparts, many Japanese car buyers never visit dealerships. The close, long-term relationships between auto salespersons and the Japanese people can be thought of as a consumer version of the *keiretsu* system discussed in Chapter 9.

Japanese car buyers expect numerous face-to-face meetings with a sales representative, during which trust is established. The relationship continues after the deal is closed; sales reps send cards and continually seek to ensure the buyer's satisfaction. American rivals such as Ford, meanwhile, try to generate showroom traffic. In the 1990s, Nobumasa Ogura managed a Ford dealership in Tokyo. "We need to come up with some ideas to sell more cars without door-to-door sales, but the reality is that we haven't come up with any," he said.[6] As it turned out, the challenge proved to be insurmountable, and Ford pulled out of the Japanese market in 2016.[7]

Another direct-selling alternative is the *manufacturer-owned store* or *independent franchise store*. One of the first successful U.S.-based international companies, Singer, established a worldwide chain of company-owned and operated outlets to sell and service sewing machines. As noted in Chapter 9, Japanese consumer electronics companies integrate stores into their distribution groups. Apple, Levi Strauss, Nike, Sony, well-known fashion design houses, and other companies with strong brands sometimes establish flagship retail stores as product showcases or as a means of obtaining marketing intelligence (see Exhibit 12-3). These stores are designed to provide an interactive shopping experience and build brand loyalty.[8] Such channels supplement, rather than replace, distribution through independent retail stores.

Exhibit 12-3 Apple operates more than 500 retail stores in 22 countries. Each store features a Genius Bar, where customers can seek one-on-one technical support with a knowledgeable employee. Many stores, such as this one in London, feature a signature glass staircase that Apple cofounder and former CEO Steve Jobs helped design. Although Jobs died of cancer in 2011, his legacy includes a far-reaching impact on global retailing strategies and tactics. Apple recently hired Angela Ahrendts, former CEO of Burberry, to head its retail operations.
Source: View Pictures/UIG via Getty Images.

Other channel structure alternatives for consumer products include various combinations of a manufacturer's sales force and wholesalers calling on independent retail outlets that, in turn, sell to customers (retailing is discussed in detail later in the chapter). For mass-market consumer products such as ice cream novelties, cigarettes, and light bulbs that are bought by millions of consumers, a channel that links the manufacturer to distributors and retailers is generally required to achieve market coverage. A cornerstone of Walmart's phenomenal growth in the United States has been its ability to achieve significant economies by buying huge volumes of goods directly from manufacturers. By contrast, some companies elect to pursue very selective distribution strategies to ensure that products are displayed in attractive surroundings. For example, menswear designer Alexandre Plokhov's collections have been available at Barney's and Selfridge's; Plokhov recently launched a new line, Nomenklatura, that will be available online only (see Exhibit 12-4).

Perishable goods impose special demands on channel members, who must ensure that the merchandise (e.g., fresh fruits and vegetables) is in satisfactory condition (form utility) at the time of customer purchase. In developed countries, either a company's own sales force or independent channel members may handle distribution of perishable food products. In either case, the distributor organization checks the stock to ensure that it is fresh. In less-developed countries, public marketplaces are important channels; they provide a convenient way for producers of vegetables, bread, and other food products to sell their goods directly. Notably, the high perishability rate for fresh produce is one of the biggest supply-chain issues in modern India.

Sometimes, a relatively simple channel innovation in a developing country can significantly increase a company's overall value proposition. In the early 1990s, for example, the Moscow Bread Company (MBC) needed to improve its distribution system. Russian consumers queue up daily to buy fresh loaves at numerous shops and kiosks. Unfortunately, MBC's staff was burdened by excessive paperwork, which resulted in the delivery of stale bread. Andersen Consulting found that as much as one-third of the bread the company produced was wasted. In developed countries, approximately 95 percent of food is sold packaged; the figure is much lower in the former Soviet Union. Whether a consumer bought bread at an outdoor market or in an enclosed store, it was displayed unwrapped. The consulting team thus devised a simple solution—plastic bags to keep the bread fresh. Russian consumers responded favorably to the change; not only do the bags guarantee freshness and significantly extend the bread's shelf life, but the bags themselves

Exhibit 12-4 Alexandre Plokhov is a menswear designer with a noir sensibility. Some of his designs—these combat boots, for example—are inspired by vintage military uniforms. After launching Cloak and the eponymous Alexandre Plokhov lines, he designed for Versace and Helmut Lang. His new venture is called Nomenklatura.
Source: © NomenklaturaStudio.

Exhibit 12-5 Brazil's middle class is growing rapidly, but reaching consumers in far-flung rural areas can be a challenge for global marketers. Nestlé's channel strategy includes a floating supermarket. Nestlé Até Você a Bordo ("Nestlé Takes You on Board") is a boat that travels the Amazon by night and welcomes shoppers in 18 different municipalities by day. Consumers who don't have access to hypermarkets can stock up on dog food, chocolates, powdered milk, and nearly 300 other Nestlé products and brands.
Source: Marcia Zoet/Bloomberg via Getty Images.

also create utility. In a country where such extras are virtually unknown, the bags constitute a reusable "gift."[9]

The retail environment in developing countries presents similar challenges for companies marketing nonperishable items. In affluent countries, Procter & Gamble (P&G), Kimberly-Clark, Unilever, Colgate-Palmolive, and other global consumer-products companies are accustomed to catering to a "buy-in-bulk" consumer mentality. By contrast, in Mexico and other emerging markets, many consumers shop for food, soft drinks, and other items several times each day at tiny, independent "mom-and-pop" stores, kiosks, and market stalls (see Exhibit 12-5). The products offered, including shampoo, disposable diapers, and laundry detergent, are packaged in single-use quantities at a relatively high per-use cost.

At P&G, these operations are known as "high-frequency stores"; in Mexico alone, an estimated 70 percent of the population shops at such stores. To motivate shopkeepers to stock more of P&G's products, the company launched a "golden store" program. In exchange for a pledge to carry at least 40 different P&G products, participating stores receive regular visits from P&G representatives, who tidy display areas and arrange promotional material in prominent places. Although P&G initially used its own sales force for these activities, it has since begun relying on independent agents who buy inventory (paying in advance) and then resell the items to shop operators.[10] P&G's experience illustrates the fact that the channel structures shown in Figure 12-1 represent strategic alternatives; firms can and should vary their strategies as market conditions change.

Industrial Products

Figure 12-2 summarizes marketing channel alternatives for an industrial or business products company. As is true with consumer channels, product and customer characteristics have an impact on channel structure. Three basic elements are involved: the manufacturer's sales force, distributors or agents, and wholesalers. A manufacturer can reach customers with its own sales force, a sales force that calls on wholesalers who sell to customers, or a combination of these two arrangements. A manufacturer can also sell directly to wholesalers without using a sales force, and wholesalers, in turn, can supply customers.

Italy's Saeco distributes its products through both b-to-c and b-to-b channels. Marketing managers responsible for domestic appliances arrange for retail distribution for consumer purchase.

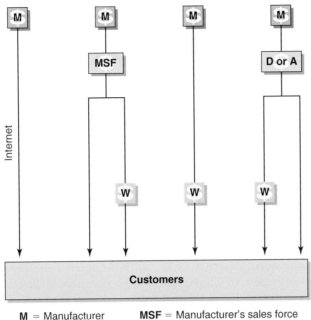

FIGURE 12-2 Marketing Channel Alternatives: Industrial Products

M = Manufacturer
W = Wholesaler
MSF = Manufacturer's sales force
D or A = Distributor or agent

The managers who service the vending and professional segments provide vending machines to organizational customers and professional espresso-making equipment to bars and cafés.

Channel innovation can be an essential element of a successful marketing strategy. Dell's rise to a leading position in the global PC industry was fueled by Michael Dell's decision to bypass conventional channels and instead sell direct and build computers to customers' specifications. Dell began life as a b-to-b marketer; its business model proved so successful that the company then began marketing directly to the home PC market.

As another example, consider Boeing aircraft: Given the price, physical size, and complexity of a jet airliner, it is easy to understand why Boeing utilizes its own sales force. Other products sold in this way include mainframe computers and large photocopy systems—both are expensive, complicated products that require both explanation and applications analysis focused on each customer's needs. A company-trained salesperson, sales engineer, or sales team is well suited for the task of creating information utility for computer buyers.

(12-2) Establishing Channels and Working With Channel Intermediaries

◀ **12-2** List the guidelines companies should follow when establishing channels and working with intermediaries in global markets.

A global company expanding across national boundaries must either utilize existing **distribution channels** or build its own. Channel obstacles are often encountered when a company enters a competitive market where brands and supply relationships are already established. If management chooses *direct involvement*, the company establishes its own sales force or operates its own retail stores.

The other option is *indirect involvement*, which entails utilizing independent agents, distributors, and retailers. In Asia, for example, Western luxury goods marketers such as Jean Paul Gaultier (France) and Harmont & Blaine (Italy) have long relied on non-exclusive, independent distributors. One such company is Hong Kong–based Fairton International Group, whose local market knowledge and network of stores are keys to success in Greater China. Similarly, as noted in Chapter 11, DeBeers uses independent intermediaries to market its diamonds in the United States.

The channel strategy used in a global marketing program must fit with the company's competitive position and overall marketing objectives in each national market. Direct involvement in distribution in a new market can entail considerable expense, as sales representatives and sales management must be hired and trained. The sales organization will inevitably be a massive loser in its early stages of operation in a new market because it will not have sufficient volume to cover its overhead costs. Therefore, any company contemplating establishing its own sales force should be prepared to underwrite its losses for a reasonable period of time.

Channel decisions are important because of the number and nature of relationships that must be managed. Channel decisions typically involve long-term legal commitments and obligations to various intermediaries. Such commitments are often extremely expensive to terminate or change, so it is imperative for companies to document the nature of the relationship with the foreign partner. As the saying goes, "The shortest pencil is better than the longest memory." At a minimum, the written agreement should include a definition of what constitutes "good cause" for termination. Also, as noted in Chapter 5, it is often preferable to settle business disputes through arbitration rather than in a local court. Thus, the distributor or agent agreement should provide for arbitration in a neutral forum in a third country. In many instances, local laws protect agents and distributors; thus, even in the absence of a formal written agreement, the law will be applied in a civil-law country. In addition to written obligations, commitments must be backed by good faith and feelings of mutual obligation. In short, the careful selection of distributors and agents in a target market is critically important.

Companies entering emerging markets for the first time must exercise particular care in choosing a channel intermediary. Typically, a local distributor is required because the market entrant lacks knowledge of local business practices and needs a partner with links to potential customers. In addition, newcomers to a particular market generally want to limit their risk and financial exposure. Sometimes, even though the initial results may be satisfactory, headquarters may eventually become dissatisfied with the local distributor's performance. In such a case, managers from the global company often intervene and attempt to take control. Harvard professor David Arnold offers seven specific guidelines to help prevent such problems from arising:[11]

1. *Select distributors. Don't let them select you.* A company may link up with a distributor by default after being approached by representatives at a trade fair. In fact, such eager candidates may already be serving a company's competitors. Their objective may be to maintain control over the product category in a given market. A proactive market entrant can identify potential distributors by requesting a list from the U.S. Department of Commerce or its equivalent in other countries. The local chamber of commerce or trade association in a country can provide similar information.

2. *Look for distributors capable of developing markets, rather than those with a few good customer contacts.* A distributor with good contacts may appear to be the "obvious" choice in terms of generating quick sales and revenues. However, a better choice is often a partner that is willing to both make the investment necessary to achieve success and draw upon the marketing experience of the global company. Such a partner may, in fact, have no prior experience with a particular product category. In this case, the distributor may devote more effort and assign the new partner a higher priority simply because taking on the product line does not represent the status quo.

3. *Treat local distributors as long-term partners, not as temporary market-entry vehicles.* A contractual agreement that provides strong financial incentives for customer acquisition, new-product sales, or other forms of business development is a signal to the distributor that the market entrant is taking a long-term perspective. Such development can take place with the input of managers from the global company.

4. *Support market entry by committing money, managers, and proven marketing ideas.* In addition to providing sales personnel and technical support, management should consider demonstrating its commitment early on by investing in a minority equity stake in an independent distributor. Of course, the risks associated with such investment should be no greater than the risks associated with independent distribution systems in the manufacturer's home country. The earlier such a commitment is made, the better the relationship that is likely to develop.

5. *From the start, maintain control over the marketing strategy.* To exploit the full potential of global marketing channels, the manufacturer should provide solid leadership for marketing in terms of which products the distributor sells and how those products are positioned. Again, it is necessary to have employees on site or to have country or regional managers monitor the distributor's performance. As one manager told the author of the study, "We used to give far too much autonomy to distributors, thinking that they knew their markets. But our value proposition is a tough one to execute, and time and again we saw distributors cut prices to compensate for failing to target the right customers or to sufficiently train salespeople." This is not to say that the intermediary should not be allowed to adapt the distribution strategy to suit local conditions. Rather, the point is that the manufacturer should take the lead.

6. *Make sure distributors provide the company with detailed market and financial performance data.* Distributor organizations are often a company's best source—and sometimes the only source—of market information. The contract between a manufacturer and a distributor should include specific language to the effect that local market information and financial data will be transferred back to the manufacturer. One sign that a successful manufacturer–distributor relationship can be established is the latter's willingness to provide such information.

7. *Build links among national distributors at the earliest opportunity.* A manufacturer should attempt to establish links between its networks of national distributors. This can be accomplished by setting up a regional corporate office or by establishing a distributor council. At any point in time, a company may have some excellent agents and distributors, others that are satisfactory, and a third group that is unsatisfactory. By creating opportunities for distributors to communicate, ideas for new product designs based on individual market results can be leveraged and overall distributor performance can be improved.

When devising a channel strategy, it is necessary to be realistic about the intermediary's motives. It is the intermediary's responsibility to implement an important element of a company's marketing strategy. Left to their own devices, however, middlemen may seek to maximize their own profit rather than the manufacturer's revenues. These agents sometimes engage in **cherry picking**, the practice of accepting orders only from manufacturers with established demand for certain products and brands. Cherry picking can also take the form of selecting only a few choice items from a vendor's product lines. The cherry picker is not interested in developing a market for a new product, which is a problem for an expanding international company.

As noted previously, a manufacturer should provide leadership and invest resources to build a solid relationship with a desired distributor. Conversely, a manufacturer with a new product or a product with a limited market share may find it more desirable to set up some arrangement for bypassing the cherry-picking channel member. In some cases, a manufacturer must incur the costs of direct involvement by setting up its own distribution organization to obtain a share of the market. When the company sales finally reach critical mass, management may decide to shift from direct involvement to a more cost-effective, independent intermediary.

An alternative method of dealing with the cherry-picking problem does not require setting up an expensive direct sales force. Rather, a company may decide to rely on a distributor's own sales force by subsidizing the cost of the sales representatives the distributor has assigned to the company's products. This approach has the advantage of holding down costs by tying the manufacture in with the distributor's existing sales management team and physical distribution system. It is possible to place managed direct-selling support and distribution support behind a product at the expense of only one salesperson per selling area. The distributor's incentive for cooperating in this kind of arrangement is that he or she obtains a "free" sales representative for a new product that has the potential to be a profitable addition to his or her line. This cooperative arrangement is ideally suited to getting a new export-sourced product into distribution in a market. Alternatively, a company may decide to provide special incentives to independent channel agents.

▶ **12-3** Describe the different categories of retail operations that are found in various parts of the world.

(12-3) Global Retailing

Global retailing is any retailing activity that crosses national boundaries. It has a long history: For centuries, entrepreneurial merchants have ventured abroad to seek out merchandise and ideas and to establish retail operations. During the nineteenth and early twentieth centuries, British, French, Dutch, Belgian, and German trading companies established retailing organizations in Africa and Asia. Indeed, international trading and retail store operations were two of the economic pillars of that era's colonial system. In the twentieth century, Dutch apparel and footwear retailer C&A expanded across Europe. In 1909, Harry Gordon Selfridge traveled from Chicago to London to open a department store that ended up reshaping retailing. That same year, another American, Frank Woolworth, took his five-and-dime concept across the Atlantic, opening his first British store in Liverpool.

Global retailers serve an important distribution function. For example, when Carrefour, Tesco, and Walmart set up shop in developing countries, they provide customers with access to more products and lower prices than were available previously. As we have noted throughout the text, when global companies expand abroad, they often encounter local competitors. The retail sector is no exception; India is a case in point. *Organized retail*, a term that is used to describe modern, branded chain stores, currently accounts for less than 5 percent of India's total market. The sector is expected to exhibit double-digit growth in the future—a rosy outlook that has attracted the giants of global retailing. Today, however, they must compete with stores operated by local retail chains. One such company is Reliance Industries; its Reliance Retail division is opening thousands of modern supermarkets across India. What's more, Reliance itself is developing plans for global expansion.[12]

In some instances, it is a local retailer, rather than a global one, that breaks new ground by transforming the shopping experience. Nakumatt, a supermarket chain in Kenya, is a case in point. As Wambui Mwangi, a political science professor at the University of Toronto, notes, "Nakumatt is where you go to show you are educated and prosperous and cognizant of larger affairs. It's an aspirational space that appeals to everyone, especially the people who can't really afford to shop there."[13]

Retail business models may undergo significant adaptation outside the country in which they originated. For example, after the first 7-Eleven Japan franchise opened in 1973, the stores quickly attracted customers seeking greater convenience in purchasing. Today, "conbinis" are ubiquitous in Japan, with tens of thousands of store locations. Seven & I Holdings, which operates 7-Eleven, is Japan's largest grocer. The convenience store operators use cutting-edge electronic point-of-sale (EPOS) data to track customer behavior and ensure that perishable products and other merchandise are delivered on a just-in-time basis during high-traffic periods. Even in the recent difficult economic environment, convenience store sales have remained strong in Japan. Now the operators are moving to further differentiate themselves: For example, 7-Eleven has Seven Bank ATMs in its stores and a lower-priced line of own-brand merchandise, Seven Premium.[14]

Today's global retailing scene is characterized by great diversity (as seen in Table 12-1, which lists the top five companies by revenue). We will begin the discussion of this area with a brief survey of some of the different forms retailing can take. Retail stores can be divided into categories according to the amount of square feet of floor space, the level of service offered, the width and depth of product offerings, or other criteria. Each represents a strategic option for a retailer considering global expansion.

TABLE 12-1 Top Five Global Retailers, 2017

Rank	Company	Country	Formats	Sales ($ millions)
1	Walmart Stores	United States	Discount store, wholesale club	$485,873
2	Carrefour	France	Hypermarket	82,996*
3	Tesco PLC	United Kingdom	Supermarket/hypermarket	69,501
4	Metro AG	Germany	Diversified	43,828
5	Aldi	Germany	Discount store	NA

* 2016 data.
Source: Company reports.

Types of Retail Operations

Department stores literally have several departments under one roof, each representing a distinct merchandise line and staffed with a limited number of salespeople. Departments in a typical store might include men's, women's, children's, beauty aids, housewares, and toys. Table 12-2 lists major department stores that have expanded outside their home-country markets. However, in most instances, the expansion is limited to a few countries. As Maureen Hinton, a retail analyst with a London-based consultancy, notes, "It's quite difficult to transfer a department store brand abroad. You have to find a city with the right demographic for your offer. If you adapt your offer to the locality, you dilute your brand name." Marvin Traub, former chief executive of Bloomingdales, has a different perspective: "Conceptually, department stores are global brands already because we live in a world with an enormous amount of travel between cities and continents," he says.[15]

Specialty retailers offer less variety than department stores; that is, they are more narrowly focused and offer a relatively narrow merchandise mix aimed at a particular target market. Specialty stores do offer a great deal of merchandise depth (e.g., many styles, colors, and sizes), high levels of service from knowledgeable staff, and a value proposition that is both clear and appealing to consumers. Gap, the Disney Store, Lululemon, Superdry, and Victoria's Secret are examples of global retail operators that have stores in many parts of the world. In some countries, local companies operate the stores. In Japan, for example, the giant Aeon Group runs The Body Shop stores and has a joint venture with Sports Authority.

Supermarkets are departmentalized, single-story retail establishments that offer a variety of food (e.g., produce, baked goods, meats) and nonfood (e.g., paper products, health and beauty aids) items, mostly on a self-service basis. On average, supermarkets occupy between 50,000 square feet and 60,000 square feet of floor space.

U.K.-based Tesco is one retailing group that expanded globally for many years. While home-country sales still account for approximately 80 percent of its overall sales, the company has operations in 11 international markets. Company officials typically study a country market for several years before choosing an entry strategy. For example, Tesco's initial entry into Japan came via the acquisition of the C Two-Network, a chain of shops in Tokyo. As former Tesco chairman David Reid once explained, Tesco has succeeded globally because it does its homework and pays attention to details. Even so, in the 2000s, Tesco's efforts to penetrate the U.S. market failed.

Although Walmart is generating headlines as it moves around the globe, American retailers lag behind the Europeans in expanding outside their home countries. One reason is the sheer size of the domestic U.S. market.[16] In fact, Walmart's lack of experience outside North America undoubtedly contributed to its failures in South Korea and Germany.

Convenience stores offer some of the same products as supermarkets, but the merchandise mix is limited to high-turnover convenience and impulse products. Prices for some products may be 15 to 20 percent higher than supermarket prices. In terms of square footage, these venues are the smallest organized retail stores discussed here. In the United States, for example, the typical 7-Eleven occupies 3,000 square feet. Most convenience stores are located in high-traffic locations and offer extended service hours to accommodate commuters, students, and other highly mobile consumers. 7-Eleven is the world's largest convenience store chain; it has more than 64,000 locations, including franchisees, licensees, and stores that the company operates itself.

TABLE 12-2 Department Stores with Global Branches

Store	Original Store Location	Global Locations
Harvey Nichols	United Kingdom	Saudi Arabia, Hong Kong, Ireland, Dubai
Saks Fifth Avenue	United States	Dubai, Bahrain, Mexico
Barneys New York	United States	Japan
Lane Crawford	Hong Kong	China, Macao, Taiwan
Mitsukoshi	Japan	United States, Europe, Asia
H&M (Hennes & Mauritz)	Sweden	Austria, Germany, Kuwait, Slovakia, United States, 20 others

The current trend in convenience store retailing is toward smaller stores placed inside malls, airports, office buildings, and in college and university buildings. As Jeff Lenard, spokesperson for the National Association of Convenience Stores, has noted, "All the good street corners are gone, and the competition is so fierce for the ones that are left."[17]

Discount retailers can be divided into several categories. The most general characteristic that they have in common is their emphasis on low prices. *Full-line discounters* typically offer a wide range of merchandise, including nonfood items and nonperishable food, in a limited-service format. As Table 12-1 clearly shows, Walmart is the reigning king of the full-line discounters. Many of its stores cover 120,000 square feet (or more) of floor space; food accounts for approximately one-third of floor space and sales. Walmart stores typically offer a folksy atmosphere and value-priced brands. This company is also a leader in the *warehouse club* segment of discount retailing; shoppers "join" the club to take advantage of low prices on a limited range of products (typically 3,000 to 5,000 different items), many of which are displayed in their shipping cartons in a "no-frills" atmosphere.

When Walmart expands into a new country market, local discounters must respond to the competitive threat it poses. In Canada, for example, Hudson Bay's Zellers is the largest discount store chain. After Walmart acquired a bankrupt Canadian chain, Zellers countered by brightening the décor in its stores, widening aisles, and catering to women with young children.[18] French discounter Tati is also going global; in addition to opening a store on New York's Fifth Avenue, Tati currently has stores in Lebanon, Turkey, Germany, Belgium, Switzerland, and the Côte d'Ivoire.

Dollar stores sell a select assortment of products at one or more low prices. In the United States, Family Dollar Stores and Dollar Tree Stores dominate the industry. However, a recent industry entrant, My Dollarstore, is experiencing rapid international growth; it now has franchises in Eastern Europe, Central America, and Asia. To succeed in global markets, My Dollarstore has adapted its U.S. business model. For example, the typical U.S. dollar store has a "bargain basement" image. By contrast, in India, My Dollarstore targets affluent, middle-class shoppers who are attracted by the lure of low prices on brands associated with "the good life" in America. Goods are priced at 99 rupees—the equivalent of $2—and the stores are decorated in red, white, and blue with the Statue of Liberty on display. In the United States, dollar stores operate on a self-service basis with lean staffs; My Dollarstore's Indian locations have significantly higher staffing levels, the better to answer customers' questions about new or unfamiliar products.[19]

Hard discounters include retailers such as Germany's Aldi and Lidl ("Where quality is cheaper!") and France's Leader Price ("Le Prix La Qualité en Plus!"). These discounters offer a limited assortment of goods—typically 1,000 to 3,000 different items—at rock-bottom prices. Starting in 1976, Aldi began opening a few stores each year in the United States (where Aldi also owns the Trader Joe's "neighborhood grocery" chain). Aldi stores have a relatively small footprint; 17,500 square feet of floor space is typical. As Jason Hart, co-president of Aldi's U.S. operation, noted recently, "We carry 1,500 of the most popular grocery items out there. When you look at the large supermarkets that may have 20,000 to 30,000 items, it's surprising to the customers how much of the shopping list we're able to fit in our smaller store."[20] The company recently announced expansion plans calling for a total of 2,500 stores in the United States by 2022.[21]

When Walmart entered the German market, Aldi and Lidl were already well entrenched. By mid-2006, after years of losses, Walmart decided to close up shop in that country. In the recent economic downturn, hard discounters thrived as cash-strapped consumers sought ways to stretch their household budgets. Hard-discount retailers, which account for approximately 10 percent of grocery sales in Europe, rely heavily on "own-label" or private brands. Some items sell for much less than well-known global brands; tight cost control and supply-chain optimization are critical to maintain the companies' profits. Carrefour and other large supermarket operators are responding to the challenges posed by hard discounters by offering more own-brand products at lower prices. A decade ago, Tesco began offering hundreds of new, cheaper products under its own brands, including tea bags, cookies, and shampoo. "If there is a war, we will win it," said Tesco's one-time commercial director, Richard Brasher.[22]

Hypermarkets are a hybrid retailing format combining the discounter, supermarket, and warehouse club approaches under a single roof. Size-wise, hypermarkets are huge, ranging from 200,000 to 300,000 square feet.

Supercenters offer a wide range of aggressively priced grocery items plus general merchandise in a space that occupies about half the size of a hypermarket. Supercenters are an important aspect of Walmart's growth strategy, both at home and abroad. Walmart opened its first supercenter in 1988; today, it operates more than 3,275 supercenters in the United States, plus hundreds of stores in Mexico and units in Argentina and Brazil. Some prices at Walmart's supercenters in Brazil are as much as 15 percent lower than competitors' prices, and some observers wondered if the company had taken the discount approach too far. Company officials insist, though, that profit margins are in the 20 to 22 percent range.[23]

Superstores (also known as **category killers** and *big-box retail*) is the label many in the retailing industry use when talking about stores such as Home Depot and IKEA (see Exhibit 12-6). The name refers to the fact that such stores specialize in selling vast assortments of specific product categories—home improvement supplies or furniture, for example—in high volumes at low prices. In short, these stores represent retailing's "900-pound gorillas," which put pressure on smaller, more traditional competitors and prompt department stores to scale down merchandise sections that are in direct competition with the bigger selections found at the superstores.

Shopping malls consist of a grouping of stores in one place. Developers assemble an assortment of retailers that will create an appealing leisure destination; typically one or more large department stores serve as anchors (see Exhibit 12-7). Shopping malls offer acres of free parking and easy access from main traffic thoroughfares. Historically, malls were enclosed, allowing

"There is a new middle class of savvy consumers in South Africa. A shopping mall in South Africa is not very different from an Australian shopping mall or a British shopping mall."[24]

Simon Susman, CEO, Woolworths Holdings

Exhibit 12-6 STIHL Inc. manufactures and markets chainsaws, trimmers, and other types of outdoor power equipment. The distribution (*P*) factor of the marketing mix is an integral part of STIHL's marketing strategy: Its products are available only at independent dealers that provide full after-sale service. STIHL also sponsors "Independent We Stand," an initiative among independent businesses to help educate consumers about the importance of "buying local."
Source: Courtesy of STIHL Inc; ad campaign from 2010-2011.

Exhibit 12-7 The LP12 Mall of Berlin opened in September 2014. Located in Leipziger Platz, the mixed-use complex features 270 stores as well as apartments.
Source: Art Kowalsky/Alamy Stock Photo.

shoppers to browse in comfort no matter the weather outside. More recently, the trend has been toward outdoor shopping centers, now called "lifestyle centers." Food courts and entertainment encourage families to spend several hours at the mall. In the United States, malls sprang up as people moved from city centers to the suburbs. Today, global mall development reflects the opportunity to serve emerging middle-class consumers who seek both convenience and entertainment.

The world's five largest malls are in Asia (see Table 12-3). The reasons for their presence in this region are clear-cut: Economic growth led to rising incomes; in addition, tourism is booming in Asia. Some industry observers warn, however, that the megamalls and their glamorous global brand offerings are luring shoppers away from markets that sell goods produced by local craftspeople. Somewhere along the way, the thrill of discovering something new has been lost. Emil Pocock, a professor of American studies at Eastern Connecticut State University, is an expert on shopping malls. As he has noted, "I find it very disconcerting that shopping malls are more or less the same wherever you go in the world. I'm not sure I want 100 international companies determining our choices for consumer goods."[25]

Outlet stores are a variation on the traditional shopping mall: retail operations that allow companies with well-known consumer brands to dispose of excess inventory, out-of-date merchandise, or factory seconds. To attract large numbers of shoppers, outlet stores are often grouped together in **outlet malls**. The United States is home to hundreds of outlet malls, such as the giant Woodbury Common mall in Central Valley, New York. Now, the concept is catching on in Europe and Asia as well. The acceptance of this type of venue reflects changing attitudes among consumers and retailers alike; in both Asia and Europe, brand-conscious consumers are eager to save money (see Exhibit 12-8).

TABLE 12-3 The World's Largest Shopping Malls (ranked by gross leasable retail space)

Rank	Mall	City/Country	Millions of Square Feet
1	New South China Mall	Dongguan, China	7.1
2	Golden Resources Mall	Beijing, China	6.0
3	SM Megamall	Philippines	5.45
4	SM City North EDSA	Philippines	5.2
5	1 Utama	Malaysia	5.0

Source: Author research.

Designer brands, always 30-70% less

Discover more online.
mcarthurglen.com

Exhibit 12-8 McArthurGlen operates several upscale designer outlets in Europe. Although the retail tenants include popular American companies such as Nike, the majority of stores represent a veritable "who's who" of exclusive European fashion brands: Fendi, Ferrari, Harmont & Blaine, Jil Sander, Prada, Salvatore Ferragamo, and Versace (to name just a few). Fashion-forward bargain hunters can find prices that represent discounts of 30 percent to 70 percent off regular retail prices.
Source: McArthurGlen Designer Outlets.

Trends in Global Retailing

Currently, a variety of environmental factors have combined to push retailers out of their home markets in search of opportunities around the globe. Saturation of the home-country market, recession or other economic factors, strict regulation on store development, and high operating costs are some of the factors that prompt management to look abroad for growth opportunities. Walmart is a case in point; its international expansion in the mid-1990s coincided with disappointing financial results in its home market.

Even as the domestic retailing environment grows more challenging for many companies, an ongoing environmental scanning effort is likely to turn up markets in other parts of the world that are underdeveloped or where competition is weak. In addition, high rates of economic growth, a growing middle class, a high proportion of young people in the population, and less stringent regulation combine to make some country markets very attractive.[26] For example, Laura Ashley, The Body Shop, Disney Stores, and other specialty retailers were lured to Japan by developers who needed established names to fill space in large, suburban, American-style shopping malls.[27] Such malls are being developed as some local and national restrictions on retail development are being eased and as consumers tire of the aggravations associated with shopping in congested urban areas.

However, the large number of unsuccessful cross-border retailing initiatives suggests that any chief executive contemplating a move into global retailing should do so with a great deal of caution and due diligence. A few years ago, Frank Blake, Home Depot's CEO, noted, "International expansion has proved to be a competitive advantage for us. In Canada, Mexico, and now, China, we've shown we can enter a market, tailor our model to the local customer and see the same sort of growth we saw in our early days here in the U.S."[28] Despite this pronouncement, by the end of 2012 Home Depot had been forced to scale back its China operations. Other failures include the following:

- Walmart pulled out of Germany and South Korea.
- Best Buy closed several stores in China.
- Mattel closed its six-story flagship Barbie store in Shanghai.
- Tesco shut down its Fresh & Easy stores in the United States after incurring $1.6 billion in losses.

These are just a few of the examples that illustrate that it's not always possible to export a retail business model that has proved successful in the domestic market. As one industry analyst noted, "It's awfully hard to operate across the water. It's one thing to open up in Mexico and Canada, but the distribution hassles are just too big when it comes to exporting an entire store concept overseas."[29]

The critical question for the would-be global retailer is, "Which advantages do we have relative to local competition?" After taking into account the existing competition, local laws governing retailing practice, distribution patterns, or other factors, the answer will often be "Nothing." Sometimes, however, a company may possess competencies that can be the basis for competitive advantage in a particular retail market. A retailer may have several attractions to offer consumers, such as selection, price, and the overall manner and condition in which the goods are offered in the store setting. Store location, parking facilities, in-store atmosphere, and customer service also contribute to the value proposition. Competencies can also be found in less visible value-chain activities such as distribution, logistics, and information technology. As Thomas Hübner, CEO of Metro Cash & Carry International, noted, "Stores are just the tip of the iceberg—90 percent of the work is under water."[30]

For example, Japanese retailers traditionally offered few extra services to their clientele. There were no special orders or returns, and stock was chosen not according to consumer demand, but rather according to the purchasing preferences of the stores. Typically, a store would buy limited quantities from each of its favorite manufacturers, leaving consumers with no recourse when the goods sold out. Instead of trying to capitalize on the huge market, many retailers simply turned a deaf ear to customer needs and desires. From the retailers' point of view, this came out fine in the end; most of their stock eventually sold because buyers were forced to purchase what was left over—they had no other choice.

Then Gap, Eddie Bauer, and other Western retailers entered Japan, often by means of joint ventures. Their stores offered liberal return policies, a willingness to take special orders, and a policy of replenishing stock; in response, many Japanese consumers switched loyalties. Also, thanks to economies of scale and modern distribution methods unknown to some Japanese department store operators, the foreign retailers offered a greater variety of goods at lower prices. Although this upscale foreign competition hurt Japanese department store operators, Japan's depressed economy was another factor. Traditional retailers are also being squeezed from below as recession-pressed consumers flock to discounters such as Uniqlo and the Y100 Shop chain.

The retailing environment continues to be challenging in many parts of the world. For example, the French Connection Group PLC closed all of its U.S. and Japanese stores, as well as underperforming stores in Europe. One problem faced by that company: higher prices relative to competitors such as Zara and H&M, without a well-known brand and the higher quality that justifies the prices. Likewise, a traditional department store such as Macy's has neither the advantages of H&M and other affordable fast-fashion retailers nor the aspirational appeal of luxury specialty retailers.[31] Even so, global opportunities still attract some companies. For example, value retailer Primark, whose product assortment ranges from lingerie and athleisure to housewares, has expanded beyond its United Kingdom base and continental Europe by opening stores in the United States.[32]

Figure 12-3 shows a matrix-based scheme for classifying global retailers.[33] One axis represents a private- or own-label focus versus a manufacturer-brand focus. The other axis differentiates between retailers specializing in relatively few product categories and retailers that offer a wide product assortment. IKEA, in quadrant A, is a good example of a global retailer with a niche focus (assemble-yourself furniture for the home) as well as an own-label focus (IKEA sells its own brand). IKEA and other retailers in quadrant A typically use extensive advertising and product innovation to build a strong brand image.

In quadrant B, the private-label focus is retained, but many more product categories are offered. This is the strategy of Marks & Spencer (M&S), the British-based department store company whose St. Michael private label is found on a broad range of clothing, food, home furnishings, jewelry, and other items. Private-label retailers that attempt to expand internationally face a double-edged challenge: They must attract customers to both the store and the branded merchandise. M&S has succeeded by virtue of an entrepreneurial management style that has evolved over the last 100-plus years. The company opened its first store outside the United Kingdom in 1974; it currently operates more than 450 stores in 54 countries, including 15 locations in Shanghai.

In 1997, then chairman Sir Richard Greenbury announced an ambitious plan to put M&S "well on its way to establishing a global business." It was his belief that consumer tastes are globalizing, at least with respect to fashion apparel. Food is a different story; because tastes are more localized, M&S executives anticipated that the proportion of revenues from global food sales would be lower than they are in Great Britain.[35]

Retailers in quadrant C of Figure 12-3 offer many well-known brands in a relatively tightly defined merchandise range. Some well-known historical examples include Toys 'R' Us, Blockbuster Video, and Virgin Megastores. A few decades ago, this type of store tended to quickly dominate smaller established retailers by out-merchandising the local competition and offering customers superior value by virtue of extensive inventories and low prices. Typically, the low prices were the result of buyer power and sourcing advantages that the local retailers lacked. As it turns out, the three companies mentioned here have virtually disappeared from the retail landscape. All fell victim to changing consumer tastes and buying habits and were slower to adapt and innovate than industry disrupters such as Netflix and Spotify and e-commerce titan Amazon.

"Apparel has always been extremely competitive and retail is one of the least consolidated sectors. Brands have to evolve or risk becoming less relevant."[34]

Jamie Merriman, analyst, Bernstein Research

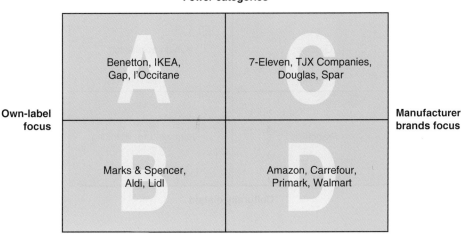

Fewer categories

A Benetton, IKEA, Gap, l'Occitane	C 7-Eleven, TJX Companies, Douglas, Spar
B Marks & Spencer, Aldi, Lidl	D Amazon, Carrefour, Primark, Walmart

Own-label focus — **Manufacturer brands focus**

Many categories

FIGURE 12-3 Global Retailing Categories
Source: Adapted from Jacques Horovitz and Nirmalya Kumar, "Strategies for Retail Globalization," *Financial Times—Mastering Global Business, Part VII* (1998), pp. 4–8.

Despite the demise of most brick-and-mortar record shops, the retailing environment in which Richard Branson originally built the Virgin Megastore chain illustrates the type of success that can be achieved through an entrepreneurial management style:

> It required little retailing expertise to see that the sleepy business practices of traditional record shops provided a tremendous opportunity. To rival the tiny neighborhood record shops, with their eclectic collections of records, a new kind of record store was coming into being. It was big; it was well-lit, and records were arranged clearly in alphabetical order by artist; it covered most tastes in pop music comprehensively; and it turned over its stock much faster than the smaller record retailer . . . . It was the musical equivalent of a supermarket.[36]

Starting with one megastore location on London's Oxford Street in 1975, Branson's Virgin retail empire once extended throughout Europe, North America, Japan, Hong Kong, and Taiwan.

Another of Branson's ventures, Virgin Atlantic Airlines, reflects the same effort to provide a different service experience. As Steve Ridgway, former CEO of Virgin Atlantic, explained, "Fundamentally it's around the value proposition and what consumers will pay for. Our single biggest innovation was always to try to wrong-foot the market. We've always positioned our products half a notch out of the convention."[37]

Amazon, Carrefour, Primark, Walmart, and other retailers in quadrant D of Figure 12-3 offer the same type of merchandise available from established local retailers. What the newcomers bring to a market, however, is competence in distribution or some other value-chain element. To date, Walmart's international division has established more than 6,360 stores outside the United States; it is already the biggest retailer in Mexico and Canada. Other store locations include Central America, South America, China, and, until recently, Germany.

Global Retailing Market Expansion Strategies

Retailers can choose from four market-entry expansion strategies when expanding outside the home country. As shown in Figure 12-4, these strategies can be diagrammed using a matrix that differentiates between (1) markets that are easy to enter versus those that are difficult to enter and (2) culturally close markets versus culturally distant ones. The upper half of the matrix encompasses quadrants A and D and represents markets in which shopping patterns and retail structures are similar to those in the home country. In the lower half of the matrix, quadrants B and C represent markets that are significantly different from the home-country market in terms of one or more cultural characteristics. The right side of the matrix, quadrants A and B, represents markets that are difficult to enter because of the presence of strong competitors, location restrictions, excessively high rent or real estate costs, or other factors. In quadrants C and D, any barriers that

FIGURE 12-4 Global Retailing Market Entry Strategy Framework

Source: Adapted from Jacques Horovitz and Nirmalya Kumar, "Strategies for Retail Globalization," *Financial Times—Mastering Global Business, Part VII* (1998), p. 5.

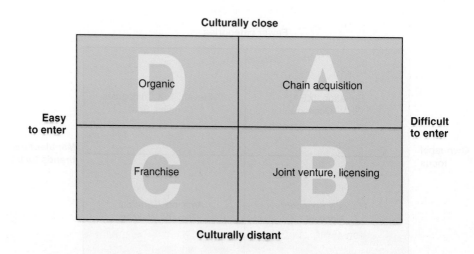

exist are relatively easy to overcome. The four entry strategies indicated by the matrix are organic, franchise, chain acquisition, and joint ventures and licensing.

Organic growth occurs when a company uses its own resources to open a store on a greenfield site or to acquire one or more existing retail facilities from another company. In 1997, for example, M&S announced plans to expand from one store to four in Germany via the purchase of three stores operated by Cramer and Meerman. When Richard Branson set up the first Virgin Megastore in Paris, he did so by investing millions of pounds in a spectacular retail space on the Champs-Élysées. From the perspectives of M&S and Virgin, the retail environments of Germany and France are both culturally close and easy to enter. The success of this strategy hinges on the availability of company resources to sustain the high cost of the initial investment.

Franchising, shown in quadrant C of Figure 12-4, is the appropriate entry strategy when barriers to entry are low, yet the market is culturally distant in terms of consumer behavior or retailing structures. As defined in Chapter 9, franchising is a contractual relationship between two companies. In this arrangement, the parent company–franchisor authorizes a franchisee to operate a business developed by the franchisor in return for a fee and adherence to franchise-wide policies and practices. The key to a successful franchise operation is the ability to transfer company know-how to new markets. Benetton, IKEA, and other focused, private-label retailers often use franchising as a market-entry strategy in combination with wholly owned stores that represent organic growth. The IKEA Group has more than 260 company-owned stores across Europe, in North America, and in China; 34 additional stores in various global locations are franchise operations.

In global retailing, **acquisition** is a market-entry strategy that entails purchasing a company with multiple retail locations in a foreign country. This strategy can provide the buyer with quick growth as well as access to existing brand suppliers, distributors, and customers. For example, when Walmart first entered the Japanese market in 2002, it did so by acquiring a 6.1 percent stake in the Seiyu retail chain. In 2007, Walmart upped its stake to 95.1 percent; the following year, Seiyu and its 414 stores became a wholly owned subsidiary. Now Walmart is seeking to expand by making additional acquisitions. As Walmart Asia CEO Scott Price explained, "We see scale as being the next level of being able to change the value proposition for Japanese customers." Organic growth is not an option, however: "We do not want to build more retail in Japan. The last thing Japan needs is more retail space," Price said.[38]

Joint ventures and **licensing** were examined in detail in Chapter 9. Global retailers frequently use these strategies to limit their risk when targeting unfamiliar, difficult-to-enter markets. For example, Barneys New York licensed its name to Barneys Japan for a period of 10 years; Saks Fifth Avenue has licensed stores in the Middle East. In some countries, local regulations mandate the use of joint ventures. For example, prior to 2005, China had regulations that required foreign retailers entering the market to have local partners. In 2005, Chinese authorities liberalized the country's retail climate, and today IKEA and other retailers that initially used joint ventures as an entry strategy are shifting to wholly owned stores in China.

Virgin Group's retail expansion in Asia provides a case study of the appropriateness of the joint venture approach. In Japan, commercial landlords typically require millions of dollars in upfront payments before they will lease retail space. Accordingly, in 1992, Virgin established a joint venture called Virgin Megastores Japan with Marui, a local retailer with a good track record of catering to the preferences of young people. The first megastore was set up in the basement of an existing Marui department store in Japan's Shinjuku district. That site and subsequent stores have been wildly successful; Virgin has duplicated the joint venture approach elsewhere in Asia, including Hong Kong, Taiwan, and South Korea. In each location, Virgin establishes a joint venture with a leading industrial group.[39]

Achieving retailing success outside the home-country market is not simply a matter of consulting a matrix and choosing the recommended entry strategy. Management must also be alert to the possibility that the merchandise mix, sourcing strategy, distribution, or other format elements will have to be adapted. Management at Crate & Barrel, for example, is hesitant to open stores in Japan. Part of the reason is research indicating that at least half the company's product line would have to be modified to accommodate local preferences. Another issue is whether the company will have the ability to transfer its expertise to new country markets.

ENTREPRENEURIAL LEADERSHIP, CREATIVE THINKING, AND THE GLOBAL STARTUP

Mr. Selfridge: An American Retailer in London

Harry Gordon Selfridge was an entrepreneur, an enthusiast, and a dreamer. Selfridge developed an innovative product, created a brand, and started a business. And not just any business: He launched Selfridge & Company, called by some "the most beautiful department store the world has ever seen." By applying the basic tools and principles of marketing decades before modern marketing had emerged as a discipline, Selfridge achieved remarkable success. As is true with many entrepreneurs, Selfridge's idea was based on his own needs, wants, and vision. He declared, "We are going to show the world how to make shopping thrilling!" (See Exhibit 12-9.)

Retailers may have a difficult time crossing borders if they fail to appreciate differences in retailing environments and consumer behavior and preferences. However, just the opposite was true when Selfridge opened his department store just off Oxford Street in London. He broke with convention on a number of fronts. Noting that there were more horse-drawn carriages than cars at the time, he moved perfume and fragrances to the front of the store, putting them front and center. This arrangement served to neutralize any foul odors from horse dung that shoppers might track in on their shoes. In traditional British stores, articles were kept behind counters and shoppers had to ask clerks for help. By contrast, Selfridge put the goods out for people to see and touch. "The customer always comes first," Selfridge declared. Londoners had never seen anything like it.

If the Selfridge story sounds fascinating, well, it is! It has been the subject of a book, *Shopping, Seduction, and Mr Selfridge*, as well as a television series that aired on ITV in Great Britain and on public television in the United States. Although ratings were higher in Britain, the series was renewed for a fourth season for American viewers. As the book and the TV series clearly demonstrate, Selfridge loved the theater, performers, and artists. Not surprisingly, there was more than a hint of theatricality in some of Selfridge's marketing tactics and publicity stunts. These included early-bird specials, an in-store appearance by Russian ballerina Anna Pavlova, and a display on the store's ground floor of the first airplane to cross the English Channel.

As it turns out, the human story ended badly; Selfridge fell victim to various demons and vices and was ousted from the company he had founded. His legacy endures, however, and in the twenty-first century, Selfridges continues to be at the forefront of retailing innovation. Its flagship London store is home to Europe's largest cosmetics department. Window displays have featured buzz-building "performances" such as humans in animal costumes modeling lingerie. As Peter Williams, CEO of Selfridges, said, "Our competitors are not just other department stores. Our competitors are restaurants, theaters, a weekend away, or other entertainment venues."

Sources: Nancy Dewolf Smith, "Tales of the Counter Culture," *The Wall Street Journal* (March 28, 2014), p. D7; Mike Hale, "Fogging up the Windows of a Big Store," *The New York Times* (March 30, 2013), p. C1; Nancy Dewolf Smith, "The Dawn of Shopping," *The Wall Street Journal* (March 29, 2013), p. D5; Vanessa O'Connell, "Department Stores Are Hard Sell Abroad," *The Wall Street Journal* (May 22, 2008), p. B3; Cecilie Rohwedder, "Harvey Nichols's Foreign Affair," *The Wall Street Journal* (February 18, 2005), p. B3; Erin White, "Dress for Success: After Long Slump, U.S. Retailers Look to Britain for Fashion Tips," *The Wall Street Journal* (April 22, 2004), pp. A1, A8; Rohwedder, "Selling Selfridges," *The Wall Street Journal* (May 5, 2003), p. B1.

Exhibit 12-9 Harry Gordon Selfridge was a marketing and retail genius. His spirit lives on today in London, where Selfridge's continues to find innovative ways to lure shoppers to the store. For example, when designer Michel Lamy launched a special collaboration with Everlast, Selfridge's installed a boxing ring in the store and invited Olympic boxing champion Nicola Adams to stop by.
Source: PA Images/Alamy Stock Photo.

(12-4) Physical Distribution, Supply Chains, and Logistics Management

◀ **12-4** Compare and contrast the six major international transportation modes and explain how they vary in terms of reliability, accessibility, and other performance metrics.

In Chapter 1, marketing was described as one of the activities in a firm's value chain. The distribution (*P*) of the marketing mix is a critical value-chain activity. After all, Coca-Cola, IKEA, Nokia, P&G, Toyota, and other global companies create value by making sure their products are available where and when customers need and want to buy them. As defined in this chapter, physical distribution consists of activities involved in moving finished goods from manufacturers to customers. However, the concept of the value chain is much broader: It is a useful tool for assessing an organization's competence as it performs value-creating activities within a broader **supply chain**. The latter includes *all* the firms that perform support activities by generating raw materials, converting them into components or finished products, and facilitating their delivery to customers.

The particular industry in which a firm competes (e.g., automobiles, consumer electronics, furniture, or pharmaceuticals) is characterized by a value chain. The specific activities an individual firm performs help define its position in the value chain. A company or activity that is somewhat removed from the final customer is said to be *upstream* in the value chain. Consider the following comment from Anders Moberg, the former CEO of IKEA: "At IKEA, we went out into the forest to see which were the right trees to pick to optimize production and cost efficiency in the saw mills."[40] That's a pretty good description of an upstream activity! A company or activity that is relatively close to customers—a retailer, for example—is said to be downstream in the value chain.

Logistics, in turn, is the management process that integrates the activities of all companies—both upstream and downstream—to ensure an efficient flow of goods through the supply chain. Logistics was not really a household term until UPS launched its global "We ♥ Logistics" advertising campaign. The TV ads utilize a catchy jingle: a Harry Warren–penned tune, "That's Amore," popularized by the 1953 motion picture *The Caddy* starring Jerry Lewis and Dean Martin. In the UPS ads, the original lyrics (e.g., "When the moon hits your eye like a big pizza pie, that's amore!") have been replaced by an ode to, well, logistics! Here's a sample:

> "When it's planes in the sky for a chain of supply, that's logistics.
> When the parts for the line come precisely on time, that's logistics."

You can find the U.S. version of the ad, plus Chinese and Spanish versions, on YouTube.

Analogy and metaphor can also help you gain a better understanding of logistics; consider the following passage from a book written in 1917:

> Strategy is to war what the plot is to the play. Tactics is represented by the role of the players; logistics furnishes the stage management, accessories, and maintenance. The audience, thrilled by the action of the play and the art of the performers, overlooks all of the cleverly hidden details of stage management.[41]

As this quote suggests, many activities associated with logistics and supply-chain management take place "behind the scenes." However, the supply chain's vital role in global marketing has become more evident in recent years. The catastrophic earthquake and tsunami that struck Japan in March 2011 resulted in a tragic loss of life—but they also disrupted supply chains for a variety of industries, including automobiles and consumer electronics.

The ongoing political upheaval in the Middle East has also highlighted the importance of flexibility in global supply-chain design. For example, in spring 2011, P&G was forced to briefly close plants in Egypt that supply products for South Africa. During the closure, production from plants in Hungary and Turkey was redirected to supply the South African market. Such incidents explain why supply-chain managers use a term borrowed from the military, VUCA, to describe places that are "volatile, uncertain, complex, and ambiguous."[42]

For decades, Walmart's mastery of logistics and supply-chain management was an important source of competitive advantage. The retailing giant's basic value proposition is simple: getting goods to people as efficiently as possible. To do this, Walmart exploited a core competency: It

ENTREPRENEURIAL LEADERSHIP, CREATIVE THINKING, AND THE GLOBAL STARTUP

Malcom McLean: Containerization Visionary

Malcom McLean was an entrepreneur. He developed an innovative industrial product and used it to help his business grow. Along the way, he revolutionized the way goods are shipped, thereby helping usher in the era of globalization. By applying the basic tools and principles of modern marketing, McLean achieved remarkable success. As is true with many entrepreneurs, McLean's idea was based on his recognition of a problem that needed to be solved and the needs of his growing business. Recognizing the significant inefficiencies in terms of the time and costs associated with loading and unloading oceangoing freight, Maclean set about devising a solution that would streamline those labor-intensive processes.

Until the mid-twentieth century, shipping goods was slow and expensive. Longshoremen would unload as many as 200,000 separate pieces of cargo from trucks or warehouses near the docks and then stow each item on an oceangoing freighter. The process was reversed at the end of the voyage. The solution seemed obvious to McLean: What if freight was preloaded in boxes, and then those boxes could be picked up and loaded on the ship—and vice versa? The solution was containerization—the use of standardized steel boxes that could be loaded with freight at the factory and shipped by rail or by truck to a port. There, the entire box would be loaded onto the deck or into the ship's hold.

As the late management guru Peter Drucker noted, innovation can occur when the wealth-producing potential of an existing resource is enhanced. This is exactly what happened when, in the 1950s, McLean helped change the definition of a "cargo vessel" from a "ship" to a "cargo-handling device." In other words, McLean was pragmatic: He didn't care about the "romance of the sea." For him, freight was just freight. For years, innovation in the industry had focused on building faster ships that used less fuel and smaller crews. However, these costs were relatively small to start with. The real cost came when the ship was sitting idle when it was docked at port. The innovative solution was quite simple, focused, and specific; McLean's insight was to uncouple the loading of freighters from the loading of the cargo.

As Marc Levinson notes in his book about McLean, the container turned the economics of location on its head. Containerization revolutionized the handling of cargo. McLean, the man who spearheaded the revolution, was originally a trucking industry magnate. His innovation—containerization—represented a profoundly disruptive technology. In the 1950s, Maclean sold his successful trucking company and bought Pan-Atlantic Steamship Company, which was renamed Sea-Land Service in 1960. Container and multimodal transportation quadrupled the productivity of oceangoing freighters and enabled the explosive growth of world trade after World War II.

As is often the case when a disruptive technology is introduced, the container revolution created both winners and losers. Among the losers: New York City's port system, which, in the 1950s, was the largest in the United States. Immortalized by Hollywood in the motion picture *On the Waterfront*, New York's port system had several disadvantages. Notably, freight arriving by rail had to be floated across the Hudson River by barge, which resulted in higher costs in terms of both money and time. In addition, wildcat strikes and cargo theft, and the fact that many piers had fallen into disrepair, made New York increasingly unattractive as a shipping center. Today, things have come full circle, and the Port of New York is bustling again (see Exhibit 12-10).

> "McLean's real achievement was in changing the system that surrounded his box: the way that ships, ports, and docks were designed."[44]
>
> Tim Harford, author, *Fifty Inventions That Shaped the Modern Economy*

Sources: Mark Levinson, Keynote Address, Moving Iowa Forward Conference, Des Moines, Iowa, October 21, 2014; Mark Levinson, *The Box: How the Shipping Container Made the World Smaller and the World Economy Bigger* (Princeton, NJ: Princeton University Press, 2008); Peter F. Drucker, *Innovation and Entrepreneurship* (New York, NY: Harper & Row, 1985).

Exhibit 12-10 Prior to 1985, the Port of New York was the busiest container port in the world. Subsequently, it went into decline as ports on the West Coast and the South courted freight lines. Now, thanks to a high tide of imports from Asia, as well as major disruptions at West Coast ports, the Port of New York is experiencing a resurgence of traffic. Giant freighters leave China and travel through the Panama Canal en route to the East Coast.
Source: Randy Duchaine/Alamy Stock Photo.

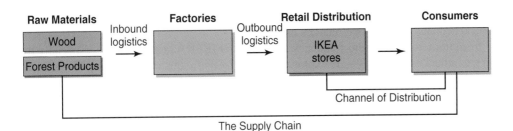

FIGURE 12-5 Supply Chain, Value Chain, and Logistics

leveraged its vast customer database to determine and anticipate what customers want and got it to them quickly and efficiently.

Today, however, the company faces significant competitive threats in both food and non-food categories. In the United States, more than two-thirds of Walmart customers also shop at dollar stores; meanwhile, Aldi is stepping up the pace of its new-store openings. Online giant Amazon has moved into brick-and-mortar grocery retail with its acquisition of Whole Foods. The shift to online shopping is gaining momentum as social media apps such as Pinterest add new functionality such as "Buy Now" buttons. In an effort to improve its e-commerce capabilities as it searches for new sources of competitive advantage, Walmart paid $3 billion to acquire Jet.com in 2016.[43]

An industry's value chain can change over time. In pharmaceuticals, for example, research, testing, and delivery were the three steps that historically defined the industry from its beginnings in the early nineteenth century. Then, starting in the mid-1960s, after Crick and Watson published their groundbreaking work on DNA, two new upstream steps in the industry's value chain emerged: basic research into genes associated with specific diseases and identification of the proteins produced by those genes. More recently, with the mapping of the human genome largely complete, value in the pharmaceuticals industry is migrating downstream to identifying, testing, and producing molecules that operate on the proteins produced by genes.[45]

The value chain, logistics, and related concepts are extremely important as supply chains stretch around the globe. As export administrator Beth Dorrell notes, "A commodity raw material from Africa can be refined in Asia, then shipped to South America to be incorporated into a component of a final product that is produced in the Middle East and then sold around the world." Figure 12-5 illustrates some of these concepts and activities at IKEA, the global furniture marketer. IKEA purchases wood and other raw material inputs from a network of suppliers located in dozens of countries; these suppliers are upstream in the value chain, and the process by which wood is transported to the factories is known as *inbound logistics*. IKEA's factories add value to the inputs by transforming them into furniture kits that are then shipped to IKEA's stores. These stores are downstream in IKEA's value chain; the activities associated with shipping furniture kits from factory to store are known as *outbound logistics*.[47]

Physical distribution and logistics are the means by which products are made available to customers when and where they want them. The most important distribution activities are order processing, warehousing, inventory management, and transportation.

Order Processing

Activities related to order processing provide information inputs that are critical in fulfilling a customer's order. **Order processing** includes *order entry*, in which the order is actually entered into the company's information system; *order handling*, which involves locating, assembling, and moving products into distribution; and *order delivery*, the process by which products are made available to the customer.

In some instances, the customer is a consumer, as is the case when you place an order with Amazon.com or Lands' End. In other instances, the customer is a channel member.

Order processing can be targeted for improvement as a means to increase a company's efficiency in distribution. For example, Pepsi Bottling Group overhauled its supply chain in an effort to eliminate out-of-stock inventory problems. The company's handheld computers lacked wireless capability and required a hookup to a landline telephone service; by upgrading the technology, sales representatives can now enter orders wirelessly. Warehouse workers are equipped with

"We are trying to take advantage of the global factory. We are a global company; we should have a supply chain that reflects our customer base."[46]

Keith Sherin, former chairman and CEO, GE Capital

barcode scanners and headsets so they can do a better job of ensuring that each pallet of drink products contains exactly what retailers ordered.[48]

In addition to using radio frequency identification (RFID) tags, retailers—especially those with e-commerce operations—are exploring the potential of industrial robots to pick out items in warehouses and distribution centers and put them in boxes for shipping. The drive to automate fulfillment holds the promise of significantly reducing the time and labor cost involved in preparing an order for shipment. The development process includes creating massive data sets and 3D renderings of individual inventory items. Meanwhile, just in the United States alone, Amazon.com and other companies are hiring hundreds of thousands of distribution center employees in an effort to keep up with the torrid pace of online sales growth.[49]

Warehousing

Warehouses are used to store goods until they are sold; another type of facility, the *distribution center*, is designed to efficiently receive goods from suppliers and then fill orders for individual stores or customers. Modern distribution and warehousing is such an automated, high-tech business today that many companies outsource this function. For example, ODW Logistics Inc. operates several warehouses on behalf of Deere & Company, Limited Brands, and other customers. Much of ODW's capacity is in Columbus, Ohio, a major U.S. port of entry for textiles.

One of the driving forces behind the growth of third-party warehousing is the need to reduce fixed costs and speed up delivery times to customers. ODW Logistics adds additional utility by tracking shipments from the time they leave the factory in, say, China, until they reach Columbus. This enables the company to alert retailers of possible delays due to weather issues or port congestion. In addition, as manufacturers ramp up adoption of RFID technology, ODW will split the cost of the new technology with its customers. As consultant John Boyd noted a decade ago, "Distribution warehousing is the next arena of corporate re-engineering and corporate cost-cutting."[50]

Inventory Management

Proper inventory management ensures that a company neither runs out of manufacturing components or finished goods nor incurs the expense and risk of carrying excessive stocks of these items. As part of this quest, order-processing costs must be balanced against inventory-carrying costs. The more often a product is ordered, the higher the order-processing costs associated with unloading, stocking, packing for shipping, and related activities. The less frequently a product is ordered, the higher the inventory-carrying costs, because more product must be kept in inventory to cover the longer period between orders.

Social media can play an important role in inventory management. For example, Vetements is a luxury fashion label founded by Guram Gvasalia in 2014. Even with eye-popping prices such as $1,300 for a pair of jeans made from recycled denim, the company quickly scaled up to $100 million in annual sales. How? For one thing, rigorous wholesale management and a digital strategy that connects the brand's nearly 2 million Instagram followers to its global inventory.[51]

Transportation

Transportation decisions concern the method, or *mode*, a company should utilize when moving products through domestic and global channels. The word *mode* implies a choice, and the major transportation mode choices are rail, truck, air, water, pipeline, and the Internet. Each of these modes has its advantages and disadvantages, as summarized in Table 12-4. However, a particular mode may be unavailable in some countries because of an underdeveloped infrastructure or geographic barriers. In addition, pipelines are highly specialized and are used only by companies transporting energy-related resources such as oil and natural gas.

Rail provides an extremely cost-effective means for moving large quantities of merchandise long distances. In the United States, carriers such as CSX and Burlington Northern Santa Fe (BNSF) account for nearly half of all cargo moved when measured by ton-miles. Rail's capability is second only to water in terms of the variety of products that can be transported. However, trains are less reliable than trucks. Poor track maintenance leads to derailments, and bottlenecks on heavily traveled lines can create delays.

By the numbers:

8.5 million barrels of oil are pumped in the United States every day. Most is transported by pipeline, but 1.6 million barrels—almost 20 percent of the total—travels by rail.

Source: US. Energy Information Agency.

TABLE 12-4 Comparison of Major International Transportation Modes

Mode	Reliability	Cost	Speed	Accessibility	Capability	Ease of Tracing
Rail	Average	Average	Average	High	High	Low
Water	Low	Low	Slow	Low	High	Low
Truck	High	Varies	Fast	High	High	High
Air	High	High	Fast	Low	Moderate	High
Pipeline	High	Low	Slow	Low	Low	Moderate
Internet	High	Low	Moderate to fast	Moderate; increasing	Low	High

Trucks are an excellent mode for both long-haul, transcontinental transport and local delivery of goods. In nations with well-developed highway systems, truck freight combines the advantage of fast delivery times with the highest level of accessibility of any mode. Thanks to modern information technology, truck shipments are also easily traced. However, in countries with poorly developed infrastructures, truck deliveries can move much more slowly. India is a case in point.

The two main types of water transportation are inland water and ocean transportation. *Inland water transportation* is an extremely low-cost mode generally used to move agricultural commodities, petroleum, fertilizers, and other goods that, by their nature, lend themselves to bulk shipping via barge. However, inland water transportation can be slow and subject to weather-related delays. Virtually any product can be shipped via *ocean transportation*. The world's deepwater ports can receive a variety of types of oceangoing vessels, such as container vessels; bulk and break-bulk vessels; and roll-on, roll-off (ro-ro) vessels. Although sailing times are not competitive with air transportation, it is generally more cost-effective to ship large quantities of merchandise via ocean than by air. Denmark's Maersk Sealand is the world's largest shipping container line (see Table 12-5).

Why is water rated "low" in reliability? In any given year, approximately 200 freighters sink due to bad weather or other factors (see Exhibit 12-11). Compounding the tragic loss of human lives is the fact that the cargo ends up on the ocean floor. Cargo can also sometimes be lost without a ship sinking. For example, in 1997 a huge wave rocked the freighter *Tokio Express* in the waters off Land's End, England. Several dozen shipping containers were tossed overboard, including one containing nearly 5 million LEGO pieces. The container was bound for Connecticut, where the pieces were to be assembled into kits. One year later, LEGO pieces began washing ashore in Florida!

Losses can occur even when the cargo remains on board and the ship doesn't sink. For example, the *Cougar Ace*, a freighter loaded with 4,700 new Mazdas, narrowly avoided sinking

TABLE 12-5 Leading Container Shipping Lines

Carrier	Number of Vessels
A. P. Moller-Maersk (Denmark)	600+
Mediterranean Shipping Company MSC (Switzerland)	458
CMA-CGM (France)	414
Evergreen Marine (Taiwan)	182
Cosco (China)	130+

Source: Compiled by authors from company reports.

Exhibit 12-11 Container ships can be lost in storms or run aground, resulting in tragic loss of life. If cargo containers can't be salvaged, they may end up on the ocean floor.
Source: Maritime New Zealand/ZUMAPRESS/Newscom.

in the Pacific in 2006. The cars were strapped down, but the ship listed at a 60-degree angle for weeks before being righted. Concerned that the cars might not be saleable, management decided to destroy the entire shipment, which was valued at $100 million.[52]

Piracy on the high seas is another factor affecting the reliability of water as a transport mode. In recent years, pirates operating in the Indian Ocean off the coast of Africa have fired upon and attempted to board dozens of commercial vessels. In some instances, the pirates have succeeded in boarding ships and hijacking the cargo. In one case, pirates captured the captain of an American-flagged ship carrying food aid to East Africa.

Air is the fastest transport mode and the carrier of choice for perishable exports such as flowers or fresh fish, but it is also the most expensive. The size and the weight of an item may indicate that it is more cost-effective to ship the product via air rather than ocean transportation. If a shipment's delivery is time sensitive, such as an emergency parts replacement, air is also the logical mode.

Thanks to the digital revolution, the *Internet* is an important transportation mode that is associated with several advantages and one major disadvantage. First, the bad news: The Internet's capability is low. As Nicolas Negroponte, former director of MIT's Media Lab, has famously observed, as long as something consists of atoms, it cannot be shipped via the Internet. However, anything that can be digitized can be sent via the Internet. Advantages of this mode include low cost and high reliability. Accessibility is increasing as the mobile revolution picks up speed; today, it is estimated that half the world's population has Internet access. Speed depends on several factors, including bandwidth. In recent years, improvements in broadband technology and cellular infrastructure have provided much of the world with on-ramps to the Internet superhighway. Facebook, Netflix, Spotify, and WhatsApp are just a few of the beneficiaries of this trend.

Channel strategy involves an analysis of each shipping mode to determine which mode, or combination of modes, will be both effective and efficient in a given situation. A number of firms specializing in third-party logistics are available to help companies with transportation logistics. For example, C. H. Robinson Worldwide matches shippers with trucking companies and other carriers in all parts of the world. One aspect of transportation technology that has revolutionized global trade is containerization—a concept that was first utilized in the United States starting in the mid-1950s. **Containerization** refers to the practice of loading oceangoing freight into steel boxes measuring 20 feet, 40 feet, or longer. Containerization offers many advantages, including flexibility in the products that can be shipped via container, as well as flexibility in shipping modes.

Intermodal transportation of goods involves a combination of land and water shipping from producer to customer.[53] In the United States alone, railroads handle more than $150 billion in seaport goods—a statistic that is a testament to intermodal transportation's growing importance. Unfortunately, lack of investment in America's rail infrastructure has resulted in delays at seaports. As Bernard LaLonde, a professor of transportation and logistics, noted two decades ago, "It's the Achilles' heel of global distribution. The ships keep getting bigger and faster. Trade keeps growing. But we don't have the rail links we need."[54]

The decision of which mode of transportation to use may be dictated by a particular market situation, by the company's overall strategy, or by conditions at the port of importation. For example, every November, winemakers from France's Beaujolais region participate in a promotion celebrating the release of the current vintage. Although wine destined for European markets may travel by rail or truck, U.S.-bound wine is shipped via air freight: Speed is of the essence when producers of Beaujolais nouveau are racing to get their products to the market. Normally, owing to weight and bulk considerations, French wine makes the transatlantic journey by water. Similarly, Acer Group ships motherboards and other high-tech components from Taiwan via air freight to ensure that the latest technology is incorporated into its computers. Bangladesh's primary port, Chittagong, is subject to congestion, frequent delays, and strikes, which forces Gap and other clothing companies to ship via air.

Every Christmas, supplies of the season's hottest-selling toys and electronics products are shipped via air from factories in Asia to ensure their just-in-time delivery by Santa Claus. Sony's PlayStation 3 is a case in point; in the fall of 2006, the company shipped hundreds of thousands of PS3 units by air to the United States. Likewise, in 2007, the first shipments of Apple's highly anticipated iPhone arrived from Asia via air freight. An estimated $1 billion is added to U.S. shipping costs each year because companies are forced to compensate for railway delays by keeping more components or parts in inventory or by shipping via air.

Logistics Management: A Brief Case Study

The term **logistics management** describes the integration of activities necessary to ensure the efficient flow of raw materials, in-process inventory, and finished goods from producers to customers. JCPenney provides a case study in the changing face of logistics, physical distribution, and retail supply chains in the twenty-first century. Several years ago, Penney's management team made a key decision to outsource most elements of its private-label shirt supply chain to TAL Apparel Ltd. of Hong Kong. Penney's North American stores carry almost no extra inventory of house-brand shirts; when an individual shirt is sold, EPOS scanner data are transmitted directly to Hong Kong. TAL's proprietary computer model then determines whether to replenish the store with the same size, color, and style. Replacement shirts are sent directly to stores without passing through Penney's warehouse system; sometimes the shirts are sent via air, sometimes by ship.

This approach represents a dramatic departure from past practices; Penney's typically carried 6 months' worth of inventory in its warehouses and 3 months' inventory in stores. By working closely with TAL, the retailer can lower its inventory costs, reduce the quantity of goods that have to be marked down, and respond more quickly to changing consumer tastes and fashion styles. However, as Wai-Chan Chan of McKinsey & Company Hong Kong noted, "You are giving away a pretty important function when you outsource your inventory management. That's something that not a lot of retailers want to part with."[55]

Summary

A *channel of distribution* is the network of agencies and institutions that links producers with users. *Physical distribution* is the movement of goods through channels. *Business-to-consumer (b-to-c) marketing* uses consumer channels; *business-to-business (b-to-b) marketing* employs industrial channels to deliver products to manufacturers or other types of organizations. *Peer-to-peer* marketing via the Internet is another channel. *Distributors* and *agents* are key intermediaries in some channels. Channel decisions are difficult to manage globally because of the variation in channel structures from country to country. Marketing channels can create *place utility*, *time utility*, *form utility*, and *information utility* for buyers. The characteristics of customers, products, middlemen, and the environment all affect channel design and strategy.

Consumer channels may be relatively direct, utilizing direct-mail or door-to-door selling, as well as manufacturer-owned stores. A combination of manufacturers' sales forces, agents/brokers, and wholesalers may also be used. Channels for industrial products are less varied, with manufacturers' sales forces, wholesalers, and dealers or agents being used.

Global retailing is a growing trend as successful retailers expand around the world in support of their growth objectives. Retail operations take many different forms, including *department stores*, *specialty retailers*, *supermarkets*, *convenience stores*, *discount retailers*, *hard discounters*, *hypermarkets*, *supercenters*, *superstores*, *shopping malls*, *outlet stores*, and *outlet malls*. Selection, price, store location, and customer service are a few of the competencies that can be used strategically to enter a new market. One way to classify retailers is by using a matrix that distinguishes companies offering few product categories with an own-label focus, many categories with an own-label focus, few categories with a manufacturer-brand focus, and many categories with a manufacturer-brand focus. Global retail expansion can be achieved via *organic growth*, *franchising*, *acquisition*, *joint venture*, and *licensing*.

Transportation and physical distribution issues are critically important in a company's value chain because of the geographical distances involved in sourcing products and serving customers in different parts of the world. A company's *supply chain* includes all the firms that perform support activities such as generating raw materials or fabricating components. *Logistics* and *logistics management* integrate the activities of all companies in a firm's value chain to ensure an efficient flow of goods through the supply chain. Important activities include *order processing*, *warehousing*, and *inventory management*. To cut costs and improve efficiency, many companies are reconfiguring their supply chains by outsourcing some or all of these activities. Six transportation modes—air, truck, water, rail, pipeline, and Internet—are widely used in global distribution. *Containerization* was a key innovation in physical distribution that facilitates *intermodal transportation*.

Discussion Questions

12-1. Explain the relationship between supply chain and logistics management.

12-2. Describe the mechanisms involved in establishing channel design and working with intermediaries.

12-3. Compare and contrast the typical channel structures for consumer products and industrial products.

12-4. Identify the various modes of transportation available to global marketers and the factors that influence the choice of the mode to utilize.

12-5. South Korean business Lotte Shopping Co. Ltd. is in 40th place in the global retail ranking. What makes it so successful?

12-6. In 2018, the global ecommerce giant Amazon made another move into the retail market in India; the Aditya Birla Group's retail chain More was acquired by Amazon and a private equity partner. Referring to Figure 12.4, what might have prompted Amazon to take this approach?

12-7. Global distribution organizations face difficult challenges, some of which can be solved by using enterprise resource planning software. What is it, and how can it help?

CASE 12-1 *continued (refer to page 393)*
Welcome to the World of Fast Fashion

So, what puts the "fast" in "fast fashion"? A behind-the-scenes peek at Zara shows how, say, a woman's winter coat can go from a designer's sketchpad to store display racks in less than one month.

The product development process begins with a designer in Spain creating a sketch that incorporates feedback from Zara's worldwide network of store managers about the latest trends (zippers? plaids? Millennial Pink?). Next, a pattern maker creates a prototype of the garment; if it's approved, a pattern is created and used to cut fabric. These steps take a total of about seven days.

Over the course of the next two weeks, pattern cutters and seamstresses physically produce the correct number of units (typically, a few thousand). It takes an additional week for the coats to be pressed; tags and labels are added, and each garment undergoes a quality inspection. The entire production lot is then transported to the company's centralized logistics center, where the items are boxed and dispatched within 48 hours. For example, orders bound for New York may be shipped by air to John F. Kennedy Airport on Long Island, and then sent by truck to various Zara stores in the metro New York area. All stores receive orders twice weekly.

As this scenario shows, one key to Zara's success has been keeping manufacturing close to its home base—if not in Spain, then in nearby Morocco, Portugal, or Turkey. Another key is flexibility; if a particular item is not selling well in one location, that inventory can be quickly shifted to another location where demand is strong. Also, production runs of even hot-selling items are limited; this helps Zara convey an air of exclusivity that translates into higher prices and fewer markdowns.

> "Think of Zara not as a brand, but as a very speedy chameleon that adapts instantly to fashion trends."[56]
>
> Anne Chrichlow, analyst, Société Générale

The production process is somewhat different at Zara's competitors. The bulk of H&M's production is ordered months ahead of time, and then shipped to warehouses. By the time an item gets to stores, however, fashion trends may have changed. Unsold stock must then be marked down for clearance, which dampens profits. The company has continued to open more brick-and-mortar stores even as the movement of consumers to online shopping gains traction.

As noted in the chapter introduction, H&M has faced other challenges in recent years. Unlike Zara, H&M's decentralized supply chain stretches to Asia, where company-approved subcontractors may redirect some orders to other factories that have not passed inspections. Such instances result in a loss of control over where products are sourced.

Uniqlo founder Tadashi Yanai has also faced challenges. After Japan's economy had suffered from more than a decade of deflation, Yanai made a strategic bet that he could raise profits by increasing prices in Uniqlo stores by 5 to 10 percent. It didn't work; as at H&M, the company had to resort to markdowns to clear out unsold inventory. In 2016, Yanai announced that Uniqlo's Japanese stores would return to "everyday low pricing." Although sales have recovered since the change in the pricing policy, the number of shoppers visiting Uniqlo stores has been falling. Taking a page from Zara's strategy book, Yanai will open a new distribution center in Japan and centralize product development in an effort to get inventory into stores more quickly.

Is Fast Fashion Sustainable?

Some observers criticize the fast-fashion business model on the grounds that it can lead to worker exploitation; that it encourages uniformity of consumption; that it feeds a culture of disposability; and that it creates waste. In addition, it breeds the perception among consumers that the prices charged by some purveyors of well-made, high-quality apparel are exorbitant ($300 Brunello Cucinelli T-shirts, anyone?).

In a 2005 book titled *The Travels of a T-Shirt in the Global Economy: An Economist Examines the Markets, Power, and Politics of World Trade*, author Pietra Rivoli examined the global apparel supply chain. Among her conclusions: While the global apparel trade has its downsides, it can also be beneficial. Elizabeth L. Cline, author of a recent book on fast fashion, frames her own critique this way:

> A half-century of competition based on low price has forced the fashion industry to cut corners on quality, construction, and detail, leaving most of us wearing very basic and crudely slapped together clothes.

Worker safety in the garment industry is a key issue in Bangladesh, which ranks as the world's number 4 clothing exporter. Bangladesh has benefited from rising wages in China that have increased the cost of manufacturing there. Indeed, approximately 80 percent of Bangladesh's export earnings comes from its network of more than 5,000 garment manufacturing operations. However, the garment industry has been roiled by a series of tragedies that have highlighted the often-dangerous conditions facing workers.

In 2010, dozens of Bangladeshis were killed in two separate fires in factories that made clothing for Western clients such as H&M, JCPenney, and Gap. In November 2012, 117 garment workers were confirmed to have died when a fire broke out at Tazreen Fashions, a clothing manufacturer in Dhaka, Bangladesh. Tazreen's clients included Walmart and other well-known global retail brands. The tragedy highlighted failures to adhere to the Bangladesh Fire and Building Safety Agreement, a contract that increasing numbers of workers, unions, and marketers have signed.

In April 2013, tragedy struck another factory in Dhaka. The death toll—most of the victims were women—ultimately came to 1,134 people. In this instance, however, fire was not the cause. Rather, the eight-story Rana Plaza building in Dhaka collapsed. The building housed garment factories that employed about 5,000 garment workers making clothing such as the Joe Fresh line for Loblaw, a Canadian retailer; Italy's Benetton was another customer.

In the aftermath of the tragedy, it was revealed that the building's owner was a local politician who had not obtained the necessary permits from Dhaka's building-safety authority. Some of the factories in the Rana Plaza building had been certified in audits conducted by the Business Social Compliance Initiative (BSCI). The BSCI was launched by the Foreign Trade Association, an agency that represents hundreds of European retailers. Its auditors were not engineers, however, and had not made recommendations regarding building safety and stability.

The response from Western retailers was swift. For example, although Walmart had forbidden its contractors from using the Tazreen factory, some of its clothing was found at the scene of the 2012 fire. Walmart has since implemented a "zero-tolerance policy" for contractors who use factories without authorization. Walmart also donated $1.6 million to provide fire-safety training to garment workers in Bangladesh.

In 2013, the owners of several global brands in the ready-made garment industry signed a five-year agreement known as the Bangladesh Accord on Fire and Safety. The purpose of the Accord was to provide factory inspections and ensure that repairs and upgrades such as fire-safety systems were being made. In 2018, H&M and Zara parent Inditex announced that the Accord would be extended for another three years.

Despite such efforts, the Workers Rights Consortium, the International Labor Organization, the Interfaith Center for Corporate Responsibility, and other groups that monitor labor issues are stepping up pressure on the companies that participate in the global garment supply chain. Too often, the activists charge, Western retailers pay lip service to concerns about factory safety; in reality, critics say, the retailers continue to focus on low prices rather than the welfare of workers. As the head of the Cambodian garment manufacturers association told the *Financial Times*, "The buyer and consumer must be willing to pay more."

The Robotics Revolution

While many labor abuses have been documented in the garment industry, it is also true that the jobs in apparel factories may be the only opportunities for employment available to some people living in developing countries. In Bangladesh alone, nearly 4 million people work in the clothing business, earning a minimum wage of about

Exhibit 12-12 Contract apparel manufacturers in India and other low-wage countries are integral to fast fashion's global supply chain. The factory shown here is "fair trade" certified, paying above-average wages and embracing sustainability practices such as using organic textiles.
Source: Joerg Boethling/Alamy Stock Photo.

Exhibit 12-13 Overproduction is a problem in the fashion industry. Sometimes, unsold merchandise ends up in landfills. India imports tons of used clothing; after processing, the majority of items are re-exported to emerging markets.

Source: Allison Joyce.

$64 per month (see Exhibit 12-12). Their jobs are not necessarily secure, however, as the industry is gradually becoming automated. Today, computerized machinery can make the same sweater for H&M or Zara that humans operating sewing machines have traditionally made. Just as advances in machine learning and artificial intelligence are making robotic inventory picking possible, so, too, can robots be trained to handle soft materials such as thread and fabric.

The upshot is that Bangladesh's garment industry is not creating enough new jobs to accommodate the country's growing labor force. As is the case in India, an estimated 1 million Bangladeshis join the work force every month. With automation threatening to take the place of low-skilled labor in the industry, many women may lose their jobs. Industry observers worry that job-retraining opportunities may not be available for these women.

Recycling and Upcycling

The myriad choices of inexpensive clothing mean that many items are donated or discarded after being worn just a few times. In many developed countries, donation bins are widely available; some

retailers, including H&M, offer discounts to shoppers who bring in donations of used clothing when they visit a store to make new purchases.

Those cast-off items find their way into a separate supply chain that winds through India and then on to Africa and other developing countries. Donations made to charity shops in the United States and elsewhere may be sold to intermediaries who bundle them into giant bales and ship them to India for recycling (see Exhibit 12-13). There, processing companies employ sorters to divide the contents of each bale into scores of different apparel categories for resale. Sometimes the sorters make valuable finds, such as vintage denim jeans or luxury brands.

Items that are damaged or stained are separated out. Some items that are in good shape can't be resold, however; this is especially true of garments that originate in the United States. The reason? In the case of men's and women's trousers, the waist sizes are often too big for customers in the rest of the world. Some items that can't be resold are broken down into rags after buttons, zippers, and other ornamentation are removed. Any remaining items are ground into fiber that can be spun into yard that is upcycled into new items.

Exhibit 12-14 Ki-Pepeo is the brainchild of Rwandan entrepreneur Priscilla Ruzibuka. After recognizing an opportunity to design and produce children's apparel locally, Ruzibuka teaches women to sew clothing and helps them become skilled tailors.
Source: JACQUES NKINZINGABO/The New York Times/Redux.

Markets Are Local, Markets Are Global

As noted in the chapter introduction, local fashion designers in India are beginning to emerge from the shadow of the global giants. A similar trend is taking shape in Rwanda, where an NGO called Fashion Hub Kigali has been established to help support designers. For example, Priscilla Ruzibuka started a label focusing on casual clothing for children (see Exhibit 12-14). Ms. Ruzibuka employs underprivileged women, some of whom suffered ill effects from the violence and genocide that occurred in Rwanda in the 1990s.

Other Rwandan designers include Muhire Patrick, an entrepreneur who established his own atelier after he couldn't find suitable attire to wear to his sister's wedding. Joselyne Umutoniwase, founder of Rwanda Clothing, creates modern African designs for both men and women. These and other designers take advantage of Made in Rwanda, a government initiative designed to support locally produced clothing and reduce the flow of imported apparel.

Discussion Questions

12-8. What is so appealing about fast-fashion brands such as H&M and Zara?

12-9. Fast fashion has been criticized on the grounds that the same "looks" are found on display racks everywhere and that the clothing itself may be poorly constructed. Do you agree?

12-10. Is the fashion industry doing enough to create sustainable supply chains? What about the issue of discarded clothing items that have never been worn or barely been worn?

Sources: Shivani Vora, "Trying to Create Many Threads That Run True," *The New York Times* (April 8, 2018), p. 10; John Emont, "Bangladesh Still Grapples with Safety Issues," *The Wall Street Journal* (March 30, 2018), p. B1; Tiffany Hsu, "How to Prevent a Racist Hoodie," *The New York Times* (March 30, 2018), pp. B1, B5; Richard Milne, "H&M Faces a New Reality in Fashion," *Financial Times* (February 9–10, 2018), p. 13; Patricia Kowsman, "A Model for Fast Fashion," *The Wall Street Journal* (December 7, 2016), pp. B1, B2; Kana Inagaki, "Uniqlo's Pricing U-Turn Pays Off," *Financial Times* (July 25, 2016), p. 14; Preetika Rana, "Indian Retailer Makes 'Fast Fashion' Local," *The Wall Street Journal* (July 22, 2016), p. B6; Eric Bellman, "Fashion Feeds a Recycling Network," *The Wall Street Journal* (June 27, 2016), pp. B1, B2; Joseph Allchin and Amy Kamzin, "Clothes Groups in Factory Safety Row," *Financial Times* (October 2, 2015), p. 16; Kate O'Keeffe, "Supply Chain Trips H&M," *The Wall Street Journal* (May 22, 2013), p. B3; Elizabeth L. Cline *"Overdressed: The Shockingly High Cost of Cheap Fashion."* Published by Portfolio/Penguin. Copyright © Elizabeth L. Cline, 2012. Wall Street Journal.

CASE 12-2
Can Walmart Crack the Retail Code in India?

Walmart, the discount retail giant whose very name can strike fear in the hearts of small-town retailers in the United States, has gone global. To reach customers around the world, the company utilizes a variety of retail formats, including discount stores, supercenters that feature a full line of groceries and general merchandise, and Sam's Club, a warehouse operation offering goods in unbroken bulk packages. As Walmart extends its reach around the globe, observers are using words such as "assault" and "invasion" to describe what it's like for a nation on which the company has fixed its sights. As the chief executive of one supplier noted, "Walmart is going to change the retailing landscape internationally exactly the same way it's done domestically."

Not surprisingly, the BRICS (Brazil, Russia, India, China, and South Africa) nations are integral to Walmart's global expansion plans. In India, for example, strict government regulations once meant that the retail market was essentially closed to foreigners, but that situation is now changing. Walmart began its foray into that country by operating a liaison office in India from which it conducted market research and lobbied Indian policymakers. India's annual retail market is worth $500 billion, and analysts expect the retail sector to grow at a rate of 7 percent over the next few years. Today, more than 90 percent of retail activity is generated by small shops, newspaper kiosks, and tea stalls (see Exhibit 12-15).

Exhibit 12-15 This Bharti-Walmart store on the outskirts of Chandigarh, India, is a wholesale supplier to India's many small shopkeepers. In 2012, India agreed to open its market to foreign retailers such as Walmart as part of an economic reform program aimed at jump-starting growth in the country's sputtering economy. The reforms mean that Walmart will be able to open retail stores.
Source: Saurabh Das/Associated Press.

Regulatory reforms passed in fall 2012 will finally allow Walmart and other foreign big-box retailers to sell directly to consumers. Yet, despite Walmart's potential to transform India's retail sector for the better, some observers have concerns about the company's presence there. Western-style, big-box retailing is anathema to many Indian activists and policymakers, who fear that Walmart will drive some of India's millions of shopkeepers out of business. Legislators are also suspicious of the company's motives—an attitude that can be traced back to the colonial era and the operations of the British East India Company. Perhaps, they fear, the foreigners will raise prices after they have driven small operators out of business.

So why does Walmart persist? Because success in India is critical to CEO Doug McMillon global marketing strategy. Confronted with saturated markets in the United States and other developed countries, McMillon understands that the company needs to establish a bigger presence and build scale in emerging markets, such as India, where modern stores make up roughly 7 percent of the country's retail industry.

Global retailers that have set their sights on India face special challenges. As noted previously in this chapter, the term *organized retail* is used to describe activity by large branded retail chains such as Woolworths, Tesco, and Walmart. Such stores currently account for only a small percentage of India's nearly $500 billion in annual retail sales.

There have been many calls for regulatory reform, and some observers believe organized retailing will grow at a rate of 30 to 35 percent in the next few years. For now, however, some members of the ruling National Congress Party are concerned about the impact of organized retail on the millions of small-scale, "mom-and-pop" stores. The vast majority of Indian retail activity is conducted in cramped stalls with approximately 50 square feet of floor space.

Modernization of the sector is inevitable, although it has been slow in coming. Until the law was changed in 2012, Walmart and other global retailers that sell multiple brands were barred from participating directly in the Indian market. In 2006, Bharti Enterprises, a local business group that operates India's largest cellular network, announced a joint-venture partnership with Walmart. However, because of restrictions in place at the time, the venture consisted of wholesale stores. When single-brand retailers such as Benetton, Nike, Pizza Hut, Reebok, and Subway first came to India, they were required to use franchising as a market-entry strategy.

The recent regulatory changes will make it easier for such companies to have a majority stake in Indian operations. Even so, the deal comes with strings attached: The government has demanded that foreign retailers invest $100 million in India, with at least half the money going to "back end" operations and infrastructure, including cold storage facilities and transportation infrastructure. For its part, the government pledged more than $4 billion in infrastructure improvements. In addition, each of India's 28 states retains the right to approve or ban foreign-owned stores.

Western retailers often have to work with local vendors to help them improve their quality. For example, when the Bharti–Walmart venture was opening its wholesale cash-and-carry supercenters that serve small retailers, it had to contend with India's poor infrastructure and inefficient supply chains, which stem from producers using outdated techniques. Produce is typically transported on open trucks, horse-drawn carts, and tractors to wholesale markets in large cities. There, it passes through the hands of traders and agents licensed by the Agriculture Produce Marketing Committee. It is then transferred to smaller markets or warehouses that are not temperature-controlled. By the time it gets to consumers, the produce has passed through as many as seven intermediaries; perhaps not surprisingly, much of it is spoiled. In fact, according to government estimates, one-third of the country's produce—worth $10 billion—spoils each year.

In India, Walmart must do much more than just set up wholesale and retail stores. For example, it is trying to transform India's agriculture sector by using its hyperefficient practices to improve productivity and speed the flow of produce and other goods. Walmart and a partner, Bayer Cropscience, are working with farmers to improve yields and quality. In addition, Walmart has begun bypassing traditional middlemen by signing up farmers and sending its own refrigerated trucks to the farms. One reason farmers like working with Walmart: The global giant pays the farmers promptly.

Meanwhile, anticipating the arrival of the global retailers, local operators in India are investing for the future. For example, Pantaloon Retail Ltd., India's largest retailer, operates the Central and Big Bazaar department store chains and Food Bazaar, a supermarket chain. Kishore Biyani, Pantaloon's chief executive, has succeeded by giving lower-middle-class shoppers a familiar retail experience: cramped stores with an environment that Western shoppers would find chaotic. Large business groups such as Reliance Industries, a petroleum refiner, and Birla Group have also entered the retail sector. Meanwhile, Hindustan Lever, the Indian unit of packaged goods giant Unilever, has launched a consultancy service to help the "mom-and-pop" retail operators become more competitive.

During his tenure as Walmart's CEO, Mike Duke was undaunted by the challenges his company faced. In his view, the Indian people are missing out on the opportunity because of supply chain inefficiencies. But he expressed faith that, over time, the process, would get worked out. Meanwhile, Duke moved ahead in other key emerging markets. In Africa, for example, Walmart spent $2.4 billion to acquire a stake in Massmart, a chain with 288 stores in South Africa and 13 other African countries. Although South Africa's population numbers only 50 million, those people have embraced shopping, and the transportation infrastructure and banking and telecommunications systems are well developed. A successful market entry in South Africa will serve as a springboard for Walmart to expand throughout the continent. Needless to say, managers at local companies that win contracts to supply the global giant are hoping that they can tag along and join the global supply chain.

Discussion Questions

12-11. What are the biggest obstacles facing Walmart and other foreign retailers in India?

12-12. Summarize some of the elements in India's political, economic, and cultural environments that can impact the market opportunity there.

12-13. Review Figure 12-4. Which quadrant of the matrix applies most directly to India? Why?

12-14. Going forward, to what degree will Walmart be required to adapt its business model in India?

Sources: Amol Sharma, "Bad Roads, Red Tape, Burly Thugs Slow Wal-Mart's Passage to India," *The Wall Street Journal* (January 12–13, 2013), pp. A1, A10; Shelly Banjo, "Japan, Ready for Wal-Mart," *The Wall Street Journal* (September 26, 2012), p. B6; Vikas Bajaj, "Skepticism and Caution Greet India's New Policy on Retailers," *The New York Times* (September 20, 2012), p. B1; Sharma, "India Revives Plan to Let in Retailers," *The Wall Street Journal* (September 15–16, 2012), p. A8; Robb M. Stewart, "Wal-Mart Checks out a New Continent," *The Wall Street Journal* (October 27, 2010), p. B1; Bajaj, "In India, Wal-Mart Goes to the Farm," *The New York Times* (April 13, 2010), p. B1; Eric Bellman and Cecilie Rohwedder, "Western Grocer Modernizes Passage to India's Markets," *The Wall Street Journal* (November 28, 2007), p. B2; Bellman, "Chaos Theory: In India, a Retailer Finds Key to Success Is Clutter," *The Wall Street Journal* (August 8, 2007), p. A8; Bellman, "India's Reliance Looks Abroad," *The Wall Street Journal* (March 16, 2007), pp. A1, A10; Jo Johnson and Jonathan Birchall, "'Mom and Pop' Stores Braced for Challenge," *Financial Times* (November 28, 2006), p. 16; Joe Leahy, "Indian Regulation Hampers Retail Growth," *Financial Times* (October 26, 2006), p. 21; Anita Jain, "The 'Crown Jewel' Sector That's Ripe for Modernization," *Financial Times Special Report—India and Globalization* (January 26, 2006), p. 16; Ann Zimmerman and Emily Nelson, "With Profits Elusive, Wal-Mart to Exit Germany," *The Wall Street Journal* (July 29/30, 2006), pp. A1, A6.

Notes

[1] Peter D. Bennett, *Dictionary of Marketing Terms* (Chicago, IL: American Marketing Association, 1988), p. 29.

[2] Nick Wingfield, "Ebay Allows Sellers to Set up Storefronts Online in Bid to Expand Beyond Auctions," *The Wall Street Journal* (June 12, 2001), p. B8.

[3] Eric Bellman, "Indonesia Serves Tasty Dish for Tupperware," *The Wall Street Journal* (April 25, 2013), p. B8.

[4] Kathy Chu, "Tupperware's Party Goes Worldwide," *The Wall Street Journal* (July 6, 2014).

[5] Terence Tsai and Shubo Liu, "Mary Kay: Developing a Salesforce in China," *Financial Times* (January 8, 2013), p. 10.

[6] Valerie Reitman, "Toyota Calling: In Japan's Car Market, Big Three Face Rivals Who Go Door-to-Door," *The Wall Street Journal* (September 28, 1994), pp. A1, A6.

[7] Yoko Kubota and Christina Rogers, "Ford to Exit Japan, Indonesia Amid Dim Prospects for Profit," *The Wall Street Journal* (January 26, 2016), p. B3.

[8] Cassell Bryan-Low and Li Yuan, "Selling Cellphone Buzz," *The Wall Street Journal* (February 23, 2006), pp. B1, B5.

[9] "Case Study: Moscow Bread Company," Andersen Consulting, 1993.

[10] Ellen Byron, "Emerging Ambitions: P&G's Global Target: Shelves of Tiny Stores," *The Wall Street Journal* (July 16, 2007), p. A1.

[11] The following discussion is adapted from David Arnold, "Seven Rules of International Distribution," *Harvard Business Review* 78, no. 6 (November–December 2000), pp. 131–137.

[12] Eric Bellman, "India's Reliance Looks Abroad," *The Wall Street Journal* (March 16, 2007), p. A8.

[13] Barney Jopson, "Consumerism for Kenya's As and Bs," *Financial Times* (July 8, 2008), p. 14.

[14] Michiyo Nakamoto, "Convenience Stores Pay Price of Success," *Financial Times Special Report—Japan* (October 14, 2008), p. 3. See also Juro Osawa, "Convenience Stores Score in Japan," *The Wall Street Journal* (August 19, 2008), p. B2.

[15] Cecilie Rohwedder, "Harvey Nichols's Foreign Affair," *The Wall Street Journal* (February 18, 2005), p. B3.

[16] Michael Flagg, "In Asia, Going to the Grocery Increasingly Means Heading for a European Retail Chain," *The Wall Street Journal* (April 24, 2001), p. A21.

[17] Kortney Stringer, "Convenience Stores Turn a New Corner," *The Wall Street Journal* (June 1, 2004), p. B5.

[18] Elena Cherney and Ann Zimmerman, "Canada's Zellers Retools Itself in Bid to Battle Walmart," *The Wall Street Journal* (December 10, 2001), p. B4.

[19] Eric Bellman, "A Dollar Store's Rich Allure in India," *The Wall Street Journal* (January 23, 2007), pp. B1, B14.

[20] Stephanie Clifford, "Where Wal-Mart Failed, Aldi Succeeds," *The New York Times* (March 30, 2011), p. B1.

[21] Heather Haddon, "Pressure on U.S. Grocers Rises," *The Wall Street Journal* (June 12, 2017), p. B1.

[22] Christina Passariello and Aaron O. Patrick, "Europe Eats on the Cheap," *The Wall Street Journal* (September 30, 2008), pp. B1, B7.

[23] Matt Moffett and Jonathan Friedland, "Walmart Won't Discount Its Prospects in Brazil, Though Its Losses Pile Up," *The Wall Street Journal* (June 4, 1996), p. A15; Wendy Zellner, "Walmart Spoken Here," *BusinessWeek* (June 23, 1997), pp. 138–139.

[24] Robb M. Stewart, "Wal-Mart Checks out a New Continent," *The Wall Street Journal* (October 27, 2010), p. B1.

[25] Stan Sesser, "The New Spot for Giant Malls: Asia," *The Wall Street Journal* (September 16/17, 2006), p. P6.

[26] Ross Davies and Megan Finney, "Retailers Rush to Capture New Markets," *Financial Times—Mastering Global Business, Part VII* (1998), pp. 2–4.

[27] Norihiko Shirouzu, "Japanese Mall Mogul Dreams of American Stores," *The Wall Street Journal* (July 30, 1997), pp. B1, B10; Norihiko Shirouzu, "Jusco Bets that U.S.-Style Retail Malls Will Revolutionize Shopping in Japan," *The Wall Street Journal* (April 21, 1997), p. A8.

[28] Ann Zimmerman, "Home Depot Chief Renovates," *The Wall Street Journal* (June 5, 2008), p. B2.

[29]Neil King, Jr., "Kmart's Czech Invasion Lurches Along," *The Wall Street Journal* (June 8, 1993), p. A11.

[30]Eric Bellman and Cecilie Rohwedder, "Western Grocer Modernizes Passage to India's Markets," *The Wall Street Journal* (November 28, 2007), p. B2.

[31]Michael J. de la Merced, "Macy's, Once a Retail Titan, Is Approached about a Buyout," The *New York Times* (February 7, 2017), p. B1.

[32]Andrea Felsted, "Reborn in the USA," *Financial Times* (June 27–28, 2015), p. 6.

[33]The discussion in this section is adapted from Jacques Horovitz and Nirmalya Kumar, "Strategies for Retail Globalization," *Financial Times—Mastering Global Business, Part VII* (1998), pp. 4–8.

[34]Scheherazade Daneshkhu, "Bricks-and-Mortar Retailers Struggle to Cope with Shift to Online Shopping," *Financial Times* (June 14, 2016), p. 19.

[35]Rufus Olins, "M&S Sets out Its Stall for World Domination," *The Sunday Times* (November 9, 1997), p. 6. See also Andrew Davidson, "The Andrew Davidson Interview: Sir Richard Greenbury," *Management Today* (November 2001), pp. 62–67; and Judi Bevan, *The Rise and Fall of Marks & Spencer* (London, UK: Profile Books, 2001).

[36]Tim Jackson, *Virgin King: Inside Richard Branson's Business Empire* (London, UK: HarperCollins, 1995), p. 277.

[37]Daniel Michaels, "No, the CEO Isn't Sir Richard Branson," *The Wall Street Journal* (July 30, 2007), pp. B1, B3.

[38]Mariko Sanchanta, "Wal-Mart Bargain Shops for Japanese Stores to Buy," *The Wall Street Journal* (November 15, 2010), p. B1.

[39]Tim Jackson, *Virgin King: Inside Richard Branson's Business Empire* (London, UK: HarperCollins, 1995), pp. 289–291.

[40]Ian Bickerton, "'It Is All about the Value Chain,'" *Financial Times* (February 24, 2006), p. 10.

[41]Lt. Col. George C. Thorpe, *Pure Logistics* (Washington, DC: National Defense University Press, 1917; 1986).

[42]Barney Jopson, "Business Diary: Keith Harrison, Procter & Gamble," *Financial Times* (March 8, 2011), p. 23.

[43]Lindsay Whipp, "Trouble in Store," *Financial Times—FT Big Read: Walmart* (April 7, 2016), p. 7.

[44]Tim Harford, *Fifty Inventions That Shaped The Modern Economy* (New York, NY: Riverhead Books, 2017).

[45]David Champion, "Mastering the Value Chain: An Interview with Mark Levin of Millennium Pharmaceuticals," *Harvard Business Review* 79, no. 6 (June 2001), pp. 108–115.

[46]Francesco Guerrera, "GE to Shift Output from U.S.," *Financial Times* (July 27, 2006), p. 27.

[47]A detailed analysis of IKEA's approach to value creation is found in Richard Normann and Rafael Ramirez, "From Value Chain to Value Constellation: Designing Interactive Strategy," *Harvard Business Review* 71, no. 4 (July–August 1993), pp. 65–77.

[48]Chad Terhune, "Supply-Chain Fix for Pepsi," *The Wall Street Journal* (June 6, 2006), p. B3.

[49]Brian Baskin, "Robots Picking, Retailers Grinning," *The Wall Street Journal* (July 24, 2017), pp. B1, B2. See also Sarah Nassauer, "Retailers Check out Automation," *The Wall Street Journal* (July 20, 2017), p. B3.

[50]Kris Maher, "Global Goods Jugglers," *The Wall Street Journal* (July 5, 2005), pp. A11, A12.

[51]Jo Ellison, "Vetements: The Gospel of Guram Gvasalia," *Financial Times* (August 3, 2017), p. 14.

[52]Joel Millman, "A Crushing Issue: How to Destroy Brand-New Cars," *The Wall Street Journal* (April 29, 2008), pp. A1, A9.

[53]For an excellent case study of the evolution of intermodal technology in the United States, see Jon R. Katzenback and Douglas K. Smith, *The Wisdom of Teams: Creating the High-Performance Organization* (New York, NY: HarperBusiness, 1994), Chapter 2.

[54]Daniel Machalaba, "Cargo Hold: As U.S. Seaports Get Busier, Weak Point Is a Surprise: Railroads," *The Wall Street Journal* (September 19, 1996), p. A1.

[55]Alexandra Harney, "Technology Takes the Wrinkles out of Textiles Manufacturing," *Financial Times* (January 11, 2006), p. 11. See also Gabriel Kahn, "Made to Measure: Invisible Supplier Has Penney's Shirts All Buttoned Up," *The Wall Street Journal* (September 11, 2003), pp. A1, A9.

[56]Patricia Kowsmann, "A Model for Fast Fashion," *The Wall Street Journal* (December 7, 2016), p. B2.

13

Global Marketing Communications Decisions I

Advertising and Public Relations

LEARNING OBJECTIVES

13-1 Define *global advertising* and identify the top-ranked companies in terms of worldwide ad spending.

13-2 Explain the structure of the advertising industry, and describe the difference between agency holding companies and individual agency brands.

13-3 Identify key ad agency personnel and describe their respective roles in creating global advertising.

13-4 Explain how media availability varies around the world.

13-5 Compare and contrast publicity and public relations and identify global companies that have recently been impacted by negative publicity.

CASE 13-1
Volkswagen's "Dieselgate" Nightmare

In May 2011, production began at Volkswagen's new $1 billion auto assembly plant in Chattanooga, Tennessee. The Passat sedans rolling off the line were a striking symbol of the German automaker's ambitious strategic goal: Volkswagen CEO Martin Winterkorn intended to overtake Toyota and become the world's number 1 automaker by 2018. The U.S. market was key to achieving the goal, and Winterkorn predicted that VW would sell 1 million cars in the United States by 2018.

VW's portfolio of brands boasts upscale nameplates such as Audi, Bentley, Bugatti, Lamborghini, and Porsche. Its mass-market brands include Skoda and SEAT, and the Volkswagen brand itself accounts for approximately 50 percent of annual revenues (see Exhibit 13-1). Volkswagen executives acknowledged that meeting the 2018 goal would require tripling the number of vehicles sold in the United States. To do that, they had design and build cars with the VW nameplate that appeal to American drivers.

Many U.S. car buyers seek eco-friendly vehicles that offer high mileage and low emissions. VW's diesel models were advertised as being "green," a selling proposition that was very attractive to American car buyers. For example, one model was called the Passat TDI (Turbocharged Direct Injection) Clean Diesel. Thanks in part to robust U.S. sales, in the first six months of 2015 VW did, in fact, outsell Toyota.

However, the good times were short-lived, as VW became embroiled in a public relations nightmare of epic proportions. In September 2015, regulators from the U.S. Environmental Protection Agency (EPA) determined that some of VW's models with two-liter diesel engines had been equipped

Exhibit 13-1 Volkswagen's 20-story "Autostadt storage tower" in Wolfsburg.
Source: John MacDougall/AFP/Getty Images/.

with special software that allowed the vehicles to pass stringent emissions tests. Subsequent tests showed that the cars' emissions of nitrous oxide (NO_x), a known pollutant, were much higher than the company claimed. Before long, it was determined that 11 million diesel cars sold worldwide had also been equipped with the so-called defeat devices. More revelations were to come, including admissions by VW officials that they had understated the carbon dioxide (CO_2) emission levels in 800,000 vehicles, including those with conventional gasoline engines.

The scandal was a public relations nightmare for the German company. Martin Winterkorn recorded a video apology in which he blamed the mistakes on "only a few." Needless to say, the video was not convincing. Winterkorn resigned, and Matthias Müller was named VW's CEO. In addition, three of the company's top engineers were suspended.

By the end of October 2015, one month after the scandal broke, it was clear that VW was caught in a perfect storm: The shrinking demand for its core VW brand was made worse by economic problems in Brazil and Russia. Concerned that the U.S. Justice Department might file criminal charges and seek penalties totaling tens of millions of dollars, investors began selling off VW stock. For more on the emissions cheating scandal and other issues, see the continuation of Case 13-1 at the end of the chapter.

The challenges facing Volkswagen in the aftermath of the emissions crisis provide a case study of the roles of advertising, public relations, and other forms of communication in the marketing program. Marketing communications—the promotion (*P*) of the marketing mix—refers to all forms of communication used by organizations to inform, remind, explain, persuade, and influence the attitudes, perceptions, and buying behavior of customers and others. The primary purpose of marketing communications is to tell customers about the benefits and values that a company, nation, product, or service offers. The elements of the promotion mix are advertising, public relations, personal selling, and sales promotion.

Global marketers can use all of these elements, either alone or in varying combinations. Volkswagen's efforts to address consumer and governmental concerns about its integrity highlight the critical importance of public relations to any entity—be it a nation or a business enterprise—that finds itself in the spotlight on the world stage. This chapter examines advertising and public relations from the perspective of the global marketer. Chapter 14 examines sales promotion, personal selling, event marketing, and sponsorships. As you study these chapters, remember: All the communication tools described here should be used in a way that reinforces a consistent message.

(13-1) Global Advertising

◀ **13-1** Define *global advertising* and identify the top-ranked companies in terms of worldwide ad spending.

The environment in which marketing communications programs and strategies are implemented varies from country to country. The challenge of effectively communicating across borders is one reason that global companies and their advertising agencies are embracing a concept known as **integrated marketing communications (IMC)**. Adherents of an IMC approach explicitly recognize that the various elements of a company's communication strategy must be carefully coordinated.[1] For example, Nike has applied the IMC concept across a variety of marketing communication channels. As Nike president Trevor Edwards noted in the mid-2000s:

> We create demand for our brand by being flexible about how we tell the story. We do not rigidly stay with one approach . . . . We have an integrated marketing model that involves all elements of the marketing mix from digital to sports marketing, from event marketing to advertising to entertainment, all sitting at the table driving ideas.[2]

Advertising is one element of an IMC program. **Advertising** is any sponsored, paid message that is communicated in a nonpersonal way, often through mass media. Some advertising messages are designed to resonate with consumers in a single country or market area. By comparison, regional or pan-regional advertising is created for audiences across several country markets, such as Europe or Latin America. **Global advertising** may be defined as messages whose art, copy, headlines, photographs, taglines, and other elements have been developed expressly for their worldwide suitability.

Companies that have used global themes include BASF ("We create chemistry"), Chevrolet ("Find new roads"), Coca-Cola ("Taste the feeling"), IBM ("Let's put smart to work"), McDonald's ("i'm lovin' it"), and Philips ("Innovation and you"). In Chapter 10, we noted that some global companies simultaneously offer local, international, and global products and brands to buyers in different parts of the world. The same is true with advertising: A global company may use single-country advertising in addition to campaigns that are regional and global in scope.

A global company possesses a critical marketing advantage with respect to marketing communications: It has the opportunity to successfully transform a domestic advertising campaign into a worldwide one. Alternatively, it can create a new global campaign from the ground up. The search for a global advertising campaign should bring together key company and ad agency personnel to share information, insights, and experience.

McDonald's "i'm lovin' it" tagline is a case in point; it was developed after global marketing chief Larry Light called a meeting of representatives from all McDonald's ad agencies. Global campaigns with unified themes can help to build long-term product and brand identities and offer significant savings by reducing the costs associated with producing ads. Regional market areas such as Europe are experiencing an influx of standardized global brands as companies position themselves for selling their products and services in a united region by making acquisitions and evaluating production plans and pricing policies. From a marketing point of view, there is a great deal of activity going on that is making brands truly pan-European. This phenomenon is accelerating the growth of global advertising.

The potential for effective global advertising also increases as companies recognize and embrace new concepts such as "product cultures." An example is the globalization of beer culture, which can be seen in the popularity of German-style beer halls in Japan and Irish-style pubs in the United States. Similarly, the globalization of coffee culture has created market opportunities for companies such as Starbucks. Marketing managers also realize that some market segments can be defined on the basis of global demography—youth culture or an emerging middle class, for example—rather than ethnic or national culture. Athletic shoes and other clothing items, for instance, can be targeted to a worldwide segment of 18- to 25-year-old males.

William Roedy, former global chairman of MTV Networks, suggests that such product cultures have clear implications for advertising. MTV is just one of the media vehicles that enable people almost anywhere to see how the rest of the world lives and to learn about the latest electronic gadgets and fashion trends. As Roedy noted in the early 1990s, "Eighteen-year-olds in Paris have more in common with 18-year-olds in New York than with their own parents. They buy the same products, go to the same movies, listen to the same music, sip the same colas. Global advertising merely works on that premise."[3]

According to data compiled by various industry groups, worldwide advertising expenditures in 2012 passed the $500 billion milestone. Because advertising is often designed to add psychological value to a product or brand, it plays a more important communications role in marketing consumer products than in marketing industrial products. Frequently purchased, low-cost products generally require heavy promotional support, which often takes the form of reminder advertising. Perhaps not surprisingly, then, consumer products companies top the list of big global advertising spenders. Procter & Gamble, Unilever, L'Oréal, and Nestlé are companies whose global scope can be inferred from the significant proportion of their advertising expenditures that are devoted to areas outside their home-country markets (see Exhibit 13-2).

Advertising Age magazine's annual ranking of global marketers in terms of advertising expenditures is shown in Table 13-1.[4] The United States is the world's top advertising market; the $176 billion that advertisers spent on major U.S. media in 2016 represents one-third of the worldwide total.

Exhibit 13-2 Procter & Gamble is the world's number 1 advertiser. One-fourth of its measured-media expenditures are allocated to the United States. (The dozen-plus categories known as measured media include television, newspaper, radio, etc.)

P&G is the top advertiser in China; overall, 25 percent of the company's measured-media spending is budgeted for the Asia-Pacific region. Europe accounts for another one-third of its measured-media expenditures; P&G is Germany's leading advertiser.

Source: Xu Ruiping/Associated Press.

Overall, emerging markets are posting solid growth numbers in terms of advertising expenditures; 2014 ad spending in Brazil totaled nearly $17 billion; Russia, $10.1 billion; India, $8 billion; China, $45.5 billion; and South Africa, $4.2 billion.[5] In fact, in 2014 China passed Japan as the world's number 2 advertising market. A close examination of Table 13-1 provides clues about the extent of a company's globalization efforts. For example, packaged-goods giants Procter & Gamble and Unilever spend significant amounts in all major world regions.

Global advertising also offers companies economies of scale in advertising as well as improved access to distribution channels. Where shelf space is at a premium, a company has to convince retailers to stock its products. A global brand supported by global advertising may be very attractive because, from the retailer's standpoint, that brand may be less likely to languish on the shelves. Landor Associates, a company specializing in brand identity and design, recently released its first-ever Global Agile Brands Study, in which the metrics included "Adaptive," "Principled," and "Global." Topping the ranking was Samsung; arch-rival Apple came in at number 6. However, standardization is not always required or even advised. Nestlé's Nescafé coffee is marketed as a global brand, even though advertising messages and product formulation vary to suit cultural differences.

Global Advertising Content: Standardization versus Adaptation

Communication experts generally agree that the overall requirements of effective communication and persuasion are fixed and do not vary from country to country. The same is true of the components of the communication process: The marketer is the source of the message; the message must be encoded, conveyed via the appropriate channel(s), and decoded by a member of the target audience. Communication takes place only when the intended meaning transfers from the source to the receiver. Four major difficulties can compromise an organization's attempt to communicate with customers in any location:

1. The message may not get through to the intended recipient. This problem may result from an advertiser's lack of knowledge about the appropriate media category or media vehicle for reaching certain types of audiences.
2. The message may reach the target audience but not be understood or even be misunderstood. This difficulty may reflect an inadequate understanding of the target audience's level of sophistication or improper encoding.
3. The message may reach the target audience and may be understood but still may not compel the recipient to take action. This problem could result from a lack of cultural knowledge about a target audience.

TABLE 13-1 Top 25 Global Marketers by Worldwide Total Ad Spending and Measured Media Spending in Selected Regions, 2016 ($ millions)

Company/Headquarters	Worldwide†	United States*	Asia and Pacific*	Europe*	Latin America*
1. Procter & Gamble (U.S.)	$10,45	$2,489	$2,36	$3,56	$413
2. Samsung Electronics (South Korea)	9,901	774	444	755	63
3. Nestlé (Switzerland)	9,228	722	577	1,380	134
4. Unilever (U.K., Netherlands)	8,559	866	2,386	1,758	560
5. L'Oréal (France)	8,302	1,288	540	2,029	143
6. Volkswagen (Germany)	6,735	652	189	2,453	99
7. Comcast Corp. (U.S.)	6,114	1,726	24	213	4
8. Anheuser-Busch InBev (Belgium)	5,933	718	61	140	202
9. General Motors Corp. (U.S.)	5,300	1,807	65	190	164
10. Daimler (Germany)	5,090	391	30	656	0
11. Amazon.com (U.S.)	5,000	921	142	607	0
12. LVMH (France)	4,696	392	96	563	0
13. Ford Motor Co. (U.S.)	4,300	1,250	132	909	**72**
14. Toyota Motor Corp. (Japan)	4,151	1,194	1,370	709	117
15. Coca-Cola Co. (U.S.)	4,004	551	1,424	1,024	240
16. Fiat Chrysler (U.K.)	3,938	1,087	25	1,035	124
17. Alphabet (Google) (U.S.)	3,868	406	234	128	0
18. Priceline (U.S.)	3,775	415	14	2.3	0
19. AT&T (U.S.)	3,768	1,592	0	0	48
20. American Express (U.S.)	3,650	469	28	58	0
21. Mars Inc. (U.S.)	3,500	710	568	725	4.5
22. McDonald's (U.S.)	3,400	774	378	780	94
23. Sony Corp. (Japan)	3,365	518	1,100	395	13
24. Bayer (Germany)	3,288	675	35	421	66
25. Pfizer (U.S.)	3,200	1,750	297	304	63

†Figures reflect total advertising spending.
*Figures reflect measured media spending by region.
Source: Adapted from "World's Largest Advertisers 2017," *Advertising Age* (December 4, 2017), p. 9. http://adage.com/datacenter/globalmarketers2017. Accessed December 1, 2017.

4. The effectiveness of the message may be impaired by noise. *Noise*, in this case, is an external influence, such as competitive advertising, other sales personnel, or confusion at the receiving end, that can detract from the ultimate effectiveness of the communication.

The key question for global marketers is whether the *specific* advertising message and media strategy must be changed from region to region or from country to country because of environmental requirements. Proponents of the "one world, one voice" approach to global advertising believe that the era of the global village has arrived and that tastes and preferences are converging worldwide. According to this standardization argument, people everywhere want the same products for the same reasons. This means that companies can achieve significant economies of scale by unifying advertising around the globe.

Advertisers who prefer the localized approach are skeptical of the global village argument. Instead, they assert that consumers still differ from country to country and must be reached by advertising tailored to their respective countries. Proponents of localization point out that most marketing communication blunders occur because advertisers have failed to understand—and adapt to—foreign cultures. Ad industry veteran Nick Brien is currently CEO of Dentsu Aegis Network Americas and U.S. As Brien observed in the late 1990s, the local/global debate does not necessarily have to be framed as an "either/or" proposition:

> As the potency of traditional media declines on a daily basis, brand building locally becomes more costly and international brand building becomes more cost-effective. The challenge for advertisers and agencies is finding ads that work in different countries and cultures. At the same time as this global tendency, there is a growing local tendency. It's becoming increasingly important to understand the requirements of both.[6]

Nils Larsson, an external communications executive at IKEA, echoes Brien's view, but leans more toward the localized side of the debate:

> If we could find one message on a global basis it could be effective, but so far there are different needs in different countries. We have been in Sweden for 60 years and in China for only 4 or 5, so our feeling is that retail is local. It is important to take advantage of local humor, and the things on people's minds.[7]

And consider this quote from Michael Conrad, former chief creative officer at Leo Burnett Worldwide:

> I can think of very few truly global ads that work. Brands are often at different stages around the world, and that means there are different advertising jobs to do.[8]

During the 1950s, the widespread opinion among advertising professionals was that effective international advertising required assigning responsibility for campaign preparation to a local agency. In the early 1960s, this idea of local delegation was challenged repeatedly. For example, Eric Elinder, head of a Swedish advertising agency, wrote: "Why should three artists in three different countries sit drawing the same electric iron and three copywriters write about what, after all, is largely the same copy for the same iron?"[9] Elinder argued that consumer differences among countries were diminishing and that he would more effectively serve a client's interest by putting top specialists to work devising a strong international campaign. The campaign would then be presented with insignificant modifications that mainly entailed translating the copy into language well suited for a particular country.

The "standardized versus localized" debate picked up tremendous momentum after the 1983 publication, noted in earlier chapters, of Professor Ted Levitt's *Harvard Business Review* article "The Globalization of Markets." Recently, global companies have embraced a technique known as **pattern advertising**, which is analogous to the concept of global product platforms discussed in Chapter 10. Representing a middle ground between 100 percent standardization and 100 percent adaptation, a pattern strategy calls for developing a basic pan-regional or global communication concept for which copy, artwork, or other elements can be adapted as required for individual country markets (see Exhibit 13-3). For example, ads in a European print campaign for Boeing shared basic design elements, but the copy and the visual elements were localized on a country-by-country basis.

Much of the research on this issue has focused on the match between advertising messages and local culture. Researcher Ali Kanso surveyed two different groups of advertising managers, those adopting localized approaches to advertising and those adopting standardized approaches. One finding was that managers who are attuned to cultural issues tend to prefer the localized approach, whereas managers who are less sensitive to cultural issues prefer a standardized approach.[10] When Bruce Steinberg was ad sales director for MTV Europe, he discovered that the people responsible for executing global campaigns locally often exhibit strong resistance to a global campaign. Steinberg reported that he sometimes had to visit as many as 20 marketing directors from the same company to get approval for a pan-European MTV ad.[11]

Exhibit 13-3 These print ads from U.K.-based TwoSides advocate for sustainable use of paper for printing magazines and books. The ads are a textbook example of pattern advertising. Overall, the layouts are consistent. The dominant visual elements are similar, but the references to a football pitch in the U.K. version and to a football field for the U.S. version are talking about two different sports. The subheads and body copy have been localized.
Source: TwoSides.

As Kanso correctly notes, the long-standing debate over advertising approaches will probably continue for years to come. Kanso's conclusion: What is needed for successful international advertising is a global commitment to local vision. In the final analysis, the decision of whether to use a global or a localized campaign depends on recognition by managers of the trade-offs involved. A global campaign will result in the substantial benefits of cost savings, increased control, and the potential creative leverage of a global **appeal**. It is also true that localized campaigns can focus on the most important attributes of a product or brand in each nation or culture.

As a practical matter, marketing managers may choose to run *both* global *and* local ads rather than adopt an "either/or" stance. For example, marketing and advertising managers at DuPont Pioneer frequently use both global and localized advertising executions. It is management's belief that some messages lend themselves to straight translation, whereas others need to be created in a way that best suits the farmers, marketplace, and style of the particular country or region.

The question of *when* to use each approach depends on the product involved and a company's objectives in a particular market. The following generalizations can serve as guidelines:

- Standardized print campaigns can be used for industrial products or for high-tech consumer products. Examples: Apple's iPhone and iPad.
- Standardized print campaigns with a strong visual appeal often travel well. Example: Johnny Walker Scotch ("Keep Walking"). Similarly, no text appears in the assembly

instructions for IKEA furniture. Picture-based instructions can be used throughout the world without translation.

• TV commercials that use voice-overs instead of actors or celebrity endorsers speaking dialogue can use standardized visuals with translated copy for the voice-over. Examples: Gillette ("The best a man can get"); GE ("Imagination at work"); UPS ("We ♥ Logistics").

(13-2) Advertising Agencies: Organizations and Brands

◀ **13-2** Explain the structure of the advertising industry, and describe the difference between agency holding companies and individual agency brands.

Advertising is a fast-paced business, and the ad agency world is fluid and dynamic. New agencies are formed, existing agencies are dismantled, and cross-border investments, spin-offs, joint ventures, and mergers and acquisitions are a fact of life. The industry is also very mobile, and executives and top talent move from one agency to another. The 20 largest global **advertising organizations** ranked by 2016 worldwide revenue are shown in Table 13-2. As you can see, there is considerable geographic diversity; agency companies can be found in China, France, Great Britain, Japan, and elsewhere (see Exhibit 13-4)

The key to understanding the table is the word *organization*; most of the firms identified in Table 13-2 are umbrella corporations or holding companies that include one or more "core" advertising agencies, as well as units specializing in direct marketing, marketing services, public

TABLE 13-2 The World's Largest Agency Companies

Organization (Headquarters)	Worldwide Revenues 2016 ($ millions)
1. WPP Group (London)	$19,379
2. Omnicom Group (New York)	15,417
3. Publicis Groupe (Paris)	10,765
4. Interpublic Group of Cos. (New York)	7,847
5. Dentsu Inc. (Tokyo)	7,246
6. Accenture's Accenture Interactive (New York)	4,412
7. PwC's PwC Digital Services (New York)	3,267
8. IBM Corp.'s IBM iX (Armonk, NY)	2,954
9. Deloitte's Deloitte Digital (New York)	2,575
10. Havas (Puteaux, France)	2,520
11. Hakuhodo DY Holdings (Tokyo)	2,205
12. Alliance Data Systems Corp.'s Epsilon (Irving, Texas)	2,155
13. BlueFocus Communication Group (Beijing)	1,872
14. MDC Partners (New York)	1,386
15. DJE Holdings (Chicago)	934
16. Acxiom Corp. (Little Rock, Arkansas)	873
17. Cheil Worldwide (Seoul, South Korea)	859
18. Experian's Experian Marketing Services (New York)	720
19. Advantage Solutions' Advantage Marketing Partners (Irvine, California)	640
20. MC Group (Media Consulta; Berlin)	583

Source: Adapted from "Agency Report 2017: Agency Companies," *Advertising Age* (May 1, 2017), p. 22.

Exhibit 13-4 Mercedes Erra is executive chairman of France's Havas Worldwide. Highly regarded by industry insiders for her insight and ingenuity, Erra has created memorable advertising for Danone, Evian, and Air France.
Source: Eric Fougere/Corbis via Getty Images.

relations, or research. A close inspection of the table reveals that IBM has gotten into the advertising business. Not surprisingly, IBM iX (ranked eighth in the world) is a digital specialist.

In 2013, the announcement of a planned merger between Omnicom and Publicis rocked the advertising world. The deal would have propelled the new entity past WPP and made it the world's largest advertising holding company. Both organizations, in turn, own several global agency networks whose clients represent a veritable "who's who" of global companies.

For example, Omnicom is home to DDB Worldwide, DDBO Worldwide, and TBWA Worldwide; its client roster includes Johnson & Johnson, Nissan, and Volkswagen. Key Publicis networks include Bartle Bogle Hegarty, Leo Burnett Worldwide, Publicis Worldwide, and Saatchi & Saatchi; L'Oréal, Unilever, and Nestlé are clients. In the end, however, the deal fell through, and currently Omnicom is searching for a mid-sized acquisition.

Table 13-3 presents the rankings of individual agencies (agency "brands") by 2016 worldwide revenue. Most of the agency brands identified in Table 13-3 are *full-service agencies*: In addition to creating advertising, they provide other services, such as market research, media buying, and direct marketing. The agencies listed in Table 13-3 are all owned by larger corporations (e.g., IBM iX) or by advertising holding companies (e.g., Young and Rubicam is owned by WPP).

Selecting an Advertising Agency in the Era of Digital Disruption

Companies can perform some advertising functions in-house, use one or more outside agencies, or combine both approaches. The advantages of using in-house marketing and advertising staffs for creative work or media planning can include greater control, superior product and brand knowledge, and lower cost. Boeing, Coca-Cola, Lego, and Nestlé are some of the global companies that rely on in-house talent for at least some of their marketing communications. When outside agencies are used, they can serve accounts on a multicountry or even global basis. It is possible to select a different local agency in each national market or a global agency with both domestic and international offices.

Sometimes, multiple agencies collaborate on a given account. For example, in 2007, Ford Motor Company created a consortium of five different agencies to work together in Detroit on the Ford account for the United States, Canada, and Mexico. J. Walter Thompson, Mindshare, Ogilvy & Mather Worldwide, Wunderman, and Young & Rubicam are all units of WPP. In 2010, three other WPP agencies—Mindshare, Ogilvy & Mather, and Wunderman—formed a European agency named Blue Hive that was styled after Team Detroit. In 2016, Team Detroit, Blue Hive,

TABLE 13-3 The World's Largest Consolidated Agency Networks

Agency	Estimated Worldwide Revenues 2016 ($ millions)
1. Accenture Interactive (Accenture)	$4,412
2. Young & Rubicam Group (WPP)	3,627
3. PwC Digital Services (PwC)	3,267
4. McCann Worldgroup (Interpublic Group)	3,193
5. IBM iX (IBM Corp.)	2,954
6. BBDO Worldwide (Omnicom Group)	2,577
7. Deloitte Digital (Deloitte)	2,575
8. Publicis.Sapient (Publicis Group)	2,402
9. Dentsu (Dentsu)	2,381
10. DDB Worldwide Communications Group (Omnicom)	2,338

Source: Adapted from "Agency Report 2017: Consolidated Networks," *Advertising Age* (May 1, 2017), p. 22.

and a third unit, Retail First, were brought together as GTB ("Global Team Blue"); the new entity provides Ford and other clients with unified global services.[12]

The digital revolution that is disrupting a wide range of industries is having an impact on the advertising business as well. Global companies such as McDonald's and Unilever are seeking new agency partners that offer digital expertise. The traditional world of the advertising agency—including approaches to advertising creativity, long-standing communication channels, and media-buying processes—is being upended as clients seek to leverage "big data" and take advantage of social media opportunities to improve segmentation and targeting strategies.

In response to the changing environment, WPP, Omnicom, Publicis, and other advertising holding companies are snapping up digital-marketing agencies and other tech specialists. One challenge facing top management in these companies is bridging the cultural divide between staff "creatives" and newer hires from the tech world.[14]

Google and Facebook now account for more than three-fourths of new online ad spending, and Snapchat is gaining traction as an advertising forum. In the United States, digital media are on track to surpass television as the biggest source of advertising revenues. It is not surprising, then, that print advertising revenues are dropping in key markets such as the United States and the United Kingdom, as print advertising budgets are shifted to digital media. As is clear from Exhibit 13-5, this state of affairs has prompted industry groups to promote the value of print-based media. Moreover, the MPA (formerly known as the Magazine Publishers Association) is promoting the value of real news from trusted print sources at a time when "fake news" is proliferating in social media.

With these changes and challenges in mind, the following are some considerations that come into play when an advertiser selects an advertising agency:

- *Company organization.* Companies that are decentralized typically allow managers at the local subsidiary to make ad agency selection decisions.
- *National responsiveness.* Is the global agency familiar with the local culture and buying habits in a particular country, or should a local agency be hired?
- *Area coverage.* Does the candidate agency cover all relevant markets?
- *Buyer perception.* Which kind of brand awareness does the company want to project? If the product needs a strong local identification, it would be best to select a national agency.
- *Digital expertise.* Does the agency have in-house computer engineering and coding talent with a proven ability to work with staff from traditional functions such as creative services and account services?

Despite an unmistakable trend toward using global agencies to support global marketing efforts, companies with geocentric orientations tend to adapt to the global market requirements

"Even in the digital era, there will always be two things that differentiate agencies from other players: the ability to understand consumers and to identify the levers that can change behavior, and the capacity to translate this intelligence into strategic and creative achievements."[13]

Mercedes Erra, Executive President, Havas Worldwide

Exhibit 13-5 In an effort to push back against social media platforms where fake news has proliferated, more than 100 magazines participated in an advertising campaign designed to raise awareness for the credible and trust-worthy editorial environment that print media provide.

Source: MPA—The Association of Magazine Media.

and select the best agency or agencies accordingly. Western agencies still find markets such as China and Japan to be very complex; Asian agencies find it just as difficult to establish a local agency presence in Western markets. One notable exception is Japan's Dentsu Inc; the Dentsu Aegis Network extends beyond Asia to North America and Europe.[15]

Advertising professionals face escalating pressure to balance the desire for creative freedom with emerging data-driven approaches. Some critics of advertising complain that agencies sometimes try to create advertising that will win awards and generate acclaim and prestige rather than advertising that serves clients' needs. Meanwhile, agency creatives are finding themselves at odds with digital talent who may be more attuned to building brands via social media than going "on location" to film a TV campaign.

The search for fresh answers to promotion challenges has prompted some client companies to look to new sources for creative ideas. For example, McDonald's historically relied on American agencies for basic creative direction. However, when Larry Light was McDonald's global marketing chief, he staged a competition that included agencies from all over the world. A German agency devised the "i'm lovin' it" tagline.[16] Leo Burnett China's ideas included a

THE CULTURAL CONTEXT

Smokers Fume about Limits on Tobacco Advertising

According to the World Health Organization (WHO), 5 million people die each year as a direct result of consuming tobacco products. A total of 172 countries are signatories to the Framework Convention on Tobacco Control (WHO FCTC), which aims to reduce global tobacco production as well as the consumption of tobacco products. The treaty entered into force in February 2005.

Even before the WHO FCTC, policymakers in various countries had taken steps to reduce the extent to which tobacco companies could promote their products and brands. In China, tobacco advertising has been banned from television and radio since 1994; the ban also extends to newspaper, magazine, and cinema ads.

With a population of 1.3 billion people, including one-third of the world's smokers, China is a massive potential market for cigarette manufacturers at a time when Western markets are shrinking. The ban was part of China's first law regulating advertisements. WHO asked Chinese leaders to launch antismoking campaigns and impose tougher controls on cigarette smuggling and higher taxes on domestic cigarette producers. China agreed to ratify the WHO FCTC. On June 1, 2015, a stronger antismoking law took effect in China, which prohibits smoking in all indoor public spaces as well as in schools and maternal health facilities.

With 100 million smokers, India ranks number 2 in the world in terms of number of smokers. A report by India's Ministry of Health and Family Welfare puts the annual economic cost of tobacco use at nearly $25 billion. In 2009, the government introduced a rule that health warnings had to cover 40 percent of the front of each cigarette pack. Effective April 2016, the government revised the law, mandating that graphic labels cover 85 percent of each cigarette pack. However, most of India smokers buy a cheaper product known as the *bidi*. Packs of *bidi* are taxed at a much lower rate than regular cigarettes, and warning labels have to appear on only one side of each pack.

The European Union (EU) spends approximately €16 million ($21 million) annually on antismoking initiatives. A tobacco ad ban proposal was introduced in mid-1991 with the aim of fulfilling the single-market rules of the Maastricht Treaty. This directive would have prohibited tobacco advertising on billboards as of July 2001; newspaper and magazine advertising was slated to end by 2002, with sports sponsorship banned by 2003 (such "world-level" sports as Formula One racing would be excluded until 2006). Not surprisingly, tobacco companies and advertising associations opposed the proposed ban. The European Commission justified the directive on the grounds that various countries had, or were considering, restrictions on tobacco advertising and that there was a need for common rules on cross-border trade. In 2012, the European Union was set to revise tobacco regulations; among the proposals was the introduction of plain packaging.

In December 2012, Australia implemented some of the world's most stringent antismoking regulations. Measures included a ban on brand logos and prominent placement of graphic photographic images of smoking-related illnesses and disfigurement on cigarette packs. Uniform packaging is required for all brands, although brand names can still appear in a standard typeface (see Exhibit 13-6).

In May 2015, government officials in the United Kingdom were set to vote on similar legislation. In response, Hands Off Our Packs, an activist group supported by the tobacco industry, encouraged smokers and nonsmokers who are "sick of being patronized by the tobacco control industry" to contact government policymakers and urge them to oppose the packaging regulations.

In November 2017, a new antismoking marketing campaign debuted in the United States. Media buys include print and television; the corrective ads acknowledge that tobacco products are addictive. The ads, which were mandated by a 1999 lawsuit brought by the U.S. Department of Justice, are being paid for by Altria Group and British American Tobacco. Critics point out that the Millennials—the intended audience for the campaign—do not watch prime-time TV and do not read newspapers. According to this view, the campaign's reach is likely to be limited because it does not extend to social media.

Sources: Jo Craven McGinty, "New Tobacco Ads Aren't Likely to Go Viral," *The Wall Street Journal* (November 18–19, 2017), p. A2; Preetika Rana, "Cigarette Output Halts in India," *The Wall Street Journal* (April 14, 2016), p. B8; "India's Real and Deadly Tobacco Problem," Editorial, *Bloomberg Businessweek* (April 4, 2016), p. 10; Peter Evans, "Cigarette Branding under Fire in U.K.," *The Wall Street Journal* (January 23, 2015), p. B3; Christopher Thompson and Neil Hume, "Big Tobacco Prepares for Plain Packaging," *Financial Times* (February 15, 2012), p. 15; Cailainn Barr, "Cigarette Factories Suck in €1.5 Million of Funds," *Financial Times* (December 2, 2010), p. 8; Rita Rubin, "Smoking Warnings More Graphic Elsewhere," *USA Today* (December 9, 2010), p. 13A; Farai Mutsaka, "Zimbabwe Enemies United on Tobacco," *The Wall Street Journal* (November 13–14, 2010), p. A8; Hugh Williamson, "Germany to Stub out Most Tobacco Adverts," *Financial Times* (June 13, 2006), p. 17; Geoffrey A. Fowler, "Treaty May Stub out Cigarette Ads in China," *The Wall Street Journal* (December 2, 2003), pp. B1, B6.

Exhibit 13-6 Plain-packaging regulations such as those proposed in the United Kingdom and Australia would erode tobacco companies' efforts to differentiate their respective brands.
Source: Rodger Tamblyn/Alamy Stock Photo.

hand signal for the McDonald's global campaign. As Light noted, "China just blew our minds. We didn't expect that kind of expression and joy. Our expectation was for more conservatism, much less individuality, and more caution."[17]

In 2016, McDonald's pulled much of its advertising business from Leo Burnett (which is a unit of Publicis Groupe) and transferred it to Omnicom. The reason? Omnicom had partnered with both Facebook and Google to form an integrated team of creative experts and data scientists. The new unit, known as We Are Unlimited, is based in Chicago. Despite losing the account, Leo Burnett did get a consolation prize: Its London office will handle global marketing communications for McDonald's new McDelivery service.

▶ **13-3** Identify key ad agency personnel and describe their respective roles in creating global advertising.

(13-3) Creating Global Advertising

As suggested earlier in the discussion of the adaptation versus standardization debate, the *message* is at the heart of advertising. What an advertising message says, and the way it is presented, will depend on the advertiser's objective. Is the ad designed to inform, entertain, remind, or persuade? Moreover, in a world characterized by information overload and multitasking, ads must break through the clutter, grab the audience's attention, and linger in their minds. This requires developing an original and effective **creative strategy**, which is simply a statement or concept of what a particular message or campaign will say.

Advertising agencies can be thought of as "idea factories"; in industry parlance, the Holy Grail in creative strategy development is something known as the **big idea**. Legendary ad man John O'Toole defined the *big idea* as "that flash of insight that synthesizes the purpose of the strategy, joins the product benefit with consumer desire in a fresh, involving way, brings the subject to life, and makes the reader or audience stop, look, and listen."[18] In his book about Subaru of America, Randall Rothenberg describes the big idea in the following way:

> The Big Idea is easier to illustrate than define, and easier to illustrate by what it is not than by what it is. It is not a "position" (although the place a product occupies in the consumer's mind may be a part of it). It is not an "execution" (although the writing or graphic style of an ad certainly contributes to it). It is not a slogan (although a tagline may encapsulate it).
>
> The Big Idea is the bridge between an advertising strategy, temporal and worldly, and an image, powerful and lasting. The theory of the Big Idea assumes that average consumers are at best bored and more likely irrational when it comes to deciding what to buy.[19]

Some of the world's most memorable advertising campaigns have achieved success because they originated from an idea that was so big that the campaign offered opportunities for a seemingly unlimited number of new executions. Such a campaign is said to have *legs* because it can be used for long periods of time. The print campaign for Absolut Vodka is a perfect example: Over the course of two decades, Absolut's agency created hundreds of two-word puns on the brand name linked with various pictorial renderings of the distinctive bottle shape. Other campaigns based on big ideas include Nike ("Just do it") and MasterCard ("There are some things in life money can't buy"). In 2003, McDonald's executives launched a search for an idea big enough to be used in multiple country markets even as the company faced disapproval in some countries from consumers who linked it to unpopular U.S. government policies (see Case 1-2 in Chapter 1).

The **advertising appeal** is the communications approach that relates to the motives of the target audience. Ads based on a **rational appeal** depend on logic and speak to the audience's intellect. Rational appeals are based on consumers' needs for information, and typically contain a great deal of copy. Prescription pharmaceuticals and financial services are two examples of this approach.

By contrast, ads using an **emotional appeal** may tug at the heartstrings or tickle the funny bone of the intended audience and evoke an emotional response that will reinforce brand attitudes and direct purchase behavior. For example, a global campaign for IKEA, the Swedish home furnishings retailer, positioned houses as homes: "It's a place for love . . . a place for memories . . . a place for laughter. Home is the most important place in the world."[20]

Or, consider the advertising tagline that the Minneapolis, Minnesota–based Carmichael Lynch agency developed for Subaru. "Love—it's what makes a Subaru, a Subaru," omits any reference to the auto brand's most salient functional attribute—namely, its dependable Symmetrical AWD (all-wheel drive) system. Plus, who can forget Subaru's "Puppy Bowl" ads that tied in to Super Bowl Sunday? And, of course, Subaru vehicles play a prominent role in the cable television comedy *Portlandia*.[21]

The message elements in a particular ad will depend, in part, on which appeal is being employed. The **selling proposition** is the promise or claim that captures the reason for buying the product or the benefit that ownership confers. Because products are frequently at different stages in their life cycles in various national markets, and because of cultural, social, and economic differences that exist in those markets, the most effective appeal or selling proposition for a product may vary from market to market.

Effective global advertising may also require developing different presentations of the product's appeal or selling proposition. The way an appeal or proposition is presented is called the **creative execution**. In other words, there can be differences between *what* one says and *how* one says it. Ad agency personnel can choose from a variety of executions, including straight sell, scientific evidence, demonstration, comparison, testimonial, slice of life, animation, fantasy, and dramatization. The responsibility for deciding on the appeal, the selling proposition, and the appropriate execution lies with **creatives**, a term that applies to art directors and copywriters.

Art Direction and Art Directors

The visual presentation of an advertisement—the "body language"—is a matter of **art direction**. The individual with general responsibility for the overall look of an ad is the **art director**. This person typically has a staff who choose graphics, images, type styles, and other visual elements that appear in an ad. Some forms of visual presentation are universally understood; others speak to specific demographics. In either case, the way information is presented shapes the way that it is perceived.

For example, the IBM logo, designed by legendary graphic artist and art director Paul Rand, conveys a sense of modernism and corporate stability. The logo design of Monster energy drink is perfectly aligned with the brand's target demographic of youthful "experiencers."[22] In 2017, when *Advertising Age* magazine was rebranded as *Ad Age*, the company commissioned a new logo to signify reinvention at a time of seismic industry change. Interest in typography has also been fueled by the recent success of the Netflix paranormal series *Stranger Things* with its now-iconic glowing red logo.

The global advertiser must make sure that visual executions are not extended inappropriately into certain markets. In the mid-1990s, Benetton's United Colors of Benetton campaign generated considerable controversy. The campaign appeared in scores of countries, primarily in print and on billboards. The art direction focused on striking, provocative interracial juxtapositions—images such as a white hand and a black hand handcuffed together. Another version of the campaign, depicting a black woman nursing a white baby, won advertising awards in France and Italy. However, because the image evoked the history of slavery in the United States, that particular creative execution was not used in the U.S. market.[23]

Copy and Copywriters

The words that are the spoken in broadcast advertising or that constitute the written communication elements in advertisements are known as **copy**. **Copywriters** are language specialists who develop the headlines, subheads, and body copy used in print advertising and the scripts containing the words that are delivered by spokespeople, actors, or hired voice talents in broadcast ads.

As a general rule, copy should be relatively short and should avoid slang and idioms. Languages vary in terms of the number of words required to convey a given message—thus the increased use of pictures and illustrations. One straightforward approach to copywriting is to find a way to incorporate the brand's name into an advertising slogan. That's the approach Illy uses for its coffee ("Live Happ*illy*"). The "I Feel **Slove**nia" national branding campaign mentioned in Chapter 10 cleverly capitalizes on the fact that the four-letter sequence "love" is part of the country name!

Some global ads feature visual appeals that convey a specific message with minimal use of copy. The low literacy rates in many countries seriously compromise the use of print as a communications device and require greater creativity in the use of audio-oriented media.

In many areas of the world, certain languages are used in multiple countries (e.g., the European Union, Latin America, and North America). Capitalizing on this fact, global advertisers can realize economies of scale by producing advertising copy with the same language and message for these markets. The success of this approach will depend in part on avoiding unintended ambiguity in the ad copy. Then again, in some situations, ad copy must be translated into the local language. Translating copy has been the subject of great debate in advertising circles. Advertising slogans often present the most difficult translation problems. The challenge of encoding and decoding slogans and taglines in different national and cultural contexts can lead to unintentional errors. For example, the Asian version of Pepsi's "Come alive" tagline was rendered as a call to bring ancestors back from the grave.

Advertising executives may elect to prepare new copy for a foreign market in the language of the target country or to translate the original copy into the target language. A third option is to leave some (or all) copy elements in the original (home-country) language. In choosing one of these alternatives, the advertiser must consider whether the intended foreign audience will be able to receive and comprehend a translated message. Anyone with knowledge of two or more languages realizes that the ability to think in another language facilitates accurate communication. For a message to be understood correctly after it is received, a person must understand the connotations of words, phrases, and sentence structures, as well as their translated meaning.

The same principle applies to advertising—perhaps to an even greater degree. A copywriter who can think in the target language and understands the consumers in the target country will be able to create the most effective appeals, organize the ideas, and craft the specific language, especially if colloquialisms, idioms, or humor are involved. For example, in southern China, McDonald's is careful not to advertise prices with multiple occurrences of the number four. The reason is simple: In Cantonese, the pronunciation of the word *four* is similar to that of the word *death*.[24] In its efforts to develop a global brand image, Citicorp discovered that translations of its slogan "Citi never sleeps" conveyed that Citibank had a sleeping disorder such as insomnia. Company executives decided to retain the slogan but use English throughout the world.[25]

Additional Cultural Considerations

Knowledge of cultural diversity, especially the symbolism associated with cultural traits, is essential for creating advertising. Local country managers can share important information, such as when to use caution in advertising creativity. Use of colors and man–woman relationships can often be stumbling blocks. For example, in Japan intimate scenes between men and women are in bad taste; they are outlawed in Saudi Arabia. Veteran adman John O'Toole offers the following insights to global advertisers:

> Transplanted American creative people always want to photograph European men kissing women's hands. But they seldom know that the nose must never touch the hand or that this rite is reserved solely for married women. And how do you know that the woman in the photograph is married? By the ring on her left hand, of course. Well, in Spain, Denmark, Holland, and Germany, Catholic women wear the wedding ring on the right hand.

ENTREPRENEURIAL LEADERSHIP, CREATIVE THINKING, AND THE GLOBAL STARTUP

Evan Sharp, Paul Sciarra, and Ben Silbermann: Pinterest

Ben Silbermann is an entrepreneur. Silbermann, along with Paul Sciarra and Evan Sharp, created a new product and started a company to market it (see Exhibit 13-7). Pinterest is a visual-search image-sharing site that allows users to post ("pin") photos that are interesting to them. Users can customize boards any way they like and share them with others, both publicly and privately. In the company's own words, Pinterest is "the world's catalog of ideas." Food and style are among the most popular categories of images shared on the Pinterest forum.

As is true with many entrepreneurs, Silbermann's creation grew out of his own childhood experience collecting various things, especially insects. Silbermann himself acknowledges that a propensity for collecting is "kind of dorky." Even so, his passion resulted in a key insight: The things a person collects say a great deal about him or her. The core motivation of Pinterest users is different from those of social media users on other sites, says Silbermann. What compels Pinterest users is the desire to "Let me find ideas for myself that serve for inspiration for where I want to take my life."

Pinterest was launched in March 2010. By September 2015, Pinterest's user base passed the 100 million mark. One year later, the company announced that 150 million people used the service at least once each month. By fall 2017, that number had increased to 200 million.

More than half the service's users ("Pinners") are outside the United States. Silbermann attributes the strong growth in part to the company's efforts to recruit users in key regions such as Western Europe, including France, Germany, and the United Kingdom, plus Brazil and Japan. Another growth driver has been increased mobile phone usage by Pinners.

Roughly two-thirds of Pinners are female. Until recently Pinterest's business model was geared toward attracting big-name advertisers including retailers and consumer-products companies hoping to reach women. Some advertisers are drawn by attractive marketing analytics: Pinterest users typically have a much higher "intent to buy" than users of social media platforms. (Silbermann thinks of Pinterest as a "visual-discovery tool," rather than a "social network.") As company executives like to point out, there is a natural link between "intent" and commerce that is stronger than the link between "interest" and commerce. Now the company is hoping to attract more male users, which in turn should bring in a wider array of advertisers.

Pinterest began selling ads in 2015. In 2017, as part of an effort to differentiate the company from Facebook, Google, Instagram, Snapchat, and Twitter, Silbermann's team launched its first print brand campaign keyed to the theme "What if." In March 2017, the company sponsored the Pinterest House at the highly influential South by Southwest Interactive conference in Austin, Texas. The following month, a Pinterest team traveled to an advertising conference in Cannes, France, to spread the word among ad professionals about Pinterest's advantages. As Silbermann explained, "The pitch to advertisers is explaining what people do on the platform. What they do is try to design their life. That's a good place to be."

Sources: Sapna Maheshwari, "Pinterest Is Ready to Run with the Big Dogs," *The New York Times* (July 3, 2017), pp. B1, B3; Alexandra Wolfe, "Weekend Confidential: Ben Silbermann," *The Wall Street Journal* (January 14–15, 2017), p. C11; Yoree Koh, "Pinterest Posts Big Increase in Users," *The Wall Street Journal* (October 14, 2016), pp. B1, B4; Yoree Koh, "Pinterest Takes a Shot with Image-Search Tools," *The Wall Street Journal* (July 7, 2016), p. B6; Hannah Kuchler, "Going Global, Modestly," *Financial Times* (April 11, 2016), p. 14.

Exhibit 13-7 Pinterest co-founders Evan Sharp and Ben Silbermann describe their app as a "visual search engine."
Source: I AM NIKOM/Shutterstock.

> When photographing a couple entering a restaurant or theater, you show the woman preceding the man, correct? No. Not in Germany and France. And this would be laughable in Japan. Having someone in a commercial hold up his hand with the back of it to you, the viewer, and the fingers moving toward him should communicate "come here." In Italy it means "good-bye."[26]

Ads that strike viewers in some countries as humorous or irritating may not necessarily be perceived that way by viewers in other countries. American ads make frequent use of spokes-people and direct product comparisons; they use logical arguments to try to appeal to the reason of audiences. Japanese advertising is more image oriented and appeals to audience sentiment. And, while Hollywood celebrities such as Brad Pitt and Arnold Schwarzenegger would never appear in American television ads, they can often be seen as television pitchmen in Japan.

In Japan, what is most important frequently is not what is stated explicitly, but rather what is implied. For example, the Aflac duck puts in an appearance in the insurance company's Japanese TV ads but, unlike its U.S. counterpart, the duck is not disruptive. Instead, in one spot, the duck does a gentle song-and-dance routine with a cat.

Nike's U.S. advertising is legendary for its irreverent, "in-your-face" style and relies heavily on celebrity sports endorsers such as Michael Jordan. In other parts of the world, where soccer is the top sport, some Nike ads are considered to be in poor taste, and its spokespeople have less relevance. Nike has responded by adjusting its approach; as Geoffrey Frost, former director of global advertising at Nike, noted more than a decade ago, "We have to root ourselves in the passions of other countries. It's part of our growing up."[27]

Some American companies have canceled television ads created for the Latin American market portraying racial stereotypes that were offensive to persons of color. Nabisco, Goodyear, and other companies are also being more careful about the shows during which they buy airtime: Some very popular Latin American programs feature content that exploits class, race, and ethnic differences.[28]

Standards vary widely with regard to the use of sexually explicit or provocative imagery. Partial nudity and same-sex couples are frequently seen in ads in Latin America and Europe. In the U.S. market, however, network television decency standards and the threat of boycotts by conservative consumer activists constrain advertisers. Some industry observers note a paradoxical situation in which the programs shown on U.S. TV are frequently racy, but the ads that air during those shows are not. As Marcio Moreira, the former worldwide chief creative officer at the McCann-Erickson agency, once noted, "Americans want titillation in entertainment but when it comes to advertising they stop being viewers and become consumers and critics."[29]

Of course, it is certainly not the case that anything goes outside the United States. Women in Monterrey, Mexico, once complained about billboards for the Playtex unit of Sara Lee Corporation that featured supermodel Eva Herzegova wearing a Wonderbra. The campaign was created by a local agency, Perez Munoz Publicidad. Playtex responded by covering up the model on the billboards in some Mexican cities. French Connection UK made waves in the United States with print ads that prominently featured the British company's initials, that is, FCUK. Public outcry prompted the company to tone down the ads by spelling out the name.

Food is the product category most likely to elicit cultural sensitivity, so marketers of food and food products must be alert to the need to localize their advertising. A good example of this is the effort by H. J. Heinz Company to develop the overseas market for ketchup. In the early 1990s, marketing managers at Heinz formulated a strategy that called for adapting both the product and the advertising to target country tastes.[30] In Greece, for example, ads showed ketchup pouring over pasta, eggs, and cuts of meat. In Japan, they instructed Japanese homemakers on using ketchup as an ingredient in Western-style foods such as omelets, sausages, and pasta.

Barry Tilley, who was general manager of Heinz's Western Hemisphere trading division based in London at the time, noted that Heinz uses focus groups to determine what consumers want in the way of taste and image. Americans like a sweet ketchup, but Europeans prefer a spicier, more piquant variety. Significantly, Heinz's international marketing efforts are most successful when the company quickly adapts to local cultural preferences. In Sweden, the made-in-America theme is so muted in Heinz's ads that "Swedes don't realize Heinz is American. They think it is German because of the name," said Tilley.

Conversely, American themes worked well in Germany. Kraft and Heinz tried to outdo each other with ads featuring strong American images. In one of Heinz's TV ads, American football players in a restaurant become very angry when the 12 steaks they ordered arrive without ketchup. The ad ends happily, of course, with plenty of Heinz ketchup to go around.[31]

In 2018, Heinz was still experimenting with the global/local taste trade-off: Managers at the Pittsburgh-based company had to decide whether to introduce a blend of mayonnaise and ketchup, which was popular in the Middle East, to American consumers. A @HeinzKetchup_US Twitter campaign with a # mayochup hashtag generated 1 million responses. The verdict? More than 500,000 people voted "Yes!"

Much academic research has been devoted to the impact of culture on advertising. For example, Tamotsu Kishii identified seven characteristics that distinguish Japanese creative strategy from its American counterpart:

1. Indirect rather than direct forms of expression are preferred in the messages. This avoidance of directness in expression is pervasive in all types of communication among the Japanese, including their advertising. Many television ads do not mention what is desirable about the brand in use and let the audience judge for themselves.
2. There is often little relationship between ad content and the advertised product.
3. Only brief dialogue or narration is used in television commercials, with minimal explanatory content. In the Japanese culture, the more a person talks, the less others will perceive the individual as trustworthy or self-confident.
4. Humor is used to create a bond of mutual feelings. Rather than slapstick, humorous dramatizations involve family members, neighbors, and office colleagues.
5. Famous celebrities appear as close acquaintances or everyday people.
6. Priority is placed on company trust rather than product quality. Japanese tend to believe that if the firm is large and has a good image, the quality of its products should also be outstanding.
7. The product name is impressed on the viewer with short, 15-second commercials.[32]

Green, Cunningham, and Cunningham conducted a cross-cultural study to determine the extent to which consumers of different nationalities use the same criteria to evaluate soft drinks and toothpaste. Their subjects were college students from the United States, France, India, and Brazil. Compared to the French and Indian respondents, the U.S. respondents placed more emphasis on subjective, as opposed to functional, product attributes. The Brazilian respondents appeared even more concerned with the subjective attributes than the Americans were. The authors concluded that advertising messages should not use the same appeal for these countries if the advertiser is concerned with communicating the most important attributes of its product in each market.[33]

(13-4) Global Media Decisions

◀ **13-4** Explain how media availability varies around the world.

The next issue facing advertisers is which medium or media to use when communicating with target audiences. Media availability can vary from country to country. Some companies use virtually the entire spectrum of available media; Coca-Cola is a good example. Other companies prefer to utilize one or two media categories. In some instances, the agency that creates the advertising also makes recommendations about media placement; however, many advertisers use the services of specialized media planning and buying organizations. The Mindshare Worldwide unit of WPP, Omnicom's OMD Worldwide, and WPP's Mediacom are three of the top media specialists.

The available alternatives can be broadly categorized as print media, electronic media, and other. Print media range from local daily and weekly newspapers to magazines and business publications with national, regional, or international audiences. Electronic media include broadcast television, cable television, radio, and the Internet. Additionally, advertisers may utilize various forms of outdoor, transit, and direct-mail advertising. Globally, media decisions must take into account country-specific regulations. For example, France bans retailers from advertising on television.

Global Advertising Expenditures and Media Vehicles

Each year, more money is spent on advertising in the United States than anywhere else in the world. As noted previously, U.S. ad spending in 2017 totaled more than $200 billion. To put this figure in context, consider that 2017 ad spending in China, now the world's second-largest advertising market, was approximately $80 billion. In addition, as one might expect, the largest per capita ad spending occurs in high-income countries.

Today, much of the geographic growth in advertising expenditures—as much as one-third—is occurring in the BRICS countries. Russia is the exception. Although top advertisers in Russia include Procter & Gamble, Nestlé, PepsiCo, and Mars, declining oil revenues and geopolitical tensions are among the factors contributing to relatively flat advertising revenue growth in that country.

Advertisers can choose from a variety of media, including broadcast (e.g., television and radio) and print (e.g., magazines and newspapers). Within each of these categories, various media vehicles are available to reach a given target audience with marketing communications. Among cable channels, BBC America and ESPN are examples of media vehicles. Likewise, *The Wall Street Journal* and *Financial Times* newspapers represent individual media vehicles.

For years, television—including broadcast, cable, and satellite—was the number 1 advertising medium, capturing between 40 percent and 50 percent of global expenditures. Newspapers ranked second on a worldwide basis, accounting for approximately 25 percent of advertising spending. Now, however, media consumption patterns are changing at a rapid pace. Spending on newspaper advertising has fallen sharply and, as noted previously, digital advertising expenditures are on track to surpass television advertising spending for the first time. In one sign of the times, Amazon recently announced that it has 100 million subscribers to its ad-free Prime Video streaming service.

The availability of media and the conditions affecting media buys also vary greatly around the world. In Mexico, an advertiser that can pay for a full-page ad may get the front page, whereas in India, paper shortages may require booking an ad 6 months in advance. In some countries, especially those where the electronic media are government owned, television and radio stations can broadcast only a restricted number of advertising messages. In Saudi Arabia, no commercial television advertising was allowed prior to May 1986; currently, ad content and visual presentations are restricted.

Worldwide, radio continues to be a less important advertising medium than print and television. However, in countries where advertising budgets are limited, radio's enormous reach can provide a cost-effective means of communicating with a large consumer market. Also, radio can be effective in countries where literacy rates are low. One clear trend is gaining traction throughout the world: Spending on customer relationship management (CRM) and Internet advertising is gaining ground at the expense of TV and print advertising.

Media Decisions

As noted previously, newspaper advertising has been in decline for several years; many papers have ceased publication or merged with others. India represents a bright spot on the global media scene: Print media are enjoying a revival as redesigned newspaper formats and glossy supplements lure a new generation of readers. India is home to hundreds of daily newspapers, including two Hindi-language titles, *Dainik Jagran* and *Dainik Bhaskar*. Other popular newspapers include the English-language *Hindustan Times* and *The Times of India*. The price per copy is as little as 5 rupees—about 10 cents.[34] An additional factor in India's evolving media environment: One-third of the population can access the Internet using mobile phones.

Billboards are a popular advertising medium in Moscow. As Thomas L. Friedman has pointed out, Moscow is a city built for approximately 30,000 cars; during the 2000s, the number of cars grew from 300,000 to 3 million.[35] The result is massive traffic jams and commuting delays. In turn, affluent businesspeople spend hours in traffic and have little time to read the newspaper or watch TV.

Even when media availability is high, its use as an advertising vehicle may be limited. For example, in Europe, television advertising is very limited in Denmark, Norway, and Sweden. Regulations concerning the content of commercials vary; Sweden bans advertising to children younger than 12 years of age. In 2001, when Sweden headed the European Union, its policymakers tried to extend the country's ban to the rest of Europe. Although the effort failed, Sweden

Exhibit 13-8 The first screening of *Black Panther* in Saudi Arabia was an invitation-only, VIP occasion. However, it was just one example of an increasing number of entertainment options available in the kingdom; Saudis are also flocking to pop and rap concerts, monster truck rallies, and theater productions.
Source: Amr Nabil/Associated Press.

retained its domestic ban. This helps explain why annual spending on print media in Sweden is three times the annual spending for television.[36]

As noted earlier, cultural considerations often affect the presentation of the advertising message. One study comparing the content of magazine advertisements in the United States with those in the Arab world found the following:

- People are depicted less often in Arabic magazine ads. However, when people do appear, there is no difference in the extent to which women are depicted. Women appearing in ads in Arab magazines wear long dresses; their presence generally is relevant to the advertised product.
- U.S. ads tend to have more information content; by contrast, brevity is considered a virtue in the Arab world. Context plays a greater role in interpreting an Arab message than in the United States.
- U.S. ads contain more price information, and are more likely to include comparative appeals than Arabic ads.[37]

Of course, cultural change is always possible. Recently, for example, Saudi Arabia lifted its ban on cinemas. In 2018, for the first time in 35 years, Saudis were able to enjoy popcorn and a movie in a movie theater in their home country. The first film to be shown, at an AMC theater in the capital city of Riyadh, was the global blockbuster *Black Panther* (see Exhibit 13-8). As more theaters are opened, opportunities for cinema advertising may become available.

(13-5) Public Relations and Publicity

13-5 Compare and contrast publicity and public relations and identify global companies that have recently been impacted by negative publicity.

In 2011, the Public Relations Society of America (PRSA) launched Public Relations Defined, an initiative to update the definition of public relations. As part of this initiative, the PRSA sought input from industry professionals, academics, and members of the general public. More than 900 definitions were submitted; according to the winning entry, **public relations (PR)** is a "strategic communication process that builds mutually beneficial relationships between organizations and their publics."[38] Public relations personnel are responsible for fostering goodwill, understanding, and acceptance among a company's various constituents and stakeholders. Along with advertising, PR is one of four variables in the promotion mix. One of the tasks of the PR practitioner is to generate favorable **publicity**. By definition, publicity is communication about a company or product for which the company does not pay. (In the PR world, publicity is sometimes referred to as *earned media*, and advertising and promotions are known as *unearned media*.)

PR professionals also play a key role in responding to unflattering media reports, crises, or controversies that arise because of a company's activities in different parts of the globe. In such instances, and especially if a company's reputation is on the line, it is good PR practice to respond promptly and provide the public with facts. The basic tools of PR include news releases, newsletters, media kits, press conferences, tours of plants and other company facilities, articles in trade or professional journals, company publications and brochures, TV and radio talk show interviews, special events, social media, and corporate Web sites.

Caterpillar's activities in China provide a textbook example of the power of public relations. The Chinese market for industrial machinery is booming because the government is spending billions of dollars on infrastructure improvements. Caterpillar hopes to sell giant wheel tractor-scrapers that are more efficient to operate than the hydraulic excavators and trucks currently in use. However, a business intelligence team that contacted 100 customers and dealers across China found low levels of awareness and acceptance of Caterpillar's machines. Survey respondents were not persuaded by data from other countries about the machines' cost savings.

To gain traction, Mike Cai, Caterpillar's man in China, staged product demonstrations—road shows—around the country. "Word-of-mouth is the best form of publicity for the construction industry in China," he says. Scott Kronick, president for Ogilvy Public Relations Worldwide/China, agrees. "Chinese customers are being introduced to a lot of products and services for the first time, so you can't advertise something that's intangible," he said. Reporters from the local and national media were invited to the demonstrations; in one instance, China Central Television ran a story that featured a clip of the tractor-scraper at work.[39]

Senior executives at some companies relish the opportunity to generate publicity. For example, Benetton's striking print and outdoor ad campaigns keyed to the "United Colors of Benetton" generate both controversy and widespread media attention. Richard Branson, the flamboyant founder of the Virgin Group, is a one-man publicity machine. His personal exploits as a hot-air balloon pilot have earned him and his company a great deal of free ink. Even so, the company continues to employ traditional media advertising. Over a long career at Virgin, Will Whitehorn's jobs included head of brand development and corporate affairs and president of Virgin Galactic. As he noted in the 1990s, "PR is the heart of the company. If we do things badly, it will reflect badly on the image of the brand more than most other companies." At Virgin, Whitehorn has said, "Advertising is a subset of PR, not the other way around."[40]

Not surprisingly, the importance of a social media presence as a PR tool is growing at many companies. PR professionals point to increasing consumer "engagement with the brand" on Facebook, Twitter, and other Web 2.0 platforms. Consider, for example, that as of mid-2018, Adidas Originals had 33 million Facebook "likes," and Heineken had 24 million.

FedEx's "I am FedEx" Facebook page features "Team Member Stories from FedEx." This communication channel allows the company's 285,000 employees to share stories about their work and home lives. Joe Becker, an executive at Ketchum Digital, believes that the conversations that take place on Facebook can be leveraged as content that can be used to enhance the FedEx brand. He says, "The primary goal is about enabling employees to tell and create stories, which influences public opinion about the brand."[41] Another advantage: Because visitors to social media sites can immediately click on a link to an e-commerce site, it is easy to track return on investment (ROI). We discuss social media in more detail in Chapter 15.

As noted earlier, a company exerts complete control over the content of its advertising and pays for message placement in the media. In contrast, members of the media typically receive many more press releases and other PR materials than they can use. Generally speaking, a company has little control over when, or if, a news story runs, nor can the company directly control the spin, slant, or tone of the story. To compensate for this lack of control over the ultimate outcome of their PR efforts, many companies utilize **corporate advertising**, which, despite the name, is generally considered part of the PR function.

As with "regular" advertising, a company or organization identified in the ad pays for corporate advertising. However, unlike regular advertising, the objective of corporate advertising is not to generate demand by informing, persuading, entertaining, or reminding customers. Instead, in the context of IMC, corporate advertising is often used to call attention to the company's other communications efforts. In addition to the examples discussed in the following pages, Table 13-4 summarizes several instances of global publicity involving well-known firms.

Image advertising enhances the public's perception of a company; creates goodwill; or announces a major change, such as a merger, acquisition, or divestiture. In 2008, for example, Anheuser-Busch InBev placed full-page ads in the business press to announce the companies' merger. Global companies frequently use image advertising in an effort to present themselves as good corporate citizens in international markets.

BASF uses advertising to raise awareness about the company's innovative products that are used in the automotive, home construction, and pharmaceutical industries. Boeing uses consumer advertising in Europe to build awareness and create goodwill. Similarly, a recent campaign from Daimler AG was designed to raise awareness of the company's eco-friendly electric drive vehicles (see Exhibit 13-10). The ad positions Daimler both as an innovator and as a responsible corporate citizen. Because the message and the associated image have worldwide appeal, this ad lends itself to an extension strategy.

In **advocacy advertising**, a company presents its point of view on a particular social, environmental, or cultural issue. The point of such communication is not to sell a particular product or service. Rather, it is to express the company's point of view or ask for support on issues that management believes are important. Examples of this type of communication include the MPA advertisement shown in Exhibit 13-5 and the New Balance ad shown in Chapter 17. A recent print campaign from the Interpublic Group of Companies (IPG) called attention to the fact that lack of access to clean water is a pressing issue in many parts of the world (see Exhibit 13-9).

Sometimes a company generates publicity simply by going about the business of global marketing activities. For example, Nike, Walmart, and other marketers have received a great deal of negative publicity regarding alleged sweatshop conditions in the factories run by their subcontractors. Today, Nike's PR team is doing a better job of counteracting the criticism by effectively communicating the positive economic impact Nike has had on the nations where it manufactures its sneakers (see Exhibit 13-11).

Any company that is increasing its activities outside its home country can utilize PR personnel as boundary spanners between the company and employees, unions, stockholders, customers, the media, financial analysts, governments, or suppliers. Many companies have their own in-house PR staff; others may choose to engage the services of an outside PR firm. During the past few years, some of the large advertising holding companies discussed previously have acquired PR agencies. For example, the Omnicom Public Relations Group consists of three agencies: FleishmanHillard, Ketchum, and Porter Novelli.

TABLE 13-4   Negative Publicity Affecting Global Marketers

Company or Brand (Home Country)	Nature of Publicity
Facebook (United States)	A privacy scandal erupted when personal data for about 87 million of Facebook's 2 billion users were shared with Cambridge Analytica, a firm that allegedly used the data to influence the 2016 U.S. presidential election.
Volkswagen (Germany)	The "Dieselgate" emissions cheating scandal involved illegal software defeat devices installed on millions of vehicles.
Samsung Electronic Co. (South Korea)	Batteries on the flagship Galaxy Note 7 overheated and in some cases caught fire. Samsung announced a massive global recall and urged all Note 7 owners to turn their phones off immediately.
Sony Corporation (Japan)	In a massive security breach, North Korean hackers leaked data, memos, and films stolen from Sony in retaliation for Sony Pictures Entertainment's *The Interview*. The Hollywood comedy, starring Seth Rogan and James Franco, concerned a CIA plot to assassinate North Korean leader Kim Jung Un.
Petrobras (Brazil)	Officials at Brazil's state-owned oil company and top politicians were accused of collaborating with contractors to receive billions in kickbacks. The scandal was dramatized in the Netflix series *The Mechanism*.

Exhibit 13-9 Because of a global water crisis, more than 800 million people lack access to clean water. The crisis especially impacts women and children. This advocacy print ad from IPG is intended to raise awareness of the issue.

Source: The Interpublic Group of Companies, Inc.

Exhibit 13-10 Daimler AG is one of the world's leading developers of emission-free and autonomous automotive technology. This corporate image advertisement is not about the company's vehicle brands per se; rather, it is about the company's ongoing efforts to create the eco-friendly car of the future.

Source: Daimler Corporation AG.

Exhibit 13-11 When making public appearances, Nike chairman Phil Knight and other executives frequently defend labor practices and policies in the Asian factories where the company's shoes are made. In the late 1990s, a protester filed a lawsuit against Nike alleging that the company's public assertions about working conditions constituted false advertising. After the California Supreme Court ruled against Nike, the company appealed. In 2003, the U.S. Supreme Court heard the case as protesters gathered outside. The Court later dismissed Nike's appeal, and the case was sent back to California. In the end, Nike settled the suit by agreeing to pay $1.5 million to worker rights group with no admission of wrongdoing.
Source: Chuck Kennedy/KRT/Newscom.

The Growing Role of PR in Global Marketing Communications

PR professionals with international responsibility must go beyond media relations and serve as more than a company mouthpiece; they are called upon to simultaneously build consensus and understanding, create trust and harmony, articulate and influence public opinion, anticipate conflicts, and resolve disputes.[42] As companies become more involved in global marketing and the globalization of industries continues, company management must recognize the value of international PR. Today, the PR industry faces a challenging business environment with a mixture of threats and opportunities. A decade ago, many PR firms saw revenues and profits decline as a result of the global recession. At the same time, the recession also increased the demand for PR services. Edelman Worldwide chief Richard Edelman recently noted that PR's status as a key input to corporate decision making has been improving. Edelman says, "We used to be the tail on the dog."[43]

Europe has a long-standing PR tradition; for example, the Deutsche Public Relations Gesellschaft (DPRG) recently commemorated its 60th anniversary. Many European PR practitioners and trade associations, including the DPRG, are members of the Confédération Européenne des Relations Publiques (www.cerp.org). The U.K.-based International Public Relations Association (www.ipra.org) has an Arabic Web site, an illustration of the way PR's importance is recognized in all parts of the world.

An important factor fueling the growth of international PR is increased governmental relations between countries. Governments, organizations, and societies are dealing with broad-based issues of mutual concern, such as the aftermath of the recent global recession, trade relations, the environment, and world peace. The technology-driven communication revolution that has ushered in the Information Age makes public relations a profession with truly global reach. Smartphones, broadband Internet connectivity, social media, satellite links, and other channel innovations allow PR professionals to be in contact with media virtually anywhere in the world.

In spite of these technological advances, PR professionals must still carry out some traditional aspects of public relations—that is, they must build good personal working relationships with journalists and other media representatives, as well as with leaders of other primary constituencies. Therefore, strong interpersonal skills are needed. One of the most basic concepts of the practice of PR is to know the audience. For the global PR practitioner, this means knowing the audiences in both the home country and the host country or countries. Specific skills needed include the ability to communicate in the language of the host country and familiarity with local customs. A PR professional who is unable to speak the language of the host country will be unable to communicate directly with a huge portion of an essential audience. Likewise, the PR professional working outside the home country must be sensitive to nonverbal communication issues so as to maintain good working relationships with host-country nationals. Commenting on the complexity of the international PR professional's job, one expert noted that, in general, audiences are becoming more hostile, more organized, more powerful, more skeptical, and more diverse. International PR practitioners can play an important role as "bridges over the shrinking chasm of the global village."[44]

How PR Practices Differ Around the World

Cultural traditions, social and political contexts, and economic environments in specific countries can affect public relations practices. As noted earlier in the chapter, the mass media and the written word are important vehicles for information dissemination in many industrialized countries. In contrast, in developing countries, the best way to communicate might be through the gong man, the town crier, the market square, or the chief's courts. In Ghana, dance, songs, and storytelling are important communication channels. In India, where half of the population cannot read, issuing press releases will not be the most effective way to communicate.[45] In Turkey, the practice of PR is thriving in spite of that country's reputation for harsh treatment of political prisoners. Although the Turkish government still asserts absolute control over the mass media in that country, as it has for generations, corporate PR and journalism are allowed to flourish so that Turkish organizations can compete globally.

Even in industrialized countries, PR practices differ. In the United States, the hometown news release may account for much of the news in a small, local newspaper. In Canada, in contrast, large metropolitan population centers have combined with Canadian economic and climatic conditions to thwart the emergence of a local press. The dearth of small newspapers means that the practice of sending out hometown news releases is almost nonexistent.[46] In the United States, PR is increasingly viewed as a separate management function. In Europe, this perspective has not been widely accepted; PR professionals are viewed as part of the marketing function rather than as distinct and separate specialists in a company. In Europe, fewer colleges and universities offer courses and degree programs in PR than in the United States. Also, European coursework in PR is more theoretical; in the United States, PR programs are often part of mass communication or journalism schools, and there is more emphasis on practical job skills.

A company that is ethnocentric in its approach to public relations will extend its home-country PR activities into host countries. The rationale behind this approach is that people everywhere are motivated and persuaded in much the same manner; thus, this approach does not take cultural considerations into account. In contrast, a company adopting a polycentric approach to PR gives the host-country practitioner more leeway to incorporate local customs and practices into the PR effort. Although such an approach has the advantage of local responsiveness, the lack of global communication and coordination can lead to a PR disaster.[47]

The ultimate test of an organization's understanding of the power and importance of PR occurs during a time of environmental turbulence, especially a potential or actual crisis. When disaster strikes, a company or industry often finds itself thrust—unwillingly—into the spotlight. A company's swift and effective handling of communications during such times can have significant implications. The best response is to be forthright and direct, reassure the public, and provide the media with accurate information.

China's ongoing trade-related friction with its trading partners highlights the need for a better PR effort on the part of the Chinese Foreign Ministry. Some sources of this friction have been discussed in earlier chapters, such as estimates that Chinese counterfeiting of copyrighted material costs foreign companies billions of dollars annually and that 98 percent of the computer software used in China is pirated. Such revelations reflect poorly on China. As Hong Kong businessman Barry C. Cheung noted in the mid-1990s, "China lacks skills in public relations generally and crisis management specifically, and that hurts them."[48] Part of the problem stems from the unwillingness of China's Communist leaders to publicly explain their views on these issues, to admit failure, and to accept advice from the West.

Summary

Marketing communications—the promotion (*P*) of the marketing mix—includes advertising, public relations, sales promotion, and personal selling. When a company embraces *integrated marketing communications (IMC)*, it recognizes that the various elements of a company's communication strategy must be carefully coordinated. *Advertising* is a sponsored, paid message that is communicated through nonpersonal channels. *Global advertising* relies on the same advertising appeals, messages, artwork, and copy in campaigns around the world. The effort required to create a global campaign forces a company to determine whether a global market exists for its product or brand. The trade-off between standardized and adapted advertising is often accomplished by means of *pattern advertising*, which can be used to create localized global advertising. Many advertising agencies are part of larger *advertising organizations*. Advertisers may place a single global agency in charge of worldwide advertising; it is also possible to use one or more agencies on a regional or local basis.

The starting point in ad development is the *creative strategy*, a statement of what the message will say. The people who create ads often seek a *big idea* that can serve as the basis for memorable, effective messages. The *advertising appeal* is the communication approach—rational or emotional—that best relates to buyer motives. *Rational appeals* speak to the mind; *emotional appeals* speak to the heart. The *selling proposition* is the promise that captures the reason for buying the product. The *creative execution* is the way an appeal or proposition is presented. *Art direction* and *copy* must be created with cultural considerations in mind. Perceptions of humor, male–female relationships, and sexual imagery vary in different parts of the world. Likewise, media availability varies considerably from country to country. When selecting media, marketers are sometimes as constrained by laws and regulations as by literacy rates.

A company utilizes *public relations (PR)* to foster goodwill and understanding among constituents both inside and outside the company. In particular, the PR department attempts to generate favorable *publicity* about the company and its products and brands. The PR department must also manage corporate communications when responding to negative publicity. Important PR tools include interviews, media kits, press releases, social media, and tours. Many global companies make use of various types of *corporate advertising*, including *image advertising* and *advocacy advertising*. PR is also responsible for providing accurate, timely information, especially in the event of a crisis.

Discussion Questions

13-1. In what ways is cultural consideration an important element in global marketing communication?

13-2. Discuss some of the key considerations in selecting an advertising agency.

13-3. Describe the roles and responsibilities of an art director and a copywriter.

13-4. Starting with Chapter 1, review the ads that appear in this text. Can you identify ads that use emotional appeals? Rational appeals? What is the communication task of each ad? To inform? To persuade? To remind? To entertain?

13-5. How do the media options available to advertisers vary in different parts of the world? What can advertisers do to cope with media limitations in certain countries?

13-6. In January 2019, Gillette received extreme negative publicity and a potential boycott over their #MeToo advertisement, a short film named "We Believe: The Best Men Can Be." Negative reactions outweighed positive ones by 2:1. What did Gillette do, and why?

CASE 13-1 *continued (refer to page 429)*

Volkswagen's "Dieselgate" Nightmare

In November 2015, VW faced even more bad news. It was revealed that some three-liter, six-cylinder engines in cars produced by Audi, one of Volkswagen AG's luxury brands, also contained defeat devices. Audi is the world's number 2 premium auto brand, behind BMW. Two Audi engineers who were suspected of designing the engine software were suspended. In the United States, the EPA began developing enforcement options.

With VW in crisis mode, its public relations team created and implemented a series of communication tactics and strategies designed to restore consumer trust. In the United States, the company bought full-page ads in national newspapers with the headline "We're working to make things right." The ads announced that the company was offering affected owners a goodwill package consisting of a $500 prepaid Visa Card, a $500 Volkswagen Dealership Card, and free roadside assistance for three years. Owners were also directed to a Web site, vwdieselinfo.com, for more information. Michael Horn, president and CEO of the Volkswagen Group of America, signed the letter at the bottom of the ad.

As the investigation expanded, some industry observers were convinced that VW's problem involved more than a handful of engineers. According to this view, the crisis was attributed to VW's insular, engineering-based corporate culture and potentially involved hundreds of people (see Exhibit 13-12).

In Europe, partial blame was directed at regulators at both the national and EU levels. The auto industry is one of Europe's biggest employers and has a powerful lobbying presence in Brussels (home of the EU headquarters) and elsewhere. The industry had successfully pushed for laboratory-based emissions tests that yielded more positive results than tests under real-world driving conditions did. Indeed, the European Union itself was pressuring automakers to produce cleaner cars; new emissions limits were established in 2007 and entered into force in 2014. Many believed that advanced diesel technology represented a promising solution. Even so, it was alleged that regulatory officials had known for years that NO_x levels under actual driving conditions exceeded the legal limits.

The Fix Is In

VW engineers created inexpensive software and hardware updates that fixed the emissions issue for the 9 million affected cars in Europe. Due to differences in emissions standards, however, a separate solution was required for the 500,000 affected cars in United States. In January 2016, regulatory officials in California rejected a proposed fix on the grounds it was "vague and inadequate." The regulators were particularly interested in the effect of any proposed fix on automotive performance and safety. Meanwhile, U.S. sales of some of Volkswagen's diesel models were suspended because a fix had not been approved. In the end, VW was forced to buy back 85 percent of the affected diesel vehicles purchased by U.S. drivers. Some drivers who qualified for free repairs and updates were offered payouts ranging from about $5,000 to nearly $10,000.

Müller, the new Volkswagen CEO, took a team to Washington, D.C., to meet with Gina McCarthy, the EPA's chief administrator. McCarthy told Müller that her agency agreed with the findings in California. For his part, Müller said his goal was to rekindle Americans' love for the Volkswagen brand and regain their trust. Meanwhile, a Volkswagen team visiting the Detroit Auto Show offered apologies for misleading American consumers and regulators.

VW Motors On

Chance played an important role in helping VW rebound from the crisis. A previous scandal involving BP and the lawsuits resulting from the Deepwater Horizon oil drilling platform tragedy had resulted in a streamlined process for consolidating claims coming from the federal,

Exhibit 13-12
Source: Jeremy Banx/Banx Cartoons.

"THERE MUST BE SOME WAY OF MAKING THESE FIGURES LOOK BETTER."

state, and consumer levels. Meanwhile, the attention of the media and the general public shifted to a new hot-button topic: the 2016 presidential campaign of Donald Trump.

Even as Volkswagen spends billions of dollars on reparations for the scandal (the final tab amounts to nearly $15 billion), it is also investing heavily on new technology. In 2016, Volkswagen launched a new division, Moia, marking the company's entry into ride-sharing and related mobility services. Volkswagen also acquired PayByPhone, a firm based in Canada that processes mobile payments for parking spaces.

As is true with most automakers, VW is investing heavily in next-generation vehicles that do not have internal combustion engines—gas or diesel. This was partly in response to the scandal, and partly in response to Tesla chief Elon Musk's vow that his company's annual production will reach 1 million electric cars by 2020. In addition, industry changes are being driven by recent announcements that the United Kingdom, France, and the Netherlands will ban the sale of conventional vehicles starting in 2030.

With sales of VW's diesel vehicles declining in the wake of the scandal, Müller announced a Vision 2025 plan to significantly cut VW's environmental impact. The CEO pledged that, by 2030, VW would offer 300 electric vehicle (EV) models across its 12 brands. The EV team took over space in the Wolfsburg plant that had been occupied by engineers for Phaeton, the first super-luxury sedan to bear the VW nameplate. Developed at a cost of $700 million, the Phaeton boasted the world's finest automotive air conditioning system and carried a price tag of more than $100,000. Müller shut down production of the vehicle.

In an interview, Müller also called for the German government to quit subsidizing diesel technology; the subsidies come in the form of lower prices for diesel fuel compared to gasoline. Müller advocated shifting those funds into electric vehicle technology. In addition, Müller negotiated a workforce reduction in Germany of approximately 30,000 employees; the move was intended to bring VW's productivity more in line with global competitors such as Toyota. The chief executive also announced that he had budgeted €50 billion for the purchase of

lithium ion EV batteries. And one more thing: Because the EV future is still a few years away, VW must still find a way to persuade consumers to keep buying its diesel cars.

A New CEO Takes Charge

In spring 2018, the diesel cheating scandal at Volkswagen continued to make news. In connection with the ongoing investigation, German police raided the offices of senior executives at luxury car maker Porsche. Volkswagen owns Porsche; allegedly, an internal investigation at Porsche revealed that some diesel engines sourced from sister company Audi contained defeat software, but the executives had failed to take action in removing the software.

In other news, Volkswagen board hired a new CEO. Herbert Diess said that he would speed up the pace of corporate reforms that were initiated by his predecessor Matthias Müller. It was also anticipated that Diess would move ahead with a separate stock market listing of Volkswagen's heavy-truck unit, a restructuring that was designed to appeal to investors.

Discussion Questions

13-7. Assess VW's response to the Dieselgate scandal in terms of the effectiveness of its marketing communications.

13-8. Some VW diesel owners were reluctant to get the emissions-control updates because they were satisfied with their cars' performance. Is it ethical for car owners to continue driving their cars even though they know the vehicles are emitting high levels of pollutants?

13-9. Do you think VW will be able to transform itself into a leader in electric vehicles? Or does Tesla have an insurmountable first-mover advantage?

Sources: Matthew Campbell, Christoph Rauwald, and Chris Reiter, "Volkswagen's Peace Offering," *Cover Story—Bloomberg Businessweek* (April 2, 2018), pp. 50–55; Danny Hakim, "VW's Crisis Response: Driving in Circles," *The New York Times* (February 28, 2016), pp. BU1, BU3; William Boston, "VW Crisis Spreads to Audi Engines," *The Wall Street Journal* (November 27, 2015), pp. B1, B2; Richard Milne, "System Failure," *Financial Times—FT Big Read: Volkswagen* (November 5, 2015), p. 7.

CASE 13-2
Coca-Cola: Using Advertising and Public Relations to Respond to a Changing World

It's often been said that "perception is reality." That's one of the problems facing the Coca-Cola Company and other soft-drink marketers as they address a variety of marketing communication issues. For example, Big Soda has been linked to the issue of obesity around the world. In addition, Coca-Cola has been singled out for criticism for its operations in key emerging markets such as China and India. And, as soft-drink consumption declines, the company must find new and authentic ways to communicate with customers.

Health experts point to scientific evidence that beverages containing sugar or other sweeteners, including Coca-Cola's core soft-drink brands, are one factor contributing to the growing obesity problem. The obesity controversy was spotlighted when New York City Mayor Michael Bloomberg launched an advertising attack on sugar-filled beverages. Print ads, created in conjunction with New York's Department of Health and Mental Hygiene, included the bold headline

"Are you pouring on the pounds?" The ads appeared on subway posters, educational brochures, and the Internet (see Exhibit 13-13).

What's more, high-end U.S. grocery chain Whole Foods Market does not stock Coke in its stores. Why? Founder and CEO John Mackey is on a mission to bring healthy food to the world, and the company emphasizes natural and organic grocery items.

Coca-Cola is one of the world's truly iconic brands: It ranks number 3 in Interbrand's annual rankings, just behind Apple and Google. However, sales of Coca-Cola have been declining as consumers switch to bottled tea, juice, and water. Perhaps that explains why, in the *Financial Times* 2016 Global Brands survey, Coca-Cola fell 5 points, to number 13. Only a year earlier, in the 2015 survey, Coca-Cola had ranked number 8.

Considering that Coke's global advertising tagline has been "Open Happiness," Coca-Cola executives knew they had to act. To counteract the negative perception and negative publicity about Big Soda, the company launched its own print ad campaign that featured smaller-format cans and bottles. Coca-Cola also created a 2-minute television spot in which the voice-over explained that people who eat more calories than they burn are bound to gain weight.

The backlash was immediate. Coca-Cola executives insisted that they wanted to be part of the conversation about obesity, and that the company welcomed any reactions, including negative ones. Even so, the tone of the conversation was turning nasty. Marion Nestle, a professor of public health at New York University, said, "The idea that Coca-Cola is a force against obesity is ludicrous."

The Coca-Cola Company is no stranger to publicity. Because of its status as the world's largest beverage company and its presence in more than 200 countries, Coca-Cola is often the target of antiglobalization protests. Water scarcity is a key issue in many countries. In India, villagers protested the company's water consumption in areas severely affected by drought (see Exhibit 13-14). In response, the company closed two bottling plants while insisting that the allegations about excessive water usage were false.

Similarly, before the 2008 Olympics in Beijing, activists and various nongovernmental groups (NGOs) such as Students for a Free Tibet and Dreams for Darfur made their voices heard. They targeted Coca-Cola and other global companies that had spent tens of millions of dollars on advertising and public relations campaigns associated with the Games and the Olympic torch relay. The activists, who were thoroughly steeped in modern PR tactics, used text messaging, blogs, and other tools to spread messages and organize protests that threatened to undermine and overshadow the carefully cultivated image of Olympic harmony. For example, some protests were staged to call attention to Beijing's crackdown on protesters in Tibet (over the latter's status as an independent nation versus a subordinate of China) and China's economic ties with the government of Sudan, the North African country where a deadly civil war was raging in the Darfur region. The activists opposed Coke's relationship with China in view of the latter's support of a repressive regime.

E. Neville Isdell, who was chairman and CEO of the Coca-Cola Company at the time, responded to activists' concerns at Coke's annual shareholder meeting and in newspaper opinion-page letters. China is

Exhibit 13-13 Advertisements that appeared in New York City were designed to address the public-health crisis centered on empty calories. The American Beverage Association objected to the campaign, as did some advertising critics.
Source: Neno Images/PhotoEdit, Inc.

an important market for the soft-drink and beverage giant: China is part of the Asia-Pacific region, Coca-Cola's second largest region by revenue. As Isdell told the *Financial Times*, "We are neither a government nor the United Nations, but we can and must be a catalyst for change through actions that are appropriate for a business to take." Those actions included committing resources to ensure that relief supplies reached Darfur and addressing the pressing need for fresh water and sanitation for residents who had been displaced by the fighting.

Prior to retiring in 2009, Isdell guided the company toward greater transparency in its global operations. Isdell also wanted to make sure that the public would perceive Coke as a global leader in corporate social responsibility. To do this, he began forging relationships and partnerships with nongovernmental organizations (NGOs) such as the Nature Conservancy and the World Wildlife Fund. The company has set a goal that by 2020 it will be replenishing global water supplies with an amount of water equal to that required to produce finished beverages.

Ad Age "Marketer of the Year"

Of course, Coca-Cola's marketing communications entail much more than public relations efforts to deal with bad publicity. In fact, *Advertising Age* magazine honored the company as Marketer of the Year in 2011. This was due in part to the fact that Diet Coke slipped past Pepsi to become the number 2 soft drink in the United States. Also, Minute Maid Pulpy, which was launched in China, had become a billion-dollar brand. And, for the entire decade of the 2000s, Coca-Cola had ranked number 1 on Interbrand's list of most-valuable global brands.

Exhibit 13-14
Source: RAVEENDRAN/AFP/Getty Images.

Coca-Cola showcased its brand at Shanghai Expo in 2010. Coca-Cola's red-and-white pavilion—"The Happiness Factory"—featured animated characters and creatures that introduced visitors to "a world refreshed by happiness." In addition, Coke showcased PlantBottle, a packaging innovation that uses plastic and plant-based material. Visitors were also treated to cans of Coke that freeze when they are opened. Why was Coke present at Expo 2010? As Ted Ryan, a manager at Coca-Cola, said, "Our goal is to be considered the premier drinks brand; who else would be there? It has got to be Coca-Cola."

The Search for a New Global Campaign

Despite such achievements and accolades, Coke missed its revenue and profit targets in 2014. A recent Gallup poll had revealed that nearly two-thirds of Americans are avoiding soda. The company's product portfolio includes nearly two dozen billion-dollar brands, including Dasani water and Minute Maid juices. Even so, because soft drinks represent 70 percent of the company's revenues, then-CEO Muhtar Kent insisted that he would spend more on marketing in an effort to boost sales. Although the "Share a Coke" advertising campaign featuring personalized names on bottles led to a sales uptick in summer 2014, overall global volume growth was flat in 2013 and 2014. Kent pledged to boost annual advertising spending by $1 billion, to more than $4 billion, by 2016.

Besides increasing the advertising budget, Kent oversaw the company's efforts to develop a new global advertising campaign. "Open Happiness" was launched in 2009 on the hit TV program *American Idol*, and Coca-Cola products were prominently displayed on the judges' tables. Coca-Cola has multiple advertising agencies on its roster. For example, Wieden+Kennedy creates advertising for Coke and Diet Coke. "Generous World," a TV spot that the Portland, Oregon, shop developed, centers on a bottle of Coke that is passed from one person to another as each deals with increasing levels of adversity (e.g., car being towed, swimmer being rescued). Other advertising agencies include Dentsu (Japan) and FCB (South Africa). These and several others were invited to pitch creative ideas for the new campaign.

The Industry Strikes Back

The World Health Organization recommends that governments tax sugared beverages. The International Council of Beverage Associations represents trade groups in various countries that are fighting to defeat tax levies on soft drinks. Besides challenging sugar's link to obesity, such groups assert that the taxes are a burden on low-income families and also lead to unemployment.

Proposed taxes on sugar-containing beverages have been defeated in several countries, including Russia and New Zealand. Nevertheless, more than two dozen countries have approved the taxes, which result in higher prices for soft drinks. The goal, obviously, is to reduce consumption.

Latin America is now the world's largest market for soft drinks. In January 2014, the Mexican government imposed a 10 percent tax—amounting to 1 peso per liter—on sugared beverages. The result? Thanks to the combined impact of the new tax and a public-health campaign, sales declined in the short term, but then rebounded. Some observers argue that if the tax were increased, its impact on consumption would be stronger.

At the end of 2016, a consumer advocacy organization in Colombia known as Educar Consumidores launched a campaign urging the country's legislature approve a 20 percent tax on sugared soft drinks. Members of the organization reported that they had been harassed and threatened; a government agency ordered a television ad that linked sugar consumption to obesity and disease off the air.

The New CEO

In 2017, James Quincey succeeded Muhtar Kent as president and CEO of the Coca-Cola Company. The new CEO is focusing on juices, teas, protein shakes, and other drinks with healthier ingredients. One of his first major decisions was to eliminate the position of chief marketing officer. Quincey defended the move, noting that Coke's advertising model had not adapted sufficiently rapidly to the digital age. In place of the CMO, Quincey established a new C-level post, Chief Growth Officer. One of the company's new initiatives, "Beverages for Life," is designed to communicate that the company offers a wide range of products and brands for consumers at various life stages.

Discussion Questions

13-10. Do you believe that soft drinks and other sugared beverages contribute to obesity, diabetes, and other health-related issues?

13-11. Assess the timing and effectiveness of Coca-Cola's response to consumer concerns about sugar intake and the obesity controversy.

13-12. Coca-Cola and its advertising agencies developed a new global campaign keyed to the tagline "Taste the feeling." Assess its potential.

Sources: Jennifer Maloney, "Coca-Cola's Plan to Move beyond Its Name," *The Wall Street Journal—Journal Report: C-Suite Strategies* (February 20, 2018), p. R4; John Arlidge, "Coke's Brit Boss: I May Turn out to Be a 'Cretin,' We'll Find Out," *The Sunday Times* (November 26, 2017), p. 6; Andrew Jacobs and Matt Richtel, "After Drug Wars, a Dangerous Battle over Soda," *The New York Times* (November 14, 2017), p. A1; Mike Esterl, "Philadelphia Approves Tax on Soft Drinks," *The Wall Street Journal* (June 17, 2016), p. B6; Scheherazade Daneshkhu and Arash Massoudi, "Coca-Cola Cans Talk of Fight against Sugar Tax," *Financial Times* (June 7, 2016), p. 12; Stephen Foley, "Buffett Fizzes in Defense of Cherry Coke," *Financial Times* (May 27, 2016), p. 16; Amy Guthrie and Mike Esterl, "Despite Tax, Mexico Soda Sales Pop," *The Wall Street Journal* (May 4, 2016), p. B1; Anne Marie Chaker, "It's the Real Thing: Spoonfuls of Sugar Help the Soda Go Down," *The Wall Street Journal* (March 31, 2016), pp. A1, A7; Margot Sanger-Katz, "Hard Times for Soft Drinks," *The New York Times Sunday Business* (October 4, 2015), pp. 1, 4+; Tamara Audi and Mike Esterl, "Soda's New Enemy: San Francisco," *The Wall Street Journal* (June 10, 2015), pp. B1, B2; Neil Munshi and Scheherazade Daneshkhu, "When Less Is More," *Financial Times* (April 21, 2015), p. 6; Mike Esterl, "What Is Coke CEO's Solution for Lost Fizz? Sell More Soda," *The Wall Street Journal* (March 1, 2015), pp. A1, A12; Alan Rappeport, "Out for the Calorie Count," *Financial Times* (January 26, 2013).

Notes

[1]Thomas R. Duncan and Stephen E. Everett, "Client Perception of Integrated Marketing Communications," *Journal of Advertising Research* (May–June 1993), pp. 119–122. See also Stephen J. Gould, Dawn B. Lerman, and Andreas F. Grein, "Agency Perceptions and Practices on Global IMC," *Journal of Advertising Research* 39, no. 1 (January–February 1999), pp. 7–20.

[2]Gavin O'Malley, "Who's Leading the Way in Web Marketing? It's Nike, of Course," *Advertising Age* (October 26, 2006), p. D3.

[3]Ken Wells, "Selling to the World: Global Ad Campaigns, after Many Missteps, Finally Pay Dividends," *The Wall Street Journal* (August 27, 1992), p. A1.

[4]To be included in the rankings, companies must report media spending on at least three continents.

[5]Adapted from "25 Largest Markets," *Advertising Age* (December 8, 2014), p. 28.

[6]Meg Carter, "Think Globally, Act Locally," *Financial Times* (June 30, 1997), p. 12.

[7]Emma Hall and Normandy Madden, "IKEA Courts Buyers with Offbeat Ideas," *Advertising Age* (April 12, 2004), p. 1.

[8]Vanessa O'Connell, "Exxon 'Centralizes' New Global Campaign," *The Wall Street Journal* (July 11, 2001), p. B6.

[9]Eric Elinder, "International Advertisers Must Devise Universal Ads, Dump Separate National Ones, Swedish Ad Man Avers," *Advertising Age* (November 27, 1961), p. 91.

[10]Ali Kanso, "International Advertising Strategies: Global Commitment to Local Vision," *Journal of Advertising Research* 32, no. 1 (January–February 1992), pp. 10–14.

[11]Ken Wells, "Selling to the World: Global Ad Campaigns, after Many Missteps, Finally Pay Dividends," *The Wall Street Journal* (August 27, 1992), p. A1.

[12]Lindsay Stein, "WPP's Team Detroit, Blue Hive Unify Globally as GTB," *Ad Age* (May 5, 2016), p. 3.

[13]Helen Barrett, "Creative Force," *FT Business School Rankings* (December 4, 2017), p. 17.

[14]Nick Kostov and David Gauthier-Villars, "Digital Revolution Upends Ad Industry," *The Wall Street Journal* (January 20–21, 2018), pp. A1, A10.

[15]Angela Doland, "How Japan's Dentsu Climbed to the Top of the Agency World," *Advertising Age* (May 5, 2015), p. 17.

[16]Erin White and Shirley Leung, "How Tiny German Shop Landed McDonald's," *The Wall Street Journal* (August 6, 2003), pp. B1, B3.

[17]Geoffrey A. Fowler, "Commercial Break: The Art of Selling," *Far Eastern Economic Review* (October 30, 2003), pp. 30–33.

[18]John O'Toole, *The Trouble with Advertising* (New York, NY: Random House, 1985), p. 131.

[19]Randall Rothenberg, *Where the Suckers Moon* (New York, NY: Vintage Books, 1995), pp. 112–113.

[20]Suzanne Vranica, "IKEA to Tug at Heartstrings," *The Wall Street Journal* (September 18, 2007), p. B6.

[21]Stuart Elliot, "Subaru's Ride with 'Portlandia' Is a Playful One," *The New York Times* (December 10, 2014), p. B6.

[22]Janet Morrissey, "Marketers Value the Wisdom of Fonts," *The New York Times* (April 1, 2018), p. B5.

[23]Janet L. Borgerson, Jonathan E. Schroeder, Martin Escudero Magnusson, and Frank Magnusson, "Corporate Communication, Ethics, and Operational Identity: A Case Study of Benetton," *Business Ethics: A European Review* 18, no. 3 (July 2009), pp. 209–223.

[24]Jeanne Whalen, "McDonald's Cooks Worldwide Growth," *Advertising Age International* (July–August 1995), p. I4.

[25]Stephen E. Frank, "Citicorp's Big Account Is at Stake as It Seeks a Global Brand Name," *The Wall Street Journal* (January 9, 1997), p. B6.

[26]John O'Toole, *The Trouble with Advertising* (New York, NY: Random House, 1985), pp. 209–210.

[27]Roger Thurow, "Shtick Ball: In Global Drive, Nike Finds Its Brash Ways Don't Always Pay Off," *The Wall Street Journal* (May 5, 1997), p. A10.

[28]Leon E. Wynter, "Global Marketers Learn to Say 'No' to Bad Ads," *The Wall Street Journal* (April 1, 1998), p. B1.

[29]Melanie Wells and Dottie Enrico, "U.S. Admakers Cover It Up; Others Don't Give a Fig Leaf," *USA Today* (June 27, 1997), pp. B1, B2.

[30]Gary Levin, "Ads Going Global," *Advertising Age* (July 22, 1991), pp. 4, 42.

[31]Gabriella Stern, "Heinz Aims to Export Taste for Ketchup," *The Wall Street Journal* (November 20, 1992), p. B1.

[32]C. Anthony di Benedetto, Mariko Tamate, and Rajan Chandran, "Developing Creative Advertising Strategy for the Japanese Marketplace," *Journal of Advertising Research* (January–February 1992), pp. 39–48. A number of studies have compared ad content in different parts of the world, including Mary C. Gilly, "Sex Roles in Advertising: A Comparison of Television Advertisements in Australia, Mexico, and the United States," *Journal of Marketing* (April 1988), pp. 75–85; and Marc G. Weinberger and Harlan E. Spotts, "A Situation View of Information Content in TV Advertising in the U.S. and UK," *Journal of Advertising* 53 (January 1989), pp. 89–94.

[33]Robert T. Green, William H. Cunningham, and Isabella C. M. Cunningham, "The Effectiveness of Standardized Global Advertising," *Journal of Advertising* (Summer 1975), pp. 25–30.

[34]John Larkin, "Newspaper Nirvana? 300 Dailies Court India's Avid Readers," *The Wall Street Journal* (May 5, 2006), pp. B1, B3.

[35]Thomas L. Friedman, "The Oil-Addicted Ayatollahs," *The New York Times* (February 2, 2007), p. A19.

[36]John Tylee, "EC Permits Sweden to Continue Child Ad Ban," *Advertising Age* (July 11, 2003), p. 6.

[37]Fahad S. Al-Olayan and Kiran Karande, "A Content Analysis of Magazine Advertisements from the United States and the Arab World," *Journal of Advertising* 29, no. 3 (Fall 2000), pp. 69–82. See also Mushtag Luqmani, Ugur Yavas, and Zahir Quraeshi, "Advertising in Saudi Arabia: Content and Regulation," *International Marketing Review* 6, no. 1 (1989), pp. 59–72.

[38]Stuart Elliot, "Public Relations Defined, after an Energetic Public Discussion," *The New York Times* (March 2, 2012), p. B2.

[39]Jason Leow, "In China, Add a Caterpillar to the Dog and Pony Show," *The Wall Street Journal* (December 10, 2007), p. B1.

[40]Elena Bowes, "Virgin Flies in Face of Conventions," *Ad Age International* (January 1997), p. I.

[41]Matthew Schwartz, "Metrics of Success: PR's New Numbers," *Advertising Age* (November 29, 2010), p. S14.

[42]Karl Nessman, "Public Relations in Europe: A Comparison with the United States," *Public Relations Journal* 21, no. 2 (Summer 1995), p. 154.

[43]"Good News: Other Firms' Suffering Has Bolstered the PR Business," *Economist* (January 14, 2010), p. 34.

[44]Larissa A. Grunig, "Strategic Public Relations Constituencies on a Global Scale," *Public Relations Review* 18, no. 2 (Summer 1992), pp. 127–136.

[45]Carl Botan, "International Public Relations: Critique and Reformulation," *Public Relations Review* 18, no. 2 (Summer 1992), pp. 150–151.

[46]Melvin L. Sharpe, "The Impact of Social and Cultural Conditioning on Global Public Relations," *Public Relations Review* 18, no. 2 (Summer 1992), pp. 103–107.

[47]Carl Botan, "International Public Relations: Critique and Reformulation," *Public Relations Review* 18, no. 2 (Summer 1992), p. 155.

[48]Marcus W. Brauchli, "A Change of Face: China Has Surly Image, But Part of the Reason Is Bad Public Relations," *The Wall Street Journal* (June 16, 1996), p. A1.

14 Global Marketing Communications Decisions II

Sales Promotion, Personal Selling, and Special Forms of Marketing Communication

---

LEARNING OBJECTIVES

14-1 Define *sales promotion* and identify the most important promotion tactics and tools used by global marketers.

14-2 List the steps in the strategic/consultative personal selling model.

14-3 Explain the contingency factors that must be considered when making decisions about sales force nationality.

14-4 Explain direct marketing's advantages and identify the most common types of direct marketing channels.

14-5 Describe how global marketers integrate support media, sponsorships, and product placement into the overall promotion mix.

CASE 14-1
Milan Expo 2015

For marketers of some of the world's biggest corporate and national brands, all roads led to Milan, Italy, in 2015. The reason? Expo Milano, the latest in a series of massive Universal Exhibitions that date back to the mid-nineteenth century. London's Great Exhibition of the Works of Industry of All Nations in 1851 was the first; others include the Exhibition Universelle in Paris (1889), the World's Columbian Exposition in Chicago (1893), the New York World's Fair (1939 and 1964), and Shanghai Expo (2010).

Even before the Expo, Milan enjoyed a reputation as "the design capital of the world." Numerous Italian companies with global reach are headquartered there, including Dolce & Gabbana, Luxottica, Pirelli, and Versace. Milan is also known to millions of visitors for the Salone Internazionale Del Mobile—the Milan Furniture Fair—that is held every April.

The theme of Expo Milano, which ran from May 1, 2015, to October 31, 2015, was "Feed the World: Energy for Life" (see Exhibit 14-1). Organizers promised "six months of multi-sensory experiences in the universe of food" spread over 250 acres. Staged at an estimated cost of $3 billion, the Expo was intended to make a lasting contribution to nutrition education and better stewardship of Earth's resources. And, following years of recession and stagnation, policymakers hoped Expo would benefit Italy's economy as well.

Exhibit 14-1 The Italian Pavilion at Milan Expo 2015 showcased Italy's excellence in manufacturing, technology, and science. The nursery symbolized the nurturing of talent and progress; the tree was a symbol of life; and the roots conveyed the connections among Italy's many regions. Expo 2020 will be held in Dubai.
Source: Giovanni Tagini/Alamy Stock Photo.

Corporate sponsors included Accenture, Coca-Cola, Ferrero, McDonald's, Samsung, and San Pellagrino. Illy Caffè, based in Trieste, Italy, was the official coffee partner for the Coffee Cluster. Other clusters included "cereals," "rice," "islands and fish," and "bio-Mediterranean." There were seven subthemes, including "Innovation in the Agro Food Supply Chain," "Food for Better Lifestyles," and "Food in the World's Cultures and Ethnic Groups."

Sixty-three countries had their own eco-friendly pavilions; smaller nations were represented in nine specific clusters. Some countries were hosted with the sponsorship of bigger countries. For example, France, Germany, and China sponsored smaller countries in their pavilions. You can read more about Milan Expo, and prospects that its impacts will last, at the end of this chapter.

Sponsorships and event marketing are critical marketing tools for global companies. When developing integrated marketing communications (IMC) solutions and strategies, global companies and advertising agencies are giving these and other special forms of promotion an increasingly prominent role in the communication mix; in the first decades of the twenty-first century, worldwide expenditures on sales promotion have been growing at double-digit rates.

Sales promotion, direct marketing, and specialized forms of marketing communication such as infomercials and the Internet are also growing in importance. Personal selling remains an important promotional tool as well. Taken together, the marketing mix elements discussed in this chapter and Chapter 13 can be used to create highly effective, integrated promotional campaigns that support global brands.

▶ **14-1** Define *sales promotion* and identify the most important promotion tactics and tools used by global marketers.

(14-1) Sales Promotion

Sales promotion refers to any paid consumer or trade communication program of limited duration that adds tangible value to a product or brand. In a *price promotion*, tangible value may take the form of a price reduction, coupon, or mail-in refund. *Nonprice promotions* may take the form of free samples, premiums, "buy one, get one free" offers, sweepstakes, and contests. **Consumer sales promotions** may be designed to make consumers aware of a new product, to stimulate nonusers to sample an existing product, or to increase overall consumer demand. **Trade sales promotions** are designed to increase product availability within distribution channels. At many companies, expenditures for sales promotion activities have surpassed expenditures for media advertising. At any level of expenditure, however, sales promotion is just one of several marketing communication tools available to enterprises. In turn, sales promotion plans and programs should be integrated and coordinated with those for advertising, public relations (PR), and personal selling.

Worldwide, several explanations have been offered for the increasing popularity of sales promotion as a marketing communication tool. In addition to providing a tangible incentive to buyers, sales promotions reduce the perceived risk that buyers may associate with purchasing the product. From the marketer's point of view, sales promotion provides accountability; the manager in charge of the promotion can immediately track its results. Overall, promotional spending is increasing at many companies as they shift advertising spending away from traditional print and broadcast advertising. Exhibit 14-2 shows how the marketing managers responsible for Axe Apollo use sales promotions; additional examples are listed in Table 14-1.

Exhibit 14-2 When it comes to iconic figures that embody heroism, nothing beats an astronaut. That's the message from brand managers for Unilever's Axe Apollo. A marketing promotion created by the London-based Bartle Bogle Hegarty advertising agency partnered Axe with legendary American astronaut Buzz Aldrin and offered 22 prize winners a free trip in space. In 1969, Aldrin piloted the Apollo 11 lunar-landing module, and he was the second human to set foot on the moon.
Source: Eugene Gologursky/Getty Images.

TABLE 14-1 Sales Promotions by Global Marketers

Company/Country Market for Promotion	Promotion
Unilever/Global	In a contest in 45 different languages covering 60 countries, marketers for Axe Apollo invited consumers to fill out an "astronaut profile." Twenty-two finalists will have the opportunity to travel into space on the Lynx suborbital airship.
Walt Disney Company/China	To fight counterfeiting, the "Disney Magical Journey" promotion was keyed to mail-in hologram stickers on genuine Disney products. Participants could win Disney DVDs, TV sets, and trips to Hong Kong Disneyland.*
Mars/Global	The Global Color Vote promotion invited consumers in 200 countries to vote on whether a new M&M candy should be purple, aqua, or pink. Purple won.
Guinness/Worldwide	The "Arthur's Day" concert series honored the 250th anniversary of the birth of Arthur Guinness, founder of the Dublin, Ireland–based Guinness brewery.

* Geoffrey A. Fowler, "Disney Fires a Broadside at Pirates," *The Wall Street Journal* (May 31, 2006), p. B3.

Sweepstakes, rebates, and other promotional tools may require consumers to divulge personal information, which companies can then add to their databases. For example, the French Ministry of Agriculture recently launched a global promotion aimed at boosting exports of French wine and cheese. Acknowledging that some consumers are intimidated by France's culinary heritage, the Ministry sponsored the promotion to demonstrate that French cuisine can be relaxed and laid back. As part of this multi-pronged promotion, Spoexa, a food-marketing company, was hired to organize cocktail parties in 19 countries, including Canada, Spain, and the United States. House Party Inc., an American marketing firm, promoted the U.S. parties through its Web site. Would-be hosts registered online (allowing their personal information to be collected); from that applicant pool, House Party chose 1,000 people. The winners received discount coupons good for purchases of French wine; In addition, they were entitled to free gifts when ordering French cheeses from select Web sites (more opportunities for data collection). Each winner also received a basket of party supplies, including a corkscrew and an apron. In return, the hosts agreed to take photos and blog about their parties. After the parties, the hosts answered questionnaires to provide sponsors with feedback about the featured food and wine (yet more data collection). Finally, in-store promotions on party-related French goods were featured at various shops and supermarkets.[1]

A global company can sometimes leverage experience gained in one country market or region and use it in another market. For example, on July 17, 2015, PepsiCo rolled out a "PepsiMoji" promotion in Canada, Russia, and Thailand. The rollout coincided with World Emoji Day; labels on the brand's soft-drink cans and bottles had special emojis. Pepsi drinkers could download an iOS8 app with a custom 35-character keyboard that let them share emojis with their social media friends. Before long, #PepsiMoji was trending as users suggested new designs. The promotion was so successful that it was expanded to more than 100 global markets in 2016. The campaign included both global and local emojis. And, in true IMC fashion, the program was supported by traditional and digital media advertising.[2]

International managers can learn about American-style promotion strategies and tactics by attending seminars such as those offered by the Promotional Marketing Association of America (PMAA). Of course, those approaches cannot always be applied without modifications outside the United States; sometimes adaptation to country-specific conditions is required. For example, TV ads in France cannot have movie tie-ins; ads must be designed to focus on the promotion rather than the movie. Such regulations may have an impact on media companies such as Disney whose film properties are distributed on a worldwide basis.

As with other aspects of marketing communication, a key issue is whether personnel at headquarters should direct promotion efforts or leave those decisions to local country managers. The authors of one study noted that Nestlé and other large companies that once had a polycentric approach to consumer and trade sales promotion have redesigned their efforts. Kashani and Quelch identify four factors that contribute to more involvement of company headquarters in the sales promotion effort:[3]

1. *Cost.* As sales promotions command ever-larger budget allocations, managers at headquarters naturally take a greater interest.
2. *Complexity.* The formulation, implementation, and follow-up of a promotion program may require skills that local managers lack.
3. *Global branding.* The increasing importance of global brands justifies headquarters' involvement to maintain consistency from country to country and to ensure that successful local promotion programs are leveraged in other markets.
4. *Transnational trade.* As mergers and acquisitions lead to increased concentration in the retail industry and as the industry globalizes, retailers will seek coordinated promotional programs from their suppliers.

The level of headquarters' involvement notwithstanding, in most cases local managers in the market know the specific local situation, so they should be consulted before a promotion is launched. A number of factors must be taken into account when determining the extent to which the promotion must be localized:

- In countries with low levels of economic development, low incomes limit the range of promotional tools available. In such countries, free samples and demonstrations are more likely to be used than coupons or on-pack premiums.
- Market maturity can be different from country to country. Consumer sampling and coupons are appropriate in growing markets, but mature markets might require trade allowances or loyalty programs.
- Local perceptions of a particular promotional tool or program can vary. Japanese consumers, for example, are reluctant to use coupons at the checkout counter. A particular premium can be a waste of money.
- Local regulations in certain countries may rule out the use of a particular promotion such as in-pack coupons or price-off coupons by mail.
- Trade structure in the retailing industry can affect the use of sales promotions. As noted in Chapter 12, in the United States and parts of Europe, the retail industry is highly concentrated (i.e., dominated by a few key players such as Walmart). This situation requires significant promotional activity at both the trade and the consumer levels. By contrast, in countries where retailing is more fragmented—Japan is a case in point—there is less pressure to engage in promotional activities.

Sampling

Sampling is a sales promotion technique that provides potential customers with the opportunity to try a product or service at no cost. As Marc Pritchard, Chief Brand Officer at Procter & Gamble (P&G), noted, "The most fundamental thing that consumers want to do is try before they buy."[4] A typical sample is an individual portion of a consumer packaged good, such as breakfast cereal, shampoo, cosmetics, or detergent, distributed through the mail, on a door-to-door basis, or at a retail location.

Fifty years ago, Kikkoman brand soy sauce was unknown in the United States. Yuzaburo Mogi, currently honorary CEO and chairman of the board of directors, took part in a sampling program that Kikkoman had started in American supermarkets. Mogi and his employees passed out free samples of food seasoned with Kikkoman; today, the U.S. market accounts for approximately 70 percent of Kikkoman's profits from international operations.[5] The company continues to make extensive use of shopper marketing as a communication tool. During grilling season, for example, Kikkoman's promotional strategy calls for dispensing recipes for marinades and coupons from shelf displays in the supermarket meat aisle. Before Thanksgiving, the strategy calls for placing turkey-brining recipes in the poultry section.[6]

The average cost per sample can range from $0.10 to $0.50; 2 to 3 million samples are distributed in a typical sampling program. Cost is one of the major disadvantages associated with sampling; another problem is that it is sometimes difficult for marketing managers to assess the contribution that a sampling program makes to return on investment. Today, many companies utilize *event marketing* and *sponsorships* to distribute samples at concerts, sports events, and special events such as food and beverage festivals attended by large numbers of people. In the Information Age, sampling may also consist of a week's free viewing of a cable TV channel or a no-cost trial subscription to an online computer service; Internet users can also request free samples through a company's Web site.

Compared with other forms of marketing communication, sampling is more likely to result in actual trials of the product. To ensure a trial, consumer products companies are increasingly using a technique known as "point-of-use" sampling. For example, Starbucks dispatches "Chill Patrols" in the summertime to pass out samples of ice-cold Frappuccinos to overheated commuters during rush hour in busy metropolitan areas. In an example of "point-of-dirt" sampling, Unilever hired a promotional marketing firm to pass out Lever2000 hand wipes in food courts and petting zoos. As Michael Murphy, director of home and personal-care promotions at Unilever, noted, "We're getting smarter. You must be much more precise in what, where, and how you deliver samples."[7]

Sampling can be especially important if consumers are not persuaded by claims made in advertising or other channels. In China, shoppers are often reluctant to buy full-sized packages of imported consumer products that they have not tried—especially because the price may be several times higher than the price of local brands.

P&G's dominance in China's shampoo market can be attributed to the company's skillful use of market segmentation coupled with an aggressive sampling program. P&G offers several shampoo brands in China: Rejoice ("soft and beautiful hair") is currently the top hair-care brand in that market, but other P&G brands in China include Pantene ("nutrition"), Head & Shoulders ("dandruff relief"), and Vidal Sassoon ("fashion").[8] P&G distributed millions of free samples of its shampoo products; after the no-risk trial, many consumers became adopters. Now, however, P&G faces a new challenge: Urban Millennials in China are favoring upmarket, niche brands at the expense of mainstream brands such as Head & Shoulders.

Couponing

A **coupon** is a printed certificate that entitles the bearer to a price reduction or some other special consideration for purchasing a particular product or service. In the United States and Great Britain, marketers rely heavily on newspapers to deliver coupons; nearly 90 percent of all coupons are distributed in a printed, ride-along vehicle known as a *free-standing insert* (FSI). Sunday papers carry the vast majority of FSIs. *On-pack coupons* are attached to, or part of, the product package; they can frequently be redeemed immediately at checkout. *In-pack coupons* are placed inside the package. Coupons can also be handed out in stores, offered on a self-service basis from on-shelf dispensers, delivered to homes by mail, or distributed electronically at the checkout counter. In addition, the number of coupons distributed via the Internet is growing.

Cross coupons are distributed with one product but redeemable for another. For example, a toothpaste coupon might be distributed with a toothbrush.

The United States leads the world in the number of coupons issued, by a wide margin. NCH Marketing Services, which tracks coupon trends, reports that nearly 300 billion coupons are distributed in the United States each year, but only 1 percent are actually redeemed. Online coupon distribution is growing at a rapid rate, with Google being one of the companies experimenting with this channel.[9]

Coupons are a favorite promotion tool of consumer packaged goods companies such as P&G and Unilever. The goal is to reward loyal users and stimulate product trials by nonusers. In the European Union, couponing is widely used in the United Kingdom and Belgium. Couponing is not as prevalent in Asia, a region where saving face is important. Although Asian consumers have a reputation for thriftiness, some are reluctant to use coupons, because doing so might bring shame upon them or their families. According to Joseph Potacki, who has taught a "Basics of Promotion" seminar for the Promotion Marketing Association (PMA), couponing is the aspect of the promotion mix for which the practices in the United States differ the most from those in other countries. In the United States, couponing accounts for 70 percent of consumer promotion spending. Elsewhere, the percentage is much lower. As Potacki explained, "It is far less—or nonexistent—in most other countries simply because the cultures don't accept couponing." According to Potacki, one reason that use of coupons has grown in importance in countries such as the United Kingdom is that retailers are learning more about its advantages.[10]

Social couponing is one of hottest online sales promotion trends today. Industry leader Groupon offers its followers deal-of-the-day coupons that are sponsored by local businesses. Followers then share their experiences via social networks. The local business gets customers, and Groupon takes a share of the coupon proceeds. Groupon has grown at a dizzying pace, expanding from 1 country to 35 countries in a single year. Much of that growth has come via acquisition. By the end of 2016, Groupon had more than 50 million users in dozens of countries. More than half of Groupon's Web site visitors live in Europe; 33 percent are in North America. A key investor in this venture is the Russian Internet investment group Digital Sky Technologies (DST). Nevertheless, as me-too companies have sprung up, Groupon has struggled in recent years. Perhaps its founders are having second thoughts about the time they rejected a $6 billion takeover offer from Google![11]

Sales Promotion: Issues and Problems

As noted earlier, many companies are being more strategic in targeting their sampling programs. In the case of coupons, retailers must bundle the redeemed coupons together and ship them to a processing point. Many times, coupons are not validated at the point of purchase; in addition, fraudulent redemption costs marketers hundreds of millions of dollars each year. Fraud can take other forms as well. For example, during the 2004 Super Bowl broadcast, PepsiCo launched a joint promotion with Apple's iTunes Music Store. Apple planned to give away 100 million songs for free (regular price: $0.99); consumers could obtain a code from the caps of Pepsi bottles and enter the code online to qualify for the download. The promotion was designed so that anyone purchasing a bottle of Pepsi had a one-in-three chance of being a winner. However, many people discovered that by tilting the bottles to one side, they could tell whether the bottle was a winner. Moreover, they could read the code without having to pay for the Pepsi![12]

Given these kinds of risks, companies must take extreme care when formulating and executing sales promotions. In some emerging markets, sales promotion efforts can raise eyebrows if companies appear to be exploiting regulatory loopholes and lack of consumer resistance to intrusion. Sales promotion in Europe is highly regulated. Sales promotions are popular in Scandinavia because of restrictions on broadcast advertising, but promotions in the Nordic countries are subject to regulations. If such regulations are relaxed and harmonized as the single market develops in Europe, companies may eventually be able to roll out pan-European promotions.

In the late 1990s, a study examined coupon usage and attitudes toward both coupons and sweepstakes in Taiwan, Thailand, and Malaysia.[13] Although it is a bit dated, this study still has relevance to global companies that are targeting these and other developing nations in Asia, where consumers have relatively little experience with coupons. The study utilized Hofstede's social values framework as a guide. All three countries in the study are collectivist, and the researchers found that positive attitudes of family members and society as a whole influenced in an individual in having a positive attitude toward coupons and coupon usage.

However, consumers in the three nations showed some distinct differences in values orientation. For example, Malaysians are characterized by higher power distance and lower uncertainty avoidance than populations in the other countries. For Malaysians, the fear of public embarrassment was a constraint on coupon usage. In all three countries, media consumption habits were also a factor in couponing; individuals who were not regular readers of magazines or newspapers were less likely to be aware that coupons were available in the periodicals. Consumers in Taiwan and Thailand looked more favorably on coupons compared to sweepstakes. The impact of religion also surprised the researchers. In Malaysia, where the population is primarily Muslim, the researchers assumed that consumers would avoid sweepstakes promotions. Sweepstakes can be likened to gambling, which is frowned on by Islam. In reality, Malaysians showed a preference for sweepstakes over coupons. In Taiwan, where Buddhism, Confucianism, and Taoism are all practiced, religion appeared to have little impact on attitudes toward promotions. One implication of this study's findings for marketing in developing countries is that, despite cultural differences, increased availability of promotions is likely to result in higher levels of consumer utilization.[14]

(14-2) Personal Selling

◀ **14-2** List the steps in the strategic/consultative personal selling model.

Personal selling is person-to-person communication between a company representative and a prospective buyer. The seller's communication effort is focused on informing and persuading the prospect, with the short-term goal of making a sale and the longer-term goal of building a relationship with that buyer. The salesperson's job is to correctly understand the buyer's needs, match those needs to the company's product(s), and then persuade the customer to buy. Because selling provides a two-way communication channel, it is especially important in marketing industrial products that may be expensive and technologically complex. Sales personnel can often provide headquarters with important customer feedback that can be used in design and engineering decisions.

Effective personal selling in a salesperson's home country requires building a relationship with the customer; global marketing presents additional challenges because the buyer and the seller may come from different national or cultural backgrounds. Nevertheless, it is difficult to overstate the importance of a face-to-face, personal selling effort for industrial products in global markets. For example, when Spain's Iberia Airlines was modernizing its long-haul fleet, salespeople from Boeing and rival Airbus met numerous times with Enrique Dupuy de Lome, Iberia's chief financial officer. At stake was a 12-plane order worth approximately $2 billion. The aircraft under consideration were the Boeing 777-300ER ("Extended Range") and the Airbus A340-600. After each sales team presented its initial bid, the negotiations began; Toby Bright, Boeing's top salesperson for jets, faced off against John Leahy of Airbus. Iberia's demands included discounts off list prices and resale value guarantees for the aircraft. After months of meetings and revised proposals, Airbus was awarded the contract.[15]

Personal selling is also a popular marketing communication tool in countries that place various restrictions on advertising. In Japan, for example, it is difficult to obtain permission to present product comparisons in any type of advertising. In such an environment, personal selling is the best way to provide hard-hitting, side-by-side comparisons of competing products. Personal selling is also used frequently in countries where low wage rates allow large local sales forces to be hired. When expanding in Central Europe, HBO built its core of subscribers in Hungary by selling the service through a door-to-door campaign.

The cost-effectiveness of personal selling in certain parts of the world has been a key driver behind the decision at many U.S.-based firms to begin marketing products and services overseas. A company is more likely to test a new territory or product if the entry price is relatively low. For example, some high-tech firms have utilized lower-cost sales personnel in Latin America to introduce new product features to their customers. Only if the response is favorable do the firms commit major resources to a U.S. rollout.

The risks inherent in establishing a personal selling structure overseas persist today. The crucial issue is not whether in-country sales and marketing people can provide more benefit than a remote force: In the vast majority of scenarios, they can. Instead, the issue is whether the country team should consist of in-country nationals or **expatriates** (also known as *expats*)—that is, employees who are sent from their respective home countries to work abroad.

Many of the environmental issues and challenges identified in earlier chapters often surface as a company completes the initial stages of implementing a personal selling strategy. These include the following factors:

- *Political risks*. Unstable or corrupt governments can completely change the rules for the sales team. Establishing new operations in a foreign country is especially tricky if a coup is imminent or if a dictator demands certain "considerations" (which has been the case in many developing countries). Today, for example, Colombia offers great market potential, and its government projects an image of openness; that was not always the case, however. In the not-so-distant past, many companies found the unspoken rules of the cabal to be inordinately burdensome.

  In a country ruled by a dictatorship, the target audience and accompanying message of the sales effort tend to be far narrower and restricted because government planners mandate how business will be conducted. Firms selling in Hong Kong, for example, were concerned that China would impose its will and dramatically alter the selling environment after the transfer of power over that territory from the United Kingdom to China in 1997. In response to such concerns, British Telecom brought many members of its Hong Kong sales staff back to London prior to the changeover. However, to the great relief of Hong Kong's business community, Chinese officials ultimately recognized that a policy of minimal intervention would be the wisest approach.

- *Regulatory hurdles*. Governments sometimes set up quota systems or impose tariffs that affect entering foreign sales forces. In part, governments consider such actions to be an easy source of revenue, but, even more important, policymakers want to ensure that sales teams from local firms retain a competitive edge in terms of what they can offer and at what price. Regulations can also take the form of rules that restrict certain types of sales activities. In 1998, for example, the Chinese government banned door-to-door selling, effectively thwarting Avon's business model. Avon responded by establishing a network of store representatives.

  When direct selling was legalized in 2006, CEO Andrea Jung expected that China would soon be adding $1 billion a year to Avon's bottom line. As it turns out however, Avon incurred losses in China in connection with the transition from stores to the direct-sales business model. Compounding the situation was a bribery scandal that originated in China and spread to other markets; the subsequent investigation tarnished the company's reputation and cost it tens of millions of dollars.[16]

- *Currency fluctuations*. In many instances, a company's sales effort has been derailed not by ineffectiveness or lack of market opportunity, but rather by fluctuating currency values. In the mid-1980s, for example, Caterpillar's global market share declined when the dollar's strength allowed Komatsu to woo U.S. customers away. Then, while Caterpillar's management team was preoccupied with domestic issues, competitors chipped away at the firm's position in global markets.

- *Market unknowns*. When a company enters a new region of the world, its selling strategy may unravel because of a lack of knowledge of market conditions, the accepted way of doing business, or the positioning of its in-country competitors. When a game plan is finally crafted to counter the obstacles, it is sometimes too late for the company to succeed. Conversely, if management devotes an inordinate amount of time to conducting market research prior to entry, it may discover that its window of opportunity has closed, with the sales being lost to a fast-moving competitor that did not fall victim to the "analysis paralysis" syndrome. Thus, it is difficult to make generalizations about the optimal time to enter a new country.

If all of these challenges can be overcome, or at least minimized, the personal selling endeavor can be implemented with the aid of a tool known as the *strategic/consultative selling model*.

The Strategic/Consultative Selling Model

Figure 14-1 depicts the **strategic/consultative selling model**, which has gained wide acceptance in the United States. This model consists of five interdependent steps, each with three prescriptions that can serve as a checklist for sales personnel.[17] Many U.S. companies that have begun developing global markets have established face-to-face sales teams either directly, using their own personnel, or indirectly, through contracted sales agents. As a result, the strategic/consultative selling model is increasingly being used on a worldwide basis. The key to ensuring that the model produces the desired outcome—quality partnerships with customers—is to implement and follow its steps on a consistent basis. This is far more difficult to achieve with international sales teams than it is with U.S.-based units, which are much more accessible to corporate headquarters.

First, a sales representative must develop a **personal selling philosophy**. This requires a commitment to the marketing concept and a willingness to take on the role of problem solver or partner in helping customers. A sales professional must also be secure in the belief that selling is a valuable activity. In addition, the representative must develop a **relationship strategy**, a game plan for establishing and maintaining high-quality relationships with prospects and customers. The relationship strategy provides a blueprint for creating the rapport and mutual trust that will serve as the basis of a lasting partnership. This step connects sales personnel directly to the concept of *relationship marketing*, an approach that stresses the importance of developing long-term partnerships with customers. Many U.S.-based companies have adopted the relationship marketing

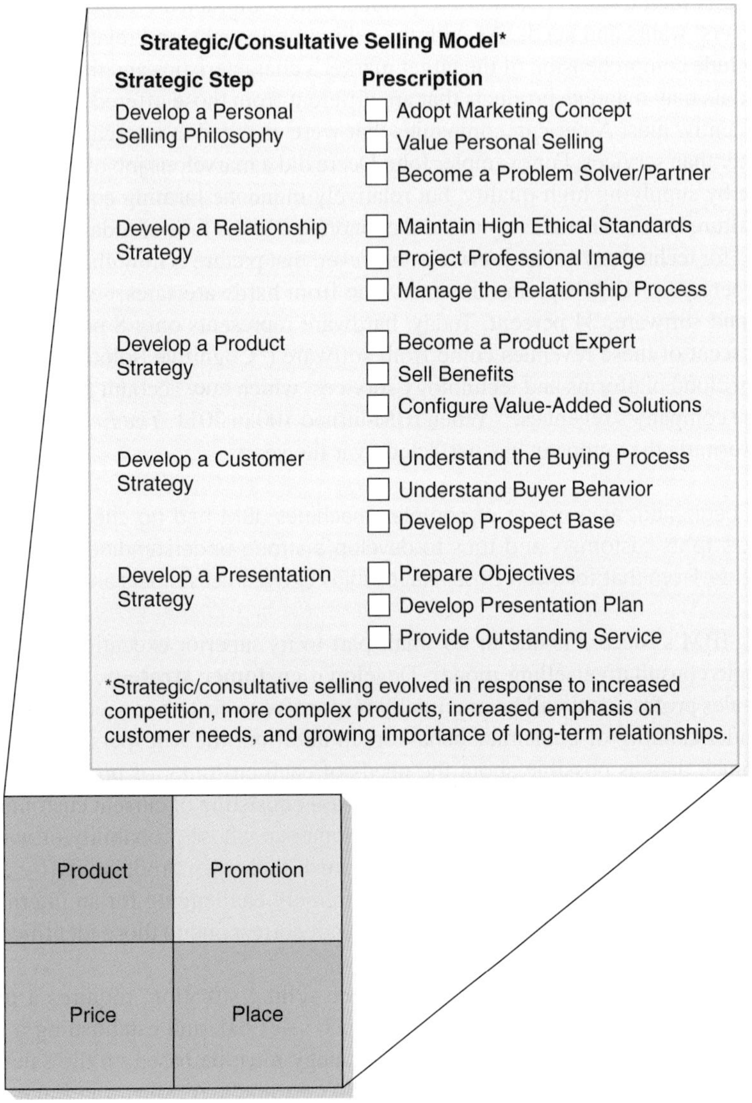

Figure 14-1 The Strategic/Consultative Selling Model

Source: Manning, Gerald L.; Ahearne, Michael; Reese, Barry L., Selling Today: Partnering to Create Value, 14th Ed., ©2018, Pearson Education, Inc.

approach to selling in the American market; it is equally relevant—perhaps even more so—to any company hoping to achieve success in global marketing.

Second, in developing personal and relationship strategies on an international level, the representative is wise to take a step back and understand how these strategies will likely fit with the foreign environment. For example, an aggressive "I'll do whatever it takes to get your business" attitude is the worst possible approach to use in some cultures, even though in many large U.S. cities it is viewed as the standard, and even preferred, practice. These variations in customers' preferences are why it is prudent for a company's sales management and sales rep teams to invest the time and energy necessary to learn about the global market in which they will be selling. In many countries, people have only a rudimentary understanding of sales techniques; acceptance of those techniques may be low as well. In turn, a sophisticated sales campaign that excels in the United States may never hit the mark in other countries. In-country experts such as consultants or agents can be excellent sources of real-world intelligence that can help a sales rep create an effective international relationship strategy. Such people are especially helpful if the sales force will include many expatriates, who will not have resident nationals as colleagues to whom they can turn for advice. Sales representatives must understand that patience and a willingness to assimilate host-country norms and customs are important attributes in developing relationships built on respect.

The third step, developing a **product strategy**, results in a plan that can assist the sales representative in selecting and positioning products that will satisfy customer needs. A sales professional must be an expert who possesses not only a deep understanding of the features and attributes of each product he or she represents, but also an understanding of the competitive offerings. That understanding is then used to position the product and communicate benefits that are relevant to the customers' wants and needs. As with the selling philosophy and relationship strategy, this step must include comprehension of the target market's characteristics and the fact that prevailing needs and wants may mandate products that are different from those offered in the home country.

Until recently, most American companies that were engaged in international selling offered products rather than services. For example, John Deere did a marvelous job of increasing its global market share by supplying high-quality, but relatively mundane farming equipment to countries where agriculture remains a mainstay of local economies. In the face of today's exploding worldwide demand for technology-related services, however, that picture is now changing. For example, in 2000, 24 percent of IBM's pretax income came from hardware sales; services accounted for 40 percent, and software, 24 percent. Today, hardware represents only 8 percent of IBM's revenues; 23 percent of these revenues come from software ("Cognitive Solutions"). A big growth area has been cloud platforms and technology services, which now account for approximately 43 percent of the company's revenues.[18] When IBM turned 100 in 2011, *The Economist* summarized the success formula the company has perfected over the years:

> From the beginning, as a maker of complex machines, IBM had no choice but to explain its products to its customers and thus to develop a strong understanding of their business requirements. From that followed close relationships between customers and supplier.[19]

In short, IBM's success is due in no small part to its superior execution of the fourth step of the strategic/consultative selling model: Develop a **customer strategy**, which is a plan that ensures the sales professional will be maximally responsive to customer needs. Doing so requires a general understanding of consumer behavior; in addition, the salesperson must collect and analyze as much data as possible about the needs of each customer or prospect. The customer strategy step also includes building a prospect database consisting of current customers as well as potential customers (or leads). A *qualified lead* is someone whose probability of wanting to buy the product is high. Many sales organizations diminish their own productivity by chasing after too many nonqualified leads. This issue can be extremely challenging for an international sales unit, because customer cues or "buying signs" may not correspond to those identified in the sales rep's home country.

The fifth and final step, the actual face-to-face selling situation, requires a **presentation strategy**. This consists of setting objectives for each sales call and establishing a presentation plan to meet those objectives. The presentation strategy must be based on the sales representative's commitment to provide outstanding service to customers. As shown in Figure 14-2, when these five strategies are integrated into an appropriate personal selling philosophy, the result is a high-quality partnership.

The **presentation plan** that is at the heart of the presentation strategy is typically divided into six stages: approach, presentation, demonstration, negotiation, closing, and servicing the sale (see Figure 14-3). The relative importance of each stage can vary by country or region. As mentioned previously, the global salesperson *must* understand cultural norms and proper protocol, from the proper technique for exchanging business cards to the proper volume of one's voice during a discussion to the proper amount of eye contact made with the decision maker. In some countries, the approach is prolonged as the buyer gets to know or takes the measure of the salesperson on a personal level, with no mention of the pending deal. In such instances, the presentation comes only after rapport has been firmly established. In some regions of Latin America and Asia, for example, rapport development may take weeks, even months. The customer may also place more importance on what occurs *following* work than on what is accomplished *during* the formal work hours of 8 A.M. to 5 P.M.

In the six-step presentation plan, the first step, *approach*, is the sales representative's initial contact with the customer or prospect. The most crucial element of this step is to completely understand the decision-making process and the role of each participant, such as decision maker, influencer, ally, or blocker. Also, it is critical to understand cross-cultural communication differences. In Britain, for example, one of the "unwritten rules" of behavior is the "no name" rule. As Kate Fox explains, the "Brash American" approach—for example, "Hi, I'm Bill, how are you?", particularly if accompanied by an outstretched hand and beaming smile—makes the English wince and cringe.[20]

In some societies, it is difficult to identify the highest-ranking individual based on observable behavior during group meetings. This crucial bit of strategic information often is uncovered only after the sales rep has spent considerable time developing rapport and getting to know the overall customer organization from various perspectives and in various contexts.

In the second step, the need discovery, the prospect's needs are assessed and matched to the company's products. To communicate effectively with a foreign audience, the style and message of the presentation must be carefully thought out. In the United States, the presentation is typically designed to sell and persuade, whereas the intent of the international version should be to educate and inform. High-pressure tactics rarely succeed in global selling, despite the fact that they are natural components of many American sales pitches. The message is equally critical because what may be regarded as fully acceptable in U.S. discussions may either offend or confuse the overseas sales audience. A humorous example of this occurred during a session between representatives from Adolph Coors Company and a foreign prospect. The first slide in the presentation contained a translation of Coors's slogan "Turn It Loose," but within seconds of this slide being shown, the audience began to chuckle. As translated, the slogan described diarrhea—obviously a message that the presenters had no desire to convey to this group!

Next comes the presentation, during which the salesperson has the opportunity to tailor the communication effort to the customer and alternately tell and show how the product can meet

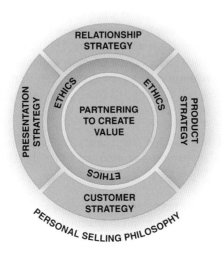

Figure 14-2 Building a High-Quality Sales Partnership

Source: Manning, Gerald L.; Ahearne, Michael; Reese, Barry L., Selling Today: Partnering to Create Value, 14th Ed., ©2018, Pearson Education, Inc.

Figure 14-3 The Six-Step Presentation Plan

Source: Manning, Gerald L.; Ahearne, Michael; Reese, Barry L., Selling Today: Partnering to Create Value, 14th Ed., ©2018, Pearson Education, Inc.

The Six-Step Presentation Plan

Step One:
Approach
- [ ] Review Strategic/Consultative Selling Model
- [ ] Initiate customer contact

Step Two:
Need Discovery
- [ ] Ask strategic questions
- [ ] Determine customer needs
- [ ] Select product Solution

Step Three:
Presentation
- [ ] Select presentation strategy
- [ ] Create presentation plan
- [ ] Initiate presentation

Step Four:
Negotiation
- [ ] Anticipate buyer concerns
- [ ] Plan negotiating methods
- [ ] Initiate win-win negotiations

Step Five:
Close
- [ ] Plan appropriate closing methods
- [ ] Recognize closing clues
- [ ] Initiate closing methods

Step Six:
Servicing the Sale
- [ ] Follow through
- [ ] Follow-up calls
- [ ] Expansion selling

Service, retail, wholesale, and manufacturer selling

the customer's needs. This third step represents one of personal selling's important advantages as a promotional tool. The prospect's senses become involved, and he or she can actually see the product in action, and touch it, taste it, or hear it, as the case may be.

During the presentation, the prospect may express concerns or objections about the product itself, the price, or some other aspect of the sale. Dealing effectively with objections in an international setting is a learned art. In some cases, this is simply part of the sales ritual, and the customer expects the representative to be prepared for a lively debate on the pros and cons of the product in question. In other instances, it is taboo to initiate an open discussion where any form of disagreement is apparent: Such conversations are to be handled in a one-to-one situation or in a small group with a few key individuals present. A common theme in sales training is the concept of *active listening*; naturally, in global sales, verbal and nonverbal communication barriers of the type discussed in Chapter 4 present special challenges. When objections are successfully overcome, serious negotiations can begin.

The fourth step, *negotiation*, is required to ensure that both the customer and the salesperson come away from the presentation as winners. Experienced American sales representatives know that persistence during the negotiation stage is one tactic often needed to win an order in the United States. In contrast, some foreign customers consider American-style persistence (implying tenacity) or arm-twisting rude and offensive. This kind of behavior can end the negotiations quickly—or, in the worst case, can be taken as a display of self-perceived American superiority. Such a perception must be countered aggressively or the pressure tactics brought to an immediate end. In her best-selling book *Watching the English*, author Kate Fox notes that, among the British:

> There is near-universal distaste for the "hard sell," for "pushiness," for the sort of brash, in-your-face approach to advertising and marketing that the English invariably describe, in contemptuous tones, as "American."[21]

Conversely, in other countries, persistence often means endurance, a willingness to patiently invest months or years before the efforts result in an actual sale. For example, a company wishing to enter the Japanese market must be prepared for negotiations to take several years.

Having completed the negotiation step, the sales representative is able to move on to the fifth step, the *close*, in which the rep asks for the order. Attitudes toward the degree of bluntness that is acceptable in making this request vary among countries. In Latin America, a bold closing statement is respected. In contrast, in Asia, the closing must be done with more deference toward the decision maker. As with objection handling and negotiation, the close is a selling skill that comes with both knowledge and experience in global business and sales.

The sixth and final step is *servicing the sale*. A sale does not end when the order is written; to ensure customer satisfaction with the purchase, an implementation process (which may include delivery and installation) must be outlined and a customer service program established (see Exhibit 14-3). Implementation can be complicated because of logistical and transportation issues as well as potential problems with the in-country resources needed to handle all the necessary steps. Transportation alternatives were discussed in Chapter 12. Decisions regarding resources for implementation and after-sale service are similar to decisions about the personal selling structure described in the following paragraphs. There are cost benefits to using in-country nationals for implementation, but quality control is more difficult to guarantee. Establishing expatriates for the primary function of implementation is costly and normally cannot be justified until international operations are more mature and profitable. Nevertheless, sending an implementation team to the host country creates a variety of expense and regulatory concerns. Even when implementation has been adequately addressed, the requirement for solid customer service raises all of the same questions again: in-country nationals, expatriates, or third-country nationals?

(14-3) Sales Force Nationality

◀ **14-3** Explain the contingency factors that must be considered when making decisions about sales force nationality.

As just noted, a basic issue for companies that sell globally is the composition of the sales force in terms of nationality. It is possible to utilize expatriate salespersons, hire host-country nationals, or recruit third-country sales personnel (see Exhibit 14-4). The staffing decision is contingent on several factors, including management's orientation, the technological sophistication of the product, and the stage of economic development exhibited by the target country. Not surprisingly, a company with an ethnocentric orientation is likely to prefer expatriates as its sales representatives and to adopt a standardized approach without regard to technology or the level of economic development in the target country. Polycentric companies selling in developed countries should opt for expatriates to sell technologically sophisticated products; a host-country sales force can be used when technological sophistication is lower. In less-developed countries, host-country

Exhibit 14-3 This pair of print advertisements for DuPont Pioneer communicates the fact that the company's global network of sales agents is dedicated to top-notch customer service. Worldwide, the Pioneer brand is associated with expert advice and customer support: It is important for farmers to have the right seeds for their particular soil and climatic conditions. Pioneer's sales agents go into the field equipped with tablet devices on which they record and store data about each farmer's needs. The agents can also search Pioneer's database for the product that will give the best yield per acre. In 2019, DuPont Pioneer's corporate name was changed to Corteva Agriscience. In 2019, DuPont Pioneer's corporate name was changed to Corteva Agriscience.
Source: Courtesy of DuPont.

Exhibit 14-4 In global marketing, sales meetings and presentations typically involve people of various nationalities. These individuals may include expatriates (from the headquarters country), host-country nationals, and third-country nationals. A successful salesperson takes the time to adapt the strategic/consultative selling model to the specific selling situation. The various elements of the six-step presentation plan may also need to be adapted. Can you think of any characteristics of your home-country communication patterns that might require adaptation?
Source: Rawpixel.com/Shutterstock.

nationals should be used for products in which technology is a factor; host-country agents should be used for low-tech products. The widest diversity of sales force nationality is found in a company in which a regiocentric orientation prevails. Except in the case of high-tech products in developed countries, third-country nationals are likely to be used in all situations.[22]

In addition to the factors just cited, management must weigh the advantages and disadvantages of each option. First, because they come from the home country, expatriates often possess a high level of product knowledge and are likely to be thoroughly versed in their company's commitment to after-sales service. They also come with corporate philosophies and culture well ingrained. In addition, they are better able to institute the acceptable practices and follow the policies of the home office, and generally there is less potential for control or loyalty issues to arise. Finally, a foreign assignment can provide employees with valuable experience that can enhance their own promotion prospects within the company's hierarchy.

Utilizing expatriates, however, has several disadvantages. If the headquarters mind-set is *too* firmly ingrained, the expat may have a difficult time understanding the foreign environment and assimilating into it. This can eventually lead to significant losses, as the sales effort may be poorly received in the market, or homesickness can lead to a costly reversal of the relocation process. Maintaining expat sales personnel is also extremely expensive: The average annual cost to post employees and their families overseas exceeds $250,000. In addition to paying expat salaries, companies must pay moving expenses, cost-of-living adjustments, and host-country taxes. Despite the high investment made in them, many expats fail to complete their assignments because of inadequate training and orientation prior to the cross-border transfer.

An alternative is to build a sales force with host-country personnel. Locals offer several advantages when it comes to selling, including intimate knowledge of the market and business environment, language skills, and superior knowledge of local culture. The last consideration can be especially important in Asia and Latin America. In addition, because in-country personnel are already in place in the target country, the company avoids the need for expensive relocations. On the downside, host-country nationals may possess work habits or selling styles that do not mesh well with those of the parent company. Furthermore, a firm's corporate sales executives tend to have less control over an operation that is dominated by host-country nationals. Headquarters executives may also experience difficulty cultivating loyalty, and host-country nationals are likely to need hefty doses of training and education regarding both the company and its products.

A third option is to hire persons who are natives of neither the headquarters country nor the host country; such persons are known as *third-country nationals*. For example, a U.S.-based company might hire someone from Thailand to represent it in China. This option has many advantages in common with the host-country-national approach. In addition, if conflict, diplomatic tension, or some other form of disagreement has driven a wedge between the home country and the target sales country, a sales representative from a third country may be perceived as sufficiently neutral or at "arm's length" to enable the company to continue its sales effort. Even so, the third-country option has several disadvantages. For one thing, sales prospects may wonder why they have been approached by someone who is neither a local national nor a native of the headquarters country. Third-country nationals may also lack motivation if they are compensated less generously than expats or host-country sales personnel, and they may find themselves passed over for promotions as coveted assignments go to others.

After much trial and error in creating sales forces, most companies today attempt to establish a hybrid sales force composed of a balanced mix of expatriates and in-country nationals. The operative word for this approach is *balanced*, because the potential always remains for conflict to occur between the two groups. It is also the most expensive proposition in terms of upfront costs, because both relocation of expats and extensive training of in-country nationals are required. However, the short-term costs are usually deemed necessary to do business and conduct personal selling overseas.

After considering the options, management may question the appropriateness of trying to create personal selling units made up of their own people. A fourth option is to utilize the services of **sales agents**. Such agents work under contract rather than as full-time employees. From a global perspective, it often makes a great deal of sense to set up one or more agent entities to at least gain entry into a selected country or region. In some cases, because of the remoteness of the area or the lack of revenue opportunity (beyond servicing satellite operations of customers headquartered elsewhere), agents are retained on a fairly permanent level. To this day, the majority of U.S., Asian, and European companies with an Africa-based sales presence maintain agent groups to represent their interests.

Agents are less expensive than full-time, in-country national sales representatives; at the same time, they possess the same market and cultural knowledge. If agents are used initially and the sales effort gains traction, they can be phased out and replaced by the manufacturer's sales force. Conversely, a company may use its own sales force initially and then convert to agents. P&G's Golden Store program in Mexico is an excellent illustration of the various sales force options. As discussed in Chapter 12, company representatives visit participating stores to tidy display areas and arrange promotional material in prominent places. At first, P&G used its own sales force for this purpose; now it relies on independent agents, who buy inventory (paying in advance) and then resell the items to shopkeepers.

Other international personal selling approaches that fall somewhere between sales agents and full-time employee teams include the following:

- *Exclusive license arrangements* in which a firm pays commissions to an in-country company's sales force to conduct personal selling on its behalf. For example, when Canada's regulatory agency prevented U.S. telephone companies from entering the market on their own, AT&T, MCI, Sprint, and other firms crafted a series of exclusive license arrangements with Canadian telephone companies.
- *Contract manufacturing or production* with a degree of personal selling made available through warehouses or showrooms that are open to potential customers. Sears has employed this technique in various overseas markets, with the emphasis placed on manufacturing and production but with the understanding that opportunities for some sales results do exist.
- *Management-only agreements* through which a corporation manages a foreign sales force in a mode that is similar to franchising. Hilton Hotels has these types of agreements all over the world—not only for its hotel operations, but also for its personal selling efforts aimed at securing conventions, business meetings, and other large-group events.
- *Joint ventures* with an in-country (or regional) partner. Because many countries place restrictions on foreign ownership within their borders, partnerships can serve as the best way for a company to obtain both a personal sales capability and an existing base of customers.

▶ 14-4 Explain direct marketing's advantages and identify the most common types of direct marketing channels.

(14-4) Special Forms of Marketing Communications: Direct Marketing

The Direct Marketing Association defines **direct marketing** as any communication with a consumer or business recipient that is designed to generate a response in the form of an order, a request for further information, or a visit to a store or other place of business. Companies use direct mail, telemarketing, television, print, and other media to generate responses and build databases filled with purchase histories and other information about customers. By contrast, mass-marketing communications are typically aimed at broad segments of consumers with certain demographic, psychographic, or behavioral characteristics in common. Table 14-2 highlights other differences between direct marketing and "regular" marketing.

Although direct marketing dates back decades, more sophisticated techniques and tools are being used today. For example, Don Peppers and Martha Rogers advocate an approach known as **one-to-one marketing**. Building on the notion of customer relationship management (CRM), one-to-one marketing calls for treating different customers differently based on their previous purchase histories or past interactions with the company. Peppers and Rogers describe the four steps in one-to-one marketing as follows:[23]

1. *Identify* customers and accumulate detailed information about them.
2. *Differentiate* customers and rank them in terms of their value to the company.
3. *Interact* with customers and develop more cost-efficient and effective forms of interaction.
4. *Customize* the product or service offered to the customer (e.g., by personalizing direct-mail offers).

Worldwide, the popularity of direct marketing has been steadily increasing in recent years. One reason is the availability of credit cards—widespread in some countries, growing in others—as a convenient payment mechanism for direct-response purchases. (Visa, American Express, and MasterCard generate enormous revenues by sending direct-mail offers to their cardholders.) Another reason is societal: Whether in Japan, Germany, or the United States, dual-income families have money to spend but less time to shop outside the home. Technological advances have made it easier for companies to reach customers directly. For example, cable and satellite television allow advertisers to reach specific audiences on a global basis. MTV reaches hundreds of millions of households worldwide and attracts a young viewership. In contrast, a company wishing to reach businesspeople may buy time on CNN, Fox News Network, or CNBC.

Direct marketing's popularity in Europe increased sharply during the 1990s. The European Commission expects investment in direct marketing to surpass expenditures for traditional advertising in the near future. One reason is that direct marketing programs can be readily made to conform to the "think global, act local" philosophy. As Tony Coad, managing director of

TABLE 14-2 Comparison of Direct Marketing and Mass Marketing

Direct Marketing	Mass Marketing
The marketer adds value (creates place utility) by arranging for delivery of the product to the customer's door.	The product benefits do not typically include delivery to the customer's door.
The marketer controls the product all the way through to delivery.	The marketer typically loses control as the product is turned over to distribution channel intermediaries.
Direct-response advertising is used to generate an immediate inquiry or order.	Advertising is used for its cumulative effect over time to build image, awareness, loyalty, and benefit recall. Purchase action is deferred.
Repetition is used within the ad/offer.	Repetition is used over a period of time.
The customer perceives higher risk because the product is bought unseen. Recourse may be viewed as distant or inconvenient.	The customer perceives less risk due to direct contact with the product. Recourse is viewed as less distant.

a London-based direct marketing and database company, noted two decades ago, "Given the linguistic, cultural, and regional diversity of Europe, the celebrated idea of a Euro-consumer is Euro-baloney. Direct marketing's strength lies in addressing these differences and adapting to each consumer."[24] Obstacles still remain, however, including the European Commission's concerns about data protection and privacy, high postal rates in some countries, and the relatively limited development of the mailing list industry. Rainer Hengst of Deutsche Post offers the following guidelines for U.S.-based direct marketers that wish to go global:[25]

- The world is full of people who are not Americans. Be sure not to treat them like they are.
- Like politics, all marketing is local. Just because your direct-mail campaign worked in Texas, do not assume it will work in Toronto.
- Although there may be a European Union, there is no such thing as a "European."
- Pick your target, focus on one country, and do your homework.
- You will have a hard time finding customers in Paris, France, if your return address is Paris, Texas. Customers need to be able to return products locally or at least believe there are services available in their country.

Direct Mail

Direct mail uses the postal service as a vehicle for delivering a personally addressed offer to a prospect targeted by a marketer. Direct mail is popular with banks, insurance companies, and other financial services providers. As customers respond to direct-mail offers, the marketer adds their information to its database. That information, in turn, allows the marketer to refine subsequent offers and generate more precisely targeted lists. The United States is home to a well-developed mailing list industry. A company can rent a list to target virtually any type of buyer; naturally, the more selective and specialized the list, the more expensive it is. The availability of good lists and the sheer size of the market are important factors in explaining why Americans receive more direct mail than anyone else. On a per capita basis, German consumers are actually the world's leading mail-order shoppers, buying more than $500 each in merchandise annually.

Compared with the United States, mailing list availability in Europe and Japan is much more limited. The lists that are available may be lower in quality and contain more errors and duplications than lists from the United States. Despite such problems, direct mail is growing in popularity as a marketing vehicle in some parts of the world. In Europe, for example, regulators are concerned about the extent to which children are exposed to, or even targeted by, traditional cigarette advertising. Faced with the threat of increased restrictions on its advertising practices, the tobacco industry is making a strategy shift toward direct mail.

Following the economic crisis in Asia, a number of companies in that region turned to direct mail in an effort to use their advertising budgets more effectively. Historically, the Asian direct marketing sector has lagged behind its counterparts in the United States and Europe. Grey Global Group established a Kuala Lumpur office of Grey Direct Interactive in 1997; OgilvyOne Worldwide is the Malaysian subsidiary of Ogilvy & Mather Group specializing in direct marketing. Companies in the banking and telecommunications sectors have been at the forefront of direct marketing initiatives in Asia, using their extensive databases to target individual consumers by mail or Internet.

Catalogs

A **catalog** is a magazine-style publication that features photographs, illustrations, and extensive information about a company's products. (The term *magalog* is sometimes used to describe this communication medium.) The global catalog retail sector generates revenues of several hundred billion dollars each year. Catalogs have a long and illustrious history as a direct marketing tool in both Europe and the United States. The European catalog market flourished after World War II as consumers sought convenience, bargain prices, and access to a wider range of goods. U.S.-based catalog marketers include JCPenney, Lands' End, L.L. Bean, and Victoria's Secret; in Europe, Otto GmbH & Co KG (Germany) is the leading catalog retailer.

Catalogs are widely recognized as an important part of an IMC program, and many companies use catalogs in tandem with traditional retail distribution and e-commerce channels. The catalog retail sector in the United States represents approximately one-third of the total global market; however, the number of catalogs mailed each year peaked in 2007 at about 20 billion. By 2015, due in part to the increased popularity of online shopping, the number of catalogs mailed had dropped

Exhibit 14-5 Despite the surge in popularity of online shopping, some consumers still prefer the "tactile" aspect of physical catalogs. Anthropologie, the fashion, lifestyle, and home decor specialist, is one example of a retailer that distributes catalogs in an effort to build foot traffic in its stores as well as drive online sales.
Source: Kevin George/Alamy Stock Photo.

to only 12 million (see Exhibit 14-5). Felix Carbullido, chief marketing officer for Williams-Sonoma, explains how his company's view of catalogs has evolved: "Years ago, it was a selling tool. Now it's become an inspiration source. We know our customers love a tactile experience."[26]

Historically, companies selling through catalogs in the United States benefited from the ability to ship their goods from one coast to the other, with those goods crossing multiple state boundaries with relatively few regulatory hurdles. By contrast, prior to the advent of the single market, catalog sales in Europe were hindered by the fact that mail-order products passing through customs at national borders were subject to value-added taxes (VAT). Because VAT drove up prices of goods that crossed borders, catalogs tended to be targeted at intracountry buyers. In other words, Germans bought from German catalogs, French consumers bought from French catalogs, and so on. Market-entry strategies were also affected by customs regulations; catalogers' business grew by acquiring existing companies in various countries.

Today, catalogs play a diminished role in the multichannel marketing strategy of Germany's Otto GmbH & Co KG. As Theo Bendler, vice president of the Otto Group, noted recently, "In 2020 we will still have catalogs, but they will only be more of a source of information. The catalog as something to order from where we show everything we have on paper will be extinct by 2020. Catalogs can't stay valid for 6 months like they used to."[27]

Today, the single market means that mail-order goods can move freely throughout the European Union without incurring VAT charges. Also, since January 1993, VAT exemptions have been extended to goods bound for the European Free Trade Area countries (Norway, Iceland, Switzerland, and Liechtenstein). Some predict robust growth in Europe's mail-order business, thanks to the increased size of the potential catalog market and the VAT-free environment. The single market is also attracting American catalog retailers, even though they will face higher costs for paper, printing, and shipping in Europe, along with the familiar issue of whether to adapt their offerings to local tastes. Stephen Miles, former managing director for Europe at Lands' End, has taken note of these challenges: "The most difficult thing is to know in which areas to be local. We're proud that we're an American sportswear company, but that doesn't mean your average German consumer wants to pick up the phone and speak English to someone."[28]

In Japan, the domestic catalog industry is well developed. Leading catalog companies include Cecile, with $1 billion in annual sales of women's apparel and lingerie; Kukutake Publishing, which sells educational materials; and Shaddy, a general merchandise company. As noted in Chapter 12, Japan's fragmented distribution system represents a formidable obstacle to market entry by outsiders, and an increasing number of companies are using direct marketing in an attempt to circumvent this distribution bottleneck. Annual revenues for all forms of consumer and business direct-response advertising in Japan passed the $1 trillion mark in the mid-1990s; they declined to $525 billion in 2000 as Japan's economic difficulties continued. Success in this market can be achieved using different strategies. For example, Patagonia dramatically increased its sales after publishing a Japanese-language catalog, whereas L.L. Bean offers a Japanese-language insert in its traditional catalog.

Even as they continue to develop the Japanese market, Western catalogers are now turning their attention to other Asian countries. In Hong Kong and Singapore, efficient postal services, highly educated populations, wide use of credit cards, and high per capita income are attracting the attention of catalog marketers. Notes Michael Grasee, the former director of international business development at Lands' End, "We see our customer in Asia as pretty much the same customer we have everywhere. It's the time-starved, traveling, hardworking executive."[29] Catalogers are also targeting Asia's developing countries. Otto GmbH & Co KG, with 2016 revenues of €12.5 billion ($13.2 billion) and about 6 percent of global mail-order sales, is planning to enter China, South Korea, and Taiwan. Because these countries have few local mail-order companies that could be acquisition targets, executives at Otto have mapped out an entry strategy based on acquiring a majority stake in joint ventures with local retailers.

Infomercials, Teleshopping, and Interactive Television

An **infomercial** is a form of paid television programming in which a particular product is demonstrated, explained, and offered for sale to viewers who call a toll-free number shown on the screen. According to Thomas Burke, once the president of Saatchi & Saatchi's infomercial division, infomercials are the most powerful form of advertising ever created. The cost of producing a single infomercial can reach $3 million; advertisers then pay as much as $500,000 for time slots on U.S. cable and satellite systems and local TV channels. Because infomercials are typically 30 minutes in length and often feature studio audiences and celebrity announcers, many viewers believe they are watching regular talk show–type programming. Although originally associated with personal-care, fitness, and household products, such as those from legendary direct-response pitchman Ron Popeil, infomercials have gone upmarket in recent years. For example, Lexus generated more than 40,000 telephone inquiries after launching its used-car program with an infomercial; 2 percent of respondents ultimately purchased a Lexus automobile.

In Asia, infomercials generate several hundred million dollars in annual sales. Costs for a late-night time slot range from $100,000 in Japan to $20,000 in Singapore. Infomercials are also playing a part in the development of China's market. The government has given its blessing by allowing China Central Television, the state-run channel, to air infomercials and give Chinese consumers access to Western goods. Despite their generally low per-capita incomes, Chinese consumers are thought to have a savings rate as high as 40 percent because housing and health care are provided by the state; that translates into a lot of disposable income that marketers would love to tap into. China Shop-A-Vision was in the vanguard in seeking to access these potential customers through infomercials, signing up 20,000 "TV shopping members" in its first year of airing infomercials starting in the late 1990s. Nevertheless, pioneers in Chinese direct-response television had to deal with a number of barriers to success, including the limited number of private telephones at that time, low penetration of credit cards, and problems with delivery logistics in crowded cities such as Shanghai.[30] Beginning in 2013, new rules from China's state TV regulator were implemented that aimed to rein in unscrupulous operators working in this channel.

With **teleshopping**, home-shopping channels such as QVC and the Home Shopping Network (HSN) take the infomercial concept one step further: The round-the-clock programming is *exclusively* dedicated to product demonstration and selling (see Exhibit 14-6). Worldwide, this kind of home shopping is a multibillion-dollar industry. The leading home-shopping channels are also leveraging the Internet. For example, in addition to operating home-shopping channels in the United States, China, Germany, and Japan, HSN Inc. offers an online shopping experience at www.hsn.com.

QVC ("Quality, Value, and Convenience"), the U.S.-based home-shopping channel, is available in nearly 250 million homes worldwide. Shoppers can order jewelry, housewares, clothing, and other merchandise around the clock, both on QVC's cable TV channels and online. QVC has international retailing operations in China (via joint venture), Germany, Italy, Japan, and the UK. As Jeff Charney, chief marketing officer at QVC, has noted, the essence of the brand is the feeling a shopper gets when she opens the package.

QVC's agreement with Rupert Murdoch's British Sky Broadcasting (BSkyB) satellite company enables it to reach Germany, Italy, and the United Kingdom, as well as Japan. As QVC executive Francis Edwards explained, "European customers respond in different ways, though the basic premise and concept is the same. The type of jewelry is different. German consumers wouldn't buy 14-karat gold. They go for a higher karat. We can sell wine in Germany, but not in the U.S."[31] A number of local and regional teleshopping channels have also sprung up in Europe: Germany's HOT (Home Order Television) is a joint venture with Quelle Schickedanz, a mail-order company; Sweden's TV-Shop is available in more than one dozen European countries. Typically, Europeans are more discriminating than the average American teleshopping customer.

Industry observers expect the popularity of home shopping to increase during the next few years as **interactive television** (ITV or t-commerce) technology is introduced into more households. As

the term implies, ITV allows television viewers to interact with the programming content that they are viewing. ITV has a greater presence in Europe than in the United States; in the United Kingdom alone, more than half of all Pay TV subscribers make use of ITV services. The remote control units provided by Pay TV service providers in the United Kingdom have a red button that viewers press to order products from home-shopping channels, choose different camera angles during sports broadcasts, vote during audience participation shows such as *Big Brother*, or order free samples of advertised products. In 2005, Diageo tested an interactive ad for Smirnoff vodka; after the first 60 seconds, viewers were required to press the button two more times to see the ad in its entirety. Comparing traditional TV ads with the new format, James Pennefather, Smirnoff brand manager for the United Kingdom, noted, "Interactive advertising is a lot more unproven and untested, and it is a calculated risk for us. We have to do this kind of thing to learn if it will be a success or not."[32]

 14-5 Describe how global marketers integrate support media, sponsorships, and product placement into the overall promotion mix.

(14-5) Special Forms of Marketing Communications: Support Media, Sponsorship, and Product Placement

Traditional support media include transit and billboard advertising; as a category, these media are known as out-of-home (OOH) advertising. Global marketers also take advantage of a wide variety of sponsorship opportunities that enable them to align themselves with popular cultural and sports events. For example, Adidas, Coca-Cola, Russia's Gazprom, and Chinese conglomerate Wanda were some of the official sponsors of the 2018 World Cup in Russia. Finally, global marketers are placing their products and brands in popular motion picture, television, and streaming programming.

Support Media

As governments in China and other emerging markets add mass transportation systems and build and improve their highway infrastructures, advertisers are utilizing more indoor and outdoor posters and billboards to reach the buying public. Japan's population relies heavily on public transportation, with the average worker spending approximately 80 minutes total each day commuting to and from work. Consequently, spending on outdoor and transit advertising in Japan is much higher

EMERGING MARKETS BRIEFING BOOK

Billboards Banned in Brazil!

Score one for environmental activists: On January 1, 2007, *Lei Cidade Limpa* ("Clean City Law") went into effect in São Paulo, Brazil. The main effect of the law, which was championed by Mayor Gilberto Kassab, is to ban various forms of outdoor advertising in the city of 11 million people. As Kassab asserted, "The Clean City Law came about from a necessity to combat pollution . . . pollution of water, sound, air, and the visual. We decided that we should start combating pollution with the most conspicuous sector: visual pollution."

The ban means that São Paulo's giant billboards and video screens—some 15,000 in all—have come down. What is left is a mishmash of skeletal frames devoid of posters (see Exhibit 14-7). In addition, transit ads on buses and taxis are no longer allowed. Store signs are still permitted, but the maximum size of a given sign is determined by a formula based on the dimensions of the store's facade.

Applauding the ban, a local journalist wrote that the new law "is a rare victory of the public interest over private; of order over disorder; of aesthetics over ugliness; of cleanliness over trash." That view, however, was not shared by the chief economist of the 32,000-member Commercial Association of São Paulo. Denouncing the ban, Marcel Solimeo said, "This is a radical law that damages the rules of a market economy and respect for the rule of law. We live in a consumer society and the essence of capitalism is the availability of information about products."

Some advertisers acknowledge that, in Brazil, traditional outdoor advertising may not necessarily be the best communication channel.

Marcio Santoro, an executive at Agência Africa, is blunt when he describes the advertising environment before the Clean City Law went into effect. According to Santoro, there was so much clutter that advertisers had to make big advertising buys, which in turn led to more clutter. Denied access to traditional outdoor advertising for now, companies have devised a number of alternative ways to communicate with prospective customers. For example, Citibank uses the color blue in much of its advertising, so its main branch in São Paulo was painted blue to help it stand out. Innovative indoor approaches such as placing ads in elevators and bathrooms are also being adopted. Brazilians have embraced social media, so online channels are a natural fit. As Nizan Guanaes of agency network Grupo ABC says, "The Internet is the next frontier, for reasons I don't have to explain. Brazil is very sophisticated in digital and social media."

City leaders have indicated that, eventually, special zones will be created in which a limited amount of outdoor advertising will be permitted. Even so, many advertisers have adjusted to the new reality. With the vast majority of São Paulo residents supporting the ban, advertisers understand that it does not make sense to put ads where they are not welcome.

Sources: Vincent Bevins, "São Paulo Advertising Goes Underground," *Financial Times* (September 7, 2010), p. 10; David Evan Harris, "São Paulo: A City without Ads," *Adbusters*, 73 (September–October 2007), p. 7; Larry Rohter, "Billboard Ban in São Paulo Angers Advertisers," *The New York Times* (December 12, 2006), p. C1.

Exhibit 14-7 Billboards were once ubiquitous in Brazil's most populous city. Now that the Clean City Law has taken effect, empty frames are all that remain.
Source: Jean Pierre Pingoud/Getty Images.

Exhibit 14-8 Coca-Cola, Samsung, Hyundai, and Stella McCartney are just some of the brands that have advertised in the iconic Piccadilly Lights.
Source: Pajor Pawel/Shutterstock.

than in most other countries. In fact, OOH's 13 percent of total ad spending in Japan is second only to its share in Hong Kong, where OOH represents more than 18 percent of the ad market.[33]

In absolute dollar terms, the United States ranks number 1 in terms of OOH spending. Globally, OOH represents a $28 billion market, accounting for approximately 6 percent of total ad expenditures.[34] Growth in this category in recent years has been fueled by the rollout of digital billboard platforms, known as digital out-of-home (DOOH) advertising. In fact, the signage in London's Piccadilly Circus, widely regarded as the most valuable DOOH property in the world, has recently been updated to incorporate digital recognition technology (see Exhibit 14-8). The technology allows for targeted ads to be directed some of the 100 million people who pass through the intersection every year.

The two largest players in the OOH industry are Texas-based Clear Channel Outdoor Holdings, with nearly 600,000 outdoor and transit displays in 35 countries, and France's JCDecaux. JCDecaux is the market leader in Europe; overall, the company operates in about 75 different countries. Outdoor advertising is currently experiencing explosive growth in China, where JCDecaux competes with Tom Group, Clear Media, and thousands of other local companies, especially in large cities such as Beijing, Shanghai, and Guangzhou. The same trend is evident in Russia, especially in Moscow.

Sponsorship

Sponsorship is an increasingly popular form of marketing communications whereby a company pays a fee to have its name associated with a particular event, team or athletic association, or sports facility. Sponsorship combines elements of PR and sales promotion. From a PR perspective, sponsorship generally ensures that a corporate or brand name will be mentioned numerous times by on-air or public-address commentators. Large-scale events also draw considerable media attention that typically includes multiple mentions of the sponsoring company or brand in news reports or talk shows (see Exhibit 14-9). Because event sponsorship typically provides numerous contact points with large numbers of people, it is a perfect vehicle for sampling and other sales promotion opportunities.

Olympic Games or World Cup soccer sponsorships can help companies reach a global audience; sponsors are also drawn to professional team sports, car racing, hot-air balloon competitions, rodeos, music concerts, and other events that appeal to national or regional audiences. For example, the Coca-Cola Company views World Cup sponsorship as a key promotional opportunity. During the 2010 World Cup in South Africa, Coca-Cola spent an estimated $124 million for sponsorship rights plus another $475 million on advertising and promotions. The beverage giant used an IMC approach, running Africa-themed ads on TV, online, and in restaurants. When World Cup matches were broadcast, Coke's Powerade sports drink brand was featured on the electronic billboards that surrounded the pitch. Scott McCune, Coke's integrated marketing chief, predicted a 5 percent sales increase for Coke in the months leading up to the match. His company plans to invest $12 billion in Africa between now and 2020. According to McCune, "The continent is critically important to us."[35]

As the Coca-Cola Company's participation in World Cup soccer demonstrates, sponsorship can be an effective component of an IMC program. It can be used in countries where regulations limit the extent to which a company can use advertising or other forms of marketing communication. In China, for example, where tobacco advertising is prohibited, B.A.T. and Philip Morris have spent tens of millions of dollars sponsoring events such as a Hong Kong–Beijing car rally and China's national soccer tournament. However, in 2005, Chinese authorities ratified the World Health Organization's (WHO) Framework Convention on Tobacco Controls; all forms of tobacco promotion and sponsorship were phased out in 2010. Tobacco sponsorship was also popular in the United Kingdom, where Benson & Hedges paid £4 million ($6 million) for a 5-year contract to sponsor cricket matches and Rothman's spent £15 million ($23 million) annually to sponsor a Formula One racing team. However, to comply with the EU directive on tobacco advertising, tobacco sponsorship of all sports—including Formula One racing—has now been phased out.

Exhibit 14-9 Coca-Cola's low-key sponsorship of 2014 Winter Games in Sochi, Russia, included local TV spots.
Source: dpa picture alliance/Alamy Stock Photo.

Exhibit 14-10 Milan-based luxury marketer Moncler received a welcome boost after Drake wore one of the company's Maya puffer jackets in his video for *Hotline Bling*.
Source: Christopher Polk/Getty Images.

Product Placement: Motion Pictures, Television Shows, and Public Figures

Companies can achieve a unique kind of exposure by using **product placement**, in which they arrange for their products and brand names to appear in popular television programs, movies, and other types of performances. Marketers can also lend or donate products to celebrities or other public figures; the products get publicity when the celebrity appears in public using the product. Some global marketers are able to generate publicity for their brands when public figures and celebrities are seen using their favorite brands. For example, former First Lady Michelle Obama was seen wearing an expensive Moncler quilted down jacket while skiing in Aspen; the company's designer outerwear has become a fashion statement in any kind of weather (see Exhibit 14-10).[36]

This tactic is especially popular with auto manufacturers and fashion designers and is often used in conjunction with movie premieres and popular annual television events such as the Academy Awards and the Grammys that garner significant media attention. For example, Celeste Atkinson has worked as a lifestyle and entertainment manager for Audi. Her job is to create buzz by ensuring that vehicles such as the Audi A8L, the 12-cylinder A8L, and the S8 sports sedan figure in paparazzi photos.[37] And, let's not forget the Audi R8 Spyder that Robert Downey, Jr.'s Tony Stark character drives in the *Iron Man* movies! Subaru's high-performance WRX was actor Ansel Elgort's preferred getaway car in the recent hit movie *Baby Driver*. Fans of the recent hit film *Kingsman: The Golden Circle* can even buy a Tag Heuer ("Don't Crack Under Pressure") Connected Watch and clothing from the Kingsman Collection on the Mr Porter Web site.

Worldwide audiences for a blockbuster movie can number in the tens of millions of people. In many instances, product placements in such films can generate considerable media interest and result in additional publicity. Placements can be arranged in several different ways. Sometimes companies pay a fee for the placement; alternatively, a show's producers may write the product into the script in exchange for marketing and promotion support of the new production. A brand's owners can also strike a barter agreement whereby the company (Sony, for example) supplies the filmmakers with products that serve as props in exchange for licensing rights to, say, the James Bond name in retail promotions. Product placement agencies such as Propaganda, Hero Product

THE CULTURAL CONTEXT

Products Star in Bond Films

Lieutenant Commander James Bond—better known as Agent 007—first appeared on film in 1962. Fifty years later, the Bond franchise is stronger than ever, and the films have become famous for integrating well-known brand names into the action (see Exhibit 14-11). The 23 films featuring the suave British agent have grossed more than $5 billion in worldwide ticket sales. However, *Spectre*, released in 2015, cost more than $300 million to produce. The series' popularity, plus the high cost of making the films, makes Bond a perfect vehicle for showcasing products and brands.

Many companies are eager to be associated with a high-profile project like a Bond film. In 1996, when BMW introduced a sporty new Z3 convertible, it wanted to make a major global splash. BMW garnered extensive publicity by placing the Z3 in *GoldenEye*, the 18th James Bond film. In the film, gadget chief Q gives 007 a Z3 in place of his Aston Martin; the Z car also figured prominently in movie previews and print ads. BMW dealers were provided with "BMW 007 kits" that allowed prospective buyers to learn more about both the movie and the car before either was available. As *Advertising Age* observed, "BMW has shaken, not just stirred, the auto industry with unprecedented media exposure and awareness for the Z3 and BMW in the U.S."

Tomorrow Never Dies, the follow-up to *GoldenEye*, featured global brand promotional tie-ins worth an estimated $100 million. Ericsson, Heineken, Omega, Brioni, and Visa International all placed products in the film. Bond star Pierce Brosnan also appeared as Agent 007 in specially filmed television commercials. However, when *Die Another Day*, the 20th installment in the series, was released at the end of 2002, BMW took a back seat to Ford. The U.S. automaker persuaded the producers to bring back the Aston Martin (the nameplate was owned by Ford at the time); Jaguars and the new Thunderbird also appeared prominently in the film.

The 21st Bond film, *Casino Royale*, featured actor Daniel Craig in the role of 007. To avoid a backlash from fans and marketing executives, the film's producers deliberately limited the number of official global partners in the film to six: Sony Electronics, Sony Ericsson, Omega, Heineken, Ford, and Smirnoff. As Myles Romero, Ford's global brand entertainment director, noted, "It's great for brand awareness. The film takes us where we don't have marketing."

The producers' decision to cast Craig as the sixth Bond proved to be a brilliant choice. *Casino Royale* raked in nearly $600 million at the box office, making it the number 1 moneymaker in the franchise. For the next installment, 2008's *Quantum of Solace*, several companies hitched their brands to Bond for the first time. These included Coke Zero and Avon. Speaking of Coke Zero, Derk Hendriksen explained, "We're in more than 100 markets. We thought the tie-in would be very appropriate for two irreverent and global personalities." For its part, Avon coordinated the launch of Bond Girl 007 Fragrance with the film's release. Tracy Haffner, global vice president for marketing, called the film "a great platform to develop a beautiful fragrance and connect with women worldwide."

As the Bond franchise celebrated its 50th anniversary, 2012's *Skyfall* continued the product placement tradition. Heineken spent tens of millions of dollars on a product placement for its flagship beer; star Daniel Craig also appeared in television commercials for the brand. A Sony Vaio laptop and Xperia mobile phone got some screen time, too. And there were the cars: Nameplates in evidence included Audi, Jaguar, Land Rover, Volkswagen, Range Rover, and, of course, Aston Martin.

Sources: Edward Helmore, "Happy Birthday, Mr. Bond," *The Wall Street Journal* (July 7–8, 2012), p. D11; Theresa Howard, "Brands Cozy up to Bond," *USA Today* (October 20, 2008), p. 3B; Emiko Terazono, "Brand New Bond Has a License to Sell," *Financial Times* (November 14, 2006), p. 10; Tim Burt, "His Name's Bond, and He's Been Licensed to Sell," *Financial Times* (October 5–6, 2002), p. 22; Jon Rappoport, "BMW Z3," *Advertising Age* (June 24, 1996), p. S37.

Exhibit 14-11 The Aston Martin DB5 is closely identified with Agent 007. The car's big screen debut was in 1962's *Dr. No*, with Sean Connery starring as James Bond. Things came full circle in fall 2015 as Daniel Craig, the actor who has taken over the Bond role, was paired with a new model, the DB10.
Source: JSN/Lexi Jones/WENN/Newscom.

Placement, and Eon function like talent agencies for products. These agencies perform several important roles in such arrangements, including obtaining legal clearances from a brand's owners, promoting their clients' products to producers, and arranging for products to be delivered to a soundstage.

In the case of television placement, the blurring of advertising and programming content has become more evident as companies have increasingly questioned the effectiveness of traditional advertising. In fact, some evidence suggests that a prominent product placement in a television program leads to better recall than a traditional advertisement. Moreover, many viewers use digital video recorders (DVRs) to "skip" through commercials; consumers are, in effect, ignoring commercials. This trend is forcing advertisers to find new ways to expose viewers to their messages. Sometimes called *branded entertainment*, the effective integration of products and brands into entertainment can be seen on the monster TV hit *American Idol*.

In addition to the effectiveness issue, prop masters and set dressers facing budget pressures are compelled to obtain props for free whenever possible, which can drive them to seek product placements as a means to cut production costs. Moreover, as the cost of marketing major feature films has increased—it is not unusual for a studio to spend $20 to $30 million on marketing alone—studios are increasingly looking for partnerships to share these costs and attract the broadest possible viewing audience. At the same time, product placement raises an interesting issue for global marketers, especially consumer packaged goods companies. This tactic virtually dictates a product standardization approach, because once footage of a scene is shot and incorporated into a movie or television program, the image of the product is "frozen" and will be seen without adaptation everywhere in the world.[38]

For better or for worse, product placements have even reached the world of live theater and opera: In fall 2002, a Broadway production of Puccini's *La Bohème* was set in Paris circa 1957. The stage set included billboards for luxury pen maker Montblanc and Piper-Heidsieck champagne; during a crowd scene at Café Momus, Piper-Heidsieck was served. Some industry observers warn of a backlash from such efforts. In addition, ethical concerns are sometimes raised when controversial products such as cigarettes are featured prominently or glamorized. When advertising appears in conventional forms such as broadcast commercials, most consumers are aware of the fact that they are being exposed to an ad. This is not necessarily the case with product placement; in effect, viewers are being marketed to subliminally without their consent.

What constitutes proper use of product placement? As Joe Uva, an executive with Omnicom's media planning group, has noted, "It shouldn't be forced; it shouldn't be intrusive. If people say 'It's a sell-out, it's product placement,' it didn't work."[39] Eugene Secunda, a media studies professor at New York University, is also skeptical: "I think it's a very dangerous plan. The more you get the audience to distrust the content of your programming, to look at it with suspicion in terms of your real agenda, the less likely they are to be responsive to the message because they're going to be looking at everything cynically and with resistance."[40]

Summary

Sales promotion is any paid, short-term communication program that adds tangible value to a product or brand. *Consumer sales promotions* are targeted at the ultimate consumers; *trade sales promotions* are used in business-to-business marketing. *Sampling* gives prospective customers a chance to try a product or service at no cost. A *coupon* is a certificate that entitles the bearer to a price reduction or other value-enhancing consideration when purchasing a product or service.

Personal selling is face-to-face communication between a prospective buyer and a company representative. The *strategic/consultative selling model* that is widely used in the United States is also being utilized worldwide. The model's five strategic steps call for developing a *personal selling philosophy*, a *relationship strategy*, a *product strategy*, a *customer strategy*, and a *presentation strategy*. The six steps in the *presentation plan* are approach, presentation, demonstration, negotiation, close, and servicing the sale; successful global selling may require adaptation of one or more of these steps. An additional consideration in global selling is the composition of the sales force, which may include *expatriates*, *host-country natives*, or *sales agents*.

Several other forms of communication can be used in global marketing. These include *direct marketing*, a measurable system that uses one or more types of media to start or complete a sale. *One-to-one marketing* is an updated approach to direct marketing that calls for treating each customer in a distinct way based on his or her previous purchase history or past interactions with the company. *Direct mail*, *catalogs*, *infomercials*, *teleshopping*, and *interactive television* are some of the direct marketing tools that have been successfully used on a global basis. Global marketers frequently try to place their products in blockbuster movies that will reach global audiences. *Sponsorships* and *product placement* are also becoming vital communication tools that can be used on a global basis.

Discussion Questions

14-1. What is the difference between a consumer sales promotion and a trade sales promotion? Describe the various types and purposes of using coupons, like free-standing inserts and on-pack coupons.

14-2. Which potential environmental challenges must be taken into account by a company that uses personal selling as a promotional tool outside the home country?

14-3. How does management's orientation (e.g., ethnocentric, polycentric, or regiocentric) correlate with decisions about sales force nationality? Which other factors affect sales force composition?

14-4. In March 2019, the Paris-based fashion, music, and lifestyle brand Maison Kitsuné announced that it had concluded negotiations for a joint venture with JoeOne in China. The partnership is called Maison Kitsuné China Co. Ltd. and will run the brand's fashion business across mainland China, Hong Kong, and Macau. How will Maison Kitsuné benefit from this?

14-5. How do support media complement the primary media in reinforcing their messages? Discuss the potential problems of support media.

14-6. Explain the strategic/consultative selling model in relation to selling in the global context.

CASE 14-1 *Continued (refer to page 461)*

Milan Expo 2015

Not surprisingly, an event with the size and scale of Milan Expo drew its share of criticism. For example, on April 30, the day before Expo opened, thousands of protesters took to the streets in Milan (see Exhibit 14-12). Some of the anger was directed at cost overruns; the Italian pavilion itself was more than €30 million ($33 million) over budget. The protesters' ire was also aimed at a corruption scandal that involved the event's manager and several politicians who were accused of accepting bribes in exchange for contracts. Anti-globalization activists were also present: Many viewed the Expo as an example of capitalist excess and accused the organizers of skirting pressing issues such as global hunger.

Other activists focused on the issue of sponsorships. For example, the Slow Food movement was founded in northern Italy. As noted on the group's Web site (www.slowfood.com), Slow Food officials objected to McDonald's sponsorship presence at the event. The fast-food giant's participation included both a restaurant and a terrace with seating for several hundred people. Also, in conjunction with Italy's Ministry of Agriculture, McDonald's launched a project called Making

the Future. The project offered 20 Italian farmers younger than the age of 40 the opportunity to become McDonald's suppliers. According to Slow Food's statement, "The presence of McDonald's means that the planet can continue to gorge itself on fast food or junk food—call it whatever you like—without concern for our own well-being."

Despite its anticorporate stance, Slow Food was also an exhibitor at the Expo. Acclaimed Swiss architects Herzog & de Meuron created a special pavilion that took the form of a three-part wooden *cascina* (farmhouse) typical of Italy's Lombardy region. Visitors had the opportunity to taste a variety of artisanal cheeses at an area dubbed, not surprisingly, Slow Cheese. Slow Food officials hoped that, by participating in the Expo, the organization could spread the word about the importance of safeguarding biodiversity through local, small-scale, sustainable agriculture. After Expo ended, the pavilion was disassembled and repurposed as garden sheds at Italian schools.

South Korea's pavilion provided a textbook example of the way individual nations presented their respective food cultures within the overall context of the Expo. Korea's theme was "*Hansik*, Food for the

Exhibit 14-12 Anti-Expo protests in Milan in 2015.
Source: Sandro Bertola/Zuma Press/Newscom.

Future: You Are What You Eat." The pavilion's architecture was based on a traditional porcelain vessel, the moon-jar. The organizers included Korea's Ministry of Culture, Sports and Tourism and the Korea Tourism Organization.

Within Korea's pavilion, exhibits addressed several food-related issues. First, Korea presented artwork depicting the risks of overeating, excessive reliance on processed foods, and depletion of food resources. Next came an exhibit devoted to *Hansik*, a Korean concept that updates traditional Korean cuisine and involves the blending of seasonal produce, colors, and ingredients into a "symphony of food." Fermentation and storage techniques were also showcased. Visitors entering the final part of the exhibition found themselves in a circular hall dedicated to the notion that *Hansik* represents a sustainable "food for the future" that is in sync with nature. Finally, visitors had the opportunity to taste *Hansik* food offerings using natural ingredients and unusual seasonings.

Considering the theme of Milan Expo 2015, it should come as no surprise that a great deal of food was prepared and consumed at the event. In fact, an estimated 400 *tons* of food were delivered to the Expo grounds each day. Needless to say, not all of this food was used on any given day and significant quantities might be wasted—a fact not lost on members of the Milan and broader food community.

To address this issue, Michelin-starred Italian chef Massimo Bottura* collaborated with several fellow chefs, a number of noted artists and designers, and the Diocese of Milan on a project known as the Refettorio Ambrosiano (Ambrosian Refectory). Reflecting the theme of "*Non solo una mensa*" ("Not just a mess"), the Refectory was a pop-up restaurant brought to life in an abandoned community theater located in Milan's Greek neighborhood. The theater's renovation was supervised by two professors from Politecnico di Milano. The project's mission was to create meals from Milan Expo's surplus food that would otherwise go to waste. The restaurant was designed to serve and assist needy and disadvantaged individuals while offering a symbolic gesture toward food and the human experience of eating within the context of Milan Expo. Although the Refectory opened in May 2015, its creators envisioned that operations would continue after Milan Expo concluded and that the Refectory would distribute hot meals to counseling centers and the homeless shelter at Milan's Central Station. (More information can be found at www.refettorioambrosiano.it.)

Discussion Questions

14-7. Do you agree with Slow Food's objections to McDonald's sponsorship participation in Milan Expo 2015?

14-8. Do you think Milan Expo 2015 will be a "game changer" that has an impact on problems such as global hunger and sustainable food supplies?

14-9. Do you think the corporate and national pavilions at Milan Expo 2015 represent money well spent in terms of return on investment?

*Chef Massimo Bottura is featured in a new Netflix series titled *Chef's Table*.

Sources: Massimo Bottura, "One Man's Trash Is Another Man's Dinner," *The Future of Everything* (December 2015), pp. 60–61; Jay Cheshes, "Far beyond Funnel Cake," *The Wall Street Journal* (June 6–7, 2015), p. D10; Kathryn Tomasetti, "140 Ways to Feed the Planet (and Entertain 30 Million Visitors)," *EasyJet Traveller* (May 2015), pp. 32–34; Rachel Sanderson, "Italy Pins Hopes for Economic Revival on Expo," *Financial Times* (May 1, 2015); Elisabetta Povoledo, "Milan Pins Hopes on World Expo after Graft Scandal," *The New York Times* (April 23, 2015), p. A8; "Con Fattore Futuro McDonald's insieme al MiPAAF e a EXPO 2015 per sostenere l'agricoltura italiana," Press Release, February 27, 2015; Rocky Casale, "The Luxury of Leftovers," *TMagazine* (April 6, 2015), p. 35.

CASE 14-2
Red Bull

It is a safe bet that most people reading this textbook are familiar with Red Bull. The $6.4 billion company that largely created the market for energy drinks revels in its association with cultural events such as concerts and extreme sports including snowboarding and surfing. The company uses a variety of communication channels in addition to advertising and PR to promote the brand. Red Bull's Facebook page has 43 million "likes," and 2 million people follow its Twitter feed. At concerts and other events, street teams pass out free samples while driving specially modified cars with giant Red Bull cans mounted on them. The company sponsors the Infiniti Red Bull Formula One racing team, and the Red Bull Arena in Harrison, New Jersey, is home to the New York Red Bulls Major League Soccer team. In sum, Red Bull is not only high energy; it is high profile, too!

The brand's slogan, "Red Bull Gives You Wings," made Red Bull the perfect corporate partner for one of the biggest PR coups in recent years. In fall 2012, Red Bull sponsored Red Bull Stratos, otherwise known as Felix Baumgartner's death-defying skydive from the edge of space (see Exhibit 14-13). After seven years of planning, Baumgartner jumped from a helium-filled balloon at an altitude of 24 miles. As a worldwide audience watched on television and YouTube, Baumgartner plummeted toward Earth at speeds as high as Mach 1.24 (834 miles per hour) before landing safely. Needless to say, the Red Bull logo was prominently displayed on his uniform, and the event received extensive publicity in the press.

The success of the Red Bull Stratos project helped the Red Bull brand stand out from a crowded field of competitors that include Monster and Rockstar. As brand strategist Roger Addis noted, "It's a smart move because it's such a singular event. If the logo is buried in a sea of logos on a NASCAR car, you're completely diluted by all the others." The ad industry seems to agree; Red Bull topped *Advertising Age* magazine's 2012 Best of Creativity rankings in the integrated/interactive category.

Dietrich Mateschitz, Red Bull's creator, trusted his entrepreneurial instincts instead of relying on traditional marketing research. As Mateschitz recalls, "When we first started, we said that there is not an existing market for Red Bull, but Red Bull will create it. And this is what finally became true." In other words, Mateschitz succeeded at accomplishing one of the most basic goals in marketing: He discovered a market segment with needs that were not being met by any existing product. Today, Red Bull's blue-and-silver cans emblazoned with the iconic charging bulls logo are recognized around the globe. Mateschitz's marketing instincts have made him a wealthy man; in 2005, for example, he was featured in *Forbes* magazine's cover story on billionaires.

With typical entrepreneurial flair, Mateschitz pursues alternatives to orthodox advertising strategies and tactics. "We were always looking for a different, more creative point of view," he says. For example, Red Bull utilizes a communication tool known as marketer-produced media. *The Red Bulletin* is a monthly magazine produced by Red Bull Media House. Red Bull distributes more than 3 million copies of each issue through newsstand sales, subscriptions, and as a free iPad app. The magazine is available in Austria, Germany, Great Britain, Kuwait, New Zealand, Poland, and South Africa. In 2011, *The Red Bulletin* was launched in the United States; 1.2 million free copies were distributed in major newspapers such as *The Los Angeles Times*, *The Chicago Tribune*, and *The New York Daily News*. The first U.S. issue featured San Francisco Giants pitcher Tim Lincecum, one of hundreds of athletes

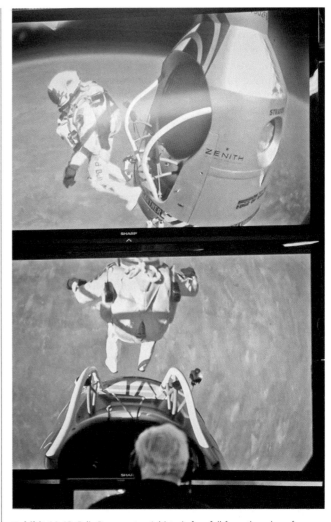

Exhibit 14-13 Felix Baumgartner's historic free fall from the edge of space was a spectacular sponsorship and PR coup for Red Bull. The project also provided a laboratory for testing new spacesuit designs and escape procedures and for assessing various contingencies that can arise when a human being breaks the sound barrier.
Source: EDB Image Archive/Alamy Stock Photo.

who are sponsored by Red Bull. As publisher Raymond Roker put it, "We are entering a new age of media in terms of what consumers of content want and expect."

Since 1998, Red Bull has been involved in another high-profile initiative. The Red Bull Music Academy is a series of concerts, workshops, art installations, and other cultural events that rotate from year to year among different international cities. Red Bull Music Academy also sponsors stages at international music festivals such as the Montreux Jazz Festival; RBMA Radio is a Web resource where listeners can access new music, live concerts, interviews, and other content. Despite the name, Red Bull plays down its participation in the Academy; according to the Web site, "The Red Bull Music Academy is not a sponsored event, but a long-term music initiative, commit[t]ed to fostering creative exchange amongst those who have made and continue to make a difference in the world of sound." Needless to say, the Red Bull logo is visible everywhere, and coolers filled with the drink are placed in strategic locations at the music events.

In its first two years of existence, the Academy was held in Berlin; subsequent host cities have included Dublin, Rome, London, Cape Town, and New York City. Songwriters, DJs, producers, and musicians are invited to apply to the Academy; out of thousands of applicants, 62 people are selected to participate each year. The participants attend workshops and lectures during the day; in the evenings, they break into teams to write and record music. Red Bull makes no ownership claims on any music that is produced at the Academy. Indeed, Torsten Schmidt, one of the Academy's founders, downplays the brand's sponsorship role; in his view, the event offers participants a chance to be inspired.

In 2013, the Red Bull Music Academy returned to New York City for the first time since 2001. Many of the workshops and lectures were open to the public; for example, a panel discussion featuring veteran music producers Nile Rodgers, Tony Visconti, and Ken Scott was devoted to David Bowie's studio recordings. There were presentations and performances by industry legends such as ambient music pioneer Brian Eno and Giorgio Moroder, who was Donna Summer's producer.

One enthusiastic alumnus of the Academy explained its impact and importance by noting that, from the artists' point of view, there are fewer "suits" to deal with ("suits" being a term that refers to noncreative industry types). Still, there are some dissenting voices. Matthew Herbert is a British electronic musician whose recordings include "One Pig," an album cataloging the life (and death) of, well, one pig. He has participated in the Red Bull Music Academy in the past, but has no plans to do so in the future. In Herbert's view, at the end of the day the event is still mainly about building the Red Bull brand, no matter what the organizers say.

Nirmalya Kumar, a marketing professor at the London Business School, has written a case study on Red Bull titled "The Anti-Brand Brand." Kumar gives Red Bull high marks for its nontraditional marketing communication strategy. As Kumar explains, a great company excels at communicating its brand's essence to consumers in an authentic manner. In Kumar's view, both the Music Academy and the Baumgartner tie-in accomplish this task for Red Bull.

Discussion Questions

14-10. What is the critical-thinking issue raised by the case?

14-11. Summarize the different types of marketing communications that Red Bull uses. Are these "traditional" or "nontraditional"?

14-12. Which communication goal does each of Red Bull's marketing communication tools accomplish? Are you familiar with any additional brand touch points that are not mentioned in the case?

14-13. What is the risk of sponsoring a special event such as Felix Baumgartner's historic skydive?

14-14. Red Bull and other energy drinks have generated negative publicity regarding their possible health hazards. Discuss.

14-15. What makes Red Bull, in Professor Kumar's words, an "anti-brand brand"?

Sources: Ben Sesario, "Live Music and a Canned Patron," *The New York Times* (April 26, 2013), p. C1; William M. Welch, "Skydiver's Space Jump Pays off for Red Bull," *USA Today* (October 21, 2012), p. 1B; Nat Ives, "Red Bull Brings Its Monthly Magazine, *Red Bulletin*, to the U.S.," *Advertising Age* (May 8, 2011), p. 17; Kerry A. Dolan, "The Soda with Buzz," *Forbes* (March 28, 2005), pp. 126–130.

Notes

[1] Max Colchester, "French Recipe for Launching 1,000 Parties," *The Wall Street Journal* (April 24, 2009), p. B7.

[2] E.J. Schultz and Jessica Wohl, "Pepsi Preps Global Emoji Can and Bottle Campaign," *Ad Age* (February 19, 2016), p. 2.

[3] Kamran Kashani and John A. Quelch, "Can Sales Promotion Go Global?" *Business Horizons* 33, no. 3 (May–June 1990), pp. 37–43.

[4] Sarah Ellison, "Taking the 'Free' out of Free Samples," *The Wall Street Journal* (September 25, 2002), p. D1.

[5] Mariko Sanchanta, "Soy Sauce Seeps into the Culture," *Financial Times* (August 10, 2006), p. 6.

[6] Andrew Adam Newman, "Taking Pickles out of the Afterthought Aisle," *The New York Times* (April 26, 2011), p. B3.

[7] Geoffrey A. Fowler, "When Free Samples Become Saviors," *The Wall Street Journal* (August 14, 2001), p. B1.

[8] "Winning the China FMCG Market," ATKearney, 2003.

[9] Steve Lohr, "Clip and Save Holds Its Own against Point and Click," *The New York Times* (August 30, 2006), p. C1.

[10] Leslie Ryan, "Sales Promotion: Made in America," *Brandweek* (July 31, 1995), p. 28.

[11] Kunur Patel, "What's Next for Groupon?" *Advertising Age* (December 13, 2010), p. 3.

[12] Ina Fried, "Pepsi's iTunes Promotion Goes Flat," *cnetNews* (April 28, 2004). www.news.cnet.com. Accessed June 1, 2010.

[13] Lenard C. Huff and Dana L. Alden, "An Investigation of Consumer Response to Sales Promotions in Developing Markets: A Three Country Analysis," *Journal of Advertising Research* 38, no. 3 (May/June 1998), pp. 47–57.

[14] Lenard C. Huff and Dana L. Alden, "An Investigation of Consumer Response to Sales Promotions in Developing Markets: A Three Country Analysis," *Journal of Advertising Research* 38, no. 3 (May/June 1998), pp. 47–57.

[15] Daniel Michaels, "Dogfight: In the Secret World of Airplane Deals, One Battle up Close," *The Wall Street Journal* (March 10, 2003), pp. A1, A9.

[16] Ellen Byron, "Avon Bribery Investigation Widens," *The Wall Street Journal* (May 5, 2011), p. B1.

[17] Manning, Gerald L.; Ahearne, Michael; Reese, Barry L., Selling Today: Partnering to Create Value, 14th Ed., ©2018, Pearson Education, Inc.

[18] *IBM 2017 Annual Report* (Armonk, NY), p. 35.

[19] "1100100 and Counting," *The Economist* (June 11, 2011), p. 60.

[20] Kate Fox, *Watching the English: The Hidden Rules of English Behavior* (Boston, MA: Nicholas Brealey, 2014), p. 52.

[21] Kate Fox, *Watching the English: The Hidden Rules of English Behavior* (Boston, MA: Nicholas Brealey, 2014), p. 284.

[22] Earl D. Honeycutt, Jr., and John B. Ford, "Guidelines for Managing an International Sales Force," *Industrial Marketing Management* 24 (March 1995), p. 139.

[23] Don Peppers, Martha Rogers, and Bob Dorf, "Is Your Company Ready for One-to-One Marketing?" *Harvard Business Review* 77, no. 1 (January–February 1999).

[24] Bruce Crumley, "European Market Continues to Soar," *Advertising Age* (February 21, 1994), p. 22.

[25] Rainer Hengst, "Plotting Your Global Strategy," *Direct Marketing* 63, no. 4 (August 2000), pp. 52–57.

[26]Rebecca R. Ruiz, "Catalogs Rewrite the Book," *The New York Times* (January 25, 2015), p. B1.

[27]Katie Evans, "Otto Group's Progress from Catalogs to Clicks," *Internet Retailer* (March 19, 2014). Accessed June 1, 2015. https://www.digitalcommerce360.com/2014/03/19/how-otto-group-progressed-catalogs-clicks/

[28]Cecilie Rohwedder, "U.S. Mail-Order Firms Shake up Europe," *The Wall Street Journal* (January 6, 1998), p. A15.

[29]James Cox, "Catalogers Expand in Asia," *USA Today* (October 18, 1996), p. 4B.

[30]Jon Hilsenrath, "In China, a Taste of Buy-Me TV," *The New York Times* (November 17, 1996), Section 3, pp. 1, 11.

[31]Michelle Pentz, "Teleshopping Gets a Tryout in Europe But Faces Cultural and Legal Barriers," *The Wall Street Journal* (September 9, 1996), p. A8.

[32]Aaron O. Patrick, "Selling Vodka with an Interactive Twist," *The Wall Street Journal* (October 11, 2005), p. B3. See also "Europe Wants Its ITV," *Chain Store Age* 77, no. 7 (July 2001), pp. 76–78.

[33]Geoffrey A. Fowler and Sebastian Moffett, "Adidas's Billboard Ads Give a Kick to Japanese Pedestrians," *The Wall Street Journal* (August 29, 2003), pp. B1, B4.

[34]"OOH around the Globe," Outdoor Advertising Association of America (August 14, 2017). Accessed March 1, 2018. https://www.magnaglobal.com/wp-content/uploads/2017/08/OutdoorOutlook_081517-.pdf

[35]Valerie Baurlein and Robb M. Stewart, "Coca-Cola Hopes to Score with World Cup Campaign," *The Wall Street Journal* (June 29, 2010), pp. B1, B2.

[36]Robert Williams, "When Cold-Weather Coats Get Too Hot," *Bloomberg Businessweek* (April 23, 2018), pp. 20–21.

[37]Chris Woodyard, "Audi Works the Ropes to Put Stars in Its Cars," *USA Today* (February 22, 2007), p. 3B.

[38]Stephen J. Gould, Pola B. Gupta, and Sonja Grabner-Krauter, "Product Placements in Movies: A Cross-Cultural Analysis of Austrian, French and American Consumers' Attitudes toward This Emerging, International Promotional Medium," *Journal of Advertising* 29, no. 4 (Winter 2000), pp. 41–58.

[39]Richard Tompkins, "How Hollywood Brings Brands into Your Home," *Financial Times* (November 5, 2002), p. 15.

[40]Richard Tompkins, "How Hollywood Brings Brands into Your Home," *Financial Times* (November 5, 2002), p. 15.

15 Global Marketing and the Digital Revolution

LEARNING OBJECTIVES

15-1 List the major innovations and trends that contributed to the digital revolution.

15-2 Define "convergence" and give an example.

15-3 Define *value network* and explain the differences between sustaining technologies and disruptive technologies.

15-4 Identify current trends in global e-commerce and explain how global companies are expanding their presence on the Web.

15-5 Explain the key issues facing a global company when designing and implementing a Web site.

15-6 Identify the most important new products and services that have been introduced in the past decade.

CASE 15-1
How Do You Like Your Reality? Virtual? Augmented? Mixed?

Every January, tens of thousands of tech enthusiasts and journalists converge in Las Vegas for a trade show known as International CES. There, attendees test out the hottest tech gadgets and get briefed about the latest industry trends. For the past few years, virtual reality (VR) headsets and software have been among the most buzz-worthy new products on display. (Artificial intelligence [AI] has also generated a lot of buzz at CES.)

Many different companies, including well-known tech giants, have showcased their wares at CES. For example, Facebook demonstrated the $600 Oculus Rift at the show. Sony's VR entry was the PlayStation VR ($400); Samsung's offering was Gear VR. Among lesser-known brands, the HTC Vive ($800) and VR units from Tsinghua Tongfang have also been introduced at CES.

To fully appreciate the VR experience, users don goggles and hold a set of handles. Then, in an area equipped with laser sensors, they are immersed in a 360-degree virtual world (see Exhibit 15-1). That world can be anything from the bottom of the Indian Ocean, where a person might come face-to-face with a shark, to the top of Mount Everest.

Advocates believe that a new user interface is on the horizon, and that VR and augmented reality (AR) have the potential to replace our phones, our TVs, and our desktop computers. But there's more! Have you heard of "mixed reality" (MR)? Some industry experts have even started using terms such as "personal reality" and "preferred reality" (PR) to describe this new experiential world. To find out more about the opportunities and challenges facing companies marketing and activating immersive

Exhibit 15-1 Virtual reality (VR) technology allows people to immerse themselves in a digital experience that replaces reality.
Source: Kobby Dagan/Shutterstock.

technologies and the potential uses of VR, AR, and variants such as MR, turn to the continuation of Case 15-1 at the end of the chapter.

VR and AR are just two examples of the way that the digital revolution is driving the creation of new companies, industries, and markets. It is also contributing to the transformation—and, in some cases, the destruction—of companies, industries, and markets. In short, this revolution is dramatically transforming the world in which we live. As the digital revolution gains traction and picks up speed, global marketers will be forced to adapt to an evolutionary world in which cell phone tablets and other mobile devices play an important role.

This chapter appears after the five-chapter sequence devoted to the marketing mix. Why? Because all the elements of the marketing mix—the four Ps—converge in the world of Internet connectivity and commerce. For example, the product (*P*) includes Facebook, Google, Pinterest, Snapchat, Twitter, Wikipedia, and the myriad other Web sites that can be accessed worldwide. The Web also functions as a distribution channel, and a very efficient one at that. Case in point: iTunes, Pandora, Spotify, and YouTube are rewriting the rules of music and video distribution.

The Internet has also become a key communication platform. Today, almost every company and organization has a presence in the online space. The Internet can be used as an advertising channel, as a public relations (PR) tool, as a means for running a contest or sales promotion, and as support for the personal selling effort.

Finally, there is price. Comparison-shopping Web sites make it easy to check and compare prices for products and services. Moreover, the marginal cost of storing and distributing digitized products—music files, for example—is practically nothing. This has led to some interesting pricing strategy experiments. For example, Radiohead, the innovative rock band from Oxford, England, was one of the first to harness the efficiency of the Web by offering free downloads of its 2007 album *In Rainbows*.

We begin by briefly reviewing the key innovations that served as precursors to the digital revolution. In the next two sections, convergence and the disruptive nature of Internet technology, and their effects on global companies, are discussed. Key e-commerce issues that face global marketers are then examined. The discussion continues with an overview of Web site design issues as they pertain to global marketing. The final section of the chapter examines some of the products and service innovations that are driving the digital revolution.

(15-1) The Digital Revolution: A Brief History

◀ **15-1** List the major innovations and trends that contributed to the digital revolution.

The **digital revolution** is a paradigm shift resulting from technological advances that allow for the digitization (i.e., conversion to binary code) of analog sources of information, sounds, and images. The origins of the digital revolution can be traced back to the mid-twentieth century. Over a five-year period between 1937 and 1942, John Vincent Atanasoff and Clifford Berry developed the world's first electromechanical digital computer at Iowa State University. The Atanasoff–Berry Computer (ABC) incorporated several major innovations in computing, including the use of binary arithmetic, regenerative memory, parallel processing, and separation of the memory and computing functions.

In 1947, William Shockley and two colleagues at AT&T's Bell Laboratories invented a "solid state amplifier," or **transistor** (the term was coined by information theorist John R. Pierce). This was a critical innovation, because the vacuum tubes used in computers and electronics products at that time were large, consumed a large amount of power, and generated a great deal of heat. Shockley and his collaborators John Bardeen and William Brattain were awarded the Nobel Prize in physics in 1956 for their invention.

In 1948, a Bell Labs researcher named Claude Shannon wrote a technical report titled "A Mathematical Theory of Communication" in which he proposed that all information media could be encoded in *binary digits*, or bits. Eight years earlier, in 1940, Shannon had argued in his doctoral dissertation that the logical values "true" and "false" could be denoted by "1" and "0," respectively, and that streams of 1s and 0s could transmit media over a wire. Thanks to his pioneering work, Shannon is regarded as the inventor of information theory.

In the early 1950s, Sony licensed the transistor from Bell Labs; Sony engineers boosted the yield of the transistor and created the market for transistor radios. The sound was "lo-fi" but the devices were portable and stylish, which is what consumers—especially teenagers— wanted. Also during the 1950s, Robert Noyce and Jack Kilby independently invented the silicon chip, also known as the **integrated circuit (IC)**.[1] In essence, the IC put the various parts of an electrical circuit—including resistors, diodes, and capacitors—on a single piece of material. The IC gave the transistor its modern form and allowed its power to be harnessed in a reliable, low-cost way.

The IC and the concept of binary code permitted the development of the **personal computer (PC)**, a compact, affordable device whose advent marked the next phase of the digital revolution. Pivotal events and people associated with this era have become the stuff of legend. Seminal research in the early 1970s by Robert Taylor and Alan Kay at the Xerox Palo Alto Research Center (PARC) in California permitted the development of the first PCs. Taylor led a team that created a prototype PC called the Alto. Kay, the director of the Learning Research Group, developed software based on a "desktop metaphor" that used graphical icons.[2]

Taylor and Kay's breakthroughs at Xerox PARC had a strong impact on Steve Jobs, who, with partner Steve Wozniak, started Apple Computer in a garage in the late 1970s. The company's Apple II is widely regarded as the first "true" PC; the Apple II's popularity received a big boost in 1979 when a spreadsheet program known as VisiCalc was introduced. A computer **spreadsheet** is an electronic ledger that automatically calculates the effect of a change to one number on other entries across rows and down columns; previously, these changes had to be done manually. Although such powerful, time-saving functionality is taken for granted today, VisiCalc was a true milestone in the digital revolution.[3]

IBM brought its first PC to market in 1981; Bill Gates initially declined an offer to create an **operating system**—the software code that provides basic instructions—for IBM's new machine. Gates later changed his mind and developed the Microsoft Disk Operating System (MS-DOS). In 1984, Apple introduced the revolutionary Macintosh, with its user-friendly graphical interface and point-and-click mouse. A few years later, Microsoft replaced MS-DOS with Windows. Meanwhile, component manufacturers were innovating as well; Intel began marketing the 286 microprocessor in 1982. This chip was followed in quick succession by the 386 and 486 versions; in 1993, Intel unveiled the Pentium processor.

The rise of the Internet and the World Wide Web marks the next phase of the digital revolution. The Internet's origins can be traced back to an initiative by the **Defense Advanced Research Projects Agency (DARPA)**, which created a computer network that could maintain lines of communication in the event of a war. Robert Taylor, whose work at Xerox PARC has already been mentioned, was director of the Information Processing Techniques Office at the Pentagon in 1966. It was Taylor who secured the funding to create a single computer network that could connect separate computer research projects. In 1969, the ARPANET was unveiled; this network linked computer research centers at colleges and universities. E-mail within a computer network was made possible by the creation of a file-transfer program in 1972.

There was a problem, however: It was not possible to send e-mail that was created on one network to a computer on a different network. This problem was solved the following year when Vinton Cerf and Robert Kahn created a software framework known as TCP/IP (Transmission Control

Protocol/Internet Protocol) (see Exhibit 15-2). Launched in 1973, this cross-network protocol was the extended architecture that paved the way for a "network of networks." In December 1974, the term "Internet transmission control" appeared in a technical paper for the first time, and the **Internet** was born.

The ability to exchange e-mail messages on the Internet had a revolutionary impact on society, as technology guru Stewart Brand noted in the late 1980s:

> Marshall McLuhan used to remark, "Gutenberg made everybody a reader. Xerox made everybody a publisher." Personal computers are making everybody an author. E-mail, word processing programs that make revising as easy as thinking, and laser printers collapse the whole writing–publishing–distributing process into one event controlled entirely by the individual. If, as alleged, the only real freedom of the press is to own one, the fullest realization of the First Amendment is being accomplished by technology, not politics.[4]

Of course, the Internet revolution did not end with the advent of e-mail. More hardware and software innovations were yet to come. As America Online (AOL) cofounder Steve Case has noted, the "first wave" of the Internet revolution began in the mid-1980s as companies such as Cisco Systems and Xilinx created the core technologies (e.g., routers) that were the infrastructure or "on ramps" to the Internet.[5]

In 1990, a software consultant named Tim Berners-Lee invented the **Uniform Resource Locator (URL)**, an Internet site's address on the World Wide Web; **Hypertext Markup Language (HTML)**, a format language that controls the appearance of Web pages; and **Hypertext Transfer Protocol (HTTP)**, which enables hypertext files to be transferred across the Internet.[6] These innovations allowed Web sites to be linked and visually rich content to be posted and accessed. In short, Berners-Lee is the father of the **World Wide Web**.

In 1992, the U.S. government authorized the use of the Internet for commercial purposes. At the time, it was believed that programmers and scientists would be the heaviest users of this network. In the mid-1990s, however, a computer scientist at the University of Illinois named Marc Andreessen developed a Web browser; called Mosaic, it combined images and words together on the same screen and allowed users to search for and view resources on the Web. Andreessen joined forces with Jim Clark, one of the founders of Silicon Graphics, to form Mosaic Communications. Renamed Netscape Communications, the company became one of the brightest stars in the dot-com era, as commercial demand for the Netscape browser software exploded. As Thomas L. Friedman notes, "Marc Andreessen did not invent the Internet, but he did as much as any single person to bring it alive and popularize it."[8]

"There are certain limitations that are part of the network, and we are struggling with that. We're worried that in the zeal to address localization that people will not be able to communicate any more. If someone gives you a business card with the e-mail address in Chinese, what are you to do?"[7]

Vinton G. Cerf, Internet pioneer, former chairman of ICANN, and Chief Internet Evangelist, Google

Exhibit 15-2 Vint Cerf is Chief Internet Evangelist at Google. He is widely considered to be one of the fathers of the Internet. In March 2017, Cerf appeared at the SXSW Interactive Festival in Austin, Texas, where he discussed a new initiative called People-Centered Internet.
Source: Diego Donamaria/Getty Images.

Within five years of the Web's debut, the user base had increased from 600,000 users to 40 million. Although computer makers were slow to add modems to PCs, fledgling online services such as America Online were exhibiting robust subscriber growth. Thanks in part to a direct-mail marketing campaign in which millions of software discs were sent to prospective customers, AOL grew from 5 million subscribers in 1996 to 20 million subscribers in 1999. And, of course, the company's iconic sign-on greeting, "You've got mail," became a part of popular culture.

During the second wave of the Internet revolution, which Case describes as running from 2000 to 2014, the focus shifted from building the Internet to building on top of it. Search engines such as Yahoo! and Google emerged, and encryption and security features were built into the Web. Social media companies, including Facebook, YouTube, and Twitter, exploded onto the scene, and the iPhone launched the "app economy."

Case envisions the third wave as a time when the Internet is seamlessly integrated into everyday life. He also anticipates a period of reinvention and disruption in key economic sectors, including major changes in health care, education, financial services, and transportation. Some of this integration and disruption is already occurring, as evidenced by the popularity of ride-sharing services such as Uber and Lyft. And, as the impact of Uber, Lyft, and other ride-sharing services on traditional industry sectors such as auto manufacturing demonstrates, the third wave is likely to be characterized by an ongoing dialog between attackers and defenders of disruption and revolution.

Case foresees four trends during the third wave. Case describes the first trend as "capital for all," with global crowdfunding sites such GoFundMe, Indiegogo, and Kickstarter growing in importance. The second trend is the reemergence of partnerships; whether in health care or education, *who* a company partners with will be just as important as what the company does. A third trend is the launch of social enterprises that link profit and purpose. Warby Parker, Tesla, and TOMS are three examples (see Exhibit 15-3). Case dubs the fourth trend the "rise of the rest," as the globalization of entrepreneurship gains traction on a regional basis, far from startup hotbeds such as Silicon Valley.

Today, almost 3 billion people—nearly half of the world's population—use the Internet. As noted in Chapter 10, because residents in developing countries lag in terms of Internet access, Google is working to build wireless networks in those areas, especially outside large cities, that are beyond the reach of wired networks.[9]

Despite the promise embodied by the digital revolution, the technology's powerful capabilities and increasing importance have also resulted in a backlash that has manifested itself in various ways. For example, the Chinese government, alarmed by the free flow of information across the Internet, closely monitors the content on Web sites that its citizens access. Facebook, Twitter, and numerous other social media sites are blocked in China.

Exhibit 15-3 Warby Parker is an innovative online purveyor of prescription eyewear. Its direct-sales business model has disrupted the traditional eyewear industry. Warby Parker's commitment to social responsibility is embodied in its buy-a-pair, give-a-pair philosophy.
Source: CrowdSpark/Alamy Stock Photo.

Who controls the Internet? Good question! The first Internet Governance Forum (IGF) was held in Athens, Greece, in 2006. The IGF was charged with guiding "the development and application by governments, the private sector, and civil society, in their respective roles, of shared principles, norms, rules, decision-making procedures, and programs that shape the evolution and use of the Internet." Some people in the global Internet community are concerned about the inclusion of the word "governments" in this statement.

The nonprofit Internet Corporation for Assigned Names and Numbers (ICANN) is based in Marina del Ray, California. ICANN maintains a database of Web addresses, approves new suffixes for Web addresses (e.g., .info and .tv), and performs other behind-the-scenes procedures that are critical for keeping the Internet functioning properly. ICANN's advisory body includes international members, but the U.S. Department of Commerce retains veto power over all decisions. For example, after ICANN tentatively approved the domain name .xxx for pornography sites, the U.S. Department of Commerce blocked the decision.

Policymakers in some countries are concerned about U.S. control of the Internet. For example, China, India, Brazil, and the European Union (EU) have taken the position that, because the Internet is global, no single country should be in control of it. Accordingly, these nations have sought to have the United Nations assume a role in Internet governance.[10]

Privacy is another issue. As Amazon, Facebook, Google, and myriad other companies continue to exploit "conversation commerce" by using the Internet to gather vast amounts of information about customers, privacy issues are becoming a focal point of concern among policymakers and the general public. For example, Russia and China have new cyber-security laws requiring that all data about customers in their respective countries be stored on in-country servers. More than 2,000 U.S. companies have pledged to comply with European data protection standards by signing Privacy Shield, an agreement between the United States and the EU. Moreover, effective in 2018, the General Data Protection Regulation (GPDR) requires all companies conducting business in the EU to comply with strict guidelines for gathering, storing, and using data provided by customers.[11]

(15-2) Convergence

◄ **15-2** Define "convergence" and give an example.

The digital revolution is causing dramatic, disruptive changes in industry structures. Writing in *The New York Times* at the beginning of 2010, columnist Jon Pareles summarized some of these changes as follows:

> The 2000s were the broadband decade, the disintermediation decade, the file-sharing decade, the digital recording (and image) decade, the iPod decade, the long-tail decade, the blog decade, the user-generated decade, the on-demand decade, the all-access decade. Inaugurating the new millennium, the Internet swallowed culture whole and delivered it back—cheaper, faster, and smaller—to everyone who can get online.[12]

Convergence is a term that refers to the coming together of previously separate industries and product categories (see Figure 15-1). New technologies often affect the business sector(s) in which a company competes. Which business is Sony in? Originally, Sony was a consumer electronics company best known for innovative products such as transistor radios, Trinitron televisions, VCRs, stereo components, and the Walkman line of personal music players. Then, Sony entered new businesses by acquiring CBS Records and Columbia Motion Pictures. These acquisitions themselves did not represent convergence because they occurred in the early days of the digital revolution, when motion pictures, recorded music, and consumer electronics were still separate industries. Today, however, Sony is in the "bits" business: Its core businesses incorporate digital technology and involve digitizing and distributing sound, images, and data. Now, Sony's competitors include Apple (music players, smartphones), Dell (computers), Canon (cameras), and Nokia (smartphones).

Which kinds of challenges does convergence present? Consider the case of Kodak, the undisputed leader in photography-related products for more than a century. The company struggled to remake its business model as its sales of digital-related products grew from zero to $1 billion in five years. Through convergence, Kodak's competitors came to include companies such as Dell and Hewlett-Packard. Moreover, Kodak's core businesses—film, photographic paper, and

"I think there will be an increasing convergence between content and commerce, that it will be about following consumers instead of making consumers come to you, and I am especially excited about the various platforms that will allow more and more access to customers."[13]

Natalie Massenet, founder, Net-a-Porter

FIGURE 15-1
Industry Convergence

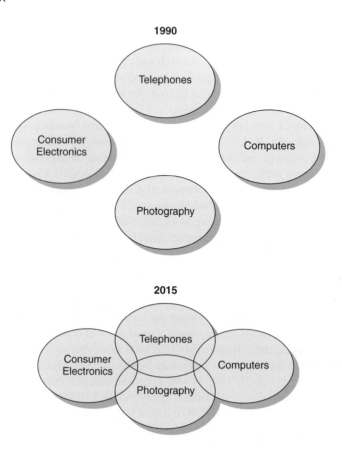

chemicals—were disrupted. Competition for Kodak also came from the telecommunications industry. The cell phone camera was invented in 1997; a key benefit of this innovation was the ability to download digital photos from the camera and post them on the Web or e-mail them to friends. Motorola, a key player in the cell phone business, could have been one of the first companies to market a cell phone camera, but its management's attention was distracted by the ill-fated launch of the Iridium satellite phone. Instead, inventor Philippe Kahn took his idea to Japan, where the first cell phone cameras were introduced in 1999.[14] In 2010, annual sales of camera-equipped phones passed the 1-billion-unit mark.

▶ **15-3** Define *value network* and explain the differences between sustaining technologies and disruptive technologies.

(15-3) Value Networks and Disruptive Technologies

As noted in the chapter introduction, the digital revolution has created both opportunities and threats.[15] Dell, IBM, Kodak, Motorola, Xerox, and Sony are just a few examples of global companies that have struggled to remake their businesses in the face of technological innovation. IBM missed out on the minicomputer market, in part because the company's management believed minicomputers promised lower profit margins and represented a smaller market opportunity. DEC, Data General, and Prime created the minicomputer market, but these companies then missed the PC revolution. This time, however, IBM's executive team demonstrated that it had learned its lesson: It set up an independent organizational unit to create the company's first PC. However, IBM subsequently was slow to recognize the growing market demand for laptops; new entrants included Apple, Dell, Toshiba, Sharp, and Zenith. Recently, IBM exited the PC market altogether.

How is it that the managers at so many companies fail to respond to change in a timely manner? According to Harvard professor Clayton Christensen, the problem is that executives become so committed to a current, profitable technology that they fail to provide adequate levels of investment in new, apparently riskier technologies. Indeed, companies may fall into this trap precisely because they adhere too closely to the prevailing marketing orthodoxy—that is, they listen to and respond to the needs of established customers, rather than seeking out new opportunities. Christensen calls this situation the **innovator's dilemma**.

ENTREPRENEURIAL LEADERSHIP, CREATIVE THINKING, AND THE GLOBAL STARTUP

Jack Ma, Alibaba

Jack Ma is an entrepreneur. He has developed several innovative products and services, created new brands, and started companies to market his creations. By applying the basic tools and principles of modern marketing, Ma has achieved remarkable success.

As is true with many of today's entrepreneurs, Ma's key innovation was based on his insights into the possibilities and opportunities provided by the Internet. Today, nearly 80 percent of China's e-commerce is channeled through Alibaba, the company Ma founded in 1999. Not surprisingly, Ma is a billionaire many times over; he is also the richest man in China (see Exhibit 15-4).

In 2003, Ma launched a consumer site called Taobao (Chinese for "search for treasure") as an alternative to eBay. At the time, eBay and its Chinese partner, EachNet, dominated the market. Undeterred, Ma famously remarked at the time, "eBay is a shark in the ocean; we are a crocodile in the Yangtze River. If we fight in the ocean we will lose, but if we fight in the river we will win."

Initially, Taobao set itself apart from eBay by not charging sales commissions or listing fees. Ma was convinced that global Internet companies entering China were making three kinds of mistakes. First, they underestimated the differences between China and the U.S. market. Second, they incurred higher costs than local Chinese operators. Third, they pursued global expansion too quickly. Ma's instincts were correct. In less than five years, eBay's share of the Chinese market was down to single digits, while Taobao dominated the market with an 85 percent share. Another service spun off from Taobao, Tmall, is a mass-market shopping site for Chinese consumers.

In 2005, Yahoo paid $1 billion for a 40 percent share of Alibaba, and Ma became chief executive of Yahoo's Chinese operations. In 2014, Alibaba made history when its $25 billion initial public offering on the New York Stock Exchange set a record for both the United States and the world. Ma is also preparing to launch 11 Main, a site specifically targeting American shoppers. Alibaba is making selective investments in innovative startups, including Lyft, the ride-sharing service that competes with Uber. Acknowledging that consumer awareness of Alibaba is low in the United States, company executives are approaching the U.S. market with caution.

Despite the "go-slow" market entry strategy in the United States, by 2016 Alibaba was selling nearly 15 billion items per year—three times more than Amazon. Now Ma has set an ambitious long-term goal for his company: 2 billion global customers by 2025. Ma envisions that the company's AliExpress sales platform will be the main driver of growth, and will lead to a new data-driven business model for e-commerce that he has dubbed Globalization 2.0. Ma hopes that Singles Day, an online shopping event that takes place in China every November 11, will be embraced by shoppers in the rest of the world.

However, Ma's company faces a thorny problem: Some of the Chinese companies that sell on AliExpress are offering counterfeit goods. These can range from fake Nike Air Jordan sneakers to fake Rolex watches to fake Ray-Ban sunglasses. The International Anti-Counterfeiting Coalition estimates that, in 2015 alone, worldwide sales of fake goods totaled $1.7 trillion.

Alibaba uses data analytics to combat the counterfeiters and protect intellectual property rights. Millions of product listings on Alibaba are scanned each day, and each year the company has been able to close down tens of thousands of stores selling counterfeit goods. Working with brand rights holders and law enforcement, Alibaba has also helped shut down hundreds of facilities that manufacture the fakes.

In 2016, Ma announced the formation of the Alibaba Big Data Anti-Counterfeiting Alliance to address this ongoing problem. The Alliance includes some two dozen companies with well-known brand names. A statement issued by the company indicated that Louis Vuitton, Swarovski, and other alliance members would share data and expertise with the goal of authenticating intellectual property and removing listings on Alibaba that infringe IP rights.

Sources: Louise Lucas, "Do-It-Yourself Globalization: Alibaba," *FT Big Read—Financial Times* (May 23, 2017), p. 9; Marco della Cava, "Alibaba Puts Heat on $1.7T Fake Goods Market," *USA Today* (January 28, 2017), p. 5B; Gillian Wong, "Counterfeits Test Alibaba's Goals," *The Wall Street Journal* (November 15, 2015), p. B8; David Barboza, "The Jack Ma Way," *The New York Times Sunday* Business (September 7, 2014), pp. 1, 4–5; David Gelles, Hiroko Tabuchi, and Michael J. de la Merced, "Alibaba's American Aspirations," *The New York Times* (May 24, 2014), pp. B1, B5.

Exhibit 15-4 Alibaba founder Jack Ma is a fan of Chinese kung fu novels. His company dominates the e-commerce sector in China, where Alibaba uses VR and AR to drive traffic to both physical and virtual stores.
Source: HOANG DINH NAM/AFP/ Getty Images.

"The incumbent leaders never see it coming. They focus on their best customers and try to provide what they need, but the customers who first defect to new technology are usually the least profitable."[16]

Clayton Christenson, commenting on the problems facing retailer J. Crew

In every industry, companies are embedded in a **value network**. Each value network has a cost structure associated with it that dictates the margins needed to achieve profitability. The boundaries of the network are defined, in part, by the unique rank ordering of the importance of various product performance attributes. Parallel value networks, each built around a different definition of what makes a product valuable, may exist within the same broadly defined industry. Each network has its own "metrics of value." For example, for laptop computers, the metrics are small size, low weight, minimal power consumption, and rugged design. During the 1980s, customers who bought portable computers were willing to pay a premium for smaller size; buyers of mainframe computers did not value this attribute. Conversely, mainframe buyers valued (i.e., were willing to pay more for) memory capacity as measured by megabytes; portable computer buyers placed less value on this attribute. In short, the value networks for mainframe computers and portable computers are different.

As firms gain experience within a given network, they are likely to develop capabilities, organizational structures, and cultures tailored to the distinctive requirements of their respective value networks. The industry's dominant firms—typically those with reputations as "well-managed" firms—lead in developing and/or adopting **sustaining technologies**, which comprise incremental or radical innovations that improve product performance. According to Christensen, most new technologies developed by established companies are sustaining in nature; indeed, the vast majority of innovations are of this type.

In contrast, new entrants to an industry lead in developing **disruptive technologies** that redefine performance. The benefits associated with disruptive technologies go beyond enhancing product performance—these technologies enable something to be done that was previously deemed impossible. Disruptive technologies typically enable new markets to emerge. As Christensen explains, "An innovation that is disrupting to one firm can be sustaining to another firm. The Internet was sustaining technology to Dell, which already sold PCs via direct marketing channels. But it was disruptive technology to Compaq, whose major distribution channel was retailers."[17]

To help managers recognize the innovator's dilemma and develop appropriate responses to environmental change, Christensen has developed five principles of disruptive innovations:

1. Companies depend on customers and investors for resources. As management guru Rosabeth Moss Kanter points out, the best innovations are user driven; paradoxically, however, if management listens to established customers, opportunities for disruptive innovation may be missed.[18]

2. Small markets don't solve the growth needs of large companies. Small organizations can most easily respond to the opportunities for growth in a small market. This fact may require large organizations to create independent units to pursue new technologies, as IBM did in developing its PC.

3. Markets that don't exist can't be analyzed. Christensen recommends that companies embrace *agnostic marketing*. This is the explicit assumption that *no one*—not company personnel, not the company's customers—can know whether, how, or in what quantities a disruptive product can or will be used before they have experienced using it.

4. An organization's capabilities define its disabilities. For example, Microsoft was once an industry trendsetter. Today, while it remains firmly committed to its Windows operating system, Microsoft lags behind new industry entrants in high-growth, consumer-oriented areas such as search and social networking.[19]

5. Technology supply may not equal market demand. Some products offer a greater degree of sophistication than the market requires. For example, developers of accounting software for small businesses overshot the functionality required by the market, creating an opportunity for a disruptive software technology that provided adequate, not superior, functionality and was simple and more convenient to use. This was the opportunity seized by Scott Cook, developer of Quicken and QuickBooks.

(15-4) Global E-Commerce

The term **e-commerce** refers to the general exchange of goods and services using the Internet or a similar online network as a marketing channel. Global e-commerce sales surpassed $1.3 trillion in 2014, the same year that China surpassed the United States as the world's largest e-commerce market. Hundreds of millions of Chinese consumers are shopping online with greater frequency as smartphone penetration ramps up. The U.S. Census Bureau reported that U.S. online retail sales revenues totaled $390 billion in 2016, a figure that represents a 100 percent increase since 2011. By comparison, Chinese online retail transactions in 2016 were an estimated $750 billion—almost twice the U.S. figure.

Internet penetration in some world regions is in the low single digits; this is especially true in Africa. For example, penetration is less than 10 percent in Eritrea, Burundi, Sierra Leone, Somalia, and other low-income countries. By contrast, in several countries, including South Korea, the Netherlands, Greenland, the United Arab Emirates, Bahrain, and Qatar, more than 90 percent of the population is online. Consider the following statistics:

- Between 2003 and 2014, the number of Internet users in China increased from 68 million to 640 million. More than 600 million Chinese people shop online, making China the world's largest e-commerce market. Local companies such as Alibaba and JD.Com dominate the market.
- According to Forrester Research, online retail in Western Europe will grow at a compound annual rate of 11.3 percent between 2017 and 2022. Eighty-five percent of surveyed European mobile phone owners access the Internet at least weekly on a mobile phone.[21]

E-commerce activities can be divided into three broad categories: business-to-consumer (B2C or b-to-c), business-to-business (B2B or b-to-b), and consumer-to-consumer (peer-to-peer: P2P or p-to-p). People often associate e-commerce with well-known consumer-oriented sites such as Amazon.com, Apple's iTunes Store, and eBay.

As noted in Chapter 14, Germany's Otto Group is the world's second-largest B2C e-commerce retailer. Indeed, according to Forrester Research, Germany, France and the United Kingdom together account for more than two-thirds of online retail sales in Western Europe (see Figure 15-2). More recently, consumers in Italy and Spain have begun to embrace online shopping, contributing to rapid growth in those countries. Overall, online purchases of clothing outpace other types of purchases by a two-to-one ratio. However, online sales of consumer electronics, watches, and jewelry are growing as well.[22]

In general, B2B commerce constitutes the biggest share of the Internet economy and will likely continue to do so for the foreseeable future. Industry forecasts call for global B2B revenues to reach $6.7 trillion by 2020, at which point B2C is expected to be $3.2 trillion.[23]

Web sites can be classified by purpose: **Promotion sites** provide marketing communications about a company's goods or services, **content sites** provide news and entertainment and support a company's PR efforts, and **transaction sites** are online retail operations that allow customers to purchase goods and services. Typically, Web sites combine the three functions.

Web sites can also be categorized in terms of content and audience focus. For example, international students at your college or university may have learned about your school via the Internet, even though home-country prospective students constitute the primary target audience for the Web site.

Similarly, Pandora, the online music service, serves only American listeners; Deezer, the French online music-streaming company, is operational in 160 countries. Prior to 2015, Deezer was not available in the United States. Why? For one thing, international copyright laws make it difficult to license performance rights for songs. However, in 2015, Deezer launched a partnership with hi-fi marketers Sonos and Bose, making Deezer Elite available for U.S. customers. As former Pandora CEO Joe Kennedy once remarked, "The good news is that the Internet is global, but the bad news is that copyright law is country by country."[24] Apple's iTunes Store began as a U.S.-only retailer. During the next decade, the service was rolled out in dozens of countries. Netflix, the online movie distributor, has evolved from domestic to international in a similar way.

◀ **15-4** Identify current trends in global e-commerce and explain how global companies are expanding their presence on the Web.

"This is the definition of disruption. This is Netflix replacing Blockbuster. This is Uber replacing taxis."[20]

Brendan Witcher, Vice President and Principal Analyst, Forrester Research, commenting on the potential impact of Amazon's Just Walk Out stores on retailing

FIGURE 15-2

Western European Online Retail Sales, 2017–2022 (€ billions)

Source: Adapted from Michelle Beeson and Claudia Tajima, *Online Retail Will Drive Overall European Retail Sales Growth Through 2022*, Forrester Research (December 5, 2017), p. 2.

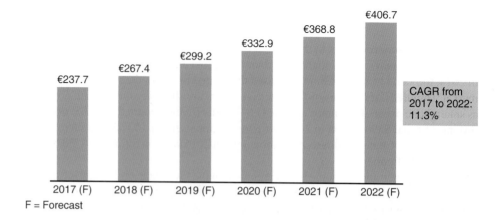

€237.7 — 2017 (F)
€267.4 — 2018 (F)
€299.2 — 2019 (F)
€332.9 — 2020 (F)
€368.8 — 2021 (F)
€406.7 — 2022 (F)

CAGR from 2017 to 2022: 11.3%

F = Forecast

Companies such as FedEx and Gucci are global in scope, and the Internet constitutes a powerful, cost-effective communication tool for these firms. Similarly, the interactive marketing staff at Unilever understands that the Web represents an important low-cost medium for promoting products. Unilever's vast archive of TV commercials has been digitized; Web surfers can download the videos for products such as Salon Selectives shampoo and watch them anytime. A decade ago Unilever launched a 12-week series on Yahoo! Food titled *In Search of Real Food.* Hosted by Food Network TV star David Lieberman, the show was created around Hellman's mayonnaise. As Doug Scott, executive director of entertainment at the Ogilvy & Mather ad agency explained, "Content for broadband costs significantly less than TV productions and it allows you to distribute to a much larger audience."[25]

Companies can also seek e-commerce transactions with customers on a worldwide basis. Amazon.com is the most successful example of this transaction business model. Online book shoppers can choose from millions of book titles on its Web site; many carry discounted prices. And, of course, today Amazon offers a vast range of products.

In the mid-1990s, after assessing a number of potential products in terms of their suitability for online sales, company founder Jeffrey Bezos settled on books for two reasons. First, there were too many titles for any one "brick-and-mortar" store to carry. The second reason was related to industry structure: The publishing industry is highly fragmented, with thousands of publishers found in the United States alone. As a consequence, no single publisher has a high degree of supplier power. Bezos's instincts proved sound: Sales exploded after Amazon's Web site became operational in mid-1995. Within a year, orders were coming in from dozens of countries.

Today, Amazon.com is the world's largest online retail site, with hundreds of millions of annual visitors. The company's 12 international sites generate between 40 percent and 50 percent of its total sales, with Germany, Japan, and the United Kingdom being Amazon's three biggest markets outside the United States. The company employees more than 500,000 people, and Bezos is the world's richest person, with an estimated net worth of $100 billion.

Online retail in the United States passed the $400 billion mark in 2017, including orders from abroad. Abercrombie & Fitch, Aéropostale, J. Crew, Macy's, Timberland, and Saks Fifth Avenue are just some of the U.S. retailers targeting foreign buyers by adding international shipping services to their Web sites. The dollar's strength, which translates into higher prices for shoppers paying in euros or other currencies, has prompted more U.S. consumers to order from abroad. Delivery giants FedEx, UPS, and DHL are making key acquisitions and partnering with other firms to help ensure seamless, frictionless ordering and delivery experiences for online shoppers.[26]

Some products are inherently not suitable candidates for sale via the Internet; for example, McDonald's doesn't sell hamburgers from its Web site. In addition, some global marketers make the strategic decision to establish a presence on the Web without offering transaction opportunities, even though the product could be sold that way. Instead, such companies limit their Web activities to promotion and information in support of offline retail distribution channels.

Companies may pursue this strategy for several reasons. First, they may lack the infrastructure necessary to process orders from individual customers. Second, it can cost anywhere from $20 million to $30 million to establish a fully functioning e-commerce site. Other, product-specific factors may also underlie the decision to forgo Web-based sales. The Web site for Godin Guitars, for example, provides a great deal of product information and a directory of the company's worldwide dealer network. But company founder Robert Godin believes that the best way for a person to select a guitar is to play one, and that requires a visit to a music store.

For consumer products giant Procter & Gamble (P&G), the Internet represents a global promotion and information channel that is an integral part of its brand strategy. For example, Pampers is P&G's number 1 brand, with annual global sales of $10 billion. Pampers' online presence at www.pampers.com represents a new conceptualization of the brand. Previously, brand managers viewed Pampers disposable diapers as a way of keeping babies happy; the new view is that the Pampers brand is a child development aid. Visitors to the Pampers Village online community can read advice from the Pampers Parenting Institute as well as tips from mothers. Discount coupons are also available.

P&G launched www.thankyoumom.com to position P&G as "a proud sponsor of moms." In 2010, P&G used the site to award $100,000 in travel vouchers to help mothers reunite with their families. P&G has also launched a retail Web site to sell Pantene shampoo, Pampers baby products, and other brands to consumers. This online strategy change brings P&G into direct competition with Walmart, Target, and other retailers that complement brick-and-mortar stores with Internet selling.[27]

Until recently, visitors to the Web sites for most luxury goods purveyors were not given the opportunity to buy. The reason is simple: Top design houses strive to create an overall retail shopping experience that enhances the brand. This objective is basically at odds with e-commerce. As Forrester Research analyst Sucharita Mulpuru explained, "There was a belief that there was no way you could communicate your brand essence online."[28] This belief is now changing, and some luxury goods marketers have developed smartphone and iPad apps to help consumers shop. Burberry, Chanel, Coach, Gucci, and other luxury brands are cultivating official online communities on Facebook. According to Reggie Bradord, CEO of a social media management company, they are doing the right thing. He says, "Luxury brands should be thinking about 'how can we create a dialogue and get consumers connecting with our brand?'"[29]

As the Internet has developed into a crucial global communication tool, decision makers in virtually all organizations are realizing that they must include this new medium in their communications planning. Many companies purchase banner ads on popular Web sites; the ads are linked to the company's home page or product- or brand-related sites. Advertisers pay when users click the link. Although creative possibilities are limited with banner ads and **click-through rates**—the percentage of users who click on an advertisement that has been presented—are typically low, the number of companies that use the Web as a medium for global advertising is expected to increase dramatically over the next few years.

One of the most interesting aspects of the digital revolution has been noted by Chris Anderson, the editor of *Wired* magazine and author of *The Long Tail*. The title of Anderson's book refers to the use of the efficient economics of online retail to aggregate a large number of relatively slow-selling products. *The Long Tail* helps explain the success of eBay, Amazon.com, Netflix, and iTunes, all of which offer far more variety and choice than traditional retailers can. As Anderson explains, "The story of the Long Tail is really about the economics of abundance—what happens when the bottlenecks that stand between supply and demand in our culture start to disappear and everything becomes available to everyone." Anderson notes that "below-the-radar" products—for example, obscure books, movies, and music—are driving revenues at e-commerce merchants such as Amazon.com, Netflix, and iTunes. He says, "These millions of fringe sales are an efficient, cost-effective business. . . . For the first time in history, hits and niches are on equal economic footing."[30]

▶ **15-5** Explain the key issues facing a global company when designing and implementing a Web site.

(15-5) Web Site Design and Implementation

To fully exploit the Internet's potential, company executives must be willing to integrate interactive media into their marketing mixes.[31] Web sites can be developed in-house, or an outside firm can be contracted to do the job. During the past few years, a new breed of interactive advertising agency has emerged to help companies globalize their Internet offerings (see Table 15-1). Some of these agencies are independent; others are affiliated with other advertising agency brands and holding companies (see Chapter 13). Whether Web development is handled in-house or by an outside agency, several issues must be addressed when setting up for global e-commerce—for example, choosing domain names, arranging payment, localizing sites, addressing privacy issues, and setting up a distribution system.

A critical first step is registering a country-specific domain name. For example, Amazon.com has a family of different domain names, one for each country in which it operates (see Table 15-3). Although it is certainly possible for European consumers to browse Amazon.com's U.S. site, they may prefer a direct link to a site with a local domain name. From both a marketing perspective and a consumer perspective, this makes sense: For European consumers, the Web site of choice will be one that quotes prices in euros rather than dollars, offers a product selection tailored to local tastes, and ships from local distribution points. However, as noted earlier, the weak dollar may make it less expensive for shoppers in, say, Europe, to order from U.S. online retailers.

Moreover, research suggests that visitors spend more time at sites that are in their own language; they also tend to view more pages and make more purchases. Many people will seek information about sites on local versions of well-known search engines. For example, in France, Yahoo!'s local site is http://fr.Yahoo.com. The same principle applies to non-U.S. companies targeting the American online consumer market. For example, Waterford Wedgwood, Harrods,

TABLE 15-1 Top Five Digital Agency Networks by 2016 Interactive Marketing Revenues

Agency (Parent Company)	Headquarters	Selected Clients
Accenture Interactive (Accenture)	New York	L'Oréal; SKY Cable
IBM iX (IBM)	Armonk, New York	Atlanta Falcons; Knorr; Migros
Deloitte Digital (Deloitte)	New York	Vodaphone Malta; PepsiCo; Estée Lauder
Publicis.Sapient (Publicis)	Boston	McDonald's
PwC Digital Services (PwC)	New York	Hire Heroes USA

Source: Adapted from "Digital Networks: Worldwide," *Ad Age* (Mary 1, 2017), p. 17.

TABLE 15-2 Selected Amazon.com Domain Names

Domain Name	Country
amazon.com.br	Brazil
amazon.ca	Canada
amazon.cn	China
amazon.fr	France
amazon.de	Germany
amazon.it	Italy
amazon.co.jp	Japan
amazon.es	Spain
amazon.co.uk	United Kingdom

Johnnie Boden, and other well-known companies have acquired U.S. domain names and created sites with prices listed in dollars.[32]

While registering a ".com" domain name is a relatively straightforward procedure in the United States, requirements can vary elsewhere. In some countries, a company must establish a legal entity before it can register a site with a local domain-name extension. **Cybersquatting**— the practice of registering a particular domain name for the express purpose of reselling it to the company that should rightfully use it—is also a problem. Avon, Panasonic, and Starbucks are some of the companies that have been victims of cybersquatting.

Payment can be another problem for e-commerce transactions; in some countries, including China, credit card use is low. In such situations, e-commerce operators must arrange payment by bank check or postal money order; cash on delivery is also an option. Another issue is credit card fraud; Indonesia, Russia, Croatia, and Bosnia are among the countries where fraud is rampant. Extra identity measures may have to be taken, such as requiring buyers to fax a photo of the actual credit card they are using as well as photo IDs.[33] In Japan, consumers pay for online purchases at convenience stores (*konbini*). After selecting an item online, the buyer goes to a nearby convenience store (e.g., a 7-Eleven) and pays cash for the item; the clerk transfers the money to the online seller's account. However, foreign companies can't participate in the *konbini* system, which means that a foreign online retailer must establish an alliance with a local company.

Ideally, each country-specific site should reflect local culture, language usage, customs, and aesthetic preferences. Logos and other elements of brand identity should be included on the site, with adjustments for color preferences and meaning differences when necessary. For example, the shopping cart icon is familiar to online shoppers in the United States and many European countries, but online companies must determine whether that icon is appropriate in all country markets. Subtle but important language differences can also occur even in English-speaking countries. For example, www.figleaves.com and www.figleaves.com/uk are, respectively, the American and British Web addresses for a UK-based lingerie marketer. However, the U.S. site refers to "panties," whereas the U.K. site has a listing for "briefs." When two or more different languages are involved, translators should be used to ensure that the copy reflects current language usage. It is also important not to "reinvent the wheel" by translating the same terms over and over again. Local translators should have access to an in-house dictionary that contains preferred translations of company-specific terms. The database system should be capable of identifying content that has already been translated and then reusing that content.

After Yao Ming joined the Houston Rockets in 2002, the NBA's Chinese Web site was launched in conjunction with www.SOHU.com, China's leading Internet portal. Written entirely in Chinese characters, the site is designed to capitalize on basketball's increasing popularity in the world's largest market. The NBA has also launched country-specific English-language sites in Africa, Australia, Canada, India, New Zealand, the Philippines, and the United Kingdom. In addition, sites have been developed in several other languages, including German, Greek, Hebrew, Italian, Portuguese, and Spanish.

As the NBA's Chinese site illustrates, it is not enough to simply translate a Web site from the home-country language into other languages. Thus, another basic step is localizing a Web site in the native language and business nomenclature of the target country. From a technical point of view, Web sites designed to support English, French, German, and other languages that use the Latin alphabet store only a maximum of 256 characters in the American Standard Code for Information Interchange (ASCII) format. Even so, there are language-specific needs; for example, a German-language Web site requires more than double the capacity of an English-language site because German copy takes more space.[34] In contrast, languages such as Japanese and Chinese require a database that supports double-ASCII. For this reason, it is wise to start with a double-ACSII platform when designing a Web site's architecture. The site's architecture should also be flexible enough to allow different date, currency, and money formatting. For example, to someone living in the United Kingdom, "7/10/16" means October 7, 2016. To an American, it means July 10, 2016.

Another critical global e-commerce issue is privacy. The EU's regulations related to protection of personal data are among the world's strictest: Companies are limited in terms of how much personal information—a customer's age, marital status, and buying patterns, for example—can be gathered and how long the information can be retained. In 2012, EU Justice Commissioner Viviane Reding announced an overhaul of the EU's data collection rules (see Exhibit 15-5). These rules will apply to companies based outside the EU—Apple, Google, and Facebook, for example—if they offer services to EU citizens. Customers living in the EU also have the "right to be forgotten"; that is, they can request to have their personal data deleted. Moreover, EU citizens must give explicit consent before companies can share their data.[35] By contrast, the U.S. government has been reluctant to issue privacy protection rules in part due to First Amendment issues and in part due to national security concerns stemming from the terrorist attacks of 2001. To help ensure compliance with privacy laws, some American companies have created a new executive-level job position: chief privacy officer.[36]

A number of e-commerce issues are related to physical distribution decisions. As online sales increase in a particular country or region, it may be necessary to establish local warehouse facilities to speed delivery and reduce shipping costs. In the United States, such a step has tax implications, because the marketer may have to collect sales tax. To allay consumer concerns about ordering merchandise online, companies may opt to waive shipping fees and offer free returns and money-back guarantees.

▶ **15-6** Identify the most important new products and services that have been introduced in the past decade.

(15-6) New Products and Services

The digital revolution has spurred innovations in many different industries. Companies in all parts of the world are developing a new generation of products, services, and technologies. These include broadband networks, mobile commerce, wireless connectivity, and smartphones. For example, GoDaddy is used by many entrepreneurs who need help establishing domain names and hosting Web sites. (see Exhibit 15-6).

Broadband

A **broadband** communication system is one that has sufficient capacity to carry multiple voice, data, or video channels simultaneously. *Bandwidth* determines the range of frequencies that can pass over a given transmission channel. For example, traditional telephone networks offered quite limited bandwidth compared with state-of-the-art digital telephone networks. As a result, a

Exhibit 15-5 Viviane Reding is the European Commissioner for Justice, Fundamental Rights, and Citizenship. In her official capacity, Reding has spoken out about data privacy issues. One concern in the European Union is the widespread corporate practice of gathering and using consumer data without permission. The new GDPR will ensure that consumers have the "right to be forgotten," by requiring companies such as Google to delete user data if requested to do so.
Source: GEORGES GOBET/AFP/Getty Images.

Make your idea a reality.

Get everything you need to thrive online, all baked into one simple toolkit.

GoDaddy

Exhibit 15-6 GoDaddy has raised awareness for its Web hosting and Internet domain registration services with various advertising campaigns. Its Super Bowl ads sometimes courted controversy; recent print ads have been much more straightforward.
Source: GoDaddy.

traditional telephone call sounds "lo-fi." Bandwidth is measured in units of bits per second (bps); a full page of English text is approximately 16,000 bits. An old-school, 56 Kpbs dial-up modem connected to a conventional telephone line could move 16,000 bits per second; by comparison, today's broadband Internet connections that utilize coaxial cable or DSL (digital subscriber line) technology can move data at speeds measured in gigabits per second.

South Korea currently boasts the world's fastest average Internet speeds. However, technology upgrades currently under way will mean even higher speeds: The government intends to ensure that every Korean household has a 1-gigabit Internet connection. As Choi Gwang-gi, the engineer overseeing the project, explains, "A lot of Koreans are early adopters, and we thought we needed to be prepared for things like 3D TV, Internet Protocol TV, high-definition multimedia, gaming and videoconferencing, ultra-high definition TV, and cloud computing."[38] Consumers won't be the only beneficiaries of the upgrade; corporations will also be able to harness gigabit Internet connections for high-definition global videoconferencing and other applications.

As South Korea and other countries forge ahead with massive investments in broadband infrastructure upgrades, politicians and union leaders in laggard countries are taking a keen interest in the issue. A recent study declared that South Korea and several other countries are "ready for tomorrow" in terms of Internet speed. A second tier of countries falls into the category "below today's applications threshold." The United States, Germany, and Hong Kong all fall into this category.[39] U.S. President Barack Obama responded to this situation in 2011 by promising to spend tens of billions of dollars to improve America's broadband network.

Why are policymakers following the broadband race so closely? Broadband offers multiple marketing opportunities to companies in a variety of industries. It also allows Internet users to access **streaming media** such as **streaming audio** and **streaming video**. Personalized radio services such as Apple Music, Pandora, Spotify, and Tidal allow users to list their favorite artists and songs; Pandora then uses a proprietary technology called the Music Genome Project to make recommendations for new music that are similar to a listener's current favorites. Streaming media are also having a profound impact on the television industry, with Amazon.com, iTunes, Netflix, YouTube, and other services offering movie and TV show downloads and streaming as viewing options.

Streaming media represent a major market opportunity for the video game industry, which includes electronics companies (e.g., Microsoft and Sony), game publishers (e.g., Electronic Arts),

"Increased broadband penetration is opening up possibilities that didn't exist even 2 years ago . . . . We need to realize that online is now an important part of the overall communications mix . . . . We are not an online business. We're a beverage business. But we have to develop compelling marketing platforms that are relevant to the lives of young people."[37]

Tim Kopp, former vice president of global interactive marketing, Coca-Cola and Internet portals (e.g., Google). Gamers in different locations, even different countries, can compete against one another using PCs or Xbox or PlayStation consoles. These shared gaming experiences are sometimes called *massively multiplayer online games* (MMOG); the most popular MMOG is *World of Warcraft*. How popular are Internet-based video games? Microsoft's Xbox Live service has more than 48 million subscribers worldwide. Consumer interest in online gaming has been fueled by powerful next-generation game consoles such as Microsoft's Xbox One and Sony's PlayStation 4.

Cloud Computing

In the preceding section, *cloud computing* was referenced as one driver of higher broadband speeds. This term refers to next-generation computing that is performed "in the cloud." With this approach, rather than installing software such as iTunes or Microsoft Office on a computer hard drive, such applications are delivered through a Web browser. Cloud computing means that archives—including music and movie files, photos, and documents—are stored on massive remote servers and data centers rather than on individual users' computers. Computer files can be accessed remotely, via the Internet, from any location and from any computer.

Google's Chrome operating system, which has been described as "a new computing paradigm," is designed to exploit the opportunities of cloud computing. Amazon.com's Amazon Web Services (AWS) provides cloud-computing resources for businesses. AWS is a variation on the outsourcing trend that was discussed in Chapter 8; Netflix, Foursquare, and thousands of other companies use the service instead of running their own data centers. Cloud computing is expected to grow at an annual torrid pace of 25 percent over the next several years.[40]

Smartphones

Cell phones have been one of the biggest new-product success stories of the digital revolution. Worldwide, 1.5 billion smartphones were shipped in 2017. Soaring demand has boosted the fortunes of manufacturers such as Apple, Huawei, Oppo, and Samsung, as well as AT&T, Deutsche Telekom, U.S. Cellular, Verizon, and other service providers. New features and functionality give consumers a reason to upgrade their handsets on a regular basis. Conventional cell phones (sometimes called feature phones) allow text messaging via **short message service (SMS)**, a globally accepted wireless standard for sending alphanumeric messages of up to 160 characters. SMS is the technology platform that is the basis for Twitter's microblogging service. Industry experts expect marketers to integrate SMS with communication via other digital channels, such as interactive digital TV, the Internet, and e-mail.

Smartphones have much greater functionality than feature phones, incorporating many of the capabilities of computers. Case in point: Apple's wildly successful iPhone comes equipped with a full-blown version of the company's iOS and Web browser. Worldwide, smartphones represent about one-fourth of all cell phone sales. The popularity of smartphones is due, in part, to the availability of apps such as Action Movie FX, Angry Birds, Pinterest, and Uber. In 2013, Apple's iTunes store sold its 50 billionth iPhone app. Apple commemorated the milestone with a "50 Billion Apps Download Promotion": The lucky person who downloaded the 50 billionth app won a $10,000 gift card—to be redeemed on iTunes, of course! Many of Apple's rivals use Android, a mobile operating system developed by Google.

Mobile Advertising and Mobile Commerce

Mobile advertising and **mobile commerce (m-commerce)** are terms that describe the use of cell phones as channels for delivering advertising messages and conducting product and service transactions. Most smartphone and tablet users can access the Internet via **Wi-Fi**, a type of wireless network; in addition, cell phone service providers typically offer data plans that allow Internet connections via 3G or 4G networks. This allows Apple, AOL, Crisp Media, Google, Medialets, Mobext, and other companies to offer clients mobile ad services. For example, Unilever, Nissan, and other companies use Apple's iAd service to place interactive ads inside iPhone and iPod apps.[41]

Total worldwide spending for mobile ads was only about $1 billion in 2007; according to eMarketer, that figure had passed $100 billion by the end of 2016. The United States leads all other nations in this kind of spending, with eMarketer reporting that 2017 mobile advertising totaled $49.9 billion.[42] Mobile search and mobile display advertising are growing in importance

$1 billion

The amount Facebook paid to acquire Instagram in 2012

800 million

The number of Instagram users as of September 2017

75 percent

Instagram users outside the United States

ENTREPRENEURIAL LEADERSHIP, CREATIVE THINKING, AND THE GLOBAL STARTUP

Reed Hastings, Netflix

Reed Hastings is an entrepreneur. He developed an innovative service, created a brand, and started a company to market it. By applying the basic tools and principles of modern marketing, Hastings has achieved remarkable success.

Today, Netflix is the global leader in video streaming. Canada was Netflix's first international market entry, with operations commencing in 2010. In 2011, 43 countries in Latin America were added, and in 2012 the United Kingdom, Ireland, Denmark, Finland, Norway, and Sweden came online as well.

Such global expansion has proved expensive. Copyright laws require licensing content on a country-by-country basis, and marketing costs are significant as well. One of Hastings's goals is to negotiate worldwide licensing deals that will provide better terms than the country-by-country approach. Another problem: Latin America's Internet infrastructure is underdeveloped, so subscriber growth and viewership in Brazil and elsewhere were low. To address the problem, Netflix deployed a team to install local networks of web servers to ensure coverage.

Another challenge in global markets is billing. In Brazil, for example, many consumers do not have credit cards. Those who do are often distrustful about disclosing credit card information on company Web sites. As new subscribers began signing up for the service on mobile devices, Netflix responded by adding mobile payment options such as iTunes and Google Play.

In January 2016, Netflix service was rolled out in 130 additional international markets. Irrespective of location, streaming subscribers pay roughly the equivalent of the U.S. subscription rate—between $5.00 and $8.00 per month. Netflix content can also be accessed on more hundreds of different devices, including smartphones, tablets, and, of course, televisions.

As its global footprint has expanded, Netflix is adjusting the algorithm that powers its content recommendations. For example, when Netflix first launched in Britain, the algorithm generated recommendations that reflected the preferences of British viewers only. Now, the service aggregates data from users in all parts of the world when making recommendations.

Netflix is also discovering that some locally produced programming has global appeal. One example is *Narcos*, a series about a notorious Colombian drug cartel and its kingpin, Pablo Escobar. The series is a French production, shot on location in Colombia and starring Brazilian actor Wagner Moura. Another original series, *3%*, is a science fiction show shot in Sao Paolo and starring Brazilian telenovela star Bianca Comparato. In November 2016, Netflix launched the first eight episodes in 191 countries—and the show proved to be a smash hit.

Netflix is also working to stay aligned to the consumer shift to mobile viewing. One challenge: Presenting viewing recommendations on small screens, where the faces of movie and TV stars may be hard to recognize. Instead of scaling down the artwork, which may make the screen cluttered and hard to read, Netflix offers fewer choices on each screen.

Anticipating a day with international subscribers will represent 75 percent of Netflix viewers, Hastings says, "To be a successful global service, we need to be more than Hollywood to the world. We need to be a company that shares stories from all around the world."

Sources: Lucas Shaw, "Building a World of Binge-Watchers [Cover story]," *Bloomberg Businessweek* (January 16, 2017), pp. 40–45; Shalini Ramachandran, "What's New on Netflix: A Big Push to Go Global," *The Wall Street Journal: Journal Report—C-Suite Strategies* (October 3, 2016), p. R6; Resty Woro Yuniar, "Netflix Hits Hurdle in Indonesia," *The Wall Street Journal* (January 28, 2016) p. B4; Emily Steel, "Netflix Accelerates Ambitious Global Expansion as U.S. Growth Slows," *The New York Times* (January 21, 2015), p. B3; Sam Schechner, "Netflix Tries to Woo a Wary Europe," *The Wall Street Journal* (September 8, 2014), p. B1; Ashlee Vance, "The Man Who Ate the Internet [Cover story]," *Bloomberg Businessweek* (May 13, 2013), pp. 56–60; Amol Sharma and Nathalie Tadena, "Viewers Stream to Netflix," *The Wall Street Journal* (April 23, 2013), pp. B1, B4.

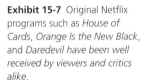

Exhibit 15-7 Original Netflix programs such as *House of Cards*, *Orange Is the New Black*, and *Daredevil* have been well received by viewers and critics alike.
Source: Ethan Miller/Getty Images.

as consumers migrate away from their desktop computers and spend more time on mobile devices. In fact, Google recently announced that it was tweaking its vaunted search algorithms to favor "mobile-friendly sites" with text that can be read on small screens and content that fits the screen. Web sites that are not optimized for mobile use will be demoted in the search process.

A smartphone that is equipped with a **global positioning system (GPS)** can determine the user's exact geographic position. This capability has created new opportunities for location-based mobile platforms, such as Foursquare and Uber. The popularity of GPS-equipped mobile devices is also driving interest in *location-based advertising*. For example, Alcatel-Lucent, the French telecommunications equipment manufacturer, has launched a service that sends tailored text messages when smartphone users are near a specific location, such as a store, hotel, or restaurant. The service, which is managed by San Francisco–based 1020 Placecast, provides addresses and telephone numbers of the businesses and can also provide links to coupons or other types of sales promotions. Users "opt in" by signing up to receive ads.

NAVTEQ Media Solutions is a digital map data company owned by Nokia. NAVTEQ provides location-based advertising services using the company's proprietary technology, LocationPoint Advertising (see Exhibit 15-8). NAVTEQ's global clients include Best Western Germany, Domino's Pizza India, and McDonald's Finland. Recent campaigns for a variety of clients have demonstrated that mobile campaigns can provide marketers with important metrics that can be used to calculate return on investment (ROI).

In one campaign, mobile users who were within a 5-mile radius of any McDonald's location in Finland received an offer to buy a cheeseburger for 1 euro. The result was a 7 percent click-through rate. Of those users, 39 percent used the ad's click-to-navigate option to request walking or driving directions to the nearest McDonald's. In India, a campaign to reach existing and prospective Domino's customers was also successful. Ads were delivered to smartphone users; banner ads were placed on Nokia's Ovi Services portal as well. The results were impressive: 22.6 percent of users clicked for the map, 10.8 percent clicked to call for home-delivery options, and 8 percent used the ad to access Domino's Web site.[43]

Cell phone usage is exploding in India. As Manoj Dawane, CEO of Mumbai software company People Infocom, explains, "In India, mobile phone penetration is high compared to other forms of media like television or the Internet. You can't have a better place than India for mobile advertising." One factor driving mobile ads in India is the low rates that subscribers pay—as little as 2 cents per minute. Demographics play an important role, too. Nearly two-thirds of the Indian population lives in rural areas where television ownership and newspaper readership are low.

Exhibit 15-8 NAVTEQ provides digital map data for location-based devices such as smartphones. NAVTEQ data are also used in vehicle navigation devices from Garmin.

Source: Krisztian Bocsi/Bloomberg via Getty Images.

Cellular operators such as BPL Mobile have built networks that reach tens of thousands of Indian villages. Arif Ali, head of brand communications at BPL, has ideas that will keep subscriber costs low. "We are thinking of providing 30- to 60-second commercials over the phone where we will pass on some kind of benefit," he said.[44]

Bluetooth mobile communication technology has the advantage of consuming less power than Wi-Fi.[45] This makes Bluetooth well suited for use with cell phones. On the downside, Bluetooth works over shorter distances than Wi-Fi. Both Bluetooth and Wi-Fi technology are being incorporated into automobiles and home appliances such as refrigerators, lighting systems, and microwave ovens. In short, the "Internet of Things" (IoT) is rapidly coming into being.

Autonomous Mobility

The Internet-connected car is becoming a reality as automakers rush to incorporate technology into their vehicles. Indeed, many drivers view their cars as the "ultimate mobile device" that is an extension of their digital selves. Apps now permit drivers to interact with their vehicles in new ways. For example, several automakers have developed Apple Watch apps that enable drivers to remotely check, say, whether the doors are locked and the windows are up. Electric car owners can also check whether their cars' batteries are fully charged.

With a new era of self-driving "robocars," electric vehicles, and shared-mobility services rapidly approaching, most global automakers and suppliers have established research laboratories in California's Silicon Valley tech hub. Tesla seized the industry lead in 2015 with the launch of Autopilot functions that include Autosteer.

Dieter Zetsche, chairman of the board of management at Daimler AG and head of Mercedes-Benz, uses the acronym CASE when summarizing trends in his industry: connected, autonomous, shared, and electric (see Exhibit 15-9). The latest generation of Mercedes-Benz vehicles incorporate vehicle-to-infrastructure (V2X) cloud-based functionality that allows cars to seek out available parking spots. One key component of the system: high-definition mapping.

Other car companies are quickly adapting as well. Investor concern about Ford Motor's lagging efforts to develop electric and self-driving cars cost CEO Mark Fields his job in mid-2017. At BMW, staffers have received briefings warning that the company trails newcomer Tesla as well as longtime rival Mercedes-Benz.[46] To speed up its development efforts, BMW has partnered with several firms, including Israel's Mobileye, Intel, and Delphi, to develop software for self-driving cars.

Exhibit 15-9 Dieter Zetsche, chairman of the board of management at Daimler AG and head of Mercedes-Benz, delivered the keynote address at the 2015 International Consumer Electronics Show in Las Vegas. In his remarks, Zetsche discussed the future of autonomous vehicle technology and other innovations. As of 2017, 7 million Mercedes-Benz vehicles were equipped with sensors that allow the company to gather data that will benefit drivers.
Source: VanderWolf Images/Shutterstock.

Mobile Music

Because of rampant illegal sharing of music files, music companies were forced to search for new sources of revenue—and they found them, thanks to technology convergence. Today, the new generation of smartphones is driving changes in the mobile music industry. **Mobile music** is music that is played on a smartphone or other mobile device.

For more than a decade, the market for paid, legal, full-track music downloads was dominated by Apple's iTunes Store. Music purchased from iTunes was played back on computers and mobile devices such as Apple's iPod, iPhone, and iPad. In 2006, iTunes reached a milestone of 1 billion downloads; today, Apple is the world's number 1 music seller, with a cumulative total of 25 billion downloads. (The 25 billionth song was downloaded in Germany in 2013, and the lucky iTunes customer won a €10,000 Apple Gift Card.) Apple's competitors tried, without much success, to develop music players and download services to rival the iPod/iTunes combination.

The market for paid downloads matured rapidly, however, as consumers opted for streaming services such as Spotify and Pandora. According to figures compiled by the International Federation for the Phonographic Industry (IFPI), annual global download revenues peaked in 2012 at approximately $4 billion. Streaming revenues totaled about $3.9 billion in 2016 and, with streaming's robust growth as the driver, global recorded music revenues rebounded to $15.7 billion.

Responding to the changing market, Apple launched Apple Music, a new subscription-only service, in 2015. Some streaming sites—Spotify, for example—offer a free tier as well as a paid, "premium" level of service. The difference is that the paid tier is ad-free while the free tier requires users to listen to mobile ads. Apple Music executives believe their service will be able to offer better personalization features and superior artist recommendations compared to the competing services.[48]

Cloud computing, which was discussed earlier in the chapter, is expected to have a major impact on the mobile music business. Cloud-based music services represent a hybrid of the subscription and online store business models; the new approach addresses some of the shortcomings of the existing methods. For example, iPod owners had to sync their iPods to their computers or other devices. Also, the pricing schemes for the various subscription services can be confusing. By contrast, cloud-based music services, including iTunes Match, Google Play, and Amazon Cloud Player, offer users a music locker; the locker is "in the cloud," and music files that have been purchased or uploaded can be accessed from a variety of mobile devices.

Mobile Gaming

Mobile gaming is gaining in popularity; revenues from this industry were expected to exceed $100 billion in 2017, up from $3.77 billion in 2010. Until mid-2016, *Game of War: Fire Age* and *Clash of Clans* were two of the most widely played mobile games. However, on July 6, 2016, Nintendo's *Pokémon GO* took the mobile gaming world by storm. The game incorporates augmented reality technology with a smartphone's camera and GPS; players hunt for, and try to capture, "pocket monsters." In record time, the game ("Gotta catch 'em all!") topped the "most downloaded apps" rankings in the Apple and Android apps stores in Australia, New Zealand, and the United States. One week later, *Pokémon GO* was launched in Japan, the world's biggest market for mobile games.

The Asia-Pacific region represents more than half of the global games market. China is home to 600 million players, whose annual game-related spending exceeds $25 billion. The most popular mobile game is *Honor of Kings*, from Chinese Internet giant Tencent. With WeChat and QQZone, Tencent dominates the social network space in a market where Facebook and WhatsApp are blocked.[49]

Some games, including Pokémon GO, are available on a free-to-play basis; others, such as *Super Mario Run*, are available for free on a trial basis while the full game costs several dollars. How can a marketer monetize a free game? For a small fee, free games can be upgraded to premium versions. In addition, many games offer users the opportunity to make in-app purchases of virtual goods. *Game of War* is a case in point: It generates $1 million in revenue every day for parent company Machine Zone. Similarly, *Honor of Kings* is available as a free download, but players spend freely to customize their characters. Indeed, the word "free" can be misleading, as network operators typically charge fees for downloading the games.[50]

Online Gaming and e-Sports

In the past few years, online gaming has morphed into a spectator sport. In fact, the term **e-sports** has been coined to describe video game competitions in which professional gamers and teams compete for cash prizes that can reach $10 million. Examples include the November 2017 League of Legends World Championship, which was held at Bird's Nest stadium in Beijing (see Exhibit 15-10).

In the United States, fan can watch the matches from locations such as the Ignite lounge in Chicago, the Staples Center in Los Angeles, and the new Blizzard Arena in California's Burbank Studios. Top players with global name recognition include Faker (from South Korea), KuroKy (Germany), and Neo (Poland). Members of leagues such as Overwatch are paid six-figure salaries. E-sports revenues total nearly $700 million annually; the industry's business model includes money from media rights, advertising, sponsorships, and ticket sales.

Fans of e-sports—some 200 million of them—log 6 billion viewing hours each year. Legions of video game fans use Twitch, a mobile-streaming site that provides video coverage of professional e-sports as well as streams of ordinary people ("variety streamers") playing video games. In 2014, Amazon outmaneuvered Google by paying $970 million to buy Twitch. Streamers often interact with viewers; some streamers actually earn their livelihoods by sharing revenues from commercials that run on Twitch and from subscription fees.[51]

Mobile Payments

Mobile payments—that is, payments made via smartphones—received a major boost when Apple launched Apple Pay in conjunction with the iPhone 6 in 2014. To make these payments, users first link their smartphones to their bank accounts; a technology called **near-field communication (NFC)** then allows users to "swipe" their phones near a point-of-sale terminal to complete a purchase. Alphabet's Android Pay is also vying for market acceptance as a mobile payment platform.

Mobile payments have exploded in China, where users make purchases as well as transfer money to family and friends through their mobile devices. The mobile payments volume in China has passed the $9 trillion mark in a market dominated by Alibaba's Alipay and Tencent's Tenpay platforms. As the Chinese market matures, both Alibaba and Tencent are targeting emerging markets where merchants lack point-of-sale machines that can process payments using conventional credit cards or mobile apps such as Apple Pay and Android Pay. In India, for example, Alibaba has provided financing for the Paytm mobile-payments platform, which has benefited

> "We think e-sports can have truly global appeal. There isn't anything inherently sociocultural that would make it appeal more in one region than another."[52]
>
> Chris Hopper, head of league operations, Riot Games

Exhibit 15-10 E-sports are exploding in popularity as thousands of fans pack arenas to watch competitive video gaming.
Source: STR/AFP/Getty Images.

greatly from the Indian government's currency reforms (see Chapter 2); Paytm relies on QR code technology.[53]

$1.3 billion

Number of people who tune into YouTube each day

5 billion

Number of videos viewed on YouTube each day

300

Number of hours of new content uploaded to YouTube every minute

Streaming Video

Global penetration of broadband Internet service has fueled the growing popularity of global digital video services such as YouTube. Other players operating in this space include Facebook, Instagram, Twitter, and, as discussed in the "Global Startup" sidebar, Netflix. One recent innovation is Meerkat, a streaming app that allows users to stream live video using their Twitter accounts. Some industry observers predict that Meerkat and similar apps will lead to major changes in the way people consume news and live events such as sports.

Internet Phone Service

For the telecommunications industry, Internet telephone service is the "next big thing." **Voice over Internet Protocol (VoIP)** technology allows the human voice to be digitized and broken into data packets that can be transmitted over the Internet and then converted back into normal speech. If a call is placed to a conventional phone, it must be switched from the Internet to a traditional phone network; local telephone companies generally own the lines into residences and businesses. In contrast, if the call is made between two subscribers to the same VoIP provider, it bypasses the traditional network altogether. The implications are clear: VoIP has the potential to render the current telecommunications infrastructure—consisting primarily of twisted copper and fiber-optic cable—obsolete.

Currently, VoIP accounts for only a small percentage of global calls. Nevertheless, it has the potential to be a disruptive innovation that will upset the balance of power in the telecommunications industry. The promise of a global growth market has resulted in soaring stock values for startups. In Europe, Niklas Zennström, cofounder of the Kazaa music file-sharing service, started Skype Ltd. to offer Internet telephone service. As hundreds of thousands of new users—many in China, India, and Sweden—joined each day, Skype became a global phenomenon. In 2005, eBay acquired Skype for $2.6 billion. However, eBay struggled to create synergies between the communication system and the company's core auction business. In 2009, eBay spun off Skype as a separate company; two years later, Microsoft bought Skype for $8.6 billion.

Digital Books and Electronic Reading Devices

The digital revolution has had a dramatic impact on traditional print media such as newspapers and magazines. Publishers are experiencing dramatic downturns in readership as people spend more time online. At the same time, the global recession has forced many companies to cut back on print advertising. Caught in a squeeze, magazines are folding and newspapers are declaring bankruptcy. However, electronic readers (e-readers), such as Amazon.com's Kindle, Barnes & Noble's Nook, and Apple's iPad, may help lure subscribers back.

Amazon.com sold the first Kindle for $359; prices for the latest-generation Kindle Fire HD start at $99 (see Exhibit 15-11). Amazon.com has taken the Kindle global with the launch of a smaller, less expensive version that can be used in more than 100 countries. Apple launched the iPad in March 2010; by the end of the year, 15 million units had been sold. By mid-2014, Apple had sold more than 200 million of the devices.

Industry observers think that colleges and universities will be instrumental in building awareness and encouraging adoption of e-readers and e-books. The reason is simple: Electronic versions of textbooks represent a huge market opportunity. For example, the textbook you are reading right now is available directly from the publisher in the form of an electronic "subscription" at www.coursesmart.com. The online version requires users to be connected to the Internet; the text can be accessed from an unlimited number of computers. Buyers can use the e-book for 180 days before the subscription expires. The price is approximately half of what bookstores charge for a new copy of the physical textbook. Usually, students can print as many as 10 pages at a time; it is also possible to cut and paste content, highlight items, and take notes directly on the computer.

As is the case with music and movies, digital piracy is a growing problem with e-books. A number of Web sites and file-sharing services distribute unauthorized copies of popular copyrighted material. What do authors themselves think of the problem? Some view digital piracy as a way to gain new readers. Others simply want fair compensation for their work. A third camp includes authors who don't think pursuing the pirates is worth the effort. As best-selling author Stephen King once remarked, "The question is, how much time and energy do I want to spend chasing these guys? And to what end? My sense is that most of them live in basements floored with carpeting remnants, living on Funions and discount beer."[54]

Wearables

When supermodel Karolina Kurkova attended the Metropolitan Museum of Art's Met Gala in 2016, she made quite a fashion statement. Her "cognitive dress," by high-end womenswear brand Marchesa, was connected to IBM's Watson supercomputer. When people attending the gala tweeted, the dress changed colors! Some observers noted that the event marked a moment when wearable technology—including fitness bands, the Apple Watch, and other products and brands—reached a tipping point in terms of fashionability and sales growth. Technology research firm IDC predicts that annual sales of such products will reach 113 million units by 2018, up from 6 million units in 2013.

It is perhaps no surprise that new strategic partnerships, such as the collaboration between Marchesa and IBM, are key to turning these dreams into reality. For example, Google has partnered with Levi's "Eureka" innovation lab to create a smart denim cycling jacket (see Exhibit 15-12). As Paul Dillinger, head of global product innovation at Levi's, commented wryly, "We are not very good at technology and they [Google] are not very good at garments."[55]

Exhibit 15-12 The Eureka Lab is an initiative by venerable Levi Strauss to rethink how denim jeans are made.
Source: Matt Edge/The New York Times/Redux.

Summary

The *digital revolution* has created a global electronic marketplace. This revolution has gained momentum over the course of 75-plus years, during which time technological breakthroughs included the digital mainframe computer; the *transistor*; the *integrated circuit (IC)*; the *personal computer (PC)*; the *spreadsheet*; the PC *operating system*; and the *Internet*, which originated as an initiative of the *Defense Advanced Research Projects Agency (DARPA)*. Three key innovations by Tim Berners-Lee—*URLs*, HTTP, and HTML—led to the creation in the early 1990s of the *World Wide Web*.

The digital revolution has resulted in a process known as *convergence*, in which previously separate industries and markets come together. In this environment, the *innovator's dilemma* means that company management must decide whether to invest in current technologies or try to develop new technologies. Although leading firms in an industry often develop *sustaining technologies* that result in improved product performance, the revolution has also unleashed a wave of *disruptive technologies* that are creating new markets and reshaping industries and *value networks*.

E-commerce is growing in importance for both consumer and industrial goods marketers. Generally, commercial Web sites can have a domestic or a global focus; in addition, they can be classified as *promotion sites*, *content sites*, or *transaction sites*. Global marketers must take care when designing Web sites. Country-specific domain names must be registered and local-language sites developed. In addition to addressing issues of technology and functionality, content must reflect local culture, customs, and aesthetic preferences. *Cybersquatting* can hinder a company's effort to register its corporate name as an Internet destination.

The Internet is a powerful tool for advertisers; *click-through rates* are one measure of effectiveness. Another Internet-related trend is *paid search advertising*. New products and services spawned by the digital revolution include *broadband*, which permits transmission of *streaming media* over the Internet; *mobile commerce (m-commerce)*, which is made possible by *Wi-Fi*, *Bluetooth*, and other forms of wireless connectivity; *global positioning systems (GPS)*; and *short message service (SMS)*. *Smartphones* are creating new markets for *mobile music* downloads and streaming; these devices can also be used for mobile gaming and Internet phone service using *VoIP*.

Discussion Questions

15-1. Briefly review the key innovations that culminated in the digital revolution. What is the basic technological process that made the revolution possible?

15-2. What is convergence? How is convergence affecting Sony? Kodak? Nokia?

15-3. What is the innovator's dilemma? What is the difference between a sustaining technology and a disruptive technology? Briefly review Christensen's five principles of disruptive innovation.

15-4. Explain some of the main issues involved in setting up a global e-commerce business.

15-5. Review the key products and services that have emerged during the digital revolution. What are some new products and services that are not mentioned in the chapter?

15-6. Disruptive technologies and business models continue to have a huge impact on markets. What are the current trends and predictions?

15-7. The digital revolution may lead to the creation of cashless societies where payments are conducted digitally using smartphones. Discuss some of the benefits and problems of a cashless payment system in relation to global marketing.

CASE 15-1   *(Continued refer to page 493)*

How Do You Like Your Reality: Virtual? Augmented? Mixed?

VR technology was developed decades ago; in fact, a computer engineer and author named Jeron Lanier coined the term "virtual reality" in 1987. That was two years after Lanier left his job at Atari to start VPL Research, the first company to manufacture and sell VR goggles.

The early user experience with VR was not satisfactory for a mainstream consumer product: Users often experienced motion sickness and nausea. Those issues do not concern Hollywood filmmakers, however. *Minority Report*, Tom Cruise's 2002 movie based on a novel by sci-fi writer Philip K. Dick, provided one tantalizing glimpse of the future (Jeron Lanier served as advisor to the authors of the screenplay). In the film, Cruise uses hand gestures to interface with large virtual video screens. More than a decade later, Steven Spielberg's 2018 film *Ready Player One* envisioned a dystopia in which a VR world called the Oasis offers respite for beleaguered citizens in the year 2045.

The future depicted by sci-fi visionaries is still a long way off. Today, however, anticipating strong demand, software developers are rushing to create VR applications to harness the potential of the hardware. VRTIFY ("the world's first and largest virtual & mixed reality music platform") is a social network that specializes in rock concerts. Liquor brands, concert promotion company Live Nation, and iHeartMedia are just a few of the companies partnering with artists such as Deadmau5, Duran Duran, U2, the Weeknd and others to produce 360-degree concert videos.

More mundane applications of VR technology are also possible. For example, real estate agents can provide their clients with virtual tours of property listings. Retailers such as home-improvement specialist Lowe's can use VR to help customers overcome the "fear of the unknown." The problem: Potential do-it-yourselfers have trouble visualizing the results of a home renovation, so they never start the project. No project, no sale! Lowe's appeals to those customers by inviting them to "design your home" using VR.

Despite the growing number of uses for VR, critics such as University of Southern California professor Dmitri Williams point out that the current generation of headsets is bulky and expensive, requires a cable connection to a powerful hardware unit, and isolates the users. In general, detractors suggest that "VR 1.0" is unlikely to achieve mass-market consumer adoption because it does not provide a seamless, frictionless user experience.

Make Room for Augmented Reality

As it turns out, augmented reality (AR) technology addresses the isolation issue. AR allows users to see the real world around them on lightweight headsets or mobile screens with an added layer of digital graphics. One well-known application is Pokémon GO; Microsoft's HoloLens headset running Windows Holographic software is another. The early AR headsets are wireless and lightweight, and respond to both hand and voice commands. One application: anatomy labs for medical students.

Facebook CEO Mark Zuckerberg is one person who anticipates a future in which AR has myriad uses. In 2014, Zuckerberg paid $3 billion to acquire Oculus, a VR headset company started in a garage by a teenager named Palmer Luckey. Although Zuckerberg made an expensive bet with the acquisition, he is convinced that AR will become a mainstream communication technology even sooner than VR. The reason is simple: In contrast to the equipment purchases associated with VR, AR users can take advantage of a piece of gear they already own—namely, their smartphones.

Most of today's AR applications are relatively primitive, including filters and frames in the images. Nevertheless, some, such as the Nike+ Run Club smartphone app, show the technology's potential. Zuckerberg envisions that comfortable, lightweight eyeglass frames will eventually feature lenses that overlay various types of virtual content and information on whatever part of the physical world the wearer is looking at.

China's Alibaba is showing how AR and VR have the potential to transform retail. In 2016, the 11.11 Global Shopping Festival incorporated a number of innovations on the Tmall and Taobao platforms. For example, in the weeks leading up to the event, AR was used to drive foot traffic to offline, brick-and-mortar retailers. Tens of thousands of retailers, including KFC and Starbucks, participated in a "Catch the Tmall Cat" AR game. On the VR side, consumers were able to "sample" and purchase items from retailers in various parts of the world. Alibaba created a special Buy+ shopping channel; participating retailers included Target, Macy's, and CostCo.

Meanwhile, given the relatively high costs associated with VR equipment for home use, media and tech companies have been grappling with some basic new-product marketing issues. For one thing, traditional television and print advertising is not a good vehicle for conveying the essence of the VR experience. Also, how can marketers give potential customers the opportunity to try before they buy?

With these and other issues in mind, companies are migrating the VR experience to new locations outside the home, such as shopping malls and movie theaters. That, in turn, is good news for theater operators such as IMAX, which are seeking ways to increase foot traffic in the era of instant Amazon downloads, streaming video, overnight home deliveries, and decreasing consumer interest in visiting shopping malls.

The Void, Dreamscape, and other startups are partnering with theater operators to open VR centers in select cities such as New York and Los Angeles. There, customers are provided with full-body sensors, headsets, and computers; they can engage with other users in virtual space. That functionality is reminiscent of the virtual mall shopping sequence in the 2017 French sci-fi extravaganza *Valerian* and addresses one of the basic drawbacks of VR—namely, the sense of isolation. As Walter Parkes, cofounder of Dreamscape, explains, "We are social animals and we consume entertainment socially. If you are isolated in virtual space, it will never become a mainstream entertainment form."

The VR "arcade" experience, as it has been called, has proved especially popular in Japan. In Great Britain, a company called Other Worlds VR is sponsoring arcade pop-ups in London and other cities; its arcades are equipped with HTC Vive hardware.

What about Mixed Reality?

VR pioneers have discovered that sound is critical for maintaining the immersive experience. Also, there is considerable excitement about taking top-quality VR and incorporating the real world into it. Imagine, for example, entering a purpose-built entertainment site based on a TV show where live actors interact with VR users. Instead of "replacing" reality, which VR does, or "augmenting" it (AR), this new mixed reality (MR) experience creates a purpose-built, custom-tailored space.

One recent project involved the popular FX Network cable show *Legion*. In the show, David Haller (played by Dan Stevens) can absorb other peoples' consciousness. (Spoiler alert: David is the undocumented son of Professor Xavier of X-Men fame!) FX Networks partnered with Microsoft HoloLens and the Moving Picture Company (MPC) to create an MR experience based *Legion*.

The event was staged at the 2017 San Diego Comic-Con International in San Diego. Participants were treated to an immersive, 15-minute experience during which the actors triggered events from iPads. Thanks to the HoloLens goggles and directional audio sound design, participants felt that they could stop time with their minds and make things levitate. In other words, they got inside David Haller's head! Justin Denton of VR production company Here Be Dragons directed *Sessions: The Legion Mixed Reality Experience*. The goal, he said, was to "hit all of your senses at once in a curated way."

Discussion Questions

15-8. What are the differences between VR, AR, and VR?

15-9. Which technology do you think will be the first to reach mass-market acceptance: VR, AR, or MR?

15-10. What experiences have you had with VR? AR?

Sources: Justin Denton, Tim Dillon, Lucas Matney, and Jacqueline Bosnjak, "The Next Phase of VR: Moving to MR," Panel Discussion, SXSW Interactive, Film and Music Conference (March 15, 2018); Tim Bradshaw and Peter Wells, "VR Returns to Malls and Movies for Mass Launch," *Financial Times* (September 28, 2017), p. 16; Jessica Guyunn, "Inside Mark Zuckerberg's Vision for Your Facebook Augmented Reality," *USA Today* (April 19, 2017), pp. 1B, 2B; Brooks Barnes, "Virtual Reality's Next Trick," *The New York Times* (February 20, 2017), pp. B1, B3; Gregory Schmidt, "Virtual Reality Waits for the Music to Catch Up," *The New York Times* (July 26, 2016), p. C3; Jack Nicas and Cat Zakrzewski, "Augmented Reality Beyond Pokémon," *The Wall Street Journal* (July 14, 2016), pp. B1, B4; Tim Bradshaw, "Virtual Reality in Search for Killer Gaming App," *Financial Times* (September 26–27, 2015), p. 14.

CASE 15-2
Africa 3.0

Have you heard of the Cheetah generation? Here's a hint: It's the opposite of the Hippo generation. As you might infer, we are talking about Africa, a continent with 54 countries and a population of 1.03 billion. According to Ghanaian economist George Ayittey, the Cheetah generation is composed of fast-moving African citizens who don't accept corruption and who believe that democracy and transparency lead to better governance. Cell phones are powerful tools for the Cheetahs; notes Michael Joseph, founder and former CEO of Kenya's Safaricom, "The mobile phone has revolutionized lives and transformed society."

Deregulation of the telecommunications sector has been driving that transformation, and market liberalization helps explain why Africa's gross domestic product (GDP) growth rate is averaging between 5 and 6 percent. Overall, there are more than 650 million mobile phone subscribers in Africa; between 2000 and 2011, mobile use grew at an average annual rate of 41 percent. This explosive growth is easy to understand: Cell phones make life easier. In villages that lack running water and electricity, a cell phone is a person's most important possession (see Exhibit 15-13). Improved communication has also led to increased economic activity; for example, a peasant farmer can check crop prices to determine where and when to sell his harvest. Africa's widespread adoption of the cell phone and the explosive growth of the telecom sector there have also corrected a common misperception among global marketers—namely, that the market opportunity in Africa is limited because the people are "too poor" and it is "too risky to do business there."

Investment in telecommunications and other sectors in Africa is being driven by a variety of factors, including demographic trends. For example, nearly half the population is younger than the age of 15. The World Bank reports that half the population lives on $1.25 per day.

Exhibit 15-13 Africa's economy has rebounded from the global financial crisis faster than the economies in the developed world. This is particularly true in sub-Saharan Africa, where the widespread adoption of cell phones has spawned mobile-banking networks and other innovations.
Source: Trevor Snapp/Bloomberg via Getty Images.

However, according to a study by the African Development Bank, Africa's middle class now includes 34 percent of the population, some 313 million people in all. The report defines "middle class" as those who spend between $2 and $20 per day; a narrower definition would include the 120 million people (21 percent) who spend between $4 and $20 per day.

Demand from this emerging middle class has been a boon to telecommunications companies. Between 2006 and 2010, compound revenue growth in the sector averaged 40 percent. Kenya, for example, is home to more than 21 million active phone numbers among a total population of 40 million people. In most parts of Africa, mobile networks suffer service interruptions. As a result, many people use more than one cell phone and have multiple providers.

Key industry players include Safaricom, Kenya's leading mobile phone service provider and the largest, most profitable company in East Africa. South Africa's MTN Group is the continent's leading mobile provider in terms of subscribers. MTN gained prominence in 2010 when it became the first African company to have a sponsorship for World Cup soccer. Globacon is a major service provider in Nigeria.

One of the biggest African success stories involves Celtel International, a telecom created by Sudanese businessman Mo Ibrahim. In 2005, Ibraham sold the company to Zain, based in Kuwait, for $3.4 billion. In 2010, India's Bharti Airtel paid $10.7 billion for Zain's African assets. Zain has operations in 15 African countries, including Malawi, Chad, and Zambia. The acquisition makes Bharti the world's largest mobile provider—165 million subscribers in all—with operations only in emerging markets.

Not surprisingly, the market opportunity afforded by Africa is also attracting investment from other global telecom operators. For example, France Telecom has tens of millions of users in 22 countries in Africa and the Middle East. Executives are extending the company's African reach to span the entire continent; the goal is to become the "champion of rural Africa" by rolling out a range of new, low-cost mobile services under the Orange brand. For example, France Telecom's E-Recharge service lets users exchange credits via text messaging. Price discounts of up to 99 percent for off-peak calls are also very popular.

Kenya has become a key battleground for mobile telecommunications, as service providers cut prices to attract customers. Airtel Kenya has squared off against Safaricom, Orange Kenya, and other rivals; the company recently cut its rates by 50 percent, to $0.03 per minute for voice calls and $0.01 for text messages. Parent company Bharti Airtel had previously used this tactic in India, where customers are making longer calls because airtime is less expensive. Despite the competition, Safaricom is the dominant player in Kenya, with nearly 75 percent market share in mobile.

Going forward, Safaricom CEO Robert Collymore says his company will focus on data and mobile banking services. Collymore is planning for cross-border expansion both to the east and the west. Ethiopia, with a population of 100 million people and the largest economy (GDP of $73 billion) in the region, represents an appealing market opportunity. Safaricom's e-commerce platform, Masoko, is modeled after Alibaba. It is intended to serve as an e-commerce hub for both B2B and B2C transactions.

Perhaps the biggest mobile innovation in Africa is M-Pesa (M for "mobile"; *pesa* is Swahili for "money"). M-Pesa is a mobile phone–based money transfer service developed by Safaricom Kenya and Vodaphone, with backing from Britain's Department for International Development. In 2014, Safaricom partnered with KCB, Kenya's biggest bank.

Today, M-Pesa is the dominant mobile money platform and a case study of the way telecommunications companies are transforming the banking industry in Africa. Safaricom has data on the 19 million Kenyans who use M-Pesa regularly, and whose daily transactions add up to tens of millions of dollars. For example, Kenyans use M-Pesa to get cash and make payments for bills, school fees, and airline tickets. Safaricom's service boasts a network of more than 100,000 agents. As competitors across the continent enter the mobile payments space, interoperability between service providers will increase in importance.

Just a decade ago, many mainstream banks would not have found it feasible to do business with low-income customers; the meager returns did not justify opening branch networks or setting up ATMs. As a result, a person with a city job would have to give money to a friend or a bus driver to deliver to relatives at home. Needless to say, highway robbery was a constant threat.

Today, banks can work with shopkeepers and bar owners who dispense or collect cash and then credit or debit a customer's mobile phone account. The target market is the "unbanked"—that is, people who do not have bank accounts. In Kenya alone, the majority of adults have access to financial services today, compared with only 5 percent in 2006. In Nigeria, a country of 150 million people, only 20 percent of the population has a bank account. Nigeria's Central Bank (CBN) is taking the lead in reaching out to the unbanked members of this population, by creating a system in which telecommunications companies will provide the infrastructure for offering financial services. This approach is necessary because there are several dominant cell phone service providers in Nigeria.

Price wars are just one of the challenges of doing business on the continent. Africa is at the bottom of the World Bank's "Ease of Doing Business" rankings. Widespread corruption is part of the problem. As Sudanese telecom magnate Ibrahim puts it, "There is a crisis of leadership and governance in Africa and we must face it." Moreover, he notes, "These guys know that millions of children are going to bed without dinner. The blood of those children is on the hands of those who spend the money on arms and private jets."

Data compiled by Global Financial Integrity, a nongovernmental organization, support Ibrahim's assessment of the business environment. According to a recent report, more than $350 billion flowed out of Africa as a result of corruption and illicit deals.

Discussion Questions

15-11. The United States and Latin America have been far slower than countries in Africa and Europe in adopting mobile payments technology. Why is this the case?

15-12. Further economic liberalization in Africa depends, in part, on government leaders overcoming suspicions that foreign companies want to exploit Africa. How quickly is this likely to happen?

15-13. If marketers "think local and act local," what are some of the new products and services that are likely to emerge from Africa in the next few years?

Sources: John Aglionby, "Safaricom Eyes the Prize of Cross-Border E-Commerce," *Financial Times* (September 6, 2017), p. 17; John Aglionby, "Visa Sets Sights on Safaricom's Mpesa in Battle for Kenya," *Financial Times* (September 15, 2016), p. 14; Katrina Manson and Jude Webber, "Simple Phone Technology Promises to Revolutionise Access to Finance," *Financial Times* (January 30, 2015), p. 14; Nichole Sobecki, "Making Change: Mobile Pay in Africa," *The Wall Street Journal* (January 2, 2015), p. B6; Chad Bray and Reuben Kyama, "Tap to Pay (Not So Much in the U.S.)," *The New York Times* (April 2, 2014), pp. F1, F8; Kevin J. O'Brien, "Microsoft and Huawei of China to Unite to Sell Low-Cost Windows Smartphones in Africa," *The New York Times* (February 5, 2013), p. B2; Peter Wonacott, "A New Class of Consumers Grows in Africa," *The Wall Street Journal* (May 2, 2011), p. A8; Sarah Childress, "Telecom Giants Battle for Kenya," *The Wall Street Journal* (January 14, 2011), pp. B1, B7; Ben Hall, "France Telecom Targets Rural Africa for Growth," *Financial Times* (November 10, 2010), p. 16; Parselelo Kantai, "Telecoms: Mobile May Be the Future of Banking," *Financial Times* (September 29, 2010), p. 3; Gordon Brown, "To Combat Poverty, Get Africa's Children to School," *Financial Times* (September 20, 2010), p. 9; William Wallis and Tom Burgis, "Attitudes Change to Business in Region," *Financial Times* (June 4, 2010), p. 6; Wallis, "Outlook Brightens for Frontier Market," *Financial Times* (June 2, 2010), p. 7; Robb M. Stewart and Will Connors, "For Bharti, Africa Potential Outweighs Hurdles," *The Wall Street Journal* (February 17, 2010), pp. B1, B2; Jamie Anderson, Martin Kupp, and Ronan Moaligou, "Lessons from the Developing World," *The Wall Street Journal* (August 17, 2009), p. R6; Tom Burgis, "Case Study: Text Messages Give Shopkeepers the Power to Bulk Buy," *Financial Times Special Report: Digital Business* (May 29, 2009), p. 8; Cassell Bryan-Low, "New Frontiers for Cellphone Service," *The Wall Street Journal* (February 13, 2007), pp. B1, B5.

Notes

[1]Noyce founded Fairchild Semiconductor and, later, Intel. His Intel cofounder was Gordon Moore, who is famous for formulating "Moore's law," which states that computer power doubles every 18 months. Kilby was the founder of Texas Instruments. See Evan Ramstad, "At the End of an Era, Two Tech Pioneers Are Remembered," *The Wall Street Journal* (August 15, 2005), p. B1.

[2]John Markoff, "Innovator Who Helped Create PC, Internet and the Mouse," *The New York Times* (April 15, 2017), pp. A1, A14.

[3]For more on the development of VisiCalc, see Dan Bricklin, "Natural Born Entrepreneur," *Harvard Business Review* 79, no. 8 (September 2001), pp. 53–59.

[4]Stewart Brand, *The Media Lab: Inventing the Future at MIT* (New York, NY: Penguin Books, 1988), p. 253.

[5]Steve Case, "Pardon the Disruption: Steve Case on Entrepreneurs." Keynote address presented at SXSW Music, Film, and Interactive, March 14, 2015. See also Nick Summers, "Steve Case's Second Life," *Bloomberg Businessweek* (August 26, 2013), pp. 52–57.

[6]Hypertext is any text that contains links to other documents.

[7]John Markoff, "Control the Internet? A Futile Pursuit, Some Say," *The New York Times* (November 24, 2005), p. C4.

[8]Thomas L. Friedman, *The World Is Flat* (New York, NY: Farrar, Straus and Giroux, 2005), p. 58.

[9]Amir Efrati, "Google Pushes into Emerging Markets," *The Wall Street Journal* (May 25–26, 2013), pp. B1, B2.

[10]Christopher Rhoads, "EU, Developing Nations Challenge U.S. Control of Internet," *The Wall Street Journal* (October 25, 2005), pp. B1, B2. See also "A Free Internet," *Financial Times* (November 14, 2003), p. 15.

[11]Barney Thompson, "GDPR: Crackdowns and Conflict on Personal Privacy," *Financial Times: Tomorrow's Global Business, Part Five—Rule of Law* (November 16, 2017), pp. 2–3.

[12]Jon Pareles, "A World of Megabeats and Megabytes," *The New York Times* (January 3, 2010), p. AR1.

[13]Vanessa Friedman, "Ready for the Next Chapter in E-Tailing," *Financial Times* (April 5, 2010), p. 18.

[14]Kevin Maney, "Baby's Arrival Inspires Birth of Cell Phone Camera—and Societal Evolution," *USA Today* (January 24, 2007), p. 3B.

[15]Much of the material in this section is adapted from Clayton Christensen, *The Innovator's Dilemma* (New York, NY: HarperBusiness, 2003). See also Simon London, "Digital Discomfort: Companies Struggle to Deal with the 'Inevitable Surprise' of the Transition from Atoms to Bits," *Financial Times* (December 17, 2003), p. 17.

[16]Cited in Khadeeja Safdar, "J. Crew's Slip: Trusting in Design over Tech," *The Wall Street Journal* (May 25, 2017), p. A12.

[17]Simon London, "Why Disruption Can Be Good for Business," *Financial Times* (October 3, 2003), p. 8.

[18]Rosabeth Moss Kanter, John Kao, and Fred Wiersema, *Innovation: Breakthrough Thinking at 3M, DuPont, GE, Pfizer, and Rubbermaid* (New York, NY: HarperBusiness, 1997), p. 24.

[19]"Middle-Aged Blues," *The Economist* (June 11, 2011), p. 59.

[20]Elizabeth Weise, "No Checkout Line: Amazon Go Store Opens to Public," *USA Today* (January 22, 2018), p. 1B.

[21]Michelle Beeson and Claudia Tajima, *Online Retail Will Drive Overall European Retail Sales Growth Through 2022*, Forrester Research (December 5, 2017), p. 3.

[22]Michelle Beeson and Claudia Tajima, *Online Retail Will Drive Overall European Retail Sales Growth Through 2022*, Forrester Research (December 5, 2017), p. 3.

[23]Sarwant Singh, "B2B e-Commerce Market Worth $6.7 Trillion by 2020; Alibaba and China the Frontrunners," *Forbes* (November 6, 2014), p. 34.

[24]Joe Mullin, "Pandora CEO: The Complexity of International Copyright Law Is a Big Problem," PaidContent.org (March 30, 2011). Accessed June 1, 2011. https://gigaom.com/2011/03/30/419-pandora-ceo-international-copyright-law-is-intractable-problem/

[25]Susanne Vranica, "Hellmann's Targets Yahoo for Its Spread," *The Wall Street Journal* (June 27, 2007), p. B4.

[26]Laura Stevens, "Borders Matter Less and Less in E-Commerce," *The Wall Street Journal* (June 24, 2015), p. B8. See also Stephanie Clifford, "U.S. Stores Learn How to Ship to Foreign Shoppers," *The New York Times* (March 21, 2012), pp. B1, B7.

[27]Ellen Byron, "P&G Goes on the Defensive for Pampers," *The Wall Street Journal* (June 15, 2010), p. B5.

[28]David Gelles, "Innovation Brings a Touch of Class to Online Shopping," *Financial Times Special Report: Business of Luxury* (June 14, 2010), p. 7.

[29]David Gelles, "Social Media: Tarnish the Brand or Build an Aspirational Following?" *Financial Times* (June 14, 2010), p. 23. See also Gary Silverman, "How May I Help You?" *Financial Times* (February 4–5, 2006), p. W2.

[30]Chris Anderson, *The Long Tail: Why the Future of Business Is Selling Less of More* (New York, NY: Hyperion, 2006), p. 13.

[31]Much of the discussion in this section is adapted from Alexis D. Gutzman, *The E-Commerce Arsenal* (New York, NY: Amacom, 2001).

[32]Jessica Vascellaro, "Foreign Shopping Sites Cater to U.S. Customers," *The Wall Street Journal* (October 12, 2005), pp. D1, D14.

[33]Peter Loftus, "Internet Turns Firms into Overseas Businesses," *The Wall Street Journal* (December 16, 2003), p. B4. See also Matt Richtel, "Credit Card Theft Is Thriving Online as Global Market," *The New York Times* (May 13, 2002), p. A1.

[34]Patricia Riedman, "Think Globally, Act Globally," *Advertising Age* (June 19, 2000), p. 48.

[35]Frances Robinson, "EU Unveils Web-Privacy Rules," *The Wall Street Journal* (January 26, 2012), p. B9.

[36]David Scheer, "For Your Eyes Only: Europe's New High-Tech Role: Playing Privacy Cop to the World," *The Wall Street Journal* (October 10, 2003), p. A1.

[37]Andrew Ward, "Coke Taps into Brand New Internet Craze," *Financial Times* (August 8, 2006), p. 15.

[38]Mark McDonald, "Home Internet May Get Even Faster in South Korea," *The New York Times* (February 22, 2011), p. B3.

[39]Alan Cane, "Leaders Look to Future in Broadband Race," *Financial Times* (October 23, 2009).

[40]Steve Lohr, "Amazon's Trouble Raises Cloud Computing Doubts," *The New York Times* (April 23, 2011), p. B1.

[41]Yukari Iwatani Kane and Emily Steel, "Apple's iAd Helping Rivals," *The Wall Street Journal* (November 11, 2010), p. B4.

[42]Felicia Greiff, "Global Mobile Ad Spending Will Rise to $100 Billion in 2016," *Advertising Age* (April 2, 2015).

[43]Sara Silver and Emily Steel, "Alcatel Gets into Mobile Ads," *The Wall Street Journal* (May 21, 2009), p. B9; NAVTEQ, "Domino's," http://navteqmedia.com/mobile/case-studies/dominos (accessed May 24, 2011); NAVTEQ, "McDonald's," http://navteqmedia.com/mobile/case-studies/mcdonalds (accessed May 24, 2011).

[44]Eric Bellman and Tariq Engineer, "India Appears Ripe for Cell Phone Ads," *The Wall Street Journal* (March 10, 2008), p. B3.

[45]*Bluetooth* is the Anglicized version of a Scandinavian epithet for Harald Blatand, a Danish Viking and king who lived in the tenth century.

[46]Elisabeth Behrman, "BMW to Staff: Be Afraid, Be Very Afraid," *Bloomberg Businessweek* (May 1, 2017), p. 25.

[47]Patrick McGee, "Is It the End of the Road for the Motor Car Marque?" *Financial Times* (June 27, 2017), p. 15.

[48]Tim Bradshaw and Matthew Garrahan, "Apple Streaming Service Leaves iTunes Behind," *Financial Times* (June 6/7, 2015), p. 10.

[49]Tom Hancock, Yingzhi Yang and Yuan Yang, "Tencent Rests Easy at Top of Biggest Gaming Market," *Financial Times* (October 4, 2017), p. 18.

[50]Daisuke Wakabayashi and Spencer E. Ante, "Mobile Game Fight Goes Global," *The Wall Street Journal* (June 14, 2012), p. B1.

[51]Seth Stevenson, "A Chat Star Is Born," *WSJ Magazine* (March 2016), p. 60.

[52]Leo Lewis and Tim Bradshaw, "Esports Move into Big League," *Financial Times Big Read: Entertainment* (November 6, 2017), p. 11.

[53]Newley Pernell, "Chinese Lead the Way in Mobile Payment," *The Wall Street Journal* (September 23–24, 2017), pp. B1, B2.

[54]Motoko Rich, "New Target for Digital Pirates: The Printed Word," *The New York Times* (May 12, 2009), p. A1.

[55]Hannah Kuchler, "The Race to Make Wearables Cool," *Financial Times* (September 24/25, 2016), p. 5.

16 Strategic Elements of Competitive Advantage

LEARNING OBJECTIVES

16-1 Identify the forces that shape competition in an industry, and illustrate each force with a specific company or industry example.

16-2 Define *competitive advantage* and identify the key conceptual frameworks that guide decision makers in the strategic planning process.

16-3 Explain how a nation can achieve competitive advantage, and list the forces that may be present in a national "diamond."

16-4 Define *hypercompetitive industry* and list the key arenas in which dynamic strategic interactions take place.

CASE 16-1
IKEA

When IKEA founder Ingvar Kamprad passed away in early 2018 at the age of 91, the world lost a retailing legend and an icon of entrepreneurship. IKEA has been called "one of the most extraordinary success stories in the history of postwar European business." As an enterprising teenager in rural Sweden, Kamprad sold pencils and other merchandise by mail. He later bought an abandoned factory and began making furniture. The next step was opening a showroom in the town of Almhult. By the time of Kamprad's death, IKEA had evolved from its humble beginnings as a mail-order business into a $38 billion global furniture powerhouse with more than 400 stores in 49 countries (see Exhibit 16-1).

Today, the company's Billy bookcases, Ektorp sofas, and Hemnes bedroom suites are bestsellers, popular with students, young families, and other budget-conscious shoppers. Thrifty by nature, Kamprad flew economy class and took public transportation when he traveled. IKEA's success reflects Kamprad's "social ambition" of selling a wide range of stylish, functional home furnishings at prices so low that the majority of people can afford to buy them.

Kamprad's frugal ways also applied to the company's finances. To minimize tax liabilities, he split the company into two parts: Inter Ikea owns the brand and the concept, while Ikea Group runs the retailing operations. Both units are now headquartered in the Netherlands rather than Sweden, where taxes are higher. Ikea Group pays Inter Ikea a royalty fee for use of the brand; this somewhat unorthodox arrangement has attracted the attention of the European Commission's tax authorities.

The essence of marketing strategy is successfully relating the strengths of an organization to its environment. As the horizons of marketers have expanded from domestic to regional and global, so,

Exhibit 16-1 In 2018, IKEA celebrated the 20th anniversary of its entry into China. The Swedish company currently has 24 stores in China; the Xu Hui store in Shanghai is one of the top performers by revenues.
Source: WorldFoto/Alamy Stock Photo.

too, have the horizons of competitors. Global competition is the reality in almost every industry today—a fact of life that puts organizations under increasing pressure to master techniques for conducting industry analysis and competitor analysis and understanding competitive advantage at both the industry and the national levels. This chapter covers these topics in detail. For more on the way that top management at IKEA is accomplishing this feat, turn to the continuation of Case 16-1 at the end of the chapter.

(16-1) Industry Analysis: Forces Influencing Competition

◀ **16-1** Identify the forces that shape competition in an industry, and illustrate each force with a specific company or industry example.

A useful way of gaining insight into competitors is through industry analysis. As a working definition, an *industry* can be defined as a group of firms that produce products that are close substitutes for each other. In any industry, competition works to drive down the rate of return on invested capital toward the rate that would be earned in the economist's "perfectly competitive" industry. Rates of return that are greater than this "competitive" rate will stimulate an inflow of capital either from new entrants or from existing competitors making additional investments. The global smartphone industry is a case in point: Apple's success with the iPhone prompted Samsung and other companies to enter this market. Rates of return below the competitive rate will result in withdrawal from the industry and a decline in the levels of activity and competition.

Harvard University's Michael E. Porter, a leading authority on competitive strategy, has developed a **five forces model** that explains competition in an industry. The five forces comprise the threat of new entrants, the threat of substitute products or services, the bargaining power of buyers, the bargaining power of suppliers, and the competitive rivalry among current members of the industry. In industries such as soft drinks, pharmaceuticals, and cosmetics, the favorable nature of the five forces has resulted in attractive returns for competitors. However, pressure from any of the forces can limit profitability, as evidenced by the recent fortunes of some competitors in the PC and semiconductor industries. A discussion of each of the five forces follows.

Threat of New Entrants

New entrants to an industry bring new capacity; a desire to gain market share and position; and, quite often, new approaches to serving customer needs. The decision to become a new entrant in an industry is often accompanied by a major commitment of resources. New players mean prices will be pushed downward and margins squeezed, resulting in reduced industry profitability in the long run. Porter describes eight major sources of barriers to entry, whose presence or absence determines the extent of threat by new industry entrants.[1]

The first barrier, **economies of scale**, refers to the decline in per-unit product costs as the absolute volume of production per period increases. Although the concept of scale economies is frequently associated with manufacturing, it is also applicable to research and development (R&D), general administration, marketing, and other business functions. Honda's efficiency at engine R&D, for example, results from the wide range of products it produces that feature gasoline-powered engines. When existing firms in an industry achieve significant economies of scale, it becomes difficult for potential new entrants to be competitive.

Product differentiation, the second major entry barrier, is the extent of a product's perceived uniqueness—in other words, whether it is a commodity. Differentiation can be achieved as a result of unique product attributes or effective marketing communications, or both. Product differentiation and brand loyalty "raise the bar" for would-be industry entrants who are required to make substantial investments in R&D or advertising. For example, Intel achieved differentiation and erected a barrier in the microprocessor industry with its "Intel Inside" advertising campaign and logo that appears on many brands of PCs.

A third entry barrier relates to *capital requirements*. Capital is required not only for manufacturing facilities (fixed capital), but also for financing R&D, advertising, field sales and service, customer credit, and inventories (working capital). The enormous capital requirements in such industries as pharmaceuticals, mainframe computers, chemicals, and mineral extraction present formidable entry barriers.

A fourth barrier to entry is the one-time *switching costs* resulting from the need to change suppliers and products. These might include retraining costs, ancillary equipment costs, the cost of evaluating a new source, and so on. The perceived cost to customers of switching to a new competitor's product may present an insurmountable obstacle, preventing industry newcomers from achieving success. For example, Microsoft's huge installed base of Windows operating systems and applications presented a formidable entry barrier to would-be competitors for many years.

A fifth barrier to entry is access to *distribution channels*. If channels are full or unavailable, the cost of entry is substantially increased because a new entrant must invest time and money to gain access to existing channels or to establish new channels. Some Western companies have encountered this barrier to market entry in Japan.

Government policy, the sixth barrier, is frequently a major entry barrier. In some cases, the government will restrict competitive entry. This is true in a number of industries, especially those outside the United States, that have been designated as "national" industries by their respective governments. Japan's postwar industrialization strategy was based on a policy of preserving and protecting national industries in their development and growth phases. The result was a market that proved difficult for non-Japanese competitors to enter, an issue that was targeted by U.S. President Bill Clinton's administration. During that era, American business executives in a wide range of industries urged adoption of a government policy that would reduce some of these barriers and open the Japanese market to more U.S. companies.

Established firms may also enjoy *cost advantages independent of scale economies* that present a seventh barrier to entry. Access to raw materials, a large pool of low-cost labor, favorable locations, and government subsidies are several examples.

Finally, expected *competitor response* can be a major entry barrier. If new entrants expect existing competitors to strongly oppose their entry into the market, the entrants' expectations about the rewards of entry will certainly be affected. Indeed, a potential competitor's belief that entry into an industry or market will be an unpleasant experience may serve as a strong deterrent to its participation. Bruce Henderson, former president of the Boston Consulting Group, used the term "brinkmanship" to describe a recommended approach for deterring competitive entry. Brinkmanship occurs when industry leaders convince potential competitors that any market-entry effort

"Thirty years ago, you had to surmount two powerful barriers to entry. One was getting word out about your product without a massive advertising budget. And the second one was getting listed with one of the key retailers. Because of the digital change, once new entrants have the product, making it to market has become faster and cheaper."[2]

Mark Schneider, CEO, Nestlé, commenting on consumer use of e-commerce to bypass traditional retail channels will be countered with vigorous and unpleasant responses. For example, Microsoft has used this approach many times to maintain its dominance in software operating systems and applications.

In the three decades since Porter first described the five forces model, the digital revolution appears to have altered the entry barriers in many industries. First and foremost, technology has lowered the cost for new entrants. For example, Barnes & Noble watched an entrepreneurial upstart, Amazon.com, storm the barriers protecting traditional brick-and-mortar booksellers. Amazon.com founder Jeff Bezos identified and exploited a glaring inefficiency in book distribution: Bookstores ship unsold copies of books back to publishers to be shredded and turned into pulp. Amazon.com's centralized operations and increasingly personalized online service enable customers to select from millions of different titles at discount prices and have them delivered to their homes within days. For a growing number of book-buying consumers, Amazon.com eclipses the value proposition of local bookstores that offer "only" a few thousand titles and gourmet coffee bars.

Barnes & Noble responded to the threat posed by Amazon.com by entering the online book market itself, even as it continues to be profitable in its traditional brick-and-mortar business. In the meantime, Bezos has repositioned Amazon.com as an Internet superstore selling electronics and general merchandise. Since Bezos founded Amazon.com in 1995, the company's annual sales have grown to more than $100 billion and it has expanded into new product lines, including CDs, DVDs, streaming movies and music, e-books, and the Echo smart speaker. The company has also entered the enterprise sector: Amazon Web Services, the cloud-computing unit, is a significant revenue source. Today, Amazon.com serves tens of millions of customers in more than 160 countries.

Threat of Substitute Products

A second force influencing competition in an industry is the threat of substitute products. The availability of substitute products places limits on the prices that market leaders can charge in an industry; high prices may induce buyers to switch to the substitute.

Once again, the digital revolution is dramatically altering industry structures in regard to substitute products. In addition to lowering entry barriers, the digital movement means that certain types of products can be converted to bits and distributed in pure digital form. For example, the development of the MP3 file format for music was accompanied by the increased popularity of peer-to-peer (p-to-p or P2P) file swapping among music fans. Napster and other online music services offered a substitute to consumers who were tired of paying $15 or more for a CD. Although a U.S. court severely curtailed Napster's activities, other services—including several outside the United States—sprang up in its place. The top players in the music industry were taken by surprise, and today, Sony Music Entertainment, Warner Music Group, and Universal Music Group are still struggling to develop new strategies in response to the changing business environment.

Bargaining Power of Buyers

In Porter's model, the term "buyers" refers to manufacturers (e.g., General Motors [GM]) and retailers (e.g., Walmart and Amazon) rather than consumers. The ultimate aim of such buyers is to pay the lowest possible price to obtain the products or services that they require. To achieve this goal, buyers try to drive down profitability in the supplier industry. First, however, the buyers have to gain leverage over their vendors.

One way they can do this is to purchase goods and services in such large quantities that supplier firms become highly dependent on the buyers' business. For example, Amazon has tremendous bargaining power over delivery companies. The reason is simple: In the United States alone, Amazon has roughly 44 percent of all Internet retail business. Second, when the suppliers' products are viewed as commodities—that is, as standard or undifferentiated—buyers are likely to bargain hard for low prices because many firms can meet their needs. Buyers will also bargain hard when the supplier industry's products or services represent a significant portion of the buying firm's costs. A fourth source of buyer power is the willingness and ability to achieve backward integration.

For example, because it purchases massive quantities of goods for resale, Walmart is in a position to dictate terms to any vendor wishing to distribute its products through the retail giant's stores. Walmart's influence also extends to the recorded music industry; the company refuses to stock CDs bearing parental advisory stickers for explicit lyrics or violent imagery. Recording artists who want their recordings to be sold by Walmart have the option of altering lyrics and song titles or deleting offending tracks. Likewise, artists are sometimes asked to change album cover art

Exhibit 16-2 Walmart refused to stock Green Day's politically charged CD *21st Century Breakdown*. More recently, the band has complied with Walmart's requirements, so that its newer releases are now carried by the retail giant. Slipknot, a Grammy-winning metal band from Des Moines, Iowa, has had a similar experience with Walmart.

Source: Hector Acevedo/ZUMAPRESS.com/ Alamy Stock Photo.

"Walmart is the 800-pound gorilla. You're going to want to do more things for a customer who is growing as fast as Walmart is."[4]

Ted Taft, Meridian Consulting Group

if Walmart deems it offensive. For example, the retailer wouldn't stock Green Day's *21st Century Breakdown* CD in 2009 after the band refused to alter some lyrics so the CD wouldn't carry a parental advisory sticker (see Exhibit 16-2). In 2017, Green Day changed its tune and released a "clean" version of its *¡Uno! ¡Dos! ¡Tres!* trilogy so that fans could purchase it at Walmart.[3]

Bargaining Power of Suppliers

Supplier power in an industry is the converse of buyer power. If suppliers have enough leverage over industry firms, they can raise prices high enough to significantly influence the profitability of their organizational customers. Several factors determine suppliers' ability to gain leverage over industry firms. First, suppliers will have the advantage if they are large and relatively few in number. Second, when the suppliers' products or services are important inputs to user firms, are highly differentiated, or carry switching costs, the suppliers will have considerable leverage over buyers. Suppliers will also enjoy bargaining power if alternative products do not threaten their business. A fourth source of supplier power is these companies' willingness and ability to develop their own products and brand names if they are unable to get satisfactory terms from industry buyers.

In the tech world, Microsoft and Intel are two companies with substantial supplier power. Because about 90 percent of the world's more than 1 billion PCs run on Microsoft's operating systems and 80 percent use Intel's microprocessors, the two companies enjoy a great deal of leverage relative to Dell, Hewlett-Packard, and other computer manufacturers. Microsoft's industry dominance prompted both the U.S. government and the European Union to launch separate antitrust investigations of its business practices. Today, the tech world's focus is shifting to new electronic devices such as smartphones, netbooks, and tablets. Many of these new products use the Apple, Android, or Linux operating systems instead of Windows; the chips come from competitors such as Qualcomm and Texas Instruments. As these trends take hold, Microsoft and Intel will find their supplier power diminishing.[5]

Rivalry among Competitors

"The only way to gain lasting competitive advantage is to leverage your capabilities around the world so that the company as a whole is greater than the sum of its parts. Being an international company—selling globally, having global brands or operations in different countries—isn't enough."[6]

David Whitwam, former CEO, Whirlpool

Rivalry among firms refers to all the actions taken by firms in an industry to improve their positions and gain advantage over each other. Rivalry manifests itself in price competition, advertising battles, product positioning, and attempts at differentiation. To the extent that rivalry among firms forces companies to rationalize costs, it is a positive force. To the extent that it drives down prices (and therefore profitability) and creates instability in the industry, it is a negative factor.

Several factors can create intense rivalry. First, once an industry becomes mature, firms focus on market share and how it can be gained at the expense of other firms. Second, industries characterized by high fixed costs are always under pressure to keep production at full capacity to cover those costs. Once the industry accumulates excess capacity, the drive to fill capacity will push prices—and profitability—down. A third factor affecting rivalry is lack of differentiation or an absence of switching costs, which encourages buyers to treat the products or services as commodities and shop for the best prices. Again, this factor places downward pressure on prices and profitability. Fourth, firms with high strategic stakes in achieving success in an industry generally are destabilizing forces because they may be willing to accept below-average profit margins to establish themselves, hold their positions, or expand their operations.

(16-2) Competitive Advantage

◀ **16-2** Define *competitive advantage* and identify the key conceptual frameworks that guide decision makers in the strategic planning process.

Competitive advantage exists when there is a match between a firm's distinctive competencies and the factors critical for success within its industry. Any superior match between a company's competencies and customers' needs permits the firm to outperform its competitors. Competitive advantage can be achieved in two ways. First, a firm can pursue a low-cost strategy that enables it to offer products at lower prices compared to competitors' products. Second, competitive advantage may be gained by differentiating products so that customers perceive them as having unique benefits, and perhaps as warranting a premium price. Note that both strategies have the same effect: They contribute to the firm's overall value proposition. Porter explored these issues in two landmark books, *Competitive Strategy* (1985) and *Competitive Advantage* (1990); the latter is widely considered to be one of the most influential management books in recent years.

Ultimately, customer perception decides the quality of a firm's strategy. Operating results such as sales and profits are measures that depend on the level of psychological value created for customers: The greater the perceived consumer value, the better the strategy. A firm may market a better mousetrap, but the ultimate success of the product depends on customers deciding for themselves whether to buy it. Value is like beauty: It's in the eye of the beholder. In sum, creating more value than the competition does achieves competitive advantage, and customer perception defines value.

Two different models of competitive advantage have received considerable attention. The first model offers "generic strategies," four routes or paths through which organizations choose to offer superior value and achieve competitive advantage. Critics of this model insist that generic strategies alone did not account for the astonishing success of many Japanese companies in the 1980s and 1990s. Thus, the second, more recent model, which is based on the concept of "strategic intent," proposes four different sources of competitive advantage. Both models are discussed in the following paragraphs.

Generic Strategies for Creating Competitive Advantage

In addition to the five forces model of industry competition, Porter has developed a framework of so-called generic business strategies based on the two types or sources of competitive advantage mentioned previously: *low cost* and *differentiation*. The relationship of these two sources with the scope of the target market served (narrow or broad) or product mix width (narrow or wide) yields four **generic strategies**: *cost leadership, product differentiation, cost focus,* and *focused differentiation.*

Generic strategies aiming at the achievement of competitive advantage or superior marketing strategy demand that a firm make choices. These choices concern the *type of competitive advantage* the firm seeks to attain (based on cost or differentiation) and the *market scope* or *product mix width* within which competitive advantage will be attained.[7] The nature of the choice between types of advantage and market scope is a gamble, and it is the nature of every gamble that it entails *risk*: By choosing a given generic strategy, a firm always risks making the wrong choice.

BROAD MARKET STRATEGIES: COST LEADERSHIP AND DIFFERENTIATION Cost leadership is competitive advantage based on a firm's position as the industry's low-cost producer, in broadly defined markets or across a wide mix of products. This strategy has achieved widespread appeal in recent years as a result of the popularization of the experience curve concept. In general, a firm that bases its competitive strategy on overall cost leadership must construct the most efficient facilities (in terms of scale or technology) and obtain the largest share of market so that its cost per unit is the lowest in the industry. These advantages, in turn, give the producer a substantial lead in terms of experience with building the product. Experience then leads to more refinements of the entire process of production, delivery, and service, which lead to further cost reductions.

Whatever its source, a cost leadership advantage can be the basis for offering lower prices (and more value) to customers in the late, more-competitive stages of the product life cycle. In Japan, companies in a range of industries—photography and imaging, consumer electronics and entertainment equipment, motorcycles, and automobiles—have achieved cost leadership on a worldwide basis.

Nevertheless, cost leadership will be a sustainable source of competitive advantage only if barriers exist that prevent competitors from achieving the same low costs. In an era of increasing technological improvements in manufacturing, manufacturers constantly leapfrog over one another in pursuit of lower costs. At one time, for example, IBM enjoyed the low-cost advantage in the production of computer printers. Then its Japanese rivals adopted the same technology and, after reducing production costs and improving product reliability, gained the low-cost advantage in the printer market. IBM fought back by constructing a highly automated printer plant in North Carolina, where the number of component parts was slashed by more than 50 percent and robots were used to snap many components into place. Despite these changes, IBM ultimately chose to exit the business.

When a firm's product has an actual or perceived uniqueness in a broad market, it is said to have achieved competitive advantage by **differentiation**. This can be an extremely effective strategy for defending market position and obtaining superior financial returns; unique products often command premium prices (see Exhibit 16-3). Examples of successful differentiation

> "We're living in a very polarized world now. You're either an absolute price leader—you're a Ryanair, a Southwest Airlines, a Walmart, and you're just hugely efficient and you will not be touched on price or cost. Or you're over on the quality end of the market with the Guccis and the Pradas and you're a quality leader."[8]
>
> Steve Ridgway, CEO of Virgin Atlantic Airways

Exhibit 16-3 Munich-based Siemens AG is a key global player in a variety of engineering sectors. Worldwide, public interest in energy-related issues has increased significantly. In 2011 the company's U.S. unit opened a new plant in Hutchinson, Kansas, to manufacture components for wind turbines.
Source: Siemens AG.

include Maytag in large home appliances, Caterpillar in construction equipment, and almost any successful branded consumer product. IBM traditionally has differentiated itself with a strong sales/service organization and the security of the IBM standard in a world of rapid obsolescence. Among athletic shoe manufacturers, Nike has positioned itself as the technological leader thanks to unique product features found in a wide array of shoes.

NARROW TARGET STRATEGIES: COST FOCUS AND FOCUSED DIFFERENTIATION The preceding discussion of cost leadership and differentiation considered only the impact on broad markets. By contrast, strategies to achieve a narrow-focus advantage target a narrowly defined market or customer. This advantage is based on an ability to create more customer value for a narrowly targeted segment and results from a better understanding of customer needs and wants. A narrow-focus strategy can be combined with either cost- or differentiation-advantage strategies. In other words, whereas a *cost focus* means offering low prices to a narrow target market, a firm pursuing *focused differentiation* will offer a narrow target market the perception of product uniqueness at a premium price.

Germany's *Mittelstand* companies (small and medium-sized firms) have been extremely successful in pursuing **focused differentiation** strategies backed by a strong export effort. The world of "high-end" audio equipment offers another example of focused differentiation. A few hundred small companies design speakers, amplifiers, and related hi-fi gear that cost thousands of dollars per component. While audio components represent a $21 billion market worldwide, annual sales in the high-end segment are only about $1.1 billion. American companies such as Audio Research, Conrad-Johnson, Krell, Mark Levinson, Martin-Logan, and Thiel dominate the segment, which also includes hundreds of smaller enterprises with annual sales of less than $10 million (see Exhibit 16-4). The state-of-the-art equipment that these companies offer is distinguished by superior craftsmanship and performance and is highly sought after by audiophiles in Asia (especially Japan and Hong Kong) and Europe. Even so, market growth has slowed in recent years, as technological advances have enabled makers of inexpensive gear to offer improved sound quality in their products. Also, many audiophiles are turning their attention to other components such as flat-screen televisions and multi-room wireless speaker systems.

The final strategy is **cost focus**, in which a firm's lower-cost position enables it to focus on a narrow target market and offer lower prices than the competition (see Exhibit 16-5). In the ship-building industry, for example, Polish and Chinese shipyards offer simple, standard vessel types at low prices that reflect low production costs.[9] Germany's Aldi, a no-frills "hard discounter" with grocery store operations in numerous countries, offers a very limited selection of household goods at extremely low prices. In 1976, Aldi opened its first U.S. stores in southeastern Iowa. It expanded slowly, opening a handful of stores each year. Private-label products help keep costs and prices down, allowing Aldi to expand in the key U.S. markets despite the recent poor economic climate. Recently, Aldi opened its first store in New York City.[10]

IKEA, the Swedish furniture company, has grown into a successful global company by using the cost-focus strategy (see Case 16-1). As George Bradley, president of Levitz Furniture in Boca Raton, Florida, noted a quarter century ago, "[IKEA] has really made a splash. They're going to capture their niche in every city they go into." Such a strategy can be risky. As Bradley explained, "Their market is finite because it is so narrow. If you don't want contemporary, knock-down furniture, it's not for you. So it takes a certain customer to buy it. And remember, fashions change."[11]

The issue of sustainability is central to this strategy concept. As noted, cost leadership is a sustainable source of competitive advantage only if barriers exist that prevent competitors from achieving the same low costs. Sustained differentiation depends on continued perceived value and the absence of imitation by competitors.[12] Several factors determine whether focus can be sustained as a source of competitive advantage. First, a cost focus is sustainable if a firm's competitors are defining their target markets more broadly. A company with a cost focus doesn't try to be all things to all people. Thus, competitors may diminish their advantage by trying to satisfy the needs of a broader market segment—a strategy that, by definition, means a blunter focus. Second, a firm's differentiation focus advantage is sustainable only if competitors cannot define the segment even more narrowly. Also, focus can be sustained if competitors cannot overcome barriers that prevent imitation of the focus strategy, and if consumers in the target segment do not migrate to other segments that the more focused company doesn't serve.

Exhibit 16-4 In keeping with the aesthetics of high-end audio gear, Theta Digital's Prometheus monoblock power amplifier is the epitome of classic, minimalist design. A pair of these beauties—one for each stereo channel—will set you back $12,000.
Source: Mr. Buzz Delano/Theta Digital.

Exhibit 16-5 For more than 100 years, Germany's Aldi has offered shoppers a tightly focused assortment of unbranded merchandise at very low prices in a no-frills setting. Now, taking a cue from its Trader Joe's unit in the United States, Aldi is making major improvements in its home-country market. German shoppers want more than low prices; they also want a nice ambience and a more appealing atmosphere.
Source: ZUMA Press Inc/Alamy Stock Photo.

Creating Competitive Advantage via Strategic Intent

An alternative framework for understanding competitive advantage focuses on competitiveness as a function of the pace at which a company implants new advantages deep within its organization. This framework identifies **strategic intent**, growing out of ambition and obsession with winning, as the means for achieving competitive advantage. Writing in the *Harvard Business Review*, Gary Hamel and C. K. Prahalad note:

> Few competitive advantages are long lasting. Keeping score of existing advantages is not the same as building new advantages. The essence of strategy lies in creating tomorrow's competitive advantages faster than competitors mimic the ones you possess today. An organization's capacity to improve existing skills and learn new ones is the most defensible competitive advantage of all.[13]

This approach is founded on the principles espoused by W. Edwards Deming, who stressed that a company must commit itself to continuing improvement if it expects to be a winner in a competitive struggle. For years, Deming's message fell on deaf ears in the United States, while the Japanese heeded his message and benefited tremendously. Japan's most prestigious business award is named after Deming. Eventually, however, U.S. auto manufacturers responded, and Detroit's current resurgence is evidence that those automakers have made much progress.

The significance of Hamel and Prahalad's framework becomes evident when comparing Caterpillar and Komatsu. As noted earlier, Caterpillar is a classic example of differentiation: The company became the largest manufacturer of earthmoving equipment in the world because it was fanatical about quality and service. Caterpillar's success as a global marketer has enabled it to achieve a 40 percent share of the worldwide market for earthmoving equipment, more than half of which represents sales to developing countries. The differentiation advantage was achieved with product durability, global spare parts service (including guaranteed parts delivery anywhere in the world within 48 hours), and a strong network of loyal dealers.

Over the last several decades, Caterpillar has faced a very challenging set of environmental pressures. Many of Caterpillar's plants were closed by a lengthy strike in the early 1980s; a worldwide recession at the same time caused a downturn in the construction industry. This hurt companies that were Caterpillar customers. In addition, the strong dollar gave a cost advantage to foreign rivals.

Compounding Caterpillar's problems was a new competitive threat from Japan. Komatsu was the world's number 2 construction equipment company and had been competing with Caterpillar in the Japanese market for years. Komatsu's products were generally acknowledged to offer a lower level of quality. The rivalry took on a new dimension after Komatsu adopted the slogan "*Maru-c*," meaning "encircle Caterpillar." Emphasizing quality and taking advantage of low labor costs and the strong dollar, Komatsu surpassed Caterpillar to become number 1 in earthmoving equipment in Japan and made serious inroads in the United States and other markets. Even after it achieved world-class quality, Komatsu continued to develop new sources of competitive advantage. For example, new-product development cycles were shortened and manufacturing was rationalized. Caterpillar struggled to sustain its competitive advantage because many customers found that Komatsu's combination of quality, durability, and lower price created compelling value. Yet even as the recession and a strong yen put new pressure on Komatsu, the company sought new opportunities by diversifying into machine tools and robots.[14]

The Komatsu/Caterpillar saga illustrates the fact that global competitive battles can be shaped by factors other than the pursuit of generic strategies. Many firms have gained competitive advantage by *disadvantaging* rivals through "competitive innovation." Hamel and Prahalad define *competitive innovation* as "the art of containing competitive risks within manageable proportions" and identify four successful approaches used by Japanese competitors: *building layers of advantage*, *searching for loose bricks*, *changing the rules of engagement*, and *collaborating*.

LAYERS OF ADVANTAGE A company faces less risk in competitive encounters if it has a wide portfolio of advantages. Successful companies steadily build such portfolios by establishing layers of advantage on top of one another. Komatsu is an excellent example of this approach. Another is the TV industry in Japan. By 1970, Japan was not only the world's largest producer of black-and-white TV sets, but also well on its way to becoming the leader in producing color sets. The main competitive advantage for such companies as Matsushita at that time was low labor costs.

Because they realized that their cost advantage might be temporary, Japanese companies added another layer of *quality and reliability* advantages by building plants large enough to serve world markets. Much of this output did not carry the manufacturer's brand name. For example, Matsushita Electric sold products to other companies such as RCA, which then marketed them under their own brand names. Matsushita was pursuing a simple idea: A product sold was a product sold, no matter whose label it carried.[15]

To build the next layer of advantage, Japanese firms spent the 1970s investing heavily in marketing channels and Japanese brand names to gain recognition. This strategy added yet another layer of competitive advantage: the *global brand franchise*—that is, a global customer base. By the late 1970s, channels and brand awareness were established well enough to support the introduction of new products that could benefit from global marketing—VCRs and photocopy machines, for example. Finally, many companies have invested in *regional manufacturing* so their products can be differentiated and better adapted to customer needs in individual markets.

The process of building layers illustrates how a company can move along the value chain to strengthen its competitive advantage. The Japanese companies began with manufacturing (an upstream value activity) and moved on to marketing (a downstream value activity) and then back upstream to basic R&D. All of these sources of competitive advantage represent mutually reinforcing layers that accumulate over time.

LOOSE BRICKS A second approach takes advantage of the "loose bricks" left in the defensive walls of competitors whose attention is narrowly focused on a market segment or a geographic area to the exclusion of others. For example, Caterpillar's attention was focused elsewhere when Komatsu made its first foray into the Eastern Europe market. Similarly, Taiwan's Acer prospered by following founder Stan Shih's strategy of approaching the world computer market from the periphery. Shih's inspiration was the Asian board game *Go*, in which the winning player successfully surrounds opponents. Shih gained experience and built market share in countries overlooked by competitors such as IBM and Compaq. By the time Acer was ready to target the United States in earnest, it was already the number 1 PC brand in key countries in Latin America, Southeast Asia, and the Middle East.

Intel's loose brick was its narrow focus on complex microprocessors for PCs. The world's biggest chip maker in terms of sales, it currently commands approximately 80 percent of the global market for PC processors. However, even as it built its core business, demand for non-PC consumer electronics products began to explode. The new non-PC products, such as set-top boxes for televisions, digital cameras, smartphones, and tablets, require chips that are cheaper and use less power than those produced by Intel. Competitors such as LSI Logic and Arm Holdings recognized the opportunity and beat Intel into an important new market. Intel has responded by developing new chips incorporating 3D technology that use half as much power as current designs.[16]

CHANGING THE RULES A third approach involves **changing the rules of engagement** and refusing to play by the rules set by industry leaders. For example, in the copier market, IBM and Kodak imitated the marketing strategies used by market leader Xerox. Meanwhile, Canon, a Japanese challenger, wrote a new rulebook.

While Xerox built a wide range of copiers, Canon built standardized machines and components, reducing manufacturing costs. While Xerox employed a huge direct-sales force, Canon chose to distribute its copiers through office-product dealers. Canon also designed serviceability and reliability into its products, so that it could rely on dealers when service was needed rather than incurring the expense required to create a national service network. In addition, the company decided to sell rather than lease its machines, freeing the company from the burden of financing the lease base. In another major departure, Canon targeted its copiers at secretaries and department managers rather than at the heads of corporate duplicating operations.[17]

Canon introduced the first full-color copiers and the first copiers with "connectivity"—the ability to print images from such sources as video camcorders and computers. The Canon example shows how an innovative marketing strategy—with fresh approaches to the product, pricing, distribution, and selling—can lead to overall competitive advantage in the marketplace. Canon is not invulnerable, however: In 1991, Tektronix, a U.S. company, leapfrogged past Canon in the color copier market by introducing a plain-paper color copier that offered sharper copies at a much lower price.[18]

COLLABORATING A final source of competitive advantage is using know-how developed by other companies. Such *collaboration* may take the form of licensing agreements, joint ventures, or partnerships. History has shown that Japanese firms have excelled at using the collaborating strategy to achieve industry leadership. One of the legendary licensing agreements of modern business history is Sony's licensing of transistor technology from AT&T's Bell Labs subsidiary in the 1950s for $25,000. This agreement gave Sony access to the transistor and allowed the company to become a world leader. Building on its initial successes in the manufacturing and marketing of portable radios, Sony has grown into a superb global marketer whose name is synonymous with a wide assortment of high-quality consumer electronics products.

More recent examples of Japanese collaboration are found in the aircraft industry. Today, Mitsubishi Heavy Industries and other Japanese companies manufacture airplanes under license to U.S. firms and also work as subcontractors for aircraft parts and systems. Many observers fear that the future of the American aircraft industry may be jeopardized as the Japanese gain technological expertise. The next section discusses various examples of "collaborative advantage."[19]

(16-3) Global Competition and National Competitive Advantage

◀ **16-3** Explain how a nation can achieve competitive advantage, and list the forces that may be present in a national "diamond."

An inevitable consequence of the expansion of global marketing activities is the growth of competition on a global basis.[20] In industry after industry, global competition is a critical factor affecting success. As Yoshino and Rangan have explained, **global competition** occurs when a firm takes a global view of competition and sets about maximizing profits worldwide, rather than on a country-by-country basis. If, when expanding abroad, a company encounters the same rival in market after market, then it is engaged in global competition.[21] In some industries, global companies have virtually excluded all other companies from their markets. An example is the detergent industry, in which three companies—Colgate, Unilever, and Procter & Gamble—dominate an increasing number of detergent markets in Latin America and the Pacific Rim. Many companies can make a quality detergent, but brand-name muscle and the skills required for quality packaging overwhelm the local competition in market after market.[22]

The automobile industry has also become fiercely competitive on a global basis. Part of the reason for the initial success of foreign automakers in the United States was the reluctance—or inability—of U.S. manufacturers to design and manufacture high-quality, inexpensive small cars. The resistance of U.S. manufacturers was based on the economics of car production: Bigger cars equaled bigger profits. Under this formula, small cars meant smaller unit profits. Sadly, U.S. car manufacturers mostly ignored the increasing preference of U.S. drivers for smaller cars, a classic case of ethnocentrism and management myopia. European and Japanese manufacturers always offered cars smaller than those made in the United States, in part because market conditions were much different: less space, higher taxes on engine displacement and fuel, and greater market interest in functional design and engineering innovations.

First Volkswagen, and then Japanese automakers such as Nissan and Toyota, discovered a growing demand for their cars in the U.S. market. For most of the past 20 years, the Toyota Camry has been the best-selling passenger car in North America. Ironically, the Camry plants are located in Kentucky and Indiana, and Cars.com rates the Camry as "the most American car" in its American-Made Index! But the competitive environment continues to evolve. Today, South Korea's Hyundai and Kia have joined the ranks of world-class automakers. Meanwhile, Korea's Automobile Journalist Association named Camry the "Korea Car of the Year" for 2013; however, those Korea-bound Camrys come from U.S. plants. Doubly ironic! And, as noted in Case 13-1, Volkswagen's drive to become the world's top automaker has faltered in the face of an emissions-cheating scandal.

The effect of global competition has been highly beneficial to consumers around the world. In the two examples cited, detergents and automobiles, consumers have benefited. In Central America, detergent prices have fallen as a result of global competition. Global automakers provide consumers with the models, performance, and price characteristics they want. If smaller, lower-priced imported cars had not been available, it is unlikely that Detroit's manufacturers would have responded as quickly to the changing market conditions. What is true for automobiles in the United States is true for every product category around the world: Global competition expands the range of products available and increases the likelihood that consumers will get what they want.

The downside of global competition is its impact on the producers of goods and services. Global competition creates value for consumers, but it also has the potential to destroy jobs and profits. When a company—Toyota, for example—offers consumers in other countries a better product at a lower price, it takes customers away from domestic firms such as GM. Unless the domestic firm can create new sources of value and find new customers, the jobs and livelihoods of the domestic supplier's employees are threatened.

This section addresses the following issue: Why is a particular nation a good home base for specific industries? Why, for example, is the United States the home base for the leading competitors in tablets and smartphones, software, credit cards, and filmed entertainment? Why is Germany home to so many world leaders in printing presses, chemicals, and luxury cars? Why are so many leading pharmaceutical, chocolate/confectionery, and trading companies located in Switzerland? How does one account for Italy's success in wool textiles, knitwear, and apparel?

Harvard professor Michael E. Porter explored these issues in his groundbreaking 1990 book *The Competitive Advantage of Nations*. The book was hailed as a valuable guide for shaping national policies on competitiveness. According to Porter, the presence or absence of particular attributes in individual countries influences industry development, not just the ability of individual firms to create core competencies and competitive advantage.[23] Porter describes these attributes in terms of a national "diamond." You can visualize these attributes relative to a baseball diamond: Demand conditions are on "first base"; firm strategy, structure, and rivalry occupy "second base"; factor conditions are on "third base"; and related and supporting industries are at "home plate." The diamond shapes the environment in which firms compete. Activity in any one of the four points of the diamond impacts all the other points, and vice versa.

Factor Conditions

Factor conditions comprise a country's endowment with resources. Those resources may have been created or inherited. *Basic factors* may be inherited or created without much difficulty; because they can be replicated in other nations, they are not sustainable sources of **national advantage**. Specialized factors, by contrast, are more advanced and provide a more sustainable source for advantage. Porter describes five categories of factor conditions: human, physical, knowledge, capital, and infrastructure.

HUMAN RESOURCES The quantity of workers available, the skills possessed by these workers, the wage levels, and the overall work ethic of the workforce together constitute a nation's human resources factor. Countries with a plentiful supply of low-wage workers have an obvious advantage in the production of labor-intensive products. Conversely, such countries may be at a disadvantage when it comes to the production of sophisticated products requiring highly skilled workers capable of working without extensive supervision.

PHYSICAL RESOURCES The availability, quantity, quality, and cost of land, water, minerals, and other natural resources determine a country's or region's physical resources. As Porter discusses in *The Competitive Advantage of Nations*, Italy's strength as an exporter is due in part to clusters of successful industries including textiles and apparel; glass, ceramics, and stone products; and many others (see Exhibit 16-6). A country's size and location are also included in this category, because proximity to markets and sources of supply, as well as transportation costs, are strategic considerations. These factors are important advantages—or disadvantages—to industries dependent on natural resources. Brazil is a case in point. With a large landmass, temperate climate, and abundant water supply, Brazil is a leading producer of agricultural commodities, including coffee, soybeans, and sugar.

KNOWLEDGE RESOURCES When a significant portion of a country's population has scientific, technical, and market-related knowledge, that nation is considered to be endowed with knowledge

Exhibit 16-6 Impruneta, a city in the Italian province of Florence, is a source of top-quality terracotta. The high iron content of the area's clay means that the finished pieces can withstand temperatures as low as −20°F. Many artisan designs are rolled by hand, including those imported for the U.S. market by Seibert & Rice.
Source: Seibert & Rice.

resources. The presence of this factor is usually a function of the number of research facilities and universities—both government and private—operating in the country. This factor is important to success in sophisticated products and services, and to doing business in sophisticated markets. This factor speaks directly to Germany's leadership in chemicals; today, BASF is the world's largest producer of chemicals. For the past 200 years, Germany has been home to top university chemistry programs, advanced scientific journals, and apprenticeship programs.

CAPITAL RESOURCES Countries vary in the availability, amount, cost, and types of capital available to their industries. A nation's savings rate, interest rates, tax laws, and government deficit all affect the availability of this factor. The advantage enjoyed by industries in countries with low capital costs versus those located in nations with relatively high capital costs is sometimes decisive. Firms paying high capital costs are frequently unable to stay in a market where the competition comes from a nation with low capital costs. Those firms with a low cost of capital can keep their prices low and force the firms paying high costs to either accept low returns on investment or leave the industry.

INFRASTRUCTURE RESOURCES Infrastructure includes a nation's banking system, health care system, transportation system, and communications system, as well as the availability and cost of using these systems. More sophisticated industries are more dependent on advanced infrastructures for success.

Competitive advantage accrues to a nation's industry if the mix of factors available to the industry is such that it facilitates pursuit of a generic strategy (i.e., low-cost production or the production of a highly differentiated product or service). Nations that have selective factor *disadvantages* may also indirectly create competitive advantage. For example, the absence of suitable labor may force firms to develop forms of mechanization or automation that give the nation an advantage. High transportation costs may motivate firms to develop new materials that are less expensive to transport.

Demand Conditions

The nature of home demand conditions for the firm's or industry's products and services is important because it determines the rate and nature of improvement and innovation by the firms in the nation. **Demand conditions** are the factors that either train firms for world-class competition or fail to adequately prepare them to compete in the global marketplace. Four characteristics of home demand are particularly important to the creation of competitive advantage: the composition of home demand, the size and pattern of the growth of home demand, rapid home-market growth, and the means by which a nation's home demand pushes or pulls the nation's products and services into foreign markets.

ENTREPRENEURIAL LEADERSHIP, CREATIVE THINKING, AND THE GLOBAL STARTUP

Italian Entrepreneurs Combine Fashion and Function, Part 1: Leonardo del Vecchio, Luxottica

As Michael Porter notes in *The Competitive Advantage of Nations*:

> Entrepreneurship thrives in Italy, feeding rivalry in existing industries and the formation of clusters. Italians are risk takers. Many are individualistic and desire independence. They aspire to have their own company. They like to work with people they know well, as in the family, and not as part of a hierarchy. . . . Recently, the entrepreneur has become celebrated in Italy, and a number of business magazines are full of nothing but profiles of successful entrepreneurs. (p. 447)

Leonardo del Vecchio is an entrepreneur. He developed an innovative approach to an existing product and, in 1961, founded a company that manufactures and markets it. By applying the basic tools and principles of modern marketing, del Vecchio has achieved remarkable success.

Del Vecchio grew up in an orphanage, but today he is one of Europe's richest men. His insight: Although eyeglasses are critical for vision, they also reflect the wearer's personality. As a product, then, eyeglass frames serve two purposes; one is functional, the other is aesthetic. This insight fueled the growth of del Vecchio's company, Luxottica, and turned it into the world's top producer of eyeglass frames.

Luxottica has 78,000 employees worldwide, and is vertically integrated. It designs and manufactures frames in its own factories, and also is involved in distribution through fully owned chains such as Sunglass Hut, LensCrafters, and Pearle Vision (see Exhibit 16-7). It owns top eyewear brands including Oakley, Ray-Ban, and Vogue. The company also produces frames under license for a veritable who's who of luxury brands: Burberry, Dolce & Gabbana, Donna Karan, Prada, Ralph Lauren, Versace, and many others. Ray-Ban is Luxottica's biggest-selling brand, with more than €2 billion ($2.2 billion) in sales each year.

By 2016, Luxottica commanded nearly 14 percent of the $90 billion global eyewear market. However, demographic trends and new industry entrants are presenting significant opportunities and challenges. Following the departure of longtime chief executive Andrea Guerra, Leonardo del Vecchio, at the age of 80, returned to the company he founded.

In 2017, Del Vecchio announced that Luxottica was merging with Essilor, a lens manufacturer based in France. The new company, Essilor-Luxottica, will have annual revenues of €15 billion (about $17.5 billion) and market products in 150 countries. Commenting on the deal, Del Vecchio said, "We have the brand. What was missing was the quality of the lenses." Another plus: Essilor has been granted several patents for connected glasses. A new product, MyEye, consists of frames equipped with a camera and earphones so that users can listen to scanned text while doing something else.

Meanwhile, other entrepreneurial startups have recognized new opportunities in the eyewear sector. Italia Independent is a brand created by Lapo Elkann, a billionaire heir to the family that owns Ferrari. It's been said that Elkann's company created the "mass cool" segment. Italia Independent is known for using innovative materials such as carbon fiber in its frames; the brand is especially popular with Millennials.

Sources: Rachel Sanderson, "The Far-Sighted Dealmaker of Milan," *Financial Times* (January 21–22, 2017), p. 7; Michael Stothard and Rachel Sanderson, "Luxottica and Essilor Set out Their €50bn Growth Vision," *Financial Times* (January 17, 2017), p. 15; Rachel Sanderson, "Let's Launch in . . . Milan, Italy," *Financial Times* (June 29, 2016), p. 12; Rachel Sanderson, "Designers Open Eyes to Latest Fashion Spectacle," *Financial Times* (April 9–10, 2016), p. 12; Bill Emmott, *Good Italy, Bad Italy: Why Italy Must Conquer Its Demons to Face the Future* (New Haven, CT: Yale University Press, 2012), Chapter 7; Christina Passariello, "Fitting Shades for Chinese," *The Wall Street Journal* (April 21, 2011), p. B5; Rachel Sanderson, "The Real Value of Being 'Made in Italy,'" *Financial Times* (January 19, 2011); Emanuela Scarpellini, *Material Nation: A Consumer's History of Modern Italy* (New York, NY: Oxford University Press, 2011); David Segal, "Is Italy Too Italian?" *The New York Times* (August 1, 2010), p. B1; Michael E. Porter, *The Competitive Advantage of Nations* (New York, NY: Free Press, 1990), Chapter 8.

Exhibit 16-7 Luxottica, the world's leading eyewear manufacturer, also owns and operates retail chains in key global markets. Generally speaking, customers in the United States tend to emphasize function (e.g., brands such as Ray-Ban and Oakley) and are somewhat more conservative and traditional in their tastes. By contrast, European and Asian customers share the desire for an emotional connection with the things they buy—including eyeglass frames. The company is ramping up efforts to expand in Brazil, India, Turkey, and China.
Source: Kris Tripplaar/SIPA/Newscom.

COMPOSITION OF HOME DEMAND This demand element determines how firms perceive, interpret, and respond to buyer needs. Competitive advantage can be achieved when the home demand sets the quality standard and gives local firms a better picture of buyer needs, at an earlier time, than the perspective that is available to foreign rivals. This advantage is enhanced when home buyers pressure the nation's firms to innovate quickly and frequently. The basis for advantage is the fact that the nation's firms can stay ahead of the market when the firms are more sensitive and more responsive to home demand and when that demand, in turn, reflects or anticipates world demand.

SIZE AND PATTERN OF GROWTH OF HOME DEMAND These are important only if the composition of the home demand is sophisticated and anticipates foreign demand. Large home markets offer opportunities to achieve economies of scale and learning while dealing with familiar, comfortable markets. There is less apprehension about investing in large-scale production facilities and expensive R&D programs when the home market is sufficient to absorb the increased capacity. If the home demand accurately reflects or anticipates foreign demand, and if the firms do not become content with serving just the home market, the existence of large-scale facilities and programs will be an advantage in global competition.

RAPID HOME-MARKET GROWTH Rapid growth in the local market is yet another incentive to invest in and adopt new technologies faster and to build large, efficient facilities. The best example of this factor is seen in Japan, where rapid home-market growth provided the incentive for Japanese firms to invest heavily in modern, automated facilities. *Early home demand*, especially if it anticipates international demand, gives local firms the advantage of getting established in an industry sooner than their foreign rivals. Equally important is *early market saturation*, which puts pressure on a company to expand into international markets and innovate. Market saturation is especially important if it coincides with rapid growth in foreign markets.

MEANS BY WHICH A NATION'S PRODUCTS AND SERVICES ARE PUSHED OR PULLED INTO FOREIGN COUNTRIES The issue here is whether a nation's people and businesses go abroad and then demand the home nation's products and services in those second countries. For example, when the U.S. auto companies set up operations in foreign countries, the auto parts industry followed. The same is true for the Japanese auto industry. Similarly, when overseas demand for the services of U.S. engineering firms skyrocketed after World War II, those firms, in turn, established demand for U.S. heavy construction equipment. This provided an impetus for Caterpillar to establish foreign operations.

A related issue is that of a nation's people going abroad for training, pleasure, business, or research. After returning home, they are likely to demand the products and services with which they became familiar while abroad. Similar effects can result from professional, scientific, and political relationships between nations. Those involved in the relationships begin to demand the products and services of the recognized leaders.

It is the interplay of demand conditions that produces competitive advantage. Of special importance are those conditions that lead to initial and continuing incentives to invest and innovate and to continuing competition in increasingly sophisticated markets.

Related and Supporting Industries

A nation has an advantage when it is home to globally competitive companies in business sectors that comprise **related and supporting industries**. Globally competitive supplier industries provide inputs to downstream industries. The latter, in turn, are likely to be globally competitive in terms of price and quality, thereby gaining competitive advantage from this situation. Downstream industries will have easier access to these inputs and the technology that produced them, and to the managerial and organizational structures that made them competitive. Access is a function of proximity in terms of both physical distance and cultural similarity. It is not the inputs themselves that give advantage, but rather the *contact* and *coordination* with the suppliers, which give home-country firms the opportunity to structure the value chain so that linkages with suppliers are optimized. These opportunities may not be available to foreign firms.

Similar advantages are present when globally competitive, related industries operate within a nation. In such a case, opportunities are available for coordinating and sharing value chain activities. Consider, for example, the opportunities for sharing between computer hardware manufacturers and software developers. Related industries also create "pull through" opportunities, as described previously. For example, non-U.S. sales of PCs from Hewlett-Packard, Lenovo, Dell, Acer, and others have bolstered demand for software from Microsoft and other U.S. companies. Porter notes that the development of the Swiss pharmaceuticals industry can be attributed, in part, to Switzerland's large synthetic dye industry; the discovery of the therapeutic effects of dyes, in turn, led to the development of pharmaceutical companies.[24]

Firm Strategy, Structure, and Rivalry

The **nature of firm strategy, structure, and rivalry** is the final determinant of a nation's diamond. Domestic rivalry in a single national market is a powerful influence on competitive advantage. The PC industry in the United States is a good example of how a strong domestic rivalry keeps an industry dynamic and creates continual pressure to improve and innovate. The rivalry among Dell, Hewlett-Packard, and Apple forces all the players to develop new products, improve existing ones, lower costs and prices, develop new technologies, and continually improve quality and service to keep customers happy. Rivalry with foreign firms, by contrast, may lack this intensity. Domestic rivals have to fight each other not just for market share, but also for employee talent, R&D breakthroughs, and prestige in the home market. Eventually, strong domestic rivalry will push firms to seek international markets to support their expansions in scale and R&D investments, as the case of Japan amply demonstrates. In contrast, the absence of significant domestic rivalry can engender complacency in the home firms and eventually cause them to become noncompetitive in the world markets.

It is not the number of domestic rivals that is important, but rather the intensity of the competition and the quality of the competitors that make the difference. In addition, a fairly high rate of new business formation is necessary to create new competitors and prevent the older companies from becoming too comfortable with their market positions and products and services. As noted earlier in the discussion of the five forces model, new industry entrants bring new perspectives and new methods to the market. They frequently define and serve new market segments that established companies have failed to recognize.

Differences in management styles, organizational skills, and strategic perspectives also create advantages and disadvantages for firms competing in different types of industries, as do differences in the intensity of domestic rivalry. In Germany, for example, company structure and management style tend to be hierarchical. Managers tend to come from technical backgrounds and to be most successful when dealing with industries that demand highly disciplined structures, such as chemicals and precision machinery. Italian firms, in contrast, tend to look like, and be run like, small family businesses that stress customized over standardized products, niche markets, and substantial flexibility in meeting market demands.

Well known and highly esteemed in its own country, India's Tata Group participates in a variety of industries, including heavy vehicles, cars, department stores, and tea. Now the group's management team is hoping to maintain that brand image as an international strategy is implemented. Historically, Tata's Group's competitive advantage was based on scouring the globe to find the lowest-cost, highest-quality production inputs—be they raw materials or skilled labor—and then selling them in the global marketplace at a substantial profit. Not every deal works out as planned, however. In 2006, for example, the Group's Taj Hotels Resorts and Palaces subsidiary bought the Ritz-Carlton Hotel in Boston for $170 million and renamed it Taj Boston. A decade later, in 2016, a local real estate investment group, New England Development, agreed to buy Taj Boston. The price? A reported $125 million.

There are two final external variables to consider in the evaluation of national competitive advantage—chance and government.

Chance

Chance events may sometimes play a role in shaping the competitive environment. Chance events are occurrences that are beyond the control of firms, industries, and usually governments. Included in this category are such issues as wars and their aftermaths; major technological breakthroughs; sudden, dramatic shifts in a factor or an input cost, like an oil crisis; dramatic swings in exchange rates; and so on.

Chance events are important because they create major discontinuities in technologies that allow nations and firms that were not competitive to leapfrog over former competitors and become competitive—perhaps even leaders—in the changed industry. For example, the development of microelectronics allowed many Japanese firms to overtake U.S. and German firms in industries that had been based on electromechanical technologies—areas traditionally dominated by the Americans and Germans.

From a systemic perspective, the importance of chance events lies in the fact that they alter conditions in the diamond. The nation with the most favorable "diamond," however, will be the one most likely to take advantage of these chance events and convert them into competitive advantage. For example, Canadian researchers were the first to isolate insulin, but they could not convert this breakthrough into a globally competitive product. In contrast, firms in the United States and Denmark were able to make that conversion because of their respective national "diamonds."

Government

Although it is often argued that government is a major determinant of national competitive advantage, in actuality, government is not a determinant but rather an influence on determinants. Government influences determinants by virtue of its roles as a buyer of products and services and a maker of policies on labor, education, capital formation, natural resources, and product standards. It also influences determinants through its role as a regulator of commerce—for example, by telling banks and telephone companies what they can and cannot do.

By reinforcing determinants in industries where a nation has competitive advantage, government improves the competitive position of the nation's firms. Governments devise legal systems that influence competitive advantage by means of tariffs and nontariff barriers and laws requiring local content and labor. In the United States, for example, the dollar's decline over the past decade has been due, in part, to a deliberate policy to enhance U.S. export flows and stem imports. In other words, government can improve or lessen competitive advantage, but it cannot create it.

(16-4) Current Issues in Competitive Advantage

◀ **16-4** Define *hypercompetitive industry* and list the key arenas in which dynamic strategic interactions take place.

Porter's work on national competitive advantage has stimulated a great deal of further research. The Geneva-based World Economic Forum issues an annual report ranking countries in terms of their competitiveness. The Lausanne, Switzerland–based International Institute for Management Development (IMD) compiles similar rankings. In a recent study by IMD, the United States ranked first, thanks to big tech companies such as Amazon, Apple, Facebook, Google, and Netflix (see Table 16-1). Fine Swiss watches, Novartis and other pharmaceutical firms, and food-giant Nestlé are a few of the sources of Switzerland's competitiveness in the runner-up position.[25]

Hypercompetitive Industries

In a book published in the mid-1990s, Dartmouth College professor Richard D'Aveni suggested that the Porter strategy frameworks fail to adequately address the dynamics of competition in the 1990s and the new millennium.[26] D'Aveni took a different approach in analyzing issues related to competitive advantage. He noted that the business environment at the time was characterized by short product life cycles, short product design cycles, new technologies, and globalization. All of these factors and forces interacted to undermine market stability. The result? An escalation and acceleration of competitive forces.

In light of these changes, D'Aveni believed the goal of strategy was shifting from sustaining advantages to disrupting advantages. The limitation of the Porter models, D'Aveni argued, is that they are static; that is, they provide a snapshot of competition at a given point in time. Acknowledging that Hamel and Prahalad broke new ground in recognizing that few advantages are sustainable, D'Aveni aimed to build upon their work to shape "a truly dynamic approach to the creation and destruction of traditional advantages." D'Aveni used the term **hypercompetition** to describe a dynamic competitive world in which no action or advantage can be sustained for long. In such a world, D'Aveni argued, "everything changes" because of the dynamic maneuvering and strategic interactions by hypercompetitive firms such as Microsoft and Gillette.

According to D'Aveni's model, competition unfolds in a series of dynamic strategic interactions in four areas: cost and quality, timing and know-how, entry barriers, and deep pockets. Each of these arenas is "continuously destroyed and recreated by the dynamic maneuvering of hypercompetitive firms." Also, according to D'Aveni, the only source of a truly sustainable competitive

ENTREPRENEURIAL LEADERSHIP, CREATIVE THINKING, AND THE GLOBAL STARTUP

Italian Entrepreneurs Combine Fashion and Function, Part 2
Diego Della Valle, Tod's; Mario Moretti Polegato, Geox

Diego Della Valle is an entrepreneur. He developed an innovative approach to an existing product and then leveraged his family's business to manufacture and market it. By applying the basic tools and principles of modern marketing, Della Valle and his family have achieved remarkable success.

As is true with many entrepreneurs, Della Valle's idea was based on his recognition that "there had to be a better way." While visiting the United States as a young man, he spotted "these strange, very badly made shoes from Portugal" at a flea market in New York. They were marketed as a driving accessory. Diego brought a pair back to Italy and showed his father, Dorino. The elder Della Valle thought they were "horrible" and told his son to throw them away. Dorino Della Valle then reconsidered. His son says, "He changed the way we think about shoes. In the past, expensive shoes were rigid, heavy. So he had the idea of making them soft, to fit like a glove, using the best quality leather."

Today, Tod's S.p.A., the family business that was started in the 1920s, is closely identified with its iconic driving shoe. Called the Gommino, each pair requires 35 pieces of leather and 100 steps to fabricate. Integral to the design is the Leo Clamp, a decorative band across the front of the shoe. Prices start at about $350 per pair. The company's strategic focus extends to handbags as well; total annual sales are $1 billion. CEO Diego Della Valle says, "We want to guarantee our customers we're giving them the best." The CEO continues, "Pure Italian style is identifiable anywhere in the world. When I am walking in Central Park, I recognize the Italians because an Italian, even when he jogs, he's dressed perfect."

One of the company's most recent endeavors was a collaboration with five young designers whose backgrounds include art and architecture. Each designer created a limited-edition version of the Gommino. The project, called Looking at Tod's Leo, was headed by Italian architect Giulio Cappellini. One group created a shoe with leather that had been treated to give the impression it was marble; other teams incorporated unusual materials including ceramics and wood.

The need to maintain a quality image is one reason that all Tod's production—including six sewing factories—takes place in Italy. Analyst Davide Vimercati notes, "Tod's is proof that if you manage your brand consistently and you build brand equity over the years, you reach a stage where demand remains strong, even in tough times."

Della Valle is keenly aware that the world of luxury fashion is being impacted by the digital revolution. For many consumers—especially younger ones—brand loyalty is being replaced by the urge to buy "the next big thing" online. Even as Tod's embraces classic designs, Della Valle is leveraging social media. Streams of its catwalk shows attract millions of viewers.

Another Italian entrepreneur, Mario Moretti Polegato, is targeting a very different aspect of the shoe market—the mass-market footwear segment. Polegato's strategic insight was simple: Shoes with conventional rubber soles are bad for your feet! While on a business trip to Las Vegas, Polegato went for a run in the Nevada desert. When he got back to his hotel, his feet were bruised and sweaty. It occurred to him that holes in the soles would allow feet to breathe. As Polegato recalls, "I went looking for breathable soles in sports shops all around Italy, and I couldn't find them. I thought, 'Is it possible that nobody has thought of this yet?' And nobody had."

Of course, it hardly makes sense to walk around with holes in one's shoes, because they let in dirt and water. So Polegato was faced with a technological challenge: how to make a waterproof shoe with holes in the soles. Polegato persevered, and today the Geox brand's signature product is mid-price casual shoes with perforations in the soles that allow feet to "breathe." How? A special membrane based on Japanese technology makes each shoe waterproof but allows sweat to evaporate (see Exhibit 16-8. In short, "The shoe that breathes!" To keep prices competitive, much of the production is outsourced to low-wage countries such as Romania. Polegato has clearly hit upon a successful strategy: Today there are more than 30,000 Geox employees worldwide, and the company has more than 1,000 stores.

Sources: Rachel Sanderson, "Tod's Owner Diego Della Valle: 'Millennials Are Not for Everyone,'" *Financial Times* (February 15, 2018), p. 23; Stephen Doig, "If the Shoe Fits: Tod's at Salone de Mobile," *The Telegraph* (April 15, 2016), p. 9; Rachel Sanderson, "'Move over, We Will Do It,'" *Financial Times* (September 23, 2015), p. 10; Liz Alderman, "A Shoemaker That Walks But Never Runs," *The New York Times* (October 10, 2010), p. B1; Vincent Boland, "Italy's Entrepreneur with Sole," *Financial Times* (April 22, 2009), p. 17; "Employment, Italian Style," *The Wall Street Journal* (June 26, 2012), p. A14.

Exhibit 16-8 Geox's competitive advantage stems from a patented technology that allows for "breathability" in the soles of its shoes. "Respira!"

Source: george photo cm/Shutterstock.

TABLE 16-1 The World's Most Competitive Countries

Rank	Country
1.	United States
2.	Switzerland
3.	Hong Kong
4.	Sweden
5.	Singapore
6.	Norway
7.	Canada
8.	United Arab Emirates
9.	Germany
10.	Qatar

advantage is a company's ability to manage its dynamic strategic interactions with competitors by means of frequent movements and counter-movements that maintain a relative position of strength in each of the four arenas (see Table 16-2).

COST AND QUALITY Competition in the first arena, cost and quality, occurs via seven dynamic strategic interactions: price wars, quality and price positioning, "the middle path," "cover all niches," outflanking and niching, the move toward an ultimate value marketplace, and escaping from the ultimate value marketplace by restarting the cycle. D'Aveni cites the global watch industry as an example of hypercompetitive behavior in the cost and quality arena. In the 1970s, the center of the watch industry shifted from its traditional home in Switzerland to Japan as the Japanese created high-quality quartz watches that could be sold cheaply.

In the early 1980s, the merger of two Swiss companies to form Société Suisse Microélectronique et d'Horlogerie SA (SMH) was followed by a highly automated manufacturing innovation that allowed a quartz movement to be integrated into a stylish plastic case. As a result of this innovation and a strong marketing effort in support of the Swatch brand, the center of the watch industry shifted back to Switzerland. In 2013, for the company's 30th anniversary, Swatch announced the Sistem51, the world's first watch built entirely by automation. The Sistem51 line currently produces 4,000 watches per day.[28]

Today, the Swatch Group is the world's largest watchmaker (see Exhibit 16-9). The watch industry continues to be highly segmented, with prestige brands competing on reputation and exclusivity; as with many other luxury goods, higher prices are associated with higher perceived quality. In the low-cost segment, brands compete on price and value.

TIMING AND KNOW-HOW The second arena for hypercompetition is based on organizational advantages derived from timing and know-how. As described by D'Aveni, a firm that has the skills to be a "first mover" and arrive first in a market has achieved a *timing advantage*. A *know-how advantage* is the technological knowledge—or other knowledge of a new method of doing business—that allows a firm to create an entirely new product or market.[29]

D'Aveni identifies six dynamic strategic interactions that drive competition in this arena: capturing first-mover advantages, imitation and improvement by followers, creating impediments to imitation, overcoming the impediments, transformation or leapfrogging, and downstream vertical integration. As the consumer electronics industry has globalized, Sony and its competitors have exhibited hypercompetitive behavior in this second arena. Sony has an enviable history of first-mover achievements based on its know-how in audio technology: first pocket-sized transistor radio, first consumer videocassette recorder (VCR), first portable personal stereo, and first compact disc player.

Although each of these innovations literally created an entirely new market, Sony fell victim to the risks associated with being a first mover. The second dynamic strategic interaction—imitation and improvement by followers—can be seen in the successful efforts of JVC and Matsushita in the late 1970s to enter the home VCR market a few months after Sony's Betamax launch. VHS

"The three digital giants [Apple, Facebook, and Google] have signaled to Hollywood that they are serious about entering a television landscape that Netflix and Amazon shook up just a few years ago. Their arrival will make an already hypercompetitive industry even more ferocious."[27]

John Koblin, media reporter, *The New York Times*

TABLE 16-2　Dynamic Strategic Interactions in Hypercompetitive Industries

Arena	Dynamic Strategic Interaction
1. Cost and quality	1. Price wars
	2. Quality and price positioning
	3. "The middle path"
	4. "Cover all niches"
	5. Outflanking and niching
	6. The move toward an ultimate value marketplace
	7. Escaping from the ultimate value marketplace by restarting the cycle
2. Timing and know-how	1. Capturing first-mover advantages
	2. Imitation and improvement by followers
	3. Creating impediments to imitation
	4. Overcoming the impediments
	5. Transformation or leapfrogging
	6. Downstream vertical integration
3. Entry barriers	1. Building a geographic stronghold by creating and reinforcing entry barriers
	2. Targeting the product market strongholds of competitors in other countries
	3. Incumbents make short-term counter-responses to guerrilla attacks
	4. Incumbents realize they must respond fully to the invaders by making strategic responses to create new hurdles
	5. Competitors react to new hurdles
	6. Long-run counter-responses via defensive or offensive moves
	7. Competition between the incumbent and entrant is exported to entrant's home turf
	8. An unstable standoff between the competitors is established
4. Deep pockets	1. "Drive 'em out"
	2. Smaller competitors use courts or Congress to derail deep-pocketed firm
	3. Large firm thwarts antitrust suit
	4. Small firms neutralize the advantage of the deep pocket
	5. The rise of a countervailing power

technology offered longer recording times and was the dominant consumer format worldwide until the advent of the DVD era.

After years of moves and countermoves among Sony and its imitators, Sony progressed to downstream vertical integration with the 1988 purchase of CBS Records for $2 billion and then, later, the purchase of Columbia Pictures. The acquisitions, which represent the sixth dynamic strategic interaction, were intended to complement Sony's core "hardware" businesses (e.g., TVs, VCRs, and hi-fi equipment) with "software" (e.g., videocassettes and CDs). However, Matsushita quickly imitated Sony by paying $6 billion for MCA Inc. Initially, neither Sony nor Matsushita proved successful at managing their acquisitions. More recently, however, Sony Pictures Entertainment has enjoyed huge successes with the *Spider-Man* movies and *Spectre*, the 2015 James Bond film.

Sony is also facing serious challenges to its core electronics businesses. The digital revolution rendered Sony's core competencies in analog audio technology obsolete. The company must develop new know-how resources if it is to continue to lead in the Information Age. Sony has found technological leaps harder to achieve, as evidenced by the fact that Apple's iPod is now the world's best-selling portable music player. Sony was also slow to grasp the speed with which consumers would embrace flat-panel TV technology; its home entertainment and sound businesses

Exhibit 16-9 Swatch Group has been an Official Partner of the Venice Biennale International Art Exposition for the past several years. Swatch often commissions new styles from well-known artists. Nick Hayek, the son of Swatch founder Nicolas Hayek, is the company's current CEO. Nayla Hayek, Nick's sister, is the group's chairwoman. Swatch recently introduced a new mechanical watch, the Sistem51. Each watch is produced by automated machines in less than 30 seconds.
Source: Fabrice Coffrini/AFP/Getty Images.

have been losing money for years. In fact, a hedge fund manager has called for top management to spin off a portion of the entertainment business to boost profitability.[30]

Hypercompetition is showing up in other ways, too. For example, after 20 years on the market, sales of Sony's Handycam camcorders started to decline. Meanwhile, an inexpensive device called the Flip from startup Pure Digital Technologies quickly became a best seller after its launch in 2006. Belatedly, Sony rolled out the Webbie Internet-ready camcorder. During the product's development, the U.S.-based marketing director for the design team asked Tokyo for permission to make the camcorder available in orange and purple—colors that the team thought would appeal to American consumers.[31] Today, of course, most consumers use their smartphones to capture and share video images, rendering stand-alone camcorder devices unnecessary.

ENTRY BARRIERS Industries in which barriers to entry have been built up constitute the third arena in which hypercompetitive behavior is exhibited. As described earlier in the chapter, these barriers may include economies of scale, product differentiation, capital investments, switching costs, access to distribution channels, cost advantages other than scale, and government policies. D'Aveni describes how aggressive competitors erode these traditional entry barriers via eight strategic interactions. For example, a cornerstone of Dell's global success in the PC industry is a direct-sales approach that bypasses dealers and other distribution channels.

The first dynamic strategic interaction arises as a company builds a geographic "stronghold" by creating and reinforcing barriers. After securing a market—especially the home-country market—competitors begin to seek markets outside their initial stronghold. Thus, the second dynamic strategic interaction takes place when companies target the product market strongholds of competitors in other countries. Honda's geographic expansion outside Japan with motorcycles and automobiles—a series of forays utilizing guerrilla tactics—is a case in point. The third dynamic strategic interaction develops when incumbents make short-term counter-responses to the guerrilla attacks. Strong incumbents may try to turn back the invader with price wars, factory investment, or product introductions; alternatively, they may adopt a wait-and-see attitude before responding. In the case of both Harley-Davidson and the Detroit-based U.S. auto industry, management originally underestimated and rationalized away the full potential of the threat from Honda and other Japanese companies. Realizing that its company was a weak incumbent, Harley-Davidson management then had little choice but to appeal for government protection from the new competitors. The resulting "breathing room" allowed Harley to put its house in order. Similarly, the U.S. government heeded Detroit's pleas for relief and imposed tariffs and quotas on Japanese auto imports. This move gave the Big Three time to develop higher-quality, fuel-efficient models to offer U.S. consumers.

The fourth dynamic strategic interaction occurs when the incumbent realizes it must respond fully to the invader by making strategic responses to create new hurdles. U.S. automakers, for example, waged a PR campaign urging U.S. citizens to "Buy American." The fifth dynamic strategic interaction takes place when competitors react to these new hurdles. In an effort to circumvent import quotas as well as co-opt the "Buy American" campaign, the Japanese automakers built plants in the United States. The sixth dynamic strategic interaction consists of long-run counter-responses to the attack via defensive or offensive moves. GM's 1990 introduction of Saturn is a good illustration of a well-formulated and -executed defensive move. As the second decade of the twenty-first century continues, GM is launching another defensive move: In an effort to defend its Cadillac nameplate from Lexus, Acura, and Infiniti, GM is developing a global strategy for Cadillac.

Competition in the third arena may then continue to escalate; in the seventh dynamic strategic interaction, competition between the incumbent and the entrant is exported to the entrant's home turf. President Clinton's threat of trade sanctions against Japanese automakers in 1995 was intended to send a message that Japan needed to open its auto market. In 1997, GM intensified its assault on Japan by exporting right-hand-drive Saturns to the Japanese market. The eighth and final dynamic strategic interaction in this arena consists of an unstable standoff between the competitors. Over time, the stronghold erodes as entry barriers are overcome, leading competitors to the fourth arena.

As the preceding discussion shows, the irony and paradox of the hypercompetition framework is that to achieve a sustainable advantage, companies must seek a series of *unsustainable* advantages! In this sense, the model proposed by D'Aveni is in agreement with that offered by the late Peter Drucker, who long counseled that the roles of marketing are innovation and the creation of new markets. Innovation begins with abandonment of the old and obsolete. Sumantra Ghoshal and Christopher Bartlett make a similar point in *The Individualized Corporation*:

> Managers are forced to refocus their attention from a preoccupation with defining defensible product-market positions to a newly awakened interest in how to develop the organizational capability to sense and respond rapidly and flexibly to change. . . . Managers worldwide have begun to focus less on the task of forecasting and planning for the future and more on the challenge of being highly sensitive to emerging changes. Their broad objective is to create an organization that is constantly experimenting with appropriate responses, then is able to quickly diffuse the information and knowledge gained so it can be leveraged by the entire organization. The age of strategic planning is fast evolving into the era of organizational learning.[32]

Likewise, D'Aveni urges managers to reconsider and reevaluate the use of old strategic tools and maxims. Overcommitment to a given strategy or course of action carries dangers, he warns, because the flexible, unpredictable player may have an advantage over the inflexible, committed opponent. D'Aveni notes that, in hypercompetition, pursuit of generic strategies results in short-term advantage, at best. The winning companies are the ones that successfully move up the ladder of escalating competition, rather than the ones that lock into a fixed position. D'Aveni is also critical of the five forces model. The best entry barrier, he argues, is one that maintains the initiative, instead of mounting a defensive attempt to exclude new entrants.

The Flagship Firm: The Business Network with Five Partners

According to Professors Alan Rugman and Joseph D'Cruz, Porter's model is too simplistic given the complexity of today's global environment.[33] To remedy what they see as that model's shortcomings, Rugman and D'Cruz have developed an alternative framework based on business networks that they call the **flagship model**. Japanese vertical *keiretsu* and Korean *chaebol* have succeeded, Rugman and D'Cruz argue, by adopting strategies that are mutually reinforcing within a business system and by fostering a collective long-term outlook among partners in the system. Moreover, the authors note, "long-term competitiveness in global industries is less a matter of rivalry between firms and more a question of competition between business systems."

A major difference between the flagship model and Porter's model is that the latter is based on the notion of corporate individualism and individual business transactions. For example, as discussed previously, Microsoft's tremendous supplier power allows it to dictate to, and even prosper at the expense of, the computer manufacturers it supplies with operating systems and applications. The flagship model, by contrast, is evident in the strategies of Ford, Volkswagen, and other global automakers; Sweden's IKEA and Italy's Benetton are additional examples.

Luciano Benetton is one of four siblings who founded the Italian fashion company that bears the family's name. Luciano recently stepped down as chairman of the Benetton Group and turned over control of the company to son Alessandro. The change comes as Benetton faces increased competition from fleet-footed global rivals such as Sweden's Hennes & Mauritz (H&M) and Spain's Zara. Some industry observers note that Benetton's business model, which involves partnerships with regional sales agents, will need to be adjusted to reflect the business environments in key emerging markets such as China and India (see Exhibit 16-10).

In the model developed by Rugman and D'Cruz, the flagship firm is at the center of a collection of five partners; together, they form a business system that consists of two types of relationships. The flagship firm provides the leadership, vision, and resources to "lead the network in a successful global strategy." *Key suppliers* perform some value-creating activities, such as manufacturing of critical components, better than the flagship. Together with the flagship firm, these suppliers form a network relationship, with a sharing of strategies, resources, and responsibility for the success of the network. Other suppliers, in contrast, are kept at "arm's length."

Likewise, the flagship has network relationships with *key customers* and more traditional, arm's-length commercial relationships with *key consumers*. In the case of Volkswagen, for example, dealers are its key customers while individual car buyers are its key consumers; in other words, strictly speaking, Volkswagen sells to dealers, and dealers sell to consumers. Similarly, Benetton's key customers are its retail outlets while the individual clothes shopper is the key consumer.

Selected competitors are companies with which the flagship develops alliances, such as those described at the end of Chapter 9. The fifth partner is the *non-business infrastructure* (NBI), composed of universities, governments, trade unions, and other entities that can supply the network with intangible inputs such as intellectual property and technology. In the flagship model, flagship firms often play a role in the development of a country's industrial policy.

Benetton's success in the global fashion industry illustrates the flagship model. Benetton is the world's largest purchaser of wool, and its centralized buying enables the company to reap scale economies. The core activities of cutting and dyeing are retained in-house, and Benetton has made substantial investments in computer-assisted design and manufacturing. However, Benetton is linked to approximately 400 subcontractors that produce finished garments in exclusive supply relationships with the company. In turn, a network of 80 agents who find investors, train managers, and assist with merchandising link the subcontractors to the 6,000 Benetton retail shops. As Rugman and D'Cruz note, "Benetton is organized to reward cooperation and relationship building and the company's structure has been created to capitalize on the benefits of long-term relationships."

Exhibit 16-10 The Benetton Group embodies many of the qualities of entrepreneurial enterprises that thrive in northern Italy's Veneto region.
Source: Agence Opale/Alamy Stock Photo.

Blue Ocean Strategy

One of the most important recent strategy frameworks was proposed by Professors Renée Mauborgne and Kim Chan. In books and articles devoted to the "Blue Ocean Strategy," the authors define two categories of competitive spaces: red oceans and blue oceans. Red oceans are, in essence, existing markets or industries with well-defined boundaries where the "rules" are understood by all players. By contrast, blue oceans are markets or industries that do not currently exist.[34]

Mauborgne and Chan advise company executives to avoid getting bloodied in a "red ocean" of cost cutting and imitation. A far better choice, they assert, is for a company to create a new space, a blue ocean of "uncontested market space," where hypercompetitive forces don't operate. The authors cite eBay as one example: Founder Pierre Omidyar created a completely new industry. Cirque du Soleil is another example; in this instance, however, founder Guy Laliberté innovated within the boundaries of an existing industry—the circus. Likewise, while Sony and Microsoft were ramping up speed and power with their PlayStation and Xbox gaming systems, Nintendo created a blue ocean with the low-tech, lower-priced Wii console and family-oriented games. Launched in 2006, Wii emphasized "fun, magic, and joy" rather than processing power.[35]

Additional Research on Competitive Advantage

Other researchers have challenged Porter's thesis that a firm's home-base country is the main source of core competencies and innovation. For example, Indiana University Professor Alan Rugman has argued that the success of companies based in small economies such as Canada and New Zealand stems from the "diamonds" found in a particular set or combination of home and related countries. For example, a company based in an EU nation may rely on the national "diamond" of one of the 27 (or 26, post-Brexit) other EU members. Similarly, one impact of the North American Free Trade Agreement (NAFTA) on Canadian firms is to make the U.S. "diamond" relevant to competency creation. Rugman argues that, in such cases, the distinction between the home nation and the host nation becomes blurred. He proposes that Canadian managers must look to a "double-diamond" and assess the attributes of both Canada and the United States when formulating corporate strategy.[36] In other words, for smaller countries, the nation is not the relevant unit of analysis in formulating strategy. Rather, corporate strategists must look beyond the nation to the region or to sets of closely linked countries.

Other critics have argued that Porter generalized inappropriately from the American experience, while confusing industry-level competition with trade at the national level. In the *Journal of Management Studies*, Howard Davies and Paul Ellis assert that nations can, in fact, achieve sustained prosperity without becoming innovation driven; these authors also note the absence of strong diamonds in the home bases of many global industries.[37]

As for Michael Porter, his views on corporate strategy and competitive advantage have evolved during the last three decades. In a 1997 interview with the *Financial Times*, he emphasized the difference between operational efficiency and corporate strategy. The former, in Porter's view, concerns improvement via time-based competition or total quality management; the latter entails "making choices." Porter explains, "'Choice' arises from doing things differently from the rival. And strategy is about trade-offs, where you decide to do this and not that. Strategy is the deliberate choice not to respond to some customers, or choosing which customer needs you are going to respond to." Porter is not convinced of the validity of competitive advantage models based on core competency or hypercompetitive industries. Instead, he suggests, a nation has an advantage when it is home to globally competitive companies in business sectors that are related and supporting industries.

In 2008, Porter revisited his five forces model in an article in the *Harvard Business Review*. Despite all the changes and challenges brought about in the world's markets by the global financial crisis, Porter believes his model is as relevant and robust as ever. As he told the *Financial Times* in 2011, the five forces are

> more and more and more fundamentally important and visible, because a lot of the barriers and the distortions that would blunt or mitigate these distortions and the need for strategy and competitive advantage . . . have been swept away.

The factors contributing to this, Porter says, are globalization, increased transparency of information, and the reduction in trade barriers.[38]

Summary

In this chapter, we focused on the factors that help industries and countries achieve *competitive advantage*. According to Porter's *five forces model*, industry competition is a function of the threat of new entrants, the threat of substitutes, the bargaining power of suppliers and buyers, and the rivalry among existing competitors. Managers can use Porter's *generic strategies* model to conceptualize possible sources of competitive advantage. A company can pursue broad market strategies of *cost leadership* and *differentiation* or the more targeted approaches of *cost focus* and *focused differentiation*. Rugman and D'Cruz have developed a framework known as the *flagship model* to explain how networked business systems have achieved success in global industries. In regard to pursuing competitive advantage, Hamel and Prahalad have proposed an alternative framework that grows out of a firm's *strategic intent* and use of competitive innovation. A firm can build *layers of advantage*, search for *loose bricks* in a competitor's defensive walls, *change the rules of engagement*, or *collaborate with competitors* and utilize their technology and know-how.

Today, *global competition* is a reality in many industry sectors. Thus, competitive analysis must be carried out on a global scale. Global marketers, however, must also have an understanding of national sources of competitive advantage. Porter has described four determinants of *national advantage*. *Factor conditions* include human, physical, knowledge, capital, and infrastructure resources. *Demand conditions* include the composition, size, and growth pattern of home demand. The rate of home-market growth and the means by which a nation's products are pulled into foreign markets also affect demand conditions. The final two determinants are the presence of *related and supporting industries* and the *nature of firm strategy, structure, and rivalry*. Porter notes that chance and government actions also influence a nation's competitive advantage. Porter's work has been the catalyst for promising new research into strategy issues, including D'Aveni's work on *hypercompetition*, Rugman's *double-diamond framework* for national competitive advantage, and Mauborgne and Chan's *blue ocean* framework.

Discussion Questions

16-1. Outline Porter's five forces model of industry competition. How are the various barriers to entry relevant to global marketing?

16-2. With competition increasing among institutions of higher learning, how should a university utilize the layers of advantage strategy?

16-3. What are the benefits and downsides of global competition?

16-4. How can a nation achieve competitive advantage?

16-5. According to current research on competitive advantage, what are some of the shortcomings of Porter's model?

16-6. What is the relationship between the "Blue Ocean Strategy" framework and the notion of competitive advantages?

CASE 16-1   *(Continued refer to page 523)*

IKEA

IKEA's Business Model

The store exteriors are painted bright blue and yellow, Sweden's national colors. Shoppers view furniture on the main floor in scores of realistic-looking settings arranged throughout the cavernous warehouses. At IKEA, shopping is a self-service activity. Store layouts ensure that visitors have ample opportunity to drop grab-and-go impulse purchases into their $.99 blue Frakta shopping bags as they browse each showroom and write down the names of desired items.

The lower level of a typical IKEA store contains a restaurant, a housewares department, a grocery store called the Swede Shop, a supervised play area for children, and a baby care room. Finally, after shoppers have paid for their purchases on the lower level, they pick up their furniture and drive away.

Most furniture is in "flat pack" kit form; one of the cornerstones of IKEA's low-cost strategy is having customers take their purchases home in their own vehicles and assemble the furniture themselves. Kamprad arrived at this crucial insight early in his career after watching an employee at the original Almhult store take the legs off a table and tuck them under the tabletop so the unit would be easier to transport.

Over the years, IKEA has become integrated into global consumer culture. Kamprad's insight about the advantages of selling knocked-down furniture has given rise to something called the "Ikea effect." Writing in the *Journal of Consumer Psychology*, a team of researchers showed that successfully completing a task such as assembling IKEA furniture leads to perceptions of high value by the consumer. French fashion house Balenciaga even paid IKEA the ultimate compliment by recreating the Frakta bag as a luxury item. Balenciaga's blue "Arena Extra-Large Shopper" carries a price tag of $2,145!

IKEA's unconventional approach to the furniture business has enabled it to rack up impressive growth in an industry in which overall sales have been flat. Sourcing furniture from a network of more than 1,600 suppliers in 55 countries helps the company maintain its low-cost, high-quality position. During the 1990s, IKEA expanded into Central and Eastern Europe. Because consumers in those regions had relatively little purchasing power, the stores offered a smaller selection of goods; some furniture was designed specifically for the cramped living styles typical in former Soviet bloc countries.

Europe

Throughout Europe, IKEA benefits from the perception that Sweden is a source of high-quality products and efficient service. Currently, Germany and the United Kingdom are IKEA's top two markets; Germany is the company's largest market, with 50 stores. The United Kingdom represents IKEA's fastest-growing market in Europe. Although Brits initially viewed the company's less-is-more approach as cold and "too Scandinavian," they were eventually won over. IKEA currently has 18 stores in the United Kingdom, and plans call for opening more in this decade. As Allan Young, creative director of London's St. Luke's advertising agency, noted, "IKEA is anticonventional. It does what it shouldn't do. That's the overall theme for all IKEA ads: liberation from tradition."

Japan

In 2005, IKEA opened two stores near Tokyo; more stores are on the way as the company expands in Asia. IKEA's first attempt to develop the Japanese market in the mid-1970s resulted in failure. Why? As Tommy Kullberg, former chief executive of IKEA Japan, explained, "In 1974, the Japanese market from a retail point of view was closed. Also, from the Japanese point of view, I do not think they were ready for IKEA, with our way of doing things, with flat packages and asking the consumers to put things together and so on." However, demographic and economic trends are much different today. After years of recession, consumers are seeking alternatives to paying high prices for quality goods. Also, IKEA's core customer segment—post–baby boomers in their thirties—grew nearly 10 percent between 2000 and 2010. In Japan, IKEA will offer home delivery and an assembly service option.

India and China

India presents special challenges for IKEA. Although a 2012 law allows 100 percent foreign ownership of retail operations, the regulations also mandate that approximately one-third of foreign retail sales revenues must come from items sourced locally. That target must be reached within five years after a company opens its first store. Finding locally made products has proved to be a difficult task; Ikea's procurement teams have found chemical contaminants in various housewares, ranging from table-tops to dinner plates.

Some global companies, including Carrefour and Walmart, have abandoned plans to operate retail stores in India. IKEA opened its first store in 2018; that means the company has until 2023 to comply with the sourcing regulations. The company's managers understand that they will have to find ways to offer shoppers in India even lower prices

on merchandise if they are to attract masses of customers. If the India launch is successful, it may pave the way for additional store openings in low-income areas such as sub-Saharan Africa.

In keeping with IKEA's standardized global retail concept, the Chinese stores are spacious and clean. All locations feature restaurants where visitors can enjoy Swedish meatballs and other meal items. In some cases, the restaurants have also become a favorite meeting place for dating clubs that allow older Chinese to socialize.

> "The ideal IKEA leader is not the great flamboyant personalities but leaders that fit into the IKEA down-to-earth culture of humbleness."[39]
>
> Steen Kanter, former IKEA executive

Leadership Challenges and the Drive for Sustainability

The first two decades of the twenty-first century have been difficult for IKEA. The euro's strength dampened financial results, as did the economic downturn in Central Europe. The company faces increasing competition from hypermarkets, "do-it-yourself" home-improvement chains such as Lowe's and Wickes, and supermarkets that are expanding into home furnishings. The growing popularity of e-commerce is another threat. Across a variety of retail sectors, consumer behavior is also changing.

During his tenure as IKEA's CEO from 1999 to 2009, Anders Dahlvig stressed three areas for improvement: product assortment, customer service, and product availability. By the time Mikael Ohlsson was named CEO in 2009, he had spent several years running the company's operations in Canada. It was there that he pioneered the idea of "home visits," during which company representatives stop by customer's homes to see how furniture and furnishings fit into their lives. Ohlsson also stressed sustainability and safe working conditions at factories in Bangladesh and elsewhere.

One takeaway: a realization that a straight product extension strategy, while economical, didn't always work. For example, Ohlsson noticed that IKEA's sheets and mattresses didn't fit beds in North America. Likewise, European-style drinking glasses were deemed too small; shoppers bought vases instead and used them as glasses! That's why, today, between 20 and 30 percent of IKEA's products are adapted to local market preferences.

Peter Agnefjäll, the company's chief executive from 2013 to 2017, retreated from his predecessor's goal of opening as many as 25 new stores per year. Agnefjäll continued the company's sustainability initiatives, including ideas such as leasing kitchens to consumers. As Steve Howard, chief sustainability officer, has said, "We want a smarter consumption, and maybe people are less attached to ownership." Management has set a revenue target of €50 billion by 2020; reaching that target will be a key goal for new CEO Jesper Brodin.

One challenge for Brodin: Getting potential customers who live in urban areas to drive to IKEA stores, which are typically located away from city centers. Top management must also deal with the trend among Millennial and Gen Z customers to shun car ownership. As an experiment, the company opened a pop-up store in central Stockholm that features only kitchens. Customers can make appointments for design consultations. Consumer response has been very positive, and the program has been extended to include a bedroom pop-up in Madrid.

Some observers question IKEA's sustainability bona fides, noting that its low-priced furniture contributes to a "throw it away" mentality when a piece breaks. Critics also point out that requiring customers to drive long distances to and from the stores can contribute to environmental pollution. Howard responds to such criticism by noting, "People have needs to be met—they need wardrobes, sofas, kitchens. The most important thing is to meet those needs in the most sustainable way possible." For example, in France, one factory sources half its wood from recycled IKEA products that are ground up and repurposed as bookshelves, tables, and other new products.

Discussion Questions

16-7. Review the characteristics of global and transnational companies described in Chapter 1. Based on your reading of the case, would IKEA be described as a global firm or a transnational firm?

16-8. In Chapter 11, it was noted that managers of IKEA stores have a great deal of discretion when it comes to setting prices. In terms of the ethnocentric/polycentric/regiocentric/geocentric (EPRG) framework, which management orientation is in evidence at IKEA?

16-9. What does it mean to say that, in terms of Porter's generic strategies, IKEA pursues a strategy of "cost focus"?

Sources: Richard Milne, "What Will Ikea Build Next?" [Cover story], *Financial Times Magazine* (February 3–4, 2018), pp. 12–15+; Preetika Rana, "Ikea's India Bet Hits Thicket of Rules," *The Wall Street Journal* (February 24, 2016), pp. A1, A14; Richard Milne, "Ikea Store Planners Think outside the Big Box," *Financial Times* (December 5–6, 2015), p. 14; Richard Milne, "Ikea Looks to Be Sitting Comfortably Again," *Financial Times* (September 11, 2015), p. 14; Richard Milne, "Against the Grain," *Financial Times* (November 14, 2012), p. 7; Richard Milne, "IKEA Eyes Kitchen Recycling in Green Push," *Financial Times* (October 23, 2012), p. 19; Mei Fong, "IKEA Hits Home in China," *The Wall Street Journal* (March 3, 2006), pp. B1, B4; Richard Tomkins, "How IKEA Has Managed to Treat Us Mean and Keep Us Keen," *Financial Times* (January 14–15, 2006), p. 7; Kerry Capell, "IKEA: How the Swedish Retailer Became a Global Cult Brand," *BusinessWeek* (November 14, 2005), pp. 96–106; Theresa Howard, "IKEA Builds on Furnishings Success," *USA Today* (December 29, 2004), p. 3B; Mariko Sanchanta, "IKEA's Second Try at Japan's Flat-Pack Fans," *Financial Times* (March 4, 2004), p. 11; Paula M. Miller, "IKEA with Chinese Characteristics," *The China Business Review* (July–August, 2004), pp. 36–38; Christopher Brown-Humes, "An Empire Built on a Flat Pack," *Financial Times* (November 24, 2003), p. 8.

CASE 16-2
"Everything Is Awesome, Everything Is Cool" at LEGO

When Jørgen Vig Knudstorp stepped down as the CEO of LEGO in January 2017, he was widely regarded as one of the world's best corporate leaders. After becoming CEO in 2004, Knudstorp had moved quickly to turn around the fortunes of the maker of the iconic children's play blocks.

The LEGO Company is a $5 billion global business built out of the humblest of materials: interlocking plastic toy bricks. From its base in Billund, Denmark, the family-owned LEGO empire extends around the world and has at times included theme parks, clothing, and computer-controlled toys. Each year, the company produces approximately 15 billion molded plastic blocks as well as tiny human figures to populate towns and operate gizmos that spring from the imaginations of young people (see Exhibit 16-11). LEGO products, which are especially popular with boys, are available in more than 130 countries; in the key North American market, the company's overall share of the construction-toy market has been as high as 85 percent.

Kjeld Kirk Kristiansen, the grandson of the company's founder as well as the main shareholder, served as CEO from 1979 until 2004. Kristiansen says that LEGO products stand for "exuberance, spontaneity, self-expression, concern for others, and innovation." (The company's name comes from the Danish phrase *leg godt*, which translates as "play well.") Kristiansen also attributes his company's success to the esteem the brand enjoys among parents. "Parents consider LEGO not as just a toy company but as providing products that help learning and developing new skills," he says.

LEGO has always been an innovator. For example, Mybots was a $70 toy set that included blocks with computer chips embedded to provide lights and sound. A $200 Mindstorms Robotics Invention System allows users to build computer-controlled creatures. To further leverage the LEGO brand, the company also formed alliances with Walt Disney Company and Lucasfilms, creator of the popular *Star Wars* series. For several years, sales of licensed merchandise relating to the popular *Harry Potter* and *Star Wars* movie franchises sold extremely well.

The company has not always enjoyed nonstop success. After a disappointing Christmas 2003 season, LEGO was left with millions of dollars' worth of unsold goods. The difficult retail situation was compounded by the dollar's weakness relative to the Danish krone; LEGO posted a record loss of $166 million for 2003. The company then unveiled a number of new initiatives aimed at restoring profitability. A new line, Quattro, consisting of large, soft bricks, was targeted directly at the preschool market. Clikits was a line of pastel-colored bricks targeted at young girls who want to create jewelry.

In 2004, after LEGO had posted several years of losses, Jørgen Vig Knudstorp succeeded Kristiansen as LEGO's chief executive. Knudstorp convened a task force consisting of company executives and outside consultants to review the company's operations and business model. The task force discovered that LEGO's sources of competitive advantage—creativity, innovation, and superior quality—were also sources of weakness. The company had become overly complex, with 12,500 stock-keeping units (SKUs), a palette of 100 different block colors, and 11,000 suppliers.

Exhibit 16-11
Source: Amy Sancetta/Associated Press.

Acknowledging that the company's forays into theme parks, children's clothing, and software games had been the wrong strategy, Knudstorp launched a restructuring initiative known as "Shared Vision." Within a few months, cross-functional teams collaborated to reduce the number of SKUs to 6,500; the number of color options was slashed by 50 percent. Production was outsourced to a Singaporean company with production facilities in Mexico and the Czech Republic, resulting in the elimination of more than 2,000 jobs. The theme parks and computer games businesses were sold.

Knudstorp also decided to focus on the company's retail customers, including Toys 'R' Us, Metro, Karstadt, and Galeria. After surveying these customers, Knudstorp and his task force learned that the customers do not require express product deliveries. This insight prompted a change to once-weekly deliveries of orders that are placed in advance. The result: improved customer service and lower costs. In the three-year period from 2005 to 2008, on-time deliveries increased by 62 percent to 92 percent. LEGO also logged improvements in other key performance indicators such as package quality and quantity. In 2008, LEGO was awarded the European Supply Chain Excellence Award in the category "Logistics and Fulfillment."

In terms of competitive advantage, Knudstorp has noted, "A bucket of bricks is the core of the core." Still, he adds, "There's more to being a global successful company than being able to build a plastic brick." Evidence of the company's magic touch can be found in LEGO Friends, a new theme targeting girls that has sold extremely well. One advantage of the new line: Because it was developed in-house, LEGO does not have to pay licensing fees.

Moreover, the company's forays into video games such as *Lego Batman 2*, *The Lego Ideas Book* and other children's books, and TV series on the Cartoon Network have proved successful as well. *The Lego Movie*, released in 2014, was a global blockbuster with ticket sales of nearly $500 million.

By 2015, under Knudstorp's capable leadership, LEGO ranked as the world's number 1 toymaker, ahead of industry heavyweights Mattel and Hasbro. In less than a decade, LEGO's revenues had tripled, and its net profit soared. Knudstorp credits his brief stint as a trainee kindergarten teacher with helping him hone his leadership skills. One key decision as the new CEO: listening to a marketing executive who advocated focusing on "back-to-basics" toys such as fire engines and police stations.

In 2015, after a three-year development process, Knudstorp launched *Lego Dimensions*. This product represented LEGO's first attempt to target a game category known as "toys-to-life." The $100 game kit can be used in conjunction with the Sony PlayStation, Microsoft Xbox, or Nintendo Wii consoles. The game also comes with several hundred pieces for building a controller, plus Batman, Gandalf, and Wyldstyle. The game incorporates *Doctor Who*, *Back to the Future*, and a variety of other popular TV and motion picture brands.

Going forward, Knudstorp will be chairman of LEGO and head up a new entity, LEGO Brand Group. According to Knudstorp, "The LEGO Brand Group will focus on things that are additive and are not being done today." One challenge facing Bali Padda, the new CEO, is to sustain the explosive pace of sales and earnings growth achieved by his predecessor.

Discussion Questions

16-10. Jørgen Vig Knudstorp became CEO of LEGO in 2004. Assess the key strategic decisions he made, including outsourcing and divesting the theme parks.

16-11. LEGO's movie-themed products, keyed to popular film franchises such as *Harry Potter*, *Lord of the Rings*, and *Spider-Man*, include detailed construction plans. Do you think this is the right strategy?

16-12. Using Porter's generic strategies framework, assess LEGO in terms of the company's pursuit of competitive advantage.

16-13. What risk, if any, is posed by LEGO's movement into multi-media categories such as video games and television?

Sources: Richard Milne, "LEGO Quick off the Blocks to Avoid Stock Shortfalls," *Financial Times* (December 23, 2016), p. 19; Richard Milne, "LEGO Builds New Dimension with Digital Vision," *Financial Times* (September 28, 2015), p. 12; Richard Milne, "LEGO's Saviour Builds on Success," *Financial Times* (September 6-7, 2015), p. 7; Clemens Bomsdorf, "Lego Building up Its Mexico Plant," *The Wall Street Journal* (June 21–22, 2014), p. B4; Jens Hansegard, "What It Takes to Build a Lego Hobbit (and Gollum and More)," *The Wall Street Journal* (December 20, 2012), p. D1; Matt Richtel and Jesse McKinley, "Has Lego Sold Out?" *The New York Times* (December 23, 2012), p. SR4; Carlos Cordon, Ralf Seifert, and Edwin Wellian, "Case Study: LEGO," *Financial Times* (November 24, 2010), p. 10; Kim Hjelmgaard, "Lego, Refocusing on Bricks, Builds an Image," *The Wall Street Journal* (December 24, 2009), p. B1; David Robertson and Per Hjuler, "Innovating a Turnaround at LEGO," *Harvard Business Review* (September 2009), pp. 20-27; John Tagliabue, "Taking Their Blocks and Playing Toymaker Elsewhere," *The New York Times* (November 20, 2006), p. A4; Lauren Foster and David Ibison, "Spike the Robot Helps LEGO Rebuild Strategy," *Financial Times* (June 22, 2006), p. 18; Ian Austen, "Building a Legal Case, Block by Block," *The New York Times* (February 2, 2005), p. C6; Joseph Pereira and Christopher J. Chipello, "Battle of the Block Makers," *The Wall Street Journal* (February 4, 2004), pp. B1, B4; Clare MacCarthy, "Deputy Chief Sacked as LEGO Tries to Rebuild," *Financial Times* (January 9, 2004), p. 19; Majken Schultz and Mary Jo Hatch, "The Cycles of Corporate Branding: The Case of the LEGO Company," *California Management Review* 46, no. 1 (Fall 2003), pp. 6–26; Meg Carter, "Building Blocks of Success," *Financial Times* (October 30, 2003), p. 8.

Notes

[1] Michael E. Porter, *Competitive Strategy* (New York, NY: Free Press, 1980), pp. 7–33.

[2] Anna Nicolaou and Scheherazade Deneshkkhu, "FT Big Read: Consumer Goods," *Financial Times* (October 14–15, 2017), p. 9.

[3] Melissa Webster, "Green Day Changes Its Stance on Walmart and Censorship," *Huffington Post* (December 6, 2017). Accessed April 1, 2018. https://www.huffingtonpost.com/melissa-webster/green-day-walmart-censorship_b_1844276.html.

[4] Melanie Warner, "Its Wish, Their Command," *The New York Times* (March 3, 2006), p. C1.

[5] Olga Kharif, Peter Burrows, and Cliff Edwards, "Windows and Intel's Digital Divide," *BusinessWeek* (February 23, 2009), p. 58.

[6] Regina Fazio Maruca, "The Right Way to Go Global: An Interview with Whirlpool CEO David Whitwam," *Harvard Business Review* 72, no. 2 (March–April 1994), p. 135.

[7] Michael E. Porter, *Competitive Advantage: Creating and Sustaining Superior Performance* (New York, NY: Free Press, 1985), p. 12.

[8] Daniel Michaels, "No, the CEO Isn't Sir Richard Branson," *The Wall Street Journal* (July 30, 2007), pp. B1, B3.

[9] Michael E. Porter, *The Competitive Advantage of Nations* (New York, NY: Free Press, 1990), p. 39.

[10] Cecilie Rohwedder and David Kesmodel, "Aldi Looks to U.S. for Growth," *The Wall Street Journal* (January 13, 2009), p. B1. For an excellent discussion of Aldi's corporate history, see Michael J. Silverstein, *Treasure Hunt: Inside the Mind of the New Consumer* (New York, NY: Portfolio, 2006), pp. 66–75.

[11] Jeffrey A. Trachtenberg, "Home Economics: IKEA Furniture Chain Pleases with Its Prices, Not with Its Service," *The Wall Street Journal* (September 17, 1991), pp. A1, A5.

[12]Michael E. Porter, *Competitive Advantage: Creating and Sustaining Superior Performance* (New York, NY: Free Press, 1985), p. 158.

[13]Gary Hamel and C. K. Prahalad, "Strategic Intent," *Harvard Business Review* 67, no. 3 (May–June 1989), pp. 63–76. See also Hamel and Prahalad, "The Core Competence of the Corporation," *Harvard Business Review* 68, no. 3 (May–June 1990), pp. 79–93.

[14]Robert L. Rose and Masayoshi Kanabayashi, "Komatsu Throttles Back on Construction Equipment," *The Wall Street Journal* (May 13, 1992), p. B4.

[15]James Lardner, *Fast Forward: Hollywood, the Japanese, and the VCR Wars* (New York, NY: New American Library, 1987), p. 135.

[16]Chris Nuttal, Robin Kwong, and Maija Palmer, "Intel Wants to Get a Grip on Mobile Market," *Financial Times* (May 6, 2011), p. 17.

[17]Gary Hamel and C. K. Prahalad, "Strategic Intent," *Harvard Business Review* 67, no. 3 (May–June 1989), p. 69.

[18]G. Pascal Zachary, "Color Printer Gives Tektronix Jump on Canon," *The Wall Street Journal* (June 14, 1991), p. B1.

[19]Hamel and Prahalad have continued to refine and develop the concept of strategic intent since it was first introduced in their groundbreaking 1989 article. During the 1990s, the authors outlined five broad categories of resource leverage that managers can use to achieve their aspirations: concentrating resources on strategic goals via convergence and focus; accumulating resources more efficiently via extracting and borrowing; complementing one resource with another by blending and balancing; conserving resources by recycling, co-opting, and shielding; and rapid recovery of resources in the marketplace. Gary Hamel and C. K. Prahalad, "Strategy as Stretch and Leverage," *Harvard Business Review* 71, no. 2 (March–April 1993), pp. 75–84.

[20]This section draws heavily on Chapter 3, "Determinants of National Competitive Advantage," and Chapter 4, "The Dynamics of National Advantage," in Porter, *The Competitive Advantage of Nations*, 1990. For an extended country analysis based on Porter's framework, see Michael Enright, Antonio Francés, and Edith Scott Assavedra, *Venezuela: The Challenge of Competitiveness* (New York, NY: St. Martin's Press, 1996).

[21]Michael Y. Yoshino and U. Srinivasa Rangan, *Strategic Alliances: An Entrepreneurial Approach to Globalization* (Boston, MA: Harvard Business School Press, 1995), p. 56.

[22]See Joseph Kahn, "Cleaning up: P&G Viewed China as a National Market and Is Conquering It," *The Wall Street Journal* (September 12, 1995), pp. A1, A6.

[23]Michael E. Porter, *The Competitive Advantage of Nations* (New York, NY: Free Press, 1990).

[24]Michael E. Porter, *The Competitive Advantage of Nations* (New York, NY: Free Press, 1990), p. 324.

[25]Susan Adams, "The World's Most Competitive Countries," *Forbes* (May 30, 2013), p. 18.

[26]Richard D'Aveni, *Hypercompetition: Managing the Dynamics of Strategic Maneuvering* (New York, NY: Free Press, 1994), p. 71.

[27]John Koblin, "Tech Firms Make Push toward TV," *The New York Times* (August 21, 2017), p. B1.

[28]Robin Swithinbank, "Manufactured, Assembled and Decorated—in 28.5 Seconds," *Financial Times Special Report—Watches and Jewellery* (June 5, 2015), p. 8.

[29]Richard D'Aveni, *Hypercompetition: Managing the Dynamics of Strategic Maneuvering* (New York, NY: Free Press, 1994), p. 71.

[30]Hiroko Tabuchi, "Investor's Next Target Is Sony," *The New York Times* (May 15, 2013), p. B1.

[31]Daisuke Wakabayashi and Christopher Lawton, "At Sony, Culture Shift Yields a Low-Cost Video Camera," *The Wall Street Journal* (April 16, 2009), p. B1.

[32]Sumantra Ghoshal and Christopher Bartlett, *The Individualized Corporation* (New York, NY: HarperBusiness, 1997), p. 71.

[33]The following discussion is adapted from Alan M. Rugman and Joseph R. D'Cruz, *Multinationals as Flagship Firms* (Oxford, UK: Oxford University Press, 2000).

[34]Renée Mauborgne and Kim Chan, "Blue Ocean Strategy," *Harvard Business Review* 82, no. 10 (October 2004), pp. 76–84.

[35]John Gapper, "Nintendo's Wizards Put the Magic into Video Games," *Financial Times* (July 16, 2015), p. 9.

[36]Alan M. Rugman and Lain Verbeke, "Foreign Subsidiaries and Multinational Strategic Management: An Extension and Correction of Porter's Single Diamond Framework," *Management International Review* 3, no. 2 (1993), pp. 71–84.

[37]Howard Davies and Paul Ellis, "Porter's Competitive Advantage of Nations: Time for the Final Judgment?" *Journal of Management Studies* 37, no. 8 (December 2000), pp. 1189–1213.

[38]Andrew Hill, "An Academic Who Shares His Values," *Financial Times* (September 25, 2011), p. 14.

[39]Marina Strauss, "What IKEA CEO Mikael Ohlsson Learned From Canada," *The Globe and Mail* (May 31, 2013), p. 13.

17 Leadership, Organization, and Corporate Social Responsibility

LEARNING OBJECTIVES

17-1 Identify the names and nationalities of the chief executives at five global companies discussed in the text.

17-2 Describe the different organizational structures that companies can adopt as they grow and expand globally.

17-3 Discuss the attributes of lean production, and identify some of the companies that have been pioneers in this organizational form.

17-4 List some of the lessons regarding corporate social responsibility that global marketers can take away from Starbucks' experience with Global Exchange.

CASE 17-1
A Changing of the Guard at Unilever

Unilever, the global food and consumer packaged goods powerhouse, markets a brand portfolio that includes such well-known names as Axe, Ben & Jerry's, Dove, Hellmann's, Lipton, and Magnum. The company has approximately 167,000 employees and 2016 sales of €52.7 billion (about $60 billion); Unilever can trace its roots, in part, to the northern English town of Port Sunlight on the River Mersey. There, in 1888, Lever Brothers founder William Hesketh Lever created a garden village for the benefit of his employees.

Before retiring at the end of 2008, Unilever Group chief executive Patrick Cescau wanted to reconnect the company with its heritage of sustainability and concern for the environment. These and other values reflect Unilever's philosophy of "doing well by doing good." One example: the "Campaign for Real Beauty," which was launched by managers at the company's Dove brand. To prepare for their first presentation to management, Dove team members videotaped interviews with teen girls who talked about the pressures they felt to conform to a certain look and body type. The interviewees included Cescau's daughter as well as the daughters of Unilever's directors.

Later, when the CEO recalled watching the video, he explained, "It suddenly becomes personal. You realize your own children are impacted by the beauty industry, and how stressed they are by this image of unattainable beauty which is imposed on them every day." The Dove team was given the green light to launch a new advertising campaign based on this insight; in the years since, Dove has won numerous awards and accolades for the positive body image campaign.

Cescau's vision of "doing well by doing good" manifested itself in other ways, too. For example, he guided the company's detergent business toward using fewer chemicals and less water, plastic,

Exhibit 17-1 Former Unilever CEO Patrick Cescau put corporate social responsibility at the top of his agenda. Paul Polman, the company's chief executive from 2009 to 2019, built on Cescau's initiatives while expanding into key emerging markets.
Sources: Hindustan Times/Newscom.

and packaging. In addition, he recognized that today's "conscience consumers" look to a company's reputation when deciding which brands to purchase.

Paul Polman, Cescau's successor, built on another of the former chief executive's priorities: business opportunities in emerging markets such as India and China (see Exhibit 17-1). However, Polman also took the top job in the middle of the recent global recession. He is set to retire in 2019; to find out more about Unilever's commitment to global social responsibility and the challenges facing Polman's successor, turn to Case 17-1 at the end of the chapter.

This chapter focuses on the integration of each element of the marketing mix into a total plan that addresses opportunities and threats in the global marketing environment. Cescau's achievements as the head of Unilever illustrate some of the challenges facing business leaders in the twenty-first century: They must be able to articulate a coherent global vision and strategy that integrate global efficiency, local responsiveness, and leverage. The leader is also the architect of an organizational design that is appropriate for the company's strategy. For large global enterprises such as ASEA Brown Boveri (ABB), General Electric (GE), Koninklijke Philips, Tesco, Toyota, and Unilever, the leader must ensure that size and scale are assets that can be leveraged rather than encumbrances that slow response times and stifle innovation. Finally, the leader must ensure that the organization takes a proactive approach to corporate social responsibility.

Leadership

◀ **17-1** Identify the names and nationalities of the chief executives at five global companies discussed in the text.

Global marketing demands exceptional leadership. As noted throughout this book, the hallmark of a global company is its capacity to formulate and implement global strategies that leverage worldwide learning, respond fully to local needs and wants, and draw on the talent and energy of every member of the organization. This daunting task requires global vision and sensitivity to local needs. Overall, the leader's challenge is to direct the efforts and creativity of everyone in the company toward a global effort that best utilizes organizational resources to exploit global opportunities. As Carly Fiorina, former CEO of Hewlett-Packard, said in her 2002 commencement address at the Massachusetts Institute of Technology:

Leadership is not about hierarchy or title or status: It is about having influence and mastering change. Leadership is not about bragging rights or battles or even the accumulation of wealth; it's about connecting and engaging at multiple levels. It's about challenging minds and capturing hearts. Leadership in this new era is about empowering others to decide for themselves. Leadership is about empowering others to reach their full potential. Leaders can no longer view strategy and execution as abstract concepts, but must realize that both elements are ultimately about people.[1]

An important leadership task is articulating beliefs, values, policies, and the intended geographic scope of a company's activities. Using the mission statement or similar document as a reference and guide, members of each operating unit must address their immediate responsibilities and at the same time cooperate with functional, product, and country experts in different locations. Of course, it is one thing to spell out a vision, and another thing entirely to secure commitment to that vision throughout the organization. As noted in Chapter 1, global marketing also entails engaging in significant business activities outside the home country, which means exposure to different languages and cultures. In addition, global marketing involves the skillful application of specific concepts, insights, and strategies. Such endeavors may represent substantial change, especially in U.S. companies with a long tradition of a domestic focus. When the "go global" initiative is greeted with skepticism, the CEO must be a change agent who prepares and motivates employees.

Former Whirlpool CEO David Whitwam described his own efforts in this regard in the early 1990s after he had approved the acquisition of Royal Philips Electronics' European home appliance division:

> When we announced the Philips acquisition, I talked with our people, explained why it was so important. Most opposed the move. They thought, "We're spending a billion dollars on a company that has been losing money for 10 years? We're going to take resources we could use right here and ship them across the Atlantic because we think this is becoming a 'global' industry? What the hell does that mean?"[2]

Jack Welch encountered similar resistance when he was chief executive at GE: "The lower you are in the organization, the less clear it is that globalization is great," he said. As Paolo Fresco, a former GE vice chairman, explained:

> To certain people, globalization is a threat without rewards. You look at the engineer for X-ray in Milwaukee and there is no upside on this one for him. He runs the risk of losing his job, he runs the risk of losing authority—he might find his boss is a guy who does not even know how to speak his language.[3]

In addition to "selling" their visions, top management at Boeing, Coca-Cola, GE, Unilever, Whirlpool, Tata Group, and other companies face the formidable task of building and maintaining organizational cultures that emphasize good corporate governance and reward creativity and nimbleness. A new generation of CEOs are making their mark by upending the strategic decisions that their predecessors made.

For example, former Coca-Cola CEO Muhtar Kent was intent on putting more "fizz" into sales of Coke's flagship cola. By contrast, James Quincey, the new CEO, is focusing on juices, teas, protein shakes, and other drinks with healthier ingredients. Some observers denounced Quincey's decision to eliminate the position of chief marketing officer as "cretinous"; Quincey defended the move, noting that Coke's advertising model had not adapted sufficiently rapidly to the digital age. In place of the CMO, Quincey established a new C-level post, chief growth officer.[4]

The Coca-Cola example underscores the fact that corporate leaders in all parts of the world face challenges that include dealing with fast-moving changes in consumer behavior. The rejection of mature brands in favor of more on-trend, exciting ones is just one example. Add to this the increased fragmentation of markets and the dismantling of previously defensible barriers to industry entry, and today's corporate chiefs have plenty to keep them awake at night!

Top Management Nationality

Many globally minded companies realize that the best person for a top management job or board position is not necessarily someone born in the home country. Coca-Cola's James Quincey is a case in point: He is British. Speaking of U.S. companies, Christopher Bartlett of the Harvard Business School has noted:

> Companies are realizing that they have a portfolio of human resources worldwide, that their brightest technical person might come from Germany, or their best financial manager from England. They are starting to tap their worldwide human resources. And as they do, it will not be surprising to see non-Americans rise to the top.[5]

Exhibit 17-2 Indra Nooyi, chair and chief executive of PepsiCo, is faced with rising commodity prices and weak demand for carbonated soft drinks in the United States. Despite these threats, Nooyi believes the snack-and-beverage giant's current strategy is on track. In recent quarters, the strongest results have come from PepsiCo's fast-growing international division. Snack sales are particularly strong in Mexico and Russia; international sales volume for beverage brands is also increasing, particularly in the Middle East, Argentina, China, and Brazil.
Source: Manish Swarup/Associated Press.

The ability to speak foreign languages is one difference between managers born and raised in the United States and those born and raised elsewhere. For example, the U.S. Department of Education has reported that 200 million Chinese children are studying English; by contrast, only 24,000 American children are studying Chinese! Fluency in English is a prerequisite for managerial success in many global organizations, irrespective of the language of the headquarters country. A decade ago, Yong Nam, CEO of LG Electronics, stipulated that English would be required throughout the company. He explained:

> English is essential. The speed of innovation that is required to compete in the world mandates that we must have seamless communication. We cannot depend on a small group of people who are holding the key to all communication throughout the world. That really impedes information sharing and decision making. I want everybody's wisdom instead of just a few.[6]

Sigismundus W. W. Lubsen, the former president and CEO of Quaker Chemical Corporation, is a good example of today's cosmopolitan executive. Born in the Netherlands and educated in Rotterdam as well as New York, Lubsen speaks Dutch, English, French, and German. He recalled, "I was lucky to be born in a place where if you drove for an hour in any direction, you were in a different country, speaking a different language. It made me very comfortable traveling in different cultures."[7] PepsiCo's Indra Nooyi is also bilingual (see Exhibit 17-2). Table 17-1 gives other examples of corporate leaders who are not native to the headquarters country.

Generally speaking, Japanese companies have been reluctant to place non-Japanese nationals in top positions. For years, only Sony, Mazda, and Mitsubishi had foreigners on their boards. Recently, some Japanese companies have made hiring and promotion decisions aimed at increasing the diversity of their top-management ranks. For example, Didier Leroy recently became the most-senior non-Japanese executive at Toyota; an American, Julie Hamp, is the company's first Western female senior executive.[8]

Similarly, after Renault SA bought a 36.8 percent stake in Nissan Motor in 1999, the French company installed Carlos Ghosn as Nissan's president. Born in Brazil, raised in Lebanon, and educated in France, Ghosn's outsider status at the Japanese company enabled him to move aggressively to cut costs and make drastic changes in the organizational structure. He also introduced two new words into Nissan's lexicon: *speed* and *commitment*. Ghosn's turnaround efforts have been so successful that his life story and exploits are featured in *Big Comic Story*, a comic that is popular with Japan's salarymen. Today, Ghosn is chairman and CEO of Groupe Renault as well as chairman of both Nissan Motor and Mitsubishi Motors.[9] Taken together, these companies form a global strategic partnership known as the Renault–Nissan–Mitsubishi Alliance.

TABLE 17-1 Who's in Charge? Executives of 2017

Company (Headquarters Country)	Executive/Nationality	Position
3M (United States)	Inge G. Thulin (Sweden)	CEO
ABB (Switzerland)	Ulrich Spiesshofer (Germany)	CEO
Adidas (Germany)	Kasper Rorsted (Denmark)	CEO
Chrysler (United States)	Sergio Marchionne (Italy)	CEO
Coca-Cola (United States)	James Quincey (United Kingdom–England)	CEO
Microsoft (United States)	Satya Nadella (India)	CEO
Monsanto (United States)	Hugh Grant (United Kingdom–Scotland)	Chairman, CEO, and president
Nissan Motor (Japan)	Carlos Ghosn (Brazil)	Chairman, president, and CEO
PepsiCo (United States)	Indra K. Nooyi (India)	CEO
Reckitt Benckiser (United Kingdom)	Rakesh Kapoor (India)	CEO
Tapestry (United States)	Victor Luis (Portugal)	CEO
Wolters Kluwer NV (Netherlands)	Nancy McKinstry (United States)	Chairman and CEO

Leadership and Core Competence

In the 1980s, many business executives were assessed on their ability to reorganize their corporations. In the 1990s, global strategy experts C. K. Prahalad and Gary Hamel suggested that executives would be better judged on their abilities to identify, nurture, and exploit the core competencies that make growth possible. Simply put, a **core competence** is something that an organization can do better than its competitors. According to Prahalad and Hamel, a core competence has three characteristics:

- It provides potential access to a wide variety of markets.
- It makes a significant contribution to perceived customer benefits.
- It is difficult for competitors to imitate.

Few companies are likely to build world leadership in more than five or six fundamental competencies. In the long run, an organization derives its global competitiveness from its ability to bring high-quality, low-cost products to market faster than its competitors do. To achieve this goal, an organization must be viewed as a portfolio of competencies rather than as a portfolio of businesses. In some instances, a company has the technical resources to build competencies, but key executives lack the vision to do so. Sometimes the vision is present, but is rigidly focused on existing competencies even as market conditions are changing rapidly.

For example, in the early 2000s, Jorma Ollila, then chairman of Finland's Nokia, noted, "Design is a fundamental building block of the [Nokia] brand. It is central to our product creation and is a core competence integrated into the entire company."[10] The chairman was right— 10 years ago. Design did help Nokia secure its position as the worldwide leader in handset sales. But Apple's introduction of the game-changing iPhone in 2007 caught Nokia off guard. Nokia clung to its proprietary Symbian operating system even as smartphones running Google's Android operating system exploded in popularity. Nokia responded by launching new, mid-priced smartphone models; in addition, new CEO Steven Elop announced an alliance with Microsoft to develop new phones using Windows OS. Despite these moves, by early 2011 Nokia was issuing profit warnings. In 2014, Microsoft acquired Nokia's handset business and Elop was named executive vice president of the newly formed Devices Group. In 2016, the Nokia brand reverted back to Finnish ownership when Microsoft sold it to a new venture called HMD.

Nokia's reversal of fortune in the wake of innovations introduced by Apple and Google underscores the fact that today's executives must rethink the concept of the corporation if they wish to operationalize the concept of core competencies. In addition, the task of management must be viewed as building both competencies and the administrative means for assembling resources

TABLE 17-2 Responsibility for Global Marketing

Company (Headquarters Country)	Executive	Position/Title
Amway (United States)	Su Jung Bae	Chief marketing officer
Apple (United States)	Phil Schiller	Senior vice president of worldwide marketing
Coca-Cola (United States)	Francisco Crespo	Chief growth officer
Facebook (United States)	Rebecca Van Dyck	Chief marketing officer, augmented reality/virtual reality
Ford (United States)	Kumar Galhotra	Chief marketing officer
General Motors (United States)	Deborah Wahl	Global chief marketing officer
Levi's (United States)	Jennifer Sey	Global chief marketing officer
L'Oréal (France)	Gretchen Saegh-Fleming	Chief marketing officer
McDonald's (United States)	Morgan Flatley	Global chief brand officer
Procter & Gamble (United States)	Marc Pritchard	Global marketing officer
Starbucks (United States)	Sharon Rothstein	Global chief marketing officer

spread across multiple businesses.[11] Table 17-2 lists some of the individuals currently responsible for global marketing at selected companies.

(17-2) Organizing For Global Marketing

◄ **17-2** Describe the different organizational structures that companies can adopt as they grow and expand globally.

The goal in **organizing for global marketing** is to find a structure that enables the company to respond to relevant market environment differences while ensuring that corporate knowledge and experience from national markets becomes diffused throughout the entire corporate system. The struggle between the value of centralized knowledge and coordination and the need for individualized response to the local situation creates a constant tension in the global marketing organization. A key issue in any global organization is how to achieve a balance between autonomy and integration. Subsidiaries need autonomy to adapt to their local environments, but the business as a whole needs to be integrated to implement global strategy.[12]

When management at a domestic company decides to pursue international expansion, the issue of how to organize arises immediately. Who should be responsible for this expansion? Should product divisions operate independently or should an international division be established? Should individual countries' subsidiaries report directly to the company president or should a special corporate officer be appointed to take full-time responsibility for international activities?

After the firm reaches a decision about how it will organize the initial international operations, a growing company is faced with a number of reappraisal points during the development of its international business activities. Should the company abandon its international division, and, if so, which alternative structure should be adopted? Should it form an area or regional headquarters? What should be the relationships among staff executives at the corporate, regional, and subsidiary offices? Specifically, how should the company organize the marketing function? To what extent should regional and corporate marketing executives become involved in subsidiary marketing management?

Even companies with years of experience competing around the globe find it necessary to adjust their organizational designs in response to environmental changes. It is perhaps not surprising that, during his tenure at Quaker Chemical, Sigismundus Lubsen favored a global approach to organizational design over a domestic/international approach. He advised Peter A. Benoliel, his predecessor CEO, to have units in the Netherlands, France, Italy, Spain, and England report to a regional vice president in Europe. "I saw that it would not be a big deal to put all of the European units under one common denominator," Lubsen recalled.[13]

As markets globalize and as Japan opens its own market to more competition from overseas, more Japanese companies are likely to break from their traditional organization patterns. Many of the Japanese companies discussed in this text qualify as global or transnational companies because they serve world markets, source globally, or do both. Typically, knowledge is created at these companies' headquarters in Japan and then transferred to other country units.

For example, Canon enjoys a strong reputation for world-class, innovative imaging products such as bubble-jet printers and laser printers. In the past two decades, Canon's management has shifted more control to subsidiaries, hired more non-Japanese staff and management personnel, and assimilated more innovations that were not developed in Japan. In 1996, for example, research and development (R&D) responsibility for software was shifted from Tokyo to the United States, responsibility for telecommunication products to France, and computer-language translation to Great Britain. As Canon president Fujio Mitarai explained, "The Tokyo headquarters cannot know everything. Its job should be to provide low-cost capital, to move top management between regions, and come up with investment initiatives. Beyond that, the local subsidiaries must assume total responsibility for management. We are not there yet, but we are moving step by step in that direction." Toru Takahashi, director of R&D, shared this view: "We used to think that we should keep research and development in Japan, but that has changed," he said. Despite these changes, Canon's board of directors includes only Japanese nationals.[14]

No single correct organizational structure exists for global marketing. Even within a particular industry, worldwide companies have developed different strategic and organizational responses to changes in their environments.[15] Even so, it is possible to make some generalizations. Leading-edge global competitors share one key organizational design characteristic: Their corporate structure is flat and simple, rather than tall and complex. The message is clear: The world is complicated enough, so there is no need to add to the confusion with complex internal structure. Simple structures increase the speed and clarity of communication and allow organizational energy and valuable resources to concentrate on learning, rather than on controlling, monitoring, and reporting.[16] According to David Whitwam, former CEO of Whirlpool, "You must create an organization whose people are adept at exchanging ideas, processes, and systems across borders, people who are absolutely free of the 'not-invented-here' syndrome, people who are constantly working together to identify the best global opportunities and the biggest global problems facing the organization."[17]

A geographically dispersed company cannot limit its knowledge to product, function, and the home territory. Instead, company personnel must acquire knowledge of the complex set of social, political, economic, and institutional arrangements that exist within each international market. Many companies start with ad hoc arrangements, such as having all foreign subsidiaries report to a designated vice president or to the company president. Eventually, such companies establish an international division to manage their geographically dispersed new businesses. It is clear, however, that the international division in the multiproduct company is an unstable organizational arrangement. As a company grows, this initial organizational structure frequently gives way to various alternative structures.

In the fast-changing, competitive global environment of the twenty-first century, corporations will have to find new, more creative ways to organize. New forms of flexibility, efficiency, and responsiveness are required to meet the demands of globalizing markets. In particular, today's global realities include the need to be cost-effective, to be customer driven, to deliver the best quality, and to deliver that quality quickly.

Over the past quarter century, several authors have described new organizational designs that represent responses to today's competitive environment. These designs acknowledge the need to find more responsive and flexible structures, to flatten the organization, and to employ teams. There is also recognition of the need to develop networks, to develop stronger relationships among participants, and to exploit technology. The new designs reflect an evolution in approaches to organizational effectiveness. Early in the twentieth century, Frederick Taylor claimed that all managers had to see the world the same way. Then came the contingency theorists, who said that effective organizations design themselves to match their conditions. These two basic theories are reflected in today's popular management writings. As Henry Mintzberg observed, "To Michael Porter, effectiveness resides in strategy, while to Tom Peters it is the operations that count—executing any strategy with excellence."[18]

Kenichi Ohmae has written extensively on the implications of globalization on organization design. He recommends a type of "global superstructure" at the highest level that provides a view of the world as a single unit. The staff members at this level are responsible for ensuring that work is performed in the best location and coordinating efficient movement of information

THE CULTURAL CONTEXT

Can New Leaders Reinvent Sony, the "Apple of the 1980s," in the Twenty-First Century?

Sony Corporation is a legend in the global consumer electronics industry whose reputation for innovation and engineering has made it the envy of rivals. For decades, quality-conscious consumers paid premium prices for the company's Trinitron color televisions. In 1979, Sony created the personal stereo category with its iconic Walkman.

By the early 2000s, however, Sony's vaunted innovation and marketing machine was faltering. The company had not anticipated the rapid consumer acceptance of flat-panel, wide-screen TV sets, and the Sony Walkman was eclipsed by Apple's iPod and iTunes Store. In 2005, tumbling stock prices resulted in the resignation of chairman and CEO Nobuyuki Idei. Sir Howard Stringer, a Welsh-born American who had been knighted in 2000, was named as Idei's replacement.

One of Stringer's first priorities was to bridge the divide between Sony's media businesses, which included music, games, and motion pictures, and its hardware businesses. As Stringer himself declared, "We've got to get the relationship between content and devices seamlessly managed."

Management writers often use terms like *silos*, *stovepipes*, or *chimneys* to describe an organization in which autonomous business units operate with their own agendas and a minimum of horizontal interdependence. This was the situation at Sony, where the internal rivalries between different engineering units—the PC and Walkman groups, for example—were ingrained in the corporate culture and regarded as healthy. As Osamu Katayama, author of several books about Sony, notes, "Instead of working together, the managers of the different businesses fought to keep their independence."

Because Sony's consumer products businesses have historically accounted for a significant proportion of the company's worldwide sales, breathing new life into the home entertainment and mobile products units was important. To do this, Stringer developed a restructuring plan: He cut 28,000 jobs, reduced the number of manufacturing sites, and eliminated some unprofitable products.

Cost cutting was only part of the story. Boosting revenues with new products was also crucial to Sony's recovery. Stringer was convinced that Sony's TV business would recover, thanks in part to the new Bravia line of HDTVs. As it turned out, the television business continued to lose money. The company also launched an e-book reader and, in 2006, the PlayStation 3 (PS3) game console.

After seven years, it was clear Stringer's turnaround effort was still a work in progress. He had successfully negotiated Sony's withdrawal from a smartphone partnership with Sweden's Ericsson. He had restructured the TV business and ended an expensive LCD screen partnership with Samsung. Sony's Blu-ray DVD format had gained widespread acceptance, but Sony, Sharp, Panasonic, and other Japanese manufacturers were all experiencing declining sales of traditional electronics products. Meanwhile, Apple and Samsung had risen to prominence in the competitive landscape once dominated by the Japanese.

In 2012, Stringer relinquished the chief executive role to Kazuo Hirai (see Exhibit 17-3). One problem facing the company going forward is that Sony has lost its lead in flat-panel television technology to Samsung. In addition, the one–two punch of Apple's iPod/iTunes combination has upstaged Sony's Walkman personal stereo brand. Contributing to its status as a laggard in these markets was the reality that Sony's various divisions—for example, Home Entertainment and Sound; Mobile Products and Communication; and Entertainment—did not work well together.

In 2013, Hirai presided over the launch of the Xperia Z smartphone, an event that provided tangible evidence of a reduction in divisional rivalries. In 2018, new CEO Kenichiro Yoshida took on the task of returning the company to profitability by infusing employees with entrepreneurial spirit while trimming the bureaucracy and speeding up decision making.

Sources: Eric Pfanner and Takashi Mochizuki, "Sony Pares down before Rebuilding," *The Wall Street Journal* (November 17, 2014), pp. B1, B4; Daisuke Wakabayashi, "Japan's Electronics under Siege," *The Wall Street Journal* (May 15, 2013), pp. B1, B4; Andrew Edgecliffe-Johnson and Jonathan Soble, "Channels to Choose," *Financial Times* (February 28, 2012), p. 9; Jonathan Soble, "Sony Chief Looks to Secure Legacy," *Financial Times* (May 23, 2011), p. 11; Yukari Iwatani Kane, "Sony Expects to Trim PS3 Losses, Plans More Games, Online Features," *The Wall Street Journal* (May 18, 2007), p. B4; Phred Dvorak, "Sony Aims to Cut Costs, Workers to Revive Its Electronics Business," *The Wall Street Journal* (September 23, 2005), p. A5; Dvorak, "Out of Tune: At Sony, Rivalries Were Encouraged; Then Came iPod," *The Wall Street Journal* (June 29, 2005), pp. A1, A6; Lorne Manly and Andrew Ross Sorkin, "Choice of Stringer Aims to Prevent Further Setbacks," *The New York Times* (March 8, 2005), pp. C1, C8.

Exhibit 17-3 In 2012, Kazuo Hirai (shown at right) was named president and CEO of Sony Corporation. The new boss faced many challenges, as Japan's once-vaunted electronics industry had fallen behind in the fast-changing tech world. In 2018, Kenichiro Yoshida became president and CEO.
Source: Agencja Fotograficzna Caro/Alamy Stock Photo.

and products across borders. Below this level, Ohmae envisions organizational units assigned to regions "governed by economies of service and economies of scale in information." In Ohmae's view of the world, there are 30 regions with populations ranging from 5 million to 20 million people. For example, China would be viewed as several distinct regions; the same would be true of the United States. The first task of the CEO in such an organization is to become oriented to the single unit that is the borderless business sphere, much as an astronaut might view the earth from space. Then, zooming in, the CEO attempts to identify differences. As Ohmae explained:

> A CEO has to look at the entire global economy and then put the company's resources where they will capture the biggest market share of the most attractive regions. Perhaps as you draw closer from outer space you see a region around the Pacific Northwest, near Puget Sound, that is vibrant and prosperous. . . . In parts of New England you will see regions that are strong centers for health care and biotechnology. As a CEO, that's where you put your resources and shift your emphasis.[19]

Your authors believe that successful companies, the real global winners, must have both good strategies and good execution.

Patterns of International Organizational Development

Organizations vary in terms of the size and potential of targeted global markets and local management competence in different country markets. Conflicting pressures may arise from the need for product and technical knowledge; functional expertise in marketing, finance, and operations; and area and country knowledge. Because the constellation of pressures that shape organizations is never exactly the same, no two organizations pass through organizational stages in exactly the same way, nor do they arrive at precisely the same organizational pattern. Nevertheless, some general patterns hold.

A company engaging in limited export activities often has a small in-house export department as a separate functional area. Most domestically oriented companies undertake initial foreign expansion by means of foreign sales offices or subsidiaries that report directly to the company president or other designated company officer. This person carries out his or her responsibilities without assistance from a headquarters staff group. Many other design options are available to companies that seek to extend their reach internationally without creating separate divisions. For example, Des Moines, Iowa–based Meredith Corporation participates in international markets by means of licensing agreements developed and managed by the Corporate Development group, and further supported by various operating departments within the company (see Exhibit 17-4).

INTERNATIONAL DIVISION STRUCTURE   As a company's international business grows, the complexity of coordinating and directing this activity extends beyond the scope of a single person. Pressure is created to assemble a staff that will have responsibility for coordination and direction of the growing international activities of the organization. Eventually, this process leads to the creation of the international division, as illustrated in Figure 17-1. Best Buy, Hershey, Levi Strauss, Under Armour, Walmart, and Walt Disney are some examples of companies whose structures include international divisions.

When Hershey announced the creation of its international division in 2005, J. P. Bilbrey, the division's senior vice president, noted that Hershey would no longer utilize the extension strategy of exporting its chocolate products from the United States. Instead, the company would tailor products to local markets and also manufacture locally. As Bilbrey explained, "We're changing our business model in Asia. The product was not locally relevant and it also got there at an unattractive cost."[20] Currently, international sales make up only 15 percent of Hershey's sales; the company's strategic goal is to boost that figure to 25 percent in the near future.

China is the world's fastest-growing candy market, so it is no surprise that Hershey is ramping up efforts to penetrate the Middle Kingdom. Until recently, Hershey had only about a 2.2 percent share of China's chocolate market; by contrast, Mars commands 43 percent of this market

Exhibit 17-4 With more than 7 million U.S. subscribers, *Better Homes and Gardens* is the flagship publication of Des Moines, Iowa–based Meredith Corporation. Meredith licenses *BH&G* and other titles in numerous international markets, including Europe, the Middle East, and Asia. Shown here is the Chinese edition of the magazine, published under license by SEEC Media.

Source: November 2012 *Better Homes and Gardens*® Magazine China edition. Photo courtesy of Meredith Corporation ©2017. All rights reserved.

with its M&M's and Dove brands. In 2013, Hershey rolled out a new line of condensed-milk candies specifically targeting China's premium candy segment. Lancaster (as in "Lancaster, Pennsylvania," the company's hometown) is the English-language name; in Chinese, the brand is Yo-man (see Exhibit 17-5). Hershey has opened its second-largest R&D facility, Asia Innovation Center, in Shanghai.[21]

Several factors contribute to the establishment of an international division. First, top management's commitment to global operations has increased enough to justify an organizational unit headed by a senior manager. Second, the complexity of international operations requires a single organizational unit whose management has sufficient authority to make its own determinations on important issues such as which market-entry strategy to employ. Third, an international division is frequently formed when the firm has recognized the need for internal specialists to deal with

FIGURE 17-1

Functional Corporate Structure, Domestic Corporate Staff Orientation, and International Division

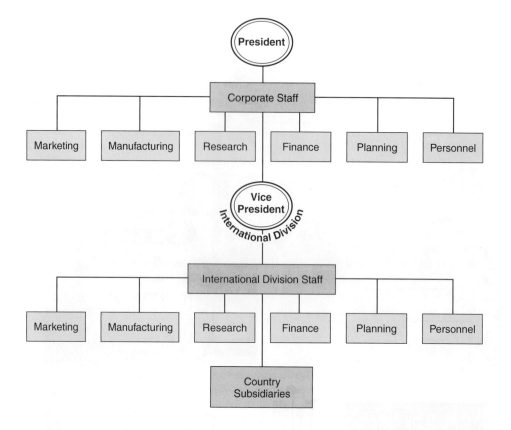

the special demands of global operations. A fourth contributing factor is management's recognition of the importance of strategically scanning the global horizon for opportunities and aligning them with company resources, rather than simply responding on an ad hoc basis to opportunities as they arise.

REGIONAL MANAGEMENT CENTERS   When business is conducted in a single region that is characterized by similarities in economic, social, geographic, and political conditions, there is both justification and need for a management center. Thus, another stage of organizational evolution is the emergence of an area or regional headquarters as a management layer between the country organization and the international division headquarters.

Exhibit 17-5 Hershey has rolled out its Lancaster brand in China. Flavors include Original Pure Nai Bei, Pure Nai Bei filled with Rich Nai Bei, and Pure Nai Bei with Strawberry. "Nai Bei" refers to a slow-cooking process using imported milk.

Lancaster is the first completely new brand launched outside the United States in Hershey's 120-year history. Lancaster was recently introduced in the United States as well.
Source: Daniel Acker/Bloomberg via Getty Images.

For example, the increasing importance of the European Union as a regional market prompted a number of companies to change their organizational structures by setting up regional headquarters there. In the mid-1990s, Quaker Oats established its European headquarters in Brussels; Electrolux, the Swedish home appliance company, has also regionalized its European operations.[22] Two decades later, Procter & Gamble (P&G) began to shift its global skin, cosmetics, and personal-care unit from Cincinnati to Singapore; Asia-Pacific countries account for approximately half of the $100 billion global skin-care market.[23]

A regional center typically coordinates decisions on pricing, sourcing, and other matters. Executives at the regional center also participate in the planning and control of each country's operations with an eye toward applying company knowledge on a regional basis and optimally utilizing corporate resources on a regional basis. This organizational design is illustrated in Figure 17-2.

Regional management can offer a company several advantages. First, many regional managers agree that an on-the-scene regional management unit makes sense where there is a real need for coordinated, pan-regional decision making. Coordinated regional planning and control are becoming necessary as the national subsidiary continues to lose its relevance as an independent operating unit. Regional management can probably achieve the best balance of geographic, product, and functional considerations required to implement corporate objectives effectively. By shifting operations and decision making to the region, the company is better able to maintain an insider advantage.[24]

Of course, a major disadvantage of a regional center is its cost. The cost of a two-person office can be as much as $500,000 per year. The scale of regional management must also be in line

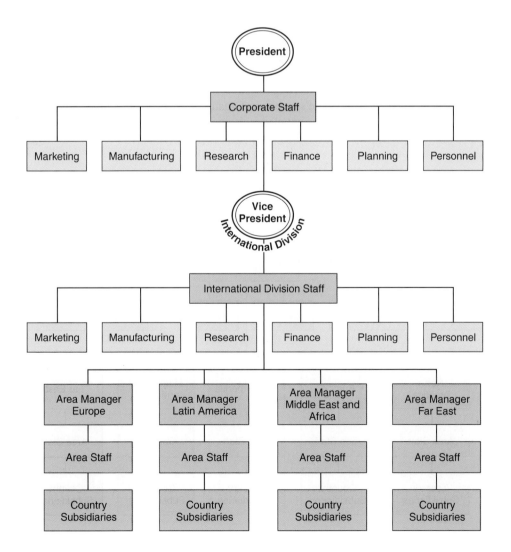

FIGURE 17-2 Functional Corporate Structure, Domestic Corporate Staff Orientation, International Division, and Area Divisions

with the scale of operations in a region. A regional headquarters is inappropriate if the size of the operations it manages is inadequate to cover the costs of the additional layer of management. The basic issue with regard to the regional headquarters is "Does it contribute enough to organizational effectiveness to justify its cost and the complexity of another layer of management?"

GEOGRAPHIC AND PRODUCT DIVISION STRUCTURES   As a company becomes more global, management frequently faces the dilemma of whether to organize by geography or by product lines. The geographically organized structure involves the assignment of operational responsibility for geographic areas of the world to line managers. The corporate headquarters retains responsibility for worldwide planning and control, and each area of the world—including the "home" or base market—is organizationally equal.

Take the case of a company with French origins. France is simply another geographic market under this organizational arrangement. This structure is most common in companies with closely related product lines that are sold in similar end-use markets around the world. For example, the major international oil companies utilize the geographic structure, which is illustrated in Figure 17-3. McDonald's organizational design integrates the international division and geographic structures. McDonald's U.S. has three geographic operating divisions, and McDonald's International has three.

When an organization assigns regional or worldwide product responsibility to its product divisions, manufacturing standardization can result in significant economies. For example, Whirlpool recently reorganized its European operations, switching from a geographic or country orientation to one based on product lines. One potential disadvantage of the product approach is that local input from individual country managers may be ignored, with the result that products are not sufficiently tailored to local markets. The essence of the Ford 2000 reorganization initiated in 1995 was to integrate the automaker's North American and European operations. Over a three-year period, the company saved $5 billion in development costs. However, by 2000, Ford's European market share had slipped nearly 5 percent. In a shift back toward the geographic model, then CEO Jacques Nasser returned to regional executives some of the authority they had lost.[25]

The challenges associated with devising the structure that is best suited to improving global sales can be seen in Procter & Gamble's ambitious Organization 2005 plan. Initiated by then CEO Durk Jager in 1999, this reorganization entailed replacing separate country organizations with five global business units for key product categories such as paper products and feminine hygiene.

FIGURE 17-3 Geographic Corporate Structure, World Corporate Staff Orientation, and Area Divisions Worldwide

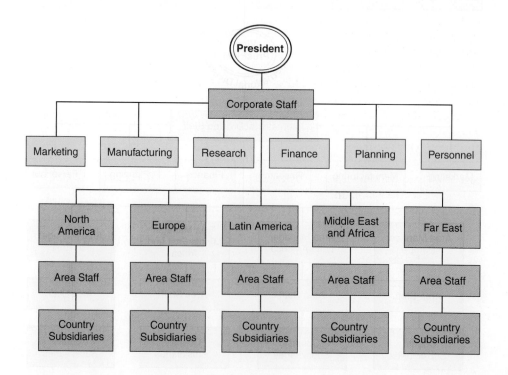

A number of executives were reassigned; in Europe alone, 1,000 staff members were transferred to Geneva, Switzerland. Many managers, upset about the transfers and news that P&G intended to cut 15,000 jobs worldwide, quit the company, and the resulting upheaval cost Jager his job. To appease middle managers, new CEO A. G. Lafley restored some of the company's previous geographic focus.[26]

THE MATRIX DESIGN   In the fully developed large-scale global company, product or business, function, area, and customer know-how are simultaneously focused on the organization's worldwide marketing objectives. This type of total competence underlies the **matrix organization**. Management's task in the matrix organization is to achieve an organizational balance that brings together different perspectives and skills to accomplish the organization's objectives.

In 1998, both Gillette and Ericsson announced plans to reorganize into matrix organizations. Ericsson's matrix is focused on three customer segments: network operators, private consumers, and commercial enterprises.[28] Gillette's matrix structure separates product-line management from geographic sales and marketing responsibility.[29] Likewise, Boeing has reorganized its commercial transport design and manufacturing engineers into a matrix organization built around five platform or aircraft model–specific groups. Previously, Boeing was organized along functional lines; the new design was expected to lower costs and accelerate updates and problem solving. It was also expected to unite essential design, engineering, and manufacturing processes between Boeing's commercial transport factories and component plants, thereby enhancing product consistency.[30]

> "GE is managing its worldwide organization as a network, not a centralized hub with foreign appendages."[27]
>
> Christopher A. Bartlett, Emeritus professor, Harvard Business School

Why are executives at these and other companies implementing matrix designs? The matrix form of organization is well suited to global companies because it can be used to establish a multiple-command structure that gives equal emphasis to functional and geographic departments.

Professor John Hunt of the London Business School has suggested four considerations regarding the matrix organizational design. First, the matrix is appropriate when the market is demanding and dynamic. Second, employees must accept higher levels of ambiguity and understand that policy manuals cannot cover every eventuality. Third, in country markets where the command-and-control model persists, it is best to overlay matrices on only small portions of the workforce. Finally, management must be able to clearly state what each axis of the matrix can and cannot do, albeit without creating a bureaucracy.[31]

Having established that the matrix is appropriate, management can expect the matrix to integrate four basic competencies on a worldwide basis:

1. *Geographic knowledge.* An understanding of the basic economic, social, cultural, political, and governmental market and competitive dimensions of a country is essential. The country subsidiary is the major structural device employed today to enable the corporation to acquire geographic knowledge.
2. *Product knowledge and know-how.* Product managers with a worldwide responsibility can achieve this level of competence on a global basis. Another way of achieving global product competence is simply to duplicate product management organizations in domestic and international divisions, thereby achieving high competence in both organizational units.
3. *Functional competence in such fields as finance, production, and, especially, marketing.* Corporate functional staff with worldwide responsibility contribute to the development of functional competence on a global basis. In some companies, the corporate functional manager, who is responsible for the development of his or her functional activity on a global basis, reviews the appointment of country subsidiary functional managers.
4. *A knowledge of the customer or industry and its needs.* Certain large and extremely sophisticated global companies have staff with the responsibility for serving industries on a global basis to assist the line managers in the country organizations in their efforts to penetrate specific customer markets.

Under the matrix arrangement, instead of designating national organizations or product divisions as profit centers, both are responsible for profitability—the national organization for country profits and the product divisions for national and worldwide product profitability.

Figure 17-4 illustrates the matrix organization. This organizational chart starts with a bottom section that represents a single-country responsibility level, moves to representing the area

FIGURE 17-4 The Matrix Structure

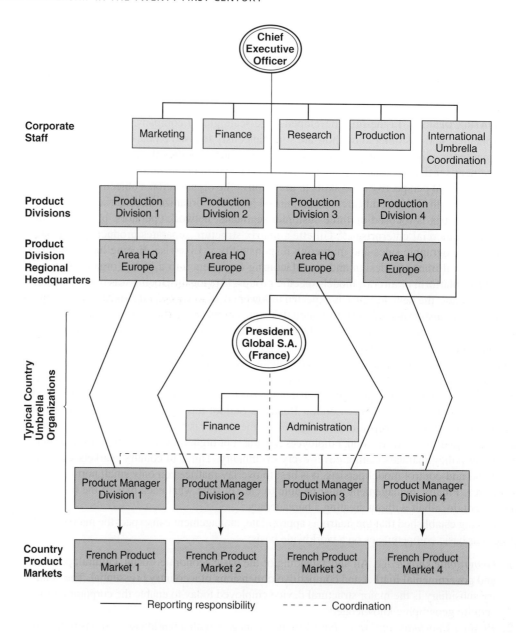

or international level, and finally moves to representing global responsibility from the product divisions, to the corporate staff, to the chief executive at the top of the structure.

At Whirlpool, North American operations are organized in matrix form. Whirlpool managers from traditional functions such as operations, marketing, and finance also work in teams devoted to specific products, such as dishwashers or ovens. To encourage interdependence and integration, the cross-functional teams are headed by "brand czars," such as the brand chief for Whirlpool or Kenmore. As Whitwam explained, "The Whirlpool-brand czar still worries about the Whirlpool name. But he also worries about all the refrigerator brands that we make because he heads that product team. It takes a different mind-set."[32]

The key to successful matrix management is ensuring that managers are able to resolve conflicts and achieve integration of organization programs and plans. The mere adoption of a matrix design or structure does not create a true matrix organization. Instead, evolution of a matrix organization requires fundamental changes in management behavior, organizational culture, and technical systems. In a matrix, influence is based on technical competence and interpersonal sensitivity, not on formal authority. Moreover, managers in a matrix culture recognize the absolute need to resolve issues and choices at the lowest possible level and do not rely on higher authority for making decisions.

The matrix structure is not always appropriate, however. Indeed, some companies are moving away from the matrix in response to changing competitive conditions. Heineken and EMI are two examples; ABB is another.[33] For nearly a decade, ABB was a matrix organized along regional lines. Local business units—factories that make motors or power generators, for example—reported both to a country manager and to a business area manager who set strategy for the whole world. This structure allowed ABB to execute global strategies while still thriving in local markets. But in 1998, new chairman Göran Lindahl dissolved the matrix. As the chairman explained in a press release, "This is an aggressive move aimed at greater speed and efficiency by further focusing and flattening the organization. This step is possible now thanks to our strong, decentralized presence in all local and global markets around the world."

In January 2001, Lindahl stepped down and his successor, Jorgen Centerman, revamped the organizational structure yet again. The new design was intended to improve the focus on industries and large corporate customers; Centerman wanted to ensure that all of ABB's products were designed to the same systems standards. In 2002, with the chief executive under pressure to sell assets, ABB's board replaced Centerman with Jürgen Dorman. Dorman stepped down in 2005 and was succeeded by Fred Kindle. Although ABB returned to profitability under his leadership, Kindle left after three years. The official reason: irreconcilable differences about the best way to lead the company. Michel Demaré, ABB's chief financial officer, was named interim CEO.

Then, in fall 2008, Joe Hogan was selected as ABB's new CEO. Hogan, an American, was a 23-year veteran of GE whose most recent assignment had been running GE Healthcare. ABB's board was impressed by Hogan's performance at the U.S. industrial giant: During his 8 years at GE Healthcare, the unit's sales more than doubled, from $7 billion to $18 billion. These results were due, in part, to several major acquisitions engineered by Hogan.[34] By the time Hogan stepped down as CEO of ABB in 2013, he had made a number of acquisitions to position the company as a leader in industrial automation (see Exhibit 17-6).

In the twenty-first century, an important task of top management is to eliminate a one-dimensional approach to decisions and to encourage the development of multiple management perspectives and an organization that will sense and respond to a complex and fast-changing world. The challenges facing Sony, discussed earlier, are a case in point. By thinking in terms of changing behavior rather than changing structural design, management can free itself from the limitations of the structural chart and focus instead on achieving the best possible results with the available resources.

Exhibit 17-6 Industrial robots such as ABB's YuMi are playing an increasingly important role in factories in China and elsewhere.
Source: CTK/Alamy Stock Photo.

▶ **17-3** Discuss the attributes of lean production, and identify some of the companies that have been pioneers in this organizational form.

(17-3) Lean Production: Organizing The Japanese Way

In the automobile industry, a comparison of early craft production processes, mass production, and modern "lean" production provides an interesting case study of the effectiveness of new organizational structures in the twenty-first century.[35] Dramatic productivity differences existed between craft and mass producers in the first part of the twentieth century. The mass producers—most notably Ford Motor Company—gained their substantial advantage by changing their value chains so that each worker was able to do far more work each day than was possible with the craft producers. The innovation that supported this workflow was the moving assembly line, which required the originators to conceptualize the production process in a totally new way. The assembly line also required a new approach to organizing people, production machinery, and supplies. By rearranging their value chain activities, the mass producers were able to achieve substantial reductions in effort compared with the craft producers. These productivity improvements provided an obvious competitive advantage.

The advantage of the mass producers lasted until the Japanese auto companies further revised the value chain and created **lean production**, thereby gaining for themselves the kinds of dramatic competitive advantages that mass producers had previously gained over craft producers. For example, the Toyota Production System (TPS), as the Japanese company's manufacturing methods are known, achieves efficiencies of approximately 50 percent over typical mass production systems. TPS is based on two concepts. First is *jidoka*, which involves visualizing potential problems. *Jidoka* also means that quality is built into the company's vehicles during the manufacturing process. Just-in-time (JIT), the second pillar of the TPS, means that Toyota produces only what is needed, when it is needed, in the amount that is needed. Toyota's training programs ensure that all employees understand the Toyota Way. Future factory workers attend the Toyota Technical Skills Academy in Toyota City, Japan. Executive training takes place at the Toyota Institute.

Even with the reduced assembly time, the lean producer's vehicles have significantly fewer defects than mass-produced vehicles. The lean producer also uses approximately 40 percent less factory space and maintains only a fraction of the inventory stored by the mass producer. Again, the competitive advantages conferred by these outcomes are obvious. Whether the strategy is based on differentiation or low cost, the lean producer has the advantage.

To achieve these gains at Toyota, production gurus Taiichi Ohno and Shigeo Shingo challenged several assumptions traditionally associated with automobile manufacturing. First, they made changes to operations within the auto company itself, such as reducing setup times for machinery. The changes also applied to operations within supplier firms, as well as to the interfaces between Toyota and its suppliers and to the interfaces with distributors and dealers. Ohno and Shingo's innovations have been widely embraced in the industry; as a result, individual producers' value chains have been modified, and interfaces between producers and suppliers have been optimized to create more effective and efficient value systems.

Assembler Value Chains

Employee ability is emphasized in a lean production environment. Before being hired, people seeking jobs with Toyota participate in the Day of Work, a 12-hour assessment test to determine who has the right mix of physical dexterity, team attitude, and problem-solving ability. Once hired, workers receive considerable training to enable them to perform any job in their section of the assembly line or area of the plant, and they are assigned to teams in which all members must be able to perform the functions of all other team members. Workers are also empowered to make suggestions and to take actions aimed at improving quality and productivity. Quality control is achieved through *kaizen*, a devotion to continuous improvement that ensures every flaw is isolated, examined in detail to determine the ultimate cause, and then corrected.

Mechanization, and particularly flexible mechanization, is a hallmark of lean production. For example, a single assembly line in Georgetown, Kentucky, that produces Toyota's Camry sedan also produces the Sienna minivan. The Sienna and Camry share the same basic chassis and 50 percent of their parts. Of the 300 different stations on the line, only 26 stations require different parts to assemble minivans. Similarly, Honda has invested hundreds of millions of dollars to introduce flexible production technology in its U.S. plants. In an era of volatile gasoline prices and fluctuating exchange rates, production flexibility becomes a source of competitive advantage. For example, when the weak dollar put pressure on margins for vehicles imported into the United States, Honda shifted production of CR-V crossovers from the United Kingdom to a plant in Ohio. Within a matter of minutes, Honda can switch from producing Civic compacts to CR-V crossovers as demand or other market conditions dictate.[36]

In contrast to the lean producers, U.S. mass producers typically maintain operations with greater direct labor content, less mechanization, and much less flexible mechanization. They also divide their employees into a large number of discrete specialties with no overlap. Employee initiative and teamwork are not encouraged. In addition, quality control is expressed as an acceptable number of defects per vehicle.

Even when the comparisons are based on industry averages, the Japanese lean producers continue to enjoy substantial productivity and quality advantages. Again, these advantages put the lean producers in a better position to exploit low-cost or differentiation strategies. They are getting better productivity out of their workers and machines, and they are making better use of their factory floor space. The relatively small size of the repair area reflects the higher quality of their products. A high number of "suggestions per employee" provides some insight into why lean producers outperform mass producers. First, they invest a great deal more in the training of their workers. They also rotate all workers through all jobs for which their teams are responsible. Finally, all workers are encouraged to make suggestions, and management acts on those suggestions. These changes to the value chain translate into major improvements in the value of the lean producers' products.

It should come as no surprise that many of the world's automakers studied lean production methods and introduced them in both existing and new plants throughout the world. In 1999, for example, General Motors (GM) announced plans to spend nearly $500 million to overhaul its Adam Opel plant in Germany. Pressure for this change came from several sources, including increasingly intense rivalry in Europe's car market, worldwide overcapacity, and a realization that price transparency in the euro zone would exert downward pressure on prices. GM's goal was to transform the plant into a state-of-the-art lean production facility with a 40 percent workforce reduction. As GM Europe president Michael J. Burns said at the time, "Pricing is more difficult today. . . . You have to work on product costs, structural costs. . . everything."[37] Even so, despite nearly two decades of investment in new models and new, cleaner engines, GM's European business was a money loser. In 2017, GM sold the Opel business to Peugeot.

Downstream Value Chains

The differences between lean producers and U.S. mass producers in the way they deal with their respective dealers, distributors, and customers are as dramatic as the differences in the way they deal with their suppliers. U.S. mass producers follow the basic industry model and maintain an "arm's-length" relationship with dealers that is often characterized by a lack of cooperation and even open hostility. There is often no sharing of information because there is no incentive to do so. In many cases, the manufacturer tries to force on the dealer models that the dealer knows will not sell. The dealer, in turn, often tries to pressure the customer into buying a model he or she does not want. All parties are trying to hide information about what they really want from their supposed partners. This kind of disingenuous behavior does little to ensure that the industry is responsive to market needs.

The problem starts with the market research, which is often in error. The faulty research is compounded by lack of feedback from dealers regarding real customer desires. Matters continue to worsen when the product-planning divisions make changes to the models without consulting the marketing divisions or the dealers. This process invariably results in production of models that are unpopular and almost impossible to sell. The manufacturer then uses incentives and other schemes, such as making a dealer accept one unpopular model for every five hot-selling models it orders, to persuade the dealers to market the unpopular models. The dealer then has the problem of persuading customers to buy the unpopular models.

Within the mass assembler's value chain, the linkage between the marketing elements and the product planners is broken. The external linkage between the sales divisions and the dealers is also broken. The production process portion of the value chain is broken as well, in that it relies on the production of thousands of models that won't sell and that will then sit on dealer lots, at enormous cost, while the dealer works to find customers.

Within the dealerships, there are even more problems. The relationship between the salesperson and the customer is based on sparring and trying to outsmart each other on price. When the salesperson gets the upper hand, the customer gets stung. It is very much like the relationship between the dealer and the manufacturer. Each is withholding information from the other party in the hope of outsmarting the other. Too often, salespeople do not investigate customers' real needs and try to find the best product to satisfy those needs. Rather, they provide only as much information as is needed to close the deal. Once the deal is closed, the salesperson has essentially no further contact with the customer. No attempt is made to optimize the linkage between dealers and manufacturers or the linkage between dealers and customers.

The contrast with the lean producer is again striking. In Japan, the dealer's employees are true product specialists. They know their products and deal with all aspects of those products, including financing, service, maintenance, insurance, registration and inspection, and delivery. A customer deals with one person in the dealership, and that person takes care of everything from the initial contact through eventual trade-in and replacement and all the problems in between. Further, dealer representatives are included on the manufacturer's product development teams and provide continuous input regarding customer desires. The linkages between dealers, marketing divisions, and product development teams are totally optimized.

The stress caused by large inventories of unsold cars is also absent. A car is not built until a customer places an order for it. Each dealer has only a stock of models for the customer to view. Once the customer has decided on the car he or she wants, the order is sent to the factory and in a matter of weeks, the salesperson delivers the car to the customer's house.

Once a Japanese dealership gets a customer, it is absolutely determined to hang on to that customer for life. It is also determined to acquire all of that customer's family members as customers. A joke among the Japanese says that the only way to escape the salesperson who sold a person a car is to leave the country. Japanese dealers maintain extensive databases on actual and potential customers; the databases include both demographic data and preference data. Customers are encouraged to help keep the information in the database current, and they do so.

This extensive store of data becomes an integral part of the market research effort and helps ensure that products match customer desires. There are no inventories of unpopular models because every car is custom ordered for each customer. This factor, combined with the dealer's detailed data on the needs and desires of its customers, changes the whole nature of the interaction between the customer and the dealer. The customer decides which car she or he wants and can afford, and the company then builds that car to order. There is no need for the salesperson and the customer to try to outsmart each other.

The differences between U.S. mass producers and Japanese lean producers reflect their fundamental differences in business objectives. U.S. producers focus on short-term income and return on investment. Today's sale is a discrete event that is not connected to upstream activities in the value chain and has no value in tomorrow's activities. Efforts are made to reduce the cost of the sales activities. In contrast, Japanese automakers see the process in terms of the long-term perspective. There are two major goals of the sales process: to maximize the income stream from each customer over time, and to use the linkage with the production processes to reduce production and inventory costs and to maximize quality and therefore differentiation.

▶ **17-4** List some of the lessons regarding corporate social responsibility that global marketers can take away from Starbucks' experience with Global Exchange.

ⓘ17-4 Ethics, Corporate Social Responsibility, and Social Responsiveness in the Globalization Era

Today's chief executive must be a proactive steward of the reputation of the company he or she is leading. This entails, in part, understanding and responding to the concerns and interests of a variety of stakeholders. A **stakeholder** is any group or individual that is affected by, or takes an interest in, the policies and practices adopted by an organization.[38] Top management, employees, customers, persons or institutions that own the company's stock, and suppliers constitute a company's *primary stakeholders*. *Secondary stakeholders* include the media, the general business community, local community groups, and **nongovernmental organizations (NGOs)**. NGOs focus on human rights, political justice, and environmental issues; examples include Global Exchange,

Exhibit 17-7 Product (RED) has a number of stakeholders, including the companies that market (RED)-branded products, the customers who buy them, and the people who benefit from the funds raised. To date, the initiative has raised $500 million to fight disease in Africa.
Source: Tony Cenicola/The New York Times/Redux Pictures.

Greenpeace, Oxfam, and others. **Stakeholder analysis** is the process of formulating a "win–win" outcome for all stakeholders.[39]

U2 singer Bono and Bobby Shriver are cofounders of Product (RED), a partnership with well-known global companies to raise money to fight disease in Africa. Apple, American Express, Emporio Armani, Converse, Gap, and Motorola all offer (RED)-themed merchandise and services to their customers. The partners are demonstrating their commitment to corporate social responsibility by pledging to donate a percentage of the profits generated to the Global Fund to Fight AIDS, Tuberculosis, and Malaria. To launch its (RED) line, Gap's advertising campaign used celebrities and one-word headlines consisting of verbs that end in "-red." For example, one ad featured the word "INSPI(RED)" superimposed over a photo of director Steven Spielberg wearing a Product (RED) leather jacket (see Exhibit 17-7).

The leaders of global companies must practice **corporate social responsibility (CSR)**, which can be defined as a company's obligation to pursue goals and policies that are in society's best interests. A key issue for a company contemplating its CSR is whose interests come first. That is, how does a company find the right balance between competing points of view? Peter Brabeck, former chairman and CEO of Nestlé, summarized the situation this way: "The unique role of business is to create social, economic and environmental value for the countries where we operate."[40]

Organizations can demonstrate their commitment to CSR in a variety of ways, including cause-marketing efforts or a commitment to sustainability. Subaru, a unit of Japan's Fuji Heavy Industries, enjoys strong demand in North America for its Crosstrek hatchback and Forester SUV. Subaru's Indiana plant currently produces 400,000 vehicles per year; part of the brand's appeal is its reputation for eco-awareness and family-friendly values. The company maintains a zero landfill approach to manufacturing (see Exhibit 17-8).

In some companies, such policies play an important internal role with primary stakeholders, especially employees drawn from the ranks of Generation Y. As Kevin Havelock, president of refreshment at Unilever, has noted:

> We are seeing, particularly with the new generation of young businesspeople and young marketers, that they are only attracted to companies that fit with their own value set. And the value set of the new generation is one that says this company must take a positive and global view on the global environment. . . . The ethical positions we take on brands like Dove, the positions we take on not using [fashion] models of size zero across any of our brands, the positions we take in terms of adding back to communities. . . these all underpin an attractive proposition for marketers.[41]

Exhibit 17-8 The Subaru nameplate is synonymous with the brand's Symmetrical All-Wheel Drive and Partial Zero Emissions Vehicle (PZEV) engineering. The company's U.S. assembly plant, Subaru of Indiana Automotive, Inc., has been awarded ISO 140001 and ISO 50001 certification for its energy management systems and environmental management systems.
Source: Subaru of America.

Similarly, Starbucks founder and CEO Howard Schultz's enlightened human resources policies have played a key part in the company's success. Partners, as the company's employees are known, who work 20 hours or more per week are offered health benefits; partners can also take advantage of an employee stock option plan known as Bean Stock. As noted on the company's Web site:

> Consumers are demanding more than "product" from their favorite brands. Employees are choosing to work for companies with strong values. Shareholders are more inclined to invest in businesses with outstanding corporate reputations. Quite simply, being socially responsible is not only the right thing to do; it can distinguish a company from its industry peers.

Schultz takes advantage of every opportunity to repeat his message. In interviews and personal appearances, CSR is a constant theme. Here's a typical example, from a 2005 interview with *Financial Times*:

> Perhaps we have the opportunity to be a different type of global company, a global brand that can build a different model, a company that is a global business, that makes a profit, but at the same time demonstrates a social conscience and gives back to the local market.[42]

As noted in Chapter 1, one of the forces restraining the growth of global business and global marketing is resistance to globalization. In a wired world, a company's reputation can quickly be tarnished if activists target its policies and practices. The anti-globalization movement constitutes an important secondary stakeholder for global companies; this movement takes a variety of forms and finds expression in various ways. In developed countries, its concerns and agenda include cultural imperialism (e.g., the French backlash against McDonald's), the loss of jobs due to offshoring and outsourcing (e.g., the furniture industry in the United States), and a distrust of global institutions (e.g., anti-globalization protests).

In developing countries, globalization's opponents accuse companies of undermining local cultures, placing intellectual property rights ahead of human rights, promoting unhealthy diets and unsafe food technologies, and pursuing unsustainable consumption.[44] Environmental degradation and labor exploitation are also key issues for activists (see Exhibit 17-9).

In a socially responsible firm, employees conduct business in an ethical manner. In other words, they are guided by moral principles that enable them to distinguish between right and wrong. At many companies, a formal statement or **code of ethics** summarizes core ideologies, corporate values, and expectations. GE, Boeing, and United Technologies Corp. are some of the American companies offering training programs that specifically address ethics issues. For many years, Jack Welch, the legendary former CEO of GE, challenged his employees to take an informal "mirror test." The challenge: "Can you look in the mirror every day and feel proud of what you're doing?"[45] Today, GE uses more formal approaches to ethics and compliance; it has produced training videos and instituted an online training program, and also provides employees with a 64-page guide to ethical conduct titled *The Spirit & The Letter*. The document provides guidance on potentially illegal payments, security and crisis management, and other issues.

At Johnson & Johnson (J&J), the ethics statement is known as "Our Credo"; first introduced in 1943, the credo has been translated into dozens of languages for Johnson & Johnson employees around the world (see Figure 17-5 and the Appendix at the end of this chapter). As management guru Jim Collins notes in his book *Built to Last*, J&J's credo is a "codified ideology" that guides managerial actions. J&J operationalizes the credo in various ways, including through its organizational structure and its planning and decision-making processes. The credo also serves as a crisis management guide. For example, during the Tylenol crisis of the early 1980s, J&J's adherence to the credo enabled the company to mount a swift, decisive, and transparent response to what might have been a devastating blow to its business.

As we have seen, the issue of corporate social responsibility becomes complicated for the global company with operations in multiple markets. When the chief executive of a global firm in a developed country or government policymakers attempt to act in "society's best interests," the question arises: Which society? That of the home-country market (see Exhibit 17-10)? Other developed countries? Developing countries? For example, in the late 1990s, in an effort to address the issue of child labor, the U.S. government threatened trade sanctions against the garment industry in Bangladesh. Thousands of child workers lost their jobs, and their plight worsened. Whose interests were served by this turn of events? In addition, as noted in Chapter 1, companies that do business around the globe may be in different stages of evolution. Thus, a multinational firm may rely on individual country managers to address CSR issues on an ad hoc basis, while a global or transnational firm may create a policy at headquarters.

Consider the following facts:

- The fashion industry has come under fire from critics who allege poor working conditions are rampant in the factories that make clothes for well-known brands.
- Walmart has been the target of criticism for a variety of reasons. In particular, activists have targeted the company, urging management to pay higher wages to hourly employees. Walmart CEO Doug McMillan has responded by raising the minimum wages of its employees and launching a number of eco-friendly initiatives.
- CEO pay in the United States is rising faster than average salaries and much faster than inflation. A study by the Economic Policy Institute found that, in 2016, CEOs were paid 271 times more than the average worker.[46]

> "Coke has become a whipping boy for globalization, just as Nike and McDonald's have been for years."[43]
>
> Tom Pirko, president, BevMark

FIGURE 17-5

Johnson & Johnson Credo

Johnson & Johnson's credo is woven into the fabric of the company's organizational structure, planning and decision-making processes. The credo also serves as a crisis management guide.

Source: Courtesy of Johnson & Johnson.

Our Credo

We believe our first responsibility is to the doctors, nurses and patients, to mothers and fathers and all others who use our products and services. In meeting their needs everything we do must be of high quality. We must constantly strive to reduce our costs in order to maintain reasonable prices. Customers' orders must be serviced promptly and accurately. Our suppliers and distributors must have an opportunity to make a fair profit.

We are responsible to our employees, the men and women who work with us throughout the world. Everyone must be considered as an individual. We must respect their dignity and recognize their merit. They must have a sense of security in their jobs. Compensation must be fair and adequate, and working conditions clean, orderly and safe. We must be mindful of ways to help our employees fulfill their family responsibilities. Employees must feel free to make suggestions and complaints. There must be equal opportunity for employment, development and advancement for those qualified. We must provide competent management, and their actions must be just and ethical.

We are responsible to the communities in which we live and work and to the world community as well. We must be good citizens – support good works and charities and bear our fair share of taxes. We must encourage civic improvements and better health and education. We must maintain in good order the property we are privileged to use, protecting the environment and natural resources.

Our final responsibility is to our stockholders. Business must make a sound profit. We must experiment with new ideas. Research must be carried on, innovative programs developed and mistakes paid for. New equipment must be purchased, new facilities provided and new products launched. Reserves must be created to provide for adverse times. When we operate according to these principles, the stockholders should realize a fair return.

Johnson & Johnson

What is the best way for a global firm to respond to such issues? Table 17-3 provides several examples. Using Starbucks as a case study, Paul A. Argenti explains how global companies can work collaboratively with NGOs to arrive at a "win–win" outcome. As previously noted, with no external prompting, Starbucks CEO Schultz uses enlightened compensation and benefits packages to attract and retain employees. Despite the fact that Starbucks is widely admired for such forward-thinking management policies, Global Exchange pressed the company to further demonstrate its commitment to social responsibility by selling Fair Trade coffee. Schultz was faced with three options: ignore Global Exchange's demands, fight back, or capitulate. In the end, Schultz pursued a middle ground: He agreed to offer Fair Trade coffee in Starbucks' company-owned U.S. stores. He also launched several other initiatives, including establishing long-term, direct relationships with suppliers. Argenti offers seven lessons from the Starbucks case study:[47]

- Realize that socially responsible companies are likely targets but also attractive candidates for collaboration.
- Don't wait for a crisis to collaborate.
- Think strategically about relationships with NGOs.
- Recognize that collaboration involves some compromise.
- Appreciate the value of the NGOs' independence.
- Understand that building relationships with NGOs takes time and effort.
- Think more like an NGO by using communication strategically.

In an article in *Business Ethics Quarterly*, Arthaud-Day proposed a three-dimensional framework for analyzing the social behavior of international, multinational, global, and transnational firms.[48] These different stages of development constitute the first dimension. The second

Exhibit 17-9 Designer Stella McCartney created one of the fashion world's first socially conscious luxury brands. She does not use fur or leather as materials in her collections; also, McCartney is an advocate for a "circular economy" that reduces energy use and minimizes waste.
Source: Victor VIRGILE/Gamma-Rapho via Getty Images.

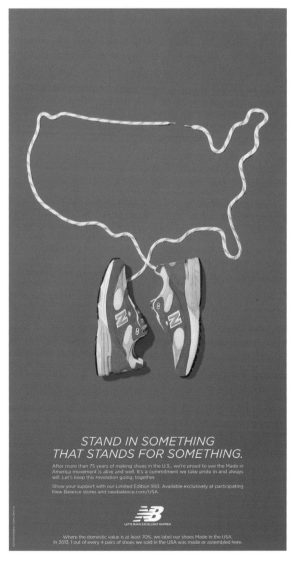

Exhibit 17-10 New Balance Athletic Shoe is the only major footwear company in the United States that manufactures athletic shoes domestically. Management believes that creating jobs at home is an important aspect of corporate citizenship. As a company spokesman has noted, if maximizing profit were the sole objective, it would be more advantageous to source shoes in low-wage countries. This corporate image print ad encourages other U.S. companies to follow New Balance's example.
Source: New Balance Athletic, Inc.

TABLE 17-3 Global Marketing and Corporate Social Responsibility

Company (Headquarters Country)	Nature of CSR Initiative
IKEA (Sweden)	IKEA's primary carpet supplier in India monitors subcontractors to ensure that they do not employ children. IKEA also helps lower-caste Indian women reduce their indebtedness to moneylenders. In an effort to create a more child-friendly environment in Indian villages, IKEA sponsors "bridge schools" to increase literacy so young people—including girls and untouchables—can enroll in regular schools.*
Avon (United States)	The company's Breast Cancer Awareness Crusade has raised hundreds of millions of dollars for cancer research. The money funds research in 50 countries.
Subaru (Japan)	Subaru's assembly plant in Indiana is the first "zero landfill" auto plant in the United States. More than 99 percent of the packaging taken in by the plant is recycled. Subaru also partners with key organizations such as the Leave No Trace Center for Outdoor Ethics and United By Blue, the ocean-friendly apparel brand.

*Edward Luce, "IKEA's Grown-up Plan to Tackle Child Labor," *Financial Times* (September 15, 2004), p. 7.

dimension of the model includes CSR's three "content domains": human rights, labor, and the environment. These are the universal concerns for global companies established by the United Nations Global Compact. The third dimension in Arthaud-Day's framework consists of three perspectives. The *ideological dimension* of CSR pertains to the things a firm's management believes it should be doing; the *societal dimension* consists of the expectations held by the firm's external stakeholders; and the *operational dimension* includes the actions and activities actually taken by the firm. The interactions among the dimensions can result in several conflict scenarios. Conflict may arise if there is an incongruity between those things a company's leadership believes it should be doing and the expectations of stakeholders. Conflict can also arise when there is an incongruity between those things a company's leadership believes it should be doing and the things it actually is doing. Finally, conflict can arise from an incongruity between society's expectations and actual corporate practices and activities.

Summary

To respond to the opportunities and threats in the global marketing environment, organizational leaders must develop a global vision and strategy. Leaders must also be able to communicate that vision throughout the organization and build *core competencies* on a worldwide basis. Global companies are increasingly realizing that the "right" person for a top job is not necessarily a home-country national.

In *organizing* for the global marketing effort, the goal is to create a structure that enables the company to respond to significant differences in international market environments and to extend valuable corporate knowledge. Alternatives include an international division structure, regional management centers, geographic structure, regional or worldwide product division structure, and the *matrix organization*. Whichever form of organization is chosen, balance between autonomy and integration must be established. Many companies are adopting the organizational principle of *lean production* that was pioneered by Japanese automakers.

Many global companies are paying attention to the issue of *corporate social responsibility (CSR)*. A company's *stakeholders* may include *nongovernmental organizations (NGOs)*; *stakeholder analysis* can help identify others. Consumers throughout the world expect that the brands and products they buy and use will be marketed by companies that conduct business in an ethical, socially responsible way. Socially conscious companies should include human rights, labor, and environmental issues in their agendas. These values may be spelled out in a *code of ethics*. Ideological, societal, and organizational perspectives can all be brought to bear on CSR.

Discussion Questions

17-1. Some 52 percent of all CEOs of the largest Swiss companies are from overseas. Why might this be the case?

17-2. Why does it seem that the growth of global business and global marketing is almost inevitably associated with ethical issues and corporate social responsibility?

17-3. Mechanistic and bureaucratic structures can offer big advantages. What are they?

17-4. In what ways is exceptional leadership an important and daunting role in global marketing?

17-5. Identify some features of the Japanese "lean production" concept that could be implemented in a non-automobile industry.

CASE 17-1   *(Continued refer to page 553)*

Unilever

After Cescau was elevated to the top job, Unilever's board streamlined the company's management structure. Now there is a single chief executive; previously, there had been one in Rotterdam and one in London. Cescau asserted that, with a single chief executive, the need for consensus was replaced by speed at making decisions. As noted, many of those decisions concerned "doing good." However, some observers were skeptical of Cescau's determination to operationalize a responsible business philosophy. Cescau recalled, "The company was not doing well. There was an article saying that I was draping myself in a flag of corporate social responsibility to excuse poor performance. I was so angry with that."

Cescau's commitment was put to the test in 2008, his final year as CEO. Greenpeace launched an advertising campaign alleging that Unilever's purchases of Indonesian palm oil were contributing to rain forest destruction. Palm oil, a key ingredient in Dove soap, Magnum ice cream bars, and Vaseline lotion, comes from oil palm trees that grow in Indonesia and Malaysia. Unilever is the world's biggest palm oil customer, buying approximately 1.4 million tons each year. Rising world prices for the commodity prompted Indonesian farmers to cut down large swaths of old-growth rain forest and plant fast-growing oil palms. Specifically, Greenpeace identified the operations of Sinar Mas, an Indonesian company that is a major palm oil supplier, as contributing to deforestation.

The media strategy for the Greenpeace campaign included newspaper ads in London and a video on YouTube. Fliers parodied Unilever's Campaign for Real Beauty; for example, they showed pictures of orangutans juxtaposed with the headline "Gorgeous or gone?" John Sauven, executive director of Greenpeace, explained why his organization had targeted Unilever: "Everyone has heard of those brands. They are the public face of the company" (see Exhibit 17-11).

Cescau responded by calling for a moratorium on rain forest destruction by Indonesian oil producers. The Unilever chief also pledged that his company would buy palm oil only from producers who could prove that the rain forest had not been sacrificed in the production process. The move allied Unilever with the Roundtable on Sustainable Palm Oil (RSPO), an organization that certifies palm oil producers. A Unilever spokesperson also indicated that the proposed change in Unilever's palm oil sourcing strategy had been in the works for months. Nevertheless, Greenpeace and other NGOs claimed victory.

Unilever brought its message to the public with a print ad campaign featuring the headline "What you buy in the supermarket can change the world." The body copy outlined Unilever's pledge that "by 2015 all our palm oil will come from sustainable sources." The ads ended with the tagline "Small actions, big difference." By 2011, however, only 2 percent of Unilever's palm oil purchases were coming from traceable sources. Even so, as chief procurement officer Marc Engel said, "I'm not aware of anyone else who has made that commitment, particularly on our scale." In an effort to achieve its goals, Unilever began buying GreenPalm certificates, which are sold by growers certified by the RSPO.

"Doing well" is also part of the leadership equation at Unilever. Cescau understood the importance of improving Unilever's profitability. To this end, he continued a restructuring drive that was initiated by his predecessor, co-chairman Niall FitzGerald. Specific actions included reducing Unilever's bureaucracy by removing several management layers. Cescau also reduced the top management head count from 25 people to 7 and narrowed the vertical distance between management and marketing. In addition, the company shed hundreds of brands and closed dozens of factories in France, Germany, and elsewhere. In Cescau's view, the new, leaner structure would translate into a more rapid response to changing market trends and consumer preferences and ensure quicker rollouts of new products.

Cescau also bet heavily on emerging markets to jump-start sales growth. Rising incomes mean that many people purchase consumer packaged goods for the first time. One scenario: As increasing numbers of people in developing countries buy their first washing machines, they will need to buy laundry detergent. To capitalize on such trends, Cescau shifted budgetary resources out of mature markets such as Europe, instead using those funds to support research in India and other emerging markets. Brand managers were instructed to innovate by taking a "clean slate" approach to developing new products for emerging markets. As Steph Carter, packaging director for deodorant brands, noted, "Traditionally, we would have taken existing products and then tried to fathom how to adapt them for the developing world. Our thinking has changed."

The Polman Decade Begins

Paul Polman took over as CEO in January 2009; a former Nestlé executive, he was the first outsider to lead Unilever in its 80-year history. In his first months on the job, Polman initiated a shift in Unilever's core strategy. In the past, the company had generated sales growth by increasing prices. Noting that this was the wrong strategy for recessionary times, Polman said the new priority would be to increase sales volumes. The change entailed some risk: Holding the line on prices

Exhibit 17-11 Unilever has been targeted by activist groups concerned about sustainability issues. For example, palm oil is a key ingredient in several of Unilever's brands, but orangutan habitat in Indonesia has been cleared to make room for oil palm plantations. Greenpeace and other NGOs have staged protests; here, an activist dressed as an orangutan is shown outside Unilever House in London. Unilever has pledged that, by 2020, all its palm oil will come from sustainable sources.
Source: Stephen Hird/Reuters.

could put pressure on margins, given the trend of rising costs for the agricultural commodities that are key ingredients in Unilever's products.

Polman was also keenly aware that many budget-conscious shoppers were choosing less expensive, private-label supermarket products instead of well-known name brands. Polman vowed to improve product quality across the board and to boost marketing and advertising spending. To support the increased investment, he accelerated some of the cost-cutting measures that his predecessor had initiated. For example, the timetable for planned factory closures and job cuts was moved up; Polman also froze executive salaries and changed the bonus policy. He established 30-day action plans for managers of brands with flagging sales. He also replaced nearly one-third of Unilever's top 100 executives, including the chief marketing officer.

When it came to demonstrating Unilever's commitment to its customers, Polman sent clear signals to his employees. He spent about 50 percent of his time on the road, with regular stops in Asia, Latin America, and, of course, Europe. In a recent interview, he noted that he would meet with consumers in every country that he visited. Polman believes strongly that the leader must set an example from the top of the organization.

That passion is evident in a flurry of marketing activities orchestrated by Polman. One is the quick pace of new-product rollouts, especially in emerging markets. For example, Unilever's home care unit was the first to market with liquid laundry detergent in China; it also introduced a dishwashing liquid in Turkey in less than 30 days. In addition, innovation has become a key element for shoring up the value proposition of Unilever's brands, with existing brands such as Surf laundry detergent getting an upgrade in the African market.

Driving growth in the personal-care category has been another priority for Polman. By itself, the global deodorant segment represents an estimated $17 billion in annual sales. To tap into that market, the Dove brand has been extended to men's products. Dove for Men has been rolled out in dozens of countries.

Meanwhile, Dove's product managers devised a new strategy for persuading women to switch deodorant brands. Dove Ultimate Go Sleeveless resulted from company research designed to discover insights about consumer attitudes toward underarms. What the researchers learned is that 93 percent of women think their armpits are not attractive. Dove Ultimate Go Sleeveless is formulated with moisturizers that, the company claims, will result in nicer-looking underarms after just a few days' use.

The ice cream and beverage unit is also on the move. Unilever's Magnum brand premium ice cream bars are the world's top-selling ice cream novelty. Although Magnum enjoys great popularity in Europe, it was not introduced in the United States until 2011. Häagen-Dazs and Mars were already entrenched in the market; undaunted, the Magnum marketing team is confident its brand will stand out. One manager explained that an important part of the brand's equity is the loud cracking sound heard when someone bites through Magnum's thick chocolate shell. It must be helping: In its first year on the U.S. market, Magnum rang up $100 million in sales.

Between 2015 and 2017, Polman presided over an ambitious schedule of mergers and acquisitions. Many of the 18 acquisitions represented relatively small investments in fast-growing niche businesses. Case in point: Unilever paid $1 billion for Dollar Shave Club, the upstart e-commerce company offering personal products by subscription that disrupted a sleepy consumer category dominated by Gillette. Other investments such as Carver Korea are bringing Unilever into regional and local markets around the globe.

Meanwhile, Unilever itself became the target of a takeover bid. Polman turned down Kraft Heinz's offer of £115 billion ($143 billion) on the grounds that the bid "drastically undervalued" Unilever's assets. Analysts wondered whether Unilever's new CEO would seek a major acquisition such as Colgate-Palmolive or Estée Lauder.

And, as Brexit talks continued, Unilever postponed the decision regarding streamlining its corporate structure. For years, the company commonly known as the "Anglo-Dutch consumer products giant" consisted of two parent companies and headquarters locations in both London and Rotterdam. In addition, Unilever stock was listed on two separate European exchanges. This dual structure was due in part to differing regulations in the United Kingdom and the Netherlands concerning taxation of investor dividends. By 2017, as the Dutch government undertook tax reform to attract more foreign investment, top management at Unilever prepared to shift to a unified structure headquartered in one country only. The question was: Which one?

Renewing the Commitment to Sustainability

Even while overseeing these and other management and marketing activities, Polman has made sure that former CEO Cescau's commitment to corporate social responsibility is maintained. Summarizing his views on sustainability and environmental impact, Polman said:

> [T]he road to well-being doesn't go via reduced consumption. It has to be done via more responsible consumption. . . . So that's why we're taking such a stand on moving the world to sustainable palm oil. That's why we work with small-hold farmers, to be sure that people who don't have sufficient nutrition right now have a chance to have a better life.

In 2012, Unilever announced plans to build a $100 million palm oil processing plant in Indonesia. Having a company-controlled plant near the source should make the task of tracing oil to sustainable sources easier. It is currently common practice at processing plants to combine oil from different sources—both sustainable and not—in the same vat. That makes it difficult to trace any individual batch of oil to its origins.

Marc Engel, chief supply chain officer, draws an analogy between palm oil processing and crude oil processing used to make gasoline. "When you actually want to know where the gas in your car is coming from—from which oil well—it's very hard to see," he says. To hedge its bets, Unilever has also invested in Solazyme, a California-based company that produces oil from algae. What kind of potential does this technology hold? "We've made all kinds of food products," says Solazyme CEO and cofounder Jonathan Wolfson. "We've used the oil for frying. We've made mayonnaises, ice creams. And they work, taste good and are functional."

Discussion Questions

17-6. If a company such as Unilever has to make trade-offs between being a good corporate citizen and making a profit, which should be the higher priority?

17-7. Assess Cescau's response to the Greenpeace palm oil protest. Was it appropriate? Which types of relationships should Unilever cultivate with Greenpeace and other NGOs in the future?

17-8. Do you think that a streamlined management structure and emphasis on emerging markets and niche acquisitions will help a big company like Unilever increase revenue growth by a significant amount? Or, will a much larger acquisition be required?

17-9. As you read this, has Unilever decided on a single headquarters country? If so, which one, and why?

Sources: Saabira Chaudhuri, "Nipped by Upstarts, Unilever Decides to Imitate Them," *The Wall Street Journal* (January 3, 2018), pp. A1, A8; Scheherazade Daneshkhu, "Unilever Uses Deals Strategy to Enter Niche Markets," *Financial Times* (December 1, 2017), p. 18; Michael Skapinker and Scheherazade Daneshkhu, "Man on a Mission," *Financial Times* (October 1–2, 2016), p. 20; Paul Sonne, "Unilever Takes Palm Oil in Hand," *The Wall Street Journal* (April 24, 2012), p. B3; Louise Lucas, "Growing Issue for Palm Oil Producers," *Financial Times* (May 23, 2011), p. 22; Ellen Byron, "Unilever Takes on the Ugly Underarm," *The Wall Street Journal* (March 30, 2011), p. B1; Paul Sonne, "To Wash Hands of Palm Oil, Unilever Embraces Algae," *The Wall Street Journal* (September 7, 2010), p. B1; Louise Lucas, "Investors Skeptical as Unilever Pursues Bold Growth Plan," *Financial Times* (November 16, 2010), p. 20; Stefan Stern, "The Outsider in a Hurry to Shake up His Company," *Financial Times* (April 5, 2010), p. 4; Jenny Wiggins, "Unilever Vows to Focus on Cheaper Products," *Financial Times* (August 7, 2009), p. 17; Jenny Wiggins, "Unilever's New Chief Prepares to Brew up Changes," *Financial Times* (February 6, 2009), p. 15; Michael Skapinker, "Taking a Hard Line on Soft Soap," *Financial Times* (July 7, 2008), p. 12; Aaron O. Patrick, "After Protests, Unilever Does an About-Face on Palm Oil," *The Wall Street Journal* (May 2, 2008), p. B1.

APPENDIX

Johnson & Johnson Credos: Brazil, Russia, India, and China

Nosso Credo

Cremos que nossa primeira responsabilidade é para com os médicos, enfermeiras e pacientes,
para com as mães, pais e todos os demais que usam nossos produtos e serviços.
Para atender suas necessidades, tudo que fizermos deve ser de alta qualidade.
Devemos constantemente nos esforçar para reduzir nossos custos,
a fim de manter preços razoáveis.
Os pedidos de nossos clientes devem ser pronta e corretamente atendidos.
Nossos fornecedores e distribuidores devem ter a oportunidade
de auferir um lucro justo.

Somos responsáveis por nossos empregados,
homens e mulheres que conosco trabalham em todo o mundo.
Todos devem ser considerados em sua individualidade.
Devemos respeitar sua dignidade e reconhecer o seu mérito.
Eles devem se sentir seguros em seus empregos.
A remuneração pelo seu trabalho deve ser justa e adequada
e o ambiente de trabalho limpo, ordenado e seguro.
Devemos ter em mente maneiras de ajudar nossos empregados
a atender as suas responsabilidades familiares.
Os empregados devem se sentir livres para fazer sugestões e reclamações.
Deve haver igual oportunidade de emprego, desenvolvimento
e progresso para os qualificados.
Devemos ter uma administração competente,
e suas ações devem ser justas e éticas.

Somos responsáveis perante as comunidades nas quais vivemos e trabalhamos,
bem como perante a comunidade mundial.
Devemos ser bons cidadãos – apoiar boas obras sociais e de caridade
e pagar corretamente os tributos.
Devemos encorajar o desenvolvimento do civismo e a melhoria da saúde e da educação.
Devemos manter em boa ordem
as propriedades que temos o privilégio de usar,
protegendo o meio ambiente e os recursos naturais.

Nossa responsabilidade final é para com os acionistas.
Os negócios devem proporcionar lucros adequados.
Devemos experimentar novas idéias.
Pesquisas devem ser levadas avante. Programas inovadores desenvolvidos
e os erros corrigidos.
Novos equipamentos devem ser adquiridos, novas fábricas construídas
e novos produtos lançados.
Reservas devem ser criadas para enfrentar tempos adversos.
Ao operarmos de acordo com esses princípios,
nossos acionistas devem
receber justa recompensa.

Johnson & Johnson

Наше Кредо

Наша основная ответственность – перед врачами и медицинскими сёстрами,
перед пациентами, перед отцами и матерями, перед всеми,
кто пользуется нашей продукцией и услугами. В соответствии с их
потребностями мы должны обеспечивать высокие стандарты качества во всём,
что мы делаем. Мы должны постоянно стремиться к снижению затрат,
чтобы поддерживать приемлемый уровень цен. Заказы клиентов должны
выполняться точно и в срок. Наши поставщики и дистрибьюторы
должны иметь возможность получать достойную прибыль.

Мы несём ответственность перед нашими сотрудниками,
мужчинами и женщинами, которые работают у нас по всему миру.
Мы должны ценить индивидуальность в каждом из них.
Мы должны уважать их достоинство и признавать их заслуги:
нам важно поддерживать в них чувство уверенности в завтрашнем дне.
Вознаграждение должно быть справедливым и соразмерным,
а условия труда обеспечивать чистоту, порядок и безопасность.
Нам важно, чтобы сотрудники имели возможность заботиться о семье.
Сотрудники должны чувствовать, что они могут свободно
выступать с предложениями и замечаниями.
У всех квалифицированных специалистов должны быть
равные возможности для получения работы, развития и продвижения.
Мы должны обеспечивать компетентное управление,
действия руководителей должны быть справедливыми и этичными.

Мы несём ответственность перед обществом,
в котором живём и работаем, а также перед мировым сообществом.
Мы должны выполнять свой гражданский долг:
поддерживать добрые начинания и благотворительные акции,
честно платить налоги. Мы должны содействовать улучшениям
в социальной сфере, здравоохранении и образовании.
Мы должны бережно относиться к вверенной нам собственности,
сохраняя природные ресурсы и защищая окружающую среду.

И, наконец, мы несём ответственность перед нашими акционерами.
Бизнес должен приносить существенную прибыль.
Мы должны экспериментировать с новыми идеями,
вести научно-исследовательскую работу,
внедрять инновации, учиться на своих ошибках.
Мы должны приобретать новое оборудование, обеспечивать современные
условия работы и выводить на рынок новую продукцию.
Мы должны быть готовы к сложным ситуациям и иметь резервы
для их решения. Придерживаясь этих принципов,
мы обеспечим нашим акционерам достойный доход.

हमारी नीति

हम यह मानते हैं कि हमारी पहली जिम्मेदारी डाक्टरों, नर्सों, रोगियों, माताओं, पिताओं तथा
उन सभी लोगों के प्रति है जो हमारे उत्पादनों और सेवाओं का उपयोग करते हैं।
उनकी आवश्यकताओं की पूर्ति के लिए जो कुछ भी हम करें, वह उत्तम दर्जे का हो।
हमें अपने उत्पादनों की कीमत घटाने की लगातार कोशिश करनी चाहिए
ताकि वे उचित कीमतों में उपलब्ध हों।
ग्राहकों की मांगी सही तौर पर तथा तत्परता से पूरी की जानी चाहिए।
हमारे विक्रेताओं और वितरकों को उचित लाभ मिलने का अवसर मिले।

हम अपने उन सभी और पुरुष कर्मचारियों के प्रति
जिम्मेदार हैं जो हमारे साथ संसार के हर देश में काम करते हैं।
हर व्यक्ति को व्यक्तिगत रूप से देखा जाय।
हमें उनकी प्रतिष्ठा और योग्यता का आदर करना चाहिए।
उन्हें अपनी नौकरी का सुरक्षा का विश्वास रहे।
उनका वेतन उचित और पर्याप्त हो।
काम करने का वातावरण स्वच्छ, सुव्यवस्थित और सुरक्षित हो।
पारिवारिक जिम्मेदारियां निभानेके लिए हमें अपने कर्मचारियोंको दक्षतापूर्वक मार्ग दिखाने चाहिए।
कर्मचारियों को उनके सुझाव और शिकायतें उचित ढंग से प्रस्तुत करने की स्वतंत्रता हो।
योग्य लोगों को सेवा, प्रगति और विकास का समान अवसर मिले।
हमारा व्यवस्थापन निपुण हो और प्रबंधकों की कृति उचित और न्यायपूर्ण हो।

हम जिस समाज में रहते और काम करते हैं और जिस विश्व समाज के हम भाग हैं
उस समाज के प्रति हमारी जिम्मेदारी है।
हमें अच्छा नागरिक होना चाहिए – दान, धर्म और दूसरे अच्छे कार्यों में
भाग लेना चाहिए तथा अपने हिस्से के कर बराबर चुकाने चाहिए।
हम नगर-सुधार, स्वास्थ्य और शिक्षा को प्रोत्साहन करें।
वातावरण और नैसर्गिक उपलब्धियों को सुरक्षित रखते हुए, जिस संपत्ति का उपयोग
करने का हमें सुअवसर मिला है इसे हम अच्छी तरह संभाल कर रखें।

हमारी आखरी जिम्मेदारी भागधारकों के प्रति है।
व्यापार में पर्याप्त लाभ होना चाहिए।
हमें नये-नये विचारों को अमल में लाना चाहिए।
अनुसंधान किए जाएं, आभिनव योजनाओं का विकास किया जाए और
भूलों से हुई हानि का मूल्य चुकाया जाए।
नये यंत्र खरिदे जाएं, नई सुविधाओं उपलब्ध हों और नये उत्पादनों का
निर्माण किया जाए ताकि बुरे दिनों के लिए प्रबंध हो।
यदि हम उन सिद्धान्तों के अनुसार कार्य करते हैं तो
भागधारकों को पर्याप्त लाभ मिल सकता है।

जॉनसन ॲण्ड जॉनसन

我们的信条

我们相信我们的首先要对医生、护士和病人,
对父母亲以及所有使用我们的产品和接受我们服务的人负责。
为了满足他们的需求,我们所做的一切都必须是高质量的。
我们必须不断致力于降低成本,以保持合理的价格。
客户的订货必须迅速而准确地供应。
我们的供应商和经销商应该有机会获得合理的利润。

我们要对世界各地和我们一起从事的男女同仁负责。
每一位同仁都应被作为独立的个体。
我们必须维护他们的尊严,赞赏他们的优点。
要使他们对其工作有一种安全感。
薪酬必须公平合理。
工作环境必须清洁、整齐和安全。
我们必须设法帮助员工履行他们对家庭的责任。
必须让员工在提出建议和申诉时无所顾虑。
对于合格的人必须给予平等的聘用、发展和升迁的机会,
我们必须具备称职的管理人员,
他们的行为必须公正并符合道德。

我们要对我们所生活和工作的社会,对整个世界负责。
我们必须做好公民 – 支持对社会有益的活动和慈善事业,
缴纳我们应付的税款。
我们必须鼓励公民进步,促进健康和教育事业。
我们必须很好地维护我们所使用的财产,
保护环境和自然资源。

最后,我们要对全体股东负责。
企业经营必须获取可靠的利润。
我们必须尝试新的构想。
必须坚持研究工作,开发革新项目。
承担错误的代价并加以改正。
必须购置新设备,提供新设施,推出新产品。
必须设立储备金,以备不时之需。
如果我们的业务运作是按照这些原则进行经营
股东们就会获得合理的回报。

Johnson & Johnson

Notes

[1]Carleton "Carly" S. Fiorina, Commencement Address, Massachusetts Institute of Technology, Cambridge, MA, June 2, 2002. See also Carly S. Fiorina, "It's Death If You Stop Trying New Things," *Financial Times* (November 20, 2003), p. 8.

[2]William C. Taylor and Alan M. Webber, *Going Global: Four Entrepreneurs Map the New World Marketplace* (New York: Penguin Books USA, 1996), p. 12.

[3]Noel M. Tichy and Stratford Sherman, *Control Your Destiny or Someone Else Will* (New York: HarperBusiness, 1994), p. 227.

[4]John Arlidge, "Coke's Brit Boss: I May Turn out to Be a 'Cretin,' We'll Find Out," *The Sunday Times* (November 26, 2017), p. 6.

[5]Kerry Peckter, "The Foreigners Are Coming," *International Business* (September 1993), p. 53.

[6]Evan Ramstad, "CEO Broadens Vistas at LG," *The Wall Street Journal* (May 21, 2008), pp. B1, B2.

[7]Kerry Peckter, "The Foreigners Are Coming," *International Business* (September 1993), p. 58.

[8]Kana Inagaki, "Rise of Leroy Signals Toyota's Global Goals," *Financial Times* (June 19, 2015), p. 17.

[9]Monte Reel, Kae Inoue, Jihn Lippert, Jie Ma, and Ania Nussbaum, "Globalism Is Alive and Well," *Bloomberg Businessweek* (July 24, 2017), pp. 50–55.

[10]Neil McCartney, "Squaring up to Usability at Nokia," *Financial Times—IT Review Telecom World* (October 13, 2003), p. 4.

[11]C. K. Prahalad and Gary Hamel, "The Core Competence of the Corporation," *Harvard Business Review* 68, no. 3 (May–June 1990), pp. 79–86.

[12]George S. Yip, *Total Global Strategy* (Upper Saddle River, NJ: Prentice Hall, 1992), p. 179.

[13]Kerry Peckter, "The Foreigners Are Coming," *International Business* (September 1993), p. 58.

[14]William Dawkins, "Time to Pull Back the Screen," *Financial Times* (November 18, 1996), p. 12. See also Sumantra Ghoshal and Christopher A. Bartlett, *The Individualized Corporation* (New York, NY: Harper Perennial, 1999), pp. 179–181.

[15]Christopher Bartlett and Sumantra Ghoshal, *Managing across Borders: The Transnational Solution* (Boston, MA: Harvard Business School Press, 1989), p. 3.

[16]Vladimir Pucik, "Globalization and Human Resource Management," in V. Pucik, N. Tichy, and C. Barnett (eds.), *Globalizing Management: Creating and Leading the Competitive Organization* (New York, NY: John Wiley & Sons, 1992), p. 70.

[17]Regina Fazio Maruca, "The Right Way to Go Global: An Interview with Whirlpool CEO David Whitwam," *Harvard Business Review* 72, no. 2 (March–April 1994), p. 137.

[18]Henry Mintzberg, "The Effective Organization: Forces and Forms," *Sloan Management Review* 32, no. 2 (Winter 1991), pp. 54–55.

[19]William C. Taylor and Alan M. Webber, *Going Global: Four Entrepreneurs Map the New World Marketplace* (New York, NY: Penguin, 1996), pp. 48–58.

[20]Jeremy Grant, "Hershey Chews over Growth Strategy," *Financial Times* (December 14, 2005), p. 23.

[21]Colum Murphy and Laurie Burkitt, "Hershey Launches New Brand in China," *The Wall Street Journal* (May 21, 2013), p. B8.

[22]". . . And Other Ways to Peel the Onion," *The Economist* (January 7, 1995), pp. 52–53.

[23]Emily Glazer, "P&G Unit Bids Goodbye to Cincinnati, Hello to Asia," *The Wall Street Journal* (May 11, 2012), p. B1.

[24]Allen J. Morrison, David A. Ricks, and Kendall Roth, "Globalization versus Regionalization: Which Way for the Multinational?", *Organizational Dynamics* (Winter 1991), pp. 17–29.

[25]Joann S. Lublin, "Division Problem: Place vs. Product: It's Tough to Choose a Management Model," *The Wall Street Journal* (June 27, 2001), pp. A1, A4.

[26]Emily Nelson, "Rallying the Troops at P&G: New CEO Lafley Aims to End Upheaval by Revamping Program of Globalization," *The Wall Street Journal* (August 31, 2000), pp. B1, B4.

[27]Claudia Deutsch, "At Home in the World," *The New York Times* (February 14, 2008), p. C1.

[28]"Ericsson to Simplify Business Structure," *Financial Times* (September 29, 1998), p. 21.

[29]Mark Maremont, "Gillette to Shut 14 of Its Plants, Lay off 4,700," *The Wall Street Journal* (September 29, 1998), pp. A3, A15.

[30]Paul Proctor, "Boeing Shifts to 'Platform Teams,'" *Aviation Week & Space Technology* (May 17, 1999), pp. 63–64.

[31]John W. Hunt, "Is Matrix Management a Recipe for Chaos?" *Financial Times* (January 12, 1998), p. 10.

[32]William C. Taylor and Alan M. Webber, *Going Global: Four Entrepreneurs Map the New World Marketplace* (New York, NY: Penguin USA, 1996), p. 25.

[33]Andrew Edgecliffe-Johnson, "Case Study: EMI," *Financial Times* (September 23, 2011), p. 4.

[34]Haig Simonian, "The GE Man Who Generated a Buzz," *Financial Times* (June 8, 2009), p. 17.

[35]This section is adapted from the following sources: James P. Womack, Daniel T. Jones, and Daniel Roos, *The Machine That Changed the World: The Story of Lean Production* (New York, NY: HarperCollins, 1990); Ranganath Nayak and John M. Ketteringham, *Breakthroughs!* (San Diego, CA: Pfeiffer, 1994), Chapter 9; and Michael Williams, "Back to the Past: Some Plants Tear out Long Assembly Lines, Switch to Craft Work," *The Wall Street Journal* (October 24, 1994), pp. A1, A4.

[36]Kate Linebaugh, "Honda's Flexible Plants Provide Edge," *The Wall Street Journal* (September 23, 2008), p. B1.

[37]Joseph B. White, "GM Plans to Invest $445 Million, Cut Staff," *The Wall Street Journal* (May 27, 1999), p. A23.

[38]The English term *stakeholder* is sometimes hard to convey in different languages, especially in developing countries. See Neil King, Jr., and Jason Dean, "Untranslatable Word in U.S. Aide's Speech Leaves Beijing Baffled," *The Wall Street Journal* (December 7, 2005), pp. A1, A8.

[39]Archie B. Carroll and Ann K. *Buchholtz, Business and Society: Ethics and Stakeholder Management*, 5th ed. (Cincinnati, OH: South-Western, 2003).

[40]Haig Simonian, "Nestlé Charts Low-Income Territory," *Financial Times* (July 14, 2006), p. 15.

[41]Jack Neff, "Unilever, P&G War Over Which Is Most Ethical," *Advertising Age* (March 3, 2008), p. 67.

[42]John Murray Brown and Jenny Wiggins, "Coffee Empire Expands Reach by Pressing Its Luck in Ireland," *Financial Times* (December 15, 2005), p. 21.

[43]Andrew Ward, "Coke Struggles to Defend Positive Reputation," *Financial Times* (January 6, 2006), p. 15.

[44]Terrence H. Witkowski, "Antiglobal Challenges to Marketing in Developing Countries: Exploring the Ideological Divide," *Journal of Public Policy and Marketing* 24, no. 1 (Spring 2005), pp. 7–23.

[45]Stratford Sherman and Noel Tichy, *Control Your Destiny or Someone Else Will* (New York: HarperBusiness, 2001), Chapter 9, "The Mirror Test."

[46]Jena McGregor, "Major Company CEOs Made 271 Times the Typical U.S. Worker in 2016," *The Washington Post* (July 20, 2017), p. 4.

[47]Paul A. Argenti, "Collaborating with Activists: How Starbucks Works with NGOs," *California Management Review* 47, no. 1 (Summer 2004), pp. 91–116.

[48]Marne Arthaud-Day, "Transnational Corporate Social Responsibility: A Tri-dimensional Approach to International CSR Research," *Business Ethics Quarterly* 15, no. 1 (January 2005), pp. 1–22.

Glossary

The chapter number(s) follow(s) the definition.

80/20 rule In behavioral market segmentation, the rule of thumb that 20 percent of a company's products or customers account for 80 percent of revenues or profits. (7)

achievement The fourth dimension in Hofstede's social values framework that describes a society in which men are expected to be assertive, competitive, and concerned with material success and women fulfill the role of nurturer and are concerned with issues such as the welfare of children. (4)

acquisition A market-entry strategy that entails investing in assets outside the home country. (12)

adaptation strategy A global market approach that involves changing elements of design, function, or packaging in response to needs or conditions in particular country markets. (10)

adopter categories In the adoption process developed by Everett Rogers, a typology of buyers at different stages of the "adoption" or product life cycle. The categories are innovators, early adopters, early majority, late majority, and laggards. (4)

adoption process A model developed by Everett Rogers that describes the "adoption" or purchase decision process. The stages consist of awareness, interest, evaluation, trial, and adoption. (4)

ad valorem duty A duty that is expressed as a percentage of the value of goods. (8)

advertising Any sponsored, paid message that is communicated through a nonpersonal channel. Advertising is one of the four variables in the promotion mix. (13)

advertising appeal The communications approach that relates to the motives of the target audience. (13)

advertising organization A corporation or holding company that includes one or more "core" advertising agencies, as well as units specializing in direct marketing, marketing services, public relations, or research. (13)

advocacy advertising A form of corporate advertising in which a company presents its point of view on a particular issue. (13)

aesthetics A shared sense within a culture of what is beautiful as opposed to not beautiful and what represents good taste as opposed to tastelessness. (4)

agent An intermediary who negotiates transactions between two or more parties but does not take title to the goods being purchased or sold. (12)

Andean Community A customs union comprised of Bolivia, Colombia, Ecuador, and Peru. (3)

antidumping duties Duties imposed on products whose prices government officials deem too low. (8)

appeal The creative approach used in advertising to attract the attention of the target audience. Rational appeals and emotional appeals are two common approaches. (13)

arbitration A negotiation process between two or more parties to settle a dispute outside of the court system. (5)

art direction The visual presentation of an advertisement. (13)

art director An ad agency "creative" with general responsibility for the overall look of an advertisement. The art director chooses graphics, pictures, type styles, and other visual elements. (13)

Association of Southeast Asian Nations (ASEAN) A trade bloc comprised of Brunei, Cambodia, Indonesia, Malaysia, Laos, Myanmar, the Philippines, Singapore, Thailand, and Vietnam. (3)

attitude In culture, a learned tendency to respond in a consistent way to a given object or entity. (4)

balance of payments The record of all economic transactions between the residents of a country and the rest of the world. (2)

barter The least complex and oldest form of bilateral, non-monetized countertrade consisting of a direct exchange of goods or services between two parties. (11)

behavior segmentation The process of performing market segmentation utilizing user status, usage rate, or some other measure of product consumption. (7)

belief In culture, an organized pattern of knowledge that an individual holds to be true about the world. (4)

benefit segmentation The process of segmenting markets on the basis of the benefits sought by buyers. (7)

big data Extremely large data sets that can be subjected to computational analysis to reveal patterns and trends. (6)

big idea A concept that can serve as the basis for a memorable, effective advertising message. (13)

Bluetooth Technology that permits access to the Internet from a cell phone when the user is within the range of a hotspot. (15)

brand A representation of a promise by a particular company about a particular product; a complex bundle of images and experiences in the customer's mind. (10)

brand equity The reflection of the brand's value to a company as an intangible asset. (10)

brand extensions A strategy that uses an established brand name as an umbrella when entering new businesses or developing new product lines that represent new categories to the company. (10)

brand image A single, but often complex, mental image about both the physical product and the company that markets it. (10)

bribery The corrupt business practice of demanding or offering some type of consideration—typically a cash payment—when negotiating a cross-border deal. (5)

broadband A digital communication system with sufficient capacity to carry multiple voice, data, or video channels simultaneously. (15)

business-to-business (b-to-b or B2B) marketing Marketing products and services to other companies and organizations. Contrasts with business-to-consumer (b-to-c or B2C) marketing. (12)

business-to-consumer (b-to-c or B2C) marketing Marketing products and services to people for their own use. Contrasts with business-to-business (b-to-b or B2B) marketing. (12)

Byrd Amendment Law that calls for antidumping revenues to be paid to U.S. companies harmed by imported goods sold at below-market prices. (11)

call centers Sophisticated telephone operations that provide customer support and other services to in-bound callers from around the world. May also provide outsourcing services such as telemarketing. (8)

call option The right to buy a specified amount of foreign currency at a fixed price, up to the option's expiration date. (2)

capital account In a country's balance of payments, the record of all long-term direct investment, portfolio investment, and other short- and long-term capital flows. (2)

cartel A group of separate companies or countries that collectively set prices, control output, or take other actions to maximize profits. (5)

cash with order (CWO) A form of trade financing that presents the least transaction risk to the exporter. (8)

catalog A magazine-style publication that features photographs, illustrations, and extensive information about a company's products. (14)

category killer A store that specializes in a particular product category and offers a vast selection at low prices. (12)

Central American Integration System A customs union comprised of El Salvador, Honduras, Guatemala, Nicaragua, Costa Rica, and Panama. (3)

centrally planned capitalism An economic system characterized by command resource allocation and private resource ownership. (2)

centrally planned socialism An economic system characterized by command resource allocation and state resource ownership. (2)

CFR (cost and freight) A contract in which the seller is not responsible for risk or loss at any point outside the factory. (11)

changing the rules of engagement A strategy for creating competitive advantage that involves breaking these rules and refusing to play by the rules set by industry leaders. (16)

channel of distribution An organized network of agencies and institutions that, in combination, perform all the activities required to link producers with users to accomplish the marketing task. (12)

characteristics of innovations One element of Everett Rogers' diffusion of innovations framework. The other elements in the framework are the five-stage innovation adoption process and innovation adopter categories. (4)

cherry picking In distribution, a situation in which a channel intermediary such as a distributor accepts new lines only from manufacturers whose products and brands already enjoy strong demand. (12)

CIF (cost, insurance, freight) named port The Incoterm for a contract requiring the seller to retain responsibility and liability for goods until they have physically passed over the rail of a ship. (11)

civil-law country A country in which the legal system reflects the structural concepts and principles of the Roman Empire in the sixth century. (5)

click-through rate The percentage of visitors to an Internet site who click on an advertisement link presented on the computer screen. (15)

cluster analysis In market research, a quantitative data analysis technique that groups variables into clusters that maximize within-group similarities and between-group differences. Can be used in psychographic segmentation. (6)

co-branding A variation of combination branding in which two or more different company or product brands are featured prominently on product packaging or in advertising. (10)

code of ethics A formal statement that summarizes a company's core ideologies, corporate values, and expectations. (17)

collectivist culture In Geert Hofstede's social values typology, a culture in which group cohesiveness and harmony are emphasized. A shared concern for the well-being of all members of society is also evident. (4)

combination branding A strategy in which a corporate name is combined with a product brand name; also called tiered or umbrella branding. (10)

Common Agricultural Policy (CAP) Legislation adopted by European countries after World War II to aid and protect the interests of farmers. (8)

common external tariff (CET) A tariff agreed upon by members of a preferential trading bloc. Implementation of a CET marks the transition from a free trade area to a customs union. (3)

common-law country A country in which the legal system relies on past judicial decisions (cases) to resolve disputes. (5)

common market A preferential trade agreement that builds on the foundation of economic integration provided by a free trade area and a customs union. (3)

Common Market of the South (Mercosur) A customs union comprised of Argentina, Brazil, Paraguay, and Uruguay. (3)

compensation trading (buyback) A countertrade deal typically involving the sale of plant equipment or technology licensing in which the seller or licensor agrees to take payment in the form of the products produced using the equipment or technology for a specified number of years. (11)

competitive advantage The result of a match between a firm's distinctive competencies and the factors critical for creating superior customer value in an industry. (1, 16)

confirmed irrevocable letter of credit An L/C that provides an extra layer of financing protection by stipulating that an exporter's bank will pay if importer's bank cannot perform. (8)

confiscation Governmental seizure of a company's assets without compensation. (5)

conjoint analysis In market research, a quantitative data analysis technique that can be used to gain insights into the combination of product features that will be attractive to potential buyers. (6)

consumer panel Primary data collection using a sample of consumers or households whose behavior is tracked over time; frequently used for television audience measurement. (6)

consumer sales promotions Promotion designed to make consumers aware of a new product, to stimulate nonusers to sample an existing product, or to increase overall consumer demand. (14)

containerization In physical distribution, the practice of loading oceangoing freight into steel boxes measuring 20 feet, 40 feet, or longer. (12)

content site A Web site that provides news and entertainment and supports a company's PR efforts. (15)

continuous innovation A product that is "new and improved" and requires little research and development (R&D) expenditure to develop, causes minimal disruption in existing consumption patterns, and requires the least amount of learning on the part of buyers. (10)

contract manufacturing A licensing arrangement in which a global company provides technical specifications to a subcontractor or local manufacturer. (9)

convenience stores A form of retail distribution that offers some of the same products as supermarkets, but the merchandise mix is limited to high-turnover convenience products. (12)

convergence The aspect of the digital revolution that pertains to the merging, overlapping, or coming together of previously distinct industries or product categories. (15)

cooperative exporter An export organization of a manufacturing company retained by other independent manufacturers to sell their products in some or all foreign markets. (8)

copy The words that are the spoken or written communication elements in advertisements. (13)

copyright The establishment of ownership of a written, recorded, performed, or filmed creative work. (5)

copywriters Language specialists who develop the headlines, subheads, and body copy used in print advertising and the scripts containing the words that are delivered by spokespeople, actors, or hired voice talents in broadcast ads. (13)

core competence Something that an organization can do better than its competitors. (17)

corporate advertising Advertising that is not designed to directly stimulate demand for a specific product. Image advertising and advocacy advertising are two types of corporate advertising. (13)

corporate social responsibility (CSR) A company's obligation and commitment to the pursuit of goals and policies that are in society's best interests. (17)

cost-based pricing Pricing based on an analysis of internal costs (e.g., materials, labor, etc.) and external costs. (11)

cost-based transfer pricing A transfer pricing policy that uses costs as a basis for setting prices in intracorporate transfers. (11)

cost focus In Michael Porter's generic strategies framework, one of four options for building competitive advantage. When a firm that serves a small (niche) market has a lower cost structure than its competitors, it can offer customers the lowest prices in the industry. (16)

cost leadership A competitive advantage based on a firm's position as the industry's low-cost competitor. (16)

counterfeiting The unauthorized copying and production of a product. (5)

counterpurchase A monetized countertrade deal in which the seller agrees to purchase products of equivalent value that it must then sell in order to realize revenue from the original deal. (11)

countertrade An export transaction in which a sale results in product flowing in one direction to a buyer, and a separate stream of products and services, often flowing in the opposite direction. (11)

countervailing duties (CVDs) Additional duties levied to offset subsidies granted in the exporting country. (8)

country and market concentration A market expansion strategy that involves targeting a limited number of customer segments in a few countries. (9)

country and market diversification The corporate market expansion strategy of a global, multibusiness company. (9)

country concentration and market diversification A market expansion strategy in which a company serves many markets in a few countries. (9)

country diversification and market concentration A market expansion strategy whereby a company seeks out the world market for a product. (9)

country-of-origin effect Perceptions of, and attitudes toward, products or brands on the basis of the country of origin or manufacture. (10)

coupon A sales promotion tool consisting of a printed certificate that entitles the bearer to a price reduction or some other value-enhancing consideration when purchasing a particular product or service. (14)

creative execution In advertising, the way an appeal or selling proposition is presented. Creative execution is the "how," and creative strategy is the "what." (13)

creatives An advertising agency term that applies to art directors and copywriters. (13)

creative strategy A statement or concept of what a particular advertising message or campaign will say. (13)

culture A society's ways of living transmitted from one generation to another. Culture's manifestations include attitudes, beliefs, values, aesthetics, dietary customs, and language. (4)

current account A record of all recurring trade in merchandise and services, private gifts, and public aid transactions between countries. (2)

customer relationship management (CRM) The process of storing and analyzing data collected from customer "touchpoints" for the purpose of identifying a firm's best customers and serving their needs as efficiently, effectively, and profitably as possible. (6)

customer strategy A sales representative's plan for collecting and analyzing information about the needs of each customer or prospect. (14)

customs union A preferential trade bloc whose members agree to seek a greater degree of economic integration than is provided by a free trade agreement. In addition to reducing tariffs and quotas, a customs union is characterized by a common external tariff (CET). (3)

cybersquatting The practice of registering a particular domain name for the express purpose of reselling it to the company that should rightfully use it. (15)

data warehouse A database, part of a company's MIS, that is used to support management decision making. (6)

Defense Advanced Research Projects Agency (DARPA) Agency that created a computer network that could maintain lines of communication in the event of a war. (15)

delivered duty paid (DDB) A type of contract in which the seller has agreed to deliver the goods to the buyer at the place the buyer names in the country of import, with all costs, including duties, paid. (11)

demand conditions In Michael Porter's framework for national competitive advantage, conditions that determine the rate and nature of improvement and innovations by the firms in the nation. (16)

demographic segmentation The process of segmenting markets on the basis of measurable characteristics such as country, income, population, age, or some other measure. (7)

department store A category of retail operations characterized by multiple sections or areas under one roof, each representing a distinct merchandise line and staffed with a limited number of salespeople. (12)

devaluation The decline in value of a currency relative to other currencies. (2)

developed countries Countries that can be assigned to the high-income category. (2)

developing countries Countries that can be assigned to the upper ranks of the low-income category, the lower-middle-income category, or the upper-middle-income category. (2)

differentiated global marketing A strategy that calls for targeting two or more distinct market segments with multiple marketing mix offerings. (7)

differentiation In Porter's generic strategies framework, one of four options for building competitive advantage. Differentiation advantage is present when a firm serves a broad market and its products are perceived as unique; this allows the firm to charge premium prices compared with the competition. (16)

diffusion of innovations A framework developed by Everett Rogers to explain the way that new products are adopted by a culture over time. The framework includes the five-stage innovation adoption process, characteristics of innovations, and innovation adopter categories. (4)

digital revolution The paradigm shift resulting from technological advances allowing for the digitization (i.e., conversion to binary code) of analog sources of information, sounds, and images. (15)

direct mail A direct marketing technique that uses the postal service as a vehicle for delivering an offer to prospects targeted by a marketer. (14)

direct marketing Any communication with a consumer or business recipient that is designed to generate a response in the form of an order, a request for further information, and/or a visit to a store or other place of business. (14)

discontinuous innovation A new product that, when it is widely adopted, creates new markets and new consumption patterns. (10)

discount retailers A category of retail operations that emphasizes low merchandise prices. (12)

discriminatory procurement policies Policies that can take the form of government rules and administrative regulations, as well as formal or informal company policies that discriminate against foreign suppliers. (8)

disruptive technology A technology that redefines product or industry performance and enables new markets to emerge. (15)

distribution channels A barrier to entry into an industry created by the need to create and establish new channels. (12)

distributor A channel intermediary, frequently a wholesaler, that aggregates products from manufacturers and delivers them to retail channel members. (12)

documentary collection A form of trade financing that is less risky than sales on open account but more risky and less burdensome than sales using an L/C. (8)

dumping The sale of a product in an export market at a price lower than that normally charged in the domestic market or country of origin. (8, 11)

duties Rate schedule; can sometimes be thought of as a tax that punishes "individuals for making choices of which their governments disapprove." (8)

dynamically continuous innovation An intermediate category of newness that is somewhat disruptive and requires a moderate amount of learning on the part of consumers. (10)

e-commerce The general exchange of goods and services using the Internet or a similar online network as a marketing channel. (15)

Economic Community of West African States (ECOWAS) An association of 16 nations that includes Benin, Burkina Faso, Cape Verde, Gambia, Ghana, Guinea, Guinea-Bissau, Ivory Coast, Liberia, Mali, Mauritania, Niger, Nigeria, Senegal, Sierra Leone, and Togo. (3)

economic union A highly evolved form of cross-border economic integration involving reduced tariffs and quotas, a common external tariff, reduced restrictions on the movement of labor and capital, and the creation of unified economic policies and institutions such as a central bank. (3)

economies of scale The decline in per-unit product costs as the absolute volume of production per period increases. (16)

efficient consumer response (ECR) An MIS tool that enables retailers to work more closely with vendors to facilitate stock replenishment. (6)

electronic data interchange (EDI) An MIS tool that allows a company's business units to submit orders, issue invoices, and conduct business electronically with other company units as well as with outside companies. (6)

electronic point of sale (EPOS) Purchase data gathered by checkout scanners that help retailers identify product sales patterns and the extent to which consumer preferences vary with geography. (6)

emic analysis Global market research that analyzes a country in terms of its local system of meanings and values. (6)

emotional appeal In advertising, an appeal intended to evoke an emotional response (as opposed to an intellectual response) that will direct purchase behavior. (13)

enabling conditions Structural market characteristics whose presence or absence can determine whether the marketing model can succeed. (7)

environmental sensitivity A measure of the extent to which products must be adapted to the culture-specific needs of different country markets. Generally, consumer products show a higher degree of environmental sensitivity than industrial products. (4)

equity stake Market-entry strategy involving foreign direct investment for the purpose of establishing partial ownership of a business. (9)

e-sports multiplayer videogame competition, often presented in front of a live audience. (15)

ethnocentric orientation The first level in the EPRG framework: the conscious or unconscious belief that one's home country is superior. (1)

ethnocentric pricing The practice of extending a product's home-country price to all country markets. Also known as extension pricing. (11)

etic analysis Global market research that analyzes a country from an outside perspective. (6)

euro zone Nineteen countries that use the euro: Austria, Belgium, Cyprus, Estonia, Finland, Ireland, the Netherlands, France, Germany, Greece, Italy, Latvia, Lithuania, Luxembourg, Malta, Portugal, Slovakia, Slovenia, and Spain. (3)

expatriate An employee who is sent from his or her home country to work abroad. (14)

export broker A broker who receives a fee for bringing together the seller and the overseas buyer. (8)

export commission representative Representative assigned to all or some foreign markets by the manufacturer. (8)

export distributor An individual or organization that has the exclusive right to sell a manufacturer's products in all or some markets outside the country of origin. (8)

export management company (EMC) Term used to designate an independent export firm that acts as the export department for more than one manufacturer. (8)

export marketing Exporting using the product offered in the home market as a starting point and modifying it as needed to meet the preferences of international target markets. (8)

export merchants Merchants who seek out needs in foreign markets and make purchases in world markets to fill these needs. (8)

export price escalation The increase in an imported product's price due to expenses associated with transportation, currency fluctuations, etc. (11)

export selling Exporting without tailoring the product, the price, or the promotional material to suit individual country requirements. (8)

express warranty A written guarantee that assures a buyer that he or she is getting what was paid for or provides recourse in the event that a product's performance falls short of expectations. (10)

expropriation Governmental seizure of a company's assets in exchange for compensation that is generally lower than market value. (5)

extension strategy A global strategy of offering a product virtually unchanged (i.e., "extending" it) in markets outside the home country. (10)

ex-works (EXW) A type of contract in which the seller places goods at the disposal of the buyer at the time specified in the contract. (11)

factor analysis In market research, a computerized quantitative data analysis technique that is used to perform data reduction. Responses from questionnaires that contain multiple items about a product's benefits serve as input; the computer generates factor loadings that can be used to cre- ate a perceptual map. (6)

factor conditions A country's endowment with resources. (16)

FAS (free alongside ship) named port The Incoterm for a contract that calls for the seller to place goods alongside, or available to, the vessel or other mode of transportation and pay all charges up to that point. (11)

first-mover advantage Orthodox marketing wisdom suggesting that the first company to enter a country market has the best chance of becoming the market leader. (7)

five forces model Model developed by Michael Porter that explains competition in an industry: the threat of new entrants, the threat of substitute products or services, the bargaining power of buyers, the bargaining power of suppliers, and the competitive rivalry among current members of the industry. (16)

flagship model A model of competitive advantage developed by Alan Rugman and Joseph D'Cruz that describes how networked business systems can create competitive advantage in global industries. (16)

FOB (free on board) named port The Incoterm for a contract in which the responsibility and liability of the seller do not end until the goods have actually been placed aboard a ship. (11)

focus The concentration of resources on a core business or competence. (1)

focused differentiation In Michael Porter's generic strategies framework, one of four options for building competitive advantage. When a firm serves a small (niche) market and its products are perceived as unique, the firm can charge premium prices. (16)

focus group Primary data collection method involving a trained moderator who facilitates discussion among the members of a group at a specially equipped research facility. (6)

foreign consumer culture positioning (FCCP) A positioning strategy that seeks to differentiate a product, brand, or company by associating it with its country or culture of origin. (7)

Foreign Corrupt Practices Act (FCPA) A law that makes it illegal for U.S. corporations to bribe an official of a foreign government or political party to obtain or retain business. (5)

foreign direct investment (FDI) The market-entry strategy in which companies invest in or acquire plants, equipment, or other assets outside the home country. (9)

foreign purchasing agents Purchasing agents who operate on behalf of, and are compensated by, an overseas customer. (8)

foreign sales corporation (FSC) Provision in the U.S. tax code that allowed American exporters to exclude 15 percent of international sales from reported earnings. (8)

form utility The availability of the product processed, prepared, in proper condition, and/or ready to use. (12)

forward market A mechanism for buying and selling currencies at a preset price for future delivery. (2)

franchising A contract between a parent company–franchisor and franchisee that allows the franchisee to operate a business developed by the franchisor in return for a fee and adherence to franchise-wide policies and practices. This is an appropriate entry strategy when barriers to entry are low yet the market is culturally distant in terms of consumer behavior or retailing structures. (9, 12)

free carrier (FCA) The Incoterm for a contract where transfer from seller to buyer is effected when the goods are delivered to a specified carrier at a specified destination. (11)

free trade agreement (FTA) An agreement that leads to the creation of a free trade area (also abbreviated FTA). A FTA represents a relatively low level of economic integration. (3)

free trade area (FTA) A preferential trade bloc whose members have signed a free trade agreement (also abbreviated FTA) that entails reducing or eliminating tariffs and quotas. (3)

free trade zone (FTZ) A geographical entity that may include a manufacturing facility and a warehouse. (8)

freight forwarders Specialists in traffic operations, customs clearance, and shipping tariffs and schedules. (8)

full ownership Market-entry strategy involving foreign direct investment for the purpose of establishing 100 percent control of a business. (9)

General Agreement on Tariffs and Trade (GATT) The organization established at the end of World War II to promote free trade; also, the treaty signed by member nations. (3)

generic strategies Michael Porter's model describing four different options for achieving competitive advantage: cost leadership, product differentiation, cost focus, focused differentiation. (16)

geocentric orientation The fourth level in the EPRG framework: the understanding that the company should seek market opportunities throughout the world. Management also recognizes that country markets may be characterized by both similarities and differences. (1)

geocentric pricing The practice of using both extension and adaptation pricing policies in different country markets. (11)

global advertising An advertising message whose art, copy, headlines, photographs, taglines, and other elements have been developed expressly for their worldwide suitability. (13)

global brand A brand that has the same name and a similar image and positioning throughout the world. (10)

global brand leadership The act of allocating brand-building resources globally with the goal of creating global synergies and developing a global brand strategy that coordinates and leverages country brand strategies. (10)

global competition A success strategy in which a firm takes a global view of competition and sets about maximizing profits worldwide, rather than on a country-by-country basis. (16)

global consumer culture positioning (GCCP) A positioning strategy that seeks to differentiate a product, brand, or company as a symbol of, or association with, a global culture or a global market segment. (4, 7)

global elite A global market segment comprised of well-traveled, affluent consumers who spend heavily on prestige or luxury products and brands that convey an image of exclusivity. (7)

global industry An industry in which competitive advantage can be achieved by integrating and leveraging operations on a worldwide scale. (1)

global marketing The commitment of organizational resources to pursuing global market opportunities and responding to environmental threats in the global marketplace. (1)

global marketing strategy (GMS) A firm's blueprint for pursuing global market opportunities that addresses four issues: whether a standardization approach or a localization approach will be used; whether key marketing activities will be concentrated in relatively few countries or widely dispersed around the globe; the guidelines for coordinating marketing activities around the globe; and the scope of global market participation. (1)

global market research The project-specific gathering and analysis of data on a global basis or in one or more markets outside the home country. (6)

global market segmentation The process of identifying specific segments of potential customers with homogeneous attributes who are likely to exhibit similar buying behavior irrespective of their countries of residence. (7)

global positioning system (GPS) A digital communication system that uses satellite feeds to determine the geographic position of a mobile device. (15)

global product A product that satisfies the wants and needs of buyers in all parts of the world. (10)

global retailing Engaging in or owning retail operations in multiple national markets. (12)

global strategic partnerships (GSPs) A sophisticated market-entry strategy via an alliance with one or more business partners for the purpose of serving the global market. (9)

global teens A global market segment comprised of persons 12 to 19 years old whose shared interests in fashion, music, and youthful lifestyle issues shape purchase behavior. (7)

gray market goods Products that are exported from one country to another without authorization from the trademark owner. (11)

greenfield investment A market-entry strategy that entails foreign direct investment in a factory, retail outlet, or some other form of new operations in a target country. Also known as greenfield operations. (9)

gross domestic product (GDP) A measure of a nation's economic activity calculated by adding consumer spending (C), investment spending (I), government purchases (G), and net exports (NX): $C + I + G + NX = \text{GDP}$. (2)

gross national income (GNI) A measure of a nation's economic activity that includes gross domestic product (GDP) plus income generated by nonresident sources. (2)

Group of Eight (G-8) Eight nations—the United States, Japan, Germany, France, Great Britain, Canada, Italy, and Russia— whose representatives met regularly to deal with global economic issues. Russian was dropped from the group in 2014. (2)

Group of Seven (G-7) Seven nations—the United States, Japan, Germany, France, Great Britain, Canada, and Italy— whose representatives meet regularly to deal with global economic issues. (2)

Group of Twenty (G-20) Twenty nations whose representatives meet regularly to discuss global economic and financial issues. Objectives include restoring global economic growth and strengthening the global financial system. (2)

Gulf Cooperation Council (GCC) An association of oil-producing states that includes Bahrain, Kuwait, Oman, Qatar, Saudi Arabia, and the United Arab Emirates. (3)

hard discounter A retailer that sells a tightly focused selection of goods at very low prices, often relying heavily on private brands. (12)

harmonization The coming together of varying standards and regulations that affect the marketing mix. (3)

Harmonized Tariff System (HTS) A system in which importers and exporters have to determine the correct classification number for a given product or service that will cross borders. (8)

hedging An investment made to protect a company from possible financial losses due to fluctuating currency exchange rates. (2)

high-context culture A culture in which a great deal of information and meaning reside in the context of communication, including the background, associations, and basic values of the communicators. (4)

high-income country A country in which per capita gross national income (GNI) is \$12,236 or greater. (2)

hypercompetition A strategy framework developed by Richard D'Aveni that views competition and the quest for competitive advantage in terms of the dynamic maneuvering and strategic interactions by hypercompetitive firms in an industry. (16)

hypermarket A category of retail operations characterized by very large-scale facilities that combine elements of discount store, supermarket, and warehouse club approaches. (12)

hypertext markup language (HTML) A format language that controls the appearance of Web pages. (15)

hypertext transfer protocol (HTTP) A protocol that enables hypertext files to be transferred across the Internet. (15)

image advertising A type of corporate advertising that informs the public about a major event, such as a name change, merger, etc. (13)

incipient market A market in which demand will materialize if particular economic, demographic, political, or sociocultural trends continue. (6)

Incoterms Internationally accepted terms of trade that impact prices. (11)

individualist culture In Geert Hofstede's social values typology, a society in which each member is primarily concerned with his or her interests and those of the immediate family. (4)

infomercial A form of paid television programming in which a particular product is demonstrated, explained, and offered for sale to viewers who call a toll-free number shown on the screen. (14)

information technology (IT) An organization's processes for creating, storing, exchanging, using, and managing information. (6)

information utility The availability of answers to questions and general communication about useful product features and benefits. (12)

innovation The process of endowing resources with a new capacity to create value. (10)

innovator's dilemma Executives become so committed to a current, profitable technology that they fail to provide adequate levels of investment in new, apparently riskier technologies. (15)

integrated circuit (IC) The silicon chip that gave modern form to the transistor and represented a milestone in the digital revolution. (15)

integrated marketing communications (IMC) An approach to the promotion element of the marketing mix that values coordination and integration of a company's marketing communication strategy. (13)

interactive television (ITV) Allows television viewers to interact with the programming content that they are viewing. (14)

intermodal transportation The aspect of physical distribution that involves transferring shipping containers between land and water transportation modes. (12)

international brand A brand that is available throughout a particular world region. Also known as an international product. (10)

international law The body of international law that pertains to noncommercial disputes between nations. (5)

Internet A network of computer networks across which e-mail and other digital files can be sent. (15)

intranet An electronic system that allows authorized company personnel or outsiders to share information electronically in a secure fashion while reducing the amount of paper generated. (6)

irrevocable letter of credit A common form of trade financing in which the importer's bank cannot cancel or modify the terms of a L/C without approval from both the importer and exporter. (8)

Islamic law A legal system used in the Middle East that is based on a comprehensive code known as *sharia*. (5)

joint venture A market-entry strategy in which two companies share ownership of a newly created business entity. (9, 12)

jurisdiction The aspect of a country's legal environment that deals with a court's authority to rule on particular types of controversies arising outside of a nation's borders or exercise power over individuals or entities from different countries. (5)

latent market An undiscovered market segment in which demand for a product would materialize if an appropriate product were offered. (6)

law of one price A market in which all customers have access to the best product at the best price. (11)

lean production An extremely effective, efficient, and streamlined manufacturing system such as the Toyota Production System. (17)

least-developed countries (LDCs) Terminology adopted by the United Nations to refer to the 50 countries that rank lowest in per capita gross national product (GNP). (2)

letter of credit (L/C) A payment method in export/import in which a bank substitutes its creditworthiness for that of the importer-buyer. (8)

leverage Some type of advantage—for example, experience transfers, know-how, or scale economies—that a company enjoys by accumulating experience in multiple country markets. (1)

licensing A contractual market-entry strategy whereby one company makes an asset available to another company in exchange for royalties or some other form of compensation. (9, 12)

line extension A variation of an existing product such as a new flavor or new design. (10)

local brand A brand that is available in a single country market. Also known as a local product. (10)

local consumer culture positioning A positioning strategy that seeks to differentiate a product, brand, or company in terms of its association with local culture, local production, or local consumption. (7)

localization (adaptation) approach The pursuit of global market opportunities using an adaptation strategy of significant marketing mix variations in different countries. (1)

logistics management The management activity responsible for planning, implementing, and controlling the flow of components and finished goods between the point of origin and the point of assembly or final consumption. (12)

long-term orientation (LTO) The fifth dimension in Geert Hofstede's social values framework, LTO is a reflection of a society's concern with immediate gratification versus persistence and thrift over the long term. (4)

low-context culture A culture in which messages and knowledge are more explicit and words carry most of the information in communication. (4)

lower-middle-income country A country with gross national income (GNI) per capita between $1,006 and $3,955. (2)

low-income country A country with per capita gross national income (GNI) of less than or equal to $1,005. (2)

Maastricht Treaty The 1991 treaty that set the stage for the transition from the European monetary system to an economic and monetary union. (3)

Madrid Protocol A system of trademark protection that allows intellectual property registration in multiple countries with a single application and fee. (5)

management information system (MIS) A system that provides managers and other decision makers with a continuous flow of information about company operations. (6)

manufacturer's export agent (MEA) One who can act as an export distributor or as an export commission representative. (8)

market-based transfer price A transfer pricing policy that sets prices for intracorporate transactions at levels that are competitive in the global market. (11)

market capitalism An economic system characterized by market allocation of resources and private resource ownership. (2)

market expansion strategy The particular combination of product-market and geographic alternatives that management chooses when expanding company operations outside the home country. (9)

market holding strategy A pricing strategy that allows management to maintain market share; prices are adjusted up or down as competitive or economic conditions change. (11)

marketing The activity, set of institutions, and processes for creating, communicating, delivering, and exchanging offerings that have value for customers, clients, partners, and society at large. (1)

marketing mix The four factors—product, price, place, and promotion—that represent strategic variables controlled by the marketer. (1)

marketing model drivers Key elements or factors that must be taken into account when evaluating countries as potential target markets. (7)

market penetration pricing strategy A pricing strategy that calls for setting price levels that are low enough to quickly build market share. (11)

market research The project-specific, systematic gathering of data in the search scanning mode. (6)

market skimming A pricing strategy designed to reach customers willing to pay a premium price for a particular brand or for a specialized product. (11)

market socialism An economic system characterized by limited market resource allocation within an overall environment of state ownership. (2)

Maslow's needs hierarchy A classic framework for understanding how human motivation is linked to needs. (10)

matrix organization A pattern of organization design in which management's task is to achieve an organizational balance that brings together different perspectives and skills to accomplish the organization's objectives. (17)

merchandise trade In balance of payments statistics, entries that pertain to manufactured goods. (2)

mobile advertising Persuasive or informative communication that uses a smartphone or other handheld device as the channel. (15)

mobile commerce (m-commerce) Conducting commercial transactions using wireless handheld devices such as smartphones and tablets. (15)

mobile music Music that is purchased and played on a smartphone or tablet. (15)

multidimensional scaling (MDS) In market research, a quantitative data analysis technique that can be used to create perceptual maps. MDS helps marketers gain insights into consumer perceptions when a large number of products or brands are available. (6)

multisegment targeting A marketing strategy that entails targeting two or more distinct market segments with multiple marketing mix offerings. (7)

national advantage Strategy guru Michael Porter's competitive advantage framework for analysis at the nation-state level. The degree to which a nation develops competitive advantage depends on four elements: factor conditions, demand conditions, the presence of related and supporting industries, and the nature of firm strategy. (16)

nationalization Broad transfer of industry management and ownership in a particular country from the private sector to the government. (5)

nature of firm strategy, structure, and rivalry In Michael Porter's framework for national competitive advantage, the fourth determinant of a national "diamond." (16)

near-field communication (NFC) A set of communication protocols underlying Apple Pay and other mobile payments platforms that allows smartphones or other electronic devices to establish a communcation link with a point-of-sale terminal. (15)

negotiated transfer price A transfer pricing policy that establishes prices for intracorporate transactions on the basis of the organization's affiliations. (11)

newly industrializing economies (NIEs) Upper-middle-income countries with high rates of economic growth. (2)

niche A single, narrowly targeted segment of the global market. (7)

nongovernmental organization (NGO) A secondary stakeholder that focuses on human rights, political justice, and environmental issues. (17)

nontariff barriers (NTBs) Any restriction besides taxation that restricts or prevents the flow of goods across borders, ranging from "buy local" campaigns to bureaucratic obstacles that make it difficult for companies to gain access to some individual country and regional markets. (1, 8)

normal trade relations (NTR) A trading stratus under World Trade Organization (WTO) rules that entitles a country to low tariff rates. (8)

North American Free Trade Agreement (NAFTA) A free trade area encompassing Canada, the United States, and Mexico. In 2018, replaced with the US-Mexico-Canada Agreement. (3)

"not invented here" (NIH) syndrome An error made in choosing a strategy by ignoring decisions made by subsidiary or affiliate managers. (10)

nurturing Describes a society in which the social roles of men and women overlap, with neither gender exhibiting overly ambitious or competitive behavior. (4)

observation A method of primary data collection using trained observers who watch and record the behavior of actual or prospective customers. (6)

offset A countertrade deal in which a government recoups hard-currency expenditures by requiring some form of cooperation from the seller, such as importing products or transferring technology. (11)

one-to-one marketing An updated framework for direct marketing that calls for treating each customer in a distinct way based on his or her previous purchase history or past interactions with the company. (14)

open account a type of payment that presents the greatest transaction risk to the exporter. (8)

operating system A software code that provides basic instructions for a computer. (15)

option In foreign currency trading, a contract confirming the right to buy or sell a specific amount of currency at a fixed price. (2)

order processing The aspect of physical distribution that includes order entry, order handling, and order delivery. (12)

organic growth In global retailing, a market expansion strategy whereby a company uses its own resources to open a store on a greenfield site or to acquire one or more existing retail facilities or sites from another company. (12)

Organization for Economic Cooperation and Development (OECD) A group of 34 nations that work together to aid in the development of economic systems based on market capitalism and pluralistic democracy. (2)

organizing for global marketing The managerial process of creating departments, business units, lines of reporting, and systems of coordination to ensure that a firm's global strategy can be executed. (17)

outlet mall A grouping of outlet stores. (12)

outlet store A category of retail operations that allows marketers of well-known consumer brands to dispose of excess inventory, out-of-date merchandise, or factory seconds. (12)

outsourcing Shifting jobs or work assignments to another company to cut costs. When the work moves abroad to a low-wage country such as India or China, the term *offshoring* is sometimes used. (8)

parallel importing The act of importing goods from one country to another without authorization from the trademark owner. Parallel import schemes exploit price differentials among country markets. (11)

patent A formal legal document that gives an inventor the exclusive right to make, use, and sell an invention for a specified period of time. (5)

pattern advertising A communication strategy that calls for developing a basic pan-regional or global concept for which copy, artwork, or other elements can be adapted as required for individual country markets. (13)

peer-to-peer (p-to-p) marketing A marketing model whereby individual consumers market products to other individuals. (12)

peoplemeter An electronic device used by companies such as Nielsen to collect national television audience data. (6)

personal computer (PC) A compact, affordable computing device whose advent marked the next phase of the digital revolution. (15)

personal selling One of four variables in the promotion mix; face-to-face communication between a prospective buyer and a company sales representative. (14)

personal selling philosophy A sales representative's commitment to the marketing concept coupled with a willingness to take on the role of problem solver or partner in helping customers. The first step in the strategic/consultative selling model. (14)

place utility The availability of a product or service in a location that is convenient to a potential customer. (12)

platform A core product design element or component that can be quickly and cheaply adapted to various country markets. (10)

political environment The set of governmental institutions, political parties, and organizations that are the expression of the people in the nations of the world. (5)

political risk The risk of a change in political environment or government policy that would adversely affect a company's ability to operate effectively and profitably. (5)

polycentric orientation The second level in the EPRG framework: the view that each country in which a company does business is unique. In global marketing, this orientation results in high levels of marketing mix adaptation, often implemented by autonomous local managers in each country market. (1)

polycentric pricing The practice of setting different price levels for a given product in different country markets. Also known as adaptation pricing. (11)

positioning The act of differentiating a product or brand in the minds of customers or prospects relative to competing products or brands. (7)

power distance In Geert Hofstede's social values typology, the cultural dimension that reflects the extent to which it is acceptable for power to be distributed unequally in a society. (4)

preferential tariff A reduced tariff rate applied to imports from certain countries. (8)

preferential trade agreement (PTA) A trade agreement between a relatively small number of signatory nations, often on a regional or subregional basis. Different levels of economic integration can characterize such trade agreements. (3)

presentation plan In personal selling, the heart of the presentation strategy. The plan has six stages: approach, need discovery, presentation, negotiation, closing, and servicing the sale. (14)

presentation strategy Setting objectives for each sales call and establishing a presentation plan to meet those objectives. (14)

price fixing Secret agreements between representatives of two or more companies to set prices. (11)

price transparency Euro-denominated prices for goods and services that enable consumers and organizational buyers to comparison shop across Europe. (11)

primary data In market research, data gathered through research pertaining to the particular problem, decision, or issue under study. (6)

product One of the four Ps of the marketing mix: a good, service, or idea with tangible and/or intangible attributes that collectively create value for a buyer or user. (10)

product adaptation–communication extension A strategy of extending, with minimal change, the basic home-market communications strategy while adapting the product to local use or preference conditions. (10)

product-communication adaptation (dual adaptation) A dual-adaptation strategy that uses a combination of marketing conditions. (10)

product-communication extension A strategy for pursuing opportunities outside the home market. (10)

product extension–communications adaptation The strategy of marketing an identical product by adapting the marketing communications program. (10)

product invention In global marketing, developing new products with the world market in mind. (10)

product placement A marketing communication tool that involves a company paying a fee to have one or more products and brand names appear in popular television programs, movies, and other types of performances. (14)

product saturation level The percentage of customers or households that own a product in a particular country market; a measure of market opportunity. (2)

product strategy In personal selling, a sales representative's plan for selecting and positioning products that will satisfy customer needs. The third step in the strategic/consultative selling model. (14)

product transformation When a product that has been introduced into multiple country markets via a product extension–communication adaptation strategy serves a different function or use than originally intended. (10)

pro forma invoice A document that sets an export/import transaction into motion. The document specifies the amount and the means by which an exporter-seller wants to be paid; it also specifies the items to be purchased. (8)

promotion site A Web site that provides marketing communications about a company's goods or services. (15)

psychographic segmentation The process of assigning people to market segments on the basis of their attitudes, interests, opinions, and lifestyles. (7)

publicity Communication about a company or product for which the company does not pay. (13)

public relations (PR) One of four variables in the promotion mix. Within an organization, the department or function responsible for evaluating public opinion about, and attitudes toward, the organization and its products and brands. PR personnel also are responsible for fostering goodwill, understanding, and acceptance among a company's various constituents and the public. (13)

put option The right to sell a specified number of foreign currency units at a fixed price, up to the option's expiration date. (2)

quota Government-imposed limit or restriction on the number of units or the total value of a particular product or product category that can be imported. (8)

rational appeal In advertising, an appeal to the target audience's logic and intellect. (13)

regiocentric orientation The third level in the EPRG framework: the view that similarities as well as differences characterize specific regions of the world. In global marketing, a regiocentric orientation is evident when a company develops an integrated strategy for a particular geographic area. (1)

regulatory environment Governmental and nongovernmental agencies and organizations that enforce laws or establish guidelines for conducting business. (5)

related and supporting industries In Michael Porter's framework for national competitive advantage, one of the four determinants of a national "diamond." (16)

relationship strategy In personal selling, a sales representative's game plan for establishing and maintaining high-quality relationships with prospects and customers. The second step in the Strategic/Consultative Selling Model. (14)

restrictive administrative and technical regulations Regulations that can create barriers to trade; they may take the form of antidumping, size, or safety and health regulations. (8)

revaluation The strengthening of a country's currency. (2)

rules of origin A system of certification that verifies the country of origin of a shipment of goods. (3)

sales agent An agent who works under contract rather than as a full-time employee. (14)

sales promotion One of the four elements of the promotion mix. A paid, short-term communication program that adds tangible value to a product or brand. (14)

sampling A sales promotion technique that provides potential customers with the opportunity to try a product or service at no cost. (14)

secondary data Existing data in personal files, published sources, and databases. (6)

self-reference criterion (SRC) The unconscious human tendency to interpret the world in terms of one's own cultural experience and values. (4)

selling proposition In advertising, the promise or claim that captures the reason for buying the product or the benefit that product ownership confers. (13)

services trade The buying and selling of intangible, experience-based economic output. (2)

shopping mall A group of stores in one place, typically with one or more large department stores serving as anchors and with easy access and free parking. (12)

short message service (SMS) A globally accepted wireless standard for sending alphanumeric messages of up to 160 characters. (15)

short-term orientation One of the dimensions in Geert Hofstede's social values typology. Contrasts with long-term orientation. (4)

single-column tariff A schedule of duties in which the rate applies to imports from all countries on the same basis; the simplest type of tariff. (8)

smartphone A phone that offers some of the capabilities of computers, such as a Web browser. (15)

sourcing decision A strategic decision that determines whether a company makes a product itself or buys products from other manufacturers as well as where it makes or buys its products. (8)

Southern African Development Community (SADC) An association whose member states are Angola, Botswana, Democratic Republic of Congo, Lesotho, Malawi, Mauritius, Mozambique, Namibia, Seychelles, South Africa, Swaziland, Tanzania, Zambia, and Zimbabwe. (3)

sovereignty A country's supreme and independent political authority. (5)

special economic zone (SEZ) A geographic entity that offers manufacturers simplified customs procedures, operational flexibility, and a general environment of relaxed regulations. (8)

specialty retailer A category of retail operations characterized by a more narrow focus than a department store and offering a relatively narrow merchandise mix aimed at a particular target market. (12)

sponsorship A form of marketing communication that involves payment of a fee by a company to have its name associated with a particular event, team or athletic association, or sports facility. (14)

spreadsheet A software application in the form of an electronic ledger that automatically calculates the effect of changes made to figures entered in rows and columns. (15)

stakeholder Any group or individual that is affected by, or takes an interest in, the policies and practices adopted by an organization. (17)

stakeholder analysis The process of formulating a "win-win" outcome for all stakeholders. (17)

standardized (extension) approach The pursuit of a global market opportunity using an extension strategy of minimal marketing mix variation in different countries. (1)

standardized global marketing A target market strategy that calls for creating the same marketing mix for a broad mass market of potential buyers. (7)

strategic alliance A partnership among two or more firms created to minimize risk while maximizing leverage in the marketplace. (9)

strategic/consultative selling model A five-step framework for approaching the personal selling task: personal selling philosophy, relationship strategy, product strategy, customer strategy, and presentation strategy. (14)

strategic intent A competitive advantage framework developed by strategy experts Gary Hamel and C. K. Prahalad. (16)

strategic international alliances A form of mutually beneficial collaboration among two or more companies doing business globally. The goal is to leverage complementary resources and competencies in order to achieve competitive advantage. (9)

streaming audio Transmission that allows users to listen to Internet radio stations. (15)

streaming media The transmission of combined audio and video content via a broadband network. (15)

streaming video Video sent via the Internet and displayed on a computer, tablet, smartphone, or television screen. (15)

subculture Within a culture, a small group of people with their own shared subset of attitudes, beliefs, and values. (4)

subsidies Direct or indirect financial contributions or incentives that benefit producers. (8)

supercenter A category of retail operations that combines elements of discount stores and supermarkets in a space that occupies about half the size of a hypermarket. (12)

supermarket A category of retail operations characterized by a departmentalized, single-story retail establishment that offers a variety of food and nonfood items on a self-service basis. (12)

superstore A store that specializes in selling vast assortments of a particular product category in high volumes at low prices. (12)

supply chain A group of firms that perform support activities by generating raw materials, converting them into components or finished goods, and making them available to buyers. (12)

survey research Primary data collection via questionnaire-based studies designed to generate qualitative responses, quantitative responses, or both. (6)

sustaining technologies Incremental or radical innovations that improve product performance. (15)

switch trading A transaction in which a professional switch trader, switch trading house, or bank steps into a simple barter arrangement or other countertrade arrangement in which one of the parties is not willing to accept all the goods received in the transaction. (11)

targeting The process of evaluating market segments and focusing marketing efforts on a country, region, or group of people. (7)

tariffs The rules, rate schedules (duties), and regulations of individual countries affecting goods that are imported. (8)

teleshopping Round-the-clock programming exclusively dedicated to product demonstration and selling. (14)

temporary surcharge Surcharges introduced from time to time to provide additional protection for local industry and, in particular, in response to balance of payments deficits. (8)

tiered branding A strategy in which a corporate name is combined with a product brand name; also called combination or umbrella branding. (10)

time utility The availability of a product or service when desired by a customer. (12)

trade deficit A negative number in the balance of payments showing that the value of a country's imports exceeds the value of its exports. (2)

trademark A distinctive mark, motto, device, or emblem that a manufacturer affixes to a particular product or package to distinguish it from goods produced by other manufacturers. (5)

trade mission A state- or federally sponsored show outside the home country organized around a product, a group of products, an industry, or an activity at which company personnel can learn about new markets as well as competitors. (8)

trade sales promotion Promotion designed to increase product availability in distribution channels. (14)

trade show A gathering of company representatives organized around a product, a group of products, or an industry, at which company personnel can meet with prospective customers and gather competitor intelligence. (8)

trade surplus A positive number in the balance of payments showing that the value of a country's exports exceeds the value of its imports. (2)

transaction site A cyberspace retail operation that allows customers to purchase goods and services. (15)

transfer pricing The pricing of goods, services, and intangible property bought and sold by operating units or divisions of a company doing business with an affiliate in another jurisdiction. (11)

transistor A "solid state amplifier" that replaced vacuum tubes in electronics products; it was a milestone in the digital revolution. (15)

transparency Openness in business dealings, financial disclosures, pricing, or other situations where the goal is to remove layers of secrecy or other obstacles to clear the way for understanding and decision making. (3)

two-column tariff General duties plus special duties indicating reduced rates determined by tariff negotiations with other countries. (8)

uncertainty avoidance In Geert Hofstede's social values framework, the extent to which members of a culture are uncomfortable with unclear, ambiguous, or unstructured situations. (4)

uniform resource locator (URL) An Internet site's address on the World Wide Web. (15)

upper-middle-income country A country with gross national income (GNI) per capita between \$3,956 and \$12,235. (2)

US-Mexico-Canada Agreement The 2018 replacement for NAFTA. (3)

usage rate In behavioral market segmentation, an assessment of the extent to which a person uses a product or service. (7)

user status In behavioral market segmentation, an assessment of whether a person is a present user, potential user, non-user, former user, etc. (7)

value chain The various activities that a company performs (e.g., research and development, manufacturing, marketing, physical distribution, and logistics) in order to create value for customers. (1)

value equation $V = B/P$, where V stands for "perceived value," B stands for "product, price, and place," and P stands for "price." (1)

value network The cost structure in a particular industry that dictates the margins needed to achieve profitability. A broadly defined industry (e.g., computers) may have parallel value networks, each with its own metrics of value. (15)

values In culture, enduring beliefs or feelings that a specific mode of conduct is personally or socially preferable to another mode of conduct. (4)

variable import levies A system of levies applied to certain categories of imported agricultural products. (8)

Voice over Internet Protocol (VoIP) Technology that allows the human voice to be digitized and broken into data packets that can be transmitted over the Internet and converted back into normal speech. (15)

Wi-Fi (wireless fidelity) Technology based on a low-power radio signal that permits access to the Internet from a laptop computer or smartphone when the user is within range of a base station transmitter ("hotspot"). (15)

World Trade Organization (WTO) The successor to the General Agreement on Tariffs and Trade (GATT). (3)

World Wide Web Global computer network connecting Internet sites that contain text, graphics, and streaming audio and video resources. (15)

Author/Name Index

Page numbers with e, f, or t represent exhibits, figures, and tables respectively.

A

Aaker, David A., 265n49, 333, 334, 355n24
Abkowitz, Alyssa, 262, 265n38
Adams, Susan, 551n25
Adamy, Janet, 56
Addis, Roger, 489
Adese, Carlos, 388
Adler, Allen, 376
Aeppel, Timothy, 356n43
Agarwal, Amit, 240
Agins, Teri, 390
Aglionby, John, 92n19, 92n20, 264n16, 520
Agnefjäll, Peter, 548
Agon, Jean-Paul, 211
Agunnaryd, Ingvar Kamprad Elmtaryd, 335t
Ahearne, Michael, 469f, 471f, 472f, 490n17
Ahrendts, Angela, 33, 57, 59n25, 396e
Ajami, Riad, 323n22
al-Assad, Bashar, 117, 193
Alden, Dana L., 265n52, 490n13, 490n14
Alderman, Liz, 540
Aldrin, Buzz, 462
Alexander, Dan, 91
Alford, William P., 195n20
Ali, Arif, 511
Allchin, Joseph, 423
Al-Olayan, Fahad S., 459n37
Alpert, Luca I., 305
Alpert, Lukas I., 92n38
Alyokhina, Maria, 192
Anderson, Chris, 503, 521n30
Anderson, Jamie, 520
Andreessen, Marc, 495
Andrews, Edmund L., 293n4
Angier, Natalie, 157n8
Anholt, Simon, 340, 356n38
Ante, Spencer E, 521n50
Anthony, Myrvin L., 127n15
Antia, Kersi D., 391n36
Argenti, Paul A., 574, 581n47
Arlidge, John, 458, 581n4
Arnau, Michelle, 213
Arnault, Bernard, 388, 389
Arnold, David, 209, 221, 250e, 323n1, 425n11
Arnold, Wayne, 195n10
Arthaud-Day, Marne, 581n48
Ashcroft, Elizabeth, 59n16
Aspden, Peter, 356n37
Assavedra, Edith Scott, 551n20
Atanasoff, John Vincent, 493
Atkinson, Celeste, 484
Audi, Tamara, 458
Austen, Ian, 550
Ayal, I., 323n57
Ayittey, George, 518

B

Bae, Su Jung, 557t
Bahardeen, Fazal, 243
Bailey, Christopher, 34
Bajaj, Vikas, 322, 386, 425
Ball, Deborah, 59n49, 158n47, 230n34, 355n5, 355n16, 356n55, 356n56, 356n57, 390
Ballard, John, 373
Banjo, Shelly, 425
Bannon, Lisa, 390, 391n28
Barber, Tony, 59n18, 195n19
Barboza, David, 262, 499
Bardeen, John, 494
Bariyo, Nicolas, 320
Barkley, Tom, 126
Barnes, Brooks, 518
Barney, Jay, 59n9
Barr, Cailainn, 439
Barrett, Amy, 157n32
Barrett, Craig, 77
Barrett, Helen, 458n13
Barta, Patrick, 74
Bartlett, Christopher A., 265n42, 341, 356n42, 356n60, 544, 551n32, 565, 581n14, 581n15
Baskin, Brian, 426n49
Bata, Thomas, 205
Batra, Rajeev, 265n52
Baumgartner, Felix, 489, 490e
Baurlein, Valerie, 491n35
Beattie, Alan, 127n12
Beatty, Sally, 264n29, 356n58
Beccari, Pietro, 389
Beck, Ernest, 92n30
Becker, Joe, 448
Beeson, Michelle, 502, 520n21, 520n22
Behrman, Elisabeth, 521n46
Belge, Antoine, 389
Bell, Charlie, 55
Bell, Daniel, 79
Bellman, Eric, 265n37, 388, 423, 425, 425n3, 425n12, 425n19, 426n30, 521n44
Bendler, Theo, 478
Bennett, Peter D., 425n1
Benoit, Bertrand, 92n43, 356n35
Benoliel, Peter A., 557
Bergen, Mark, 57, 391n36
Berners-Lee, Tim, 495
Berry, Clifford, 493
Bevins, Vincent, 481
Bevins, Viñcent, 127n11
Bezos, Jeff, 34, 502, 515e, 525
Bhagwati, Jagdish, 28, 59n10
Bhattacharya, Arindam K., 239, 264n17, 294n20
Bickerton, Ian, 426n40
Bilbrey, J. P., 560

Bilefsky, Dan, 157n20, 195n9, 321, 356n46
Bilkey, Warren J., 293n1
Bingaman, Anne, 181
Birchall, Jonathan, 425
Biyani, Kishore, 393, 425
Bizzari, Marco, 362
Blake, Frank, 408
Bland, Ben, 356n34
Blatand, Harald, 521n45
Bleakley, Fred R., 391n20
Bloomberg, Michael, 455
Blumenstein, Rebecca, 60n53, 356n66
Boden, Johnnie, 505
Boland, Vincent, 166, 540
Bomsdorf, Clemens, 550
Bond, Michael Harris, 157n2, 158n35
Bond, Shannon, 265n33
Bonn, Hans Riegel Sr., 335t
Bono, 571
Booth, Lewis, 322
Borchardt, Klaus-Dieter, 195n49
Borgerson, Janet L., 458n23
Borrus, Amy, 195n42, 356n59
Bosnjak, Jacqueline, 518
Boston, William, 305, 455
Botan, Carl, 459n45, 459n47
Bottura, Massimo, 488
Bourgeois, Jacques C., 158n45
Bové, Jose, 54
Bowes, Elena, 356n67, 459n40
Bowie, David, 490
Boyd, John, 416
Brabeck, Peter, 571
Brabeck-Letmathe, Peter, 331
Bradley, George, 529
Bradord, Reggie, 503
Bradshaw, Tim, 58, 518, 521n48, 521n52
Bradsher, Keith, 390n11
Brand, Stewart, 495, 520n4
Branson, Richard, 248, 249e, 265n39, 332, 410, 411, 448
Brasher, Philip, 391n41
Brasher, Richard, 404
Brat, Ian, 355n7
Brattain, William, 494
Brauchli, Marcus W., 294n21, 459n48
Bray, Chad, 520
Bream, Rebecca, 195n41
Bricklin, Dan, 520n3
Bricklin, Malcolm, 285
Brien, Nick, 433
Brin, Sergei, 324
Brinkley, Douglas, 41, 60n52
Britt, Bill, 157n6
Brodin, Jesper, 548

Subject/Organization Index

Page numbers with e, f, or t represent exhibits, figures, and tables respectively.

A

ABB, 47, 553, 556t, 567, 567e
Abercrombie & Fitch, 502
AB InBev, 319–321
Abstract culture, 130
Accenture, 435t, 437t, 461, 504t
Acer Group, 419
Achievement, in Hofstede's cultural typology, 141
Acquisition, 420
Action Movie FX, 508
Active listening, 472
Acura, 225t, 544
Acxiom Corp., 435t
Adam Opel AG, 330
Adaptation approach, 40, 50
Adaptation pricing, 376
Adaptation strategy, 342, 343f, 346
Adaptation *versus* standardization, 31, 34
  in global advertising, 415–419
Adidas, 200, 258, 387, 448, 556t
Admiration, in needs hierarchy, 338, 339f
Adolph Coors Company, 471
Adopter categories, 147–148, 147f
Adoption process, 146
Ad valorem duty, 279
Advanced countries, 73
Advanced Micro Devices (AMD), 178e
Advantage Solutions' Advantage Marketing
  Partners, 435t
Advertising
  defined, 429
  pattern, 433
Advertising Age magazine, 56, 172e, 376, 437, 441
Advertising agencies, 435–440
  merger between Omnicom and Publicis, 436
  organizations and brands, 435–440
  selecting, 436–440
  world's largest global advertising agency
    companies, 437t
Advertising appeal, 440
Advertising organizations, 435–440. *See also*
  Advertising agencies
Advisory, Conciliation and Arbitration Service
  (ACAS), 186
Advocacy advertising, 449
Aeon Group, 403
Aéropostale, 502
AES Corporation, 167
Aesthetics
  culture and, 132–133
  packaging, 326–327
  in web site design and implementation, 504–506
Aesthetic styles, 132, 328
Affiliation needs, in needs hierarchy, 338, 339f
Affluent Materialists, 244

Africa, 119–121
  digital revolution, 518–520
  East African Community, 119, 120f
  ECOWAS, 119
  marketing issues in, 120–121
  nations in, 119
  outsourcing in, 287t
  SADC, 120
Africa, cell phones in, 518–519
African Development Bank, 519
African Growth and Opportunities Act (AGOA), 120
Aftermath Entertainment, 366
Agência Africa, 481
Agent, 394
Age segmentation, 240–241
Agreement on Customs Valuations, 278–279
Airberlin, 310t
AirBnB, 160, 166
Airbus Industries, 252, 312, 467
Air Canada, 252
Airtel, 363
Airtel Kenya, 519
Air transportation, 417
Alcatel-Lucent, 46
Aldi, 333, 335t, 415, 529, 530e
Alibaba, 499, 499e, 501, 513, 517
Alliance Data Systems Corp., 435t
Allied Domecq, 300, 330
Alphabet, 324–325
Aluswiss, 384
Amazing Race, The, 78
Amazon.com, 77, 190, 201, 334t, 398e, 409f, 410,
  415, 432t, 497, 501–502, 504t, 512, 514
  Amazon Cloud Player, 512
  Amazon Web Services (AWS), 525
  Kindle, 514, 515e
Ambrosian Refectory, 488
American Airlines, 252, 309e, 310t
American Apparel, 259, 340
American Arbitration Association (AAA), 185, 186
American Association of Publishers, 376
American Automobile Labeling Act, 328
American Express, 241, 432t, 476, 571
American Idol, 366, 457, 486
American Marketing Association, 205, 393
American Standard Code for Information
  Interchange (ASCII), 505
America Online (AOL), 495, 496, 508
Amstel, 320
Amway, 396, 557t
Analogy, 220–221
Analysis, data. *See* Data analysis
Analysis of variance (ANOVA), 217
Analytics manager, 227–230
Andean Community, 98, 102–109, 105f

Andersen Consulting, 397
Android, 42
Android operating system, 57, 353, 508, 513,
  526, 556
Anglo-Saxon model, 66t
Angry Birds, 508
Anheuser-Busch/InBev, 48, 70, 137, 179t, 307,
  320, 432t, 449
Animals, 55
Antidumping duties, 279
Antitrust, 177–181, 179t
APMEA, 53
A.P. Moller/Maersk, 181, 417t
Appeal, global, 434
Apple, 24, 193, 214, 241, 259, 262, 329, 333, 334t,
  343, 349, 350, 353, 363, 396, 431, 455, 494,
  497, 501, 556, 557t, 559, 571
  Apple Gift Card, 512
  Apple II, 56, 494
  Apple Music, 507
  Apple Pay, 55, 58, 513
  Apple Store, 56
  Apple Watch, 259, 511
  Beats Music, 366
  CarPlay, 354
  iAd service, 508
  iOS, 354, 508
  iPad, 56, 57, 349, 434, 503, 512
  iPhone, 56–58, 193, 241, 259, 349, 353, 363,
    434, 496, 508, 512, 556
  iPod, 259, 349, 366, 497, 508, 512, 559, 559e
  iTunes, 25, 56, 214, 493, 501, 503, 559e
  iTunes Match, 512
  iTunes Music Store, 466
  iTunes Store, 501, 508, 512, 559
  Macintosh, 56, 57, 494
  Music, 507, 512
Apple's App Store, 42
Approach, in presentation plan, 471
Arab Cooperation Council (ACC), 118
Arab League, 118
Arab Maghreb Union (AMU), 118
Arbitration, 185
Arbitration Institute of the Stockholm Chamber of
  Commerce, 186
Armani, 389
Arm Holdings, 532
ARPANET, 494
Arrival terms, 367
Art direction, 441
Art directors, 441
Artificial intelligence (AI), 492
Asahi, 360
ASEAN Economic Community (AEC), 109, 110
ASEAN Free Trade Area (AFTA), 109